Financial Aid for Veterans, Military Personnel, and Their Families 2010-2012

RSP FINANCIAL AID DIRECTORIES
OF INTEREST TO VETERANS,
MILITARY PERSONNEL & THEIR FAMILIES

College Student's Guide to Merit and Other No-Need Funding, 2010-2012
More than 1,200 merit and other no-need funding opportunities for currently-enrolled or returning college students are described in this highly-praised directory. Named by *Choice* as one of the "Outstanding Titles of the Year." 470 pages. ISBN 1-58841-212-1. $32.50, plus $7 shipping.

Directory of Financial Aids for Women, 2009-2011
Called "the cream of the crop" by *School Library Journal,* this award-winning directory describes more than 1,400 scholarships, fellowships, grants, awards, and internships set aside specifically for women. 552 pages. ISBN 1-58841-194-X. $45, plus $7 shipping.

Financial Aid for African Americans, 2009-2011
Selected as *Reference Books Bulletin's* "Editor's Choice," this directory describes in detail more than 1,250 scholarships, fellowships, grants, and internships open to African Americans at all levels (high school seniors through professionals and postdoctorates). 500 pages. ISBN 1-58841-177-X. $42.50, plus $7 shipping.

Financial Aid for Asian Americans, 2009-2011
This is the source to use if you are looking for financial aid for Asian Americans; more than 1,000 sources of free money are described and thoroughly indexed. 406 pages. ISBN 1-58841-178-8. $40, plus $7 shipping.

Financial Aid for Hispanic Americans, 2009-2011
Nearly 1,200 funding programs open to Americans of Mexican, Puerto Rican, Central American, or other Latin American heritage are described here. 474 pages. ISBN 1-58841-179-6. $42.50, plus $7 shipping.

Financial Aid for Native Americans, 2009-2011
Detailed information is provided on 1,200 funding opportunities open to American Indians, Native Alaskans, and Native Pacific Islanders. 526 pages. ISBN 1-58841-180-X. $45, plus $7 shipping.

Financial Aid for Research and Creative Activities Abroad, 2010-2012
Described here are more than 1,000 scholarships, fellowships, grants, etc. available to support research, professional, or creative activities abroad. 422 pages. ISBN 1-58841-206-7. $45, plus $7 shipping.

Financial Aid for Study and Training Abroad, 2010-2012
This directory, which the reviewers call "invaluable," describes nearly 1,000 financial aid opportunities available to support study abroad. 362 pages. ISBN 1-58841-205-9. $40, plus $7 shipping.

Financial Aid for the Disabled and Their Families, 2010-2012
Named one of the "Best Reference Books of the Year" by *Library Journal,* this directory describes in detail more than 1,200 funding opportunities. 530 pages. ISBN 1-58841-204-0. $40, plus $7 shipping.

Financial Aid for Veterans, Military Personnel, and Their Families, 2010-2012
According to *Reference Book Review,* this directory (with its 1,100 entries) is "the most comprehensive guide available on the subject." 436 pages. ISBN 1-58841-209-1. $40, plus $7 shipping.

High School Senior's Guide to Merit and Other No-Need Funding, 2010-2012
Here's your guide to 1,100 funding programs that *never* look at income level when making awards to college-bound high school seniors. 416 pages. ISBN 1-58841-212-1. $29.95, plus $7 shipping.

How to Pay for Your Degree in Nursing, 2010-2012
You'll find 900 scholarships, fellowships, loans, grants, and awards here that can be used for study, research, professional, or other nursing activities. 250 pages. ISBN 1-58841-207-5. $30, plus $7 shipping.

Kaplan Scholarships, 2010
Given 5 stars (highest rating) on Amazon.com, this directory identifies 3,000 of the best scholarships and other sources of "free" money for beginning and continuing undergraduate students. 576 pages. ISBN 1-4195-5308-9. $22.50, plus $7 shipping.

Money for Christian College Students, 2010-2012
This is the only directory to describe nearly 800 funding opportunities available to support Christian students working on an undergraduate or graduate degree. 275 pages. ISBN 1-58841-196-6. $30, plus $7 shipping.

Money for Graduate Students in the Social & Behavioral Sciences, 2010-2012
If you are looking for money for a graduate degree in the social/behavioral sciences, this is the source to use. Described in this award-winning directory are the 1,000 biggest and best fellowships, grants, and awards available. 316 pages. ISBN 1-58841-201-6. $42.50, plus $7 shipping.

Financial Aid for Veterans, Military Personnel, and Their Families 2010-2012

Gail Ann Schlachter
R. David Weber

A List of: Scholarships, Fellowships/Grants, Loans, and Grants-in-Aid, Set Aside Primarily or Exclusively for Veterans, Military Personnel, and Their Family Members, Plus a Set of Six Indexes

Reference Service Press
El Dorado Hills, California

ISBN 10: 1588412091
ISBN 13: 9781588412096
ISSN: 0896-7792

10 9 8 7 6 5 4 3 2 1

Reference Service Press (RSP) began in 1977 with a single financial aid publication *(Directory of Financial Aids for Women)* and now specializes in the development of financial aid resources in multiple formats, including books, large print books, disks, CD-ROMs, print-on-demand reports, eBooks, and online sources. Long recognized as a leader in the field, RSP has been called, by the *Simba Report on Directory Publishing,* "a true success in the world of independent directory publishers." Both Kaplan Educational Centers and Military.com have hailed RSP as "the leading authority on scholarships."

Reference Service Press
El Dorado Hills Business Park
5000 Windplay Drive, Suite 4
El Dorado Hills, CA 95762
> **(916) 939-9620**
> **Fax: (916) 939-9626**
> **E-mail: info@rspfunding.com**
Visit our web site: www.rspfunding.com

Previously issued as *Financial Aid for Veterans, Military Personnel, and Their Dependents*
Manufactured in the United States of America
Price: $40.00, plus $7 shipping.

ACADEMIC INSTITUTIONS, LIBRARIES, ORGANIZATIONS, AND OTHER QUANTITY BUYERS:
Discounts on this book are available for bulk purchases. Write or call for information on our discount programs.

Contents

Introduction

WHY THIS DIRECTORY IS NEEDED

More than one third of America's population today has either direct or indirect ties to the armed services. This includes more than 25 million veterans, 3 million active-duty military personnel, and millions of their family members (including spouses, parents, children, grandchildren, and other descendants).

Over the years, a number of organizations have attempted to reward the members of these groups in a variety of ways. In 1944, Congress established the Veterans Administration (now called the Department of Veterans Affairs) to develop programs for the benefit of the men and women who served in previous wars. Today, the DVA provides a wide variety of funding opportunities to veterans and their families. Many state governments have also established or expanded programs that complement federal benefits. In addition, voluntary and other private organizations (most notably the American Legion) have raised millions of dollars to provide financial aid to their members, other veterans or military personnel, or their family members. Similarly, to recruit, retain, and reward their personnel (especially since the advent of the all-volunteer military), the armed services have developed wide-ranging benefits for members and those who are related to them. In all, billions of dollars a year are now set aside in the form of publicly- and privately-funded scholarships, fellowships, grants-in-aid, and loans for veterans, military personnel, and their family members.

Except for *Financial Aid for Veterans, Military Personnel, and Their Families,* no single guide has ever provided comprehensive coverage of the funding available to the millions of Americans with ties to the military. Instead, the other financial aid resources have focused either on one source of funds or on a small portion of the total funding available. For example, *Need a Lift* is issued annually to identify financial aid programs sponsored by the departments and auxiliaries of the American Legion (more than one quarter of which are not intended for those affiliated with the armed services). *Federal Benefits for Veterans and Dependents,* a listing produced each year by the Department of Veterans Affairs, describes only programs sponsored by the federal government, and less than one third of those are benefits that provide financial assistance; the others involve such nonmonetary services as passports to visit overseas cemeteries and availability of burial flags. Even the general financial aid directory that does the best job of covering programs for those affiliated with the armed services, *Scholarships, Fellowships and Loans* (published by Gale Cengage), identifies less than 300 programs in its most recent edition.

That's why Gail A. Schlachter and R. David Weber put together this new edition describing funding for veterans, military personnel, and their family members. With this up-to-date listing, individuals with ties to the military will now be able to use just one source to identify the billions of dollars available to them to support study, research, creative activities, travel, career development, emergencies, and much more.

WHAT'S UNIQUE ABOUT THE DIRECTORY?

Financial Aid for Veterans, Military Personnel, and Their Families is the first and only publication to provide comprehensive information about the nearly 1,400 programs that have been set aside specifically for those with ties to the military. The listings in this book cover every major field of study, are sponsored by more than 500 different private and public agencies and organizations, and are open to all levels of applicants—from high school students, to college students, to professionals and others. By using this biennially-issued directory, the one out of three Americans eligible for military-related benefits (and the counselors, advisers, and librarians who are there to serve them) can easily identify the total array of available funding programs.

In addition to its comprehensive coverage, the 2010-2012 edition of the directory offers several other unique features. First, all funding described here is substantial; every program offers at least $1,000, and many award $20,000 or more or pay all college expenses. In addition, there are hundreds of financial aid opportunities described here that are not included in any other resource; so, even if you have searched elsewhere, you will want to look at *Financial Aid for Veterans, Military Personnel, and Their Families* for additional leads.

Second, unlike other funding directories, which generally follow a straight alphabetical arrangement, this one groups entries by both type of program (e.g., scholarships, grants-in-aid) and recipient (veterans, military personnel, and their family members)—thus making it easy to pinpoint appropriate programs. The same convenience is offered in the indexes, where the entries are similarly subdivided by program type and recipient group. With this arrangement, users with one set of characteristics (e.g., veterans) will be able to find all programs set aside specifically for them—and not be distracted or have to waste time sorting through descriptions of programs intended for members of the other groups.

In fact, everything about the directory has been designed to make your search for funding as easy as possible. You can identify programs not only by recipient group, but by program title, sponsoring organizations, where you live, where you want to spend the money, individual subject areas, and even deadline date (so fundseekers working within specific time constraints can locate programs that are still open). Plus, you'll find all the information you need to decide if a program is a match for you: purpose, eligibility requirements, financial data, duration, special features, limitations, number awarded, and application date. You even get fax numbers, toll-free numbers, e-mail addresses, and web site locations (when available), along with complete contact information, to make your requests for applications proceed smoothly.

The unique value of *Financial Aid for Veterans, Military Personnel, and Their Families* has been consistently praised by the reviewers. *Reference Book Review* wrote, "This is the most comprehensive guide available on the subject of financial aid for those with ties to the military." The directory was "enthusiastically reviewed" by *American Reference Books Annual* (which judged it to be "exceptionally useful"), was called "comprehensive" and "authoritative" by *Midwest Book Review,* and was pronounced "easy to use" by *College & Research Library News.* In the view of *Booklist,* "This book fills a noteworthy gap" and libraries across the country "should make this well-conceived and useful information source a part of their reference collection." Perhaps Military.com summed it up best: "the definitive source."

WHAT'S EXCLUDED?

The focus of the directory is on "portable" (noninstitution-based) programs designed primarily or exclusively for veterans, military personnel, and their family members. Excluded from this list are:

Awards open equally to all segments of the population.   See the list of Reference Service Press titles opposite the directory's title page for publications that identify these unrestricted programs.

Financial aid programs administered by academic institutions solely for the benefit of their currently-enrolled students. Financial aid seekers should contact individual schools directly for this information.

Service programs for veterans, military personnel, and their family members. To obtain information about these benefits (e.g., job counseling, medical and dental care, treatment for alcohol or drug dependency), check with your state veteran's agency, your local DVA office, or the most recent annual edition of the DVA's *Federal Benefits for Veterans and Dependents.*

Nonmonetary benefits (such as burial flags, presidential certificates, and complimentary licenses for hunting and fishing). To obtain information, check with your state veteran's agency, your local DVA office, or the most recent annual edition of the DVA's *Federal Benefits for Veterans and Dependents.*

Indirect aid programs, where funds go to military-related agencies rather than directly to veterans, military personnel, or their family members. To obtain information, check with your state veteran's agency or your local DVA office.

Money for study or research outside the United States. Since there are comprehensive and up-to-date directories that describe all available funding for study and research abroad (particularly Reference Service Press's biennial *Financial Aid for Study and Training Abroad* and *Financial Aid for Research and Creative Activities Abroad),* only programs that support study, research, or other activities in the United States are covered here.

Very restrictive programs. In general, programs are excluded if they are open only to residents of a narrow geographic area (anything below the state level). To get information on these geographically restrictive programs, contact Reference Service Press directly or use *RSP FundingFinder,* Reference Service Press's subscription-based online funding database.

Programs offering limited financial support. Comprehensive coverage is provided for programs that can substantively impact the financial situation of veterans, military personnel, and their family members. Scholarships, fellowships, loans, and grants-in-aid must pay at least $1,000 a year or they are not included here. Also excluded are programs that offer military personnel the opportunity to pursue college training but do not provide any financial support beyond their current salary. For information on these more limited programs, contact Reference Service Press directly or use *RSP FundingFinder*, Reference Service Press's subscription-based online funding database.

EXTENT OF UPDATING IN THE 2010-2012 EDITION

The preparation of each new edition of *Financial Aid for Veterans, Military Personnel, and Their Families* involves extensive updating and revision. To insure that the information included in the directory is both reliable and current, the editors at Reference Service Press 1) review and update all programs requiring military affiliation currently in our funding database and 2) search exhaustively for new program leads in a variety of sources, including printed directories, news reports, journals, newsletters, house organs, annual reports, and sites on the Internet. Our policy is to write program descriptions only from information supplied in print or online by the sponsoring organization (no information is ever taken from secondary sources). When that information could not be found, we sent up to four collection letters (followed by up to three telephone inquiries, if necessary) to those sponsors. Despite our best efforts, however, some sponsoring organizations still failed to respond and, as a result, their programs are not included in this edition of the directory.

The 2010-2012 edition of the directory completely revises and updates the earlier biennial edition. Programs that have ceased operations have been dropped. Profiles of continuing programs have been rewritten to reflect operations in 2010-2012; nearly 85% of these programs reported substantive changes in their locations, requirements (particularly application deadline), or benefits since 2008. In addition, more than 400 new entries have been added to the program section of the directory. The resulting listing presents nearly 1,400 profiles of available scholarships, fellowships/grants, loans, and grants-in-aid.

HOW THE DIRECTORY IS ORGANIZED

The directory is divided into two separate sections: 1) a descriptive list of financial aid programs designed primarily or exclusively for veterans, military personnel, and their family members; and 2) a set of six indexes to help you find the funding you need.

Funding Available to Veterans, Military Personnel, and Their Families. The first section of the directory describes 1,397 financial aid programs set aside primarily or exclusively for veterans, military personnel, and their family members. Entries in this section are grouped into the following four categories to guide readers in their search for a specific kind of financial assistance (e.g., a scholarship for undergraduate courses, a grant-in-aid for emergency assistance).

- **Scholarships:** Programs that support studies at the undergraduate level in the United States. Usually no repayment is required, provided stated requirements are met.

- **Fellowships/Grants:** Programs that support graduate or postdoctoral study, research, or projects in the United States. Usually no repayment is required, provided stated requirements are met.

- **Loans:** Programs that provide money for a variety of purposes (e.g., education, personal assistance, purchases) but eventually must be repaid—with or without interest. Scholarship/loans, forgivable loans, loans-for-service, and loan repayment programs are covered here as well.

- **Grants-in-Aid:** Programs that provide financial assistance for property and income tax liabilities, travel, emergency situations, service in dangerous military zones, or burial costs.

Each of these four categories is further divided into three population groupings: veterans, military personnel, and family members of veterans or military personnel (children, spouses, parents, grandchildren, other relatives, etc.). Within each of the subdivisions, entries appear alphabetically by program title. Programs that supply more than one type of assistance or assistance to more than one specific group are listed in any relevant subsection. For example, both undergraduate *and* graduate students may apply for the Air Force Spouse Scholarships, so that program is described in both the scholarship *and* in the fellowship chapters.

Each program entry has been designed to provide a concise profile that includes information (when available) on program title, organization address, telephone numbers, fax and toll-free numbers, e-mail address, web site, purpose, eligibility, money awarded, duration, special features, limitations, number of awards, and application deadline. (Refer to the sample on page 9).

Each entry in the directory has been written using information provided by the sponsoring organizations (in print or online) through the first half of 2010. While the listing is intended to cover available funding as comprehensively as possible, some sponsoring organizations did not respond to our research inquiries and, consequently, are not included in this edition of the directory.

Indexes.   The directory's six indexes make it easy to search for appropriate financial aid opportunities. Program Title, Sponsoring Organization, Residency, Tenability, Subject, and Calendar Indexes follow a word-by-word alphabetical arrangement and refer the user to the appropriate entry by number.

Program Title Index.   This index lists alphabetically all program titles and variant names of the scholarships, fellowships/grants, loans, and grants-in-aid covered in the first section of the directory. Since one program can be listed in more than one subsection (e.g., a program providing assistance to veterans at both the undergraduate and graduate levels is listed in two subsections), each entry number in the index has been coded to indicate program type (e.g., scholarship, loan) and availability (veterans, military personnel, or family members). By using this coding system, readers can turn directly to the programs that match their financial needs and eligibility characteristics.

Sponsoring Organization Index.   This index provides an alphabetical listing of the more than 500 organizations sponsoring financial aid programs listed in the first section of the directory. As in the Program Title Index, entry numbers have been coded to indicate program type and availability.

Residency Index.   This index identifies the residency requirements of the programs listed in the directory. Index entries (state, region, country) are arranged alphabetically. To facilitate access, the geographic terms in the index are subdivided by program type and availability group. Use this index when you are looking for money set aside for veterans, military personnel, and members of their families in a particular geographic area.

Tenability Index.   This index identifies the geographic locations where the funding described in the directory may be used. Index entries (city, county, state, region, country) are arranged alphabetically and subdivided by program type and availability group. Use this index when you or your family members are looking for money to support research, study, or other activities in a particular geographic area.

SAMPLE ENTRY

(1) **[25]**

(2) **MILITARY ORDER OF THE PURPLE HEART SCHOLARSHIP PROGRAM**

(3) Military Order of the Purple Heart
Attn: Scholarships
5413-B Backlick Road
Springfield, VA 22151-3960
(703) 642-5360   Toll-free: (888) 668-1656
Fax: (703) 642-2054
E-mail: scholarship@purpleheart.org
Web: www.purpleheart.org

(4) **Summary**   To provide financial assistance for college or graduate school to members of the Military Order of the Purple Heart (MOPH) and their families.

(5) **Eligibility**   This program is open to 1) members of the MOPH; 2) direct descendants (children, stepchildren, adopted children, grandchildren, and great-grandchildren) of veterans who are MOPH members or who were members at the time of death; 3) direct descendants of veterans killed in action or who died of wounds but did not have the opportunity to join the order; and 4) spouses and widows of MOPH members, veterans killed in action, and veterans who died of wounds. Applicants must be graduating seniors or graduates of an accredited high school who are enrolled or accepted for enrollment in a full-time program of study in a college, trade school, or graduate school. They must have a GPA of 2.75 or higher. U.S. citizenship is required. Along with their application, they must submit an essay of 200 to 300 words on "What it means to be an American." Financial need is not considered in the selection process.

(6) **Financial data**   The stipend is $3,000 per year.

(7) **Duration**   1 year; may be renewed up to 2 additional years.

(8) **Additional information**   Membership in MOPH is open to all veterans who received a Purple Heart Medal and were discharged under conditions other than dishonorable. A processing fee of $15 is required.

(9) **Number awarded**   Varies each year; recently, 50 of these scholarships were awarded.

(10) **Deadline**   February of each year.

DEFINITION

(1) **Entry number:** Consecutive number assigned to each funding program and used to index the entry.

(2) **Program title:** Title of scholarship, fellowship, loan, or grant-in-aid.

(3) **Sponsoring organization:** Name, address, telephone number, toll-free number, fax number, e-mail address, and web site (when information was supplied) for organization sponsoring the program.

(4) **Summary:** Identifies the major program requirements; read the rest of the entry for additional detail.

(5) **Eligibility:** Describes qualifications required of applicants, application procedures, and selection criteria.

(6) **Financial data:** Financial details of the program, including fixed sum, average amount, or range of funds offered, expenses for which funds may and may not be applied, and cash-related benefits supplied (e.g., room and board).

(7) **Duration:** Period for which support is provided; renewal prospects.

(8) **Additional information:** Any unusual (generally nonmonetary) benefits, restrictions, or requirements associated with the program.

(9) **Number awarded:** Total number of recipients each year or other specified period.

(10) **Deadline:** The month by which applications must be submitted.

Subject Index. This index allows the reader to use more than 200 subject headings to access the financial aid programs designed primarily or exclusively for veterans, military personnel, and their families listed in the first section of the directory. The extensive "see" and "see also" references provided there can aid in the search for appropriate funding.

Calendar Index. To assist fundseekers who often must work within specific time constraints, the Calendar Index identifies financial aid programs by filing date. The Calendar Index is arranged by group and divided according to program type (e.g., scholarship, loan) and month during which the deadline falls. Filing dates can and quite often do vary from year to year; consequently, this index should be used only as a guide for deadlines beyond 2012. It is important to note that not all sponsoring organizations supplied information on application deadline, so some of the programs described in the directory are not listed here.

TIPS TO HELP YOU USE THE DIRECTORY

To Locate Programs Offering a Particular Type of Assistance. If you are looking for programs offering a particular type of financial aid (e.g., a scholarship for undergraduate courses, a grant-in-aid for emergency situations), turn to the appropriate category in the first section (scholarships, fellowships/grants, loans, or grants-in-aid) and read through all the entries in the subsection that applies (i.e., veterans, military personnel, or family members). Since programs with multiple purposes are listed in every appropriate location, each of the three target population subsections functions as a self-contained entity. In fact, you can browse through any of the sections or subsections in the directory without first consulting an index.

To Locate a Particular Financial Aid Program. If you know the name of a particular financial aid program and the type of assistance offered by the program (scholarship, grant-in-aid, etc.) and the availability (veterans, military personnel, or family members), then go directly to the appropriate category in the first section of the directory, where you will find the program profiles arranged alphabetically by title. But be careful: program titles can be misleading. The Air Force Health Professions Scholarship Program is available only to graduate students and therefore is listed under Fellowships/Grants not Scholarships. The Anne M. Gannett Award for Veterans is actually a scholarship, as is the Massachusetts Public Service Grant Program. Consequently, if you are looking for a specific program and do not find it in the subsection you have checked, be sure to refer to the Program Title Index to see if it is covered elsewhere in the directory. To save time, always check the Program Title Index first if you know the name of a specific award but are not sure under which subsection it would be listed.

To Browse Quickly Through the Listings. Turn to the type of funding and recipient categories that interest you and read the "Summary" field in each entry. In seconds, you'll know if this is an opportunity that might apply to you. If it is, read the rest of the information in the entry to make sure you meet all of the program requirements before writing or going online for an application form. Remember: don't apply if you don't qualify!

To Locate Programs Sponsored by a Particular Organization. The Sponsoring Organization Index makes it easy to determine groups that provide financial assistance to veterans, military personnel, and their families, or to identify specific financial aid programs offered by a particular organization. Each entry number in the index is coded to identify program type and availability, thus enabling users to target appropriate entries.

To Locate Programs Open to Residents of or Tenable in a Particular Area. The Residency Index identifies financial aid programs open to residents of a particular state, region, or country. The Tenability Index shows where the money can be spent. In both indexes, "see" and "see also" references are used liberally, and index entries for a particular geographic area are divided by both program type and eligible group.

To Locate Financial Aid Programs for Veterans, Military Personnel, and Their Families in a Particular Subject Area. Turn to the Subject Index first if you are interested in identifying financial aid programs for veterans, military personnel, or their family members in a particular subject area. To help you structure your search, the type of funding indexed (scholarships, fellowships/grants, loans, or grants-in-aid) and the eligible group (veterans, military personnel, family members) are clearly identified. Extensive cross-references are provided.

To Locate Financial Aid Programs for Veterans, Military Personnel, or Their Families by Deadline Date. If you are working with specific time constraints and want to weed out the financial aid programs whose filing dates you won't be able to meet, turn first to the Calendar Index and check the program references listed under the appropriate group, program type, and month. To identify every relevant financial aid program, regardless of filing dates, read through all the entries in each of the program categories (scholarships, loans, etc.) and availability subsections (veterans, military personnel, family members) that apply.

To Locate Information on Geographically Restricted or Financially Limited Funding Programs. Only programs aimed at large segments of the population (at least a state) or offering significant awards (at least $1,000) are covered in this directory. To get information on the other, more limited programs, contact Reference Service Press to search its comprehensive database directly.

PLANS TO UPDATE THE DIRECTORY

This volume, covering 2010-2012, is the twelfth biennial edition of *Financial Aid for Veterans, Military Personnel, and Their Families.* The next edition will cover the years 2012-2014 and will be released in the first half of 2012.

OTHER RELATED PUBLICATIONS

In addition to *Financial Aid for Veterans, Military Personnel, and Their Families,* Reference Service Press publishes several other titles dealing with fundseeking, including the biennially-issued *Directory of Financial Aids for Women* and *College Student's Guide to Merit and Other No-Need Funding.* For more information on these and other related publications, you can 1) write to Reference Service Press' Marketing Department at 5000 Windplay Drive, Suite 4, El Dorado Hills, CA 95762; 2) call us at (916) 939-9620; 3) send us an e-mail message at info@rspfunding.com; 4) fax us at (916) 939-9626; or 5) visit us on the web: www.rspfunding.com.

ACKNOWLEDGEMENTS

A debt of gratitude is owed all the organizations that contributed information to this edition of *Financial Aid for Veterans, Military Personnel, and Their Families.* Their generous cooperation has helped to make this publication a current and comprehensive survey of awards.

ABOUT THE AUTHORS

Dr. Gail Ann Schlachter has worked for more than three decades as a library manager, a library educator, and an administrator of library-related publishing companies. Among the reference books to her credit are the biennially-issued *Money for Graduate Students in the Social & Behavioral Sciences* and two award-winning bibliographic guides: *Minorities and Women: A Guide to Reference Literature in the Social Sciences* (which was chosen as an "Outstanding Reference Title of the Year" by *Choice*) and *Reference Sources in Library and Information Services* (which won the first Knowledge Industry Publications "Award for Library Literature"). She was the reference book review editor for *RQ* (now *Reference and User Services Quarterly*) for 10 years, is a past president of the American Library Association's Reference and User Services Association (RUSA, formerly RASD), is serving her fifth elected term on the American Library Association's governing council, and is a former editor-in-chief of *Reference and User Services Quarterly*. In recognition of her outstanding contributions to reference service, Dr. Schlachter was named the "Outstanding Alumna" by the University of Wisconsin School of Library and Information Studies and has been awarded both the Isadore Gilbert Mudge Citation and the Louis Shores/Oryx Press Award.

Dr. R. David Weber taught history and economics at Los Angeles Harbor College (in Wilmington, California) for many years and continues to teach history as an emeritus professor. During his years of full-time teaching there, and at East Los Angeles College, he directed the Honors Program and was frequently selected as the "Teacher of the Year." Dr. Weber is the author of a number of critically-acclaimed reference works, including *Dissertations in Urban History* and the three-volume *Energy Information Guide*. With Gail Schlachter, he is the author of Reference Service Press's award-winning *Financial Aid for Hispanic Americans* and a number of other financial aid titles, including *How to Pay for Your Engineering Degree* and *Financial Aid for the Disabled and Their Families*, which was selected as one of the "Best Reference Books of the Year" by *Library Journal*.

Financial Aid Programs for Veterans, Military Personnel and Their Families

Scholarships ●

Fellowships/Grants ●

Loans ●

Grants-in-Aid ●

Scholarships

Veterans ●

Military Personnel ●

Family Members ●

Described here are 765 programs designed primarily or exclusively for veterans, military personnel, and their family members that are to be used to pursue studies on the undergraduate level in the United States. Usually no repayment will be required, provided stated requirements are met. Of these listings, 122 are set aside specifically for veterans, 242 for military personnel, and 401 for their family members (spouses, children, grandchildren, parents, and other relatives). If you are looking for a particular program and don't find it in this section, be sure to check the Program Title Index to see if it is covered elsewhere in the directory.

Veterans

[1]
11TH ARMORED CAVALRY VETERANS OF VIETNAM AND CAMBODIA SCHOLARSHIP

11th Armored Cavalry Veterans of Vietnam and Cambodia
Attn: National Headquarters
P.O. Box 1948
Plainview, TX 79073-1948
Web: www.11thcavnam.com/scholar.html

Summary To provide financial assistance for college to members of the 11th Armored Cavalry Veterans of Vietnam and Cambodia (11ACVVC) and to their children.

Eligibility This program is open to 1) current members of the 11ACVVC; 2) children and stepchildren of current members of the 11ACVVC; 3) children whose legal guardian is a current member of the 11ACVVC; and 4) children of 11th Armored Cavalry troopers who were killed in action, died of wounds, or died as a result of service in Vietnam or Cambodia. Applicants must be enrolled or planning to enroll as an undergraduate student. Along with their application, they must submit brief essays on 1) the field of study they plan to enter and why; and 2) why they would be a worthy recipient of this scholarship. Selection is based on the essays and grades; financial need is not considered. Priority is given to children of members who were killed in action or died of wounds.

Financial Data The stipend is $3,000; funds are paid directly to the recipient's school, in 2 equal installments.

Duration 1 year; nonrenewable.

Additional data This program was established in 1997. Recipients must use the awarded money within 20 months of being notified.

Number awarded Varies each year; recently, 19 of these scholarships were awarded. Since the program was established, it has awarded a total of 245 scholarships with a value of $705,000.

Deadline May of each year.

[2]
AAAA SCHOLARSHIPS

Army Aviation Association of America Scholarship
Foundation
Attn: AAAA Scholarship Foundation
755 Main Street, Suite 4D
Monroe, CT 06468-2830
(203) 268-2450   Fax: (203) 268-5870
E-mail: Scholarship@quad-a.org
Web: www.quad-a.org/scholarship.htm

Summary To provide financial aid for undergraduate or graduate study to members of the Army Aviation Association of America (AAAA) and their relatives.

Eligibility This program is open to AAAA members and their spouses, unmarried siblings, unmarried children, and unmarried grandchildren. Applicants must be enrolled or accepted for enrollment as an undergraduate or graduate student at an accredited college or university. Graduate students must include a 250-word essay on their life experiences, work history, and aspirations. Some scholarships are specifically reserved for enlisted, warrant officer, company grade, and Department of the Army civilian members. Selection is based on academic merit and personal achievement.

Financial Data Most stipends range from $1,000 to $4,000. Special scholarships are $11,000.

Duration Scholarships may be for 1 year, 2 years, or 4 years.

Additional data This program includes 3 special scholarships: the GEN Hamilton H. Howze Memorial Scholarship, the Helen Cribbins Memorial Scholarship, and the Joseph P. Cribbins Scholarship.

Number awarded Varies each year; recently, $268,500 in scholarships was awarded to 171 students. Since the program began in 1963, the foundation has awarded more than $3.3 million to nearly 2,000 qualified applicants.

Deadline April of each year.

[3]
ADRIENNE ALIX SCHOLARSHIP

American Legion Auxiliary
Department of New Hampshire
State House Annex
25 Capitol Street, Room 432
Concord, NH 03301-6312
(603) 271-2212   Toll Free: (800) 778-3816
Fax: (603) 271-5352 E-mail: nhalasec@amlegion.state.nh.us
Web: www.nhlegion.org

Summary To provide financial assistance to New Hampshire residents, including those recently discharged from the military, who wish to refresh or upgrade their skills at a school in any state.

Eligibility This program is open to New Hampshire residents who are 1) reentering the work force or upgrading skills; 2) displaced from the work force; or 3) recently discharged honorably from the military. Applicants must be interested in taking a refresher course or advancing their knowledge or techniques needed in today's work force at a school in any state. Along with their application, they must submit a 500-word essay explaining their career goals and objectives.

Financial Data The stipend is $1,000.

Duration 1 year.

Number awarded 1 each year.

Deadline April of each year.

[4]
AMVETS NATIONAL SCHOLARSHIPS FOR VETERANS

AMVETS National Headquarters
Attn: Scholarships
4647 Forbes Boulevard
Lanham, MD 20706-3807
(301) 459-9600   Toll Free: (877) 7-AMVETS, ext. 3043
Fax: (301) 459-7924   E-mail: amvets@amvets.org
Web: www.amvets.org/programs/scholarships.html

Summary To provide financial assistance for college or graduate school to certain veterans who are members of AMVETS.

Eligibility This program is open to AMVETS members who are veterans and U.S. citizens. Applicants must be interested in working full time on an undergraduate degree, graduate degree, or certification from an accredited technical/trade school. They must have exhausted all other government aid. Selection is based on financial need, academic promise, military duty and awards, volunteer activities, community services, jobs held during the past 4 years, and an essay of 50 to 100 words on "What a Higher Education Means to Me."

Financial Data The stipend is $1,000 per year.

Duration Up to 4 years.

Additional data Requests for applications must be accompanied by a self-addressed stamped envelope.

Number awarded 3 each year.

Deadline April of each year.

[5]
ANDREW J. ZABIEREK MEMORIAL SCHOLARSHIPS

Andrew J. Zabierek Foundation
P.O. Box 533
Chelmsford, MA 01824
(978) 726-2913   E-mail: info@ajzfoundation.org
Web: www.ajzfoundation.org

Summary   To provide financial assistance to veterans from Massachusetts who are working on an undergraduate degree.

Eligibility   This program is open to residents of Massachusetts who are honorably discharged veterans. Applicants must be working on a postsecondary or technical degree. Along with their application, they must submit a 500-word personal reflection essay on how their service has impacted them personally, how they will continue to serve their community and country in the future, and their educational and professional goals after they complete their education. Financial need is considered in the selection process.

Financial Data   The stipend is $1,500.

Duration   1 year.

Additional data   This program was established in 2004 to honor Lance Corporal Andrew J. Zabierek, who was killed in action in Al Anbar provide of Iraq.

Number awarded   2 each year.

Deadline   May of each year.

[6]
ANGELFIRE SCHOLARSHIP

Datatel Scholars Foundation
4375 Fair Lakes Court
Fairfax, VA 22033
(703) 968-9000, ext. 4549   Toll Free: (800) 486-4332
Fax: (703) 968-4625   E-mail: scholars@datatel.com
Web: www.datatelscholars.org

Summary   To provide financial assistance to graduating high school seniors, continuing college students, and graduate students who will be studying at a Datatel client school and are veterans, veterans' dependents, or refugees from southeast Asia.

Eligibility   This program is open to 1) veterans who served in the Asian theater (Vietnam, Cambodia, or Laos) between 1964 and 1975; 2) their spouses and children; 3) refugees from Vietnam, Cambodia, or Laos; and 4) veterans who served in Operation Desert Storm, Operation Enduring Freedom, and/or Operation Iraqi Freedom. Applicants must attend a Datatel client college or university during the upcoming school year. They must first apply to their institution, which selects 2 semifinalists and forwards their applications to the sponsor. Along with their application, they must include a 1,000-word personal statement that discusses how the conflict has affected them personally, summarizes how the conflict has impacted their educational goals, and describes how being awarded this scholarship will help them achieve their goals. Selection is based on the quality of the personal statement (40%), academic merit (30%), achievements and civic involvement (20%), and 2 letters of recommendation (10%).

Financial Data   The stipend is $1,700. Funds are paid directly to the institution.

Duration   1 year.

Additional data   Datatel, Inc. produces advanced information technology solutions for higher education. It has more than 725 client sites in the United States and Canada. This scholarship was created to commemorate those who lost their lives in Vietnam or Iraq and is named after a memorial administered by the Disabled American Veterans Association in Angelfire, New Mexico.

Number awarded   Varies each year. Recently, 10 of these scholarships were awarded.

Deadline   Students must submit online applications to their institution or organization by January of each year.

[7]
ANNE M. GANNETT AWARD FOR VETERANS

National Federation of Music Clubs
1646 Smith Valley Road
Greenwood, IN 46142
(317) 882-4003   Fax: (317) 882-4019
E-mail: info@nfmc-music.org
Web: www.nfmc-music.org

Summary   To provide financial assistance for undergraduate education to members of the National Federation of Music Clubs (NFMC) whose careers have been delayed or interrupted as a result of their service in the U.S. armed forces.

Eligibility   This program is open to undergraduate students who are majoring in music and whose musical careers were interrupted by military service. Applicants must be student members of the federation and U.S. citizens. Along with their application, they must submit an essay on their reason for wanting this award and their future plans. Financial need is not considered in the selection process.

Financial Data   The stipend is $2,000.

Duration   1 year.

Additional data   The application fee is $20.

Number awarded   1 each year.

Deadline   February of each year.

[8]
ARMY COLLEGE FUND

U.S. Army
Human Resources Command
AHRC-PDE-EI
Attn: Education Incentives and Counseling Branch
200 Stovall Street, Suite 3N17
Alexandria, VA 22332-0472
(703) 325-0285   Toll Free: (800) 872-8272
Fax: (703) 325-6599   E-mail: pdeei@hoffman.army.mil
Web: www.goarmy.com/benefits/education_money.jsp

Summary   To provide financial assistance for college to Army enlistees after they have completed their service obligation.

Eligibility   Eligible for this program are high school seniors or graduates who enlist in an approved military occupational specialty (MOS) for at least 2 years, score 50 or above on the Armed Forces Qualification Test (AFQT), enroll in the Montgomery GI Bill, and attend a Department of Veterans Affairs-approved postsecondary educational institution on a full-time basis after completion of their service obligation.

Financial Data   The Army College Fund (ACF) provides money for college in addition to that which the enlistee receives under the Montgomery GI Bill. The maximum benefit, depending on MOS, is $44,028 for a 2-year enlistment, $63,756 for a 3-year enlistment, $70,956 for a 4-year enlistment, $78,156 for a 5-year enlistment, or $81,756 for a 6-year enlistment.

Duration   36 months; funds must be utilized within 10 years of leaving the Army.

Additional data   Applications and further information are available from local Army recruiters.

Number awarded   Varies each year.

Deadline   Applications may be submitted at any time.

[9]
ARMY NURSE CORPS ASSOCIATION SCHOLARSHIPS

Army Nurse Corps Association
Attn: Education Committee
P.O. Box 39235
San Antonio, TX 78218-1235
(210) 650-3534   Fax: (210) 650-3494
E-mail: education@e-anca.org
Web: e-anca.org/ANCAEduc.htm

Summary   To provide financial assistance to students who have a connection to the Army and are interested in working on an undergraduate or graduate degree in nursing.

Eligibility   This program is open to students attending colleges or universities that have accredited programs offering associate, bachelor's, master's, or doctoral degrees in nursing. Applicants must be 1) nursing students who plan to enter the active Army, Army National Guard, or Army Reserve and are not participating in a program funded by the active Army, Army National Guard, or Army Reserve; 2) nursing students who have previously served in the active Army, Army National Guard, or Army Reserve; 3) Army Nurse Corps officers enrolled in an undergraduate or graduate nursing program not funded by the active Army, Army National Guard, or Army Reserve; 4) Army enlisted soldiers in the active Army, Army National Guard, or Army Reserve who are working on a baccalaureate degree in nursing not funded by the active Army, Army National Guard, or Army Reserve; or 5) nursing students whose parent(s) or spouse are serving or have served in the active Army, Army National Guard, or Army Reserve. Along with their application, they must submit a personal statement on their professional career objectives, reasons for applying for this scholarship, financial need, special considerations, personal and academic interests, and why they are preparing for a nursing career.

Financial Data   The stipend is $3,000. Funds are sent directly to the recipient's school.

Duration   1 year.

Additional data   Although the sponsoring organization is made up of current, retired, and honorably discharged officers of the Army Nurse Corps, it does not have an official affiliation with the Army. Therefore, students who receive these scholarships do not incur any military service obligation.

Number awarded   1 or more each year.

Deadline   March of each year.

[10]
BART LONGO MEMORIAL SCHOLARSHIPS

National Chief Petty Officers' Association
c/o Marjorie Hays, Treasurer
1014 Ronald Drive
Corpus Christi, TX 78412-3548
Web: www.goatlocker.org/ncpoa/scholarship.htm

Summary   To provide financial assistance for college or graduate school to members of the National Chief Petty Officers' Association (NCPOA) and their families.

Eligibility   This program is open to members of the NCPOA and the children, stepchildren, and grandchildren of living or deceased members. Applicants may be high school seniors or graduates entering a college or university or students currently enrolled full time as undergraduate or graduate students. Selection is based on academic achievement and participation in extracurricular activities; financial need is not considered.

Financial Data   The stipend is $1,000.

Duration   1 year.

Additional data   Membership in the NCPOA is limited to men and women who served or are serving as Chief Petty Officers in the U.S. Navy, U.S. Coast Guard, or their Reserve components for at least 30 days.

Number awarded   2 each year: 1 to a high school senior or graduate and 1 to an undergraduate or graduate student.

Deadline   May of each year.

[11]
BETTER CHANCE SCHOLARSHIP

Associates of Vietnam Veterans of America
Attn: Scholarship Program
8719 Colesville Road, Suite 100
Silver Spring, MD 20910
(301) 585-4000   Toll Free: (800) VVA-1316
Fax: (301) 585-0519
Web: www.avva.org/Welcome%20Page/programs.htm

Summary   To provide financial assistance for college to members of Vietnam Veterans of America (VVA) and Associates of Vietnam Veterans of America (AVVA), their families, and the families of Vietnam veterans killed or missing in action.

Eligibility   This program is open to members of VVA and AVVA; their spouses, children, and grandchildren; and the spouses, children, and grandchildren of Vietnam veterans killed in action (KIA) or missing in action (MIA). Especially encouraged to apply are average students who are not eligible for academic scholarships but who can demonstrate financial need. Applicants must submit essays on their long-term goals, work experience, organizations or activities, and community service.

Financial Data   Stipends are $1,000, $750, or $500.

Duration   1 year.

Additional data   This program was established in 1998.

Number awarded   3 each year: 1 at $1,000, 1 at $750, and 1 at $500.

Deadline   June of each year.

[12]
CALIFORNIA FEE WAIVER PROGRAM FOR RECIPIENTS OF THE MEDAL OF HONOR AND THEIR CHILDREN

California Department of Veterans Affairs
Attn: Division of Veterans Services
1227 O Street, Room 101
Sacramento, CA 95814
(916) 503-8397   Toll Free: (800) 952-LOAN (within CA)
Fax: (916) 653-2563   TDD: (800) 324-5966
E-mail: ruckergl@cdva.ca.gov
Web: www.cdva.ca.gov/VetService/Waivers.aspx

Summary   To provide financial assistance for college to veterans in California who received the Medal of Honor and their children.

Eligibility   This program is open to recipients of the Medal of Honor and their children younger than 27 years of age who are residents of California. Applicants must be attending or planning to attend a community college, branch of the California State University system, or campus of the University of California.

Financial Data   Full-time college students receive a waiver of tuition and registration fees at any publicly-supported community or state college or university in California.

Duration   1 year; may be renewed.

Number awarded   Varies each year.

Deadline   Deadline not specified.

[13]
CALIFORNIA LEGION AUXILIARY PAST PRESIDENTS' PARLEY NURSING SCHOLARSHIPS

American Legion Auxiliary
Department of California
Veterans War Memorial Building
401 Van Ness Avenue, Room 113
San Francisco, CA 94102-4586
(415) 861-5092   Fax: (415) 861-8365
E-mail: calegionaux@calegionaux.org
Web: www.calegionaux.org/scholarships.htm

Summary To provide financial assistance to California residents who are current military personnel, veterans, or members of their families and interested in studying nursing at a school in the state.

Eligibility This program is open to California residents who are currently serving on active military duty, veterans who served during war time, or the spouse, widow(er), or child of such a veteran. Applicants must be entering or continuing students of nursing at an accredited institution of higher learning in California. Financial need is considered in the selection process.

Financial Data Stipends range up to $2,000.

Duration 1 year.

Number awarded Varies each year.

Deadline April of each year.

[14]
CALIFORNIA LEGION AUXILIARY SCHOLARSHIPS FOR CONTINUING AND/OR REENTRY STUDENTS

American Legion Auxiliary
Department of California
Veterans War Memorial Building
401 Van Ness Avenue, Room 113
San Francisco, CA 94102-4586
(415) 861-5092   Fax: (415) 861-8365
E-mail: calegionaux@calegionaux.org
Web: www.calegionaux.org/scholarships.htm

Summary To provide financial assistance to California residents who are active-duty military personnel, veterans, or children of veterans and require assistance to continue their education.

Eligibility This program is open to California residents who are 1) active-duty military personnel; 2) veterans of World War I, World War II, Korea, Vietnam, Grenada/Lebanon, Panama, or Desert Shield/Desert Storm; and 3) children of veterans who served during those periods of war. Applicants must be continuing or reentry students at a college, university, or business/trade school in California. Financial need is considered in the selection process.

Financial Data The stipend is $1,000 or $500.

Duration 1 year.

Additional data This program includes 1 scholarship designated as the Mel Foronda Memorial Scholarship.

Number awarded 5 each year: 3 at $1,000 and 2 at $500.

Deadline March of each year.

[15]
COLORADO LEGION AUXILIARY PAST PRESIDENT'S PARLEY NURSE'S SCHOLARSHIP

American Legion Auxiliary
Department of Colorado
7465 East First Avenue, Suite D
Denver, CO 80230
(303) 367-5388   Fax: (303) 367-5388
E-mail: ala@impactmail.net
Web: www.freewebs.com/ala-colorado

Summary To provide financial assistance to wartime veterans and their descendants in Colorado who are interested in attending school in the state to prepare for a career in nursing.

Eligibility This program is open to 1) daughters, sons, spouses, granddaughters, and great-granddaughters of veterans, and 2) veterans who served in the armed forces during eligibility dates for membership in the American Legion. Applicants must be Colorado residents who have been accepted by an accredited school of nursing in the state. Along with their application, they must submit a 500-word essay on the topic, "Americanism." Selection is based on scholastic ability (25%), financial need (25%), references (13%), a 500-word essay on Americanism (25%), and dedication to chosen field (12%).

Financial Data Stipends range from $500 to $1,000.

Duration 1 year; nonrenewable.

Number awarded Varies each year, depending on the availability of funds.

Deadline April of each year.

[16]
COMMANDER'S SCHOLARSHIPS

American Legion
Department of Missouri
P.O. Box 179
Jefferson City, MO 65102-0179
(573) 893-2353   Toll Free: (800) 846-9023
Fax: (573) 893-2980   E-mail: info@missourilegion.org
Web: www.missourilegion.org

Summary To provide financial assistance to veterans in Missouri who are interested in attending college in the state.

Eligibility This program is open to residents of Missouri who served at least 90 days in the U.S. armed forces and received an honorable discharge. Applicants must be enrolled or planning to enroll full time at an accredited vocational/technical school, college, or university in Missouri.

Financial Data The stipend is $1,000.

Duration 1 year.

Number awarded 2 each year.

Deadline April of each year.

[17]
CONNECTICUT TUITION WAIVER FOR VETERANS

Connecticut Department of Higher Education
Attn: Education and Employment Information Center
61 Woodland Street
Hartford, CT 06105-2326
(860) 947-1816   Toll Free: (800) 842-0229 (within CT)
Fax: (860) 947-1310   E-mail: veterans@ctdhe.org
Web: www.ctdhe.org/SFA/default.htm

Summary To provide financial assistance for college to certain Connecticut veterans and military personnel and their dependents.

Eligibility This program is open to 1) honorably-discharged Connecticut veterans who served at least 90 days during specified periods of wartime; 2) active members of the Connecticut Army and Air National Guard; 3) Connecticut residents who are a dependent child or surviving spouse of a member of the armed forces killed in action on or after September 11, 2001 who was also a Connecticut resident; and 4) Connecticut residents who are dependent children or a person officially declared missing in action or a prisoner of war while serving in the armed forces after January 1, 1960. Applicants must be attending or planning to attend a public college or university in the state.

Financial Data The program provides a waiver of 100% of tuition for general fund courses at Connecticut public colleges or universities, 50% of tuition for extension and summer courses at campuses of Connecticut State University, and 50% of part-time fees at OnlineCSU.

Duration Up to 4 years.
Additional data This is an entitlement program; applications are available at the respective college financial aid offices.
Number awarded Varies each year.
Deadline Deadline not specified.

[18]
DARLENE HOOLEY SCHOLARSHIP FOR OREGON VETERANS

Oregon Student Assistance Commission
Attn: Grants and Scholarships Division
1500 Valley River Drive, Suite 100
Eugene, OR 97401-2146
(541) 687-7395   Toll Free: (800) 452-8807, ext. 7395
Fax: (541) 687-7414   TDD: (800) 735-2900
E-mail: awardinfo@osac.state.or.us
Web: www.osac.state.or.us/osac_programs.html

Summary To provide financial assistance to veterans in Oregon who served during the Global War on Terror and are interested in working on an undergraduate or graduate degree at a college in the state.
Eligibility This program is open to Oregon veterans who served during the Global War on Terror; there is no minimum length of service requirement. Applicants must be enrolled or planning to enroll at least half time as an undergraduate or graduate student at a college or university in Oregon.
Financial Data A stipend is awarded (amount not specified).
Duration 1 year; recipients may reapply.
Additional data This program is administered by the Oregon Student Assistance Commission (OSAC) with funds provided by the Oregon Community Foundation, 1221 S.W. Yamhill, Suite 100, Portland, OR 97205, (503) 227-6846, Fax: (503) 274-7771.
Number awarded Varies each year.
Deadline February of each year.

[19]
DISABLED WAR VETERANS SCHOLARSHIPS

Armed Forces Communications and Electronics Association
Attn: AFCEA Educational Foundation
4400 Fair Lakes Court
Fairfax, VA 22033-3899
(703) 631-6149   Toll Free: (800) 336-4583, ext. 6149
Fax: (703) 631-4693   E-mail: scholarship@afcea.org
Web: www.afcea.org

Summary To provide financial assistance to disabled military personnel and veterans who are majoring in specified scientific fields in college.
Eligibility This program is open to active-duty service personnel and honorably discharged U.S. military veterans, Reservists, and National Guard members who are disabled because of wounds received during service in Enduring Freedom (Afghanistan) or Iraqi Freedom operations. Applicants must be enrolled full or part time at an accredited 2- or 4-year college or university or in a distance learning or online degree program. They must be working toward a degree in engineering (aerospace, computer, electrical, or systems), computer science, computer engineering technology, computer network systems, computer information systems, electronics engineering technology, mathematics, physics, science or mathematics education, information systems management, information systems security, technology management, or other field directly related to the support of U.S. intelligence or national security enterprises. Selection is based on demonstrated academic excellence, leadership, and financial need.
Financial Data The stipend is $2,500.
Duration 1 year.
Number awarded 2 each year: 1 for spring and 1 for fall.
Deadline March of each year for fall; November of each year for spring.

[20]
DONALD D. FRIZZELL MEMORIAL SCHOLARSHIPS

First Command Educational Foundation
Attn: Scholarship Programs Manager
1 FirstComm Plaza
Fort Worth, TX 76109-4999
(817) 569-2634   Toll Free: (877) 872-8289
Fax: (817) 569-2970   E-mail: aymcmanus@fcef.com
Web: www.fcef.com/direct-apply-scholarship.php

Summary To provide financial assistance to students, especially those with ties to the military, entering or attending college.
Eligibility This program is open to 2 categories of applicants: 1) traditional students, including high school seniors and students already enrolled at a college, university, or accredited trade school; and 2) nontraditional students, including those defined by their institution as nontraditional and adult students planning to return to a college, university, or accredited trade school. Traditional students must have a GPA of 3.0 or higher. Special consideration is given to applicants with a connection to the military. Along with their application, they must submit 1-page essays on 1) their active involvement in community service programs, 2) the impact of financial literacy on their future, and 3) why they need this scholarship. Selection is based primarily on the essays, academic merit, and financial need.
Financial Data Stipends are $5,000 or $2,500. Funds are disbursed directly to the recipient's college, university, or trade school.
Duration 1 year.
Additional data The sponsoring organization was formerly known as the USPA & IRA Educational Foundation, founded in 1983 to provide scholarships to the children of active, retired, or deceased military personnel. In addition to these scholarships, for which students may apply directly, it supports scholarships offered by a number of partner organizations. Since its establishment, it has awarded scholarships worth nearly $4 million.
Number awarded 6 each year: 2 at $5,000 and 4 at $2,500. Awards are split evenly between the 2 categories.
Deadline The online application process begins in February of each year and continues until 200 applications have been received in each category.

[21]
DR. AURELIO M. CACCOMO FAMILY FOUNDATION MEMORIAL SCHOLARSHIP

AMVETS National Headquarters
Attn: Scholarships
4647 Forbes Boulevard
Lanham, MD 20706-3807
(301) 459-9600   Toll Free: (877) 7-AMVETS, ext. 3043
Fax: (301) 459-7924   E-mail: amvets@amvets.org
Web: www.amvets.org/programs/programs_scholarships.html

Summary To provide financial assistance for college to veterans and members of the National Guard and Reserves who are members of AMVETS.
Eligibility This program is open to AMVETS members who are veterans or currently serving in the National Guard or Reserves. Applicants must be interested in working full or part time on an undergraduate degree or certification from an accredited technical/trade school. They must have exhausted all other government aid. U.S. citizenship is required. Selection is based on financial need, academic promise, military duty and awards, volunteer activities, community services, jobs held during the past 4 years, and an essay of 50 to 100 words on "This award will help me achieve my career/vocational goal, which is..."
Financial Data The stipend is $3,000.
Duration 1 year; nonrenewable.
Additional data Requests for applications must be accompanied by a self-addressed stamped envelope.

Number awarded 1 each year.
Deadline April of each year.

[22]
EDWARD T. CONROY MEMORIAL SCHOLARSHIP PROGRAM

Maryland Higher Education Commission
Attn: Office of Student Financial Assistance
839 Bestgate Road, Suite 400
Annapolis, MD 21401-3013
(410) 260-4563   Toll Free: (800) 974-1024, ext. 4563
Fax: (410) 260-3200   TDD: (800) 735-2258
E-mail: lasplin@mhec.state.md.us
Web: www.mhec.state.md.us

Summary To provide financial assistance for college or graduate school in Maryland to children and spouses of victims of the September 11, 2001 terrorist attacks and specified categories of veterans, public safety employees, and their children or spouses.
Eligibility This program is open to entering and continuing undergraduate and graduate students in the following categories: 1) children and surviving spouses of victims of the September 11, 2001 terrorist attacks who died in the World Trade Center in New York City, the Pentagon in Virginia, or United Airlines Flight 93 in Pennsylvania; 2) veterans who have, as a direct result of military service, a disability of 25% or greater and have exhausted or are no longer eligible for federal veterans' educational benefits; 3) children of armed forces members whose death or 100% disability was directly caused by military service; 4) POW/MIA veterans of the Vietnam Conflict and their children; 5) state or local public safety officers or volunteers who became 100% disabled in the line of duty; and 6) children and unremarried surviving spouses of state or local public safety employees or volunteers who died or became 100% disabled in the line of duty. The parent, spouse, veteran, POW, or public safety officer or volunteer must have been a resident of Maryland at the time of death or when declared disabled. Financial need is not considered.
Financial Data The amount of the award is equal to tuition and fees at a Maryland postsecondary institution, to a maximum of $19,000 for children and spouses of the September 11 terrorist attacks or $9,000 for all other recipients.
Duration Up to 5 years of full-time study or 8 years of part-time study.
Additional data Recipients must enroll at a 2-year or 4-year Maryland college or university as a full-time or part-time degree-seeking undergraduate or graduate student or attend a private career school.
Number awarded Varies each year.
Deadline July of each year.

[23]
E.E. MIXON SECOND DRAGOON FOUNDATION SCHOLARSHIPS

E.E. Mixon Second Dragoon Foundation
c/o Scott C. Pierce
217 Painted Fall Way
Cary, NC 27513
(203) 979-7083   E-mail: scott@2nddragoons.org
Web: 2nddragoons.org/index/?q=node/15

Summary To provide financial assistance for college to former members of the U.S. Army's Second Cavalry Regiment and the children of current and former members.
Eligibility This program is open to former members of the Second Cavalry Regiment and the children of current or former members. Members of other Army units and their children may also be considered, especially if they have a previous connection with the Second Cavalry Regiment or other U.S. Cavalry Regiments. Applicants must submit a 500-word essay on 1 of the following topics: 1) how our military presence in Europe contributed to the

end of the Cold War; 2) the role of the non-commissioned officer corps in the U.S. military; or 3) what America means to them. They must be attending or planning to attend a college or university. Selection is based on the essay and a statement of their educational goals, projected or current field of study, and personal or family affiliation with a cavalry unit.
Financial Data Stipends range from $250 to $1,000 per year. Funds are deposited directly into the recipient's college tuition account.
Duration 1 semester; may be renewed.
Number awarded Varies each year; recently, 6 of these scholarships were awarded.
Deadline July of each year.

[24]
EXEMPTION FOR TEXAS VETERANS

Texas Higher Education Coordinating Board
Attn: Grants and Special Programs
1200 East Anderson Lane
P.O. Box 12788, Capitol Station
Austin, TX 78711-2788
(512) 427-6340   Toll Free: (800) 242-3062
Fax: (512) 427-6127   E-mail: grantinfo@thecb.state.tx.us
Web: www.collegeforalltexans.com

Summary To exempt Texas veterans from payment of tuition for undergraduate or graduate study at public universities in the state.
Eligibility This program is open to veterans who were legal residents of Texas at the time they entered the U.S. armed forces and served for at least 181 days of active military duty, excluding basic training, during specified periods of war time. Applicants must have received an honorable discharge or separation or a general discharge under honorable conditions. They must be enrolled at a public college or university in Texas and all their other federal veterans education benefits (not including Pell and SEOG grants) may not exceed the value of this exemption. If they are in default on a student loan made or guaranteed by the state of Texas or on a federal education loan that affects their eligibility for GI education benefits, they are not eligible.
Financial Data Veterans who are eligible for this benefit are entitled to free tuition and fees at state-supported colleges and universities in Texas.
Duration Exemptions may be claimed up to a cumulative total of 150 credit hours, including undergraduate and graduate study.
Additional data This program was established under provisions of the Hazlewood Act, and is also referred to as Hazlewood Exemption for Texas Veterans.
Number awarded Varies each year; recently, 8,885 of these awards were granted.
Deadline Deadline not specified.

[25]
FLEET RESERVE ASSOCIATION SCHOLARSHIP

Fleet Reserve Association
Attn: Scholarship Administrator
125 North West Street
Alexandria, VA 22314-2754
(703) 683-1400   Toll Free: (800) FRA-1924
Fax: (703) 549-6610   E-mail: fra@fra.org
Web: www.fra.org

Summary To provide financial assistance for college or graduate school to members of the Fleet Reserve Association (FRA), as well as their spouses, children, and grandchildren.
Eligibility This program is open to members of the FRA and their dependent children, grandchildren, and spouses. The children, grandchildren, and spouses of deceased FRA members are also eligible. Applicants must submit an essay on their life experiences, career objectives, and what motivated them to select

those objectives. Selection is based on academic record, financial need, extracurricular activities, leadership skills, and participation in community activities. U.S. citizenship is required.

Financial Data The stipend is $5,000 per year.

Duration 1 year; may be renewed.

Additional data Membership in the FRA is restricted to active-duty, retired, and reserve members of the Navy, Marines, and Coast Guard.

Number awarded 6 each year.

Deadline April of each year.

[26]
FORCE RECON ASSOCIATION SCHOLARSHIPS

Force Recon Association
P.O. Box 425
Rowe, MA 01367
E-mail: commchief@forcerecon.com
Web: www.forcerecon.com

Summary To provide financial assistance for college to members of the Force Recon Association and their dependents.

Eligibility This program is open to members of the Force Recon Association and family members of a relative who served both in the U.S. Marine Corps and was or is assigned to a Force Reconnaissance Company. The relative must be either an active or deceased member of the Force Recon Association. Family members include wives and widows, sons and daughters (including adopted and stepchildren), grandchildren, and great-grandchildren. Applicants may be pursuing scholastic, vocational, or technical education. Along with their application, they must submit a personal statement on why they desire this scholarship, their proposed course of study, their progress in their current course of study, and their long-range career goals. Selection is based on academic achievement, letters of recommendation, demonstrated character, and the written statements.

Financial Data A stipend is awarded (amount not specified).

Duration 1 year; may be renewed.

Number awarded 1 or more each year.

Deadline Applications must be received at least 2 weeks prior to the annual meeting of the Force Recon Association.

[27]
GENERAL EMMETT PAIGE SCHOLARSHIPS

Armed Forces Communications and Electronics Association
Attn: AFCEA Educational Foundation
4400 Fair Lakes Court
Fairfax, VA 22033-3899
(703) 631-6149   Toll Free: (800) 336-4583, ext. 6149
Fax: (703) 631-4693   E-mail: scholarship@afcea.org
Web: www.afcea.org

Summary To provide financial assistance to veterans, military personnel, and their family members who are majoring in specified scientific fields in college.

Eligibility This program is open to veterans, persons on active duty in the uniformed military services, and their spouses or dependents who are currently enrolled full time in an accredited 4-year college or university in the United States. Graduating high school seniors are not eligible, but veterans entering college as freshmen may apply. Spouses or dependents must be sophomores or juniors. Applicants must be U.S. citizens, be of good moral character, have demonstrated academic excellence, be motivated to complete a college education, and be working toward a degree in engineering (aerospace, chemical, electrical, or systems), mathematics, physics, science or mathematics education, management information systems, technology management, computer science, or other field directly related to the support of U.S. intelligence enterprises or national security. They must have a GPA of 3.0 or higher. Along with their application, they must provide a copy of Discharge Form DD214, Certificate of

Service, or facsimile of their current Department of Defense or Coast Guard Identification Card. Financial need is not considered in the selection process.

Financial Data The stipend is $2,000 per year.

Duration 1 year; may be renewed.

Number awarded Varies each year; recently, 9 of these scholarships were awarded.

Deadline February of each year.

[28]
GEORGE WASHINGTON CHAPTER AUSA SCHOLARSHIPS

Association of the United States Army-George Washington Chapter
c/o Bobbie Williams, Scholarship Committee
79 Brush Everard Court
Stafford, VA 22554
(703) 697-6340   E-mail: Bobbie.Williams@us.army.mil
Web: www.gwcausa.org/Scholarship/index.htm

Summary To provide financial assistance for undergraduate or graduate study at a school in any state to members of the George Washington Chapter of the Association of the United States Army (AUSA) and their families.

Eligibility This program is open to active members of the AUSA George Washington Chapter (which serves the Washington, D.C. area) and the families of active members. Applicants must have a GPA of 2.5 or higher and be working on an undergraduate or advanced degree at a college or university in any state. Along with their application, they must submit a letter describing any family circumstances they believe are relevant and explaining why they deserve the scholarship. Members must also submit a favorable recommendation from their supervisor. Membership in AUSA is open to Army personnel (including Reserves and National Guard) who are either active or retired, ROTC cadets, or civilian employees of the Army.

Financial Data Stipends range up to $1,000.

Duration 1 year.

Number awarded Varies each year; recently, 15 of these scholarships were awarded.

Deadline April of each year.

[29]
HOWARD R. HARPER SCHOLARSHIPS

Enlisted Association of the National Guard of Iowa
c/o Jerald D. Hansen, Secretary
1409 East Coolbaugh Street
Red Oak, IA 51566
(712) 623-2804
Web: www.eangi.com/index-4.html

Summary To provide financial assistance to members of the Enlisted Association of the National Guard of Iowa (EANGI) and their dependents who are interested in attending college in any state.

Eligibility This program is open to EANGI members and their spouses and children. Applicants must be attending or accepted at a VA-approved college or vocational/technical school in any state. Along with their application, they must submit a copy of their transcript, a letter with specific facts as to their desire to continue their education and why financial assistance is required, 3 letters of recommendation, and 1 academic reference.

Financial Data The stipend is $1,000.

Duration 1 year.

Additional data Membership in EANGI is open to enlisted members of the Iowa Army or Air National Guard, active component members assigned to the Iowa Army or Air National Guard, and enlisted personnel who are retired or honorably discharged from the Iowa Army or Air National Guard.

Number awarded 4 each year.
Deadline January of each year.

[30]
IDAHO LEGION AUXILIARY NURSES SCHOLARSHIP

American Legion Auxiliary
Department of Idaho
905 Warren Street
Boise, ID 83706-3825
(208) 342-7066 Fax: (208) 342-7066
E-mail: idalegionaux@msn.com

Summary To provide financial assistance to Idaho veterans and their children who are interested in studying nursing at a school in any state.
Eligibility This program is open to student nurses who are veterans or the children or grandchildren of veterans and have resided in Idaho for 5 years prior to application. Applicants must be attending or planning to attend a school of nursing in any state. They must be between 17 and 35 years of age. Selection is based on financial need, scholarship, and deportment.
Financial Data The stipend is $1,000.
Duration 1 year.
Number awarded 1 each year.
Deadline May of each year.

[31]
ILLINOIS LEGION AUXILIARY SPECIAL EDUCATION SCHOLARSHIP

American Legion Auxiliary
Department of Illinois
2720 East Lincoln Street
P.O. Box 1426
Bloomington, IL 61702-1426
(309) 663-9366 Fax: (309) 663-5827
E-mail: staff@ilala.org
Web: illegion.org/auxiliary/scholar.html

Summary To provide financial assistance to Illinois veterans and their descendants who are attending college in any state to prepare for a career as a special education teacher.
Eligibility This program is open to veterans who served during designated periods of war time and their children, grandchildren, and great-grandchildren. Applicants must be currently enrolled in their second or third year at a college or university in any state and studying teaching retarded or disabled children. They must be residents of Illinois or members of the American Legion Family, Department of Illinois. Along with their application, they must submit a 1,000-word essay on "What my education will do for me." Selection is based on that essay (25%) character and leadership (25%), scholarship (25%), and financial need (25%).
Financial Data The stipend is $1,000.
Duration 1 year.
Additional data Applications may be obtained only from a local unit of the American Legion Auxiliary.
Number awarded 1 or more each year.
Deadline March of each year.

[32]
ILLINOIS LEGION AUXILIARY STUDENT NURSE SCHOLARSHIP

American Legion Auxiliary
Department of Illinois
2720 East Lincoln Street
P.O. Box 1426
Bloomington, IL 61702-1426
(309) 663-9366 Fax: (309) 663-5827
E-mail: staff@ilala.org
Web: illegion.org/auxiliary/scholar.html

Summary To provide financial assistance to Illinois veterans and their descendants who are attending college in any state to prepare for a career as a nurse.
Eligibility This program is open to veterans who served during designated periods of war time and their children, grandchildren, and great-grandchildren. Applicants must be currently enrolled at a college or university in any state and studying nursing. They must be residents of Illinois or members of the American Legion Family, Department of Illinois. Along with their application, they must submit a 1,000-word essay on "What my education will do for me." Selection is based on that essay (25%) character and leadership (25%), scholarship (25%), and financial need (25%).
Financial Data The stipend is $1,000.
Duration 1 year.
Additional data Applications may be obtained only from a local unit of the American Legion Auxiliary.
Number awarded 1 or more each year.
Deadline April of each year.

[33]
ILLINOIS NATIONAL GUARD GRANT PROGRAM

Illinois Student Assistance Commission
Attn: Scholarship and Grant Services
1755 Lake Cook Road
Deerfield, IL 60015-5209
(847) 948-8550 Toll Free: (800) 899-ISAC
Fax: (847) 831-8549 TDD: (800) 526-0844
E-mail: collegezone@isac.org
Web: www.collegezone.com/studentzone/407_626.htm

Summary To provide financial assistance to current or former members of the Illinois National Guard who are interested in attending college or graduate school in the state.
Eligibility This program is open to members of the Illinois National Guard who are 1) currently active or 2) have been active for at least 5 consecutive years, have been called to federal active duty for at least 6 months, and are within 12 months after their discharge date. Applicants must also be enrolled at an Illinois public 2- or 4-year college or university and have served at least 1 full year in the Guard.
Financial Data Recipients are eligible for payment of tuition and some fees for either undergraduate or graduate study at an Illinois state-supported college or university.
Duration This assistance extends for 8 semesters or 12 quarters (or the equivalent in part-time study).
Number awarded Varies each year.
Deadline September of each year for the academic year; February of each year for spring semester, winter quarter, or spring quarter; June of each year for summer term.

[34]
ILLINOIS VETERAN GRANT PROGRAM

Illinois Student Assistance Commission
Attn: Scholarship and Grant Services
1755 Lake Cook Road
Deerfield, IL 60015-5209
(847) 948-8550 Toll Free: (800) 899-ISAC
Fax: (847) 831-8549 TDD: (800) 526-0844
E-mail: collegezone@isac.org
Web: www.collegezone.com/studentzone/407_629.htm

Summary To provide financial assistance to Illinois veterans Guard who are interested in attending college or graduate school in the state.
Eligibility This program is open to Illinois residents who served in the U.S. armed forces (including members of the Reserves and the Illinois National Guard) for at least 1 year on active duty and have been honorably discharged. The 1-year service requirement does not apply to veterans who 1) served in a foreign country in a time of hostilities in that country, 2) were medically discharged

for service-related reasons, or 3) were discharged prior to August 11, 1967. Applicants must have been Illinois residents for at least 6 months before entering service and they must have returned to Illinois within 6 months after separation from service. Current members of the Reserve Officer Training Corps are not eligible.

Financial Data This program pays all tuition and certain fees at all Illinois public colleges, universities, and community colleges.

Duration This scholarship may be used for the equivalent of up to 4 years of full-time enrollment, provided the recipient maintains the minimum GPA required by their college or university.

Additional data This is an entitlement program; once eligibility has been established, no further applications are necessary.

Number awarded Varies each year.

Deadline Applications may be submitted at any time.

[35]
IMAGINE AMERICA MILITARY AWARD PROGRAM

Career College Association
Attn: Imagine America Foundation
1101 Connecticut Avenue, N.W., Suite 901
Washington, DC 20036
(202) 336-6719   Fax: (202) 408-8102
E-mail: torianb@imagine-america.org
Web: www.imagine-america.org

Summary To provide financial assistance to veterans and military personnel interested in attending a participating career college.

Eligibility This program is open to active-duty, reservist, honorably-discharged, and retired veterans of a U.S. military service branch. Applicants must be interested in attending 1 of more than 300 participating career colleges. They must have access to tuition assistance and government-supported financial aid through the GI Bill and other programs. All applications are submitted online to the college where the student wishes to enroll. Selection is based on the likelihood of successfully completing postsecondary education and financial need.

Financial Data The stipend is $1,000. Funds must be used for payment of tuition at a participating career college.

Duration 1 year.

Additional data The Imagine America Foundation (originally known as the Career College Foundation) established this program in 2004.

Number awarded Varies each year.

Deadline June of each year.

[36]
IOWA LEGION AUXILIARY PAST PRESIDENTS SCHOLARSHIP

American Legion Auxiliary
Department of Iowa
Attn: Education Committee
720 Lyon Street
Des Moines, IA 50309-5457
(515) 282-7987   Fax: (515) 282-7583
E-mail: alasectreas@ialegion.org
Web: ialegion.org/ala/scholarships.htm

Summary To provide financial assistance for nursing education to dependents of Iowa veterans and to veterans who are members of the American Legion.

Eligibility This program is open to members of the American Legion and the American Legion Auxiliary and the children or grandchildren of veterans of World War I, World War II, Korea, Vietnam, Grenada, Lebanon, Panama, or the Persian Gulf. Applicants must reside in Iowa and be enrolled or planning to enroll in a nursing program in that state. Selection is based on character, Americanism, activities, and financial need.

Financial Data The amount of this scholarship depends on the contributions received from past unit, county, district, department, or national presidents.

Duration 1 year.

Number awarded 1 each year.

Deadline May of each year.

[37]
JOHN J. GUENTHER MERIT SCHOLARSHIP

Marine Corps Intelligence Association, Inc.
Attn: Marine Corps Intelligence Educational Foundation
P.O. Box 1028
Quantico, VA 22134-1028
E-mail: mcia@mcia-inc.org
Web: www.mcia-inc.org

Summary To provide financial assistance for college to members of the Marine Corps Intelligence Association (MCIA) and their dependent children.

Eligibility This program is open to current MCIA members, their dependent children, and their survivors. Applicants must be attending or planning to attend an accredited 4-year college or university as a full-time student. They must submit a 300-word essay on a risk that has led to a significant change in their personal or intellectual life, the most challenging obstacles they have had to overcome and what they learned from the experience, and where they envision themselves in 10 years. Selection is based on the essay, academic achievement, extracurricular activities, and work experience. Financial need is not considered.

Financial Data The stipend is $2,000.

Duration 1 year.

Additional data Membership in the MCIA is open to Marine Corps intelligence personnel, including active duty, Reserve, and retired.

Number awarded At least 1 each year.

Deadline July of each year.

[38]
JOHN KEYS KENTUCKY SONS OF THE AMERICAN LEGION SCHOLARSHIP

Sons of the American Legion
Detachment of Kentucky
c/o Kent Kelso
Independence Squadron 275
P.O. Box 18791
Erlanger, KY 41018-0791
E-mail: SAL275@fuse.net
Web: www.SAL275.com

Summary To provide financial assistance for college to members of Kentucky squadrons of the Sons of the American Legion and to veterans who are residents of Kentucky.

Eligibility This program is open to 1) members of the Sons of the American Legion who belong to a squadron in Kentucky, and 2) honorably-discharged veterans of the U.S. armed forces who are residents of Kentucky. Applicants must be enrolled (and have completed some course work) at a postsecondary institution in Kentucky or an adjoining state (Illinois, Indiana, Missouri, Ohio, Tennessee, Virginia, or West Virginia).

Financial Data The stipend varies, depending on the availability of funds; recently, they averaged $1,000. Awards are made directly to the recipient's institution.

Duration 1 year.

Additional data This program began in 1988.

Number awarded 1 or 2 each year; since the program began, it has awarded 27 scholarships.

Deadline March of each year.

[39]
JOSEPH A. McALINDEN DIVERS' SCHOLARSHIP

Navy-Marine Corps Relief Society
Attn: Education Division
875 North Randolph Street, Suite 225
Arlington, VA 22203-1757
(703) 696-4960   Fax: (703) 696-0144
E-mail: education@nmcrs.org
Web: www.nmcrs.org/education.html

Summary To provide financial assistance to current and former Navy and Marine Corps divers and their families who are interested in working on an undergraduate or graduate degree in a field related to ocean agriculture.

Eligibility This program is open to Navy and Marine Corps active-duty and retired divers and members of their families. Applicants must be enrolled full time in an undergraduate or graduate program in oceanography, ocean agriculture, aquaculture, or a related field; they may also be engaged in advanced diver training, certification, or recertification. Financial need is considered in the selection process.

Financial Data The stipend ranges from $500 to $3,000, depending on the need of the recipient.

Duration 1 year.

Number awarded 1 or more each year.

Deadline Applications may be submitted at any time.

[40]
JOSEPH P. AND HELEN T. CRIBBINS SCHOLARSHIP

Association of the United States Army
Attn: National Secretary
2425 Wilson Boulevard
Arlington, VA 22201
(703) 841-4300, ext. 655 Toll Free: (800) 336-4570, ext. 655
E-mail: ausa-info@ausa.org
Web: www3.ausa.org/webpub/depthome.nsf/byid/kcat-6fcq8s

Summary To provide financial assistance to active-duty and honorably-discharged soldiers interested in studying engineering in college.

Eligibility This program is open to 1) soldiers currently serving in the active Army, Army Reserve, or Army National Guard of any rank; and 2) honorably-discharged soldiers from any component of the total Army. Applicants must have been accepted at an accredited college or university to work on a degree in engineering or a related field (e.g., computer science, biotechnology). Along with their application, they must submit a 1-page autobiography, 2 letters of recommendation, and a transcript of high school or college grades (depending on which they are currently attending). Selection is based on academic merit and personal achievement. Financial need is not normally a selection criterion but in some cases of extreme need it may be used as a factor; the lack of financial need, however, is never a cause for non-selection.

Financial Data The stipend is $2,000; funds are sent directly to the recipient's college or university.

Duration 1 year.

Number awarded 1 or more each year.

Deadline June of each year.

[41]
KANSAS MILITARY SERVICE SCHOLARSHIPS

Kansas Board of Regents
Attn: Student Financial Assistance
1000 S.W. Jackson Street, Suite 520
Topeka, KS 66612-1368
(785) 296-3517   Fax: (785) 296-0983
E-mail: dlindeman@ksbor.org
Web: www.kansasregents.org/financial_aid/awards.html

Summary To provide financial assistance for college to residents of Kansas who have served or are still serving in the military.

Eligibility This program is open to students who graduated from high school in Kansas or received a GED credential and have been a resident of the state for at least 2 years. Applicants must have served in the U.S. armed forces in Iraq or Afghanistan, or in international waters or on foreign soil in support of military operations in Iraq or Afghanistan, for at least 90 days after September 11, 2001 or for less than 90 days because of injuries received during such service. They must still be in military service or have received an honorable discharge with orders that indicate they served after September 11, 2001 in Operations Enduring Freedom, Nobel Eagle, and/or Iraqi Freedom. Qualified veterans and military personnel may enroll at a public postsecondary institution in Kansas, including area vocational schools, area vocational/technical schools, community colleges, the municipal university, state educational institutions, or technical colleges. They are not required to demonstrate financial need.

Financial Data Qualifying students are permitted to enroll at an approved Kansas institution without payment of tuition or fees. If they receive any federal military tuition assistance, that money must be applied to their tuition and fees and they are eligible only for the remaining balance in scholarship assistance.

Duration 1 year; may be renewed for a total of 10 semesters as long as the recipient remains in good academic standing.

Additional data This program was established in 2007.

Number awarded Varies each year.

Deadline April of each year.

[42]
KANSAS TUITION WAIVER FOR PRISONERS OF WAR

Kansas Board of Regents
Attn: Student Financial Assistance
1000 S.W. Jackson Street, Suite 520
Topeka, KS 66612-1368
(785) 296-3517   Fax: (785) 296-0983
E-mail: dlindeman@ksbor.org
Web: www.kansasregents.org/financial_aid/awards.html

Summary To provide financial assistance for college to residents of Kansas who have been a prisoner of war.

Eligibility This program is open to current residents of Kansas who entered active service in the U.S. armed forces as a resident of the state. Applicants must have been declared a prisoner of war after January 1, 1960 while serving in the armed forces. They must be enrolled or planning to enroll at a public educational institution in Kansas, including area vocational/technical schools and colleges, community colleges, the state universities, and Washburn University.

Financial Data Qualifying students are permitted to enroll at an approved Kansas institution without payment of tuition or fees. They are responsible for other costs, such as books, room, and board.

Duration 1 year; may be renewed for a total of 10 semesters of undergraduate study.

Additional data This program was established in 2005.

Number awarded Varies each year.

Deadline Deadline not specified.

[43]
LDRSHIP AWARDS

Career College Association
Attn: Imagine America Foundation
1101 Connecticut Avenue, N.W., Suite 901
Washington, DC 20036
(202) 336-6743   Fax: (202) 408-8102
E-mail: jennyf@career.org
Web: www.imagine-america.org/06-LDRSHIP.asp

Summary   To provide financial assistance to veterans and military personnel who are attending a career college that is a member of the Career College Association.

Eligibility   This program is open to active-duty, reservist, honorably-discharged, and retired veterans of a U.S. military service branch. Applicants must currently be attending 1 of more than 300 participating career colleges. They must have maintained a GPA of 3.5 or higher and an attendance record of at least 95%. Along with their application, they must submit a recommendation from a faculty member or administrator at their college and a copy of their current college transcript.

Financial Data   The stipend is $5,000. Funds must be used for payment of tuition at a participating career college.

Duration   1 year.

Additional data   The Imagine America Foundation (originally known as the Career College Foundation) established this program in 2004. It stands for Loyalty, Duty, Respect, Selfless Service, Honor, Integrity and Personal Courage. Sponsorship is provided by Ambassador College Bookstores, Military.com, and Lockheed Martin.

Number awarded   Varies each year; recently, 4 of these scholarships were granted.

Deadline   April of each year.

[44]
LILLIAN CAMPBELL MEDICAL SCHOLARSHIP

Wisconsin Veterans of Foreign Wars
214 North Hamilton Street
P.O. Box 1623
Madison, WI 53701-1623
(608) 255-6655   Fax: (608) 255-0652
E-mail: qm@wi.vfwwebmail.com
Web: vfwwebcom.org/wisconsin

Summary   To provide financial assistance to students working on a degree in a medical field in Wisconsin who served in the military or are related to a person who did.

Eligibility   This program is open to students who have completed at least 1 year of study in Wisconsin in a program in nursing, pharmacy, physician assistant, medical or surgical technology, physical or occupational therapy, dental assisting, radiology, or other related medical profession. Applicants or a member of their immediate family (parent, sibling, child, spouse, or grandparent) must have served in the military. They must have a high school diploma or GED but may be of any age. Along with their application, they must submit a 200-word essay on their goals for studying this medical profession. Financial need is considered in the selection process.

Financial Data   The stipend is $1,000.

Duration   1 year.

Number awarded   1 or more each year.

Deadline   April of each year.

[45]
LUCILLE PARRISH WARD VETERAN'S AWARD

National Federation of Music Clubs
1646 Smith Valley Road
Greenwood, IN 46142
(317) 882-4003   Fax: (317) 882-4019
E-mail: info@nfmc-music.org
Web: www.nfmc-music.org

Summary   To provide financial assistance to undergraduate student members of the National Federation of Music Clubs (NFMC) whose careers have been delayed or interrupted as a result of their service in the U.S. armed forces.

Eligibility   This program is open to undergraduate students who are majoring in music and whose musical careers were interrupted by service in the armed forces. Veterans who served overseas receive preference. Student membership in the federation and U.S. citizenship are required. Selection is based on worthiness, character, background, musical talent, potential ability, and financial need.

Financial Data   The stipend is $1,600.

Duration   1 year; may be renewed if the recipient maintains a GPA of 3.0 or higher.

Number awarded   1 each year.

Deadline   February of each year.

[46]
MAJOR GENERAL DUANE L. "DUKE" CORNING MEMORIAL SCHOLARSHIP

South Dakota National Guard Enlisted Association
c/o Bruce Anderson, Executive Director
25790 Country Lane
Renner, SD 57055
(605) 988-5414   E-mail: bcres@sio.midco.net
Web: www.sdngea.com/scholarship.html

Summary   To provide financial assistance to current and retired members of the South Dakota National Guard Enlisted Association (SDNGEA), the National Guard Association of South Dakota (NGASD), and their dependents who are interested in attending college in any state.

Eligibility   This program is open to current and retired members of the SDNGEA and the NGASD and the dependents of current and retired members of those associations. Applicants must be graduating high school seniors or full-time undergraduate students at a college or university in any state. They must submit a 300-page autobiography that includes their experiences to date and their hopes and plans for the future. Selection is based on the essay; awards, honors, and offices in high school, college, or trade school; GPA and ACT/SAT scores; letters of recommendation; and extracurricular and community activities and honors.

Financial Data   The stipend is $1,000.

Duration   1 year; nonrenewable.

Number awarded   1 each year.

Deadline   March of each year.

[47]
MARIA C. JACKSON/GENERAL GEORGE A. WHITE SCHOLARSHIP

Oregon Student Assistance Commission
Attn: Grants and Scholarships Division
1500 Valley River Drive, Suite 100
Eugene, OR 97401-2146
(541) 687-7395   Toll Free: (800) 452-8807, ext. 7395
Fax: (541) 687-7414   TDD: (800) 735-2900
E-mail: awardinfo@osac.state.or.us
Web: www.osac.state.or.us/osac_programs.html

Summary   To provide financial assistance to veterans and children of veterans and military personnel in Oregon who are interested in attending college or graduate school in the state.

Eligibility This program is open to residents of Oregon who served, or whose parents are serving or have served, in the U.S. armed forces. Applicants or their parents must have resided in Oregon at the time of enlistment. They must be enrolled or planning to enrolled in a college or graduate school in the state. College and university undergraduates must have a GPA of 3.75 or higher, but there is no minimum GPA requirement for graduate students or those attending a technical school. Selection is based on scholastic ability and financial need.

Financial Data A stipend is awarded (amount not specified).

Number awarded Varies each year.

Deadline February of each year.

[48]
MARINE CORPS LEAGUE SCHOLARSHIPS

Marine Corps League
Attn: National Executive Director
P.O. Box 3070
Merrifield, VA 22116-3070
(703) 207-9588　　　　Toll Free: (800) MCL-1775
Fax: (703) 207-0047　　　E-mail: mcl@mcleague.org
Web: www.mcleague.org

Summary To provide college aid to students whose parents served in the Marines and to members of the Marine Corps League or Marine Corps League Auxiliary.

Eligibility This program is open to 1) children of Marines who lost their lives in the line of duty; 2) spouses, children, grandchildren, great-grandchildren, and stepchildren of active Marine Corps League and/or Auxiliary members; and 3) members of the Marine Corps League and/or Marine Corps League Auxiliary who are honorably discharged and in need of rehabilitation training not provided by government programs. Applicants must be seeking further education and training as a full-time student and be recommended by the commandant of an active chartered detachment of the Marine Corps League or the president of an active chartered unit of the Auxiliary. They must have a GPA of 3.0 or higher. Financial need is not considered in the selection process.

Financial Data A stipend is awarded (amount not specified). Funds are paid directly to the recipient.

Duration 1 year; may be renewed up to 3 additional years (all renewals must complete an application and attach a transcript from the college or university).

Number awarded Varies, depending upon the amount of funds available each year.

Deadline June of each year.

[49]
MARINE CORPS SGT. JEANNETTE L. WINTERS MEMORIAL SCHOLARSHIP

Armed Forces Communications and Electronics Association
Attn: AFCEA Educational Foundation
4400 Fair Lakes Court
Fairfax, VA 22033-3899
(703) 631-6149　　　　Toll Free: (800) 336-4583, ext. 6149
Fax: (703) 631-4693　　　E-mail: scholarship@afcea.org
Web: www.afcea.org

Summary To provide funding to members and veterans of the U.S. Marine Corps (USMC) who are majoring in specified fields in college.

Eligibility This program is open to USMC personnel currently on active duty, in the Reserves, or honorably-discharged veterans who are enrolled full or part time in an accredited college or university in the United States. Applicants must be U.S. citizens, be of good moral character, have demonstrated academic excellence, be motivated to complete a college education, and be working on a bachelor's degree in engineering (aerospace, chemical, electrical, or systems), electronics, mathematics, physics, science or mathematics education, management information

systems, technology management, computer science, or other field directly related to the support of U.S. intelligence enterprises or national security. They must provide a copy of Discharge Form DD214, Certificate of Service, or facsimile of their current Department of Defense Identification Card.

Financial Data The stipend is $2,000.

Duration 1 year.

Additional data This program was established in 2002 to honor a Marine who died when her KC-130 aircraft crashed in Pakistan.

Number awarded 1 each year.

Deadline August of each year.

[50]
MARYLAND SCHOLARSHIPS FOR VETERANS OF THE AFGHANISTAN AND IRAQ CONFLICTS

Maryland Higher Education Commission
Attn: Office of Student Financial Assistance
839 Bestgate Road, Suite 400
Annapolis, MD 21401-3013
(410) 260-4563　　　　Toll Free: (800) 974-1024, ext. 4563
Fax: (410) 260-3200　　　TDD: (800) 735-2258
E-mail: lasplin@mhec.state.md.us
Web: www.mhec.state.md.us

Summary To provide financial assistance for college to residents of Maryland who served in the armed forces in Afghanistan or Iraq and their children and spouses.

Eligibility This program is open to Maryland residents who are 1) a veteran who served at least 60 days in Afghanistan on or after October 24, 2001 or in Iraq on or after March 19, 2003; 2) an active-duty member of the armed forces who served at least 60 days in Afghanistan or Iraq on or after those dates; 3) a member of a Reserve component of the armed forces or the Maryland National Guard who was activated as a result of the Afghanistan or Iraq conflicts and served at least 60 days; and 4) the children and spouses of such veterans, active-duty armed forces personnel, or members of Reserve forces or Maryland National Guard. Applicants must be enrolled or accepted for enrollment in a regular undergraduate program at an eligible Maryland institution. In the selection process, veterans are given priority over dependent children and spouses.

Financial Data The stipend is equal to 50% of the annual tuition, mandatory fees, and room and board of a resident undergraduate at a 4-year public institution within the University System of Maryland, currently capped at $9,026 per year. The total amount of all state awards may not exceed the cost of attendance as determined by the school's financial aid office or $19,000, whichever is less.

Duration 1 year; may be renewed for an additional 4 years of full-time study or 7 years of part-time study, provided the recipient remains enrolled in an eligible program with a GPA of 2.5 or higher.

Additional data This program is scheduled to expire in 2016.

Number awarded Varies each year.

Deadline February of each year.

[51]
MASSACHUSETTS VETERANS TUITION WAIVER PROGRAM

Massachusetts Office of Student Financial Assistance
454 Broadway, Suite 200
Revere, MA 02151
(617) 727-9420　　　　　　Fax: (617) 727-0667
E-mail: osfa@osfa.mass.edu
Web: www.osfa.mass.edu/default.asp?page=categoricalwaiver

Summary To provide financial assistance for college to Massachusetts residents who are veterans.

Eligibility Applicants for these scholarships must have been permanent legal residents of Massachusetts for at least 1 year and veterans who served actively during the Spanish-American War, World War I, World War II, Korea, Vietnam, the Lebanese peace keeping force, the Grenada rescue mission, the Panamanian intervention force, the Persian Gulf, or Operation Restore Hope in Somalia. They may not be in default on any federal student loan.

Financial Data Eligible veterans are exempt from any tuition payments for an undergraduate degree or certificate program at public colleges or universities in Massachusetts.

Duration Up to 4 academic years, for a total of 130 semester hours.

Additional data Recipients may enroll either part or full time in a Massachusetts publicly-supported institution.

Number awarded Varies each year.

Deadline Deadline not specified.

[52]
MG EUGENE C. RENZI, USA (RET.)/MANTECH INTERNATIONAL CORPORATION TEACHER'S SCHOLARSHIP

Armed Forces Communications and Electronics Association
Attn: AFCEA Educational Foundation
4400 Fair Lakes Court
Fairfax, VA 22033-3899
(703) 631-6149   Toll Free: (800) 336-4583, ext. 6149
Fax: (703) 631-4693   E-mail: scholarship@afcea.org
Web: www.afcea.org

Summary To provide financial assistance to undergraduate and graduate students (especially veterans) who are preparing for a career as a teacher of science and mathematics.

Eligibility This program is open to full-time juniors, seniors, and graduate students at accredited colleges and universities in the United States. Applicants must be U.S. citizens preparing for a career as a teacher of science, mathematics, or information technology at a middle or secondary school. They must have a GPA of 3.0 or higher. In the selection process, first consideration is given to wounded or disabled veterans, then to honorably discharged veterans. Financial need is not considered.

Financial Data The stipend is $2,500.

Duration 1 year.

Additional data This program was established in 2008 with support from ManTech International Corporation.

Number awarded 1 each year.

Deadline May of each year.

[53]
MIKE NASH MEMORIAL SCHOLARSHIP FUND

Vietnam Veterans of America
Attn: Mike Nash Scholarship Program
8719 Colesville Road, Suite 100
Silver Spring, MD 20910-3919
(301) 585-4000   Toll Free: (800) VVA-1316
Fax: (301) 585-0519   E-mail: finance@vva.org
Web: www.vva.org/scholarship.html

Summary To provide financial assistance for college to members of Vietnam Veterans of America (VVA), their families, and the families of other Vietnam veterans.

Eligibility This program is open to 1) members of VVA; 2) the spouses, children, stepchildren, and grandchildren of VVA members; and 3) the spouses, children, stepchildren, and grandchildren of MIA, KIA, or deceased Vietnam veterans. Applicants must be enrolled or planning to enroll at least half time at an accredited college, university, or technical institution. Along with their application, they must submit high school or college transcripts; SAT, ACT, or other recognized test scores; a letter of recommendation from a VVA state council, chapter, or national; 2 letters of recommendation; a letter describing their current educational goals and objectives, individual accomplishments, and any other personal

information that may assist in the selection process; and documentation of financial need.

Financial Data The stipend is $1,000 per year.

Duration 1 year; may be renewed for up to 3 additional years.

Additional data This program was established in 1991 and given its current name in 1997.

Number awarded Varies each year; recently, 9 of these scholarships were awarded.

Deadline May of each year.

[54]
MILDRED R. KNOLES SCHOLARSHIPS

American Legion Auxiliary
Department of Illinois
2720 East Lincoln Street
P.O. Box 1426
Bloomington, IL 61702-1426
(309) 663-9366   Fax: (309) 663-5827
E-mail: staff@ilala.org
Web: illegion.org/auxiliary/scholar.html

Summary To provide financial assistance to Illinois veterans and their descendants who are attending college in any state.

Eligibility This program is open to veterans who served during designated periods of war time and their children, grandchildren, and great-grandchildren. Applicants must be currently enrolled at a college or university in any state and studying any field except nursing. They must be residents of Illinois or members of the American Legion Family, Department of Illinois. Along with their application, they must submit a 1,000-word essay on "What my education will do for me." Selection is based on that essay (25%) character and leadership (25%), scholarship (25%), and financial need (25%).

Financial Data Stipends are $1,200 or $800.

Duration 1 year.

Additional data Applications may be obtained only from a local unit of the American Legion Auxiliary.

Number awarded Varies; each year 1 scholarship at $1,200 and several at $800 are awarded.

Deadline March of each year.

[55]
MILITARY EDUCATION SCHOLARSHIP PROGRAM

VA Mortgage Center.com
2101 Chapel Plaza Court, Suite 107
Columbia, MO 65203
(573) 876-2729   Toll Free: (800) 405-6682
Web: www.vamortgagecenter.com/scholarships.html

Summary To provide financial assistance for college to students who have a tie to the military.

Eligibility This program is open to 1) current and prospective ROTC program students; 2) active-duty military personnel with plans to attend college; 3) honorably-discharged veterans of the U.S. military; and 4) children of veterans or active-duty military. Applicants must be attending or planning to attend college. Selection is based primarily on an essay.

Financial Data The stipend is $1,500.

Duration 1 year.

Additional data This program was established in 2007.

Number awarded 10 each year: 5 each term.

Deadline April or October of each year.

[56]
MILITARY INTELLIGENCE CORPS ASSOCIATION SCHOLARSHIPS

Military Intelligence Corps Association
Attn: Scholarship Chair
P.O. Box 13020
Fort Huachuca, AZ 85670-3020
(520) 533-1174
Web: micorps.org

Summary To provide financial assistance for college to members of the Military Intelligence Corps Association (MICA) and their immediate family.

Eligibility This program is open to active-duty, Reserve, National Guard, and retired military intelligence soldiers who are MICA members and to their immediate family (spouses, children, or other relatives living with and supported by the MICA member). Applicants must be attending or accepted for attendance at an accredited college, university, vocational school, or technical institution. Along with their application, they must submit a 1-page essay on their reasons for applying for the scholarship, including their educational plans, ambitions, goals, and personal attributes or experiences they feel will enable them to reach their goals. Financial need is not considered in the selection process.

Financial Data Stipend amounts vary depending on the availability of funds and the number of qualified applicants, but are awarded in increments of $500 and $1,000. Funds are to be used for tuition, books, and classroom fees; support is not provided for housing, board, travel, or administrative purposes.

Duration 1 year; recipients may reapply.

Number awarded Varies each year.

Deadline May of each year.

[57]
MILITARY NONRESIDENT TUITION WAIVER FOR MEMBERS, SPOUSES OR CHILDREN WHO REMAIN CONTINUOUSLY ENROLLED IN HIGHER EDUCATION IN TEXAS

Texas Higher Education Coordinating Board
Attn: Grants and Special Programs
1200 East Anderson Lane
P.O. Box 12788, Capitol Station
Austin, TX 78711-2788
(512) 427-6340   Toll Free: (800) 242-3062
Fax: (512) 427-6127   E-mail: grantinfo@thecb.state.tx.us
Web: www.collegeforalltexans.com

Summary To waive nonresident tuition at Texas public colleges and universities for members of the armed forces and their families who are no longer in the military.

Eligibility Eligible for these waivers are members of the U.S. armed forces, commissioned officers of the Public Health Service, their spouses, and their children. Applicants must have previously been eligible to pay tuition at the resident rate while enrolled in a degree or certificate program at a Texas public college or university. They must remain continuously enrolled in the same degree or certificate program in subsequent terms or semesters.

Financial Data The student's eligibility to pay tuition and fees at the rate provided for Texas students does not terminate because the member, spouse, or parent is no longer in the service.

Duration 1 year.

Additional data This program became effective in September 2003.

Number awarded Varies each year.

Deadline Deadline not specified.

[58]
MILITARY ORDER OF THE PURPLE HEART SCHOLARSHIP PROGRAM

Military Order of the Purple Heart
Attn: Scholarships
5413-B Backlick Road
Springfield, VA 22151-3960
(703) 642-5360   Toll Free: (888) 668-1656
Fax: (703) 642-2054   E-mail: scholarship@purpleheart.org
Web: www.purpleheart.org/Scholarships/Default.aspx

Summary To provide financial assistance for college or graduate school to members of the Military Order of the Purple Heart (MOPH) and their families.

Eligibility This program is open to 1) members of the MOPH; 2) direct descendants (children, stepchildren, adopted children, grandchildren, and great-grandchildren) of veterans who are MOPH members or who were members at the time of death; 3) direct descendants of veterans killed in action or who died of wounds but did not have the opportunity to join the order; and 4) spouses and widows of MOPH members, veterans killed in action, and veterans who died of wounds. Applicants must be graduating seniors or graduates of an accredited high school who are enrolled or accepted for enrollment in a full-time program of study in a college, trade school, or graduate school. They must have a GPA of 2.75 or higher. U.S. citizenship is required. Along with their application, they must submit an essay of 200 to 300 words on "What it means to be an American." Financial need is not considered in the selection process.

Financial Data The stipend is $3,000 per year.

Duration 1 year; may be renewed up to 2 additional years.

Additional data Membership in MOPH is open to all veterans who received a Purple Heart Medal and were discharged under conditions other than dishonorable. A processing fee of $15 is required.

Number awarded Varies each year; recently, 50 of these scholarships were awarded.

Deadline February of each year.

[59]
MINNESOTA G.I. BILL PROGRAM

Minnesota Office of Higher Education
Attn: Manager of State Financial Aid Programs
1450 Energy Park Drive, Suite 350
St. Paul, MN 55108-5227
(651) 642-0567   Toll Free: (800) 657-3866
Fax: (651) 642-0675   TDD: (800) 627-3529
E-mail: Ginny.Dodds@state.mn.us
Web: www.ohe.state.mn.us

Summary To provide financial assistance for college or graduate school in the state to residents of Minnesota who served in the military after September 11, 2001 and the families of deceased or disabled military personnel.

Eligibility This program is open to residents of Minnesota enrolled at colleges and universities in the state as undergraduate or graduate students. Applicants must be 1) a veteran who is serving or has served honorably in a branch of the U.S. armed forces at any time on or after September 11, 2001; 2) a non-veteran who has served honorably for a total of 5 years or more cumulatively as a member of the Minnesota National Guard or other active or Reserve component of the U.S. armed forces, and any part of that service occurred on or after September 11, 2001; or 3) a surviving child or spouse of a person who has served in the military at any time on or after September 11, 2001 and who has died or has a total and permanent disability as a result of that military service. Financial need is also considered in the selection process.

Financial Data The stipend is $1,000 per semester for full-time study or $500 per semester for part-time study.

Duration 1 year; may be renewed up to 4 additional years, provided the recipient continues to make satisfactory academic progress.

Additional data This program was established by the Minnesota Legislature in 2007.

Number awarded Varies each year.

Deadline Deadline not specified.

[60]
MONTANA HONORABLY DISCHARGED VETERAN WAIVER

Montana Guaranteed Student Loan Program
2500 Broadway
P.O. Box 203101
Helena, MT 59620-3101
(406) 444-0638   Toll Free: (800) 537-7508
Fax: (406) 444-1869 E-mail: scholarships@mgslp.state.mt.us
Web: www.mgslp.state.mt.us

Summary To provide financial assistance for undergraduate or graduate studies to selected Montana veterans.

Eligibility This program is open to honorably-discharged veterans who served with the U.S. armed forces and who are residents of Montana. Only veterans who at some time qualified for U.S. Department of Veterans Affairs (VA) educational benefits, but who are no longer eligible or have exhausted their benefits, are entitled to this waiver. Veterans who served any time prior to May 8, 1975 are eligible to work on undergraduate or graduate degrees. Veterans whose service began after May 7, 1975 are eligible only to work on their first undergraduate degree. They must have received an Armed Forces Expeditionary Medal for service in Lebanon, Grenada, or Panama; served in a combat theater in the Persian Gulf between August 2, 1990 and April 11, 1991 and received the Southwest Asia Service Medal; were awarded the Kosovo Campaign Medal; or served in a combat theater in Afghanistan or Iraq after September 11, 2001 and received the Global War on Terrorism Expeditionary Medal, the Afghanistan Campaign Medal, or the Iraq Campaign Medal. Financial need must be demonstrated.

Financial Data Veterans eligible for this benefit are entitled to attend any unit of the Montana University System without payment of registration or incidental fees.

Duration Students are eligible for continued fee waiver as long as they make reasonable academic progress as full-time students.

Number awarded Varies each year.

Deadline Deadline not specified.

[61]
MONTGOMERY GI BILL (ACTIVE DUTY)

Department of Veterans Affairs
Attn: Veterans Benefits Administration
810 Vermont Avenue, N.W.
Washington, DC 20420
(202) 418-4343   Toll Free: (888) GI-BILL1
Web: www.gibill.va.gov/GI_Bill_Info/benefits.htm

Summary To provide financial assistance for college, graduate school, and other types of postsecondary schools to new enlistees in any of the armed forces after they have completed their service obligation.

Eligibility This program is open to veterans who received an honorable discharge and have a high school diploma, a GED, or, in some cases, up to 12 hours of college credit; veterans who already have a bachelor's degree are eligible to work on a master's degree or higher. Applicants must also meet the requirements of 1 of the following categories: 1) entered active duty for the first time after June 30, 1985, had military pay reduced by $100 per month for the first 12 months, and continuously served for 3 years, or 2 years if that was their original enlistment, or 2 years if they entered Selected Reserve within a year of leaving active duty and served 4 years (the 2 by 4 program); 2) entered active duty before January 1, 1977, had remaining entitlement under the Vietnam Era GI Bill on December 31, 1989, served at least 1 day between October 19, 1984 and June 30, 1985, and stayed on active duty through June 30, 1988 (or June 30, 1987 if they entered Selected Reserve within 1 year of leaving active duty and served 4 years); 3) on active duty on September 30, 1990 and separated involuntarily after February 2, 1991, involuntarily separated on or after November 30, 1993, or voluntarily separated under either the Voluntary Separation Incentive (VSI) or Special Separation Benefit (SSB) program, and before separation had military pay reduced by $1,200; or 4) on active duty on October 9, 1996, had money remaining in an account from the Veterans Educational Assistance Program (VEAP), elected Montgomery GI Bill (MGIB) by October 9, 1997, and paid $1,200. Certain National Guard members may also qualify under category 4 if they served on full-time active duty between July 1, 1985 and November 28, 1989, elected MGIB between October 9, 1996 and July 8, 1997, and paid $1,200. Following completion of their service obligation, participants may enroll in colleges or universities for associate, bachelor, or graduate degrees; in courses leading to a certificate or diploma from business, technical, or vocational schools; for apprenticeships or on-the-job training programs; in correspondence courses; in flight training; for preparatory courses necessary for admission to a college or graduate school; for licensing and certification tests approved for veterans; or in state-approved teacher certification programs. Veterans who wish to enroll in certain high-cost technology programs (life science, physical science, engineering, mathematics, engineering and science technology, computer specialties, and engineering, science, and computer management) may be eligible for an accelerated payment.

Financial Data For veterans in categories 1, 3, and 4 who served on active duty for 3 years or more, the current monthly stipend for college or university work is $1,368 for full-time study, $1,026 for three-quarter time study, $684 for half-time study, or $342 for quarter-time study or less; for apprenticeship and on-the-job training, the monthly stipend is $1,026 for the first 6 months, $752.40 for the second 6 months, and $478.80 for the remainder of the program. For enlistees whose initial active-duty obligation was less than 3 years, the current monthly stipend for college or university work is $1,111 for full-time study, $833.25 for three-quarter time study, $550.50 for half-time study, or $275.75 for quarter-time study or less; for apprenticeship and on-the-job training, the monthly stipend is $833.25 for the first 6 months, $611.05 for the second 6 months, and $388.85 for the remainder of the program. For veterans in category 2 with remaining eligibility, the current monthly stipend for institutional study full time is $1,556 for no dependents, $1,592 with 1 dependent, $1,623 with 2 dependents, and $16 for each additional dependent; for three-quarter time study, the monthly stipend is $1,167.50 for no dependents, $1,194 with 1 dependent, $1,217.50 with 2 dependents, and $12 for each additional dependent; for half-time study, the monthly stipend is $778 for no dependents, $796 with 1 dependent, $811.50 with 2 dependents, and $8.50 for each additional dependent. For those veterans pursuing an apprenticeship or on-the-job training, the current monthly stipend for the first 6 months is $1,128.75 for no dependents, $1,141.13 with 1 dependent, $1,152 with 2 dependents, and $5.25 for each additional dependent; for the second 6 months, the current monthly stipend is $808.78 for no dependents, $818.13 with 1 dependent, $825.83 with 2 dependents, and $3.85 for each additional dependent; for the third 6 months, the current monthly stipend is $502.60 for no dependents, $508.73 with 1 dependent, $513.45 with 2 dependents, and $2.45 for each additional dependent; for the remainder of the training period, the current monthly stipend is $490.70 for no dependents, $496.48 with 1 dependent, $501.73 with 2 dependents, and $2.45 for each additional dependent. Other rates apply for less than half-time study, cooperative education, correspondence courses, and flight training. Veterans who qualify for the accelerated payment and whose entitlement does not cover 60% of tuition and fees receive an additional lump sum payment to make up the difference between their entitlement and 60% of tuition and fees.

Duration 36 months; active-duty servicemembers must utilize the funds within 10 years of leaving the armed services; Reservists may draw on their funds while still serving.

Additional data Further information is available from local armed forces recruiters. This was the basic VA education program, referred to as Chapter 30, until the passage of the Post-9/11 GI Bill in 2009. Veterans who have remaining benefits available from this program may utilize those or transfer to the new program.

Number awarded Varies each year.

Deadline Deadline not specified.

[62]
NATIONAL 4TH INFANTRY (IVY) DIVISION ASSOCIATION SCHOLARSHIP

National 4th Infantry (IVY) Division Association
c/o Don Kelby, Executive Director
P.O. Box 1914
St. Peters, MO 63376-0035
(314) 606-1969   E-mail: 4thidaed@swbell.net
Web: www.4thinfantry.org

Summary To provide financial assistance for college to members of the National 4th Infantry (IVY) Division Association and their families.

Eligibility This program is open to association members in good standing and all blood relatives of active association members in good standing. Recipients are chosen by lottery.

Financial Data The stipend is $1,000.

Duration 1 year; may be renewed.

Additional data The trust fund from which these scholarships are awarded was created by the officers and enlisted men of the 4th Infantry Division as a living memorial to the men of the division who died in Vietnam. Originally, it was only open to children of members of the division who died in the line of duty while serving in Vietnam between August 1, 1966 and December 31, 1977. When all those eligible had completed college, it adopted its current requirements.

Number awarded 1 or more each year.

Deadline June of each year.

[63]
NAVAL HELICOPTER ASSOCIATION UNDERGRADUATE SCHOLARSHIPS

Naval Helicopter Association
Attn: Scholarship Fund
P.O. Box 180578
Coronado, CA 92178-0578
(619) 435-7139   Fax: (619) 435-7354
E-mail: info@nhascholarship.org
Web: www.nhascholarship.org/nhascholarshipfund/index.html

Summary To provide financial assistance for college to students who have an affiliation with the rotary wing activities of the sea services.

Eligibility This program is open to high school seniors and current undergraduates who are 1) children, grandchildren, or spouses of current or former Navy, Marine Corps, or Coast Guard rotary wing aviators or aircrewmen; 2) individuals who are serving or have served in maintenance or support billets in rotary wing squadrons or wings and their spouses and children. Applicants must provide information on their rotary wing affiliation and a personal statement on their educational plans and future goals. Selection is based on that statement, academic proficiency, scho-

lastic achievements and awards, extracurricular activities, employment history, and letters of recommendation.

Financial Data Stipends are $3,000, $2,500, or $2,000.

Duration 1 year.

Additional data This program includes the DPA Thousand Points of Light Award (sponsored by D.P. Associates Inc. and L3 Communications), the Sergei Sikorsky Scholarship, the Ream Memorial Scholarship, and a scholarship sponsored by Raytheon Corporation.

Number awarded Varies each year; recently, 9 of these scholarships were awarded: 3 at $3,000, 1 at $2,500, and 5 at $2,000.

Deadline January of each year.

[64]
NAVY COLLEGE FUND

U.S. Navy
Attn: Navy Personnel Command (PERS-675)
5720 Integrity Drive
Millington, TN 38055-6040
(901) 874-4258   Toll Free: (866) U-ASK-NPC
Fax: (901) 874-2052   E-mail: MILL_MGIB@navy.mil
Web: www.navyjobs.com/benefits/education/earnmoney

Summary To provide financial assistance for college to Navy enlistees during and after they have completed their service obligation.

Eligibility Eligible for this program are high school seniors and graduates between 17 and 35 years of age who enlist in the Navy for 3 to 4 years of active duty. They must score 50 or above on the ASVAB and also enroll in the Montgomery GI Bill. Sailors currently on active duty in selected Navy ratings with critical personnel shortages are also eligible. Applicants must be interested in attending a Department of Veterans Affairs-approved postsecondary educational institution on a full-time basis after completion of their service obligation.

Financial Data The Navy College Fund provides, in addition to the Montgomery GI Bill, up to $15,000 for college tuition and expenses.

Duration Enlistees may begin using this educational benefit on a part-time basis after 2 years of continuous active duty. Funds must be utilized within 10 years of leaving the Navy.

Number awarded Varies each year.

Deadline Applications may be submitted at any time.

[65]
NEW MEXICO VIETNAM VETERANS SCHOLARSHIPS

New Mexico Department of Veterans' Services
Attn: Benefits Division
407 Galisteo Street, Room 142
Santa Fe, NM 87504
(505) 827-6374   Toll Free: (866) 433-VETS
Fax: (505) 827-6372   E-mail: alan.martinez@state.nm.us
Web: www.dvs.state.nm.us/benefits.html

Summary To provide financial assistance to Vietnam veterans in New Mexico who are interested in working on an undergraduate or master's degree at a public college in the state.

Eligibility This program is open to Vietnam veterans who have been residents of New Mexico for at least 10 years. Applicants must have been honorably discharged and have been awarded the Vietnam Service Medal or the Vietnam Campaign Medal. They must be planning to attend a state-supported college, university, or community college in New Mexico to work on an undergraduate or master's degree. Awards are granted on a first-come, first-served basis.

Financial Data The scholarships provide full payment of tuition and purchase of required books at any state-funded postsecondary institution in New Mexico.

Duration 1 year.

Deadline Deadline not specified.

[66]
NEW YORK STATE MILITARY SERVICE RECOGNITION SCHOLARSHIPS

New York State Higher Education Services Corporation
Attn: Student Information
99 Washington Avenue
Albany, NY 12255
(518) 473-1574   Toll Free: (888) NYS-HESC
Fax: (518) 473-3749   TDD: (800) 445-5234
E-mail: webmail@hesc.com
Web: www.hesc.com

Summary To provide financial assistance to disabled veterans and the family members of deceased or disabled veterans who are residents of New York and interested in attending college in the state.

Eligibility This program is open to New York residents who served in the armed forces of the United States or state organized militia at any time on or after August 2, 1990 and became severely and permanently disabled as a result of injury or illness suffered or incurred in a combat theater or combat zone or during military training operations in preparation for duty in a combat theater or combat zone of operations. Also eligible are the children, spouses, or financial dependents of members of the armed forces of the United States or state organized militia who at any time after August 2, 1990 1) died, became severely and permanently disabled as a result of injury or illness suffered or incurred, or are classified as missing in action in a combat theater or combat zone of operations, 2) died as a result of injuries incurred in those designated areas, or 3) died or became severely and permanently disabled as a result of injury or illness suffered or incurred during military training operations in preparation for duty in a combat theater or combat zone of operations. Applicants must be attending or accepted at an approved program of study as full-time undergraduates at a public college or university or private institution in New York.

Financial Data At public colleges and universities, this program provides payment of actual tuition and mandatory educational fees; actual room and board charged to students living on campus or an allowance for room and board for commuter students; and allowances for books, supplies, and transportation. At private institutions, the award is equal to the amount charged at the State University of New York (SUNY) for 4-year tuition and average mandatory fees (or the student's actual tuition and fees, whichever is less) plus allowances for room, board, books, supplies, and transportation.

Duration This program is available for 4 years of full-time undergraduate study (or 5 years in an approved 5-year bachelor's degree program).

Number awarded Varies each year.

Deadline April of each year.

[67]
NEW YORK VETERANS TUITION AWARDS

New York State Higher Education Services Corporation
Attn: Student Information
99 Washington Avenue
Albany, NY 12255
(518) 473-1574   Toll Free: (888) NYS-HESC
Fax: (518) 473-3749   TDD: (800) 445-5234
E-mail: webmail@hesc.com
Web: www.hesc.com

Summary To provide tuition assistance to eligible veterans enrolled in an undergraduate or graduate program in New York.

Eligibility This program is open to veterans who served in the U.S. armed forces in 1) Indochina between February 28, 1961 and May 7, 1975; 2) hostilities that occurred after February 28, 1961 as evidenced by receipt of an Armed Forces Expeditionary Medal, Navy Expeditionary Medal, or Marine Corps Expeditionary Medal; 3) the Persian Gulf on or after August 2, 1990; or 4) Afghanistan on or after September 11, 2001. Applicants must have been discharged from the service under honorable conditions, must be a New York resident, must be a U.S. citizen or eligible non-citizen, must be enrolled full or part time at an undergraduate or graduate degree-granting institution in New York State or in an approved vocational training program in the state, must be charged at least $200 tuition per year, and must apply for a New York Tuition Assistance Program (TAP) award.

Financial Data For full-time study, the maximum stipend is 98% of tuition or $4,895.10, whichever is less. For part-time study, the stipend is based on the number of credits certified and the student's actual part-time tuition.

Duration For undergraduate study, up to 8 semesters, or up to 10 semesters for a program requiring 5 years for completion; for graduate study, up to 6 semesters; for vocational programs, up to 4 semesters. Award limits are based on full-time study or equivalent part-time study.

Additional data If a TAP award is also received, the combined academic year award cannot exceed tuition costs. If it does, the TAP award will be reduced accordingly.

Number awarded Varies each year.

Deadline April of each year.

[68]
NGAM SCHOLARSHIPS

National Guard Association of Maryland
Attn: Scholarship Committee
P.O. Box 16675
Baltimore, MD 21221-0675
(410) 557-2606   Toll Free: (800) 844-1394
Fax: (410) 893-7529   E-mail: executivedirector@ngam.net
Web: www.ngam.net/NGAM-BenefitsScholarships.htm

Summary To provide financial assistance to current and former members of the Maryland National Guard and their dependents who are interested in attending college in any state.

Eligibility This program is open to active and retired members of the Maryland National Guard and their spouses, sons, and daughters. Applicants must be enrolled or planning to enroll in an accredited college, university, or vocational/technical school in any state on either a part-time or full-time basis. They must submit a resume in which they outline their academic background, activities in which they have participated, and honors they have received; 3 letters of recommendation; the name of the college; and information on financial need.

Financial Data The stipend is $1,000. Funds may be used for tuition, fees, and books.

Duration 1 year; recipients may reapply.

Number awarded Varies each year; recently, 6 of these scholarships were awarded.

Deadline March of each year.

[69]
NGANH SCHOLARSHIPS

National Guard Association of New Hampshire
Attn: Scholarship Committee
1 Minuteman Way
Concord, NH 03301
(603) 540-9608   E-mail: info@nganh.org
Web: www.nganh.org

Summary To provide financial assistance to members of the National Guard Association of New Hampshire and their dependents who are interested in attending college in any state.

Eligibility This program is open to current members of the National Guard Association of New Hampshire (officer, enlisted, or retired) and their dependents. Applicants must be attending or planning to attend an accredited college or university in any state. Along with their application, they must submit a 1-page essay on a topic that changes annually; recently, they were asked to give their thoughts on whether or not United States efforts to support and stabilize democratic governments in Afghanistan and Iraq will lead to greater stability in the Southwest Asian region.

Financial Data The stipend is $1,000.

Duration 1 year.

Number awarded 1 each year.

Deadline April of each year.

[70]
NGASC SCHOLARSHIPS

National Guard Association of South Carolina
Attn: NGASC Scholarship Foundation
132 Pickens Street
Columbia, SC 29205
(803) 254-8456   Toll Free: (800) 822-3235
Fax: (803) 254-3869   E-mail: nginfo@ngasc.org
Web: www.ngasc.org/ngasc_scholarship_foundation.htm

Summary To provide financial assistance to current and former South Carolina National Guard members and their dependents who are interested in attending college or graduate school in any state.

Eligibility This program is open to undergraduate students who are 1) current, retired, or deceased members of the South Carolina National Guard; 2) their dependents; and 3) members of the National Guard Association of South Carolina (NGASC). Graduate students are also eligible if they are members of the South Carolina National Guard. Applicants must be attending or interested in attending a college or university in any state as a full-time student. Several of the scholarships include additional restrictions on school or academic major; some are granted only for academic excellence, but most are based on both academics and financial need.

Financial Data The stipend is $1,500 or $1,000.

Duration 1 year; may be renewed up to 3 additional years.

Additional data Among the named scholarships included in this program recently were the BG (Ret) C. Norwood Gayle Memorial Scholarship Award, the CMSgt Jim Burgess Scholarship Award, the Mrs. Kaye Helgeson Memorial Scholarship Award, the LTC (Ret) Glenny J. (Jeff) Matthews Memorial Scholarship Awards, the Ron McNair Memorial Scholarship Award, the Darla Moore Scholarship Award, the Sergeants Major Watson Scholarship Award, the SCANG Chiefs Council Scholarship Award, the Chief Shepherd Pitney Bowes Scholarship Award, the Fallen Soldiers' Memorial Scholarship Award, and the South Carolina National Guard Federal Credit Union Awards.

Number awarded Varies each year. Recently, 48 of these scholarships were awarded: 1 at $1,500 and 47 at $1,000. The $1,500 scholarship and 1 of the $1,000 scholarships were based on academic excellence; the remaining $1,000 scholarships were based on both academics and financial need.

Deadline January of each year.

[71]
NGAT SCHOLARSHIP PROGRAM

National Guard Association of Texas
Attn: NGAT Educational Foundation
3706 Crawford Avenue
Austin, TX 78731-6803
(512) 454-7300   Toll Free: (800) 252-NGAT
Fax: (512) 467-6803   E-mail: rlindner@ngat.org
Web: www.ngat.org

Summary To provide financial assistance to members and dependents of members of the National Guard Association of Texas who are interested in attending college or graduate school in any state.

Eligibility This program is open to annual and life members of the association and their spouses and children (associate members and their dependents are not eligible). Applicants may be high school seniors, undergraduate students, or graduate students, either enrolled or planning to enroll at an institution of higher education in any state. Along with their application, they must submit an essay on their desire to continue their education. Selection is based on scholarship, citizenship, and leadership.

Financial Data Stipends range from $500 to $5,000.

Duration 1 year (nonrenewable).

Additional data This program includes the following named scholarships: the Thomas F. Berry Memorial Scholarship, the Len and Jean Tallas Memorial Scholarship, the Texas Military Forces Retirees Scholarship, the T-Mates Scholarship, the LTC Gary W. Parrish Memorial Scholarship, the 1SG Harry E. Lux Memorial Scholarship, the Gloria Jenell and Marlin E. Mote Endowed Scholarship, the Chief Master Sergeants Scholarship, the Sergeants Major Scholarship, and the Texas USAA Scholarship (sponsored by USAA Insurance Corporation).

Number awarded Varies each year. Recently, 10 of these scholarships were awarded: 1 at $5,000, 3 at $2,500, 1 at $2,000, 2 at $1,250, 2 at $1,000, and 1 at $500.

Deadline February of each year.

[72]
NGATN SCHOLARSHIP PROGRAM

National Guard Association of Tennessee
Attn: Scholarship Committee
4332 Kenilwood Drive
Nashville, TN 37204-4401
(615) 833-9100   Toll Free: (888) 642-8448 (within TN)
Fax: (615) 833-9173   E-mail: larry@ngatn.org
Web: www.ngatn.org

Summary To provide financial assistance for college to members or dependents of members of the National Guard Association of Tennessee (NGATN).

Eligibility This program is open to active Tennessee National Guard members and to active annual or life members of the NGATN. If no active Guard or association member qualifies, the scholarships may be awarded to the child of a Guard or association member, including life members who have retired or are deceased. All applicants must be high school seniors or graduates who meet entrance or continuation requirements at a Tennessee college or university. Selection is based on leadership in school and civic activities, motivation for continued higher education, academic achievement in high school and/or college, and financial need.

Financial Data The stipends are $1,500.

Duration 1 year.

Number awarded 6 each year: 1 to an active National Guard member; 2 to current association members or their dependents; 2 to active National Guard members or their dependents; and 1 to a current Guard member who was mobilized for Operations Desert Storm, Noble Eagle, Enduring Freedom, or Iraqi Freedom.

Deadline June of each year.

[73]
NMIA/NMIF SCHOLARSHIP PROGRAM

National Military Intelligence Association
Attn: Scholarship Committee
256 Morris Creek Road
Cullen, VA 23934
(434) 542-5929   Fax: (703) 738-7487
E-mail: admin@nmia.org
Web: www.nmia.org/about/scholarshipprogram.html

Summary To provide financial assistance to undergraduate and graduate students majoring in a field of interest to the intelligence community.

Eligibility This program is open to full- and part-time juniors, seniors, and graduate students who are preparing for a career in a field related to the intelligence community. Applicants must list special activities, internships, prior or current military service, or other activities that provide tangible evidence of career aspirations to serve as a member of the intelligence community. Along with their application, they must submit a 1,000-word essay that covers 1) their intelligence community career goals and objectives; 2) the relationship between courses completed, courses planned, extracurricular activities, and prior work experience (including military service) to identified career goals and objectives; and 3) how this scholarship will make a difference to their efforts to realize their career goals and aspirations. Selection is based primarily on past academic success; financial need is not considered.

Financial Data The stipend is $3,000 for full-time students or $2,000 for part-time students.

Duration 1 year; nonrenewable.

Additional data This program is offered jointly by the National Military Intelligence Association (NMIA) and the National Military Intelligence Foundation (NMIF), P.O. Box 6844, Arlington, VA 22206, E-mail: ffrank54@comcast.net

Number awarded 6 each year: 3 for full-time students and 3 for part-time students.

Deadline November each year.

[74]
NONRESIDENT TUITION WAIVERS FOR VETERANS AND THEIR DEPENDENT WHO MOVE TO TEXAS

Texas Higher Education Coordinating Board
Attn: Grants and Special Programs
1200 East Anderson Lane
P.O. Box 12788, Capitol Station
Austin, TX 78711-2788
(512) 427-6340   Toll Free: (800) 242-3062
Fax: (512) 427-6127   E-mail: grantinfo@thecb.state.tx.us
Web: www.collegeforalltexans.com

Summary To exempt veterans who move to Texas and their dependents from the payment of nonresident tuition at public institutions of higher education in the state.

Eligibility Eligible for these waivers are former members of the U.S. armed forces and commissioned officers of the Public Health Service who are retired or have been honorably discharged, their spouses, and dependent children. Applicants must have moved to Texas upon separation from the service and be attending or planning to attend a public college or university in the state. They must have indicated their intent to become a Texas resident by registering to vote and doing 1 of the following: owning real property in Texas, registering an automobile in Texas, or executing a will indicating that they are a resident of the state.

Financial Data Although persons eligible under this program are still classified as nonresidents, they are entitled to pay the resident tuition at Texas institutions of higher education on an immediate basis.

Duration 1 year.

Number awarded Varies each year.

Deadline Deadline not specified.

[75]
NON-TRADITIONAL STUDENTS SCHOLARSHIP

American Legion Auxiliary
8945 North Meridian Street
Indianapolis, IN 46260
(317) 569-4500   Fax: (317) 569-4502
E-mail: alahq@legion-aux.org
Web: www.legion-aux.org

Summary To provide financial assistance for college to nontraditional students affiliated with the American Legion.

Eligibility This program is open to members of the American Legion, American Legion Auxiliary, or Sons of the American Legion who have paid dues for the 2 preceding years and the calendar year in which application is being made. Applicants must be nontraditional students who are either 1) returning to school after some period of time during which their formal education was interrupted, or 2) just beginning their education at a later point in life. Selection is based on scholastic standing and academic achievement (25%), character and leadership (25%), initiative and goals (25%), and financial need (25%).

Financial Data The stipend is $1,000, paid directly to the school.

Duration 1 year.

Additional data Applications are available from the president of the candidate's own unit or from the secretary or education chair of the department.

Number awarded 5 each year: 1 in each division of the American Legion Auxiliary.

Deadline Applications must be submitted to the unit president by February of each year.

[76]
OHIO LEGION SCHOLARSHIPS

American Legion
Department of Ohio
60 Big Run Road
P.O. Box 8007
Delaware, OH 43015
(740) 362-7478   Fax: (740) 362-1429
E-mail: legion@ohiolegion.com
Web: www.ohiolegion.com/scholarships/info.htm

Summary To provide financial assistance to residents of Ohio who are members of the American Legion, their families, or dependents of deceased military personnel and interested in attending college in any state.

Eligibility This program is open to residents of Ohio who are Legionnaires, direct descendants of living or deceased Legionnaires, or surviving spouses or children of deceased U.S. military personnel who died on active duty or of injuries received on active duty. Applicants must be attending or planning to attend colleges, universities, or other approved postsecondary schools in any state with a vocational objective. Selection is based on academic achievement as measured by course grades, scholastic test scores, difficulty of curriculum, participation in outside activities, and the judging committee's general impression.

Financial Data Stipends are at least $2,000.

Duration 1 year.

Number awarded Varies each year; recently, 14 of these scholarships were awarded.

Deadline April of each year.

[77]
OHIO NATIONAL GUARD ENLISTED ASSOCIATION SCHOLARSHIP PROGRAM

Ohio National Guard Enlisted Association
1299 Virginia Avenue
Columbus, OH 43212
(740) 574-5932   Toll Free: (800) 642-6642
Fax: (614) 486-2216   E-mail: ongea@juno.com
Web: www.ongea.org

Summary To provide financial assistance to members of the Ohio National Guard Enlisted Association (ONGEA) and children of members of the ONGEA Auxiliary who are interested in attending college in any state.

Eligibility This program is open to 1) sons and daughters of ONGEA Auxiliary members (spouse must have at least 1 year remaining on his/her enlistment following the completion of the school year for which the application is submitted); 2) unmarried dependent sons and daughters of deceased ONGEA and ONGEA Auxiliary members who were in good standing the time of their death; and 3) ONGEA members. Spouses of ONGEA members must also be a member of the ONGEA Auxiliary in order for a dependent to be considered for this award (unless the ONGEA member is a single parent). Applicants must be enrolling as full-time undergraduate students at a college, university, trade school, or business school in any state. Graduate students are not eligible. All applications must be accompanied by a transcript of high school and (if appropriate) college credits, a letter from the applicant describing educational goals and financial need, 3 letters of recommendation, and a copy of the current membership cards of both parents or current membership card of the single parent. Selection is based on academic record, character, leadership, and financial need.

Financial Data Stipends are $1,000 or $500. After verification of enrollment is provided, checks are sent to the recipient and made out to the recipient's school.

Duration 1 year; nonrenewable.

Additional data This program is sponsored jointly by ONGEA, the ONGEA Auxiliary, USAA Insurance Corporation, and the First Cleveland Cavalry Association.

Number awarded 5 to 10 each year, depending upon the availability of funds.

Deadline February of each year.

[78]
OKLAHOMA TUITION WAIVER FOR PRISONERS OF WAR, PERSONS MISSING IN ACTION, AND DEPENDENTS

Oklahoma State Regents for Higher Education
Attn: Director of Scholarship and Grant Programs
655 Research Parkway, Suite 200
P.O. Box 108850
Oklahoma City, OK 73101-8850
(405) 225-9239   Toll Free: (800) 858-1840
Fax: (405) 225-9230   E-mail: studentinfo@osrhe.edu
Web: www.okhighered.org

Summary To provide financial assistance for college to Oklahoma residents (or their dependents) who were declared prisoners of war or missing in action.

Eligibility Applicants for this assistance must be veterans who were declared prisoners of war or missing in action after January 1, 1960 and were residents of Oklahoma at the time of entrance into the armed forces or when declared POW/MIA. Dependent children of those veterans are also eligible as long as they are under 24 years of age. Selection is based on financial need, academic aptitude and achievement, student activity participation, academic level, and academic discipline or field of study.

Financial Data Eligible applicants are entitled to receive free tuition at any Oklahoma state-supported postsecondary educational, technical, or vocational school.

Duration Assistance continues for 5 years or until receipt of a bachelor's degree, whichever occurs first.

Additional data This assistance is not available to persons eligible to receive federal benefits.

Number awarded Varies each year.

Deadline Deadline not specified.

[79]
OREGON EDUCATIONAL AID FOR VETERANS

Oregon Department of Veterans' Affairs
Attn: Educational Aid Program
700 Summer Street N.E., Suite 150
Salem, OR 97301-1285
(503) 373-2085   Toll Free: (800) 692-9666 (within OR)
Fax: (503) 373-2362   TDD: (503) 373-2217
E-mail: orvetsbenefits@odva.state.or.us
Web: www.oregon.gov

Summary To provide financial assistance for college to certain Oregon veterans.

Eligibility This program is open to veterans who served on active duty in the U.S. armed forces for not less than 90 days during the Korean War or subsequent to June 30, 1958. Applicants must be residents of Oregon released from military service under honorable conditions. They must be enrolled or planning to enroll in classroom instruction, home study courses, or vocational training from an accredited educational institution. U.S. citizenship is required.

Financial Data Full-time students are entitled to receive up to $150 per month and part-time students up to $100 per month.

Duration Benefits are paid for as many months as the veteran spent in active service, up to a maximum of 36 months. One month of entitlement will be charged for each month paid, regardless of the amount paid.

Additional data Educational Aid will not be paid if the veteran is receiving federal GI training benefits for that course. School officials are required to certify the amount that the student paid for tuition, lab fees, books, and supplies; payments for each month or portion of a month are made only if the actual cost of the course is equal to or greater than the payment amount.

Number awarded Varies each year.

Deadline Applications must be submitted at the time of enrollment.

[80]
PENNSYLVANIA GRANTS FOR VETERANS

Pennsylvania Higher Education Assistance Agency
Attn: State Grant and Special Programs
1200 North Seventh Street
P.O. Box 8114
Harrisburg, PA 17105-8114
(717) 720-2800   Toll Free: (800) 692-7392
TDD: (800) 654-5988   E-mail: info@pheaa.org
Web: www.pheaa.org/specialprograms/index.shtml

Summary To provide financial assistance to Pennsylvania veterans who are interested in attending college in any state.

Eligibility This program is open to veterans who served on active duty with the U.S. armed services (or were a cadet or midshipman at a service academy); were released or discharged under conditions other than dishonorable, bad conduct, uncharacterized, or other than honorable; have resided in Pennsylvania for at least 12 months immediately preceding the date of application; graduated from high school; and are enrolled on at least a half-time basis in an approved program of study that is at least 2 academic years in length. First priority is given to veterans who have separated from active duty after January 1 of the current year. All veterans are considered without regard to the financial status of their parents.

Financial Data The amount of the award depends on the financial need of the recipient, up to a maximum of $3,500 at a Pennsylvania school or $800 at a school outside of Pennsylvania that is approved for participation in the program.

Duration 1 year; may be renewed for 3 additional years.

Additional data With certain exceptions, recipients may attend any accredited college in the United States. Excluded from coverage are 2-year public colleges located outside Pennsylvania and schools in states bordering on Pennsylvania that do not allow their state grant recipients to attend Pennsylvania schools (i.e., New York, Maryland, and New Jersey).

Number awarded Varies each year.

Deadline April of each year for renewal applicants and any non-renewals who will enroll in a baccalaureate degree program; July of each year for nonrenewals who will enroll in a 2-year or 3-year terminal program.

[81]
PETER CONNACHER MEMORIAL AMERICAN EX-PRISONER OF WAR SCHOLARSHIPS

Oregon Student Assistance Commission
Attn: Grants and Scholarships Division
1500 Valley River Drive, Suite 100
Eugene, OR 97401-2146
(541) 687-7395   Toll Free: (800) 452-8807, ext. 7395
Fax: (541) 687-7414   TDD: (800) 735-2900
E-mail: awardinfo@osac.state.or.us
Web: www.osac.state.or.us/osac_programs.html

Summary To provide financial assistance for college or graduate school to ex-prisoners of war and their descendants.

Eligibility Applicants must be U.S. citizens who 1) were military or civilian prisoners of war or 2) are the descendants of ex-prisoners of war. They may be undergraduate or graduate students. A copy of the ex-prisoner of war's discharge papers from the U.S. armed forces must accompany the application. In addition, written proof of POW status must be submitted, along with a statement of the relationship between the applicant and the ex-prisoner of war (father, grandfather, etc.). Selection is based on academic record and financial need. Preference is given to Oregon residents or their dependents.

Financial Data The stipend amount varies; recently, it was at least $1,150.

Duration 1 year; may be renewed for up to 3 additional years for undergraduate students or 2 additional years for graduate students. Renewal is dependent on evidence of continued financial need and satisfactory academic progress.

Additional data This program is administered by the Oregon Student Assistance Commission (OSAC) with funds provided by the Oregon Community Foundation, 1221 S.W. Yamhill, Suite 100, Portland, OR 97205, (503) 227-6846, Fax: (503) 274-7771. Funds are also provided by the Columbia River Chapter of the American Ex-prisoners of War, Inc. Recipients must attend college on a full-time basis.

Number awarded Varies each year; recently, 4 of these scholarships were awarded.

Deadline February of each year.

[82]
POST-9/11 GI BILL

Department of Veterans Affairs
Attn: Veterans Benefits Administration
810 Vermont Avenue, N.W.
Washington, DC 20420
(202) 418-4343   Toll Free: (888) GI-BILL1
Web: www.gibill.va.gov

Summary To provide financial assistance to veterans or military personnel who entered service on or after September 11, 2001.

Eligibility This program is open to current and former military who served on active duty for at least 90 aggregate days after September 11, 2001. Applicants must be planning to enroll at an accredited college or university as an undergraduate or graduate student; study in a certificate program, on-the-job training, apprenticeship program, flight training, and non-college degree course study do not qualify for support.

Financial Data Active-duty personnel receive payment of tuition and fees, up to the level of tuition and fees at the most expensive public institution of higher learning in their state of residence; the actual amount depends on the state of residence and the length of service completed. Veterans also receive a monthly housing allowance based on the Basic Allowance for Housing (BAH) for an E-5 with dependents if the location of the school they are attending is in the United States (or $1,333 per month at schools in foreign countries); an annual book allowance of $1,000; and (for participants who live in a rural county remote from an educational institution) a rural benefit payment of $500 per year.

Duration Most participants receive up to 36 months of entitlement under this program.

Additional data This program began in 2009 as a replacement for previous educational programs for veterans and military personnel (e.g., Montgomery GI Bill, REAP). Current participants in those programs may be able to utilize benefits under those programs and this new plan. Further information is available from local armed forces recruiters. This is the latest VA education program, referred to as Chapter 33.

Number awarded Varies each year.

Deadline Deadline not specified.

[83]
PPQ WILLIAM F. HELMS STUDENT SCHOLARSHIP PROGRAM

Department of Agriculture
Animal and Plant Health Inspection Service
Attn: Human Resources/Recruitment
1400 Independence Avenue, S.W., Room 1710
Washington, DC 20250
(202) 690-4759
Web: www.aphis.usda.gov/plant_health/helms/index.shtml

Summary To provide financial assistance and work experience to college students (particularly veterans) who are majoring in the agricultural or biological sciences.

Eligibility This program is open to college sophomores and juniors who are attending an accredited college or university, are majoring in an agricultural or biological science (such as biology, plant pathology, entomology, virology, bacteriology, mycology, or ecology), are interested in a career in plant protection and quarantine, and are U.S. citizens. Applicants must submit a personal letter that describes their interests, goals, and chosen career plans; explains how they envision their ability to contribute to the sponsor's mission; and outlines why they should be selected over other candidates for this program. A preference is given to veterans of the U.S. armed forces.

Financial Data The stipend is $5,000 per year.

Duration 1 year; may be renewed if the recipient maintains a GPA of 2.5 or higher.

Additional data This program is sponsored by the U.S. Department of Agriculture's (USDA) Animal and Plant Health Inspection Service (APHIS), the agency responsible for protecting America's agriculture base; Plant Protection and Quarantine (PPQ) is the program within APHIS that deals with plant health issues. In addition to financial assistance, the Helms Student Scholarship Program also offers tutoring assistance, mentoring, paid work experience during vacation periods, career exploration, and possible employment upon graduation.

Number awarded Several each year.

Deadline February of each year.

[84]
PVA EDUCATIONAL SCHOLARSHIP PROGRAM

Paralyzed Veterans of America
Attn: Education and Training Foundation
801 18th Street, N.W.
Washington, DC 20006-3517
(202) 416-7651   Fax: (202) 416-7641
TDD: (202) 416-7622   E-mail: foundations@pva.org
Web: www.pva.org

Summary To provide financial assistance for college to members of the Paralyzed Veterans of America (PVA) and their families.

Eligibility This program is open to PVA members, spouses of members, and unmarried dependent children of members under 24 years of age. Applicants must be attending or planning to attend an accredited U.S. college or university. They must be U.S. citizens. Along with their application, they must submit a personal statement explaining why they wish to further their education, short- and long-term academic goals, how this will meet their career objectives, and how it will affect their PVA membership. Selection is based on that statement, academic records, letters of recommendation, and extracurricular and community activities.

Financial Data Stipends are $1,000 for full-time students or $500 for part-time students.

Duration 1 year.

Additional data This program was established in 1986.

Number awarded Varies each year; recently 14 full-time and 3 part-time students received these scholarships. Since this program was established, it has awarded more than $300,000 in scholarships.

Deadline May of each year.

[85]
RHODE ISLAND EDUCATIONAL BENEFITS FOR DISABLED AMERICAN VETERANS

Division of Veterans Affairs
480 Metacom Avenue
Bristol, RI 02809-0689
(401) 254-8350   Fax: (401) 254-2320
TDD: (401) 254-1345   E-mail: devangelista@dhs.ri.gov
Web: www.dhs.ri.gov/VeteransServices/tabid/307/Default.aspx

Summary To provide assistance to disabled veterans in Rhode Island who wish to pursue higher education at a public institution in the state.

Eligibility This program is open to permanent residents of Rhode Island who have been verified by the Department of Veterans Affairs (DVA) as having a disability of at least 10% resulting from military service.

Financial Data Eligible veterans are entitled to take courses at any public institution of higher education in Rhode Island without the payment of tuition, exclusive of other fees and charges.

Number awarded Varies each year.

Deadline Deadline not specified.

[86]
ROSAMOND P. HAEBERLE MEMORIAL SCHOLARSHIP

Daughters of the American Revolution-Michigan State Society
c/o Toni Barger, Memorial Scholarship Committee
130 Lake Region Circle
Winter Haven, FL 33881-9535
(863) 326-1687   E-mail: tonibarger@aol.com
Web: www.michigandar.org/scholarships.htm

Summary To provide financial assistance to Michigan veterans and military personnel interested in attending college in the state.

Eligibility This program is open to residents of Michigan who have served on active duty in the U.S. armed forces (including Reserves and National Guard) for at least 6 continuous months and are either currently serving in the armed forces or have received a separation from active duty under honorable conditions. Applicants must be currently accepted to and/or enrolled at a 2-year or 4-year accredited college, university, or technical/trade school in Michigan. They must be enrolled at least half time and have a cumulative high school or undergraduate GPA of 2.5 or higher. Along with their application, they must submit a 1-page essay on what serving their country has meant to them and how it has influenced their future goals and priorities. Selection is based on academic performance, extracurricular activities, community service, potential to succeed in an academic environment, financial need, and military service record.

Financial Data The stipend is $1,500.

Duration 1 year.

Additional data This program was established in 2007.

Number awarded 1 each year.

Deadline March of each year.

[87]
RSF MEMORIAL SCHOLARSHIP

Missouri Society of Professional Engineers
Attn: MSPE Educational Foundation
200 East McCarty Street, Suite 200
Jefferson City, MO 65101-3113
(573) 636-4861   Toll Free: (888) 666-4861
Fax: (573) 636-5475   E-mail: marladay@mspe.org
Web: www.mspe.org/edfoundation.html

Summary To provide financial assistance to military personnel and veterans who are residents of any state and currently studying engineering at selected universities in Missouri.

Eligibility This program is open to military personnel (including active, National Guard, and Reserves), ROTC cadets, and veterans who are residents of any state. Applicants must be sophomores or juniors currently enrolled in or planning to transfer to an engineering program at 1 of the following institutions in Missouri: University of Missouri, College of Engineering, Columbia; University of Missouri, School of Engineering, Kansas City; Missouri University of Science and Technology, School of Engineering, Rolla; Missouri University of Science and Technology, School of Materials, Energy, and Earth Resources, Rolla; University of Missouri St. Louis/Washington University Joint Undergraduate Engineering Program; Southeast Missouri State University, Engineering Physics Program, Cape Girardeau; and Washington University, School of Engineering and Applied Sciences, St. Louis. Along with their application, they must submit a 1,000-word essay on their interest in engineering, their major area of study and area of specialization, the occupation they propose to pursue after graduation, their long-term goals, and how they hope to achieve those. Selection is based on the essay (10 points), academic achievement (5 points), extracurricular college or community activities (5 points), work experience (10 points), recommendations (10 points), and financial need (10 points). U.S. citizenship is required.

Financial Data The stipend is $2,000.

Duration 1 year.
Number awarded 1 each year.
Deadline December of each year.

[88]
RUBY LORRAINE PAUL SCHOLARSHIP FUND

American Legion Auxiliary
Department of Nebraska
P.O. Box 5227
Lincoln, NE 68505-0227
(402) 466-1808   Fax: (402) 466-0182
E-mail: neaux@windstream.net
Web: www.nebraskalegionaux.net/scholarships.htm

Summary To provide financial assistance to students in Nebraska who have a connection to the American Legion and plan to attend college in any state and study any field except nursing.

Eligibility Applicants must have been residents of Nebraska for at least 3 years and either 1) have been a member for at least 2 years of the American Legion, American Legion Auxiliary, or Sons of the American Legion, or 2) be the child, grandchild, or great-grandchild of an American Legion or American Legion Auxiliary member who has been a member for at least 2 years. They must be high school seniors or graduates who maintained a GPA of 3.0 or higher during the last 2 semesters of high school and have been accepted at an accredited college or university in any state to study any field except nursing. Financial need is considered in the selection process.

Financial Data A stipend is awarded (amount not specified).
Duration 1 year.
Number awarded 1 each year.
Deadline February of each year.

[89]
SAN FRANCISCO BAY AREA NDTA VETERANS MERIT SCHOLARSHIP

National Defense Transportation Association-San Francisco
  Bay Area Chapter
Attn: Scholarship Committee
2750 North Texas Street, Suite 140
Fairfield, CA 94533
E-mail: c_madison@msn.com
Web: ndta-sf.com/scholarship_information

Summary To provide financial assistance to veterans and military personnel in California who are majoring in a field related to transportation at a school in any state.

Eligibility This program is open to military personnel on active duty and veterans who have been on active duty within the past 5 years. Applicants must be residents of California and enrolled or planning to enroll in an undergraduate or vocational program at an accredited institution in any state with a major in transportation, logistics, business, marketing, engineering, planning, or environment. They must be preparing for a career related to transportation. Along with their application, they must submit a certified copy of their high school or college transcript, 3 letters of recommendation, and a 1-page essay detailing their career goals and ambitions (with an emphasis on transportation and related areas). Selection is based on academic ability, professional interest, and community involvement.

Financial Data The stipend is $1,000.
Duration 1 year.
Number awarded 1 or more each year.
Deadline May of each year.

[90]
SAUL T. WILSON, JR. SCHOLARSHIP

Department of Agriculture
Animal and Plant Health Inspection Service
Attn: Human Resources/Recruitment
1400 Independence Avenue, S.W., Room 1710
Washington, DC 20250
(202) 690-4759
Web: www.aphis.usda.gov

Summary To provide scholarship/loans and work experience to undergraduate and graduate students (particularly veterans) who are interested in preparing for a career in veterinary medicine and biomedical sciences.

Eligibility This program is open to U.S. citizens enrolled in an accredited college or university in the United States as a full-time student. Undergraduates must have completed at least 2-years of a 4-year preveterinary medicine or other biomedical science program. Graduate students must have completed not more than 1 year of study in veterinary medicine. All applicants must submit a 500-word essay on why they should receive this scholarship and what contributions they would make to veterinary services of the Animal and Plant Health Inspection Service (APHIS). Preference is given to veterans of the U.S. armed forces. Financial need is not considered in the selection process.

Financial Data The maximum stipend is $5,000 per year for undergraduates or $10,000 per year for graduate students. Funds must be used for tuition, books, tutors, and laboratory fees. During summers and school breaks, scholars receive paid employment as a veterinary student trainee with APHIS at a salary that ranges from $9 to $13 per hour, depending on the student's qualifications. After 640 hours of study-related work with APHIS in the career experience program and graduation with a D.V.M. degree, and at the option of APHIS, the student must become a full-time employee for at least 1 calendar year for each school year of support from this scholarship. If scholarship recipients refuse to accept an APHIS offer of employment, they must reimburse the agency for all financial assistance received. If recipients fail to serve the entire length of the mandatory APHIS employment period, they must reimburse APHIS a prorated share of scholarship funds used.
Duration 1 year; may be renewed.
Number awarded 1 or more each year.
Deadline February of each year.

[91]
SCHNEIDER-EMANUEL AMERICAN LEGION SCHOLARSHIPS

American Legion
Department of Wisconsin
2930 American Legion Drive
P.O. Box 388
Portage, WI 53901-0388
(608) 745-1090   Fax: (608) 745-0179
E-mail: info@wilegion.org
Web: www.wilegion.org

Summary To provide financial assistance to members of the American Legion in Wisconsin and their children or grandchildren who plan to attend college in any state.

Eligibility This program is open to seniors and graduates from accredited Wisconsin high schools. Applicants must be at least 1 of the following 1) a child whose father, mother, or legal guardian is a member of the Department of Wisconsin of the American Legion, American Legion Auxiliary, or Sons of the American Legion; 2) a grandchild whose grandfather, grandmother, or legal guardian is a member of the Department of Wisconsin of the American Legion, American Legion Auxiliary, or Sons of the American Legion; 3) a member of the Sons of the American Legion, American Legion Auxiliary, or Junior American Legion Auxiliary; or 4) a veteran and an American Legion member in Wisconsin. Applicants must have participated in Legion and Auxiliary youth programs. They must be planning to attend a college or university in any state. Selection is based on moral character; scholastic excellence (GPA of 3.0 or higher); participation and accomplishment in American Legion affiliated activities; and personality, leadership, and participation in general extracurricular activities.

Financial Data The stipend is $1,000.

Duration 1 year.

Number awarded 3 each year.

Deadline February of each year.

[92]
SCHUYLER S. PYLE SCHOLARSHIP

Fleet Reserve Association
Attn: Scholarship Administrator
125 North West Street
Alexandria, VA 22314-2754
(703) 683-1400 Toll Free: (800) FRA-1924
Fax: (703) 549-6610 E-mail: fra@fra.org
Web: www.fra.org

Summary To provide financial assistance for college or graduate school to members of the Fleet Reserve Association (FRA) who are current or former naval personnel and their spouses and children.

Eligibility This program is open to dependent children, grandchildren, and spouses of FRA members who are in good standing (or were at the time of death, if deceased). FRA members are also eligible. Applicants must be working on or planning to work on an undergraduate or graduate degree. Along with their application, they must submit an essay on their life experiences, career objectives, and what motivated them to select those objectives. Selection is based on academic record, financial need, extracurricular activities, leadership skills, and participation in community activities. U.S. citizenship is required.

Financial Data The stipend is $5,000 per year.

Duration 1 year; may be renewed.

Additional data Membership in the FRA is restricted to active-duty, retired, and Reserve members of the Navy, Marine Corps, and Coast Guard.

Number awarded 1 each year.

Deadline April of each year.

[93]
SERGEANT MAJOR DOUGLAS R. DRUM MEMORIAL SCHOLARSHIP

American Military Retirees Association, Inc.
Attn: Scholarship Committee
5436 Peru Street, Suite 1
Plattsburgh, NY 12901
(518) 563-9479 Toll Free: (800) 424-2969
Fax: (518) 324-5204 E-mail: info@amra1973.org
Web: www.amra1973.org/scholarship.asp

Summary To provide financial assistance for college to members of the American Military Retirees Association (AMRA) and their dependents.

Eligibility This program is open to current members of AMRA and their dependents, children, and grandchildren. Applicants must be attending or planning to attend an accredited college or university. Along with their application, they must submit a 500-word essay on why they deserve this scholarship. Selection is based on academic achievement, leadership abilities, character, citizenship, and community service.

Financial Data The stipend is $1,000.

Duration 1 year.

Additional data Membership in AMRA is open to all retired members of the armed forces, regardless of rank.

Number awarded Varies each year; recently, 24 of these scholarships were awarded.

Deadline February of each year.

[94]
SFC CURTIS MANCINI MEMORIAL SCHOLARSHIPS

Association of the United States Army-Rhode Island Chapter
c/o CSM (Ret) Anthony Ferri, Secretary
47 Spokane Street
Providence, RI 02904
(401) 861-2997 E-mail: afnf458673755@aol.com
Web: www.ausari.org/index.html

Summary To provide financial assistance to members of the Rhode Island Chapter of the Association of the United States Army (AUSA) and their families who are interested in attending college or graduate school in any state.

Eligibility This program is open to members of the AUSA Rhode Island Chapter and their family members (spouses, children, and grandchildren). Applicants must be high school seniors or graduates accepted at an accredited college, university, or vocational/technical school in any state or current undergraduate or graduate students. Along with their application, they must submit a 250-word essay on why they feel their achievements should qualify them for this award. Selection is based on academic and individual achievements; financial need is not considered. Membership in AUSA is open to current and retired Army personnel (including Reserves and National Guard), ROTC cadets, or civilian employees of the Army.

Financial Data The stipend is $1,000.

Duration 1 year.

Number awarded 2 each year.

Deadline March of each year.

[95]
SOCIETY OF SPONSORS OF THE UNITED STATES NAVY CENTENNIAL SCHOLARSHIP

Navy-Marine Corps Relief Society
Attn: Education Division
875 North Randolph Street, Suite 225
Arlington, VA 22203-1757
(703) 696-4960 Fax: (703) 696-0144
E-mail: education@nmcrs.org
Web: www.nmcrs.org/education.html

Summary To provide financial assistance to wounded Navy and Marine Corps veterans of Operation Iraqi Freedom (OIF) and Operation Enduring Freedom (OEF) who are interested in preparing to become a teacher.

Eligibility This program is open to Navy and Marine Corps veterans who were injured in combat in Iraq or Afghanistan. Applicants must have at least an associate degree or equivalent and be enrolled full time in an undergraduate program leading to a bachelor's degree and teacher licensure. They must have a GPA of 2.0 or higher. Financial need is considered in the selection process.

Financial Data The stipend is $3,000 per year.

Duration 1 year; may be renewed 1 additional year.

Additional data The Society of Sponsors of the United States Navy, an organization of women who serve as sponsors of ships, established this program in 2008 to honor the centennial of its founding.

Number awarded 5 each year.

Deadline Applications may be submitted at any time.

[96]
SOUTH DAKOTA FREE TUITION FOR VETERANS AND OTHERS WHO PERFORMED WAR SERVICE

South Dakota Board of Regents
Attn: Scholarship Committee
306 East Capitol Avenue, Suite 200
Pierre, SD 57501-2545
(605) 773-3455   Fax: (605) 773-2422
E-mail: info@sdbor.edu
Web: www.sdbor.edu

Summary To provide free tuition at South Dakota public colleges and universities to certain veterans.

Eligibility This program is open to current residents of South Dakota who have been discharged from the military forces of the United States under honorable conditions. Applicants must meet 1 of the following criteria: 1) served on active duty at any time between August 2, 1990 and March 3, 1991; 2) received an Armed Forces Expeditionary Medal, Southwest Asia Service Medal, or other U.S. campaign or service medal for participation in combat operations against hostile forces outside the boundaries of the United States: or 3) have a service-connected disability rating of at least 10%. They may not be eligible for any other educational assistance from the U.S. government. Qualifying veterans must apply for this benefit within 20 years after the date proclaimed for the cassation of hostilities or within 6 years from and after the date of their discharge from military service, whichever is later.

Financial Data Eligible veterans are entitled to attend any South Dakota state-supported institution of higher education or state-supported technical or vocational school free of tuition and mandatory fees.

Duration Eligible veterans are entitled to receive 1 month of free tuition for each month of qualifying service, from a minimum of 1 year to a maximum of 4 years.

Number awarded Varies each year.

Deadline Deadline not specified.

[97]
SSGT BENTON MEMORIAL SCHOLARSHIP

California State University
CSU Foundation
Attn: Director, Foundation Programs and Services
401 Golden Shore, Sixth Floor
Long Beach, CA 90802-4210
(562) 951-4768   E-mail: abrown@calstate.edu
Web: www.calstate.edu/foundation/scholarship.shtml

Summary To provide financial assistance to veterans of the U.S. Marine Corps who are enrolled at campuses of the California State University (CSU) system.

Eligibility This program is open to students currently enrolled at CSU campuses who have served in the U.S. Marine Corps. Applicants must be able to demonstrate financial need and merit, including academic achievement.

Financial Data The stipend is $2,500.

Duration 1 year.

Number awarded 2 each year.

Deadline Deadline not specified.

[98]
TAILHOOK EDUCATIONAL FOUNDATION SCHOLARSHIPS

Tailhook Educational Foundation
9696 Businesspark Avenue
P.O. Box 26626
San Diego, CA 92196-0626
(858) 689-9223   Toll Free: (800) 322-4665
E-mail: tag@tailhook.net
Web: www.tailhook.org/Foundation.html

Summary To provide financial assistance for college to personnel associated with naval aviation and their children.

Eligibility This program is open to 1) the children (natural, step, and adopted) of current or former U.S. Navy or Marine Corps personnel who served as an aviator, flight officer, or air crewman, or 2) personnel and children of personnel who are serving or have served on board a U.S. Navy aircraft carrier as a member of the ship's company or air wing. Applicants must be enrolled or accepted for enrollment at an accredited college or university. Selection is based on educational and extracurricular achievements, merit, and citizenship.

Financial Data The stipend ranges from $1,500 to $15,000.

Duration 1 to 2 years.

Number awarded Varies each year; recently, 85 of these scholarships were awarded.

Deadline March of each year.

[99]
TENNESSEE HELPING HEROES GRANTS

Tennessee Student Assistance Corporation
Parkway Towers
404 James Robertson Parkway, Suite 1510
Nashville, TN 37243-0820
(615) 741-1346   Toll Free: (800) 342-1663
Fax: (615) 741-6101   E-mail: TSAC.Aidinfo@tn.gov
Web: www.tn.gov/collegepays/mon_college/hh_grant.htm

Summary To provide financial assistance to veterans and current Reservists or National Guard members who are residents of Tennessee and enrolled at a college or university in the state.

Eligibility This program is open to residents of Tennessee who are veterans honorably discharged from the U.S. armed forces and former or current members of a Reserve or Tennessee National Guard unit who were called into active military service. Applicants must have been awarded, on or after September 11, 2001, the Iraq Campaign Medal, the Afghanistan Campaign Medal, or the Global War on Terrorism Expeditionary Medal. They must be enrolled at least half time at an eligible college or university in Tennessee and receive no final failing grade in any course. No academic standard or financial need requirements apply.

Financial Data Grants are $1,000 per semester for full-time study or $500 per semester for part-time study. Funds are awarded after completion of each semester of work.

Duration Grants are awarded until completion of the equivalent of 8 full semesters of work, completion of a baccalaureate degree, or the eighth anniversary of honorable discharge from military service, whichever comes first.

Additional data This program was added as a component of the Tennessee Education Lottery Scholarship Program in 2005.

Number awarded Varies each year.

Deadline August of each year for fall enrollment, January of each year for spring, or April of each year for summer.

[100]
THE FUND FOR VETERANS' EDUCATION SCHOLARSHIP

The Fund for Veterans' Education
Attn: Program Director
111 Radio Circle
Mount Kisco, NY 10549
(914) 242-2377   Fax: (914) 241-7328
E-mail: scholarships@veteransfund.org
Web: www.veteransfund.org

Summary To provide financial assistance for college to veterans who served in Afghanistan or Iraq.

Eligibility This program is open to veterans of all branches of the armed forces (Army, Navy, Air Force, Marines), Coast Guard, National Guard, and Reserves who served at least 60 days in Afghanistan or Iraq (or less because of a service-connected injury of condition) after September 11, 2001. Applicants must be enrolled as a full-time or part-time undergraduate student at an accredited 2-year or 4-year college, university, or technical school. They must have applied for and accepted all federal, state, and institutional need-based grants and all available military educational benefits. U.S. citizenship is not required as long as all other eligibility requirements, including military service, are met. Selection is based primarily on financial need, although length of military service is also considered.

Financial Data Awards are intended to cover any unmet financial need, according to standard federal procedures. Funds may be used for tuition, fees, books, supplies, and required equipment.

Duration 1 year; recipients may reapply.

Additional data These scholarships were first awarded in 2008. The program is administered by Scholarship Management Services, a division of Scholarship America, P.O. Box 297, One Scholarship Way, St. Peter, MN 56082, (507) 931-1682, (800) 537-4180.

Number awarded Up to 2 from each state, U.S. territory, and the District of Columbia. A total of $1 million is available for this program each year.

Deadline October of each year.

[101]
TILLMAN MILITARY SCHOLARSHIPS FOR SERVICEMEMBERS

Pat Tillman Foundation
2121 South Mill Avenue, Suite 214
Tempe, AZ 85282
(480) 621-4074   Fax: (480) 621-4075
E-mail: scholarships@pattillmanfoundation.org
Web: www.pattillmanfoundation.org

Summary To provide financial assistance to veterans and active servicemembers who are interested in working on an undergraduate or graduate degree.

Eligibility This program is open to veterans and active servicemembers of all branches of the armed forces from both the pre- and post-September 11 era whose educational benefits have run out or are insufficient to meet their need. Applicants must be interested in starting, finishing, or furthering their undergraduate, graduate, or postgraduate education at a 2-year, 4-year, or vocational institution (public or private). Along with their application, they must submit 1-page essays on 1) their specific financial need, including any gap in educational benefits they may already be receiving and their reason for applying for this scholarship; 2) their motivation and decision to serve in the U.S. armed forces; and 3) their educational and career goals, how they will incorporate their military service into those goals, and how they intend to continue their service to others and the community. Selection is based on those essays, educational and career ambitions, length of service, record of personal achievement, demonstration of service to others in the community and a desire to continue such service, and unmet financial need.

Financial Data Stipends vary; recently, total awards (including multi-year awards) averaged $12,800.

Duration 1 year; may be renewed, provided the recipient maintains a GPA of 3.0 or higher, remains enrolled full time, and documents participation in civic action or community service.

Additional data This program was established in 2009. The foundation administers the program directly for students at colleges and universities nationwide; it also acts in partnership with 4 universities (the University of Maryland, the University of Arkansas, the University of Idaho, and Mississippi State University) which award scholarships directly to their students.

Number awarded Varies each year; recently, 52 students received a total of $665,820 in these scholarships

Deadline May of each year.

[102]
TONY LOPEZ SCHOLARSHIP PROGRAM

Louisiana National Guard Enlisted Association
c/o SGM Milton J. Billberry
202 Dean Lane
Pineville, LA 71360
(318) 623-2464   E-mail: Milton.billberry@us.army.mil
Web: www.langea.org

Summary To provide financial assistance to members of the Louisiana National Guard Enlisted Association (LANGEA) and their dependents who plan to attend college in any state.

Eligibility This program is open to members of the association, their spouses and unmarried dependent children, and the unremarried spouses and unmarried dependent children of deceased members who were in good standing at the time of their death. The qualifying LANGEA members must have at least 1 year remaining on their enlistment following completion of the school year for which the application is submitted or have served 20 years of more in the Louisiana National Guard. Applicants must be enrolled or planning to enroll full time at an accredited college, university, trade school, or business school in any state. Graduate students are not eligible. Selection is based on academic achievement, character, leadership, and financial need.

Financial Data The stipend is $2,000.

Duration 1 year; nonrenewable.

Number awarded 3 each year.

Deadline February of each year.

[103]
U.S. ARMY WOMEN'S FOUNDATION LEGACY SCHOLARSHIPS

U.S. Army Women's Foundation
Attn: Scholarship Committee
P.O. Box 5030
Fort Lee, VA 23801-0030
(804) 734-3078   E-mail: info@awfdn.org
Web: www.awfdn.org/programs/legacyscholarships.shtml

Summary To provide financial assistance for college to women who are serving or have served in the Army and their children.

Eligibility This program is open to 1) women who have served or are serving honorably in the U.S. Army, U.S. Army Reserve, or Army National Guard; and 2) children of women who served honorably in the U.S. Army, U.S. Army Reserve, or Army National Guard. Applicants must be entering their junior or senior year at an accredited college or university and have a GPA of 3.0 or higher. Along with their application, they must submit a 2-page essay on why they should be considered for this scholarship, their future plans as related to their program of study, and information about their community service, activities, and work experience. Selection is based on merit, academic potential, community service, and financial need.

Financial Data The stipend is $2,500.

Duration 1 year.

Additional data This program includes scholarships named after Lt. Col. Juanita L. Warman, Sgt. Amy Krueger, and Pvt. Francheska Velez, all of whom lost their lives in the tragedy at Fort Hood, Texas on November 5, 2009.

Number awarded 5 to 10 each year.

Deadline February of each year.

[104]
USS LAKE CHAMPLAIN (CG-57) SCHOLARSHIP FUND

USS Lake Champlain Foundation
c/o Captain Ralph K. Martin, USN (ret)
P.O. Box 233
Keeseville, NY 12944-0233
(518) 834-7660

Summary To provide financial assistance for college to naval personnel who are (or have been) attached to the *USS Lake Champlain* and to their dependents.

Eligibility Eligible to apply are 1) past and present crewmembers of the *USS Lake Champlain;* 2) spouses and dependent children of officers and enlisted personnel currently serving aboard the *USS Lake Champlain;* and 3) spouses and dependent children of officers and enlisted personnel on active duty, retired with pay, or deceased who were previously assigned to the *USS Lake Champlain* since commissioning on August 12, 1988. Applicants must submit an essay on their career objectives, why they are interested in that career, and how furthering their education will lead to their accomplishing their career objective. Selection is based on that essay, financial need, high school and/or college transcripts, 2 letters of recommendation, extracurricular activities and awards, and work experience.

Financial Data Stipends range from $100 to $1,000. Scholarships greater than $250 are paid in 2 installments: 1 at the beginning of the fall semester and 1 at the beginning of the second semester upon verification of satisfactory completion of the first semester and continued enrollment. Funds are paid directly to the academic institution.

Duration 1 year.

Number awarded Varies each year. Recently, 11 of these scholarships were awarded: 5 at $1,000, 3 at $250, and 3 at $100.

Deadline May of each year.

[105]
UTAH TUITION WAIVER FOR PURPLE HEART RECIPIENTS

Utah Division of Veteran's Affairs
Attn: Director
550 Foothill Boulevard, Room 202
Salt Lake City, UT 84108
(801) 326-2372   Toll Free: (800) 894-9497 (within UT)
Fax: (801) 326-2369   E-mail: veterans@utah.gov
Web: veterans.utah.gov/homepage/stateBenefits/index.html

Summary To provide a tuition waiver to veterans in Utah who received a Purple Heart award and are attending a public institution in the state.

Eligibility This program is open to residents of Utah who received a Purple Heart award as a result of military service. Applicants must be working on an undergraduate or master's degree at a public college or university in the state.

Financial Data Tuition at the rate for residents of the state is waived for qualified veterans.

Duration Tuition is waived until completion of a bachelor's or master's degree.

Number awarded Varies each year.

Deadline Deadline not specified.

[106]
VADM ROBERT L. WALTERS SCHOLARSHIP

Surface Navy Association
2550 Huntington Avenue, Suite 202
Alexandria, VA 22303
(703) 960-6800   Toll Free: (800) NAVY-SNA
Fax: (703) 960-6807   E-mail: navysna@aol.com
Web: www.navysna.org/awards/index.html

Summary To provide financial assistance for college or graduate school to members of the Surface Navy Association (SNA) and their dependents.

Eligibility This program is open to SNA members and their children, stepchildren, wards, and spouses. The SNA member must 1) be in the second or subsequent consecutive year of membership; 2) be serving, retired, or honorably discharged; 3) be a Surface Warfare Officer or Enlisted Surface Warfare Specialist; and 4) have served for at least 3 years on a surface ship of the U.S.

Navy or Coast Guard. Applicants must be studying or planning to study at an accredited undergraduate or graduate institution. Along with their application, they must submit a 200-word essay about themselves; a list of their extracurricular activities, community service activities, academic honors and/or positions of leadership that represent their interests, with an estimate of the amount of time involved with each activity; and 3 letters of reference. High school seniors should also include a transcript of high school grades and a copy of ACT or SAT scores. Applicants who are on active duty or drilling Reservists should also include a letter from their commanding officer commenting on their military service and leadership potential, a transcript of grades from their most recent 4 semesters of school, a copy of their ACT or SAT scores if available, and an indication of whether they have applied for or are enrolled in the Enlisted Commissioning Program. Applicants who are not high school seniors, active-duty servicemembers, or drilling Reservists should also include a transcript of the grades from their most recent 4 semesters of school and a copy of ACT or SAT test scores (unless they are currently attending a college or university). Selection is based on demonstrated leadership, community service, academic achievement, and commitment to pursuing higher educational objectives.

Financial Data The stipend is $2,000 per year.

Duration 4 years, provided the recipient maintains a GPA of 3.0 or higher.

Number awarded Varies each year.

Deadline February of each year.

[107]
VADM SAMUEL L. GRAVELY, JR., USN (RET.) MEMORIAL SCHOLARSHIPS

Armed Forces Communications and Electronics Association
Attn: AFCEA Educational Foundation
4400 Fair Lakes Court
Fairfax, VA 22033-3899
(703) 631-6149   Toll Free: (800) 336-4583, ext. 6149
Fax: (703) 631-4693   E-mail: scholarship@afcea.org
Web: www.afcea.org

Summary To provide funding to students, especially veterans and military personnel, who are majoring in specified scientific fields at an Historically Black College or University (HBCU).

Eligibility This program is open to sophomores and juniors enrolled full or part time at an accredited 2- or 4-year HBCU or in a distance learning or online degree program affiliated with those institutions. They must be working toward a degree in engineering (aerospace, computer, electrical, or systems), computer science, computer engineering technology, computer information systems, mathematics, physics, information systems management, or other field directly related to the support of U.S. intelligence or homeland security enterprises. Special consideration is given to military enlisted personnel and veterans.

Financial Data The stipend is $5,000.

Duration 1 year; may be renewed.

Additional data This program was established in 2009 with support from American Systems.

Number awarded At least 2 each year.

Deadline October of each year.

[108]
VETERAN'S CAUCUS SCHOLARSHIPS

American Academy of Physician Assistants-Veterans Caucus
Attn: Veterans Caucus
P.O. Box 362
Danville, PA 17821-0362
(570) 271-0292   Fax: (570) 271-5850
E-mail: admin@veteranscaucus.org
Web: www.veteranscaucus.org

Summary To provide financial assistance to veterans and Reserve component personnel who are studying to become physician assistants.

Eligibility This program is open to U.S. citizens who are currently enrolled in a physician assistant program. The program must be approved by the Commission on Accreditation of Allied Health Education. Applicants must be honorably discharged members of a uniformed service of the United States or an active member of the Guard or Reserve of a uniformed service of the United States. Selection is based on military honors and awards received, civic and college honors and awards received, professional memberships and activities, and GPA. An electronic copy of the applicant's DD Form 214 must accompany the application.

Financial Data The stipend is $2,000.

Duration 1 year.

Additional data This program includes the following named scholarships: the Donna Jones Moritsugu Memorial Award, the SGT Craig Ivory Memorial Scholarships, the Society of Air Force Physician Assistants Scholarship, the Society of Army Physician Assistants Scholarship, the Naval Association of Physician Assistants Scholarship, the Tim and Jackie Egan Scholarship, the Ken Gartzke Scholarship, the David H. Gwinn Memorial Scholarship, and the Vicki Moritsugu Memorial Scholarship.

Number awarded Varies each year; recently, 11 of these scholarships were awarded.

Deadline February of each year.

[109]
VETERANS EDUCATIONAL ASSISTANCE PROGRAM (VEAP)

Department of Veterans Affairs
Attn: Veterans Benefits Administration
810 Vermont Avenue, N.W.
Washington, DC 20420
(202) 418-4343   Toll Free: (888) GI-BILL1
Web: www.gibill.va.gov/GI_Bill_Info/benefits.htm

Summary To provide financial assistance for college to veterans who first entered active duty between January 1, 1977 and June 30, 1985.

Eligibility Veterans who served and military servicemembers currently serving are eligible if they 1) entered active duty between January 1, 1977 and June 30, 1985; 2) were released under conditions other than dishonorable or continue on active duty; 3) served for a continuous period of 181 days or more (or were discharged earlier for a service-connected disability); and 4) have satisfactorily contributed to the program. No individuals on active duty could enroll in this program after March 31, 1987. Veterans who enlisted for the first time after September 7, 1980 or entered active duty as an office or enlistee after October 16, 1981 must have completed 24 continuous months of active duty. Benefits are available for the pursuit of an associate, bachelor, or graduate degree at a college or university; a certificate or diploma from a business, technical, or vocational school; apprenticeship or on-the-job training programs; cooperative courses; correspondence school courses; tutorial assistance; remedial, refresher, and deficiency training; flight training; study abroad programs leading to a college degree; nontraditional training away from school; and work-study for students enrolled at least three-quarter time.

Financial Data Participants contribute to the program, through monthly deductions from their military pay, from $25 to $100 monthly, up to a maximum of $2,700. They may also, while on active duty, make a lump sum contribution to the training fund. At the time the eligible participant elects to use the benefits to pursue an approved course of education or training, the Department of Veterans Affairs (VA) will match the contribution at the rate of $2 for every $1 made by the participant.

Duration Participants receive monthly payments for the number of months they contributed, or for 36 months, whichever is less. The amount of the payments is determined by dividing the number of months benefits will be paid into the participant's training fund total. Participants have 10 years from the date of last discharge or release from active duty within which to use these benefits.

Additional data A participant may leave this program at the end of any 12-consecutive-month period of participation and those who do so may have their contributions refunded. Ineligible courses include bartending or personality development courses; farm cooperative courses; non-accredited independent study courses; any course given by radio; self-improvement courses such as reading, speaking, woodworking, basic seamanship, and English as a second language; audited courses; any course that is avocational or recreational in character; courses not leading to an educational, professional, or vocational objective; courses taken and successfully completed previously; courses taken by a federal government employee and paid for under the Government Employees' Training Act; courses paid for in whole or in part by the armed forces while on active duty; and courses taken while in receipt of benefits for the same program from the Office of Workers' Compensation Programs.

Number awarded Varies each year.

Deadline Applications may be submitted at any time.

[110]
VETERANS OF ENDURING FREEDOM (AFGHANISTAN) AND IRAQI FREEDOM SCHOLARSHIP

Armed Forces Communications and Electronics Association
Attn: AFCEA Educational Foundation
4400 Fair Lakes Court
Fairfax, VA 22033-3899
(703) 631-6149   Toll Free: (800) 336-4583, ext. 6149
Fax: (703) 631-4693   E-mail: scholarship@afcea.org
Web: www.afcea.org

Summary To provide financial assistance to veterans and military personnel who served in Afghanistan or Iraq and are working on an undergraduate degree in fields related to the support of U.S. intelligence enterprises.

Eligibility This program is open to active-duty and honorably discharged U.S. military members (including Reservists and National Guard personnel) who served in Enduring Freedom (Afghanistan) or Iraqi Freedom operations. Applicants must be enrolled at a 2- or 4-year institution in the United States and working on an undergraduate degree in computer engineering technology, computer information systems, computer network systems, computer science, electronics engineering technology, engineering (aerospace, computer, electrical, or systems), information systems management, information systems security, mathematics, physics, science or mathematics education, technology management, or other field directly related to the support of U.S. intelligence enterprises or national security. Along with their application, they must submit an essay that includes a brief synopsis of relevant work experience (including military assignments), a brief statement of career goals after graduation, and a explanation of how their academic and career goals will contribute to the areas related to communications, intelligence and/or information systems, and the mission of the Armed Forces Communications and Electronics Association (AFCEA). Financial need is also considered in the selection process.

Financial Data The stipend is $2,500.

Duration 1 year.

Additional data This program was established in 2005 with funding from the Northern Virginia Chapter of AFCEA.

Number awarded 6 each year: 3 for the fall semester and 3 for the spring semester.

Deadline March of each year for fall semester; October of each year for spring semester.

[111]
VII CORPS DESERT STORM VETERANS ASSOCIATION SCHOLARSHIP

VII Corps Desert Storm Veterans Association
Attn: Scholarship Committee
Army Historical Foundation
2425 Wilson Boulevard
Arlington, VA 22201
(703) 604-6565   E-mail: viicorpsdsva@aol.com
Web: www.desertstormvets.org/Scholarship/html

Summary To provide financial assistance for college to students who served, or are the spouses or other family members of individuals who served, with VII Corps in Operations Desert Shield, Desert Storm, or related activities.

Eligibility Applicants must have served, or be a family member of those who served, with VII Corps in Operations Desert Shield/Desert Storm, Provide Comfort, or 1 of the support base activities. Scholarships are limited to students entering or enrolled in accredited technical institutions (trade or specialty), 2-year colleges, and 4-year colleges or universities. Awards will not be made to individuals receiving military academy appointments or full 4-year scholarships. Letters of recommendation and a transcript are required. Selection is not based solely on academic standing; consideration is also given to extracurricular activities and other self-development skills and abilities obtained through on-the-job training or correspondence courses. Priority is given to survivors of VII Corps soldiers who died during Operations Desert Shield/Desert Storm or Provide Comfort, veterans who are also members of the VII Corps Desert Storm Veterans Association, and family members of veterans who are also members of the VII Corps Desert Storm Veterans Association.

Financial Data The stipend is $5,000 per year. Funds are paid to the recipients upon proof of admission or registration at an accredited institution, college, or university.

Duration 1 year; recipients may reapply.

Additional data This program began in 1998.

Number awarded Approximately 3 each year.

Deadline January of each year.

[112]
VIRGINIA ARMY/AIR NATIONAL GUARD ENLISTED ASSOCIATION SCHOLARSHIP

Virginia Army/Air National Guard Enlisted Association
Attn: Scholarship Chair
P.O. Box 5826
Roanoke, VA 24012
(540) 366-5133   Fax: (540) 362-4417
E-mail: Scholarship@vaaangea.org
Web: www.vaaangea.org

Summary To provide financial assistance to members of the Virginia Army/Air National Guard Enlisted Association (VaA/ANGEA) and their families who are interested in attending college in any state.

Eligibility This program is open to 1) enlisted soldiers or enlisted airmen currently serving as a member of the Virginia National Guard (VNG) who are also a member of the VaA/ANGEA; 2) retired enlisted soldiers or retired enlisted airmen of the VNG who are also a member of the VaA/ANGEA; 3) spouses of current enlisted soldiers or enlisted airmen of the VNG who are also a member of the VaA/ANGEA; 4) spouses of retired enlisted soldiers or retired enlisted airmen of the VNG who are also a member of the VaA/ANGEA; and 5) dependents of current or retired enlisted soldiers or airmen of the VNG (a copy of the dependency decree may be required) who are also a member of the VaA/ANGEA. Applicants must submit a copy of their school transcript (high school or college), a letter with specific facts about their desire to continue their education and their need for assistance, 3 letters of recommendation, a letter of academic reference, and a photocopy of their VaA/ANGEA membership card.

Selection is based on academics (15 points), personal statement (15 points), letters of recommendation (16 points), school involvement (15 points), community involvement (15 points), responsibility (15 points), and financial need (9 points).

Financial Data Generally, stipends are either $1,000 or $500.

Duration 1 year; recipients may reapply.

Number awarded Generally, 2 scholarships at $1,000 and 4 scholarships at $500 are awarded each year.

Deadline March of each year.

[113]
VOCATIONAL REHABILITATION FOR DISABLED VETERANS

Department of Veterans Affairs
Attn: Veterans Benefits Administration
Vocational Rehabilitation and Employment Service
810 Vermont Avenue, N.W.
Washington, DC 20420
(202) 418-4343   Toll Free: (800) 827-1000
Web: www.vba.va.gov/bin/vre/index.htm

Summary To provide vocational rehabilitation to certain categories of veterans with disabilities.

Eligibility This program is open to veterans who have a service-connected disability of 1) at least 10% and a serious employment handicap, or 2) at least 20% and an employment handicap. They must have been discharged or released from military service under other than dishonorable conditions. The Department of Veterans Affairs (VA) must determine that they would benefit from a training program that would help them prepare for, find, and keep suitable employment. The program may be 1) institutional training at a certificate, 2-year college, 4-year college or university, or technical program; 2) unpaid on-the-job training in a federal, state, or local agency or a federally-recognized Indian tribal agency, training in a home, vocational course in a rehabilitation facility or sheltered workshop, independent instruction, or institutional non-farm cooperative; or 3) paid training through a farm cooperative, apprenticeship, on-the-job training, or on-the-job non-farm cooperative.

Financial Data While in training and for 2 months after, eligible disabled veterans may receive subsistence allowances in addition to their disability compensation or retirement pay. For most training programs, the current full-time monthly rate is $547.54 with no dependents, $679.18 with 1 dependent, $800.36 with 2 dependents, and $58.34 for each additional dependent; proportional rates apply for less than full-time training. The VA also pays the costs of tuition, books, fees, supplies, and equipment; it may also pay for special supportive services, such as tutorial assistance, prosthetic devices, lipreading training, and signing for the deaf. If during training or employment services the veteran's disabilities cause transportation expenses that would not be incurred by nondisabled persons, the VA will pay for at least a portion of those expenses. If the veteran encounters financial difficulty during training, the VA may provide an advance against future benefit payments.

Duration Up to 48 months of full-time training or its equivalent in part-time training. If a veteran with a serious disability receives services under an extended evaluation to improve training potential, the total of the extended evaluation and the training phases of the rehabilitation program may exceed 48 months. Usually, the veteran must complete a rehabilitation program within 12 years from the date of notification of entitlement to compensation by the VA. Following completion of the training portion of a rehabilitation program, a veteran may receive counseling and job search and adjustment services for 18 months.

Additional data The program may also provide employment assistance, self-employment assistance, training in a rehabilitation facility, or college and other training. Veterans who are seriously disabled may receive services and assistance to improve their ability to live more independently in their community. After completion of the training phase, the VA will assist the veteran to find and have a suitable job.

Number awarded Varies each year.

Deadline Applications are accepted at any time.

[114]
VVNW NATIONAL SCHOLARSHIP PROGRAM

Veterans of the Vietnam War, Inc.
Attn: Assistance in Education Program
805 South Township Boulevard
Pittston, PA 18640-3327
(570) 603-9740   Fax: (570) 603-9741
Web: www.vvnw.org

Summary To provide financial assistance for college to members of Veterans of the Vietnam War (VVnW) and their families.

Eligibility This program is open to members of the VVnW in good standing for at least 1 year and their spouses, children, adopted children, foster children, and other immediate descendants. Applicants must be enrolled in or accepted to a program of postsecondary education. Selection is based on a random drawing; financial need, merit, and course of study are not considered.

Financial Data The stipend is $1,000. Funds are paid directly to the recipient.

Duration 1 year.

Number awarded 1 or more each year, depending on the availability of funds.

Deadline October of each year.

[115]
WILMA D. HOYAL/MAXINE CHILTON SCHOLARSHIPS

American Legion Auxiliary
Department of Arizona
4701 North 19th Avenue, Suite 100
Phoenix, AZ 85015-3727
(602) 241-1080   Fax: (602) 604-9640
E-mail: amlegauxaz@mcleodusa.net
Web: www.azlegion.org/scholar3.txt

Summary To provide financial assistance to veterans, the dependents of veterans, and other students who are majoring in selected subjects at Arizona public universities.

Eligibility This program is open to second-year or upper-division full-time students majoring in political science, public programs, or special education at public universities in Arizona (the University of Arizona, Northern Arizona University, or Arizona State University). Applicants must have been Arizona residents for at least 1 year. They must have a GPA of 3.0 or higher. U.S. citizenship is required. Honorably-discharged veterans and immediate family members of veterans receive preference. Selection is based on scholarship (20%), financial need (40%), character (25%), and initiative (15%).

Financial Data The stipend is $1,000.

Duration 1 year; renewable.

Number awarded 3 each year: 1 to each of the 3 universities.

Deadline May of each year.

[116]
WISCONSIN G.I. BILL TUITION REMISSION PROGRAM

Wisconsin Department of Veterans Affairs
30 West Mifflin Street
P.O. Box 7843
Madison, WI 53707-7843
(608) 266-1311   Toll Free: (800) WIS-VETS
Fax: (608) 267-0403   E-mail: WDVAInfo@dva.state.wi.us
Web: www.dva.state.wi.us/Ben_education.asp

Summary To provide financial assistance for college or graduate school to Wisconsin veterans and their dependents.

Eligibility This program is open to current residents of Wisconsin who 1) were residents of the state when they entered or reentered active duty in the U.S. armed forces, or 2) have moved to the state and have been residents for any consecutive 12-month period after entry or reentry into service. Applicants must have served on active duty for at least 2 continuous years or for at least 90 days during specified wartime periods. Also eligible are 1) qualifying children and unremarried surviving spouses of Wisconsin veterans who died in the line of duty or as the direct result of a service-connected disability; and 2) children and spouses of Wisconsin veterans who have a service-connected disability rated by the U.S. Department of Veterans Affairs as 30% or greater. Children must be between 17 and 25 years of age (regardless of the date of the veteran's death or initial disability rating) and be a Wisconsin resident for tuition purposes. Spouses remain eligible for 10 years following the date of the veteran's death or initial disability rating; they must be Wisconsin residents for tuition purposes but they may enroll full or part time. Students may attend any institution, center, or school within the University of Wisconsin (UW) System or the Wisconsin Technical College System (WCTS). There are no income limits, delimiting periods following military service during which the benefit must be used, or limits on the level of study (e.g., vocational, undergraduate, professional, or graduate).

Financial Data Veterans who qualify as a Wisconsin resident for tuition purposes are eligible for a remission of 100% of standard academic fees and segregated fees at a UW campus or 100% of program and material fees at a WCTS institution. Veterans who qualify as a Wisconsin veteran for purposes of this program but for other reasons fail to meet the definition of a Wisconsin resident for tuition purposes at the UW system are eligible for a remission of 100% of non-resident fees. Spouses and children of deceased or disabled veterans are entitled to a remission of 100% of tuition and fees at a UW or WCTS institution.

Duration Up to 8 semesters or 128 credits, whichever is greater.

Additional data This program was established in 2005 as a replacement for Wisconsin Tuition and Fee Reimbursement Grants.

Number awarded Varies each year.

Deadline Applications must be submitted within 14 days from the office start of the academic term: in October for fall, March for spring, or June for summer.

[117]
WISCONSIN JOB RETRAINING GRANTS

Wisconsin Department of Veterans Affairs
30 West Mifflin Street
P.O. Box 7843
Madison, WI 53707-7843
(608) 266-1311   Toll Free: (800) WIS-VETS
Fax: (608) 267-0403   E-mail: WDVAInfo@dva.state.wi.us
Web: www.dva.state.wi.us/Ben_retraininggrants.asp

Summary To provide funds to recently unemployed Wisconsin veterans or their families who need financial assistance while being retrained for employment.

Eligibility This program is open to current residents of Wisconsin who 1) were residents of the state when they entered or reentered active duty in the U.S. armed forces, or 2) have moved to the state and have been residents for any consecutive 12-month period after entry or reentry into service. Applicants must have served on active duty for at least 2 continuous years or for at least 90 days during specified wartime periods. Unremarried spouses and minor or dependent children of deceased veterans who would have been eligible for the grant if they were living today may also be eligible. The applicant must, within the year prior to the date of application, have become unemployed (involuntarily laid off or discharged, not due to willful misconduct) or underemployed (experienced an involuntary reduction of income). Underemployed applicants must have current annual income from employment that does not exceed federal poverty guidelines. All applicants must be retraining at accredited schools in Wisconsin or in a structured on-the-job program. Course work toward a college degree does not qualify. Training does not have to be full time, but the program must be completed within 2 years and must reasonably be expected to lead to employment.

Financial Data The maximum grant is $3,000 per year; the actual amount varies, depending upon the amount of the applicant's unmet need. In addition to books, fees, and tuition, the funds may be used for living expenses.

Duration 1 year; may be renewed 1 additional year.

Number awarded Varies each year.

Deadline Applications may be submitted at any time.

[118]
WISCONSIN VETERANS EDUCATION (VETED) REIMBURSEMENT GRANTS

Wisconsin Department of Veterans Affairs
30 West Mifflin Street
P.O. Box 7843
Madison, WI 53707-7843
(608) 266-1311   Toll Free: (800) WIS-VETS
Fax: (608) 267-0403   E-mail: WDVAInfo@dva.state.wi.us
Web: www.dva.state.wi.us/Ben_VetEd.asp

Summary To provide financial assistance for undergraduate education to Wisconsin veterans.

Eligibility This program is open to current residents of Wisconsin who 1) were residents of the state when they entered or reentered active duty in the U.S. armed forces, or 2) have moved to the state and have been residents for any consecutive 12-month period after entry or reentry into service. Applicants must have served on active duty for at least 2 continuous years or for at least 90 days during specified wartime periods. They must be working full or part time on a degree, certificate of graduation, or course completion at an eligible campus of the University of Wisconsin, technical college, or approved private institution of higher education in Wisconsin or Minnesota. Their household income must be below $50,000 plus $1,000 for each dependent in excess of 2 dependents. Veterans seeking reimbursement through this program must first apply for Wisconsin G.I. Bill benefits. To qualify for reimbursement, they must achieve at least a 2.0 GPA or an average grade of "C" in the semester for which reimbursement is requested. Veterans may use this program up to 10 years after leaving active duty. Once a veteran reaches the 10-year delimiting date, he or she may "bank" up to 60 unused credits for part-time study.

Financial Data Eligible veterans are entitled to reimbursement of 100% of the costs of tuition and fees not covered by other grants, scholarships, or remissions, to a maximum of the UW-Madison rate for the same number of credits.

Duration The amount of reimbursement depends on the time the veteran served on active duty: 30 credits or 2 semesters for 90 to 180 days of active service, 60 credits or 4 semesters for 181 to 730 days of active service, or 120 credits or 8 semesters for 731 days or more of active service.

Additional data This program was established in 2005 as a replacement for the former Wisconsin Part-Time Study Grants. Reimbursement is not provided to students for payment amounts for which they are eligible under other programs, including the Wisconsin G.I. Bill.

Number awarded Varies each year.

Deadline Applications must be received within 60 days of the start of the course, semester, or term.

[119]
WMA SCHOLARSHIP PROGRAM

Women Marines Association
P.O. Box 377
Oaks, PA 19456-0377
Toll Free: (888) 525-1943 E-mail: wma@womenmarines.org
Web: www.womenmarines.org/scholarships.aspx

Summary To provide financial assistance for college or graduate school to students sponsored by members of the Women Marines Association (WMA).

Eligibility Applicants must be sponsored by a WMA member and fall into 1 of the following categories: 1) have served or are serving in the U.S. Marine Corps, regular or Reserve; 2) are a direct descendant by blood, legal adoption, or stepchild of a Marine on active duty or who has served honorably in the U.S. Marine Corps, regular or Reserve; 3) are a sibling or a descendant of a sibling by blood, legal adoption, or stepchild of a Marine on active duty or who has served honorably in the U.S. Marine Corps, regular or Reserve; or 4) have completed 2 years in a Marine Corps JROTC program. WMA members may sponsor an unlimited number of applicants per year. High school seniors must submit transcripts (GPA of 3.0 or higher) and SAT or ACT scores. Undergraduate and graduate students must have a GPA of 3.0 or higher.

Financial Data The stipend is $1,500 per year.

Duration 1 year; may be renewed 1 additional year.

Additional data This program includes the following named scholarships: the WMA Memorial Scholarships, the Lily H. Gridley Memorial Scholarship, the Ethyl and Armin Wiebke Memorial Scholarship, the Maj. Megan Malia McClung Memorial Scholarship, and the LaRue A. Ditmore Music Scholarships. Applicants must know a WMA member to serve as their sponsor; the WMA will not supply listings of the names or addresses of chapters or individual members.

Number awarded Varies each year.

Deadline March of each year.

[120]
WNGEA COLLEGE GRANT PROGRAM

Wisconsin National Guard Enlisted Association
Attn: Executive Director
2400 Wright Street
Madison, WI 53704
(608) 242-3112   E-mail: WNGEA@yahoo.com
Web: www.wngea.org/MAIN/PROG/prosch.htm

Summary To provide financial assistance to members of the Wisconsin National Guard Enlisted Association (WNGEA) and their spouses and children who are interested in attending college or graduate school in any state.

Eligibility This program is open to WNGEA members, the unmarried children of WNGEA members, the spouses of WNGEA members, and the unmarried children and spouses of deceased WNGEA members. WNGEA member applicants, as well as the parents or guardians of unmarried children who are applicants, must have at least 1 year remaining on their enlistment following completion of the school year for which application is submitted (or they must have 20 or more years of service). Applicants must be enrolled at a college, university, graduate school, trade school, or business school in any state. Selection is based on financial need, leadership, and moral character.

Financial Data Stipends are $1,000 or $500 per year.

Duration 1 year; recipients may not reapply for 2 years.

Additional data This program includes 1 scholarship sponsored by the USAA Insurance Corporation.

Number awarded Varies each year. Recently, 4 of these scholarships were awarded: the Raymond A. Matera Scholarship at $1,000 and 3 others at $500 each.

Deadline May of each year.

[121]
WYOMING OVERSEAS COMBAT VETERAN TUITION BENEFIT

Wyoming Veterans Commission
Attn: Executive Director
5500 Bishop Boulevard
Cheyenne, WY 82009
(307) 772-5145   Toll Free: (866) 992-7641, ext. 5145
Fax: (307) 772-5202   E-mail: lbartt@state.wy.us
Web: www.wy.ngb.army.mil/benefits

Summary To provide financial assistance to Wyoming veterans who served in overseas combat anytime except during the Vietnam era and are interested in attending college in the state.

Eligibility This program is open to Wyoming veterans who served anytime except during the Vietnam era and were residents of Wyoming for at least 1 year before entering military service. Applicants must have received an honorable discharge and have been awarded the armed forces expeditionary medal or other authorized service or campaign medal indicating service to the United States in an armed conflict in a foreign country. They must enroll at the University of Wyoming or a community college in the state within 10 years following completion of military service.

Financial Data Qualifying veterans are eligible for free resident tuition at the University of Wyoming or at any of the state's community colleges.

Duration Up to 10 semesters.

Additional data Applications may be obtained from the institution the applicant is attending or planning to attend.

Number awarded Varies each year.

Deadline Applications may be submitted at any time, but they should be received 2 or 3 weeks before the beginning of the semester.

[122]
WYOMING VIETNAM VETERAN TUITION BENEFIT

Wyoming Veterans Commission
Attn: Executive Director
5500 Bishop Boulevard
Cheyenne, WY 82009
(307) 772-5145   Toll Free: (866) 992-7641, ext. 5145
Fax: (307) 772-5202   E-mail: lbartt@state.wy.us
Web: www.wy.ngb.army.mil/benefits

Summary To provide financial assistance to Wyoming veterans who served during the Vietnam era and are interested in attending college in the state.

Eligibility This program is open to Wyoming veterans who 1) served on active duty with the U.S. armed forces between August 5, 1964 and May 7, 1975; 2) received a Vietnam service medal between those dates; 3) received an honorable discharge; 4) have lived in Wyoming for at least 1 year; and 5) have exhausted their veterans' benefits entitlement or for some other reason are no longer eligible for U.S. Department of Veterans Affairs benefits. Applicants must be attending or planning to attend the University of Wyoming or a community college in the state.

Financial Data Qualifying veterans are eligible for free resident tuition at the University of Wyoming or at any of the state's community colleges.

Duration Up to 10 semesters.

Additional data Applications may be obtained from the institution the applicant is attending or planning to attend.

Number awarded Varies each year.

Deadline Applications may be submitted at any time, but they should be received 2 or 3 weeks before the beginning of the semester.

Military Personnel

[123]
AAAA SCHOLARSHIPS

Army Aviation Association of America Scholarship
   Foundation
Attn: AAAA Scholarship Foundation
755 Main Street, Suite 4D
Monroe, CT 06468-2830
(203) 268-2450   Fax: (203) 268-5870
E-mail: Scholarship@quad-a.org
Web: www.quad-a.org/scholarship.htm

Summary To provide financial aid for undergraduate or graduate study to members of the Army Aviation Association of America (AAAA) and their relatives.

Eligibility This program is open to AAAA members and their spouses, unmarried siblings, unmarried children, and unmarried grandchildren. Applicants must be enrolled or accepted for enrollment as an undergraduate or graduate student at an accredited college or university. Graduate students must include a 250-word essay on their life experiences, work history, and aspirations. Some scholarships are specifically reserved for enlisted, warrant officer, company grade, and Department of the Army civilian members. Selection is based on academic merit and personal achievement.

Financial Data Most stipends range from $1,000 to $4,000. Special scholarships are $11,000.

Duration Scholarships may be for 1 year, 2 years, or 4 years.

Additional data This program includes 3 special scholarships: the GEN Hamilton H. Howze Memorial Scholarship, the Helen Cribbins Memorial Scholarship, and the Joseph P. Cribbins Scholarship.

Number awarded Varies each year; recently, $268,500 in scholarships was awarded to 171 students. Since the program began in 1963, the foundation has awarded more than $3.3 million to nearly 2,000 qualified applicants.

Deadline April of each year.

[124]
ADMIRAL MIKE BOORDA SCHOLARSHIP PROGRAM

Navy-Marine Corps Relief Society
Attn: Education Division
875 North Randolph Street, Suite 225
Arlington, VA 22203-1757
(703) 696-4960   Fax: (703) 696-0144
E-mail: education@nmcrs.org
Web: www.nmcrs.org/boorda.html

Summary To provide supplemental assistance to Navy or Marine Corps personnel selected for or enrolled in enlisted commissioning programs.

Eligibility Eligible for this assistance are active-duty members of the Navy or Marine Corps selected for or enrolled in the Marine Enlisted Commissioning Education Program (MECEP), the Navy's Medical Enlisted Commissioning Program (MECP), or the Marine Meritorious Commissioning Program (MCP). Participants in the Navy's Seaman to Admiral-21 program are not eligible. Applicants must be planning to enroll as a full-time undergraduate in a traditional classroom setting at a college or university. They must have a GPA of 2.0 or higher and be able to demonstrate financial need.

Financial Data Grants range from $500 to $3,000 per year, depending on need.

Duration 1 year; may be renewed up to 3 additional years.

Number awarded Varies each year.

Deadline April of each year.

[125]
AIR FORCE ASSOCIATION FIRST COMMAND EDUCATIONAL FOUNDATION ROTC SCHOLARSHIP

Air Force Association
Attn: Scholarship Manager
1501 Lee Highway
Arlington, VA 22209-1198
(703) 247-5800, ext. 4807
Toll Free: (800) 727-3337, ext. 4807
Fax: (703) 247-5853   E-mail: LCross@afa.org
Web: www.afa.org/aef/aid/afa-fcef-rotc.asp

Summary To provide financial assistance to Air Force ROTC cadets who are entering their junior or senior year of college and majoring in a field of science, technology, engineering, or mathematics (STEM).

Eligibility This program is open to Air Force ROTC cadets entering their junior or senior year as full-time students and majoring in a STEM discipline. Selection is based on academic merit and financial need.

Financial Data The stipend is $5,000.

Duration 1 year.

Additional data This program was established in 2008 by the Air Force Association in partnership with the First Command Educational Foundation and is administered by Air Force ROTC headquarters.

Number awarded 2 each year.

Deadline Deadline not specified.

[126]
AIR FORCE ENHANCED ROTC HISPANIC SERVING INSTITUTION SCHOLARSHIP PROGRAM

U.S. Air Force
Attn: Headquarters AFROTC/RRUC
551 East Maxwell Boulevard
Maxwell AFB, AL 36112-5917
(334) 953-2091   Toll Free: (866) 4-AFROTC
Fax: (334) 953-6167   E-mail: afrotc1@maxwell.af.mil
Web: afrotc.com

Summary To provide financial assistance to students at designated Hispanic Serving Institutions (HSIs) who are willing to join Air Force ROTC in college and serve as Air Force officers following completion of their bachelor's degree.

Eligibility This program is open to U.S. citizens who are at least 17 years of age and currently enrolled at 1 of 5 designated HSIs that have an Air Force ROTC unit on campus. Applicants do not need to be Hispanic, as long as they are enrolled at the university and have a cumulative GPA of 2.5 or higher. At the time of commissioning, they may be no more than 31 years of age. They must be able to pass the Air Force Officer Qualifying Test (AFOQT) and the Air Force ROTC Physical Fitness Test. Currently, the program is accepting applications from students with any major.

Financial Data Awards are type 2 AFROTC scholarships that provide for payment of tuition and fees, to a maximum of $18,000 per year, plus an annual book allowance of $900. Recipients are also awarded a tax-free subsistence allowance for 10 months of each year that is $350 per month during the sophomore year, $450 during the junior year, and $500 during the senior year.

Duration Up to 3 and a half years (beginning as early as the spring semester of the freshman year).

Additional data The designated universities are California State University at San Bernardino, New Mexico State University, the University of Puerto Rico at Rio Piedras, the University of Puerto Rico at Mayaguez, and the University of Texas at San Antonio. While scholarship recipients can major in any subject, they must complete 4 years of aerospace studies courses. They

must also attend a 4-week summer training camp at an Air Force base, usually between their sophomore and junior years; 2-year scholarship awardees attend in the summer after their junior year. Current military personnel are eligible for early release from active duty in order to enter the Air Force ROTC program. Following completion of their bachelor's degree, scholarship recipients earn a commission as a second lieutenant in the Air Force and serve at least 4 years.

Number awarded Up to 75 each year: 15 at each of the participating AFROTC units.

Deadline Applications may be submitted at any time.

[127]
AIR FORCE ENHANCED ROTC HISTORICALLY BLACK COLLEGES AND UNIVERSITIES SCHOLARSHIP PROGRAM

U.S. Air Force
Attn: Headquarters AFROTC/RRUC
551 East Maxwell Boulevard
Maxwell AFB, AL 36112-5917
(334) 953-2091   Toll Free: (866) 4-AFROTC
Fax: (334) 953-6167   E-mail: afrotc1@maxwell.af.mil
Web: afrotc.com

Summary To provide financial assistance to students at designated Historically Black Colleges and Universities (HBCUs) who are willing to join Air Force ROTC and serve as Air Force officers following completion of their bachelor's degree.

Eligibility This program is open to U.S. citizens at least 17 years of age who are currently enrolled as freshmen at 1 of the 7 HBCUs that has an Air Force ROTC unit on campus. Applicants do not need to be African American, as long as they are attending an HBCU and have a cumulative GPA of 2.5 or higher. At the time of commissioning, they may be no more than 31 years of age. They must be able to pass the Air Force Officer Qualifying Test (AFOQT) and the Air Force ROTC Physical Fitness Test. Currently, the program is accepting applications from students with any major.

Financial Data Awards are type 2 AFROTC scholarships that provide for payment of tuition and fees, to a maximum of $18,000 per year, plus an annual book allowance of $900. Recipients are also awarded a tax-free subsistence allowance for 10 months of each year that is $350 per month during the sophomore year, $450 during the junior year, and $500 during the senior year.

Duration Up to 3 and a half years (beginning as early as the spring semester of the freshman year).

Additional data The participating HBCUs are Tuskegee University (Tuskegee, Alabama), Alabama State University (Montgomery, Alabama), Howard University (Washington, D.C.), North Carolina A&T State University (Greensboro, North Carolina), Fayetteville State University (Fayetteville, North Carolina), Tennessee State University (Nashville, Tennessee), and Jackson State University (Jackson, Mississippi). While scholarship recipients can major in any subject, they must complete 4 years of aerospace studies courses at 1 of the HBCUs that have an Air Force ROTC unit on campus. Recipients must also attend a 4-week summer training camp at an Air Force base, usually between their sophomore and junior years; 2-year scholarship awardees attend in the summer after their junior year. Current military personnel are eligible for early release from active duty in order to enter the Air Force ROTC program. Following completion of their bachelor's degree, scholarship recipients earn a commission as a second lieutenant in the Air Force and serve at least 4 years.

Number awarded Up to 105 each year: 15 at each of the participating AFROTC units.

Deadline Applications may be submitted at any time.

[128]
AIR FORCE EXCELLENCE SCHOLARSHIPS

Air Force Association
Attn: Scholarship Manager
1501 Lee Highway
Arlington, VA 22209-1198
(703) 247-5800, ext. 4807
Toll Free: (800) 727-3337, ext. 4807
Fax: (703) 247-5853   E-mail: LCross@afa.org
Web: www.afa.org/aef/aid/afa-fcef-rotc.asp

Summary   To provide financial assistance for college or graduate school to Air Force personnel and their dependents.

Eligibility   This program is open to Air Force active duty, Reserve, or Air National Guard personnel and their spouses and dependent children. Applicants must be entering or enrolled at an accredited college or university to work on an associate, bachelor's, or master's degree. In the selection process, no consideration is given to race, creed, color, sex, religious belief, national origin, rank, length of service, or financial need.

Financial Data   The stipend is $3,000.

Duration   1 year.

Additional data   This program was established in 2008 by the Air Force Association in partnership with the First Command Educational Foundation.

Number awarded   5 each year.

Deadline   April of each year.

[129]
AIR FORCE REGULAR ROTC HISPANIC SERVING INSTITUTION SCHOLARSHIP PROGRAM

U.S. Air Force
Attn: Headquarters AFROTC/RRUC
551 East Maxwell Boulevard
Maxwell AFB, AL 36112-5917
(334) 953-2091   Toll Free: (866) 4-AFROTC
Fax: (334) 953-6167   E-mail: afrotc1@maxwell.af.mil
Web: afrotc.com

Summary   To provide financial assistance to students at Hispanic Serving Institutions (HSIs) who are willing to join Air Force ROTC in college and serve as Air Force officers following completion of their bachelor's degree.

Eligibility   This program is open to U.S. citizens at least 17 years of age who are currently enrolled at an HSI that has an Air Force ROTC unit on campus or that has a cross-enrollment agreement with another school that hosts a unit. Applicants do not need to be Hispanic, as long as they are attending an HSI and have a cumulative GPA of 2.5 or higher. At the time of commissioning, they may be no more than 31 years of age. They must be able to pass the Air Force Officer Qualifying Test (AFOQT) and the Air Force ROTC Physical Fitness Test. Currently, the program is accepting applications from students with any major.

Financial Data   Awards are type 2 AFROTC scholarships that provide for payment of tuition and fees, to a maximum of $18,000 per year, plus an annual book allowance of $900. Recipients are also awarded a tax-free subsistence allowance for 10 months of each year that is $350 per month during the sophomore year, $450 during the junior year, and $500 during the senior year.

Duration   2 to 3 years, beginning during the current term.

Additional data   While scholarship recipients can major in any subject, they must complete 4 years of aerospace studies courses. They must also attend a 4-week summer training camp at an Air Force base, usually between their sophomore and junior years; 2-year scholarship awardees attend in the summer after their junior year. Current military personnel are eligible for early release from active duty in order to enter the Air Force ROTC program. Following completion of their bachelor's degree, scholarship recipients earn a commission as a second lieutenant in the Air Force and serve at least 4 years.

Number awarded   Varies each year. AFROTC units at every HSI may nominate an unlimited number of cadets to receive these scholarships.

Deadline   Applications may be submitted at any time.

[130]
AIR FORCE REGULAR ROTC HISTORICALLY BLACK COLLEGES AND UNIVERSITIES SCHOLARSHIP PROGRAM

U.S. Air Force
Attn: Headquarters AFROTC/RRUC
551 East Maxwell Boulevard
Maxwell AFB, AL 36112-5917
(334) 953-2091   Toll Free: (866) 4-AFROTC
Fax: (334) 953-6167   E-mail: afrotc1@maxwell.af.mil
Web: afrotc.com

Summary   To provide financial assistance to students at Historically Black Colleges and Universities (HBCUs) who are willing to serve as Air Force officers following completion of their bachelor's degree.

Eligibility   This program is open to U.S. citizens at least 17 years of age who are currently enrolled at an HBCU that has an Air Force ROTC unit on campus or that has a cross-enrollment agreement with another school that hosts a unit. Applicants do not need to be African American, as long as they are attending an HBCU and have a cumulative GPA of 2.5 or higher. At the time of commissioning, they may be no more than 31 years of age. They must be able to pass the Air Force Officer Qualifying Test (AFOQT) and the Air Force ROTC Physical Fitness Test. Currently, the program is accepting applications from students with any major.

Financial Data   Awards are type 2 AFROTC scholarships that provide for payment of tuition and fees, to a maximum of $18,000 per year, plus an annual book allowance of $900. Recipients are also awarded a tax-free subsistence allowance for 10 months of each year that is $350 per month during the sophomore year, $450 during the junior year, and $500 during the senior year.

Duration   2 to 3 years, beginning during the current term.

Additional data   While scholarship recipients can major in any subject, they must complete 4 years of aerospace studies courses at 1 of the HBCUs that have an Air Force ROTC unit on campus. Recipients must also attend a 4-week summer training camp at an Air Force base, usually between their sophomore and junior years; 2-year scholarship awardees attend in the summer after their junior year. Current military personnel are eligible for early release from active duty in order to enter the Air Force ROTC program. Following completion of their bachelor's degree, scholarship recipients earn a commission as a second lieutenant in the Air Force and serve at least 4 years.

Number awarded   Varies each year. AFROTC units at every HBCU may nominate an unlimited number of cadets to receive these scholarships.

Deadline   Applications may be submitted at any time.

[131]
AIR FORCE RESERVE TUITION ASSISTANCE

U.S. Air Force Reserve
Attn: Air Reserve Personnel Center
Directorate of Personnel Services
6760 East Irvington Place
Denver, CO 80280-4000
(303) 676-7037   Toll Free: (800) 525-0102
Fax: (478) 327-2215
E-mail: arpc.contactcenter@arpc.denver.af.mil
Web: www.arpc.afrc.af.mil/library/education/index.asp

Summary   To provide financial assistance for college or graduate school to members of the Air Force Reserve.

Eligibility This program is open to Air Force Reserve members interested in working on an undergraduate or graduate degree either through distance learning or on-campus courses from an accredited postsecondary institution. Applicants must be actively participating (for pay and points) and in good standing (not have a UIF, not placed on a control roster, not pending or issued an Article 15, and/or not pending court martial). They must submit a degree plan specifying all classes for which they are seeking assistance. Enlisted students must have retainability that extends beyond the last course approved for assistance or they must extend or re-enlist; commissioned officers must have a mandatory separation date of not less than 24 months of service commitment starting at the end of the last course completed.

Financial Data Undergraduates receive 100% of tuition, to a maximum of $250 per semester hour or $4,500 per year; graduate students receive 75% of tuition, to a maximum of $250 per semester hour or $4,500 per year.

Duration 1 year; may be renewed.

Number awarded Varies each year.

Deadline Applications may be submitted at any time.

[132]
AIR FORCE ROTC BIOMEDICAL SCIENCES CORPS

U.S. Air Force
Attn: Headquarters AFROTC/RRUC
551 East Maxwell Boulevard
Maxwell AFB, AL 36112-5917
(334) 953-2091   Toll Free: (866) 4-AFROTC
Fax: (334) 953-6167   E-mail: afrotc1@maxwell.af.mil
Web: afrotc.com

Summary To provide financial assistance to students who are interested in joining Air Force ROTC in college and preparing for a career as a physical therapist, optometrist, or pharmacist.

Eligibility This program is open to U.S. citizens who are freshmen or sophomores in college and interested in a career as a physical therapist, optometrist, or pharmacist. Applicants must have a GPA of 2.0 or higher and meet all other academic and physical requirements for participation in AFROTC. At the time of their Air Force commissioning, they may be no more than 31 years of age. They must agree to serve for at least 4 years as nonline active-duty Air Force officers following graduation from college.

Financial Data Awards are type 2 AFROTC scholarships that provide for payment of tuition and fees, to a maximum of $18,000 per year, plus an annual book allowance of $900. All recipients are also awarded a tax-free subsistence allowance for 10 months of each year that is $350 per month during their sophomore year, $450 during their junior year, and $500 during their senior year.

Duration 2 or 3 years, provided the recipient maintains a GPA of 2.0 or higher.

Additional data Recipients must also complete 4 years of aerospace studies courses at 1 of the 144 colleges and universities that have an Air Force ROTC unit on campus or 1 of the 984 colleges that have cross-enrollment agreements with those institutions. They must also attend a 4-week summer training camp at an Air Force base, usually between their sophomore and junior years. Following completion of their bachelor's degree, scholarship recipients earn a commission as a second lieutenant in the Air Force and serve at least 4 years.

Deadline June of each year.

[133]
AIR FORCE ROTC EXPRESS SCHOLARSHIPS

U.S. Air Force
Attn: Headquarters AFROTC/RRUC
551 East Maxwell Boulevard
Maxwell AFB, AL 36112-5917
(334) 953-2091   Toll Free: (866) 4-AFROTC
Fax: (334) 953-6167   E-mail: afrotc1@maxwell.af.mil
Web: afrotc.com/scholarships/in-college/express-scholarships

Summary To provide financial assistance to students who are interested in joining Air Force ROTC and majoring in critical Air Force officer technical fields in college.

Eligibility This program is open to U.S. citizens who are entering their junior or senior year of college and are working on a degree in technical fields that may change annually but are of critical interest to the Air Force; currently, the eligible fields are computer, electrical, and environmental engineering. Applicants must have a GPA of 2.5 or higher and meet all other academic and physical requirements for participation in AFROTC. At the time of their Air Force commissioning, they may be no more than 31 years of age. They must be able to pass the Air Force Officer Qualifying Test (AFOQT) and the Air Force ROTC Physical Fitness Test.

Financial Data Awards are type 1 AFROTC scholarships that provide for full payment of tuition and fees plus an annual book allowance of $900. All recipients are also awarded a tax-free monthly subsistence allowance that is $450 for juniors and $500 for seniors.

Duration 1 or 2 years, until completion of a bachelor's degree.

Additional data Following completion of their bachelor's degree, scholarship recipients earn a commission as a second lieutenant in the Air Force and serve at least 4 years.

Deadline Deadline not specified.

[134]
AIR FORCE ROTC FOREIGN LANGUAGE MAJORS SCHOLARSHIPS

U.S. Air Force
Attn: Headquarters AFROTC/RRUC
551 East Maxwell Boulevard
Maxwell AFB, AL 36112-5917
(334) 953-2091   Toll Free: (866) 4-AFROTC
Fax: (334) 953-6167   E-mail: afrotc1@maxwell.af.mil
Web: afrotc.com

Summary To provide financial assistance to students who are interested in joining Air Force ROTC and majoring in specified foreign languages of importance to the Air Force.

Eligibility This program is open to U.S. citizens who are entering their junior or senior year of college and are working on a degree in foreign languages that may change annually but are of interest to the Air Force; currently, those are Arabic, Azeri, Bengali, Cambodian, Chinese, Hausa, Hindi, Indonesian, Japanese, Kazakh, Kurdish, Malay, Pashto, Persian-Iranian, Persian-Afghan, Russian, Serbo-Croatian, Swahili, Thai, Turkish, Uighar, Urdu/Punjabi, Uzbek, or Vietnamese. Applicants must have a GPA of 2.5 or higher and meet all other academic and physical requirements for participation in AFROTC. At the time of their Air Force commissioning, they may be no more than 31 years of age. They must be able to pass the Air Force Officer Qualifying Test (AFOQT) and the Air Force ROTC Physical Fitness Test.

Financial Data Awards are type 1 AFROTC scholarships that provide for full payment of tuition and fees plus an annual book allowance of $900. All recipients are also awarded a tax-free monthly subsistence allowance that is $450 for juniors and $500 for seniors.

Duration 1 or 2 years, until completion of a bachelor's degree.

Additional data Following completion of their bachelor's degree, scholarship recipients earn a commission as a second lieutenant in the Air Force and serve at least 4 years.

Deadline Deadline not specified.

[135]
AIR FORCE ROTC GENERAL MILITARY COURSE INCENTIVE

U.S. Air Force
Attn: Headquarters AFROTC/RRUC
551 East Maxwell Boulevard
Maxwell AFB, AL 36112-5917
(334) 953-2091   Toll Free: (866) 4-AFROTC
Fax: (334) 953-6167   E-mail: afrotc1@maxwell.af.mil
Web: afrotc.com/learn-about/programs-and-scholarships

Summary To provide financial assistance to college sophomores interested in joining Air Force ROTC and serving as Air Force officers following completion of their bachelor's degree.

Eligibility This program is open to U.S. citizens who are entering the spring semester of their sophomore year in the general military course at a college or university with an Air Force ROTC unit on campus or a college with a cross-enrollment agreement with such a school. Applicants must be full-time students, have a GPA of 2.0 or higher both cumulatively and during the prior term, be enrolled in both the Aerospace Studies 200 class and the Leadership Laboratory, pass the Air Force Officer Qualifying Test, meet Air Force physical fitness and weight requirements, and be able to be commissioned before they become 31 years of age. They must agree to serve for at least 4 years as active-duty Air Force officers following graduation from college.

Financial Data Selected cadets receive up to $1,500 for tuition and a stipend of $250 per month.

Duration 1 semester (the spring semester of junior year); nonrenewable.

Additional data Upon successful completion of their sophomore year, recipients of these scholarships may upgrade to the Professional Officer Course Incentive. They also remain eligible to apply for other AFROTC in-college scholarship programs.

Deadline Deadline not specified.

[136]
AIR FORCE ROTC HIGH SCHOOL SCHOLARSHIPS

U.S. Air Force
Attn: Headquarters AFROTC/RRUC
551 East Maxwell Boulevard
Maxwell AFB, AL 36112-5917
(334) 953-2091   Toll Free: (866) 4-AFROTC
Fax: (334) 953-6167   E-mail: afrotc1@maxwell.af.mil
Web: afrotc.com/scholarships/high-school

Summary To provide financial assistance to high school seniors or graduates who are interested in joining Air Force ROTC in college and are willing to serve as Air Force officers following completion of their bachelor's degree.

Eligibility This program is open to high school seniors who are U.S. citizens at least 17 years of age and have been accepted at a college or university with an Air Force ROTC unit on campus or a college with a cross-enrollment agreement with such a college. Applicants must have a cumulative GPA of 3.0 or higher, a class rank in the top 40%, and an ACT composite score of 24 or higher or an SAT score of 1100 or higher (mathematics and critical reading portion only). At the time of their commissioning in the Air Force, they must be no more than 31 years of age. They must agree to serve for at least 4 years as active-duty Air Force officers following graduation from college. Recently, scholarships were offered to students planning to major (in order or priority) in 1) the science and technical fields of architecture, chemistry, computer science, engineering (aeronautical, aerospace, astronautical, architectural, civil, computer, electrical, environmental, or mechanical), mathematics, meteorology and atmospheric sciences, operations research, or physics; 2) foreign languages (Arabic, Azeri, Bengali, Cambodian, Chinese, Hausa, Hindi, Indonesian, Japanese, Kazakh, Kurdish, Malay, Pashto, Persian-Iranian, Persian-Afghan, Russian, Serbo-Croatian, Swahili, Thai, Turkish, Uighar, Urdu/Punjabi, Uzbek, or Vietnamese); 3) all other fields.

Financial Data Type 1 scholarships provide payment of full tuition and most laboratory fees, as well as $900 per year for books. Type 2 scholarships pay the same benefits except tuition is capped at $18,000 per year; students who attend an institution where tuition exceeds $18,000 must pay the difference. Type 7 scholarships pay full tuition and most laboratory fees, but students must attend a public college or university where they qualify for the in-state tuition rate or a college or university where the tuition is less than the in-state rate; they may not attend an institution with higher tuition and pay the difference. Approximately 5% of scholarship offers are for Type 1, approximately 20% are for Type 2, and approximately 75% are for type 7. All recipients are also awarded a tax-free subsistence allowance for 10 months of each year that is $300 per month as a freshman, $350 per month as a sophomore, $450 per month as a junior, and $500 per month as a senior.

Duration 4 years.

Additional data While scholarship recipients can major in any subject, they must enroll in 4 years of aerospace studies courses at 1 of the 144 colleges and universities that have an Air Force ROTC unit on campus; students may also attend 984 other colleges that have cross-enrollment agreements with the institutions that have an Air Force ROTC unit on campus. Recipients must attend a 4-week summer training camp at an Air Force base, usually between their sophomore and junior years. Most cadets incur a 4-year active-duty commitment. Pilots incur a 10-year active-duty service commitment after successfully completing Specialized Undergraduate Pilot Training and navigators incur a 6-year commitment after successfully completing Specialized Undergraduate Navigator Training. The minimum service obligation for intelligence and Air Battle Management career fields is 5 years.

Number awarded Approximately 2,000 each year.

Deadline November of each year.

[137]
AIR FORCE ROTC IN-COLLEGE SCHOLARSHIP PROGRAM

U.S. Air Force
Attn: Headquarters AFROTC/RRUC
551 East Maxwell Boulevard
Maxwell AFB, AL 36112-5917
(334) 953-2091   Toll Free: (866) 4-AFROTC
Fax: (334) 953-6167   E-mail: afrotc1@maxwell.af.mil
Web: afrotc.com/scholarships/in-college/programs

Summary To provide financial assistance to undergraduate students who are willing to join Air Force ROTC in college and serve as Air Force officers following completion of their bachelor's degree.

Eligibility This program is open to U.S. citizens enrolled as freshmen or sophomores at 1 of the 144 colleges and universities that have an Air Force ROTC unit on campus. Applicants must have a cumulative GPA of 2.5 or higher and be able to pass the Air Force Officer Qualifying Test and the Air Force ROTC Physical Fitness Test. At the time of commissioning, they may be no more than 31 years of age. They must agree to serve for at least 4 years as active-duty Air Force officers following graduation from college. Phase 1 is open to students enrolled in the Air Force ROTC program who do not currently have a scholarship but now wish to apply. Phase 2 is open to Phase 1 nonselects and students not enrolled in Air Force ROTC. Phase 3 is open only to Phase 2 nonselects.

Financial Data Cadets selected in Phase 1 are awarded type 2 AFROTC scholarships that provide for payment of tuition and fees, to a maximum of $18,000 per year. A limited number of cadets selected in Phase 2 are also awarded type 2 AFROTC scholarships, but most are awarded type 3 AFROTC scholarships with tuition capped at $9,000 per year. Cadets selected in Phase 3 are awarded type 6 AFROTC scholarships with tuition capped at $3,000 per year. All recipients are also awarded a book allowance of $900 per year and a tax-free subsistence allowance for 10 months of each year that is $350 per month during the sophomore year, $450 during the junior year, and $500 during the senior year.

Duration 3 years for students selected as freshmen or 2 years for students selected as sophomores.

Additional data While scholarship recipients can major in any subject, they must complete 4 years of aerospace studies courses at 1 of the 144 colleges or universities that have an Air Force ROTC unit on campus; students may also attend 984 other colleges that have cross-enrollment agreements with the institutions that have an Air Force ROTC unit on campus. Recipients must also attend a 4-week summer training camp at an Air Force base, usually between their sophomore and junior years; 2-year scholarship awardees attend in the summer after their junior year. Current military personnel are eligible for early release from active duty in order to enter the Air Force ROTC program. Following completion of their bachelor's degree, scholarship recipients earn a commission as a second lieutenant in the Air Force and serve at least 4 years.

Number awarded Varies each year.

Deadline February of each year.

[138]
AIR FORCE ROTC NURSING SCHOLARSHIPS

U.S. Air Force
Attn: Headquarters AFROTC/RRUC
551 East Maxwell Boulevard
Maxwell AFB, AL 36112-5917
(334) 953-2091   Toll Free: (866) 4-AFROTC
Fax: (334) 953-6167   E-mail: afrotc1@maxwell.af.mil
Web: afrotc.com/admissions/professional-programs/nursing

Summary To provide financial assistance to college students who are interested in a career as a nurse, are interested in joining Air Force ROTC, and are willing to serve as Air Force officers following completion of their bachelor's degree.

Eligibility This program is open to U.S. citizens who are freshmen or sophomores in college and interested in a career as a nurse. Applicants must have a cumulative GPA of 2.5 or higher at the end of their freshman year and meet all other academic and physical requirements for participation in AFROTC. They must be interested in working on a nursing degree from an accredited program. At the time of Air Force commissioning, they may be no more than 31 years of age. They must be able to pass the Air Force Officer Qualifying Test (AFOQT) and the Air Force ROTC Physical Fitness Test.

Financial Data Awards are type 1 AFROTC scholarships that provide for full payment of tuition and fees plus an annual book allowance of $900. All recipients are also awarded a tax-free subsistence allowance for 10 months of each year that is $350 per month during their sophomore year, $450 during their junior year, and $500 during their senior year.

Duration 2 or 3 years, provided the recipient maintains a GPA of 2.5 or higher.

Additional data Recipients must also complete 4 years of aerospace studies courses at 1 of the 144 colleges and universities that have an Air Force ROTC unit on campus or 1 of the 984 colleges that have cross-enrollment agreements with those institutions. They must also attend a 4-week summer training camp at an Air Force base, usually between their sophomore and junior years. Following completion of their bachelor's degree, scholar-

ship recipients earn a commission as a second lieutenant in the Air Force and serve at least 4 years.

Deadline June of each year.

[139]
AIR FORCE ROTC PROFESSIONAL OFFICER CORPS INCENTIVE

U.S. Air Force
Attn: Headquarters AFROTC/RRUC
551 East Maxwell Boulevard
Maxwell AFB, AL 36112-5917
(334) 953-2091   Toll Free: (866) 4-AFROTC
Fax: (334) 953-6167   E-mail: afrotc1@maxwell.af.mil
Web: afrotc.com/learn-about/programs-and-scholarships

Summary To provide financial assistance for undergraduate and graduate studies to individuals who have completed 2 years of college and who are willing to join Air Force ROTC and serve as Air Force officers following completion of their degree.

Eligibility Applicants must be U.S. citizens who have completed 2 years of the general military course at a college or university with an Air Force ROTC unit on campus or a college with a cross-enrollment agreement with such a college. They must be full-time students, have a GPA of 2.0 or higher both cumulatively and for the prior term, be enrolled in both Aerospace Studies class and Leadership Laboratory, pass the Air Force Officer Qualifying Test, meet Air Force physical fitness and weight requirements, and be able to be commissioned before they become 31 years of age. They must agree to serve for at least 4 years as active-duty Air Force officers following graduation from college with either a bachelor's or graduate degree.

Financial Data This scholarship provides $3,000 per year for tuition and a monthly subsistence allowance of $450 as a junior or $500 as a senior.

Duration Until completion of a graduate degree.

Additional data Scholarship recipients must complete 4 years of aerospace studies courses at 1 of the 144 colleges and universities that have an Air Force ROTC unit on campus; students may also attend 984 other colleges that have cross-enrollment agreements with the institutions that have an Air Force ROTC unit on campus. Recipients must also attend a 4-week summer training camp at an Air Force base between their junior and senior year.

Number awarded Varies each year.

Deadline Deadline not specified.

[140]
AIR FORCE SERVICES CLUB MEMBERSHIP SCHOLARSHIP PROGRAM

Air Force Services Agency
Attn: HQ AFSVA/SVOFT
10100 Reunion Place, Suite 501
San Antonio, TX 78216-4138
(210) 652-6312   Toll Free: (800) 443-4834
Fax: (210) 652-7041
E-mail: web.clubs-operations@randolph.af.mil
Web: www.afclubs.net/CN_Scholarship.htm

Summary To recognize and reward, with academic scholarships, Air Force Club members and their families who submit outstanding essays.

Eligibility This program is open to Air Force Club members and their spouses, children, and stepchildren who have been accepted by or are enrolled at an accredited college or university. Grandchildren are eligible if they are the dependent of a club member. Applicants may be undergraduate or graduate students enrolled full or part time. They must submit an essay of up to 500 words on a topic that changes annually; a recent topic was "The High Cost of Freedom" Applicants must also include a 1-page summary of their long-term career and life goals and previous accomplishments, including civic, athletic, and academic awards.

Financial Data Awards are $1,000 scholarships.

Duration The competition is held annually.

Additional data This competition, first held in 1997, is sponsored by Chase Bank and the Coca-Cola Company.

Number awarded 25 each year.

Deadline Entries must be submitted to the member's base services commander or division chief by June of each year.

[141]
AIR FORCE TUITION ASSISTANCE PROGRAM

U.S. Air Force
Attn: Air Force Personnel Center
Headquarters USAF/DPPAT
550 C Street West, Suite 10
Randolph AFB, TX 78150-4712
Fax: (210) 565-2328
Web: www.airforce.com/opportunities/enlisted/education

Summary To provide financial assistance for college or graduate school to active-duty Air Force personnel.

Eligibility Eligible to apply for this program are active-duty Air Force personnel who have completed 2 years of their service obligation.

Financial Data Air Force personnel chosen for participation in this program continue to receive their regular Air Force pay. The Air Force will pay 100% of the tuition costs in an approved program, to a maximum of $4,500 per year or $250 per semester hour, whichever is less.

Duration Up to 4 years.

Additional data Applications and further information about this program are available from counselors at the education centers on Air Force bases. Most Air Force personnel who receive tuition assistance participate in the Community College of the Air Force; there, participants earn a 2-year associate degree by combining on-the-job technical training or attendance at Air Force schools with enrollment in college courses at a civilian institution during off-duty hours. In addition, each Air Force base offers at least 4 subject areas in which selected Air Force personnel can receive tuition assistance for study leading to a bachelor's degree, and 2 disciplines in which they can pursue graduate study.

Number awarded Varies each year.

Deadline Deadline not specified.

[142]
AIRMAN EDUCATION AND COMMISSIONING PROGRAM

U.S. Air Force
Attn: Headquarters AFROTC/RRUE
Enlisted Commissioning Section
551 East Maxwell Boulevard
Maxwell AFB, AL 36112-6106
(334) 953-2091   Toll Free: (866) 4-AFROTC
Fax: (334) 953-6167   E-mail: enlisted@afrotc.com
Web: www.afoats.af.mil/AFROTC/EnlistedComm/AECP.asp

Summary To allow selected enlisted Air Force personnel to earn a bachelor's degree in approved majors by providing financial assistance for full-time college study while remaining on active duty.

Eligibility Eligible to participate in this program are enlisted members of the Air Force who have been accepted at a university or college (or approved crosstown institution) that is associated with AFROTC and that offers an approved major. The majors currently supported are computer science, all ABET-accredited engineering fields (not engineering technology), foreign area studies (limited to Middle East, Africa, Asia, and Russia/Eurasia), foreign languages (limited to Arabic, Azeri, Chinese, French, Georgian, Hebrew, Hindi, Indonesian, Japanese, Kazakh, Korean, Pashto, Persian Farsi, Portuguese, Russian, Swahili, Turkish, Urdu, and Vietnamese), mathematics, meteorology, nursing, and physics.

Applicants must have completed at least 1 year of time-in-service and 1 year of time-on-station. They must have scores on the Air Force Officer Qualifying Test of at least 15 on the verbal and 10 on the quantitative and be able to pass the Air Force ROTC Physical Fitness Test. Normally they should have completed at least 30 semester hours of college study with a GPA of 2.75 or higher. They must be younger than 31 years of age (39 for nursing students) or otherwise able to be commissioned before they become 35 years of age (42 for nursing students).

Financial Data While participating in this program, cadets remain on active duty in the Air Force and receive their regular salary and benefits. They also receive payment of tuition and fees up to $15,000 per year and an annual textbook allowance of $600.

Duration 1 to 3 years, until completion of a bachelor's degree.

Additional data While attending college, participants in this program attend ROTC classes at their college or university. Upon completing their degree, they are commissioned to serve in the Air Force in their area of specialization with an active-duty service commitment of at least 4 years. Further information is available from base education service officers or an Air Force ROTC unit. This program does not provide for undergraduate flying training.

Number awarded Approximately 60 each year.

Deadline February of each year.

[143]
AIRMAN SCHOLARSHIP AND COMMISSIONING PROGRAM

U.S. Air Force
Attn: Headquarters AFROTC/RRUE
Enlisted Commissioning Section
551 East Maxwell Boulevard
Maxwell AFB, AL 36112-6106
(334) 953-2091   Toll Free: (866) 4-AFROTC
Fax: (334) 953-6167   E-mail: enlisted@afrotc.com
Web: www.afoats.af.mil/AFROTC/EnlistedComm/ASCP.asp

Summary To allow selected enlisted Air Force personnel to separate from the Air Force and earn a bachelor's degree in approved majors by providing financial assistance for full-time college study, especially in designated fields.

Eligibility This program is open to active-duty enlisted members of the Air Force who have completed at least 1 year of continuous active duty and at least 1 year on station. Applicants normally must have completed at least 24 semester hours of graded college credit with a cumulative college GPA of 2.5 or higher. If they have not completed 24 hours of graded college credit, they must have an ACT score of 24 or higher or an SAT combined critical reading and mathematics score of 1100 or higher. They must also have scores on the Air Force Officer Qualifying Test (AFOQT) of 15 or more on the verbal scale and 10 or more on the quantitative scale and be able to pass the Air Force ROTC Physical Fitness Test. Applicants must have been accepted at a college or university (including cross-town schools) offering the AFROTC 4-year program. When they complete the program and receive their commission, they may not be 31 years of age or older. U.S. citizenship is required. Recently, priority was given to students in the following technical majors: architecture, chemistry, computer science, engineering (especially aeronautical, aerospace, architectural, astronautical, civil, computer, electrical, environmental, and mechanical), mathematics, meteorology/atmospheric sciences, operations research, and physics.

Financial Data Awards are type 2 AFROTC scholarships that provide for payment of tuition and fees, to a maximum of $18,000 per year, plus an annual book allowance of $900. All recipients are also awarded a tax-free subsistence allowance of $350 to $500 per month.

Duration 2 to 4 years, until completion of a bachelor's degree.

Additional data Selectees separate from the active-duty Air Force, join an AFROTC detachment, and become full-time students. Upon completing their degree, they are commissioned as officers and returned to active duty in the Air Force with a service obligation of 4 years of active duty and 4 years of Reserves. Further information is available from base education service officers or an Air Force ROTC unit.

Number awarded   Varies each year.

Deadline   October of each year.

[144]
ALABAMA NATIONAL GUARD EDUCATIONAL ASSISTANCE PROGRAM

Alabama Commission on Higher Education
Attn: Grants Coordinator
100 North Union Street
P.O. Box 302000
Montgomery, AL 36130-2000
(334) 242-2273   Fax: (334) 242-0268
E-mail: cheryl.newton@ache.alabama.gov
Web: www.ache.alabama.gov/StudentAsst/Programs.htm

Summary   To provide financial assistance to members of the Alabama National Guard interested in attending college or graduate school in the state.

Eligibility   This program is open to Alabama residents who are enrolled in an associate, baccalaureate, master's, or doctoral program at a public college, university, community college, technical college, or junior college in the state; are making satisfactory academic progress as determined by the eligible institution; and are members in good standing of the Alabama National Guard who have completed basic training and advanced individual training. Applicants may be receiving federal veterans benefits, but they must show a cost less aid amount of at least $25.

Financial Data   Scholarships cover tuition, educational fees, books, and supplies, up to a maximum of $1,000 per year. All Alabama Student Grant program proceeds for which the student is eligible are deducted from this award.

Duration   Up to 12 years after the date of the first grant payment to the student through this program.

Number awarded   Varies each year; awards are determined on a first-in, first-out basis as long as funds are available.

Deadline   July of each year.

[145]
ALASKA NATIONAL GUARD STATE TUITION REIMBURSEMENT PROGRAM

Alaska National Guard
Attn: Education Services Officer
P.O. Box 5800
Fort Richardson, AK 99505-5800
(907) 428-6477   Fax: (907) 428-6929
E-mail: les.poletzky@us.army.mil
Web: veterans.alaska.gov/state_benefits.htm

Summary   To provide financial assistance to members of the Alaska National Guard who wish to attend a college or university in the state other than the University of Alaska.

Eligibility   This program is open to members of the Alaska National Guard (Air and Army) and Naval Militia who are attending a university program in Alaska, other than the University of Alaska. First priority is given to undergraduates; if funding is available, students working on a second bachelor's degree or a master's degree may be supported. Non-prior servicemembers must complete Initial Active Duty for Training (IADT); prior servicemembers are eligible immediately.

Financial Data   Recipients are entitled to reimbursement of 100% of the cost of tuition and fees, to a maximum of $2,000 per fiscal year.

Duration   1 semester; may be renewed.

Number awarded   Varies each year.

Deadline   Applications may be submitted at any time.

[146]
ALASKA NATIONAL GUARD UNIVERSITY OF ALASKA TUITION SCHOLARSHIPS

Alaska National Guard
Attn: Education Services Officer
P.O. Box 5800
Fort Richardson, AK 99505-5800
(907) 428-6477   Fax: (907) 428-6929
E-mail: les.poletzky@us.army.mil
Web: veterans.alaska.gov/state_benefits.htm

Summary   To provide financial assistance to members of the Alaska National Guard who wish to take classes at a campus or branch of the University of Alaska.

Eligibility   This program is open to members of the Alaska National Guard (Air and Army) and Naval Militia who are interested in attending any institution within the University of Alaska system to work on an associate, bachelor's, or master's degree. Applicants must have completed Initial Active Duty for Training (IADT).

Financial Data   Recipients are entitled to reimbursement of 100% of the cost of tuition and fees, to a maximum of 15 undergraduate course units per semester or 9 graduate course units per semester.

Duration   1 semester; may be renewed as long as undergraduates maintain a GPA of 2.0 or higher and graduate students maintain a GPA of 3.0 or higher.

Number awarded   Varies each year.

Deadline   August of each year for fall semester; December of each year for spring semester.

[147]
AMEDD ENLISTED COMMISSIONING PROGRAM (AECP)

U.S. Army
Attn: Recruiting Command, RCHS-SVD-AECP
1307 Third Avenue
Fort Knox, KY 40121-2726
(502) 626-0381   Toll Free: (800) 223-3735, ext. 60381
Fax: (502) 626-0952   E-mail: aecp@usarec.army.mil
Web: www.usarec.army.mil/AECP

Summary   To provide financial assistance to enlisted Army personnel who are interested in completing a bachelor's degree in nursing and becoming a commissioned officer.

Eligibility   This program is open to enlisted Army personnel in the active component, Reserves, or National Guard who have at least 3 but no more than 10 years of active federal service. Applicants must be interested in enrolling full time at an accredited school of nursing to work on a bachelor's degree and becoming a licensed registered nurse. They must be U.S. citizens, have a GPA of 2.5 or higher overall and in mathematics and science courses, be between 21 and 42 years of age, be eligible to become a commissioned officer in the active component following licensure, and agree to fulfill a 3-year additional service obligation.

Financial Data   The stipend is $9,000 per year for tuition and $1,000 for books. Participants are not allowed to attend a school whose tuition exceeds $9,000. They continue to draw their regular pay and allowances while attending nursing school.

Duration   Participants must be able to complete all degree requirements in 24 consecutive months or less.

Number awarded   Up to 100 each year.

Deadline   January of each year

[148]
AOC ENLISTED TUITION GRANTS

Association of Old Crows
Attn: AOC Educational Foundation
1000 North Payne Street
Alexandria, VA 22314-1652
(703) 549-1600 Fax: (703) 549-2589
Web: www.crows.org/aef/scholarship-a-grants.html

Summary To provide financial assistance to military enlisted personnel who are pursuing off-duty college-level education programs in fields related to electronics.

Eligibility This program is open to military enlisted personnel (rank of E-4 and above) who are utilizing the tuition assistance programs of the services to study physics, engineering, or other field related to electronic warfare or information superiority during their off-duty hours. Selection is based on academic excellence and financial need.

Financial Data Support is provided to supplement the funding available through the tuition assistance programs.

Duration 1 semester; may be renewed.

Additional data Funding is provided by local chapters of this organization, which was founded by World War II veterans who had engaged in electronic warfare to disrupt enemy communications and radars. The program was code-named "Raven" and its operators became known as Old Crows. For information on a chapter in your area, contact the AOC Educational Foundation.

Number awarded Varies each year; recently, a total of $160,000 per year was available for this program.

Deadline Deadline not specified.

[149]
ARIZONA NATIONAL GUARD SCHOLARSHIP

National Guard Association of Arizona
5640 East McDowell Road
Phoenix, AZ 85008
(602) 275-8305 Fax: (602) 275-9254
E-mail: ngaofaz@aol.com
Web: www.ngaaz.org

Summary To provide financial assistance to members of the Arizona National Guard who are interested in attending college in the state.

Eligibility This program is open to active members of the Arizona National Guard who are enrolled for at least 12 hours in an undergraduate degree program. Selection is based on current GPA, academic honors or awards, military decorations and awards, unit involvement, community involvement as a National Guard representative, and potential for future contribution to the National Guard.

Financial Data The program provides up to $500 per semester ($1,000 per year) to cover tuition at any state college or university in Arizona.

Duration Up to 4 years, as long as the recipient maintains a GPA of 3.0 or higher.

Number awarded Varies each year.

Deadline March of each year.

[150]
ARIZONA NATIONAL GUARD STATE EDUCATION REIMBURSEMENT PROGRAM

Arizona Army National Guard
Soldier Support Center
Attn: Education Services Officer
5636 East McDowell Road
Phoenix, AZ 85008-3495
(602) 267-2618 Fax: (602) 267-2912
E-mail: azsoldiersupportcenter@us.army.mil
Web: www.azguard.gov

Summary To provide financial assistance for college to members of the Arizona Army or Air National Guard.

Eligibility This program is open to members of the Arizona Army and Air National Guard who have completed Advanced Infantry Training (AIT) or Officer Basic Course (OBC). Applicants must have attended annual training or equivalent training and may not have any AWOLs. They must be working on a college degree or certification at an Arizona institution.

Financial Data Recipients are reimbursed for the actual cost of completed education, to a maximum of $250 per credit hour, $2,296 per semester, or $6,500 per state fiscal year.

Duration 1 year; may be renewed if the recipient maintains satisfactory drill performance.

Number awarded Varies each year.

Deadline Applications for reimbursement must be submitted no later than 15 calendar days after the start of school.

[151]
ARKANSAS NATIONAL GUARD TUITION INCENTIVE PROGRAM

Arkansas National Guard
Attn: Education Services Officer
DCSPER-ED
Camp Robinson
North Little Rock, AR 72199-9600
(501) 212-4021 Fax: (501) 212-4039
E-mail: Education@ar.ngb.army.mil
Web: www.arguard.org/Education/ta.asp

Summary To provide financial assistance for college to members of the Arkansas National Guard.

Eligibility This program is open to members of the Arkansas National Guard who have 10 years or less of service. Applicants must have a sufficient score on the standard military entrance examination to be rated as Category IIIA or higher (i.e., AFQT score of at least 50 or equivalent). They must be enrolled or accepted for enrollment in an undergraduate program at a participating college or university in Arkansas. Non-prior service applicants must enlist in the Arkansas National Guard for at least 6 year; enlisted members must reenlist or extend for at least 3 years; warrant and commissioned officers must commit to at least 2 years of service.

Financial Data The stipend is $2,500 per semester for fall or spring semester or $1,250 for summer term; the maximum award in a fiscal year is $5,000.

Duration 1 semester; may be renewed if the recipient maintains a GPA of 2.0 or higher.

Number awarded Varies each year.

Deadline August of each year for fall semester; December of each year for spring semester; May of each year for first summer term; June of each year for second summer term.

[152]
ARMED FORCES COMMUNICATIONS AND ELECTRONICS ASSOCIATION ROTC SCHOLARSHIPS

Armed Forces Communications and Electronics Association
Attn: AFCEA Educational Foundation
4400 Fair Lakes Court
Fairfax, VA 22033-3899
(703) 631-6149 Toll Free: (800) 336-4583, ext. 6149
Fax: (703) 631-4693 E-mail: scholarship@afcea.org
Web: www.afcea.org/education/scholarships/rotc/rotc1.asp

Summary To provide financial assistance to ROTC cadets who are majoring in fields related to communications and electronics.

Eligibility This program is open to ROTC cadets majoring in electronics, engineering (aerospace, chemical, computer, electrical, or systems), mathematics, computer science, physics, science or mathematics education, technology management, foreign languages, global security and intelligence studies, security and intelligence, international studies, or other fields directly related to the support of U.S. national security enterprises. Applicants must be nominated by their ROTC professor, be entering their junior or senior year, be U.S. citizens, be of good moral character, have demonstrated academic excellence, be motivated to complete a college education and serve as officers in the U.S. armed forces, and be able to demonstrate financial need.

Financial Data The stipend is $2,000.

Duration 1 year; may be renewed.

Number awarded 36 each year, divided equally among Army, Navy/Marine Corps, and Air Force ROTC programs; for each service, 6 are awarded to rising juniors, 6 to rising seniors.

Deadline February of each year.

[153]
ARMY FUNDED NURSE EDUCATION PROGRAM (FNEP)

U.S. Army
Attn: Recruiting Command, RCHS-SVD-FNEP
1307 Third Avenue
Fort Knox, KY 40121-2726
(502) 626-0364 Toll Free: (800) 223-3735, ext. 60364
Fax: (502) 626-0952 E-mail: fnep@usarec.army.mil
Web: www.usarec.army.mil/AECP

Summary To provide financial assistance to Army officers who are interested in completing a bachelor's or master's degree in nursing and continuing to serve in the Army Nurse Corps.

Eligibility This program is open to active component Army officers who are currently in grade O-3 and have completed at least 38 months but no more than 7 years of active federal service. Applicants must be interested in enrolling full time at an accredited school of nursing to work on a bachelor's or entry-level master's degree. They must agree to serve an additional 2 years for each year of support received for a bachelor's degree or an additional 3 years for the first year of support for a master's degree plus 1 year for each additional 6 months of support. U.S. citizenship is required.

Financial Data The stipend is $12,000 per year, including $11,000 for tuition and fees and $1,000 for books. Participants are not allowed to pay tuition in excess of $11,000 per year from other sources. If the university's tuition is more than $11,000, it must either waive the additional amount or direct the participant to another school. Army officers continue to draw their regular pay and allowances while attending nursing school.

Duration Participants must be able to complete all degree requirements in 24 consecutive months or less. They must remain enrolled full time and maintain a GPA of 2.5 or higher.

Number awarded Up to 25 each year.

Deadline February of each year.

[154]
ARMY NATIONAL GUARD TUITION ASSISTANCE

U.S. Army National Guard
c/o DANTES
6490 Saufley Field Road
Pensacola, FL 32509-5243
(850) 452-1085 Fax: (850) 452-1161
E-mail: tahelp@voled.doded.mil
Web: www.nationalguard.com/education/payingfor.php

Summary To provide financial assistance for college or graduate school to members of the Army National Guard in each state.

Eligibility This program is open to members of the Army National Guard in every state who are interested in attending a college, community college, or university within the state. Applicants must have sufficient time to complete the course before their Expiration Time of Service (ETS) date. They must be interested in working on a high school diploma or equivalent (GED),

certificate, associate degree, bachelor's degree, master's degree, or first professional degree, including those in architecture, Certified Public Accountant (C.P.A.), podiatry, dentistry (D.D.S. or D.M.D.), medicine (M.D.), optometry, osteopathic medicine, pharmacy (Pharm.D.), or theology (M.Div. or M.H.L.). Commissioned officers must agree to remain in the Guard for at least 4 years following completion of the course for which assistance is provided, unless they are involuntarily separated from the service.

Financial Data Assistance provides up to 100% of tuition (to a maximum of $250 per semester hour or $4,500 per person per fiscal year).

Duration Participants in Office Candidate School (OCS), Warrant Officer Candidate School (WOCS), and ROTC Simultaneous Membership Program (SMP) may enroll in up to 15 semester hours per year until completion of a baccalaureate degree. Warrant Officers are funded to complete an associate degree.

Additional data Tuition assistance may be used along with federal Pell Grants but not with Montgomery GI Bill benefits. State tuition assistance programs can be used concurrently with this program, but not to exceed 100% of tuition costs.

Number awarded Varies each year; recently, more than 22,000 Guard members received tuition assistance.

Deadline Deadline not specified.

[155]
ARMY NURSE CORPS ASSOCIATION SCHOLARSHIPS

Army Nurse Corps Association
Attn: Education Committee
P.O. Box 39235
San Antonio, TX 78218-1235
(210) 650-3534 Fax: (210) 650-3494
E-mail: education@e-anca.org
Web: e-anca.org/ANCAEduc.htm

Summary To provide financial assistance to students who have a connection to the Army and are interested in working on an undergraduate or graduate degree in nursing.

Eligibility This program is open to students attending colleges or universities that have accredited programs offering associate, bachelor's, master's, or doctoral degrees in nursing. Applicants must be 1) nursing students who plan to enter the active Army, Army National Guard, or Army Reserve and are not participating in a program funded by the active Army, Army National Guard, or Army Reserve; 2) nursing students who have previously served in the active Army, Army National Guard, or Army Reserve; 3) Army Nurse Corps officers enrolled in an undergraduate or graduate nursing program not funded by the active Army, Army National Guard, or Army Reserve; 4) Army enlisted soldiers in the active Army, Army National Guard, or Army Reserve who are working on a baccalaureate degree in nursing not funded by the active Army, Army National Guard, or Army Reserve; or 5) nursing students whose parent(s) or spouse are serving or have served in the active Army, Army National Guard, or Army Reserve. Along with their application, they must submit a personal statement on their professional career objectives, reasons for applying for this scholarship, financial need, special considerations, personal and academic interests, and why they are preparing for a nursing career.

Financial Data The stipend is $3,000. Funds are sent directly to the recipient's school.

Duration 1 year.

Additional data Although the sponsoring organization is made up of current, retired, and honorably discharged officers of the Army Nurse Corps, it does not have an official affiliation with the Army. Therefore, students who receive these scholarships do not incur any military service obligation.

Number awarded 1 or more each year.

Deadline March of each year.

[156]
ARMY RESERVE TUITION ASSISTANCE

U.S. Army Reserve
Attn: Director, USAR Education
ARPC-PS
1 Reserve Way
St. Louis, MO 63132-5200
Toll Free: (800) 452-0201
Web: www.goarmy.com/reserve/nps/education.jsp

Summary To provide financial assistance for college or graduate school to specified members of the U.S. Army Reserve (USAR).

Eligibility This program is open to USAR soldiers in the following categories: TPU, JRU, IMA, ROTC Simultaneous Membership Program Cadets (non-scholarship holders), and Chaplain Candidates. Members of the Active Guard Reserve (AGR) are covered by Regular Army tuition assistance and are not eligible for this program. Soldiers who have been flagged for weight control or because of the results of their Army Physical Fitness Test (APFT) are still eligible, but soldiers who have been flagged for adverse actions cannot receive this assistance. Applicants must be working on their first credential at the diploma, certificate associate, baccalaureate, or graduate level. Commissioned officers must agree to participate actively for 4 years in the Selected Reserve from the date of completion of the course for which tuition assistance is provided. Enlisted soldiers must certify that sufficient time remains within their Time In Service (TIS) to complete the course before their Expiration Term of Service (ETS).

Financial Data Assistance is provided at the rate of $250 per credit hour, to a maximum of $4,500 per fiscal year.

Duration 1 year; may be renewed.

Number awarded Varies each year.

Deadline Applications may be submitted at any time.

[157]
ARMY ROTC 4-YEAR SCHOLARSHIPS

U.S. Army
ROTC Cadet Command
Attn: ATCC-OP-I-S
55 Patch Road, Building 56
Fort Monroe, VA 23651-1052
(757) 788-4559   Toll Free: (800) USA-ROTC
Fax: (757) 788-4643   E-mail: atccps@usacc.army.mil
Web: www.goarmy.com/rotc/high_school_students.jsp

Summary To provide financial assistance to high school seniors or graduates who are interested in enrolling in Army ROTC in college.

Eligibility Applicants for this program must 1) be U.S. citizens; 2) be at least 17 years of age by October of the year in which they are seeking a scholarship; 3) be able to complete a college degree and receive their commission before their 31st birthday; 4) score at least 920 on the combined mathematics and critical reading SAT or 19 on the ACT; 5) have a high school GPA of 2.5 or higher; and 6) meet medical and other regulatory requirements. Current college or university students may apply if their school considers them beginning freshmen with 4 academic years remaining for a bachelor's degree.

Financial Data This scholarship provides financial assistance of up to $20,000 per year for college tuition and educational fees or for room and board, whichever the student selects. In addition, a flat rate of $1,200 per year is provided for the purchase of textbooks, classroom supplies, and equipment. Recipients are also awarded a stipend for up to 10 months of each year that is $300 per month during their freshman year, $350 per month during their sophomore year, $450 per month during their junior year, and $500 per month during their senior year.

Duration 4 years, until completion of a baccalaureate degree.

Additional data Scholarship recipients participate in the Army ROTC program as part of their college curriculum by enrolling in 4 years of military science classes and attending a 6-week summer camp between the junior and senior years. Following graduation, they receive a commission as a Regular Army, Army Reserve, or Army National Guard officer. Scholarship winners must serve in the military for 8 years. That service obligation may be fulfilled 1) by serving on active duty for 4 years followed by service in the Army National Guard (ARNG), the United States Army Reserve (USAR), or the Inactive Ready Reserve (IRR) for the remainder of the 8 years; or 2) by serving 8 years in an ARNG or USAR troop program unit that includes a 3- to 6-month active-duty period for initial training.

Number awarded Approximately 1,500 each year.

Deadline November of each year.

[158]
ARMY ROTC ADVANCED COURSE

U.S. Army
ROTC Cadet Command
Attn: ATCC-OP-I-S
55 Patch Road, Building 56
Fort Monroe, VA 23651-1052
(757) 788-4559   Toll Free: (800) USA-ROTC
Fax: (757) 788-4643   E-mail: atccps@usacc.army.mil
Web: www.goarmy.com/rotc/ar_advanced_course.jsp

Summary To provide financial assistance to non-scholarship participants in the Army ROTC Program who have qualified for the Advanced Course.

Eligibility Non-scholarship cadets in the ROTC Program are eligible to apply for this program if they have qualified for the ROTC Advanced Course. The Advanced Course is usually taken during the final 2 years of college.

Financial Data Participants receive a stipend of $450 per month during their junior year and $500 per month during their senior year, as well as pay for attending the 6-week advanced camp during the summer between the junior and senior years of college.

Duration 2 years.

Additional data Non-scholarship graduates may serve 3 years on active duty and 5 years in the Reserve Forces, or they may select or be selected to serve all 8 years on Reserve Forces Duty (RFD). If RFD is selected, graduates attend an Officer Basic Course and spend the remainder of their 8-year obligation in the Reserve Forces.

Number awarded Varies each year.

Deadline Deadline not specified.

[159]
ARMY ROTC CIVILIAN SPONSORED SCHOLARSHIP PROGRAM

U.S. Army
ROTC Cadet Command
Attn: ATCC-OP-I-S
55 Patch Road, Building 56
Fort Monroe, VA 23651-1052
(757) 788-3473   Toll Free: (800) USA-ROTC
Fax: (757) 788-4643   E-mail: atccps@usacc.army.mil
Web: www.goarmy.com/rotc/college_students.jsp

Summary To provide additional financial assistance to Army ROTC cadets.

Eligibility This program is open to Army ROTC cadets entering the fourth year of college. Both scholarship and non-scholarship cadets are eligible. The program currently includes the following named awards: the General Creighton W. Abrams Scholarships, the United Services Automobile Association Scholarships, the Armed Forces Insurance General Melvin Zais Scholarships, the LTG Timothy J. Maude Foundation Scholarship, the First Command Educational Foundation ROTC Scholarships, and the Army and Air Force Mutual Aid Association Scholarships. Each of those awards has additional specific requirements.

Financial Data Stipends are $1,500 or $1,000.

Duration 1 year.

Additional data Applications must be made through professors of military science at 1 of the schools hosting the Army ROTC program. All scholarships are sponsored by civilian organizations, including the United Services Automobile Association (USAA), the First Command Educational Foundation, the Armed Forces Insurance Company, and the Army and Air Force Mutual Aid Association.

Number awarded Varies each year. Recently, 48 of these scholarships were awarded: 3 at $1,500 and 45 at $1,000.

Deadline June of each year.

[160]
ARMY ROTC COLLEGE SCHOLARSHIP PROGRAM

U.S. Army
ROTC Cadet Command
Attn: ATCC-OP-I-S
55 Patch Road, Building 56
Fort Monroe, VA 23651-1052
(757) 788-4559 Toll Free: (800) USA-ROTC
Fax: (757) 788-4643 E-mail: atccps@usacc.army.mil
Web: www.goarmy.com/rotc/college_students.jsp

Summary To provide financial assistance to students who are or will be enrolled in Army ROTC.

Eligibility This program is open to U.S. citizens between 17 and 27 years of age who have already completed 1 or 2 years in a college or university with an Army ROTC unit on campus or in a college with a cross-enrollment agreement with a college with an Army ROTC unit on campus. Applicants must have 2 or 3 years remaining for their bachelor's degree (or 4 years of a 5-year bachelor's program) and must be able to complete that degree before their 31st birthday. They must have a GPA of 2.5 or higher in their previous college study and scores of at least 920 on the combined mathematics and critical reading SAT or 19 on the ACT.

Financial Data These scholarships provide financial assistance for college tuition and educational fees, up to an annual amount of $20,000. In addition, a flat rate of $1,200 is provided for the purchase of textbooks, classroom supplies, and equipment. Recipients are also awarded a stipend for up to 10 months of each year that is $350 per month during their sophomore year, $450 per month during their junior year, and $500 per month during their senior year.

Duration 2 or 3 years, until the recipient completes the bachelor's degree.

Additional data Applications must be made through professors of military science at 1 of the schools hosting the Army ROTC program. Preference is given to students who have already enrolled as non-scholarship students in military science classes at 1 of the more than 270 institutions with an Army ROTC unit on campus, at 1 of the 75 college extension centers, or at 1 of the more than 1,000 colleges with cross-enrollment or extension agreements with 1 of the colleges with an Army ROTC unit. Scholarship winners must serve in the military for 8 years. That service obligation may be fulfilled 1) by serving on active duty for 4 years followed by service in the Army National Guard (ARNG), the United States Army Reserve (USAR), or the Inactive Ready Reserve (IRR) for the remainder of the 8 years; or 2) by serving 8 years in an ARNG or USAR troop program unit that includes a 3- to 6-month active-duty period for initial training.

Number awarded Varies each year; a recent allocation provided for 700 4-year scholarships, 1,800 3-year scholarships, and 2,800 2-year scholarships.

Deadline December of each year.

[161]
ARMY ROTC NURSE PROGRAM

U.S. Army
ROTC Cadet Command
Attn: ATCC-OP-I-S
55 Patch Road, Building 56
Fort Monroe, VA 23651-1052
(757) 788-4552 Toll Free: (800) USA-ROTC
Fax: (757) 788-4643 E-mail: atccps@usacc.army.mil
Web: www.goarmy.com/rotc/nurse_program.jsp

Summary To provide financial assistance to high school seniors or graduates who are interested in enrolling in Army ROTC and majoring in nursing in college.

Eligibility Applicants for the Army Reserve Officers' Training Corps (ROTC) Nurse program must 1) be U.S. citizens; 2) be at least 17 years of age by October of the year in which they are seeking a scholarship; 3) be no more than 27 years of age when they graduate from college after 4 years; 4) score at least 1050 on the combined mathematics and critical reading SAT or 21 on the ACT; 5) have a high school GPA of 3.0 or higher; and 6) meet medical and other regulatory requirements. This program is open to ROTC scholarship applicants who wish to enroll in a nursing program at 1 of approximately 100 designated partner colleges and universities and become Army nurses after graduation.

Financial Data This scholarship provides financial assistance toward college tuition and educational fees up to an annual amount of $17,000. In addition, a flat rate of $1,000 is provided for the purchase of textbooks, classroom supplies, and equipment. Recipients are also awarded a stipend for up to 10 months of each year that is $300 per month during their freshman year, $350 per month during their sophomore year, $450 per month during their junior year, and $500 per month during their senior year.

Duration 4 years, until completion of a baccalaureate degree. A limited number of 2-year and 3-year scholarships are also available to students who are already attending an accredited B.S.N. program on a campus affiliated with ROTC.

Additional data This program was established in 1996 to ensure that ROTC cadets seeking nursing careers would be admitted to the upper-level division of a baccalaureate program. The 56 partnership nursing schools affiliated with Army ROTC have agreed to guarantee upper-level admission to students who maintain an established GPA during their first 2 years. During the summer, participants have the opportunity to participate in the Nurse Summer Training Program, a paid 3- to 4-week clinical elective at an Army hospital in the United States, Germany, or Korea. Following completion of their baccalaureate degree, participants become commissioned officers in the Army Nurse Corps. Scholarship winners must serve in the military for 8 years. That service obligation may be fulfilled 1) by serving on active duty for 4 years followed by service in the Army National Guard (ARNG), the United States Army Reserve (USAR), or the Inactive Ready Reserve (IRR) for the remainder of the 8 years; or 2) by serving 8 years in an ARNG or USAR troop program unit that includes a 3- to 6-month active-duty period for initial training.

Number awarded A limited number each year.

Deadline November of each year.

[162]
ARMY SPECIALIZED TRAINING ASSISTANCE PROGRAM (STRAP)

U.S. Army
Human Resources Command, Health Services Division
Attn: AHRC-OPH-AN
200 Stovall Street, Room 9N47
Alexandria, VA 22332-0417
(703) 325-2330 Toll Free: (800) USA-ARMY
Fax: (703) 325-2358
Web: www.goarmy.com/amedd/postgrad.jsp

Summary To provide funding for service to members of the United States Army Reserve (USAR) or Army National Guard (ARNG) who are engaged in additional training in designated health care fields that are considered critical for wartime medical needs.

Eligibility This program is open to members of the USAR or ARNG who are currently 1) medical residents (in orthopedic surgery, family practice, emergency medicine, general surgery, obstetrics/gynecology, or internal medicine); 2) dental residents (in oral surgery, prosthodontics, or comprehensive dentistry); 3) nursing students working on a master's degree in critical care or nurse anesthesia; or 4) associate degree or diploma nurses working on a bachelor's degree. Applicants must agree to a service obligation of 1 year for every 6 months of support received.

Financial Data This program pays a stipend of $1,992 per month.

Additional data During their obligated period of service, participants must attend Extended Combat Training (ECT) at least 12 days each year and complete the Officer Basic Leadership Course (OBLC) within the first year.

Number awarded Varies each year.

Deadline Applications may be submitted at any time.

[163]
ARMY TUITION ASSISTANCE BENEFITS

U.S. Army
Human Resources Command
AHRC-PDE-EI
Attn: Education Incentives and Counseling Branch
200 Stovall Street, Suite 3N17
Alexandria, VA 22332-0472
(703) 325-0285   Toll Free: (800) 872-8272
Fax: (703) 325-6599   E-mail: pdeei@hoffman.army.mil
Web: www.goarmy.com/benefits/education_taking_classes.jsp

Summary To provide financial assistance to Army personnel interested in working on an undergraduate or graduate degree.

Eligibility This program is open to active-duty Army personnel, including members of the Army National Guard and Army Reserve on active duty. Applicants must first visit an education counselor to declare an educational goal and establish an educational plan. Applicants may enroll in up to 15 semester hours of academic courses.

Financial Data Those selected for participation in this program receive their regular Army pay and 100% of tuition at the postsecondary educational institution of their choice, but capped at $4,500 per year or $250 per semester hour, whichever is less.

Duration Until completion of a bachelor's or graduate degree.

Additional data This program is part of the Army Continuing Education System (ACES). Further information is available from counselors at the education centers at all Army installations with a troop strength of 750 or more.

Number awarded Varies each year.

Deadline Deadline not specified.

[164]
BART LONGO MEMORIAL SCHOLARSHIPS

National Chief Petty Officers' Association
c/o Marjorie Hays, Treasurer
1014 Ronald Drive
Corpus Christi, TX 78412-3548
Web: www.goatlocker.org/ncpoa/scholarship.htm

Summary To provide financial assistance for college or graduate school to members of the National Chief Petty Officers' Association (NCPOA) and their families.

Eligibility This program is open to members of the NCPOA and the children, stepchildren, and grandchildren of living or deceased members. Applicants may be high school seniors or graduates entering a college or university or students currently

enrolled full time as undergraduate or graduate students. Selection is based on academic achievement and participation in extracurricular activities; financial need is not considered.

Financial Data The stipend is $1,000.

Duration 1 year.

Additional data Membership in the NCPOA is limited to men and women who served or are serving as Chief Petty Officers in the U.S. Navy, U.S. Coast Guard, or their Reserve components for at least 30 days.

Number awarded 2 each year: 1 to a high school senior or graduate and 1 to an undergraduate or graduate student.

Deadline May of each year.

[165]
BG BENJAMIN B. TALLEY SCHOLARSHIP

Society of American Military Engineers-Anchorage Post
Attn: BG B.B. Talley Scholarship Endowment Fund
P.O. Box 6409
Anchorage, AK 99506-6409
E-mail: william_kontess@urscorp.com
Web: www.sameanchorage.org/h_about/scholinfo.html

Summary To provide financial assistance to student members of the Society of American Military Engineers (SAME) from Alaska who are working on a bachelor's or master's degree in designated fields of engineering or the natural sciences.

Eligibility This program is open to members of the Anchorage Post of SAME who are residents of Alaska, attending college in Alaska, an active-duty military member stationed in Alaska, or a dependent of an active-duty military member stationed in Alaska. Applicants must be 1) sophomores, juniors, or seniors majoring in engineering, architecture, construction or project management, natural sciences, physical sciences, applied sciences, or mathematics at an accredited college or university; or 2) students working on a master's degree in those fields. They must have a GPA of 2.5 or higher. U.S. citizenship is required. Along with their application, they must submit an essay of 250 to 500 words on their career goals. Selection is based on that essay, academic achievement, participation in school and community activities, and work/family activities; financial need is not considered.

Financial Data Stipends range up to $3,000.

Duration 1 year.

Additional data This program was established in 1997.

Number awarded Varies each year; at least 1 scholarship is reserved for a master's degree students.

Deadline December of each year.

[166]
BRYCE ROWEN MEMORIAL SCHOLARSHIP

New Mexico Engineering Foundation
Attn: Scholarship Chair
P.O. Box 3828
Albuquerque, NM 87190-3828
(505) 615-1800   E-mail: info@nmef.net
Web: www.nmef.net/?section=scholarship

Summary To provide financial assistance to residents of any state working on a degree in engineering at specified universities in New Mexico.

Eligibility This program is open to juniors and seniors working on a degree in engineering at the University of New Mexico, New Mexico State University, or New Mexico Institute of Mining and Technology. Preference is given to non-scholarship ROTC students. Financial need is considered in the selection process.

Financial Data The stipend is $1,000.

Duration 1 year; nonrenewable.

Additional data This program is offered by the Albuquerque Post of the Society of American Military Engineers.

Number awarded 1 or more each year.

Deadline March of each year.

[167]
CALIFORNIA LEGION AUXILIARY PAST PRESIDENTS' PARLEY NURSING SCHOLARSHIPS

American Legion Auxiliary
Department of California
Veterans War Memorial Building
401 Van Ness Avenue, Room 113
San Francisco, CA 94102-4586
(415) 861-5092   Fax: (415) 861-8365
E-mail: calegionaux@calegionaux.org
Web: www.calegionaux.org/scholarships.htm

Summary To provide financial assistance to California residents who are current military personnel, veterans, or members of their families and interested in studying nursing at a school in the state.

Eligibility This program is open to California residents who are currently serving on active military duty, veterans who served during war time, or the spouse, widow(er), or child of such a veteran. Applicants must be entering or continuing students of nursing at an accredited institution of higher learning in California. Financial need is considered in the selection process.

Financial Data Stipends range up to $2,000.

Duration 1 year.

Number awarded Varies each year.

Deadline April of each year.

[168]
CALIFORNIA LEGION AUXILIARY SCHOLARSHIPS FOR CONTINUING AND/OR REENTRY STUDENTS

American Legion Auxiliary
Department of California
Veterans War Memorial Building
401 Van Ness Avenue, Room 113
San Francisco, CA 94102-4586
(415) 861-5092   Fax: (415) 861-8365
E-mail: calegionaux@calegionaux.org
Web: www.calegionaux.org/scholarships.htm

Summary To provide financial assistance to California residents who are active-duty military personnel, veterans, or children of veterans and require assistance to continue their education.

Eligibility This program is open to California residents who are 1) active-duty military personnel; 2) veterans of World War I, World War II, Korea, Vietnam, Grenada/Lebanon, Panama, or Desert Shield/Desert Storm; and 3) children of veterans who served during those periods of war. Applicants must be continuing or reentry students at a college, university, or business/trade school in California. Financial need is considered in the selection process.

Financial Data The stipend is $1,000 or $500.

Duration 1 year.

Additional data This program includes 1 scholarship designated as the Mel Foronda Memorial Scholarship.

Number awarded 5 each year: 3 at $1,000 and 2 at $500.

Deadline March of each year.

[169]
CIVIL ENGINEER CORPS OPTION OF THE SEAMAN TO ADMIRAL-21 PROGRAM

U.S. Navy
Attn: Commander, Naval Service Training Command
250 Dallas Street, Suite A
Pensacola, FL 32508-5268
(850) 452-9563   Fax: (850) 452-2486
E-mail: PNSC_STA21@navy.mil
Web: www.sta-21.navy.mil

Summary To allow outstanding enlisted Navy personnel to complete a bachelor's degree and receive a commission in the Civil Engineer Corps (CEC).

Eligibility This program is open to U.S. citizens who are currently serving on active duty in the Navy as enlisted personnel in any rating. Applicants must have completed at least 4 years of active duty, of which at least 3 years were in an other than formal training environment. They must be high school graduates (or GED recipients) who are able to complete requirements for a professional Accreditation Board for Engineering and Technology (ABET) engineering degree or National Architectural Accrediting Board (NAAB) architectural degree within 36 months or less. Preferred specialties are civil, electrical, mechanical, or ocean engineering. When applicants complete their degree requirements, they must be younger than 42 years of age. Within the past 3 years, they must have taken the SAT test (and achieved scores of at least 500 on the mathematics section and 500 on the critical reading section) or the ACT test (and achieved a score of 41 or higher, including at least 21 on the mathematics portion and 20 on the English portion).

Financial Data Awardees continue to receive their regular Navy pay and allowances while they attend college on a full-time basis. They also receive reimbursement for tuition, fees, and books up to $10,000 per year. If base housing is available, they are eligible to live there. Participants are not eligible to receive benefits under the Navy's Tuition Assistance Program (TA), the Montgomery GI Bill (MGIB), the Navy College Fund, or the Veterans Educational Assistance Program (VEAP).

Duration Selectees are supported for up to 36 months of full-time, year-round study or completion of a bachelor's degree, as long as they maintain a GPA of 3.0 or higher.

Additional data This program was established in 2001 as a replacement for the Civil Engineer Corps Enlisted Commissioning Program (CECECP). Upon acceptance into the program, selectees attend the Naval Science Institute (NSI) in Newport, Rhode Island for an 8-week program in the fundamental core concepts of being a naval officer (navigation, engineering, weapons, military history and justice, etc.). They then enter a college or university with an NROTC unit that is designated for the CEC to work full time on a bachelor's degree. They become members of and drill with the NROTC unit. When they complete their degree, they are commissioned as ensigns in the United States Naval Reserve and assigned to initial training as an officer in the CEC. After commissioning, 5 years of active service are required.

Number awarded Varies each year.

Deadline June of each year.

[170]
CIVIL ENGINEER CORPS SCHOLARSHIPS

U.S. Navy
Bureau of Navy Personnel
BUPERS-314E
5720 Integrity Drive
Millington, TN 38055-4630
(901) 874-4034   Toll Free: (866) CEC-NAVY
Fax: (901) 874-2681   E-mail: p4413d@persnet.navy.mil
Web: portal.navfac.navy.mil/portal/page/portal/cec/accessions

Summary To provide financial assistance to undergraduate and graduate students in architecture and engineering who are interested in serving in the Navy's Civil Engineer Corps (CEC) following graduation.

Eligibility   This program is open to undergraduate and master's degree students who are U.S. citizens between 19 and 35 years of age. Applicants must be enrolled in an engineering program accredited by the Accreditation Board for Engineering and Technology (ABET) or an architecture program accredited by the National Architectural Accrediting Board (NAAB) with a GPA of 3.0 or higher. Eligible majors include civil engineering, electrical engineering, mechanical engineering, ocean engineering, or architecture. For the Exceptional Student Program, they must apply at the end of their sophomore year. For the Collegiate Program, they must apply at the end of their junior year. For the Graduate Program, they must apply upon acceptance to an accredited graduate school and when they are within 6 months of completing a bachelor's degree in engineering. Preference is given to applicants who have engineering or architecture work experience and registration as a Professional Engineer (P.E.) or Engineer-in-Training (EIT). Students majoring in mathematics, physics, non-engineering programs, and engineering or architectural technology are not eligible. Applicants must also be able to meet the Navy's physical fitness requirements.

Financial Data   Students accepted as undergraduates receive E-3 pay (approximately $2,000 per month), an allowance, and benefits; after completing 12 months of the program or being referred to other specified programs, they may be advanced to E-4 or E-5 levels. Graduate students receive payment of tuition and fees plus full officers' salary and allowances.

Duration   Up to 24 months for the Exceptional Student Program, up to 12 months for the Collegiate Program, and up to 18 months (6 months of undergraduate school plus 12 months of graduate school) for the Graduate Program.

Additional data   While in college, selectees have no uniforms, drills, or military duties. After graduation with a bachelor's or master's degree, they enter the Navy and attend 13 weeks at Officer Candidate School (OCS) in Pensacola, Florida, followed by 15 weeks at Civil Engineer Corps Officers School (CECOS) in Port Hueneme, California. They then serve 4 years in the CEC, rotating among public works, contract management, and the Naval Construction Force (Seabees).

Number awarded   Varies each year.

Deadline   Deadline not specified.

[171]
CIVILIAN MARKSMANSHIP PROGRAM UNDERGRADUATE ROTC SCHOLARSHIPS

Corporation for the Promotion of Rifle Practice and Firearms Safety, Inc.
Attn: Civilian Marksmanship Program
Camp Perry Training Site, Building 3
P.O. Box 576
Port Clinton, OH 43452
(419) 635-2141, ext. 1109   Fax: (419) 635-2573
E-mail: programs@odcmp.com
Web: www.odcmp.com/Programs/Scholarship.htm

Summary   To provide financial assistance to rifle shooters who are high school seniors involved in a JROTC program or college undergraduates enrolled in an ROTC program.

Eligibility   This program is open to 1) high school seniors involved in Army, Marine Corps, Navy, or Air Force JROTC who will attend a 4-year college or university and enroll in an ROTC program; and 2) undergraduates enrolled in Army, Air Force, or Navy ROTC or Marine Corps Platoon Leaders Course at a 4-year college or university. Applicants must be able to demonstrate excellence in rifle team programs at their high school or college, good moral character, academic achievement (GPA of 2.5 or higher), financial need, and motivation to complete a college education and serve as an officer of the armed services of the United States. U.S. citizenship is required.

Financial Data   The stipend is $1,000 per year.

Duration   1 year; may be renewed up to 3 additional years, provided the recipient remains enrolled in ROTC, maintains a GPA of 2.5 or higher, continues to participate in ROTC or college rifle team activities, and continues to meet the moral character standards for eligibility.

Additional data   Information on Army ROTC or JROTC is available from the Commanding General, U.S. Army Cadet Command, Attn: ATTCC-OI, 55 Patch Road, Building 56, Fort Monroe, VA 23651-1052. Information on Marine Corps JROTC is available from Commanding General, Training and Education Command (C 46JR), 1019 Elliot Road, Quantico, VA 22134-5001. Information on Navy ROTC or JROTC is available from Naval Service Training Command (NJROTC), 250 Dallas Street, Suite A, Pensacola, FL 32508-5268. Information on Air Force ROTC or JROTC is available from Headquarters AFROTC/RRUC, 551 East Maxwell Boulevard, Building 500, Maxwell AFB, AL 36112-5917.

Number awarded   100 each year.

Deadline   March of each year.

[172]
COAST GUARD RESERVE USAA SCHOLARSHIP

U.S. Coast Guard
Attn: COMDT CG-1313
1900 Half Street, S.W.
Washington, DC 20593-0001
(202) 475-5461   E-mail: Greg.P.Hunton@uscg.mil
Web: www.uscg.mil/RESERVE/docs/pay_benefits/usaa.asp

Summary   To provide financial assistance for college or graduate school to members of the Coast Guard Reserves and their dependents.

Eligibility   This program is open to Coast Guard enlisted reservists (SELRES or IRR) and their dependents who are registered in the Defense Enrollment Eligibility Reporting System (DEERS). Applicants must be enrolled or accepted for enrollment at 1) an accredited institution in a program leading to an associate, bachelor's, master's, or doctoral degree; or 2) a 2- or 4-year course of study at an accredited technical or vocational training school. Along with their application, they must submit a 1-page essay on how the participation of themselves, their spouse, or their parent in the Coast Guard Reserve has contributed to their success.

Financial Data   The stipend is $1,000.

Duration   1 year.

Additional data   This program is sponsored by the United States Automobile Association (USAA) Insurance Corporation.

Number awarded   6 each year.

Deadline   July of each year.

[173]
COAST GUARD TUITION ASSISTANCE PROGRAM

U.S. Coast Guard Institute
Attn: Commanding Officer
5900 S.W. 64th Street, Room 233
Oklahoma City, OK 73169-6990
(405) 954-1360   Fax: (405) 954-7245
E-mail: CGI-PF-Tuition_Assistance@uscg.mil
Web: www.uscg.mil/hq/cgi/cfa/ta.asp

Summary   To provide financial assistance to members and employees of the Coast Guard who are interested in pursuing additional education during their off-duty hours.

Eligibility   This program is open to Coast Guard members who are interested in pursuing additional education at the high school, vocational/technical, undergraduate, graduate, or professional level. Civilian employees with at least 90 days of Coast Guard service and Selected Reservists are also eligible. Enlisted members must have at least 12 months remaining on their active-duty contracts or Selected Reserve obligation after completion of the course. Active-duty officers must agree to fulfill a 2-year service obligation following completion of the course; officers of the selected reserve must agree to fulfill a 4-year service obligation following completion of the course. Civilian employees must agree to retain employment with the Coast Guard for 1 month for each completed course credit hour. For military personnel, the command education services officer (ESO) must certify that the course of instruction is Coast Guard mission or career related. The supervisor of civilian employees must certify that the education is career related. All courses must be related to the mission of the Coast Guard or the individual's career or professional development.

Financial Data Active-duty, Reserve, and civilian Coast Guard members receive full payment of all expenses for completion of a high school degree or equivalent. For college courses (vocational/technical, undergraduate, and graduate), 100% of the cost of tuition is reimbursed, to a maximum of $250 per semester hour or $4,500 per fiscal year.

Duration Until completion of a bachelor's or graduate degree.

Additional data Graduate students must earn a grade of "B" or higher to receive reimbursement; undergraduates must earn a grade of "D" or higher.

Number awarded Varies each year; recently, more than 10,000 Coast Guard active-duty members, Reservists, and civilian employees received tuition assistance worth approximately $14.5 million.

Deadline Applications may be submitted at any time.

[174]
COLLEGE STUDENT PRE-COMMISSIONING INITIATIVE

U.S. Coast Guard
Attn: Recruiting Command
2300 Wilson Boulevard, Suite 500
Arlington, VA 22201
(703) 235-1775　　　　Toll Free: (877) NOW-USCG
Fax: (703) 235-1881　E-mail: Margaret.A.Jackson@uscg.mil
Web: www.gocoastguard.com/find-your-fit/officer-opportunities

Summary To provide financial assistance to college students at minority institutions willing to serve in the Coast Guard following graduation.

Eligibility This program is open to students entering their junior or senior year at a college or university designated as an Historically Black College or University (HBCU), Hispanic Serving Institution (HSI), Tribal College or University (TCU), or an institution located in Guam, Puerto Rico, or the U.S. Virgin Islands. Applicants must be U.S. citizens; have a GPA of 2.5 or higher; have scores of 1100 or higher on the critical reading and mathematics SAT, 23 or higher on the ACT, or 109 or higher on the ASVAB GT; be between 19 and 27 years of age; have no more than 2 dependents; and meet all physical requirements for a Coast Guard commission. They must agree to attend the Coast Guard Officer Candidate School following graduation and serve on active duty as an officer for at least 3 years.

Financial Data Those selected to participate receive full payment of tuition, books, and fees; monthly housing and food allowances; medical and life insurance; special training in leadership, management, law enforcement, navigation, and marine science; 30 days paid vacation per year; and a monthly salary of up to $2,200.

Duration Up to 2 years.
Number awarded Varies each year.
Deadline February of each year.

[175]
COLORADO NATIONAL GUARD STATE TUITION ASSISTANCE

Department of Military and Veterans Affairs
Attn: CODAG-TA
6848 South Revere Parkway
Centennial, CO 80112-6703
(720) 250-1550　　　　　　　　Fax: (720) 250-1559
E-mail: tuition@dmva.state.co.us
Web: www.dmva.state.co.us/page/ta

Summary To provide financial assistance for college or graduate school to members of the Colorado National Guard.

Eligibility This program is open to members of the Colorado National Guard who have completed at least 6 months of military service and are currently in drilling status. Applicants must be enrolled or planning to enroll at a public institution of higher education in Colorado to work on an associate, bachelor's, or master's degree.

Financial Data This program provides payment of up to 100% of the in-state tuition at public institutions in Colorado.

Duration 1 semester; may be renewed as long as the recipient remains an active member of the Guard and maintains a GPA of 2.0 or higher. Assistance is limited to a total of 132 semester hours.

Additional data Recipients must serve 1 year in the Guard for each semester or quarter of assistance received.

Number awarded Varies each year.

Deadline June of each year for the fall semester; November of each year for the spring semester; April of each year for the summer term.

[176]
CONGRESSMAN DAVID L. HOBSON CIVIL ENGINEERING SCHOLARSHIP

Army Engineer Association
Attn: Washington DC Operations
P.O. Box 30260
Alexandria, VA 22310-8260
(703) 428-7084　　　　　　　　Fax: (703) 428-6043
E-mail: DCOps@armyengineer.com
Web: www.armyengineer.com/AEA_scholarships.html

Summary To provide financial assistance to members of the Army Engineer Association (AEA) and their families interested in studying civil engineering in college.

Eligibility This program is open to AEA members and their families who are U.S. citizens. Applicants must be enrolled full time at an accredited college or university and working on a bachelor's degree in civil engineering. Along with their application, they must submit a 600-word essay that lists their academic and professional goals, extracurricular activities, and military service (if applicable). Selection is based on that essay, scholastic aptitude, and letters of recommendation.

Financial Data The stipend is $3,000.
Duration 1 year; nonrenewable.
Additional data This program is sponsored by the engineering firm, Trimble.
Number awarded 4 each year.
Deadline July of each year.

[177]
CONNECTICUT NATIONAL GUARD EDUCATIONAL ASSISTANCE PROGRAM

Connecticut National Guard
Attn: Education Service Officer
360 Broad Street
Hartford, CT 06105-3795
(860) 524-4816
Web: www.ng.mil/CT/default.aspx

Summary To provide financial assistance for college to members of the Connecticut National Guard.
Eligibility This program is open to active members of the Connecticut National Guard who are interested in working on an undergraduate degree at any branch of the University of Connecticut, any of the 4 state universities, or any of the 13 community/technical colleges in Connecticut. Applicants must have been residents of the state and a satisfactory Guard participant for at least 12 months.
Financial Data The program provides a full waiver of tuition at state colleges or universities in Connecticut.
Duration 1 year; may be renewed.
Number awarded Varies each year.
Deadline Deadline not specified.

[178]
CONNECTICUT NATIONAL GUARD FOUNDATION SCHOLARSHIPS

Connecticut National Guard Foundation, Inc.
Attn: Scholarship Committee
360 Broad Street
Hartford, CT 06105-3795
(860) 241-1550　　　　　　　　　　Fax: (860) 293-2929
E-mail: ctngfi@sbcglobal.net
Web: www.ctngfoundation.org/Scholarship.asp
Summary To provide financial assistance for college to members of the Connecticut National Guard and their families.
Eligibility This program is open to members of the Connecticut Army National Guard and Organized Militia, their children, and their spouses. Applicants must be enrolled or planning to enroll in an accredited college or technical program. Along with their application, they must submit a letter of recommendation, a list of extracurricular activities, high school or college transcripts, and a 200-word statement on their educational and future goals. Selection is based on achievement and citizenship.
Financial Data Stipends are $2,000 or $1,000.
Duration 1 year.
Number awarded 5 each year: 2 at $2,000 and 3 at $1,000.
Deadline March of each year.

[179]
CONNECTICUT TUITION WAIVER FOR VETERANS

Connecticut Department of Higher Education
Attn: Education and Employment Information Center
61 Woodland Street
Hartford, CT 06105-2326
(860) 947-1816　　　　　Toll Free: (800) 842-0229 (within CT)
Fax: (860) 947-1310　　　　　E-mail: veterans@ctdhe.org
Web: www.ctdhe.org/SFA/default.htm
Summary To provide financial assistance for college to certain Connecticut veterans and military personnel and their dependents.
Eligibility This program is open to 1) honorably-discharged Connecticut veterans who served at least 90 days during specified periods of wartime; 2) active members of the Connecticut Army and Air National Guard; 3) Connecticut residents who are a dependent child or surviving spouse of a member of the armed forces killed in action on or after September 11, 2001 who was also a Connecticut resident; and 4) Connecticut residents who are dependent children or a person officially declared missing in action or a prisoner of war while serving in the armed forces after January 1, 1960. Applicants must be attending or planning to attend a public college or university in the state.
Financial Data The program provides a waiver of 100% of tuition for general fund courses at Connecticut public colleges or universities, 50% of tuition for extension and summer courses at campuses of Connecticut State University, and 50% of part-time fees at OnlineCSU.

Duration Up to 4 years.
Additional data This is an entitlement program; applications are available at the respective college financial aid offices.
Number awarded Varies each year.
Deadline Deadline not specified.

[180]
CSM ROBERT W. ELKEY AWARD

Army Engineer Association
Attn: Washington DC Operations
P.O. Box 30260
Alexandria, VA 22310-8260
(703) 428-7084　　　　　　　　　　Fax: (703) 428-6043
E-mail: DCOps@armyengineer.com
Web: www.armyengineer.com/AEA_scholarships.html
Summary To provide financial assistance for college or graduate school to enlisted members of the Army Engineer Association (AEA).
Eligibility This program is open to AEA members serving in an active, Reserve, or National Guard component Army Engineer unit, school, or organization within the Corps of Engineers of the United States Army. Applicants must be enlisted personnel (PVT, PFC, SPC, CPL, SGT, or SSG). They must be working on or planning to work on an associate, bachelor's, or master's degree at an accredited college or university. Selection is based primarily on financial need, although potential for academic success and standards of conduct as supported by personal references are also considered.
Financial Data The stipend is $1,000.
Duration 1 year.
Number awarded 3 each year.
Deadline June of each year.

[181]
CSM VINCENT BALDASSARI MEMORIAL SCHOLARSHIPS

Enlisted Association National Guard of New Jersey
Attn: Scholarship Committee
101 Eggert Crossing Road
Lawrenceville, NJ 08648-2805
(609) 562-0207　　　　　　　　　　Fax: (609) 562-0283
Web: www.eang-nj.org/scholarships.html
Summary To provide financial assistance to New Jersey National Guard members and their children who are interested in attending college in any state.
Eligibility This program is open to 1) children of New Jersey National Guard members who are also members of the Enlisted Association National Guard of New Jersey, and 2) drilling Guard members who are also members of the Association. Applicants must be attending or planning to attend a college or university in any state. Along with their application, they must submit 1) information on their church, school, and community activities; 2) a list of honors they have received; 3) letters of recommendation; 4) transcripts; and 5) a letter with specific facts about their desire to continue their education and specifying their career goals. Financial need is not considered in the selection process.
Financial Data The stipend is $1,000.
Duration 1 year.
Number awarded Varies each year; recently, 4 of these scholarships were awarded.
Deadline May of each year.

[182]
CSM VIRGIL R. WILLIAMS SCHOLARSHIP PROGRAM

Enlisted Association of the National Guard of the United States
3133 Mount Vernon Avenue
Alexandria, VA 22305-2640
(703) 519-3846   Toll Free: (800) 234-EANG
Fax: (703) 519-3849   E-mail: eangus@eangus.org
Web: www.eangus.org

Summary To provide financial assistance to National Guard members and their dependents who are members of the Enlisted Association of the National Guard of the United States (EANGUS) and entering or continuing in college.

Eligibility This program is open to high school seniors and currently-enrolled college students. They must be 1) National Guard members who belong to EANGUS; 2) unmarried sons and daughters of EANGUS members; 3) spouses of EANGUS members; or 4) unremarried spouses and unmarried dependent children of deceased EANGUS members who were in good standing at the time of their death. Honorary, associate, or corporate membership alone does not qualify. Graduate students are not eligible. Applicants must submit a copy of their school transcript, 3 letters of recommendation, a letter of academic reference (from their principal, dean, or counselor), a photocopy of the qualifying state and/or national membership card (parent's, spouse's or applicant's), and a personal letter with specific facts as to their desire to continue their education and why financial assistance is necessary. Application packets must be submitted to the state EANGUS association; acceptable packets are then sent to the national offices for judging. Selection is based on academic achievement, character, leadership, and financial need.

Financial Data The stipend is $2,000.

Duration 1 year; nonrenewable.

Additional data Recipients must enroll full time.

Number awarded 2 or more each year.

Deadline Applications must first be verified by the state office and then submitted by June to the national office.

[183]
DAEDALIAN ACADEMIC MATCHING SCHOLARSHIP PROGRAM

Daedalian Foundation
Attn: Scholarship Committee
55 Main Circle (Building 676)
P.O. Box 249
Randolph AFB, TX 78148-0249
(210) 945-2113   Fax: (210) 945-2112
E-mail: icarus2@daedalians.org
Web: www.daedalians.org/foundation/scholarships.htm

Summary To provide financial assistance to ROTC and other college students who wish to become military pilots.

Eligibility Eligible are students who are attending or have been accepted at an accredited 4-year college or university and have demonstrated the desire and potential to become a commissioned military pilot. Usually, students in ROTC units of all services apply to local chapters (Flights) of Daedalian; if the Flight awards a scholarship, the application is forwarded to the Daedalian Foundation for 1 of these matching scholarships. College students not part of a ROTC program are eligible to apply directly to the Foundation if their undergraduate goals and performance are consistent with Daedalian criteria. Selection is based on intention to pursue a career as a military pilot, demonstrated moral character and patriotism, scholastic and military standing and aptitude, and physical condition and aptitude for flight. Financial need may also be considered. Additional eligibility criteria may be set by a Flight Scholarship Selection Board.

Financial Data The amount awarded varies but is intended to serve as matching funds for the Flight scholarship. Generally, the maximum awarded is $2,000.

Number awarded Up to 99 each year.

Deadline Students who are members of Daedalian Flights must submit their applications by November of each year; students who apply directly to the Daedalian Foundation must submit their applications by July of each year.

[184]
DEDARNG SCHOLARSHIPS

U.S. Army
ROTC Cadet Command
Attn: ATCC-OP-I-S
55 Patch Road, Building 56
Fort Monroe, VA 23651-1052
(757) 788-4551   Toll Free: (800) USA-ROTC
Fax: (757) 788-4643 E-mail: william.daniels@usaac.army.mil
Web: www.rotc.monroe.army.mil

Summary To provide financial assistance to college and graduate students who are interested in enrolling in Army ROTC and serving in the Army National Guard following graduation.

Eligibility This program is open to full-time students entering their sophomore or junior year of college with a GPA of 2.5 or higher. High school seniors are also eligible if they plan to attend a military junior college (MJC), have a GPA of 2.5 or higher, and have scores of at least 19 on the ACT or 920 on the combined mathematics and critical reading SAT. Graduate students may also be eligible if they have only 2 years remaining for completion of their degree. Students who have been awarded an ROTC campus-based scholarship may apply to convert to this program during their freshman year. Applicants must meet all medical and moral character requirements for enrollment in Army ROTC. They must be willing to enroll in the Simultaneous Membership Program (SMP) of an ROTC unit on their campus; the SMP requires simultaneous membership in Army ROTC and the Army National Guard.

Financial Data Participants receive full reimbursement of tuition, a grant of $1,200 per year for books, plus an ROTC stipend for 10 months of the year at $450 per month during their junior year and $500 per month during their senior year. As a member of the Army National Guard, they also receive weekend drill pay at the pay grade of E-5 during their junior year or E-6 during their senior year.

Duration 2 or 3 years for college students; 2 years for high school seniors entering an MJC.

Additional data After graduation, participants serve 3 to 6 months on active duty in the Officer Basic Course (OBC). Following completion of OBC, they are released from active duty and are obligated to serve 8 years in the Army National Guard.

Number awarded 594 each year (11 in each state or U.S. territory).

Deadline Deadline not specified.

[185]
DELAWARE NATIONAL GUARD EDUCATION ASSISTANCE PROGRAM

Delaware National Guard
Attn: Education Services Officer
State Tuition Reimbursement Program
First Regiment Road
Wilmington, DE 19808-2191
(302) 326-7012   Fax: (302) 326-7029
Web: www.delawarenationalguard.com

Summary To provide financial assistance to members of the Delaware National Guard who plan to attend college in the state.

Eligibility This program is open to active members of the Delaware National Guard who are interested in working on an associate or bachelor's degree at a school in Delaware. Applicants must have made satisfactory progress in their assigned military career field, may not have missed more than 6 periods of scheduled unit training assembly periods in the preceding 12 months, and must have avoided all adverse personnel actions. They must earn a grade of 2.0 or higher in all courses to qualify for tuition reimbursement.

Financial Data Participants receive reimbursement of 100% of the tuition at state-supported colleges and universities in Delaware, to a maximum of $1,236 per semester at Delaware Technical and Community college, $4,270 per semester at the University of Delaware, or $3,240.50 at Delaware State University. Students who attend a Delaware private college are reimbursed up to $243 per credit hour. If total funding appropriated by the legislature is insufficient for all qualified applicants, the available funds are distributed among recipients according to a maximum allowable fair percentage formula. Recipients must complete 6 years of satisfactory membership in the Delaware National Guard (before, during, and after participation in the program) or repay the funds received.

Duration 1 semester; may be renewed. Guard members are eligible for this assistance only for 10 years after the date on which they begin the first course for which reimbursement was granted.

Number awarded Varies each year. Recently, a total of $490,000 was available for this program.

Deadline September of each year for fall semester; January of each year for winter semester; March of each year for spring semester; June of each year for summer semester.

[186]
DISABLED WAR VETERANS SCHOLARSHIPS

Armed Forces Communications and Electronics Association
Attn: AFCEA Educational Foundation
4400 Fair Lakes Court
Fairfax, VA 22033-3899
(703) 631-6149   Toll Free: (800) 336-4583, ext. 6149
Fax: (703) 631-4693   E-mail: scholarship@afcea.org
Web: www.afcea.org

Summary To provide financial assistance to disabled military personnel and veterans who are majoring in specified scientific fields in college.

Eligibility This program is open to active-duty service personnel and honorably discharged U.S. military veterans, Reservists, and National Guard members who are disabled because of wounds received during service in Enduring Freedom (Afghanistan) or Iraqi Freedom operations. Applicants must be enrolled full or part time at an accredited 2- or 4-year college or university or in a distance learning or online degree program. They must be working toward a degree in engineering (aerospace, computer, electrical, or systems), computer science, computer engineering technology, computer network systems, computer information systems, electronics engineering technology, mathematics, physics, science or mathematics education, information systems management, information systems security, technology management, or other field directly related to the support of U.S. intelligence or national security enterprises. Selection is based on demonstrated academic excellence, leadership, and financial need.

Financial Data The stipend is $2,500.

Duration 1 year.

Number awarded 2 each year: 1 for spring and 1 for fall.

Deadline March of each year for fall; November of each year for spring.

[187]
DISTRICT OF COLUMBIA NATIONAL GUARD TUITION ASSISTANCE

District of Columbia National Guard
Attn: Education Services Office
2001 East Capitol Street
Washington, DC 20003-1719
(202) 685-9825   Fax: (202) 685-9815
E-mail: joanne.thweatt@dc.ngb.army.mil
Web: states.ng.mil/sites/DC/education/Pages/tuition.aspx

Summary To provide financial assistance for college to current members of the District of Columbia National Guard.

Eligibility This program is open to traditional, technician, and AGR members of the District of Columbia Air and Army National Guard. Applicants must have a high school diploma or equivalency and currently be working on an associate, bachelor's, or master's degree at an accredited postsecondary education institution. In some instances, support may also be available for an M.D., D.O., P.A., or J.D. degree.

Financial Data Army National Guard members are eligible for up to $4,500 per year in federal tuition assistance; they may supplement that with up to $1,500 per year in District tuition assistance. Air National Guard members do not have access to federal tuition assistance, so they may receive up to $6,000 in District tuition assistance. Funds must be used to pay for tuition, fees, and/or books.

Duration 1 semester; recipients may reapply.

Number awarded Varies each year.

Deadline July of each year for the fall session, October of each year for the spring session, or April of each year for the summer session.

[188]
DIVISION COMMANDER'S HIP POCKET SCHOLARSHIPS

U.S. Army
ROTC Cadet Command
Attn: ATCC-OP-I-S
55 Patch Road, Building 56
Fort Monroe, VA 23651-1052
(757) 788-3341   Toll Free: (800) USA-ROTC
Fax: (757) 788-5781   E-mail: atccps@usacc.army.mil
Web: www.goarmy.com/rotc/pocket_scholarship.jsp

Summary To enable soldiers who are nominated by their Division Commanding General to obtain an early discharge from the Army and return to college to participate in the Army Reserve Officers' Training Corps (ROTC).

Eligibility Enlisted soldiers who have served at least 2 but less than 10 years on active duty are eligible for this program. They must be nominated by their Division Commanding General to obtain an early discharge in order to enroll in a baccalaureate degree program. Nominees must have a cumulative high school or college GPA of 2.5 or higher, a score of at least 19 on the ACT or 920 on the combined mathematics and critical reading SAT, a General Technical (GT) score of 110 or higher, and a recent (within the past 6 months) Army Physical Fitness Test (APFT) score of 180 or higher (including 60 points in each event). They may not have a spouse who is also in the military or dependent children under 18 years of age (those requirements may be waived). At the time they graduate and are commissioned , they must be under 31 years of age. Selection is made by the Division Commanding General; no additional review is made by Cadet Command Headquarters.

Financial Data Scholarship winners receive full payment of tuition, a grant of $1,200 per year for books and supplies, a monthly stipend of up to $500 per month (depending on academic status) for 10 months per year, and pay for attending the 6-week Leader Development and Assessment Course (LDAC) during the summer between the junior and senior year of college.

Duration 2, 3, or 4 years.

Additional data Recipients who had previously qualified for benefits from the Army College Fund and/or the Montgomery GI Bill are still entitled to receive those in addition to any benefits from this program. Upon graduation from college, scholarship winners are commissioned as second lieutenants and are required to serve in the military for 8 years. That obligation may be fulfilled by serving 4 years on active duty followed by 4 years in the Inactive Ready Reserve (IRR).

Number awarded Varies each year.

Deadline March of each year.

[189]
DONALD D. FRIZZELL MEMORIAL SCHOLARSHIPS

First Command Educational Foundation
Attn: Scholarship Programs Manager
1 FirstComm Plaza
Fort Worth, TX 76109-4999
(817) 569-2634   Toll Free: (877) 872-8289
Fax: (817) 569-2970   E-mail: aymcmanus@fcef.com
Web: www.fcef.com/direct-apply-scholarship.php

Summary To provide financial assistance to students, especially those with ties to the military, entering or attending college.

Eligibility This program is open to 2 categories of applicants: 1) traditional students, including high school seniors and students already enrolled at a college, university, or accredited trade school; and 2) nontraditional students, including those defined by their institution as nontraditional and adult students planning to return to a college, university, or accredited trade school. Traditional students must have a GPA of 3.0 or higher. Special consideration is given to applicants with a connection to the military. Along with their application, they must submit 1-page essays on 1) their active involvement in community service programs, 2) the impact of financial literacy on their future, and 3) why they need this scholarship. Selection is based primarily on the essays, academic merit, and financial need.

Financial Data Stipends are $5,000 or $2,500. Funds are disbursed directly to the recipient's college, university, or trade school.

Duration 1 year.

Additional data The sponsoring organization was formerly known as the USPA & IRA Educational Foundation, founded in 1983 to provide scholarships to the children of active, retired, or deceased military personnel. In addition to these scholarships, for which students may apply directly, it supports scholarships offered by a number of partner organizations. Since its establishment, it has awarded scholarships worth nearly $4 million.

Number awarded 6 each year: 2 at $5,000 and 4 at $2,500. Awards are split evenly between the 2 categories.

Deadline The online application process begins in February of each year and continues until 200 applications have been received in each category.

[190]
DR. AURELIO M. CACCOMO FAMILY FOUNDATION MEMORIAL SCHOLARSHIP

AMVETS National Headquarters
Attn: Scholarships
4647 Forbes Boulevard
Lanham, MD 20706-3807
(301) 459-9600   Toll Free: (877) 7-AMVETS, ext. 3043
Fax: (301) 459-7924   E-mail: amvets@amvets.org
Web: www.amvets.org/programs/programs_scholarships.html

Summary To provide financial assistance for college to veterans and members of the National Guard and Reserves who are members of AMVETS.

Eligibility This program is open to AMVETS members who are veterans or currently serving in the National Guard or Reserves.

Applicants must be interested in working full or part time on an undergraduate degree or certification from an accredited technical/trade school. They must have exhausted all other government aid. U.S. citizenship is required. Selection is based on financial need, academic promise, military duty and awards, volunteer activities, community services, jobs held during the past 4 years, and an essay of 50 to 100 words on "This award will help me achieve my career/vocational goal, which is..."

Financial Data The stipend is $3,000.

Duration 1 year; nonrenewable.

Additional data Requests for applications must be accompanied by a self-addressed stamped envelope.

Number awarded 1 each year.

Deadline April of each year.

[191]
DR. JON L. BOYES, VICE ADMIRAL, USN (RET.) MEMORIAL SCHOLARSHIP

Armed Forces Communications and Electronics Association
Attn: AFCEA Educational Foundation
4400 Fair Lakes Court
Fairfax, VA 22033-3899
(703) 631-6149   Toll Free: (800) 336-4583, ext. 6149
Fax: (703) 631-4693   E-mail: scholarship@afcea.org
Web: www.afcea.org/education/scholarships/rotc/Boyes.asp

Summary To provide financial assistance to Navy ROTC midshipmen who are majoring in electrical engineering.

Eligibility This program is open to Navy ROTC midshipmen enrolled full time at an accredited degree-granting 4-year college or university in the United States. Applicants must be sophomores or juniors at the time of application and have a GPA of 3.0 or higher with a major in electrical engineering. Their application must be endorsed by the professor of naval science at their institution. Selection is based on demonstrated dedication, superior performance, and potential to serve as an officer in the United States Navy. Financial need is not considered in the selection process.

Financial Data The stipend is $3,000.

Duration 1 year.

Number awarded 1 each year.

Deadline February of each year.

[192]
ENLISTED ASSOCIATION OF THE NATIONAL GUARD OF KANSAS SCHOLARSHIPS

Enlisted Association of the National Guard of Kansas
Attn: Executive Director
P.O. Box 841
Topeka, KS 66601-0841
(785) 242-5678   Fax: (785) 242-3765
E-mail: eangks@earthlink.net
Web: www.eangks.org

Summary To provide financial assistance to members of the Enlisted Association National Guard of Kansas and their families who are interested in attending college in any state.

Eligibility This program is open to members of the association who are also currently serving in the Kansas National Guard and their families. Spouses and dependents of associate members are not eligible. Applicants must submit high school and/or college transcripts, 3 letters of recommendation, and a letter describing their educational goals, future plans, and financial situation. They must be enrolled or planning to enroll full time at an accredited institution of higher learning in any state.

Financial Data Stipends are normally approximately $1,000.

Duration 1 year.

Additional data This program is supported, in part, by USAA Insurance Corporation.

Number awarded Varies each year.
Deadline May of each year.

[193]
ENLISTED ASSOCIATION OF THE NATIONAL GUARD OF TENNESSEE SCHOLARSHIP PROGRAMS

Enlisted Association of the National Guard of Tennessee
Attn: Scholarship Committee
4332 Kenilwood Drive, Suite B
Nashville, TN 37204-4401
(615) 781-2000 Fax: (615) 833-9173
E-mail: betty@eangtn.org
Web: www.eangtn.org/Scholarships.htm

Summary To provide financial assistance to members of the Enlisted Association of the National Guard of Tennessee (EANGTN) and to their dependents who are interested in attending college in any state.

Eligibility This program is open to students who are members of both the Tennessee National Guard and EANGTN or the dependent son, daughter, or spouse of a member in good standing. Children must be unmarried, unless they are also a member of the National Guard. Applicants must be entering or continuing at a college or university in any state. Along with their application, they must submit a transcript, a letter with specific facts as to their desire to continue their education and why financial assistance is required, 3 letters of recommendation, and a letter of academic reference.

Financial Data The stipend is $1,000. Funds are paid to the recipient's school once enrollment is confirmed.

Duration 1 year.

Additional data In 1985, the National Guard Association of Tennessee (NGAT) agreed that the EANGTN would fund the scholarships of both associations. Additional funding is also provided by USAA Insurance Corporation.

Number awarded 6 each year.

Deadline January of each year.

[194]
ENLISTED ASSOCIATION OF THE NATIONAL GUARD OF UTAH SCHOLARSHIP

Enlisted Association of the National Guard of Utah
Attn: Scholarship Committee
12953 Minuteman Drive
P.O. Box 1776
Draper, UT 84020-1776
(801) 523-4493 Fax: (801) 523-4659
E-mail: Derek.dimond1@us.army.mil
Web: www.eangut.org/scholarships.html

Summary To provide financial assistance to National Guard members who are active members of the Enlisted Association National Guard of Utah (EANGUT) and their families entering or continuing in college in the state.

Eligibility This program is open to members of EANGUT, their spouses, and their children who are attending or planning to attend a college, university, or vocational/technical school in Utah. Priority may be given to members of the National Guard. Applicants must have a GPA of 2.5 or higher and be able to demonstrate financial need. Along with their application, they must submit a brief statement on their desire to continue their education and their anticipated occupation or profession. Selection is based on academic achievement, citizenship, and financial need.

Financial Data A stipend is awarded (amount not specified).

Duration 1 year.

Number awarded 1 or more each year.

Deadline January of each year.

[195]
FALCON FOUNDATION SCHOLARSHIPS

Falcon Foundation
3116 Academy Drive, Suite 200
USAF Academy, CO 80840-4480
(719) 333-4096 Fax: (719) 333-3669
Web: www.falconfoundation.org/about_ff.htm

Summary To provide financial assistance to people who require additional training for possible admission to the U.S. Air Force Academy.

Eligibility This program is open to individuals who have applied for admission to the Air Force Academy and are considered qualified but not competitive. Applicants must be U.S. citizens, high school seniors or graduates, of good moral character, between 17 and 21 years of age on July 1 of the year of potential admission to the Academy, in good physical condition, unmarried, and with no dependent children. They must be interested in attending a selected junior college or preparatory school to enable them to meet Air Force Academy requirements. Selection is based on motivation to enter and graduate from the USAF Academy and then follow a career as an Air Force officer; scholastic achievements; qualities of maturity, truthfulness, courage, kindliness, unselfishness, fellowship, and devotion to duty; exhibition of moral force of character and leadership instincts, with an interest in others; and physical vigor, as shown by a fondness for, and participation and success in, sports.

Financial Data Amounts of the scholarships depend on the availability of funds but are intended to provide a large portion of the cost of room, board, and tuition at a preparatory school or junior college selected by the foundation.

Additional data Students who meet the basic requirements but may have academic deficiencies that might disqualify them from admission to the Academy may enroll in preparatory school training to correct the deficiencies. Completion of the preparatory school training does not guarantee admission to the Academy. The Falcon Foundation recognizes that these scholarships may provide the student with additional education if the applicant fails to receive an appointment at the Academy.

Number awarded Varies each year; recently, 90 of these scholarships were awarded for study at 5 junior colleges and preparatory schools: Marion Military Institute (Marion, Alabama), New Mexico Military Institute (Roswell, New Mexico), Northwestern Preparatory School (Santa Barbara, California), Valley Forge Military College (Wayne, Pennsylvania), and Wentworth Military Academy (Lexington, Missouri).

Deadline April of each year.

[196]
FIRST CAVALRY DIVISION ASSOCIATION SCHOLARSHIPS

First Cavalry Division Association
Attn: Foundation
302 North Main Street
Copperas Cove, TX 76522-1703
(254) 547-6537 Fax: (254) 547-8853
E-mail: firstcav@1cda.org
Web: www.1cda.org

Summary To provide financial assistance for undergraduate education to soldiers currently or formerly assigned to the First Cavalry Division and their families.

Eligibility This program is open to children of soldiers who died or have been declared totally and permanently disabled from injuries incurred while serving with the First Cavalry Division during any armed conflict; children of soldiers who died while serving in the First Cavalry Division during peacetime; and active-duty soldiers currently assigned or attached to the First Cavalry Division and their spouses and children.

Financial Data The stipend is $1,200 per year. The checks are made out jointly to the student and the school and may be used for whatever the student needs, including tuition, books, and clothing.

Duration 1 year; may be renewed up to 3 additional years.

Additional data Requests for applications must be accompanied by a self-addressed stamped envelope.

Number awarded Varies each year. Since the program was established, it has awarded more than $640,500 to 444 children of disabled and deceased Cavalry members and more than $184,500 to 224 current members of the Division and their families.

Deadline June of each year.

[197]
FIRST SERGEANT DOUGLAS AND CHARLOTTE DEHORSE SCHOLARSHIP

Catching the Dream
8200 Mountain Road, N.E., Suite 203
Albuquerque, NM 87110-7835
(505) 262-2351   Fax: (505) 262-0534
E-mail: NScholarsh@aol.com
Web: www.catchingthedream.org

Summary To provide financial assistance to American Indians who have ties to the military and are working on an undergraduate or graduate degree.

Eligibility This program is open to American Indians who 1) have completed 1 year of an Army, Navy, or Air Force Junior Reserve Officer Training (JROTC) program; 2) are enrolled in an Army, Navy, or Air Force Reserve Officer Training (ROTC) program; or 3) are a veteran of the U.S. Army, Navy, Air Force, Marines, Merchant Marine, or Coast Guard. Applicants must be enrolled in an undergraduate or graduate program of study. Along with their application, they must submit a personal essay, high school transcripts, and letters of recommendation.

Financial Data A stipend is awarded (amount not specified).

Duration 1 year.

Additional data This program was established in 2007.

Number awarded 1 or more each year.

Deadline April of each year for fall semester or quarter; September of each year for spring semester or winter quarter.

[198]
FLEET RESERVE ASSOCIATION SCHOLARSHIP

Fleet Reserve Association
Attn: Scholarship Administrator
125 North West Street
Alexandria, VA 22314-2754
(703) 683-1400   Toll Free: (800) FRA-1924
Fax: (703) 549-6610   E-mail: fra@fra.org
Web: www.fra.org

Summary To provide financial assistance for college or graduate school to members of the Fleet Reserve Association (FRA), as well as their spouses, children, and grandchildren.

Eligibility This program is open to members of the FRA and their dependent children, grandchildren, and spouses. The children, grandchildren, and spouses of deceased FRA members are also eligible. Applicants must submit an essay on their life experiences, career objectives, and what motivated them to select those objectives. Selection is based on academic record, financial need, extracurricular activities, leadership skills, and participation in community activities. U.S. citizenship is required.

Financial Data The stipend is $5,000 per year.

Duration 1 year; may be renewed.

Additional data Membership in the FRA is restricted to active-duty, retired, and reserve members of the Navy, Marines, and Coast Guard.

Number awarded 6 each year.

Deadline April of each year.

[199]
FLORIDA NATIONAL GUARD EDUCATIONAL DOLLARS FOR DUTY (EDD) PROGRAM

Department of Military Affairs
Attn: Education Services Officer
82 Marine Street
St. Augustine, FL 32084-5039
(904) 823-0417   Toll Free: (800) 342-6528
Web: www.dma.state.fl.us

Summary To provide financial assistance for college to members of the Florida National Guard.

Eligibility This program is open to current members of the Florida National Guard. Applicants must be attending or planning to attend a college or university in Florida to work on an undergraduate or master's degree. College preparatory and vocational/technical programs also qualify. Guard members who already have a master's degree are not eligible.

Financial Data The program provides for payment of 100% of tuition and fees at a public college or university or an equivalent amount at a private institution.

Duration 1 year; may be renewed.

Number awarded Varies each year; recently, approximately 765 Florida National Guard members utilized this program.

Deadline Deadline not specified.

[200]
FORCE RECON ASSOCIATION SCHOLARSHIPS

Force Recon Association
P.O. Box 425
Rowe, MA 01367
E-mail: commchief@forcerecon.com
Web: www.forcerecon.com

Summary To provide financial assistance for college to members of the Force Recon Association and their dependents.

Eligibility This program is open to members of the Force Recon Association and family members of a relative who served both in the U.S. Marine Corps and was or is assigned to a Force Reconnaissance Company. The relative must be either an active or deceased member of the Force Recon Association. Family members include wives and widows, sons and daughters (including adopted and stepchildren), grandchildren, and great-grandchildren. Applicants may be pursuing scholastic, vocational, or technical education. Along with their application, they must submit a personal statement on why they desire this scholarship, their proposed course of study, their progress in their current course of study, and their long-range career goals. Selection is based on academic achievement, letters of recommendation, demonstrated character, and the written statements.

Financial Data A stipend is awarded (amount not specified).

Duration 1 year; may be renewed.

Number awarded 1 or more each year.

Deadline Applications must be received at least 2 weeks prior to the annual meeting of the Force Recon Association.

[201]
GENERAL EDWARD W. WALDON SCHOLARSHIP PROGRAM

Grand Lodge of Minnesota, A.F. & A.M.
Attn: Grand Secretary
11501 Masonic Home Drive
Bloomington, MN 55437-3699
(952) 948-6700   Toll Free: (800) 245-6050 (within MN)
Fax: (952) 948-6710   E-mail: grandlodge@qwest.net
Web: www.mn-masons.org/page931.aspx

Summary To provide financial assistance to members of the National Guard and Reserve units in Minnesota who have deployed to combat zones since September 11, 2001 and plan to attend college in any state.

Eligibility This program is open to members of the Minnesota National Guard and Minnesota Reserve units who have deployed in combat zones since September 11, 2001. Applicants must be interested in attending college in any state and be seeking funding either to help pay for tuition or to assist with the administrative fee for the Montgomery GI Bill. Awards are not based on grades or past results as a student. If there are more applicants than available scholarships, recipients are selected in a random drawing.

Financial Data The stipend is $1,000.

Duration 1 year.

Additional data This program was established in 2007.

Number awarded 100 each year.

Deadline September of each year.

[202]
GENERAL EMMETT PAIGE SCHOLARSHIPS

Armed Forces Communications and Electronics Association
Attn: AFCEA Educational Foundation
4400 Fair Lakes Court
Fairfax, VA 22033-3899
(703) 631-6149   Toll Free: (800) 336-4583, ext. 6149
Fax: (703) 631-4693   E-mail: scholarship@afcea.org
Web: www.afcea.org

Summary To provide financial assistance to veterans, military personnel, and their family members who are majoring in specified scientific fields in college.

Eligibility This program is open to veterans, persons on active duty in the uniformed military services, and their spouses or dependents who are currently enrolled full time in an accredited 4-year college or university in the United States. Graduating high school seniors are not eligible, but veterans entering college as freshmen may apply. Spouses or dependents must be sophomores or juniors. Applicants must be U.S. citizens, be of good moral character, have demonstrated academic excellence, be motivated to complete a college education, and be working toward a degree in engineering (aerospace, chemical, electrical, or systems), mathematics, physics, science or mathematics education, management information systems, technology management, computer science, or other field directly related to the support of U.S. intelligence enterprises or national security. They must have a GPA of 3.0 or higher. Along with their application, they must provide a copy of Discharge Form DD214, Certificate of Service, or facsimile of their current Department of Defense or Coast Guard Identification Card. Financial need is not considered in the selection process.

Financial Data The stipend is $2,000 per year.

Duration 1 year; may be renewed.

Number awarded Varies each year; recently, 9 of these scholarships were awarded.

Deadline February of each year.

[203]
GEORGE WASHINGTON CHAPTER AUSA SCHOLARSHIPS

Association of the United States Army-George Washington
   Chapter
c/o Bobbie Williams, Scholarship Committee
79 Brush Everard Court
Stafford, VA 22554
(703) 697-6340   E-mail: Bobbie.Williams@us.army.mil
Web: www.gwcausa.org/Scholarship/index.htm

Summary To provide financial assistance for undergraduate or graduate study at a school in any state to members of the George Washington Chapter of the Association of the United States Army (AUSA) and their families.

Eligibility This program is open to active members of the AUSA George Washington Chapter (which serves the Washington, D.C.

area) and the families of active members. Applicants must have a GPA of 2.5 or higher and be working on an undergraduate or advanced degree at a college or university in any state. Along with their application, they must submit a letter describing any family circumstances they believe are relevant and explaining why they deserve the scholarship. Members must also submit a favorable recommendation from their supervisor. Membership in AUSA is open to Army personnel (including Reserves and National Guard) who are either active or retired, ROTC cadets, or civilian employees of the Army.

Financial Data Stipends range up to $1,000.

Duration 1 year.

Number awarded Varies each year; recently, 15 of these scholarships were awarded.

Deadline April of each year.

[204]
GEORGIA'S HERO SCHOLARSHIP PROGRAM

Georgia Student Finance Commission
Attn: Scholarships and Grants Division
2082 East Exchange Place, Suite 200
Tucker, GA 30084-5305
(770) 724-9000   Toll Free: (800) 505-GSFC
Fax: (770) 724-9089   E-mail: gsfcinfo@gsfc.org
Web: www.gacollege411.org

Summary To provide financial assistance for college to members of the National Guard or Reserves in Georgia and the children and spouses of deceased or disabled Guard or Reserve members.

Eligibility This program is open to Georgia residents who are active members of the Georgia National Guard or U.S. Military Reserves, were deployed outside the United States for active-duty service on or after February 1, 2003 to a location designated as a combat zone, and served in that combat zone for at least 181 consecutive days. Also eligible are 1) the children, younger than 25 years of age, of Guard and Reserve members who completed at least 1 term of service (of 181 days each) overseas on or after February 1, 2003; 2) the children, younger than 25 years of age, of Guard and Reserve members who were killed or totally disabled during service overseas on or after February 1, 2003, regardless of their length of service; and 3) the spouses of Guard and Reserve members who were killed in a combat zone, died as a result of injuries, or became 100% disabled as a result of injuries received in a combat zone during service overseas on or after February 1, 2003, regardless of their length of service. Applicants must be interested in attending a unit of the University System of Georgia, a unit of the Georgia Department of Technical and Adult Education, or an eligible private college or university in Georgia.

Financial Data The stipend is $2,000 per academic year, not to exceed $8,000 during an entire program of study.

Duration 1 year; may be renewed (if satisfactory progress is maintained) for up to 3 additional years.

Additional data This program, which stands for Helping Educate Reservists and their Offspring, was established in 2005.

Number awarded Varies each year.

Deadline June of each year.

[205]
GETCHELL AND ROTC SCHOLARSHIPS

Daedalian Foundation
Attn: Scholarship Committee
55 Main Circle (Building 676)
P.O. Box 249
Randolph AFB, TX 78148-0249
(210) 945-2113   Fax: (210) 945-2112
E-mail: icarus2@daedalians.org
Web: www.daedalians.org/foundation/scholarships.htm

Summary To provide financial assistance to ROTC students who wish to become military pilots.
Eligibility This program is open to students who are currently enrolled in an ROTC program at their college or university. Applicants must be interested in preparing for a career as a military pilot. They must apply through their ROTC detachment. Selection is based on intention to pursue a career as a military pilot, demonstrated moral character and patriotism, scholastic and military standing and aptitude, and physical condition and aptitude for flight. Financial need may also be considered.
Financial Data The stipend is $2,000.
Duration 1 year.
Number awarded 19 each year: 5 designated as Getchell Scholarships, 8 for Air Force ROTC cadets, 3 for Army ROTC cadets, and 3 for Navy/Marine ROTC midshipmen.
Deadline November of each year.

[206]
GLADYS MCPARTLAND SCHOLARSHIPS

United States Marine Corps Combat Correspondents
  Association
Attn: Executive Director
110 Fox Court
Wildwood, FL 34785
(352) 748-4698   E-mail: usmccca@cfl.rr.com
Web: www.usmccca.org/awards/gladys

Summary To provide financial assistance for college or graduate school to regular members of the U.S. Marine Corps Combat Correspondents Association (USMCCCA) or their children.
Eligibility Eligible are active-duty Marines and certain Marine Corps Reservists who are regular members of the USMCCCA, or the dependent children of such members, as long as the member is in a "dues-paid" status, or died in such status, or is listed as a prisoner of war or missing in action and was in a "dues-paid" status when so listed. Applicants must be high school seniors or graduates, seeking at least a bachelor's degree. Preference is given to students working on degrees in disciplines that will lead to careers in mass media communications, although applications are accepted in any field.
Financial Data The stipend is $1,000; funds are to be used exclusively for tuition, books, and/or fees.
Duration 1 year; may be renewed, provided the recipient maintains a GPA of 2.0 or higher.
Additional data Funds for this scholarship were originally provided by a contribution from Kathryne Timmons in honor of her sister, Gladys McPartland, who served as executive secretary of the USMCCCA from its founding until her death in 1985.
Number awarded 1 or more each year.
Deadline June of each year.

[207]
GREEN TO GOLD ACTIVE DUTY OPTION

U.S. Army
ROTC Cadet Command
Attn: ATCC-OP-I-S
55 Patch Road, Building 56
Fort Monroe, VA 23651-1052
(757) 788-3341   Toll Free: (800) USA-ROTC
Fax: (757) 788-5781   E-mail: atccps@usacc.army.mil
Web: www.goarmy.com/rotc/green_to_gold_active_duty.jsp

Summary To provide an opportunity for soldiers to remain in the Army while they return to college to participate in the Army Reserve Officers' Training Corps (ROTC).
Eligibility This program is open to enlisted soldiers who have served at least 2 but less than 10 years on active duty and have also completed at least 2 years of college so they can complete a bachelor's or master's degree within 21 months. Applicants must have a cumulative high school or college GPA of 2.5 or higher, a

General Technical (GT) score of 110 or higher, and a recent (within the past 6 months) Army Physical Fitness Test (APFT) score of 180 or higher (including 60 points in each event). They must be under 35 years of age when they graduate. Soldiers who participate in this program remain on active duty while they attend a college or university that has an Army ROTC unit on campus.
Financial Data Participants continue to receive their current pay and allowances; they are responsible for payment of all educational expenses.
Duration Up to 21 months; may be extended to 24 months upon petition.
Additional data Cadets who had previously qualified for benefits from the Army College Fund and/or the Montgomery GI Bill are still entitled to receive those in addition to any benefits from this program. They are not, however, eligible for Army Tuition Assistance. While in college, participants must successfully complete the prescribed military science classes, professional military education subjects, the Leader Development and Assessment Course (normally between their junior and senior years), and any other requirements for commissioning. Upon graduation, they are commissioned as second lieutenants and are required to serve in the military for 8 years. That obligation may be fulfilled by serving 3 years on active duty and 5 years in the Army National Guard (ARNG), the United States Army Reserve (USAR), or the Inactive Ready Reserve (IRR).
Number awarded Up to 200 each year.
Deadline March of each year.

[208]
GREEN TO GOLD NON-SCHOLARSHIP PROGRAM

U.S. Army
ROTC Cadet Command
Attn: ATCC-OP-I-S
55 Patch Road, Building 56
Fort Monroe, VA 23651-1052
(757) 788-3341   Toll Free: (800) USA-ROTC
Fax: (757) 788-5781   E-mail: atccps@usacc.army.mil
Web: www.goarmy.com/rotc/green_to_gold_nonscholarship.jsp

Summary To provide financial assistance to soldiers who wish to obtain an early discharge from the Army and return to college to participate in the Army Reserve Officers' Training Corps (ROTC).
Eligibility This program is open to enlisted soldiers who have served at least 2 years on active duty and have also completed at least 2 years of college with a GPA of 2.0 or higher. Applicants must be under 30 years of age when they graduate (waivers up to 32 years of age are available). They apply for this program to obtain an early discharge from active duty in order to enroll in a baccalaureate degree program.
Financial Data Cadets receive a stipend for 10 months of the year that is $450 per month during their junior year and $500 per month during their senior year, as well as pay for attending the 6-week Leader Development and Assessment Course (LDAC) during the summer between the junior and senior year of college.
Duration 2 years.
Additional data Cadets who had previously qualified for benefits from the Army College Fund and/or the Montgomery GI Bill are still entitled to receive those in addition to any benefits from this program. Cadets are also entitled to participate in the Simultaneous Membership Program and serve with pay in a drilling unit of the Army Reserve or Army National Guard. Upon graduation from college, cadets are commissioned as second lieutenants and are required to serve in the military for 8 years. That obligation may be fulfilled by serving 3 years on active duty and 5 years in the Inactive Ready Reserve (IRR).
Number awarded Varies each year.
Deadline March or September of each year.

[209]
GREEN TO GOLD SCHOLARSHIP PROGRAM

U.S. Army
ROTC Cadet Command
Attn: ATCC-OP-I-S
55 Patch Road, Building 56
Fort Monroe, VA 23651-1052
(757) 788-3341   Toll Free: (800) USA-ROTC
Fax: (757) 788-5781   E-mail: atccps@usacc.army.mil
Web: www.goarmy.com/rotc/green_to_gold_scholarship.jsp

Summary To provide scholarships and other payments to soldiers who wish to obtain an early discharge from the Army and return to college to participate in the Army Reserve Officers' Training Corps (ROTC).

Eligibility Enlisted soldiers who have served at least 2 but less than 10 years on active duty may apply for this program to obtain an early discharge in order to enroll in a baccalaureate degree program. Applicants must have a cumulative high school or college GPA of 2.5 or higher, a General Technical (GT) score of 110 or higher, and a recent (within the past 6 months) Army Physical Fitness Test (APFT) score of 180 or higher (including 60 points in each event). They may have no more than 3 dependents including a spouse (that requirement may be waived) and must be under 31 years of age when they graduate and are commissioned. Applicants who have no college experience must have an ACT score of at least 19 or a combined mathematics and critical reading SAT score of at least 920. U.S. citizenship is required.

Financial Data Scholarship winners receive up to $20,000 per year as support for tuition and fees or for room and board, whichever the recipient selects; additional support up to $1,200 per year for textbooks, supplies, and equipment; a stipend for 10 months of the year that is $350 per month during their sophomore year, $450 per month during their junior year, and $500 per month during their senior year; and pay for attending the 6-week Leader Development and Assessment Course (LDAC) during the summer between the junior and senior year of college.

Duration Scholarships are for 2, 3, or 4 years; soldiers without prior college credit or whose colleges accept them as academic freshmen are eligible for 4-year scholarships; soldiers with 1 year of college completed are eligible for 3-year scholarships; soldiers with 2 years of college completed are eligible for 2-year scholarships.

Additional data Recipients who had previously qualified for benefits from the Army College Fund and/or the Montgomery GI Bill are still entitled to receive those in addition to any benefits from this program. Upon graduation from college, scholarship winners are commissioned as second lieutenants and are required to serve in the military for 8 years. That obligation may be fulfilled by serving 4 years on active duty followed by 4 years in the Inactive Ready Reserve (IRR).

Number awarded Varies each year; recently, 224 of these scholarships were awarded, including 76 for 2 years, 91 for 3 years, 51 for 4 years, and 6 for graduate study.

Deadline March or September of each year.

[210]
GRFD SCHOLARSHIPS

U.S. Army
ROTC Cadet Command
Attn: ATCC-OP-I-S
55 Patch Road, Building 56
Fort Monroe, VA 23651-1052
(757) 788-2782   Toll Free: (800) USA-ROTC
Fax: (757) 788-4643   E-mail: nancy.davis@usaac.army.mil
Web: www.rotc.monroe.army.mil

Summary To provide financial assistance to college and graduate students who are willing to enroll in Army ROTC and serve in a Reserve component of the Army following graduation.

Eligibility This program is open to full-time students entering their junior year of college with a GPA of 2.5 or higher. High school seniors are also eligible if they plan to attend a military junior college (MJC), have a GPA of 2.5 or higher, and have scores of at least 19 on the ACT or 920 on the combined mathematics and critical reading SAT. Graduate students are also eligible if they have only 2 years remaining before completion of their graduate degree. Applicants must meet all other medical and moral character requirements for enrollment in Army ROTC. They must be willing to enroll in the Simultaneous Membership Program (SMP) of an ROTC unit on their campus; the SMP requires simultaneous membership in Army ROTC and either the Army National Guard or Army Reserve.

Financial Data Participants receive full reimbursement of tuition, a grant of $1,200 per year for books, plus an ROTC stipend for 10 months of the year at $450 per month during their junior year and $500 per month during their senior year. As a member of the Army National Guard or Army Reserve, they also receive weekend drill pay at the pay grade of E-5 during their junior year or E-6 during their senior year.

Duration 2 years.

Additional data After graduation, participants serve 3 to 6 months on active duty in the Officer Basic Course (OBC). Following completion of OBC, they are released from active duty and are obligated to serve 8 years in the Army National Guard or Army Reserve.

Number awarded Currently, 416 of these scholarships are awarded each year: 108 (2 in each state or U.S. territory) for members of the Army National Guard, 223 for members of the Army Reserve, and 85 for MJC students (17 at each approved school).

Deadline Deadline not specified.

[211]
HAWAII NATIONAL GUARD ENLISTED ASSOCIATION SCHOLARSHIP

Hawaii National Guard Enlisted Association
c/o MSG Mara L. Bacon Chang, Scholarship Committee
  Chair
45-251 Kulauli Street
Kaneohe, HI 96744
E-mail: mara.bacon@us.army.mil
Web: www.hngea.net/Scholarship%20Webpage.htm

Summary To provide financial assistance for college to members of the Hawaii National Guard Enlisted Association (HNGEA) and their dependents.

Eligibility This program is open to HNGEA members and their dependents. Applicants must be attending or interested in attending a college or university in Hawaii as an undergraduate student. They must have a GPA of at least 2.5 for the current semester and 2.0 overall. Along with their application, they must submit a letter describing their educational goals and need for the scholarship. Selection is based on that letter (10 points), academic achievement (50 points), participation in the organization (10 points), and financial need (30 points).

Financial Data Stipends range from $500 to $1,000.

Duration 1 year.

Number awarded Varies each year; a total of $2,000 is available for this program annually.

Deadline June of each year.

[212]
HISTORICALLY BLACK COLLEGE SCHOLARSHIPS

U.S. Navy
Attn: Naval Education and Training Command
NSTC OD2
250 Dallas Street, Suite A
Pensacola, FL 32508-5268
(850) 452-4941, ext. 25166
Toll Free: (800) NAV-ROTC, ext. 25166
Fax: (850) 452-2486
E-mail: PNSC_NROTC.scholarship@navy.mil
Web: www.nrotc.navy.mil/hist_black.aspx

Summary To provide financial assistance to students at specified Historically Black Colleges or Universities (HBCUs) who are interested in joining Navy ROTC.

Eligibility This program is open to students attending or planning to attend 1 of 15 specified HBCUs with a Navy ROTC unit on campus. Applicants must be nominated by the professor of naval science at their institution and meet academic requirements set by each school. They must be U.S. citizens between 17 and 23 years of age who are willing to serve for 4 years as active-duty Navy officers following graduation from college. They must not have reached their 27th birthday by the time of college graduation and commissioning; applicants who have prior active-duty military service may be eligible for age adjustments for the amount of time equal to their prior service, up to a maximum of 36 months. The qualifying scores for the Navy option are 530 critical reading and 520 mathematics on the SAT or 22 on both English and mathematics on the ACT; for the Marine Corps option they are 1000 composite on the SAT or 22 composite on the ACT. Current enlisted and former military personnel are also eligible if they will complete the program by the age of 30.

Financial Data These scholarships provide payment of full tuition and required educational fees, as well as a specified amount for textbooks, supplies, and equipment. The program also provides a stipend for 10 months of the year that is $250 per month as a freshman, $300 per month as a sophomore, $350 per month as a junior, and $400 per month as a senior.

Duration Up to 4 years.

Additional data Students may apply for either a Navy or Marine Corps option scholarship, but not for both. Recipients must complete 4 years of study in naval science classes as students at 1 of the following HBCUs: Clark Atlanta University, Dillard University, Florida A&M University, Hampton University, Howard University, Huston-Tillotson University, Morehouse College, Norfolk State University, Prairie View A&M University, Savannah State University, Southern University and A&M College, Spelman College, Tennessee State University, Tuskegee University, or Xavier University. After completing the program, all participants are commissioned as ensigns in the Naval Reserve or second lieutenants in the Marine Corps Reserve with an 8-year service obligation, including 4 years of active duty. Current military personnel who are accepted into this program are released from active duty and are not eligible for active-duty pay and allowances, medical benefits, or other active-duty entitlements.

Number awarded Varies each year.

Deadline January of each year.

[213]
HOWARD R. HARPER SCHOLARSHIPS

Enlisted Association of the National Guard of Iowa
c/o Jerald D. Hansen, Secretary
1409 East Coolbaugh Street
Red Oak, IA 51566
(712) 623-2804
Web: www.eangi.com/index-4.html

Summary To provide financial assistance to members of the Enlisted Association of the National Guard of Iowa (EANGI) and

their dependents who are interested in attending college in any state.

Eligibility This program is open to EANGI members and their spouses and children. Applicants must be attending or accepted at a VA-approved college or vocational/technical school in any state. Along with their application, they must submit a copy of their transcript, a letter with specific facts as to their desire to continue their education and why financial assistance is required, 3 letters of recommendation, and 1 academic reference.

Financial Data The stipend is $1,000.

Duration 1 year.

Additional data Membership in EANGI is open to enlisted members of the Iowa Army or Air National Guard, active component members assigned to the Iowa Army or Air National Guard, and enlisted personnel who are retired or honorably discharged from the Iowa Army or Air National Guard.

Number awarded 4 each year.

Deadline January of each year.

[214]
HUMAN RESOURCES OPTION OF THE SEAMAN TO ADMIRAL-21 PROGRAM

U.S. Navy
Attn: Commander, Naval Service Training Command
250 Dallas Street, Suite A
Pensacola, FL 32508-5268
(850) 452-9563   Fax: (850) 452-2486
E-mail: PNSC_STA21@navy.mil
Web: www.sta-21.navy.mil

Summary To allow outstanding enlisted Navy personnel to complete a bachelor's degree and receive a commission as a human resources officer.

Eligibility This program is open to U.S. citizens who are currently serving on active duty in the U.S. Navy or Naval Reserve, including Full Time Support (FTS), Selected Reserves (SELRES), and Navy Reservists on active duty except for those on active duty for training (ACDUTRA). Applicants must be high school graduates (or GED recipients) who are able to complete requirements for a baccalaureate degree in 36 months or less. They must be planning to work on a degree in human resources/personnel, financial management, manpower systems analysis, operations analysis, business administration, education/training management, or a related field. When they complete their degree requirements, they must be younger than 29 years of age. Within the past 3 years, they must have taken the SAT test (and achieved scores of at least 500 on the mathematics section and 500 on the critical reading section) or the ACT test (and achieved a score of 41 or higher, including at least 21 on the mathematics portion and 20 on the English portion).

Financial Data Awardees continue to receive their regular Navy pay and allowances while they attend college on a full-time basis. They also receive reimbursement for tuition, fees, and books up to $10,000 per year. If base housing is available, they are eligible to live there. Participants are not eligible to receive benefits under the Navy's Tuition Assistance Program (TA), the Montgomery GI Bill (MGIB), the Navy College Fund, or the Veterans Educational Assistance Program (VEAP).

Duration Selectees are supported for up to 36 months of full-time, year-round study or completion of a bachelor's degree, as long as they maintain a GPA of 2.5 or higher.

Additional data Upon acceptance into the program, selectees attend the Naval Science Institute (NSI) in Newport, Rhode Island for an 8-week program in the fundamental core concepts of being a naval officer (navigation, engineering, weapons, military history and justice, etc.). They then enter a college or university with an NROTC unit or affiliation to work full time on a bachelor's degree. They become members of and drill with the NROTC unit. When they complete their degree, they are commissioned as ensigns in the United States Naval Reserve and assigned to initial training as a human resources officer. After commissioning, 5 years of active service are required.

Number awarded Varies each year.

Deadline June of each year.

[215]
IDAHO ENLISTED ASSOCIATION YOUNG PATRIOT SCHOLARSHIP

Idaho Enlisted Association of the National Guard of the
United States
c/o Chris Brearley, President
1501 Shoshone Street
Boise, ID 83705
(208) 422-5489   E-mail: chris_brearley@hotmail.com
Web: eangusidaho.org/Scholarships.php

Summary To provide financial assistance to members of the Idaho Enlisted Association of the National Guard of the United States and their family who are interested in attending college in any state.

Eligibility This program is open to 1) members of the association; 2) dependent children of members; 3) spouses of members; and 4) unmarried spouses and unmarried dependent children of deceased members who were in good standing at the time of death. Association members must also be enlisted members of the Idaho National Guard with at least 1 year remaining on their enlistment or have 20 or more years of military service. Applicants must be enrolled or planning to enroll full time at a college, university, trade school, or business school in any state. Along with their application, they must submit a 2-page essay about an activity or interest that has been meaningful to them, a personal letter providing information about themselves and their families, 2 letters of recommendation, an academic letter of recommendation, and a copy of the sponsor's current membership card or number. Family income is considered in the selection process.

Financial Data The stipend is $1,500.

Duration 1 year; nonrenewable.

Number awarded 1 each year.

Deadline January of each year.

[216]
ILLINOIS NATIONAL GUARD GRANT PROGRAM

Illinois Student Assistance Commission
Attn: Scholarship and Grant Services
1755 Lake Cook Road
Deerfield, IL 60015-5209
(847) 948-8550   Toll Free: (800) 899-ISAC
Fax: (847) 831-8549   TDD: (800) 526-0844
E-mail: collegezone@isac.org
Web: www.collegezone.com/studentzone/407_626.htm

Summary To provide financial assistance to current or former members of the Illinois National Guard who are interested in attending college or graduate school in the state.

Eligibility This program is open to members of the Illinois National Guard who are 1) currently active or 2) have been active for at least 5 consecutive years, have been called to federal active duty for at least 6 months, and are within 12 months after their discharge date. Applicants must also be enrolled at an Illinois public 2- or 4-year college or university and have served at least 1 full year in the Guard.

Financial Data Recipients are eligible for payment of tuition and some fees for either undergraduate or graduate study at an Illinois state-supported college or university.

Duration This assistance extends for 8 semesters or 12 quarters (or the equivalent in part-time study).

Number awarded Varies each year.

Deadline September of each year for the academic year; February of each year for spring semester, winter quarter, or spring quarter; June of each year for summer term.

[217]
IMAGINE AMERICA MILITARY AWARD PROGRAM

Career College Association
Attn: Imagine America Foundation
1101 Connecticut Avenue, N.W., Suite 901
Washington, DC 20036
(202) 336-6719   Fax: (202) 408-8102
E-mail: torianb@imagine-america.org
Web: www.imagine-america.org

Summary To provide financial assistance to veterans and military personnel interested in attending a participating career college.

Eligibility This program is open to active-duty, reservist, honorably-discharged, and retired veterans of a U.S. military service branch. Applicants must be interested in attending 1 of more than 300 participating career colleges. They must have access to tuition assistance and government-supported financial aid through the GI Bill and other programs. All applications are submitted online to the college where the student wishes to enroll. Selection is based on the likelihood of successfully completing postsecondary education and financial need.

Financial Data The stipend is $1,000. Funds must be used for payment of tuition at a participating career college.

Duration 1 year.

Additional data The Imagine America Foundation (originally known as the Career College Foundation) established this program in 2004.

Number awarded Varies each year.

Deadline June of each year.

[218]
INDIANA NATIONAL GUARD SUPPLEMENTAL GRANT PROGRAM

State Student Assistance Commission of Indiana
Attn: Grant Division
150 West Market Street, Suite 500
Indianapolis, IN 46204-2811
(317) 232-2350   Toll Free: (888) 528-4719 (within IN)
Fax: (317) 232-3260   E-mail: grants@ssaci.state.in.us
Web: www.in.gov/ssaci/2339.htm

Summary To provide financial assistance to members of the Indiana National Guard who are interested in attending designated colleges in the state.

Eligibility This program is open to members of the Indiana Air and Army National Guard who are in active drilling status and have not been AWOL at any time during the preceding 12 months. Applicants must be high school graduates seeking their first associate or bachelor's degree. Allowances may be made for students who earned a GED certificate or were home schooled, but only on a case-by-case basis following a written appeal. As part of the application process, students must file the Free Application for Federal Student Aid (FAFSA). If they qualify as dependent students based on FAFSA data, their parents must be residents of Indiana; if the FAFSA standards define them as independent students, they must be Indiana residents.

Financial Data The award provides payment of 100% of the tuition costs at state-funded colleges and universities in Indiana. No funding is provided for books, room, or board.

Duration 1 year; may be renewed.

Additional data This assistance may be used only at the following state funded colleges and universities: Ball State University, Indiana State University, Indiana University, Ivy Tech State College, Purdue University, University of Southern Indiana, and Vincennes University.

Number awarded Varies each year.

Deadline March of each year.

[219]
IOWA NATIONAL GUARD EDUCATIONAL ASSISTANCE PROGRAM

Iowa National Guard
Joint Forces Headquarters Iowa
Attn: JFHQ-IA-DCSPER-ESO
7105 N.W. 70th Avenue
Johnston, IA 50131-1824
(515) 252-4468   Toll Free: (800) 294-6607, ext. 4468
Fax: (515) 252-4656   E-mail: educationia@ngb.army.mil
Web: www.iowanationalguard.com

Summary To provide financial assistance to members of the Iowa National Guard who wish to attend college.

Eligibility This program is open to residents of Iowa who are members of an Iowa Army or Air National Guard unit. Applicants must have satisfactorily completed Initial Entry Training (Basic Training and Advanced Individual Training), have maintained satisfactory performance of duty (including attending a minimum 90% of scheduled drill dates and scheduled annual training in the preceding 12 months), have maintained satisfactory academic progress as determined by their academic institution, and have not completed their baccalaureate degree. They may be seeking to attend a state-supported university, community college, or participating private accredited institution of postsecondary education located in Iowa.

Financial Data Awards provide payment of at least 50% of the tuition rate at Iowa Board of Regents schools or 50% of the tuition rate at the institution attended by the National Guard member, whichever is less. Recently, available funding permitted payment of the full Regents rate, or a maximum of $3,210 per semester for full-time enrollment or $231 per semester hour for part-time enrollment. Funds may be used for any educational expense, including tuition, room, board, supplies, books, fees, and other associated costs.

Duration 1 year; may be renewed.

Additional data This program was established in 1999.

Number awarded Varies each year, depending on the availability of funds. Assistance is provided on a first-come, first-served basis.

Deadline August of each year for fall term or December of each year for spring term.

[220]
JOHN AND ALICE EGAN MULTI-YEAR MENTORING SCHOLARSHIP PROGRAM

Daedalian Foundation
Attn: Scholarship Committee
55 Main Circle (Building 676)
P.O. Box 249
Randolph AFB, TX 78148-0249
(210) 945-2113   Fax: (210) 945-2112
E-mail: icarus2@daedalians.org
Web: www.daedalians.org/foundation/scholarships.htm

Summary To provide financial assistance to college students who are participating in a ROTC program and wish to become military pilots.

Eligibility This program is open to students who have completed at least the freshman year at an accredited 4-year college or university and have a GPA of 3.0 or higher. Applicants must be participating in an ROTC program and be medically qualified for flight training. They must plan to apply for and be awarded a military pilot training allocation at the appropriate juncture in their ROTC program. Selection is based on intention to prepare for a career as a military pilot, demonstrated moral character and patriotism, scholastic and military standing and aptitude, and physical condition and aptitude for flight. Financial need may also be considered.

Financial Data The stipend is $2,500 per year.

Duration 1 year; may be renewed up to 2 or 3 additional years, provided the recipient maintains a GPA of 3.0 or higher and is enrolled in an undergraduate program.

Additional data This program began in 2003. It includes a mentoring component.

Number awarded Up to 11 each year.

Deadline July of each year.

[221]
JOHN CORNELIUS/MAX ENGLISH MEMORIAL SCHOLARSHIP AWARD

Marine Corps Tankers Association
P.O. Box 20761
El Cajon, CA 92021
Web: www.usmarinetankers.org/scholarship-program

Summary To provide financial assistance for college or graduate school to children and grandchildren of Marines who served in a tank unit.

Eligibility This program is open to high school seniors and graduates who are children, grandchildren, or under the guardianship of an active, Reserve, retired, or honorably discharged Marine who served in a tank unit. Marine or Navy Corpsmen currently assigned to tank units are also eligible. Applicants must be enrolled or planning to enroll full time at a college or graduate school. Their sponsor must be a member of the Marine Corps Tankers Association or, if not a member, must join if the application is accepted. Along with their application, they must submit an essay on their educational goals, future aspirations, and concern for the future of our society and for the peoples of the world. Selection is based on that essay, academic record, school activities, leadership potential, and community service.

Financial Data The stipend is at least $2,000 per year.

Duration 1 year; recipients may reapply.

Number awarded 8 to 12 each year.

Deadline March of each year.

[222]
JOHN J. GUENTHER MERIT SCHOLARSHIP

Marine Corps Intelligence Association, Inc.
Attn: Marine Corps Intelligence Educational Foundation
P.O. Box 1028
Quantico, VA 22134-1028
E-mail: mcia@mcia-inc.org
Web: www.mcia-inc.org

Summary To provide financial assistance for college to members of the Marine Corps Intelligence Association (MCIA) and their dependent children.

Eligibility This program is open to current MCIA members, their dependent children, and their survivors. Applicants must be attending or planning to attend an accredited 4-year college or university as a full-time student. They must submit a 300-word essay on a risk that has led to a significant change in their personal or intellectual life, the most challenging obstacles they have had to overcome and what they learned from the experience, and where they envision themselves in 10 years. Selection is based on the essay, academic achievement, extracurricular activities, and work experience. Financial need is not considered.

Financial Data The stipend is $2,000.

Duration 1 year.

Additional data Membership in the MCIA is open to Marine Corps intelligence personnel, including active duty, Reserve, and retired.

Number awarded At least 1 each year.

Deadline July of each year.

[223]
JOSEPH A. MCALINDEN DIVERS' SCHOLARSHIP

Navy-Marine Corps Relief Society
Attn: Education Division
875 North Randolph Street, Suite 225
Arlington, VA 22203-1757
(703) 696-4960   Fax: (703) 696-0144
E-mail: education@nmcrs.org
Web: www.nmcrs.org/education.html

Summary To provide financial assistance to current and former Navy and Marine Corps divers and their families who are interested in working on an undergraduate or graduate degree in a field related to ocean agriculture.

Eligibility This program is open to Navy and Marine Corps active-duty and retired divers and members of their families. Applicants must be enrolled full time in an undergraduate or graduate program in oceanography, ocean agriculture, aquaculture, or a related field; they may also be engaged in advanced diver training, certification, or recertification. Financial need is considered in the selection process.

Financial Data The stipend ranges from $500 to $3,000, depending on the need of the recipient.

Duration 1 year.

Number awarded 1 or more each year.

Deadline Applications may be submitted at any time.

[224]
JOSEPH P. AND HELEN T. CRIBBINS SCHOLARSHIP

Association of the United States Army
Attn: National Secretary
2425 Wilson Boulevard
Arlington, VA 22201
(703) 841-4300, ext. 655   Toll Free: (800) 336-4570, ext. 655
E-mail: ausa-info@ausa.org
Web: www3.ausa.org/webpub/depthome.nsf/byid/kcat-6fcq8s

Summary To provide financial assistance to active-duty and honorably-discharged soldiers interested in studying engineering in college.

Eligibility This program is open to 1) soldiers currently serving in the active Army, Army Reserve, or Army National Guard of any rank; and 2) honorably-discharged soldiers from any component of the total Army. Applicants must have been accepted at an accredited college or university to work on a degree in engineering or a related field (e.g., computer science, biotechnology). Along with their application, they must submit a 1-page autobiography, 2 letters of recommendation, and a transcript of high school or college grades (depending on which they are currently attending). Selection is based on academic merit and personal achievement. Financial need is not normally a selection criterion but in some cases of extreme need it may be used as a factor; the lack of financial need, however, is never a cause for non-selection.

Financial Data The stipend is $2,000; funds are sent directly to the recipient's college or university.

Duration 1 year.

Number awarded 1 or more each year.

Deadline June of each year.

[225]
KANSAS MILITARY SERVICE SCHOLARSHIPS

Kansas Board of Regents
Attn: Student Financial Assistance
1000 S.W. Jackson Street, Suite 520
Topeka, KS 66612-1368
(785) 296-3517   Fax: (785) 296-0983
E-mail: dlindeman@ksbor.org
Web: www.kansasregents.org/financial_aid/awards.html

Summary To provide financial assistance for college to residents of Kansas who have served or are still serving in the military.

Eligibility This program is open to students who graduated from high school in Kansas or received a GED credential and have been a resident of the state for at least 2 years. Applicants must have served in the U.S. armed forces in Iraq or Afghanistan, or in international waters or on foreign soil in support of military operations in Iraq or Afghanistan, for at least 90 days after September 11, 2001 or for less than 90 days because of injuries received during such service. They must still be in military service or have received an honorable discharge with orders that indicate they served after September 11, 2001 in Operations Enduring Freedom, Nobel Eagle, and/or Iraqi Freedom. Qualified veterans and military personnel may enroll at a public postsecondary institution in Kansas, including area vocational schools, area vocational/technical schools, community colleges, the municipal university, state educational institutions, or technical colleges. They are not required to demonstrate financial need.

Financial Data Qualifying students are permitted to enroll at an approved Kansas institution without payment of tuition or fees. If they receive any federal military tuition assistance, that money must be applied to their tuition and fees and they are eligible only for the remaining balance in scholarship assistance.

Duration 1 year; may be renewed for a total of 10 semesters as long as the recipient remains in good academic standing.

Additional data This program was established in 2007.

Number awarded Varies each year.

Deadline April of each year.

[226]
KANSAS NATIONAL GUARD EDUCATIONAL ASSISTANCE

Kansas Board of Regents
Attn: Student Financial Assistance
1000 S.W. Jackson Street, Suite 520
Topeka, KS 66612-1368
(785) 296-3517   Fax: (785) 296-0983
E-mail: dlindeman@ksbor.org
Web: www.kansasregents.org/financial_aid/awards.html

Summary To provide financial assistance to members of the Kansas National Guard who wish to take additional college courses.

Eligibility This program is open to members of the Kansas National Guard (Air or Army) who are interested in working on a vocational, associate, or bachelor's degree. Applicants must be newly enlisted or reenlisted Guard member with no more than 15 years of service. They must agree to complete their current service obligation plus 3 months of additional service for each semester of assistance received.

Financial Data The program reimburses up to 100% of tuition and fees at public and designated private institutions in Kansas. Recent maximums were $2,388.25 for a 4-year university, $1,155 for a community college, or $2,570 for a technical school.

Duration 1 semester; may be renewed.

Number awarded Varies each year; recently, approximately 300 of these awards were granted each semester.

Deadline September of each year for fall semester; February of each year for spring semester.

[227]
KENTUCKIANA POST SAME SCHOLARSHIP

Society of American Military Engineers-Kentuckiana Post
c/o Erin Hall, Scholarship Committee Co-Chair
Messer Construction Company
11001 Plantside Drive
Louisville, KY 40299
(502) 261-9775   E-mail: ehall@messer.com
Web: posts.same.org/kentuckiana

Summary To provide financial assistance to students in Indiana and Kentucky (especially those with ties to the military) who are interested in majoring in engineering in college.

Eligibility This program is open to students who fall into 1 of the following categories: a dependent of a current Society of American Military Engineers (SAME) Kentuckiana Post member; an employee or dependent of an employee of a Kentuckiana Post sustaining member firm; an employee or dependent of an employee of the Louisville District Corps of Engineers; a current student member of the Kentuckiana Post; a student whose permanent home address is within the Kentuckiana Post's geographic boundary (Kentucky and Indiana) and who is enrolled in an ROTC program or military academy; or an individual on active duty or the dependent of an individual on active duty who is assigned to an installation within the Kentuckiana Post's geographic boundary. Applicants must be U.S. citizens accepted at an undergraduate ABET-accredited engineering program; undergraduates enrolled in engineering technology programs are not eligible. Along with their application, they must submit an essay of 300 to 500 words on a topic that changes annually; recently, applicants were invited to write on their definition of engineering, how they plan to practice engineering, and how winning this scholarship will sustain their drive toward a career in engineering. Financial need is not considered in the selection process.

Financial Data The stipend is $3,000 per year.

Duration 1 year; may be renewed 1 additional year.

Additional data Recipients are required to attend the scholarship luncheon ceremony in Louisville in May.

Number awarded Up to 5 each year.

Deadline March of each year.

[228]
LARRY STRICKLAND LEADERSHIP AWARD AND SCHOLARSHIP

Association of the United States Army
Attn: Strickland Memorial Scholarship Fund
2425 Wilson Boulevard
Arlington, VA 22201
(703) 841-4300, ext. 693 Toll Free: (800) 336-4570, ext. 693
E-mail: jspencer@ausa.org
Web: www.ausa.org

Summary To recognize and reward, with funding for additional education, Army noncommissioned officers who demonstrate outstanding leadership.

Eligibility This award is presented to a noncommissioned officer who best exemplifies "the Army's vision and influences others in shaping future leaders." Candidates must also be interested in obtaining additional education.

Financial Data The award consists of a plaque and $4,000 to assist in covering educational costs that Army tuition assistance does not pay, such as instructional fees, laboratory fees, and books.

Duration The award is presented annually.

Additional data This award was established in 2003 to honor SGM Larry L. Strickland, who was killed in the Pentagon on September 11, 2001.

Number awarded 1 each year.

Deadline Deadline not specified.

[229]
LDRSHIP AWARDS

Career College Association
Attn: Imagine America Foundation
1101 Connecticut Avenue, N.W., Suite 901
Washington, DC 20036
(202) 336-6743   Fax: (202) 408-8102
E-mail: jennyf@career.org
Web: www.imagine-america.org/06-LDRSHIP.asp

Summary To provide financial assistance to veterans and military personnel who are attending a career college that is a member of the Career College Association.

Eligibility This program is open to active-duty, reservist, honorably-discharged, and retired veterans of a U.S. military service branch. Applicants must currently be attending 1 of more than 300 participating career colleges. They must have maintained a GPA of 3.5 or higher and an attendance record of at least 95%. Along with their application, they must submit a recommendation from a faculty member or administrator at their college and a copy of their current college transcript.

Financial Data The stipend is $5,000. Funds must be used for payment of tuition at a participating career college.

Duration 1 year.

Additional data The Imagine America Foundation (originally known as the Career College Foundation) established this program in 2004. It stands for Loyalty, Duty, Respect, Selfless Service, Honor, Integrity and Personal Courage. Sponsorship is provided by Ambassador College Bookstores, Military.com, and Lockheed Martin.

Number awarded Varies each year; recently, 4 of these scholarships were granted.

Deadline April of each year.

[230]
LOUISIANA NATIONAL GUARD STATE TUITION EXEMPTION PROGRAM

Louisiana National Guard
Attn: Education Services Office
Military Development (DMP-XD)
Jackson Barracks
New Orleans, LA 70146-0330
(504) 278-8304   Toll Free: (800) 899-6355
E-mail: dmp-xd@la.ngb.army.mil
Web: www.la.ngb.army.mil

Summary To provide financial assistance to members of the Louisiana National Guard who are interested in attending college in the state.

Eligibility This program is open to active drilling members of the Louisiana Army National Guard or Air National Guard. Guard members are ineligible if they have been disqualified by their unit commander for any adverse action, have already obtained a bachelor's degree, are placed on academic probation or suspension, test positive on a drug/alcohol test or declare themselves as a self-referral, are separated or transfer to the Inactive National Guard, or have 9 or more AWOLs. Applicants must have been accepted for admission or be enrolled in a Louisiana public institution of higher learning, either part time or full time.

Financial Data Recipients are exempt from all tuition charges at Louisiana state-funded colleges, universities, or community colleges.

Duration The exemption may be claimed for 5 separate academic years or until the receipt of a bachelor's degree, whichever occurs first.

Additional data The state legislature established this program in 1974.

Number awarded Varies each year.

Deadline Deadline not specified.

[231]
LTG AND MRS. JOSEPH M. HEISER SCHOLARSHIP

U.S. Army Ordnance Corps Association
Attn: Heiser Scholarship
P.O. Box 377
Aberdeen Proving Ground, MD 21005-0377
(410) 272-8540   Fax: (410) 272-8425
Web: www.usaocaweb.org/scholarships.htm

Summary To provide financial assistance for college to soldiers serving in the U.S. Army Ordnance Corps and members of the U.S. Army Ordnance Corps Association (OCA) and their families.

Eligibility This program is open to Ordnance soldiers (active and reserve), OCA members, and immediate family of OCA members. Applicants must be entering or attending a college or university to work on an associate or baccalaureate degree. Along with their application, they must submit 1) an essay of 1,000 to 1,500 words on the missions, heritage, or history of the U.S. Army Ordnance Corps; and 2) an essay of 300 to 500 words on their reasons for seeking this scholarship and why they feel they merit its award. Selection is based on the essays, scholastic aptitude, and grades.

Financial Data The stipend is $1,000.

Duration 1 year.

Number awarded Varies each year; recently, 4 of these scholarships were awarded.

Deadline June of each year.

[232]
MAINE NATIONAL GUARD EDUCATION ASSISTANCE PROGRAM

Maine National Guard
Attn: Education
Camp Keyes
Augusta, ME 04333-0033
(207) 626-4370   Toll Free: (800) 462-3101 (within ME)
Fax: (207) 626-4509
Web: www.me.ngb.army.mil

Summary To provide financial assistance for undergraduate or graduate study to members of the Maine National Guard.

Eligibility This program is open to active members of the Maine National Guard who are interested in working on an undergraduate or graduate degree or certificate at a college or university within the state. Applicants must be Maine residents who have successfully completed basic training or received a commission. They may not have any unsatisfactory record of participation in the Guard. First priority is given to Guard members who do not have a baccalaureate degree and are working on a degree; second priority is given to members without a graduate degree who are working on a degree, teacher certification, principal certification, or superintendent certification; third priority is for all others.

Financial Data This program provides payment of up to 100% of tuition and fees at a Maine accredited public postsecondary institution. Recipients may also attend a private college or university in Maine, but the benefit is capped at the tuition rates at the University of Maine.

Duration 1 semester; may be renewed for a total of 150 credit hours, as long as the recipient maintains satisfactory participation in the Guard and an academic GPA of 2.0 or higher.

Number awarded Varies each year.

Deadline October of each year for college terms beginning from January through April; February of each year for college terms beginning from May through July; June of each year for college terms beginning in August or September.

[233]
MAJOR GENERAL DUANE L. "DUKE" CORNING MEMORIAL SCHOLARSHIP

South Dakota National Guard Enlisted Association
c/o Bruce Anderson, Executive Director
25790 Country Lane
Renner, SD 57055
(605) 988-5414   E-mail: bcres@sio.midco.net
Web: www.sdngea.com/scholarship.html

Summary To provide financial assistance to current and retired members of the South Dakota National Guard Enlisted Association (SDNGEA), the National Guard Association of South Dakota (NGASD), and their dependents who are interested in attending college in any state.

Eligibility This program is open to current and retired members of the SDNGEA and the NGASD and the dependents of current and retired members of those associations. Applicants must be graduating high school seniors or full-time undergraduate students at a college or university in any state. They must submit a 300-page autobiography that includes their experiences to date and their hopes and plans for the future. Selection is based on the essay; awards, honors, and offices in high school, college, or trade school; GPA and ACT/SAT scores; letters of recommendation; and extracurricular and community activities and honors.

Financial Data The stipend is $1,000.

Duration 1 year; nonrenewable.

Number awarded 1 each year.

Deadline March of each year.

[234]
MARINE CORPS SGT. JEANNETTE L. WINTERS MEMORIAL SCHOLARSHIP

Armed Forces Communications and Electronics Association
Attn: AFCEA Educational Foundation
4400 Fair Lakes Court
Fairfax, VA 22033-3899
(703) 631-6149   Toll Free: (800) 336-4583, ext. 6149
Fax: (703) 631-4693   E-mail: scholarship@afcea.org
Web: www.afcea.org

Summary To provide funding to members and veterans of the U.S. Marine Corps (USMC) who are majoring in specified fields in college.

Eligibility This program is open to USMC personnel currently on active duty, in the Reserves, or honorably-discharged veterans who are enrolled full or part time in an accredited college or university in the United States. Applicants must be U.S. citizens, be of good moral character, have demonstrated academic excellence, be motivated to complete a college education, and be working on a bachelor's degree in engineering (aerospace, chemical, electrical, or systems), electronics, mathematics, physics, science or mathematics education, management information systems, technology management, computer science, or other field directly related to the support of U.S. intelligence enterprises or national security. They must provide a copy of Discharge Form DD214, Certificate of Service, or facsimile of their current Department of Defense Identification Card.

Financial Data The stipend is $2,000.

Duration 1 year.

Additional data This program was established in 2002 to honor a Marine who died when her KC-130 aircraft crashed in Pakistan.

Number awarded 1 each year.

Deadline August of each year.

[235]
MARINE CORPS TUITION ASSISTANCE PROGRAM

U.S. Marine Corps
Attn: Lifelong Learning Center
3098 Range Road
Quantico, VA 22134-5028
(703) 784-9550   E-mail: vernon.taylor@usmc.mil
Web: www.usmc-mccs.org/education/mta.cfm

Summary   To provide financial assistance for undergraduate or graduate study to Marine Corps personnel.

Eligibility   Eligible for assistance under this program are active-duty Marines who wish to take college courses for academic credit during off-duty time. Funding is available for vocational/technical, undergraduate, graduate, undergraduate development, independent study, and distance learning programs. Commissioned officers must agree to remain on active duty for 2 years after the completion of any funded courses. All students must successfully complete their courses with a satisfactory grade.

Financial Data   Those selected for participation in this program receive their regular Marine Corps pay and 100% of tuition at the postsecondary educational institution of their choice, but capped at $4,500 per year or $250 per semester hour, whichever is less.

Duration   Until completion of a bachelor's or graduate degree.

Number awarded   Varies each year; in recent years, approximately 20,000 Marines availed themselves of this funding.

Deadline   Deadline not specified.

[236]
MARYLAND NATIONAL GUARD STATE TUITION ASSISTANCE

Maryland National Guard
Attn: Education Services Office
Fifth Regiment Armory
29th Division Street, Room D24
Baltimore, MD 21201-2288
(410) 576-1467   Toll Free: (800) 492-2526
Fax: (410) 576-6082
E-mail: mdng_education@md.ngb.army.mil
Web: www.mdarmyguard.com/moneyforcollege.htm

Summary   To provide tuition reimbursement to members of the Maryland National Guard.

Eligibility   This program is open to members of the Maryland National Guard in grades E-1 through O-4 who have at least 24 months of service remaining in the Guard from the start of the course date. Applicants must be attending or planning to attend a state-supported college or university in Maryland to work on an undergraduate degree.

Financial Data   Eligible Guard members receive an amount equal to 50% of their college/university tuition and related course fees, to a maximum of $5,000 per fiscal year.

Duration   1 semester; recipients may reapply.

Additional data   Individuals must apply for reimbursement within 45 days after their course is completed. They must have earned at least a grade of "C" in the course to qualify for reimbursement.

Number awarded   Varies each year.

Deadline   Deadline not specified.

[237]
MARYLAND NATIONAL GUARD STATE TUITION WAIVER

Maryland National Guard
Attn: Education Services Office
Fifth Regiment Armory
29th Division Street, Room D24
Baltimore, MD 21201-2288
(410) 576-1467   Toll Free: (800) 492-2526
Fax: (410) 576-6082
E-mail: mdng_education@md.ngb.army.mil
Web: www.mdarmyguard.com/moneyforcollege.htm

Summary   To waive tuition for members of the Maryland National Guard at colleges and universities in the state.

Eligibility   All state-supported colleges and universities in Maryland have developed a tuition waiver program for members of the National Guard who are taking graduate or university courses.

Financial Data   The amount of the waiver ranges from 25% to 50%.

Duration   1 semester; recipients may reapply.

Additional data   Some schools also limit the number of credits for which a Guard member can receive waivers during any semester.

Number awarded   Varies each year.

Deadline   Deadline not specified.

[238]
MARYLAND SCHOLARSHIPS FOR VETERANS OF THE AFGHANISTAN AND IRAQ CONFLICTS

Maryland Higher Education Commission
Attn: Office of Student Financial Assistance
839 Bestgate Road, Suite 400
Annapolis, MD 21401-3013
(410) 260-4563   Toll Free: (800) 974-1024, ext. 4563
Fax: (410) 260-3200   TDD: (800) 735-2258
E-mail: lasplin@mhec.state.md.us
Web: www.mhec.state.md.us

Summary   To provide financial assistance for college to residents of Maryland who served in the armed forces in Afghanistan or Iraq and their children and spouses.

Eligibility   This program is open to Maryland residents who are 1) a veteran who served at least 60 days in Afghanistan on or after October 24, 2001 or in Iraq on or after March 19, 2003; 2) an active-duty member of the armed forces who served at least 60 days in Afghanistan or Iraq on or after those dates; 3) a member of a Reserve component of the armed forces or the Maryland National Guard who was activated as a result of the Afghanistan or Iraq conflicts and served at least 60 days; and 4) the children and spouses of such veterans, active-duty armed forces personnel, or members of Reserve forces or Maryland National Guard. Applicants must be enrolled or accepted for enrollment in a regular undergraduate program at an eligible Maryland institution. In the selection process, veterans are given priority over dependent children and spouses.

Financial Data   The stipend is equal to 50% of the annual tuition, mandatory fees, and room and board of a resident undergraduate at a 4-year public institution within the University System of Maryland, currently capped at $9,026 per year. The total amount of all state awards may not exceed the cost of attendance as determined by the school's financial aid office or $19,000, whichever is less.

Duration   1 year; may be renewed for an additional 4 years of full-time study or 7 years of part-time study, provided the recipient remains enrolled in an eligible program with a GPA of 2.5 or higher.

Additional data   This program is scheduled to expire in 2016.

Number awarded Varies each year.
Deadline February of each year.

[239]
MASSACHUSETTS ARMED FORCES TUITION WAIVER PROGRAM

Massachusetts Office of Student Financial Assistance
454 Broadway, Suite 200
Revere, MA 02151
(617) 727-9420   Fax: (617) 727-0667
E-mail: osfa@osfa.mass.edu
Web: www.osfa.mass.edu/default.asp?page=categoricalwaiver

Summary To waive tuition at Massachusetts public colleges and universities for members of the armed forces.

Eligibility Applicants for this assistance must have been permanent legal residents of Massachusetts for at least 1 year and stationed in Massachusetts as members of the Army, Navy, Marine Corps, Air Force, or Coast Guard. They may not be in default on any federal student loan. They must enroll in at least 3 undergraduate credits per semester.

Financial Data Eligible military personnel are exempt from any tuition payments toward an undergraduate degree or certificate program at public colleges or universities in Massachusetts.

Duration Up to 4 academic years, for a total of 130 semester hours.

Additional data Recipients may enroll either part or full time in a Massachusetts publicly-supported institution.

Number awarded Varies each year.
Deadline April of each year.

[240]
MASSACHUSETTS NATIONAL GUARD EDUCATIONAL ASSISTANCE PROGRAM

Massachusetts National Guard
Attn: Education Services Office
50 Maple Street
Milford, MA 01757-3604
Toll Free: (888) 301-3103, ext. 6753   Fax: (508) 233-6781
E-mail: ma-education@ng.army.mil
Web: www.mass.gov/guard/education/index.htm

Summary To provide financial assistance to members of the Massachusetts National Guard interested in working on an undergraduate or graduate degree at a college in the state.

Eligibility This program is open to actively participating members of the Army or Air National Guard in Massachusetts. Applicants must have less than 9 AWOLs (Absence Without Leave) at all times and must not ETS (Expiration of Term of Service) during the period enrolled. They must be accepted for admission or enrolled at 1 of 28 Massachusetts public colleges, universities, or community colleges and working on an associate, bachelor's, master's, or doctoral degree. The institution must have a vacancy after all tuition-paying students and all students who are enrolled under any scholarship or tuition waiver provisions have enrolled.

Financial Data Eligible Guard members are exempt from any tuition payments at colleges or universities operated by the Commonwealth of Massachusetts and funded by the Massachusetts Board of Higher Education.

Duration Up to a total of 130 semester hours.

Additional data Recipients may enroll either part or full time in a Massachusetts state-supported institution. This program, commonly referred to as the 100% Tuition Waiver Program, is funded through the Massachusetts Board of Higher Education.

Number awarded Varies each year.
Deadline Deadline not specified.

[241]
MEDAL OF HONOR AFCEA ROTC SCHOLARSHIPS

Armed Forces Communications and Electronics Association
Attn: AFCEA Educational Foundation
4400 Fair Lakes Court
Fairfax, VA 22033-3899
(703) 631-6149   Toll Free: (800) 336-4583, ext. 6149
Fax: (703) 631-4693   E-mail: scholarship@afcea.org
Web: www.afcea.org

Summary To provide financial assistance to ROTC cadets who demonstrate outstanding leadership performance and potential.

Eligibility This program is open to ROTC cadets enrolled full time at an accredited degree-granting 4-year college or university in the United States. Applicants must be sophomores or juniors at the time of application and have a GPA of 3.0 or higher with a major in an academic discipline. They must be U.S. citizens. Selection is based on demonstrated leadership performance and potential and strong commitment to serve in the U.S. armed forces.

Financial Data The stipend is $4,000.

Duration 1 year.

Additional data This program, established in 2005, is sponsored by the Congressional Medal of Honor Foundation in partnership with the Armed Forces Communications and Electronics Association (AFCEA) Educational Foundation.

Number awarded 4 each year: 1 each for Army, Navy, Marine Corps, and Air Force ROTC students.

Deadline February of each year.

[242]
MEDICAL CORPS OPTION OF THE SEAMAN TO ADMIRAL-21 PROGRAM

U.S. Navy
Attn: Commander, Naval Service Training Command
250 Dallas Street, Suite A
Pensacola, FL 32508-5268
(850) 452-9563   Fax: (850) 452-2486
E-mail: PNSC_STA21@navy.mil
Web: www.sta-21.navy.mil

Summary To allow outstanding enlisted Navy personnel to complete a bachelor's degree, be accepted to medical school, earn an M.D. or D.O. degree, and be commissioned in the Navy Medical Corps.

Eligibility This program is open to U.S. citizens who are currently serving on active duty in the U.S. Navy or Naval Reserve, including Full Time Support (FTS), Selected Reserves (SEL-RES), and Navy Reservists on active duty except for those on active duty for training (ACDUTRA). Applicants must be high school graduates (or GED recipients) who are able to complete requirements for baccalaureate and medical degrees and then be able to complete 20 years of active commissioned service as a physician by age 62. Within the past 3 years, they must have taken the SAT test (and achieved scores of at least 500 on the mathematics section and 500 on the critical reading section) or the ACT test (and achieved a score of 41 or higher, including at least 21 on the mathematics portion and 20 on the English portion).

Financial Data Awardees continue to receive their regular Navy pay and allowances while they attend college on a full-time basis. They also receive reimbursement for tuition, fees, and books up to $10,000 per year. If base housing is available, they are eligible to live there. Participants are not eligible to receive benefits under the Navy's Tuition Assistance Program (TA), the Montgomery GI Bill (MGIB), the Navy College Fund, or the Veterans Educational Assistance Program (VEAP).

Duration Selectees are supported for up to 36 months of full-time, year-round study or completion of a bachelor's degree, as long as they maintain a GPA of 3.0 or higher. They are then supported until completion of a medical degree.

Additional data Upon acceptance into the program, selectees attend the Naval Science Institute (NSI) in Newport, Rhode Island for an 8-week program in the fundamental core concepts of being a naval officer (navigation, engineering, weapons, military history and justice, etc.). They then enter an NROTC affiliated college or university with a pre-medical program that confers an accredited B.S. degree to pursue full-time study. They become members of and drill with the NROTC unit. After they complete their bachelor's degree, they are commissioned as an ensign in the Naval Reserve. They must apply to and be accepted at medical school, either the Uniformed Services University of Health Sciences (USUSH) or a civilian medical school through the Health Professions Scholarship Program (HPSP). Following completion of medical school, they are promoted to lieutenant and assigned to active duty in the Medical Corps. Selectees incur a service obligation of 5 years for their baccalaureate degree support plus whatever obligation they incur for medical degree support (usually 7 years if they attend USUSH or 4 years if they attend a civilian institution through HPSP).

Number awarded Varies each year.

Deadline June of each year.

[243]
MEDICAL SERVICE CORPS INSERVICE PROCUREMENT PROGRAM (MSC-IPP)

U.S. Navy
Attn: Navy Medicine Manpower, Personnel, Education and Training Command
Code O3C
8901 Wisconsin Avenue, 16th Floor, Tower 1
Bethesda, MD 20889-5611
(301) 319-4520   Fax: (301) 295-1783
E-mail: mscipp@nmetc.med.navy.mil
Web: www.med.navy.mil

Summary To provide funding to Navy and Marine enlisted personnel who wish to earn an undergraduate or graduate degree in selected health care specialties while continuing to receive their regular pay and allowances.

Eligibility This program is open to enlisted personnel who are serving on active duty in any rating in pay grade E-5 through E-9 of the U.S. Navy, U.S. Marine Corps, and the Marine Corps Reserve serving on active duty (including Full Time Support of the Reserve). Applicants must be interested in working on a degree to become commissioned in the following medical specialties: health care administration, physician assistant, radiation health, pharmacy, environmental health, industrial hygiene, or entomology. If they plan to work on a graduate degree, they must have scores of at least 1000 on the GRE or 500 on the GMAT; if they plan to work on a bachelor's or physician assistant degree, they must have scores of at least 1000 on the SAT (including 460 on the mathematics portion) or 42 on the ACT. They must be U.S. citizens who can be commissioned before they reach their 42nd birthday.

Financial Data Participants receive payment of tuition, mandatory fees, a book allowance, and full pay and allowances for their enlisted pay grade. They are eligible for advancement while in college.

Duration 24 to 48 months of full-time, year-round study, until completion of a relevant degree.

Additional data Following graduation, participants are commissioned in the Medical Service Corps and attend Officer Indoctrination School.

Number awarded Varies each year. Recently, 36 of these positions were available: 20 in health care administration, 10 in physician assistant, 2 in pharmacy, 2 in environmental health, 1 in industrial hygiene, and 1 in entomology.

Deadline August of each year.

[244]
MG LEIF J. SVERDRUP AWARD

Army Engineer Association
Attn: Washington DC Operations
P.O. Box 30260
Alexandria, VA 22310-8260
(703) 428-7084   Fax: (703) 428-6043
E-mail: DCOps@armyengineer.com
Web: www.armyengineer.com/AEA_scholarships.html

Summary To provide financial assistance for college or graduate school to officers who are members of the Army Engineer Association (AEA).

Eligibility This program is open to AEA members serving in an active, Reserve, or National Guard component Army Engineer unit, school, or organization within the Corps of Engineers of the United States Army. Applicants must be commissioned officers (2LT, 1LT, or CPT) or warrant officers (WO1 or WO2). They must be working on or planning to work on an associate, bachelor's, or master's degree at an accredited college or university. Selection is based primarily on financial need, although potential for academic success and standards of conduct as supported by personal references are also considered.

Financial Data The stipend is $1,000.

Duration 1 year.

Number awarded 1 or 2 each year.

Deadline June of each year.

[245]
MICHIGAN NATIONAL GUARD UNIVERSITY AND COLLEGE TUITION GRANTS

Department of Military and Veterans Affairs
Attn: State Education Office
2500 South Washington Avenue
Lansing, MI 48913-5101
(517) 481-7646   Toll Free: (800) 292-1386
E-mail: serpmich@michigan.gov
Web: www.michigan.gov/dmva

Summary To provide financial assistance to members of the Michigan National Guard who are enrolled at designated universities in the state.

Eligibility This program is open to all members of the Michigan National Guard who are in good standing with their unit and have completed basic training. Applicants must be enrolled full time at 1 of the following institutions: Baker College, Cleary University, Cornerstone University, Davenport University, Eastern Michigan University, Ferris State University, Kalamazoo Valley Community College, Kirtland Community College, Lansing Community College, Lawrence Tech University, Mid Michigan Community College, Miller College, Northern Michigan University, Oakland University, Olivet College, Rochester College, Siena Heights University, Spring Arbor University, University of Detroit Mercy, University of Phoenix, Walsh College, or Western Michigan University.

Financial Data The amount of the grant varies at each participating institution.

Duration 1 semester; may be renewed for a total of 4 years.

Additional data These grants are in addition to funds received through the Michigan National Guard State Education Reimbursement Program.

Number awarded Varies each year.

Deadline Deadline not specified.

[246]
MILITARY EDUCATION SCHOLARSHIP PROGRAM

VA Mortgage Center.com
2101 Chapel Plaza Court, Suite 107
Columbia, MO 65203
(573) 876-2729   Toll Free: (800) 405-6682
Web: www.vamortgagecenter.com/scholarships.html

Summary To provide financial assistance for college to students who have a tie to the military.

Eligibility This program is open to 1) current and prospective ROTC program students; 2) active-duty military personnel with plans to attend college; 3) honorably-discharged veterans of the U.S. military; and 4) children of veterans or active-duty military. Applicants must be attending or planning to attend college. Selection is based primarily on an essay.

Financial Data The stipend is $1,500.

Duration 1 year.

Additional data This program was established in 2007.

Number awarded 10 each year: 5 each term.

Deadline April or October of each year.

[247]
MILITARY INTELLIGENCE CORPS ASSOCIATION SCHOLARSHIPS

Military Intelligence Corps Association
Attn: Scholarship Chair
P.O. Box 13020
Fort Huachuca, AZ 85670-3020
(520) 533-1174
Web: micorps.org

Summary To provide financial assistance for college to members of the Military Intelligence Corps Association (MICA) and their immediate family.

Eligibility This program is open to active-duty, Reserve, National Guard, and retired military intelligence soldiers who are MICA members and to their immediate family (spouses, children, or other relatives living with and supported by the MICA member). Applicants must be attending or accepted for attendance at an accredited college, university, vocational school, or technical institution. Along with their application, they must submit a 1-page essay on their reasons for applying for the scholarship, including their educational plans, ambitions, goals, and personal attributes or experiences they feel will enable them to reach their goals. Financial need is not considered in the selection process.

Financial Data Stipend amounts vary depending on the availability of funds and the number of qualified applicants, but are awarded in increments of $500 and $1,000. Funds are to be used for tuition, books, and classroom fees; support is not provided for housing, board, travel, or administrative purposes.

Duration 1 year; recipients may reapply.

Number awarded Varies each year.

Deadline May of each year.

[248]
MILITARY NONRESIDENT TUITION WAIVER FOR MEMBERS, SPOUSES OR CHILDREN ASSIGNED TO DUTY IN TEXAS

Texas Higher Education Coordinating Board
Attn: Grants and Special Programs
1200 East Anderson Lane
P.O. Box 12788, Capitol Station
Austin, TX 78711-2788
(512) 427-6340   Toll Free: (800) 242-3062
Fax: (512) 427-6127   E-mail: grantinfo@thecb.state.tx.us
Web: www.collegeforalltexans.com

Summary To exempt military personnel stationed in Texas and their dependents from the payment of nonresident tuition at public institutions of higher education in the state.

Eligibility Eligible for these waivers are members of the U.S. armed forces and commissioned officers of the Public Health Service from states other than Texas, their spouses, and dependent children. Applicants must be assigned to Texas and attending or planning to attend a public college or university in the state.

Financial Data Although persons eligible under this program are classified as nonresidents, they are entitled to pay the resi-

dent tuition at Texas institutions of higher education, regardless of their length of residence in Texas.

Duration 1 year; may be renewed.

Number awarded Varies each year; recently, 11,600 students received these waivers.

Deadline Deadline not specified.

[249]
MILLER/CURRY/JACKSON LEADERSHIP AND EXCELLENCE SCHOLARSHIP

National Naval Officers Association-Washington, D.C.
  Chapter
Attn: Scholarship Program
2701 Park Center Drive, A1108
Alexandria, VA 22302
(703) 566-3840   Fax: (703) 566-3813
E-mail: Stephen.Williams@Navy.mil
Web: dcnnoa.memberlodge.com/Default.aspx?pageId=309002

Summary To provide financial assistance to African American and Hispanic high school seniors from the Washington, D.C. area who are interested in attending a college or university in any state and enrolling in the Navy Reserve Officers Training Corps (NROTC) program.

Eligibility This program is open to African American and Hispanic seniors graduating from high schools in the Washington, D.C. metropolitan area who plan to enroll full time at an accredited 2-year or 4-year college or university in any state. Applicants must be planning to enroll in the NROTC program. They must have a GPA of 3.0 or higher and be U.S. citizens or permanent residents. Selection is based on academic achievement, community involvement, and financial need.

Financial Data The stipend is $1,500.

Duration 1 year; nonrenewable.

Additional data If the recipient fails to enroll in the NROTC unit, all scholarship funds must be returned.

Number awarded 1 each year.

Deadline March of each year.

[250]
MINNESOTA G.I. BILL PROGRAM

Minnesota Office of Higher Education
Attn: Manager of State Financial Aid Programs
1450 Energy Park Drive, Suite 350
St. Paul, MN 55108-5227
(651) 642-0567   Toll Free: (800) 657-3866
Fax: (651) 642-0675   TDD: (800) 627-3529
E-mail: Ginny.Dodds@state.mn.us
Web: www.ohe.state.mn.us

Summary To provide financial assistance for college or graduate school in the state to residents of Minnesota who served in the military after September 11, 2001 and the families of deceased or disabled military personnel.

Eligibility This program is open to residents of Minnesota enrolled at colleges and universities in the state as undergraduate or graduate students. Applicants must be 1) a veteran who is serving or has served honorably in a branch of the U.S. armed forces at any time on or after September 11, 2001; 2) a non-veteran who has served honorably for a total of 5 years or more cumulatively as a member of the Minnesota National Guard or other active or Reserve component of the U.S. armed forces, and any part of that service occurred on or after September 11, 2001; or 3) a surviving child or spouse of a person who has served in the military at any time on or after September 11, 2001 and who has died or has a total and permanent disability as a result of that military service. Financial need is also considered in the selection process.

Financial Data The stipend is $1,000 per semester for full-time study or $500 per semester for part-time study.

Duration 1 year; may be renewed up to 4 additional years, provided the recipient continues to make satisfactory academic progress.

Additional data This program was established by the Minnesota Legislature in 2007.

Number awarded Varies each year.

Deadline Deadline not specified.

[251]
MINNESOTA NATIONAL GUARD STATE TUITION REIMBURSEMENT

Department of Military Affairs
Attn: Education Services Officer
JFMN-J1-ARED
20 West 12th Street
St. Paul, MN 55155-2098
(651) 282-4125   Toll Free: (800) 657-3848
Fax: (651) 282-4694   E-mail: education@mn.ngb.army.mil
Web: www.minnesotanationalguard.org

Summary To provide financial assistance for college or graduate school to members of the Minnesota National Guard.

Eligibility Eligible for this program are members of the Minnesota Army or Air National Guard in grades E-1 through O-5 (including warrant officers) who are enrolled as undergraduate or graduate students at colleges or universities in Minnesota. Reimbursement is provided only for undergraduate courses completed with a grade of "C" or better or for graduate courses completed with a grade of "B" or better. Guard members who served on federal active status or federally-funded state active service after September 11, 2001 are eligible for this assistance for up to 2 years after completion of their service contract (or up to 8 years if they were separated or discharged because of a service-connected injury, disease, or disability).

Financial Data The maximum reimbursement rate is 100% of the undergraduate tuition rate at the University of Minnesota Twin Cities campus (currently, $326.92 per credit to a maximum of $4,250 per term).

Duration 1 semester, to a maximum of 18 credits per semester; may be renewed.

Number awarded Varies each year.

Deadline Deadline not specified.

[252]
MISSISSIPPI NATIONAL GUARD STATE EDUCATIONAL ASSISTANCE PROGRAM

Mississippi Military Department
Attn: Education Services and Incentives Office
JFH-MS-J1-ED
1410 Riverside Drive
P.O. Box 5027
Jackson, MS 39296-5027
(601) 313-6248   Fax: (601) 313-6151
E-mail: msedu@ng.army.mil
Web: www.ngms.state.ms.us/edu/Pages/SEAP.aspx

Summary To provide financial assistance to members of the Mississippi National Guard who are interested in attending college in the state.

Eligibility This program is open to members of the Mississippi Army or Air National Guard who have completed basic training and are in good standing. Applicants must be registered to vote in Mississippi and be enrolled or accepted for enrollment at an accredited college or university (public or private) in the state. They may not currently be receiving federal tuition assistance.

Financial Data Stipends cover the actual cost of tuition, to a maximum of $4,500 per year or $250 per hour.

Duration 1 year; may be renewed until the Guard member earns a bachelor's degree, as long as the member maintains a

minimum GPA of 2.0. The full benefit must be utilized within a 10-year period.

Number awarded Varies each year.

Deadline Applications must be submitted not later than 2 weeks after the start date of the semester.

[253]
MISSOURI NATIONAL GUARD STATE TUITION ASSISTANCE PROGRAM

Office of the Adjutant General
Attn: JFMO-PER-INC (State TA)
2302 Militia Drive
Jefferson City, MO 65101-1203
(573) 638-9500, ext. 7650   Toll Free: (888) 526-MONG
Fax: (573) 638-9620
Web: www.moguard.com/DisplayPage.aspx?PageID=68

Summary To provide financial assistance for college to members of the Missouri National Guard.

Eligibility This program is open to members of the Missouri National Guard who are participating satisfactorily in required training. Applicants must be enrolled or accepted for enrollment as a full-time or part-time undergraduate at an approved public or private institution of higher learning. If they have already completed some college courses, they must have earned a GPA of 2.5 or higher. As recently structured, priority is given to personnel in the following order: 1) officers who do not have a bachelor's degree, regardless of their length of service; 2) non-prior service enlistees accessed to fill a valid unit vacancy; 3) prior service transfers access to fill a valid unit vacancy; and 4) prior service beyond first term with less than 10 years total military service.

Financial Data The program provide 100% tuition assistance for Guard members with 10 years or less of service and 50% tuition for those with more than 10 and less than 17 years of service. Tuition is paid at the rate of $245.60 per semester hour and may not exceed 39 hours per state fiscal year.

Duration Support is provided for 10 semesters, 150 credit hours, or completion of a bachelor's degree, whichever comes first. Recipients must maintain a GPA of 2.5 or higher.

Additional data This program was established in 1998.

Number awarded Varies each year, depending on the availability of funds.

Deadline Applications are due no later than 30 days from the start date of class.

[254]
MONTANA NATIONAL GUARD SCHOLARSHIPS

Montana National Guard
Attn: Education Service Officer
P.O. Box 4789
Fort Harrison, MT 59636-4789
(406) 324-3238
Web: www.montanaguard.com/rrwebsite/ed_mtscholarship.htm

Summary To provide financial assistance for college to members of the Montana National Guard.

Eligibility This program is open to members of the Montana National Guard who are enrolled or accepted for enrollment at a college, university, vocational/technical college, or other VA-approved training program in the state. Applicants must be in pay grades E-1 through E-7, W-1 through W-3, or O-1 through O-2; have completed Initial Active Duty for Training; have a high school diploma or GED; be eligible for Montgomery GI Bill Selected Reserve Benefits or be under a 6-year obligation to the Montana National Guard; and not have completed more than 16 years of military service. Funds are awarded on a first-come, first-served basis until exhausted.

Financial Data Support is provided at the rate of $100 per credit, up to $1,000 per semester, to assist with tuition and books.

Duration 1 year; may be renewed.
Number awarded Varies each year.
Deadline Deadline not specified.

[255]
MONTGOMERY GI BILL (SELECTED RESERVE)

Department of Veterans Affairs
Attn: Veterans Benefits Administration
810 Vermont Avenue, N.W.
Washington, DC 20420
(202) 418-4343   Toll Free: (888) GI-BILL1
Web: www.gibill.va.gov/GI_Bill_Info/benefits.htm

Summary To provide financial assistance for college or graduate school to members of the Reserves or National Guard.
Eligibility Eligible to apply are members of the Reserve elements of the Army, Navy, Air Force, Marine Corps, and Coast
Guard, as well as the Army National Guard and the Air National
Guard. To be eligible, a Reservist must 1) have a 6-year obligation
to serve in the Selected Reserves signed after June 30, 1985 (or,
if an officer, to agree to serve 6 years in addition to the original
obligation); 2) complete Initial Active Duty for Training (IADT); 3)
meet the requirements for a high school diploma or equivalent
certificate before completing IADT; and 4) remain in good standing in a drilling Selected Reserve unit. Reservists who enlisted
after June 30, 1985 can receive benefits for undergraduate
degrees, graduate training, or technical courses leading to certificates at colleges and universities. Reservists whose 6-year commitment began after September 30, 1990 may also use these
benefits for a certificate or diploma from business, technical, or
vocational schools; cooperative training; apprenticeship or on-
the-job training; correspondence courses; independent study
programs; tutorial assistance; remedial, deficiency, or refresher
training; flight training; or state-approved alternative teacher certification programs.
Financial Data The current monthly rate is $333 for full-time
study, $249 for three-quarter time study, $169 for half-time study,
or $83.25 for less than half-time study. For apprenticeship and on-
the-job training, the monthly stipend is $249.75 for the first 6
months, $183.15 for the second 6 months, and $116.55 for the
remainder of the program. Other rates apply for cooperative education, correspondence courses, and flight training.
Duration Up to 36 months for full-time study, 48 months for
three-quarter study, 72 months for half-time study, or 144 months
for less than half-time study.
Additional data This program is frequently referred to as Chapter 1606 (formerly Chapter 106). Reservists who are enrolled for
three-quarter or full-time study are eligible to participate in the
work-study program. The Department of Defense periodically
offers "kickers" of additional benefits on behalf of individuals in
critical military fields, as deemed necessary to encourage enlistment. Information on currently-available "kickers" is available
from Reserve and National Guard recruiters. Benefits end 10
years from the date the Reservist became eligible for the program. The Department of Veterans Affairs (VA) may extend the
10-year period if the individual could not train because of a disability caused by Selected Reserve service. Certain individuals
separated from the Selected Reserve due to downsizing of the
military between October 1, 1991 and September 30, 1999 will
also have the full 10 years to use their benefits.
Number awarded Varies each year.
Deadline Applications may be submitted at any time.

[256]
MONTGOMERY GI BILL TUITION ASSISTANCE TOP-UP

Department of Veterans Affairs
Attn: Veterans Benefits Administration
810 Vermont Avenue, N.W.
Washington, DC 20420
(202) 418-4343   Toll Free: (888) GI-BILL1
Web: www.gibill.va.gov/GI_Bill_Info/benefits.htm

Summary To supplement the tuition assistance provided by the
military services to their members.
Eligibility This program is open to military personnel who have
served at least 2 full years on active duty and are approved for
tuition assistance by their military service. Applicants must be
participating in the Montgomery GI Bill (MGIB) Active Duty program and be eligible for MGIB benefits. This assistance is available to servicemembers whose military service does not pay
100% of tuition and fees.
Financial Data This program pays the difference between what
the military services pay for tuition assistance and the full amount
of tuition and fees, to a maximum of $1,075 per month.
Duration Up to 36 months of payments are available.
Additional data This program was established in 2000.
Number awarded Varies each year.
Deadline Deadline not specified.

[257]
NATIONAL GUARD ASSOCIATION OF CALIFORNIA SCHOLARSHIPS

National Guard Association of California
Attn: Scholarship Committee
3336 Bradshaw Road, Suite 230
Sacramento, CA 95827-2615
(916) 362-3411   Toll Free: (800) 647-0018
Fax: (916) 362-3707
Web: www.ngac.org

Summary To provide financial assistance for college or graduate school to members of the National Guard Association of California.
Eligibility This program is open to members of the association
who are also currently serving in the California National Guard.
Applicants must be attending or planning to attend a college, university, graduate school, business school, or trade school in California. They may have no record of AWOL or unsatisfactory performance for the previous year or since enlistment. Selection is
based on academic merit and financial need.
Financial Data The amount of the award depends on the availability of funds.
Duration 1 year; recipients are ineligible for 2 successive
awards.
Number awarded Varies each year; recently, 4 of these scholarships were awarded.
Deadline Applications may be submitted at any time, but recipients are selected in October and April of each year.

[258]
NATIONAL GUARD ASSOCIATION OF COLORADO SCHOLARSHIP PROGRAM

National Guard Association of Colorado
Attn: Education Foundation, Inc.
P.O. Box 440889
Aurora, CO 80044-0889
(303) 677-8387   Fax: (303) 677-8823
E-mail: ed.foundation@earthlink.net
Web: www.ngaco-edufoundation.org

Summary To provide financial assistance to members of the
National Guard Association of Colorado (NGACO) and the Colo-

rado National Guard and their families who are interested in attending college or graduate school in any state.

Eligibility This program is open to 1) current and retired members of the Colorado National Guard and the NGACO; 2) dependent unmarried children of current and retired members of the Colorado National Guard and the NGACO; 3) spouses of current and retired members of the Colorado National Guard and the NGACO; and 4) unremarried spouses and unmarried dependent children of deceased members of the Colorado National Guard and the NGACO. Applicants must be enrolled or planning to enroll full or part time at a college, university, trade school, business school, or graduate school in any state. Along with their application, they must submit an essay, up to 2 pages in length, on their desire to continue their education, what motivates them, their financial need, their commitment to academic excellence, and their current situation.

Financial Data Stipends are $1,000, $750, or $500 per year.

Duration 1 year; may be renewed.

Additional data Members of the Colorado National Guard must perform at least 1 year of service following the completion of the school year for which the scholarship was received.

Number awarded Varies each year. Recently, 11 of these scholarships were awarded: 4 at $1,000 to members of the NGACO, 2 at $750 to dependents of members of the NGACO, 2 at $500 to current enlisted members of the Colorado National Guard, 2 at $500 to current officer members of the Colorado National Guard, and 1 at $1,000 to a Colorado National Guard member or dependent working on a graduate degree.

Deadline August of each year for fall semester; January of each year for spring semester.

[259]
NATIONAL GUARD ASSOCIATION OF MASSACHUSETTS SCHOLARSHIPS

National Guard Association of Massachusetts
Attn: Scholarship Committee
50 Maple Street
Milford, MA 01757
(508) 735-6544   E-mail: feedback@ngama.org
Web: www.ngama.org

Summary To provide financial assistance for college to members of the Massachusetts National Guard and their dependents.

Eligibility This program is open to 1) current members of the Massachusetts National Guard; 2) children and spouses of current members of the National Guard Association of Massachusetts (NGAMA); and 3) children and spouses of current members of the Massachusetts National Guard. Applicants must be enrolled in or planning to enroll in an accredited college or technical program. Along with their application, they must submit a letter of recommendation, a list of extracurricular activities and other significant accomplishments, high school or college transcripts, and an essay on a topic that changes annually but relates to the National Guard; recently, applicants were asked to give their ideas on the best operational use for the National Guard as the country takes a new direction under a new President.

Financial Data The stipend is $1,000.

Duration 1 year.

Number awarded 5 each year: 2 to members of the Massachusetts National Guard, 2 to dependents of NGAMA members, and 1 to a dependent of a Massachusetts National Guard member.

Deadline March of each year.

[260]
NATIONAL GUARD ASSOCIATION OF MICHIGAN TUITION GRANTS

National Guard Association of Michigan
Attn: Scholarships
P.O. Box 810
Cadillac, MI 49601
Toll Free: (800) 477-1644   Fax: (231) 775-7906
E-mail: NGAM@charter.net
Web: www.ngam.org/grants.php

Summary To provide financial assistance to members of the National Guard Association of Michigan who are interested in attending college in any state.

Eligibility This program is open to members of the association who are also current members of the Michigan National Guard. Applicants may be enlisted members of any rank, warrant officers through CW3, or commissioned officers through the rank of captain. They must be attending or planning to attend a college, university, or trade school in any state. Along with their application, they must submit a 100-word statement on their educational and military goals and the path they expect to take to achieve their goals. Financial need is not considered in the selection process.

Financial Data A stipend is awarded (amount not specified).

Duration 1 semester; may be renewed.

Number awarded Varies each year; recently, 5 of these grants were awarded.

Deadline June of each year for the fall term/semester; November of each year for the winter term/semester.

[261]
NATIONAL GUARD OF GEORGIA SCHOLARSHIP FUND FOR COLLEGES OR UNIVERSITIES

Georgia Guard Insurance Trust
P.O. Box 889
Mableton, GA 30126
(770) 739-9651   Toll Free: (800) 229-1053
Fax: (770) 745-0673   E-mail: director@ngaga.org
Web: www.ngaga.org/scholarship.html

Summary To provide financial assistance to members of the Georgia National Guard and their spouses, children, and grandchildren who are interested in attending college in any state.

Eligibility This program is open to policyholders with the Georgia Guard Insurance Trust (GGIT) who are members of the National Guard Association of Georgia (NGAGA) or the Enlisted Association of the National Guard of Georgia (EANGGA); spouses, children, and grandchildren of NGAGA and EANGGA members; and unremarried widow(er)s, children, and grandchildren of deceased NGAGA and EANGGA members. Applicants must be enrolled or planning to enroll full time at a college or university in any state. High school seniors must have a combined mathematics and critical reading SAT score of at least 1000 or a GPA of 3.0 or higher. Students already enrolled in a college or university must have a cumulative GPA of 3.0 or higher. Along with their application, they must submit transcripts, a letter with personal specific facts regarding their desire to continue their education, 2 letters of recommendation, a letter of academic reference, and an agreement to retain insurance with the GGIT for at least 2 years following completion of the school year for which the scholarship is awarded.

Financial Data The stipend is $1,000.

Duration 1 year.

Number awarded Up to 3 each year.

Deadline April of each year.

[262]
NATIONAL GUARD OF GEORGIA SCHOLARSHIP FUND FOR VOCATIONAL OR BUSINESS SCHOOLS

Georgia Guard Insurance Trust
P.O. Box 889
Mableton, GA 30126
(770) 739-9651   Toll Free: (800) 229-1053
Fax: (770) 745-0673   E-mail: director@ngaga.org
Web: www.ngaga.org/scholarship.html

Summary To provide financial assistance to members of the Georgia National Guard and their spouses, children, and grandchildren who are interested in attending business or vocational school in any state.

Eligibility This program is open to policyholders with the Georgia Guard Insurance Trust (GGIT) who are members of the National Guard Association of Georgia (NGAGA) or the Enlisted Association of the National Guard of Georgia (EANGGA); spouses, children, and grandchildren of NGAGA and EANGGA members; and unremarried widow(er)s, children, and grandchildren of deceased NGAGA and EANGGA members. Applicants must be interested in enrolling full time in day or evening classes at a business or vocational school in any state. They must be able to meet program-specific admission standards and institutional requirements and complete all admission procedures for admission to a degree/diploma program in regular program status. Along with their application, they must submit transcripts, a letter with personal specific facts regarding their desire to continue their education, 2 letters of recommendation, and an agreement to retain insurance with the GGIT for at least 2 years following completion of the school year for which the scholarship is awarded.

Financial Data The stipend is $1,000.

Duration 1 year.

Number awarded Up to 3 each year.

Deadline April of each year.

[263]
NAVAL FLIGHT OFFICER OPTION OF THE SEAMAN TO ADMIRAL-21 PROGRAM

U.S. Navy
Attn: Commander, Naval Service Training Command
250 Dallas Street, Suite A
Pensacola, FL 32508-5268
(850) 452-9563   Fax: (850) 452-2486
E-mail: PNSC_STA21@navy.mil
Web: www.sta-21.navy.mil

Summary To allow outstanding enlisted Navy personnel to complete a bachelor's degree and receive a commission as a naval flight officer (NFO).

Eligibility This program is open to U.S. citizens who are currently serving on active duty in the U.S. Navy or Naval Reserve, including Full Time Support (FTS), Selected Reserves (SELRES), and Navy Reservists on active duty except for those on active duty for training (ACDUTRA). Applicants must be high school graduates (or GED recipients) who are able to complete requirements for a baccalaureate degree in 36 months or less. When they complete their degree requirements, they must be younger than 27 years of age (may be adjusted to 31 years of age for prior active-duty service). Within the past 3 years, they must have taken the SAT test (and achieved scores of at least 500 on the mathematics section and 500 on the critical reading section) or the ACT test (and achieved a score of 41 or higher, including at least 21 on the mathematics portion and 20 on the English portion). They must also achieve a score of at least the following: AQR (4), FOFAR (5) on the Aviation Selection Test Battery.

Financial Data Awardees continue to receive their regular Navy pay and allowances while they attend college on a full-time basis. They also receive reimbursement for tuition, fees, and books up to $10,000 per year. If base housing is available, they are eligible to live there. Participants are not eligible to receive benefits under the Navy's Tuition Assistance Program (TA), the Montgomery GI Bill (MGIB), the Navy College Fund, or the Veterans Educational Assistance Program (VEAP).

Duration Selectees are supported for up to 36 months of full-time, year-round study or completion of a bachelor's degree, as long as they maintain a GPA of 2.5 or higher.

Additional data This program was established in 2001 as a replacement for the Aviation Enlisted Commissioning Program (AECP). Upon acceptance into the program, selectees attend the Naval Science Institute (NSI) in Newport, Rhode Island for an 8-week program in the fundamental core concepts of being a naval officer (navigation, engineering, weapons, military history and justice, etc.). They then enter a college or university with an NROTC unit or affiliation to work full time on a bachelor's degree. They become members of and drill with the NROTC unit. When they complete their degree, they are commissioned as ensigns in the United States Naval Reserve and assigned to flight training. After commissioning, participants incur an active-duty obligation of 6 years after designation as a Naval Flight Officer or 6 years from the date of disenrollment from flight training.

Number awarded Varies each year.

Deadline June of each year.

[264]
NAVAL HELICOPTER ASSOCIATION UNDERGRADUATE SCHOLARSHIPS

Naval Helicopter Association
Attn: Scholarship Fund
P.O. Box 180578
Coronado, CA 92178-0578
(619) 435-7139   Fax: (619) 435-7354
E-mail: info@nhascholarship.org
Web: www.nhascholarship.org/nhascholarshipfund/index.html

Summary To provide financial assistance for college to students who have an affiliation with the rotary wing activities of the sea services.

Eligibility This program is open to high school seniors and current undergraduates who are 1) children, grandchildren, or spouses of current or former Navy, Marine Corps, or Coast Guard rotary wing aviators or aircrewmen; 2) individuals who are serving or have served in maintenance or support billets in rotary wing squadrons or wings and their spouses and children. Applicants must provide information on their rotary wing affiliation and a personal statement on their educational plans and future goals. Selection is based on that statement, academic proficiency, scholastic achievements and awards, extracurricular activities, employment history, and letters of recommendation.

Financial Data Stipends are $3,000, $2,500, or $2,000.

Duration 1 year.

Additional data This program includes the DPA Thousand Points of Light Award (sponsored by D.P. Associates Inc. and L3 Communications), the Sergei Sikorsky Scholarship, the Ream Memorial Scholarship, and a scholarship sponsored by Raytheon Corporation.

Number awarded Varies each year; recently, 9 of these scholarships were awarded: 3 at $3,000, 1 at $2,500, and 5 at $2,000.

Deadline January of each year.

[265]
NAVY ADVANCED EDUCATION VOUCHER PROGRAM

U.S. Navy
Naval Education and Training Command
Center for Personal and Professional Development
Attn: AEV Program Office
6490 Saufley Field Road
Pensacola, FL 32509-5204
(850) 452-7271   Fax: (850) 452-1272
E-mail: rick.cusimano@navy.mil
Web: www.navycollege.navy.mil/aev/aev_home.cfm

Summary To provide financial assistance to Navy enlisted personnel who are interested in earning an undergraduate or graduate degree during off-duty hours.

Eligibility This program is open to senior enlisted Navy personnel in ranks E-7 and E-8. Applicants should be transferring to, or currently on, shore duty with sufficient time ashore to complete a bachelor's or master's degree. Personnel at rank E-7 may have no more than 16 years time in service and E-8 no more than 18 years. The area of study must be certified by the Naval Postgraduate School as Navy-relevant.

Financial Data This program covers 100% of education costs (tuition, books, and fees). For a bachelor's degree, the maximum is $6,700 per year or a total of $20,000 per participant. For a master's degree, the maximum is $20,000 per year or a total of $40,000 per participant.

Duration Up to 36 months from the time of enrollment for a bachelor's degree; up to 24 months from the time of enrollment for a master's degree.

Additional data Recently approved majors for bachelor's degrees included human resources, construction management, information technology, emergency and disaster management, paralegal, engineering, business administration, leadership and management, nursing, strategic foreign languages, and electrical/electronic technology. Approved fields of study for master's degrees included business administration, education and training management, emergency and disaster management, engineering and technology, homeland defense and security, human resources, information technology, leadership and management, project management, and systems analysis. Recipients of this assistance incur an obligation to remain on active duty following completion of the program for a period equal to 3 times the number of months of education completed, to a maximum obligation of 36 months.

Number awarded Varies each year. Recently, 20 of these vouchers were awarded: 15 for bachelor's degrees and 5 for master's degrees.

Deadline February of each year.

[266]
NAVY COLLEGE FUND

U.S. Navy
Attn: Navy Personnel Command (PERS-675)
5720 Integrity Drive
Millington, TN 38055-6040
(901) 874-4258   Toll Free: (866) U-ASK-NPC
Fax: (901) 874-2052   E-mail: MILL_MGIB@navy.mil
Web: www.navyjobs.com/benefits/education/earnmoney

Summary To provide financial assistance for college to Navy enlistees during and after they have completed their service obligation.

Eligibility Eligible for this program are high school seniors and graduates between 17 and 35 years of age who enlist in the Navy for 3 to 4 years of active duty. They must score 50 or above on the ASVAB and also enroll in the Montgomery GI Bill. Sailors currently on active duty in selected Navy ratings with critical personnel shortages are also eligible. Applicants must be interested in attending a Department of Veterans Affairs-approved postsec-

ondary educational institution on a full-time basis after completion of their service obligation.

Financial Data The Navy College Fund provides, in addition to the Montgomery GI Bill, up to $15,000 for college tuition and expenses.

Duration Enlistees may begin using this educational benefit on a part-time basis after 2 years of continuous active duty. Funds must be utilized within 10 years of leaving the Navy.

Number awarded Varies each year.

Deadline Applications may be submitted at any time.

[267]
NAVY NURSE CANDIDATE PROGRAM

U.S. Navy
Attn: Navy Medicine Manpower, Personnel, Education and
    Training Command
Code OH
8901 Wisconsin Avenue, Building 1, Tower 13, Room 13132
Bethesda, MD 20889-5611
(301) 295-1217   Toll Free: (800) USA-NAVY
Fax: (301) 295-1811   E-mail: OH@med.navy.mil
Web: www.med.navy.mil

Summary To provide financial assistance for nursing education to students interested in serving in the Navy.

Eligibility This program is open to full-time students in a bachelor of science in nursing program who are U.S. citizens under 40 years of age. Prior to or during their junior year of college, applicants must enlist in the U.S. Navy Nurse Corps Reserve. Following receipt of their degree, they must be willing to serve on active duty as a nurse in the Navy.

Financial Data This program pays a $10,000 initial grant upon enlistment (paid in 2 installments of $5,000 each) and a stipend of $1,000 per month. Students are responsible for paying all school expenses.

Duration Up to 24 months.

Additional data Students who receive support from this program for 1 to 12 months incur an active-duty service obligation of 4 years; students who receive support for 13 to 24 months have a service obligation of 5 years.

Number awarded Varies each year.

Deadline Deadline not specified.

[268]
NAVY NURSE CORPS NROTC SCHOLARSHIP PROGRAM

U.S. Navy
Attn: Naval Education and Training Command
NSTC OD2
250 Dallas Street, Suite A
Pensacola, FL 32508-5268
(850) 452-4941, ext. 25166
Toll Free: (800) NAV-ROTC, ext. 25166
Fax: (850) 452-2486
E-mail: PNSC_NROTC.scholarship@navy.mil
Web: www.nrotc.navy.mil/nurse.aspx

Summary To provide financial assistance to graduating high school seniors who are interested in joining Navy ROTC and majoring in nursing in college.

Eligibility Eligible to apply for these scholarships are graduating high school seniors who have been accepted at a college with a Navy ROTC unit on campus or a college with a cross-enrollment agreement with such a college. Applicants must be U.S. citizens between the ages of 17 and 23 who plan to study nursing in college and are willing to serve for 4 years as active-duty Navy officers in the Navy Nurse Corps following graduation from college. They must not have reached their 27th birthday by the time of college graduation and commissioning; applicants who have prior active-duty military service may be eligible for age adjustments for the amount of time equal to their prior service, up to a maximum of 36 months. They must have minimum SAT scores of 530 in critical reading and in 520 mathematics or minimum ACT scores of 22 in English and 21 in mathematics.

Financial Data This scholarship provides payment of full tuition and required educational fees, as well as $375 per semester for textbooks, supplies, and equipment. The program also provides a stipend for 10 months of the year that is $250 per month as a freshman, $300 per month as a sophomore, $350 per month as a junior, and $400 per month as a senior.

Duration 4 years.

Number awarded Varies each year.

Deadline January of each year.

[269]
NAVY TUITION ASSISTANCE PROGRAM

U.S. Navy
Attn: Naval Education and Training Command
Center for Personal and Professional Development
Code N725
6490 Saufley Field Road
Pensacola, FL 32509-5241
(850) 452-7271   Toll Free: (877) 253-7122
Fax: (850) 452-1149   E-mail: ncc@navy.mil
Web: www.navycollege.navy.mil/nta.cfm

Summary To provide financial assistance for high school, vocational, undergraduate, or graduate studies to Navy personnel.

Eligibility This program is open to active-duty Navy officers and enlisted personnel, including Naval Reservists on continuous active duty, enlisted Naval Reservists ordered to active duty for 120 days or more, and Naval Reservist officers ordered to active duty for 2 years or more. Applicants must register to take courses at accredited civilian schools during off-duty time. They must be working on their first associate, bachelor's, master's, doctoral, or professional degree. Tuition assistance is provided for courses taken at accredited colleges, universities, vocational/technical schools, private schools, and through independent study/distance learning (but not for flight training).

Financial Data Those selected for participation in this program receive their regular Navy pay and 100% of tuition at the postsecondary educational institution of their choice, but capped at $250 per semester hour and 12 semester hours per fiscal year (the 12-semester hour limit may be waived upon application), or a total of $4,500 per fiscal year.

Duration Until completion of a bachelor's or graduate degree.

Additional data Officers must agree to remain on active duty for at least 2 years after completion of courses funded by this program.

Number awarded Varies each year.

Deadline Deadline not specified.

[270]
NAVY-MARINE CORPS ROTC 2-YEAR SCHOLARSHIPS

U.S. Navy
Attn: Naval Education and Training Command
NSTC OD2
250 Dallas Street, Suite A
Pensacola, FL 32508-5268
(850) 452-4941, ext. 25166
Toll Free: (800) NAV-ROTC, ext. 25166
Fax: (850) 452-2486
E-mail: PNSC_NROTC.scholarship@navy.mil
Web: www.nrotc.navy.mil/scholarships.aspx

Summary To provide financial assistance to upper-division students who are interested in joining Navy ROTC in college.

Eligibility This program is open to students who have completed at least 2 years of college (or 3 years if enrolled in a 5-year

program) with a GPA of 2.5 or higher overall and 2.0 or higher in calculus and physics. Preference is given to students at colleges with a Navy ROTC unit on campus or at colleges with a cross-enrollment agreement with a college with an NROTC unit. Applicants must be U.S. citizens between the ages of 17 and 21 who plan to pursue an approved course of study in college and complete their degree before they reach the age of 27. Former and current enlisted military personnel are also eligible if they will complete the program by the age of 30.

Financial Data These scholarships provide payment of full tuition and required educational fees, as well as a specified amount for textbooks, supplies, and equipment. The program also provides a stipend for 10 months of the year that is $350 per month as a junior and $400 per month as a senior.

Duration 2 years, until the recipient completes the bachelor's degree.

Additional data Applications must be made through professors of naval science at 1 of the schools hosting the Navy ROTC program. Prior to final selection, applicants must attend, at Navy expense, a 6-week summer training course at the Naval Science Institute at Newport, Rhode Island. Recipients must also complete 4 years of study in naval science classes as students either at 1 of the 70 colleges with NROTC units or at 1 of the more than 100 institutions with cross-enrollment agreements (in which case they attend their home college for their regular academic courses but attend naval science classes at a nearby school with an NROTC unit). After completing the program, all participants are commissioned as ensigns in the Naval Reserve or second lieutenants in the Marine Corps Reserve with an 8-year service obligation, including 4 years of active duty.

Number awarded Approximately 800 each year.

Deadline March of each year.

[271]
NAVY-MARINE CORPS ROTC 4-YEAR SCHOLARSHIPS

U.S. Navy
Attn: Naval Education and Training Command
NSTC OD2
250 Dallas Street, Suite A
Pensacola, FL 32508-5268
(850) 452-4941, ext. 25166
Toll Free: (800) NAV-ROTC, ext. 25166
Fax: (850) 452-2486
E-mail: PNSC_NROTC.scholarship@navy.mil
Web: www.nrotc.navy.mil/scholarships.aspx

Summary To provide financial assistance to graduating high school seniors who are interested in joining Navy ROTC in college.

Eligibility This program is open to graduating high school seniors who have been accepted at a college with a Navy ROTC unit on campus or a college with a cross-enrollment agreement with such a college. Applicants must be U.S. citizens between 17 and 23 years of age who are willing to serve for 4 years as active-duty Navy officers following graduation from college. They must not have reached their 27th birthday by the time of college graduation and commissioning; applicants who have prior active-duty military service may be eligible for age adjustments for the amount of time equal to their prior service, up to a maximum of 36 months. The qualifying scores for the Navy option are 530 critical reading and 520 mathematics on the SAT or 22 on both English and mathematics on the ACT; for the Marine Corps option they are 1000 composite on the SAT or 22 composite on the ACT. Current enlisted and former military personnel are also eligible if they will complete the program by the age of 30.

Financial Data These scholarships provide payment of full tuition and required educational fees, as well as a specified amount for textbooks, supplies, and equipment. The program also provides a stipend for 10 months of the year that is $250 per month as a freshman, $300 per month as a sophomore, $350 per month as a junior, and $400 per month as a senior.

Duration 4 years.

Additional data Students may apply for either a Navy or Marine Corps option scholarship but not for both. Navy option applicants apply through Navy recruiting offices; Marine Corps applicants apply through Marine Corps recruiting offices. Recipients must also complete 4 years of study in naval science classes as students either at 1 of the 70 colleges, universities, and maritime institutes with NROTC units or at 1 of the more than 100 institutions with cross-enrollment agreements (in which case they attend their home college for their regular academic courses but attend naval science classes at a nearby school with an NROTC unit). After completing the program, all participants are commissioned as ensigns in the Naval Reserve or second lieutenants in the Marine Corps Reserve with an 8-year service obligation, including 4 years of active duty. Current military personnel who are accepted into this program are released from active duty and are not eligible for active-duty pay and allowances, medical benefits, or other active-duty entitlements.

Number awarded Approximately 2,200 each year.

Deadline January of each year.

[272]
NAVY-MARINE CORPS ROTC COLLEGE PROGRAM

U.S. Navy
Attn: Naval Education and Training Command
NSTC OD2
250 Dallas Street, Suite A
Pensacola, FL 32508-5268
(850) 452-4941, ext. 25166
Toll Free: (800) NAV-ROTC, ext. 25166
Fax: (850) 452-2486
E-mail: PNSC_NROTC.scholarship@navy.mil
Web: www.nrotc.navy.mil/scholarships.aspx

Summary To provide financial assistance to lower-division students who are interested in joining Navy ROTC in college.

Eligibility Applicants must be U.S. citizens between the ages of 17 and 21 who are already enrolled as non-scholarship students in naval science courses at a college or university with a Navy ROTC program on campus. They must apply before the spring of their sophomore year. All applications must be submitted through the professors of naval science at the college or university attended.

Financial Data Participants in this program receive free naval science textbooks, all required uniforms, and a stipend for 10 months of the year that is $350 per month as a junior and $400 per month as a senior.

Duration 2 or 4 years.

Additional data Following acceptance into the program, participants attend the Naval Science Institute in Newport, Rhode Island for 6 and a half weeks during the summer between their sophomore and junior year. During the summer between their junior and senior year, they participate in an additional training program, usually at sea for Navy midshipmen or at Quantico, Virginia for Marine Corps midshipmen. After graduation from college, they are commissioned ensigns in the Naval Reserve or second lieutenants in the Marine Corps Reserve with an 8-year service obligation, including 3 years of active duty.

Deadline March of each year.

[273]
NDNGEA SCHOLARSHIPS

North Dakota National Guard Enlisted Association
c/o MSG Joe Lovelace
4900 107th Avenue S.E.
Minot, ND 58701-9207
E-mail: joseph.m.lovelace@us.army.mil
Web: www.ndngea.org

Summary To provide financial assistance to members of the North Dakota National Guard Enlisted Association (NDNGEA) and their families who are interested in attending college in any state.

Eligibility This program is open to association members who have at least 1 year remaining on their enlistment or have completed 20 or more years in service. Also eligible are their unmarried dependent children, spouses, and the unremarried spouses and unmarried dependent children of a deceased NDNGEA member who was in good standing at the time of death. Applicants must be attending or planning to attend a university, college, or trade/business school in any state. Graduate students are not eligible. Selection is based on academic achievement, leadership, character, and financial need.

Financial Data The stipend is $1,000. Funds are sent directly to the school in the recipient's name.

Duration 1 year.

Number awarded 1 or more each year.

Deadline November of each year.

[274]
NEBRASKA NATIONAL GUARD TUITION ASSISTANCE PROGRAM

Nebraska Military Department
Attn: Nebraska National Guard
1300 Military Road
Lincoln, NE 68508-1090
(402) 309-7210
Web: www.neguard.com/NMD/tuition/index.html

Summary To provide an opportunity for enlisted members of the Nebraska National Guard to pursue additional education.

Eligibility Eligible for this benefit are members of the Nebraska National Guard who are enrolled in a Nebraska university, college, or community college. Commissioned and warrant officers and enlisted personnel who already have a baccalaureate degree are not eligible. Guard members must apply for this assistance within 10 years of the date of initial enlistment. The credit is not available for graduate study or noncredit courses. Priority is given to Guard members who have previously received these benefits.

Financial Data Students at state-supported institutions are exempted from payment of 75% of the tuition charges at their schools. Students at independent, nonprofit, accredited colleges and universities in Nebraska receive a credit equal to the amount they would receive if they attended the University of Nebraska at Lincoln. All funds are paid directly to the school.

Duration 1 year; may be renewed.

Additional data Any member of the Nebraska National Guard who receives this assistance must agree to serve in the Guard for 3 years after completion of the courses for which assistance was given.

Number awarded Up to 1,200 each year.

Deadline June of each year for academic terms beginning between July and September; September of each year for academic terms beginning between October and December; December of each year for academic terms beginning between January and March; March of each year for academic terms beginning between April and June.

[275]
NEBRASKA TUITION CREDIT FOR ACTIVE RESERVISTS

Department of Veterans' Affairs
State Office Building
301 Centennial Mall South, Sixth Floor
P.O. Box 95083
Lincoln, NE 68509-5083
(402) 471-2458   Fax: (402) 471-2491
E-mail: john.hilgert@nebraska.gov
Web: www.vets.state.ne.us

Summary To provide financial assistance for college to members of Nebraska units of the active Reserves.

Eligibility Nebraska residents who are enlisted members of a Nebraska-based unit of the active selected Reserve are eligible for this benefit. They must have at least 2 years remaining on their enlistment, have agreed to serve at least 3 years in the Reserves, not have completed the tenth year of total service in the U.S. armed forces (including active and Reserve time), and be working on a degree at a state-supported college or university or an equivalent level of study in a technical community college.

Financial Data Reservists who meet the requirements may receive a credit for 50% of the tuition charges at any state-supported university or college in Nebraska, including any technical community college.

Duration 1 year; may be renewed until receipt of the degree or completion of the course of study.

Number awarded Varies each year; recently 87 of these awards were granted.

Deadline Deadline not specified.

[276]
NEVADA NATIONAL GUARD STATE TUITION WAIVER PROGRAM

Nevada National Guard
Attn: Education Officer
2460 Fairview Drive
Carson City, NV 89701-6807
(775) 887-7326   Fax: (775) 887-7279
Web: www.nv.ngb.army.mil/education.cfm

Summary To provide financial assistance to Nevada National Guard members who are interested in attending college or graduate school in the state.

Eligibility This program is open to active members of the Nevada National Guard who are interested in attending a public community college, 4-year college, or university in the state. Applicants must be residents of Nevada. Independent study, correspondence courses, and study at the William S. Boyd School of Law, the University of Nevada School of Medicine, and the UNLV School of Dental Medicine are not eligible.

Financial Data This program provides a waiver of 100% of tuition at state-supported community colleges, colleges, or universities in Nevada.

Duration 1 year; may be renewed.

Additional data This program was established on a pilot basis in 2003 and became permanent in 2005. Recipients must attain a GPA of at least 2.0 or refund all tuition received.

Number awarded Varies each year.

Deadline Applications must be received at least 3 weeks prior to the start of classes.

[277]
NEW HAMPSHIRE NATIONAL GUARD TUITION WAIVER PROGRAM

Office of the Adjutant General
Attn: Education Office
State Military Reservation
4 Pembroke Road
Concord, NH 03301-5652
(603) 227-1550   Fax: (603) 225-1257
TDD: (800) 735-2964 E-mail: education@nharmyguard.com
Web: www.nh.ngb.army.mil/members/education

Summary To provide financial assistance to members of the New Hampshire National Guard who are interested in attending college or graduate school in the state.

Eligibility This program is open to active members of the New Hampshire National Guard who have completed advanced individual training or commissioning and have at least a 90% attendance rate at annual training and drill assemblies. Applicants may be working on any type of academic degree at public institutions in New Hampshire. They must apply for financial aid from their school, for the New Hampshire National Guard Scholarship Program, and for federal tuition assistance.

Financial Data The program provides full payment of tuition.

Duration 1 year; may be renewed.

Additional data This program began in 1996.

Number awarded Varies each year, depending on availability of space.

Deadline Deadline not specified.

[278]
NEW JERSEY NATIONAL GUARD TUITION PROGRAM

New Jersey Department of Military and Veterans Affairs
Attn: New Jersey Army National Guard Education Center
3650 Saylors Pond Road
Fort Dix, NJ 08640-7600
(609) 562-0654   Toll Free: (888) 859-0352
Fax: (609) 562-0201
Web: www.state.nj.us/military/education/NJNGTP.htm

Summary To provide financial assistance for college or graduate school to New Jersey National Guard members and the surviving spouses and children of deceased members.

Eligibility This program is open to active members of the New Jersey National Guard who have completed Initial Active Duty for Training (IADT). Applicants must be New Jersey residents who have been accepted into a program of undergraduate or graduate study at any of 31 public institutions of higher education in the state. The surviving spouses and children of deceased members of the Guard who had completed IADT and were killed in the performance of their duties while a member of the Guard are also eligible if the school has classroom space available.

Financial Data Tuition for up to 15 credits per semester is waived for full-time recipients in state-supported colleges or community colleges in New Jersey.

Duration 1 semester; may be renewed.

Number awarded Varies each year.

Deadline Deadline not specified.

[279]
NEW JERSEY USAA SCHOLARSHIP

Enlisted Association National Guard of New Jersey
Attn: Scholarship Committee
101 Eggert Crossing Road
Lawrenceville, NJ 08648-2805
(609) 562-0207   Fax: (609) 562-0283
Web: www.eang-nj.org/scholarships.html

Summary To provide financial assistance to New Jersey National Guard members interested in attending college in any state.

Eligibility This program is open to drilling members of the New Jersey National Guard. Membership in the Enlisted Association National Guard of New Jersey (EANGNJ) is not required. Applicants must be attending or planning to attend a college or university in any state. Along with their application, they must submit 1) information on their church, school, and community activities; 2) a list of honors they have received; 3) letters of recommendation; 4) transcripts; and 5) a letter with specific facts about their desire to continue their education and specifying their career goals. Financial need is not considered in the selection process.

Financial Data The stipend is $1,000.

Duration 1 year.

Additional data This program is administered by EANGNJ and funded by USAA Insurance Corporation.

Number awarded 1 each year.

Deadline May of each year.

[280]
NEW MEXICO NATIONAL GUARD TUITION SCHOLARSHIP PROGRAM

New Mexico National Guard
Attn: Education Services Officer
47 Bataan Boulevard
Santa Fe, NM 87508
(505) 474-1245   Fax: (505) 474-1243
E-mail: EducationNM@nm.ngb.army.mil
Web: www.nm.ngb.army.mil/education.html

Summary To provide financial assistance to members of the New Mexico National Guard who are working on an undergraduate degree at a school in the state.

Eligibility This program is open to members of the New Mexico National Guard who are working on their first degree at the undergraduate or vocational school level. Applicants must be attending a state-supported school in New Mexico.

Financial Data This program provides payment of 100% of the cost of tuition, including instructional fees in lieu of tuition and laboratory shop fees that are specifically required.

Duration 1 semester; may be renewed for up to 130 semester hours of undergraduate or vocational study.

Number awarded Varies each year, depending on the availability of funds.

Deadline June of each year for fall semester; November of each year for spring semester; April of each year for summer school.

[281]
NEW YORK RECRUITMENT INCENTIVE AND RETENTION PROGRAM

New York State Division of Military and Naval Affairs
Attn: New York National Guard Education Office
NYARNG MNP-ED
1 Buffington Street, Building 25
Watervliet, NY 12189-4000
(518) 272-4051   E-mail: education@ny.ngb.army.mil
Web: www.dmna.state.ny.us

Summary To provide financial assistance to members of the New York State Military Forces who are interested in attending college in the state.

Eligibility This program is open to members of the New York Army National Guard, New York Air National Guard, and New York Naval Militia in good military and academic standing. Applicants must have been enrolled in a degree program for a minimum of 6 credit hours per semester, have been legal residents of New York state for at least 186 days prior to using the program for the first time and 186 days per year (excluding periods of active

federal service), and be enrolled in their first baccalaureate degree program. They must have completed Initial Active Duty for Training (IADT), naval enlisted code (NEC) training, or a commissioning program.

Financial Data The program pays for the cost of tuition (up to $4,350 or the maximum cost of the State University of New York undergraduate tuition) for credit bearing courses, or courses that are required as a prerequisite within the declared degree program.

Duration Up to 8 semesters of full-time study, or the equivalent of 4 academic years, are supported; if the undergraduate program normally requires 5 academic years of full-time study, then this program will support 10 semesters of full-time study or the equivalent of 5 academic years. For part-time (from 6 to 11 semester hours per semester) study, the program provides up to 16 semesters of support.

Additional data This program became effective in 1997.

Number awarded Varies each year.

Deadline August of each year for fall semester; December of each year for spring semester.

[282]
NGACT SCHOLARSHIP PROGRAM

National Guard Association of Connecticut
Attn: Scholarship Committee
360 Broad Street
Hartford, CT 06105-3795
(860) 247-5000   Fax: (860) 247-5000
E-mail: ngact2005@yahoo.com
Web: ngact.com/scholarships.html

Summary To provide financial assistance to members and the family of members of the National Guard Association of Connecticut (NGACT) who are interested in attending college in any state.

Eligibility This program is open to 1) NGACT members; 2) unmarried children and grandchildren of NGACT members; 3) spouses of NGACT members; and 4) unremarried spouses and unmarried dependent children and grandchildren of deceased NGACT members who were members in good standing at the time of their death. Applicants must be attending or planning to attend, on a part- or full-time basis, a college, university, trade school, or business school in any state. Graduate students are not eligible to apply. Along with their application, they must submit: an official transcript, a letter on their desire to continue their education and why financial assistance is required, 2 letters of recommendation, and 1 letter of academic reference. Selection is based on academic record, character, leadership, and need.

Financial Data A stipend is awarded (amount not specified). Funds are sent to the recipient but are made payable to the recipient's choice of school. To receive the awards, proof of enrollment must be presented.

Duration 1 year.

Number awarded Varies each year.

Deadline June of each year.

[283]
NGAI EDUCATIONAL GRANTS

National Guard Association of Indiana
Attn: Educational Grant Committee
2002 South Holt Road, Building 9
Indianapolis, IN 46241-4839
(317) 247-3196   Toll Free: (800) 219-2173
Fax: (317) 247-3575   E-mail: director@ngai.net
Web: ngai.net/index.php?main_page=page&id=16

Summary To provide financial assistance to members of the National Guard Association of Indiana (NGAI) and their dependents who plan to attend college in any state.

Eligibility This program is open to NGAI members who are currently serving in the Indiana National Guard and their dependents. Children and widow(er)s of former Guard members killed or permanently disabled while on duty with the Indiana National Guard are also eligible. Applicants must be attending or planning to attend a college or university in any state. Along with their application, they must submit 2 letters of recommendation, a copy of high school or college transcripts, SAT or ACT scores (if taken), a letter of acceptance from a college or university (if not currently attending college), and an essay on the educational program they intend to pursue and the goals they wish to attain. Selection is based on academic achievement, commitment and desire to achieve, extracurricular activities, accomplishments, goals, and financial need.

Financial Data The stipend is $1,000.

Duration 1 year; recipients may reapply.

Number awarded A limited number are awarded each year.

Deadline February of each year.

[284]
NGAM SCHOLARSHIPS

National Guard Association of Maryland
Attn: Scholarship Committee
P.O. Box 16675
Baltimore, MD 21221-0675
(410) 557-2606   Toll Free: (800) 844-1394
Fax: (410) 893-7529   E-mail: executivedirector@ngam.net
Web: www.ngam.net/NGAM-BenefitsScholarships.htm

Summary To provide financial assistance to current and former members of the Maryland National Guard and their dependents who are interested in attending college in any state.

Eligibility This program is open to active and retired members of the Maryland National Guard and their spouses, sons, and daughters. Applicants must be enrolled or planning to enroll in an accredited college, university, or vocational/technical school in any state on either a part-time or full-time basis. They must submit a resume in which they outline their academic background, activities in which they have participated, and honors they have received; 3 letters of recommendation; the name of the college; and information on financial need.

Financial Data The stipend is $1,000. Funds may be used for tuition, fees, and books.

Duration 1 year; recipients may reapply.

Number awarded Varies each year; recently, 6 of these scholarships were awarded.

Deadline March of each year.

[285]
NGANH SCHOLARSHIPS

National Guard Association of New Hampshire
Attn: Scholarship Committee
1 Minuteman Way
Concord, NH 03301
(603) 540-9608   E-mail: info@nganh.org
Web: www.nganh.org

Summary To provide financial assistance to members of the National Guard Association of New Hampshire and their dependents who are interested in attending college in any state.

Eligibility This program is open to current members of the National Guard Association of New Hampshire (officer, enlisted, or retired) and their dependents. Applicants must be attending or planning to attend an accredited college or university in any state. Along with their application, they must submit a 1-page essay on a topic that changes annually; recently, they were asked to give their thoughts on whether or not United States efforts to support and stabilize democratic governments in Afghanistan and Iraq will lead to greater stability in the Southwest Asian region.

Financial Data The stipend is $1,000.

Duration 1 year.

Number awarded 1 each year.

Deadline April of each year.

[286]
NGANJ SCHOLARSHIP PROGRAM

National Guard Association of New Jersey
Attn: Executive Director
P.O. Box 266
Wrightstown, NJ 08562
(973) 541-6776   Fax: (973) 541-6909
E-mail: jose.maldonado@njdmava.state.nj.us
Web: www.nganj.org

Summary To provide financial assistance to New Jersey National Guard members or their dependents who are interested in attending college or graduate school in any state.

Eligibility This program is open to active members of the New Jersey National Guard; the spouses, children, legal wards, and grandchildren of active members; and the children, legal wards, and grandchildren of retired (with at least 20 years of service) or deceased members. Applicants must be currently attending or entering an approved community college, school of nursing, or 4-year college in any state as a full-time undergraduate or graduate student. Selection is based on academic accomplishment, leadership, and citizenship.

Financial Data Stipends up to $1,000 are available.

Duration 1 year; nonrenewable.

Number awarded Varies each year; recently, 10 of these scholarships were awarded.

Deadline March of each year.

[287]
NGASC SCHOLARSHIPS

National Guard Association of South Carolina
Attn: NGASC Scholarship Foundation
132 Pickens Street
Columbia, SC 29205
(803) 254-8456   Toll Free: (800) 822-3235
Fax: (803) 254-3869   E-mail: nginfo@ngasc.org
Web: www.ngasc.org/ngasc_scholarship_foundation.htm

Summary To provide financial assistance to current and former South Carolina National Guard members and their dependents who are interested in attending college or graduate school in any state.

Eligibility This program is open to undergraduate students who are 1) current, retired, or deceased members of the South Carolina National Guard; 2) their dependents; and 3) members of the National Guard Association of South Carolina (NGASC). Graduate students are also eligible if they are members of the South Carolina National Guard. Applicants must be attending or interested in attending a college or university in any state as a full-time student. Several of the scholarships include additional restrictions on school or academic major; some are granted only for academic excellence, but most are based on both academics and financial need.

Financial Data The stipend is $1,500 or $1,000.

Duration 1 year; may be renewed up to 3 additional years.

Additional data Among the named scholarships included in this program recently were the BG (Ret) C. Norwood Gayle Memorial Scholarship Award, the CMSgt Jim Burgess Scholarship Award, the Mrs. Kaye Helgeson Memorial Scholarship Award, the LTC (Ret) Glenny J. (Jeff) Matthews Memorial Scholarship Awards, the Ron McNair Memorial Scholarship Award, the Darla Moore Scholarship Award, the Sergeants Major Watson Scholarship Award, the SCANG Chiefs Council Scholarship Award, the Chief Shepherd Pitney Bowes Scholarship Award, the Fallen Soldiers' Memorial Scholarship Award, and the South Carolina National Guard Federal Credit Union Awards.

Number awarded Varies each year. Recently, 48 of these scholarships were awarded: 1 at $1,500 and 47 at $1,000. The $1,500 scholarship and 1 of the $1,000 scholarships were based on academic excellence; the remaining $1,000 scholarships were based on both academics and financial need.

Deadline January of each year.

[288]
NGAT SCHOLARSHIP PROGRAM

National Guard Association of Texas
Attn: NGAT Educational Foundation
3706 Crawford Avenue
Austin, TX 78731-6803
(512) 454-7300   Toll Free: (800) 252-NGAT
Fax: (512) 467-6803   E-mail: rlindner@ngat.org
Web: www.ngat.org

Summary To provide financial assistance to members and dependents of members of the National Guard Association of Texas who are interested in attending college or graduate school in any state.

Eligibility This program is open to annual and life members of the association and their spouses and children (associate members and their dependents are not eligible). Applicants may be high school seniors, undergraduate students, or graduate students, either enrolled or planning to enroll at an institution of higher education in any state. Along with their application, they must submit an essay on their desire to continue their education. Selection is based on scholarship, citizenship, and leadership.

Financial Data Stipends range from $500 to $5,000.

Duration 1 year (nonrenewable).

Additional data This program includes the following named scholarships: the Thomas F. Berry Memorial Scholarship, the Len and Jean Tallas Memorial Scholarship, the Texas Military Forces Retirees Scholarship, the T-Mates Scholarship, the LTC Gary W. Parrish Memorial Scholarship, the 1SG Harry E. Lux Memorial Scholarship, the Gloria Jenell and Marlin E. Mote Endowed Scholarship, the Chief Master Sergeants Scholarship, the Sergeants Major Scholarship, and the Texas USAA Scholarship (sponsored by USAA Insurance Corporation).

Number awarded Varies each year. Recently, 10 of these scholarships were awarded: 1 at $5,000, 3 at $2,500, 1 at $2,000, 2 at $1,250, 2 at $1,000, and 1 at $500.

Deadline February of each year.

[289]
NGATN SCHOLARSHIP PROGRAM

National Guard Association of Tennessee
Attn: Scholarship Committee
4332 Kenilwood Drive
Nashville, TN 37204-4401
(615) 833-9100   Toll Free: (888) 642-8448 (within TN)
Fax: (615) 833-9173   E-mail: larry@ngatn.org
Web: www.ngatn.org

Summary To provide financial assistance for college to members or dependents of members of the National Guard Association of Tennessee (NGATN).

Eligibility This program is open to active Tennessee National Guard members and to active annual or life members of the NGATN. If no active Guard or association member qualifies, the scholarships may be awarded to the child of a Guard or association member, including life members who have retired or are deceased. All applicants must be high school seniors or graduates who meet entrance or continuation requirements at a Tennessee college or university. Selection is based on leadership in school and civic activities, motivation for continued higher education, academic achievement in high school and/or college, and financial need.

Financial Data The stipends are $1,500.

Duration 1 year.

Number awarded 6 each year: 1 to an active National Guard member; 2 to current association members or their dependents; 2 to active National Guard members or their dependents; and 1 to a current Guard member who was mobilized for Operations Desert Storm, Noble Eagle, Enduring Freedom, or Iraqi Freedom.

Deadline June of each year.

[290]
NGAUT "MINUTEMAN" SCHOLARSHIPS

National Guard Association of Utah
12953 South Minuteman Drive, Room 198
Draper, UT 84020-9286
(801) 631-6314   E-mail: ngautah@ngaut.org
Web: www.ngaut.org/Scholarship.php

Summary To provide financial assistance to members of the Utah National Guard and their dependents who are interested in attending college in the state.

Eligibility This program is open to members of the Utah National Guard and their dependents who are enrolled for at least 6 credit hours at a college or university in the state. Applicants must submit 1) a 150-word description of their educational and career goals; 2) a 200- to 300-word description of leadership and extracurricular activities that they may have had or currently enjoy; 3) a 1-page cover letter or resume; and 4) 2 letters of reference.

Financial Data The stipend is $1,000. Funds are sent to the recipient's school and must be used for tuition, laboratory fees, and curriculum-required books and supplies.

Duration 1 year.

Number awarded 5 each year.

Deadline January of each year.

[291]
NGAVT SCHOLARSHIPS

National Guard Association of Vermont
Attn: Capt John Geno, President
P.O. Box 694
Essex Junction, VT 05452
(802) 338-3397   E-mail: john.geno@us.army.mil
Web: www.ngavt.org/scholarInfo.shtml

Summary To provide financial assistance to members of the Vermont National Guard (VTNG) and their children or spouses who are interested in attending college in any state.

Eligibility This program is open to current members of the VTNG, their spouses, and their unmarried children. Applicants must be working, or planning to work, on an associate, undergraduate, or technical degree as a full-time student at a school in any state. Along with their application, they must submit an essay on their commitment to selfless public service or their plan for pursuing it in the future. Selection is based on academic performance, overall potential for a commitment to selfless public service, and financial need.

Financial Data The stipend is $1,000. Funds are sent directly to the recipient.

Duration 1 year; recipients may reapply.

Number awarded 2 each year.

Deadline June of each year.

[292]
NGOA-FL AND ENGAF SCHOLARSHIP PROGRAM

National Guard Association of Florida
Attn: Scholarship Committee
P.O. Box 3446
St. Augustine, FL 32085-3446
(904) 823-0628   Fax: (904) 839-2068
E-mail: mary.e.paul@us.army.mil
Web: www.floridaguard.org/Scholarships/Scholarships.htm

Summary To provide financial assistance to members of the Florida National Guard and their families who are also members of either the National Guard Association of Florida (NGOA-FL) or the Enlisted National Guard Association of Florida (ENGAF) and interested in attending college in the state.

Eligibility This program is open to active members of the Florida National Guard (enlisted, officer, and warrant officer), their spouses, and children, but preference is given to Guard members. Applicants must be residents of Florida attending a college, university, or vocational/technical school in the state. They must also be a member, spouse of a member, or child of a member of their respective association. Selection is based on academic achievement, civic and moral leadership, character, and financial need.

Financial Data Scholarships are $1,000 for full-time students or $500 for part-time students; funds are paid directly to the recipient's institution.

Duration 1 year; may be renewed.

Additional data This program is jointly sponsored by the respective associations.

Number awarded 15 each year.

Deadline May of each year.

[293]
NICHOLAS CARUSO MEMORIAL SCHOLARSHIP

Enlisted Association National Guard of New Jersey
Attn: Scholarship Committee
101 Eggert Crossing Road
Lawrenceville, NJ 08648-2805
(609) 562-0207   Fax: (609) 562-0283
Web: www.eang-nj.org/scholarships.html

Summary To provide financial assistance to New Jersey National Guard members and their children who are interested in attending college in any state.

Eligibility This program is open to 1) children of New Jersey National Guard members who are also members of the Enlisted Association National Guard of New Jersey, and 2) drilling Guard members who are also members of the association. Applicants must be attending or planning to attend a college or university in any state. Along with their application, they must submit 1) information on their church, school, and community activities; 2) a list of honors they have received; 3) letters of recommendation; 4) transcripts; and 5) a letter with specific facts about their desire to continue their education and specifying their career goals. Financial need is not considered in the selection process.

Financial Data The stipend is $1,000.

Duration 1 year.

Number awarded 1 each year.

Deadline May of each year.

[294]
NMIA/NMIF SCHOLARSHIP PROGRAM

National Military Intelligence Association
Attn: Scholarship Committee
256 Morris Creek Road
Cullen, VA 23934
(434) 542-5929   Fax: (703) 738-7487
E-mail: admin@nmia.org
Web: www.nmia.org/about/scholarshipprogram.html

Summary To provide financial assistance to undergraduate and graduate students majoring in a field of interest to the intelligence community.

Eligibility This program is open to full- and part-time juniors, seniors, and graduate students who are preparing for a career in a field related to the intelligence community. Applicants must list special activities, internships, prior or current military service, or other activities that provide tangible evidence of career aspirations to serve as a member of the intelligence community. Along

with their application, they must submit a 1,000-word essay that covers 1) their intelligence community career goals and objectives; 2) the relationship between courses completed, courses planned, extracurricular activities, and prior work experience (including military service) to identified career goals and objectives; and 3) how this scholarship will make a difference to their efforts to realize their career goals and aspirations. Selection is based primarily on past academic success; financial need is not considered.

Financial Data The stipend is $3,000 for full-time students or $2,000 for part-time students.

Duration 1 year; nonrenewable.

Additional data This program is offered jointly by the National Military Intelligence Association (NMIA) and the National Military Intelligence Foundation (NMIF), P.O. Box 6844, Arlington, VA 22206, E-mail: ffrank54@comcast.net

Number awarded 6 each year: 3 for full-time students and 3 for part-time students.

Deadline November each year.

[295]
NORTH CAROLINA NATIONAL GUARD TUITION ASSISTANCE PROGRAM

North Carolina National Guard
Attn: Education Services Office
4105 Reedy Creek Road
Raleigh, NC 27607-6410
(919) 664-6272   Toll Free: (800) 621-4136
Fax: (919) 664-6520   E-mail: nceso@ng.army.mil
Web: www.nc.ngb.army.mil

Summary To provide financial assistance to members of the North Carolina National Guard who plan to attend college or graduate school in the state.

Eligibility This program is open to active members of the North Carolina National Guard (officer, warrant officer, or enlisted) who have at least 2 years of enlistment remaining after the end of the academic period for which tuition assistance is provided. Applicants must be enrolled in an eligible business or trade school, private institution, or public college/university in North Carolina. They may be working on a vocational, undergraduate, graduate, or doctoral degree.

Financial Data The maximum stipend is based on the highest tuition and fees at the University of North Carolina at Chapel Hill.

Duration 1 year; may be renewed.

Number awarded Varies each year.

Deadline Deadline not specified.

[296]
NORTH DAKOTA NATIONAL GUARD FEE WAIVER

North Dakota University System
Attn: Director of Financial Aid
State Capitol, Tenth Floor
600 East Boulevard Avenue, Department 215
Bismarck, ND 58505-0230
(701) 328-4114   Fax: (701) 328-2961
E-mail: ndus.office@ndus.nodak.edu
Web: www.ndus.nodak.edu

Summary To waive tuition and fees for members of the National Guard at public institutions in North Dakota.

Eligibility Eligible for this benefit are members of the North Dakota National Guard who meet the limitations and rules established by the Guard. Applicants must be attending or planning to attend a public college or university in North Dakota.

Financial Data Qualified members are entitled to a waiver of all tuition and fees (except fees charged to retire outstanding bonds).

Duration 1 academic year; renewable.

Number awarded Varies each year.

Deadline Deadline not specified.

[297]
NORTH DAKOTA NATIONAL GUARD TUITION ASSISTANCE PROGRAM

North Dakota National Guard
Attn: Education Services Office
P.O. Box 5511
Bismarck, ND 58506-5511
(701) 333-3064   E-mail: ngndj1esos@ng.army.mil
Web: www.ndguard.ngb.army.mil

Summary To provide financial assistance to members of the North Dakota National Guard who plan to attend college or graduate school in the state.

Eligibility This program is open to members of the North Dakota National Guard who have a record of satisfactory participation (no more than 9 unexcused absences in the past 12 months) and service remaining after completion of the class for which they are requesting assistance. Applicants must be seeking support for trade or vocational training or work on an associate, baccalaureate, or graduate degree. They must be attending or planning to attend a North Dakota higher education public institution or a participating private institution (currently, Jamestown College, University of Mary in Bismarck, MedCenter One College of Nursing, Rasmussen College, or Trinity Bible College). Full-time AGR personnel do not qualify for this program. This is an entitlement program, provided all requirements are met.

Financial Data Participating colleges and universities waive 25% of tuition for eligible courses (undergraduate only), up to 25% of the tuition at the University of North Dakota. This program provides reimbursement of 75% of tuition for eligible courses (undergraduate and graduate), or up to 75% of the tuition at the University of North Dakota. The program also reimburses 100% of all regular fees, not to exceed 100% of the regular fees charged by the University of North Dakota.

Duration Benefits are available for up to 144 semester credit hours or the completion of an undergraduate or graduate degree, provided the recipient earns a grade of "C" or higher in each undergraduate course or "B" or higher in each graduate course.

Number awarded Varies each year.

Deadline Applications should be submitted at least 30 days before the semester begins.

[298]
NUCLEAR PROPULSION OFFICER CANDIDATE (NUPOC) PROGRAM

U.S. Navy
Attn: Navy Personnel Command
5722 Integrity Drive
Millington, TN 38054-5057
(901) 874-3070   Toll Free: (888) 633-9674
Fax: (901) 874-2651   E-mail: nukeprograms@cnrc.navy.mil
Web: www.cnrc.navy.mil/nucfield/college/officer_options.htm

Summary To provide financial assistance to college juniors and seniors who wish to serve in the Navy's nuclear propulsion training program following graduation.

Eligibility This program is open to U.S. citizens who are entering their junior or senior year of college as a full-time student. Strong technical majors (mathematics, physics, chemistry, or an engineering field) are encouraged but not required. Applicants must have completed at least 1 year of calculus and 1 year of physics and must have earned a grade of "C" or better in all mathematics, science, and technical courses. Normally, they must be 26 years of age or younger at the expected date of commissioning, although applicants for the design and research specialty may be up to 29 years old.

Financial Data Participants become Active Reserve enlisted Navy personnel and receive a salary of up to $2,500 per month; the exact amount depends on the local cost of living and other fac-

tors. A bonus of $10,000 is also paid at the time of enlistment and another $2,000 upon completion of nuclear power training.

Duration Up to 30 months, until completion of a bachelor's degree.

Additional data Following graduation, participants attend Officer Candidate School in Pensacola, Florida for 4 months and receive their commissions. They have a service obligation of 8 years (of which at least 5 years must be on active duty), beginning with 6 months at the Navy Nuclear Power Training Command in Charleston, South Carolina and 6 more months of hands-on training at a nuclear reactor facility. Further information on this program is available from a local Navy recruiter or the Navy Recruiting Command, 801 North Randolph Street, Arlington, VA 22203-1991.

Number awarded Varies each year.

Deadline Deadline not specified.

[299]
NUCLEAR (SUBMARINE AND SURFACE) OPTION OF THE SEAMAN TO ADMIRAL-21 PROGRAM

U.S. Navy
Attn: Commander, Naval Service Training Command
250 Dallas Street, Suite A
Pensacola, FL 32508-5268
(850) 452-9563   Fax: (850) 452-2486
E-mail: PNSC_STA21@navy.mil
Web: www.sta-21.navy.mil

Summary To allow outstanding enlisted Navy personnel to complete a bachelor's degree and receive a commission in the nuclear officer community.

Eligibility This program is open to U.S. citizens who are currently serving on active duty in the U.S. Navy or Naval Reserve, including Full Time Support (FTS), Selected Reserves (SELRES), and Navy Reservists on active duty except for those on active duty for training (ACDUTRA). Only personnel currently enrolled in the Naval Nuclear Power School or Naval Nuclear Power Training Unit or assigned there as staff pickup instructors or sea returnee instructors are eligible. Applicants must be high school graduates (or GED recipients) who are able to complete requirements for a baccalaureate degree in 36 months or less. When they complete their degree requirements, they must be younger than 26 years of age. Sea returnee staff instructors must finish prior to their 31st birthday. Applicants must have taken the SAT or ACT test within the past 3 years and achieved a score of 1140 or higher on the new SAT or 50 or higher on the ACT. Their proposed college major must be in a technical area. The program is open to men and women, but women are not assigned to submarines.

Financial Data Awardees continue to receive their regular Navy pay and allowances while they attend college on a full-time basis. They also receive reimbursement for tuition, fees, and books up to $10,000 per year. If base housing is available, they are eligible to live there. Participants are not eligible to receive benefits under the Navy's Tuition Assistance Program (TA), the Montgomery GI Bill (MGIB), the Navy College Fund, or the Veterans Educational Assistance Program (VEAP).

Duration Selectees are supported for up to 36 months of full-time, year-round study or completion of a bachelor's degree, as long as they maintain a GPA of 3.0 or higher.

Additional data This program was established in 2001 as a replacement for the Nuclear Enlisted Commissioning Program (NECP). Upon acceptance into the program, selectees attend the Naval Science Institute (NSI) in Newport, Rhode Island for an 8-week program in the fundamental core concepts of being a naval officer (navigation, engineering, weapons, military history and justice, etc.). They then enter 1 of 18 universities with an NROTC nuclear unit (University of Arizona, Auburn University, The Citadel, University of Idaho, University of Illinois, University of Kansas, University of New Mexico, North Carolina State University, Oregon State University, Pennsylvania State University, Purdue University, Southern University and A&M College, SUNY Maritime College, University of South Carolina, University of Texas, University of Utah, University of Washington, or University of Wisconsin) to work full time on a bachelor's degree. They become members of and drill with the NROTC unit. When they complete their degree, they are commissioned as ensigns in the United States Naval Reserve and assigned to initial training for their nuclear officer community. After commissioning, participants incur an active-duty obligation of 5 years.

Number awarded Varies each year.

Deadline June of each year.

[300]
NURSE CORPS OPTION OF THE SEAMAN TO ADMIRAL-21 PROGRAM

U.S. Navy
Attn: Commander, Naval Service Training Command
250 Dallas Street, Suite A
Pensacola, FL 32508-5268
(850) 452-9563   Fax: (850) 452-2486
E-mail: PNSC_STA21@navy.mil
Web: www.sta-21.navy.mil

Summary To allow outstanding enlisted Navy personnel to complete a bachelor's degree and receive a commission in the Nurse Corps.

Eligibility This program is open to U.S. citizens who are currently serving on active duty in the U.S. Navy or Naval Reserve, including Full Time Support (FTS), Selected Reserves (SEL-RES), and Navy Reservists on active duty except for those on active duty for training (ACDUTRA). Applicants must be high school graduates (or GED recipients) who are able to complete requirements for a baccalaureate degree in nursing in 36 months or less. They must have completed at least 30 semester units in undergraduate nursing prerequisite courses with a GPA of 2.5 or higher. They must be at least 18 years of age and able to complete degree requirements and be commissioned prior to age 42. Within the past 3 years, they must have taken the SAT test (and achieved scores of at least 500 on the mathematics section and 500 on the critical reading section) or the ACT test (and achieved a score of 41 or higher, including at least 21 on the mathematics portion and 20 on the English portion).

Financial Data Awardees continue to receive their regular Navy pay and allowances while they attend college on a full-time basis. They also receive reimbursement for tuition, fees, and books up to $10,000 per year. If base housing is available, they are eligible to live there. Participants are not eligible to receive benefits under the Navy's Tuition Assistance Program (TA), the Montgomery GI Bill (MGIB), the Navy College Fund, or the Veterans Educational Assistance Program (VEAP).

Duration Selectees are supported for up to 36 months of full-time, year-round study or completion of a bachelor's degree, as long as they maintain a GPA of 2.5 or higher.

Additional data This program was established in 2001 as a replacement for the Fleet Accession to Naval Reserve Officer Training Corps (NROTC) Nurse Option. Upon acceptance into the program, selectees attend the Naval Science Institute (NSI) in Newport, Rhode Island for an 8-week program in the fundamental core concepts of being a naval officer (navigation, engineering, weapons, military history and justice, etc.). They then enter an NROTC affiliated college or university with a nursing program that confers an accredited baccalaureate degree in nursing to pursue full-time study. They become members of and drill with the NROTC unit. When they complete their bachelor's degree in nursing, they are commissioned as ensigns in the United States Naval Reserve and assigned to initial training as an officer in the Nurse Corps. After commissioning, 5 years of active service are required.

Number awarded Varies each year.

Deadline June of each year.

[301]
OHIO NATIONAL GUARD ENLISTED ASSOCIATION SCHOLARSHIP PROGRAM

Ohio National Guard Enlisted Association
1299 Virginia Avenue
Columbus, OH 43212
(740) 574-5932   Toll Free: (800) 642-6642
Fax: (614) 486-2216   E-mail: ongea@juno.com
Web: www.ongea.org

Summary To provide financial assistance to members of the Ohio National Guard Enlisted Association (ONGEA) and children of members of the ONGEA Auxiliary who are interested in attending college in any state.

Eligibility This program is open to 1) sons and daughters of ONGEA Auxiliary members (spouse must have at least 1 year remaining on his/her enlistment following the completion of the school year for which the application is submitted); 2) unmarried dependent sons and daughters of deceased ONGEA and ONGEA Auxiliary members who were in good standing the time of their death; and 3) ONGEA members. Spouses of ONGEA members must also be a member of the ONGEA Auxiliary in order for a dependent to be considered for this award (unless the ONGEA member is a single parent). Applicants must be enrolling as full-time undergraduate students at a college, university, trade school, or business school in any state. Graduate students are not eligible. All applications must be accompanied by a transcript of high school and (if appropriate) college credits, a letter from the applicant describing educational goals and financial need, 3 letters of recommendation, and a copy of the current membership cards of both parents or current membership card of the single parent. Selection is based on academic record, character, leadership, and financial need.

Financial Data Stipends are $1,000 or $500. After verification of enrollment is provided, checks are sent to the recipient and made out to the recipient's school.

Duration 1 year; nonrenewable.

Additional data This program is sponsored jointly by ONGEA, the ONGEA Auxiliary, USAA Insurance Corporation, and the First Cleveland Cavalry Association.

Number awarded 5 to 10 each year, depending upon the availability of funds.

Deadline February of each year.

[302]
OHIO NATIONAL GUARD SCHOLARSHIP PROGRAM

Adjutant General's Department
Attn: ONG Scholarship Program Office
2825 West Dublin Granville Road
Columbus, OH 43235-2789
(614) 336-7032   Toll Free: (888) 400-6484
Fax: (614) 336-7318   E-mail: ongsp@ongsp.org
Web: www.ongsp.org

Summary To provide financial assistance to members of the Ohio National Guard interested in working on a college degree.

Eligibility This program is open to members of the Ohio Army and Air National Guard attending a 2- or 4-year public college or university in the state. Applicants must commit to and/or complete a 6-year enlistment in the Ohio Guard. New enlistees must complete basic training and obtain a military job skill.

Financial Data The program covers 100% of the tuition and general fee charges at state-assisted 2- and 4-year colleges and universities in Ohio.

Duration The grant is limited to 12 quarters or 8 semesters and participants must remain enrolled as a full-time undergraduate student for that time. Enrollment in the institution of higher education must begin not later than 12 months after the completion of Initial Active Duty for Training (IADT), or date of reenlistment, or date of extension of current enlistment.

Additional data This program was established in 1999. Grant assistance is not available for an additional baccalaureate degree, for postgraduate courses, or for courses not applicable to a degree.

Number awarded Grants are limited to the annual average student load of 4,000 full-time equivalent students per term.

Deadline June for fall term; October for winter quarter or spring semester; January for spring quarter; and March for summer term.

[303]
OKLAHOMA NATIONAL GUARD TUITION WAIVER PROGRAM

Oklahoma State Regents for Higher Education
Attn: Director of Scholarship and Grant Programs
655 Research Parkway, Suite 200
P.O. Box 108850
Oklahoma City, OK 73101-8850
(405) 225-9239 Toll Free: (800) 858-1840
Fax: (405) 225-9230 E-mail: studentinfo@osrhe.edu
Web: www.okhighered.org

Summary To provide financial assistance to members of the Oklahoma National Guard who plan to attend college in the state.

Eligibility This program is open to current members in good standing of the Oklahoma National Guard who do not have any other baccalaureate or graduate degree. Applicants must be attending or planning to attend a state-supported college or university in Oklahoma to work on an associate or baccalaureate degree. They must have submitted a plan for completion of their degree to the Guard. Courses leading to a certification, continuing education courses, and career technology courses that are not counted towards a degree at another institution are not covered.

Financial Data Under this program, all tuition is waived.

Duration 1 year; may be renewed as long as the Guard member remains in good standing both in the unit and in the college or university, to a maximum of 6 years from the date of first application.

Number awarded Varies each year.

Deadline Deadline not specified.

[304]
OREGON NATIONAL GUARD ASSOCIATION SCHOLARSHIPS

Oregon National Guard Association
Attn: Scholarship Committee
1776 Militia Way, S.E.
P.O. Box 14350
Salem, OR 97309-5047
(503) 584-3030 Fax: (503) 584-3052
E-mail: info@ornga.org
Web: ornga.org/scholar_apply.htm

Summary To provide financial assistance to members of the Oregon National Guard, the Oregon National Guard Association (ORNGA), and their children and spouses who are interested in attending college in any state.

Eligibility This program is open to active members of the Oregon Army and Air National Guard, members of the ORNGA, and their children and spouses. Applicants must be high school seniors, graduates, or GED recipients and interested in working on an undergraduate degree at a college or university in any state. The parent, spouse, or applicant must have an ETS date beyond the end of the academic year for which the scholarship is used. Selection is based on participation in school and civic activities,

motivation for continued higher education, and academic achievement in high school and/or college.

Financial Data The stipend is $1,000.

Duration 1 year.

Number awarded 1 or more each year.

Deadline January of each year.

[305]
PENNSYLVANIA NATIONAL GUARD EDUCATIONAL ASSISTANCE PROGRAM

Pennsylvania Higher Education Assistance Agency
Attn: State Grant and Special Programs
1200 North Seventh Street
P.O. Box 8114
Harrisburg, PA 17105-8114
(717) 720-2800 Toll Free: (800) 692-7392
TDD: (800) 654-5988 E-mail: info@pheaa.org
Web: www.pheaa.org

Summary To provide scholarship/loans for college or graduate school to Pennsylvania National Guard members.

Eligibility This program is open to active members of the Pennsylvania National Guard who are Pennsylvania residents and serving as enlisted personnel, warrant officers, or commissioned officers of any grade. Applicants must accept an obligation to serve in the Pennsylvania National Guard for a period of 6 years from the date of entry into the program. Students who do not possess a baccalaureate degree must be enrolled full or part time in an approved program of education at an approved institution of higher learning in Pennsylvania. Master's degree students are supported on a part-time basis only. Guard members receiving an ROTC scholarship of any type are not eligible.

Financial Data Full-time undergraduate students receive payment of 100% of tuition at a state-owned university (recently, $5,554 per year). Part-time students receive either actual tuition charged or two-thirds of the full-time tuition charged to a Pennsylvania resident at a state-owned university (recently, $3,702 per year), whichever is less. Graduate students receive either half the actual tuition charged or one-third of the full-time tuition charged to a Pennsylvania resident at a state-owned university (recently, $1,851 per year), whichever is less. Recipients who fail to fulfill the service obligation must repay all funds received within 10 years, including interest at 7%.

Duration Up to 5 years.

Additional data This program, first offered in 1997, is jointly administered by the Pennsylvania Department of Military and Veterans Affairs and the Pennsylvania Higher Education Assistance Agency. Support for summer and graduate school is available only if funding permits.

Number awarded Varies each year; recently, 1,789 members of the Pennsylvania National Guard were enrolled in this program.

Deadline June of each year for fall semester; October of each year for spring semester; May of each year for summer school.

[306]
PENNSYLVANIA NATIONAL GUARD SCHOLARSHIP FUND

Pennsylvania National Guard Associations
Attn: Executive Director
Biddle Hall
Fort Indiantown Gap
Annville, PA 17003-5002
(717) 865-9631 Toll Free: (800) 997-8885
Fax: (717) 861-5560 E-mail: oswalddean@aol.com
Web: www.pngas.net/member.htm

Summary To provide financial assistance to Pennsylvania National Guard members and the children of disabled or deceased members who are interested in attending college in any state.

Eligibility This program is open to active members of the Pennsylvania Army or Air National Guard. Children of members of the Guard who died or were permanently disabled while on Guard duty are also eligible. Applicants must be entering their first year of higher education as a full-time student or presently attending a college or vocational school in any state as a full-time student. Along with their application, they must submit an essay that outlines their military and civilian plans for the future. Selection is based on that essay, academic achievement, leadership abilities, and contributions to citizenship.

Financial Data Stipends are $1,000 or $400.

Duration 1 year.

Additional data The sponsoring organization includes the National Guard Association of Pennsylvania and the Pennsylvania National Guard Enlisted Association. This program began in 1977.

Number awarded 23 each year: 3 at $1,000 and 20 at $400.

Deadline June of each year.

[307]
PILOT OPTION OF THE SEAMAN TO ADMIRAL-21 PROGRAM

U.S. Navy
Attn: Commander, Naval Service Training Command
250 Dallas Street, Suite A
Pensacola, FL 32508-5268
(850) 452-9563　　　　　　　Fax: (850) 452-2486
E-mail: PNSC_STA21@navy.mil
Web: www.sta-21.navy.mil

Summary To allow outstanding enlisted Navy personnel to complete a bachelor's degree and receive a commission as a pilot.

Eligibility This program is open to U.S. citizens who are currently serving on active duty in the U.S. Navy or Naval Reserve, including Full Time Support (FTS), Selected Reserves (SEL-RES), and Navy Reservists on active duty except for those on active duty for training (ACDUTRA). Applicants must be high school graduates (or GED recipients) who are able to complete requirements for a baccalaureate degree in 36 months or less. When they complete their degree requirements, they must be younger than 27 years of age (may be adjusted to 29 years of age for prior active-duty service). Within the past 3 years, they must have taken the SAT test (and achieved scores of at least 500 on the mathematics section and 500 on the critical reading section) or the ACT test (and achieved a score of 41 or higher, including at least 21 on the mathematics portion and 20 on the English portion). They must also achieve a score of at least the following: AQR (4), PFAR (5) on the Pilot Flight Aptitude Rating (PFAR) portions of the Aviation Selection Test Battery.

Financial Data Awardees continue to receive their regular Navy pay and allowances while they attend college on a full-time basis. They also receive reimbursement for tuition, fees, and books up to $10,000 per year. If base housing is available, they are eligible to live there. Participants are not eligible to receive benefits under the Navy's Tuition Assistance Program (TA), the Montgomery GI Bill (MGIB), the Navy College Fund, or the Veterans Educational Assistance Program (VEAP).

Duration Selectees are supported for up to 36 months of full-time, year-round study or completion of a bachelor's degree, as long as they maintain a GPA of 2.5 or higher.

Additional data This program was established in 2001 as a replacement for the Aviation Enlisted Commissioning Program (AECP). Upon acceptance into the program, selectees attend the Naval Science Institute (NSI) in Newport, Rhode Island for an 8-week program in the fundamental core concepts of being a naval officer (navigation, engineering, weapons, military history and justice, etc.). They then enter a college or university with an NROTC unit or affiliation to work full time on a bachelor's degree. They become members of and drill with the NROTC unit. When they complete their degree, they are commissioned as ensigns in the United States Naval Reserve and assigned to flight training. After commissioning, participants incur an active-duty obligation of 8 years after designation as a Naval Aviator or 6 years from the date of disenrollment from flight training.

Number awarded Varies each year.

Deadline June of each year.

[308]
PLATOON LEADERS CLASS MARINE CORPS TUITION ASSISTANCE PROGRAM

U.S. Marine Corps
Attn: Marine Corps Recruiting Command
3280 Russell Road
Quantico, VA 22134-5103
(703) 784-9449　　　　　　　Fax: (703) 784-9859
E-mail: wendelrf@mcrc.usmc.mil
Web: www.usmc.mil

Summary To provide financial assistance to members of the Marine Corps Reserves interested in working on a bachelor's or law degree.

Eligibility This program is open to members of the Marine Corps Reserves enrolled full time in a bachelor's or law (J.D. or equivalent) degree program. Applicants must be a member of the Marine Corps Platoon Leader Class (PLC) Program and have completed 6 weeks (or more) of military training required by that program. They must agree to accept a commission in the active-duty Marine Corps and serve 5 years following completion of their degree.

Financial Data This program provides reimbursement of tuition, books, and required fees, up to a maximum of $5,200 per academic year. If participants are also members of the Marine Corps Reserves, they may use any Montgomery GI Bill benefits to which they are entitled.

Duration Up to 3 consecutive years, or completion of a bachelor's or law degree.

Additional data Participants who successfully obtain a bachelor's or law degree and complete officer candidate training are commissioned as second lieutenants in the Regular Marine Corps. This program was established in 1999.

Number awarded Up to 1,200 each year.

Deadline December of each year.

[309]
POST-9/11 GI BILL

Department of Veterans Affairs
Attn: Veterans Benefits Administration
810 Vermont Avenue, N.W.
Washington, DC 20420
(202) 418-4343　　　　　　　Toll Free: (888) GI-BILL1
Web: www.gibill.va.gov

Summary To provide financial assistance to veterans or military personnel who entered service on or after September 11, 2001.

Eligibility This program is open to current and former military who served on active duty for at least 90 aggregate days after September 11, 2001. Applicants must be planning to enroll at an accredited college or university as an undergraduate or graduate student; study in a certificate program, on-the-job training, apprenticeship program, flight training, and non-college degree course study do not qualify for support.

Financial Data Active-duty personnel receive payment of tuition and fees, up to the level of tuition and fees at the most expensive public institution of higher learning in their state of residence; the actual amount depends on the state of residence and the length of service completed. Veterans also receive a monthly housing allowance based on the Basic Allowance for Housing (BAH) for an E-5 with dependents if the location of the school they are attending is in the United States (or $1,333 per month at schools in foreign countries); an annual book allowance of $1,000; and (for participants who live in a rural county remote from an educational institution) a rural benefit payment of $500 per year.

Duration Most participants receive up to 36 months of entitlement under this program.

Additional data This program began in 2009 as a replacement for previous educational programs for veterans and military personnel (e.g., Montgomery GI Bill, REAP). Current participants in those programs may be able to utilize benefits under those programs and this new plan. Further information is available from local armed forces recruiters. This is the latest VA education program, referred to as Chapter 33.

Number awarded Varies each year.

Deadline Deadline not specified.

[310]
PROFESSIONAL OFFICER COURSE EARLY RELEASE PROGRAM

U.S. Air Force
Attn: Headquarters AFROTC/RRUE
Enlisted Commissioning Section
551 East Maxwell Boulevard
Maxwell AFB, AL 36112-5917
(334) 953-2091   Toll Free: (866) 4-AFROTC
Fax: (334) 953-6167   E-mail: enlisted@afrotc.com
Web: www.afoats.af.mil

Summary To allow selected enlisted Air Force personnel to earn a baccalaureate degree by providing financial assistance for full-time college study as an ROTC cadet.

Eligibility Eligible to participate in this program are enlisted members of the Air Force under the age of 30 (or otherwise able to be commissioned before becoming 35 years of age) who have completed at least 1 year on continuous active duty, have served on station for at least 1 year, and have no more than 2 years remaining to complete their initial baccalaureate degree. Scholarship applicants must be younger than 31 years of age when they graduate and earn their commission. All applicants must have been accepted at a college or university offering the AFROTC 4-year program and must have a cumulative college GPA of 2.5 or higher. Their Air Force Officer Qualifying Test (AFOQT) scores must be at least 15 on the verbal and 10 on the quantitative. Applicants who have not completed 24 units of college work must have an ACT composite score of 24 or higher or an SAT combined critical reading and mathematics score of 1100 or higher. U.S. citizenship is required. Recently, priority was given to students in the following technical majors: architecture, chemistry, computer science, engineering (especially aeronautical, aerospace, architectural, astronautical, civil, computer, electrical, environmental, and mechanical), mathematics, meteorology/atmospheric sciences, operations research, and physics.

Financial Data Participants receive a stipend of $450 to $500 per month and an allowance of $900 per year for books. No other scholarship funding is provided.

Duration 2 years (no more and no less).

Additional data Upon completing their degree, selectees are commissioned as officers in the Air Force with a 4-year service obligation. Further information is available from base education service officers or an Air Force ROTC unit. Recipients must attend a school with annual tuition and fees less than $15,000 per year. They are not allowed to pay the difference to attend a higher cost school.

Number awarded Varies each year.

Deadline October of each year.

[311]
REAR ADMIRAL BENJAMIN T. HACKER, USN MEMORIAL SCHOLARSHIP

National Naval Officers Association-Washington, D.C.
  Chapter
Attn: Scholarship Program
2701 Park Center Drive, A1108
Alexandria, VA 22302
(703) 566-3840   Fax: (703) 566-3813
E-mail: Stephen.Williams@Navy.mil
Web: dcnnoa.memberlodge.com/Default.aspx?pageId=309002

Summary To provide financial assistance to minority high school seniors from the Washington, D.C. area who are interested in attending an Historically Black College or University (HBCU) in any state and enrolling in the Navy Reserve Officers Training Corps (NROTC) program.

Eligibility This program is open to minority seniors graduating from high schools in the Washington, D.C. metropolitan area who plan to enroll full time at an HBCU in any state that has an NROTC program; they may enroll at another college or university that shares the NROTC unit located at an HBCU. Applicants must have a GPA of 2.5 or higher and be U.S. citizens or permanent residents. Selection is based on academic achievement, community involvement, and financial need.

Financial Data The stipend is $1,500.

Duration 1 year; nonrenewable.

Additional data If the recipient fails to enroll in the NROTC unit, all scholarship funds must be returned.

Number awarded 1 each year.

Deadline March of each year.

[312]
REDUCED TUITION FOR SOUTH DAKOTA NATIONAL GUARD MEMBERS

South Dakota Board of Regents
Attn: Scholarship Committee
306 East Capitol Avenue, Suite 200
Pierre, SD 57501-2545
(605) 773-3455   Fax: (605) 773-2422
E-mail: info@sdbor.edu
Web: www.sdbor.edu

Summary To provide financial assistance for college to members of the South Dakota National Guard.

Eligibility Eligible to apply for this assistance are members of the South Dakota Army or Air National Guard who are South Dakota residents, have satisfactorily completed Initial Active Duty for Training (IADT), meet the entrance requirements at 1 of the 6 state educational institutions or 4 state vocational/technical schools, attend 90% of drills and training periods, and maintain a satisfactory academic grade level.

Financial Data Qualifying Guard members are eligible for a 50% reduction in tuition at any state-supported postsecondary institution in South Dakota.

Duration This assistance is available for up to 4 academic years.

Additional data Students participating in the Army Continuing Education Systems (ACES) or the Montgomery GI Bill are not authorized to use this program.

Number awarded Varies each year.

Deadline Deadline not specified.

[313]
RESERVE EDUCATIONAL ASSISTANCE PROGRAM

Department of Veterans Affairs
Attn: Veterans Benefits Administration
810 Vermont Avenue, N.W.
Washington, DC 20420
(202) 418-4343   Toll Free: (888) GI-BILL1
Web: www.gibill.va.gov/GI_Bill_Info/benefits.htm

Summary To provide financial assistance for college or graduate school to members of the Reserves or National Guard who are called to active duty during a period of national emergency.

Eligibility Eligible to apply are members of the Reserve elements of the Army, Navy, Air Force, Marine Corps, and Coast Guard, as well as the Army National Guard and the Air National Guard. To be eligible, a Reservist must 1) have a 6-year obligation to serve in the Selected Reserves signed after June 30, 1985 (or, if an officer, agree to serve 6 years in addition to the original obligation); 2) complete Initial Active Duty for Training (IADT); 3) meet the requirements for a high school diploma or equivalent certificate before completing IADT; and 4) remain in good standing in a drilling Selected Reserve unit. Reservists who enlisted after June 30, 1985 can receive benefits for undergraduate degrees, graduate training, or technical courses leading to certificates at colleges and universities. Reservists whose 6-year commitment began after September 30, 1990 may also use these benefits for a certificate or diploma from business, technical, or vocational schools; cooperative training; apprenticeship or on-the-job training; correspondence courses; independent study programs; tutorial assistance; remedial, deficiency, or refresher training; flight training; or state-approved alternative teacher certification programs.

Financial Data For full-time study at a college or university, the current monthly rate is $528.40 for personnel with consecutive service of 90 days but less than 1 year, $792.60 for personnel with consecutive service of more than 1 year but less than 2 years, or $1,056.80 for those with consecutive service of 2 years or more. Reduced rates apply for part-time college or university study, apprenticeship and on-the-job training, licensing and certification training, cooperative education, correspondence courses, and flight training.

Duration Up to 36 months for full-time study, 48 months for three-quarter study, 72 months for half-time study, or 144 months for less than half-time study.

Additional data This program is frequently referred to as Chapter 1607. Benefits end 10 years from the date the Reservist became eligible for the program. The Department of Veterans Affairs (VA) may extend the 10-year period if the individual could not train because of a disability caused by Selected Reserve service. Certain individuals separated from the Selected Reserve due to downsizing of the military between October 1, 1991 and September 30, 1999 will also have the full 10 years to use their benefits.

Number awarded Varies each year.

Deadline Applications may be submitted at any time.

[314]
RHODE ISLAND NATIONAL GUARD STATE TUITION ASSISTANCE PROGRAM

Rhode Island National Guard
Joint Force Headquarters
Attn: Education Service Officer
645 New London Avenue
Cranston, RI 02920-3097
(401) 275-4109   Fax: (401) 275-4014
E-mail: NGRIeduc@ngb.army.mil
Web: states.ng.mil/sites/RI/education/default.aspx

Summary To provide financial support to members of the National Guard in Rhode Island interested in attending college or graduate school in the state.

Eligibility This program is open to active members of the Rhode Island National Guard in good standing who are currently satisfactorily participating in all unit training assemblies and annual training periods. Applicants must have at least 1 year of service remaining. They must be enrolled in or planning to enroll in an associate, bachelor's, or master's degree program at a public institution in the state.

Financial Data Qualified Guard members receive payment of tuition for up to 5 courses per semester.

Duration 1 semester; may be renewed.

Additional data This program was established in 1999.

Number awarded Varies each year.

Deadline Deadline not specified.

[315]
RHODE ISLAND NATIONAL GUARD STATE TUITION EXEMPTION PROGRAM

Rhode Island National Guard
Joint Force Headquarters
Attn: Education Service Officer
645 New London Avenue
Cranston, RI 02920-3097
(401) 275-4109   Fax: (401) 275-4014
E-mail: NGRIeduc@ngb.army.mil
Web: states.ng.mil/sites/RI/education/default.aspx

Summary To provide financial support to members of the Rhode Island National Guard who attend public institutions in the state.

Eligibility This program is open to active members of the Rhode Island National Guard who attend all required unit training assemblies and annual training. Applicants must be residents of Rhode Island working toward an associate, bachelors, or master's degree at a designated public institution in the state. They must pass the Guard's height and weight standards, weapons qualification, and the APFT. They may not have more than 4 unexcused absences from military duty within a 12-month period or have tested positive for any illegal drug.

Financial Data Qualified Guard members are entitled to tuition-free classes at public institutions in Rhode Island. The waiver does not cover books or fees.

Duration Upon enrollment, Guard members are entitled to 2 tuition-free classes per year.

Additional data This program was established in 1994. The designated institutions are the University of Rhode Island, Rhode Island College, and the Community College of Rhode Island.

Number awarded Varies each year.

Deadline Deadline not specified.

[316]
ROBERT H. CONNAL EDUCATION AWARDS

Enlisted Association of the New York National Guard, Inc.
Attn: Education Awards Chair
330 Old Niskayuna Road
Latham, NY 12110-2224
(518) 344-2670   E-mail: awards@eanyng.org
Web: www.eanyng.org/AwardsandScholarships.html

Summary To provide financial assistance to members of the Enlisted Association of the New York National Guard (EANYNG) and their families who are interested in attending college in any state.

Eligibility This program is open to EANYNG members and their spouses, children, and grandchildren. Applicants must be high school seniors or current undergraduate at a college or university in any state. The applicant or sponsor must have belonged to EANYNG for more than 1 year. Membership in EANYNG is limited to enlisted personnel in the New York Air or Army National Guard. Selection is based on academic achievement, community service, extracurricular activities, and leadership abilities.

Financial Data Stipends are $1,000 or $500.
Duration 1 year.
Additional data Funding for this program is provided by the production of the association's yearly journal, members' dues, and a donation from USAA Insurance Corporation.
Number awarded 7 each year: 1 statewide scholarship at $1,000 and 6 at $500 in each region of the state.
Deadline February of each year.

[317]
ROSAMOND P. HAEBERLE MEMORIAL SCHOLARSHIP

Daughters of the American Revolution-Michigan State
  Society
c/o Toni Barger, Memorial Scholarship Committee
130 Lake Region Circle
Winter Haven, FL 33881-9535
(863) 326-1687   E-mail: tonibarger@aol.com
Web: www.michigandar.org/scholarships.htm

Summary To provide financial assistance to Michigan veterans and military personnel interested in attending college in the state.
Eligibility This program is open to residents of Michigan who have served on active duty in the U.S. armed forces (including Reserves and National Guard) for at least 6 continuous months and are either currently serving in the armed forces or have received a separation from active duty under honorable conditions. Applicants must be currently accepted to and/or enrolled at a 2-year or 4-year accredited college, university, or technical/trade school in Michigan. They must be enrolled at least half time and have a cumulative high school or undergraduate GPA of 2.5 or higher. Along with their application, they must submit a 1-page essay on what serving their country has meant to them and how it has influenced their future goals and priorities. Selection is based on academic performance, extracurricular activities, community service, potential to succeed in an academic environment, financial need, and military service record.
Financial Data The stipend is $1,500.
Duration 1 year.
Additional data This program was established in 2007.
Number awarded 1 each year.
Deadline March of each year.

[318]
RSF MEMORIAL SCHOLARSHIP

Missouri Society of Professional Engineers
Attn: MSPE Educational Foundation
200 East McCarty Street, Suite 200
Jefferson City, MO 65101-3113
(573) 636-4861   Toll Free: (888) 666-4861
Fax: (573) 636-5475   E-mail: marladay@mspe.org
Web: www.mspe.org/edfoundation.html

Summary To provide financial assistance to military personnel and veterans who are residents of any state and currently studying engineering at selected universities in Missouri.
Eligibility This program is open to military personnel (including active, National Guard, and Reserves), ROTC cadets, and veterans who are residents of any state. Applicants must be sophomores or juniors currently enrolled in or planning to transfer to an engineering program at 1 of the following institutions in Missouri: University of Missouri, College of Engineering, Columbia; University of Missouri, School of Engineering, Kansas City; Missouri University of Science and Technology, School of Engineering, Rolla; Missouri University of Science and Technology, School of Materials, Energy, and Earth Resources, Rolla; University of Missouri St. Louis/Washington University Joint Undergraduate Engineering Program; Southeast Missouri State University, Engineering Physics Program, Cape Girardeau; and Washington University, School of Engineering and Applied Sciences, St. Louis.

Along with their application, they must submit a 1,000-word essay on their interest in engineering, their major area of study and area of specialization, the occupation they propose to pursue after graduation, their long-term goals, and how they hope to achieve those. Selection is based on the essay (10 points), academic achievement (5 points), extracurricular college or community activities (5 points), work experience (10 points), recommendations (10 points), and financial need (10 points). U.S. citizenship is required.
Financial Data The stipend is $2,000.
Duration 1 year.
Number awarded 1 each year.
Deadline December of each year.

[319]
SAN FRANCISCO BAY AREA NDTA VETERANS MERIT SCHOLARSHIP

National Defense Transportation Association-San Francisco
  Bay Area Chapter
Attn: Scholarship Committee
2750 North Texas Street, Suite 140
Fairfield, CA 94533
E-mail: c_madison@msn.com
Web: ndta-sf.org/scholarship_information

Summary To provide financial assistance to veterans and military personnel in California who are majoring in a field related to transportation at a school in any state.
Eligibility This program is open to military personnel on active duty and veterans who have been on active duty within the past 5 years. Applicants must be residents of California and enrolled or planning to enroll in an undergraduate or vocational program at an accredited institution in any state with a major in transportation, logistics, business, marketing, engineering, planning, or environment. They must be preparing for a career related to transportation. Along with their application, they must submit a certified copy of their high school or college transcript, 3 letters of recommendation, and a 1-page essay detailing their career goals and ambitions (with an emphasis on transportation and related areas). Selection is based on academic ability, professional interest, and community involvement.
Financial Data The stipend is $1,000.
Duration 1 year.
Number awarded 1 or more each year.
Deadline May of each year.

[320]
SCHOLARSHIPS FOR OUTSTANDING AIRMEN TO ROTC (SOAR)

U.S. Air Force
Attn: Headquarters AFROTC/RRUE
Enlisted Commissioning Section
551 East Maxwell Boulevard
Maxwell AFB, AL 36112-5917
(334) 953-2091   Toll Free: (866) 4-AFROTC
Fax: (334) 953-6167   E-mail: enlisted@afrotc.com
Web: www.afoats.af.mil/AFROTC/EnlistedComm/SOAR.asp

Summary To allow selected enlisted Air Force personnel to earn a bachelor's degree by providing financial assistance for full-time college study.
Eligibility Eligible to participate in this program are enlisted members of the Air Force who have completed from 1 to 6 years of active duty and have at least 1 year time-on-station. Candidates must be nominated by their commanding officers and be accepted at a college or university offering the AFROTC 4-year program. Airmen with 24 semester hours or more of graded college credit must have a cumulative GPA of 2.5 or higher; airmen with less than 24 semester hours must have an ACT score of 24 or higher or an SAT combined mathematics and critical reading

score of 1100 or higher. All applicants must earn Air Force Officer Qualifying Test (AFOQT) scores of 15 or more on the verbal scale and 10 or more on the quantitative scale. U.S. citizenship is required. When the recipients complete the program, they may be no more than 31 years of age. All academic majors are eligible.

Financial Data Selectees receive a tuition and fees scholarship of up to $18,000 per year, an annual textbook allowance of $900, and a monthly nontaxable stipend of $300 to $500.

Duration 2 to 4 years.

Additional data Upon completing their degree, selectees are commissioned as officers in the Air Force with a 4-year service obligation. Further information is available from base education service officers or an Air Force ROTC unit.

Number awarded Approximately 50 each year.

Deadline September of each year.

[321]
SCHUYLER S. PYLE SCHOLARSHIP

Fleet Reserve Association
Attn: Scholarship Administrator
125 North West Street
Alexandria, VA 22314-2754
(703) 683-1400   Toll Free: (800) FRA-1924
Fax: (703) 549-6610   E-mail: fra@fra.org
Web: www.fra.org

Summary To provide financial assistance for college or graduate school to members of the Fleet Reserve Association (FRA) who are current or former naval personnel and their spouses and children.

Eligibility This program is open to dependent children, grandchildren, and spouses of FRA members who are in good standing (or were at the time of death, if deceased). FRA members are also eligible. Applicants must be working on or planning to work on an undergraduate or graduate degree. Along with their application, they must submit an essay on their life experiences, career objectives, and what motivated them to select those objectives. Selection is based on academic record, financial need, extracurricular activities, leadership skills, and participation in community activities. U.S. citizenship is required.

Financial Data The stipend is $5,000 per year.

Duration 1 year; may be renewed.

Additional data Membership in the FRA is restricted to active-duty, retired, and Reserve members of the Navy, Marine Corps, and Coast Guard.

Number awarded 1 each year.

Deadline April of each year.

[322]
SEAMAN TO ADMIRAL-21 PROGRAM

U.S. Navy
Attn: Commander, Naval Service Training Command
250 Dallas Street, Suite A
Pensacola, FL 32508-5268
(850) 452-9563   Fax: (850) 452-2486
E-mail: PNSC_STA21@navy.mil
Web: www.sta-21.navy.mil

Summary To allow outstanding enlisted Navy personnel to complete a bachelor's degree and receive a commission.

Eligibility This program is open to U.S. citizens who are currently serving on active duty in the U.S. Navy or Naval Reserve, including Full Time Support (FTS), Selected Reserves (SEL-RES), and Navy Reservists on active duty except for those on active duty for training (ACDUTRA). Applicants must be high school graduates (or GED recipients) who are able to complete requirements for a baccalaureate degree in 36 months or less. When they complete their degree requirements, they must be younger than 31 years of age. Within the past 3 years, they must have taken the SAT test (and achieved scores of at least 500 on

the mathematics section and 500 on the critical reading section) or the ACT test (and achieved a score of 41 or higher, including at least 21 on the mathematics portion and 20 on the English portion).

Financial Data Awardees continue to receive their regular Navy pay and allowances while they attend college on a full-time basis. They also receive reimbursement for tuition, fees, and books up to $10,000 per year. If base housing is available, they are eligible to live there. Participants are not eligible to receive benefits under the Navy's Tuition Assistance Program (TA), the Montgomery GI Bill (MGIB), the Navy College Fund, or the Veterans Educational Assistance Program (VEAP).

Duration Selectees are supported for up to 36 months of full-time, year-round study or completion of a bachelor's degree, as long as they maintain a GPA of 2.5 or higher.

Additional data This program was established in 2001 as a replacement for the Seaman to Admiral Program (established in 1994), the Enlisted Commissioning Program, and other specialized programs for sailors to earn a commission. Upon acceptance into the program, selectees attend the Naval Science Institute (NSI) in Newport, Rhode Island for an 8-week program in the fundamental core concepts of being a naval officer (navigation, engineering, weapons, military history and justice, etc.). They then enter a college or university with an NROTC unit or affiliation to work full time on a bachelor's degree. They become members of and drill with the NROTC unit. When they complete their degree, they are commissioned as ensigns in the United States Naval Reserve and assigned to initial training for their officer community. After commissioning, 5 years of active service are required.

Number awarded Varies each year.

Deadline June of each year.

[323]
SFC CURTIS MANCINI MEMORIAL SCHOLARSHIPS

Association of the United States Army-Rhode Island Chapter
c/o CSM (Ret) Anthony Ferri, Secretary
47 Spokane Street
Providence, RI 02904
(401) 861-2997   E-mail: afnf458673755@aol.com
Web: www.ausari.org/index.html

Summary To provide financial assistance to members of the Rhode Island Chapter of the Association of the United States Army (AUSA) and their families who are interested in attending college or graduate school in any state.

Eligibility This program is open to members of the AUSA Rhode Island Chapter and their family members (spouses, children, and grandchildren). Applicants must be high school seniors or graduates accepted at an accredited college, university, or vocational/technical school in any state or current undergraduate or graduate students. Along with their application, they must submit a 250-word essay on why they feel their achievements should qualify them for this award. Selection is based on academic and individual achievements; financial need is not considered. Membership in AUSA is open to current and retired Army personnel (including Reserves and National Guard), ROTC cadets, or civilian employees of the Army.

Financial Data The stipend is $1,000.

Duration 1 year.

Number awarded 2 each year.

Deadline March of each year.

[324]
SIMULTANEOUS MEMBERSHIP PROGRAM (SMP)

U.S. Army
ROTC Cadet Command
Attn: ATCC-OP-I-S
55 Patch Road, Building 56
Fort Monroe, VA 23651-1052
(757) 788-2782   Toll Free: (800) USA-ROTC
Fax: (757) 788-4643   E-mail: nancy.davis@usaac.army.mil
Web: www.rotc.monroe.army.mil

Summary To provide financial assistance to individuals who serve simultaneously in the Army National Guard or Army Reserve and the Army Reserve Officers' Training Corps (ROTC) while they are in college.

Eligibility Students who are members of the Army National Guard or the Army Reserve and Army ROTC at the same time are eligible for this assistance. Applicants must have completed basic training or the equivalent, have at least 4 years remaining on their current military obligation, be full-time college juniors, have a GPA of 2.0 or higher, and be U.S. citizens.

Financial Data Advanced ROTC Simultaneous Membership Program (SMP) participants are paid at the rate of at least a Sergeant E-5 for their Guard or Reserve training assemblies (recently, $226 to $315 per month, depending on the number of years of service), plus an ROTC stipend for 10 months of the year at $450 per month during their junior year and $500 per month during their senior year.

Duration Up to 2 years.

Additional data Participants serve as officer trainees in their Guard or Reserve units and, under the close supervision of a commissioned officer, perform duties commensurate with those of a second lieutenant. Cadets who successfully complete the SMP program graduate with a commission as a second lieutenant. Once commissioned, they may continue to serve in their Guard or Reserve units, or they may apply for active duty in the U.S. Army.

Number awarded Varies each year.

Deadline Deadline not specified.

[325]
SOUTH CAROLINA NATIONAL GUARD COLLEGE ASSISTANCE PROGRAM

South Carolina Commission on Higher Education
Attn: Director of Student Services
1333 Main Street, Suite 200
Columbia, SC 29201
(803) 737-2144   Toll Free: (877) 349-7183
Fax: (803) 737-2297   E-mail: mbrown@che.sc.gov
Web: www.che.sc.gov/New_Web/GoingToCollege/FinAsst.htm

Summary To provide financial assistance to members of the South Carolina National Guard who are interested in attending college in the state.

Eligibility This program is open to members of the South Carolina National Guard who are in good standing and have not already received a bachelor's or graduate degree. Applicants must be admitted, enrolled, and classified as a degree-seeking full- or part-time student at an eligible institution in South Carolina. They may not be taking continuing education or graduate course work. U.S. citizenship or permanent resident status is required.

Financial Data This program provides full payment of the cost of attendance, including tuition, fees, and textbooks. The cumulative total of all benefits received from this program may not exceed $18,000.

Duration Support is provided for up to 130 semester hours of study, provided the Guard member maintains satisfactory academic progress as defined by the institution.

Additional data This program is administered by the South Carolina Commission on Higher Education in consultation with the state Adjutant General. The General Assembly established this program in 2007 as a replacement for the South Carolina National Guard Student Loan Repayment Program. Enlisted personnel are required to continue their service in the National Guard during all terms of courses covered by the benefit received. Officers must continue their service with the National Guard for at least 4 years after completion of the most recent award or degree completion.

Number awarded Varies each year.

Deadline Deadline not specified.

[326]
SPECIAL DUTY OFFICER (INFORMATION WARFARE) OPTION OF THE SEAMAN TO ADMIRAL-21 PROGRAM

U.S. Navy
Attn: Commander, Naval Service Training Command
250 Dallas Street, Suite A
Pensacola, FL 32508-5268
(850) 452-9563   Fax: (850) 452-2486
E-mail: PNSC_STA21@navy.mil
Web: www.sta-21.navy.mil

Summary To allow outstanding enlisted Navy personnel to complete a bachelor's degree and receive a commission as a special duty officer (information warfare).

Eligibility This program is open to U.S. citizens who are currently serving on active duty in the U.S. Navy or Naval Reserve, including Full Time Support (FTS), Selected Reserves (SELRES), and Navy Reservists on active duty except for those on active duty for training (ACDUTRA). Applicants must be high school graduates (or GED recipients) who are at least 18 years of age and able to complete requirements for a baccalaureate degree in 36 months or less. Sailors in all ratings are eligible, but preference is given to cryptologic technicians, intelligence specialists, and information professionals. When they complete their degree requirements, they must be younger than 35 years of age. Within the past 3 years, they must have taken the SAT test (and achieved scores of at least 500 on the mathematics section and 500 on the critical reading section) or the ACT test (and achieved a score of 41 or higher, including at least 21 on the mathematics portion and 20 on the English portion). They must also meet relevant medical standards. Although technical degrees are preferred, the program does not specify required majors; instead, it seeks officers who possess strong analytical ability and communication skills (both oral and written).

Financial Data Awardees continue to receive their regular Navy pay and allowances while they attend college on a full-time basis. They also receive reimbursement for tuition, fees, and books up to $10,000 per year. If base housing is available, they are eligible to live there. Participants are not eligible to receive benefits under the Navy's Tuition Assistance Program (TA), the Montgomery GI Bill (MGIB), the Navy College Fund, or the Veterans Educational Assistance Program (VEAP).

Duration Selectees are supported for up to 36 months of full-time, year-round study or completion of a bachelor's degree, as long as they maintain a GPA of 2.5 or higher.

Additional data This program was established in 2001 as a replacement for the Seaman to Admiral Program (established in 1994), the Enlisted Commissioning Program, and other specialized programs for sailors to earn a commission. Upon acceptance into the program, selectees attend the Naval Science Institute (NSI) in Newport, Rhode Island for an 8-week program in the fundamental core concepts of being a naval officer (navigation, engineering, weapons, military history and justice, etc.). They then enter a college or university with an NROTC unit or affiliation to work full time on a bachelor's degree. They become members of and drill with the NROTC unit. When they complete their degree, they are commissioned as ensigns in the United States Naval Reserve and assigned to initial training as a special duty officer (information warfare); that designation was formerly special duty officer (cryptologic). After commissioning, 5 years of active service are required.

Number awarded Varies each year.

Deadline June of each year.

[327]
SPECIAL DUTY OFFICER (INTELLIGENCE) OPTION OF THE SEAMAN TO ADMIRAL-21 PROGRAM

U.S. Navy
Attn: Commander, Naval Service Training Command
250 Dallas Street, Suite A
Pensacola, FL 32508-5268
(850) 452-9563   Fax: (850) 452-2486
E-mail: PNSC_STA21@navy.mil
Web: www.sta-21.navy.mil

Summary To allow outstanding enlisted Navy personnel to complete a bachelor's degree and receive a commission as a special duty officer (intelligence).

Eligibility This program is open to U.S. citizens who are currently serving on active duty in the U.S. Navy or Naval Reserve, including Full Time Support (FTS), Selected Reserves (SELRES), and Navy Reservists on active duty except for those on active duty for training (ACDUTRA). Applicants must be high school graduates (or GED recipients) who are at least 18 years of age and able to complete requirements for a baccalaureate degree in 36 months or less. They may currently have any rating. When they complete their degree requirements, they must be younger than 35 years of age. Within the past 3 years, they must have taken the SAT test (and achieved scores of at least 500 on the mathematics section and 500 on the critical reading section) or the ACT test (and achieved a score of 41 or higher, including at least 21 on the mathematics portion and 20 on the English portion). They must also meet relevant medical standards. Although technical degrees are preferred, the program does not specify required majors; instead, it seeks officers who possess strong analytical ability and communication skills (both oral and written).

Financial Data Awardees continue to receive their regular Navy pay and allowances while they attend college on a full-time basis. They also receive reimbursement for tuition, fees, and books up to $10,000 per year. If base housing is available, they are eligible to live there. Participants are not eligible to receive benefits under the Navy's Tuition Assistance Program (TA), the Montgomery GI Bill (MGIB), the Navy College Fund, or the Veterans Educational Assistance Program (VEAP).

Duration Selectees are supported for up to 36 months of full-time, year-round study or completion of a bachelor's degree, as long as they maintain a GPA of 2.5 or higher.

Additional data This program was established in 2001 as a replacement for the Seaman to Admiral Program (established in 1994), the Enlisted Commissioning Program, and other specialized programs for sailors to earn a commission. Upon acceptance into the program, selectees attend the Naval Science Institute (NSI) in Newport, Rhode Island for an 8-week program in the fundamental core concepts of being a naval officer (navigation, engineering, weapons, military history and justice, etc.). They then enter a college or university with an NROTC unit or affiliation to work full time on a bachelor's degree. They become members of and drill with the NROTC unit. When they complete their degree, they are commissioned as ensigns in the United States Naval Reserve and assigned to initial training as a special duty officer (intelligence). After commissioning, 5 years of active service are required.

Number awarded Varies each year.

Deadline June of each year.

[328]
SPECIAL OPERATIONS OPTION OF THE SEAMAN TO ADMIRAL-21 PROGRAM

U.S. Navy
Attn: Commander, Naval Service Training Command
250 Dallas Street, Suite A
Pensacola, FL 32508-5268
(850) 452-9563   Fax: (850) 452-2486
E-mail: PNSC_STA21@navy.mil
Web: www.sta-21.navy.mil

Summary To allow outstanding enlisted Navy personnel to complete a bachelor's degree and receive a commission as a special operations officer.

Eligibility This program is open to U.S. citizens who are currently serving on active duty in the U.S. Navy or Naval Reserve, including Full Time Support (FTS), Selected Reserves (SELRES), and Navy Reservists on active duty except for those on active duty for training (ACDUTRA). Applicants must have 1 of the following NECs: 5332, 5333, 5334, 5335, 5336, 5337, 5342, 5343 and 8493 or 8494. They must be high school graduates (or GED recipients) who are able to complete requirements for a baccalaureate degree in 36 months or less. When they complete their degree requirements, they must be younger than 29 years of age. That age limitation may be adjusted upward for active service on a month for month basis up to 24 months, and waivers are considered for enlisted personnel who possess particularly exceptional qualifications if they can complete their degree prior to their 35th birthday. Within the past 3 years, they must have taken the SAT test (and achieved scores of at least 500 on the mathematics section and 500 on the critical reading section) or the ACT test (and achieved a score of 41 or higher, including at least 21 on the mathematics portion and 20 on the English portion). They must also meet physical regulations that include qualification for diving duty and/or combat swimmer. Preference is given to applicants who plan to major in a technical field (e.g., chemistry, computer science, engineering, mathematics, oceanography, operations analysis, physical sciences, or physics).

Financial Data Awardees continue to receive their regular Navy pay and allowances while they attend college on a full-time basis. They also receive reimbursement for tuition, fees, and books up to $10,000 per year. If base housing is available, they are eligible to live there. Participants are not eligible to receive benefits under the Navy's Tuition Assistance Program (TA), the Montgomery GI Bill (MGIB), the Navy College Fund, or the Veterans Educational Assistance Program (VEAP).

Duration Selectees are supported for up to 36 months of full-time, year-round study or completion of a bachelor's degree, as long as they maintain a GPA of 2.5 or higher.

Additional data This program was established in 2001 as a replacement for the Seaman to Admiral Program (established in 1994), the Enlisted Commissioning Program, and other specialized programs for sailors to earn a commission. Upon acceptance into the program, selectees attend the Naval Science Institute (NSI) in Newport, Rhode Island for an 8-week program in the fundamental core concepts of being a naval officer (navigation, engineering, weapons, military history and justice, etc.). They then enter a college or university with an NROTC unit or affiliation to work full time on a bachelor's degree. They become members of and drill with the NROTC unit. When they complete their degree, they are commissioned as ensigns in the United States Naval Reserve and assigned to initial training as a special operations officer. After commissioning, 5 years of active service are required.

Number awarded Varies each year.

Deadline June of each year.

[329]
SPECIAL WARFARE OPTION OF THE SEAMAN TO ADMIRAL-21 PROGRAM

U.S. Navy
Attn: Commander, Naval Service Training Command
250 Dallas Street, Suite A
Pensacola, FL 32508-5268
(850) 452-9563   Fax: (850) 452-2486
E-mail: PNSC_STA21@navy.mil
Web: www.sta-21.navy.mil

Summary To allow outstanding enlisted Navy personnel to complete a bachelor's degree and receive a commission as a special warfare officer.

Eligibility This program is open to U.S. citizens who are currently serving on active duty in the U.S. Navy or Naval Reserve, including Full Time Support (FTS), Selected Reserves (SEL-RES), and Navy Reservists on active duty except for those on active duty for training (ACDUTRA). Only males are eligible for this option. They must have 1 of the following NECs: 5323, 5326, 8491, or 8492. Applicants must be high school graduates (or GED recipients) who are able to complete requirements for a baccalaureate degree in 36 months or less. When they complete their degree requirements, they must be younger than 29 years of age. That age limitation may be adjusted upward for active service on a month for month basis up to 24 months, and waivers are considered for enlisted personnel who possess particularly exceptional qualifications if they can complete their degree prior to their 35th birthday. Within the past 3 years, they must have taken the SAT test (and achieved scores of at least 500 on the mathematics section and 500 on the critical reading section) or the ACT test (and achieved a score of 41 or higher, including at least 21 on the mathematics portion and 20 on the English portion). They must also meet physical regulations that include qualification for diving duty and/or combat swimmer. Preference is given to applicants who plan to major in a technical field (e.g., chemistry, computer science, engineering, mathematics, oceanography, operations analysis, physical sciences, or physics).

Financial Data Awardees continue to receive their regular Navy pay and allowances while they attend college on a full-time basis. They also receive reimbursement for tuition, fees, and books up to $10,000 per year. If base housing is available, they are eligible to live there. Participants are not eligible to receive benefits under the Navy's Tuition Assistance Program (TA), the Montgomery GI Bill (MGIB), the Navy College Fund, or the Veterans Educational Assistance Program (VEAP).

Duration Selectees are supported for up to 36 months of full-time, year-round study or completion of a bachelor's degree, as long as they maintain a GPA of 2.5 or higher.

Additional data This program was established in 2001 as a replacement for the Seaman to Admiral Program (established in 1994), the Enlisted Commissioning Program, and other specialized programs for sailors to earn a commission. Upon acceptance into the program, selectees attend the Naval Science Institute (NSI) in Newport, Rhode Island for an 8-week program in the fundamental core concepts of being a naval officer (navigation, engineering, weapons, military history and justice, etc.). They then enter a college or university with an NROTC unit or affiliation to work full time on a bachelor's degree. They become members of and drill with the NROTC unit. When they complete their degree, they are commissioned as ensigns in the United States Naval Reserve and assigned to initial training as a special warfare officer. After commissioning, 5 years of active service are required.

Number awarded Varies each year.

Deadline June of each year.

[330]
SUPPLY CORPS OPTION OF THE SEAMAN TO ADMIRAL-21 PROGRAM

U.S. Navy
Attn: Commander, Naval Service Training Command
250 Dallas Street, Suite A
Pensacola, FL 32508-5268
(850) 452-9563   Fax: (850) 452-2486
E-mail: PNSC_STA21@navy.mil
Web: www.sta-21.navy.mil

Summary To allow outstanding enlisted Navy personnel to complete a bachelor's degree in business, engineering, or mathematics and receive a commission in the Supply Corps.

Eligibility This program is open to U.S. citizens who are currently serving on active duty in the U.S. Navy or Naval Reserve, including Full Time Support (FTS), Selected Reserves (SEL-RES), and Navy Reservists on active duty except for those on active duty for training (ACDUTRA). Applicants must be high school graduates (or GED recipients) who are able to complete requirements for a baccalaureate degree in a business, engineering, or mathematics related field in 36 months or less. When they complete their degree requirements, they must be younger than 31 years of age. Within the past 3 years, they must have taken the SAT test (and achieved scores of at least 500 on the mathematics section and 500 on the critical reading section) or the ACT test (and achieved a score of 41 or higher, including at least 21 on the mathematics portion and 20 on the English portion).

Financial Data Awardees continue to receive their regular Navy pay and allowances while they attend college on a full-time basis. They also receive reimbursement for tuition, fees, and books up to $10,000 per year. If base housing is available, they are eligible to live there. Participants are not eligible to receive benefits under the Navy's Tuition Assistance Program (TA), the Montgomery GI Bill (MGIB), the Navy College Fund, or the Veterans Educational Assistance Program (VEAP).

Duration Selectees are supported for up to 36 months of full-time, year-round study or completion of a bachelor's degree, as long as they maintain a GPA of 2.5 or higher.

Additional data This program was established in 2001 as a replacement for the Seaman to Admiral Program (established in 1994), the Enlisted Commissioning Program, and other specialized programs for sailors to earn a commission. Upon acceptance into the program, selectees attend the Naval Science Institute (NSI) in Newport, Rhode Island for an 8-week program in the fundamental core concepts of being a naval officer (navigation, engineering, weapons, military history and justice, etc.). They then enter a college or university with an NROTC unit or affiliation to work full time on a bachelor's degree. They become members of and drill with the NROTC unit. When they complete their degree, they are commissioned as ensigns in the United States Naval Reserve and assigned to initial training as an officer in the Supply Corps. After commissioning, 5 years of active service are required.

Number awarded Varies each year.

Deadline June of each year.

[331]
SURFACE WARFARE OFFICER/ENGINEER OPTION OF THE SEAMAN TO ADMIRAL-21 PROGRAM

U.S. Navy
Attn: Commander, Naval Service Training Command
250 Dallas Street, Suite A
Pensacola, FL 32508-5268
(850) 452-9563   Fax: (850) 452-2486
E-mail: PNSC_STA21@navy.mil
Web: www.sta-21.navy.mil

Summary To allow outstanding enlisted Navy personnel to complete a bachelor's degree and receive a commission as a surface warfare officer/engineering.

Eligibility This program is open to U.S. citizens who are currently serving on active duty in the U.S. Navy or Naval Reserve, including Full Time Support (FTS), Selected Reserves (SEL-RES), and Navy Reservists on active duty except for those on active duty for training (ACDUTRA). Applicants must be high school graduates (or GED recipients) who are able to complete requirements for a baccalaureate degree in 36 months or less. When they complete their degree requirements, they must be younger than 35 years of age. Within the past 3 years, they must have taken the SAT test (and achieved scores of at least 500 on the mathematics section and 500 on the critical reading section) or the ACT test (and achieved a score of 41 or higher, including at least 21 on the mathematics portion and 20 on the English portion). They must also pass relevant medical standards. No specific academic major is required, but applicants are encouraged to work on a technical degree in engineering or physical sciences.

Financial Data Awardees continue to receive their regular Navy pay and allowances while they attend college on a full-time basis. They also receive reimbursement for tuition, fees, and books up to $10,000 per year. If base housing is available, they are eligible to live there. Participants are not eligible to receive benefits under the Navy's Tuition Assistance Program (TA), the Montgomery GI Bill (MGIB), the Navy College Fund, or the Veterans Educational Assistance Program (VEAP).

Duration Selectees are supported for up to 36 months of full-time, year-round study or completion of a bachelor's degree, as long as they maintain a GPA of 2.5 or higher.

Additional data Upon acceptance into the program, selectees attend the Naval Science Institute (NSI) in Newport, Rhode Island for an 8-week program in the fundamental core concepts of being a naval officer (navigation, engineering, weapons, military history and justice, etc.). They then enter a college or university with an NROTC unit or affiliation to work full time on a bachelor's degree. They become members of and drill with the NROTC unit. When they complete their degree, they are commissioned as ensigns in the United States Naval Reserve and assigned to initial training as a special duty officer (engineering duty). After commissioning, 5 years of active service are required.

Number awarded Varies each year.

Deadline June of each year.

[332]
SURFACE WARFARE OFFICER/INFORMATION PROFESSIONAL OPTION OF THE SEAMAN TO ADMIRAL-21 PROGRAM

U.S. Navy
Attn: Commander, Naval Service Training Command
250 Dallas Street, Suite A
Pensacola, FL 32508-5268
(850) 452-9563　　　　　Fax: (850) 452-2486
E-mail: PNSC_STA21@navy.mil
Web: www.sta-21.navy.mil

Summary To allow outstanding enlisted Navy personnel to complete a bachelor's degree and receive a commission as a surface warfare officer/information professional (SWO/IP).

Eligibility This program is open to U.S. citizens who are currently serving on active duty in the U.S. Navy or Naval Reserve, including Full Time Support (FTS), Selected Reserves (SEL-RES), and Navy Reservists on active duty except for those on active duty for training (ACDUTRA). Applicants must be high school graduates (or GED recipients) who are able to complete requirements for a baccalaureate degree in 36 months or less. When they complete their degree requirements, they must be younger than 28 years of age. Within the past 3 years, they must have taken the SAT test (and achieved scores of at least 500 on the mathematics section and 500 on the critical reading section) or the ACT test (and achieved a score of 41 or higher, including at least 21 on the mathematics portion and 20 on the English portion). They must also pass relevant medical standards. No spe-

cific academic major is required, but applicants are encouraged to work on a technical degree in computer science, computer or electrical engineering, mathematics, physics, information systems, or operations.

Financial Data Awardees continue to receive their regular Navy pay and allowances while they attend college on a full-time basis. They also receive reimbursement for tuition, fees, and books up to $10,000 per year. If base housing is available, they are eligible to live there. Participants are not eligible to receive benefits under the Navy's Tuition Assistance Program (TA), the Montgomery GI Bill (MGIB), the Navy College Fund, or the Veterans Educational Assistance Program (VEAP).

Duration Selectees are supported for up to 36 months of full-time, year-round study or completion of a bachelor's degree, as long as they maintain a GPA of 2.5 or higher.

Additional data Upon acceptance into the program, selectees attend the Naval Science Institute (NSI) in Newport, Rhode Island for an 8-week program in the fundamental core concepts of being a naval officer (navigation, engineering, weapons, military history and justice, etc.). They then enter a college or university with an NROTC unit or affiliation to work full time on a bachelor's degree. They become members of and drill with the NROTC unit. When they complete their degree, they are commissioned as ensigns in the United States Naval Reserve and assigned to initial training as a special duty officer (information professional). After commissioning, 5 years of active service are required.

Number awarded Varies each year.

Deadline June of each year.

[333]
SURFACE WARFARE OFFICER/OCEANOGRAPHY OPTION OF THE SEAMAN TO ADMIRAL-21 PROGRAM

U.S. Navy
Attn: Commander, Naval Service Training Command
250 Dallas Street, Suite A
Pensacola, FL 32508-5268
(850) 452-9563　　　　　Fax: (850) 452-2486
E-mail: PNSC_STA21@navy.mil
Web: www.sta-21.navy.mil

Summary To allow outstanding enlisted Navy personnel to complete a bachelor's degree and receive a commission as a surface warfare officer/oceanography.

Eligibility This program is open to U.S. citizens who are currently serving on active duty in the U.S. Navy or Naval Reserve, including Full Time Support (FTS), Selected Reserves (SEL-RES), and Navy Reservists on active duty except for those on active duty for training (ACDUTRA). Applicants must be high school graduates (or GED recipients) who are able to complete requirements for a baccalaureate degree in 36 months or less. They must be planning to work on a technical degree in chemistry, computer science, engineering, geospatial information systems, hydrography, marine science, mathematics, meteorology, oceanography, operational analysis, physical sciences, or physics. When they complete their degree requirements, they must be younger than 28 years of age. Within the past 3 years, they must have taken the SAT test (and achieved scores of at least 500 on the mathematics section and 500 on the critical reading section) or the ACT test (and achieved a score of 41 or higher, including at least 21 on the mathematics portion and 20 on the English portion). They must also pass relevant medical standards.

Financial Data Awardees continue to receive their regular Navy pay and allowances while they attend college on a full-time basis. They also receive reimbursement for tuition, fees, and books up to $10,000 per year. If base housing is available, they are eligible to live there. Participants are not eligible to receive benefits under the Navy's Tuition Assistance Program (TA), the Montgomery GI Bill (MGIB), the Navy College Fund, or the Veterans Educational Assistance Program (VEAP).

Duration Selectees are supported for up to 36 months of full-time, year-round study or completion of a bachelor's degree, as long as they maintain a GPA of 2.5 or higher.

Additional data Upon acceptance into the program, selectees attend the Naval Science Institute (NSI) in Newport, Rhode Island for an 8-week program in the fundamental core concepts of being a naval officer (navigation, engineering, weapons, military history and justice, etc.). They then enter a college or university with an NROTC unit or affiliation to work full time on a bachelor's degree. They become members of and drill with the NROTC unit. When they complete their degree, they are commissioned as ensigns in the United States Naval Reserve and assigned to initial training as a special duty officer (oceanography). After commissioning, 5 years of active service are required.

Number awarded Varies each year.

Deadline June of each year.

[334]
SURFACE WARFARE OFFICER OPTION OF THE SEAMAN TO ADMIRAL-21 PROGRAM

U.S. Navy
Attn: Commander, Naval Service Training Command
250 Dallas Street, Suite A
Pensacola, FL 32508-5268
(850) 452-9563   Fax: (850) 452-2486
E-mail: PNSC_STA21@navy.mil
Web: www.sta-21.navy.mil

Summary To allow outstanding enlisted Navy personnel to complete a bachelor's degree and receive a commission as a surface warfare officer (SWO).

Eligibility This program is open to U.S. citizens who are currently serving on active duty in the U.S. Navy or Naval Reserve, including Full Time Support (FTS), Selected Reserves (SEL-RES), and Navy Reservists on active duty except for those on active duty for training (ACDUTRA). Applicants must be high school graduates (or GED recipients) who are able to complete requirements for a baccalaureate degree in 36 months or less. When they complete their degree requirements, they must be younger than 28 years of age. Within the past 3 years, they must have taken the SAT test (and achieved scores of at least 500 on the mathematics section and 500 on the critical reading section) or the ACT test (and achieved a score of 41 or higher, including at least 21 on the mathematics portion and 20 on the English portion). They must also meet relevant medical standards. Preference is given to applicants who plan to major in a technical field (e.g., chemistry, computer science, engineering, mathematics, oceanography, operations analysis, physical sciences, or physics).

Financial Data Awardees continue to receive their regular Navy pay and allowances while they attend college on a full-time basis. They also receive reimbursement for tuition, fees, and books up to $10,000 per year. If base housing is available, they are eligible to live there. Participants are not eligible to receive benefits under the Navy's Tuition Assistance Program (TA), the Montgomery GI Bill (MGIB), the Navy College Fund, or the Veterans Educational Assistance Program (VEAP).

Duration Selectees are supported for up to 36 months of full-time, year-round study or completion of a bachelor's degree, as long as they maintain a GPA of 2.5 or higher.

Additional data This program was established in 2001 as a replacement for the Seaman to Admiral Program (established in 1994), the Enlisted Commissioning Program, and other specialized programs for sailors to earn a commission. Upon acceptance into the program, selectees attend the Naval Science Institute (NSI) in Newport, Rhode Island for an 8-week program in the fundamental core concepts of being a naval officer (navigation, engineering, weapons, military history and justice, etc.). They then enter a college or university with an NROTC unit or affiliation to work full time on a bachelor's degree. They become members of

and drill with the NROTC unit. When they complete their degree, they are commissioned as ensigns in the United States Naval Reserve and assigned to initial training as a surface warfare officer. After commissioning, 5 years of active service are required.

Number awarded Varies each year.

Deadline June of each year.

[335]
TAILHOOK EDUCATIONAL FOUNDATION SCHOLARSHIPS

Tailhook Educational Foundation
9696 Businesspark Avenue
P.O. Box 26626
San Diego, CA 92196-0626
(858) 689-9223   Toll Free: (800) 322-4665
E-mail: tag@tailhook.net
Web: www.tailhook.org/Foundation.html

Summary To provide financial assistance for college to personnel associated with naval aviation and their children.

Eligibility This program is open to 1) the children (natural, step, and adopted) of current or former U.S. Navy or Marine Corps personnel who served as an aviator, flight officer, or air crewman, or 2) personnel and children of personnel who are serving or have served on board a U.S. Navy aircraft carrier as a member of the ship's company or air wing. Applicants must be enrolled or accepted for enrollment at an accredited college or university. Selection is based on educational and extracurricular achievements, merit, and citizenship.

Financial Data The stipend ranges from $1,500 to $15,000.

Duration 1 to 2 years.

Number awarded Varies each year; recently, 85 of these scholarships were awarded.

Deadline March of each year.

[336]
TENNESSEE HELPING HEROES GRANTS

Tennessee Student Assistance Corporation
Parkway Towers
404 James Robertson Parkway, Suite 1510
Nashville, TN 37243-0820
(615) 741-1346   Toll Free: (800) 342-1663
Fax: (615) 741-6101   E-mail: TSAC.Aidinfo@tn.gov
Web: www.tn.gov/collegepays/mon_college/hh_grant.htm

Summary To provide financial assistance to veterans and current Reservists or National Guard members who are residents of Tennessee and enrolled at a college or university in the state.

Eligibility This program is open to residents of Tennessee who are veterans honorably discharged from the U.S. armed forces and former or current members of a Reserve or Tennessee National Guard unit who were called into active military service. Applicants must have been awarded, on or after September 11, 2001, the Iraq Campaign Medal, the Afghanistan Campaign Medal, or the Global War on Terrorism Expeditionary Medal. They must be enrolled at least half time at an eligible college or university in Tennessee and receive no final failing grade in any course. No academic standard or financial need requirements apply.

Financial Data Grants are $1,000 per semester for full-time study or $500 per semester for part-time study. Funds are awarded after completion of each semester of work.

Duration Grants are awarded until completion of the equivalent of 8 full semesters of work, completion of a baccalaureate degree, or the eighth anniversary of honorable discharge from military service, whichever comes first.

Additional data This program was added as a component of the Tennessee Education Lottery Scholarship Program in 2005.

Number awarded Varies each year.

Deadline August of each year for fall enrollment, January of each year for spring, or April of each year for summer.

[337]
TEXAS NATIONAL GUARD TUITION ASSISTANCE PROGRAM

Texas Higher Education Coordinating Board
Attn: Grants and Special Programs
1200 East Anderson Lane
P.O. Box 12788, Capitol Station
Austin, TX 78711-2788
(512) 427-6323   Toll Free: (800) 242-3062, ext. 6323
Fax: (512) 427-6127   E-mail: grantinfo@thecb.state.tx.us
Web: www.collegeforalltexans.com

Summary To provide financial assistance for college, technical school, or graduate school to members of the Texas National Guard.

Eligibility This program is open to Texas residents who are active, drilling members of the Texas National Guard, the Texas Air Guard, or the State Guard. Applicants must be attending, enrolled at, or planning to attend a public, private, or independent institution of higher education in Texas for undergraduate, vocational, or technical courses.

Financial Data Eligible Guard members receive exemption from tuition at Texas public colleges and universities. For students who attend a private, nonprofit institution, the award is based on public university tuition charges for 12 semester credit hours at the resident rate.

Duration Tuition assistance is available for up to 12 credit hours per semester for up to 10 semesters or 5 academic years, whichever occurs first.

Number awarded Varies each year; recently, 864 Guard members participated in this program.

Deadline June of each year for the fall semester; November of each year for the spring semester.

[338]
TILLMAN MILITARY SCHOLARSHIPS FOR SERVICEMEMBERS

Pat Tillman Foundation
2121 South Mill Avenue, Suite 214
Tempe, AZ 85282
(480) 621-4074   Fax: (480) 621-4075
E-mail: scholarships@pattillmanfoundation.org
Web: www.pattillmanfoundation.org

Summary To provide financial assistance to veterans and active servicemembers who are interested in working on an undergraduate or graduate degree.

Eligibility This program is open to veterans and active servicemembers of all branches of the armed forces from both the pre- and post-September 11 era whose educational benefits have run out or are insufficient to meet their need. Applicants must be interested in starting, finishing, or furthering their undergraduate, graduate, or postgraduate education at a 2-year, 4-year, or vocational institution (public or private). Along with their application, they must submit 1-page essays on 1) their specific financial need, including any gap in educational benefits they may already be receiving and their reason for applying for this scholarship; 2) their motivation and decision to serve in the U.S. armed forces; and 3) their educational and career goals, how they will incorporate their military service into those goals, and how they intend to continue their service to others and the community. Selection is based on those essays, educational and career ambitions, length of service, record of personal achievement, demonstration of service to others in the community and a desire to continue such service, and unmet financial need.

Financial Data Stipends vary; recently, total awards (including multi-year awards) averaged $12,800.

Duration 1 year; may be renewed, provided the recipient maintains a GPA of 3.0 or higher, remains enrolled full time, and documents participation in civic action or community service.

Additional data This program was established in 2009. The foundation administers the program directly for students at colleges and universities nationwide; it also acts in partnership with 4 universities (the University of Maryland, the University of Arkansas, the University of Idaho, and Mississippi State University) which award scholarships directly to their students.

Number awarded Varies each year; recently, 52 students received a total of $665,820 in these scholarships

Deadline May of each year.

[339]
TONY LOPEZ SCHOLARSHIP PROGRAM

Louisiana National Guard Enlisted Association
c/o SGM Milton J. Billberry
202 Dean Lane
Pineville, LA 71360
(318) 623-2464   E-mail: Milton.billberry@us.army.mil
Web: www.langea.org

Summary To provide financial assistance to members of the Louisiana National Guard Enlisted Association (LANGEA) and their dependents who plan to attend college in any state.

Eligibility This program is open to members of the association, their spouses and unmarried dependent children, and the unremarried spouses and unmarried dependent children of deceased members who were in good standing at the time of their death. The qualifying LANGEA members must have at least 1 year remaining on their enlistment following completion of the school year for which the application is submitted or have served 20 years of more in the Louisiana National Guard. Applicants must be enrolled or planning to enroll full time at an accredited college, university, trade school, or business school in any state. Graduate students are not eligible. Selection is based on academic achievement, character, leadership, and financial need.

Financial Data The stipend is $2,000.

Duration 1 year; nonrenewable.

Number awarded 3 each year.

Deadline February of each year.

[340]
TWEEDALE SCHOLARSHIPS

U.S. Navy
Attn: Naval Education and Training Command
NSTC OD2
250 Dallas Street, Suite A
Pensacola, FL 32508-5268
(850) 452-4941, ext. 25166
Toll Free: (800) NAV-ROTC, ext. 25166
Fax: (850) 452-2486
E-mail: PNSC_NROTC.scholarship@navy.mil
Web: www.nrotc.navy.mil/tweedale.aspx

Summary To provide financial assistance to currently-enrolled college students who are interested in joining Navy ROTC and majoring in a technical field in college.

Eligibility This program is open to students who have completed at least 1 but not more than 4 academic terms with a cumulative GPA that places them above their peer mean or 3.0, whichever is higher, and a grade of "C" or better in all classes attempted. They must have a strong mathematics and science background in high school (with a grade of "B" or higher in calculus, if taken) and completed at least 1 academic term of college-level mathematics or science. They must be majoring in specified technical fields (recently, those were chemistry, computer science, engineering, mathematics, and physics). Students must be interviewed by the professor of naval science (PNS) at their college or university and must comply with standards of leadership potential and military/physical fitness. They must submit a plan indicating that they will complete the introductory naval science course as soon as possible and be able to complete all naval science requirements and graduate on time with their class.

Financial Data These scholarships provide payment of full tuition and required educational fees, as well as a specified amount for textbooks, supplies, and equipment. The program also provides a stipend for 10 months of the year that is $300 per month as a sophomore, $350 per month as a junior, and $400 per month as a senior.

Duration 2 or 3 years, until the recipient completes the bachelor's degree.

Additional data Applications must be made through the PNS at 1 of the 70 schools hosting the Navy ROTC program. Prior to final selection, applicants must attend, at Navy expense, a 6-week summer training course at the Naval Science Institute at Newport, Rhode Island. After completing the program, all participants are commissioned as ensigns in the Naval Reserve or second lieutenants in the Marine Corps Reserve with an 8-year service obligation, including 4 years of active duty.

Number awarded Approximately 140 each year: 2 at each college and university with a Navy ROTC unit.

Deadline March of each year.

[341]
UNITED STATES FIELD ARTILLERY ASSOCIATION SCHOLARSHIPS

United States Field Artillery Association
Attn: Scholarship Committee
Building 758, McNair Avenue
P.O. Box 33027
Fort Sill, OK 73503-0027
(580) 355-4677   Toll Free: (866) 355-4677
Fax: (580) 355-8745   E-mail: amy@fieldartillery.org
Web: www.fieldartillery.org/usfaa_scholarship/index.html

Summary To provide financial assistance for college to members of the United States Field Artillery Association (USFAA) and their immediate family.

Eligibility This program is open to 3 categories of students: USFAA members (officer or enlisted), immediate family of enlisted members, and immediate family of officer members. Applicants must have been accepted for admission as an undergraduate at an accredited college, university, or vocational program of study. Along with their application, they must submit an essay explaining their educational goals and how this scholarship will help meet those goals. Financial need is also considered in the selection process.

Financial Data The stipend is $1,000.

Duration 1 year.

Additional data The USFAA services the field artillery branch of the military.

Number awarded 6 each year.

Deadline March of each year.

[342]
U.S. ARMY WOMEN'S FOUNDATION LEGACY SCHOLARSHIPS

U.S. Army Women's Foundation
Attn: Scholarship Committee
P.O. Box 5030
Fort Lee, VA 23801-0030
(804) 734-3078   E-mail: info@awfdn.org
Web: www.awfdn.org/programs/legacyscholarships.shtml

Summary To provide financial assistance for college to women who are serving or have served in the Army and their children.

Eligibility This program is open to 1) women who have served or are serving honorably in the U.S. Army, U.S. Army Reserve, or Army National Guard; and 2) children of women who served honorably in the U.S. Army, U.S. Army Reserve, or Army National Guard. Applicants must be entering their junior or senior year at an accredited college or university and have a GPA of 3.0 or higher. Along with their application, they must submit a 2-page

essay on why they should be considered for this scholarship, their future plans as related to their program of study, and information about their community service, activities, and work experience. Selection is based on merit, academic potential, community service, and financial need.

Financial Data The stipend is $2,500.

Duration 1 year.

Additional data This program includes scholarships named after Lt. Col. Juanita L. Warman, Sgt. Amy Krueger, and Pvt. Francheska Velez, all of whom lost their lives in the tragedy at Fort Hood, Texas on November 5, 2009.

Number awarded 5 to 10 each year.

Deadline February of each year.

[343]
USS LAKE CHAMPLAIN (CG-57) SCHOLARSHIP FUND

USS Lake Champlain Foundation
c/o Captain Ralph K. Martin, USN (ret)
P.O. Box 233
Keeseville, NY 12944-0233
(518) 834-7660

Summary To provide financial assistance for college to naval personnel who are (or have been) attached to the *USS Lake Champlain* and to their dependents.

Eligibility Eligible to apply are 1) past and present crewmembers of the *USS Lake Champlain;* 2) spouses and dependent children of officers and enlisted personnel currently serving aboard the *USS Lake Champlain;* and 3) spouses and dependent children of officers and enlisted personnel on active duty, retired with pay, or deceased who were previously assigned to the *USS Lake Champlain* since commissioning on August 12, 1988. Applicants must submit an essay on their career objectives, why they are interested in that career, and how furthering their education will lead to their accomplishing their career objective. Selection is based on that essay, financial need, high school and/or college transcripts, 2 letters of recommendation, extracurricular activities and awards, and work experience.

Financial Data Stipends range from $100 to $1,000. Scholarships greater than $250 are paid in 2 installments: 1 at the beginning of the fall semester and 1 at the beginning of the second semester upon verification of satisfactory completion of the first semester and continued enrollment. Funds are paid directly to the academic institution.

Duration 1 year.

Number awarded Varies each year. Recently, 11 of these scholarships were awarded: 5 at $1,000, 3 at $250, and 3 at $100.

Deadline May of each year.

[344]
USS LITTLE ROCK ASSOCIATION NROTC SCHOLARSHIP PROGRAM

USS Little Rock Association
c/o Kent Siegel, Scholarship Committee Chair
8508 Conover Place
Alexandria, VA 22308-2042
703) 360-8948   E-mail: ksiegel@cox.net
Web: www.usslittlerock.org/scholarship.html

Summary To provide financial assistance to Naval ROTC midshipmen who have a personal or family connection to the sea services or are members of the USS Little Rock Association.

Eligibility This program is open to students entering their third academic year of an NROTC program (scholarship, college program, Marine Enlisted Commissioning Program, or Seaman to Admiral). Applicants must 1) be the children or direct descendants of active, retired, or honorably discharged members of the sea services (U.S. Navy, U.S. Marine Corps, or U.S. Coast Guard) or their Reserve components; 2) themselves be serving or have served in any of the regular or Reserve sea services; or 3) have been Junior Associate members of the USS Little Rock Association for at least 2 years. They must have a GPA of 3.0 or higher and have demonstrated superior leadership qualities and aptitude for service in all of their NROTC activities. Along with their application, they must submit a 500-word letter describing why they consider themselves worthy of the award.

Financial Data The stipend is $1,000 per year.

Duration 1 year; may be renewed 1 additional year.

Additional data This program was initiated in 2001.

Number awarded 1 or 2 each year.

Deadline May of each year.

[345]
UTAH NATIONAL GUARD STATE TUITION ASSISTANCE PROGRAM

Utah Army National Guard
Attn: UT-G1-ESO
12953 South Minuteman Drive
P.O. Box 1776
Draper, UT 84020-1776
(801) 523-4534   E-mail: dorothy.blakely@us.army.mil
Web: www.ut.ngb.army.mil/education2

Summary To provide tuition assistance to currently-enrolled members of the Utah National Guard.

Eligibility This program is open to Utah residents who are MOS/AFSC qualified members of the Utah National Guard. Applicants must have been accepted as a student at a college or university in the state. Enlisted personnel must have remaining obligation on their existing enlistment contract that will extend to or beyond the last date of course enrollment for these funds. Officers must have at least 4 years of Selected Reserve service remaining from the date of completion of the course for which this funding is provided.

Financial Data Support is provided for 100% of the cost of tuition, to a maximum of $250 per hour or a maximum of $4,500 per year.

Duration 1 semester; recipients may renew.

Additional data Members of the Utah Air National Guard should contact the 151st MSF-DPH, 765 North 2200 West, Salt Lake City, UT 84116. Recipients of this funding may continue to receive any GI Bill funding to which they are entitled, but they may not simultaneously apply for this and federal Tuition Assistance benefits.

Number awarded Varies each year. Recently, a total of $750,000 was available for this program.

Deadline March of each year for summer term; August of each year for fall term; November of each year for winter or spring term.

[346]
UTAH NATIONAL GUARD STATE TUITION WAIVER

Utah Army National Guard
Attn: UT-G1-ESO
12953 South Minuteman Drive
P.O. Box 1776
Draper, UT 84020-1776
(801) 523-4537   E-mail: gerald.white2@us.army.mil
Web: www.ut.ngb.army.mil/education2

Summary To waive tuition for members of the Utah National Guard at public institutions in the state.

Eligibility This program is open to Utah residents who are MOS/AFSC qualified members of the Utah National Guard. Applicants must have been accepted as a full-time student at a public college or university in the state. They may not currently be on active duty and may not already have a 4-year degree. Along with their application, they must submit a short essay describing the difference between a Strategic Reserve Force and an Operational Reserve Force.

Financial Data This program provides waiver of tuition at Utah public colleges and universities.

Duration 1 semester; recipients may renew.

Additional data Members of the Utah Air National Guard should contact the 151st MSF-DPH, 765 North 2200 West, Salt Lake City, UT 84116. Recipients of these waivers may continue to receive any GI Bill funding to which they are entitled and they may utilize state Tuition Assistance or federal Tuition Assistance to pay for fees or credits not covered by this program.

Number awarded Varies each year. Each Utah public college and university is required to set aside 2.5% of its scholarship funds for members of the National Guard.

Deadline May of each year.

[347]
VADM ROBERT L. WALTERS SCHOLARSHIP

Surface Navy Association
2550 Huntington Avenue, Suite 202
Alexandria, VA 22303
(703) 960-6800   Toll Free: (800) NAVY-SNA
Fax: (703) 960-6807   E-mail: navysna@aol.com
Web: www.navysna.org/awards/index.html

Summary To provide financial assistance for college or graduate school to members of the Surface Navy Association (SNA) and their dependents.

Eligibility This program is open to SNA members and their children, stepchildren, wards, and spouses. The SNA member must 1) be in the second or subsequent consecutive year of membership; 2) be serving, retired, or honorably discharged; 3) be a Surface Warfare Officer or Enlisted Surface Warfare Specialist; and 4) have served for at least 3 years on a surface ship of the U.S. Navy or Coast Guard. Applicants must be studying or planning to study at an accredited undergraduate or graduate institution. Along with their application, they must submit a 200-word essay about themselves; a list of their extracurricular activities, community service activities, academic honors and/or positions of leadership that represent their interests, with an estimate of the amount of time involved with each activity; and 3 letters of reference. High school seniors should also include a transcript of high school grades and a copy of ACT or SAT scores. Applicants who are on active duty or drilling Reservists should also include a letter from their commanding officer commenting on their military service and leadership potential, a transcript of grades from their most recent 4 semesters of school, a copy of their ACT or SAT scores if available, and an indication of whether they have applied for or are enrolled in the Enlisted Commissioning Program. Applicants who are not high school seniors, active-duty servicemembers, or drilling Reservists should also include a transcript of the grades from their most recent 4 semesters of school and a copy of ACT or SAT test scores (unless they are currently attending a college or university). Selection is based on demonstrated leadership, community service, academic achievement, and commitment to pursuing higher educational objectives.

Financial Data The stipend is $2,000 per year.

Duration 4 years, provided the recipient maintains a GPA of 3.0 or higher.

Number awarded Varies each year.

Deadline February of each year.

[348]
VADM SAMUEL L. GRAVELY, JR., USN (RET.) MEMORIAL SCHOLARSHIPS

Armed Forces Communications and Electronics Association
Attn: AFCEA Educational Foundation
4400 Fair Lakes Court
Fairfax, VA 22033-3899
(703) 631-6149   Toll Free: (800) 336-4583, ext. 6149
Fax: (703) 631-4693   E-mail: scholarship@afcea.org
Web: www.afcea.org

Summary   To provide funding to students, especially veterans and military personnel, who are majoring in specified scientific fields at an Historically Black College or University (HBCU).

Eligibility   This program is open to sophomores and juniors enrolled full or part time at an accredited 2- or 4-year HBCU or in a distance learning or online degree program affiliated with those institutions. They must be working toward a degree in engineering (aerospace, computer, electrical, or systems), computer science, computer engineering technology, computer information systems, mathematics, physics, information systems management, or other field directly related to the support of U.S. intelligence or homeland security enterprises. Special consideration is given to military enlisted personnel and veterans.

Financial Data   The stipend is $5,000.

Duration   1 year; may be renewed.

Additional data   This program was established in 2009 with support from American Systems.

Number awarded   At least 2 each year.

Deadline   October of each year.

[349]
VETERAN'S CAUCUS SCHOLARSHIPS

American Academy of Physician Assistants-Veterans Caucus
Attn: Veterans Caucus
P.O. Box 362
Danville, PA 17821-0362
(570) 271-0292   Fax: (570) 271-5850
E-mail: admin@veteranscaucus.org
Web: www.veteranscaucus.org

Summary   To provide financial assistance to veterans and Reserve component personnel who are studying to become physician assistants.

Eligibility   This program is open to U.S. citizens who are currently enrolled in a physician assistant program. The program must be approved by the Commission on Accreditation of Allied Health Education. Applicants must be honorably discharged members of a uniformed service of the United States or an active member of the Guard or Reserve of a uniformed service of the United States. Selection is based on military honors and awards received, civic and college honors and awards received, professional memberships and activities, and GPA. An electronic copy of the applicant's DD Form 214 must accompany the application.

Financial Data   The stipend is $2,000.

Duration   1 year.

Additional data   This program includes the following named scholarships: the Donna Jones Moritsugu Memorial Award, the SGT Craig Ivory Memorial Scholarships, the Society of Air Force Physician Assistants Scholarship, the Society of Army Physician Assistants Scholarship, the Naval Association of Physician Assistants Scholarship, the Tim and Jackie Egan Scholarship, the Ken Gartzke Scholarship, the David H. Gwinn Memorial Scholarship, and the Vicki Moritsugu Memorial Scholarship.

Number awarded   Varies each year, recently, 11 of these scholarships were awarded.

Deadline   February of each year.

[350]
VETERANS OF ENDURING FREEDOM (AFGHANISTAN) AND IRAQI FREEDOM SCHOLARSHIP

Armed Forces Communications and Electronics Association
Attn: AFCEA Educational Foundation
4400 Fair Lakes Court
Fairfax, VA 22033-3899
(703) 631-6149   Toll Free: (800) 336-4583, ext. 6149
Fax: (703) 631-4693   E-mail: scholarship@afcea.org
Web: www.afcea.org

Summary   To provide financial assistance to veterans and military personnel who served in Afghanistan or Iraq and are working on an undergraduate degree in fields related to the support of U.S. intelligence enterprises.

Eligibility   This program is open to active-duty and honorably discharged U.S. military members (including Reservists and National Guard personnel) who served in Enduring Freedom (Afghanistan) or Iraqi Freedom operations. Applicants must be enrolled at a 2- or 4-year institution in the United States and working on an undergraduate degree in computer engineering technology, computer information systems, computer network systems, computer science, electronics engineering technology, engineering (aerospace, computer, electrical, or systems), information systems management, information systems security, mathematics, physics, science or mathematics education, technology management, or other field directly related to the support of U.S. intelligence enterprises or national security. Along with their application, they must submit an essay that includes a brief synopsis of relevant work experience (including military assignments), a brief statement of career goals after graduation, and a explanation of how their academic and career goals will contribute to the areas related to communications, intelligence and/or information systems, and the mission of the Armed Forces Communications and Electronics Association (AFCEA). Financial need is also considered in the selection process.

Financial Data   The stipend is $2,500.

Duration   1 year.

Additional data   This program was established in 2005 with funding from the Northern Virginia Chapter of AFCEA.

Number awarded   6 each year: 3 for the fall semester and 3 for the spring semester.

Deadline   March of each year for fall semester; October of each year for spring semester.

[351]
VICE ADMIRAL JERRY O. TUTTLE, USN (RET.) AND MRS. BARBARA A. TUTTLE SCIENCE AND TECHNOLOGY SCHOLARSHIPS

Armed Forces Communications and Electronics Association
Attn: AFCEA Educational Foundation
4400 Fair Lakes Court
Fairfax, VA 22033-3899
(703) 631-6149   Toll Free: (800) 336-4583, ext. 6149
Fax: (703) 631-4693   E-mail: scholarship@afcea.org
Web: www.afcea.org

Summary   To provide financial assistance to undergraduate students (especially military personnel) who are working on a degree in a science or technology-related field.

Eligibility   This program is open to full-time students entering their junior or senior year at an accredited 4-year technological institute in the United States. Applicants must be U.S. citizens working toward a degree in computer engineering technology, computer network systems, information systems security, or electronics engineering technology. Primary consideration is given to candidates who are military enlisted personnel. Selection is based on a statement of career goals, school and community activities, and financial need.

Financial Data The stipend is $2,000.

Duration 1 year; may be renewed.

Number awarded 1 or 2 each year.

Deadline November of each year.

[352]
VIRGINIA ARMY/AIR NATIONAL GUARD ENLISTED ASSOCIATION SCHOLARSHIP

Virginia Army/Air National Guard Enlisted Association
Attn: Scholarship Chair
P.O. Box 5826
Roanoke, VA 24012
(540) 366-5133   Fax: (540) 362-4417
E-mail: Scholarship@vaaangea.org
Web: www.vaaangea.org

Summary To provide financial assistance to members of the Virginia Army/Air National Guard Enlisted Association (VaA/ANGEA) and their families who are interested in attending college in any state.

Eligibility This program is open to 1) enlisted soldiers or enlisted airmen currently serving as a member of the Virginia National Guard (VNG) who are also a member of the VaA/ANGEA; 2) retired enlisted soldiers or retired enlisted airmen of the VNG who are also a member of the VaA/ANGEA; 3) spouses of current enlisted soldiers or enlisted airmen of the VNG who are also a member of the VaA/ANGEA; 4) spouses of retired enlisted soldiers or retired enlisted airmen of the VNG who are also a member of the VaA/ANGEA; and 5) dependents of current or retired enlisted soldiers or airmen of the VNG (a copy of the dependency decree may be required) who are also a member of the VaA/ANGEA. Applicants must submit a copy of their school transcript (high school or college), a letter with specific facts about their desire to continue their education and their need for assistance, 3 letters of recommendation, a letter of academic reference, and a photocopy of their VaA/ANGEA membership card. Selection is based on academics (15 points), personal statement (15 points), letters of recommendation (16 points), school involvement (15 points), community involvement (15 points), responsibility (15 points), and financial need (9 points).

Financial Data Generally, stipends are either $1,000 or $500.

Duration 1 year; recipients may reapply.

Number awarded Generally, 2 scholarships at $1,000 and 4 scholarships at $500 are awarded each year.

Deadline March of each year.

[353]
VIRGINIA NATIONAL GUARD TUITION ASSISTANCE PROGRAM

Virginia National Guard
Attn: Educational Services Officer
Fort Pickett, Building 316
Blackstone, VA 23824-6316
(434) 298-6222   Toll Free: (888) 483-2682
Fax: (434) 298-6296   E-mail: djuana.goodwin@us.army.mil
Web: vko.va.ngb.army.mil/VirginiaGuard

Summary To provide financial assistance to members of the Virginia National Guard who are interested in attending college or graduate school in the state.

Eligibility This program is open to active members of the Virginia National Guard who are residents of Virginia and interested in attending college or graduate school in the state. Awards are presented in the following priority order: 1) enlisted personnel who have previously received assistance through this program; 2) officers who need to complete a bachelor's degree in order to be eligible for promotion to captain; 3) warrant officers working on an associate or bachelor's degree; 4) any member working on an undergraduate degree; and 4) any member working on a graduate degree.

Financial Data The program provides reimbursement of tuition at approved colleges, universities, and vocational/technical schools in Virginia, to a maximum of $2,000 per semester or $6,000 per year. Bookstore grants up to $350 per semester are also provided.

Duration 1 semester; may be renewed.

Additional data This program was established in 1983. Recipients must remain in the Guard for at least 2 years after being funded.

Number awarded Varies each year.

Deadline March of each year for summer session; June of each year for fall semester; October of each year for spring semester.

[354]
VIRGINIA PENINSULA POST SAME SCHOLARSHIPS

Society of American Military Engineers-Virginia Peninsula
    Post
c/o Jeffrey Pitchford, Scholarship Co-Chair
CDM
825 Diligence Drive, Suite 205
Newport News, VA 23606
(757) 873-8850   Fax: (757) 596-2694
E-mail: pitchfordjl@cdm.com
Web: posts.same.org/VAPeninsula

Summary To provide financial assistance to students at universities in Virginia and dependents of members of the Virginia Peninsula Post of the Society of American Military Engineers (SAME) who have a commitment to future military service and are majoring in engineering or architecture.

Eligibility This program is open to students enrolled in an engineering or architecture program at the sophomore level or above. Applicants must be 1) attending a college or university in Virginia, or 2) the dependent of a SAME Virginia Peninsula Post member attending anywhere. They must have demonstrated commitment to future military service by enrolling in an ROTC program, a commissioning program, or an extended enlistment. Selection is based on financial need, academic standing, and involvement in university and community programs.

Financial Data The stipend is $1,500.

Duration 1 year.

Number awarded 4 each year.

Deadline March of each year.

[355]
VNGA SCHOLARSHIP

Virginia National Guard Association
Attn: Scholarship Committee
5901 Beulah Road
Sandston, VA 23150-6112
(804) 328-0037   Toll Free: (888) 703-0037
Fax: (804) 328-3020   E-mail: res003dm@gte.net
Web: www.vnga.org/scholarship.shtml

Summary To provide financial assistance to members of the Virginia National Guard Association (VNGA) and their families who are interested in attending college in any state.

Eligibility Applicants must have been enrolled in a college or university in any state for 1 year and qualify under 1 of the following conditions: 1) an officer or warrant officer in the Virginia National Guard and a VNGA member; 2) the dependent child or spouse of an officer or warrant officer in the Virginia National Guard who is a VNGA member; 3) the dependent child or spouse of a retired officer or warrant officer who is a VNGA member; 4) the dependent child or spouse of a deceased retired officer or warrant officer, or 5) the dependent child or spouse of a Virginia National Guard officer or warrant officer who died while in the Virginia National Guard. Along with their application, they must submit a brief description of their educational and/or military objectives, a list of their leadership positions and honors, and a brief statement of their financial need.

Financial Data A stipend is awarded; the amount is determined annually.

Duration 1 year; may be renewed for 2 additional years.

Additional data The association also offers a special scholarship in memory of CW4 William C. Singletary who, in rescuing 2 elderly women from drowning, gave his own life.

Number awarded Varies each year.

Deadline September of each year.

[356]
WASHINGTON ADMIRAL'S FUND SCHOLARSHIP

National Naval Officers Association-Washington, D.C.
  Chapter
Attn: Scholarship Program
2701 Park Center Drive, A1108
Alexandria, VA 22302
(703) 566-3840   Fax: (703) 566-3813
E-mail: Stephen.Williams@Navy.mil
Web: dcnnoa.memberlodge.com/Default.aspx?pageId=309002

Summary To provide financial assistance to minority high school seniors from the Washington, D.C. area who are interested in attending a college or university in any state and enrolling in the Navy Reserve Officers Training Corps (NROTC) program.

Eligibility This program is open to minority seniors graduating from high schools in the Washington, D.C. metropolitan area who plan to enroll full time at an accredited 2-year or 4-year college or university in any state. Applicants must be planning to enroll in the NROTC program. They must have a GPA of 2.5 or higher and be U.S. citizens or permanent residents. Selection is based on academic achievement, community involvement, and financial need.

Financial Data The stipend is $1,000.

Duration 1 year; nonrenewable.

Additional data If the recipient fails to enroll in the NROTC unit, all scholarship funds must be returned.

Number awarded 1 each year.

Deadline March of each year.

[357]
WASHINGTON NATIONAL GUARD SCHOLARSHIP PROGRAM

Washington National Guard
Attn: Education Services Office
Building 15, G1-ED
Camp Murray, WA 98498
(253) 512-8899   Toll Free: (800) 606-9843 (within WA)
Fax: (253) 512-8941   E-mail: education@wa.ngb.army.mil
Web: washingtonguard.org/edu

Summary To provide forgivable loans to members of the Washington National Guard who wish to attend college or graduate school in the state.

Eligibility This program is open to members of the Washington National Guard who have already served for at least 1 year and have at least 2 years remaining on their current contract. Applicants must have a rank between E1 and O3. They must be attending an accredited college as a resident of Washington state and must already have utilized all available federal educational benefits. Army Guard members must have completed BCT/AIT and awarded initial MOS; Air Guard members must have completed BMT/initial tech school and been awarded "3-Level" AFSC. Graduate students are eligible, but undergraduates receive preference as long as they are making satisfactory progress toward a baccalaureate degree. The minimum GPA requirement is 2.5 for undergraduates or 3.0 for graduate students.

Financial Data This program provides a stipend that is based on the number of credits completed but does not exceed the amount required for tuition, books, and fees at the University of Washington. Recipients incur a service obligation of 1 additional year in the Guard for the initial scholarship award and 1 additional year for each full year of academic credit completed with this assistance. The grant serves as a loan which is forgiven if the recipient completes the contracted service time in the Washington National Guard. Failure to meet the service obligation requires the recipient to repay the loan plus 8% interest.

Duration 1 year; may be renewed.

Number awarded Varies each year. A total of $100,000 is available for this program annually; scholarships are awarded on a first-come, first-served basis as long as funds are available.

Deadline June of each year.

[358]
WASHINGTON STATE EMPLOYEE TUITION WAIVER

Washington National Guard
Attn: Education Services Office
Building 15, G1-ED
Camp Murray, WA 98498
(253) 512-8899   Toll Free: (800) 606-9843 (within WA)
Fax: (253) 512-8941   E-mail: education@wa.ngb.army.mil
Web: washingtonguard.org/edu

Summary To enable members of the Washington National Guard to attend public colleges and universities in the state without payment of tuition.

Eligibility This program is open to members of the Washington National Guard who are interested in attending state universities, regional universities, and community colleges in Washington.

Financial Data Participating colleges and universities waive all or a portion of tuition and fees for members of the Washington National Guard on a space available basis.

Duration 1 class; depending on the school, additional waivers may be granted.

Additional data This program, also known as the House Bill 1601 Program, was established in 1996 when the state legislature expanded existing law, which applied to state employees, to include members of the National Guard. Each public college and university in the state decides if it wishes to support the program and terms under which it does so.

Number awarded Varies each year.

Deadline Each participating college and university determines the deadline for its applicants.

[359]
WEST VIRGINIA NATIONAL GUARD EDUCATIONAL ENCOURAGEMENT PROGRAM

Office of the Adjutant General
Attn: Education Officer
1703 Coonskin Drive
Charleston, WV 25311-1085
(304) 561-6306   Toll Free: (866) 986-4326
Fax: (304) 561-6307   E-mail: kathy.kidd@us.army.mil
Web: www.wv.ngb.army.mil/education/benefits/default.aspx

Summary To provide financial assistance to members of the National Guard in West Virginia who are interested in attending college or graduate school in the state.

Eligibility This program is open to active members of the West Virginia National Guard who are residents of West Virginia and interested in attending a public or private college in the state. Applicants must have maintained satisfactory participation (90% attendance) in the Guard. They must be interested in working on a vocational, associate, bachelor's, or master's degree. In some instances, support may also be available to Guard members who are interested in working on an M.D., D.O., P.A., or J.D. degree.

Financial Data The program provides payment of 100% of the tuition and fees at participating colleges and universities in West Virginia, to a maximum of $6,000 per year.

Duration   1 academic year; may be renewed.
Number awarded   Varies each year.
Deadline   Deadline not specified.

[360]
WISCONSIN NATIONAL GUARD TUITION GRANT

Wisconsin Department of Military Affairs
Attn: Education Services Office
WIAR-PA-ED
P.O. Box 8111
Madison, WI 53708-8111
(608) 242-3159   Toll Free: (800) 292-9464, ext. 2
Fax: (608) 242-3154
Web: dma.wi.gov/dma/dma/education.asp

Summary   To provide financial assistance for college to members of the Wisconsin National Guard.

Eligibility   Eligible to apply for these grants are enlisted members and warrant officers in good standing in the Wisconsin National Guard who wish to work on an undergraduate degree. Applicants may not have been flagged for unexcused absences or failing to meet Guard standards. They must be attending or planning to attend an extension division or campus of the University of Wisconsin system, a public institution of higher education under the Minnesota-Wisconsin student reciprocity agreement, a campus of the Wisconsin Technical College System, or an accredited institution of higher education located within Wisconsin.

Financial Data   This program offers assistance based on the undergraduate tuition rate of the University of Wisconsin at Madison (recently, that was $8,313 per year for full-time study).

Duration   8 semesters of full-time study or completion of a bachelor's degree.

Number awarded   Varies each year.

Deadline   Applications may be submitted at any time, but they must be received at least 30 days prior to the beginning of the course.

[361]
WMA SCHOLARSHIP PROGRAM

Women Marines Association
P.O. Box 377
Oaks, PA 19456-0377
Toll Free: (888) 525-1943   E-mail: wma@womenmarines.org
Web: www.womenmarines.org/scholarships.aspx

Summary   To provide financial assistance for college or graduate school to students sponsored by members of the Women Marines Association (WMA).

Eligibility   Applicants must be sponsored by a WMA member and fall into 1 of the following categories: 1) have served or are serving in the U.S. Marine Corps, regular or Reserve; 2) are a direct descendant by blood, legal adoption, or stepchild of a Marine on active duty or who has served honorably in the U.S. Marine Corps, regular or Reserve; 3) are a sibling or a descendant of a sibling by blood, legal adoption, or stepchild of a Marine on active duty or who has served honorably in the U.S. Marine Corps, regular or Reserve; or 4) have completed 2 years in a Marine Corps JROTC program. WMA members may sponsor an unlimited number of applicants per year. High school seniors must submit transcripts (GPA of 3.0 or higher) and SAT or ACT scores. Undergraduate and graduate students must have a GPA of 3.0 or higher.

Financial Data   The stipend is $1,500 per year.

Duration   1 year; may be renewed 1 additional year.

Additional data   This program includes the following named scholarships: the WMA Memorial Scholarships, the Lily H. Gridley Memorial Scholarship, the Ethyl and Armin Wiebke Memorial Scholarship, the Maj. Megan Malia McClung Memorial Scholarship, and the LaRue A. Ditmore Music Scholarships. Applicants must know a WMA member to serve as their sponsor; the WMA

will not supply listings of the names or addresses of chapters or individual members.

Number awarded   Varies each year.

Deadline   March of each year.

[362]
WNGEA COLLEGE GRANT PROGRAM

Wisconsin National Guard Enlisted Association
Attn: Executive Director
2400 Wright Street
Madison, WI 53704
(608) 242-3112   E-mail: WNGEA@yahoo.com
Web: www.wngea.org/MAIN/PROG/prosch.htm

Summary   To provide financial assistance to members of the Wisconsin National Guard Enlisted Association (WNGEA) and their spouses and children who are interested in attending college or graduate school in any state.

Eligibility   This program is open to WNGEA members, the unmarried children of WNGEA members, the spouses of WNGEA members, and the unmarried children and spouses of deceased WNGEA members. WNGEA member applicants, as well as the parents or guardians of unmarried children who are applicants, must have at least 1 year remaining on their enlistment following completion of the school year for which application is submitted (or they must have 20 or more years of service). Applicants must be enrolled at a college, university, graduate school, trade school, or business school in any state. Selection is based on financial need, leadership, and moral character.

Financial Data   Stipends are $1,000 or $500 per year.

Duration   1 year; recipients may not reapply for 2 years.

Additional data   This program includes 1 scholarship sponsored by the USAA Insurance Corporation.

Number awarded   Varies each year. Recently, 4 of these scholarships were awarded: the Raymond A. Matera Scholarship at $1,000 and 3 others at $500 each.

Deadline   May of each year.

[363]
WOMEN'S OVERSEAS SERVICE LEAGUE SCHOLARSHIPS FOR WOMEN

Women's Overseas Service League
Attn: Scholarship Committee
P.O. Box 7124
Washington, DC 20044-7124
E-mail: carolhabgood@sbcglobal.net
Web: www.wosl.org/scholarships.htm

Summary   To provide financial assistance for college to women who are committed to a military or other public service career.

Eligibility   This program is open to women who are committed to a military or other public service career. Applicants must have completed at least 12 semester or 18 quarter hours of postsecondary study with at a GPA of 2.5 or higher. They must be working on an academic degree (the program may be professional or technical in nature) and must agree to enroll for at least 6 semester or 9 quarter hours of study each academic period. Along with their application, they must submit an official transcript, a 1-page essay on their career goals, 3 current letters of reference, and a brief statement describing sources of financial support and the need for scholarship assistance. They must also provide information on their educational background, employment experience, civic and volunteer activities, and expected degree completion date.

Financial Data   Stipends range from $500 to $1,000 per year.

Duration   1 year; may be renewed 1 additional year.

Additional data   The Women's Overseas Service League is a national organization of women who have served overseas in or with the armed forces.

Deadline   February of each year.

[364]
WYOMING NATIONAL GUARD EDUCATIONAL ASSISTANCE PLAN

Wyoming National Guard
Attn: Education Services Officer
5500 Bishop Boulevard
Cheyenne, WY 82009-3320
(307) 772-5053   Toll Free: (800) 832-1959, ext. 5053
Fax: (307) 772-5132   E-mail: poconn@state.wy.us
Web: www.wy.ngb.army.mil/Tuition/assistance.asp

Summary To provide financial assistance to members of the Wyoming National Guard who are interested in attending college or graduate school in the state.

Eligibility This program is open to members of the Wyoming Army National Guard and the Wyoming Air National Guard who have spent at least 6 years in the Guard or are currently serving under their initial 6-year enlistment period. New enlistees who commit to serving 6 years are also eligible. Applicants may be pursuing, or planning to pursue, a degree at any level at the University of Wyoming, a Wyoming community college, or an approved technical institution in Wyoming.

Financial Data The program provides full payment of tuition at eligible institutions.

Duration Guard members may continue to receive these benefits as long as they maintain a GPA of 2.0 or higher, keep up with Guard standards for drill attendance, and remain in good standing with the Guard.

Additional data The Wyoming legislature created this program in 2001. Recipients must agree to serve in the Guard for at least 2 years after they graduate or stop using the plan.

Number awarded Varies each year.

Deadline Deadline not specified.

Family Members

[365]
100TH INFANTRY BATTALION MEMORIAL SCHOLARSHIP FUND

Hawai'i Community Foundation
Attn: Scholarship Department
1164 Bishop Street, Suite 800
Honolulu, HI 96813
(808) 566-5570   Toll Free: (888) 731-3863
Fax: (808) 521-6286   E-mail: scholarships@hcf-hawaii.org
Web: www.hawaiicommunityfoundation.org

Summary To provide financial assistance for college or graduate school to descendants of 100th Infantry Battalion World War II veterans.

Eligibility This program is open to entering and continuing full-time undergraduate and graduate students at 2- and 4-year colleges and universities. Applicants must be a direct descendant of a World War II veteran of the 100th Infantry Battalion (which was comprised of Americans of Japanese descent). They must be able to demonstrate academic achievement (GPA of 3.5 or higher), an active record of extracurricular activities and community service, a willingness to promote the legacy of the 100th Infantry Battalion of World War II, and financial need. Along with their application, they must submit a short statement indicating their reasons for attending college, their planned course of study, and their career goals. Current residency in Hawaii is not required.

Financial Data The amounts of the awards depend on the availability of funds and the need of the recipient; recently, stipends averaged $4,250.

Duration 1 year.

Number awarded Varies each year; recently, 2 of these scholarships were awarded.

Deadline February of each year.

[366]
10TH MOUNTAIN DIVISION DESCENDANT MERIT SCHOLARSHIP

10th Mountain Division Descendants, Inc.
c/o Don Perkins, Treasurer
P.O. Box 20011
New York, NY 10017-0001
E-mail: admin@10thmtndivdesc.org
Web: www.10thmtndivdesc.org/?cat=3

Summary To provide financial assistance for college to descendants of former members of the 10th Mountain Division.

Eligibility Eligible to apply for these scholarships are the descendants of veterans who served in the 10th Mountain Division during World War II. Applicants must be entering their first year of college. Selection is based on service to the World War II 10th Mountain Division (e.g., assisting at local chapter functions, involved in activities that support the legacy of the division, assisting at memorial services to the division, visiting veterans and/or wives or widows in nursing or private homes). Financial need is not considered. Membership in 10th Mountain Division Descendants, Inc. is not required, but it is recommended that the applicant or a parent be a member.

Financial Data The stipend is $1,000.

Duration 1 year.

Number awarded 1 each year.

Deadline April each year.

[367]
11TH ARMORED CAVALRY VETERANS OF VIETNAM AND CAMBODIA SCHOLARSHIP

11th Armored Cavalry Veterans of Vietnam and Cambodia
Attn: National Headquarters
P.O. Box 1948
Plainview, TX 79073-1948
Web: www.11thcavnam.com/scholar.html

Summary To provide financial assistance for college to members of the 11th Armored Cavalry Veterans of Vietnam and Cambodia (11ACVVC) and to their children.

Eligibility This program is open to 1) current members of the 11ACVVC; 2) children and stepchildren of current members of the 11ACVVC; 3) children whose legal guardian is a current member of the 11ACVVC; and 4) children of 11th Armored Cavalry troopers who were killed in action, died of wounds, or died as a result of service in Vietnam or Cambodia. Applicants must be enrolled or planning to enroll as an undergraduate student. Along with their application, they must submit brief essays on 1) the field of study they plan to enter and why; and 2) why they would be a worthy recipient of this scholarship. Selection is based on the essays and grades; financial need is not considered. Priority is given to children of members who were killed in action or died of wounds.

Financial Data The stipend is $3,000; funds are paid directly to the recipient's school, in 2 equal installments.

Duration 1 year; nonrenewable.

Additional data This program was established in 1997. Recipients must use the awarded money within 20 months of being notified.

Number awarded Varies each year; recently, 19 of these scholarships were awarded. Since the program was established, it has awarded a total of 245 scholarships with a value of $705,000.

Deadline May of each year.

[368]
25TH INFANTRY DIVISION ASSOCIATION EDUCATIONAL MEMORIAL SCHOLARSHIP AWARD

25th Infantry Division Association
P.O. Box 7
Flourtown, PA 19031-0007
E-mail: TropicLtn@aol.com
Web: www.25thida.com/associat.html

Summary To provide financial assistance for college to descendants of members of the 25th Infantry Division Association and of deceased members of the 25th Infantry Division.

Eligibility This program is open to 1) children and grandchildren of active members of the association; and 2) children of former members of the division deceased during active combat with the division or as a result of it. Applicants must be enrolling in the freshman year of an accredited 4-year college or university and intending to work toward a baccalaureate degree by enrolling in at least 12 semester hours of study each semester. They must submit 1) a personal letter describing the reasons for their request, future plans, school interests and activities, and financial situation; 2) a transcript of high school credits; 3) their most recent ACT or SAT scores; 4) 3 letters of recommendation; 5) a letter of acceptance from the institution they plan to attend; and 6) a photograph.

Financial Data Stipends up to $1,500 are available.

Duration Each grant is a 1-time award, which may be spent over any period of time.

Additional data This program includes the George and Rosemary Murray Scholarship Award.

Number awarded Varies each year.

Deadline March of each year.

[369]
AAAA SCHOLARSHIPS

Army Aviation Association of America Scholarship
  Foundation
Attn: AAAA Scholarship Foundation
755 Main Street, Suite 4D
Monroe, CT 06468-2830
(203) 268-2450   Fax: (203) 268-5870
E-mail: Scholarship@quad-a.org
Web: www.quad-a.org/scholarship.htm

Summary To provide financial aid for undergraduate or graduate study to members of the Army Aviation Association of America (AAAA) and their relatives.

Eligibility This program is open to AAAA members and their spouses, unmarried siblings, unmarried children, and unmarried grandchildren. Applicants must be enrolled or accepted for enrollment as an undergraduate or graduate student at an accredited college or university. Graduate students must include a 250-word essay on their life experiences, work history, and aspirations. Some scholarships are specifically reserved for enlisted, warrant officer, company grade, and Department of the Army civilian members. Selection is based on academic merit and personal achievement.

Financial Data Most stipends range from $1,000 to $4,000. Special scholarships are $11,000.

Duration Scholarships may be for 1 year, 2 years, or 4 years.

Additional data This program includes 3 special scholarships: the GEN Hamilton H. Howze Memorial Scholarship, the Helen Cribbins Memorial Scholarship, and the Joseph P. Cribbins Scholarship.

Number awarded Varies each year; recently, $268,500 in scholarships was awarded to 171 students. Since the program began in 1963, the foundation has awarded more than $3.3 million to nearly 2,000 qualified applicants.

Deadline April of each year.

[370]
AAFES RETIRED EMPLOYEES ASSOCIATION SCHOLARSHIPS

AAFES Retired Employees Association
Attn: Scholarship Committee
7045 Rembrandt Drive
Plano, TX 75093
(972) 862-8099   E-mail: gall.tom@verizon.net
Web: www.aafes.com/area/docs/programs.htm

Summary To provide financial assistance for college to high school seniors who have a tie to the Army and Air Force Exchange Service (AAFES).

Eligibility This program is open to high school seniors who are 1) the child of an active, retired, or deceased AAFES employee; 2) the child of assigned military personnel; or 3) an AAFES employee. Military retirees must have retired while on assignment with AAFES. Deceased parents must have died while an active or retired AAFES employee or military assignee. All retired parents must be members of the AAFES Retired Employees Association. Students who quality as an AAFES employee must have been employed for at least 1 year. At least 1 qualifying parent must have been an AAFES employee or on military assignment for at least 1 year. Applicants must be planning to attend an accredited college or university or a U.S. military academy. They must have scores of at least 1750 on the SAT or 25 on the ACT. Along with their application, they must submit an essay on why they should be awarded this scholarship. Selection is based on that essay; academic honors and other recognition received; school activity participation; outside activities, hobbies, and special talents; and letters of recommendation.

Financial Data Stipends range from $2,500 to $5,000.

Duration 1 year.

Additional data These scholarships were first awarded in 1985.

Number awarded Varies each year. Recently, 12 of these scholarships were awarded: 2 at $5,000, 1 at $4,000, and 9 at $2,500. Since the program began, it has awarded 221 scholarships, worth $388,795.

Deadline March of each year.

[371]
ADA MUCKLESTONE MEMORIAL SCHOLARSHIPS

American Legion Auxiliary
Department of Illinois
2720 East Lincoln Street
P.O. Box 1426
Bloomington, IL 61702-1426
(309) 663-9366   Fax: (309) 663-5827
E-mail: staff@ilala.org
Web: illegion.org/auxiliary/scholar.html

Summary To provide financial assistance to high school seniors in Illinois who are the descendants of veterans and planning to attend college in any state.

Eligibility This program is open to the children, grandchildren, or great-grandchildren of veterans who served during eligibility dates for membership in the American Legion. Applicants must be high school seniors or graduates who have not yet attended an institution of higher learning and are planning to attend college in any state. They must be residents of Illinois or members of the American Legion Family, Department of Illinois. Along with their application, they must submit a 1,000-word essay on "What my education will do for me." Selection is based on that essay (25%)

character and leadership (25%), scholarship (25%), and financial need (25%).

Financial Data The first winner receives a scholarship of $1,200, the second winner a scholarship of $1,000, and several other winners each receive $800.

Duration 1 year.

Number awarded Varies each year.

Deadline March of each year.

[372]
AFOWC OF WASHINGTON, D.C. CONTINUING EDUCATION SCHOLARSHIPS FOR AIR FORCE DEPENDENTS

Air Force Officers' Wives' Club of Washington, D.C.
Attn: Scholarship Committee
P.O. Box 8490
Washington, DC 20032
E-mail: scholarship@afowc.com
Web: www.afowc.com/making-difference.html

Summary To provide financial assistance for undergraduate or graduate education in any state to the dependents of Air Force members in the Washington, D.C. area.

Eligibility This program is open to the dependents of Air Force members residing in the Washington, D.C. metropolitan area in the following categories: active duty, retired, MIA/POW, or deceased. Dependents are eligible if their Air Force sponsor is assigned remote from the area or reassigned during the current school year and the student has remained behind to continue school. Applicants must be currently enrolled full time at an accredited college or university in any state and have a GPA of 3.0 or higher. Along with their application, they must submit a 500-word essay on a topic that changes annually; recently, applicants were asked to write on which book is required reading for all students and why. Selection is based on academic and citizenship achievements; financial need is not considered. Applicants who receive an appointment to a service academy are not eligible.

Financial Data A stipend is awarded (amount not specified). Funds may be used only for payment of tuition or academic fees.

Duration 1 year.

Number awarded Varies each year.

Deadline February of each year.

[373]
AFOWC OF WASHINGTON, D.C. CONTINUING EDUCATION SCHOLARSHIPS FOR NON-MILITARY AIR FORCE SPOUSES

Air Force Officers' Wives' Club of Washington, D.C.
Attn: Scholarship Committee
P.O. Box 8490
Washington, DC 20032
E-mail: scholarship@afowc.com
Web: www.afowc.com/making-difference.html

Summary To provide financial assistance for undergraduate or graduate study in any state to the non-military spouses of Air Force members in the Washington, D.C. area.

Eligibility This program is open to the non-military spouses of Air Force members residing in the Washington, D.C. metropolitan area in the following categories: active duty, retired, MIA/POW, or deceased. Spouses whose Air Force sponsor is assigned remote from the area or reassigned during the current school year are also eligible if they remained behind to continue their education. Applicants must be enrolled or planning to enroll as an undergraduate or graduate student at a college or university in any state. Along with their application, they must submit a 500-word essay on a topic that changes annually; recently, applicants were asked to write on which book is required reading for all students and why. Selection is based on academic and citizenship achievements; financial need is not considered.

Financial Data A stipend is awarded (amount not specified). Funds may be used only for payment of tuition or academic fees.

Duration 1 year.

Number awarded Varies each year.

Deadline February of each year.

[374]
AFSA SCHOLARSHIPS

Air Force Sergeants Association
Attn: Scholastic Program Coordinator
5211 Auth Road
Suitland, MD 20746
(301) 899-3500, ext. 230   Toll Free: (800) 638-0594, ext. 230
Fax: (301) 899-8136   E-mail: staff@hqafsa.org
Web: www.hqafsa.org

Summary To provide financial assistance for undergraduate education to the dependent children of Air Force enlisted personnel.

Eligibility This program is open to the unmarried children (including stepchildren and legally adopted children) of active-duty, retired, or veteran members of the U.S. Air Force, Air National Guard, or Air Force Reserves. Applicants must be attending or planning to attend an accredited academic institution. They must have an unweighted GPA of 3.5 or higher. Their parent must be a member of the Air Force Sergeants Association or its auxiliary. Along with their application, they must submit 1) a paragraph on their life objectives and what they plan to do with the education they receive; and 2) an essay on the most urgent problem facing society today. High school seniors must also submit a transcript of all high school grades and a record of their SAT or ACT scores. Selection is based on academic record, character, leadership skills, writing ability, versatility, and potential for success. Financial need is not a consideration.

Financial Data Stipends range from $1,500 to $2,500 per year. Funds may be used for tuition, room and board, fees, books, supplies, and transportation.

Duration 1 year; may be renewed if the student maintains full-time enrollment.

Additional data This program began in 1968.

Number awarded Varies each year. Recently, 11 of these scholarships were awarded: 5 at $2,500 (designated the Frank C. Fini, Hardy B. Abbott, Claude Klobus, James Staton, and Richard M. "Rick" Dean Scholarships); 3 at $2,000 (designated the Frank W. Garner, Richard D. Rousher, and Dr. Harry R. Page Scholarships); and 3 at $1,500. Since the program began, it has awarded more than 500 scholarships worth more than $700,000.

Deadline March of each year.

[375]
AIR FORCE EXCELLENCE SCHOLARSHIPS

Air Force Association
Attn: Scholarship Manager
1501 Lee Highway
Arlington, VA 22209-1198
(703) 247-5800, ext. 4807
Toll Free: (800) 727-3337, ext. 4807
Fax: (703) 247-5853   E-mail: LCross@afa.org
Web: www.afa.org/aef/aid/afa-fcef-rotc.asp

Summary To provide financial assistance for college or graduate school to Air Force personnel and their dependents.

Eligibility This program is open to Air Force active duty, Reserve, or Air National Guard personnel and their spouses and dependent children. Applicants must be entering or enrolled at an accredited college or university to work on an associate, bachelor's, or master's degree. In the selection process, no consideration is given to race, creed, color, sex, religious belief, national origin, rank, length of service, or financial need.

Financial Data The stipend is $3,000.

Duration 1 year.

Additional data This program was established in 2008 by the Air Force Association in partnership with the First Command Educational Foundation.

Number awarded 5 each year.

Deadline April of each year.

[376]
AIR FORCE OFFICERS' WIVES' CLUB OF WASHINGTON, D.C. HIGH SCHOOL SCHOLARSHIPS FOR AIR FORCE DEPENDENTS

Air Force Officers' Wives' Club of Washington, D.C.
Attn: Scholarship Committee
P.O. Box 8490
Washington, DC 20032
E-mail: scholarship@afowc.com
Web: www.afowc.com/making-difference.html

Summary To provide financial assistance for college to high school seniors who are dependents of Air Force members in the Washington, D.C. area.

Eligibility This program is open to high school seniors residing in the Washington, D.C. metropolitan area who are dependents of Air Force members in the following categories: active duty, retired, MIA/POW, or deceased. Also eligible are dependents whose Air Force sponsor is assigned remote from the area or reassigned during the current school year and they have remained behind to graduate. Applicants must be 1) high school seniors planning to work full time on an accredited undergraduate degree at a college or university in any state; or 2) high school seniors with a learning disability who plan to work full time on an undergraduate degree at a college or university in any state. Along with their application, they must submit a 500-word essay on a topic that changes annually; recently, applicants were asked to write on which book is required reading for all students and why. Selection is based on academic and citizenship achievements; financial need is not considered. Applicants who receive an appointment to a service academy are not eligible.

Financial Data A stipend is awarded (amount not specified). Funds may be used only for payment of tuition or academic fees.

Duration 1 year.

Number awarded Varies each year.

Deadline February of each year.

[377]
AIR FORCE SERGEANTS ASSOCIATION INTERNATIONAL AUXILIARY EDUCATION GRANTS

Air Force Sergeants Association
Attn: Scholastic Program Coordinator
5211 Auth Road
Suitland, MD 20746
(301) 899-3500, ext. 230   Toll Free: (800) 638-0594, ext. 230
Fax: (301) 899-8136   E-mail: staff@hqafsa.org
Web: www.hqafsa.org

Summary To provide financial assistance for college to members of the Air Force Sergeants Association (AFSA) Auxiliary.

Eligibility This program is open to AFSA Auxiliary members who need assistance to enhance their income potential through formal education and/or training. Applicants must be seeking to obtain effective education and/or training to acquire improved marketable skills.

Financial Data Stipends up to $2,000 per year are available. Funds are sent directly to the recipient's school to be used for tuition, room and board, fees, books, supplies, child care, meals, and transportation.

Duration 1 year; may be renewed if the student maintains full-time enrollment.

Additional data This program began in 1990.

Number awarded Varies each year. Since the program began, it has awarded grants worth more than $120,000.

Deadline March of each year.

[378]
AIR FORCE SERVICES CLUB MEMBERSHIP SCHOLARSHIP PROGRAM

Air Force Services Agency
Attn: HQ AFSVA/SVOFT
10100 Reunion Place, Suite 501
San Antonio, TX 78216-4138
(210) 652-6312   Toll Free: (800) 443-4834
Fax: (210) 652-7041
E-mail: web.clubs-operations@randolph.af.mil
Web: www.afclubs.net/CN_Scholarship.htm

Summary To recognize and reward, with academic scholarships, Air Force Club members and their families who submit outstanding essays.

Eligibility This program is open to Air Force Club members and their spouses, children, and stepchildren who have been accepted by or are enrolled at an accredited college or university. Grandchildren are eligible if they are the dependent of a club member. Applicants may be undergraduate or graduate students enrolled full or part time. They must submit an essay of up to 500 words on a topic that changes annually; a recent topic was "The High Cost of Freedom" Applicants must also include a 1-page summary of their long-term career and life goals and previous accomplishments, including civic, athletic, and academic awards.

Financial Data Awards are $1,000 scholarships.

Duration The competition is held annually.

Additional data This competition, first held in 1997, is sponsored by Chase Bank and the Coca-Cola Company.

Number awarded 25 each year.

Deadline Entries must be submitted to the member's base services commander or division chief by June of each year.

[379]
AIR FORCE SPOUSE SCHOLARSHIPS

Air Force Association
Attn: Scholarship Manager
1501 Lee Highway
Arlington, VA 22209-1198
(703) 247-5800, ext. 4807
Toll Free: (800) 727-3337, ext. 4807
Fax: (703) 247-5853   E-mail: LCross@afa.org
Web: www.afa.org/aef/aid/spouse.asp

Summary To provide financial assistance for undergraduate or graduate study to spouses of Air Force members.

Eligibility This program is open to spouses of active-duty Air Force, Air National Guard, or Air Force Reserve members. Spouses who are themselves military members or in ROTC are not eligible. Applicants must have a GPA of 3.5 or higher in college (or high school if entering college for the first time) and be able to provide proof of acceptance into an accredited undergraduate or graduate degree program. They must submit a 2-page essay on their academic and career goals, the motivation that led them to that decision, and how Air Force and other local community activities in which they are involved will enhance their goals. Selection is based on the essay and 2 letters of recommendation.

Financial Data The stipend is $2,500; funds are sent to the recipients' schools to be used for any reasonable cost related to working on a degree.

Duration 1 year; nonrenewable.

Additional data This program was established in 1995.

Number awarded Varies each year; recently, 7 of these scholarships were awarded.

Deadline April of each year.

[380]
AIRMEN MEMORIAL FOUNDATION SCHOLARSHIP PROGRAM

Air Force Sergeants Association
Attn: Scholastic Program Coordinator
5211 Auth Road
Suitland, MD 20746
(301) 899-3500, ext. 230   Toll Free: (800) 638-0594, ext. 230
Fax: (301) 899-8136   E-mail: staff@hqafsa.org
Web: www.hqafsa.org

Summary To provide financial assistance for college to the dependent children of enlisted Air Force personnel.

Eligibility This program is open to the unmarried children (including stepchildren and legally adopted children) of active-duty, retired, or veteran members of the U.S. Air Force, Air National Guard, or Air Force Reserves. Applicants must be attending or planning to attend an accredited academic institution. They must have an unweighted GPA of 3.5 or higher. Along with their application, they must submit 1) a paragraph on their life objectives and what they plan to do with the education they receive; and 2) an essay on the most urgent problem facing society today. High school seniors must also submit a transcript of all high school grades and a record of their SAT or ACT scores. Selection is based on academic record, character, leadership skills, writing ability, versatility, and potential for success. Financial need is not a consideration.

Financial Data Stipends are $3,000, $2,000, $1,500, or $1,000; funds may be used for tuition, room and board, fees, books, supplies, and transportation.

Duration 1 year; may be renewed if the recipient maintains full-time enrollment.

Additional data The Air Force Sergeants Association administers this program, which began in 1987, on behalf of the Airmen Memorial Foundation.

Number awarded Varies each year. Recently, 21 of these scholarships were awarded: 2 at $3,000 (designated the Richard Howard Scholarship and the Julene Howard Scholarship), 2 at $2,000 (designated the Sharon Piccoli Memorial Scholarship and the Sgt. James R. Seal Memorial Scholarship), 1 at $1,500, and 16 at $1,000 (including the Audrey Andrews Memorial Scholarship plus 3 sponsored by the United Services Automobile Association (USAA) Insurance Corporation). Since this program began, it has awarded more than $400,000 in financial aid.

Deadline March of each year.

[381]
AL AND WILLAMARY VISTE SCHOLARSHIP PROGRAM

101st Airborne Division Association
32 Screaming Eagle Boulevard
P.O. Box 929
Fort Campbell, KY 42223-0929
(931) 431-0199   Fax: (931) 431-0195
E-mail: 101stairbornedivisionassociation@comcast.net
Web: www.screamingeagle.org

Summary To provide financial assistance to the spouses, children, and grandchildren of members of the 101st Airborne Division Association who are upper-division or graduate students working on a degree in science.

Eligibility This program is open to college juniors, seniors, and graduate students who maintained a GPA of 3.75 or higher during the preceding school year and whose parent, grandparent, or spouse is (or, if deceased, was) a regular or life (not associate) member of the 101st Airborne Division. Preference is given to students working on a degree in a physical science, medical science, or other scientific research field. Applicants must submit a 500-word essay on what it means to be an American and a letter on their course of study, community service, hobbies, interests, personal achievements, and how a higher education for them in their

chosen field can benefit our nation. Selection is based on the letter, career objectives, academic record, and letters of recommendation.

Financial Data A stipend is awarded (amount not specified).

Duration 1 year; may be renewed.

Number awarded At least 1 each year.

Deadline May of each year.

[382]
ALABAMA G.I. DEPENDENTS' SCHOLARSHIP PROGRAM

Alabama Department of Veterans Affairs
770 Washington Avenue, Suite 530
Montgomery, AL 36102-1509
(334) 242-5077   Fax: (334) 242-5102
E-mail: willie.moore@va.state.al.us
Web: www.va.state.al.us/scholarship.htm

Summary To provide educational benefits to the dependents of disabled, deceased, and other Alabama veterans.

Eligibility Eligible are spouses, children, stepchildren, and unremarried widow(er)s of veterans who served honorably for 90 days or more and 1) are currently rated as 20% or more service-connected disabled or were so rated at time of death; 2) were a former prisoner of war; 3) have been declared missing in action; 4) died as the result of a service-connected disability; or 5) died while on active military duty in the line of duty. The veteran must have been a permanent civilian resident of Alabama for at least 1 year prior to entering active military service; veterans who were not Alabama residents at the time of entering active military service may also qualify if they have a 100% disability and were permanent residents of Alabama for at least 5 years prior to filing the application for this program or prior to death, if deceased. Children and stepchildren must be under the age of 26, but spouses and unremarried widow(er)s may be of any age.

Financial Data Eligible dependents may attend any state-supported Alabama institution of higher learning or enroll in a prescribed course of study at any Alabama state-supported trade school without payment of any tuition, book fees, or laboratory charges.

Duration This is an entitlement program for 4 years of full-time undergraduate or graduate study or part-time equivalent. Spouses and unremarried widow(er)s whose veteran spouse is rated between 20% and 90% disabled, or 100% disabled but not permanently so, may attend only 2 standard academic years.

Additional data Benefits for children, spouses, and unremarried widow(er)s are available in addition to federal government benefits. Assistance is not provided for noncredit courses, placement testing, GED preparation, continuing educational courses, pre-technical courses, or state board examinations.

Number awarded Varies each year.

Deadline Applications may be submitted at any time.

[383]
ALASKA FREE TUITION FOR SPOUSES AND DEPENDENTS OF ARMED SERVICES MEMBERS

Department of Military and Veterans Affairs
Attn: Office of Veterans Affairs
P.O. Box 5800
Fort Richardson, AK 99505-5800
(907) 428-6016   Fax: (907) 428-6019
E-mail: jerry_beale@ak-prepared.com
Web: veterans.alaska.gov/state_benefits.htm

Summary To provide financial assistance for college to dependents and spouses in Alaska of servicemembers who died or were declared prisoners of war or missing in action.

Eligibility Eligible for this benefit are the spouses and dependent children of Alaska residents who died in the line of duty, died of injuries sustained in the line of duty, or were listed by the

Department of Defense as a prisoner of war or missing in action. Applicants must be in good standing at a state-supported educational institution in Alaska.

Financial Data Those eligible may attend any state-supported educational institution in Alaska without payment of tuition or fees.

Duration 1 year; may be renewed.

Additional data Information is available from the financial aid office of state-supported universities in Alaska.

Number awarded Varies each year.

Deadline Deadline not specified.

[384]
ALASKA LEGION AUXILIARY SCHOLARSHIP

American Legion Auxiliary
Department of Alaska
Attn: Secretary/Treasurer
1392 Sixth Avenue
Fairbanks, AK 99701
(907) 455-4420   Fax: (907) 474-3040
E-mail: akaladep@ptialaska.net
Web: www.alaskalegion.org/Auxiliary.htm

Summary To provide financial assistance to veterans' children in Alaska who plan to attend college in any state.

Eligibility This program is open to the children of veterans who served during eligibility dates for membership in the American Legion. Applicants must be between 17 and 24 years of age, high school seniors or graduates who have not yet attended an institution of higher learning, and residents of Alaska. They must be planning to attend a college or university in any state.

Financial Data The stipend is $1,500, half of which is payable each semester toward tuition, matriculation, laboratory, or similar fees.

Duration 1 year.

Number awarded 1 each year.

Deadline March of each year.

[385]
ALASKA SEA SERVICES SCHOLARSHIPS

Navy League of the United States
Attn: Scholarships
2300 Wilson Boulevard, Suite 200
Arlington, VA 22201-5424
(703) 528-1775   Toll Free: (800) 356-5760
Fax: (703) 528-2333   E-mail: scholarships@navyleague.org
Web: www.navyleague.org/scholarship

Summary To provide financial assistance to spouses and dependent children of naval personnel in Alaska who are interested in attending college in any state.

Eligibility This program is open to the spouses and dependent children of active-duty, inactive-duty, and retired (with or without pay) members of the regular and Reserve Navy, Marine Corps, or Coast Guard who are residents of Alaska. Applicants must be enrolled or planning to enroll full time at an accredited 4-year college or university in any state to work on an undergraduate degree. Selection is based on academic proficiency, character, leadership ability, community involvement, and financial need.

Financial Data The stipend is $1,000 per year; funds are paid directly to the academic institution for tuition, books, and fees.

Duration 1 year; may be renewed 1 additional year.

Number awarded Up to 4 each year.

Deadline February of each year.

[386]
ALBERT M. LAPPIN SCHOLARSHIP

American Legion
Department of Kansas
1314 S.W. Topeka Boulevard
Topeka, KS 66612-1886
(785) 232-9315   Fax: (785) 232-1399
Web: www.ksamlegion.org/programs.htm

Summary To provide financial assistance to the children of members of the Kansas American Legion or American Legion Auxiliary who plan to attend college in the state.

Eligibility This program is open to high school seniors and college freshmen and sophomores who are attending or planning to attend an approved Kansas college, university, or trade school. At least 1 of their parents must be a veteran and have been a member of an American Legion post or Auxiliary in Kansas for the past 3 consecutive years. Along with their application, they must submit an essay of 250 to 500 words on "Why I Want to Go to College." Financial need is also considered in the selection process.

Financial Data The stipend is $1,000.

Duration 1 year.

Number awarded 1 each year.

Deadline February of each year.

[387]
ALBERT T. MARCOUX MEMORIAL SCHOLARSHIP

American Legion
Department of New Hampshire
State House Annex
25 Capitol Street, Room 431
Concord, NH 03301-6312
(603) 271-2211   Toll Free: (800) 778-3816
Fax: (603) 271-5352
E-mail: adjutantnh@amlegion.state.nh.us
Web: www.nhlegion.org

Summary To provide financial assistance to the children of members of the New Hampshire Department of the American Legion or American Legion Auxiliary who are interested in studying education at a college in any state.

Eligibility This program is open to residents of New Hampshire who are entering their first year at an accredited 4-year college or university in any state to work on a bachelor's degree in the field of education. Applicant's parent must be a member of the American Legion or its Auxiliary (or if deceased have been a member at time of death). They must have a GPA of 3.0 or higher in their junior and senior high school years. Financial need is considered in the selection process.

Financial Data The stipend is $1,000.

Duration 1 year.

Number awarded 1 each year.

Deadline April of each year.

[388]
ALEXANDER KREIGLOW NAVY AND MARINE CORPS DEPENDENTS EDUCATION FOUNDATION SCHOLARSHIP

Navy League of the United States-San Diego Council
Attn: Scholarship Committee
2115 Park Boulevard
San Diego, CA 92101
(619) 230-0301   Fax: (619) 230-0302
Web: www.navyleague-sd.com/Scholarship.htm

Summary To provide financial assistance to high school seniors in California who are children of Naval Service personnel and interested in attending college in any state.

Eligibility This program is open to seniors graduating from high schools in California in the top 10% of their class. Applicants must be the dependent child of an active-duty, retired, or deceased member of the Naval Service (U.S. Navy or U.S. Marine Corps). They must be planning to enroll at an accredited 4-year college or university in any state. Along with their application, they must submit an essay of 1 to 2 pages describing their high school experience and accomplishments and how those will help them as they pursue a college education. Financial need is considered in the selection process.

Financial Data The stipend ranges up to $15,000 per year.

Duration 1 year; may be renewed up to 3 additional years.

Number awarded 1 each year.

Deadline March of each year.

[389]
ALLIE MAE ODEN MEMORIAL SCHOLARSHIP

Ladies Auxiliary of the Fleet Reserve Association
Attn: Administrator
P.O. Box 490678
Everett, MA 02149-0012
(617) 548-1191   E-mail: msakathy@live.com
Web: www.la-fra.org/scholarship.html

Summary To provide financial assistance for college to the children and grandchildren of members of the Fleet Reserve Association (FRA) or its ladies auxiliary (LA FRA).

Eligibility This program is open to the children and grandchildren of FRA or LA FRA members. Applicants must submit an essay on their life experiences, career objectives, and what motivated them to select those objectives. Selection is based on academic record, financial need, extracurricular activities, leadership skills, and participation in community activities. U.S. citizenship is required.

Financial Data The stipend is $2,500.

Duration 1 year; may be renewed.

Additional data Membership in the FRA is open to active-duty, retired, and Reserve members of the Navy, Marine Corps, and Coast Guard.

Number awarded 1 each year.

Deadline April of each year.

[390]
AMERICAL DIVISION VETERANS ASSOCIATION SCHOLARSHIP

Americal Division Veterans Association
c/o Ron Green, Scholar Fund Chair
P.O. Box 830662
Oconee, TN 37361
E-mail: ron_green46@yahoo.com
Web: www.americal.org/scholar.shtml

Summary To provide financial assistance for college to the dependents of members of the Americal Division Veterans Association.

Eligibility This program is open to the children and grandchildren of members of the Americal Division Veterans Association and to the children of Americal Division veterans who were killed in action or died while on active duty with the Division. Applicants must submit an essay of 200 to 300 words on subjects pertaining to Americal Division history, national pride, loyalty to the nation, patriotism, or a related topic. Financial need is not considered in the selection process.

Financial Data Recently, stipends ranged from $500 to $3,000 per year.

Duration 1 year; recipients may reapply.

Number awarded Varies each year. Recently, 33 of these scholarships were available: 1 at $3,000, 2 at $1,500, 10 at $1,000, and 20 at $500.

Deadline April of each year.

[391]
AMERICAN LEGACY SCHOLARSHIPS

American Legion
Attn: Americanism and Children & Youth Division
700 North Pennsylvania Street
P.O. Box 1055
Indianapolis, IN 46206-1055
(317) 630-1202   Fax: (317) 630-1223
E-mail: acy@legion.org
Web: www.legion.org/programs/resources/scholarships

Summary To provide financial assistance for college to children of U.S. military personnel killed on active duty on or after September 11, 2001.

Eligibility This program is open to the children (including adopted children and stepchildren) of active-duty U.S. military personnel (including federalized National Guard and Reserve members) who died on active duty on or after September 11, 2001. Applicants must be high school seniors or graduates planning to enroll full time at an accredited institution of higher education in the United States. Selection is based on academic achievement, school and community activities, leadership skills, and financial need.

Financial Data The stipend depends on the availability of funds.

Duration 1 year; may be renewed.

Additional data This program was established in 2003.

Number awarded Varies each year.

Deadline April of each year.

[392]
AMERICAN LEGION AUXILIARY EMERGENCY FUND

American Legion Auxiliary
8945 North Meridian Street
Indianapolis, IN 46260
(317) 569-4500   Fax: (317) 569-4502
E-mail: alahq@legion-aux.org
Web: www.legion-aux.org

Summary To provide funding to members of the American Legion Auxiliary who are facing temporary emergency needs.

Eligibility This program is open to members of the American Legion Auxiliary who have maintained their membership for the immediate past 2 consecutive years and have paid their dues for the current year. Applicants must need emergency assistance for the following purposes: 1) food, shelter, and utilities during a time of financial crisis; 2) food and shelter because of weather-related emergencies and natural disasters; or 3) educational training because of the death of a spouse, divorce, separation, or the need to become the main source of support for their family. They must have exhausted all other sources of financial assistance, including funds and/or services available through the local Post and/or Unit, appropriate community welfare agencies, or state and federal financial aid for education. Grants are not available to settle already existing or accumulated debts, handle catastrophic illness, resettle disaster victims, or other similar problems.

Financial Data The maximum grant is $2,400. Payments may be made directly to the member or to the mortgage company or utility. Educational grants may be paid directly to the educational institution.

Duration Grants are expended over no more than 3 months.

Additional data This program was established in 1969. In 1981, it was expanded to include the Displaced Homemaker Fund (although that title is no longer used).

Number awarded Varies each year.

Deadline Applications may be submitted at any time.

[393]
AMERICAN LEGION AUXILIARY NATIONAL PRESIDENT'S SCHOLARSHIP

American Legion Auxiliary
8945 North Meridian Street
Indianapolis, IN 46260
(317) 569-4500   Fax: (317) 569-4502
E-mail: alahq@legion-aux.org
Web: www.legion-aux.org

Summary To provide financial assistance for college to the children of war veterans.

Eligibility This program is open to children of veterans who served during wartime. Applicants must be high school seniors who have completed at least 50 hours of volunteer service within the community. Each Department (state) organization of the American Legion Auxiliary nominates 1 candidate for the National President's Scholarship annually. Nominees must submit a 1,000-word essay on a topic that changes annually; recently, students were asked to write on "Answering the Call to Serve My Community and Our Veterans." Selection is based on the essay (20%), character and leadership (20%), scholarship, (40%), and financial need (20%).

Financial Data Stipends are $2,500, $2,000, or $1,500. Funds are paid directly to the recipient's school.

Duration 1 year; recipients may not reapply.

Additional data Applications are available from the local Unit or from the Department Secretary or Department Education Chair of the state in which the applicant resides.

Number awarded 15 each year: in each of the 5 divisions of the Auxiliary, 1 scholarship at $2,500, 1 at $2,000, and 1 at $1,500 are awarded.

Deadline February of each year.

[394]
AMERICAN PATRIOT SCHOLARSHIPS

Military Officers Association of America
Attn: Educational Assistance Program
201 North Washington Street
Alexandria, VA 22314-2539
(703) 549-2311   Toll Free: (800) 234-MOAA
Fax: (703) 838-5819   E-mail: edassist@moaa.org
Web: www.moaa.org/about_scholarship_aboutfund/index.htm

Summary To provide financial assistance for undergraduate education to children of members of the uniformed services who have died.

Eligibility This program is open to children under 24 years of age of active, Reserve, and National Guard uniformed service personnel (Army, Navy, Air Force, Marines, Coast Guard, Public Health Service, or National Oceanographic and Atmospheric Administration) whose parent has died on active service. Applicants must be working on an undergraduate degree. They must have a GPA of 3.0 or higher. Selection is based on academic ability, activities, and financial need.

Financial Data The stipend is at least $2,500 per year.

Duration 1 year; may be renewed up to 4 additional years.

Additional data The MOAA was formerly named The Retired Officers Association (TROA). It established this program in 2002 in response to the tragic events of September 11, 2001.

Number awarded Varies each year; recently, 60 students were receiving support from this program.

Deadline February of each year.

[395]
AMVETS JROTC SCHOLARSHIPS

AMVETS National Headquarters
Attn: Scholarships
4647 Forbes Boulevard
Lanham, MD 20706-3807
(301) 459-9600   Toll Free: (877) 7-AMVETS, ext. 3043
Fax: (301) 459-7924   E-mail: amvets@amvets.org
Web: www.amvets.org/programs/scholarships.html

Summary To provide financial assistance for college to the children and grandchildren of members of AMVETS who have participated in Junior Reserve Officers' Training Corps (JROTC) in high school.

Eligibility This program is open to graduating high school seniors who are JROTC cadets and the children or grandchildren of an AMVETS member or of a deceased veteran who would have been eligible to be an AMVETS member. U.S. citizenship is required. Applicants must be interested in working full time on an undergraduate degree at an accredited college, university, or technical/trade school. Selection is based on financial need, academic promise (GPA of 3.0 or higher), involvement in extracurricular activities, and an essay of 50 to 100 words on "What a Higher Education Means to Me."

Financial Data The stipend is $1,000 per year.

Duration 1 year; nonrenewable.

Additional data Requests for applications must be accompanied by a self-addressed stamped envelope.

Number awarded 1 each year.

Deadline April of each year.

[396]
AMVETS NATIONAL LADIES AUXILIARY SCHOLARSHIPS

AMVETS National Ladies Auxiliary
Attn: Scholarship Officer
4647 Forbes Boulevard
Lanham, MD 20706-4380
(301) 459-6255   Fax: (301) 459-5403
E-mail: auxhdqs@amvets.org
Web: amvetsaux.org/about_us.htm

Summary To provide financial assistance to members and certain dependents of members of AMVETS Auxiliary who are already enrolled in college.

Eligibility Applicants must belong to AMVETS Auxiliary or be the child or grandchild of a member. They must be in at least the second year of undergraduate study at an accredited college or university. Applications must include 3 letters of recommendation and an essay (from 200 to 500 words) about their past accomplishments, career and educational goals, and objectives for the future. Selection is based on the letters of reference (15%), academic record (15%), the essay (25%), and financial need (45%).

Financial Data Scholarships are $1,000 or $750 each.

Duration 1 year.

Number awarded Up to 7 each year: 2 at $1,000 and 5 at $750.

Deadline June of each year.

[397]
AMVETS NATIONAL SCHOLARSHIPS FOR ENTERING COLLEGE FRESHMEN

AMVETS National Headquarters
Attn: Scholarships
4647 Forbes Boulevard
Lanham, MD 20706-3807
(301) 459-9600   Toll Free: (877) 7-AMVETS, ext. 3043
Fax: (301) 459-7924   E-mail: amvets@amvets.org
Web: www.amvets.org/programs/scholarships.html

Summary To provide financial assistance to the children and grandchildren of members of AMVETS who are entering college.

Eligibility This program is open to graduating high school seniors who are the children or grandchildren of an AMVETS member or of a deceased veteran who would have been eligible to be an AMVETS member. U.S. citizenship is required. Selection is based on financial need, academic promise (GPA of 3.0 or higher), involvement in extracurricular activities, and an essay of 50 to 100 words on "What a Higher Education Means to Me."

Financial Data The stipend is $1,000 per year.

Duration 4 years (provided the recipient maintains a GPA of 2.0 or higher).

Additional data Requests for applications must be accompanied by a self-addressed stamped envelope.

Number awarded 6 each year (1 in each AMVETS national district).

Deadline April of each year.

[398]
ANCHOR SCHOLARSHIP FOUNDATION AWARD

Anchor Scholarship Foundation
P.O. Box 9535
Norfolk, VA 23505-0505
(757) 374-3769   E-mail: admin@nchorscholarship.com
Web: www.anchorscholarship.com

Summary To provide financial assistance for college to dependents of active-duty or retired personnel serving in the Naval Surface Forces.

Eligibility This program is open to dependents of active-duty or retired personnel who have served at least 6 years (need not be consecutive) in a unit under the administrative control of Commanders, Naval Surface Forces, U.S. Atlantic Fleet or U.S. Pacific Fleet. Applicants must be attending or planning to attend an accredited 4-year college or university to work on a bachelor's degree as a full-time student. Selection is based on academic proficiency, extracurricular activities, character, all-around ability, and financial need.

Financial Data Stipends range up to $2,000.

Duration 1 year; may be renewed.

Additional data This foundation was established in 1980 and limited to personnel who had served in the Atlantic Fleet. Its program was originally known as the SURFLANT Scholarship Foundation Award. In 2004, the program was expanded to include those who served in the Pacific Fleet and the current name was adopted. Requests for applications must be accompanied by a self-addressed stamped envelope.

Number awarded Varies each year; recently, 43 of these scholarships were awarded.

Deadline March of each year.

[399]
ANGELFIRE SCHOLARSHIP

Datatel Scholars Foundation
4375 Fair Lakes Court
Fairfax, VA 22033
(703) 968-9000, ext. 4549   Toll Free: (800) 486-4332
Fax: (703) 968-4625   E-mail: scholars@datatel.com
Web: www.datatelscholars.org

Summary To provide financial assistance to graduating high school seniors, continuing college students, and graduate students who will be studying at a Datatel client school and are veterans, veterans' dependents, or refugees from southeast Asia.

Eligibility This program is open to 1) veterans who served in the Asian theater (Vietnam, Cambodia, or Laos) between 1964 and 1975; 2) their spouses and children; 3) refugees from Vietnam, Cambodia, or Laos; and 4) veterans who served in Operation Desert Storm, Operation Enduring Freedom, and/or Operation Iraqi Freedom. Applicants must attend a Datatel client college or university during the upcoming school year. They must first apply to their institution, which selects 2 semifinalists and forwards their applications to the sponsor. Along with their application, they must include a 1,000-word personal statement that discusses how the conflict has affected them personally, summarizes how the conflict has impacted their educational goals, and describes how being awarded this scholarship will help them achieve their goals. Selection is based on the quality of the personal statement (40%), academic merit (30%), achievements and civic involvement (20%), and 2 letters of recommendation (10%).

Financial Data The stipend is $1,700. Funds are paid directly to the institution.

Duration 1 year.

Additional data Datatel, Inc. produces advanced information technology solutions for higher education. It has more than 725 client sites in the United States and Canada. This scholarship was created to commemorate those who lost their lives in Vietnam or Iraq and is named after a memorial administered by the Disabled American Veterans Association in Angelfire, New Mexico.

Number awarded Varies each year. Recently, 10 of these scholarships were awarded.

Deadline Students must submit online applications to their institution or organization by January of each year.

[400]
ANNA GEAR JUNIOR SCHOLARSHIP

American Legion Auxiliary
Department of Virginia
Attn: Education Chair
1708 Commonwealth Avenue
Richmond, VA 23230
(804) 355-6410   Fax: (804) 353-5246

Summary To provide financial assistance to junior members of the American Legion Auxiliary in Virginia who plan to attend college in any state.

Eligibility This program is open to seniors graduating from high schools in Virginia and planning to attend college in any state. Applicants must have held junior membership in the American Legion Auxiliary for the 3 previous years. They must have completed at least 30 hours of volunteer service within their community and submit a 500-word article on "The Value of Volunteering in the Community."

Financial Data The stipend is $1,000.

Duration 1 year.

Number awarded 1 each year.

Deadline March of each year.

[401]
AOG DEPENDENT SCHOLARSHIPS

Association of Graduates
Attn: Vice President of Services
3116 Academy Drive, Suite 100
USAF Academy, CO 80840-4475
(719) 472-0300   Fax: (719) 333-4194
E-mail: Wayne.Taylor@aogusafa.org
Web: www.usafa.org/membership/GDS.aspx

Summary To provide financial assistance for undergraduate education to children of Association of Graduates (AOG) members.

Eligibility This program is open to children of graduates of the U.S. Air Force Academy who either are paid-in-full life members or have maintained annual membership for at least the 5 consecutive years immediately preceding submission of the application package. Applicants must be either the graduate's natural child or legally adopted child (although they need not be financially dependent upon the graduate or his/her surviving spouse). They must have a GPA of 3.0 or higher and be working or planning to work full time on an undergraduate degree. Along with their application, they must submit an essay of 400 to 600 words on their educational goals and an essay of 200 to 400 words on the importance of this scholarship to the continuance of their education. Selection is based on overall demonstrated merit, although financial need may also receive some consideration.

Financial Data   Stipends range from $500 to $2,000 per year. Funds are paid directly to the recipient.

Duration   1 year; recipients may reapply and be awarded 3 additional scholarships.

Number awarded   Varies each year; recently, 18 of these scholarships were awarded.

Deadline   February of each year.

[402]
A-OK STUDENT REWARD PROGRAM

U.S. Navy
Attn: Navy Exchange Service Command
3280 Virginia Beach Boulevard
Virginia Beach, VA 23452-5724
Toll Free: (800) NAV-EXCH
Web: www.navy-nex.com

Summary   To provide financial assistance for college to children of active and retired military personnel who shop at Navy Exchange (NEX) stores.

Eligibility   This program is open to dependent children of active-duty military members, Reservists, and military retirees who are enrolled in grades 1-12 and have a GPA of 3.0 or higher. Applicants submit an entry at the service desk of their NEX store. Winners are selected in a drawing.

Financial Data   Winners receive savings bonds for $5,000, $3,000, $2,000, or $1,000. Funds are intended to help pay expenses of college.

Duration   Drawings are held 4 times a year (in February, May, August, and November).

Additional data   This program was established in 1997.

Number awarded   16 each year: at each drawing, 1 savings bond for each of the 4 denominations is awarded.

Deadline   Deadline not specified.

[403]
AOWCGWA SCHOLARSHIP PROGRAM

Army Officers' Wives' Club of the Greater Washington Area
c/o Fort Myer Thrift Shop
Attn: Mary Pawlow, Scholarship Committee Chair
P.O. Box 1124
Fort Myer, VA 22211
(703) 764-9656   E-mail: aowcgwascholarship@gmail.com
Web: www.aowcgwa.org/scholarshippage.html

Summary   To provide financial assistance for college to the children and spouses of U.S. Army personnel and veterans in the Washington, D.C. metropolitan area.

Eligibility   This program is open to 1) high school seniors who are children of Army personnel, 2) college students under 22 years of age who are children of Army personnel; and 3) spouses of Army personnel. High school seniors and spouses must reside with their sponsor in the Washington metropolitan area; the sponsor of college students must reside in that area. Sponsors may be active-duty, retired, or deceased, and officer or enlisted. Applicants must submit an essay of 200 to 300 words on a topic that changes annually but relates to their experience as the member of an Army family; a list of extracurricular activities, honors, church activities, community service, and employment; an official transcript that includes (for high school seniors) their SAT or ACT scores; and a letter of recommendation. Students who plan to attend a service academy or receive another full scholarship are not eligible. Selection is based on scholastic merit and community involvement; financial need is not considered.

Financial Data   The maximum stipend is $2,000.

Duration   1 year.

Additional data   The Washington metropolitan area is defined to include the Virginia cities of Alexandria, Fairfax, Falls Church, Manassas, and Manassas Park; the Virginia counties of Arlington, Fairfax, Fauquier, Loudoun, Prince William, and Stafford; the Maryland counties of Calvert, Charles, Frederick, Montgomery, and Prince George's; and the District of Columbia. This program is supported in part by the First Command Educational Foundation.

Number awarded   1 or more each year.

Deadline   March of each year.

[404]
ARKANSAS MILITARY DEPENDENTS' SCHOLARSHIP PROGRAM

Arkansas Department of Higher Education
Attn: Financial Aid Division
114 East Capitol Avenue
Little Rock, AR 72201-3818
(501) 371-2050   Toll Free: (800) 54-STUDY
Fax: (501) 371-2001   E-mail: finaid@adhe.edu
Web: www.adhe.edu/divisions/financialaid/Pages/fa_mds.aspx

Summary   To provide financial assistance for educational purposes to dependents of certain categories of Arkansas veterans.

Eligibility   This program is open to the natural children, adopted children, stepchildren, and spouses of Arkansas residents who have been declared to be a prisoner of war, killed in action, missing in action, killed on ordnance delivery, or 100% totally and permanently disabled during, or as a result of, active military service. Applicants and their parent or spouse must be residents of Arkansas. They must be working on, or planning to work on, a bachelor's degree or certificate of completion at a public college, university, or technical school in Arkansas.

Financial Data   The program pays for tuition, general registration fees, special course fees, activity fees, room and board (if provided in campus facilities), and other charges associated with earning a degree or certificate.

Duration   1 year; undergraduates may obtain renewal as long as they make satisfactory progress toward a baccalaureate degree; graduate students may obtain renewal as long as they maintain a minimum GPA of 2.0 and make satisfactory progress toward a degree.

Additional data   This program was established in 1973 as the Arkansas Missing in Action/Killed in Action Dependents Scholarship Program to provide assistance to the dependents of veterans killed in action, missing in action, or declared a prisoner of war. In 2005, it was amended to include dependents of disabled veterans and given its current name. Applications must be submitted to the financial aid director at an Arkansas state-supported institution of higher education or state-supported technical/vocational school.

Number awarded   Varies each year; recently, 4 of these scholarships were awarded.

Deadline   July of each year for fall term, November of each year for spring or winter term, April of each year for first summer session, or June of each year for second summer session.

[405]
ARMY EMERGENCY RELIEF STATESIDE SPOUSE EDUCATION ASSISTANCE PROGRAM

Army Emergency Relief
200 Stovall Street
Alexandria, VA 22332-0600
(703) 428-0000   Toll Free: (866) 878-6378
Fax: (703) 325-7183   E-mail: aer@aerhq.org
Web: www.aerhq.org

Summary   To provide financial assistance for college to the dependent spouses of Army personnel living in the United States.

Eligibility   This program is open to spouses of Army soldiers on active duty, widow(er)s of soldiers who died while on active duty, spouses of retired soldiers, and widow(er)s of soldiers who died while in a retired status. Applicants must be residing in the United States. They must be enrolled or accepted for enrollment as a full-time student at an approved postsecondary or vocational institution. Study for a second undergraduate or graduate degree is not supported. Financial need is considered in the selection process.

Financial Data The maximum stipend is $2,800 per academic year.

Duration 1 year; may be renewed up to 3 additional years.

Additional data Army Emergency Relief is a private nonprofit organization dedicated to "helping the Army take care of its own." Its primary mission is to provide financial assistance to Army people and their dependents in time of valid emergency need; its educational program was established as a secondary mission to meet a need of Army people for their dependents to pursue vocational training, preparation for acceptance by service academies, or an undergraduate college education.

Number awarded Varies each year; recently, 546 spouses received $1,517,400 in support.

Deadline February of each year.

[406]
ARMY ENGINEER MEMORIAL AWARDS

Army Engineer Officers' Wives' Club
c/o Nancy Temple, Chair
P.O. Box 6332
Alexandria, VA 22306-6332
E-mail: scholarships@aeowc.com
Web: www.aeowc.com/scholarships.html

Summary To provide financial assistance for college to the children of officers who served in the Army Corps of Engineers.

Eligibility This program is open to children of U.S. Army Corps of Engineers officers and warrant officers who are currently on active duty, retired, or deceased while on active duty or after retiring from active duty. Applicants must be high school seniors planning to attend a college, university, or technical/vocational school. Along with their application, they must submit an essay of 300 to 400 words on the event that has had the greatest impact on their life so far and how they think it will affect them in the future. Selection is based on academic and extracurricular achievement during high school.

Financial Data Stipends are $2,000 or $1,000.

Duration 1 year.

Additional data This program was established in 1967.

Number awarded Varies each year. Recently, 4 of these scholarships were awarded.

Deadline February of each year.

[407]
ARMY NURSE CORPS ASSOCIATION SCHOLARSHIPS

Army Nurse Corps Association
Attn: Education Committee
P.O. Box 39235
San Antonio, TX 78218-1235
(210) 650-3534   Fax: (210) 650-3494
E-mail: education@e-anca.org
Web: e-anca.org/ANCAEduc.htm

Summary To provide financial assistance to students who have a connection to the Army and are interested in working on an undergraduate or graduate degree in nursing.

Eligibility This program is open to students attending colleges or universities that have accredited programs offering associate, bachelor's, master's, or doctoral degrees in nursing. Applicants must be 1) nursing students who plan to enter the active Army, Army National Guard, or Army Reserve and are not participating in a program funded by the active Army, Army National Guard, or Army Reserve; 2) nursing students who have previously served in the active Army, Army National Guard, or Army Reserve; 3) Army Nurse Corps officers enrolled in an undergraduate or graduate nursing program not funded by the active Army, Army National Guard, or Army Reserve; 4) Army enlisted soldiers in the active Army, Army National Guard, or Army Reserve who are working on a baccalaureate degree in nursing not funded by the active Army, Army National Guard, or Army Reserve; or 5) nursing students whose parent(s) or spouse are serving or have served in the active Army, Army National Guard, or Army Reserve. Along with their application, they must submit a personal statement on their professional career objectives, reasons for applying for this scholarship, financial need, special considerations, personal and academic interests, and why they are preparing for a nursing career.

Financial Data The stipend is $3,000. Funds are sent directly to the recipient's school.

Duration 1 year.

Additional data Although the sponsoring organization is made up of current, retired, and honorably discharged officers of the Army Nurse Corps, it does not have an official affiliation with the Army. Therefore, students who receive these scholarships do not incur any military service obligation.

Number awarded 1 or more each year.

Deadline March of each year.

[408]
ARNOLD SOBEL SCHOLARSHIPS

Coast Guard Foundation
Commandant (G-1112)
Attn: Scholarship Program Manager
2100 Second Street, S.W., Jemal 9-0733
Washington, DC 20593-0001
(202) 475-5159   Toll Free: (800) 872-4957
E-mail: yvette.d.wright@uscg.mil
Web: coastguardfoundation.org/pages/Scholarship-Guide.html

Summary To provide financial assistance for college to the dependent children of Coast Guard enlisted personnel.

Eligibility This program is open to the dependent children of enlisted members of the U.S. Coast Guard on active duty, retired, or deceased and of enlisted personnel in the Coast Guard Reserve currently on extended active duty 180 days or more. Applicants must be attending or planning to attend a college, university, or vocational school as a full-time undergraduate student. Along with their application, they must submit their SAT or ACT scores, a letter of recommendation, transcripts, and a financial information statement.

Financial Data The stipend is $5,000 per year.

Duration 1 year; may be renewed up to 3 additional years.

Number awarded 4 each year.

Deadline March of each year.

[409]
ASSOCIATION OF THE UNITED STATES NAVY EDUCATION ASSISTANCE PROGRAM

Association of the United States Navy
Attn: Education Assistance Program
1619 King Street
Alexandria, VA 22314-2793
(703) 548-5800   Toll Free: (877) NAVY-411
Fax: (866) 683-3647   E-mail: cfo@ausn.org
Web: www.ausn.org/?tabid=79

Summary To provide financial assistance for college to dependents of members of the Association of the United States Navy (formerly the Naval Reserve Association).

Eligibility This program is open to 1) dependent children under 24 years of age of association members and 2) widows or widowers of deceased members. Applicants must be enrolled or planning to enroll full time at a college, university, or technical school. They must be U.S. citizens. Preference is given to applicants who have demonstrated an interest in the "hard sciences" (e.g., mathematics, medicine, engineering). Selection is based on academic and leadership ability, potential, character, personal qualities, and financial need.

Financial Data The amounts of the stipends vary but recently averaged more than $4,000 per year.

Duration 1 year; may be renewed 1 additional year.

Additional data The Association of the United States Navy was formed in 2009 as a successor to the Naval Reserve Association.

Number awarded Varies each year.

Deadline April of each year.

[410]
BART LONGO MEMORIAL SCHOLARSHIPS

National Chief Petty Officers' Association
c/o Marjorie Hays, Treasurer
1014 Ronald Drive
Corpus Christi, TX 78412-3548
Web: www.goatlocker.org/ncpoa/scholarship.htm

Summary To provide financial assistance for college or graduate school to members of the National Chief Petty Officers' Association (NCPOA) and their families.

Eligibility This program is open to members of the NCPOA and the children, stepchildren, and grandchildren of living or deceased members. Applicants may be high school seniors or graduates entering a college or university or students currently enrolled full time as undergraduate or graduate students. Selection is based on academic achievement and participation in extracurricular activities; financial need is not considered.

Financial Data The stipend is $1,000.

Duration 1 year.

Additional data Membership in the NCPOA is limited to men and women who served or are serving as Chief Petty Officers in the U.S. Navy, U.S. Coast Guard, or their Reserve components for at least 30 days.

Number awarded 2 each year: 1 to a high school senior or graduate and 1 to an undergraduate or graduate student.

Deadline May of each year.

[411]
BETTER CHANCE SCHOLARSHIP

Associates of Vietnam Veterans of America
Attn: Scholarship Program
8719 Colesville Road, Suite 100
Silver Spring, MD 20910
(301) 585-4000   Toll Free: (800) VVA-1316
Fax: (301) 585-0519
Web: www.avva.org/Welcome%20Page/programs.htm

Summary To provide financial assistance for college to members of Vietnam Veterans of America (VVA) and Associates of Vietnam Veterans of America (AVVA), their families, and the families of Vietnam veterans killed or missing in action.

Eligibility This program is open to members of VVA and AVVA; their spouses, children, and grandchildren; and the spouses, children, and grandchildren of Vietnam veterans killed in action (KIA) or missing in action (MIA). Especially encouraged to apply are average students who are not eligible for academic scholarships but who can demonstrate financial need. Applicants must submit essays on their long-term goals, work experience, organizations or activities, and community service.

Financial Data Stipends are $1,000, $750, or $500.

Duration 1 year.

Additional data This program was established in 1998.

Number awarded 3 each year: 1 at $1,000, 1 at $750, and 1 at $500.

Deadline June of each year.

[412]
BG BENJAMIN B. TALLEY SCHOLARSHIP

Society of American Military Engineers-Anchorage Post
Attn: BG B.B. Talley Scholarship Endowment Fund
P.O. Box 6409
Anchorage, AK 99506-6409
E-mail: william_kontess@urscorp.com
Web: www.sameanchorage.org/h_about/scholinfo.html

Summary To provide financial assistance to student members of the Society of American Military Engineers (SAME) from Alaska who are working on a bachelor's or master's degree in designated fields of engineering or the natural sciences.

Eligibility This program is open to members of the Anchorage Post of SAME who are residents of Alaska, attending college in Alaska, an active-duty military member stationed in Alaska, or a dependent of an active-duty military member stationed in Alaska. Applicants must be 1) sophomores, juniors, or seniors majoring in engineering, architecture, construction or project management, natural sciences, physical sciences, applied sciences, or mathematics at an accredited college or university; or 2) students working on a master's degree in those fields. They must have a GPA of 2.5 or higher. U.S. citizenship is required. Along with their application, they must submit an essay of 250 to 500 words on their career goals. Selection is based on that essay, academic achievement, participation in school and community activities, and work/family activities; financial need is not considered.

Financial Data Stipends range up to $3,000.

Duration 1 year.

Additional data This program was established in 1997.

Number awarded Varies each year; at least 1 scholarship is reserved for a master's degree students.

Deadline December of each year.

[413]
BLACKHORSE SCHOLARSHIP

Blackhorse Association
P.O. Box 630141
Nacogdoches, TX 75963-0141
E-mail: info@blackhorse.org
Web: www.blackhorse.org/blackhorse-programs/scholarships

Summary To provide financial assistance for college to children of members of the Blackhorse Association who are currently serving or have served with the 11th Armored Cavalry Regiment (ACR).

Eligibility This program is open to the natural and adopted children of current or former 11th ACR solders who are also members of the association. Applicants must be attending or planning to attend college. In the selection process, first priority is given to children who lost a parent in service of the regiment; second priority is given to children of those incapacitated by wounds or injury while serving the regiment; third priority is given based on financial need of the applicant and family.

Financial Data The stipend is $3,000 per year.

Duration 1 year; may be renewed.

Additional data The Blackhorse Association was founded in 1970 by veterans of the 11th ACR who had served in Vietnam.

Number awarded Varies each year; recently, 3 of these scholarships were awarded. Since this program was established, it has awarded more than $300,000 in scholarships.

Deadline March of each year.

[414]
BOOZ ALLEN HAWAII SCHOLARSHIP FUND

Hawai'i Community Foundation
Attn: Scholarship Department
1164 Bishop Street, Suite 800
Honolulu, HI 96813
(808) 566-5570   Toll Free: (888) 731-3863
Fax: (808) 521-6286   E-mail: scholarships@hcf-hawaii.org
Web: www.hawaiicommunityfoundation.org

Summary To provide financial assistance to residents of Hawaii and dependents of military personnel stationed in the state who are interested in attending college in any state.

Eligibility This program is open to residents of Hawaii and dependents of military personnel stationed in the state. Applicants must be attending or planning to attend a 4-year accredited college or university in any state as a full-time undergraduate student. They must be able to demonstrate academic achievement (GPA of 3.0 or higher), good moral character, and financial need. Along with their application, they must include a personal statement describing their participation in community service projects or activities.

Financial Data The amounts of the awards depend on the availability of funds and the need of the recipient.

Duration 1 year.

Additional data Recipients may attend college in Hawaii or on the mainland.

Number awarded Varies each year.

Deadline February of each year.

[415]
BOWFIN MEMORIAL SCHOLARSHIPS

Pearl Harbor Submarine Officers' Wives' Club
c/o Lana Vargas
Pearl Harbor Submarine Memorial Association
11 Arizona Memorial Drive
Honolulu, HI 96818
(808) 423-1341   Fax: (808) 422-5201
E-mail: submariescholarships@ymail.com
Web: www.phsowc.org/PHSOWC/Scholarships.html

Summary To provide financial assistance to the children of submarine force personnel who live in Hawaii and plan to attend college in any state.

Eligibility This program is open to the children of submarine force personnel (active duty, retired, or deceased) who are under 23 years of age. Applicants may attend school anywhere in the United States, but their submarine sponsor or surviving parent must live in Hawaii. Selection is based on academic achievement, extracurricular activities, community involvement, motivation and goals, and financial need.

Financial Data Stipends range from $250 to $5,000 per year.

Duration 1 year; may be renewed upon annual reapplication.

Additional data This program was established in 1985 to honor the 3,505 submariners and 52 submarines lost during World War II.

Number awarded Varies each year; recently, 11 of these scholarships were awarded.

Deadline February of each year.

[416]
CALIFORNIA FEE WAIVER PROGRAM FOR CHILDREN OF VETERANS

California Department of Veterans Affairs
Attn: Division of Veterans Services
1227 O Street, Room 105
Sacramento, CA 95814
(916) 503-8397   Toll Free: (800) 952-LOAN (within CA)
Fax: (916) 653-2563   TDD: (800) 324-5966
E-mail: ruckergl@cdva.ca.gov
Web: www.cdva.ca.gov/VetService/Waivers.aspx

Summary To provide financial assistance for college to the children of disabled or deceased veterans in California.

Eligibility Eligible for this program are the children of veterans who 1) died of a service-connected disability; 2) had a service-connected disability at the time of death; or 3) currently have a service-connected disability of any level of severity. Applicants must plan to attend a community college in California, branch of the California State University system, or campus of the University of California. Their income, including the value of support received from parents, cannot exceed $11,201. California veteran status is not required for this program. Dependents in college who are eligible to receive federal education benefits from the U.S. Department of Veterans Affairs are not eligible for these fee waivers.

Financial Data This program provides for waiver of registration fees to students attending any publicly-supported community or state college or university in California.

Duration 1 year; may be renewed.

Number awarded Varies each year.

Deadline Deadline not specified.

[417]
CALIFORNIA FEE WAIVER PROGRAM FOR DEPENDENTS OF DECEASED OR DISABLED NATIONAL GUARD MEMBERS

California Department of Veterans Affairs
Attn: Division of Veterans Services
1227 O Street, Room 105
Sacramento, CA 95814
(916) 503-8397   Toll Free: (800) 952-LOAN (within CA)
Fax: (916) 653-2563   TDD: (800) 324-5966
E-mail: ruckergl@cdva.ca.gov
Web: www.cdva.ca.gov/VetService/Waivers.aspx

Summary To provide financial assistance for college to dependents of disabled and deceased members of the California National Guard.

Eligibility Eligible for this program are spouses, children, and unremarried widow(er)s of members of the California National Guard who, in the line of duty and in the active service of the state, were killed, died of a disability, or became permanently disabled. Applicants must be attending or planning to attend a community college, branch of the California State University system, or campus of the University of California.

Financial Data Full-time college students receive a waiver of tuition and registration fees at any publicly-supported community or state college or university in California.

Duration 1 year; may be renewed.

Number awarded Varies each year.

Deadline Deadline not specified.

[418]
CALIFORNIA FEE WAIVER PROGRAM FOR DEPENDENTS OF TOTALLY DISABLED VETERANS

California Department of Veterans Affairs
Attn: Division of Veterans Services
1227 O Street, Room 105
Sacramento, CA 95814
(916) 503-8397   Toll Free: (800) 952-LOAN (within CA)
Fax: (916) 653-2563   TDD: (800) 324-5966
E-mail: ruckergl@cdva.ca.gov
Web: www.cdva.ca.gov/VetService/Waivers.aspx

Summary   To provide financial assistance for college to dependents of disabled and other California veterans.

Eligibility   Eligible for this program are spouses (including registered domestic partners), children, and unremarried widow(er)s of veterans who are currently totally service-connected disabled (or are being compensated for a service-connected disability at a rate of 100%) or who died of a service-connected cause or disability. The veteran parent must have served during a qualifying war period and must have been discharged or released from military service under honorable conditions. The child cannot be over 27 years of age (extended to 30 if the student was in the military); there are no age limitations for spouses or surviving spouses. This program does not have an income limit. Dependents in college are not eligible if they are qualified to receive educational benefits from the U.S. Department of Veterans Affairs. Applicants must be attending or planning to attend a community college, branch of the California State University system, or campus of the University of California.

Financial Data   Full-time college students receive a waiver of tuition and registration fees at any publicly-supported community or state college or university in California.

Duration   Children of eligible veterans may receive postsecondary benefits until the needed training is completed or until the dependent reaches 27 years of age (extended to 30 if the dependent serves in the armed forces). Widow(er)s and spouses are limited to a maximum of 48 months' full-time training or the equivalent in part-time training.

Number awarded   Varies each year.

Deadline   Deadline not specified.

[419]
CALIFORNIA FEE WAIVER PROGRAM FOR RECIPIENTS OF THE MEDAL OF HONOR AND THEIR CHILDREN

California Department of Veterans Affairs
Attn: Division of Veterans Services
1227 O Street, Room 101
Sacramento, CA 95814
(916) 503-8397   Toll Free: (800) 952-LOAN (within CA)
Fax: (916) 653-2563   TDD: (800) 324-5966
E-mail: ruckergl@cdva.ca.gov
Web: www.cdva.ca.gov/VetService/Waivers.aspx

Summary   To provide financial assistance for college to veterans in California who received the Medal of Honor and their children.

Eligibility   This program is open to recipients of the Medal of Honor and their children younger than 27 years of age who are residents of California. Applicants must be attending or planning to attend a community college, branch of the California State University system, or campus of the University of California.

Financial Data   Full-time college students receive a waiver of tuition and registration fees at any publicly-supported community or state college or university in California.

Duration   1 year; may be renewed.

Number awarded   Varies each year.

Deadline   Deadline not specified.

[420]
CALIFORNIA LEGION AUXILIARY EDUCATIONAL ASSISTANCE

American Legion Auxiliary
Department of California
Veterans War Memorial Building
401 Van Ness Avenue, Room 113
San Francisco, CA 94102-4586
(415) 861-5092   Fax: (415) 861-8365
E-mail: calegionaux@calegionaux.org
Web: www.calegionaux.org/scholarships.htm

Summary   To provide financial assistance to high school seniors in California who are the children of veterans or military personnel and require assistance to continue their education.

Eligibility   This program is open to seniors graduating from high schools in California who are the children of active-duty military personnel or veterans who served during war time. Applicants must be planning to continue their education at a college, university, or business/trade school in California. Financial need is considered in the selection process. Each high school in California may nominate only 1 student for these scholarships; the faculty selects the nominee if more than 1 student wishes to apply. Financial need is considered in the selection process.

Financial Data   Stipends are $1,000 or $500 per year.

Duration   1 year; 1 of the scholarships may be renewed 1 additional year.

Number awarded   8 each year: 1 at $1,000 that may be renewed, 4 at $1,000 that are nonrenewable, and 3 at $500 that are nonrenewable.

Deadline   March of each year.

[421]
CALIFORNIA LEGION AUXILIARY PAST DEPARTMENT PRESIDENT'S JUNIOR SCHOLARSHIP

American Legion Auxiliary
Department of California
Veterans War Memorial Building
401 Van Ness Avenue, Room 113
San Francisco, CA 94102-4586
(415) 861-5092   Fax: (415) 861-8365
E-mail: calegionaux@calegionaux.org
Web: www.calegionaux.org/scholarships.htm

Summary   To provide financial assistance for college to the daughters and other female descendants of California veterans who are active in the American Legion Junior Auxiliary.

Eligibility   This program is open to the daughters, granddaughters, and great-granddaughters of veterans who served during war time. Applicants must be in their senior year at an accredited high school, must have been members of the Junior Auxiliary for at least 3 consecutive years, and must be residents of California (if eligibility for Junior Auxiliary membership is by a current member of the American Legion or Auxiliary in California, the applicant may reside elsewhere). They must be planning to attend college in California. Selection is based on scholastic merit (20%); active participation in Junior Auxiliary (15%); record of service or volunteerism within the applicant's community, school, and/or unit (35%); a brief description of the applicant's desire to pursue a higher education (15%); and 3 letters of reference (15%).

Financial Data   The stipend depends on the availability of funds but ranges from $300 to $1,000.

Duration   1 year.

Number awarded   1 each year.

Deadline   April of each year.

[422]
CALIFORNIA LEGION AUXILIARY PAST PRESIDENTS' PARLEY NURSING SCHOLARSHIPS

American Legion Auxiliary
Department of California
Veterans War Memorial Building
401 Van Ness Avenue, Room 113
San Francisco, CA 94102-4586
(415) 861-5092   Fax: (415) 861-8365
E-mail: calegionaux@calegionaux.org
Web: www.calegionaux.org/scholarships.htm

Summary To provide financial assistance to California residents who are current military personnel, veterans, or members of their families and interested in studying nursing at a school in the state.

Eligibility This program is open to California residents who are currently serving on active military duty, veterans who served during war time, or the spouse, widow(er), or child of such a veteran. Applicants must be entering or continuing students of nursing at an accredited institution of higher learning in California. Financial need is considered in the selection process.

Financial Data Stipends range up to $2,000.

Duration 1 year.

Number awarded Varies each year.

Deadline April of each year.

[423]
CALIFORNIA LEGION AUXILIARY SCHOLARSHIPS FOR CONTINUING AND/OR REENTRY STUDENTS

American Legion Auxiliary
Department of California
Veterans War Memorial Building
401 Van Ness Avenue, Room 113
San Francisco, CA 94102-4586
(415) 861-5092   Fax: (415) 861-8365
E-mail: calegionaux@calegionaux.org
Web: www.calegionaux.org/scholarships.htm

Summary To provide financial assistance to California residents who are active-duty military personnel, veterans, or children of veterans and require assistance to continue their education.

Eligibility This program is open to California residents who are 1) active-duty military personnel; 2) veterans of World War I, World War II, Korea, Vietnam, Grenada/Lebanon, Panama, or Desert Shield/Desert Storm; and 3) children of veterans who served during those periods of war. Applicants must be continuing or reentry students at a college, university, or business/trade school in California. Financial need is considered in the selection process.

Financial Data The stipend is $1,000 or $500.

Duration 1 year.

Additional data This program includes 1 scholarship designated as the Mel Foronda Memorial Scholarship.

Number awarded 5 each year: 3 at $1,000 and 2 at $500.

Deadline March of each year.

[424]
CANDY HOWARTH SCHOLARSHIP

American Legion Auxiliary
Department of New Jersey
c/o Lucille M. Miller, Secretary/Treasurer
1540 Kuser Road, Suite A-8
Hamilton, NJ 08619
(609) 581-9580   Fax: (609) 581-8429
E-mail: newjerseyala@juno.com
Web: www.alanj.org

Summary To provide financial assistance to New Jersey residents who are the descendants of veterans and planning to attend college in any state.

Eligibility This program is open to the children, grandchildren, and great-grandchildren of veterans who served in the U.S. armed forces during specified periods of war time. Applicants must be graduating high school seniors who have been residents of New Jersey for at least 2 years. They must be planning to attend a college or university in any state. Along with their application, they must submit a 1,000-word essay on a topic that changes annually; recently, students were asked to write on the topic, "Honoring Our Promise Everyday-How I Can Serve My Country and Our Veterans." Selection is based on academic achievement (40%), character (15%), leadership (15%), Americanism (15%), and financial need (15%).

Financial Data Stipends range from $1,000 to $2,500.

Duration 1 year; nonrenewable.

Number awarded 1 each year.

Deadline April of each year.

[425]
CAPTAIN CALIENDO COLLEGE ASSISTANCE FUND SCHOLARSHIP

U.S. Coast Guard Chief Petty Officers Association
Attn: CCCAF Scholarship Committee
5520-G Hempstead Way
Springfield, VA 22151-4009
(703) 941-0395   Fax: (703) 941-0397
E-mail: cgcpoa@aol.com
Web: www.uscgcpoa.org

Summary To recognize and reward, with college scholarships, children of members or deceased members of the U.S. Coast Guard Chief Petty Officers Association (CPOA) or the Coast Guard Enlisted Association (CGEA) who submit outstanding essays.

Eligibility This competition is open to children of members or deceased members of the CPOA or CGEA who are attending or planning to attend a college, university, or vocational school. Applicants may not be older than 24 years of age (the age limit does not apply to disabled children). They must submit an essay, up to 500 words, on a topic that changes annually; a recent topic was "If I could travel anywhere in the world, where would it be and why?" The author of the essay judged most outstanding receives this scholarship.

Financial Data The award is a $5,000 scholarship.

Duration The competition is held annually.

Number awarded 1 each year.

Deadline February of each year.

[426]
CHAPPIE HALL MEMORIAL SCHOLARSHIP PROGRAM

101st Airborne Division Association
32 Screaming Eagle Boulevard
P.O. Box 929
Fort Campbell, KY 42223-0929
(931) 431-0199   Fax: (931) 431-0195
E-mail: 101stairbornedivisionassociation@comcast.net
Web: www.screamingeagle.org

Summary To provide financial assistance for college to the spouses, children, and grandchildren of members of the 101st Airborne Division Association.

Eligibility This program is open to graduating high school seniors and current college students who maintained a GPA of 2.0 or higher during the preceding school year and whose parent, grandparent, or spouse is (or, if deceased, was) a regular or life (not associate) member of the 101st Airborne Division. Applicants must submit a 150-word essay on patriotism and a letter on their career objectives, community service, hobbies, interests, personal achievements, and how a higher education for them in their chosen field can benefit our nation. Selection is based on the letter, career objectives, academic record, and letters of recommendation.

Financial Data   A stipend is awarded (amount not specified).

Duration   1 year; may be renewed.

Number awarded   At least 1 each year.

Deadline   May of each year.

[427]
CHARLES C. BLANTON AFBA FAMILY SURVIVOR COLLEGE SCHOLARSHIP

Armed Forces Benefit Association
AFBA Building
909 North Washington Street
Alexandria, VA 22314-1556
(703) 549-4455   Toll Free: (800) 776-2322
E-mail: info@afba.com
Web: www.afba.com

Summary   To provide financial assistance for college to surviving spouses and children of members of the Armed Forces Benefit Association (AFBA) who were killed on duty.

Eligibility   This program is open to surviving spouses and children of deceased members of AFBA. Membership in AFBA is open to active-duty, National Guard, or Reserve members of the armed forces; those who are retired or separated from service; and emergency service providers (law enforcement officers, fire fighters, and emergency medical service providers). The AFBA member's death must have been in a combat zone, as a result of combat action, as a result of acts of foreign or domestic terrorism, or at an event to which an emergency service provider is dispatched in a situation where there is the potential for loss of life. Applicants must be attending or planning to attend an undergraduate college or university.

Financial Data   The stipend is $10,000 per year.

Duration   1 year; may be renewed for up to 3 additional years.

Number awarded   1 or more each year.

Deadline   Deadline not specified.

[428]
CHARLES W. AND ANNETTE HILL SCHOLARSHIP FUND

American Legion
Department of Kansas
1314 S.W. Topeka Boulevard
Topeka, KS 66612-1886
(785) 232-9315   Fax: (785) 232-1399
Web: www.ksamlegion.org/programs.htm

Summary   To provide financial assistance for college to the children of members of the Kansas American Legion, particularly those interested in majoring in the sciences or business.

Eligibility   This program is open to graduating seniors at high schools in Kansas who have a GPA of 3.0 or higher. Applicants must be a descendant of a member of the American Legion. Preference is given to applicants planning to major in science, engineering, or business administration at a Kansas college, university, junior college, or trade school. Selection is based on high school transcripts, 3 letters of recommendation, an essay of 250 to 500 words on "Why I Want to Go to College," and financial need.

Financial Data   The stipend is $1,000 per year.

Duration   1 year; may be renewed if the recipient maintains a GPA of 3.0 or higher.

Number awarded   1 each year.

Deadline   February of each year.

[429]
CHIEF MASTER SERGEANTS OF THE AIR FORCE SCHOLARSHIPS

Air Force Sergeants Association
Attn: Scholarship Coordinator
P.O. Box 50
Temple Hills, MD 20757
(301) 899-3500, ext. 237   Toll Free: (800) 638-0594
Fax: (301) 899-8136   E-mail: staff@hqafsa.org
Web: www.hqafsa.org

Summary   To provide financial assistance for college to the dependent children of enlisted Air Force personnel.

Eligibility   This program is open to the unmarried children (including stepchildren and legally adopted children) of active-duty, retired, or veteran members of the U.S. Air Force, Air National Guard, or Air Force Reserves. Applicants must be attending or planning to attend an accredited academic institution. They must have an unweighted GPA of 3.5 or higher. Along with their application, they must submit 1) a paragraph on their life objectives and what they plan to do with the education they receive; and 2) an essay on the most urgent problem facing society today. High school seniors must also submit a transcript of all high school grades and a record of their SAT or ACT scores. Selection is based on academic record, character, leadership skills, writing ability, versatility, and potential for success. Financial need is not a consideration. A unique aspect of these scholarships is that applicants may supply additional information regarding circumstances that entitle them to special consideration; examples of such circumstances include student disabilities, financial hardships, parent disabled and unable to work, parent missing in action/killed in action/prisoner of war, or other unusual extenuating circumstances.

Financial Data   Stipends are $3,000, $2,000, or $1,000; funds may be used for tuition, room and board, fees, books, supplies, and transportation.

Duration   1 year; may be renewed if the recipient maintains full-time enrollment.

Additional data   The Air Force Sergeants Association administers this program on behalf of the Airmen Memorial Foundation. It was established in 1987 and named in honor of CMSAF Richard D. Kisling, the late third Chief Master Sergeant of the Air Force. In 1997, following the deaths of CMSAF's (Retired) Andrews and Harlow, it was given its current name.

Number awarded   12 each year: 1 at $3,000, 1 at $2,000, and 10 at $1,000. Since this program began, it has awarded more than $250,000 in scholarships.

Deadline   March of each year.

[430]
CLAIRE OLIPHANT MEMORIAL SCHOLARSHIP

American Legion Auxiliary
Department of New Jersey
c/o Lucille M. Miller, Secretary/Treasurer
1540 Kuser Road, Suite A-8
Hamilton, NJ 08619
(609) 581-9580   Fax: (609) 581-8429
E-mail: newjerseyala@juno.com
Web: www.alanj.org

Summary   To provide financial assistance to New Jersey residents who are the descendants of veterans and planning to attend college in any state.

Eligibility   This program is open to the children, grandchildren, and great-grandchildren of veterans who served in the U.S. armed forces during specified periods of war time. Applicants must be graduating high school seniors who have been residents of New Jersey for at least 2 years. They must be planning to attend a college or university in any state. Along with their application, they must submit a 1,000-word essay on a topic that changes annually; recently, students were asked to write on the topic, "Honoring Our Promise Everyday-How I Can Serve My Country and Our Veterans." Selection is based on academic achievement (40%), character (15%), leadership (15%), Americanism (15%), and financial need (15%).

Financial Data The stipend is $1,800.

Duration 1 year.

Number awarded 1 each year.

Deadline April each year.

[431]
COAST GUARD EXCHANGE SYSTEM SCHOLARSHIP PROGRAM

Coast Guard Exchange System
Attn: Scholarship Committee
870 Greenbrier Circle, Tower II, Suite 502
Chesapeake, VA 23320-2681
(757) 420-2480, ext. 3019   Fax: (757) 420-7185
E-mail: JSias@cg-exchange.com
Web: www.uscg.mil/mwr/hqrec/CGESScholarshipProgram.asp

Summary To provide financial assistance for college to high school seniors whose parent is affiliated with the Coast Guard.

Eligibility This program is open to graduating high school seniors and students in the final year of home schooling who are planning to enroll full time at an accredited college or university. Applicants must be the dependent children of active and Reserve Coast Guard members, retired Coast Guard members, civilian employees of the Coast Guard, or members of the Coast Guard Auxiliary. Along with their application, they must submit a 1-page essay explaining what they hope to achieve in their college career, including their educational, professional, and personal goals. Selection is based on that essay, SAT and/or ACT scores, GPA, class ranking, participation in school-oriented and other activities, demonstrated leadership qualities, personal accomplishments and interests, and letters of recommendation.

Financial Data Stipends are $1,500 or $500.

Duration 1 year.

Number awarded 3 each year: 1 at $1,500 and 2 at $500.

Deadline February of each year.

[432]
COAST GUARD FALLEN HEROES SCHOLARSHIP

Coast Guard Foundation
Commandant (G-1112)
Attn: Scholarship Program Manager
2100 Second Street, S.W., Jemal 9-0733
Washington, DC 20593-0001
(202) 475-5159   Toll Free: (800) 872-4957
E-mail: yvette.d.wright@uscg.mil
Web: coastguardfoundation.org/pages/Scholarship-Guide.html

Summary To provide financial assistance for college to families of Coast Guard personnel who died in the line of duty.

Eligibility This program is open to spouses and children of members of the U.S. Coast Guard who died in the line of duty. Applicants must be attending or planning to attend a 4-year college or university. Along with their application, they must submit college entrance scores, a letter of recommendation from a high school official or a college transcript signed by a college official, a letter to the president of the selection committee, and information on financial need.

Financial Data The stipend is $2,500 per year.

Duration 1 year; may be renewed up to 3 additional years.

Additional data This program was established in 2005.

Number awarded 1 or more each year.

Deadline Deadline not specified.

[433]
COAST GUARD FOUNDATION SCHOLARSHIPS

Coast Guard Foundation
Commandant (G-1112)
Attn: Scholarship Program Manager
2100 Second Street, S.W., Jemal 9-0733
Washington, DC 20593-0001
(202) 475-5159   Toll Free: (800) 872-4957
E-mail: yvette.d.wright@uscg.mil
Web: coastguardfoundation.org/pages/Scholarship-Guide.html

Summary To provide financial assistance for college to the dependent children of Coast Guard enlisted personnel.

Eligibility This program is open to the dependent children of enlisted members of the U.S. Coast Guard on active duty, retired, or deceased and of enlisted personnel in the Coast Guard Reserve currently on extended active duty 180 days or more. Applicants must be attending or planning to attend a college, university, or vocational school as a full-time undergraduate student. Along with their application, they must submit their SAT or ACT scores, a letter of recommendation, transcripts, and a financial information statement.

Financial Data The stipend is $5,000 per year.

Duration 1 year; may be renewed up to 3 additional years.

Number awarded Varies each year; recently, 14 of these scholarships were awarded.

Deadline March of each year.

[434]
COAST GUARD RESERVE USAA SCHOLARSHIP

U.S. Coast Guard
Attn: COMDT CG-1313
1900 Half Street, S.W.
Washington, DC 20593-0001
(202) 475-5461   E-mail: Greg.P.Hunton@uscg.mil
Web: www.uscg.mil/RESERVE/docs/pay_benefits/usaa.asp

Summary To provide financial assistance for college or graduate school to members of the Coast Guard Reserves and their dependents.

Eligibility This program is open to Coast Guard enlisted reservists (SELRES or IRR) and their dependents who are registered in the Defense Enrollment Eligibility Reporting System (DEERS). Applicants must be enrolled or accepted for enrollment at 1) an accredited institution in a program leading to an associate, bachelor's, master's, or doctoral degree; or 2) a 2- or 4-year course of study at an accredited technical or vocational training school. Along with their application, they must submit a 1-page essay on how the participation of themselves, their spouse, or their parent in the Coast Guard Reserve has contributed to their success.

Financial Data The stipend is $1,000.

Duration 1 year.

Additional data This program is sponsored by the United States Automobile Association (USAA) Insurance Corporation.

Number awarded 6 each year.

Deadline July of each year.

[435]
COASTAL NORTH CAROLINA AFCEA CHAPTER UNDERGRADUATE SCHOLARSHIPS

Armed Forces Communications and Electronics Association-
  Coastal North Carolina Chapter
c/o Daniel Egge, Secretary
201 South Shore Drive
Jacksonville, NC 28540-5633
(910) 451-8835   E-mail: daniel.egge@usmc.mil

Summary To provide financial assistance to dependents and spouses of veterans and military personnel in North Carolina who are interested in studying a technical field at a college in any state.

Eligibility This program is open to residents of North Carolina who are dependents or spouses of active-duty, retired, or honorably discharged military personnel. Applicants must be working on or planning to work on a technical degree at a school in any state in the following or related fields: electrical, chemical, systems, or aerospace engineering; mathematics; physics; science or mathematics education; computer science; or technology management. They must be U.S. citizens who can demonstrate academic excellence, moral character, dedication to completing their education, leadership abilities, and financial need.

Financial Data Stipends range from $500 to $2,000.

Duration 1 year.

Number awarded 1 or more each year.

Deadline March of each year.

[436]
COLONEL HAROLD M. BEARDSLEE MEMORIAL SCHOLARSHIP AWARDS

Army Engineer Association
Attn: Fort Leonard Wood Operations
P.O. Box 634
Fort Leonard Wood, MO 65473
(573) 329-6678   Fax: (573) 329-3203
E-mail: flw@armyengineer.com
Web: www.armyengineer.com/AEA_scholarships.html

Summary To provide financial assistance for college to children and spouses of members of the Army Engineer Association (AEA).

Eligibility This program is open to spouses and children of AEA members in the following 4 categories: 1) graduating high school seniors who are children of active-duty or civilian members (including active-duty retired); 2) graduating high school seniors who are children of Reserve or National Guard members (including Reserve or National Guard retired); 3) children and spouses of members in the second, third, or fourth year of a baccalaureate degree program; and 4) the next best qualified applicant, regardless of category, not receiving any of those awards. Applicants must be enrolled or planning to enroll full time at an accredited college or university. Along with their application, they must submit an essay on their reasons for seeking this award. Selection is based on the essay, scholastic aptitude, and letters of recommendation.

Financial Data The stipend is $1,000.

Duration 1 year; nonrenewable.

Number awarded 5 each year, including at least 1 in each category.

Deadline April of each year.

[437]
COLONEL HAZEL ELIZABETH BENN, USMC SCHOLARSHIP

Fleet Reserve Association
Attn: Scholarship Administrator
125 North West Street
Alexandria, VA 22314-2754
(703) 683-1400   Toll Free: (800) FRA-1924
Fax: (703) 549-6610   E-mail: scholars@fra.org
Web: www.fra.org

Summary To provide financial assistance for college to children of members of the Fleet Reserve Association (FRA) serving in the Navy as an enlisted medical rating assigned to the United States Marine Corps (USMC).

Eligibility This program is open to the dependent children of members of the association or persons who were members at the time of death. Applicants must be entering their freshman or sophomore year of college. Their parent must be serving and have served in the U.S. Navy as an enlisted medical rating assigned to the USMC. Selection is based on academic record,

financial need, extracurricular activities, leadership skills, and participation in community activities. U.S. citizenship is required.

Financial Data The stipend is $2,000.

Duration 1 year.

Number awarded 1 or more each year.

Deadline April of each year.

[438]
COLORADO DEPENDENTS TUITION ASSISTANCE PROGRAM

Colorado Commission on Higher Education
1560 Broadway, Suite 1600
Denver, CO 80202
(303) 866-2723   Fax: (303) 866-4266
E-mail: cche@state.co.us
Web: highered.colorado.gov

Summary To provide financial assistance for college to the dependents of disabled or deceased Colorado National Guardsmen, law enforcement officers, and fire fighters.

Eligibility Eligible for the program are dependents of Colorado law enforcement officers, fire fighters, and National Guardsmen disabled or killed in the line of duty, as well as dependents of prisoners of war or service personnel listed as missing in action. Students must be Colorado residents under 22 years of age enrolled at 1) a state-supported 2- or 4-year Colorado college or university; 2) a private college, university, or vocational school in Colorado approved by the commission; or 3) an out-of-state 4-year college. Financial need is considered in the selection process.

Financial Data Eligible students receive free tuition at Colorado public institutions of higher education. If the recipient wishes to attend a private college, university, or proprietary school, the award is limited to the amount of tuition at a comparable state-supported institution. Students who have applied to live in a dormitory, but have not been accepted because there is not enough space, may be provided supplemental assistance. Students who choose to live off-campus are not eligible for room reimbursement or a meal plan. Students who attend a nonresidential Colorado institution and do not live at home are eligible for a grant of $1,000 per semester to assist with living expenses. Students who attend an out-of-state institution are eligible for the amount of tuition equivalent to that at a comparable Colorado public institution, but they are not eligible for room and board.

Duration Up to 6 years or until completion of a bachelor's degree, provided the recipient maintains a GPA of 2.5 or higher.

Additional data Recipients must attend accredited postsecondary institutions in Colorado.

Number awarded Varies each year; recently, nearly $365,000 was allocated to this program.

Deadline Deadline not specified.

[439]
COLORADO LEGION AUXILIARY DEPARTMENT PRESIDENT'S SCHOLARSHIP FOR JUNIOR AUXILIARY MEMBERS

American Legion Auxiliary
Department of Colorado
7465 East First Avenue, Suite D
Denver, CO 80230
(303) 367-5388   Fax: (303) 367-5388
E-mail: ala@impactmail.net
Web: www.freewebs.com/ala-colorado

Summary To provide financial assistance to junior members of the American Legion Auxiliary in Colorado who plan to attend college in the state.

Eligibility This program is open to seniors at high schools in Colorado who have been junior members of the auxiliary for the past 3 years. Applicants must be Colorado residents planning to attend college in the state. Along with their application, they must submit a 1,000-word essay on the topic, "My Obligations as an American." Selection is based on character (20%), Americanism (20%), leadership (20%), scholarship (20%), and financial need (20%).

Financial Data The stipend is $1,000.

Duration 1 year; nonrenewable.

Number awarded 1 each year.

Deadline March of each year.

[440]
COLORADO LEGION AUXILIARY DEPARTMENT PRESIDENT'S SCHOLARSHIPS

American Legion Auxiliary
Department of Colorado
7465 East First Avenue, Suite D
Denver, CO 80230
(303) 367-5388   Fax: (303) 367-5388
E-mail: ala@impactmail.net
Web: www.freewebs.com/ala-colorado

Summary To provide financial assistance to children and grandchildren of veterans in Colorado who plan to attend college in the state.

Eligibility This program is open to children and grandchildren of veterans who served in the armed forces during wartime eligibility dates for membership in the American Legion. Applicants must be residents of Colorado who are high school seniors planning to attend a college in the state. Along with their application, they must submit a 1,000-word essay on the topic, "My Obligations as an American." Selection is based on character (15%), Americanism (15%), leadership (15%), scholarship (15%), and financial need (40%).

Financial Data Stipends are $1,000 or $500.

Duration 1 year.

Number awarded 3 each year: 1 at 1,000 and 2 at $500.

Deadline March of each year.

[441]
COLORADO LEGION AUXILIARY PAST PRESIDENT'S PARLEY NURSE'S SCHOLARSHIP

American Legion Auxiliary
Department of Colorado
7465 East First Avenue, Suite D
Denver, CO 80230
(303) 367-5388   Fax: (303) 367-5388
E-mail: ala@impactmail.net
Web: www.freewebs.com/ala-colorado

Summary To provide financial assistance to wartime veterans and their descendants in Colorado who are interested in attending school in the state to prepare for a career in nursing.

Eligibility This program is open to 1) daughters, sons, spouses, granddaughters, and great-granddaughters of veterans, and 2) veterans who served in the armed forces during eligibility dates for membership in the American Legion. Applicants must be Colorado residents who have been accepted by an accredited school of nursing in the state. Along with their application, they must submit a 500-word essay on the topic, "Americanism." Selection is based on scholastic ability (25%), financial need (25%), references (13%), a 500-word essay on Americanism (25%), and dedication to chosen field (12%).

Financial Data Stipends range from $500 to $1,000.

Duration 1 year; nonrenewable.

Number awarded Varies each year, depending on the availability of funds.

Deadline April of each year.

[442]
COMMANDER DANIEL J. CHRISTOVICH SCHOLARSHIP

Coast Guard Foundation
Commandant (G-1112)
Attn: Scholarship Program Manager
2100 Second Street, S.W., Jemal 9-0733
Washington, DC 20593-0001
(202) 475-5159   Toll Free: (800) 872-4957
E-mail: yvette.d.wright@uscg.mil
Web: coastguardfoundation.org/pages/Scholarship-Guide.html

Summary To provide financial assistance for college to the dependent children of Coast Guard enlisted personnel.

Eligibility This program is open to the dependent children of enlisted members of the U.S. Coast Guard on active duty, retired, or deceased and of enlisted personnel in the Coast Guard Reserve currently on extended active duty 180 days or more. Applicants must be attending or planning to attend a college, university, or vocational school as a full-time undergraduate student. Along with their application, they must submit their SAT or ACT scores, a letter of recommendation, transcripts, and a financial information statement.

Financial Data The stipend is $2,500.

Duration 1 year.

Number awarded 1 each year.

Deadline March of each year.

[443]
COMMANDER RONALD J. CANTIN SCHOLARSHIP

Coast Guard Foundation
Commandant (G-1112)
Attn: Scholarship Program Manager
2100 Second Street, S.W., Jemal 9-0733
Washington, DC 20593-0001
(202) 475-5159   Toll Free: (800) 872-4957
E-mail: yvette.d.wright@uscg.mil
Web: coastguardfoundation.org/pages/Scholarship-Guide.html

Summary To provide financial assistance for college to the dependent children of Coast Guard enlisted personnel.

Eligibility This program is open to the dependent children of enlisted members of the U.S. Coast Guard on active duty, retired, or deceased and of enlisted personnel in the Coast Guard Reserve currently on extended active duty 180 days or more. Applicants must be attending or planning to attend a college, university, or vocational school as a full-time undergraduate student. Along with their application, they must submit their SAT or ACT scores, a letter of recommendation, transcripts, and a financial information statement.

Financial Data The stipend is $2,500.

Duration 1 year.

Number awarded 1 each year.

Deadline March of each year.

[444]
COMMANDER WILLIAM S. STUHR SCHOLARSHIPS

Commander William S. Stuhr Scholarship Fund
Attn: Executive Director
P.O. Box 1138
Kitty Hawk, NC 27949-1138
(252) 255-3013   Fax: (252) 255-3014
E-mail: stuhrstudents@earthlink.net

Summary To provide financial assistance for college to the dependent children of retired or active-duty military personnel.

Eligibility This program is open to the dependent children of military personnel who are serving on active duty or retired with pay after 20 years' service (not merely separated from service). Applicants must be high school seniors who rank in the top 10% of their class and have an SAT score of at least 1250 or an ACT score of at least 27. They must plan to attend a 4-year accredited college. Selection is based on academic performance, extracurricular activities, demonstrated leadership potential, and financial need.

Financial Data   The stipend is $1,200 per year.

Duration   4 years, provided the recipient makes the dean's list at their college at least once during their first 2 years.

Additional data   This program was established in 1965. Recipients and their families attend a scholarship awards function in late May or early June; the fund pays air transportation to the event. Applications may be obtained only by writing and enclosing a self-addressed stamped envelope. The fund does not respond to telephone, fax, or e-mail inquiries.

Number awarded   6 each year: 1 for a child of a military service-member from each of the 6 branches (Air Force, Army, Coast Guard, Marine Corps, Navy, and Reserves/National Guard).

Deadline   February of each year.

[445]
CONGRESSIONAL MEDAL OF HONOR SOCIETY SCHOLARSHIPS

Congressional Medal of Honor Society
40 Patriots Point Road
Mt. Pleasant, SC 29464
(843) 884-8862   Fax: (843) 884-1471
E-mail: medalhq@earthlink.net
Web: www.cmohs.org

Summary   To provide financial assistance to dependents of Congressional Medal of Honor winners who are interested in pursuing postsecondary education.

Eligibility   Sons and daughters of Congressional Medal of Honor recipients are eligible to apply if they are high school seniors or graduates and have been accepted by an accredited college or university.

Financial Data   The stipend is $2,000 per year.

Duration   1 year; may be renewed for up to 3 additional years.

Number awarded   Varies; approximately 15 each year.

Deadline   August or December of each year.

[446]
CONNECTICUT EAGLE SCOUT OF THE YEAR SCHOLARSHIP

American Legion
Department of Connecticut
287 West Street
P.O. Box 208
Rocky Hill, CT 06067
(860) 721-5942   E-mail: deptadj@ctlegion.necoxmail.com
Web: www.ct.legion.org/?programs

Summary   To recognize and reward, with scholarships for college in any state, Eagle Scouts who are members of a troop associated with the American Legion in Connecticut or a son or grandson of a member of the Legion in the state.

Eligibility   Applicants for this award must be either 1) a registered, active member of a Boy Scout Troop, Varsity Scout Team, or Venturing Crew chartered to an American Legion Post, Auxiliary Unit, or Sons of the American Legion Squadron in Connecticut, or 2) a registered active member of a Boy Scout Troop, Varsity Scout Team, or Venturing Crew and also the son or grandson of a member of the American Legion or American Legion Auxiliary in Connecticut. Candidates must also 1) have received the Eagle Scout Award; 2) be active members of their religious institution and have received the appropriate religious emblem; 3) have demonstrated practical citizenship in church, school, Scouting, and community; 4) be at least 15 years of age and enrolled in high school; and 5) submit at least 4 letters of recommendation, including 1 each from leaders of their religious institution, school,

community, and Scouting. They must be planning to attend college in any state.

Financial Data   The stipend is $1,000, presented in the form of a savings bond which the recipient may use whenever he attends college.

Duration   The award is presented annually.

Number awarded   1 each year.

Deadline   February of each year.

[447]
CONNECTICUT NATIONAL GUARD FOUNDATION SCHOLARSHIPS

Connecticut National Guard Foundation, Inc.
Attn: Scholarship Committee
360 Broad Street
Hartford, CT 06105-3795
(860) 241-1550   Fax: (860) 293-2929
E-mail: ctngfi@sbcglobal.net
Web: www.ctngfoundation.org/Scholarship.asp

Summary   To provide financial assistance for college to members of the Connecticut National Guard and their families.

Eligibility   This program is open to members of the Connecticut Army National Guard and Organized Militia, their children, and their spouses. Applicants must be enrolled or planning to enroll in an accredited college or technical program. Along with their application, they must submit a letter of recommendation, a list of extracurricular activities, high school or college transcripts, and a 200-word statement on their educational and future goals. Selection is based on achievement and citizenship.

Financial Data   Stipends are $2,000 or $1,000.

Duration   1 year.

Number awarded   5 each year: 2 at $2,000 and 3 at $1,000.

Deadline   March of each year.

[448]
CONNECTICUT TUITION WAIVER FOR VETERANS

Connecticut Department of Higher Education
Attn: Education and Employment Information Center
61 Woodland Street
Hartford, CT 06105-2326
(860) 947-1816   Toll Free: (800) 842-0229 (within CT)
Fax: (860) 947-1310   E-mail: veterans@ctdhe.org
Web: www.ctdhe.org/SFA/default.htm

Summary   To provide financial assistance for college to certain Connecticut veterans and military personnel and their dependents.

Eligibility   This program is open to 1) honorably-discharged Connecticut veterans who served at least 90 days during specified periods of wartime; 2) active members of the Connecticut Army and Air National Guard; 3) Connecticut residents who are a dependent child or surviving spouse of a member of the armed forces killed in action on or after September 11, 2001 who was also a Connecticut resident; and 4) Connecticut residents who are dependent children or a person officially declared missing in action or a prisoner of war while serving in the armed forces after January 1, 1960. Applicants must be attending or planning to attend a public college or university in the state.

Financial Data   The program provides a waiver of 100% of tuition for general fund courses at Connecticut public colleges or universities, 50% of tuition for extension and summer courses at campuses of Connecticut State University, and 50% of part-time fees at OnlineCSU.

Duration   Up to 4 years.

Additional data   This is an entitlement program; applications are available at the respective college financial aid offices.

Number awarded   Varies each year.

Deadline   Deadline not specified.

[449]
COUDRET TRUST SCHOLARSHIPS

American Legion
Department of Arkansas
702 Victory Street
P.O. Box 3280
Little Rock, AR 72203
(501) 375-1104   Toll Free: (877) 243-9799
Fax: (501) 375-4236   E-mail: alegion@swbell.net
Web: www.arlegion.org/Scholarship_Coudret_Trust.html

Summary   To provide financial assistance for college to descendants of members of the American Legion in Arkansas.

Eligibility   This program is open to the children, grandchildren, and great-grandchildren of living or deceased members of the American Legion in Arkansas. Applicants must be high school seniors or graduates of a 2-year college in Arkansas. They must sign a drug free pledge and a declaration of support for the Preamble to the Constitution of the American Legion. Selection is based on American spirit, character, leadership quality, scholastic endeavor, and financial need.

Financial Data   The stipend is $1,000.

Duration   1 year.

Number awarded   4 each year.

Deadline   March of each year.

[450]
CSM VINCENT BALDASSARI MEMORIAL SCHOLARSHIPS

Enlisted Association National Guard of New Jersey
Attn: Scholarship Committee
101 Eggert Crossing Road
Lawrenceville, NJ 08648-2805
(609) 562-0207   Fax: (609) 562-0283
Web: www.eang-nj.org/scholarships.html

Summary   To provide financial assistance to New Jersey National Guard members and their children who are interested in attending college in any state.

Eligibility   This program is open to 1) children of New Jersey National Guard members who are also members of the Enlisted Association National Guard of New Jersey, and 2) drilling Guard members who are also members of the Association. Applicants must be attending or planning to attend a college or university in any state. Along with their application, they must submit 1) information on their church, school, and community activities; 2) a list of honors they have received; 3) letters of recommendation; 4) transcripts; and 5) a letter with specific facts about their desire to continue their education and specifying their career goals. Financial need is not considered in the selection process.

Financial Data   The stipend is $1,000.

Duration   1 year.

Number awarded   Varies each year; recently, 4 of these scholarships were awarded.

Deadline   May of each year.

[451]
CSM VIRGIL R. WILLIAMS SCHOLARSHIP PROGRAM

Enlisted Association of the National Guard of the United
   States
3133 Mount Vernon Avenue
Alexandria, VA 22305-2640
(703) 519-3846   Toll Free: (800) 234-EANG
Fax: (703) 519-3849   E-mail: eangus@eangus.org
Web: www.eangus.org

Summary   To provide financial assistance to National Guard members and their dependents who are members of the Enlisted Association of the National Guard of the United States (EANGUS) and entering or continuing in college.

Eligibility   This program is open to high school seniors and currently-enrolled college students. They must be 1) National Guard members who belong to EANGUS; 2) unmarried sons and daughters of EANGUS members; 3) spouses of EANGUS members; or 4) unremarried spouses and unmarried dependent children of deceased EANGUS members who were in good standing at the time of their death. Honorary, associate, or corporate membership alone does not qualify. Graduate students are not eligible. Applicants must submit a copy of their school transcript, 3 letters of recommendation, a letter of academic reference (from their principal, dean, or counselor), a photocopy of the qualifying state and/or national membership card (parent's, spouse's or applicant's), and a personal letter with specific facts as to their desire to continue their education and why financial assistance is necessary. Application packets must be submitted to the state EANGUS association; acceptable packets are then sent to the national offices for judging. Selection is based on academic achievement, character, leadership, and financial need.

Financial Data   The stipend is $2,000.

Duration   1 year; nonrenewable.

Additional data   Recipients must enroll full time.

Number awarded   2 or more each year.

Deadline   Applications must first be verified by the state office and then submitted by June to the national office.

[452]
DAEDALIAN FOUNDATION DESCENDANTS' SCHOLARSHIP PROGRAM

Daedalian Foundation
Attn: Scholarship Committee
55 Main Circle (Building 676)
P.O. Box 249
Randolph AFB, TX 78148-0249
(210) 945-2113   Fax: (210) 945-2112
E-mail: icarus2@daedalians.org
Web: www.daedalians.org/foundation/scholarships.htm

Summary   To provide financial assistance to descendants of members of the Order of Daedalians who wish to prepare for a career in military aviation or space.

Eligibility   This program is open to descendants of members of the order who are working on or planning to work on a baccalaureate or higher degree. Applicants must be interested in and willing to commit to a career as a commissioned military pilot, flight crew member, astronaut, or commissioned officer in 1 of the armed forces of the United States in a discipline directly supporting aeronautics or astronautics. They must be physically and mentally qualified for flight and/or space; if they intend to pursue a non-flying career as a commissioned officer in a scientific or engineering discipline supporting aviation or space, they must pass a physical examination qualifying for active commissioned duty in the U.S. armed forces. Nominations must be submitted by a local chapter (Flight) of Daedalian. Selection is based on academic achievement and recognition, extracurricular activities, honors, and employment experience. Financial need may be considered if all other factors are equal.

Financial Data   The stipend is $2,000.

Additional data   The Order of Daedalians was founded in 1934 as an organization of the nearly 14,000 aviators who served as military pilots during World War I and are still listed and designated as Founder Members. In the 1950s, the organization expanded eligibility to include 1) on a sponsorship basis, current and former commissioned military pilots from all services, and 2) on a hereditary basis, descendants of Founder Members.

Number awarded   Up to 3 each year.

Deadline   July of each year.

[453]
DANIEL E. LAMBERT MEMORIAL SCHOLARSHIP

American Legion
Department of Maine
P.O. Box 900
Waterville, ME 04903-0900
(207) 873-3229   Fax: (207) 872-0501
E-mail: legionme@mainelegion.org
Web: www.mainelegion.org/pages/programs/scholarships.php

Summary   To provide financial assistance to the children of veterans in Maine who plan to attend college in any state.

Eligibility   This program is open to residents of Maine who are the child or grandchild of a veteran. Applicants must be attending or planning to attend an accredited college or vocational/technical school in any state. They must have demonstrated, by their past behavior, that they believe in the American way of life. U.S. citizenship is required. Financial need is considered in the selection process.

Financial Data   The stipend is $1,000.

Duration   1 year.

Number awarded   1 each year.

Deadline   April of each year.

[454]
DAUGHTERS OF THE CINCINNATI SCHOLARSHIP PROGRAM

Daughters of the Cincinnati
Attn: Scholarship Administrator
20 West 44th Street, Suite 508
New York, NY 10036
(212) 991-9945   E-mail: scholarships@daughters1894.org
Web: www.daughters1894.org

Summary   To provide financial assistance for college to high school seniors who are the daughters of active-duty, deceased, or retired military officers.

Eligibility   This program is open to high school seniors who are the daughters of career commissioned officers of the regular Army, Navy, Air Force, Coast Guard, or Marine Corps on active duty, deceased, or retired. Applicants must be planning to enroll at a college or university in any state. Along with their application, they must submit an official school transcript, SAT or ACT scores, a letter of recommendation, and documentation of financial need.

Financial Data   Scholarship amounts have recently averaged $4,000 per year. Funds are paid directly to the college of the student's choice.

Duration   1 year; may be renewed up to 3 additional years, provided the recipient remains in good academic standing.

Additional data   This program was originally established in 1906.

Number awarded   Approximately 12 each year.

Deadline   March of each year.

[455]
DECA SCHOLARSHIPS FOR MILITARY CHILDREN

Defense Commissary Agency
Attn: SSP
1300 E Avenue
Fort Lee, VA 23801-1800
(804) 734-8410   E-mail: info@militaryscholar.org
Web: www.militaryscholar.org

Summary   To provide financial assistance for college to the children of veterans and military personnel.

Eligibility   This program is open to sons and daughters of U.S. military servicemembers (including active duty, retirees, Guard/Reserves, and survivors of deceased members) who are enrolled or accepted for enrollment at a college or university. Applicants must be younger than 23 years of age and enrolled in the Defense Enrollment Eligibility Reporting System (DEERS). They must have a GPA of 3.0 or higher. Along with their application, they must submit a 500-word essay on a topic that changes annually; recently, students were asked to write on "You can travel back in time, however, you cannot change events. What point in history would you visit and why." Selection is based on merit.

Financial Data   The stipend is $1,500.

Duration   1 year; recipients may reapply.

Additional data   This program, established in 2001, is supported by the Fisher House Foundation. Recipients must enroll as a full-time undergraduate student.

Number awarded   At least 1 scholarship is allocated for each of the commissaries worldwide operated by the Defense Commissary Agency (DeCA).

Deadline   February of each year.

[456]
DELAWARE EDUCATIONAL BENEFITS FOR CHILDREN OF DECEASED VETERANS AND OTHERS

Delaware Higher Education Commission
Carvel State Office Building, Fifth Floor.
820 North French Street
Wilmington, DE 19801-3509
(302) 577-5240   Toll Free: (800) 292-7935
Fax: (302) 577-6765   E-mail: dhec@doe.k12.de.us
Web: www.doe.k12.de.us

Summary   To provide financial assistance for undergraduate education to dependents of deceased Delaware veterans, state police officers, and Department of Transportation employees and members of the armed forces declared prisoners of war or missing in action.

Eligibility   Applicants for this assistance must have been Delaware residents for at least 3 consecutive years and be the children, between 16 and 24 years of age, of members of the armed forces 1) whose cause of death was service-related, 2) who are being held or were held as a prisoner of war, or 3) who are officially declared missing in action. The parent must have been a resident of Delaware at the time of death or declaration of missing in action or prisoner of war status. Also eligible are children of Delaware state police officers whose cause of death was service-related and employees of the state Department of Transportation routinely employed in job-related activities upon the state highway system whose cause of death was job related. U.S. citizenship or eligible non-citizen status is required.

Financial Data   Eligible students receive full tuition at any state-supported institution in Delaware or, if the desired educational program is not available at a state-supported school, at any private institution in Delaware. If the desired educational program is not offered at either a public or private institution in Delaware, this program pays the full cost of tuition at the out-of-state school the recipient attends. Students who wish to attend a private or out-of-state school even though their program is offered at a Delaware public institution receive the equivalent of the average tuition and fees at the state school, recently set at $6,980 per year.

Duration   1 year; may be renewed for 3 additional years.

Number awarded   Varies each year.

Deadline   Applications may be submitted at any time, but they must be received at least 4 weeks before the beginning of classes.

[457]
DELLA VAN DEUREN MEMORIAL SCHOLARSHIPS

American Legion Auxiliary
Department of Wisconsin
Attn: Education Chair
2930 American Legion Drive
P.O. Box 140
Portage, WI 53901-0140
(608) 745-0124   Toll Free: (866) 664-3863
Fax: (608) 745-1947   E-mail: alawi@amlegionauxwi.org
Web: www.amlegionauxwi.org/Scholarships.htm

Summary To provide financial assistance to Wisconsin residents who are members or children of members of the American Legion Auxiliary and interested in attending college in any state.

Eligibility This program is open to members and children of members of the American Legion Auxiliary. Applicants must be high school seniors or graduates with a GPA of 3.5 or higher and be able to demonstrate financial need. They must be Wisconsin residents, although they are not required to attend school in the state. Along with their application, they must submit a 300-word essay on "Education—An Investment in the Future."

Financial Data The stipend is $1,000.

Duration 1 year; nonrenewable.

Number awarded 2 each year.

Deadline March of each year.

[458]
DFCS SCHOLARSHIPS

Distinguished Flying Cross Society
Attn: Scholarship Program
P.O. Box 530250
San Diego, CA 92153
Toll Free: (866) DFC-MEDAL
Web: www.dfcsociety.org

Summary To provide financial assistance for college to descendants of members of the Distinguished Flying Cross Society (DFCS).

Eligibility This program is open to descendants (including legally adopted children) of DFCS members. Applicants must be working on an undergraduate degree at an accredited institution of higher education. Along with their application, they must submit a list of memberships in school-related organizations, a list of elected leadership positions they have held, information on activities that demonstrate community involvement, transcripts (including SAT scores), and a 500-word essay on why they feel they deserve this scholarship.

Financial Data The stipend is $1,000.

Duration 1 year.

Additional data Membership in the sponsoring organization, founded in 1994, is limited to members of the U.S. armed forces who have been awarded the Distinguished Flying Cross as a result of deeds accomplished during aerial flight.

Number awarded 4 each year.

Deadline November of each year.

[459]
DOLPHIN SCHOLARSHIPS

Dolphin Scholarship Foundation
Attn: Scholarship Administrator
4966 Euclid Road, Suite 109
Virginia Beach, VA 23462
(757) 671-3200, ext. 111   Fax: (757) 671-3330
E-mail: scholars@dolphinscholarship.org
Web: www.dolphinscholarship.org

Summary To provide financial assistance for college to the children of members or former members of the Submarine Force.

Eligibility This program is open to the unmarried children and stepchildren under 24 years of age of 1) members or former members of the Submarine Force who qualified in submarines and served in the submarine force for at least 8 years; 2) Navy members who served in submarine support activities for at least 10 years; and 3) Submarine Force members who died on active duty. Applicants must be working or intending to work toward a bachelor's degree at an accredited 4-year college or university. Selection is based on academic proficiency, commitment and excellence in school and community activities, and financial need.

Financial Data The stipend is $3,400 per year.

Duration 1 year; may be renewed for 3 additional years.

Additional data Since this program was established in 1961, it has awarded more than $4.2 million to more than 750 students (that number includes awards previously offered by U.S. Submarine Veterans of World War II). In 1991, that organization agreed to turn over its funds to the Dolphin Scholarship Foundation with the stipulation that it would award 3 scholarships each year, designated the U.S. Submarine Veterans of World War II Scholarship, the Wives of the U.S. Submarine Veterans of World War II Scholarship, and the Arnold Krippendorf Scholarship.

Number awarded The foundation awards 137 new and renewal scholarships every year. The number of new awards depends on the attrition and graduation of current scholars. Recently, 31 new scholarships were awarded, including 21 to high school seniors and 10 to college students.

Deadline March of each year.

[460]
DONALD D. FRIZZELL MEMORIAL SCHOLARSHIPS

First Command Educational Foundation
Attn: Scholarship Programs Manager
1 FirstComm Plaza
Fort Worth, TX 76109-4999
(817) 569-2634   Toll Free: (877) 872-8289
Fax: (817) 569-2970   E-mail: aymcmanus@fcef.com
Web: www.fcef.com/direct-apply-scholarship.php

Summary To provide financial assistance to students, especially those with ties to the military, entering or attending college.

Eligibility This program is open to 2 categories of applicants: 1) traditional students, including high school seniors and students already enrolled at a college, university, or accredited trade school; and 2) nontraditional students, including those defined by their institution as nontraditional and adult students planning to return to a college, university, or accredited trade school. Traditional students must have a GPA of 3.0 or higher. Special consideration is given to applicants with a connection to the military. Along with their application, they must submit 1-page essays on 1) their active involvement in community service programs, 2) the impact of financial literacy on their future, and 3) why they need this scholarship. Selection is based primarily on the essays, academic merit, and financial need.

Financial Data Stipends are $5,000 or $2,500. Funds are disbursed directly to the recipient's college, university, or trade school.

Duration 1 year.

Additional data The sponsoring organization was formerly known as the USPA & IRA Educational Foundation, founded in 1983 to provide scholarships to the children of active, retired, or deceased military personnel. In addition to these scholarships, for which students may apply directly, it supports scholarships offered by a number of partner organizations. Since its establishment, it has awarded scholarships worth nearly $4 million.

Number awarded 6 each year: 2 at $5,000 and 4 at $2,500. Awards are split evenly between the 2 categories.

Deadline The online application process begins in February of each year and continues until 200 applications have been received in each category.

[461]
DOROTHY KELLERMAN SCHOLARSHIP

American Legion Auxiliary
Department of New Jersey
c/o Lucille M. Miller, Secretary/Treasurer
1540 Kuser Road, Suite A-8
Hamilton, NJ 08619
(609) 581-9580   Fax: (609) 581-8429
E-mail: newjerseyala@juno.com
Web: www.alanj.org

Summary   To provide financial assistance to New Jersey residents who are the descendants of veterans and planning to attend college in any state.

Eligibility   This program is open to the children, grandchildren, and great-grandchildren of veterans who served in the U.S. armed forces during specified periods of war time. Applicants must be graduating high school seniors who have been residents of New Jersey for at least 2 years. They must be planning to attend a college or university in any state. Along with their application, they must submit a 1,000-word essay on a topic that changes annually; recently, students were asked to write on the topic, "Honoring Our Promise Everyday-How I Can Serve My Country and Our Veterans." Selection is based on academic achievement (40%), character (15%), leadership (15%), Americanism (15%), and financial need (15%).

Financial Data   Stipends range from $1,000 to $2,500.

Duration   1 year; nonrenewable.

Number awarded   1 each year.

Deadline   April of each year.

[462]
DR. HANNAH K. VUOLO MEMORIAL SCHOLARSHIP

American Legion
Department of New York
112 State Street, Suite 1300
Albany, NY 12207
(518) 463-2215   Toll Free: (800) 253-4466
Fax: (518) 427-8443   E-mail: info@nylegion.org
Web: www.ny.legion.org/scholar.htm

Summary   To provide financial assistance to descendants of members of the American Legion in New York who are interested in becoming secondary school teachers.

Eligibility   This program is open to the natural or adopted direct descendants of members or deceased members of the American Legion's New York Department. Applicants must be high school seniors or graduates under 21 years of age entering an accredited college in any state as freshmen with a commitment to earning a degree in secondary education. Preference is given to residents of New York state. Selection is based on financial need (11 points), academic record (10 points), Americanism (9 points), participation in projects to help the elderly, needy, or disabled (8 points), self-help as demonstrated by work record (7 points), participation in social, political, religious, or athletic groups (6 points), neatness and correctness of letter (5 points), and New York State residency (4 points).

Financial Data   The stipend is $1,000.

Duration   1 year.

Number awarded   1 each year.

Deadline   April of each year.

[463]
DR. KATE WALLER BARRETT GRANT

American Legion Auxiliary
Department of Virginia
Attn: Education Chair
1708 Commonwealth Avenue
Richmond, VA 23230
(804) 355-6410   Fax: (804) 353-5246

Summary   To provide financial assistance to Virginia residents who are children of veterans or of members of the American Legion Auxiliary and planning to attend college in the state.

Eligibility   This program is open to the children of veterans or of members of the American Legion Auxiliary who are high school seniors in Virginia planning to attend an accredited educational institution in the state. Along with their application, they must submit a 500-word essay on their responsibilities as a citizen of the United States. Selection is based on citizenship (20%), leadership (20%), scholarship (40%), and financial need (20%).

Financial Data   The stipend is $1,000.

Duration   1 year.

Number awarded   1 each year.

Deadline   March of each year.

[464]
E.A. BLACKMORE SCHOLARSHIP

American Legion
Department of Wyoming
1320 Hugur Avenue
Cheyenne, WY 82001
(307) 634-3035   Fax: (307) 635-7093
E-mail: wylegion@qwest.net
Web: www.wylegion.org

Summary   To provide financial assistance to the children and grandchildren of members of the American Legion in Wyoming who are interested in attending college in any state.

Eligibility   This program is open to the children and grandchildren of members and deceased members of the American Legion in Wyoming. Applicants must rank in the top 20% of their high school graduating class and be able to demonstrate financial need.

Financial Data   The stipend is $1,000 per year. Funds, paid directly to the recipient's school, may be used for tuition, room and board, textbooks, and other fees.

Duration   1 year; may be renewed up to 3 additional years.

Number awarded   1 each year.

Deadline   April of each year.

[465]
EAGLE SCOUT OF THE YEAR

American Legion
Attn: Americanism and Children & Youth Division
700 North Pennsylvania Street
P.O. Box 1055
Indianapolis, IN 46206-1055
(317) 630-1202   Fax: (317) 630-1223
E-mail: acy@legion.org
Web: www.legion.org/programs/resources/scholarships

Summary   To recognize and reward, with college scholarships, Eagle Scouts who are members of a troop associated with the American Legion or a son or grandson of a member of the Legion.

Eligibility   Applicants for this award must be either 1) a registered, active member of a Boy Scout Troop, Varsity Scout Team, or Venturing Crew chartered to an American Legion Post, Auxiliary Unit, or Sons of the American Legion Squadron, or 2) a registered active member of a Boy Scout Troop, Varsity Scout Team, or Venturing Crew and also the son or grandson of a member of the American Legion or American Legion Auxiliary. They must also 1) have received the Eagle Scout Award; 2) be active members of their religious institution and have received the appropriate religious emblem; 3) have demonstrated practical citizenship in church, school, Scouting, and community; 4) be at least 15 years of age and enrolled in high school; and 5) submit at least 4 letters of recommendation, including 1 each from leaders of their religious institution, school, community, and Scouting.

Financial Data   The Scout of the Year receives $10,000; each runner-up receives $2,500.

Duration The awards are presented annually; recipients are eligible to receive their scholarships immediately upon graduation from an accredited high school and must utilize the award within 4 years of their graduation date.

Additional data The recipients may use the scholarships at any school of their choice, provided it is accredited for education above the high school level and located within the United States or its possessions.

Number awarded 1 Scout of the Year and 3 runners-up are selected each year.

Deadline Nominations must be received by the respective department headquarters by the end of February of each year and by the national headquarters before the end of March.

[466]
EDWARD T. CONROY MEMORIAL SCHOLARSHIP PROGRAM

Maryland Higher Education Commission
Attn: Office of Student Financial Assistance
839 Bestgate Road, Suite 400
Annapolis, MD 21401-3013
(410) 260-4563   Toll Free: (800) 974-1024, ext. 4563
Fax: (410) 260-3200   TDD: (800) 735-2258
E-mail: lasplin@mhec.state.md.us
Web: www.mhec.state.md.us

Summary To provide financial assistance for college or graduate school in Maryland to children and spouses of victims of the September 11, 2001 terrorist attacks and specified categories of veterans, public safety employees, and their children or spouses.

Eligibility This program is open to entering and continuing undergraduate and graduate students in the following categories: 1) children and surviving spouses of victims of the September 11, 2001 terrorist attacks who died in the World Trade Center in New York City, the Pentagon in Virginia, or United Airlines Flight 93 in Pennsylvania; 2) veterans who have, as a direct result of military service, a disability of 25% or greater and have exhausted or are no longer eligible for federal veterans' educational benefits; 3) children of armed forces members whose death or 100% disability was directly caused by military service; 4) POW/MIA veterans of the Vietnam Conflict and their children; 5) state or local public safety officers or volunteers who became 100% disabled in the line of duty; and 6) children and unremarried surviving spouses of state or local public safety employees or volunteers who died or became 100% disabled in the line of duty. The parent, spouse, veteran, POW, or public safety officer or volunteer must have been a resident of Maryland at the time of death or when declared disabled. Financial need is not considered.

Financial Data The amount of the award is equal to tuition and fees at a Maryland postsecondary institution, to a maximum of $19,000 for children and spouses of the September 11 terrorist attacks or $9,000 for all other recipients.

Duration Up to 5 years of full-time study or 8 years of part-time study.

Additional data Recipients must enroll at a 2-year or 4-year Maryland college or university as a full-time or part-time degree-seeking undergraduate or graduate student or attend a private career school.

Number awarded Varies each year.

Deadline July of each year.

[467]
E.E. MIXON SECOND DRAGOON FOUNDATION SCHOLARSHIPS

E.E. Mixon Second Dragoon Foundation
c/o Scott C. Pierce
217 Painted Fall Way
Cary, NC 27513
(203) 979-7083   E-mail: scott@2nddragoons.org
Web: 2nddragoons.org/index/?q=node/15

Summary To provide financial assistance for college to former members of the U.S. Army's Second Cavalry Regiment and the children of current and former members.

Eligibility This program is open to former members of the Second Cavalry Regiment and the children of current or former members. Members of other Army units and their children may also be considered, especially if they have a previous connection with the Second Cavalry Regiment or other U.S. Cavalry Regiments. Applicants must submit a 500-word essay on 1 of the following topics: 1) how our military presence in Europe contributed to the end of the Cold War; 2) the role of the non-commissioned officer corps in the U.S. military; or 3) what America means to them. They must be attending or planning to attend a college or university. Selection is based on the essay and a statement of their educational goals, projected or current field of study, and personal or family affiliation with a cavalry unit.

Financial Data Stipends range from $250 to $1,000 per year. Funds are deposited directly into the recipient's college tuition account.

Duration 1 semester; may be renewed.

Number awarded Varies each year; recently, 6 of these scholarships were awarded.

Deadline July of each year.

[468]
EIRO YAMADA MEMORIAL SCHOLARSHIP

Go For Broke Memorial Education Center
P.O. Box 2590
Gardena, CA 90247
(310) 328-0907   Fax: (310) 222-5700
E-mail: Julia@goforbroke.org
Web: www.goforbroke.org

Summary To provide financial assistance for college or graduate school to residents of any state who are descendants of World War II Japanese American veterans.

Eligibility This program is open to residents of any state who are attending or planning to attend a trade school, community college, or 4-year college or university on the undergraduate or graduate school level. Applicants must be 1) a direct descendant of a Japanese American World War II veteran, or 2) a descendant once-removed (such as a grand-niece or a grand-nephew) of a Japanese American serviceman or servicewoman killed in action during World War II. Along with their application, they must submit a short essay on "The Values I Have Learned from My Japanese American Forefathers" or their personal reflections on the Japanese American experience during World War II.

Financial Data Stipends range from $500 to $1,000.

Duration 1 year.

Number awarded Varies each year; recently, 6 of these scholarships were awarded.

Deadline March of each year.

[469]
ELSIE BAILEY SCHOLARSHIP

American Legion Auxiliary
Department of New Jersey
c/o Lucille M. Miller, Secretary/Treasurer
1540 Kuser Road, Suite A-8
Hamilton, NJ 08619
(609) 581-9580   Fax: (609) 581-8429
E-mail: newjerseyala@juno.com
Web: www.alanj.org

Summary   To provide financial assistance to New Jersey residents who are the descendants of veterans and planning to attend college in any state.

Eligibility   This program is open to the children, grandchildren, and great-grandchildren of veterans who served in the U.S. armed forces during specified periods of war time. Applicants must be graduating high school seniors who have been residents of New Jersey for at least 2 years. They must be planning to attend a college or university in any state. Along with their application, they must submit a 1,000-word essay on a topic that changes annually; recently, students were asked to write on the topic, "Honoring Our Promise Everyday-How I Can Serve My Country and Our Veterans." Selection is based on academic achievement (40%), character (15%), leadership (15%), Americanism (15%), and financial need (15%).

Financial Data   Stipends range from $1,000 to $2,500.

Duration   1 year; nonrenewable.

Number awarded   1 each year.

Deadline   April of each year.

[470]
ENLISTED ASSOCIATION OF THE NATIONAL GUARD OF KANSAS SCHOLARSHIPS

Enlisted Association of the National Guard of Kansas
Attn: Executive Director
P.O. Box 841
Topeka, KS 66601-0841
(785) 242-5678   Fax: (785) 242-3765
E-mail: eangks@earthlink.net
Web: www.eangks.org

Summary   To provide financial assistance to members of the Enlisted Association National Guard of Kansas and their families who are interested in attending college in any state.

Eligibility   This program is open to members of the association who are also currently serving in the Kansas National Guard and their families. Spouses and dependents of associate members are not eligible. Applicants must submit high school and/or college transcripts, 3 letters of recommendation, and a letter describing their educational goals, future plans, and financial situation. They must be enrolled or planning to enroll full time at an accredited institution of higher learning in any state.

Financial Data   Stipends are normally approximately $1,000.

Duration   1 year.

Additional data   This program is supported, in part, by USAA Insurance Corporation.

Number awarded   Varies each year.

Deadline   May of each year.

[471]
ENLISTED ASSOCIATION OF THE NATIONAL GUARD OF TENNESSEE SCHOLARSHIP PROGRAMS

Enlisted Association of the National Guard of Tennessee
Attn: Scholarship Committee
4332 Kenilwood Drive, Suite B
Nashville, TN 37204-4401
(615) 781-2000   Fax: (615) 833-9173
E-mail: betty@eangtn.org
Web: www.eangtn.org/Scholarships.htm

Summary   To provide financial assistance to members of the Enlisted Association of the National Guard of Tennessee (EANGTN) and to their dependents who are interested in attending college in any state.

Eligibility   This program is open to students who are members of both the Tennessee National Guard and EANGTN or the dependent son, daughter, or spouse of a member in good standing. Children must be unmarried, unless they are also a member of the National Guard. Applicants must be entering or continuing at a college or university in any state. Along with their application, they must submit a transcript, a letter with specific facts as to their desire to continue their education and why financial assistance is required, 3 letters of recommendation, and a letter of academic reference.

Financial Data   The stipend is $1,000. Funds are paid to the recipient's school once enrollment is confirmed.

Duration   1 year.

Additional data   In 1985, the National Guard Association of Tennessee (NGAT) agreed that the EANGTN would fund the scholarships of both associations. Additional funding is also provided by USAA Insurance Corporation.

Number awarded   6 each year.

Deadline   January of each year.

[472]
ENLISTED ASSOCIATION OF THE NATIONAL GUARD OF THE UNITED STATES AUXILIARY SCHOLARSHIP PROGRAM

Enlisted Association of the National Guard of the United
  States
Attn: Auxiliary
3133 Mount Vernon Avenue
Alexandria, VA 22305-2640
(703) 519-3846   Toll Free: (800) 234-EANG
Fax: (703) 519-3849   E-mail: eangus@eangus.org
Web: www.eangus.org

Summary   To provide financial assistance to members of the Auxiliary of the Enlisted Association of the National Guard of the United States (EANGUS) and their dependents who are entering or continuing in college.

Eligibility   This program is open to high school seniors and currently-enrolled college students who are EANGUS Auxiliary members, their unmarried children, or their spouses. Applicants must be enrolled or planning to enroll at a college, university, business school, or trade school and taking at least 8 accredited hours. Graduate students are not eligible. Along with their application, they must submit a copy of their school transcript, 3 letters of recommendation, a letter of academic reference (from their principal, dean, or counselor), and a letter with specific goals for continuing their education and why financial assistance is necessary. The sponsor's State Auxiliary must have made a donation to the EANGUS Auxiliary Scholarship fund for the current and prior years. Selection is based on academic achievement, character, leadership, and financial need.

Financial Data   Stipends are $1,250 or $1,000.

Duration   1 year; nonrenewable.

Additional data   This program includes 1 scholarship donated by USAA Insurance Corporation.

Number awarded   4 each year: 1 at $1,250 and 3 at $1,000.

Deadline   June of each year.

[473]
ENLISTED ASSOCIATION OF THE NATIONAL GUARD OF UTAH SCHOLARSHIP

Enlisted Association of the National Guard of Utah
Attn: Scholarship Committee
12953 Minuteman Drive
P.O. Box 1776
Draper, UT 84020-1776
(801) 523-4493   Fax: (801) 523-4659
E-mail: Derek.dimond1@us.army.mil
Web: www.eangut.org/scholarships.html

Summary   To provide financial assistance to National Guard members who are active members of the Enlisted Association National Guard of Utah (EANGUT) and their families entering or continuing in college in the state.

Eligibility   This program is open to members of EANGUT, their spouses, and their children who are attending or planning to attend a college, university, or vocational/technical school in Utah. Priority may be given to members of the National Guard. Applicants must have a GPA of 2.5 or higher and be able to demonstrate financial need. Along with their application, they must submit a brief statement on their desire to continue their education and their anticipated occupation or profession. Selection is based on academic achievement, citizenship, and financial need.

Financial Data   A stipend is awarded (amount not specified).

Duration   1 year.

Number awarded   1 or more each year.

Deadline   January of each year.

[474]
EOD MEMORIAL SCHOLARSHIPS

Explosive Ordnance Disposal Memorial
Attn: Executive Director
7040 CR 772
Webster, FL 33597
(813) 389-0351   E-mail: scholarship@eodmemorial.org
Web: www.eodmemorial.org/scholarship.html

Summary   To provide financial assistance for college to spouses and other family members of technicians or military officers who have worked in explosive ordnance disposal.

Eligibility   This program is open to children, stepchildren, spouses, grandchildren and other recognized dependents of graduates of Naval School Explosive Ordnance Disposal (NAVSCOLEOD) who served or are serving in the Army, Navy, Air Force, or Marine Corps. Active-duty personnel and NAVSCOLEOD graduates are not eligible. Selection is based on GPA, community involvement and volunteerism, extracurricular activities, awards, paid employment, an essay, future goals, letters of recommendation, and overall impression.

Financial Data   A stipend is awarded (amount not specified). Funds are paid directly to the academic institution for the student's tuition, books, fees, and on-campus housing.

Duration   1 year; may be renewed up to 3 additional years.

Number awarded   Varies each year.

Deadline   March of each year.

[475]
ESSAY COMPETITION FOR CHILDREN OF PUBLIC EMPLOYEES

Civil Service Employees Insurance Group
Attn: Scholarship Contest
P.O. Box 8041
Walnut Creek, CA 94596-8041
Toll Free: (800) 282-6848
Web: www.cse-insurance.com/scholarship.htm

Summary   To recognize and reward, with college scholarships, the best essays written on teenage automobile safety by the children of full-time public employees (including military personnel) in selected states.

Eligibility   This competition is open to high school seniors in 3 geographic regions: southern California, northern California, and Arizona/Nevada. Applicants must have been accepted as a full-time student at an accredited 4-year college, university, or trade school in the United States. Applicants must have a cumulative GPA of 3.0 or higher. Their parent or legal guardian must be currently employed full time (or if retired or deceased, must have been employed full time) by a government entity, including, but not limited to, peace officers, fire fighters, educators, postal employees, military personnel, or federal, state, and local government workers. Qualified students are invited to write an essay (up to 500 words) that discusses the ways the teenage automobile accident rate can be reduced. Essays are evaluated on the basis of originality, creativity, and writing proficiency. Also required in the application process are an official transcript and letters of recommendation.

Financial Data   Prizes in each region are $1,500 scholarships for first place, $1,000 scholarships for second place, and $500 scholarships each for third through fifth places.

Duration   The prizes are awarded annually.

Number awarded   15 each year: 5 in each region.

Deadline   April of each year.

[476]
EXEMPTION FOR DEPENDENTS OF TEXAS VETERANS

Texas Higher Education Coordinating Board
Attn: Grants and Special Programs
1200 East Anderson Lane
P.O. Box 12788, Capitol Station
Austin, TX 78711-2788
(512) 427-6340   Toll Free: (800) 242-3062
Fax: (512) 427-6127   E-mail: grantinfo@thecb.state.tx.us
Web: www.collegeforalltexans.com

Summary   To exempt children of disabled or deceased veterans of the U.S. military from payment of tuition at public universities in Texas.

Eligibility   This program is open to residents of Texas whose parent was a resident of the state at the time of entry into the U.S. military and who died or became totally disabled as a result of service-related injury or illness. Applicants may not be in default on a loan made or guaranteed by the state of Texas or in default on a federal education loan if that default affects their eligibility for GI education benefits. They must be attending or planning to attend a public college or university in the state.

Financial Data   Eligible students are exempt from payment of tuition, dues, fees, and charges at state-supported colleges and universities in Texas.

Duration   1 year; may be renewed.

Additional data   This program was established under provisions of the Hazlewood Act, and is also referred to as Hazlewood Exemption for Dependents of Texas Veterans.

Number awarded   Varies each year; recently, 9 of these awards were granted.

Deadline   Deadline not specified.

[477]
EXEMPTION FOR ORPHANS OF TEXAS MEMBERS OF THE U.S. ARMED FORCES OR NATIONAL GUARD

Texas Higher Education Coordinating Board
Attn: Grants and Special Programs
1200 East Anderson Lane
P.O. Box 12788, Capitol Station
Austin, TX 78711-2788
(512) 427-6340   Toll Free: (800) 242-3062
Fax: (512) 427-6127   E-mail: grantinfo@thecb.state.tx.us
Web: www.collegeforalltexans.com

Summary   To exempt residents of Texas whose parent died in service to the U.S. military or National Guard from payment of tuition at public universities in the state.

Eligibility   This program is open to residents of Texas who are the dependent children of a parent who died as a result of injury or illness directly related to service in the U.S. military or the National Guard. Applicants must have used up all federal educational benefits for which they are eligible. They must be attending or planning to attend a public college or university in the state.

Financial Data   Eligible students are exempt from payment of tuition, dues, fees, and charges at state-supported colleges and universities in Texas.

Duration   1 year; may be renewed.

Number awarded   Varies each year.

Deadline   Deadline not specified.

[478]
EXEMPTION FROM TUITION FEES FOR DEPENDENTS OF KENTUCKY VETERANS

Kentucky Department of Veterans Affairs
Attn: Division of Field Operations
321 West Main Street, Room 390
Louisville, KY 40202
(502) 595-4447   Toll Free: (800) 928-4012 (within KY)
Fax: (502) 595-4448   E-mail: Pamela.Cypert@ky.gov
Web: www.veterans.ky.gov/benefits/tuitionwaiver.htm

Summary   To provide financial assistance for undergraduate or graduate studies to the children or unremarried widow(er)s of deceased Kentucky veterans.

Eligibility   This program is open to the children, stepchildren, adopted children, and unremarried widow(er)s of veterans who were residents of Kentucky when they entered military service or joined the Kentucky National Guard. The qualifying veteran must have been killed in action during a wartime period or died as a result of a service-connected disability incurred during a wartime period. Applicants must be attending or planning to attend a state-supported college or university in Kentucky to work on an undergraduate or graduate degree.

Financial Data   Eligible dependents and survivors are exempt from tuition and matriculation fees at any state-supported institution of higher education in Kentucky.

Duration   There are no age or time limits on the waiver.

Number awarded   Varies each year.

Deadline   Deadline not specified.

[479]
FIRST CAVALRY DIVISION ASSOCIATION SCHOLARSHIPS

First Cavalry Division Association
Attn: Foundation
302 North Main Street
Copperas Cove, TX 76522-1703
(254) 547-6537   Fax: (254) 547-8853
E-mail: firstcav@1cda.org
Web: www.1cda.org

Summary   To provide financial assistance for undergraduate education to soldiers currently or formerly assigned to the First Cavalry Division and their families.

Eligibility   This program is open to children of soldiers who died or have been declared totally and permanently disabled from injuries incurred while serving with the First Cavalry Division during any armed conflict; children of soldiers who died while serving in the First Cavalry Division during peacetime; and active-duty soldiers currently assigned or attached to the First Cavalry Division and their spouses and children.

Financial Data   The stipend is $1,200 per year. The checks are made out jointly to the student and the school and may be used for whatever the student needs, including tuition, books, and clothing.

Duration   1 year; may be renewed up to 3 additional years.

Additional data   Requests for applications must be accompanied by a self-addressed stamped envelope.

Number awarded   Varies each year. Since the program was established, it has awarded more than $640,500 to 444 children of disabled and deceased Cavalry members and more than $184,500 to 224 current members of the Division and their families.

Deadline   June of each year.

[480]
FIRST LIEUTENANT MICHAEL L. LEWIS, JR. MEMORIAL FUND SCHOLARSHIP

American Legion Auxiliary
Department of New York
112 State Street, Suite 1310
Albany, NY 12207
(518) 463-1162   Toll Free: (800) 421-6348
Fax: (518) 449-5406   E-mail: alanyterry@nycap.rr.com
Web: www.deptny.org/Scholarships.htm

Summary   To provide financial assistance to members of the American Legion Auxiliary in New York who plan to attend college in any state.

Eligibility   This program is open to 1) junior members of the New York Department of the American Legion Auxiliary who are high school seniors or graduates younger than 20 years of age; and 2) senior members who are continuing their education to further their studies or update their job skills. Applicants must be attending or planning to attend college in any state. Along with their application, they must submit a 200-word essay on "Why a college education is important to me," or "Why I want to continue my post high school education in a business or trade school." Selection is based on character (25%), Americanism (25%), leadership (25%), and scholarship (25%).

Financial Data   A stipend is awarded (amount not specified).

Duration   1 year.

Number awarded   2 each year: 1 to a junior member and 1 to a senior member. If no senior members apply, both scholarships are awarded to junior members.

Deadline   March of each year.

[481]
FIRST MARINE DIVISION ASSOCIATION SCHOLARSHIPS

First Marine Division Association
410 Pier View Way
Oceanside, CA 92054
(760) 967-8561   Toll Free: (877) 967-8561
Fax: (760) 967-8567   E-mail: oldbreed@sbcglobal.net
Web: www.1stmarinedivisionassociation.org/scholarships.php

Summary   To provide financial assistance for college to dependents of deceased or disabled veterans of the First Marine Division.

Eligibility This program is open to dependents of veterans who served in the First Marine Division or in a unit attached to that Division, are honorably discharged, and now are either totally and permanently disabled or deceased from any cause. Applicants must be attending or planning to attend an accredited college, university, or trade school as a full-time undergraduate student. Graduate students and students still in high school or prep school are not eligible.

Financial Data The stipend is $1,750 per year.

Duration 1 year; may be renewed up to 3 additional years.

Additional data Award winners who marry before completing the course or who drop out for non-scholastic reasons must submit a new application before benefits can be resumed.

Number awarded Varies each year; since the program began, more than 520 students have received more than $1.5 million in tuition assistance.

Deadline Deadline not specified.

[482]
FIRST SERGEANT DOUGLAS AND CHARLOTTE DEHORSE SCHOLARSHIP

Catching the Dream
8200 Mountain Road, N.E., Suite 203
Albuquerque, NM 87110-7835
(505) 262-2351   Fax: (505) 262-0534
E-mail: NScholarsh@aol.com
Web: www.catchingthedream.org

Summary To provide financial assistance to American Indians who have ties to the military and are working on an undergraduate or graduate degree.

Eligibility This program is open to American Indians who 1) have completed 1 year of an Army, Navy, or Air Force Junior Reserve Officer Training (JROTC) program; 2) are enrolled in an Army, Navy, or Air Force Reserve Officer Training (ROTC) program; or 3) are a veteran of the U.S. Army, Navy, Air Force, Marines, Merchant Marine, or Coast Guard. Applicants must be enrolled in an undergraduate or graduate program of study. Along with their application, they must submit a personal essay, high school transcripts, and letters of recommendation.

Financial Data A stipend is awarded (amount not specified).

Duration 1 year.

Additional data This program was established in 2007.

Number awarded 1 or more each year.

Deadline April of each year for fall semester or quarter; September of each year for spring semester or winter quarter.

[483]
FLEET RESERVE ASSOCIATION SCHOLARSHIP

Fleet Reserve Association
Attn: Scholarship Administrator
125 North West Street
Alexandria, VA 22314-2754
(703) 683-1400   Toll Free: (800) FRA-1924
Fax: (703) 549-6610   E-mail: fra@fra.org
Web: www.fra.org

Summary To provide financial assistance for college or graduate school to members of the Fleet Reserve Association (FRA), as well as their spouses, children, and grandchildren.

Eligibility This program is open to members of the FRA and their dependent children, grandchildren, and spouses. The children, grandchildren, and spouses of deceased FRA members are also eligible. Applicants must submit an essay on their life experiences, career objectives, and what motivated them to select those objectives. Selection is based on academic record, financial need, extracurricular activities, leadership skills, and participation in community activities. U.S. citizenship is required.

Financial Data The stipend is $5,000 per year.

Duration 1 year; may be renewed.

Additional data Membership in the FRA is restricted to active-duty, retired, and reserve members of the Navy, Marines, and Coast Guard.

Number awarded 6 each year.

Deadline April of each year.

[484]
FLORIDA AMERICAN LEGION GENERAL SCHOLARSHIPS

American Legion
Department of Florida
Attn: Programs Director
1912A Lee Road
P.O. Box 547859
Orlando, FL 32854-7859
(407) 295-2631   Fax: (407) 299-0901
E-mail: fal@fllegion.newsouth.net
Web: www.floridalegion.org

Summary To provide financial assistance to the descendants of American Legion members in Florida who plan to attend college in any state.

Eligibility This program is open to the direct descendants (children, grandchildren, great-grandchildren, and legally adopted children) of a member of the American Legion's Department of Florida or of a deceased U.S. veteran who would have been eligible for membership in the American Legion. Applicants must be seniors attending a Florida high school and planning to attend an accredited college or university in any state. Financial need is not considered in the selection process.

Financial Data Stipends are $2,500, $1,500, $1,000, or $500.

Duration 1 year; nonrenewable.

Number awarded 7 each year: 1 at $2,500, 1 at $1,500, 1 at $1,000, and 4 at $500.

Deadline February of each year.

[485]
FLORIDA BOYS STATE SCHOLARSHIP

American Legion
Department of Florida
Attn: Programs Director
1912A Lee Road
P.O. Box 547859
Orlando, FL 32854-7859
(407) 295-2631   Fax: (407) 299-0901
E-mail: fal@fllegion.newsouth.net
Web: www.floridalegion.org

Summary To provide financial assistance for college to the descendants of veterans who participate in Florida Boys State.

Eligibility This program is open to the direct descendants (sons, grandsons, great-grandsons, and legally adopted sons) of American war veterans who are selected as delegates to Florida Boys State.

Financial Data The stipend is $1,000.

Duration 1 year; nonrenewable.

Additional data In addition to this scholarship. which can be used at the college or university of the recipient's choice, Tallahassee Community College (TCC) and Florida State University (FSU) offer 5 scholarships to Boys State delegates who attend TCC for 2 years followed by 2 years at FSU.

Number awarded 1 each year.

Deadline Deadline not specified.

[486]
FLORIDA EAGLE SCOUT OF THE YEAR SCHOLARSHIPS

American Legion
Department of Florida
1912A Lee Road
P.O. Box 547859
Orlando, FL 32854-7859
(407) 295-2631   Fax: (407) 299-0901
E-mail: fal@fllegion.newsouth.net
Web: www.floridalegion.org

Summary To recognize and reward, with scholarships for college in any state, Eagle Scouts who are members of a troop associated with the American Legion in Florida or a son or grandson of a member of the Legion in the state.

Eligibility This program is open to Florida high school students who have earned the Eagle Scout award and religious emblem. Applicants must 1) be a registered, active member of a Boy Scout troop, Varsity Scout team, or Venturing Crew chartered to an American Legion Post or Auxiliary unit; or 2) be a registered active member of a duly chartered Boy Scout troop, Varsity Scout team, or Venturing Crew and the son or grandson of a Legionnaire or Auxiliary member. Applicants must be interested in attending a college or university in any state. They must be able to demonstrate practical citizenship in church, school, Scouting, and community.

Financial Data The winner receives a $2,500 scholarship, first runner-up a $1,500 scholarship, second runner-up a $1,000 scholarship, and third runner-up a $500 scholarship.

Duration The awards are presented annually.

Number awarded 4 each year.

Deadline February of each year.

[487]
FLORIDA LEGION AUXILIARY DEPARTMENT SCHOLARSHIP

American Legion Auxiliary
Department of Florida
1912A Lee Road
P.O. Box 547917
Orlando, FL 32854-7917
(407) 293-7411   Fax: (407) 299-6522
E-mail: contact@alafl.org
Web: alafl.org

Summary To provide financial assistance to the children of Florida veterans who are interested in attending college in the state.

Eligibility This program is open to children and stepchildren of honorably-discharged veterans who are Florida residents. Applicants must be attending or planning to attend a postsecondary school in the state on a full-time basis. Financial need is considered in the selection process.

Financial Data The stipends are up to $2,000 for a 4-year university or up to $1,000 for a community college or vocational/technical school. All funds are paid directly to the institution.

Duration 1 year; may be renewed if the recipient needs further financial assistance and has maintained a GPA of 2.5 or higher.

Number awarded Varies each year, depending on the availability of funds.

Deadline January of each year.

[488]
FLORIDA LEGION AUXILIARY MEMORIAL SCHOLARSHIP

American Legion Auxiliary
Department of Florida
1912A Lee Road
P.O. Box 547917
Orlando, FL 32854-7917
(407) 293-7411   Fax: (407) 299-6522
E-mail: contact@alafl.org
Web: alafl.org

Summary To provide financial assistance to members and female dependents of members of the Florida American Legion Auxiliary who are interested in attending college in the state.

Eligibility Applicants must be members of the Florida Auxiliary or daughters or granddaughters of members who have at least 3 years of continuous membership. They must be sponsored by their local units, be Florida residents, and be enrolled or planning to enroll full time at a college, university, community college, or vocational/technical school in the state. Selection is based on academic record and financial need.

Financial Data The stipends are up to $2,000 for a 4-year university or up to $1,000 for a community college or vocational/technical school. All funds are paid directly to the institution.

Duration 1 year; may be renewed if the recipient needs further financial assistance and has maintained at least a 2.5 GPA.

Number awarded Varies each year, depending on the availability of funds.

Deadline January of each year.

[489]
FLORIDA SCHOLARSHIPS FOR CHILDREN AND SPOUSES OF DECEASED OR DISABLED VETERANS

Florida Department of Education
Attn: Office of Student Financial Assistance
325 West Gaines Street
Tallahassee, FL 32399-0400
(850) 410-5160   Toll Free: (888) 827-2004
Fax: (850) 487-1809   E-mail: osfa@fldoe.org
Web: www.floridastudentfinancialaid.org

Summary To provide financial assistance for college to the children and spouses of Florida veterans who are disabled, deceased, or officially classified as prisoners of war (POW) or missing in action (MIA).

Eligibility This program is open to residents of Florida who are the dependent children or spouses of veterans or service members who 1) died as a result of service-connected injuries, diseases, or disabilities sustained while on active duty during a period of war; 2) have a service-connected 100% total and permanent disability; or 3) were classified as POW or MIA by the U.S. armed forces or as civilian personnel captured while serving with the consent or authorization of the U.S. government during wartime service. The veteran or service member must have been a resident of Florida for at least 1 year before death, disability, or POW/MIA status. Children must be between 16 and 22 years of age. Spouses of deceased veterans or service members must be unremarried and must apply within 5 years of their spouse's death. Spouses of disabled veterans must have been married for at least 1 year. The official military and residency status of the veteran parent or spouse must be verified by the Florida Department of Veterans' Affairs.

Financial Data Stipends are $126 per semester hour for students at 4-year institutions, $78 per semester hour for students at 2-year institutions, $87 per semester hour for students enrolled in community college baccalaureate programs, or $64 per semester hour for students at career and technical centers.

Duration 1 quarter or semester; may be renewed for up to 110% of the required credit hours of an initial baccalaureate or certificate program, provided the student maintains a GPA of 2.0 or higher.

Number awarded Varies each year; recently, 295 new and 331 renewal scholarships were awarded.

Deadline March of each year.

[490]
FOLDS OF HONOR SCHOLARSHIPS

Folds of Honor Foundation
7030 South Yale, Suite 600
Tulsa, OK 74136
(918) 591-2406   Fax: (918) 494-9826
E-mail: lhromas@foldsofhonor.org
Web: www.foldsofhonor.com/scholarships.php

Summary To provide financial assistance for college to the spouses and children of service members killed or disabled as a result of service in the Global War on Terror.

Eligibility This program is open to the spouses and children of 1) an active-duty or Reserve component soldier, sailor, airman, Marine, or Coast Guardsman killed or disabled in the Global War on Terror; 2) an active-duty or Reserve component soldier, sailor, airman, Marine, or Coast Guardsman who is currently classified as a POW or MIA; 3) a veteran who died from any cause while such service-connected disability was in existence; 4) a service member missing in action or captured in the line of duty by a hostile force; 5) a service member forcibly detained or interned in the line of duty by a foreign government or power; or 6) a service member who received a Purple Heart medal. Immediate-use scholarships are available to spouses or dependents currently attending or accepted into a 2- or 4-year college or university or a vocational, technical, or other certification program. Future-use scholarships are available to young children of service members and held for them until they are ready to attend college.

Financial Data Stipends range from $2,000 to $2,500. Funds are dispersed directly to the recipient's institution.

Duration 1 year.

Additional data These scholarships were first awarded in 2008.

Number awarded Varies each year; recently, approximately 360 of these scholarships were awarded.

Deadline May of each year.

[491]
FORCE RECON ASSOCIATION SCHOLARSHIPS

Force Recon Association
P.O. Box 425
Rowe, MA 01367
E-mail: commchief@forcerecon.com
Web: www.forcerecon.com

Summary To provide financial assistance for college to members of the Force Recon Association and their dependents.

Eligibility This program is open to members of the Force Recon Association and family members of a relative who served both in the U.S. Marine Corps and was or is assigned to a Force Reconnaissance Company. The relative must be either an active or deceased member of the Force Recon Association. Family members include wives and widows, sons and daughters (including adopted and stepchildren), grandchildren, and great-grandchildren. Applicants may be pursuing scholastic, vocational, or technical education. Along with their application, they must submit a personal statement on why they desire this scholarship, their proposed course of study, their progress in their current course of study, and their long-range career goals. Selection is based on academic achievement, letters of recommendation, demonstrated character, and the written statements.

Financial Data A stipend is awarded (amount not specified).

Duration 1 year; may be renewed.

Number awarded 1 or more each year.

Deadline Applications must be received at least 2 weeks prior to the annual meeting of the Force Recon Association.

[492]
FRANCIS P. MATTHEWS AND JOHN E. SWIFT EDUCATIONAL TRUST SCHOLARSHIPS

Knights of Columbus
Attn: Department of Scholarships
P.O. Box 1670
New Haven, CT 06507-0901
(203) 752-4332   Fax: (203) 772-2696
E-mail: info@kofc.org
Web: www.kofc.org

Summary To provide financial assistance at Catholic colleges or universities to children of disabled or deceased veterans, law enforcement officers, or firemen who are/were also Knights of Columbus members.

Eligibility This program is open to children of members of the sponsoring organization who are high school seniors planning to attend a 4-year Catholic college or university. The parent must be 1) totally and permanently disabled or deceased as a result of military service during the Korean Conflict, the Vietnam War, Cyprus, the Persian Gulf War, Iraq, Afghanistan, or Pakistan; 2) a full-time law enforcement officer who became disabled or died as a result of criminal violence; or 3) a fire fighter who became disabled or deceased in the line of duty. For the children of veterans, the death or disability must have occurred during a period of conflict or within 10 years of its official termination.

Financial Data The amounts of the awards vary but are designed to cover tuition, to a maximum of $25,000 per year, at the Catholic college or university of the recipient's choice. Funds are not available for room, board, books, fees, transportation, dues, computers, or supplies.

Duration 1 year; may be renewed up to 3 additional years.

Number awarded Varies each year.

Deadline February of each year.

[493]
FREE TUITION FOR DEPENDENTS OF DISABLED OR DECEASED SOUTH DAKOTA NATIONAL GUARD MEMBERS

South Dakota Board of Regents
Attn: Scholarship Committee
306 East Capitol Avenue, Suite 200
Pierre, SD 57501-2545
(605) 773-3455   Fax: (605) 773-2422
E-mail: info@sdbor.edu
Web: www.sdbor.edu

Summary To provide financial assistance for college to the dependents of disabled and deceased members of the South Dakota National Guard.

Eligibility This program is open to the spouses and children of members of the South Dakota Army or Air National Guard who died or sustained a total and permanent disability while on state active duty, federal active duty, or any authorized duty training. Applicants must be younger than 25 years of age and proposing to work on an undergraduate degree at a public institution of higher education in South Dakota.

Financial Data Qualifying applicants are eligible to attend a state-supported postsecondary institution in South Dakota without payment of tuition.

Duration 8 semesters or 12 quarters of either full- or part-time study.

Number awarded Varies each year.

Deadline Deadline not specified.

[494]
FREEDOM ALLIANCE SCHOLARSHIPS

Freedom Alliance
Attn: Scholarship Fund
22570 Markey Court, Suite 240
Dulles, VA 20166-6915
(703) 444-7940   Toll Free: (800) 475-6620
Fax: (703) 444-9893
Web: www.freedomalliance.org

Summary   To provide financial assistance for college to the children of deceased and disabled military personnel.

Eligibility   This program is open to high school seniors, high school graduates, and undergraduate students under 26 years of age who are dependent children of military personnel (soldier, sailor, airman, Marine, or Guardsman). The military parent must 1) have been killed or permanently disabled as a result of an operational mission or training accident, or 2) be currently classified as a POW or MIA. For disabled parents, the disability must be permanent, service-connected, and rated at 100% by the U.S. Department of Veterans Affairs. Applicants must submit a 500-word essay on what their parent's service means to them.

Financial Data   A stipend is awarded (amount not specified).

Duration   1 year; may be renewed up to 3 additional years, provided the recipient remains enrolled full time with a GPA of 2.0 or higher.

Number awarded   Varies each year; recently, 167 of these scholarships were awarded.

Deadline   August of each year.

[495]
GALA SCHOLARSHIP

Disabled American Veterans-Department of New Jersey
135 West Hanover Street, Fourth Floor
Trenton, NJ 08618
(609) 396-2885   Fax: (609) 396-9562
Web: www.davnj.org

Summary   To provide financial assistance to the children and grandchildren of members of the Disabled American Veterans in New Jersey who are interested in attending college in any state.

Eligibility   This program is open to graduating high school seniors who are the child or grandchild of a member of the Disabled American Veterans in New Jersey. Applicants must be planning to attend a college or university in any state. Along with their application, they must submit 1) letters of recommendation; 2) a transcript that includes information on their GPA, SAT scores, and class rank; and 3) a 500-word article on a topic that changes regularly (recently, students were asked to present their opinion on the war in Iraq). Selection is based on character (20%), Americanism and community service (20%), leadership (20%), scholarship (20%), and need (20%).

Financial Data   The stipend is $1,000.

Duration   1 year; nonrenewable.

Number awarded   1 each year.

Deadline   March of each year.

[496]
GAMEWARDENS OF VIETNAM ASSOCIATION SCHOLARSHIP

Gamewardens of Vietnam Association, Inc.
c/o David Ajax, Scholarship Program
6630 Perry Court
Arvada, CO 80003
E-mail: dpajax@hotmail.com
Web: www.tf116.org/scholarship.html

Summary   To provide financial assistance for college to the children or grandchildren of veterans who served in Vietnam as part of the Navy's "Operation Gamewarden."

Eligibility   This program is open to the children and grandchildren of living or deceased members of the U.S. Navy River Patrol Force (TF-116) who served in Vietnam in "Operation Gamewarden" during any period from 1966 through 1971. High school students (under 21 years of age) planning to enter college as full-time students and students already enrolled in college (under 23 years of age) are eligible. Selection is based on academic merit, grades, recommendations, and financial need. Special consideration is given to applicants whose parent sponsors are members of the Gamewardens of Vietnam Association, Inc.

Financial Data   Stipends are $2,000. Awards are paid directly to the college the student is attending.

Duration   1 year.

Number awarded   1 to 4 each year.

Deadline   April of each year.

[497]
GENERAL EMMETT PAIGE SCHOLARSHIPS

Armed Forces Communications and Electronics Association
Attn: AFCEA Educational Foundation
4400 Fair Lakes Court
Fairfax, VA 22033-3899
(703) 631-6149   Toll Free: (800) 336-4583, ext. 6149
Fax: (703) 631-4693   E-mail: scholarship@afcea.org
Web: www.afcea.org

Summary   To provide financial assistance to veterans, military personnel, and their family members who are majoring in specified scientific fields in college.

Eligibility   This program is open to veterans, persons on active duty in the uniformed military services, and their spouses or dependents who are currently enrolled full time in an accredited 4-year college or university in the United States. Graduating high school seniors are not eligible, but veterans entering college as freshmen may apply. Spouses or dependents must be sophomores or juniors. Applicants must be U.S. citizens, be of good moral character, have demonstrated academic excellence, be motivated to complete a college education, and be working toward a degree in engineering (aerospace, chemical, electrical, or systems), mathematics, physics, science or mathematics education, management information systems, technology management, computer science, or other field directly related to the support of U.S. intelligence enterprises or national security. They must have a GPA of 3.0 or higher. Along with their application, they must provide a copy of Discharge Form DD214, Certificate of Service, or facsimile of their current Department of Defense or Coast Guard Identification Card. Financial need is not considered in the selection process.

Financial Data   The stipend is $2,000 per year.

Duration   1 year; may be renewed.

Number awarded   Varies each year; recently, 9 of these scholarships were awarded.

Deadline   February of each year.

[498]
GENERAL HENRY H. ARNOLD EDUCATION GRANT PROGRAM

Air Force Aid Society
Attn: Education Assistance Department
241 18th Street South, Suite 202
Arlington, VA 22202-3409
(703) 607-3072, ext. 51   Toll Free: (800) 429-9475
Fax: (703) 607-3022
Web: www.afas.org/Education/ArnoldEdGrant.cfm

Summary   To provide financial assistance for college to dependents of active-duty, retired, disabled, or deceased Air Force personnel.

Eligibility   This program is open to 1) dependent children of Air Force personnel who are active duty, Reservists on extended active duty, retired due to length of active-duty service or disability, or deceased while on active duty or in retired status; 2) spouses of active-duty Air Force members and Reservists on extended active duty; and 3) surviving spouses of Air Force members who died while on active duty or in retired status. Applicants must be enrolled or planning to enroll as full-time undergraduate students in an accredited college, university, or vocational/trade school. Spouses must be attending school within the 48 contiguous states. Selection is based on family income and education costs.

Financial Data The stipend is $2,000.

Duration 1 year; may be renewed if the recipient maintains a GPA of 2.0 or higher.

Additional data Since this program was established in the 1988-89 academic year, it has awarded more than 88,000 grants.

Number awarded Varies each year.

Deadline March of each year.

[499]
GENERAL JOHN PAUL RATAY EDUCATIONAL FUND GRANTS

Military Officers Association of America
Attn: Educational Assistance Program
201 North Washington Street
Alexandria, VA 22314-2539
(703) 549-2311   Toll Free: (800) 234-MOAA
Fax: (703) 838-5819   E-mail: edassist@moaa.org
Web: www.moaa.org/about_scholarship_aboutfund/index.htm

Summary To provide financial assistance to dependent children of surviving spouses of members of Military Officers Association of America (MOAA) who are working on an undergraduate degree.

Eligibility This program is open to children of surviving spouses of deceased retired military officers. Applicants must be younger than 24 years of age. Applicants for the MOAA Educational Assistance Program loans are automatically considered for these scholarships; no separate application is necessary. Selection is based on scholastic ability (GPA of 3.0 or higher), participation, character, leadership, and financial need.

Financial Data The stipend is $4,000 per year.

Duration 1 year; may be renewed for up to 4 additional years if the recipient remains enrolled full time and has not yet graduated.

Additional data The MOAA was formerly named The Retired Officers Association (TROA). No grants are made for graduate study.

Number awarded Varies each year.

Deadline February of each year.

[500]
GEORGE WASHINGTON CHAPTER AUSA SCHOLARSHIPS

Association of the United States Army-George Washington
   Chapter
c/o Bobbie Williams, Scholarship Committee
79 Brush Everard Court
Stafford, VA 22554
(703) 697-6340   E-mail: Bobbie.Williams@us.army.mil
Web: www.gwcausa.org/Scholarship/index.htm

Summary To provide financial assistance for undergraduate or graduate study at a school in any state to members of the George Washington Chapter of the Association of the United States Army (AUSA) and their families.

Eligibility This program is open to active members of the AUSA George Washington Chapter (which serves the Washington, D.C. area) and the families of active members. Applicants must have a GPA of 2.5 or higher and be working on an undergraduate or advanced degree at a college or university in any state. Along with their application, they must submit a letter describing any family

circumstances they believe are relevant and explaining why they deserve the scholarship. Members must also submit a favorable recommendation from their supervisor. Membership in AUSA is open to Army personnel (including Reserves and National Guard) who are either active or retired, ROTC cadets, or civilian employees of the Army.

Financial Data Stipends range up to $1,000.

Duration 1 year.

Number awarded Varies each year; recently, 15 of these scholarships were awarded.

Deadline April of each year.

[501]
GEORGIA DEPARTMENT AMERICAN LEGION SCHOLARSHIP

American Legion
Department of Georgia
3035 Mt. Zion Road
Stockbridge, GA 30281-4101
(678) 289-8883   E-mail: amerlegga@bellsouth.net
Web: www.galegion.org/school_awards.htm

Summary To provide financial assistance to children and grandchildren of members of the American Legion in Georgia who plan to attend college in any state.

Eligibility This program is open to seniors graduating from high schools in Georgia who have a GPA of 3.0 or higher in core subjects. Applicants must be children or grandchildren of members of the American Legion in the Department of Georgia who served in the military. They must be sponsored by a Georgia post of the American Legion. Financial need is not considered in the selection process.

Financial Data The stipend is $1,000.

Duration 1 year.

Number awarded 4 each year.

Deadline June of each year.

[502]
GEORGIA LEGION AUXILIARY PAST DEPARTMENT PRESIDENTS SCHOLARSHIP

American Legion Auxiliary
Department of Georgia
3035 Mt. Zion Road
Stockbridge, GA 30281-4101
(678) 289-8446   Fax: (678) 289-9496
E-mail: amlegaux@bellsouth.net
Web: www.galegion.org/auxiliary.htm

Summary To provide financial assistance to the children of Georgia veterans who plan to attend college in any state.

Eligibility This program is open to residents of Georgia who are high school seniors and children of veterans. Preference is given to children of deceased veterans. Applicants must be sponsored by a local unit of the American Legion Auxiliary in Georgia. Selection is based on a statement explaining why they want to further their education and their need for a scholarship.

Financial Data The stipend is $1,000.

Duration 1 year.

Number awarded 2 each year.

Deadline May of each year.

[503]
GEORGIA LEGION AUXILIARY PAST PRESIDENT PARLEY NURSING SCHOLARSHIP

American Legion Auxiliary
Department of Georgia
3035 Mt. Zion Road
Stockbridge, GA 30281-4101
(678) 289-8446　　　　E-mail: amlegaux@bellsouth.net
Web: www.galegion.org/auxiliary.htm

Summary　To provide financial assistance to daughters of veterans in Georgia who are interested in attending college in any state to prepare for a career in nursing.

Eligibility　This program is open to George residents who are 1) interested in nursing education and 2) the daughters of veterans. Applicants must be sponsored by a local unit of the American Legion Auxiliary. Selection is based on a statement explaining why they want to become a nurse and why they need a scholarship, a transcript of all high school or college grades, and 4 letters of recommendation (1 from a high school principal or superintendent, 1 from the sponsoring American Legion Auxiliary local unit, and 2 from other responsible people).

Financial Data　The amount of the award depends on the availability of funds.

Number awarded　Varies, depending upon funds available.

Deadline　May of each year.

[504]
GEORGIA'S HERO SCHOLARSHIP PROGRAM

Georgia Student Finance Commission
Attn: Scholarships and Grants Division
2082 East Exchange Place, Suite 200
Tucker, GA 30084-5305
(770) 724-9000　　　　Toll Free: (800) 505-GSFC
Fax: (770) 724-9089　　　E-mail: gsfcinfo@gsfc.org
Web: www.gacollege411.org

Summary　To provide financial assistance for college to members of the National Guard or Reserves in Georgia and the children and spouses of deceased or disabled Guard or Reserve members.

Eligibility　This program is open to Georgia residents who are active members of the Georgia National Guard or U.S. Military Reserves, were deployed outside the United States for active-duty service on or after February 1, 2003 to a location designated as a combat zone, and served in that combat zone for at least 181 consecutive days. Also eligible are 1) the children, younger than 25 years of age, of Guard and Reserve members who completed at least 1 term of service (of 181 days each) overseas on or after February 1, 2003; 2) the children, younger than 25 years of age, of Guard and Reserve members who were killed or totally disabled during service overseas on or after February 1, 2003, regardless of their length of service; and 3) the spouses of Guard and Reserve members who were killed in a combat zone, died as a result of injuries, or became 100% disabled as a result of injuries received in a combat zone during service overseas on or after February 1, 2003, regardless of their length of service. Applicants must be interested in attending a unit of the University System of Georgia, a unit of the Georgia Department of Technical and Adult Education, or an eligible private college or university in Georgia.

Financial Data　The stipend is $2,000 per academic year, not to exceed $8,000 during an entire program of study.

Duration　1 year; may be renewed (if satisfactory progress is maintained) for up to 3 additional years.

Additional data　This program, which stands for Helping Educate Reservists and their Offspring, was established in 2005.

Number awarded　Varies each year.

Deadline　June of each year.

[505]
GERALDINE K. MORRIS AWARD

Army Engineer Officers' Wives' Club
c/o Nancy Temple, Chair
P.O. Box 6332
Alexandria, VA 22306-6332
E-mail: scholarships@aeowc.com
Web: www.aeowc.com/scholarships.html

Summary　To provide financial assistance to the children of officers and civilians who served in the Army Corps of Engineers and are interested in studying nursing in college.

Eligibility　This program is open to children of 1) U.S. Army Corps of Engineers officers and warrant officers who are currently on active duty, retired, or deceased while on active duty or after retiring from active duty; or 2) civilians (GS1 through GS9) assigned to U.S. Army Corps of Engineers. Applicants must be high school seniors planning to enroll in a program leading to a nursing degree or certification. Selection is based on academic and extracurricular achievement during high school. U.S. citizenship is required.

Financial Data　The stipend ranges from $1,000 to $2,000.

Duration　1 year.

Additional data　This program was established in 2006.

Number awarded　1 each year.

Deadline　February of each year.

[506]
GLADYS MCPARTLAND SCHOLARSHIPS

United States Marine Corps Combat Correspondents
　Association
Attn: Executive Director
110 Fox Court
Wildwood, FL 34785
(352) 748-4698　　　　E-mail: usmccca@cfl.rr.com
Web: www.usmccca.org/awards/gladys

Summary　To provide financial assistance for college or graduate school to regular members of the U.S. Marine Corps Combat Correspondents Association (USMCCCA) or their children.

Eligibility　Eligible are active-duty Marines and certain Marine Corps Reservists who are regular members of the USMCCCA, or the dependent children of such members, as long as the member is in a "dues-paid" status, or died in such status, or is listed as a prisoner of war or missing in action and was in a "dues-paid" status when so listed. Applicants must be high school seniors or graduates, seeking at least a bachelor's degree. Preference is given to students working on degrees in disciplines that will lead to careers in mass media communications, although applications are accepted in any field.

Financial Data　The stipend is $1,000; funds are to be used exclusively for tuition, books, and/or fees.

Duration　1 year; may be renewed, provided the recipient maintains a GPA of 2.0 or higher.

Additional data　Funds for this scholarship were originally provided by a contribution from Kathryne Timmons in honor of her sister, Gladys McPartland, who served as executive secretary of the USMCCCA from its founding until her death in 1985.

Number awarded　1 or more each year.

Deadline　June of each year.

[507]
GOLD STAR SCHOLARSHIP PROGRAM FOR SURVIVING CHILDREN OF NAVAL PERSONNEL DECEASED AFTER RETIREMENT

Navy-Marine Corps Relief Society
Attn: Education Division
875 North Randolph Street, Suite 225
Arlington, VA 22203-1757
(703) 696-4960   Fax: (703) 696-0144
E-mail: education@nmcrs.org
Web: www.nmcrs.org/goldstar.html

Summary To provide financial assistance for college to the children of Navy or Marine Corps personnel who died as a result of disabilities or length of service.

Eligibility This program is open to the unmarried, dependent children, stepchildren, or legally adopted children under the age of 23 of members of the Navy or Marine Corps who died after retirement due to disability or length of service. Applicants must be enrolled or planning to enroll full time at a college, university, or vocational/technical school. They must have a GPA of 2.0 or higher and be able to demonstrate financial need.

Financial Data Stipends range from $500 to $2,500 per year. Funds are disbursed directly to the financial institution.

Duration 1 year; may be renewed up to 3 additional years.

Number awarded Varies each year.

Deadline February of each year.

[508]
GOLD STAR SCHOLARSHIP PROGRAM FOR SURVIVING CHILDREN OF NAVAL PERSONNEL DECEASED WHILE ON ACTIVE DUTY

Navy-Marine Corps Relief Society
Attn: Education Division
875 North Randolph Street, Suite 225
Arlington, VA 22203-1757
(703) 696-4960   Fax: (703) 696-0144
E-mail: education@nmcrs.org
Web: www.nmcrs.org/goldstar.html

Summary To provide financial assistance for college to the children of Navy or Marine Corps personnel who died while on active duty.

Eligibility This program is open to the unmarried, dependent children, stepchildren, or legally adopted children under the age of 23 of members of the Navy or Marine Corps who died while on active duty but not in a hostile fire zone. Applicants must be enrolled or planning to enroll full time at a college, university, or vocational/technical school. They must have a GPA of 2.0 or higher and be able to demonstrate financial need.

Financial Data Stipends range from $500 to $2,500 per year. Funds are disbursed directly to the financial institution.

Duration 1 year; may be renewed up to 3 additional years.

Number awarded Varies each year.

Deadline February of each year.

[509]
GWOT ASSISTANCE FUND

Navy-Marine Corps Relief Society
Attn: Education Division
875 North Randolph Street, Suite 225
Arlington, VA 22203-1757
(703) 696-4960   Fax: (703) 696-0144
E-mail: education@nmcrs.org
Web: www.nmcrs.org/goldstar.html

Summary To provide financial assistance for college to the spouses of deceased Navy and Marine Corps military personnel who became disabled or died during the Global War on Terrorism (GWOT).

Eligibility This program is open to the spouses of disabled or deceased sailors and Marines who were injured or died while on active duty under hostile fire in a theater of combat operations during the GWOT. Applicants must be enrolled or planning to enroll full or part time at a college, university, or vocational/technical school. They must have a GPA of 2.0 or higher and be able to demonstrate financial need.

Financial Data Stipends range from $500 to $2,500 per year. Funds are disbursed directly to the financial institution.

Duration 1 year; may be renewed up to 3 additional years.

Number awarded Varies each year.

Deadline February of each year.

[510]
HAROLD DWIGHT HARRAH SCHOLARSHIPS

Vietnam Veterans of America-Chapter 522
P.O. Box 551
Indian Rocks Beach, FL 33785-0551
(727) 278-4111
Web: www.vva522.org/scholarship.html

Summary To provide financial assistance to high school seniors in Florida who are related to a veteran and interested in attending college in any state.

Eligibility This program is open to seniors graduating from public or private high schools in Florida and planning to attend college in any state. Applicants must be U.S. citizens and related to a veteran. They must have a GPA of 3.25 and be able to document financial need and volunteer work or community service activities within the past 12 months. Along with their application, they must submit a 1,000-word essay on how this scholarship will support their educational goals.

Financial Data The stipend is $1,000. Funds are disbursed directly to the recipient's college or university.

Duration 1 year.

Additional data Chapter 522 is the Pinellas County Chapter of Vietnam Veterans of America (VVA), but the scholarship is available to all high school seniors in Florida.

Number awarded 3 each year.

Deadline March of each year.

[511]
HATTIE TEDROW MEMORIAL FUND SCHOLARSHIP

American Legion
Department of North Dakota
405 West Main Street, Suite 4A
P.O. Box 5057
West Fargo, ND 58078
(701) 293-3120   Fax: (701) 293-9951
E-mail: Programs@ndlegion.org
Web: www.ndlegion.org

Summary To provide financial assistance to high school seniors in North Dakota who are direct descendants of veterans and interested in attending college in any state.

Eligibility This program is open to seniors graduating from high schools in North Dakota and planning to attend a college, university, trade school, or technical school in any state. Applicants must be the children, grandchildren, or great-grandchildren of veterans who served honorably in the U.S. armed forces. Along with their application, they must submit a 500-word essay on why they should receive this scholarship. Selection is based on the essay and academic performance; financial need is not considered.

Financial Data The stipend is $2,000.

Duration 1 year; nonrenewable.

Number awarded 1 each year.

Deadline April of each year.

[512]
HAWAII NATIONAL GUARD ENLISTED ASSOCIATION SCHOLARSHIP

Hawaii National Guard Enlisted Association
c/o MSG Mara L. Bacon Chang, Scholarship Committee
  Chair
45-251 Kulauli Street
Kaneohe, HI 96744
E-mail: mara.bacon@us.army.mil
Web: www.hngea.net/Scholarship%20Webpage.htm

Summary   To provide financial assistance for college to members of the Hawaii National Guard Enlisted Association (HNGEA) and their dependents.

Eligibility   This program is open to HNGEA members and their dependents. Applicants must be attending or interested in attending a college or university in Hawaii as an undergraduate student. They must have a GPA of at least 2.5 for the current semester and 2.0 overall. Along with their application, they must submit a letter describing their educational goals and need for the scholarship. Selection is based on that letter (10 points), academic achievement (50 points), participation in the organization (10 points), and financial need (30 points).

Financial Data   Stipends range from $500 to $1,000.

Duration   1 year.

Number awarded   Varies each year; a total of $2,000 is available for this program annually.

Deadline   June of each year.

[513]
HELEN KLIMEK STUDENT SCHOLARSHIP

American Legion Auxiliary
Department of New York
112 State Street, Suite 1310
Albany, NY 12207
(518) 463-1162   Toll Free: (800) 421-6348
Fax: (518) 449-5406   E-mail: alanyterry@nycap.rr.com
Web: www.deptny.org/Scholarships.htm

Summary   To provide financial assistance to New York residents who are the descendants of veterans and interested in attending college in any state.

Eligibility   This program is open to residents of New York who are high school seniors or graduates and attending or planning to attend an accredited college or university in any state. Applicants must be the children, grandchildren, or great-grandchildren of veterans who served during specified periods of war time. Along with their application they must submit a 700-word statement on the significance or value of volunteerism as a resource towards the positive development of their personal and professional future. Selection is based on character (20%), Americanism (15%), volunteer involvement (20%), leadership (15%), scholarship (15%), and financial need (15%). U.S. citizenship is required.

Financial Data   The stipend is $1,000. Funds are paid directly to the recipient's school.

Duration   1 year.

Number awarded   1 each year.

Deadline   February of each year.

[514]
HEROES TRIBUTE SCHOLARSHIPS

Marine Corps Scholarship Foundation, Inc.
P.O. Box 3008
Princeton, NJ 08543-3008
(609) 921-3534   Toll Free: (800) 292-7777
Fax: (609) 452-2259   E-mail: mcsfnj@marine-scholars.org
Web: www.mcsf.com

Summary   To provide financial assistance for college to the children of Marines and Navy Corpsmen serving with the Marines who were killed on September 11, 2001 or in combat since that date.

Eligibility   This program is open to the children of 1) Marines and former Marines killed in the terrorist attacks on September 11, 2001; and 2) Marines and U.S. Navy Corpsmen serving with the Marines who were killed in combat since September 11, 2001. Applicants must be high school seniors, high school graduates, or current undergraduates in an accredited college, university, or postsecondary vocational/technical school. They must submit academic transcripts, documentation of their parent's service, and a 500-word essay on a topic that changes periodically. Only undergraduate study is supported. There is no maximum family income limitation. All qualified applicants receive scholarships.

Financial Data   The stipend is $7,500 per year.

Duration   4 years.

Number awarded   Varies each year; recently, 4 of these scholarships were awarded.

Deadline   March of each year.

[515]
HOWARD R. HARPER SCHOLARSHIPS

Enlisted Association of the National Guard of Iowa
c/o Jerald D. Hansen, Secretary
1409 East Coolbaugh Street
Red Oak, IA 51566
(712) 623-2804
Web: www.eangi.com/index-4.html

Summary   To provide financial assistance to members of the Enlisted Association of the National Guard of Iowa (EANGI) and their dependents who are interested in attending college in any state.

Eligibility   This program is open to EANGI members and their spouses and children. Applicants must be attending or accepted at a VA-approved college or vocational/technical school in any state. Along with their application, they must submit a copy of their transcript, a letter with specific facts as to their desire to continue their education and why financial assistance is required, 3 letters of recommendation, and 1 academic reference.

Financial Data   The stipend is $1,000.

Duration   1 year.

Additional data   Membership in EANGI is open to enlisted members of the Iowa Army or Air National Guard, active component members assigned to the Iowa Army or Air National Guard, and enlisted personnel who are retired or honorably discharged from the Iowa Army or Air National Guard.

Number awarded   4 each year.

Deadline   January of each year.

[516]
H.S. AND ANGELINE LEWIS SCHOLARSHIPS

American Legion Auxiliary
Department of Wisconsin
Attn: Education Chair
2930 American Legion Drive
P.O. Box 140
Portage, WI 53901-0140
(608) 745-0124   Toll Free: (866) 664-3863
Fax: (608) 745-1947   E-mail: alawi@amlegionauxwi.org
Web: www.amlegionauxwi.org/Scholarships.htm

Summary   To provide financial assistance to Wisconsin residents who are related to veterans or members of the American Legion Auxiliary and interested in working on an undergraduate or graduate degree at a school in any state.

Eligibility   This program is open to the children, wives, and widows of veterans who are high school seniors or graduates and have a GPA of 3.5 or higher. Grandchildren and great-grandchildren of members of the American Legion Auxiliary are also eligible. Applicants must be residents of Wisconsin and interested in working on an undergraduate or graduate degree at a school in any state. Along with their application, they must submit a 300-word essay on "Education-An Investment in the Future." Financial need is considered in the selection process.

Financial Data   The stipend is $1,000.

Duration   1 year; nonrenewable.

Number awarded   6 each year: 1 to a graduate student and 5 to undergraduates.

Deadline   March of each year.

[517]
IA DRANG SCHOLARSHIP PROGRAM

First Cavalry Division Association
Attn: Foundation
302 North Main Street
Copperas Cove, TX 76522-1703
(254) 547-6537   Fax: (254) 547-8853
E-mail: firstcav@1cda.org
Web: www.1cda.org

Summary   To provide financial assistance for undergraduate education to descendants of Army and Air Force personnel who fought in the battle of Ia Drang in 1965.

Eligibility   This program is open to the children and grandchildren of members of designated Army and Air Force units who actually fought in the battle of the Ia Drang valley from November 3 through 19, 1965. For a list of the qualifying units, contact the sponsor. Children and grandchildren of personnel who were assigned to a unit that fought in the battles but were themselves at other locations during the specified dates are not eligible.

Financial Data   The stipend is $1,200 per year. The checks are made out jointly to the student and the school and may be used for whatever the student needs, including tuition, books, and clothing.

Duration   1 year; may be renewed up to 3 additional years.

Additional data   This program was established in 1994. Requests for applications must be accompanied by a self-addressed stamped envelope.

Number awarded   Varies each year. Since the program was established, 130 of these scholarships, worth more than $194,500, have been awarded.

Deadline   June of each year.

[518]
IDAHO ENLISTED ASSOCIATION YOUNG PATRIOT SCHOLARSHIP

Idaho Enlisted Association of the National Guard of the
   United States
c/o Chris Brearley, President
1501 Shoshone Street
Boise, ID 83705
(208) 422-5489   E-mail: chris_brearley@hotmail.com
Web: eangusidaho.org/Scholarships.php

Summary   To provide financial assistance to members of the Idaho Enlisted Association of the National Guard of the United States and their family who are interested in attending college in any state.

Eligibility   This program is open to 1) members of the association; 2) dependent children of members; 3) spouses of members; and 4) unmarried spouses and unmarried dependent children of deceased members who were in good standing at the time of death. Association members must also be enlisted members of the Idaho National Guard with at least 1 year remaining on their enlistment or have 20 or more years of military service. Applicants must be enrolled or planning to enroll full time at a college, university, trade school, or business school in any state. Along with their application, they must submit a 2-page essay about an activity or interest that has been meaningful to them, a personal letter providing information about themselves and their

families, 2 letters of recommendation, an academic letter of recommendation, and a copy of the sponsor's current membership card or number. Family income is considered in the selection process.

Financial Data   The stipend is $1,500.

Duration   1 year; nonrenewable.

Number awarded   1 each year.

Deadline   January of each year.

[519]
IDAHO FREEDOM SCHOLARSHIPS

Idaho State Board of Education
Len B. Jordan Office Building
650 West State Street, Room 307
P.O. Box 83720
Boise, ID 83720-0037
(208) 332-1574   Fax: (208) 334-2632
E-mail: scholarshiphelp@osbe.idaho.gov
Web: www.boardofed.idaho.gov/scholarships/freedom.asp

Summary   To provide financial assistance for college to dependent children of Idaho veterans who are deceased or listed as prisoners of war or missing in action.

Eligibility   Eligible for these scholarships are dependent children of Idaho veterans who have been determined by the federal government to have been 1) killed in action or died of injuries or wounds sustained in action, 2) prisoners of war (POW), or 3) missing in action (MIA) in southeast Asia (including Korea) or any area of armed conflict in which the United States is a party.

Financial Data   Each scholarship provides a full waiver of tuition and fees at public institutions of higher education or public vocational schools within Idaho, an allowance of $500 per semester for books, and on-campus housing and subsistence.

Duration   Benefits are available for a maximum of 36 months.

Number awarded   Varies each year.

Deadline   Deadline not specified.

[520]
IDAHO LEGION AUXILIARY NURSES SCHOLARSHIP

American Legion Auxiliary
Department of Idaho
905 Warren Street
Boise, ID 83706-3825
(208) 342-7066   Fax: (208) 342-7066
E-mail: idalegionaux@msn.com

Summary   To provide financial assistance to Idaho veterans and their children who are interested in studying nursing at a school in any state.

Eligibility   This program is open to student nurses who are veterans or the children or grandchildren of veterans and have resided in Idaho for 5 years prior to application. Applicants must be attending or planning to attend a school of nursing in any state. They must be between 17 and 35 years of age. Selection is based on financial need, scholarship, and deportment.

Financial Data   The stipend is $1,000.

Duration   1 year.

Number awarded   1 each year.

Deadline   May of each year.

[521]
IDAHO LEGION SCHOLARSHIPS

American Legion
Department of Idaho
901 Warren Street
Boise, ID 83706-3825
(208) 342-7061   Fax: (208) 342-1964
E-mail: idlegion@mindspring.com
Web: idlegion.home.mindspring.com

Summary To provide financial assistance to the children and grandchildren of members of the American Legion or American Legion Auxiliary in Idaho who are planning to attend college in the state.

Eligibility This program is open to the children and grandchildren of members of the American Legion or American Legion Auxiliary in Idaho who have been members for at least 2 consecutive years. Applicants must be Idaho residents and high school seniors who plan to attend accredited colleges, universities, or vocational/technical schools within the state.

Financial Data A stipend is awarded (amount not specified).

Duration 1 year.

Number awarded Varies each year.

Deadline June of each year.

[522]
ILLINOIS AMVETS JUNIOR ROTC SCHOLARSHIPS

AMVETS-Department of Illinois
2200 South Sixth Street
Springfield, IL 62703
(217) 528-4713   Toll Free: (800) 638-VETS (within IL)
Fax: (217) 528-9896
Web: www.ilamvets.org/prog_scholarships.cfm

Summary To provide financial assistance for college to high school seniors in Illinois who have participated in Junior ROTC (JROTC), especially children and grandchildren of veterans.

Eligibility This program is open to seniors graduating from high schools in Illinois who have taken the ACT or SAT and have participated in the JROTC program. Financial need is considered in the selection process. Priority is given to children and grandchildren of veterans.

Financial Data The stipend is $3,000.

Duration 1 year; nonrenewable.

Number awarded 10 each year: 2 in each of the sponsor's 5 divisions.

Deadline February of each year.

[523]
ILLINOIS AMVETS SERVICE FOUNDATION SCHOLARSHIPS

AMVETS-Department of Illinois
2200 South Sixth Street
Springfield, IL 62703
(217) 528-4713   Toll Free: (800) 638-VETS (within IL)
Fax: (217) 528-9896
Web: www.ilamvets.org/prog_scholarships.cfm

Summary To provide financial assistance for college to high school seniors in Illinois, especially children and grandchildren of veterans.

Eligibility This program is open to seniors graduating from high schools in Illinois who have taken the ACT or SAT. Financial need is considered in the selection process. Priority is given to children and grandchildren of veterans.

Financial Data The stipend is $3,000.

Duration 1 year; nonrenewable.

Number awarded 30 each year: 6 in each of the sponsor's 5 divisions.

Deadline February of each year.

[524]
ILLINOIS AMVETS TRADE SCHOOL SCHOLARSHIPS

AMVETS-Department of Illinois
2200 South Sixth Street
Springfield, IL 62703
(217) 528-4713   Toll Free: (800) 638-VETS (within IL)
Fax: (217) 528-9896
Web: www.ilamvets.org/prog_scholarships.cfm

Summary To provide financial assistance to high school seniors in Illinois, especially children and grandchildren of veterans, who are interested in attending trade school.

Eligibility This program is open to seniors graduating from high schools in Illinois who have been accepted at an approved trade school. Financial need is considered in the selection process. Priority is given to children and grandchildren of veterans.

Financial Data The stipend is $3,000.

Duration 1 year; nonrenewable.

Number awarded 10 each year: 2 in each of the sponsor's 5 divisions.

Deadline February of each year.

[525]
ILLINOIS CHILDREN OF VETERANS SCHOLARSHIPS

Illinois Department of Veterans' Affairs
833 South Spring Street
P.O. Box 19432
Springfield, IL 62794-9432
(217) 782-6641   Toll Free: (800) 437-9824 (within IL)
Fax: (217) 524-0344   TDD: (217) 524-4645
E-mail: webmail@dva.state.il.us
Web: www.veterans.illinois.gov/benefits/education.htm

Summary To provide financial assistance for college to the children of Illinois veterans (with preference given to the children of disabled or deceased veterans).

Eligibility Each county in the state is entitled to award an honorary scholarship to the child of a veteran of World War I, World War II, the Korean Conflict, the Vietnam Conflict, or any time after August 2, 1990. Preference is given to children of disabled or deceased veterans.

Financial Data Students selected for this program receive free tuition at any branch of the University of Illinois.

Duration Up to 4 years.

Number awarded Each county in Illinois is entitled to award 1 scholarship. The Board of Trustees of the university may, from time to time, add to the number of honorary scholarships (when such additions will not create an unnecessary financial burden on the university).

Deadline Deadline not specified.

[526]
ILLINOIS FALLEN HEROES SCHOLARSHIP

Office of the State Treasurer
Attn: Bright Start Account Representative
300 West Jefferson Street
Springfield, IL 62702
(217) 558-4983   Fax: (217) 557-6439
E-mail: fallenheroes@treasurer.state.il.us
Web: www.treasurer.il.gov

Summary To provide financial assistance for college to the children of Illinois service members killed in Iraq.

Eligibility This program is open to the children of fallen Illinois service members who served in Operation Iraqi Freedom or Operation Enduring Freedom. Applicants must be U.S. citizens of any age under 30 years. They may be planning to attend an accredited college or university anywhere in the United States or at selected institutions abroad. Children of all Illinois active and Reserve servicemen and women are eligible.

Financial Data The stipend is $2,500. Funds are deposited into an age-based Bright Start portfolio (the Illinois 529 program) and are available when the student reaches college age. The older the child, the more conservative the investment becomes. Funds may be used only for tuition, fees, room, and board, and must be spent before the child reaches 30 years of age.

Duration 1 year.

Additional data This program was established in 2008.

Number awarded Varies each year.

Deadline May of each year.

[527]
ILLINOIS LEGION AUXILIARY SPECIAL EDUCATION SCHOLARSHIP

American Legion Auxiliary
Department of Illinois
2720 East Lincoln Street
P.O. Box 1426
Bloomington, IL 61702-1426
(309) 663-9366   Fax: (309) 663-5827
E-mail: staff@ilala.org
Web: illegion.org/auxiliary/scholar.html

Summary To provide financial assistance to Illinois veterans and their descendants who are attending college in any state to prepare for a career as a special education teacher.

Eligibility This program is open to veterans who served during designated periods of war time and their children, grandchildren, and great-grandchildren. Applicants must be currently enrolled in their second or third year at a college or university in any state and studying teaching retarded or disabled children. They must be residents of Illinois or members of the American Legion Family, Department of Illinois. Along with their application, they must submit a 1,000-word essay on "What my education will do for me." Selection is based on that essay (25%) character and leadership (25%), scholarship (25%), and financial need (25%).

Financial Data The stipend is $1,000.

Duration 1 year.

Additional data Applications may be obtained only from a local unit of the American Legion Auxiliary.

Number awarded 1 or more each year.

Deadline March of each year.

[528]
ILLINOIS LEGION AUXILIARY STUDENT NURSE SCHOLARSHIP

American Legion Auxiliary
Department of Illinois
2720 East Lincoln Street
P.O. Box 1426
Bloomington, IL 61702-1426
(309) 663-9366   Fax: (309) 663-5827
E-mail: staff@ilala.org
Web: illegion.org/auxiliary/scholar.html

Summary To provide financial assistance to Illinois veterans and their descendants who are attending college in any state to prepare for a career as a nurse.

Eligibility This program is open to veterans who served during designated periods of war time and their children, grandchildren, and great-grandchildren. Applicants must be currently enrolled at a college or university in any state and studying nursing. They must be residents of Illinois or members of the American Legion Family, Department of Illinois. Along with their application, they must submit a 1,000-word essay on "What my education will do for me." Selection is based on that essay (25%) character and leadership (25%), scholarship (25%), and financial need (25%).

Financial Data The stipend is $1,000.

Duration 1 year.

Additional data Applications may be obtained only from a local unit of the American Legion Auxiliary.

Number awarded 1 or more each year.

Deadline April of each year.

[529]
ILLINOIS LEGION SCHOLARSHIPS

American Legion
Department of Illinois
2720 East Lincoln Street
P.O. Box 2910
Bloomington, IL 61702-2910
(309) 663-0361   Fax: (309) 663-5783
E-mail: hdqs@illegion.org
Web: www.illegion.org/scholarship.html

Summary To provide financial assistance to the children and grandchildren of members of the American Legion in Illinois who plan to attend college in any state.

Eligibility This program is open to students graduating from high schools in Illinois who plan to further their education at an accredited college, university, technical school, or trade school in any state. Applicants must be the children or grandchildren of members of American Legion posts in Illinois. Selection is based on academic performance and financial need. U.S. citizenship is required.

Financial Data The stipend is $1,000.

Duration 1 year; nonrenewable.

Number awarded 20 each year: 4 in each of the Illinois department's 5 divisions.

Deadline March of each year.

[530]
ILLINOIS LEGION TRADE SCHOOL SCHOLARSHIPS

American Legion
Department of Illinois
2720 East Lincoln Street
P.O. Box 2910
Bloomington, IL 61702-2910
(309) 663-0361   Fax: (309) 663-5783
E-mail: hdqs@illegion.org
Web: www.illegion.org/scholarship.html

Summary To provide financial assistance to the children and grandchildren of members of the American Legion in Illinois who plan to attend trade school in any state.

Eligibility This program is open to students graduating from high schools in Illinois who plan to further their education through a private career school, on-the-job training, apprenticeship, or cooperative training at a program in any state. Applicants must be the children or grandchildren of members of American Legion posts in Illinois. Selection is based on academic performance and financial need.

Financial Data The stipend is $1,000.

Duration 1 year; nonrenewable.

Number awarded 5 each year: 1 in each of the Illinois department's 5 divisions.

Deadline March of each year.

[531]
ILLINOIS MIA/POW SCHOLARSHIP

Illinois Department of Veterans' Affairs
833 South Spring Street
P.O. Box 19432
Springfield, IL 62794-9432
(217) 782-6641   Toll Free: (800) 437-9824 (within IL)
Fax: (217) 524-0344   TDD: (217) 524-4645
E-mail: webmail@dva.state.il.us
Web: www.veterans.illinois.gov/benefits/education.htm

Summary To provide financial assistance for 1) the undergraduate education of Illinois dependents of disabled or deceased veterans or those listed as prisoners of war or missing in action, and 2) the rehabilitation or education of disabled dependents of those veterans.

Eligibility This program is open to the spouses, natural children, legally adopted children, or stepchildren of a veteran or servicemember who 1) has been declared by the U.S. Department of Defense or the U.S. Department of Veterans Affairs to be permanently disabled from service-connected causes with 100% disability, deceased as the result of a service-connected disability, a prisoner of war, or missing in action, and 2) at the time of entering service was an Illinois resident or was an Illinois resident within 6 months of entering such service. Special support is available for dependents who are disabled.

Financial Data An eligible dependent is entitled to full payment of tuition and certain fees at any Illinois state-supported college, university, or community college. In lieu of that benefit, an eligible dependent who has a physical, mental, or developmental disability is entitled to receive a grant to be used to cover the cost of treating the disability at 1 or more appropriate therapeutic, rehabilitative, or educational facilities. For all recipients, the total benefit cannot exceed the cost equivalent of 4 calendar years of full-time enrollment, including summer terms, at the University of Illinois.

Duration This scholarship may be used for a period equivalent to 4 calendar years, including summer terms. Dependents have 12 years from the initial term of study to complete the equivalent of 4 calendar years. Disabled dependents who elect to use the grant for rehabilitative purposes may do so as long as the total benefit does not exceed the cost equivalent of 4 calendar years of full-time enrollment at the University of Illinois.

Additional data An eligible child must begin using the scholarship prior to his or her 26th birthday. An eligible spouse must begin using the scholarship prior to 10 years from the effective date of eligibility (e.g., prior to August 12, 1989 or 10 years from date of disability or death).

Number awarded Varies each year.

Deadline Deadline not specified.

[532]
INDIANA AMERICAN LEGION FAMILY SCHOLARSHIP

American Legion
Department of Indiana
777 North Meridian Street
Indianapolis, IN 46204
(317) 630-1264   Fax: (317) 630-1277
Web: www.indlegion.org/ALFS%20application.htm

Summary To provide financial assistance to children and grandchildren of members of the American Legion family in Indiana who are interested in attending college in the state.

Eligibility This program is open to residents of Indiana who are the children or grandchildren of members of the American Legion, American Legion Auxiliary, Sons of the American Legion, or deceased members of those organizations who, at the time of death, were in current paid status. Applicants must be enrolled or accepted for enrollment at an Indiana college, university, junior college, community college, or technical school. Along with their application, they must submit a 500-word essay describing the reasons they wish to be considered for this scholarship, the purpose to which the funds will be put, their relationship to the Legion family and what it has meant to them, and how the citizens of Indiana and the members of the American Legion family will benefit in the future from their having achieved their educational goals with the assistance of this scholarship. Financial need is not considered in the selection process.

Financial Data Stipends usually range from $700 to $1,000.

Duration 1 year.

Number awarded 3 each year.

Deadline March of each year.

[533]
INDIANA CHILD OF VETERAN AND PUBLIC SAFETY OFFICER SUPPLEMENTAL GRANT PROGRAM

State Student Assistance Commission of Indiana
Attn: Grant Division
150 West Market Street, Suite 500
Indianapolis, IN 46204-2811
(317) 232-2350   Toll Free: (888) 528-4719 (within IN)
Fax: (317) 232-3260   E-mail: grants@ssaci.state.in.us
Web: www.in.gov/ssaci/2338.htm

Summary To provide financial assistance to residents of Indiana who are the children or spouses of specified categories of deceased or disabled veterans or public safety officers and interested in attending college or graduate school in the state.

Eligibility This program is open to 1) children of disabled Indiana veterans; 2) children and spouses of members of the Indiana National Guard killed while serving on state active duty; and 3) children and spouses of Indiana public safety officers killed in the line of duty. The veterans portion is open to Indiana residents who are the natural or adopted children of veterans who served in the active-duty U.S. armed forces during a period of wartime. Applicants may be of any age; parents must have lived in Indiana for at least 3 years during their lifetime. The veteran parent must also 1) have a service-connected disability as determined by the U.S. Department of Veterans Affairs or the Department of Defense; 2) have received a Purple Heart Medal; or 3) have been a resident of Indiana at the time of entry into the service and declared a POW or MIA after January 1, 1960. Students at the Indiana Soldiers' and Sailors' Children's Home are also eligible. The National Guard portion of this program is open to children and spouses of members of the Indiana National Guard who suffered a service-connected death while serving on state active duty. The public safety officer portion of this program is open to 1) the children and spouses of regular law enforcement officers, regular fire fighters, volunteer fire fighters, county police reserve officers, city police reserve officers, paramedics, emergency medical technicians, and advanced emergency medical technicians killed in the line of duty, and 2) the children and spouses of Indiana state police troopers permanently and totally disabled in the line of duty. Children must be younger than 23 years of age and enrolled full time in an undergraduate or graduate degree program at a public college or university in Indiana. Spouses must be enrolled in an undergraduate program and must have been married to the covered public safety officer at the time of death or disability.

Financial Data Qualified applicants receive a 100% remission of tuition and all mandatory fees for undergraduate or graduate work at state-supported postsecondary schools and universities in Indiana. Support is not provided for such fees as room and board.

Duration Up to 124 semester hours of study.

Additional data The veterans portion of this program is administered by the Indiana Department of Veterans' Affairs, 302 West Washington Street, Room E-120, Indianapolis, IN 46204-2738, (317) 232-3910, (800) 400-4520, Fax: (317) 232-7721, E-mail: jkiser@dva.state.in.us. The National Guard portion of this program is administered by Joint Forces Headquarters, Attn: Education Services Office, 9301 East 59th Street, Lawrence, IN 46216, (317) 964-7023, Fax: (317) 964-7028.

Number awarded Varies each year.

Deadline Applications must be submitted at least 30 days before the start of the college term.

[534]
INDIANA EAGLE SCOUT OF THE YEAR SCHOLARSHIPS

American Legion
Department of Indiana
777 North Meridian Street
Indianapolis, IN 46204
(317) 630-1264   Fax: (317) 630-1277
Web: www.indlegion.org/boy_scouts.htm

Summary To recognize and reward, with scholarships for college in any state, Eagle Scouts who are members of a troop associated with the American Legion in Indiana or a son or grandson of a member of the Legion in the state.

Eligibility Applicants for this award must be either 1) a registered, active member of a Boy Scout Troop, Varsity Scout Team, or Venturing Crew chartered to an Indiana American Legion Post, Auxiliary Unit, or Sons of the American Legion Squadron, or 2) a registered active member of an Indiana Boy Scout Troop, Varsity Scout Team, or Venturing Crew and also the son or grandson of a member of the American Legion or American Legion Auxiliary. Candidates must also 1) have received the Eagle Scout Award; 2) be active members of their religious institution and have received the appropriate religious emblem; 3) have demonstrated practical citizenship in church, school, Scouting, and community; 4) be at least 15 years of age and enrolled in high school; and 5) submit at least 4 letters of recommendation, including 1 each from leaders of their religious institution, school, community, and Scouting. They must be planning to attend college in any state.

Financial Data District winners receive $200 scholarships; the state winner receives a $1,000 scholarship.

Duration The awards are presented annually.

Number awarded 12 each year: 1 state winner and 11 district winners.

Deadline January of each year.

[535]
INDIANA SONS OF THE AMERICAN LEGION SCHOLARSHIP

Sons of the American Legion
Detachment of Indiana
Attn: Scholarship Committee
777 North Meridian Street, Suite 104
Indianapolis, IN 46204
(317) 630-1363   Fax: (317) 237-9891
Web: www.in-sal.org/?page_id=305

Summary To provide financial assistance to members of the Sons of the American Legion in Indiana who are interested in attending college in the state.

Eligibility This program is open to active members of a Squadron within the Indiana Detachment of the Sons of the American Legion. Applicants must be 1) seniors graduating from high school and planning to attend an accredited college, university, or trade school in Indiana, or 2) high school graduates attending or planning to attend an accredited college, university, or trade school in the state. Along with their application, they must submit an essay (up to 1,800 words) on the reasons why they feel they should receive this scholarship. Selection is based entirely on involvement in activities of the Sons of the American Legion.

Financial Data The stipend is $1,000.

Duration 1 year; nonrenewable.

Number awarded 1 each year.

Deadline May of each year.

[536]
IOWA EAGLE SCOUT OF THE YEAR SCHOLARSHIP

American Legion
Department of Iowa
720 Lyon Street
Des Moines, IA 50309-5481
(515) 282-5068   Toll Free: (800) 365-8387
Fax: (515) 282-7583   E-mail: programs@ialegion.org
Web: www.ialegion.org/eagle_scout_of_the_year.htm

Summary To recognize and reward, with scholarships for college in any state, Eagle Scouts who are members of a troop associated with the American Legion in Iowa or a son or grandson of a member of the Legion.

Eligibility Applicants for this award must be either 1) a registered, active member of a Boy Scout Troop, Varsity Scout Team, or Venturing Crew chartered to an Iowa American Legion Post, Auxiliary Unit, or Sons of the American Legion Squadron, or 2) a registered active member of an Iowa Boy Scout Troop, Varsity Scout Team, or Venturing Crew and also the son or grandson of a member of the American Legion or American Legion Auxiliary. Candidates must also 1) have received the Eagle Scout Award; 2) be active members of their religious institution and have received the appropriate religious emblem; 3) have demonstrated practical citizenship in church, school, Scouting, and community; 4) be at least 15 years of age and enrolled in high school; and 5) submit at least 4 letters of recommendation, including 1 each from leaders of their religious institution, school, community, and Scouting. They must be planning to attend college in any state.

Financial Data The first-place winner receives a $2,000 scholarship, second a $1,500 scholarship, and third a $1,000 scholarship. All awards must be used for payment of tuition at the recipient's college or university.

Duration The awards are presented annually.

Number awarded 3 each year.

Deadline January of each year.

[537]
IOWA LEGION AUXILIARY PAST PRESIDENTS SCHOLARSHIP

American Legion Auxiliary
Department of Iowa
Attn: Education Committee
720 Lyon Street
Des Moines, IA 50309-5457
(515) 282-7987   Fax: (515) 282-7583
E-mail: alasectreas@ialegion.org
Web: ialegion.org/ala/scholarships.htm

Summary To provide financial assistance for nursing education to dependents of Iowa veterans and to veterans who are members of the American Legion.

Eligibility This program is open to members of the American Legion and the American Legion Auxiliary and the children or grandchildren of veterans of World War I, World War II, Korea, Vietnam, Grenada, Lebanon, Panama, or the Persian Gulf. Applicants must reside in Iowa and be enrolled or planning to enroll in a nursing program in that state. Selection is based on character, Americanism, activities, and financial need.

Financial Data The amount of this scholarship depends on the contributions received from past unit, county, district, department, or national presidents.

Duration 1 year.

Number awarded 1 each year.

Deadline May of each year.

[538]
IOWA WAR ORPHANS EDUCATIONAL AID FOR CHILDREN OF VETERANS WHO DIED ON OR AFTER SEPTEMBER 11, 2001

Iowa Department of Veterans Affairs
Camp Dodge, Building A6A
7105 N.W. 70th Avenue
Johnston, IA 50131-1824
(515) 242-5331   Toll Free: (800) VET-IOWA
Fax: (515) 242-5659   E-mail: info@idva.state.ia.us
Web: www.iowava.org/benefits/war_orphans.html

Summary   To provide financial assistance for college in Iowa to the children of members of the armed forces from that state who died in service on or after September 11, 2001.

Eligibility   This program is open to children of veterans who died in service or as a result of such service on or after September 11, 2001. Eligibility also extends to children of deceased parents who were members of the Reserve components or of the National Guard who died or were killed while performing training or other duties. The deceased veteran must have been a resident of Iowa for at least 6 months prior to entering active military service. The child must be attending or planning to attend a university, college, junior college, school of nursing, business school, or trade school located within Iowa and approved by the Iowa Department of Veterans Affairs. Applicants must be younger than 31 years of age. This is an entitlement program. Aid is available to eligible orphans regardless of scholastic ability, number of years they plan to attend school, or marital status.

Financial Data   The amount of assistance is equal to either 1) the highest resident undergraduate tuition rate for an institution of higher education under the control of the Iowa Board of Regents, less the amount of any state or federal education benefits, grants, or scholarships, or 2) the amount of the child's established financial need, whichever is less. Payments are made directly to the school by quarter, semester, or period, not to the recipient. Part-time students receive prorated amounts.

Duration   1 year; may be renewed until the recipient has received a total amount equal to 5 times the highest resident undergraduate tuition rate for an institution of higher education under the control of the Iowa Board of Regents, or until he or she reaches 31 years of age.

Number awarded   Varies each year.

Deadline   Deadline not specified.

[539]
ISABELLA M. GILLEN MEMORIAL SCHOLARSHIP

Aviation Boatswain's Mates Association
7 Geneva Road
P.O. Box 1106
Lakehurst, NJ 08733
E-mail: Scholarship@abma-usn.org
Web: www.abma-usn.org

Summary   To provide financial assistance for college to the spouses and children of paid-up members of the Aviation Boatswains Mates Association (ABMA).

Eligibility   Applicants must be dependents whose sponsor has been an active, dues-paying member of the ABMA for at least 2 years. They must prepare a statement describing their vocational or professional goals and relating how their past, present, and future activities make the accomplishment of those goals probable. Other submissions include transcripts, SAT or ACT scores, letters of recommendation, and honors received in scholarship, leadership, athletics, dramatics, community service, or other activities. Selection is based on financial need, character, leadership, and academic achievement.

Financial Data   The stipend is $3,500 per year.

Duration   1 year; may be renewed.

Additional data   This program was established in 1976. Membership in ABMA is open to all U.S. Navy personnel (active, retired, discharged, or separated) who hold or held the rating of aviation boatswains mate.

Number awarded   1 each year.

Deadline   May of each year.

[540]
JEWELL HILTON BONNER SCHOLARSHIP

Navy League of the United States
Attn: Scholarships
2300 Wilson Boulevard, Suite 200
Arlington, VA 22201-5424
(703) 528-1775   Toll Free: (800) 356-5760
Fax: (703) 528-2333   E-mail: scholarships@navyleague.org
Web: www.navyleague.org/scholarship

Summary   To provide financial assistance for college to dependent children of sea service personnel, especially Native Americans.

Eligibility   This program is open to U.S. citizens who are 1) dependents or direct descendants of an active, Reserve, retired, or honorably discharged member of the U.S. sea service (including the Navy, Marine Corps, Coast Guard, or Merchant Marines), or 2) current active members of the Naval Sea Cadet Corps. Applicants must be entering their freshman year at an accredited college or university. They must have a GPA of 3.0 or higher. Along with their application, they must submit transcripts, 2 letters of recommendation, SAT/ACT scores, documentation of financial need, proof of qualifying sea service duty, and a 1-page personal statement on why they should be considered for this scholarship. Preference is given to applicants of Native American heritage.

Financial Data   The stipend is $2,500 per year.

Duration   4 years, provided the recipient maintains a GPA of 3.0 or higher.

Number awarded   1 each year.

Deadline   February of each year.

[541]
JOHN A. HIGH CHILD WELFARE SCHOLARSHIP ENDOWMENT FUND

American Legion
Department of New Hampshire
State House Annex
25 Capitol Street, Room 431
Concord, NH 03301-6312
(603) 271-2211   Toll Free: (800) 778-3816
Fax: (603) 271-5352
E-mail: adjutantnh@amlegion.state.nh.us
Web: www.nhlegion.org

Summary   To provide financial assistance to the sons of members of the New Hampshire Department of the American Legion or American Legion Auxiliary who plan to attend college in any state.

Eligibility   This program is open to male seniors graduating from high schools in New Hampshire who plan to attend college in any state. Applicants must be the son of a deceased veteran or of parents who have been members of the American Legion or the American Legion Auxiliary in New Hampshire for 3 continuous years. Along with their application, they must submit a 300-word essay on what this scholarship would mean to them. Selection is based on academic record (20%), Americanism (10%), financial need (50%), and character (20%).

Financial Data   The stipend is $1,000.

Duration   1 year.

Number awarded   1 each year.

Deadline   April of each year.

[542]
JOHN CORNELIUS/MAX ENGLISH MEMORIAL SCHOLARSHIP AWARD

Marine Corps Tankers Association
P.O. Box 20761
El Cajon, CA 92021
Web: www.usmarinetankers.org/scholarship-program

Summary To provide financial assistance for college or graduate school to children and grandchildren of Marines who served in a tank unit.

Eligibility This program is open to high school seniors and graduates who are children, grandchildren, or under the guardianship of an active, Reserve, retired, or honorably discharged Marine who served in a tank unit. Marine or Navy Corpsmen currently assigned to tank units are also eligible. Applicants must be enrolled or planning to enroll full time at a college or graduate school. Their sponsor must be a member of the Marine Corps Tankers Association or, if not a member, must join if the application is accepted. Along with their application, they must submit an essay on their educational goals, future aspirations, and concern for the future of our society and for the peoples of the world. Selection is based on that essay, academic record, school activities, leadership potential, and community service.

Financial Data The stipend is at least $2,000 per year.

Duration 1 year; recipients may reapply.

Number awarded 8 to 12 each year.

Deadline March of each year.

[543]
JOHN J. GUENTHER MERIT SCHOLARSHIP

Marine Corps Intelligence Association, Inc.
Attn: Marine Corps Intelligence Educational Foundation
P.O. Box 1028
Quantico, VA 22134-1028
E-mail: mcia@mcia-inc.org
Web: www.mcia-inc.org

Summary To provide financial assistance for college to members of the Marine Corps Intelligence Association (MCIA) and their dependent children.

Eligibility This program is open to current MCIA members, their dependent children, and their survivors. Applicants must be attending or planning to attend an accredited 4-year college or university as a full-time student. They must submit a 300-word essay on a risk that has led to a significant change in their personal or intellectual life, the most challenging obstacles they have had to overcome and what they learned from the experience, and where they envision themselves in 10 years. Selection is based on the essay, academic achievement, extracurricular activities, and work experience. Financial need is not considered.

Financial Data The stipend is $2,000.

Duration 1 year.

Additional data Membership in the MCIA is open to Marine Corps intelligence personnel, including active duty, Reserve, and retired.

Number awarded At least 1 each year.

Deadline July of each year.

[544]
JOHN KEYS KENTUCKY SONS OF THE AMERICAN LEGION SCHOLARSHIP

Sons of the American Legion
Detachment of Kentucky
c/o Kent Kelso
Independence Squadron 275
P.O. Box 18791
Erlanger, KY 41018-0791
E-mail: SAL275@fuse.net
Web: www.SAL275.com

Summary To provide financial assistance for college to members of Kentucky squadrons of the Sons of the American Legion and to veterans who are residents of Kentucky.

Eligibility This program is open to 1) members of the Sons of the American Legion who belong to a squadron in Kentucky, and 2) honorably-discharged veterans of the U.S. armed forces who are residents of Kentucky. Applicants must be enrolled (and have completed some course work) at a postsecondary institution in Kentucky or an adjoining state (Illinois, Indiana, Missouri, Ohio, Tennessee, Virginia, or West Virginia).

Financial Data The stipend varies, depending on the availability of funds; recently, they averaged $1,000. Awards are made directly to the recipient's institution.

Duration 1 year.

Additional data This program began in 1988.

Number awarded 1 or 2 each year; since the program began, it has awarded 27 scholarships.

Deadline March of each year.

[545]
JOSEPH A. MCALINDEN DIVERS' SCHOLARSHIP

Navy-Marine Corps Relief Society
Attn: Education Division
875 North Randolph Street, Suite 225
Arlington, VA 22203-1757
(703) 696-4960   Fax: (703) 696-0144
E-mail: education@nmcrs.org
Web: www.nmcrs.org/education.html

Summary To provide financial assistance to current and former Navy and Marine Corps divers and their families who are interested in working on an undergraduate or graduate degree in a field related to ocean agriculture.

Eligibility This program is open to Navy and Marine Corps active-duty and retired divers and members of their families. Applicants must be enrolled full time in an undergraduate or graduate program in oceanography, ocean agriculture, aquaculture, or a related field; they may also be engaged in advanced diver training, certification, or recertification. Financial need is considered in the selection process.

Financial Data The stipend ranges from $500 to $3,000, depending on the need of the recipient.

Duration 1 year.

Number awarded 1 or more each year.

Deadline Applications may be submitted at any time.

[546]
JOSEPH H. ELLINWOOD SCHOLARSHIP

American Legion
Department of Massachusetts
State House
24 Beacon Street, Suite 546-2
Boston, MA 02133-1044
(617) 727-2966   Fax: (617) 727-2969
E-mail: masslegion@verizon.net
Web: www.masslegion.org

Summary To provide financial assistance to the children and grandchildren of members of the American Legion in Massachusetts who plan to study nursing at a school in any state.

Eligibility This program is open to the children and grandchildren of current members in good standing in the American Legion's Department of Massachusetts (or members in good standing at the time of death). Applicants must be under the age of 22, entering their freshman year at a college in any state, in financial need, and preparing for a career as a nurse.

Financial Data The stipend is $1,000. Funds are paid directly to the recipient.

Duration 1 year.

Number awarded 1 each year.

Deadline March of each year.

[547]
JOSEPH P. GAVENONIS SCHOLARSHIPS

American Legion
Department of Pennsylvania
Attn: Scholarship Secretary
P.O. Box 2324
Harrisburg, PA 17105-2324
(717) 730-9100　　　　　　　Fax: (717) 975-2836
E-mail: hq@pa-legion.com
Web: www.pa-legion.com

Summary To provide financial assistance to the children of members of the American Legion in Pennsylvania who plan to attend college in the state.

Eligibility This program is open to seniors at high schools in Pennsylvania who are planning to attend a 4-year college or university in the state. Applicants must have a parent who has been in the military or is in the military and is a member of an American Legion Post in Pennsylvania. First preference is given to the children of Legion members who are deceased, killed in action, or missing in action. Financial need is considered in the selection process.

Financial Data The stipend is $1,000 per year.

Duration 4 years, provided the recipient maintains a GPA of 2.5 or higher each semester.

Number awarded 1 or more each year.

Deadline May of each year.

[548]
JUDITH HAUPT MEMBER'S CHILD SCHOLARSHIP

Navy Wives Club of America
P.O. Box 54022
Millington, TN 38053-6022
Toll Free: (866) 511-NWCA
E-mail: nwca@navywivesclubsofamerica.org
Web: www.navywivesclubsofamerica.org/scholarinfo.htm

Summary To provide financial assistance for college to the adult children of members of the Navy Wives Club of America (NWCA).

Eligibility This program is open to children of NWCA members who no longer carry a military ID card because they have reached adult status. Applicants must be attending or planning to attend an accredited college or university. Along with their application, they must submit a brief statement on why they feel they should be awarded this scholarship and any special circumstances (financial or other) they wish to have considered. Financial need is also considered in the selection process.

Financial Data A stipend is provided (amount not specified).

Duration 1 year.

Additional data Membership in the NWCA is open to spouses of enlisted personnel serving in the Navy, Marine Corps, Coast Guard, and the active Reserve units of those services; spouses of enlisted personnel who have been honorably discharged, retired, or transferred to the Fleet Reserve on completion of duty; and widows of enlisted personnel in those services.

Number awarded 1 or more each year.

Deadline May of each year.

[549]
JUNIOR GIRLS SCHOLARSHIPS

Ladies Auxiliary to the Veterans of Foreign Wars
c/o National Headquarters
406 West 34th Street
Kansas City, MO 64111
(816) 561-8655　　　　　　　Fax: (816) 931-4753
E-mail: info@ladiesauxvfw.org
Web: www.ladiesauxvfw.org/html/scholarships.html

Summary To provide financial assistance for college to outstanding members of a Junior Girls Unit of the Ladies Auxiliary to the Veterans of Foreign Wars.

Eligibility Applicants must have been active members of a unit for 1 year, have held an office in the unit, and be between 13 and 16 years of age. Previous winners are not eligible, although former applicants who did not receive scholarships may reapply. Selection is based on participation in the Junior Girls Unit (40 points), school activities (30 points), and scholastic grades (30 points).

Financial Data The winner receives a $7,500 scholarship. Funds are paid directly to the college of the recipient's choice. In addition, $100 is awarded to each Junior Girl who is selected as the department winner and entered in the national competition.

Duration 1 year.

Number awarded 1 each year.

Deadline March of each year.

[550]
JUNIOR VOLUNTEER SCHOLARSHIP AWARD

American Legion Auxiliary
8945 North Meridian Street
Indianapolis, IN 46260
(317) 569-4500　　　　　　　Fax: (317) 569-4502
E-mail: VA&R@legion-aux.org
Web: www.legion-aux.org

Summary To provide financial assistance for college to junior members of the American Legion Auxiliary who have contributed outstanding volunteer service.

Eligibility This program is open to college-bound high school seniors who are junior members of the American Legion Auxiliary. Applicants must submit documentation of the total number of volunteer hours they have served in a Veterans Administration facility and/or in combination with Field or Home Service hours. The president or education chair of their unit should submit a 500-word introduction of the candidate. Selection is based on the total number of hours served.

Financial Data The stipend is $1,000.

Duration 1 year.

Additional data Applications are available from the president of the candidate's own unit or from the secretary or education chair of the department.

Number awarded 5 each year: 1 in each division of the American Legion Auxiliary.

Deadline Applications must be submitted to the unit president by March of each year.

[551]
KANSAS LEGION AUXILIARY L.P.N. SCHOLARSHIPS

American Legion Auxiliary
Department of Kansas
1314 S.W. Topeka Boulevard
Topeka, KS 66612-1886
(785) 232-1396　　　　　　　Fax: (785) 232-1008
E-mail: alakansas@sbcglobal.net
Web: www.kslegionaux.org/edcaschol.html

Summary To provide financial assistance to veterans' dependents from Kansas who are attending a college or university in any state to prepare for a career as a Licensed Practical Nurse (L.P.N.).

Eligibility This program is open to the children, spouses, and unremarried widows of veterans who are entering college for the first time. Applicants must be residents of Kansas attending a school in any state that offers certification as an L.P.N. Financial need is considered in the selection process.

Financial Data A stipend is awarded (amount not specified).

Duration 1 year.

Number awarded 1 or more each year.

Deadline March of each year.

[552]
KANSAS TUITION WAIVER FOR DEPENDENTS AND SPOUSES OF DECEASED MILITARY PERSONNEL

Kansas Board of Regents
Attn: Student Financial Assistance
1000 S.W. Jackson Street, Suite 520
Topeka, KS 66612-1368
(785) 296-3517   Fax: (785) 296-0983
E-mail: dlindeman@ksbor.org
Web: www.kansasregents.org/financial_aid/awards.html

Summary To provide financial assistance for college to residents of Kansas whose parent or spouse died on active military service after September 11, 2001.

Eligibility This program is open to residents of Kansas who are the dependent children or spouses of members of the U.S. armed forces who died on or after September 11, 2001 while, and as a result of, serving on active military duty. The deceased military member must have been a resident of Kansas at the time of death. Applicants must be enrolled or planning to enroll at a public educational institution in Kansas, including area vocational/technical schools and colleges, community colleges, the state universities, and Washburn University.

Financial Data Qualifying students are permitted to enroll at an approved Kansas institution without payment of tuition or fees. They are responsible for other costs, such as books, room, and board.

Duration 1 year; may be renewed for a total of 10 semesters of undergraduate study.

Additional data This program was established in 2005.

Number awarded Varies each year.

Deadline Deadline not specified.

[553]
KATHERN F. GRUBER SCHOLARSHIPS

Blinded Veterans Association
477 H Street, N.W.
Washington, DC 20001-2694
(202) 371-8880   Toll Free: (800) 669-7079
Fax: (202) 371-8258   E-mail: bva@bva.org
Web: www.bva.org/services.html

Summary To provide financial assistance for undergraduate or graduate study to spouses and children of blinded veterans.

Eligibility This program is open to dependent children and spouses of blinded veterans of the U.S. armed forces. The veteran need not be a member of the Blinded Veterans Association. The veteran's blindness may be either service connected or non-service connected, but it must meet the following definition: central visual acuity of 20/200 or less in the better eye with corrective glasses, or central visual acuity of more than 20/200 if there is a field defect in which the peripheral field has contracted to such an extent that the widest diameter of visual field subtends an angular distance no greater than 20 degrees in the better eye. Applicants must have been accepted or be currently enrolled as a full-time student in an undergraduate or graduate program at an accredited institution of higher learning. Along with their application, they

must submit a 300-word essay on their career goals and aspirations. Financial need is not considered in the selection process.

Financial Data The stipend is $2,000; funds are intended to be used to cover the student's expenses, including tuition, other academic fees, books, dormitory fees, and cafeteria fees. Funds are paid directly to the recipient's school.

Duration 1 year; recipients may reapply.

Additional data Scholarships may be used for only 1 degree (vocational, bachelor's, or graduate) or nongraduate certificate (e.g., nursing, secretarial).

Number awarded 6 each year.

Deadline April of each year.

[554]
KENTUCKIANA POST SAME SCHOLARSHIP

Society of American Military Engineers-Kentuckiana Post
c/o Erin Hall, Scholarship Committee Co-Chair
Messer Construction Company
11001 Plantside Drive
Louisville, KY 40299
(502) 261-9775   E-mail: ehall@messer.com
Web: posts.same.org/kentuckiana

Summary To provide financial assistance to students in Indiana and Kentucky (especially those with ties to the military) who are interested in majoring in engineering in college.

Eligibility This program is open to students who fall into 1 of the following categories: a dependent of a current Society of American Military Engineers (SAME) Kentuckiana Post member; an employee or dependent of an employee of a Kentuckiana Post sustaining member firm; an employee or dependent of an employee of the Louisville District Corps of Engineers; a current student member of the Kentuckiana Post; a student whose permanent home address is within the Kentuckiana Post's geographic boundary (Kentucky and Indiana) and who is enrolled in an ROTC program or military academy; or an individual on active duty or the dependent of an individual on active duty who is assigned to an installation within the Kentuckiana Post's geographic boundary. Applicants must be U.S. citizens accepted at an undergraduate ABET-accredited engineering program; undergraduates enrolled in engineering technology programs are not eligible. Along with their application, they must submit an essay of 300 to 500 words on a topic that changes annually; recently, applicants were invited to write on their definition of engineering, how they plan to practice engineering, and how winning this scholarship will sustain their drive toward a career in engineering. Financial need is not considered in the selection process.

Financial Data The stipend is $3,000 per year.

Duration 1 year; may be renewed 1 additional year.

Additional data Recipients are required to attend the scholarship luncheon ceremony in Louisville in May.

Number awarded Up to 5 each year.

Deadline March of each year.

[555]
KENTUCKY VETERANS TUITION WAIVER PROGRAM

Kentucky Department of Veterans Affairs
Attn: Division of Field Operations
321 West Main Street, Room 390
Louisville, KY 40202
(502) 595-4447   Toll Free: (800) 928-4012 (within KY)
Fax: (502) 595-4448   E-mail: Pamela.Cypert@ky.gov
Web: www.veterans.ky.gov/benefits/tuitionwaiver.htm

Summary To provide financial assistance for college to the children, spouses, or unremarried widow(er)s of disabled or deceased Kentucky veterans.

Eligibility This program is open to the children, stepchildren, spouses, and unremarried widow(er)s of veterans who are residents of Kentucky (or were residents at the time of their death). The qualifying veteran must meet 1 of the following conditions: 1) died on active duty (regardless of wartime service); 2) died as a result of a service-connected disability (regardless of wartime service); 3) has a 100% service-connected disability; 4) is totally disabled (non-service connected) with wartime service; or 5) is deceased and served during wartime. The military service may have been as a member of the U.S. armed forces, the Kentucky National Guard, or a Reserve component; service in the Guard or Reserves must have been on state active duty, active duty for training, inactive duty training, or active duty with the U.S. armed forces. Children of veterans must be under 23 years of age; no age limit applies to spouses or unremarried widow(er)s. All applicants must be attending or planning to attend a 2-year, 4-year, or vocational technical school operated and funded by the Kentucky Department of Education.

Financial Data Eligible dependents and survivors are exempt from tuition and matriculation fees at any state-supported institution of higher education in Kentucky.

Duration Tuition is waived until the recipient completes 45 months of training, receives a college degree, or (in the case of children of veterans) reaches 26 years of age, whichever comes first. Spouses and unremarried widow(er)s are not subject to the age limitation.

Number awarded Varies each year.

Deadline Deadline not specified.

[556]
KOREAN WAR VETERANS ASSOCIATION SCHOLARSHIPS

Korean War Veterans Association
Attn: Scholarship Coordinator
13730 Loumont Street
Whittier, CA 90601

Summary To provide financial assistance for college to descendants of Army veterans who served in Korea during or prior to the war there.

Eligibility This program is open to the children, grandchildren, and great-grandchildren of veterans who served on active duty in the U.S. Army in Korea between August 15, 1945 and December 31, 1955. Applicants must be attending or planning to attend an accredited college or university. Selection is based on academic achievement (GPA of 2.75 or higher), extracurricular activities, and financial need.

Financial Data The stipend depends on the need of the recipient, to a maximum of $5,000 per year.

Duration 1 year; may be renewed up to 3 additional years or until completion of a bachelor's degree.

Number awarded Varies each year; recently, 5 of these scholarships were awarded.

Deadline April of each year.

[557]
LA FRA NATIONAL PRESIDENT'S SCHOLARSHIP

Ladies Auxiliary of the Fleet Reserve Association
Attn: Administrator
P.O. Box 490678
Everett, MA 02149-0012
(617) 548-1191   E-mail: msakathy@live.com
Web: www.la-fra.org/scholarship.html

Summary To provide financial assistance for college to the children and grandchildren of naval personnel.

Eligibility Eligible to apply for these scholarships are the children and grandchildren of Navy, Marine, Coast Guard, active Fleet Reserve, Fleet Marine Corps Reserve, and Coast Guard Reserve personnel on active duty, retired with pay, or deceased while on active duty or retired with pay. Applicants must submit an essay on their life experiences, career objectives, and what moti-

vated them to select those objectives. Selection is based on academic record, financial need, extracurricular activities, leadership skills, and participation in community activities. U.S. citizenship is required.

Financial Data The stipend is $2,500.

Duration 1 year; may be renewed.

Number awarded 1 each year.

Deadline April of each year.

[558]
LA FRA SCHOLARSHIP

Ladies Auxiliary of the Fleet Reserve Association
Attn: Administrator
P.O. Box 490678
Everett, MA 02149-0012
(617) 548-1191   E-mail: msakathy@live.com
Web: www.la-fra.org/scholarship.html

Summary To provide financial assistance for college to the daughters and granddaughters of naval personnel.

Eligibility Eligible to apply for these scholarships are the daughters and granddaughters of Navy, Marine, Coast Guard, active Fleet Reserve, Fleet Marine Corps Reserve, and Coast Guard Reserve personnel on active duty, retired with pay, or deceased while on active duty or retired with pay. Applicants must submit an essay on their life experiences, career objectives, and what motivated them to select those objectives. Selection is based on academic record, financial need, extracurricular activities, leadership skills, and participation in community activities. U.S. citizenship is required.

Financial Data The stipend is $2,500.

Duration 1 year; may be renewed.

Number awarded 1 each year.

Deadline April of each year.

[559]
LADIES AUXILIARY VFW CONTINUING EDUCATION SCHOLARSHIPS

Ladies Auxiliary to the Veterans of Foreign Wars
c/o National Headquarters
406 West 34th Street
Kansas City, MO 64111
(816) 561-8655   Fax: (816) 931-4753
E-mail: info@ladiesauxvfw.org
Web: www.ladiesauxvfw.org/html/scholarships.html

Summary To provide financial assistance for college to members of Ladies Auxiliary to the Veterans of Foreign Wars (VFW) and their families.

Eligibility This program is open to members of the Ladies Auxiliary VFW and their children and spouses. Applicants must be 18 years of age and planning to work on a college degree or a career direction at a technical school. Along with their application, they must submit a 300-word essay describing their commitment to their goals and how this scholarship will help them attain those goals. The qualifying member must have belonged to the Auxiliary for at least 1 year prior to application. Financial need is considered in the selection process.

Financial Data The stipend is $1,000. Funds are paid directly to the college or vocational school.

Duration 1 year.

Number awarded 4 each year: 1 in each Ladies Auxiliary VFW Conference.

Deadline February of each year.

[560]
LAURA BLACKBURN MEMORIAL SCHOLARSHIP

American Legion Auxiliary
Department of Kentucky
c/o Artie Eakins, Education Committee
3649 Rockhouse Road
Robards, KY 42452
(270) 521-7183   E-mail: arties@bellsouth.net
Web: www.kyamlegionaux.org

Summary To provide financial assistance to descendants of veterans in Kentucky who plan to attend college in any state.

Eligibility This program is open to the children, grandchildren, and great-grandchildren of veterans who served in the armed forces during eligibility dates for membership in the American Legion. Applicants must be Kentucky residents enrolled in their senior year at an accredited high school. They must be planning to attend a college or university in any state. Selection is based on academic achievement (40%), character (20%), leadership (20%), and Americanism (20%).

Financial Data The stipend is $1,000.

Duration 1 year.

Number awarded 1 each year.

Deadline March of each year.

[561]
LAWRENCE LUTERMAN MEMORIAL SCHOLARSHIPS

American Legion
Department of New Jersey
Attn: Scholarship Judges
135 West Hanover Street
Trenton, NJ 08618
(609) 695-5418   Fax: (609) 394-1532
E-mail: newjersey@legion.org
Web: www.njamericanlegion.org

Summary To provide financial assistance to the descendants of members of the New Jersey Department of the American Legion who plan to attend college in any state.

Eligibility This program is open to high school seniors who are the natural or adopted children, grandchildren, or great-grandchildren of members of the American Legion's New Jersey Department. Applicants must be planning to attend a college or university in any state. Selection is based on character (20%), Americanism (20%), leadership (20%), scholarship (20%), and financial need (20%).

Financial Data The stipend is $1,000 per year.

Duration These scholarships are for 4 years, 2 years, or 1 year.

Number awarded 7 each year: 2 for 4 years, 3 for 2 years, and 2 for 1 year.

Deadline February of each year.

[562]
LIEUTENANT GENERAL CLARENCE L. HUEBNER SCHOLARSHIPS

Society of the First Infantry Division
Attn: 1st Infantry Division Foundation
1933 Morris Road
Blue Bell, PA 19422-1422
Toll Free: (888) 324-4733   Fax: (215) 661-1934
E-mail: Fdn1ID@aol.com
Web: www.bigredone.org/foundation/scholarships.cfm

Summary To provide financial support for college to the children or grandchildren of members of the First Infantry Division.

Eligibility This program is open to high school seniors who are the children or grandchildren of soldiers who served in the First Infantry Division of the U.S. Army. Applicants must submit academic transcripts, letters of recommendation, and a 200-word essay on a major problem facing the country today and their rec-

ommendations for the solution of the problem. Selection is based on academic achievement, extracurricular activities, community service, and work experience.

Financial Data The stipend is $1,000 per year, payable to the recipient's school annually.

Duration 4 years.

Number awarded Varies each year; recently, 3 of these scholarships were awarded.

Deadline May of each year.

[563]
LILLIAN CAMPBELL MEDICAL SCHOLARSHIP

Wisconsin Veterans of Foreign Wars
214 North Hamilton Street
P.O. Box 1623
Madison, WI 53701-1623
(608) 255-6655   Fax: (608) 255-0652
E-mail: qm@wi.vfwwebmail.com
Web: vfwwebcom.org/wisconsin

Summary To provide financial assistance to students working on a degree in a medical field in Wisconsin who served in the military or are related to a person who did.

Eligibility This program is open to students who have completed at least 1 year of study in Wisconsin in a program in nursing, pharmacy, physician assistant, medical or surgical technology, physical or occupational therapy, dental assisting, radiology, or other related medical profession. Applicants or a member of their immediate family (parent, sibling, child, spouse, or grandparent) must have served in the military. They must have a high school diploma or GED but may be of any age. Along with their application, they must submit a 200-word essay on their goals for studying this medical profession. Financial need is considered in the selection process.

Financial Data The stipend is $1,000.

Duration 1 year.

Number awarded 1 or more each year.

Deadline April of each year.

[564]
LILLIE LOIS FORD SCHOLARSHIPS

American Legion
Department of Missouri
P.O. Box 179
Jefferson City, MO 65102-0179
(573) 893-2353   Toll Free: (800) 846-9023
Fax: (573) 893-2980   E-mail: info@missourilegion.org
Web: www.missourilegion.org

Summary To provide financial assistance for college to descendants of Missouri veterans who have participated in specified American Legion programs.

Eligibility This program is open to the unmarried children, grandchildren, and great-grandchildren under 21 years of age of honorably-discharged Missouri veterans who served at least 90 days on active duty. Applicants must be enrolled or planning to enroll at an accredited college or university in any state as a full-time student. Boys must have attended a complete session of Missouri Boys State or Cadet Patrol Academy. Girls must have attended a complete session of Missouri Girls State or Cadet Patrol Academy. Financial need is considered in the selection process.

Financial Data The stipend is $1,000.

Duration 1 year (the first year of college).

Number awarded 2 each year: 1 for a boy and 1 for a girl.

Deadline April of each year.

[565]
LOUISIANA EDUCATIONAL BENEFITS FOR CHILDREN, SPOUSES, AND SURVIVING SPOUSES OF VETERANS

Louisiana Department of Veterans Affairs
Attn: Education Program
1885 Wooddale Boulevard, Room 1013
P.O. Box 94095, Capitol Station
Baton Rouge, LA 70804-9095
(225) 922-0500, ext. 206   Toll Free: (877) GEAUXVA
Fax: (225) 922-0511   E-mail: Bill.Dixon@vetaffairs.la.gov
Web: vetaffairs.la.gov/education

Summary   To provide financial assistance to children, spouses, and surviving spouses of certain disabled or deceased Louisiana veterans who plan to attend college in the state.

Eligibility   This program is open to children (between 16 and 25 years of age), spouses, or surviving spouses of veterans who served during specified periods of war time and 1) were killed in action or died in active service; 2) died of a service-connected disability; 3) are missing in action (MIA) or a prisoner of war (POW); 4) sustained a disability rated as 90% or more by the U.S. Department of Veterans Affairs; or 5) have been determined to be unemployable as a result of a service-connected disability. Deceased, MIA, and POW veterans must have resided in Louisiana for at least 12 months prior to entry into service. Living disabled veterans must have resided in Louisiana for at least 24 months prior to the child's admission into the program.

Financial Data   Eligible persons accepted as full-time students at Louisiana state-supported colleges, universities, trade schools, or vocational/technical schools are admitted free and are exempt from payment of all tuition, laboratory, athletic, medical, and other special fees. Free registration does not cover books, supplies, room and board, or fees assessed by the student body on themselves (such as yearbooks and weekly papers).

Duration   Support is provided for a maximum of 4 school years, to be completed in not more than 5 years from date of original entry.

Additional data   Attendance must be on a full-time basis. Surviving spouses must remain unremarried and must take advantage of the benefit within 10 years after eligibility is established.

Number awarded   Varies each year.

Deadline   Applications must be received no later than 3 months prior to the beginning of a semester.

[566]
LT. COL. ROMEO AND JOSEPHINE BASS FERRETTI SCHOLARSHIP

Air Force Association
Attn: Scholarship Manager
1501 Lee Highway
Arlington, VA 22209-1198
(703) 247-5800, ext. 4807
Toll Free: (800) 727-3337, ext. 4807
Fax: (703) 247-5853   E-mail: LCross@afa.org
Web: www.afa.org/aef/aid/Ferretti.asp

Summary   To provide financial assistance to dependents of Air Force enlisted personnel who are high school seniors planning to attend college to major in a field of science, technology, engineering, or mathematics.

Eligibility   This program is open to dependents of Air Force active duty, Reserve, or Air National Guard enlisted personnel who are graduating high school seniors. Applicants must be planning to enroll full time at an accredited institute of higher education to work on an undergraduate degree in the areas of science, technology, engineering, or mathematics. Selection is based on academic achievement, character, and financial need.

Financial Data   The stipend is $2,500.

Duration   1 year.

Number awarded   Varies each year; recently, 4 of these scholarships were awarded.

Deadline   Deadline not specified.

[567]
LT. MICHAEL L. LEWIS, JR. MEMORIAL FUND

Sons of the American Legion
Detachment of New York
112 State Street, Suite 1300
Albany, NY 12207
(518) 463-2215   Fax: (518) 427-8443
E-mail: info@nylegion.org
Web: www.sonsdny.org

Summary   To provide financial assistance to high school seniors and graduates in New York who are members of the Sons of the American Legion and plan to attend college in any state.

Eligibility   This program is open to members of the Sons of the American Legion in New York. Applicants must be high school seniors or graduates and planning to attend college or trade school in any state. Along with their application, they must submit a 200-word essay either on why a college education is important to them or why they want to continue their postsecondary education in a business trade school. Selection is based on academics (25%), character (25%), leadership (25%), and Americanism (25%).

Financial Data   The stipend is $1,000.

Duration   1 year.

Number awarded   1 each year.

Deadline   April of each year.

[568]
LTCOL HUBERT "BLACK BART" BARTELS SCHOLARSHIP

USMC/Combat Helicopter Association
c/o Marine Corps Scholarship Foundation
P.O. Box 3008
Princeton, NJ 08543-3008
(609) 921-3534   Toll Free: (800) 292-7777
Fax: (609) 452-2259   E-mail: mcsfnj@mcsf.org
Web: www.popasmoke.com/scholarship.html

Summary   To provide financial assistance for college to the children and grandchildren of members of the USMC/Combat Helicopter Association.

Eligibility   This program is open to children and grandchildren of members of the USMC/Combat Helicopter Association who are high school seniors, high school graduates, undergraduates enrolled at an accredited college or university, or students enrolled at an accredited postsecondary vocational/technical school. Applicants must be the child or grandchild of 1) a Marine on active duty, in the Reserve, retired, or deceased; or 2) a Marine or Marine Reservist who has received an honorable discharge, medical discharge, or was killed on active duty. Along with their application, they must submit academic transcripts, a copy of their parent's or grandparent's honorable discharge (if appropriate), and a 500-word essay on a topic that changes periodically. Recently, they were invited to discuss an attribute or accomplishment that sets them apart and how it has shaped them and their beliefs, and why they want to get a college education. Only undergraduate study is supported. The family income of applicants must be less than $82,000 per year.

Financial Data   The stipend depends on the need of the recipient and the availability of funds, but generally ranges from $500 to $3,000 per year.

Duration   1 year; may be renewed for up to 3 additional years.

Additional data   This program was established in 2008.

Number awarded   1 each year.

Deadline   March of each year.

[569]
MADELINE PICKETT (HALBERT) COGSWELL NURSING SCHOLARSHIP

National Society Daughters of the American Revolution
Attn: Committee Services Office, Scholarships
1776 D Street, N.W.
Washington, DC 20006-5303
(202) 628-1776
Web: www.dar.org/natsociety/edout_scholar.cfm

Summary To provide financial assistance for nursing education to active members of the Daughters of the American Revolution (DAR) and their descendants.

Eligibility This program is open to undergraduate students currently enrolled in accredited schools of nursing who are members, eligible for membership, or descendants of a member of DAR. Applicants must have completed at least 1 year of nursing school. They must be sponsored by a local chapter of DAR. Selection is based on academic excellence, commitment to field of study, and financial need. U.S. citizenship is required.

Financial Data The stipend is $1,000.

Duration 1 year; nonrenewable.

Number awarded Varies each year.

Deadline February of each year.

[570]
MAINE VETERANS DEPENDENTS EDUCATIONAL BENEFITS

Bureau of Veterans' Services
117 State House Station
Augusta, ME 04333-0117
(207) 626-4464   Toll Free: (800) 345-0116 (within ME)
Fax: (207) 626-4471   E-mail: mainebvs@maine.gov
Web: www.maine.gov/dvem/bvs/educational_benefits.htm

Summary To provide financial assistance for undergraduate or graduate education to dependents of disabled and other Maine veterans.

Eligibility Applicants for these benefits must be children (high school seniors or graduates under 22 years of age), non-divorced spouses, or unremarried widow(er)s of veterans who meet 1 or more of the following requirements: 1) living and determined to have a total permanent disability resulting from a service-connected cause; 2) killed in action; 3) died from a service-connected disability; 4) died while totally and permanently disabled due to a service-connected disability but whose death was not related to the service-connected disability; or 5) a member of the armed forces on active duty who has been listed for more than 90 days as missing in action, captured, forcibly detained, or interned in the line of duty by a foreign government or power. The veteran parent must have been a resident of Maine at the time of entry into service or a resident of Maine for 5 years preceding application for these benefits. Children may be working on an associate or bachelor's degree. Spouses, widows, and widowers may work on an associate, bachelor's, or master's degree.

Financial Data Recipients are entitled to free tuition at institutions of higher education supported by the state of Maine.

Duration Children may receive up to 8 semesters of support; they have 6 years from the date of first entrance to complete those 8 semesters. Continuation in the program is based on their earning a GPA of 2.0 or higher each semester. Spouses are entitled to receive up to 120 credit hours of educational benefits and have 10 years from the date of first entrance to complete their program.

Additional data College preparatory schooling and correspondence courses do not qualify under this program.

Number awarded Varies each year.

Deadline Deadline not specified.

[571]
MAJOR GENERAL DUANE L. "DUKE" CORNING MEMORIAL SCHOLARSHIP

South Dakota National Guard Enlisted Association
c/o Bruce Anderson, Executive Director
25790 Country Lane
Renner, SD 57055
(605) 988-5414   E-mail: bcres@sio.midco.net
Web: www.sdngea.com/scholarship.html

Summary To provide financial assistance to current and retired members of the South Dakota National Guard Enlisted Association (SDNGEA), the National Guard Association of South Dakota (NGASD), and their dependents who are interested in attending college in any state.

Eligibility This program is open to current and retired members of the SDNGEA and the NGASD and the dependents of current and retired members of those associations. Applicants must be graduating high school seniors or full-time undergraduate students at a college or university in any state. They must submit a 300-page autobiography that includes their experiences to date and their hopes and plans for the future. Selection is based on the essay; awards, honors, and offices in high school, college, or trade school; GPA and ACT/SAT scores; letters of recommendation; and extracurricular and community activities and honors.

Financial Data The stipend is $1,000.

Duration 1 year; nonrenewable.

Number awarded 1 each year.

Deadline March of each year.

[572]
MANNERS MEMORIAL SCHOLARSHIP

Disabled American Veterans-Department of New Jersey
135 West Hanover Street, Fourth Floor
Trenton, NJ 08618
(609) 396-2885   Fax: (609) 396-9562
Web: www.davnj.org

Summary To provide financial assistance to the children of members of the Disabled American Veterans in New Jersey who are interested in attending college in any state.

Eligibility This program is open to graduating high school seniors who are the child of a member of the Disabled American Veterans in New Jersey. Applicants must be planning to attend a college or university in any state. Along with their application, they must submit 1) letters of recommendation; 2) a letter giving the reasons for their choice of vocation; 2) a transcript that includes information on their GPA, SAT scores, and class rank; and 3) a 500-word article on a topic that changes regularly (recently, students were asked to present their opinion on the war in Iraq). Selection is based on character (20%), Americanism and community service (20%), leadership (20%), scholarship (20%), and need (20%).

Financial Data The stipend is $1,000.

Duration 1 year; nonrenewable.

Number awarded 1 each year.

Deadline March of each year.

[573]
MARIA C. JACKSON/GENERAL GEORGE A. WHITE SCHOLARSHIP

Oregon Student Assistance Commission
Attn: Grants and Scholarships Division
1500 Valley River Drive, Suite 100
Eugene, OR 97401-2146
(541) 687-7395   Toll Free: (800) 452-8807, ext. 7395
Fax: (541) 687-7414   TDD: (800) 735-2900
E-mail: awardinfo@osac.state.or.us
Web: www.osac.state.or.us/osac_programs.html

Summary To provide financial assistance to veterans and children of veterans and military personnel in Oregon who are interested in attending college or graduate school in the state.

Eligibility This program is open to residents of Oregon who served, or whose parents are serving or have served, in the U.S. armed forces. Applicants or their parents must have resided in Oregon at the time of enlistment. They must be enrolled or planning to enrolled in a college or graduate school in the state. College and university undergraduates must have a GPA of 3.75 or higher, but there is no minimum GPA requirement for graduate students or those attending a technical school. Selection is based on scholastic ability and financial need.

Financial Data A stipend is awarded (amount not specified).

Number awarded Varies each year.

Deadline February of each year.

[574]
MARINE CORPS LEAGUE SCHOLARSHIPS

Marine Corps League
Attn: National Executive Director
P.O. Box 3070
Merrifield, VA 22116-3070
(703) 207-9588   Toll Free: (800) MCL-1775
Fax: (703) 207-0047   E-mail: mcl@mcleague.org
Web: www.mcleague.org

Summary To provide college aid to students whose parents served in the Marines and to members of the Marine Corps League or Marine Corps League Auxiliary.

Eligibility This program is open to 1) children of Marines who lost their lives in the line of duty; 2) spouses, children, grandchildren, great-grandchildren, and stepchildren of active Marine Corps League and/or Auxiliary members; and 3) members of the Marine Corps League and/or Marine Corps League Auxiliary who are honorably discharged and in need of rehabilitation training not provided by government programs. Applicants must be seeking further education and training as a full-time student and be recommended by the commandant of an active chartered detachment of the Marine Corps League or the president of an active chartered unit of the Auxiliary. They must have a GPA of 3.0 or higher. Financial need is not considered in the selection process.

Financial Data A stipend is awarded (amount not specified). Funds are paid directly to the recipient.

Duration 1 year; may be renewed up to 3 additional years (all renewals must complete an application and attach a transcript from the college or university).

Number awarded Varies, depending upon the amount of funds available each year.

Deadline June of each year.

[575]
MARINE CORPS SCHOLARSHIPS

Marine Corps Scholarship Foundation, Inc.
P.O. Box 3008
Princeton, NJ 08543-3008
(609) 921-3534   Toll Free: (800) 292-7777
Fax: (609) 452-2259   E-mail: mcsfnj@marine-scholars.org
Web: www.mcsf.com

Summary To provide financial assistance for college to the children of present or former members of the U.S. Marine Corps.

Eligibility This program is open to the children of 1) Marines on active duty or in the Reserves; 2) former Marines and Marine Reservists who served at least 90 days and received an honorable discharge, received a medical discharge, or were killed while serving in the U.S. Marines; 3) active-duty, Reserve, and former U.S. Navy Corpsmen who are serving or have served with the U.S. Marine Corps; and 4) U.S. Navy Corpsmen who have served with the U.S. Marine Corps and have received an honorable discharge, medical discharge, or who were killed while serving in the

U.S. Navy. Applicants must be high school seniors, high school graduates, or current undergraduates in an accredited college, university, or postsecondary vocational/technical school. They must submit academic transcripts; a written statement of service from their parent's commanding officer or a copy of their parent's honorable discharge; and a 500-word essay on a topic that changes periodically. Only undergraduate study is supported. The family income of applicants must be less than $82,000 per year.

Financial Data The stipends of most scholarships range from $500 to $2,500 per year, depending upon the recipient's financial needs and educational requirements. The Toyota Scholars Program, established in 2004 by Toyota Motor Sales, U.S.A., Inc., provides stipends of $5,000 per year. Certain named scholarships (including the Dr. Jack C. Berger and Virginia Butts Berger Memorial Cornerstone Scholarship, the General and Mrs. Graves B. Erskine Memorial Cornerstone Scholarship, the Frederick L. Swindal Cornerstone Scholarship, the Davenport Family Foundation Cornerstone Scholarship, the Captain E. Phillips Hathaway USMCR (Ret.) Memorial Cornerstone Scholarship, and the Ralph M. Parsons Foundation Cornerstone Scholarship) are for $10,000 per year.

Duration 1 year; may be renewed upon reapplication.

Number awarded Varies each year; recently, 1,405 of these scholarships, with a total value of more than $3.5 million, were awarded.

Deadline March of each year.

[576]
MARINE GUNNERY SERGEANT JOHN DAVID FRY SCHOLARSHIP

Department of Veterans Affairs
Attn: Veterans Benefits Administration
810 Vermont Avenue, N.W.
Washington, DC 20420
(202) 418-4343   Toll Free: (888) GI-BILL1
Web: www.gibill.va.gov

Summary To provide financial assistance to children of military personnel who died in the line of duty on or after September 11, 2001.

Eligibility This program is open to the children of active-duty members of the Armed Forces who have died in the line of duty on or after September 11, 2001. Applicants must be planning to enroll as undergraduates at a college or university. They must be at least 18 years of age, even if they have completed high school.

Financial Data Eligible students receive payment of tuition and fees, up to the level of tuition and fees at the most expensive public institution of higher learning in their state of residence; the actual amount depends on the state of residence. A monthly living stipend based on the military housing allowance for the zip code where the school is located and an annual book allowance of $1,000 are also provided.

Duration Participants receive up to 36 months of entitlement. They have 15 years in which to utilize the benefit.

Additional data This program began in 2009 as a component of the Post-9/11 GI Bill.

Number awarded Varies each year.

Deadline Deadline not specified.

[577]
MARY BARRETT MARSHALL SCHOLARSHIP

American Legion Auxiliary
Department of Kentucky
c/o Lois Smith, Student Loan Fund Committee
812 Madison Street
Rockport, IN 47635-1241
(812) 649-2163
Web: www.kyamlegionaux.org

Summary To provide financial assistance to female dependents of veterans in Kentucky who plan to attend college in the state.

Eligibility This program is open to the daughters, wives, sisters, widows, granddaughters, or great-granddaughters of veterans eligible for membership in the American Legion who are high school seniors or graduates and 5-year residents of Kentucky. Applicants must be planning to attend a college or university in Kentucky.

Financial Data The stipend is $1,000. The funds may be used for tuition, registration fees, laboratory fees, and books, but not for room and board.

Duration 1 year.

Number awarded 1 each year.

Deadline March of each year.

[578]
MARY PAOLOZZI MEMBER'S SCHOLARSHIP

Navy Wives Club of America
P.O. Box 54022
Millington, TN 38053-6022
Toll Free: (866) 511-NWCA
E-mail: nwca@navywivesclubsofamerica.org
Web: www.navywivesclubsofamerica.org/scholarinfo.htm

Summary To provide financial assistance for undergraduate or graduate study to members of the Navy Wives' Club of America (NWCA).

Eligibility This program is open to NWCA members who can demonstrate financial need. Applicants must be 1) a high school graduate or senior planning to attend college full time next year; 2) currently enrolled in an undergraduate program and planning to continue as a full-time undergraduate; 3) a college graduate or senior planning to be a full-time graduate student next year; or 4) a high school graduate or GED recipient planning to attend vocational or business school next year. Along with their application, they must submit a brief statement on why they feel they should be awarded this scholarship and any special circumstances (financial or other) they wish to have considered. Financial need is also considered in the selection process.

Financial Data Stipends range from $500 to $1,000 each year (depending upon the donations from the NWCA chapters).

Duration 1 year.

Additional data Membership in the NWCA is open to spouses of enlisted personnel serving in the Navy, Marine Corps, Coast Guard, and the active Reserve units of those services; spouses of enlisted personnel who have been honorably discharged, retired, or transferred to the Fleet Reserve on completion of duty; and widows of enlisted personnel in those services.

Number awarded 1 or more each year.

Deadline May of each year.

[579]
MARY ROWENA COOPER SCHOLARSHIP

Winston-Salem Foundation
Attn: Student Aid Department
860 West Fifth Street
Winston-Salem, NC 27101-2506
(336) 725-2382   Toll Free: (866) 227-1209
Fax: (336) 727-0581   E-mail: info@wsfoundation.org
Web: www.wsfoundation.org/students

Summary To provide financial assistance for college to children of veterans who served in Vietnam.

Eligibility This program is open to students currently enrolled at least half time at an accredited 2- or 4-year college, university, or vocational/technical school. Applicants must be the child of a living or deceased veteran who served in Vietnam. They must have a GPA of 2.0 or higher and be able to demonstrate financial need (income of $31,200 or less for a family of 1, ranging up to $106,800 or less for a family of 8). U.S. citizenship is required.

Financial Data A stipend is awarded (amount not specified).

Duration 1 year.

Additional data This program was established in 1991. There is a $20 application fee (waived if the applicant is unable to pay).

Number awarded 1 or more each year.

Deadline August of each year.

[580]
MARYANN K. MURTHA MEMORIAL SCHOLARSHIP

American Legion Auxiliary
Department of New York
112 State Street, Suite 1310
Albany, NY 12207
(518) 463-1162   Toll Free: (800) 421-6348
Fax: (518) 449-5406   E-mail: alanyterry@nycap.rr.com
Web: www.deptny.org/Scholarships.htm

Summary To provide financial assistance to New York residents who are the descendants of veterans and interested in attending college in any state.

Eligibility This program is open to residents of New York who are high school seniors or graduates and attending or planning to attend an accredited college or university in any state. Applicants must be the children, grandchildren, or great-grandchildren of veterans who served during specified periods of war time. Along with their application, they must submit a 700-word article describing their plans and goals for the future and how they hope to use their talent and education to help others. Selection is based on character (20%), Americanism (15%), community involvement (15%), leadership (15%), scholarship (20%), and financial need (15%). U.S. citizenship is required.

Financial Data The stipend is $1,000. Funds are paid directly to the recipient's school.

Duration 1 year.

Number awarded 1 each year.

Deadline February of each year.

[581]
MARYLAND LEGION AUXILIARY CHILDREN AND YOUTH FUND SCHOLARSHIP

American Legion Auxiliary
Department of Maryland
1589 Sulphur Spring Road, Suite 105
Baltimore, MD 21227
(410) 242-9519   Fax: (410) 242-9553
E-mail: hq@alamd.org
Web: www.alamd.org

Summary To provide financial assistance for college to the daughters of veterans who are Maryland residents and wish to study arts, sciences, business, public administration, education, or a medical field at a school in the state.

Eligibility This program is open to Maryland senior high girls with a veteran parent who wish to study arts, sciences, business, public administration, education, or a medical field other than nursing at a college or university in the state. Preference is given to children of members of the American Legion or American Legion Auxiliary. Selection is based on character (30%), Americanism (20%), leadership (10%), scholarship (20%), and financial need (20%).

Financial Data The stipend is $2,000.

Duration 1 year; may be renewed up to 3 additional years.

Number awarded 1 each year.

Deadline April of each year.

[582]
MARYLAND LEGION AUXILIARY PAST PRESIDENTS' PARLEY NURSING SCHOLARSHIP

American Legion Auxiliary
Department of Maryland
1589 Sulphur Spring Road, Suite 105
Baltimore, MD 21227
(410) 242-9519   Fax: (410) 242-9553
E-mail: hq@alamd.org
Web: www.alamd.org

Summary To provide financial assistance to the female descendants of Maryland veterans who wish to study nursing at a school in any state.

Eligibility This program is open to Maryland residents who are the daughters, granddaughters, great-granddaughters, step-daughters, step-granddaughters, or step-great-granddaughters of ex-servicewomen (or of ex-servicemen, if there are no qualified descendants of ex-servicewomen). Applicants must be interested in attending a school in any state to become a registered nurse and be able to show financial need. They must submit a 300-word essay on the topic "What a Nursing Career Means to Me."

Financial Data The stipend is $2,000. Funds are sent directly to the recipient's school.

Duration 1 year; may be renewed for up to 3 additional years if the recipient remains enrolled full time.

Number awarded 1 each year.

Deadline April of each year.

[583]
MARYLAND SCHOLARSHIPS FOR VETERANS OF THE AFGHANISTAN AND IRAQ CONFLICTS

Maryland Higher Education Commission
Attn: Office of Student Financial Assistance
839 Bestgate Road, Suite 400
Annapolis, MD 21401-3013
(410) 260-4563   Toll Free: (800) 974-1024, ext. 4563
Fax: (410) 260-3200   TDD: (800) 735-2258
E-mail: lasplin@mhec.state.md.us
Web: www.mhec.state.md.us

Summary To provide financial assistance for college to residents of Maryland who served in the armed forces in Afghanistan or Iraq and their children and spouses.

Eligibility This program is open to Maryland residents who are 1) a veteran who served at least 60 days in Afghanistan on or after October 24, 2001 or in Iraq on or after March 19, 2003; 2) an active-duty member of the armed forces who served at least 60 days in Afghanistan or Iraq on or after those dates; 3) a member of a Reserve component of the armed forces or the Maryland National Guard who was activated as a result of the Afghanistan or Iraq conflicts and served at least 60 days; and 4) the children and spouses of such veterans, active-duty armed forces personnel, or members of Reserve forces or Maryland National Guard. Applicants must be enrolled or accepted for enrollment in a regular undergraduate program at an eligible Maryland institution. In the selection process, veterans are given priority over dependent children and spouses.

Financial Data The stipend is equal to 50% of the annual tuition, mandatory fees, and room and board of a resident undergraduate at a 4-year public institution within the University System of Maryland, currently capped at $9,026 per year. The total amount of all state awards may not exceed the cost of attendance as determined by the school's financial aid office or $19,000, whichever is less.

Duration 1 year; may be renewed for an additional 4 years of full-time study or 7 years of part-time study, provided the recipient remains enrolled in an eligible program with a GPA of 2.5 or higher.

Additional data This program is scheduled to expire in 2016.

Number awarded Varies each year.

Deadline February of each year.

[584]
MASSACHUSETTS LEGION DEPARTMENT GENERAL SCHOLARSHIPS

American Legion
Department of Massachusetts
State House
24 Beacon Street, Suite 546-2
Boston, MA 02133-1044
(617) 727-2966   Fax: (617) 727-2969
E-mail: masslegion@verizon.net
Web: www.masslegion.org

Summary To provide financial assistance to the children and grandchildren of members of the American Legion in Massachusetts who are entering college in any state.

Eligibility Eligible to apply are the children and grandchildren of members in good standing in the American Legion's Department of Massachusetts (or who were members in good standing at the time of death). Applicants must be entering their freshman year at a college or university in any state. Financial need is considered in the selection process.

Financial Data Stipends are $1,000 or $500.

Duration 1 year.

Additional data The $1,000 scholarships are designated as follows: the Frank R. Kelley Scholarship, the Robert (Sam) Murphy Scholarship, the H.P. Redden Scholarship, the Mayer/Murphy/Nee Scholarship, the Legionnaire Scholarship, the Past Department Commanders Scholarship, the Daniel J. Doherty Scholarship PNC, the John P. "Jake" Comer Scholarship PNC, and the Grace Fuller Olson Scholarship.

Number awarded 19 each year: 9 at $1,000 and 10 at $500.

Deadline March of each year.

[585]
MASSACHUSETTS PUBLIC SERVICE GRANT PROGRAM

Massachusetts Office of Student Financial Assistance
454 Broadway, Suite 200
Revere, MA 02151
(617) 727-9420   Fax: (617) 727-0667
E-mail: osfa@osfa.mass.edu
Web: www.osfa.mass.edu

Summary To provide financial assistance for college to children or widow(er)s of deceased public service officers and others in Massachusetts.

Eligibility Only Massachusetts residents are eligible. They must be 1) the children or spouses of fire fighters, police officers, or corrections officers who were killed or died from injuries incurred in the line of duty; 2) children of prisoners of war or military service personnel missing in action in southeast Asia whose wartime service was credited to Massachusetts and whose service was between February 1, 1955 and the termination of the Vietnam campaign; or 3) children of veterans whose service was credited to Massachusetts and who were killed in action or died as a result of their service.

Financial Data Scholarships provide up to the cost of tuition at a state-supported college or university in Massachusetts; if the recipient attends a private Massachusetts college or university, the scholarship is equivalent to tuition at a public institution, up to $2,500.

Duration 1 year; renewable.

Number awarded Varies each year.

Deadline April of each year.

[586]
MG JAMES URSANO SCHOLARSHIP FUND

Army Emergency Relief
200 Stovall Street
Alexandria, VA 22332-0600
(703) 428-0000   Toll Free: (866) 878-6378
Fax: (703) 325-7183   E-mail: Education@aerhq.org
Web: www.aerhq.org/education_dependentchildren.asp

Summary To provide financial assistance for college to the dependent children of Army personnel.

Eligibility This program is open to dependent children under 23 years of age (including stepchildren and legally adopted children) of soldiers on active duty, retired, or deceased while on active duty or after retirement. Applicants must be unmarried and enrolled, accepted, or pending acceptance as full-time students in accredited postsecondary educational institutions. Selection is based primarily on financial need, but academic achievements and individual accomplishments are also considered.

Financial Data The amount varies, depending on the needs of the recipient, but ranges from $1,000 to $5,200 per academic year. Recently, awards averaged more than $3,000.

Duration 1 year; may be renewed for up to 3 additional years, provided the recipient maintains a GPA of 2.0 or higher.

Additional data Army Emergency Relief is a private nonprofit organization dedicated to "helping the Army take care of its own." Its primary mission is to provide financial assistance to Army people and their dependents in time of valid emergency need; its educational program was established as a secondary mission to meet a need of Army people for their dependents to pursue vocational training, preparation for acceptance by service academies, or an undergraduate education. It established this program in 1976.

Number awarded Varies each year; recently, 3,310 of these scholarships, with a value of $9,961,826, were awarded.

Deadline February of each year.

[587]
MGYSGT GEORGE T. CURTIS SCHOLARSHIP

USMC/Combat Helicopter Association
c/o Marine Corps Scholarship Foundation
P.O. Box 3008
Princeton, NJ 08543-3008
(609) 921-3534   Toll Free: (800) 292-7777
Fax: (609) 452-2259   E-mail: mcsfnj@mcsf.org
Web: www.popasmoke.com/scholarship.html

Summary To provide financial assistance for college to the children and grandchildren of members of the USMC/Combat Helicopter Association.

Eligibility This program is open to children and grandchildren of members of the USMC/Combat Helicopter Association who are high school seniors, high school graduates, undergraduates enrolled at an accredited college or university, or students enrolled at an accredited postsecondary vocational/technical school. Applicants must be the child or grandchild of 1) a Marine on active duty, in the Reserve, retired, or deceased; or 2) a Marine or Marine Reservist who has received an honorable discharge, medical discharge, or was killed on active duty. Along with their application, they must submit academic transcripts, a copy of their parent's or grandparent's honorable discharge (if appropriate), and a 500-word essay on a topic that changes periodically. Recently, they were invited to discuss an attribute or accomplishment that sets them apart and how it has shaped them and their beliefs, and why they want to get a college education. Only undergraduate study is supported. The family income of applicants must be less than $82,000 per year.

Financial Data The stipend depends on the need of the recipient and the availability of funds, but generally ranges from $500 to $3,000 per year.

Duration 1 year; may be renewed for up to 3 additional years.
Additional data This program was established in 2006.
Number awarded 1 each year.
Deadline March of each year.

[588]
MICHIGAN CHILDREN OF VETERANS TUITION GRANTS

Michigan Department of Treasury
Michigan Higher Education Assistance Authority
Attn: Office of Scholarships and Grants
P.O. Box 30462
Lansing, MI 48909-7962
(517) 373-0457   Toll Free: (888) 4-GRANTS
Fax: (517) 335-6851   E-mail: osg@michigan.gov
Web: www.michigan.gov/mistudentaid

Summary To provide financial assistance for college to the children of Michigan veterans who are totally disabled or deceased as a result of service-connected causes.

Eligibility This program is open to children of Michigan veterans who have been totally and permanently disabled as a result of a service-connected illness or injury prior to death and has now died, have died or become totally and permanently disabled as a result of a service-connected illness or injury, have been killed in action or died from another cause while serving in a war or war condition, or are listed as missing in action in a foreign country. Applicants must be between 16 and 26 years of age and must have lived in Michigan at least 12 months prior to the date of application. They must be enrolled or planning to enroll at least half time at a public institution of higher education in Michigan. U.S. citizenship or permanent resident status is required.

Financial Data Recipients are exempt from payment of the first $2,800 per year of tuition or any other fee that takes the place of tuition.

Duration 1 year; may be renewed for up to 3 additional years if the recipient maintains full-time enrollment and a GPA of 2.25 or higher.

Additional data This program was formerly known as the Michigan Veterans Trust Fund Tuition Grants, administered by the Michigan Veterans Trust Fund within the Department of Military and Veterans Affairs. It was transferred to the Office of Scholarships and Grants in 2006.

Number awarded Varies each year; recently, 400 of these grants were awarded.

Deadline Deadline not specified.

[589]
MICHIGAN LEGION AUXILIARY NATIONAL PRESIDENT'S SCHOLARSHIP

American Legion Auxiliary
Department of Michigan
212 North Verlinden Avenue
Lansing, MI 48915
(517) 267-8809   Fax: (517) 371-3698
E-mail: scholarships@michalaux.org
Web: www.michalaux.org/scholarships.htm

Summary To provide financial assistance to children of veterans in Michigan who plan to attend college in any state.

Eligibility This program is open to Michigan residents who are the children of veterans who served during designated periods of war time. Applicants must be in their senior year or graduates of an accredited high school and may not yet have attended an institution of higher learning. They must have completed 50 hours of community service during their high school years. Selection is based on scholarship, character, leadership, Americanism, and financial need. The winner competes for the American Legion National President's Scholarship. If the Michigan winners are not awarded the national scholarship, then they receive this departmental scholarship.

Financial Data   The stipend ranges from $1,000 to $2,500.

Duration   1 year.

Number awarded   1 each year.

Deadline   February of each year.

[590]
MIKE NASH MEMORIAL SCHOLARSHIP FUND

Vietnam Veterans of America
Attn: Mike Nash Scholarship Program
8719 Colesville Road, Suite 100
Silver Spring, MD 20910-3919
(301) 585-4000   Toll Free: (800) VVA-1316
Fax: (301) 585-0519   E-mail: finance@vva.org
Web: www.vva.org/scholarship.html

Summary   To provide financial assistance for college to members of Vietnam Veterans of America (VVA), their families, and the families of other Vietnam veterans.

Eligibility   This program is open to 1) members of VVA; 2) the spouses, children, stepchildren, and grandchildren of VVA members; and 3) the spouses, children, stepchildren, and grandchildren of MIA, KIA, or deceased Vietnam veterans. Applicants must be enrolled or planning to enroll at least half time at an accredited college, university, or technical institution. Along with their application, they must submit high school or college transcripts; SAT, ACT, or other recognized test scores; a letter of recommendation from a VVA state council, chapter, or national; 2 letters of recommendation; a letter describing their current educational goals and objectives, individual accomplishments, and any other personal information that may assist in the selection process; and documentation of financial need.

Financial Data   The stipend is $1,000 per year.

Duration   1 year; may be renewed for up to 3 additional years.

Additional data   This program was established in 1991 and given its current name in 1997.

Number awarded   Varies each year; recently, 9 of these scholarships were awarded.

Deadline   May of each year.

[591]
MILDRED R. KNOLES SCHOLARSHIPS

American Legion Auxiliary
Department of Illinois
2720 East Lincoln Street
P.O. Box 1426
Bloomington, IL 61702-1426
(309) 663-9366   Fax: (309) 663-5827
E-mail: staff@ilala.org
Web: illegion.org/auxiliary/scholar.html

Summary   To provide financial assistance to Illinois veterans and their descendants who are attending college in any state.

Eligibility   This program is open to veterans who served during designated periods of war time and their children, grandchildren, and great-grandchildren. Applicants must be currently enrolled at a college or university in any state and studying any field except nursing. They must be residents of Illinois or members of the American Legion Family, Department of Illinois. Along with their application, they must submit a 1,000-word essay on "What my education will do for me." Selection is based on that essay (25%) character and leadership (25%), scholarship (25%), and financial need (25%).

Financial Data   Stipends are $1,200 or $800.

Duration   1 year.

Additional data   Applications may be obtained only from a local unit of the American Legion Auxiliary.

Number awarded   Varies; each year 1 scholarship at $1,200 and several at $800 are awarded.

Deadline   March of each year.

[592]
MILITARY EDUCATION SCHOLARSHIP PROGRAM

VA Mortgage Center.com
2101 Chapel Plaza Court, Suite 107
Columbia, MO 65203
(573) 876-2729   Toll Free: (800) 405-6682
Web: www.vamortgagecenter.com/scholarships.html

Summary   To provide financial assistance for college to students who have a tie to the military.

Eligibility   This program is open to 1) current and prospective ROTC program students; 2) active-duty military personnel with plans to attend college; 3) honorably-discharged veterans of the U.S. military; and 4) children of veterans or active-duty military. Applicants must be attending or planning to attend college. Selection is based primarily on an essay.

Financial Data   The stipend is $1,500.

Duration   1 year.

Additional data   This program was established in 2007.

Number awarded   10 each year: 5 each term.

Deadline   April or October of each year.

[593]
MILITARY FAMILY SUPPORT TRUST SCHOLARSHIPS

Military Family Support Trust
1010 American Eagle Boulevard
P.O. Box 301
Sun City Center, FL 33573
(813) 634-4675   Fax: (813) 633-2412
E-mail: president@mobc-online.org
Web: www.mobc-online.org

Summary   To provide financial assistance for college to children and grandchildren of retired and deceased officers who served in the military or designated public service agencies.

Eligibility   This program is open to graduating high school seniors who have a GPA of 3.0 and a minimum score of 21 on the ACT, 900 on the 2-part SAT, or 1350 on the 3-part SAT. Applicants must have a parent, guardian, or grandparent who is 1) a retired active-duty, National Guard, or Reserve officer or former officer of the U.S. Army, Navy, Marine Corps, Air Force, Coast Guard, Public Health Service, or National Oceanic and Atmospheric Administration, at the rank of O-1 through O-10, WO-1 through WO-5, or E-5 through E-9; 2) an officer who died while on active duty in service to the country; 3) a recipient of the Purple Heart, regardless of pay grade or length of service; 4) a World War II combat veteran of the Merchant Marine; 5) a federal employee at the grade of GS-7 or higher; 6) a Foreign Service Officer at the grade of FSO-8 or lower; or 7) an honorably discharged or retired foreign military officer of friendly nations meeting the service and disability retirement criteria of the respective country and living in the United States. Applicants must have been accepted to an accredited program at a college or university. Selection is based on leadership (40%), scholarship (30%), and financial need (30%).

Financial Data   Stipends are $3,000, $2,000, $1,500, or $500 per year.

Duration   4 years, provided the recipient maintains a GPA of 3.0 or higher.

Additional data   This foundation was established in 1992 as the Military Officers' Benevolent Corporation. It changed its name in 2008 to the current usage.

Number awarded   12 each year: 2 at $3,000 per year, 4 at $2,000 per year, 2 at $1,500 per year, and 4 at $500 per year.

Deadline   February of each year.

[594]
MILITARY INTELLIGENCE CORPS ASSOCIATION SCHOLARSHIPS

Military Intelligence Corps Association
Attn: Scholarship Chair
P.O. Box 13020
Fort Huachuca, AZ 85670-3020
(520) 533-1174
Web: micorps.org

Summary To provide financial assistance for college to members of the Military Intelligence Corps Association (MICA) and their immediate family.

Eligibility This program is open to active-duty, Reserve, National Guard, and retired military intelligence soldiers who are MICA members and to their immediate family (spouses, children, or other relatives living with and supported by the MICA member). Applicants must be attending or accepted for attendance at an accredited college, university, vocational school, or technical institution. Along with their application, they must submit a 1-page essay on their reasons for applying for the scholarship, including their educational plans, ambitions, goals, and personal attributes or experiences they feel will enable them to reach their goals. Financial need is not considered in the selection process.

Financial Data Stipend amounts vary depending on the availability of funds and the number of qualified applicants, but are awarded in increments of $500 and $1,000. Funds are to be used for tuition, books, and classroom fees; support is not provided for housing, board, travel, or administrative purposes.

Duration 1 year; recipients may reapply.

Number awarded Varies each year.

Deadline May of each year.

[595]
MILITARY NONRESIDENT TUITION WAIVER AFTER ASSIGNMENT IN TEXAS

Texas Higher Education Coordinating Board
Attn: Grants and Special Programs
1200 East Anderson Lane
P.O. Box 12788, Capitol Station
Austin, TX 78711-2788
(512) 427-6340   Toll Free: (800) 242-3062
Fax: (512) 427-6127   E-mail: grantinfo@thecb.state.tx.us
Web: www.collegeforalltexans.com

Summary To provide educational assistance to the spouses and children of Texas military personnel assigned elsewhere.

Eligibility This program is open to the spouses and dependent children of members of the U.S. armed forces or commissioned officers of the Public Health Service who remain in Texas when the member is reassigned to duty outside of the state. The spouse or dependent child must reside continuously in Texas. Applicants must be attending or planning to attend a Texas public college or university.

Financial Data Eligible students are entitled to pay tuition and fees at the resident rate at publicly-supported colleges and universities in Texas.

Duration The waiver remains in effect for the duration of the member's first assignment outside of Texas.

Additional data This program became effective in 2003.

Number awarded Varies each year.

Deadline Deadline not specified.

[596]
MILITARY NONRESIDENT TUITION WAIVER FOR MEMBERS, SPOUSES OR CHILDREN ASSIGNED TO DUTY IN TEXAS

Texas Higher Education Coordinating Board
Attn: Grants and Special Programs
1200 East Anderson Lane
P.O. Box 12788, Capitol Station
Austin, TX 78711-2788
(512) 427-6340   Toll Free: (800) 242-3062
Fax: (512) 427-6127   E-mail: grantinfo@thecb.state.tx.us
Web: www.collegeforalltexans.com

Summary To exempt military personnel stationed in Texas and their dependents from the payment of nonresident tuition at public institutions of higher education in the state.

Eligibility Eligible for these waivers are members of the U.S. armed forces and commissioned officers of the Public Health Service from states other than Texas, their spouses, and dependent children. Applicants must be assigned to Texas and attending or planning to attend a public college or university in the state.

Financial Data Although persons eligible under this program are classified as nonresidents, they are entitled to pay the resident tuition at Texas institutions of higher education, regardless of their length of residence in Texas.

Duration 1 year; may be renewed.

Number awarded Varies each year; recently, 11,600 students received these waivers.

Deadline Deadline not specified.

[597]
MILITARY NONRESIDENT TUITION WAIVER FOR MEMBERS, SPOUSES OR CHILDREN WHO REMAIN CONTINUOUSLY ENROLLED IN HIGHER EDUCATION IN TEXAS

Texas Higher Education Coordinating Board
Attn: Grants and Special Programs
1200 East Anderson Lane
P.O. Box 12788, Capitol Station
Austin, TX 78711-2788
(512) 427-6340   Toll Free: (800) 242-3062
Fax: (512) 427-6127   E-mail: grantinfo@thecb.state.tx.us
Web: www.collegeforalltexans.com

Summary To waive nonresident tuition at Texas public colleges and universities for members of the armed forces and their families who are no longer in the military.

Eligibility Eligible for these waivers are members of the U.S. armed forces, commissioned officers of the Public Health Service, their spouses, and their children. Applicants must have previously been eligible to pay tuition at the resident rate while enrolled in a degree or certificate program at a Texas public college or university. They must remain continuously enrolled in the same degree or certificate program in subsequent terms or semesters.

Financial Data The student's eligibility to pay tuition and fees at the rate provided for Texas students does not terminate because the member, spouse, or parent is no longer in the service.

Duration 1 year.

Additional data This program became effective in September 2003.

Number awarded Varies each year.

Deadline Deadline not specified.

[598]
MILITARY ORDER OF THE PURPLE HEART SCHOLARSHIP PROGRAM

Military Order of the Purple Heart
Attn: Scholarships
5413-B Backlick Road
Springfield, VA 22151-3960
(703) 642-5360　　　　　　　　Toll Free: (888) 668-1656
Fax: (703) 642-2054　　E-mail: scholarship@purpleheart.org
Web: www.purpleheart.org/Scholarships/Default.aspx

Summary To provide financial assistance for college or graduate school to members of the Military Order of the Purple Heart (MOPH) and their families.

Eligibility This program is open to 1) members of the MOPH; 2) direct descendants (children, stepchildren, adopted children, grandchildren, and great- grandchildren) of veterans who are MOPH members or who were members at the time of death; 3) direct descendants of veterans killed in action or who died of wounds but did not have the opportunity to join the order; and 4) spouses and widows of MOPH members, veterans killed in action, and veterans who died of wounds. Applicants must be graduating seniors or graduates of an accredited high school who are enrolled or accepted for enrollment in a full-time program of study in a college, trade school, or graduate school. They must have a GPA of 2.75 or higher. U.S. citizenship is required. Along with their application, they must submit an essay of 200 to 300 words on "What it means to be an American." Financial need is not considered in the selection process.

Financial Data The stipend is $3,000 per year.

Duration 1 year; may be renewed up to 2 additional years.

Additional data Membership in MOPH is open to all veterans who received a Purple Heart Medal and were discharged under conditions other than dishonorable. A processing fee of $15 is required.

Number awarded Varies each year; recently, 50 of these scholarships were awarded.

Deadline February of each year.

[599]
MILITARY SPOUSE SCHOLARSHIPS FOR ALL MILITARY SPOUSES

National Military Family Association, Inc.
Attn: Spouse Scholarship Program
2500 North Van Dorn Street, Suite 102
Alexandria, VA 22302-1601
(703) 931-NMFA　　　　　　　　Toll Free: (800) 260-0218
Fax: (703) 931-4600　E-mail: scholarships@militaryfamily.org
Web: www.militaryfamily.org

Summary To provide financial assistance for postsecondary study to spouses of active and retired military personnel.

Eligibility This program is open to the spouses of military personnel (active, retired, Reserve, Guard, or survivor). Applicants must be attending or planning to attend an accredited postsecondary institution to work on an undergraduate or graduate degree, professional certification, vocational training, GED or ESL, or other postsecondary training. They may enroll part or full time and in-class or online. Along with their application, they must submit an essay on a question that changes annually; recently, applicants were asked to write about what they like most about the health care they are receiving as a military family member, what they like the least, and what they would recommend to change it. Selection is based on that essay, community involvement, and academic achievement.

Financial Data The stipend is $1,000. Funds are paid directly to the educational institution to be used for tuition, fees, and school room and board. Support is not provided for books, rent, or previous education loans.

Duration 1 year; recipients may reapply.

Additional data This program, is a component of the Joanne Holbrook Patton Military Spouse Scholarship Program, which began in 2004.

Number awarded Varies each year; recently, the program awarded a total of 293 scholarships.

Deadline January of each year.

[600]
MILITARY SPOUSE SCHOLARSHIPS FOR SPOUSES OF THE FALLEN

National Military Family Association, Inc.
Attn: Spouse Scholarship Program
2500 North Van Dorn Street, Suite 102
Alexandria, VA 22302-1601
(703) 931-NMFA　　　　　　　　Toll Free: (800) 260-0218
Fax: (703) 931-4600　E-mail: scholarships@militaryfamily.org
Web: www.militaryfamily.org

Summary To provide financial assistance for postsecondary study to spouses of military personnel have been killed as a result of service since September 11, 2001.

Eligibility This program is open to the spouses of military personnel who have been killed as a result of active-duty service since September 11, 2001. Applicants must be able to verify that the death was a result of service in support of the Global War on Terror. They must be attending or planning to attend an accredited postsecondary institution to work on an undergraduate or graduate degree, professional certification, vocational training, GED or ESL, or other postsecondary training. They may enroll part or full time and in-class or online. Along with their application, they must submit an essay on a question that changes annually; recently, applicants were asked to write about what they like most about the health care they are receiving as a military family member, what they like the least, and what they would recommend to change it. Selection is based on that essay, community involvement, and academic achievement.

Financial Data The stipend is $1,000. Funds are paid directly to the educational institution to be used for tuition, fees, and school room and board. Support is not provided for books, rent, or previous education loans.

Duration 1 year; recipients may reapply.

Additional data This program, is a component of the Joanne Holbrook Patton Military Spouse Scholarship Program, which began in 2004.

Number awarded Varies each year; recently, the program awarded a total of 293 scholarships.

Deadline January of each year.

[601]
MILITARY SPOUSE SCHOLARSHIPS FOR SPOUSES OF THE WOUNDED

National Military Family Association, Inc.
Attn: Spouse Scholarship Program
2500 North Van Dorn Street, Suite 102
Alexandria, VA 22302-1601
(703) 931-NMFA　　　　　　　　Toll Free: (800) 260-0218
Fax: (703) 931-4600　E-mail: scholarships@militaryfamily.org
Web: www.militaryfamily.org

Summary To provide financial assistance for postsecondary study to spouses of military personnel have been wounded as a result of service since September 11, 2001.

Eligibility This program is open to the spouses of military personnel who have been wounded as a result of active-duty service since September 11, 2001. Applicants must be able to verify that the wound or injury was a result of service in support of the Global War on Terror. They must be attending or planning to attend an accredited postsecondary institution to work on an undergraduate or graduate degree, professional certification, vocational training, GED or ESL, or other postsecondary training. They may enroll part or full time and in-class or online. Along with their application, they must submit an essay on a question that changes annually; recently, applicants were asked to write about what they like most about the health care they are receiving as a military family member, what they like the least, and what they would recommend to change it. Selection is based on that essay, community involvement, and academic achievement.

Financial Data The stipend is $1,000. Funds are paid directly to the educational institution to be used for tuition, fees, and school room and board. Support is not provided for books, rent, or previous education loans.

Duration 1 year; recipients may reapply.

Additional data This program, is a component of the Joanne Holbrook Patton Military Spouse Scholarship Program, which began in 2004.

Number awarded Varies each year; recently, the program awarded a total of 293 scholarships.

Deadline January of each year.

[602]
MINNESOTA G.I. BILL PROGRAM

Minnesota Office of Higher Education
Attn: Manager of State Financial Aid Programs
1450 Energy Park Drive, Suite 350
St. Paul, MN 55108-5227
(651) 642-0567   Toll Free: (800) 657-3866
Fax: (651) 642-0675   TDD: (800) 627-3529
E-mail: Ginny.Dodds@state.mn.us
Web: www.ohe.state.mn.us

Summary To provide financial assistance for college or graduate school in the state to residents of Minnesota who served in the military after September 11, 2001 and the families of deceased or disabled military personnel.

Eligibility This program is open to residents of Minnesota enrolled at colleges and universities in the state as undergraduate or graduate students. Applicants must be 1) a veteran who is serving or has served honorably in a branch of the U.S. armed forces at any time on or after September 11, 2001; 2) a non-veteran who has served honorably for a total of 5 years or more cumulatively as a member of the Minnesota National Guard or other active or Reserve component of the U.S. armed forces, and any part of that service occurred on or after September 11, 2001; or 3) a surviving child or spouse of a person who has served in the military at any time on or after September 11, 2001 and who has died or has a total and permanent disability as a result of that military service. Financial need is also considered in the selection process.

Financial Data The stipend is $1,000 per semester for full-time study or $500 per semester for part-time study.

Duration 1 year; may be renewed up to 4 additional years, provided the recipient continues to make satisfactory academic progress.

Additional data This program was established by the Minnesota Legislature in 2007.

Number awarded Varies each year.

Deadline Deadline not specified.

[603]
MINNESOTA LEGION AUXILIARY DEPARTMENT SCHOLARSHIPS

American Legion Auxiliary
Department of Minnesota
State Veterans Service Building
20 West 12th Street, Room 314
St. Paul, MN 55155-2069
(651) 224-7634   Toll Free: (888) 217-9598
Fax: (651) 224-5243   E-mail: deptoffice@mnala.org
Web: www.mnala.org/ala/scholarship.asp

Summary To provide financial assistance to the children and grandchildren of Minnesota veterans who are interested in attending college in the state.

Eligibility This program is open to the children and grandchildren of veterans who served during designated periods of war time. Applicants must be a resident of Minnesota or a member of an American Legion post, American Legion Auxiliary unit, or Sons of the American Legion detachment in the Department of Minnesota. They must be high school seniors or graduates, have a GPA of 2.0 or higher, be able to demonstrate financial need, and be planning to attend a vocational or business school, college, or university in Minnesota. Along with their application, they must submit a brief essay, telling of their plans for college, career goals, and extracurricular and community activities.

Financial Data The stipend is $1,000. Funds are to be used to pay for tuition or books and are sent directly to the recipient's school.

Duration 1 year.

Number awarded 7 each year.

Deadline March of each year.

[604]
MINNESOTA LEGION AUXILIARY PAST PRESIDENTS PARLEY HEALTH CARE SCHOLARSHIP

American Legion Auxiliary
Department of Minnesota
State Veterans Service Building
20 West 12th Street, Room 314
St. Paul, MN 55155-2069
(651) 224-7634   Toll Free: (888) 217-9598
Fax: (651) 224-5243   E-mail: deptoffice@mnala.org
Web: www.mnala.org/ala/scholarship.asp

Summary To provide financial assistance for education in health care fields to members of the American Legion Auxiliary in Minnesota.

Eligibility This program is open to residents of Minnesota who have been members of the American Legion Auxiliary for at least 3 years. Applicants must have a GPA of 2.0 or higher and be planning to study in Minnesota. Their proposed major may be in any phase of health care, including nursing assistant, registered nursing, licensed practical nurse, X-ray or other technician, physical or other therapist, dental hygienist, or dental assistant.

Financial Data The stipend is $1,000. Funds are sent directly to the recipient's school after satisfactory completion of the first quarter.

Duration 1 year.

Number awarded Up to 10 each year.

Deadline March of each year.

[605]
MINNESOTA NATIONAL GUARD SURVIVOR ENTITLEMENT TUITION REIMBURSEMENT PROGRAM

Department of Military Affairs
Attn: Education Services Officer
JFMN-J1-ARED
20 West 12th Street
St. Paul, MN 55155-2098
(651) 282-4125   Toll Free: (800) 657-3848
Fax: (651) 282-4694   E-mail: education@mn.ngb.army.mil
Web: www.minnesotanationalguard.org

Summary To provide financial assistance for college or graduate school to survivors of members of the Minnesota National Guard who were killed on active duty.

Eligibility This program is open to surviving spouses and children of members of the Minnesota Army or Air National Guard who were killed while performing military duty. Spouses remain eligible unless they remarry; dependent children are eligible until their 24th birthday. The Guard member's death must have occurred within the scope of assigned duties while in a federal duty status or on state active service. Applicants must be enrolled as undergraduate or graduate students at colleges or universities in Minnesota. Reimbursement is provided only for undergraduate courses completed with a grade of "C" or better or for graduate courses completed with a grade of "B" or better.

Financial Data The maximum reimbursement rate is 100% of the undergraduate tuition rate at the University of Minnesota Twin Cities campus (currently, $326.92 per credit to a maximum of $4,250 per term).

Duration 1 academic term, to a maximum of 18 credits per term; may be renewed for a total of 144 semester credits or 208 quarter credits.

Number awarded Varies each year.

Deadline Participants must request reimbursement within 60 days of the last official day of the term.

[606]
MINNESOTA VETERANS' DEPENDENTS ASSISTANCE PROGRAM

Minnesota Office of Higher Education
Attn: Manager of State Financial Aid Programs
1450 Energy Park Drive, Suite 350
St. Paul, MN 55108-5227
(651) 642-0567   Toll Free: (800) 657-3866
Fax: (651) 642-0675   TDD: (800) 627-3529
E-mail: Ginny.Dodds@state.mn.us
Web: www.ohe.state.mn.us

Summary To provide financial assistance for college to the dependents of Minnesota veterans and military personnel listed as POWs or MIAs.

Eligibility Eligible for this assistance are 1) spouses of a prisoner of war or person missing in action, or 2) children born before or during the period of time the parent served as a POW or was declared MIA, or 3) children legally adopted or in the legal custody of a parent prior to and during the time the parent served as a POW or was declared to be MIA. Veteran parents must have been residents of Minnesota at the time of entry into service or at the time declared to be a POW or MIA, which must have occurred after August 1, 1958.

Financial Data Students who attend private postsecondary institutions receive up to $250 per year for tuition and fees. Students who attend a Minnesota public postsecondary institution are exempt from all tuition charges.

Duration Assistance continues until the student completes a bachelor's degree or receives a certificate of completion.

Number awarded Varies each year.

Deadline Deadline not specified.

[607]
MISSISSIPPI EDUCATIONAL ASSISTANCE FOR MIA/POW DEPENDENTS

Mississippi State Veterans Affairs Board
3460 Highway 80 East
P.O. Box 5947
Pearl, MS 39288-5947
(601) 576-4850   Fax: (601) 576-4868
E-mail: grice@vab.state.ms.us
Web: www.vab.state.ms.us/booklet.htm

Summary To provide financial assistance for college to the children of Mississippi residents who are POWs or MIAs.

Eligibility This entitlement program is open to the children of members of the armed services whose official home of record and residence is in Mississippi and who are officially reported as being either a prisoner of a foreign government or missing in

action. Applicants must be attending or planning to attend a state-supported college or university in Mississippi.

Financial Data This assistance covers all costs of college attendance.

Duration Up to 8 semesters.

Number awarded Varies each year.

Deadline Deadline not specified.

[608]
MISSISSIPPI NATIONAL GUARD NONCOMMISSIONED OFFICERS ASSOCIATION SCHOLARSHIPS

Mississippi National Guard Noncommissioned Officers
  Association
Attn: Executive Director
P.O. Box 699
Brandon, MS 39043-0699
(601) 824-0304   Toll Free: (800) 205-5797
Fax: (601) 824-4970   E-mail: msngnco@bellsouth.net
Web: www.msncoa.org/Scholorships.htm

Summary To provide financial assistance to dependents of members of the Mississippi National Guard Noncommissioned Officers Association who are interested in attending college in any state.

Eligibility This program is open to the unmarried dependent children and spouses of annual, enlisted, retired, and life members of the association. Applicants must be high school seniors or undergraduate students with at least 1 full semester remaining before graduation. They must be attending or planning to attend an accredited university, college, community college, vocational/technical, business, or trade school in any state. Along with their application, they must submit a personal letter about themselves, letters of recommendation, transcripts, a copy of their sponsor's association membership card, and a copy of their ACT score.

Financial Data The stipend depends on the availability of funds.

Duration 1 year.

Number awarded Varies each year.

Deadline January of each year.

[609]
MISSOURI VIETNAM VETERANS SURVIVOR GRANT PROGRAM

Missouri Department of Higher Education
Attn: Student Financial Assistance
3515 Amazonas Drive
Jefferson City, MO 65109-5717
(573) 751-2361   Toll Free: (800) 473-6757
Fax: (573) 751-6635   E-mail: info@dhe.mo.gov
Web: www.dhe.mo.gov/vietnamveterans.shtml

Summary To provide financial to survivors of certain deceased Missouri Vietnam veterans who plan to attend college in the state.

Eligibility This program is open to surviving spouses and children of veterans who served in the military in Vietnam or the war zone in southeast Asia, who were residents of Missouri when first entering military service and at the time of death, whose death was attributed to or caused by exposure to toxic chemicals during the Vietnam conflict, and who served in the Vietnam theater between 1961 and 1972. Applicants must be Missouri residents enrolled in a program leading to a certificate, associate degree, or baccalaureate degree at an approved postsecondary institution in the state. Students working on a degree or certificate in theology or divinity are not eligible. U.S. citizenship or permanent resident status is required.

Financial Data The maximum annual grant is the lesser of 1) the actual tuition charged at the school where the recipient is enrolled, or 2) the amount of tuition charged to a Missouri undergraduate resident enrolled full time in the same class level and in the same academic major as an applicant at the Missouri public 4-year regional institutions.

Duration 1 semester; may be renewed until the recipient has obtained a baccalaureate degree or has completed 150 semester credit hours, whichever comes first.

Additional data Awards are not available for summer study.

Number awarded Up to 12 each year.

Deadline There is no application deadline, but early submission of the completed application is encouraged.

[610]
MONTANA WAR ORPHANS WAIVER

Montana Guaranteed Student Loan Program
2500 Broadway
P.O. Box 203101
Helena, MT 59620-3101
(406) 444-0638   Toll Free: (800) 537-7508
Fax: (406) 444-1869 E-mail: scholarships@mgslp.state.mt.us
Web: www.mgslp.state.mt.us

Summary To provide financial assistance for undergraduate education to the children of Montana veterans who died in the line of duty or as a result of service-connected disabilities.

Eligibility This program is open to children of members of the U.S. armed forces who served on active duty during World War II, the Korean Conflict, the Vietnam Conflict the Afghanistan Conflict, or the Iraq Conflict; were legal residents of Montana at the time of entry into service; and were killed in action or died as a result of injury, disease, or other disability while in the service. Applicants must be no older than 25 years of age. Financial need is considered in the selection process.

Financial Data Students eligible for this benefit are entitled to attend any unit of the Montana University System without payment of undergraduate registration or incidental fees.

Duration Undergraduate students are eligible for continued fee waiver as long as they maintain reasonable academic progress as full-time students.

Number awarded Varies each year.

Deadline Deadline not specified.

[611]
NANNIE W. NORFLEET SCHOLARSHIP

American Legion Auxiliary
Department of North Carolina
P.O. Box 25726
Raleigh, NC 27611-5726
(919) 832-4051   Fax: (919) 832-1888
E-mail: ala1_nc@bellsouth.net
Web: nclegion.org/auxil.htm

Summary To provide financial assistance to members of the American Legion Auxiliary in North Carolina and their children and grandchildren who plan to attend college in any state.

Eligibility This program is open to North Carolina residents who are either adult members of the American Legion Auxiliary or high school seniors (with preference to the children and grandchildren of members). Applicants must be interested in attending college in any state. They must be able to demonstrate financial need.

Financial Data The stipend is $1,000.

Duration 1 year.

Number awarded 1 each year.

Deadline March of each year.

[612]
NATIONAL 4TH INFANTRY (IVY) DIVISION ASSOCIATION SCHOLARSHIP

National 4th Infantry (IVY) Division Association
c/o Don Kelby, Executive Director
P.O. Box 1914
St. Peters, MO 63376-0035
(314) 606-1969   E-mail: 4thidaed@swbell.net
Web: www.4thinfantry.org

Summary To provide financial assistance for college to members of the National 4th Infantry (IVY) Division Association and their families.

Eligibility This program is open to association members in good standing and all blood relatives of active association members in good standing. Recipients are chosen by lottery.

Financial Data The stipend is $1,000.

Duration 1 year; may be renewed.

Additional data The trust fund from which these scholarships are awarded was created by the officers and enlisted men of the 4th Infantry Division as a living memorial to the men of the division who died in Vietnam. Originally, it was only open to children of members of the division who died in the line of duty while serving in Vietnam between August 1, 1966 and December 31, 1977. When all those eligible had completed college, it adopted its current requirements.

Number awarded 1 or more each year.

Deadline June of each year.

[613]
NATIONAL GUARD ASSOCIATION OF COLORADO SCHOLARSHIP PROGRAM

National Guard Association of Colorado
Attn: Education Foundation, Inc.
P.O. Box 440889
Aurora, CO 80044-0889
(303) 677-8387   Fax: (303) 677-8823
E-mail: ed.foundation@earthlink.net
Web: www.ngaco-edufoundation.org

Summary To provide financial assistance to members of the National Guard Association of Colorado (NGACO) and the Colorado National Guard and their families who are interested in attending college or graduate school in any state.

Eligibility This program is open to 1) current and retired members of the Colorado National Guard and the NGACO; 2) dependent unmarried children of current and retired members of the Colorado National Guard and the NGACO; 3) spouses of current and retired members of the Colorado National Guard and the NGACO; and 4) unremarried spouses and unmarried dependent children of deceased members of the Colorado National Guard and the NGACO. Applicants must be enrolled or planning to enroll full or part time at a college, university, trade school, business school, or graduate school in any state. Along with their application, they must submit an essay, up to 2 pages in length, on their desire to continue their education, what motivates them, their financial need, their commitment to academic excellence, and their current situation.

Financial Data Stipends are $1,000, $750, or $500 per year.

Duration 1 year; may be renewed.

Additional data Members of the Colorado National Guard must perform at least 1 year of service following the completion of the school year for which the scholarship was received.

Number awarded Varies each year. Recently, 11 of these scholarships were awarded: 4 at $1,000 to members of the NGACO, 2 at $750 to dependents of members of the NGACO, 2 at $500 to current enlisted members of the Colorado National Guard, 2 at $500 to current officer members of the Colorado

National Guard, and 1 at $1,000 to a Colorado National Guard member or dependent working on a graduate degree.

Deadline August of each year for fall semester; January of each year for spring semester.

[614]
NATIONAL GUARD ASSOCIATION OF MASSACHUSETTS SCHOLARSHIPS

National Guard Association of Massachusetts
Attn: Scholarship Committee
50 Maple Street
Milford, MA 01757
(508) 735-6544   E-mail: feedback@ngama.org
Web: www.ngama.org

Summary To provide financial assistance for college to members of the Massachusetts National Guard and their dependents.

Eligibility This program is open to 1) current members of the Massachusetts National Guard; 2) children and spouses of current members of the National Guard Association of Massachusetts (NGAMA); and 3) children and spouses of current members of the Massachusetts National Guard. Applicants must be enrolled in or planning to enroll in an accredited college or technical program. Along with their application, they must submit a letter of recommendation, a list of extracurricular activities and other significant accomplishments, high school or college transcripts, and an essay on a topic that changes annually but relates to the National Guard; recently, applicants were asked to give their ideas on the best operational use for the National Guard as the country takes a new direction under a new President.

Financial Data The stipend is $1,000.

Duration 1 year.

Number awarded 5 each year: 2 to members of the Massachusetts National Guard, 2 to dependents of NGAMA members, and 1 to a dependent of a Massachusetts National Guard member.

Deadline March of each year.

[615]
NATIONAL GUARD OF GEORGIA SCHOLARSHIP FUND FOR COLLEGES OR UNIVERSITIES

Georgia Guard Insurance Trust
P.O. Box 889
Mableton, GA 30126
(770) 739-9651   Toll Free: (800) 229-1053
Fax: (770) 745-0673   E-mail: director@ngaga.org
Web: www.ngaga.org/scholarship.html

Summary To provide financial assistance to members of the Georgia National Guard and their spouses, children, and grandchildren who are interested in attending college in any state.

Eligibility This program is open to policyholders with the Georgia Guard Insurance Trust (GGIT) who are members of the National Guard Association of Georgia (NGAGA) or the Enlisted Association of the National Guard of Georgia (EANGGA); spouses, children, and grandchildren of NGAGA and EANGGA members; and unremarried widow(er)s, children, and grandchildren of deceased NGAGA and EANGGA members. Applicants must be enrolled or planning to enroll full time at a college or university in any state. High school seniors must have a combined mathematics and critical reading SAT score of at least 1000 or a GPA of 3.0 or higher. Students already enrolled in a college or university must have a cumulative GPA of 3.0 or higher. Along with their application, they must submit transcripts, a letter with personal specific facts regarding their desire to continue their education, 2 letters of recommendation, a letter of academic reference, and an agreement to retain insurance with the GGIT for at least 2 years following completion of the school year for which the scholarship is awarded.

Financial Data The stipend is $1,000.

Duration 1 year.

Number awarded Up to 3 each year.

Deadline April of each year.

[616]
NATIONAL GUARD OF GEORGIA SCHOLARSHIP FUND FOR VOCATIONAL OR BUSINESS SCHOOLS

Georgia Guard Insurance Trust
P.O. Box 889
Mableton, GA 30126
(770) 739-9651   Toll Free: (800) 229-1053
Fax: (770) 745-0673   E-mail: director@ngaga.org
Web: www.ngaga.org/scholarship.html

Summary To provide financial assistance to members of the Georgia National Guard and their spouses, children, and grandchildren who are interested in attending business or vocational school in any state.

Eligibility This program is open to policyholders with the Georgia Guard Insurance Trust (GGIT) who are members of the National Guard Association of Georgia (NGAGA) or the Enlisted Association of the National Guard of Georgia (EANGGA); spouses, children, and grandchildren of NGAGA and EANGGA members; and unremarried widow(er)s, children, and grandchildren of deceased NGAGA and EANGGA members. Applicants must be interested in enrolling full time in day or evening classes at a business or vocational school in any state. They must be able to meet program-specific admission standards and institutional requirements and complete all admission procedures for admission to a degree/diploma program in regular program status. Along with their application, they must submit transcripts, a letter with personal specific facts regarding their desire to continue their education, 2 letters of recommendation, and an agreement to retain insurance with the GGIT for at least 2 years following completion of the school year for which the scholarship is awarded.

Financial Data The stipend is $1,000.

Duration 1 year.

Number awarded Up to 3 each year.

Deadline April of each year.

[617]
NAVAL HELICOPTER ASSOCIATION UNDERGRADUATE SCHOLARSHIPS

Naval Helicopter Association
Attn: Scholarship Fund
P.O. Box 180578
Coronado, CA 92178-0578
(619) 435-7139   Fax: (619) 435-7354
E-mail: info@nhascholarship.org
Web: www.nhascholarship.org/nhascholarshipfund/index.html

Summary To provide financial assistance for college to students who have an affiliation with the rotary wing activities of the sea services.

Eligibility This program is open to high school seniors and current undergraduates who are 1) children, grandchildren, or spouses of current or former Navy, Marine Corps, or Coast Guard rotary wing aviators or aircrewmen; 2) individuals who are serving or have served in maintenance or support billets in rotary wing squadrons or wings and their spouses and children. Applicants must provide information on their rotary wing affiliation and a personal statement on their educational plans and future goals. Selection is based on that statement, academic proficiency, scholastic achievements and awards, extracurricular activities, employment history, and letters of recommendation.

Financial Data Stipends are $3,000, $2,500, or $2,000.

Duration 1 year.

Additional data This program includes the DPA Thousand Points of Light Award (sponsored by D.P. Associates Inc. and L3 Communications), the Sergei Sikorsky Scholarship, the Ream

Memorial Scholarship, and a scholarship sponsored by Raytheon Corporation.

Number awarded Varies each year; recently, 9 of these scholarships were awarded: 3 at $3,000, 1 at $2,500, and 5 at $2,000.

Deadline January of each year.

[618]
NAVY LEAGUE FOUNDATION SCHOLARSHIPS

Navy League of the United States
Attn: Scholarships
2300 Wilson Boulevard, Suite 200
Arlington, VA 22201-5424
(703) 528-1775   Toll Free: (800) 356-5760
Fax: (703) 528-2333   E-mail: scholarships@navyleague.org
Web: www.navyleague.org/scholarship

Summary To provide financial assistance for college to dependent children of sea service personnel.

Eligibility This program is open to U.S. citizens who are 1) dependents or direct descendants of an active, Reserve, retired, or honorably discharged member of the U.S. sea service (including the Navy, Marine Corps, Coast Guard, or Merchant Marine), or 2) currently an active member of the Naval Sea Cadet Corps. Applicants must be entering their freshman year at an accredited college or university. They must have a GPA of 3.0 or higher. Along with their application, they must submit transcripts, 2 letters of recommendation, SAT/ACT scores, documentation of financial need, proof of qualifying sea service duty, and a 1-page personal statement on why they should be considered for this scholarship.

Financial Data The stipend is $2,500 per year.

Duration 4 years, provided the recipient maintains a GPA of 3.0 or higher.

Additional data This program includes the following named awards: the John G. Brokaw Scholarship, the Jack and Eileen Anderson Scholarship, the Anne E. Clark Foundation Scholarship, the Harold E. Wirth Scholarship, the Albert Levinson Scholarship, the CAPT Ernest G. "Scotty" Campbell, USN (Ret.) and Renee Campbell Scholarship, the CAPT Winifred Quick Collins, USN (Ret.) Scholarship, the John "Jack" Schiff Scholarship, and the Wesley C. Cameron Scholarship. Requests for applications must be accompanied by a stamped self-addressed envelope.

Number awarded Approximately 5 each year.

Deadline February of each year.

[619]
NAVY/MARINE CORPS/COAST GUARD ENLISTED DEPENDENT SPOUSE SCHOLARSHIP

Navy Wives Club of America
P.O. Box 54022
Millington, TN 38053-6022
Toll Free: (866) 511-NWCA
E-mail: nwca@navywivesclubofamerica.org
Web: www.navywivesclubofamerica.org/scholarinfo.htm

Summary To provide financial assistance for undergraduate or graduate study to spouses of naval personnel.

Eligibility This program is open to the spouses of active-duty Navy, Marine Corps, or Coast Guard members who can demonstrate financial need. Applicants must be 1) a high school graduate or senior planning to attend college full time next year; 2) currently enrolled in an undergraduate program and planning to continue as a full-time undergraduate; 3) a college graduate or senior planning to be a full-time graduate student next year; and 4) a high school graduate or GED recipient planning to attend vocational or business school next year. Along with their application, they must submit a brief statement on why they feel they should be awarded this scholarship and any special circumstances (financial or other) they wish to have considered. Financial need is also considered in the selection process.

Financial Data The stipends range from $500 to $1,000 each year (depending upon the donations from chapters of the Navy Wives Club of America).

Duration 1 year.

Number awarded 1 or more each year.

Deadline May of each year.

[620]
NAVY SUPPLY CORPS FOUNDATION MEMORIAL SCHOLARSHIPS

Navy Supply Corps Foundation
c/o CDR Jack Evans (ret), Chief Staff Officer
1425 Prince Avenue
Athens, GA 30606-2205
(706) 354-4111   Fax: (706) 354-0334
E-mail: foundation@usnscf.com
Web: www.usnscf.com/programs/scholarships.aspx

Summary To provide financial assistance for college to children of Navy Supply Corps personnel who died on active duty.

Eligibility This program is open to children of Navy Supply Corps personnel who died on active duty after 2001. The program applies to Active Duty Supply Corps Officers as well as Reserve Supply Corps Officers in the following categories: Mobilization, Active Duty for Special Work (ADSW), Active Duty for Training (ADT), Annual Training (AT), and Inactive Duty for Training (IDT). Applicants must be attending or planning to attend a 2-year or 4-year accredited college on a full-time basis and have a GPA of 2.5 or higher in high school and/or college. Selection is based on character, leadership, academic achievement, extracurricular activities, and financial need.

Financial Data The stipend is $2,500 per year.

Duration 4 years.

Number awarded Varies each year; recently, 1 of these scholarships was awarded.

Deadline March of each year.

[621]
NAVY SUPPLY CORPS FOUNDATION NIB/NISH SCHOLARSHIPS

Navy Supply Corps Foundation
c/o CDR Jack Evans (ret), Chief Staff Officer
1425 Prince Avenue
Athens, GA 30606-2205
(706) 354-4111   Fax: (706) 354-0334
E-mail: foundation@usnscf.com
Web: www.usnscf.com/programs/scholarships.aspx

Summary To provide financial assistance for college to blind or disabled relatives of current or former Navy Supply Corps personnel.

Eligibility This program is open to dependents (child, grandchild, or spouse) of a living or deceased regular, retired, reserve, or prior Navy Supply Corps officer, warrant officer, or enlisted personnel. Enlisted ratings that apply are AK (Aviation Storekeeper), SK (Storekeeper), MS (Mess Specialist), DK (Disbursing Clerk), SH (Ship Serviceman), LI (Lithographer), and PC (Postal Clerk). Applicants must be attending or planning to attend a 2-year or 4-year accredited college on a full-time basis and have a GPA of 2.5 or higher in high school and/or college. They must be able to document blindness or severe disability. Selection is based on character, leadership, academic achievement, extracurricular activities, and financial need.

Financial Data Stipends range from $1,000 to $5,000.

Duration 1 year.

Additional data This program was established in 2005 with support from National Industries for the Blind (NIB) and NISH (formerly the National Industries for the Severely Handicapped).

Number awarded 1 or more each year.

Deadline March of each year.

[622]
NAVY SUPPLY CORPS FOUNDATION SCHOLARSHIPS

Navy Supply Corps Foundation
c/o CDR Jack Evans (ret), Chief Staff Officer
1425 Prince Avenue
Athens, GA 30606-2205
(706) 354-4111   Fax: (706) 354-0334
E-mail: foundation@usnscf.com
Web: www.usnscf.com/programs/scholarships.aspx

Summary To provide financial assistance for college to relatives of current or former Navy Supply Corps personnel.

Eligibility This program is open to dependents (child, grandchild, or spouse) of a living or deceased regular, retired, Reserve, or prior Navy Supply Corps officer, warrant officer, or enlister personnel. Enlisted ratings that apply are AK (Aviation Storekeeper), SK (Storekeeper), MS (Mess Specialist), DK (Disbursing Clerk), SH (Ship Serviceman), LI (Lithographer), and PC (Postal Clerk). Applicants must be attending or planning to attend a 2-year or 4-year accredited college on a full-time basis and have a GPA of 2.5 or higher in high school and/or college. Selection is based on character, leadership, academic achievement, extracurricular activities, and financial need.

Financial Data Stipends range from $1,000 to $5,000.

Duration 1 year.

Additional data This program began in 1971.

Number awarded Varies each year. Recently, the foundation awarded 95 scholarships: 17 at $5,000, 47 at $2,500, and 31 at $1,000. Since the program was established, it has awarded 1,786 scholarships with a total value of more than $3,562,000.

Deadline March of each year.

[623]
NDNGEA SCHOLARSHIPS

North Dakota National Guard Enlisted Association
c/o MSG Joe Lovelace
4900 107th Avenue S.E.
Minot, ND 58701-9207
E-mail: joseph.m.lovelace@us.army.mil
Web: www.ndngea.org

Summary To provide financial assistance to members of the North Dakota National Guard Enlisted Association (NDNGEA) and their families who are interested in attending college in any state.

Eligibility This program is open to association members who have at least 1 year remaining on their enlistment or have completed 20 or more years in service. Also eligible are their unmarried dependent children, spouses, and the unremarried spouses and unmarried dependent children of a deceased NDNGEA member who was in good standing at the time of death. Applicants must be attending or planning to attend a university, college, or trade/business school in any state. Graduate students are not eligible. Selection is based on academic achievement, leadership, character, and financial need.

Financial Data The stipend is $1,000. Funds are sent directly to the school in the recipient's name.

Duration 1 year.

Number awarded 1 or more each year.

Deadline November of each year.

[624]
NEBRASKA WAIVER OF TUITION FOR VETERANS' DEPENDENTS

Department of Veterans' Affairs
State Office Building
301 Centennial Mall South, Sixth Floor
P.O. Box 95083
Lincoln, NE 68509-5083
(402) 471-2458   Fax: (402) 471-2491
E-mail: john.hilgert@nebraska.gov
Web: www.vets.state.ne.us

Summary To provide financial assistance for college to dependents of deceased and disabled veterans and military personnel in Nebraska.

Eligibility Eligible are spouses, widow(er)s, and children who are residents of Nebraska and whose parent, stepparent, or spouse was a member of the U.S. armed forces and 1) died of a service-connected disability; 2) died subsequent to discharge as a result of injury or illness sustained while in service; 3) is permanently and totally disabled as a result of military service; or 4) is classified as missing in action or as a prisoner of war during armed hostilities after August 4, 1964. Applicants must be attending or planning to attend a branch of the University of Nebraska, a state college, or a community college in Nebraska.

Financial Data Tuition is waived at public institutions in Nebraska.

Duration The waiver is valid for 1 degree, diploma, or certificate from a community college and 1 baccalaureate degree.

Additional data Applications may be submitted through 1 of the recognized veterans' organizations or any county service officer.

Number awarded Varies each year; recently, 311 of these grants were awarded.

Deadline Deadline not specified.

[625]
NEW HAMPSHIRE SCHOLARSHIPS FOR ORPHANS OF VETERANS

New Hampshire Postsecondary Education Commission
Attn: Financial Aid Programs Coordinator
3 Barrell Court, Suite 300
Concord, NH 03301-8543
(603) 271-2555, ext. 352   Fax: (603) 271-2696
TDD: (800) 735-2964   E-mail: jknapp@pec.state.nh.us
Web: www.nh.gov/postsecondary/financial/war_orphans.html

Summary To provide financial assistance to the children of New Hampshire veterans who died of service-connected causes and plan to attend college in the state.

Eligibility This program is open to New Hampshire residents between 16 and 25 years of age whose parent(s) died while on active duty or as a result of a service-related disability incurred during World War II, the Korean Conflict, the southeast Asian Conflict (Vietnam), or the Gulf Wars. Parents must have been residents of New Hampshire at the time of death. Applicants must be enrolled at least half time as undergraduate students at a public college or university in New Hampshire. Financial need is not considered in the selection process.

Financial Data The stipend is $2,500 per year, to be used for the payment of room, board, books, and supplies. Recipients are also eligible to receive a tuition waiver from the institution.

Duration 1 year; may be renewed for up to 3 additional years.

Additional data This program was established in 1943.

Number awarded Varies each year; recently, 2 of these scholarships were awarded.

Deadline Deadline not specified.

[626]
NEW JERSEY LEGION AUXILIARY DEPARTMENT SCHOLARSHIPS

American Legion Auxiliary
Department of New Jersey
c/o Lucille M. Miller, Secretary/Treasurer
1540 Kuser Road, Suite A-8
Hamilton, NJ 08619
(609) 581-9580   Fax: (609) 581-8429
E-mail: newjerseyala@juno.com
Web: www.alanj.org

Summary To provide financial assistance to New Jersey residents who are the descendants of veterans and planning to attend college in any state.

Eligibility This program is open to the children, grandchildren, and great-grandchildren of veterans who served in the U.S. armed forces during specified periods of war time. Applicants must be graduating high school seniors who have been residents of New Jersey for at least 2 years. They must be planning to attend a college or university in any state. Along with their application, they must submit a 1,000-word essay on a topic that changes annually; recently, students were asked to write on the topic, "Honoring Our Promise Everyday-How I Can Serve My Country and Our Veterans." Selection is based on academic achievement (40%), character (15%), leadership (15%), Americanism (15%), and financial need (15%).

Financial Data Stipends range from $1,000 to $2,500.

Duration 1 year.

Number awarded 3 each year: 1 in North Jersey, 1 in Central Jersey, and 1 in South Jersey.

Deadline April of each year.

[627]
NEW JERSEY LEGION AUXILIARY PAST PRESIDENTS' PARLEY NURSES SCHOLARSHIPS

American Legion Auxiliary
Department of New Jersey
c/o Lucille M. Miller, Secretary/Treasurer
1540 Kuser Road, Suite A-8
Hamilton, NJ 08619
(609) 581-9580   Fax: (609) 581-8429
E-mail: newjerseyala@juno.com
Web: www.alanj.org

Summary To provide financial assistance to New Jersey residents who are the descendants of veterans and interested in studying nursing at a school in any state.

Eligibility This program is open to the children, grandchildren, and great-grandchildren of veterans who served in the U.S. armed forces during specified periods of war time. Applicants must be graduating high school seniors who have been residents of New Jersey for at least 2 years. They must be planning to study nursing at a school in any state. Along with their application, they must submit a 1,000-word essay on a topic that changes annually; recently, students were asked to write on the topic, "Honoring Our Promise Everyday-How I Can Serve My Country and Our Veterans." Selection is based on academic achievement (40%), character (15%), leadership (15%), Americanism (15%), and financial need (15%).

Financial Data A stipend is awarded (amount not specified).

Duration 1 year.

Number awarded 1 or more each year.

Deadline April of each year.

[628]
NEW JERSEY NATIONAL GUARD TUITION PROGRAM

New Jersey Department of Military and Veterans Affairs
Attn: New Jersey Army National Guard Education Center
3650 Saylors Pond Road
Fort Dix, NJ 08640-7600
(609) 562-0654   Toll Free: (888) 859-0352
Fax: (609) 562-0201
Web: www.state.nj.us/military/education/NJNGTP.htm

Summary To provide financial assistance for college or graduate school to New Jersey National Guard members and the surviving spouses and children of deceased members.

Eligibility This program is open to active members of the New Jersey National Guard who have completed Initial Active Duty for Training (IADT). Applicants must be New Jersey residents who have been accepted into a program of undergraduate or graduate study at any of 31 public institutions of higher education in the state. The surviving spouses and children of deceased members of the Guard who had completed IADT and were killed in the performance of their duties while a member of the Guard are also eligible if the school has classroom space available.

Financial Data Tuition for up to 15 credits per semester is waived for full-time recipients in state-supported colleges or community colleges in New Jersey.

Duration 1 semester; may be renewed.

Number awarded Varies each year.

Deadline Deadline not specified.

[629]
NEW JERSEY POW/MIA TUITION BENEFIT PROGRAM

New Jersey Department of Military and Veterans Affairs
Attn: Division of Veterans Programs
101 Eggert Crossing Road
P.O. Box 340
Trenton, NJ 08625-0340
(609) 530-7045   Toll Free: (800) 624-0508 (within NJ)
Fax: (609) 530-7075
Web: www.state.nj.us/military/veterans/programs.html

Summary To provide financial assistance for college to the children of New Jersey military personnel reported as missing in action or prisoners of war during the southeast Asian conflict.

Eligibility Eligible to apply for this assistance are New Jersey residents attending or accepted at a New Jersey public or independent postsecondary institution whose parents were military service personnel officially declared prisoners of war or missing in action after January 1, 1960.

Financial Data This program entitles recipients to full undergraduate tuition at any public or independent postsecondary educational institution in New Jersey.

Duration Assistance continues until completion of a bachelor's degree.

Number awarded Varies each year.

Deadline February of each year for the spring term and September for the fall and spring terms.

[630]
NEW MEXICO CHILDREN OF DECEASED MILITARY AND STATE POLICE PERSONNEL SCHOLARSHIPS

New Mexico Department of Veterans' Services
Attn: Benefits Division
407 Galisteo Street, Room 142
Santa Fe, NM 87504
(505) 827-6374   Toll Free: (866) 433-VETS
Fax: (505) 827-6372   E-mail: alan.martinez@state.nm.us
Web: www.dvs.state.nm.us/benefits.html

Summary To provide financial assistance for college or graduate school to the children of deceased military and state police personnel in New Mexico.

Eligibility This program is open to the children of 1) military personnel killed in action or as a result of such action during a period of armed conflict; 2) members of the New Mexico National Guard killed while on active duty; and 3) New Mexico State Police killed on active duty. Applicants must be between the ages of 16 and 26 and enrolled in a state-supported school in New Mexico. Children of deceased veterans must be nominated by the New Mexico Veterans' Service Commission; children of National Guard members must be nominated by the adjutant general of the state; children of state police must be nominated by the New Mexico State Police Board. Selection is based on merit and financial need.

Financial Data The scholarships provide full waiver of tuition at state-funding postsecondary schools in New Mexico. A stipend of $150 per semester ($300 per year) provides assistance with books and fees.

Duration 1 year; may be renewed.

Deadline Deadline not specified.

[631]
NEW MEXICO LEGION AUXILIARY PAST PRESIDENTS PARLEY SCHOLARSHIPS

American Legion Auxiliary
Department of New Mexico
1215 Mountain Road, N.E.
Albuquerque, NM 87102
(505) 242-9918   Fax: (505) 247-0478
E-mail: alauxnm@netscape.com

Summary To provide financial assistance to residents of New Mexico who are the children of veterans and studying nursing or a related field at a school in any state.

Eligibility This program is open to New Mexico residents who are attending college in any state. Applicants must be the children of veterans who served during specified periods of war time. They must be studying nursing or a related medical field. Selection is based on scholarship, character, leadership, Americanism, and financial need.

Financial Data A stipend is awarded (amount not specified).

Deadline April of each year.

[632]
NEW YORK AMERICAN LEGION PRESS ASSOCIATION SCHOLARSHIP

New York American Legion Press Association
Attn: Awards Chair
P.O. Box 650
East Aurora, NY 14052-0650
E-mail: ddmreed2@verizon.net
Web: home.earthlink.net/~nyalpa

Summary To provide financial assistance to residents of New York who have a connection with the American Legion and are interested in careers in communications.

Eligibility This program is open to New York residents who are 1) children of members of the American Legion or American Legion Auxiliary, 2) members of the Sons of the American Legion, 3) junior members of the American Legion Auxiliary, or 4) graduates of the New York Boys State or Girls State. Applicants must be entering or attending an accredited 4-year college or university, working on a degree in communications (including public relations, journalism, reprographics, newspaper design or management, or other related fields acceptable to the scholarship committee). Along with their application, they must submit a 500-word essay on why they chose the field of communications as a future vocation. Financial need and class standing are not considered.

Financial Data The stipend is $1,000.

Duration 1 year.

Number awarded 1 each year.

Deadline April of each year.

[633]
NEW YORK EAGLE SCOUT OF THE YEAR SCHOLARSHIP

American Legion
Department of New York
112 State Street, Suite 1300
Albany, NY 12207
(518) 463-2215   Toll Free: (800) 253-4466
Fax: (518) 427-8443   E-mail: info@nylegion.org
Web: www.ny.legion.org/scouting_.htm

Summary To recognize and reward, with scholarships for college in any state, Eagle Scouts who are members of a troop associated with the American Legion in New York or a son or grandson of a member of the Legion in the state.

Eligibility The New York nominee for American Legion Scout of the Year receives this award. Applicants must be either 1) registered, active members of a Boy Scout Troop or Varsity Scout Team sponsored by an American Legion Post in New York or Auxiliary Unit in New York, or 2) registered, active members of a duly chartered Boy Scout Troop or Varsity Scout Team and the sons or grandsons of American Legion or Auxiliary members. They must be active members of their religious institution; have received the appropriate religious emblem; have demonstrated practical citizenship in church, school, Scouting, and community; have received the Eagle Scout award; be between 15 and 19 years of age; be enrolled in high school; and be planning to attend college in any state.

Financial Data The award is a $1,000 scholarship.

Duration The award is presented annually.

Number awarded 1 each year.

Deadline February of each year.

[634]
NEW YORK LEGION AUXILIARY DEPARTMENT SCHOLARSHIP

American Legion Auxiliary
Department of New York
112 State Street, Suite 1310
Albany, NY 12207
(518) 463-1162   Toll Free: (800) 421-6348
Fax: (518) 449-5406   E-mail: alanyterry@nycap.rr.com
Web: www.deptny.org/Scholarships.htm

Summary To provide financial assistance to New York residents who are the descendants of veterans and interested in attending college in any state.

Eligibility This program is open to residents of New York who are high school seniors or graduates and attending or planning to attend an accredited college or university in any state. Applicants must be the children, grandchildren, or great-grandchildren of veterans who served during specified periods of war time. Along with their application, they must submit a 500-word essay on a subject of their choice. Selection is based on character (20%), Americanism (20%), leadership (20%), scholarship (15%), and financial need (25%). U.S. citizenship is required.

Financial Data The stipend is $1,000. Funds are paid directly to the recipient's school.

Duration 1 year.

Number awarded 1 each year.

Deadline February of each year.

[635]
NEW YORK LEGION AUXILIARY DISTRICT SCHOLARSHIPS

American Legion Auxiliary
Department of New York
112 State Street, Suite 1310
Albany, NY 12207
(518) 463-1162   Toll Free: (800) 421-6348
Fax: (518) 449-5406   E-mail: alanyterry@nycap.rr.com
Web: www.deptny.org/Scholarships.htm

Summary To provide financial assistance to descendants of veterans in New York who are interested in attending college in any state to study a medical or teaching field.

Eligibility This program is open to residents of New York who are high school seniors or graduates and attending or planning to attend an accredited college or university in any state to work on a degree in a medical or teaching field. Applicants must be the children, grandchildren, or great-grandchildren of veterans who served during specified periods of war time. Along with their application they must submit a 500-word essay on a subject of their choice. Selection is based on character (20%), Americanism (20%), leadership (20%), scholarship (15%), and financial need (25%). U.S. citizenship is required.

Financial Data The stipend is $1,000. Funds are paid directly to the recipient's school.

Duration 1 year.

Number awarded 10 each year: 1 in each of the 10 judicial districts in New York state.

Deadline February of each year.

[636]
NEW YORK LEGION AUXILIARY PAST PRESIDENTS PARLEY STUDENT SCHOLARSHIP IN MEDICAL FIELD

American Legion Auxiliary
Department of New York
112 State Street, Suite 1310
Albany, NY 12207
(518) 463-1162   Toll Free: (800) 421-6348
Fax: (518) 449-5406   E-mail: alanyterry@nycap.rr.com
Web: www.deptny.org/Scholarships.htm

Summary To provide financial assistance to descendants of wartime veterans in New York who are interested in attending college in any state to prepare for a career in a medical field.

Eligibility This program is open to residents of New York who are high school seniors or graduates and attending or planning to attend an accredited college or university in any state to prepare for a career in a medical field. Applicants must be the children, grandchildren, or great-grandchildren of veterans who served during specified periods of war time. Along with their application, they must submit a 500-word essay on why they selected the medical field. Selection is based on character (30%), Americanism (20%), leadership (10%), scholarship (20%), and financial need (20%). U.S. citizenship is required.

Financial Data The stipend is $1,500. Funds are paid directly to the recipient's school.

Duration 1 year.

Number awarded 3 each year.

Deadline February of each year.

[637]
NEW YORK STATE MILITARY SERVICE RECOGNITION SCHOLARSHIPS

New York State Higher Education Services Corporation
Attn: Student Information
99 Washington Avenue
Albany, NY 12255
(518) 473-1574   Toll Free: (888) NYS-HESC
Fax: (518) 473-3749   TDD: (800) 445-5234
E-mail: webmail@hesc.com
Web: www.hesc.com

Summary To provide financial assistance to disabled veterans and the family members of deceased or disabled veterans who are residents of New York and interested in attending college in the state.

Eligibility This program is open to New York residents who served in the armed forces of the United States or state organized militia at any time on or after August 2, 1990 and became severely and permanently disabled as a result of injury or illness suffered or incurred in a combat theater or combat zone or during military training operations in preparation for duty in a combat theater or combat zone of operations. Also eligible are the children, spouses, or financial dependents of members of the armed forces of the United States or state organized militia who at any time after August 2, 1990 1) died, became severely and permanently disabled as a result of injury or illness suffered or incurred, or are classified as missing in action in a combat theater or combat zone of operations, 2) died as a result of injuries incurred in those designated areas, or 3) died or became severely and permanently disabled as a result of injury or illness suffered or incurred during military training operations in preparation for duty in a combat theater or combat zone of operations. Applicants must be attending or accepted at an approved program of study as full-time undergraduates at a public college or university or private institution in New York.

Financial Data At public colleges and universities, this program provides payment of actual tuition and mandatory educational fees; actual room and board charged to students living on campus or an allowance for room and board for commuter students; and allowances for books, supplies, and transportation. At private institutions, the award is equal to the amount charged at the State University of New York (SUNY) for 4-year tuition and average mandatory fees (or the student's actual tuition and fees, whichever is less) plus allowances for room, board, books, supplies, and transportation.

Duration This program is available for 4 years of full-time undergraduate study (or 5 years in an approved 5-year bachelor's degree program).

Number awarded Varies each year.

Deadline April of each year.

[638]
NGACT SCHOLARSHIP PROGRAM

National Guard Association of Connecticut
Attn: Scholarship Committee
360 Broad Street
Hartford, CT 06105-3795
(860) 247-5000   Fax: (860) 247-5000
E-mail: ngact2005@yahoo.com
Web: ngact.com/scholarships.html

Summary To provide financial assistance to members and the family of members of the National Guard Association of Connecticut (NGACT) who are interested in attending college in any state.

Eligibility This program is open to 1) NGACT members; 2) unmarried children and grandchildren of NGACT members; 3) spouses of NGACT members; and 4) unremarried spouses and unmarried dependent children and grandchildren of deceased NGACT members who were members in good standing at the time of their death. Applicants must be attending or planning to attend, on a part- or full-time basis, a college, university, trade school, or business school in any state. Graduate students are not eligible to apply. Along with their application, they must submit: an official transcript, a letter on their desire to continue their education and why financial assistance is required, 2 letters of recommendation, and 1 letter of academic reference. Selection is based on academic record, character, leadership, and need.

Financial Data   A stipend is awarded (amount not specified). Funds are sent to the recipient but are made payable to the recipient's choice of school. To receive the awards, proof of enrollment must be presented.

Duration   1 year.

Number awarded   Varies each year.

Deadline   June of each year.

[639]
NGAI EDUCATIONAL GRANTS

National Guard Association of Indiana
Attn: Educational Grant Committee
2002 South Holt Road, Building 9
Indianapolis, IN 46241-4839
(317) 247-3196   Toll Free: (800) 219-2173
Fax: (317) 247-3575   E-mail: director@ngai.net
Web: ngai.net/index.php?main_page=page&id=16

Summary   To provide financial assistance to members of the National Guard Association of Indiana (NGAI) and their dependents who plan to attend college in any state.

Eligibility   This program is open to NGAI members who are currently serving in the Indiana National Guard and their dependents. Children and widow(er)s of former Guard members killed or permanently disabled while on duty with the Indiana National Guard are also eligible. Applicants must be attending or planning to attend a college or university in any state. Along with their application, they must submit 2 letters of recommendation, a copy of high school or college transcripts, SAT or ACT scores (if taken), a letter of acceptance from a college or university (if not currently attending college), and an essay on the educational program they intend to pursue and the goals they wish to attain. Selection is based on academic achievement, commitment and desire to achieve, extracurricular activities, accomplishments, goals, and financial need.

Financial Data   The stipend is $1,000.

Duration   1 year; recipients may reapply.

Number awarded   A limited number are awarded each year.

Deadline   February of each year.

[640]
NGAM SCHOLARSHIPS

National Guard Association of Maryland
Attn: Scholarship Committee
P.O. Box 16675
Baltimore, MD 21221-0675
(410) 557-2606   Toll Free: (800) 844-1394
Fax: (410) 893-7529   E-mail: executivedirector@ngam.net
Web: www.ngam.net/NGAM-BenefitsScholarships.htm

Summary   To provide financial assistance to current and former members of the Maryland National Guard and their dependents who are interested in attending college in any state.

Eligibility   This program is open to active and retired members of the Maryland National Guard and their spouses, sons, and daughters. Applicants must be enrolled or planning to enroll in an accredited college, university, or vocational/technical school in any state on either a part-time or full-time basis. They must submit a resume in which they outline their academic background, activities in which they have participated, and honors they have received; 3 letters of recommendation; the name of the college; and information on financial need.

Financial Data   The stipend is $1,000. Funds may be used for tuition, fees, and books.

Duration   1 year; recipients may reapply.

Number awarded   Varies each year; recently, 6 of these scholarships were awarded.

Deadline   March of each year.

[641]
NGANH SCHOLARSHIPS

National Guard Association of New Hampshire
Attn: Scholarship Committee
1 Minuteman Way
Concord, NH 03301
(603) 540-9608   E-mail: info@nganh.org
Web: www.nganh.org

Summary   To provide financial assistance to members of the National Guard Association of New Hampshire and their dependents who are interested in attending college in any state.

Eligibility   This program is open to current members of the National Guard Association of New Hampshire (officer, enlisted, or retired) and their dependents. Applicants must be attending or planning to attend an accredited college or university in any state. Along with their application, they must submit a 1-page essay on a topic that changes annually; recently, they were asked to give their thoughts on whether or not United States efforts to support and stabilize democratic governments in Afghanistan and Iraq will lead to greater stability in the Southwest Asian region.

Financial Data   The stipend is $1,000.

Duration   1 year.

Number awarded   1 each year.

Deadline   April of each year.

[642]
NGANJ SCHOLARSHIP PROGRAM

National Guard Association of New Jersey
Attn: Executive Director
P.O. Box 266
Wrightstown, NJ 08562
(973) 541-6776   Fax: (973) 541-6909
E-mail: jose.maldonado@njdmava.state.nj.us
Web: www.nganj.org

Summary   To provide financial assistance to New Jersey National Guard members or their dependents who are interested in attending college or graduate school in any state.

Eligibility   This program is open to active members of the New Jersey National Guard; the spouses, children, legal wards, and grandchildren of active members; and the children, legal wards, and grandchildren of retired (with at least 20 years of service) or deceased members. Applicants must be currently attending or entering an approved community college, school of nursing, or 4-year college in any state as a full-time undergraduate or graduate student. Selection is based on academic accomplishment, leadership, and citizenship.

Financial Data   Stipends up to $1,000 are available.

Duration   1 year; nonrenewable.

Number awarded   Varies each year; recently, 10 of these scholarships were awarded.

Deadline   March of each year.

[643]
NGASC AUXILIARY COLLEGE SCHOLARSHIP PROGRAM

National Guard Association of South Carolina Auxiliary
c/o National Guard Association of South Carolina
132 Pickens Street
Columbia, SC 29205
(803) 254-8456   Toll Free: (800) 822-3235
Fax: (803) 254-3869   E-mail: nginfo@ngasc.org
Web: www.ngasc.org/Companion/index.htm

Summary   To provide financial assistance to members of the National Guard Association of South Carolina Auxiliary and their dependents who are interested in attending college in any state.

Eligibility   This program is open to members of the auxiliary and their dependents who are related to an active, retired, or deceased member of the South Carolina National Guard. Applicants must be attending or planning to attend a college or university in any state. Along with their application, they must submit transcripts; a list of honors and significant school activities; information on their special skills, work experience, and personal interests; and documentation of financial need.

Financial Data   A stipend is awarded (amount not specified).

Duration   1 year.

Number awarded   1 or more each year.

Deadline   January of each year.

[644]
NGASC SCHOLARSHIPS

National Guard Association of South Carolina
Attn: NGASC Scholarship Foundation
132 Pickens Street
Columbia, SC 29205
(803) 254-8456   Toll Free: (800) 822-3235
Fax: (803) 254-3869   E-mail: nginfo@ngasc.org
Web: www.ngasc.org/ngasc_scholarship_foundation.htm

Summary   To provide financial assistance to current and former South Carolina National Guard members and their dependents who are interested in attending college or graduate school in any state.

Eligibility   This program is open to undergraduate students who are 1) current, retired, or deceased members of the South Carolina National Guard; 2) their dependents; and 3) members of the National Guard Association of South Carolina (NGASC). Graduate students are also eligible if they are members of the South Carolina National Guard. Applicants must be attending or interested in attending a college or university in any state as a full-time student. Several of the scholarships include additional restrictions on school or academic major; some are granted only for academic excellence, but most are based on both academics and financial need.

Financial Data   The stipend is $1,500 or $1,000.

Duration   1 year; may be renewed up to 3 additional years.

Additional data   Among the named scholarships included in this program recently were the BG (Ret) C. Norwood Gayle Memorial Scholarship Award, the CMSgt Jim Burgess Scholarship Award, the Mrs. Kaye Helgeson Memorial Scholarship Award, the LTC (Ret) Glenny J. (Jeff) Matthews Memorial Scholarship Awards, the Ron McNair Memorial Scholarship Award, the Darla Moore Scholarship Award, the Sergeants Major Watson Scholarship Award, the SCANG Chiefs Council Scholarship Award, the Chief Shepherd Pitney Bowes Scholarship Award, the Fallen Soldiers' Memorial Scholarship Award, and the South Carolina National Guard Federal Credit Union Awards.

Number awarded   Varies each year. Recently, 48 of these scholarships were awarded: 1 at $1,500 and 47 at $1,000. The $1,500 scholarship and 1 of the $1,000 scholarships were based on academic excellence; the remaining $1,000 scholarships were based on both academics and financial need.

Deadline   January of each year.

[645]
NGAT SCHOLARSHIP PROGRAM

National Guard Association of Texas
Attn: NGAT Educational Foundation
3706 Crawford Avenue
Austin, TX 78731-6803
(512) 454-7300   Toll Free: (800) 252-NGAT
Fax: (512) 467-6803   E-mail: rlindner@ngat.org
Web: www.ngat.org

Summary   To provide financial assistance to members and dependents of members of the National Guard Association of Texas who are interested in attending college or graduate school in any state.

Eligibility   This program is open to annual and life members of the association and their spouses and children (associate members and their dependents are not eligible). Applicants may be high school seniors, undergraduate students, or graduate students, either enrolled or planning to enroll at an institution of higher education in any state. Along with their application, they must submit an essay on their desire to continue their education. Selection is based on scholarship, citizenship, and leadership.

Financial Data   Stipends range from $500 to $5,000.

Duration   1 year (nonrenewable).

Additional data   This program includes the following named scholarships: the Thomas F. Berry Memorial Scholarship, the Len and Jean Tallas Memorial Scholarship, the Texas Military Forces Retirees Scholarship, the T-Mates Scholarship, the LTC Gary W. Parrish Memorial Scholarship, the 1SG Harry E. Lux Memorial Scholarship, the Gloria Jenell and Marlin E. Mote Endowed Scholarship, the Chief Master Sergeants Scholarship, the Sergeants Major Scholarship, and the Texas USAA Scholarship (sponsored by USAA Insurance Corporation).

Number awarded   Varies each year. Recently, 10 of these scholarships were awarded: 1 at $5,000, 3 at $2,500, 1 at $2,000, 2 at $1,250, 2 at $1,000, and 1 at $500.

Deadline   February of each year.

[646]
NGATN SCHOLARSHIP PROGRAM

National Guard Association of Tennessee
Attn: Scholarship Committee
4332 Kenilwood Drive
Nashville, TN 37204-4401
(615) 833-9100   Toll Free: (888) 642-8448 (within TN)
Fax: (615) 833-9173   E-mail: larry@ngatn.org
Web: www.ngatn.org

Summary   To provide financial assistance for college to members or dependents of members of the National Guard Association of Tennessee (NGATN).

Eligibility   This program is open to active Tennessee National Guard members and to active annual or life members of the NGATN. If no active Guard or association member qualifies, the scholarships may be awarded to the child of a Guard or association member, including life members who have retired or are deceased. All applicants must be high school seniors or graduates who meet entrance or continuation requirements at a Tennessee college or university. Selection is based on leadership in school and civic activities, motivation for continued higher education, academic achievement in high school and/or college, and financial need.

Financial Data   The stipends are $1,500.

Duration   1 year.

Number awarded   6 each year: 1 to an active National Guard member; 2 to current association members or their dependents;

2 to active National Guard members or their dependents; and 1 to a current Guard member who was mobilized for Operations Desert Storm, Noble Eagle, Enduring Freedom, or Iraqi Freedom.
Deadline June of each year.

[647]
NGAUT "MINUTEMAN" SCHOLARSHIPS

National Guard Association of Utah
12953 South Minuteman Drive, Room 198
Draper, UT 84020-9286
(801) 631-6314   E-mail: ngautah@ngaut.org
Web: www.ngaut.org/Scholarship.php
Summary To provide financial assistance to members of the Utah National Guard and their dependents who are interested in attending college in the state.
Eligibility This program is open to members of the Utah National Guard and their dependents who are enrolled for at least 6 credit hours at a college or university in the state. Applicants must submit 1) a 150-word description of their educational and career goals; 2) a 200- to 300-word description of leadership and extracurricular activities that they may have had or currently enjoy; 3) a 1-page cover letter or resume; and 4) 2 letters of reference.
Financial Data The stipend is $1,000. Funds are sent to the recipient's school and must be used for tuition, laboratory fees, and curriculum-required books and supplies.
Duration 1 year.
Number awarded 5 each year.
Deadline January of each year.

[648]
NGAVT SCHOLARSHIPS

National Guard Association of Vermont
Attn: Capt John Geno, President
P.O. Box 694
Essex Junction, VT 05452
(802) 338-3397   E-mail: john.geno@us.army.mil
Web: www.ngavt.org/scholarInfo.shtml
Summary To provide financial assistance to members of the Vermont National Guard (VTNG) and their children or spouses who are interested in attending college in any state.
Eligibility This program is open to current members of the VTNG, their spouses, and their unmarried children. Applicants must be working, or planning to work, on an associate, undergraduate, or technical degree as a full-time student at a school in any state. Along with their application, they must submit an essay on their commitment to selfless public service or their plan for pursuing it in the future. Selection is based on academic performance, overall potential for a commitment to selfless public service, and financial need.
Financial Data The stipend is $1,000. Funds are sent directly to the recipient.
Duration 1 year; recipients may reapply.
Number awarded 2 each year.
Deadline June of each year.

[649]
NGOA-FL AND ENGAF SCHOLARSHIP PROGRAM

National Guard Association of Florida
Attn: Scholarship Committee
P.O. Box 3446
St. Augustine, FL 32085-3446
(904) 823-0628   Fax: (904) 839-2068
E-mail: mary.e.paul@us.army.mil
Web: www.floridaguard.org/Scholarships/Scholarships.htm
Summary To provide financial assistance to members of the Florida National Guard and their families who are also members of either the National Guard Association of Florida (NGOA-FL) or

the Enlisted National Guard Association of Florida (ENGAF) and interested in attending college in the state.
Eligibility This program is open to active members of the Florida National Guard (enlisted, officer, and warrant officer), their spouses, and children, but preference is given to Guard members. Applicants must be residents of Florida attending a college, university, or vocational/technical school in the state. They must also be a member, spouse of a member, or child of a member of their respective association. Selection is based on academic achievement, civic and moral leadership, character, and financial need.
Financial Data Scholarships are $1,000 for full-time students or $500 for part-time students; funds are paid directly to the recipient's institution.
Duration 1 year; may be renewed.
Additional data This program is jointly sponsored by the respective associations.
Number awarded 15 each year.
Deadline May of each year.

[650]
NICHOLAS CARUSO MEMORIAL SCHOLARSHIP

Enlisted Association National Guard of New Jersey
Attn: Scholarship Committee
101 Eggert Crossing Road
Lawrenceville, NJ 08648-2805
(609) 562-0207   Fax: (609) 562-0283
Web: www.eang-nj.org/scholarships.html
Summary To provide financial assistance to New Jersey National Guard members and their children who are interested in attending college in any state.
Eligibility This program is open to 1) children of New Jersey National Guard members who are also members of the Enlisted Association National Guard of New Jersey, and 2) drilling Guard members who are also members of the association. Applicants must be attending or planning to attend a college or university in any state. Along with their application, they must submit 1) information on their church, school, and community activities; 2) a list of honors they have received; 3) letters of recommendation; 4) transcripts; and 5) a letter with specific facts about their desire to continue their education and specifying their career goals. Financial need is not considered in the selection process.
Financial Data The stipend is $1,000.
Duration 1 year.
Number awarded 1 each year.
Deadline May of each year.

[651]
NONRESIDENT TUITION WAIVERS FOR VETERANS AND THEIR DEPENDENT WHO MOVE TO TEXAS

Texas Higher Education Coordinating Board
Attn: Grants and Special Programs
1200 East Anderson Lane
P.O. Box 12788, Capitol Station
Austin, TX 78711-2788
(512) 427-6340   Toll Free: (800) 242-3062
Fax: (512) 427-6127   E-mail: grantinfo@thecb.state.tx.us
Web: www.collegeforalltexans.com
Summary To exempt veterans who move to Texas and their dependents from the payment of nonresident tuition at public institutions of higher education in the state.
Eligibility Eligible for these waivers are former members of the U.S. armed forces and commissioned officers of the Public Health Service who are retired or have been honorably discharged, their spouses, and dependent children. Applicants must have moved to Texas upon separation from the service and be attending or planning to attend a public college or university in the state. They must have indicated their intent to become a Texas resident by

registering to vote and doing 1 of the following: owning real property in Texas, registering an automobile in Texas, or executing a will indicating that they are a resident of the state.

Financial Data Although persons eligible under this program are still classified as nonresidents, they are entitled to pay the resident tuition at Texas institutions of higher education on an immediate basis.

Duration 1 year.

Number awarded Varies each year.

Deadline Deadline not specified.

[652]
NON-TRADITIONAL STUDENTS SCHOLARSHIP

American Legion Auxiliary
8945 North Meridian Street
Indianapolis, IN 46260
(317) 569-4500   Fax: (317) 569-4502
E-mail: alahq@legion-aux.org
Web: www.legion-aux.org

Summary To provide financial assistance for college to nontraditional students affiliated with the American Legion.

Eligibility This program is open to members of the American Legion, American Legion Auxiliary, or Sons of the American Legion who have paid dues for the 2 preceding years and the calendar year in which application is being made. Applicants must be nontraditional students who are either 1) returning to school after some period of time during which their formal education was interrupted, or 2) just beginning their education at a later point in life. Selection is based on scholastic standing and academic achievement (25%), character and leadership (25%), initiative and goals (25%), and financial need (25%).

Financial Data The stipend is $1,000, paid directly to the school.

Duration 1 year.

Additional data Applications are available from the president of the candidate's own unit or from the secretary or education chair of the department.

Number awarded 5 each year: 1 in each division of the American Legion Auxiliary.

Deadline Applications must be submitted to the unit president by February of each year.

[653]
NORTH CAROLINA SCHOLARSHIPS FOR CHILDREN OF WAR VETERANS

Division of Veterans Affairs
Albemarle Building
325 North Salisbury Street, Suite 1065
Raleigh, NC 27603-5941
(919) 733-3851   Fax: (919) 733-2834
E-mail: ncdva.aso@ncmail.net
Web: www.doa.state.nc.us/vets/benefits-scholarships.htm

Summary To provide financial assistance to the children of disabled and other classes of North Carolina veterans who plan to attend college in the state.

Eligibility Eligible applicants come from 5 categories: Class I-A: the veteran parent died in wartime service or as a result of a service-connected condition incurred in wartime service; Class I-B: the veteran parent is rated by the U.S. Department of Veterans Affairs (VA) as 100% disabled as a result of wartime service and currently or at the time of death drawing compensation for such disability; Class II: the veteran parent is rated by the VA as much as 20% but less than 100% disabled due to wartime service, or was awarded a Purple Heart medal for wounds received, and currently or at the time of death drawing compensation for such disability; Class III: the veteran parent is currently or was at the time of death receiving a VA pension for total and permanent disability, or the veteran parent is deceased but does not qualify under any

other provisions, or the veteran parent served in a combat zone or waters adjacent to a combat zone and received a campaign badge or medal but does not qualify under any other provisions; Class IV: the veteran parent was a prisoner of war or missing in action. For all classes, applicants must 1) be under 25 years of age and have a veteran parent who was a resident of North Carolina at the time of entrance into the armed forces; or 2) be the natural child, or adopted child prior to age 15, who was born in North Carolina, has been a resident of the state continuously since birth, and is the child of a veteran whose disabilities occurred during a period of war.

Financial Data Students in Classes I-A, II, III, and IV receive $4,500 per academic year if they attend a private college or junior college; if attending a public postsecondary institution, they receive free tuition, a room allowance, a board allowance, and exemption from certain mandatory fees. Students in Class I-B receive $1,500 per academic year if they attend a private college or junior college; if attending a public postsecondary institution, they receive free tuition and exemption from certain mandatory fees.

Duration 4 academic years.

Number awarded An unlimited number of awards are made under Classes I-A, I-B, and IV. Classes II and III are limited to 100 awards each year in each class.

Deadline Applications for Classes I-A, I-B, and IV may be submitted at any time; applications for Classes II and III must be submitted by February of each year.

[654]
NORTH DAKOTA EDUCATIONAL ASSISTANCE FOR DEPENDENTS OF VETERANS

Department of Veterans Affairs
4201 38th Street S.W., Suite 104
P.O. Box 9003
Fargo, ND 58106-9003
(701) 239-7165   Toll Free: (866) 634-8387
Fax: (701) 239-7166
Web: www.nd.gov/veterans/benefits/waiver.html

Summary To provide financial assistance for college to the spouses, widow(er)s, and children of disabled and other North Dakota veterans and military personnel.

Eligibility This program is open to the spouses, widow(er)s, and dependent children of veterans who are totally disabled as a result of service-connected causes, or who were killed in action, or who have died as a result of wounds or service-connected disabilities, or who were identified as prisoners of war or missing in action. Veteran parents must have been born in and lived in North Dakota until entrance into the armed forces (or must have resided in the state for at least 6 months prior to entrance into military service) and must have served during wartime.

Financial Data Eligible dependents receive free tuition and are exempt from fees at any state-supported institution of higher education, technical school, or vocational school in North Dakota.

Duration Up to 45 months or 10 academic semesters.

Number awarded Varies each year.

Deadline Deadline not specified.

[655]
NORTH DAKOTA VETERANS DEPENDENTS FEE WAIVER

North Dakota University System
Attn: Director of Financial Aid
State Capitol, Tenth Floor
600 East Boulevard Avenue, Department 215
Bismarck, ND 58505-0230
(701) 328-4114   Fax: (701) 328-2961
E-mail: ndus.office@ndus.nodak.edu
Web: www.ndus.nodak.edu

Summary To waive tuition and fees for dependents of deceased or other veterans at public institutions in North Dakota.
Eligibility Eligible for this benefit are the dependents of veterans who were North Dakota residents when they entered the armed forces and died of service-related causes, were killed in action, were prisoners of war, or were declared missing in action. Applicants must be attending or planning to attend a public college or university in North Dakota.
Financial Data Qualified students are entitled to a waiver of all tuition and fees (except fees charged to retire outstanding bonds) at public institutions in North Dakota.
Duration 1 academic year; renewable.
Number awarded Varies each year.
Deadline Deadline not specified.

[656]
NORTHWESTERN VERMONT VIETNAM VETERANS OF AMERICA COLLEGE SCHOLARSHIPS

Northwestern Vermont Vietnam Veterans of America
Attn: Scholarship Committee
P.O. Box 965
St. Albans, VT 05478
E-mail: wemchogisle@comcast.net

Summary To recognize and reward, with college scholarships, high school seniors in Vermont who are relatives of current or former military personnel and submit outstanding essays.
Eligibility This competition is open to seniors graduating from high schools in Vermont who are relatives of a U.S. military servicemember currently serving on active duty or who has been honorably discharged or an active-duty or honorably-discharged member of the Vermont National Guard. The relative must also be a resident of Vermont. Applicants must submit an essay on a topic that changes annually.
Financial Data The award is a $1,500 scholarship for use at a college or university in any state.
Duration The competition is held annually.
Additional data This program consists of 2 named awards: the Lyndon F. Murray, Sr. College Scholarship Grant and the Michael Lawton College Scholarship Grant. The sponsoring organization is Chapter 753 of Vietnam Veterans of America. Students must request a copy of the essay topic in writing.
Number awarded 2 each year.
Deadline March of each year.

[657]
NWCA NATIONAL SCHOLARSHIPS

Navy Wives Club of America
P.O. Box 54022
Millington, TN 38053-6022
Toll Free: (866) 511-NWCA
E-mail: nwca@navywivesclubofamerica.org
Web: www.navywivesclubofamerica.org/scholarinfo.htm

Summary To provide financial assistance for college or graduate school to the children of naval personnel.
Eligibility Applicants for these scholarships must be the children (natural born, legally adopted, or stepchildren) of enlisted members of the Navy, Marine Corps, or Coast Guard on active duty, retired with pay, or deceased. Applicants must be attending or planning to attend an accredited college or university as a full-time undergraduate or graduate student. They must have a GPA of 2.5 or higher. Along with their application, they must submit an essay on their career objectives and the reasons they chose those objectives. Selection is based on academic standing, moral character, and financial need. Some scholarships are reserved for students majoring in special education, medical students, and children of members of Navy Wives Club of America (NWCA).
Financial Data The stipend is $1,500.
Duration 1 year; may be renewed up to 3 additional years.

Additional data Membership in the NWCA is open to spouses of enlisted personnel serving in the Navy, Marine Corps, Coast Guard, and the active Reserve units of those services; spouses of enlisted personnel who have been honorably discharged, retired, or transferred to the Fleet Reserve on completion of duty; and widows of enlisted personnel in those services.
Number awarded 30 each year, including at least 4 to freshmen, 4 to current undergraduates applying for the first time, 2 to medical students, 1 to a student majoring in special education, and 4 to children of NWCA members.
Deadline May of each year.

[658]
OHIO LEGION AUXILIARY DEPARTMENT PRESIDENT'S SCHOLARSHIP

American Legion Auxiliary
Department of Ohio
1100 Brandywine Boulevard, Building D
P.O. Box 2760
Zanesville, OH 43702-2760
(740) 452-8245   Fax: (740) 452-2620
E-mail: ala_katie@rrohio.com

Summary To provide financial assistance to the descendants of veterans in Ohio who are interested in attending college in any state.
Eligibility This program is open to the children, grandchildren, and great-grandchildren of living or deceased veterans who served during designated periods of war time. Applicants must be residents of Ohio, seniors at an accredited high school, and sponsored by an American Legion Auxiliary Unit. Along with their application, they must submit an original article (up to 500 words) written by the applicant on "What the American Flag Represents to Me." Selection is based on character, Americanism, leadership, scholarship, and financial need.
Financial Data Stipends are $1,500 or $1,000. Funds are paid to the recipient's school.
Duration 1 year.
Number awarded 2 each year: 1 at $1,500 and 1 at $1,000.
Deadline February of each year.

[659]
OHIO LEGION SCHOLARSHIPS

American Legion
Department of Ohio
60 Big Run Road
P.O. Box 8007
Delaware, OH 43015
(740) 362-7478   Fax: (740) 362-1429
E-mail: legion@ohiolegion.com
Web: www.ohiolegion.com/scholarships/info.htm

Summary To provide financial assistance to residents of Ohio who are members of the American Legion, their families, or dependents of deceased military personnel and interested in attending college in any state.
Eligibility This program is open to residents of Ohio who are Legionnaires, direct descendants of living or deceased Legionnaires, or surviving spouses or children of deceased U.S. military personnel who died on active duty or of injuries received on active duty. Applicants must be attending or planning to attend colleges, universities, or other approved postsecondary schools in any state with a vocational objective. Selection is based on academic achievement as measured by course grades, scholastic test scores, difficulty of curriculum, participation in outside activities, and the judging committee's general impression.
Financial Data Stipends are at least $2,000.
Duration 1 year.

Number awarded Varies each year; recently, 14 of these scholarships were awarded.
Deadline April of each year.

[660]
OHIO NATIONAL GUARD ENLISTED ASSOCIATION SCHOLARSHIP PROGRAM

Ohio National Guard Enlisted Association
1299 Virginia Avenue
Columbus, OH 43212
(740) 574-5932 Toll Free: (800) 642-6642
Fax: (614) 486-2216 E-mail: ongea@juno.com
Web: www.ongea.org

Summary To provide financial assistance to members of the Ohio National Guard Enlisted Association (ONGEA) and children of members of the ONGEA Auxiliary who are interested in attending college in any state.
Eligibility This program is open to 1) sons and daughters of ONGEA Auxiliary members (spouse must have at least 1 year remaining on his/her enlistment following the completion of the school year for which the application is submitted); 2) unmarried dependent sons and daughters of deceased ONGEA and ONGEA Auxiliary members who were in good standing the time of their death; and 3) ONGEA members. Spouses of ONGEA members must also be a member of the ONGEA Auxiliary in order for a dependent to be considered for this award (unless the ONGEA member is a single parent). Applicants must be enrolling as full-time undergraduate students at a college, university, trade school, or business school in any state. Graduate students are not eligible. All applications must be accompanied by a transcript of high school and (if appropriate) college credits, a letter from the applicant describing educational goals and financial need, 3 letters of recommendation, and a copy of the current membership cards of both parents or current membership card of the single parent. Selection is based on academic record, character, leadership, and financial need.
Financial Data Stipends are $1,000 or $500. After verification of enrollment is provided, checks are sent to the recipient and made out to the recipient's school.
Duration 1 year; nonrenewable.
Additional data This program is sponsored jointly by ONGEA, the ONGEA Auxiliary, USAA Insurance Corporation, and the First Cleveland Cavalry Association.
Number awarded 5 to 10 each year, depending upon the availability of funds.
Deadline February of each year.

[661]
OHIO SAFETY OFFICERS COLLEGE MEMORIAL FUND

Ohio Board of Regents
Attn: State Grants and Scholarships
30 East Broad Street, 36th Floor
Columbus, OH 43215-3414
(614) 466-7420 Toll Free: (888) 833-1133
Fax: (614) 466-5866
E-mail: osom_admin@regents.state.oh.us
Web: regents.ohio.gov/sgs/oso

Summary To provide financial assistance to Ohio residents who are interested in attending college in the state and whose parent or spouse was killed in the line of duty as a safety officer or member of the armed forces.
Eligibility This program is open to Ohio residents whose parent or spouse was 1) a peace officer, fire fighter, or other safety officer killed in the line of duty anywhere in the United States; or 2) a member of the U.S. armed forces killed in the line of duty during Operation Enduring Freedom, Operation Iraqi Freedom, or other designated combat zone. Applicants must be interested in attend-

ing a participating Ohio college or university. Children and spouses of military personnel are eligible for this program only if they do not qualify for the Ohio War Orphans Scholarship.
Financial Data At Ohio public colleges and universities, the program provides full payment of tuition. At Ohio private colleges and universities, the stipend is equivalent to the average amounts paid to students attending public institutions, currently $3,990 per year.
Duration 1 year; may be renewed up to 3 additional years.
Additional data Eligible institutions are Ohio state-assisted colleges and universities and Ohio institutions approved by the Board of Regents. This program was established in 1980.
Number awarded Varies each year; recently, 54 students received benefits from this program.
Deadline Application deadlines are established by each participating college and university.

[662]
OHIO WAR ORPHANS SCHOLARSHIP

Ohio Board of Regents
Attn: State Grants and Scholarships
30 East Broad Street, 36th Floor
Columbus, OH 43215-3414
(614) 752-9528 Toll Free: (888) 833-1133
Fax: (614) 466-5866
E-mail: jabdullah-simmons@regents.state.oh.us
Web: regents.ohio.gov/sgs/war_orphans

Summary To provide financial assistance to the children of deceased or disabled Ohio veterans who plan to attend college in the state.
Eligibility This program is open to residents of Ohio who are under 25 years of age and interested in enrolling full time at an eligible college or university in the state. Applicants must be the child of a veteran who 1) was a member of the U.S. armed forces, including the organized Reserves and Ohio National Guard, for a period of 90 days or more (or discharged because of a disability incurred after less than 90 days of service); 2) served during World War I, World War II, the Korean Conflict, the Vietnam era, or the Persian Gulf War; 3) entered service as a resident of Ohio; and 4) as a result of that service, either was killed or became at least 60% service-connected disabled. Also eligible are children of veterans who have a permanent and total non-service connected disability and are receiving disability benefits from the U.S. Department of Veterans Affairs. If the veteran parent served only in the organized Reserves or Ohio National Guard, the parent must have been killed or became permanently and totally disabled while at a scheduled training assembly, field training period (of any duration or length), or active duty for training, pursuant to bona fide orders issued by a competent authority. Financial need is considered in the selection process.
Financial Data At Ohio public colleges and universities, the program provides payment of 80% of tuition and fees. At Ohio private colleges and universities, the stipend is $4,400 per year (or 80% of the average amount paid to students attending public institutions).
Duration 1 year; may be renewed up to 4 additional years, provided the recipient maintains a GPA of 2.0 or higher.
Additional data Eligible institutions are Ohio state-assisted colleges and universities and Ohio institutions approved by the Board of Regents. This program was established in 1957.
Number awarded Varies, depending upon the funds available. If sufficient funds are available, all eligible applicants are given a scholarship. Recently, 861 students received benefits from this program.
Deadline June of each year.

[663]
OKLAHOMA TUITION WAIVER FOR PRISONERS OF WAR, PERSONS MISSING IN ACTION, AND DEPENDENTS

Oklahoma State Regents for Higher Education
Attn: Director of Scholarship and Grant Programs
655 Research Parkway, Suite 200
P.O. Box 108850
Oklahoma City, OK 73101-8850
(405) 225-9239   Toll Free: (800) 858-1840
Fax: (405) 225-9230   E-mail: studentinfo@osrhe.edu
Web: www.okhighered.org

Summary   To provide financial assistance for college to Oklahoma residents (or their dependents) who were declared prisoners of war or missing in action.

Eligibility   Applicants for this assistance must be veterans who were declared prisoners of war or missing in action after January 1, 1960 and were residents of Oklahoma at the time of entrance into the armed forces or when declared POW/MIA. Dependent children of those veterans are also eligible as long as they are under 24 years of age. Selection is based on financial need, academic aptitude and achievement, student activity participation, academic level, and academic discipline or field of study.

Financial Data   Eligible applicants are entitled to receive free tuition at any Oklahoma state-supported postsecondary educational, technical, or vocational school.

Duration   Assistance continues for 5 years or until receipt of a bachelor's degree, whichever occurs first.

Additional data   This assistance is not available to persons eligible to receive federal benefits.

Number awarded   Varies each year.

Deadline   Deadline not specified.

[664]
OLIVER AND ESTHER R. HOWARD SCHOLARSHIP

Fleet Reserve Association
Attn: Scholarship Administrator
125 North West Street
Alexandria, VA 22314-2754
(703) 683-1400   Toll Free: (800) FRA-1924
Fax: (703) 549-6610   E-mail: fra@fra.org
Web: www.fra.org

Summary   To provide financial assistance for college to children of members of the Fleet Reserve Association or its Ladies Auxiliary.

Eligibility   This program is open to dependent children of members of the association or its ladies auxiliary who are in good standing (or were at the time of death, if deceased). Applicants must be interested in working on an undergraduate degree. Along with their application, they must submit an essay on their life experiences, their career objectives, and what motivated them to select those objectives. Awards alternate annually between female dependents (in even-numbered years) and male dependents (in odd-numbered years). Selection is based on academic record, financial need, extracurricular activities, leadership skills, and participation in community activities. U.S. citizenship is required.

Financial Data   The amount awarded varies, depending upon the needs of the recipient and the funds available.

Duration   1 year; may be renewed.

Additional data   Membership in the Fleet Reserve Association is restricted to active-duty, retired, and Reserve members of the Navy, Marine Corps, and Coast Guard.

Number awarded   1 each year.

Deadline   April of each year.

[665]
OPERATION ENDURING FREEDOM AND OPERATION IRAQI FREEDOM SCHOLARSHIP

Vermont Student Assistance Corporation
Attn: Scholarship Programs
10 East Allen Street
P.O. Box 2000
Winooski, VT 05404-2601
(802) 654-3798   Toll Free: (888) 253-4819
Fax: (802) 654-3765   TDD: (800) 281-3341 (within VT)
E-mail: info@vsac.org
Web: services.vsac.org

Summary   To provide financial assistance for college to residents of Vermont whose parent has served or is serving in Operating Enduring Freedom in Afghanistan or Operation Iraqi Freedom.

Eligibility   This program is open to residents of Vermont who are children of a member of any branch of the armed forces or National Guard whose residence or home of record is in Vermont. Applicants must plan to enroll full time in a certificate, associate degree, or bachelor's degree program at an accredited postsecondary school. The parent must have served or currently be serving in Operation Enduring Freedom or Operation Iraqi Freedom. Preference is given to applicants whose parent was killed, wounded, or became permanently disabled as a result of their service. Along with their application, they must submit 1) a 100-word essay on any significant barriers that limit their access to education; and 2) a 250-word essay on their short- and long-term academic, educational, career, vocational, and/or employment goals. Selection is based on those essays, a letter of recommendation, and financial need.

Financial Data   The stipend ranges from $3,500 to $7,000 per year.

Duration   1 year; may be renewed up to 3 additional years.

Additional data   These scholarships were first awarded in 2007.

Number awarded   1 or more each year.

Deadline   June of each year.

[666]
OREGON LEGION AUXILIARY DEPARTMENT NURSES SCHOLARSHIP

American Legion Auxiliary
Department of Oregon
30450 S.W. Parkway Avenue
P.O. Box 1730
Wilsonville, OR 97070-1730
(503) 682-3162   Fax: (503) 685-5008
E-mail: alaor@pcez.com

Summary   To provide financial assistance to the wives, widows, and children of Oregon veterans who are interested in studying nursing at a school in any state.

Eligibility   This program is open to Oregon residents who are the wives or children of veterans with disabilities or the widows of deceased veterans. Applicants must have been accepted by an accredited hospital or university school of nursing in any state. Selection is based on ability, aptitude, character, determination, seriousness of purpose, and financial need.

Financial Data   The stipend is $1,500.

Duration   1 year; may be renewed.

Number awarded   1 each year.

Deadline   May of each year.

[667]
OREGON LEGION AUXILIARY DEPARTMENT SCHOLARSHIPS

American Legion Auxiliary
Department of Oregon
30450 S.W. Parkway Avenue
P.O. Box 1730
Wilsonville, OR 97070-1730
(503) 682-3162   Fax: (503) 685-5008
E-mail: alaor@pcez.com

Summary To provide financial assistance to the dependents of Oregon veterans who are interested in attending college in any state.

Eligibility This program is open to Oregon residents who are children or wives of disabled veterans or widows of veterans. Applicants must be interested in obtaining education beyond the high school level at a college, university, business school, vocational school, or any other accredited postsecondary school in the state of Oregon. Selection is based on ability, aptitude, character, seriousness of purpose, and financial need.

Financial Data The stipend is $1,000.

Duration 1 year; nonrenewable.

Number awarded 3 each year; 1 of these is to be used for vocational or business school.

Deadline March of each year.

[668]
OREGON LEGION AUXILIARY DEPARTMENT SPIRIT OF YOUTH SCHOLARSHIP

American Legion Auxiliary
Department of Oregon
30450 S.W. Parkway Avenue
P.O. Box 1730
Wilsonville, OR 97070-1730
(503) 682-3162   Fax: (503) 685-5008
E-mail: alaor@pcez.com

Summary To provide financial assistance to junior members of the American Legion Auxiliary in Oregon who plan to attend college in any state.

Eligibility This program is open to seniors graduating from high schools in Oregon who have been junior members of the Auxiliary for at least 3 years. Applicants must be children (including stepchildren), grandchildren, or great-grandchildren of veterans. They must be planning to attend a college, university, business school, vocational school, or any other accredited postsecondary school in any state.

Financial Data The stipend is $1,000.

Duration 1 year; nonrenewable.

Number awarded 1 each year.

Deadline February of each year.

[669]
OREGON LEGION AUXILIARY NATIONAL PRESIDENT'S SCHOLARSHIP

American Legion Auxiliary
Department of Oregon
30450 S.W. Parkway Avenue
P.O. Box 1730
Wilsonville, OR 97070-1730
(503) 682-3162   Fax: (503) 685-5008
E-mail: alaor@pcez.com

Summary To provide financial assistance to the children of war veterans in Oregon who plan to attend college in any state.

Eligibility This program is open to Oregon residents who are the children of veterans who served during specified periods of war time. Applicants must be high school seniors or graduates who have not yet attended an institution of higher learning. They must be planning to attend a college or university in any state.

Selection is based on character, Americanism, leadership, scholarship, and financial need. The winner then competes for the American Legion Auxiliary National President's Scholarship. If the Oregon winner is not awarded a national scholarship, then he or she receives the first-place award and the second winner receives the second-place award; if the Oregon winner is also a national winner, then the second-place winner in Oregon receives the first-place award and the alternate receives the second-place award.

Financial Data The first-place award is $2,000 and the second-place award is $1,500.

Duration 1 year; nonrenewable.

Number awarded 2 each year.

Deadline February of each year.

[670]
OREGON NATIONAL GUARD ASSOCIATION SCHOLARSHIPS

Oregon National Guard Association
Attn: Scholarship Committee
1776 Militia Way, S.E.
P.O. Box 14350
Salem, OR 97309-5047
(503) 584-3030   Fax: (503) 584-3052
E-mail: info@ornga.org
Web: ornga.org/scholar_apply.htm

Summary To provide financial assistance to members of the Oregon National Guard, the Oregon National Guard Association (ORNGA), and their children and spouses who are interested in attending college in any state.

Eligibility This program is open to active members of the Oregon Army and Air National Guard, members of the ORNGA, and their children and spouses. Applicants must be high school seniors, graduates, or GED recipients and interested in working on an undergraduate degree at a college or university in any state. The parent, spouse, or applicant must have an ETS date beyond the end of the academic year for which the scholarship is used. Selection is based on participation in school and civic activities, motivation for continued higher education, and academic achievement in high school and/or college.

Financial Data The stipend is $1,000.

Duration 1 year.

Number awarded 1 or more each year.

Deadline January of each year.

[671]
PAULINE LANGKAMP MEMORIAL SCHOLARSHIP

Navy Wives Club of America
P.O. Box 54022
Millington, TN 38053-6022
Toll Free: (866) 511-NWCA
E-mail: nwca@navywivesclubsofamerica.org
Web: www.navywivesclubsofamerica.org/scholarinfo.htm

Summary To provide financial assistance for college to the adult children of members of the Navy Wives Club of America (NWCA).

Eligibility This program is open to children of NWCA members who no longer carry a military ID card because they have reached adult status. Applicants must be attending or planning to attend an accredited college or university. Along with their application, they must submit a brief statement on why they feel they should be awarded this scholarship and any special circumstances (financial or other) they wish to have considered. Financial need is also considered in the selection process.

Financial Data A stipend is provided (amount not specified).

Duration 1 year.

Additional data Membership in the NWCA is open to spouses of enlisted personnel serving in the Navy, Marine Corps, Coast

Guard, and the active Reserve units of those services; spouses of enlisted personnel who have been honorably discharged, retired, or transferred to the Fleet Reserve on completion of duty; and widows of enlisted personnel in those services.

Number awarded 1 or more each year.

Deadline May of each year.

[672]
PENNSYLVANIA EDUCATIONAL GRATUITY FOR VETERANS' DEPENDENTS

Office of the Deputy Adjutant General for Veterans Affairs
Building S-0-47, FTIG
Annville, PA 17003-5002
(717) 865-8910   Toll Free: (800) 54 PA VET (within PA)
Fax: (717) 861-8589   E-mail: jamebutler@state.pa.us
Web: www.milvet.state.pa.us/DMVA/201.htm

Summary To provide financial assistance for college to the children of disabled or deceased Pennsylvania veterans.

Eligibility This program is open to children (between 16 and 23 years of age) of honorably-discharged veterans who are rated totally and permanently disabled as a result of wartime service or who have died of such a disability. Applicants must have lived in Pennsylvania for at least 5 years immediately preceding the date of application, be able to demonstrate financial need, and have been accepted or be currently enrolled in a Pennsylvania state or state-aided secondary or postsecondary educational institution.

Financial Data The stipend is $500 per semester ($1,000 per year). The money is paid directly to the recipient's school and is to be applied to the costs of tuition, board, room, books, supplies, and/or matriculation fees.

Duration The allowance is paid for up to 4 academic years or for the duration of the course of study, whichever is less.

Number awarded Varies each year.

Deadline Deadline not specified.

[673]
PENNSYLVANIA GRANTS FOR CHILDREN OF SOLDIERS DECLARED POW/MIA

Pennsylvania Higher Education Assistance Agency
Attn: State Grant and Special Programs
1200 North Seventh Street
P.O. Box 8114
Harrisburg, PA 17105-8114
(717) 720-2800   Toll Free: (800) 692-7392
TDD: (717) 720-2366
Web: www.pheaa.org

Summary To provide financial assistance for college to the children of POWs/MIAs from Pennsylvania.

Eligibility This program is open to dependent children of members or former members of the U.S. armed services who served on active duty after January 31, 1955, who are or have been prisoners of war or are or have been listed as missing in action, and who were residents of Pennsylvania for at least 12 months preceding service on active duty. Eligible children must be enrolled in a program of at least 1 year in duration on at least a half-time basis at an approved school and must demonstrate financial need.

Financial Data The amount of the award depends on the financial need of the recipient, up to a maximum of $3,500 at a Pennsylvania school or $800 at a school outside of Pennsylvania that is approved for participation in the program.

Duration 1 year; may be renewed for 3 additional years.

Additional data With certain exceptions, recipients may attend any accredited college in the United States. Excluded from coverage are 2-year public colleges located outside Pennsylvania and schools in states bordering Pennsylvania that do not allow their state grant recipients to attend Pennsylvania schools (i.e., New York, Maryland, and New Jersey).

Number awarded Varies each year.

Deadline March of each year.

[674]
PENNSYLVANIA NATIONAL GUARD SCHOLARSHIP FUND

Pennsylvania National Guard Associations
Attn: Executive Director
Biddle Hall
Fort Indiantown Gap
Annville, PA 17003-5002
(717) 865-9631   Toll Free: (800) 997-8885
Fax: (717) 861-5560   E-mail: oswalddean@aol.com
Web: www.pngas.net/member.htm

Summary To provide financial assistance to Pennsylvania National Guard members and the children of disabled or deceased members who are interested in attending college in any state.

Eligibility This program is open to active members of the Pennsylvania Army or Air National Guard. Children of members of the Guard who died or were permanently disabled while on Guard duty are also eligible. Applicants must be entering their first year of higher education as a full-time student or presently attending a college or vocational school in any state as a full-time student. Along with their application, they must submit an essay that outlines their military and civilian plans for the future. Selection is based on that essay, academic achievement, leadership abilities, and contributions to citizenship.

Financial Data Stipends are $1,000 or $400.

Duration 1 year.

Additional data The sponsoring organization includes the National Guard Association of Pennsylvania and the Pennsylvania National Guard Enlisted Association. This program began in 1977.

Number awarded 23 each year: 3 at $1,000 and 20 at $400.

Deadline June of each year.

[675]
PENNSYLVANIA POSTSECONDARY EDUCATIONAL GRATUITY PROGRAM

Pennsylvania Higher Education Assistance Agency
Attn: State Grant and Special Programs
1200 North Seventh Street
P.O. Box 8114
Harrisburg, PA 17105-8114
(717) 720-2800   Toll Free: (800) 692-7392
TDD: (800) 654-5988   E-mail: info@pheaa.org
Web: www.pheaa.org

Summary To provide financial assistance for college to the children of Pennsylvania public service personnel who died in the line of service.

Eligibility This program is open to residents of Pennsylvania who are the children of 1) Pennsylvania police officers, fire fighters, rescue and ambulance squad members, corrections facility employees, or National Guard members who died in the line of duty after January 1, 1976; or 2) Pennsylvania sheriffs, deputy sheriffs, National Guard members, and certain other individuals on federal or state active military duty who died after September 11, 2001 as a direct result of performing their official duties. Applicants must be 25 years of age or younger and enrolled or accepted at a Pennsylvania community college, state-owned institution, or state-related institution as a full-time student working on an associate or baccalaureate degree. They must have already applied for other scholarships, including state and federal grants and financial aid from the postsecondary institution to which they are applying.

Financial Data Grants cover tuition, fees, room, and board charged by the institution, less awarded scholarships and federal and state grants.

Duration Up to 5 years.

Additional data This program began in the 1998-99 winter/spring term to cover service personnel who died after January 1, 1976. It was amended in 2004 to cover additional service personnel who died after September 11, 2001.

Number awarded Varies each year.

Deadline March of each year.

[676]
PENTAGON ASSISTANCE FUND

Navy-Marine Corps Relief Society
Attn: Education Division
875 North Randolph Street, Suite 225
Arlington, VA 22203-1757
(703) 696-4960   Fax: (703) 696-0144
E-mail: education@hq.nmcrs.org
Web: www.nmcrs.org/goldstar.html

Summary To provide financial assistance for college to the children and spouses of deceased military personnel who died at the Pentagon on September 11, 2001.

Eligibility This program is open to the children and spouses of deceased military personnel who died at the Pentagon as a result of the terrorist attack of September 11, 2001. Applicants must be enrolled or planning to enroll full time (spouses may enroll part time) at a college, university, or vocational/technical school. They must have a GPA of 2.0 or higher and be able to demonstrate financial need. Children must be 23 years of age or younger. Spouses may be eligible if the service member became disabled as a result of the attack.

Financial Data Stipends range from $500 to $2,500 per year. Funds are disbursed directly to the financial institution.

Duration 1 year; may be renewed up to 3 additional years.

Number awarded Varies each year.

Deadline Children must apply by February of each year. Spouses must apply at least 2 months prior to the start of their studies.

[677]
PETER CONNACHER MEMORIAL AMERICAN EX-PRISONER OF WAR SCHOLARSHIPS

Oregon Student Assistance Commission
Attn: Grants and Scholarships Division
1500 Valley River Drive, Suite 100
Eugene, OR 97401-2146
(541) 687-7395   Toll Free: (800) 452-8807, ext. 7395
Fax: (541) 687-7414   TDD: (800) 735-2900
E-mail: awardinfo@osac.state.or.us
Web: www.osac.state.or.us/osac_programs.html

Summary To provide financial assistance for college or graduate school to ex-prisoners of war and their descendants.

Eligibility Applicants must be U.S. citizens who 1) were military or civilian prisoners of war or 2) are the descendants of ex-prisoners of war. They may be undergraduate or graduate students. A copy of the ex-prisoner of war's discharge papers from the U.S. armed forces must accompany the application. In addition, written proof of POW status must be submitted, along with a statement of the relationship between the applicant and the ex-prisoner of war (father, grandfather, etc.). Selection is based on academic record and financial need. Preference is given to Oregon residents or their dependents.

Financial Data The stipend amount varies; recently, it was at least $1,150.

Duration 1 year; may be renewed for up to 3 additional years for undergraduate students or 2 additional years for graduate stu-

dents. Renewal is dependent on evidence of continued financial need and satisfactory academic progress.

Additional data This program is administered by the Oregon Student Assistance Commission (OSAC) with funds provided by the Oregon Community Foundation, 1221 S.W. Yamhill, Suite 100, Portland, OR 97205, (503) 227-6846, Fax: (503) 274-7771. Funds are also provided by the Columbia River Chapter of the American Ex-prisoners of War, Inc. Recipients must attend college on a full-time basis.

Number awarded Varies each year; recently, 4 of these scholarships were awarded.

Deadline February of each year.

[678]
PLANNING SYSTEMS INCORPORATED SCIENCE AND ENGINEERING SCHOLARSHIP

Navy League of the United States
Attn: Scholarships
2300 Wilson Boulevard, Suite 200
Arlington, VA 22201-5424
(703) 528-1775   Toll Free: (800) 356-5760
Fax: (703) 528-2333   E-mail: scholarships@navyleague.org
Web: www.navyleague.org/scholarship

Summary To provide financial assistance to dependent children of sea service personnel or veterans who are interested in majoring in science or engineering in college.

Eligibility This program is open to U.S. citizens who are dependent children of active or honorably discharged members of the U.S. sea service (including the Navy, Marine Corps, or Coast Guard). Applicants must be entering their freshman year at an accredited college or university and planning to major in science or engineering. They must have a GPA of 3.0 or higher. Along with their application, they must submit transcripts, 2 letters of recommendation, SAT/ACT scores, documentation of financial need, proof of qualifying sea service duty, and a 1-page personal statement on why they should be considered for this scholarship.

Financial Data The stipend is $2,500 per year.

Duration 4 years, provided the recipient maintains a GPA of 3.0 or higher.

Number awarded 1 each year.

Deadline February of each year.

[679]
PRAIRIE MINUTEMAN SCHOLARSHIP

National Guard Association of Illinois
Attn: Executive Vice President
P.O. Box 8228
Melrose Park, IL 60161-8228
(708) 343-1945   Fax: (708) 343-1989
E-mail: exvpil@ngai.com
Web: www.ngai.com/service.html

Summary To provide financial assistance to dependents of members of the National Guard Association of Illinois (NGAI) who are interested in attending college in any state.

Eligibility This program is open to dependents (children and spouses) of NGAI members in good standing. Applicants may be high school seniors, high school graduates, or currently-enrolled students at a college or university in any state. They must submit a completed application form, official transcripts, 2 letters of recommendation, a verified copy of their ACT/SAT scores, and a 250-word essay on their scholastic and professional goals and aspirations. Financial need is also considered in the selection process.

Financial Data The stipend is $1,000 or $500.

Duration 1 year.

Number awarded 3 each year: 1 at $1,000 to an Illinois Army National Guard dependent, 1 at $1,000 to an Illinois Air National Guard dependent, and 1 at $500 (sponsored by USAA Insurance

Corporation) to an enlisted Illinois National Guard dependent who is also a member of NGAI.

Deadline Applications must be submitted at least 45 days prior to the sponsor's annual conference. The conference is usually in late April, so applications are due in mid-March.

[680]
PVA EDUCATIONAL SCHOLARSHIP PROGRAM

Paralyzed Veterans of America
Attn: Education and Training Foundation
801 18th Street, N.W.
Washington, DC 20006-3517
(202) 416-7651   Fax: (202) 416-7641
TDD: (202) 416-7622   E-mail: foundations@pva.org
Web: www.pva.org

Summary To provide financial assistance for college to members of the Paralyzed Veterans of America (PVA) and their families.

Eligibility This program is open to PVA members, spouses of members, and unmarried dependent children of members under 24 years of age. Applicants must be attending or planning to attend an accredited U.S. college or university. They must be U.S. citizens. Along with their application, they must submit a personal statement explaining why they wish to further their education, short- and long-term academic goals, how this will meet their career objectives, and how it will affect their PVA membership. Selection is based on that statement, academic records, letters of recommendation, and extracurricular and community activities.

Financial Data Stipends are $1,000 for full-time students or $500 for part-time students.

Duration 1 year.

Additional data This program was established in 1986.

Number awarded Varies each year; recently 14 full-time and 3 part-time students received these scholarships. Since this program was established, it has awarded more than $300,000 in scholarships.

Deadline May of each year.

[681]
RADM WILLIAM A. SULLIVAN, USN (RET.) SCHOLARSHIP

Navy League of the United States
Attn: Scholarships
2300 Wilson Boulevard, Suite 200
Arlington, VA 22201-5424
(703) 528-1775   Toll Free: (800) 356-5760
Fax: (703) 528-2333   E-mail: scholarships@navyleague.org
Web: www.navyleague.org/scholarship

Summary To provide financial assistance for college to dependent children of sea service personnel and veterans.

Eligibility This program is open to U.S. citizens who are 1) dependents or direct descendants of an active, Reserve, retired, or honorably discharged member of the U.S. sea service (including the Navy, Marine Corps, Coast Guard, or Merchant Marines), or 2) currently an active member of the Naval Sea Cadet Corps. Applicants must be entering their freshman year at an accredited college or university. They must have a GPA of 3.0 or higher. Along with their application, they must submit transcripts, 2 letters of recommendation, SAT/ACT scores, documentation of financial need, proof of qualifying sea service duty, and a 1-page personal statement on why they should be considered for this scholarship. Preference is given to applicants who reside in or near the San Diego, California area.

Financial Data The stipend is $2,500 per year.

Duration 4 years, provided the recipient maintains a GPA of 3.0 or higher.

Number awarded 1 each year.

Deadline February of each year.

[682]
RAYMOND T. WELLINGTON, JR. MEMORIAL SCHOLARSHIP

American Legion Auxiliary
Department of New York
112 State Street, Suite 1310
Albany, NY 12207
(518) 463-1162   Toll Free: (800) 421-6348
Fax: (518) 449-5406   E-mail: alanyterry@nycap.rr.com
Web: www.deptny.org/Scholarships.htm

Summary To provide financial assistance to New York residents who are the descendants of veterans and interested in attending college in any state.

Eligibility This program is open to residents of New York who are high school seniors or graduates and attending or planning to attend an accredited college or university in any state. Applicants must be the children, grandchildren, or great-grandchildren of veterans who served during specified periods of war time. Along with their application, they must submit a 700-word autobiography that includes their interests, experiences, long-range plans, and goals. Selection is based on character (15%), Americanism (15%), community involvement (15%), leadership (15%), scholarship (20%), and financial need (20%). U.S. citizenship is required.

Financial Data The stipend is $1,000. Funds are paid directly to the recipient's school.

Duration 1 year.

Number awarded 1 each year.

Deadline February of each year.

[683]
RED RIVER VALLEY FIGHTER PILOTS ASSOCIATION SCHOLARSHIP GRANT PROGRAM

Red River Valley Association Foundation
Attn: Executive Director
P.O. Box 1553
Front Royal, VA 22630-0033
(540) 639-9798   Toll Free: (866) 401-7287
Fax: (540) 636-9776   E-mail: ExecutiveOffice@river-rats.org
Web: www.river-rats.org/about_us/scholarship.php

Summary To provide financial assistance for college or graduate school to the spouses and children of selected service personnel and members of the Red River Valley Fighter Pilots Association.

Eligibility This program is open to the spouses and children of 1) servicemembers missing in action (MIA) or killed in action (KIA) in combat situations involving U.S. military forces from August 1964 through the present; 2) U.S. military aircrew members killed in a non-combat aircraft accident in which they were performing aircrew duties; and 3) current members of the association and deceased members who were in good standing at the time of their death. Scholarships are also available to students in fields related to aviation and space, even if they have no kinship relationship to a deceased aviator or member of the association. Applicants must be interested in attending an accredited college or university to work on an undergraduate or graduate degree. Selection is based on demonstrated academic achievement, college entrance examination scores, financial need, and accomplishments in school, church, civic, and social activities.

Financial Data The amount awarded varies, depending upon the need of the recipient. Recently, undergraduate stipends have ranged from $500 to $3,500 and averaged $1,725; graduate stipends have ranged from $500 to $2,000 and averaged $1,670. Funds are paid directly to the recipient's institution and are to be used for tuition, fees, books, and room and board for full-time students.

Duration 1 year; may be renewed if the recipient maintains a GPA of 2.0 or higher.

Additional data This program was established in 1970, out of concern for the families of aircrews (known as "River Rats") who were killed or missing in action in the Red River Valley of North Vietnam.

Number awarded Varies each year; since this program was established, it has awarded more than 1,000 scholarships worth more than $1,700,000.

Deadline May of each year.

[684]
REMISSION OF FEES FOR CHILDREN OF INDIANA VETERANS

Indiana Department of Veterans' Affairs
302 West Washington Street, Room E-120
Indianapolis, IN 46204-2738
(317) 232-3910   Toll Free: (800) 400-4520 (within IN)
Fax: (317) 232-7721
Web: www.in.gov/dva/2378.htm

Summary To enable the children of disabled and other Indiana veterans to attend public colleges and universities in the state without payment of tuition.

Eligibility This program is open to natural and legally-adopted children of veterans who served on active duty in the U.S. armed forces during a period of wartime and have been residents of Indiana for at least 36 consecutive months during their lifetimes. The veteran must 1) have sustained a service-connected disability as verified by the U.S. Department of Veterans Affairs or a military service; 2) have received a Purple Heart Medal; or 3) have been a resident of Indiana at the time of entry into the service and declared a prisoner of war (POW) or missing in action (MIA) after January 1, 1960. Students who were veteran-related pupils at the Indiana Soldiers' and Sailors' Children's Home are also eligible. Applicants must be attending or planning to attend a state-supported postsecondary college or university in Indiana as an undergraduate or graduate student.

Financial Data Qualified students receive remission of 100% of tuition and mandatory fees.

Duration Fees are remitted for up to 124 semester hours of education.

Number awarded Varies each year.

Deadline Requests for assistance may be submitted at any time.

[685]
RENEE FELDMAN SCHOLARSHIPS

Blinded Veterans Association Auxiliary
c/o Barbara Stocking, Scholarship Chair
3801 Coco Grove Avenue
Miami, FL 33133
(305) 446-8008

Summary To provide financial assistance for college to spouses and children of blinded veterans.

Eligibility This program is open to children and spouses of blinded veterans who are attending or planning to attend a college, university, community college, or vocational school. The veteran is not required to be a member of the Blinded Veterans Association. Applicants must submit a 300-word essay on their career goals and aspirations. Selection is based on that essay, academic achievement, and letters of reference.

Financial Data Stipends are $2,000 or $1,000. Funds are paid directly to the recipient's school to be applied to tuition, books, and general fees.

Duration 1 year.

Number awarded 5 each year: 3 at $2,000 and 2 at $1,000.

Deadline April of each year.

[686]
RICHARD T. NUSKE MEMORIAL SCHOLARSHIPS

Vietnam Veterans of America-Wisconsin State Council
c/o Virginia Nuske, Scholarship Committee Chair
N5448 Broder Road
Shawano, WI 54166
(715) 524-2487
Web: www.vva.org/vva-wisconsin.html

Summary To recognize and reward high school seniors in Wisconsin who submit outstanding essays based on an interview of a Vietnam veteran, especially if the veteran is a relative.

Eligibility This competition is open to seniors graduating from high schools in Wisconsin who plan to attend an accredited institution of higher education in any state. Applicants must submit an essay, from 3 to 5 pages in length, based on an interview of a veteran of any branch who served on active duty anywhere in the world during the Vietnam War (from January 1, 1959 to May 7, 1975). Essays are judged on originality, appearance, and elements of grammar; up to 30 points may be awarded, depending on the quality of the essay. An additional 15 points are awarded if the student is the child or grandchild of the veteran; an additional 5 points are awarded if the student is another relative (niece, cousin) of the veteran.

Financial Data The award is a $1,500 scholarship that may be used at a college or university in any state.

Duration The awards are presented annually.

Number awarded 4 each year.

Deadline January of each year.

[687]
ROBERT H. CONNAL EDUCATION AWARDS

Enlisted Association of the New York National Guard, Inc.
Attn: Education Awards Chair
330 Old Niskayuna Road
Latham, NY 12110-2224
(518) 344-2670   E-mail: awards@eanyng.org
Web: www.eanyng.org/AwardsandScholarships.html

Summary To provide financial assistance to members of the Enlisted Association of the New York National Guard (EANYNG) and their families who are interested in attending college in any state.

Eligibility This program is open to EANYNG members and their spouses, children, and grandchildren. Applicants must be high school seniors or current undergraduate at a college or university in any state. The applicant or sponsor must have belonged to EANYNG for more than 1 year. Membership in EANYNG is limited to enlisted personnel in the New York Air or Army National Guard. Selection is based on academic achievement, community service, extracurricular activities, and leadership abilities.

Financial Data Stipends are $1,000 or $500.

Duration 1 year.

Additional data Funding for this program is provided by the production of the association's yearly journal, members' dues, and a donation from USAA Insurance Corporation.

Number awarded 7 each year: 1 statewide scholarship at $1,000 and 6 at $500 in each region of the state.

Deadline February of each year.

[688]
ROSEDALE POST 346 SCHOLARSHIP FUND

American Legion
Department of Kansas
1314 S.W. Topeka Boulevard
Topeka, KS 66612-1886
(785) 232-9315   Fax: (785) 232-1399
Web: www.ksamlegion.org/programs.htm

Summary To provide financial assistance to the children of members of the Kansas American Legion or American Legion Auxiliary who are interested in attending college in any state.

Eligibility This program is open to high school seniors and college freshmen and sophomores who are attending or planning to attend an approved college, university, junior college, or trade school in any state. At least 1 of their parents must be a veteran and have been a member of an American Legion post or Auxiliary in Kansas for at least 3 consecutive years. Along with their application, they must submit an essay of 250 to 500 words on "Why I Want to Go to College." Financial need is also considered in the selection process.

Financial Data The stipend is $1,500.

Duration 1 year; nonrenewable.

Number awarded 2 each year.

Deadline February of each year.

[689]
RUBY LORRAINE PAUL SCHOLARSHIP FUND

American Legion Auxiliary
Department of Nebraska
P.O. Box 5227
Lincoln, NE 68505-0227
(402) 466-1808   Fax: (402) 466-0182
E-mail: neaux@windstream.net
Web: www.nebraskalegionaux.net/scholarships.htm

Summary To provide financial assistance to students in Nebraska who have a connection to the American Legion and plan to attend college in any state and study any field except nursing.

Eligibility Applicants must have been residents of Nebraska for at least 3 years and either 1) have been a member for at least 2 years of the American Legion, American Legion Auxiliary, or Sons of the American Legion, or 2) be the child, grandchild, or great-grandchild of an American Legion or American Legion Auxiliary member who has been a member for at least 2 years. They must be high school seniors or graduates who maintained a GPA of 3.0 or higher during the last 2 semesters of high school and have been accepted at an accredited college or university in any state to study any field except nursing. Financial need is considered in the selection process.

Financial Data A stipend is awarded (amount not specified).

Duration 1 year.

Number awarded 1 each year.

Deadline February of each year.

[690]
SAD SACKS NURSING SCHOLARSHIP

AMVETS-Department of Illinois
2200 South Sixth Street
Springfield, IL 62703
(217) 528-4713   Toll Free: (800) 638-VETS (within IL)
Fax: (217) 528-9896
Web: www.ilamvets.org/prog_scholarships.cfm

Summary To provide financial assistance for nursing education to Illinois residents, especially descendants of disabled or deceased veterans.

Eligibility This program is open to seniors at high schools in Illinois who have been accepted to an approved nursing program and students already enrolled in an approved school of nursing in Illinois. Selection is based on academic record, character, interest and activity record, and financial need. Preference is given to students in the following order: third-year students, second-year students, and first-year students.

Financial Data A stipend is awarded (amount not specified).

Duration 1 year.

Number awarded Varies each year; recently, 3 of these scholarships were awarded.

Deadline February of each year.

[691]
SAM ROSE MEMORIAL SCHOLARSHIP

Ladies Auxiliary of the Fleet Reserve Association
Attn: Administrator
P.O. Box 490678
Everett, MA 02149-0012
(617) 548-1191   E-mail: msakathy@live.com
Web: www.la-fra.org/scholarship.html

Summary To provide financial assistance for college to the children and grandchildren of deceased members of the Fleet Reserve Association (FRA).

Eligibility This program is open to children and grandchildren of deceased members of the association or those who were eligible to be members at the time of death. Applicants must submit an essay on their life experiences, career objectives, and what motivated them to select those objectives. Selection is based on academic record, financial need, extracurricular activities, leadership skills, and participation in community activities. U.S. citizenship is required.

Financial Data The stipend is $2,500.

Duration 1 year.

Additional data Membership in the FRA is open to active-duty, retired, and Reserve members of the Navy, Marine Corps, and Coast Guard.

Number awarded 1 each year.

Deadline April of each year.

[692]
SAMSUNG AMERICAN LEGION SCHOLARSHIPS

American Legion
Attn: Americanism and Children & Youth Division
700 North Pennsylvania Street
P.O. Box 1055
Indianapolis, IN 46206-1055
(317) 630-1202   Fax: (317) 630-1223
E-mail: acy@legion.org
Web: www.legion.org/programs/resources/scholarships

Summary To provide financial assistance for college to descendants of veterans who participate in Girls State or Boys State.

Eligibility This program is open to students entering their senior year of high school who are selected to participate in Girls State or Boys State, sponsored by the American Legion Auxiliary or American Legion in their state. Applicants must be the child, grandchild, or great-grandchild of a veteran who saw active-duty service during specified periods of war time. Finalists are chosen at each participating Girls and Boys State, and they are then nominated for the national awards. Selection is based on academic record, community service, involvement in school and community activities, and financial need. Special consideration is given to descendants of U.S. veterans of the Korean War.

Financial Data Stipends are $20,000 or $1,000.

Duration 4 years.

Additional data These scholarships were first presented in 1996, following a gift in July 1995 to the American Legion from Samsung Corporation of Korea, as an act of appreciation for U.S. involvement in the Korean War.

Number awarded Varies each year; recently, 10 scholarships at $20,000 and 88 at $1,000 were awarded.

Deadline Deadline not specified.

[693]
SCHNEIDER-EMANUEL AMERICAN LEGION SCHOLARSHIPS

American Legion
Department of Wisconsin
2930 American Legion Drive
P.O. Box 388
Portage, WI 53901-0388
(608) 745-1090 Fax: (608) 745-0179
E-mail: info@wilegion.org
Web: www.wilegion.org

Summary To provide financial assistance to members of the American Legion in Wisconsin and their children or grandchildren who plan to attend college in any state.

Eligibility This program is open to seniors and graduates from accredited Wisconsin high schools. Applicants must be at least 1 of the following 1) a child whose father, mother, or legal guardian is a member of the Department of Wisconsin of the American Legion, American Legion Auxiliary, or Sons of the American Legion; 2) a grandchild whose grandfather, grandmother, or legal guardian is a member of the Department of Wisconsin of the American Legion, American Legion Auxiliary, or Sons of the American Legion; 3) a member of the Sons of the American Legion, American Legion Auxiliary, or Junior American Legion Auxiliary; or 4) a veteran and an American Legion member in Wisconsin. Applicants must have participated in Legion and Auxiliary youth programs. They must be planning to attend a college or university in any state. Selection is based on moral character; scholastic excellence (GPA of 3.0 or higher); participation and accomplishment in American Legion affiliated activities; and personality, leadership, and participation in general extracurricular activities.

Financial Data The stipend is $1,000.

Duration 1 year.

Number awarded 3 each year.

Deadline February of each year.

[694]
SCHUYLER S. PYLE SCHOLARSHIP

Fleet Reserve Association
Attn: Scholarship Administrator
125 North West Street
Alexandria, VA 22314-2754
(703) 683-1400 Toll Free: (800) FRA-1924
Fax: (703) 549-6610 E-mail: fra@fra.org
Web: www.fra.org

Summary To provide financial assistance for college or graduate school to members of the Fleet Reserve Association (FRA) who are current or former naval personnel and their spouses and children.

Eligibility This program is open to dependent children, grandchildren, and spouses of FRA members who are in good standing (or were at the time of death, if deceased). FRA members are also eligible. Applicants must be working on or planning to work on an undergraduate or graduate degree. Along with their application, they must submit an essay on their life experiences, career objectives, and what motivated them to select those objectives. Selection is based on academic record, financial need, extracurricular activities, leadership skills, and participation in community activities. U.S. citizenship is required.

Financial Data The stipend is $5,000 per year.

Duration 1 year; may be renewed.

Additional data Membership in the FRA is restricted to active-duty, retired, and Reserve members of the Navy, Marine Corps, and Coast Guard.

Number awarded 1 each year.

Deadline April of each year.

[695]
SCOTT B. LUNDELL TUITION WAIVER FOR MILITARY MEMBERS' SURVIVING DEPENDENTS

Utah Division of Veteran's Affairs
Attn: Director
550 Foothill Boulevard, Room 202
Salt Lake City, UT 84108
(801) 326-2372 Toll Free: (800) 894-9497 (within UT)
Fax: (801) 326-2369 E-mail: veterans@utah.gov
Web: veterans.utah.gov/homepage/stateBenefits/index.html

Summary To provide a tuition waiver to residents of Utah who are dependents of deceased military personnel and attending a public institution in the state.

Eligibility This program is open to residents of Utah who are dependents of military members killed in the line of duty after September 11, 2001. Applicants must be working on an undergraduate degree at a public college or university in the state.

Financial Data Tuition is waived for qualified dependents.

Duration Tuition is waived until completion of a bachelor's degree.

Additional data This program was established in 2007.

Number awarded Varies each year.

Deadline Deadline not specified.

[696]
SERGEANT FELIX M. DELGRECO, JR. SCHOLARSHIP FUND

Connecticut Community Foundation
43 Field Street
Waterbury, CT 06702-1906
(203) 753-1315 Fax: (203) 756-3054
E-mail: jcarey@conncf.org
Web: www.conncf.org/scholarships

Summary To provide financial assistance to high school seniors and current college students whose parents are members of the Connecticut Army National Guard.

Eligibility This program is open to the children of members of the Connecticut Army National Guard who are attending or planning to attend college in any state. Applicants must have a GPA of "B-" or higher. Selection is based on academic motivation, extracurricular activities, work experience, a letter of recommendation, financial need, and an essay. U.S. citizenship is required.

Financial Data The stipend is $3,000 per year. Funds are paid directly to the recipient's school.

Duration 1 year; recipients may reapply up to the minimum number of years required to complete an undergraduate degree in their course of study, provided they maintain a GPA of "C+" or higher.

Additional data This program is supported by the Connecticut National Guard Foundation.

Number awarded Varies each year.

Deadline March of each year.

[697]
SERGEANT MAJOR DOUGLAS R. DRUM MEMORIAL SCHOLARSHIP

American Military Retirees Association, Inc.
Attn: Scholarship Committee
5436 Peru Street, Suite 1
Plattsburgh, NY 12901
(518) 563-9479 Toll Free: (800) 424-2969
Fax: (518) 324-5204 E-mail: info@amra1973.org
Web: www.amra1973.org/scholarship.asp

Summary To provide financial assistance for college to members of the American Military Retirees Association (AMRA) and their dependents.

Eligibility This program is open to current members of AMRA and their dependents, children, and grandchildren. Applicants must be attending or planning to attend an accredited college or university. Along with their application, they must submit a 500-word essay on why they deserve this scholarship. Selection is based on academic achievement, leadership abilities, character, citizenship, and community service.

Financial Data The stipend is $1,000.

Duration 1 year.

Additional data Membership in AMRA is open to all retired members of the armed forces, regardless of rank.

Number awarded Varies each year; recently, 24 of these scholarships were awarded.

Deadline February of each year.

[698]
SFC CURTIS MANCINI MEMORIAL SCHOLARSHIPS

Association of the United States Army-Rhode Island Chapter
c/o CSM (Ret) Anthony Ferri, Secretary
47 Spokane Street
Providence, RI 02904
(401) 861-2997   E-mail: afnf458673755@aol.com
Web: www.ausari.org/index.html

Summary To provide financial assistance to members of the Rhode Island Chapter of the Association of the United States Army (AUSA) and their families who are interested in attending college or graduate school in any state.

Eligibility This program is open to members of the AUSA Rhode Island Chapter and their family members (spouses, children, and grandchildren). Applicants must be high school seniors or graduates accepted at an accredited college, university, or vocational/technical school in any state or current undergraduate or graduate students. Along with their application, they must submit a 250-word essay on why they feel their achievements should qualify them for this award. Selection is based on academic and individual achievements; financial need is not considered. Membership in AUSA is open to current and retired Army personnel (including Reserves and National Guard), ROTC cadets, or civilian employees of the Army.

Financial Data The stipend is $1,000.

Duration 1 year.

Number awarded 2 each year.

Deadline March of each year.

[699]
SONS OF UNION VETERANS OF THE CIVIL WAR SCHOLARSHIPS

Sons of Union Veterans of the Civil War
P.O. Box 1865
Harrisburg, PA 17105
(717) 232-7000   E-mail: suvcinc@aol.com
Web: www.suvcw.org/scholar.htm

Summary To provide financial assistance for college to descendants of Union Civil War veterans.

Eligibility This program is open to high school seniors and students currently enrolled at a 4-year college or university. Applicants must 1) rank in the upper quarter of their high school graduating class (preferably in the upper tenth); 2) have a record of performance in school and community activities; 3) have an interest in and positive attitude toward college; 4) provide 3 letters of recommendation; and 5) submit an official grade transcript. Males must be a current member or associate of Sons of Union Veterans of the Civil War. Females must be the daughter or granddaughter of a current member or associate of Sons of Union Veterans of the Civil War and a current member of at least 1 of the following organizations: Woman's Relief Corps, Ladies of the Grand Army of the Republic, Daughters of Union Veterans of the Civil War

1861-1865, or Auxiliary to the Sons of Union Veterans of the Civil War. Financial need is not considered in the selection process.

Financial Data The stipend is $1,000. Funds are to be used for tuition and books. Checks are mailed directly to the recipient's school.

Duration 1 year.

Number awarded 2 each year.

Deadline March of each year.

[700]
SOUTH CAROLINA TUITION PROGRAM FOR CHILDREN OF CERTAIN WAR VETERANS

South Carolina Division of Veterans Affairs
c/o VA Regional Office Building
6437 Garners Ferry Road, Suite 1126
Columbia, SC 29209
(803) 647-2434   Fax: (803) 647-2312
E-mail: va@oepp.sc.gov
Web: www.govoepp.state.sc.us/va/benefits.html

Summary To provide free college tuition to the children of disabled and other South Carolina veterans.

Eligibility This program is open to the children of wartime veterans who were legal residents of South Carolina both at the time of entry into military or naval service and during service, or who have been residents of South Carolina for at least 1 year. Veteran parents must 1) be permanently and totally disabled as determined by the U.S. Department of Veterans Affairs; 2) have been a prisoner of war; 3) have been killed in action; 4) have died from other causes while in service; 5) have died of a disease or disability resulting from service; 6) be currently missing in action; 7) have received the Congressional Medal of Honor; 8) have received the Purple Heart Medal from wounds received in combat; or 9) now be deceased but qualified under categories 1 or 2 above. The veteran's child must be 26 years of age or younger and working on an undergraduate degree.

Financial Data Children who qualify are eligible for free tuition at any South Carolina state-supported college, university, or postsecondary technical education institution. The waiver applies to tuition only. The costs of room and board, certain fees, and books are not covered.

Duration Students are eligible to receive this support as long as they are younger than 26 years of age and working on an undergraduate degree.

Number awarded Varies each year.

Deadline Deadline not specified.

[701]
SOUTH DAKOTA FREE TUITION FOR CHILDREN OF RESIDENTS WHO DIED DURING SERVICE IN THE ARMED FORCES

South Dakota Board of Regents
Attn: Scholarship Committee
306 East Capitol Avenue, Suite 200
Pierre, SD 57501-2545
(605) 773-3455   Fax: (605) 773-2422
E-mail: info@sdbor.edu
Web: www.sdbor.edu/student/prospective/Military.htm

Summary To provide free tuition at South Dakota public colleges and universities to children of military personnel who died while in service.

Eligibility This program is open to residents of South Dakota younger than 25 years of age. The applicant's parent must have been killed in action or died of other causes while on active duty and must have been a resident of South Dakota for at least 6 months immediately preceding entry into active service.

Financial Data Eligible children are entitled to attend any South Dakota state-supported institution of higher education or state-supported technical or vocational school free of tuition and mandatory fees.

Duration 8 semesters or 12 quarters of either full- or part-time study.

Number awarded Varies each year.

Deadline Deadline not specified.

[702]
SOUTH DAKOTA FREE TUITION FOR DEPENDENTS OF PRISONERS OR MISSING IN ACTION

South Dakota Board of Regents
Attn: Scholarship Committee
306 East Capitol Avenue, Suite 200
Pierre, SD 57501-2545
(605) 773-3455   Fax: (605) 773-2422
E-mail: info@sdbor.edu
Web: www.sdbor.edu

Summary To provide free tuition at South Dakota public colleges and universities to dependents of prisoners of war (POWs) and persons missing in action (MIAs).

Eligibility This program is open to residents of South Dakota who are the spouses or children of POWs or of MIAs. Applicants may not be eligible for equal or greater benefits from any federal financial assistance program.

Financial Data Eligible dependents are entitled to attend any South Dakota state-supported institution of higher education or state-supported technical or vocational school free of tuition and mandatory fees.

Duration 8 semesters or 12 quarters of either full- or part-time study.

Additional data Recipients must attend a state-supported school in South Dakota.

Number awarded Varies each year.

Deadline Deadline not specified.

[703]
SPECIAL OPERATIONS WARRIOR FOUNDATION SCHOLARSHIPS

Special Operations Warrior Foundation
4409 El Prado Boulevard
P.O. Box 13483
Tampa, FL 33681-3483
(813) 805-9400   Toll Free: (877) 337-7693
Fax: (813) 805-0567   E-mail: warrior@specialops.org
Web: www.specialops.org/?page=ScholarshipProgram

Summary To provide financial assistance for college to the children of Special Operations personnel who died in training or operational missions.

Eligibility This program is open to the children of parents who served in Special Operations and were killed in a training accident or an operational mission. This is an entitlement program; all eligible students receive support.

Financial Data A stipend is awarded (amount not specified). Funding is based on need and is intended to ensure payment of the full cost of tuition, fees, room, board, books, and supplies.

Duration 4 years or more.

Additional data This program was established in 1980 because of the high casualty rates experienced by personnel of U.S. Special Operations Command.

Number awarded Varies each year. Recently, 125 students were receiving support from this foundation.

Deadline Applications may be submitted at any time.

[704]
SPIRIT OF YOUTH SCHOLARSHIP FOR JUNIOR MEMBERS

American Legion Auxiliary
8945 North Meridian Street
Indianapolis, IN 46260
(317) 569-4500   Fax: (317) 569-4502
E-mail: alahq@legion-aux.org
Web: www.legion-aux.org

Summary To provide financial assistance for college to junior members of the American Legion Auxiliary.

Eligibility Applicants for this scholarship must have been junior members of the Auxiliary for at least the past 3 years. They must be seniors at an accredited high school in the United States, have a GPA of 3.0 or higher, and be planning to enroll full time at a college, university, or professional or technical school that awards a certificate upon completion of an accredited course. Along with their application, they must submit a 1,000-word essay on a topic that changes annually; recently, students were asked to write on "The Future-Serving My Community and Our Veterans." Selection is based on that essay (30%), character and leadership (30%), and academic record (40%). Each unit of the Auxiliary may select a candidate for application to the department level, and each department submits a candidate for the national award.

Financial Data The stipend is $1,000 per year.

Duration 4 years.

Additional data Applications are available from the president of the candidate's own unit or from the secretary or education chair of the department.

Number awarded 5 each year: 1 in each division of the American Legion Auxiliary.

Deadline Applications must be submitted to the unit president by February of each year.

[705]
SSGT ROBERT V. MILNER MEMORIAL SCHOLARSHIP

American Academy of Physician Assistants-Veterans Caucus
Attn: Veterans Caucus
P.O. Box 362
Danville, PA 17821-0362
(570) 271-0292   Fax: (570) 271-5850
E-mail: admin@veteranscaucus.org
Web: www.veteranscaucus.org

Summary To provide financial assistance to children of past or present members of the Air Force who are studying to become physician assistants.

Eligibility This program is open to U.S. citizens who are currently enrolled in a physician assistant program. The program must be approved by the Commission on Accreditation of Allied Health Education. Applicants must be children of current members or honorably discharged members of the U.S. Air Force. Selection is based on military honors and awards received, civic and college honors and awards received, professional memberships and activities, and GPA. For children of veterans, an electronic copy of the sponsor's DD Form 214 must accompany the application.

Financial Data The stipend is $2,000.

Duration 1 year.

Number awarded 1 each year.

Deadline February of each year.

[706]
STANLEY A. DORAN MEMORIAL SCHOLARSHIPS

Fleet Reserve Association
Attn: Scholarship Administrator
125 North West Street
Alexandria, VA 22314-2754
(703) 683-1400   Toll Free: (800) FRA-1924
Fax: (703) 549-6610   E-mail: fra@fra.org
Web: www.fra.org

Summary To provide financial assistance for college or graduate school to children of members of the Fleet Reserve Association (FRA) who are current or former naval personnel.

Eligibility This program is open to the dependent children of FRA members who are in good standing (or were at the time of death, if deceased). Applicants must be working on or planning to work on an undergraduate or graduate degree. Along with their application, they must submit an essay on their life experiences, career objectives, and what motivated them to select those objectives. Selection is based on academic record, financial need, extracurricular activities, leadership skills, and participation in community activities. U.S. citizenship is required.

Financial Data The amount awarded varies, depending on the needs of the recipient and the funds available.

Duration 1 year; may be renewed.

Additional data Membership in the FRA is restricted to active-duty, retired, and Reserve members of the Navy, Marine Corps, and Coast Guard.

Number awarded 3 each year.

Deadline April of each year.

[707]
STUTZ MEMORIAL SCHOLARSHIP

American Legion
Department of New Jersey
Attn: Scholarship Judges
135 West Hanover Street
Trenton, NJ 08618
(609) 695-5418   Fax: (609) 394-1532
E-mail: newjersey@legion.org
Web: www.njamericanlegion.org

Summary To provide financial assistance to the children of members of the American Legion's New Jersey Department who plan to attend college in any state.

Eligibility This program is open to graduating high school seniors who are the natural or adopted children of members of the American Legion's New Jersey Department. Applicants must be planning to attend a college or university in any state. Selection is based on character (20%), Americanism (20%), leadership (20%), scholarship (20%), and financial need (20%).

Financial Data The stipend is $1,000 per year.

Duration 4 years.

Number awarded 1 each year.

Deadline February of each year.

[708]
SUBIC BAY-CUBI POINT SCHOLARSHIP

Navy League of the United States
Attn: Scholarships
2300 Wilson Boulevard, Suite 200
Arlington, VA 22201-5424
(703) 528-1775   Toll Free: (800) 356-5760
Fax: (703) 528-2333   E-mail: scholarships@navyleague.org
Web: www.navyleague.org/scholarship

Summary To provide financial assistance for college to dependent children of sea service personnel or veterans who were attached to U.S. Naval Facility commands in the Philippines during specified times.

Eligibility This program is open to U.S. citizens who are 1) dependents or direct descendants of an active, Reserve, retired, or honorably discharged member of the U.S. sea service (including the Navy, Marine Corps, Coast Guard, or Merchant Marines), or 2) currently an active member of the Naval Sea Cadet Corps. Applicants must be entering their freshman year at an accredited college or university. They must have a GPA of 3.0 or higher. Along with their application, they must submit transcripts, 2 letters of recommendation, SAT/ACT scores, documentation of financial need, proof of qualifying sea service duty, and a 1-page personal statement on why they should be considered for this scholarship. Preference is given to dependents of sea service personnel who were permanently attached to the U.S. Naval Facility commands at Subic Bay, Cubi Point, or San Miguel in the Philippines between January 1980 and December 1992. There is no citizenship restriction for this scholarship.

Financial Data The stipend is $2,500 per year.

Duration 4 years, provided the recipient maintains a GPA of 3.0 or higher.

Number awarded 1 each year.

Deadline February of each year.

[709]
SURVIVING DEPENDENTS OF MONTANA NATIONAL GUARD MEMBER WAIVER

Montana Guaranteed Student Loan Program
2500 Broadway
P.O. Box 203101
Helena, MT 59620-3101
(406) 444-0638   Toll Free: (800) 537-7508
Fax: (406) 444-1869 E-mail: scholarships@mgslp.state.mt.us
Web: www.mgslp.state.mt.us

Summary To provide financial assistance for undergraduate study to dependents of deceased National Guard members in Montana.

Eligibility Eligible for this benefit are residents of Montana who are surviving spouses or children of Montana National Guard members killed as a result of injury, disease, or other disability incurred in the line of duty while serving on state active duty. Financial need is considered.

Financial Data Students eligible for this benefit are entitled to attend any unit of the Montana University System without payment of undergraduate registration or incidental fees.

Duration Undergraduate students are eligible for continued fee waiver as long as they maintain reasonable academic progress as full-time students.

Additional data The waiver does not apply if the recipient is eligible for educational benefits from any governmental or private program that provides comparable benefits.

Number awarded Varies each year.

Deadline Deadline not specified.

[710]
SURVIVORS' AND DEPENDENTS' EDUCATIONAL ASSISTANCE PROGRAM

Department of Veterans Affairs
Attn: Veterans Benefits Administration
810 Vermont Avenue, N.W.
Washington, DC 20420
(202) 418-4343   Toll Free: (888) GI-BILL1
Web: www.gibill.va.gov/GI_Bill_Info/benefits.htm

Summary To provide financial assistance for undergraduate or graduate study to children and spouses of deceased and disabled veterans, MIAs, and POWs.

Eligibility Eligible for this assistance are spouses and children of 1) veterans who died or are permanently and totally disabled as the result of active service in the armed forces; 2) veterans who died from any cause while rated permanently and totally disabled from a service-connected disability; 3) servicemembers listed as missing in action or captured in the line of duty by a hostile force; 4) servicemembers listed as forcibly detained or interned by a foreign government or power; and 5) servicemembers who are hospitalized or receiving outpatient treatment for a service-connected permanent and total disability and are likely to be discharged for that disability. Children must be between 18 and 26 years of age, although extensions may be granted. Spouses and children over 14 years of age with physical or mental disabilities are also eligible.

Financial Data Monthly stipends from this program for study at an academic institution are $925 for full time, $694 for three-quarter time, or $461 for half-time. For farm cooperative work, the monthly stipends are $745 for full-time, $559 for three-quarter time, or $372 for half-time. For an apprenticeship or on-the-job training, the monthly stipend is $674 for the first 6 months, $505 for the second 6 months, $333 for the third 6 months, and $168 for the remainder of the program. For special restorative training by beneficiaries with a physical or mental disability, the monthly stipend for full-time training is $925.

Duration Up to 45 months (or the equivalent in part-time training). Spouses must complete their training within 10 years of the date they are first found eligible. For spouses of servicemembers who died on active duty, benefits end 20 years from the date of death.

Additional data Benefits may be used to work on associate, bachelor, or graduate degrees at colleges and universities, including independent study, cooperative training, and study abroad programs. Courses leading to a certificate or diploma from business, technical, or vocational schools may also be taken. Other eligible programs include apprenticeships, on-the-job training programs, farm cooperative courses, correspondence courses (for spouses only), secondary school programs (for recipients who are not high school graduates), tutorial assistance, remedial deficiency and refresher training, or work-study (for recipients who are enrolled at least three-quarter time). Eligible children who are handicapped by a physical or mental disability that prevents pursuit of an educational program may receive special restorative training that includes language retraining, lip reading, auditory training, Braille reading and writing, and similar programs. Eligible spouses and children over 14 years of age who are handicapped by a physical or mental disability that prevents pursuit of an educational program may receive specialized vocational training that includes specialized courses, alone or in combination with other courses, leading to a vocational objective that is suitable for the person and required by reason of physical or mental handicap. Ineligible courses include bartending; audited courses; non-accredited independent study courses; any course given by radio; self-improvement courses, such as reading, speaking, woodworking, basic seamanship, and English as a second language; audited courses; any course that is avocational or recreational in character; courses not leading to an educational, professional, or vocational objective; courses taken and successfully completed previously; courses taken by a federal government employee and paid for under the Government Employees' Training Act; and courses taken while in receipt of benefits for the same program from the Office of Workers' Compensation Programs.

Number awarded Varies each year.

Deadline Applications may be submitted at any time.

[711]
TAILHOOK EDUCATIONAL FOUNDATION SCHOLARSHIPS

Tailhook Educational Foundation
9696 Businesspark Avenue
P.O. Box 26626
San Diego, CA 92196-0626
(858) 689-9223   Toll Free: (800) 322-4665
E-mail: tag@tailhook.net
Web: www.tailhook.org/Foundation.html

Summary To provide financial assistance for college to personnel associated with naval aviation and their children.

Eligibility This program is open to 1) the children (natural, step, and adopted) of current or former U.S. Navy or Marine Corps personnel who served as an aviator, flight officer, or air crewman, or 2) personnel and children of personnel who are serving or have served on board a U.S. Navy aircraft carrier as a member of the ship's company or air wing. Applicants must be enrolled or accepted for enrollment at an accredited college or university. Selection is based on educational and extracurricular achievements, merit, and citizenship.

Financial Data The stipend ranges from $1,500 to $15,000.

Duration 1 to 2 years.

Number awarded Varies each year; recently, 85 of these scholarships were awarded.

Deadline March of each year.

[712]
TENNESSEE EAGLE SCOUT OF THE YEAR SCHOLARSHIP

American Legion
Department of Tennessee
215 Eighth Avenue North
Nashville, TN 37203-3583
(615) 254-0568   Fax: (615) 255-1551
E-mail: tnleg@bellsouth.net
Web: www.tennesseelegion.org/youthprograms.shtml

Summary To recognize and reward, with scholarships for college in any state, Eagle Scouts who are members of a troop associated with the American Legion in Tennessee or a son or grandson of a member of the Legion in the state.

Eligibility The Tennessee nominee for American Legion Scout of the Year receives this scholarship. Applicants must be 1) registered, active members of a Boy Scout Troop or Varsity Scout Team sponsored by an American Legion Post in Tennessee or Auxiliary Unit in Tennessee, or 2) registered, active members of a duly chartered Boy Scout Troop or Varsity Scout Team and the sons or grandsons of American Legion or Auxiliary members. Candidates must also 1) be active members of their religious institution and have received the appropriate religious emblem; 2) have demonstrated practical citizenship in church, school, Scouting, and community; and 3) be at least 15 years of age and enrolled in high school. They must be planning to attend college in any state.

Financial Data The award is a $1,500 scholarship.

Duration The award is presented annually.

Number awarded 1 each year.

Deadline Deadline not specified.

[713]
TEXAS AMERICAN LEGION AUXILIARY PAST PRESIDENT'S PARLEY SCHOLARSHIPS

American Legion Auxiliary
Department of Texas
P.O. Box 140407
Austin, TX 78714-0407
(512) 476-7278   Fax: (512) 482-8391
E-mail: alatexas@txlegion.org
Web: alatexas.org/scholarship/ppp.html

Summary   To provide financial assistance to the children and grandchildren of Texas veterans who wish to study a field related to medicine at a school in any state.

Eligibility   This program is open to the children and grandchildren of veterans who served during specified periods of war time. Applicants must be residents of Texas studying or planning to study a medical field at a postsecondary institution in any state. Selection is based on need, goals, character, citizenship, and objectives.

Financial Data   The stipend is $1,000.

Duration   1 year.

Additional data   Applications for these scholarships must be submitted through local units of the American Legion Auxiliary in Texas.

Number awarded   1 or more each year.

Deadline   May of each year.

[714]
TEXAS B-ON-TIME LOAN PROGRAM

Texas Higher Education Coordinating Board
Attn: Hinson-Hazlewood College Student Loan Program
1200 East Anderson Lane
P.O. Box 12788, Capitol Station
Austin, TX 78711-2788
(512) 427-6340   Toll Free: (800) 242-3062
Fax: (512) 427-6423   E-mail: loaninfo@thecb.state.tx.us
Web: www.hhloans.com/borrowers/BOTfactsheet.cfm

Summary   To provide forgivable loans to students in Texas who are residents of the state or entitled to pay resident tuition as a dependent child of a member of the U.S. armed forces.

Eligibility   This program is open to residents of Texas and residents of other states who are entitled to pay resident tuition as a dependent child of a member of the U.S. armed forces. Applicants must 1) have graduated from a public or accredited private high school in Texas or from a high school operated by the U.S. Department of Defense; or 2) earned an associate degree from an eligible Texas institution. They must be enrolled full time in an undergraduate degree or certificate program at an eligible college, university, junior college, or public technical college in Texas.

Financial Data   Eligible students may borrow up to $2,640 per semester ($5,280 per year) for a 4-year public or private institution, $865 per semester ($1,730 per year) for a 2-year public or private junior college, or $1,325 per semester ($2,650 per year) for a public technical college. A 3% origination fee is deducted from the loan proceeds. No interest is charged. Loans are forgiven if the students 1) graduate with a cumulative GPA of 3.0 or higher within 4 calendar years after they initially enroll; within 5 calendar years after they initially enroll in a degree program in architecture, engineering, or other field that normally requires more than 4 years for completion; or within 2 calendar years if they initially enroll in a public or private 2-year institution; or 2) graduate with a cumulative GPA of 3.0 or higher with a total number of credit hours that is no more than 6 hours beyond what is required to complete the degree or certificate.

Duration   1 year. May be renewed after the first year if the recipient makes satisfactory academic progress toward a degree or certificate. May be renewed after the second and subsequent

years if the recipient completes at least 75% of the semester credit hours attempted and has a cumulative GPA of 2.5 or higher on all course work. Loans are available for a maximum of 150 credit hours.

Number awarded   Varies each year.

Deadline   Deadline not specified.

[715]
TEXAS CHILDREN OF U.S. MILITARY WHO ARE MISSING IN ACTION OR PRISONERS OF WAR EXEMPTION PROGRAM

Texas Higher Education Coordinating Board
Attn: Grants and Special Programs
1200 East Anderson Lane
P.O. Box 12788, Capitol Station
Austin, TX 78711-2788
(512) 427-6340   Toll Free: (800) 242-3062
Fax: (512) 427-6127   E-mail: grantinfo@thecb.state.tx.us
Web: www.collegeforalltexans.com

Summary   To provide educational assistance to the children of Texas military personnel declared prisoners of war or missing in action.

Eligibility   Eligible are dependent children of Texas residents who are either prisoners of war or missing in action. Applicants must be under 21 years of age, or under 25 if they receive the majority of support from their parent(s).

Financial Data   Eligible students are exempted from the payment of all dues, fees, and tuition charges at publicly-supported colleges and universities in Texas.

Duration   Up to 8 semesters.

Number awarded   Varies each year; recently, 4 of these exemptions were granted.

Deadline   Deadline not specified.

[716]
TEXAS WAIVERS OF NONRESIDENT TUITION FOR MILITARY SURVIVORS

Texas Higher Education Coordinating Board
Attn: Grants and Special Programs
1200 East Anderson Lane
P.O. Box 12788, Capitol Station
Austin, TX 78711-2788
(512) 427-6340   Toll Free: (800) 242-3062
Fax: (512) 427-6127   E-mail: grantinfo@thecb.state.tx.us
Web: www.collegeforalltexans.com

Summary   To provide a partial tuition exemption to the surviving spouses and dependent children of deceased military personnel who move to Texas following the servicemember's death.

Eligibility   Eligible for these waivers are the surviving spouses and dependent children of members of the U.S. armed forces and commissioned officers of the Public Health Service who died while in service. Applicants must move to Texas within 60 days of the date of the death of the servicemember. They must be attending or planning to attend a public college or university in the state. Children are eligible even if the surviving parent does not accompany them to Texas.

Financial Data   Although persons eligible under this program are still classified as nonresidents, they are entitled to pay the resident tuition at Texas institutions of higher education on an immediate basis.

Duration   1 year.

Additional data   This program became effective in 2003.

Number awarded   Varies each year.

Deadline   Deadline not specified.

[717]
THE RETIRED ENLISTED ASSOCIATION NATIONAL SCHOLARSHIPS

The Retired Enlisted Association
Attn: National Scholarship Committee
1111 South Abilene Court
Aurora, CO 80012-4909
(303) 752-0660 Toll Free: (800) 338-9337
Fax: (303) 752-0835 E-mail: treahq@trea.org
Web: www.trea.org/Scholarship/index.html

Summary To provide financial assistance for college to the dependents of members of The Retired Enlisted Association (TREA).

Eligibility This program is open to dependent children and grandchildren of association or auxiliary members or deceased members who were in good standing at the time of their death. Applicants must be high school seniors or full-time college students and interested in attending a 2- or 4-year college or university. Along with their application, they must submit an essay on a topic that changes annually; recently, students were asked to explain why they chose to attend college instead of going into the military or public service. Selection is based on that essay, 2 letters of recommendation, educational accomplishments, extracurricular activities, work experience, and financial need.

Financial Data The stipend is $1,000 per year.

Duration 1 year; recipients may reapply.

Number awarded 40 each year.

Deadline April of each year.

[718]
TILLMAN MILITARY SCHOLARSHIPS FOR DEPENDENTS

Pat Tillman Foundation
2121 South Mill Avenue, Suite 214
Tempe, AZ 85282
(480) 621-4074 Fax: (480) 621-4075
E-mail: scholarships@pattillmanfoundation.org
Web: www.pattillmanfoundation.org

Summary To provide financial assistance to dependents of veterans and active servicemembers who are interested in working on an undergraduate or graduate degree.

Eligibility This program is open to the dependent children and spouses of veterans and active servicemembers whose educational benefits are not transferable from their parent or spouse, who are survivors of a servicemember, or whose transferable benefits are not sufficient to meet their needs. Their parent or spouse may have served or be serving in any branch of the armed forces from both the pre- and post-September 11 era. Applicants must be interested in starting, finishing, or furthering their undergraduate, graduate, or postgraduate education at a 2-year, 4-year, or vocational institution (public or private). Along with their application, they must submit 1-page essays on 1) their specific financial need, including any gap in educational benefits they may already be receiving and their reason for applying for this scholarship; 2) how their family member's service in the U.S. armed forces has affected their life or influenced their actions; and 3) their previous service to others and the community and how they will incorporate those service experiences into their educational and career goals. Selection is based on those essays, educational and career ambitions, family member's length of service, record of personal achievement, demonstration of service to others in the community and a desire to continue such service, and unmet financial need.

Financial Data Stipends vary; recently, total awards (including multi-year awards) averaged $12,800.

Duration 1 year; may be renewed, provided the recipient maintains a GPA of 3.0 or higher, remains enrolled full time, and documents participation in civic action or community service.

Additional data This program was established in 2009. The foundation administers the program directly for students at colleges and universities nationwide; it also acts in partnership with 4 universities (the University of Maryland, the University of Arkansas, the University of Idaho, and Mississippi State University) which award scholarships directly to their students.

Number awarded Varies each year; recently, 52 students received a total of $665,820 through this program.

Deadline May of each year.

[719]
TONY LOPEZ SCHOLARSHIP PROGRAM

Louisiana National Guard Enlisted Association
c/o SGM Milton J. Billberry
202 Dean Lane
Pineville, LA 71360
(318) 623-2464 E-mail: Milton.billberry@us.army.mil
Web: www.langea.org

Summary To provide financial assistance to members of the Louisiana National Guard Enlisted Association (LANGEA) and their dependents who plan to attend college in any state.

Eligibility This program is open to members of the association, their spouses and unmarried dependent children, and the unremarried spouses and unmarried dependent children of deceased members who were in good standing at the time of their death. The qualifying LANGEA members must have at least 1 year remaining on their enlistment following completion of the school year for which the application is submitted or have served 20 years of more in the Louisiana National Guard. Applicants must be enrolled or planning to enroll full time at an accredited college, university, trade school, or business school in any state. Graduate students are not eligible. Selection is based on academic achievement, character, leadership, and financial need.

Financial Data The stipend is $2,000.

Duration 1 year; nonrenewable.

Number awarded 3 each year.

Deadline February of each year.

[720]
TUITION WAIVER FOR DISABLED CHILDREN OF KENTUCKY VETERANS

Kentucky Department of Veterans Affairs
Attn: Division of Field Operations
321 West Main Street, Room 390
Louisville, KY 40202
(502) 595-4447 Toll Free: (800) 928-4012 (within KY)
Fax: (502) 595-4448 E-mail: Pamela.Cypert@ky.gov
Web: www.veterans.ky.gov/benefits/tuitionwaiver.htm

Summary To provide financial assistance for college to the children of Kentucky veterans who have a disability related to their parent's military service.

Eligibility This program is open to the children of veterans who have acquired a disability as a direct result of their parent's military service. The disability must have been designated by the U.S. Department of Veterans Affairs as compensable (currently defined as spina bifida). The veteran parent must 1) have served on active duty with the U.S. armed forces or in the National Guard or Reserve component on state active duty, active duty for training, or inactive duty training; and 2) be (or if deceased have been) a resident of Kentucky. Applicants must have been admitted to a state-supported university, college, or vocational training institute in Kentucky.

Financial Data Eligible children are exempt from payment of tuition at state-supported institutions of higher education in Kentucky.

Duration There are no age or time limits on the waiver.

Number awarded Varies each year.

Deadline Deadline not specified.

[721]
UNITED STATES FIELD ARTILLERY ASSOCIATION SCHOLARSHIPS

United States Field Artillery Association
Attn: Scholarship Committee
Building 758, McNair Avenue
P.O. Box 33027
Fort Sill, OK 73503-0027
(580) 355-4677   Toll Free: (866) 355-4677
Fax: (580) 355-8745   E-mail: amy@fieldartillery.org
Web: www.fieldartillery.org/usfaa_scholarship/index.html

Summary To provide financial assistance for college to members of the United States Field Artillery Association (USFAA) and their immediate family.

Eligibility This program is open to 3 categories of students: USFAA members (officer or enlisted), immediate family of enlisted members, and immediate family of officer members. Applicants must have been accepted for admission as an undergraduate at an accredited college, university, or vocational program of study. Along with their application, they must submit an essay explaining their educational goals and how this scholarship will help meet those goals. Financial need is also considered in the selection process.

Financial Data The stipend is $1,000.

Duration 1 year.

Additional data The USFAA services the field artillery branch of the military.

Number awarded 6 each year.

Deadline March of each year.

[722]
U.S. ARMY WOMEN'S FOUNDATION LEGACY SCHOLARSHIPS

U.S. Army Women's Foundation
Attn: Scholarship Committee
P.O. Box 5030
Fort Lee, VA 23801-0030
(804) 734-3078   E-mail: info@awfdn.org
Web: www.awfdn.org/programs/legacyscholarships.shtml

Summary To provide financial assistance for college to women who are serving or have served in the Army and their children.

Eligibility This program is open to 1) women who have served or are serving honorably in the U.S. Army, U.S. Army Reserve, or Army National Guard; and 2) children of women who served honorably in the U.S. Army, U.S. Army Reserve, or Army National Guard. Applicants must be entering their junior or senior year at an accredited college or university and have a GPA of 3.0 or higher. Along with their application, they must submit a 2-page essay on why they should be considered for this scholarship, their future plans as related to their program of study, and information about their community service, activities, and work experience. Selection is based on merit, academic potential, community service, and financial need.

Financial Data The stipend is $2,500.

Duration 1 year.

Additional data This program includes scholarships named after Lt. Col. Juanita L. Warman, Sgt. Amy Krueger, and Pvt. Francheska Velez, all of whom lost their lives in the tragedy at Fort Hood, Texas on November 5, 2009.

Number awarded 5 to 10 each year.

Deadline February of each year.

[723]
USO DESERT STORM EDUCATION FUND

USO World Headquarters
Attn: Scholarship Program
Washington Navy Yard, Building 198
901 M Street, S.E.
Washington, DC 20374
(202) 610-5700   Fax: (202) 610-5699
Web: www.desert-storm.com/soldiers/uso.html

Summary To provide financial assistance for academic or vocational education to spouses and children of military personnel who died in the Persian Gulf War.

Eligibility This program is open to the spouses and children of armed service personnel killed, either through accidental causes or in combat, during Operations Desert Shield and Desert Storm. Department of Defense guidelines will be used to determine those service personnel who were taking part in either of these operations at the time of their deaths. This is an entitlement program; neither financial need nor academic achievement are factors in allocating support from the fund. All eligible candidates are contacted directly.

Financial Data It is the purpose of the fund to provide as much financial support as possible to all eligible persons. To this end, USO will distribute all of the funds to the eligible persons in equal amounts.

Duration There will be a 1-time distribution of these funds.

Number awarded All eligible survivors will receive funding.

Deadline Deadline not specified.

[724]
USS COLE MEMORIAL SCHOLARSHIP FUND

Navy-Marine Corps Relief Society
Attn: Education Division
875 North Randolph Street, Suite 225
Arlington, VA 22203-1757
(703) 696-4960   Fax: (703) 696-0144
E-mail: education@hq.nmcrs.org
Web: www.nmcrs.org/goldstar.html

Summary To provide financial assistance for college to the children of deceased crewmembers of the *USS Cole*.

Eligibility This program is open to the children under 23 years of age of crewmembers of the *USS Cole* who died as a result of the terrorist attack on the ship on October 12, 2000. Applicants must be enrolled or planning to enroll full time at a college, university, or vocational/technical school. They must have a GPA of 2.0 or higher and be able to demonstrate financial need.

Financial Data Stipends range from $500 to $2,500 per year. Funds are disbursed directly to the financial institution.

Duration 1 year; may be renewed up to 3 additional years.

Number awarded Varies each year.

Deadline February of each year.

[725]
USS INTREPID FORMER CREWMEMBER SCHOLARSHIPS

USS Intrepid Association, Inc.
P.O. Box 14071
Staten Island, NY 10314
Toll Free: (800) 343-CV11 E-mail: memberscvs11@aol.com
Web: ussintrepidfcmassociation.org/default.aspx

Summary To provide financial assistance for college to the relatives of members of the USS Intrepid Former Crewmember Association.

Eligibility This program is open to the relatives (children, grandchildren, etc.) of association members.

Financial Data The stipend is $1,000.

Duration 1 year.

Number awarded Varies each year; recently, 4 of these scholarships were awarded.

Deadline Deadline not specified.

[726]
USS LAKE CHAMPLAIN (CG-57) SCHOLARSHIP FUND

USS Lake Champlain Foundation
c/o Captain Ralph K. Martin, USN (ret)
P.O. Box 233
Keeseville, NY 12944-0233
(518) 834-7660

Summary To provide financial assistance for college to naval personnel who are (or have been) attached to the *USS Lake Champlain* and to their dependents.

Eligibility Eligible to apply are 1) past and present crewmembers of the *USS Lake Champlain;* 2) spouses and dependent children of officers and enlisted personnel currently serving aboard the *USS Lake Champlain;* and 3) spouses and dependent children of officers and enlisted personnel on active duty, retired with pay, or deceased who were previously assigned to the *USS Lake Champlain* since commissioning on August 12, 1988. Applicants must submit an essay on their career objectives, why they are interested in that career, and how furthering their education will lead to their accomplishing their career objective. Selection is based on that essay, financial need, high school and/or college transcripts, 2 letters of recommendation, extracurricular activities and awards, and work experience.

Financial Data Stipends range from $100 to $1,000. Scholarships greater than $250 are paid in 2 installments: 1 at the beginning of the fall semester and 1 at the beginning of the second semester upon verification of satisfactory completion of the first semester and continued enrollment. Funds are paid directly to the academic institution.

Duration 1 year.

Number awarded Varies each year. Recently, 11 of these scholarships were awarded: 5 at $1,000, 3 at $250, and 3 at $100.

Deadline May of each year.

[727]
USS LITTLE ROCK ASSOCIATION OFFSPRING SCHOLARSHIP PROGRAM

USS Little Rock Association
c/o Kent Siegel, Scholarship Committee Chair
8508 Conover Place
Alexandria, VA 22308-2042
703) 360-8948   E-mail: ksiegel@cox.net
Web: www.usslittlerock.org/scholarship.html

Summary To provide financial assistance for college to descendants of members of the USS Little Rock Association.

Eligibility This program is open to full-time students who have completed the second year of an accredited 4-year program leading to a bachelor's degree. Applicants must be a direct descendant (child, grandchild, or great-grandchild) of a USS Little Rock veteran who is an active association member. They must have a GPA of 3.0 or higher. Along with their application, they must submit a 500-word letter describing why they consider themselves worthy of the award. Selection is based on academic achievement and motivation.

Financial Data The stipend is $1,000 per year.

Duration 1 year; may be renewed 1 additional year.

Additional data This program was initiated in 2007.

Number awarded 1 or 2 each year.

Deadline April of each year.

[728]
USS MAHAN SCHOLARSHIP

Navy League of the United States
Attn: Scholarships
2300 Wilson Boulevard, Suite 200
Arlington, VA 22201-5424
(703) 528-1775   Toll Free: (800) 356-5760
Fax: (703) 528-2333   E-mail: scholarships@navyleague.org
Web: www.navyleague.org/scholarship

Summary To provide financial assistance for college to dependent children of sea service personnel or veterans, especially those who served on the *USS Mahan.*

Eligibility This program is open to U.S. citizens who are 1) dependents or direct descendants of an active, Reserve, retired, or honorably discharged member of the U.S. sea service (including the Navy, Marine Corps, Coast Guard, or Merchant Marines), or 2) currently an active member of the Naval Sea Cadet Corps. Applicants must be entering their freshman year at an accredited college or university. They must have a GPA of 3.0 or higher. Along with their application, they must submit transcripts, 2 letters of recommendation, SAT/ACT scores, documentation of financial need, proof of qualifying sea service duty, and a 1-page personal statement on why they should be considered for this scholarship. Preference is given to direct descendants of sea service personnel who served on the *USS Mahan* and to the dependents of sea service personnel who are now serving.

Financial Data The stipend is $2,500 per year.

Duration 4 years, provided the recipient maintains a GPA of 3.0 or higher.

Number awarded 1 each year.

Deadline February of each year.

[729]
USS STARK MEMORIAL SCHOLARSHIP FUND

Navy-Marine Corps Relief Society
Attn: Education Division
875 North Randolph Street, Suite 225
Arlington, VA 22203-1757
(703) 696-4960   Fax: (703) 696-0144
E-mail: education@hq.nmcrs.org
Web: www.nmcrs.org/goldstar.html

Summary To provide financial assistance for college to the spouses and children of deceased crewmembers of the *USS Stark* (FFG 31).

Eligibility This program is open to the spouses and children of crewmembers of the *USS Stark* (FFG 31) who died as a result of the missile attack on the ship in the Persian Gulf on May 17, 1987. Applicants must be enrolled or planning to enroll full time at a college, university, or vocational/technical school. They must have a GPA of 2.0 or higher and be able to demonstrate financial need. Children must be 23 years of age or younger. Spouses may be eligible if the service member became disabled as a result of the attack.

Financial Data Stipends range from $500 to $2,500 per year. Funds are disbursed directly to the financial institution.

Duration 1 year; may be renewed up to 3 additional years.

Number awarded Varies each year.

Deadline February of each year.

[730]
USS TENNESSEE SCHOLARSHIP FUND

Navy-Marine Corps Relief Society
Attn: Education Division
875 North Randolph Street, Suite 225
Arlington, VA 22203-1757
(703) 696-4960   Fax: (703) 696-0144
E-mail: education@nmcrs.org
Web: www.nmcrs.org/spec-prgm.html

Summary   To provide financial assistance for college to children of current or former crewmembers of the *USS Tennessee.*
Eligibility   This program is open to the dependent children of active-duty and retired personnel currently or previously assigned to duty aboard the *USS Tennessee* (SSBN 734). Applicants must be enrolled or planning to enroll as an undergraduate student. Selection is based on financial need.
Financial Data   The stipend is $2,000 per year; funds may be used for any purpose, including tuition, fees, books, room, or board at a college or university offering a 2-year or 4-year course of study or at a vocational training school.
Duration   1 year; renewable.
Number awarded   Varies each year.
Deadline   February of each year.

[731]
UTAH LEGION AUXILIARY NATIONAL PRESIDENT'S SCHOLARSHIP

American Legion Auxiliary
Department of Utah
350 North State Street, Suite 80
P.O. Box 148000
Salt Lake City, UT 84114-8000
(801) 539-1015   Toll Free: (877) 345-6780
Fax: (801) 521-9191   E-mail: alaut@yahoo.com
Web: www.utlegion.org/Auxiliary/aux1.htm

Summary   To provide financial assistance to children of veterans in Utah who plan to attend college in any state.
Eligibility   This program is open to Utah residents who are the children of veterans who served during specified periods of war time. They must be high school seniors or graduates who have not yet attended an institution of higher learning. Selection is based on character, Americanism, leadership, scholarship, and financial need. The winners then compete for the American Legion Auxiliary National President's Scholarship. If the Utah winners are not awarded a national scholarship, then they receive this departmental scholarship.
Financial Data   The stipends is $1,500.
Duration   1 year.
Number awarded   1 each year.
Deadline   February of each year.

[732]
VADM ROBERT L. WALTERS SCHOLARSHIP

Surface Navy Association
2550 Huntington Avenue, Suite 202
Alexandria, VA 22303
(703) 960-6800   Toll Free: (800) NAVY-SNA
Fax: (703) 960-6807   E-mail: navysna@aol.com
Web: www.navysna.org/awards/index.html

Summary   To provide financial assistance for college or graduate school to members of the Surface Navy Association (SNA) and their dependents.
Eligibility   This program is open to SNA members and their children, stepchildren, wards, and spouses. The SNA member must 1) be in the second or subsequent consecutive year of membership; 2) be serving, retired, or honorably discharged; 3) be a Surface Warfare Officer or Enlisted Surface Warfare Specialist; and 4) have served for at least 3 years on a surface ship of the U.S. Navy or Coast Guard. Applicants must be studying or planning to study at an accredited undergraduate or graduate institution. Along with their application, they must submit a 200-word essay about themselves; a list of their extracurricular activities, community service activities, academic honors and/or positions of leadership that represent their interests, with an estimate of the amount of time involved with each activity; and 3 letters of reference. High school seniors should also include a transcript of high school grades and a copy of ACT or SAT scores. Applicants who

are on active duty or drilling Reservists should also include a letter from their commanding officer commenting on their military service and leadership potential, a transcript of grades from their most recent 4 semesters of school, a copy of their ACT or SAT scores if available, and an indication of whether they have applied for or are enrolled in the Enlisted Commissioning Program. Applicants who are not high school seniors, active-duty servicemembers, or drilling Reservists should also include a transcript of the grades from their most recent 4 semesters of school and a copy of ACT or SAT test scores (unless they are currently attending a college or university). Selection is based on demonstrated leadership, community service, academic achievement, and commitment to pursuing higher educational objectives.
Financial Data   The stipend is $2,000 per year.
Duration   4 years, provided the recipient maintains a GPA of 3.0 or higher.
Number awarded   Varies each year.
Deadline   February of each year.

[733]
VERMONT ARMED SERVICES SCHOLARSHIPS

Office of Veterans Affairs
118 State Street
Montpelier, VT 05620-4401
(802) 828-3379   Toll Free: (888) 666-9844 (within VT)
Fax: (802) 828-5932   E-mail: rhonda.boyce@state.vt.us
Web: www.va.state.vt.us

Summary   To provide financial assistance for college to the children and spouses of deceased members of the armed services in Vermont.
Eligibility   This program is open to the children and spouses of 1) members of the Vermont National Guard who have been killed since 1955 or who since January 1, 2001 have died while on active or inactive duty; 2) members in good standing of the active Reserve forces of the United States who since January 1, 2001 have died while on active or inactive duty and who were Vermont residents at the time of death; and 3) members of the active armed forces of the United States who since January 1, 2001 have died while on active duty and who, at the time of death, were Vermont residents, nonresident members of the Vermont National Guard mobilized to active duty, or nonresident active Reserve force members of a Vermont-based Reserve unit mobilized to active duty. Applicants must be residents of Vermont and attending or planning to attend a Vermont public university, college, or technical institute.
Financial Data   Full tuition, in excess of any funds the student receives from a federal Pell Grant, is paid at Vermont public institutions.
Duration   1 year; may be renewed until completion of 130 academic credits.
Number awarded   Varies each year.
Deadline   Deadline not specified.

[734]
VERMONT EAGLE SCOUT OF THE YEAR SCHOLARSHIP

American Legion
Department of Vermont
P.O. Box 396
Montpelier, VT 05601-0396
(802) 223-7131   Fax: (802) 223-7131
E-mail: alvthq@myfairpoint.net
Web: www.legionvthq.com/programs/eagle_scout.html

Summary   To recognize and reward, with scholarships for college in any state, Eagle Scouts in Vermont.
Eligibility   This award is available to residents of Vermont who are Eagle Scouts. Applicants must be between 15 and 19 years of age, be enrolled in high school, and be planning to attend college

in any state. They are not required to have an affiliation with the American Legion or to have earned a religious badge.

Financial Data The award is a $1,000 scholarship.

Duration The award is presented annually.

Number awarded 1 each year.

Deadline February of each year.

[735]
VIETNAM VETERANS GROUP OF SAN QUENTIN SCHOLARSHIPS

Vietnam Veterans Group of San Quentin
c/o Education Department
San Quentin State Prison
San Quentin, CA 94964
(415) 454-1460, ext. 5148   Fax: (415) 455-5049
Web: vvgsq.tripod.com

Summary To provide financial assistance to high school seniors in California who are interested in attending college in any state and are children of current or former members of the U.S. armed forces.

Eligibility This program is open to graduating high school seniors in California who plan to attend a college or university in any state. Applicants must have a parent or legal guardian who is currently serving in the armed forces or has been honorably discharged. Along with their application, they must submit an essay, up to 250 words in length, on the effect their parent's military service has had on their life. The Mary Manley Inspirational Award may be presented for an exceptionally inspiring essay. Financial need is not considered in the selection process.

Financial Data The scholarship stipend is $1,500. The Mary Manley Inspirational Award, if presented, is an additional $750.

Duration 1 year.

Additional data Membership in the sponsoring organization consists of Vietnam veterans who are currently incarcerated at San Quentin State Prison. Awards are presented at the annual scholarship banquet at the prison. Winners are allowed to bring up to 6 guests to accompany them for the presentation of the scholarships.

Number awarded Up to 2 each year.

Deadline May of each year.

[736]
VII CORPS DESERT STORM VETERANS ASSOCIATION SCHOLARSHIP

VII Corps Desert Storm Veterans Association
Attn: Scholarship Committee
Army Historical Foundation
2425 Wilson Boulevard
Arlington, VA 22201
(703) 604-6565   E-mail: viicorpsdsva@aol.com
Web: www.desertstormvets.org/Scholarship/html

Summary To provide financial assistance for college to students who served, or are the spouses or other family members of individuals who served, with VII Corps in Operations Desert Shield, Desert Storm, or related activities.

Eligibility Applicants must have served, or be a family member of those who served, with VII Corps in Operations Desert Shield/Desert Storm, Provide Comfort, or 1 of the support base activities. Scholarships are limited to students entering or enrolled in accredited technical institutions (trade or specialty), 2-year colleges, and 4-year colleges or universities. Awards will not be made to individuals receiving military academy appointments or full 4-year scholarships. Letters of recommendation and a transcript are required. Selection is not based solely on academic standing; consideration is also given to extracurricular activities and other self-development skills and abilities obtained through on-the-job training or correspondence courses. Priority is given to survivors of VII Corps soldiers who died during Operations Desert

Shield/Desert Storm or Provide Comfort, veterans who are also members of the VII Corps Desert Storm Veterans Association, and family members of veterans who are also members of the VII Corps Desert Storm Veterans Association.

Financial Data The stipend is $5,000 per year. Funds are paid to the recipients upon proof of admission or registration at an accredited institution, college, or university.

Duration 1 year; recipients may reapply.

Additional data This program began in 1998.

Number awarded Approximately 3 each year.

Deadline January of each year.

[737]
VIRGIN ISLAND NATIONAL GUARD GRANTS

Virgin Islands Board of Education
Dronningen Gade 60B, 61, and 62
P.O. Box 11900
St. Thomas, VI 00801
(340) 774-4546   Fax: (340) 774-3384
E-mail: stt@myviboe.com
Web: myviboe.com

Summary To provide financial assistance to the children of deceased or disabled members of the Virgin Islands National Guard who wish to attend a college in the territory or on the mainland.

Eligibility This program is open to children under 25 years of age of members of the National Guard of the Virgin Islands who have died or sustained permanent and total disability in the line of official duty while on territorial active military duty, federal active duty, or training duty. Applicants must have a GPA of 2.0 or higher and be attending or accepted for enrollment at an accredited institution of higher learning in the territory or on the mainland. They may be planning to major in any field. Financial need is considered in the selection process.

Financial Data The stipend is $2,000 per year.

Duration 1 year; may be renewed up to 3 additional years.

Additional data This program is offered as part of the Special Legislative Grants of the Virgin Islands Board of Education.

Number awarded 1 or more each year.

Deadline April of each year.

[738]
VIRGINIA ARMY/AIR NATIONAL GUARD ENLISTED ASSOCIATION SCHOLARSHIP

Virginia Army/Air National Guard Enlisted Association
Attn: Scholarship Chair
P.O. Box 5826
Roanoke, VA 24012
(540) 366-5133   Fax: (540) 362-4417
E-mail: Scholarship@vaaangea.org
Web: www.vaaangea.org

Summary To provide financial assistance to members of the Virginia Army/Air National Guard Enlisted Association (VaA/ANGEA) and their families who are interested in attending college in any state.

Eligibility This program is open to 1) enlisted soldiers or enlisted airmen currently serving as a member of the Virginia National Guard (VNG) who are also a member of the VaA/ANGEA; 2) retired enlisted soldiers or retired enlisted airmen of the VNG who are also a member of the VaA/ANGEA; 3) spouses of current enlisted soldiers or enlisted airmen of the VNG who are also a member of the VaA/ANGEA; 4) spouses of retired enlisted soldiers or retired enlisted airmen of the VNG who are also a member of the VaA/ANGEA; and 5) dependents of current or retired enlisted soldiers or airmen of the VNG (a copy of the dependency decree may be required) who are also a member of the VaA/ANGEA. Applicants must submit a copy of their school transcript (high school or college), a letter with specific facts about their desire to continue their education and their need for assistance, 3 letters of recommendation, a letter of academic reference, and a photocopy of their VaA/ANGEA membership card. Selection is based on academics (15 points), personal statement (15 points), letters of recommendation (16 points), school involvement (15 points), community involvement (15 points), responsibility (15 points), and financial need (9 points).

Financial Data Generally, stipends are either $1,000 or $500.

Duration 1 year; recipients may reapply.

Number awarded Generally, 2 scholarships at $1,000 and 4 scholarships at $500 are awarded each year.

Deadline March of each year.

[739]
VIRGINIA LEGION AUXILIARY PAST PRESIDENT'S PARLEY SCHOLARSHIP

American Legion Auxiliary
Department of Virginia
Attn: Education Chair
1708 Commonwealth Avenue
Richmond, VA 23230
(804) 355-6410   Fax: (804) 353-5246

Summary To provide financial assistance to relatives of members of the American Legion or its Auxiliary in Virginia who plan to study nursing at a college in any state.

Eligibility This program is open to seniors graduating from high schools in Virginia and planning to attend college in any state to study nursing. Applicants must be related to a member of the American Legion or the American Legion Auxiliary.

Financial Data The stipend is $1,000.

Duration 1 year.

Number awarded 1 each year.

Deadline March of each year.

[740]
VIRGINIA MILITARY SURVIVORS AND DEPENDENTS EDUCATION PROGRAM

Virginia Department of Veterans Services
270 Franklin Road, S.W., Room 503
Roanoke, VA 24011-2215
(540) 857-7101   Fax: (540) 857-7573
Web: www.dvs.virginia.gov/statebenefits.htm

Summary To provide educational assistance to the children and spouses of disabled and other Virginia veterans or service personnel.

Eligibility This program is open to residents of Virginia whose parent or spouse served in the U.S. armed forces (including the Reserves, the Virginia National Guard, or the Virginia National Guard Reserves) during any armed conflict subsequent to December 6, 1941, as a result of a terrorist act, during military operations against terrorism, or on a peacekeeping mission. The veterans must be at least 90% disabled due to an injury or disease incurred as a result of such service, has died, or is listed as a prisoner of war or missing in action. Applicants must have been accepted at a public college or university in Virginia as an undergraduate or graduate student. Children must be between 16 and 29 years of age; there are no age restrictions for spouses. The veteran must have been a resident of Virginia at the time of entry into active military service or for at least 5 consecutive years immediately prior to the date of application or death. The surviving spouse must have been a resident of Virginia for at least 5 years prior to marrying the veteran or for at least 5 years immediately prior to the date on which the application was submitted.

Financial Data The maximum allowable stipend is $1,500 per year, but current funding permits a maximum of $1,350, payable at the rate of $675 per term for full-time students, $450 per term for students enrolled at least half time but less than full time, or $225 per term for students enrolled less than half time.

Duration Entitlement extends to a maximum of 48 months.

Additional data Individuals entitled to this benefit may use it to pursue any vocational, technical, undergraduate, or graduate program of instruction. Generally, programs listed in the academic catalogs of state-supported institutions are acceptable, provided they have a clearly-defined educational objective (such as a certificate, diploma, or degree). This program was formerly known as the Virginia War Orphans Education Program.

Number awarded Varies each year; recently, funding allowed for a total of 740 of these awards.

Deadline Deadline not specified.

[741]
VIRGINIA PENINSULA POST SAME SCHOLARSHIPS

Society of American Military Engineers-Virginia Peninsula
   Post
c/o Jeffrey Pitchford, Scholarship Co-Chair
CDM
825 Diligence Drive, Suite 205
Newport News, VA 23606
(757) 873-8850   Fax: (757) 596-2694
E-mail: pitchfordjl@cdm.com
Web: posts.same.org/VAPeninsula

Summary To provide financial assistance to students at universities in Virginia and dependents of members of the Virginia Peninsula Post of the Society of American Military Engineers (SAME) who have a commitment to future military service and are majoring in engineering or architecture.

Eligibility This program is open to students enrolled in an engineering or architecture program at the sophomore level or above. Applicants must be 1) attending a college or university in Virginia, or 2) the dependent of a SAME Virginia Peninsula Post member attending anywhere. They must have demonstrated commitment to future military service by enrolling in an ROTC program, a commissioning program, or an extended enlistment. Selection is based on financial need, academic standing, and involvement in university and community programs.

Financial Data The stipend is $1,500.

Duration 1 year.

Number awarded 4 each year.

Deadline March of each year.

[742]
VNGA SCHOLARSHIP

Virginia National Guard Association
Attn: Scholarship Committee
5901 Beulah Road
Sandston, VA 23150-6112
(804) 328-0037   Toll Free: (888) 703-0037
Fax: (804) 328-3020   E-mail: res003dm@gte.net
Web: www.vnga.org/scholarship.shtml

Summary To provide financial assistance to members of the Virginia National Guard Association (VNGA) and their families who are interested in attending college in any state.

Eligibility Applicants must have been enrolled in a college or university in any state for 1 year and qualify under 1 of the following conditions: 1) an officer or warrant officer in the Virginia National Guard and a VNGA member; 2) the dependent child or spouse of an officer or warrant officer in the Virginia National Guard who is a VNGA member; 3) the dependent child or spouse of a retired officer or warrant officer who is a VNGA member; 4) the dependent child or spouse of a deceased retired officer or warrant officer, or 5) the dependent child or spouse of a Virginia National Guard officer or warrant officer who died while in the Virginia National Guard. Along with their application, they must submit a brief description of their educational and/or military objectives, a list of their leadership positions and honors, and a brief statement of their financial need.

Financial Data A stipend is awarded; the amount is determined annually.

Duration 1 year; may be renewed for 2 additional years.

Additional data The association also offers a special scholarship in memory of CW4 William C. Singletary who, in rescuing 2 elderly women from drowning, gave his own life.

Number awarded Varies each year.

Deadline September of each year.

[743]
VVNW NATIONAL SCHOLARSHIP PROGRAM

Veterans of the Vietnam War, Inc.
Attn: Assistance in Education Program
805 South Township Boulevard
Pittston, PA 18640-3327
(570) 603-9740   Fax: (570) 603-9741
Web: www.vvnw.org

Summary To provide financial assistance for college to members of Veterans of the Vietnam War (VVnW) and their families.

Eligibility This program is open to members of the VVnW in good standing for at least 1 year and their spouses, children, adopted children, foster children, and other immediate descendants. Applicants must be enrolled in or accepted to a program of postsecondary education. Selection is based on a random drawing; financial need, merit, and course of study are not considered.

Financial Data The stipend is $1,000. Funds are paid directly to the recipient.

Duration 1 year.

Number awarded 1 or more each year, depending on the availability of funds.

Deadline October of each year.

[744]
WAIVERS OF NONRESIDENT TUITION FOR DEPENDENTS OF MILITARY PERSONNEL MOVING TO TEXAS

Texas Higher Education Coordinating Board
Attn: Grants and Special Programs
1200 East Anderson Lane
P.O. Box 12788, Capitol Station
Austin, TX 78711-2788
(512) 427-6340   Toll Free: (800) 242-3062
Fax: (512) 427-6127   E-mail: grantinfo@thecb.state.tx.us
Web: www.collegeforalltexans.com

Summary To exempt dependents of military personnel who move to Texas from the payment of nonresident tuition at public institutions of higher education in the state.

Eligibility Eligible for these waivers are the spouses and dependent children of members of the U.S. armed forces and commissioned officers of the Public Health Service who move to Texas while the servicemember remains assigned to another state. Applicants must be attending or planning to attend a public college or university in the state. They must indicate their intent to become a Texas resident. For dependent children to qualify, the spouse must also move to Texas.

Financial Data Although persons eligible under this program are still classified as nonresidents, they are entitled to pay the resident tuition at Texas institutions of higher education on an immediate basis.

Duration 1 year.

Additional data This program became effective in 2003.

Number awarded Varies each year.

Deadline Deadline not specified.

[745]
WAIVERS OF NONRESIDENT TUITION FOR DEPENDENTS OF MILITARY PERSONNEL WHO PREVIOUSLY LIVED IN TEXAS

Texas Higher Education Coordinating Board
Attn: Grants and Special Programs
1200 East Anderson Lane
P.O. Box 12788, Capitol Station
Austin, TX 78711-2788
(512) 427-6340   Toll Free: (800) 242-3062
Fax: (512) 427-6127   E-mail: grantinfo@thecb.state.tx.us
Web: www.collegeforalltexans.com

Summary To provide a partial tuition exemption to the spouses and dependent children of military personnel who are Texas residents but are not assigned to duty in the state.

Eligibility Eligible for these waivers are the spouses and dependent children of members of the U.S. armed forces who are not assigned to duty in Texas but have previously resided in the state for at least 6 months. Servicemembers must verify that they remain Texas residents by designating Texas as their place of legal residence for income tax purposes, registering to vote in the state, and doing 1 of the following: owning real property in Texas, registering an automobile in Texas, or executing a will indicating that they are a resident of the state. The spouse or dependent child must be attending or planning to attend a Texas public college or university.

Financial Data Although persons eligible under this program are classified as nonresidents, they are entitled to pay the resident tuition at Texas institutions of higher education, regardless of their length of residence in Texas.

Duration 1 year.

Number awarded Varies each year.

Deadline Deadline not specified.

[746]
WALTER BEALL SCHOLARSHIP

Walter Beall Scholarship Foundation
c/o W. Ralph Holcombe, Secretary/Treasurer
4911 Fennell Court
Suffolk, VA 23435
(757) 484-7403   Fax: (757) 686-5952
E-mail: info@walterbeallscholarship.org
Web: www.walterbeallscholarship.org

Summary To provide financial assistance to members of the Fleet Reserve Association (FRA) and their families who are interested in studying engineering, aeronautical engineering, or aviation in college.

Eligibility This program is open to FRA members who have been in good standing for at least the past 2 consecutive years and their spouses, children, and grandchildren. Students in a Reserve officer candidate program receiving aid or attending a military academy are not eligible. Applicants must be enrolled at an accredited college, university, or technical institution in the United States in a program related to general engineering, aviation, or aeronautical engineering. Selection is based on GPA, scholastic aptitude test scores, curriculum goals, interests, community activities, awards, and financial need. U.S. citizenship is required.

Financial Data The amounts of the awards depend on the availability of funds and the need of the recipients; they range from $2,000 to $5,000.

Duration 1 year; recipients may reapply.

Additional data The Walter Beall Scholarship Foundation is sponsored by the Past Regional Presidents Club of the Fleet Reserve Association. Membership in the FRA is restricted to active-duty, retired, and Reserve members of the Navy, Marine Corps, and Coast Guard

Number awarded 1 or more each year.
Deadline April of each year.

[747]
WASHINGTON LEGION CHILDREN AND YOUTH SCHOLARSHIPS

American Legion
Department of Washington
3600 Ruddell Road S.E.
P.O. Box 3917
Lacey, WA 98509-3917
(360) 491-4373   Fax: (360) 491-7442
E-mail: administrator@walegion.org
Web: www.walegion.org/cy.htm

Summary To provide financial assistance to the children of members of the American Legion or American Legion Auxiliary in Washington who plan to attend college in the state.
Eligibility This program is open to sons and daughters of Washington Legionnaires or Auxiliary members, living or deceased, who are high school seniors. Applicants must be planning to attend an accredited institution of higher education, trade, or vocational school in the state of Washington. They must be able to demonstrate financial need.
Financial Data The stipend is $2,500 or $1,500, payable in equal amounts per semester.
Duration 1 year.
Number awarded 2 each year: 1 at $2,500 and 1 at $1,500.
Deadline March of each year.

[748]
WILLIAM F. JOHNSON MEMORIAL SCHOLARSHIP

Sons of the American Legion
Detachment of West Virginia
2016 Kanawha Boulevard, East
P.O. Box 3191
Charleston, WV 25332-3191
(304) 343-7591   Toll Free: (888) 534-4667
Fax: (304) 343-7592   E-mail: department@wvlegion.org
Web: www.wvlegion.org

Summary To provide financial assistance to high school seniors in West Virginia who have a family link to the American Legion and are planning to attend college in the state.
Eligibility This program is open to seniors graduating from high schools in West Virginia who are the child or grandchild of a member of the American Legion, American Legion Auxiliary, or Sons of the American Legion. The member may be a resident of any state and belong to any department of the national organization, but the student must be planning to attend a college or university in West Virginia. Along with their application, they must submit a transcript and a 500-word essay on how they can assist a veteran's family and volunteer while the soldier is deployed far from home and family.
Financial Data The stipend is $1,000 or $500. Funds are paid directly to the students, but only after they have completed their first semester of college.
Duration 1 year; nonrenewable.
Number awarded 2 each year: 1 at $1,000 and 1 at $500.
Deadline May of each year.

[749]
WILMA D. HOYAL/MAXINE CHILTON SCHOLARSHIPS

American Legion Auxiliary
Department of Arizona
4701 North 19th Avenue, Suite 100
Phoenix, AZ 85015-3727
(602) 241-1080   Fax: (602) 604-9640
E-mail: amlegauxaz@mcleodusa.net
Web: www.azlegion.org/scholar3.txt

Summary To provide financial assistance to veterans, the dependents of veterans, and other students who are majoring in selected subjects at Arizona public universities.
Eligibility This program is open to second-year or upper-division full-time students majoring in political science, public programs, or special education at public universities in Arizona (the University of Arizona, Northern Arizona University, or Arizona State University). Applicants must have been Arizona residents for at least 1 year. They must have a GPA of 3.0 or higher. U.S. citizenship is required. Honorably-discharged veterans and immediate family members of veterans receive preference. Selection is based on scholarship (20%), financial need (40%), character (25%), and initiative (15%).
Financial Data The stipend is $1,000.
Duration 1 year; renewable.
Number awarded 3 each year: 1 to each of the 3 universities.
Deadline May of each year.

[750]
WISCONSIN EAGLE SCOUT OF THE YEAR SCHOLARSHIP

American Legion
Department of Wisconsin
2930 American Legion Drive
P.O. Box 388
Portage, WI 53901-0388
(608) 745-1090   Fax: (608) 745-0179
E-mail: info@wilegion.org
Web: www.wilegion.org/programs/scholarships/?Id=228

Summary To recognize and reward, with scholarships for college in any state, Eagle Scouts who are members of a troop associated with the American Legion in Wisconsin or a son or grandson of a member of the Legion in the state.
Eligibility The Wisconsin nominee for American Legion Scout of the Year receives this scholarship. Applicants must be 1) a registered, active members of a Boy Scout Troop, Varsity Scout Team, or Explorer Post chartered to an American Legion Post in Wisconsin or Auxiliary Unit in Wisconsin, or 2) a registered, active member of a Boy Scout Troop, Varsity Scout Team, or Venturing Crew and the son or grandson of an American Legion or Auxiliary member. They must have received the Eagle Scout award; be an active member of their religious institution and have received the appropriate Boy Scout religious emblem; have demonstrated practical citizenship in church, school, Scouting, and community; have reached their 15th birthday; be enrolled in high school; and be planning to attend college in any state.
Financial Data The award is a $1,000 scholarship.
Duration The award is presented annually.
Number awarded 1 each year.
Deadline February of each year.

[751]
WISCONSIN G.I. BILL TUITION REMISSION PROGRAM

Wisconsin Department of Veterans Affairs
30 West Mifflin Street
P.O. Box 7843
Madison, WI 53707-7843
(608) 266-1311   Toll Free: (800) WIS-VETS
Fax: (608) 267-0403   E-mail: WDVAInfo@dva.state.wi.us
Web: www.dva.state.wi.us/Ben_education.asp

Summary   To provide financial assistance for college or graduate school to Wisconsin veterans and their dependents.

Eligibility   This program is open to current residents of Wisconsin who 1) were residents of the state when they entered or reentered active duty in the U.S. armed forces, or 2) have moved to the state and have been residents for any consecutive 12-month period after entry or reentry into service. Applicants must have served on active duty for at least 2 continuous years or for at least 90 days during specified wartime periods. Also eligible are 1) qualifying children and unremarried surviving spouses of Wisconsin veterans who died in the line of duty or as the direct result of a service-connected disability; and 2) children and spouses of Wisconsin veterans who have a service-connected disability rated by the U.S. Department of Veterans Affairs as 30% or greater. Children must be between 17 and 25 years of age (regardless of the date of the veteran's death or initial disability rating) and be a Wisconsin resident for tuition purposes. Spouses remain eligible for 10 years following the date of the veteran's death or initial disability rating; they must be Wisconsin residents for tuition purposes but they may enroll full or part time. Students may attend any institution, center, or school within the University of Wisconsin (UW) System or the Wisconsin Technical College System (WCTS). There are no income limits, delimiting periods following military service during which the benefit must be used, or limits on the level of study (e.g., vocational, undergraduate, professional, or graduate).

Financial Data   Veterans who qualify as a Wisconsin resident for tuition purposes are eligible for a remission of 100% of standard academic fees and segregated fees at a UW campus or 100% of program and material fees at a WCTS institution. Veterans who qualify as a Wisconsin veteran for purposes of this program but for other reasons fail to meet the definition of a Wisconsin resident for tuition purposes at the UW system are eligible for a remission of 100% of non-resident fees. Spouses and children of deceased or disabled veterans are entitled to a remission of 100% of tuition and fees at a UW or WCTS institution.

Duration   Up to 8 semesters or 128 credits, whichever is greater.

Additional data   This program was established in 2005 as a replacement for Wisconsin Tuition and Fee Reimbursement Grants.

Number awarded   Varies each year.

Deadline   Applications must be submitted within 14 days from the office start of the academic term: in October for fall, March for spring, or June for summer.

[752]
WISCONSIN JOB RETRAINING GRANTS

Wisconsin Department of Veterans Affairs
30 West Mifflin Street
P.O. Box 7843
Madison, WI 53707-7843
(608) 266-1311   Toll Free: (800) WIS-VETS
Fax: (608) 267-0403   E-mail: WDVAInfo@dva.state.wi.us
Web: www.dva.state.wi.us/Ben_retraininggrants.asp

Summary   To provide funds to recently unemployed Wisconsin veterans or their families who need financial assistance while being retrained for employment.

Eligibility   This program is open to current residents of Wisconsin who 1) were residents of the state when they entered or reentered active duty in the U.S. armed forces, or 2) have moved to the state and have been residents for any consecutive 12-month period after entry or reentry into service. Applicants must have served on active duty for at least 2 continuous years or for at least 90 days during specified wartime periods. Unremarried spouses and minor or dependent children of deceased veterans who would have been eligible for the grant if they were living today may also be eligible. The applicant must, within the year prior to the date of application, have become unemployed (involuntarily laid off or discharged, not due to willful misconduct) or underemployed (experienced an involuntary reduction of income). Underemployed applicants must have current annual income from employment that does not exceed federal poverty guidelines. All applicants must be retraining at accredited schools in Wisconsin or in a structured on-the-job program. Course work toward a college degree does not qualify. Training does not have to be full time, but the program must be completed within 2 years and must reasonably be expected to lead to employment.

Financial Data   The maximum grant is $3,000 per year; the actual amount varies, depending upon the amount of the applicant's unmet need. In addition to books, fees, and tuition, the funds may be used for living expenses.

Duration   1 year; may be renewed 1 additional year.

Number awarded   Varies each year.

Deadline   Applications may be submitted at any time.

[753]
WISCONSIN LEGION AUXILIARY DEPARTMENT PRESIDENT'S SCHOLARSHIP

American Legion Auxiliary
Department of Wisconsin
Attn: Education Chair
2930 American Legion Drive
P.O. Box 140
Portage, WI 53901-0140
(608) 745-0124   Toll Free: (866) 664-3863
Fax: (608) 745-1947   E-mail: alawi@amlegionauxwi.org
Web: www.amlegionauxwi.org/Scholarships.htm

Summary   To provide financial assistance to Wisconsin residents who are members or children of members of the American Legion Auxiliary and interested in attending college in any state.

Eligibility   This program is open to members and children of members of the American Legion Auxiliary. Applicants must be high school seniors or graduates with a GPA of 3.5 or higher and be able to demonstrate financial need. They must be Wisconsin residents, although they are not required to attend school in the state. Along with their application, they must submit a 300-word essay on "Education—An Investment in the Future."

Financial Data   The stipend is $1,000.

Duration   1 year.

Number awarded   3 each year.

Deadline   March of each year.

[754]
WISCONSIN LEGION AUXILIARY MERIT AND MEMORIAL SCHOLARSHIPS

American Legion Auxiliary
Department of Wisconsin
Attn: Education Chair
2930 American Legion Drive
P.O. Box 140
Portage, WI 53901-0140
(608) 745-0124   Toll Free: (866) 664-3863
Fax: (608) 745-1947   E-mail: alawi@amlegionauxwi.org
Web: www.amlegionauxwi.org/Scholarships.htm

Summary To provide financial assistance to Wisconsin residents who are related to veterans or members of the American Legion Auxiliary and interested in working on an undergraduate degree at a school in any state.
Eligibility This program is open to the children, wives, and widows of veterans who are high school seniors or graduates and have a GPA of 3.5 or higher. Grandchildren and great-grandchildren of members of the American Legion Auxiliary are also eligible. Applicants must be residents of Wisconsin and interested in working on an undergraduate degree at a school in any state. Along with their application, they must submit a 300-word essay on "Education: An Investment in the Future." Financial need is considered in the selection process.
Financial Data The stipend is $1,000.
Duration 1 year; nonrenewable.
Additional data This program includes the following named scholarships: the Harriet Hass Scholarship, the Adalin Macauley Scholarship, the Eleanor Smith Scholarship, the Pearl Behrend Scholarship, the Barbara Kranig Scholarship, and the Jan Pulvermacher-Ryan Scholarship.
Number awarded 7 each year.
Deadline March of each year.

[755]
WISCONSIN LEGION AUXILIARY PAST PRESIDENTS PARLEY HEALTH CAREER SCHOLARSHIPS

American Legion Auxiliary
Department of Wisconsin
Attn: Education Chair
2930 American Legion Drive
P.O. Box 140
Portage, WI 53901-0140
(608) 745-0124   Toll Free: (866) 664-3863
Fax: (608) 745-1947   E-mail: alawi@amlegionauxwi.org
Web: www.amlegionauxwi.org/Scholarships.htm

Summary To provide financial assistance for health-related education at a school in any state to the dependents and descendants of veterans in Wisconsin.
Eligibility This program is open to the children, wives, and widows of veterans who are attending or entering a hospital, university, or technical school in any state to prepare for a health-related career. Grandchildren and great-grandchildren of veterans are eligible if they are members of the American Legion Auxiliary. Applicants must be residents of Wisconsin and have a GPA of 3.5 or higher Along with their application, they must submit a 300-word essay on "The Importance of Health Careers Today." Financial need is considered in the selection process.
Financial Data The stipend is $1,200.
Duration 1 year; nonrenewable.
Number awarded 2 each year.
Deadline March of each year.

[756]
WISCONSIN LEGION AUXILIARY PAST PRESIDENTS PARLEY REGISTERED NURSE SCHOLARSHIPS

American Legion Auxiliary
Department of Wisconsin
Attn: Education Chair
2930 American Legion Drive
P.O. Box 140
Portage, WI 53901-0140
(608) 745-0124   Toll Free: (866) 664-3863
Fax: (608) 745-1947   E-mail: alawi@amlegionauxwi.org
Web: www.amlegionauxwi.org/Scholarships.htm

Summary To provide financial assistance to the dependents and descendants of Wisconsin veterans who are interested in studying nursing at a school in any state.
Eligibility This program is open to the wives, widows, and children of Wisconsin veterans who are enrolled or have been accepted in an accredited school of nursing in any state to prepare for a career as a registered nurse. Grandchildren and great-grandchildren of veterans are also eligible if they are American Legion Auxiliary members. Applicants must be Wisconsin residents and have a GPA of 3.5 or higher. Along with their application, they must submit a 300-word essay on "The Need for Trained Nurses Today." Financial need is considered in the selection process.
Financial Data The stipend is $1,200.
Duration 1 year.
Number awarded 3 each year.
Deadline March of each year.

[757]
WISCONSIN SONS OF THE AMERICAN LEGION SCHOLARSHIP

Sons of the American Legion
Detachment of Wisconsin
P.O. Box 388
Portage, WI 53901
(608) 745-1090   E-mail: adjutant@wisal.org
Web: www.wisal.org

Summary To provide financial assistance to members of the Wisconsin Detachment of the Sons of the American Legion (SAL) who plan to attend college in any state.
Eligibility This program is open to members of the SAL in Wisconsin who are seniors in high school or within 1 year of graduation from high school. Applicants must have at least 3 years of consecutive membership. They must be planning to attend a 4-year college or university or a 2-year technical school. Along with their application, they must submit a 100-word essay on their educational objectives, the life's work for which they desire to prepare by attending college, and the value and contribution this scholarship would make toward the realization of those goals. Selection is based on that essay, academic record, contributions to school and community, SAL involvement, and financial need.
Financial Data The stipend is $1,000, paid directly to the school.
Duration 1 year.
Number awarded 1 each year.
Deadline March of each year.

[758]
WMA SCHOLARSHIP PROGRAM

Women Marines Association
P.O. Box 377
Oaks, PA 19456-0377
Toll Free: (888) 525-1943 E-mail: wma@womenmarines.org
Web: www.womenmarines.org/scholarships.aspx

Summary To provide financial assistance for college or graduate school to students sponsored by members of the Women Marines Association (WMA).
Eligibility Applicants must be sponsored by a WMA member and fall into 1 of the following categories: 1) have served or are serving in the U.S. Marine Corps, regular or Reserve; 2) are a direct descendant by blood, legal adoption, or stepchild of a Marine on active duty or who has served honorably in the U.S. Marine Corps, regular or Reserve; 3) are a sibling or a descendant of a sibling by blood, legal adoption, or stepchild of a Marine on active duty or who has served honorably in the U.S. Marine Corps, regular or Reserve; or 4) have completed 2 years in a Marine Corps JROTC program. WMA members may sponsor an unlimited number of applicants per year. High school seniors

must submit transcripts (GPA of 3.0 or higher) and SAT or ACT scores. Undergraduate and graduate students must have a GPA of 3.0 or higher.

Financial Data The stipend is $1,500 per year.

Duration 1 year; may be renewed 1 additional year.

Additional data This program includes the following named scholarships: the WMA Memorial Scholarships, the Lily H. Gridley Memorial Scholarship, the Ethyl and Armin Wiebke Memorial Scholarship, the Maj. Megan Malia McClung Memorial Scholarship, and the LaRue A. Ditmore Music Scholarships. Applicants must know a WMA member to serve as their sponsor; the WMA will not supply listings of the names or addresses of chapters or individual members.

Number awarded Varies each year.

Deadline March of each year.

[759]
WNGEA COLLEGE GRANT PROGRAM

Wisconsin National Guard Enlisted Association
Attn: Executive Director
2400 Wright Street
Madison, WI 53704
(608) 242-3112   E-mail: WNGEA@yahoo.com
Web: www.wngea.org/MAIN/PROG/prosch.htm

Summary To provide financial assistance to members of the Wisconsin National Guard Enlisted Association (WNGEA) and their spouses and children who are interested in attending college or graduate school in any state.

Eligibility This program is open to WNGEA members, the unmarried children of WNGEA members, the spouses of WNGEA members, and the unmarried children and spouses of deceased WNGEA members. WNGEA member applicants, as well as the parents or guardians of unmarried children who are applicants, must have at least 1 year remaining on their enlistment following completion of the school year for which application is submitted (or they must have 20 or more years of service). Applicants must be enrolled at a college, university, graduate school, trade school, or business school in any state. Selection is based on financial need, leadership, and moral character.

Financial Data Stipends are $1,000 or $500 per year.

Duration 1 year; recipients may not reapply for 2 years.

Additional data This program includes 1 scholarship sponsored by the USAA Insurance Corporation.

Number awarded Varies each year. Recently, 4 of these scholarships were awarded: the Raymond A. Matera Scholarship at $1,000 and 3 others at $500 each.

Deadline May of each year.

[760]
WOMEN'S ARMY CORPS VETERANS' ASSOCIATION SCHOLARSHIP

Women's Army Corps Veterans' Association
P.O. Box 5577
Fort McClellan, AL 36205-5577
E-mail: info@armywomen.org
Web: www.armywomen.org

Summary To provide financial assistance for college to the relatives of Army military women.

Eligibility This program is open to high school seniors who are the children, grandchildren, nieces, or nephews of Army service women. Applicants must have a cumulative GPA of 3.5 or higher and be planning to enroll as a full-time student at an accredited college or university in the United States. They must submit a 500-word biographical sketch that includes their future goals and how the scholarship would be used. Selection is based on academic achievement, leadership ability as expressed through co-curricular activities and community involvement, the biographical

sketch, and recommendations. Financial need is not considered. U.S. citizenship is required.

Financial Data The stipend is $1,500.

Duration 1 year.

Number awarded 1 or more each year.

Deadline April of each year.

[761]
WYOMING COMBAT VETERAN SURVIVING ORPHAN TUITION BENEFIT

Wyoming Veterans Commission
Attn: Executive Director
5500 Bishop Boulevard
Cheyenne, WY 82009
(307) 772-5145   Toll Free: (866) 992-7641, ext. 5145
Fax: (307) 772-5202   E-mail: lbartt@state.wy.us
Web: www.wy.ngb.army.mil/benefits

Summary To provide financial assistance to children of deceased, POW, or MIA Wyoming veterans who are interested in attending college in the state.

Eligibility This program is open to children of veterans who had been a resident of Wyoming for at least 1 year at the time of entering service and received the armed forces expeditionary medal or a campaign medal for service in an armed conflict in a foreign country. The veteran parent must 1) have died in active service during armed conflict in a foreign country; 2) be listed officially as being a POW or MIA as a result of active service with the military forces of the United States; or 3) have been honorably discharged from the military and subsequently died of an injury or disease incurred while in service and was a Wyoming resident at the time of death. Applicants must have been younger than 21 years of age when the veteran died or was listed as POW or MIA and younger than 22 years of age when they enter college. They must be attending or planning to attend the University of Wyoming or a community college in the state.

Financial Data Qualifying veterans' children are eligible for free resident tuition at the University of Wyoming or at any of the state's community colleges.

Duration Up to 10 semesters.

Additional data Applications may be obtained from the institution the applicant is attending or planning to attend.

Number awarded Varies each year.

Deadline Applications may be submitted at any time, but they should be received 2 or 3 weeks before the beginning of the semester.

[762]
WYOMING COMBAT VETERAN SURVIVING SPOUSE TUITION BENEFIT

Wyoming Veterans Commission
Attn: Executive Director
5500 Bishop Boulevard
Cheyenne, WY 82009
(307) 772-5145   Toll Free: (866) 992-7641, ext. 5145
Fax: (307) 772-5202   E-mail: lbartt@state.wy.us
Web: www.wy.ngb.army.mil/benefits

Summary To provide financial assistance to surviving spouses of deceased, POW, or MIA Wyoming veterans who are interested in attending college in the state.

Eligibility This program is open to spouses of veterans who had been a resident of Wyoming for at least 1 year at the time of entering service and received the armed forces expeditionary medal or a campaign medal for service in an armed conflict in a foreign country. The veteran spouse must 1) have died in active service during armed conflict in a foreign country; 2) be listed officially as being a POW or MIA as a result of active service with the military forces of the United States; or 3) have been honorably discharged from the military and subsequently died of an injury or disease incurred while in service and was a Wyoming resident at the time of death. Applicants must enroll at the University of Wyoming or a community college in the state within 10 years following the death of the combat veteran.

Financial Data Qualifying veterans' spouses are eligible for free resident tuition at the University of Wyoming or at any of the state's community colleges.

Duration Up to 10 semesters.

Additional data Applications may be obtained from the institution the applicant is attending or planning to attend.

Number awarded Varies each year.

Deadline Applications may be submitted at any time, but they should be received 2 or 3 weeks before the beginning of the semester.

[763]
WYOMING VIETNAM VETERAN SURVIVING CHILD TUITION BENEFIT

Wyoming Veterans Commission
Attn: Executive Director
5500 Bishop Boulevard
Cheyenne, WY 82009
(307) 772-5145   Toll Free: (866) 992-7641, ext. 5145
Fax: (307) 772-5202   E-mail: lbartt@state.wy.us
Web: www.wy.ngb.army.mil/benefits

Summary To provide financial assistance to children of deceased, POW, or MIA Wyoming veterans of the Vietnam era who are interested in attending college in the state.

Eligibility This program is open to children of veterans who had been a resident of Wyoming for at least 1 year at the time of entering service, served some time between August 5, 1964 and May 7, 1975, and received the Vietnam service medal. The veteran parent must 1) have died as a result of service-connected causes; 2) be listed officially as being a POW or MIA as a result of active service with the military forces of the United States; or 3) have been honorably discharged from the military and subsequently died of an injury or disease incurred while in service and was a Wyoming resident at the time of death. Applicants must be attending or planning to attend the University of Wyoming or a community college in the state.

Financial Data Qualifying veterans' children are eligible for free resident tuition at the University of Wyoming or at any of the state's community colleges.

Duration Up to 10 semesters.

Additional data Applications may be obtained from the institution the applicant is attending or planning to attend.

Number awarded Varies each year.

Deadline Applications may be submitted at any time, but they should be received 2 or 3 weeks before the beginning of the semester.

[764]
WYOMING VIETNAM VETERAN SURVIVING SPOUSE TUITION BENEFIT

Wyoming Veterans Commission
Attn: Executive Director
5500 Bishop Boulevard
Cheyenne, WY 82009
(307) 772-5145   Toll Free: (866) 992-7641, ext. 5145
Fax: (307) 772-5202   E-mail: lbartt@state.wy.us
Web: www.wy.ngb.army.mil/benefits

Summary To provide financial assistance to surviving spouses of deceased, POW, or MIA Wyoming veterans of the Vietnam era who are interested in attending college in the state.

Eligibility This program is open to spouses of veterans who had been a resident of Wyoming for at least 1 year at the time of entering service, served some time between August 5, 1964 and May 7, 1975, and received the Vietnam service medal. The vet-

eran spouse must 1) have died as a result of service-connected causes; 2) be listed officially as being a POW or MIA as a result of active service with the military forces of the United States; or 3) have been honorably discharged from the military and subsequently died of an injury or disease incurred while in service and was a Wyoming resident at the time of death. Applicants must be attending or planning to attend the University of Wyoming or a community college in the state.

Financial Data Qualifying veterans' surviving spouses are eligible for free resident tuition at the University of Wyoming or at any of the state's community colleges.

Duration Up to 10 semesters.

Additional data Applications may be obtained from the institution the applicant is attending or planning to attend.

Number awarded Varies each year.

Deadline Applications may be submitted at any time, but they should be received 2 or 3 weeks before the beginning of the semester.

[765]
YANCEY SCHOLARSHIP

Disabled American Veterans-Department of New Jersey
135 West Hanover Street, Fourth Floor
Trenton, NJ 08618
(609) 396-2885   Fax: (609) 396-9562
Web: www.davnj.org

Summary To provide financial assistance to the children and grandchildren of members of the Disabled American Veterans in New Jersey who are interested in attending college in any state.

Eligibility This program is open to graduating high school seniors who are the child or grandchild of a member of the Disabled American Veterans in New Jersey. Applicants must be planning to attend a college or university in any state. Along with their application, they must submit 1) letters of recommendation; 2) a transcript that includes information on their GPA, SAT scores, and class rank; and 3) a 500-word article on a topic that changes regularly (recently, students were asked to present their opinion on the war in Iraq). Selection is based on character (20%), Americanism and community service (20%), leadership (20%), scholarship (20%), and need (20%).

Financial Data The stipend is $1,000.

Duration 1 year; nonrenewable.

Number awarded 1 each year.

Deadline March of each year.

Fellowships/Grants

Veterans ●

Military Personnel ●

Family Members ●

Described here are 224 programs designed primarily or exclusively for veterans, military personnel, and their family members that are to be used to pursue graduate or postdoctoral study or research in the United States. Usually no repayment will be required, provided stated requirements are met. Of these listings, 47 are set aside specifically for veterans, 107 for military personnel, and 70 for their family members (spouses, children, grandchildren, parents, and other relatives). If you are looking for a particular program and don't find it in this section, be sure to check the Program Title Index to see if it is covered elsewhere in the directory.

Veterans

[766]
AAAA SCHOLARSHIPS

Army Aviation Association of America Scholarship
 Foundation
Attn: AAAA Scholarship Foundation
755 Main Street, Suite 4D
Monroe, CT 06468-2830
(203) 268-2450　　　　　　　　　Fax: (203) 268-5870
E-mail: Scholarship@quad-a.org
Web: www.quad-a.org/scholarship.htm

Summary To provide financial aid for undergraduate or graduate study to members of the Army Aviation Association of America (AAAA) and their relatives.

Eligibility This program is open to AAAA members and their spouses, unmarried siblings, unmarried children, and unmarried grandchildren. Applicants must be enrolled or accepted for enrollment as an undergraduate or graduate student at an accredited college or university. Graduate students must include a 250-word essay on their life experiences, work history, and aspirations. Some scholarships are specifically reserved for enlisted, warrant officer, company grade, and Department of the Army civilian members. Selection is based on academic merit and personal achievement.

Financial Data Most stipends range from $1,000 to $4,000. Special scholarships are $11,000.

Duration Scholarships may be for 1 year, 2 years, or 4 years.

Additional data This program includes 3 special scholarships: the GEN Hamilton H. Howze Memorial Scholarship, the Helen Cribbins Memorial Scholarship, and the Joseph P. Cribbins Scholarship.

Number awarded Varies each year; recently, $268,500 in scholarships was awarded to 171 students. Since the program began in 1963, the foundation has awarded more than $3.3 million to nearly 2,000 qualified applicants.

Deadline April of each year.

[767]
AIR FORCE ROTC GRADUATE LAW PROGRAM

U.S. Air Force
Attn: Headquarters AFROTC/RRUC
551 East Maxwell Boulevard
Maxwell AFB, AL 36112-5917
(334) 953-2091　　　　　　Toll Free: (866) 4-AFROTC
Fax: (334) 953-6167　　　　E-mail: afrotc1@maxwell.af.mil
Web: afrotc.com

Summary To provide financial assistance for law school to individuals who are interested in joining Air Force ROTC and are willing to serve as Air Force officers following completion of their professional degree.

Eligibility Applicants must be U.S. citizens who are currently enrolled in the first year of law school at a college or university with an Air Force ROTC unit on campus or a college with a cross-enrollment agreement with such a school. They may be veterans, current military personnel, or first-year law students without military experience. The law school must be accredited by the American Bar Association. Applicants must agree to serve for at least 4 years as active-duty Air Force officers following graduation from law school. Selection is based on academic performance, extracurricular activities, work experience, community service, military record (if appropriate), and recommendations.

Financial Data Students are paid during summer field training and also receive a tax-free stipend of $400 per month during the

last 2 years of their legal education. No other scholarship assistance is provided.

Duration 2 years.

Additional data Participants attend a field training encampment (4 weeks for students with prior military service, 5 weeks for students with no prior military experience) during the summer between their first and second year of law school. They then complete the normal academic requirements for the 2-year AFROTC program while completing law school. After graduation, participants enter active duty as a first lieutenant (with promotion after 6 months).

Deadline March of each year.

[768]
AMVETS NATIONAL SCHOLARSHIPS FOR VETERANS

AMVETS National Headquarters
Attn: Scholarships
4647 Forbes Boulevard
Lanham, MD 20706-3807
(301) 459-9600　　　　　Toll Free: (877) 7-AMVETS, ext. 3043
Fax: (301) 459-7924　　　　E-mail: amvets@amvets.org
Web: www.amvets.org/programs/scholarships.html

Summary To provide financial assistance for college or graduate school to certain veterans who are members of AMVETS.

Eligibility This program is open to AMVETS members who are veterans and U.S. citizens. Applicants must be interested in working full time on an undergraduate degree, graduate degree, or certification from an accredited technical/trade school. They must have exhausted all other government aid. Selection is based on financial need, academic promise, military duty and awards, volunteer activities, community services, jobs held during the past 4 years, and an essay of 50 to 100 words on "What a Higher Education Means to Me."

Financial Data The stipend is $1,000 per year.

Duration Up to 4 years.

Additional data Requests for applications must be accompanied by a self-addressed stamped envelope.

Number awarded 3 each year.

Deadline April of each year.

[769]
ANGELFIRE SCHOLARSHIP

Datatel Scholars Foundation
4375 Fair Lakes Court
Fairfax, VA 22033
(703) 968-9000, ext. 4549　　　Toll Free: (800) 486-4332
Fax: (703) 968-4625　　　　　　E-mail: scholars@datatel.com
Web: www.datatelscholars.org

Summary To provide financial assistance to graduating high school seniors, continuing college students, and graduate students who will be studying at a Datatel client school and are veterans, veterans' dependents, or refugees from southeast Asia.

Eligibility This program is open to 1) veterans who served in the Asian theater (Vietnam, Cambodia, or Laos) between 1964 and 1975; 2) their spouses and children; 3) refugees from Vietnam, Cambodia, or Laos; and 4) veterans who served in Operation Desert Storm, Operation Enduring Freedom, and/or Operation Iraqi Freedom. Applicants must attend a Datatel client college or university during the upcoming school year. They must first apply to their institution, which selects 2 semifinalists and forwards their applications to the sponsor. Along with their application, they must include a 1,000-word personal statement that discusses how the conflict has affected them personally, summarizes how the conflict has impacted their educational goals, and describes how being awarded this scholarship will help them achieve their goals. Selection is based on the quality of the per sonal statement (40%), academic merit (30%), achievements and civic involvement (20%), and 2 letters of recommendation (10%).

Financial Data The stipend is $1,700. Funds are paid directly to the institution.

Duration 1 year.

Additional data Datatel, Inc. produces advanced information technology solutions for higher education. It has more than 725 client sites in the United States and Canada. This scholarship was created to commemorate those who lost their lives in Vietnam or Iraq and is named after a memorial administered by the Disabled American Veterans Association in Angelfire, New Mexico.

Number awarded Varies each year. Recently, 10 of these scholarships were awarded.

Deadline Students must submit online applications to their institution or organization by January of each year.

[770]
ARMY NURSE CORPS ASSOCIATION SCHOLARSHIPS

Army Nurse Corps Association
Attn: Education Committee
P.O. Box 39235
San Antonio, TX 78218-1235
(210) 650-3534   Fax: (210) 650-3494
E-mail: education@e-anca.org
Web: e-anca.org/ANCAEduc.htm

Summary To provide financial assistance to students who have a connection to the Army and are interested in working on an undergraduate or graduate degree in nursing.

Eligibility This program is open to students attending colleges or universities that have accredited programs offering associate, bachelor's, master's, or doctoral degrees in nursing. Applicants must be 1) nursing students who plan to enter the active Army, Army National Guard, or Army Reserve and are not participating in a program funded by the active Army, Army National Guard, or Army Reserve; 2) nursing students who have previously served in the active Army, Army National Guard, or Army Reserve; 3) Army Nurse Corps officers enrolled in an undergraduate or graduate nursing program not funded by the active Army, Army National Guard, or Army Reserve; 4) Army enlisted soldiers in the active Army, Army National Guard, or Army Reserve who are working on a baccalaureate degree in nursing not funded by the active Army, Army National Guard, or Army Reserve; or 5) nursing students whose parent(s) or spouse are serving or have served in the active Army, Army National Guard, or Army Reserve. Along with their application, they must submit a personal statement on their professional career objectives, reasons for applying for this scholarship, financial need, special considerations, personal and academic interests, and why they are preparing for a nursing career.

Financial Data The stipend is $3,000. Funds are sent directly to the recipient's school.

Duration 1 year.

Additional data Although the sponsoring organization is made up of current, retired, and honorably discharged officers of the Army Nurse Corps, it does not have an official affiliation with the Army. Therefore, students who receive these scholarships do not incur any military service obligation.

Number awarded 1 or more each year.

Deadline March of each year.

[771]
BART LONGO MEMORIAL SCHOLARSHIPS

National Chief Petty Officers' Association
c/o Marjorie Hays, Treasurer
1014 Ronald Drive
Corpus Christi, TX 78412-3548
Web: www.goatlocker.org/ncpoa/scholarship.htm

Summary To provide financial assistance for college or graduate school to members of the National Chief Petty Officers' Association (NCPOA) and their families.

Eligibility This program is open to members of the NCPOA and the children, stepchildren, and grandchildren of living or deceased members. Applicants may be high school seniors or graduates entering a college or university or students currently enrolled full time as undergraduate or graduate students. Selection is based on academic achievement and participation in extracurricular activities; financial need is not considered.

Financial Data The stipend is $1,000.

Duration 1 year.

Additional data Membership in the NCPOA is limited to men and women who served or are serving as Chief Petty Officers in the U.S. Navy, U.S. Coast Guard, or their Reserve components for at least 30 days.

Number awarded 2 each year: 1 to a high school senior or graduate and 1 to an undergraduate or graduate student.

Deadline May of each year.

[772]
CHAPLAIN SAMUEL GROVER POWELL SCHOLARSHIP

United Methodist Higher Education Foundation
Attn: Scholarships Administrator
1001 19th Avenue South
P.O. Box 340005
Nashville, TN 37203-0005
(615) 340-7385   Toll Free: (800) 811-8110
Fax: (615) 340-7330 E-mail: umhefscholarships@gbhem.org
Web: www.umhef.org/receive.php?id=chap_powell

Summary To provide funding to students interested in preparing for a career as a military chaplain.

Eligibility This program is open to middlers and seniors at accredited theological seminaries who are either involved in the chaplain candidate (seminarian) program or serving in a military Reserve component after having completed an active-duty tour in 1 of the armed forces. Preference is given to students in their senior year who plan to serve in the U.S. Air Force. However, students preparing for chaplaincy in any branch of the military are considered. Applicants must submit a letter that includes a brief personal history and a statement about their decision to choose military chaplaincy as a career, a recent photograph, undergraduate and graduate transcripts, a financial statement, and a report on their ministry in the chaplain candidate (seminarian) program.

Financial Data A stipend is awarded (amount not specified). Funds must be used to pay for tuition. Checks are mailed to the recipient's school.

Duration 1 year; recipients may reapply for 1 additional year (but new applicants are given priority each year).

Additional data This program was established in 1980. Recipients are expected to serve in the U.S. Military Chaplaincy upon completion of seminary and ordination. If this does not happen (due to factors within the recipient's control), the recipient may be asked to repay the scholarship.

Number awarded 1 or more each year.

Deadline June of each year.

[773]
DARLENE HOOLEY SCHOLARSHIP FOR OREGON VETERANS

Oregon Student Assistance Commission
Attn: Grants and Scholarships Division
1500 Valley River Drive, Suite 100
Eugene, OR 97401-2146
(541) 687-7395   Toll Free: (800) 452-8807, ext. 7395
Fax: (541) 687-7414   TDD: (800) 735-2900
E-mail: awardinfo@osac.state.or.us
Web: www.osac.state.or.us/osac_programs.html

Summary   To provide financial assistance to veterans in Oregon who served during the Global War on Terror and are interested in working on an undergraduate or graduate degree at a college in the state.

Eligibility   This program is open to Oregon veterans who served during the Global War on Terror; there is no minimum length of service requirement. Applicants must be enrolled or planning to enroll at least half time as an undergraduate or graduate student at a college or university in Oregon.

Financial Data   A stipend is awarded (amount not specified).

Duration   1 year; recipients may reapply.

Additional data   This program is administered by the Oregon Student Assistance Commission (OSAC) with funds provided by the Oregon Community Foundation, 1221 S.W. Yamhill, Suite 100, Portland, OR 97205, (503) 227-6846, Fax: (503) 274-7771.

Number awarded   Varies each year.

Deadline   February of each year.

[774]
DEPARTMENT OF HOMELAND SECURITY SMALL BUSINESS INNOVATION RESEARCH GRANTS

Department of Homeland Security
Homeland Security Advanced Research Projects Agency
Attn: SBIR Program Manager
Washington, DC 20528
(202) 254-6768   Toll Free: (800) 754-3043
Fax: (202) 254-7170   E-mail: elissa.sobolewski@dhs.gov
Web: www.dhs.gov/files/grants/gc_1247254058883.shtm

Summary   To support small businesses (especially those owned by disabled veterans, minorities, and women) that have the technological expertise to contribute to the research and development mission of the Department of Homeland Security (DHS).

Eligibility   For the purposes of this program, a "small business" is defined as a firm that is organized for profit with a location in the United States; is in the legal form of an individual proprietorship, partnership, limited liability company, corporation, joint venture, association, trust, or cooperative; is at least 51% owned and controlled by 1 or more individuals who are citizens or permanent residents of the United States; and has (including its affiliates) fewer than 500 employees. The primary employment of the principal investigator must be with the firm at the time of award and during the conduct of the proposed project. Preference is given to women-owned small business concerns, service-disabled veteran small business concerns, veteran small business concerns, and socially and economically disadvantaged small business concerns. Women-owned small business concerns are those that are at least 51% owned by a woman or women who also control and operate them. Service-disabled veteran small business concerns are those that are at least 51% owned by a service-disabled veteran and controlled by such a veteran or (for veterans with permanent and severe disability) the spouse of permanent caregiver of such a veteran. Veteran small business concerns are those that are at least 51% owned by a veteran or veterans who also control and manage them. Socially and economically disadvantaged small business concerns are at least 51% owned by an Indian tribe, a Native Hawaiian organization, a Community Development Corporation, or 1 or more socially and economically disadvan-

taged individuals (African Americans, Hispanic Americans, Native Americans, Asian Pacific Americans, or subcontinent Asian Americans). The project must be performed in the United States. Currently, DHS has 7 research priorities: explosives; border and maritime security; command, control, and interoperability; human factors; infrastructure and geophysical; chemical and biological; and domestic nuclear detection. Selection is based on the soundness, technical merit, and innovation of the proposed approach and its incremental progress toward topic or subtopic solution; the qualifications of the proposed principal investigators, supporting staff, and consultants; and the potential for commercial application and the benefits expected to accrue from this commercialization.

Financial Data   Grants are offered in 2 phases. In phase 1, awards normally range up to $100,000 (or $150,000 for domestic nuclear detection); in phase 2, awards normally range up to $750,000 (or $1,000,000 for domestic nuclear detection).

Duration   Phase 1 awards may extend up to 6 months; phase 2 awards may extend up to 2 years.

Number awarded   Varies each year. Recently, 61 Phase 1 awards were granted.

Deadline   February of each year.

[775]
DEPARTMENT OF TRANSPORTATION SMALL BUSINESS INNOVATION RESEARCH GRANTS

Department of Transportation
Attn: Research and Innovative Technology Administration
John A. Volpe National Transportation Systems Center
55 Broadway, Kendall Square
Cambridge, MA 02142-1093
(617) 494-2051   Fax: (617) 494-2370
E-mail: leisa.moniz@dot.gov
Web: www.volpe.dot.gov/sbir/index.html

Summary   To support small businesses (especially those owned by minorities, veterans, and women) that have the technological expertise to contribute to the research and development mission of the Department of Transportation.

Eligibility   For the purposes of this program, a "small business" is defined as a firm that is organized for profit with a location in the United States; is in the legal form of an individual proprietorship, partnership, limited liability company, corporation, joint venture, association, trust, or cooperative; is at least 51% owned and controlled by 1 or more individuals who are citizens or permanent residents of the United States; and has (including its affiliates) fewer than 500 employees. The primary employment of the principal investigator must be with the firm at the time of award and during the conduct of the proposed project. Preference is given to 1) women-owned small business concerns; 2) veteran-owned small businesses; and 3) socially and economically disadvantaged small business concerns. Women-owned small business concerns are those that are at least 51% owned by a woman or women who also control and operate them. Veteran-owned small businesses are those that are at least 51% owned and controlled by 1 or more veterans. Socially and economically disadvantaged small business concerns are at least 51% owned by an Indian tribe, a Native Hawaiian organization, or 1 or more socially and economically disadvantaged individuals (African Americans, Hispanic Americans, Native Americans, Asian Pacific Americans, or subcontinent Asian Americans). The project must be performed in the United States. Selection is based on scientific and technical merit, the feasibility of the proposal's commercial potential, the adequacy of the work plan, qualifications of the principal investigator, and adequacy of supporting staff and facilities, equipment, and data.

Financial Data   Support is offered in 2 phases. In phase 1, awards normally do not exceed $100,000 (for both direct and indirect costs); in phase 2, awards normally do not exceed $750,000 (including both direct and indirect costs).

Duration Phase 1 awards may extend up to 6 months; phase 2 awards may extend up to 2 years.

Number awarded Varies each year. Recently, DOT planned to award 16 of these grants: 1 to the Federal Aviation Administration, 3 to the Federal Highway Administration, 1 to the Pipeline and Hazardous Materials Safety Administration, 2 to the National Highway and Traffic Safety Administration, 3 to the Federal Transit Administration, and 6 to the Federal Railroad Administration.

Deadline November of each year.

[776]
DR. WILLIAM WALKER MEMORIAL SCHOLARSHIP

Community Foundation of the Ozarks
Attn: Scholarship Coordinator
421 East Trafficway
Springfield, MO 65806
(417) 864-6199   Toll Free: (888) 266-6815
Fax: (417) 864-8344   E-mail: jbillings@cfozarks.org
Web: www.cfozarks.org

Summary To provide financial assistance to students at medical schools in Missouri and Iowa, especially those who are veterans of the U.S. Marine Corps.

Eligibility This program is open to students entering their final year in the top 15% of their class at a medical school in Missouri or Iowa. Applicants must be natural born U.S. citizens who can demonstrate superior clinical skills and the ability to communicate with patients effectively and with empathy. Preference is given to veterans, especially U.S. Marines.

Financial Data The stipend is $3,400.

Duration 1 year.

Number awarded 1 each year.

Deadline June of each year.

[777]
EDWARD T. CONROY MEMORIAL SCHOLARSHIP PROGRAM

Maryland Higher Education Commission
Attn: Office of Student Financial Assistance
839 Bestgate Road, Suite 400
Annapolis, MD 21401-3013
(410) 260-4563   Toll Free: (800) 974-1024, ext. 4563
Fax: (410) 260-3200   TDD: (800) 735-2258
E-mail: lasplin@mhec.state.md.us
Web: www.mhec.state.md.us

Summary To provide financial assistance for college or graduate school in Maryland to children and spouses of victims of the September 11, 2001 terrorist attacks and specified categories of veterans, public safety employees, and their children or spouses.

Eligibility This program is open to entering and continuing undergraduate and graduate students in the following categories: 1) children and surviving spouses of victims of the September 11, 2001 terrorist attacks who died in the World Trade Center in New York City, the Pentagon in Virginia, or United Airlines Flight 93 in Pennsylvania; 2) veterans who have, as a direct result of military service, a disability of 25% or greater and have exhausted or are no longer eligible for federal veterans' educational benefits; 3) children of armed forces members whose death or 100% disability was directly caused by military service; 4) POW/MIA veterans of the Vietnam Conflict and their children; 5) state or local public safety officers or volunteers who became 100% disabled in the line of duty; and 6) children and unremarried surviving spouses of state or local public safety employees or volunteers who died or became 100% disabled in the line of duty. The parent, spouse, veteran, POW, or public safety officer or volunteer must have been a resident of Maryland at the time of death or when declared disabled. Financial need is not considered.

Financial Data The amount of the award is equal to tuition and fees at a Maryland postsecondary institution, to a maximum of

$19,000 for children and spouses of the September 11 terrorist attacks or $9,000 for all other recipients.

Duration Up to 5 years of full-time study or 8 years of part-time study.

Additional data Recipients must enroll at a 2-year or 4-year Maryland college or university as a full-time or part-time degree-seeking undergraduate or graduate student or attend a private career school.

Number awarded Varies each year.

Deadline July of each year.

[778]
EXEMPTION FOR TEXAS VETERANS

Texas Higher Education Coordinating Board
Attn: Grants and Special Programs
1200 East Anderson Lane
P.O. Box 12788, Capitol Station
Austin, TX 78711-2788
(512) 427-6340   Toll Free: (800) 242-3062
Fax: (512) 427-6127   E-mail: grantinfo@thecb.state.tx.us
Web: www.collegeforalltexans.com

Summary To exempt Texas veterans from payment of tuition for undergraduate or graduate study at public universities in the state.

Eligibility This program is open to veterans who were legal residents of Texas at the time they entered the U.S. armed forces and served for at least 181 days of active military duty, excluding basic training, during specified periods of war time. Applicants must have received an honorable discharge or separation or a general discharge under honorable conditions. They must be enrolled at a public college or university in Texas and all their other federal veterans education benefits (not including Pell and SEOG grants) may not exceed the value of this exemption. If they are in default on a student loan made or guaranteed by the state of Texas or on a federal education loan that affects their eligibility for GI education benefits, they are not eligible.

Financial Data Veterans who are eligible for this benefit are entitled to free tuition and fees at state-supported colleges and universities in Texas.

Duration Exemptions may be claimed up to a cumulative total of 150 credit hours, including undergraduate and graduate study.

Additional data This program was established under provisions of the Hazlewood Act, and is also referred to as Hazlewood Exemption for Texas Veterans.

Number awarded Varies each year; recently, 8,885 of these awards were granted.

Deadline Deadline not specified.

[779]
FLEET RESERVE ASSOCIATION SCHOLARSHIP

Fleet Reserve Association
Attn: Scholarship Administrator
125 North West Street
Alexandria, VA 22314-2754
(703) 683-1400   Toll Free: (800) FRA-1924
Fax: (703) 549-6610   E-mail: fra@fra.org
Web: www.fra.org

Summary To provide financial assistance for college or graduate school to members of the Fleet Reserve Association (FRA), as well as their spouses, children, and grandchildren.

Eligibility This program is open to members of the FRA and their dependent children, grandchildren, and spouses. The children, grandchildren, and spouses of deceased FRA members are also eligible. Applicants must submit an essay on their life experiences, career objectives, and what motivated them to select those objectives. Selection is based on academic record, financial need, extracurricular activities, leadership skills, and participation in community activities. U.S. citizenship is required.

Financial Data The stipend is $5,000 per year.
Duration 1 year; may be renewed.
Additional data Membership in the FRA is restricted to active-duty, retired, and reserve members of the Navy, Marines, and Coast Guard.
Number awarded 6 each year.
Deadline April of each year.

[780]
GEORGE WASHINGTON CHAPTER AUSA SCHOLARSHIPS

Association of the United States Army-George Washington
 Chapter
c/o Bobbie Williams, Scholarship Committee
79 Brush Everard Court
Stafford, VA 22554
(703) 697-6340   E-mail: Bobbie.Williams@us.army.mil
Web: www.gwcausa.org/Scholarship/index.htm

Summary To provide financial assistance for undergraduate or graduate study at a school in any state to members of the George Washington Chapter of the Association of the United States Army (AUSA) and their families.
Eligibility This program is open to active members of the AUSA George Washington Chapter (which serves the Washington, D.C. area) and the families of active members. Applicants must have a GPA of 2.5 or higher and be working on an undergraduate or advanced degree at a college or university in any state. Along with their application, they must submit a letter describing any family circumstances they believe are relevant and explaining why they deserve the scholarship. Members must also submit a favorable recommendation from their supervisor. Membership in AUSA is open to Army personnel (including Reserves and National Guard) who are either active or retired, ROTC cadets, or civilian employees of the Army.
Financial Data Stipends range up to $1,000.
Duration 1 year.
Number awarded Varies each year; recently, 15 of these scholarships were awarded.
Deadline April of each year.

[781]
GLENN F. GLEZEN SCHOLARSHIP

Fleet Reserve Association
Attn: Scholarship Administrator
125 North West Street
Alexandria, VA 22314-2754
(703) 683-1400   Toll Free: (800) FRA-1924
Fax: (703) 549-6610   E-mail: fra@fra.org
Web: www.fra.org

Summary To provide financial assistance for graduate school to members of the Fleet Reserve Association (FRA) and their spouses, children, and grandchildren.
Eligibility This program is open to the dependent children, grandchildren, and spouses of members of the association who are in good standing (or were at the time of death, if deceased). FRA members are also eligible. Applicants should be enrolled in a graduate program. Along with their application, they must submit an essay on their life experiences, career objectives, and what motivated them to select those objectives. Selection is based on academic record, financial need, extracurricular activities, leadership skills, and participation in community activities. U.S. citizenship is required.
Financial Data The stipend is $5,000 per year.
Duration 1 year; may be renewed.
Additional data Membership in the FRA is restricted to active-duty, retired, and Reserve members of the Navy, Marine Corps, and Coast Guard. This program was established in 2001.

Number awarded 1 each year.
Deadline April of each year.

[782]
ILLINOIS NATIONAL GUARD GRANT PROGRAM

Illinois Student Assistance Commission
Attn: Scholarship and Grant Services
1755 Lake Cook Road
Deerfield, IL 60015-5209
(847) 948-8550   Toll Free: (800) 899-ISAC
Fax: (847) 831-8549   TDD: (800) 526-0844
E-mail: collegezone@isac.org
Web: www.collegezone.com/studentzone/407_626.htm

Summary To provide financial assistance to current or former members of the Illinois National Guard who are interested in attending college or graduate school in the state.
Eligibility This program is open to members of the Illinois National Guard who are 1) currently active or 2) have been active for at least 5 consecutive years, have been called to federal active duty for at least 6 months, and are within 12 months after their discharge date. Applicants must also be enrolled at an Illinois public 2- or 4-year college or university and have served at least 1 full year in the Guard.
Financial Data Recipients are eligible for payment of tuition and some fees for either undergraduate or graduate study at an Illinois state-supported college or university.
Duration This assistance extends for 8 semesters or 12 quarters (or the equivalent in part-time study).
Number awarded Varies each year.
Deadline September of each year for the academic year; February of each year for spring semester, winter quarter, or spring quarter; June of each year for summer term.

[783]
ILLINOIS VETERAN GRANT PROGRAM

Illinois Student Assistance Commission
Attn: Scholarship and Grant Services
1755 Lake Cook Road
Deerfield, IL 60015-5209
(847) 948-8550   Toll Free: (800) 899-ISAC
Fax: (847) 831-8549   TDD: (800) 526-0844
E-mail: collegezone@isac.org
Web: www.collegezone.com/studentzone/407_629.htm

Summary To provide financial assistance to Illinois veterans Guard who are interested in attending college or graduate school in the state.
Eligibility This program is open to Illinois residents who served in the U.S. armed forces (including members of the Reserves and the Illinois National Guard) for at least 1 year on active duty and have been honorably discharged. The 1-year service requirement does not apply to veterans who 1) served in a foreign country in a time of hostilities in that country, 2) were medically discharged for service-related reasons, or 3) were discharged prior to August 11, 1967. Applicants must have been Illinois residents for at least 6 months before entering service and they must have returned to Illinois within 6 months after separation from service. Current members of the Reserve Officer Training Corps are not eligible.
Financial Data This program pays all tuition and certain fees at all Illinois public colleges, universities, and community colleges.
Duration This scholarship may be used for the equivalent of up to 4 years of full-time enrollment, provided the recipient maintains the minimum GPA required by their college or university.
Additional data This is an entitlement program; once eligibility has been established, no further applications are necessary.
Number awarded Varies each year.
Deadline Applications may be submitted at any time.

[784]
JOSEPH A. MCALINDEN DIVERS' SCHOLARSHIP

Navy-Marine Corps Relief Society
Attn: Education Division
875 North Randolph Street, Suite 225
Arlington, VA 22203-1757
(703) 696-4960   Fax: (703) 696-0144
E-mail: education@nmcrs.org
Web: www.nmcrs.org/education.html

Summary   To provide financial assistance to current and former Navy and Marine Corps divers and their families who are interested in working on an undergraduate or graduate degree in a field related to ocean agriculture.

Eligibility   This program is open to Navy and Marine Corps active-duty and retired divers and members of their families. Applicants must be enrolled full time in an undergraduate or graduate program in oceanography, ocean agriculture, aquaculture, or a related field; they may also be engaged in advanced diver training, certification, or recertification. Financial need is considered in the selection process.

Financial Data   The stipend ranges from $500 to $3,000, depending on the need of the recipient.

Duration   1 year.

Number awarded   1 or more each year.

Deadline   Applications may be submitted at any time.

[785]
JOSEPH R. BARANSKI EMERITUS SCHOLARSHIP

Fleet Reserve Association
Attn: Scholarship Administrator
125 North West Street
Alexandria, VA 22314-2754
(703) 683-1400   Toll Free: (800) FRA-1924
Fax: (703) 549-6610   E-mail: fra@fra.org
Web: www.fra.org

Summary   To provide financial assistance for graduate school to members of the Fleet Reserve Association (FRA) and their spouses, children, and grandchildren.

Eligibility   This program is open to the dependent children, grandchildren, and spouses of members of the association who are in good standing (or were at the time of death, if deceased). FRA members are also eligible. Applicants should be enrolled in a graduate program. Along with their application, they must submit an essay on their life experiences, career objectives, and what motivated them to select those objectives. Selection is based on academic record, financial need, extracurricular activities, leadership skills, and participation in community activities. U.S. citizenship is required.

Financial Data   The stipend is $5,000.

Duration   1 year; may be renewed.

Additional data   Membership in the FRA is restricted to active-duty, retired, and Reserve members of the Navy, Marine Corps, and Coast Guard. This program was established in 2001.

Number awarded   1 each year.

Deadline   April of each year.

[786]
MARIA C. JACKSON/GENERAL GEORGE A. WHITE SCHOLARSHIP

Oregon Student Assistance Commission
Attn: Grants and Scholarships Division
1500 Valley River Drive, Suite 100
Eugene, OR 97401-2146
(541) 687-7395   Toll Free: (800) 452-8807, ext. 7395
Fax: (541) 687-7414   TDD: (800) 735-2900
E-mail: awardinfo@osac.state.or.us
Web: www.osac.state.or.us/osac_programs.html

Summary   To provide financial assistance to veterans and children of veterans and military personnel in Oregon who are interested in attending college or graduate school in the state.

Eligibility   This program is open to residents of Oregon who served, or whose parents are serving or have served, in the U.S. armed forces. Applicants or their parents must have resided in Oregon at the time of enlistment. They must be enrolled or planning to enrolled in a college or graduate school in the state. College and university undergraduates must have a GPA of 3.75 or higher, but there is no minimum GPA requirement for graduate students or those attending a technical school. Selection is based on scholastic ability and financial need.

Financial Data   A stipend is awarded (amount not specified).

Number awarded   Varies each year.

Deadline   February of each year.

[787]
MG EUGENE C. RENZI, USA (RET.)/MANTECH INTERNATIONAL CORPORATION TEACHER'S SCHOLARSHIP

Armed Forces Communications and Electronics Association
Attn: AFCEA Educational Foundation
4400 Fair Lakes Court
Fairfax, VA 22033-3899
(703) 631-6149   Toll Free: (800) 336-4583, ext. 6149
Fax: (703) 631-4693   E-mail: scholarship@afcea.org
Web: www.afcea.org

Summary   To provide financial assistance to undergraduate and graduate students (especially veterans) who are preparing for a career as a teacher of science and mathematics.

Eligibility   This program is open to full-time juniors, seniors, and graduate students at accredited colleges and universities in the United States. Applicants must be U.S. citizens preparing for a career as a teacher of science, mathematics, or information technology at a middle or secondary school. They must have a GPA of 3.0 or higher. In the selection process, first consideration is given to wounded or disabled veterans, then to honorably discharged veterans. Financial need is not considered.

Financial Data   The stipend is $2,500.

Duration   1 year.

Additional data   This program was established in 2008 with support from ManTech International Corporation.

Number awarded   1 each year.

Deadline   May of each year.

[788]
MILITARY ORDER OF THE PURPLE HEART SCHOLARSHIP PROGRAM

Military Order of the Purple Heart
Attn: Scholarships
5413-B Backlick Road
Springfield, VA 22151-3960
(703) 642-5360   Toll Free: (888) 668-1656
Fax: (703) 642-2054   E-mail: scholarship@purpleheart.org
Web: www.purpleheart.org/Scholarships/Default.aspx

Summary   To provide financial assistance for college or graduate school to members of the Military Order of the Purple Heart (MOPH) and their families.

Eligibility   This program is open to 1) members of the MOPH; 2) direct descendants (children, stepchildren, adopted children, grandchildren, and great- grandchildren) of veterans who are MOPH members or who were members at the time of death; 3) direct descendants of veterans killed in action or who died of wounds but did not have the opportunity to join the order; and 4) spouses and widows of MOPH members, veterans killed in action, and veterans who died of wounds. Applicants must be graduating seniors or graduates of an accredited high school who are enrolled or accepted for enrollment in a full-time program of study in a college, trade school, or graduate school. They must have a GPA of 2.75 or higher. U.S. citizenship is required. Along with their application, they must submit an essay of 200 to 300 words on "What it means to be an American." Financial need is not considered in the selection process.

Financial Data The stipend is $3,000 per year.

Duration 1 year; may be renewed up to 2 additional years.

Additional data Membership in MOPH is open to all veterans who received a Purple Heart Medal and were discharged under conditions other than dishonorable. A processing fee of $15 is required.

Number awarded Varies each year; recently, 50 of these scholarships were awarded.

Deadline February of each year.

[789]
MINNESOTA G.I. BILL PROGRAM

Minnesota Office of Higher Education
Attn: Manager of State Financial Aid Programs
1450 Energy Park Drive, Suite 350
St. Paul, MN 55108-5227
(651) 642-0567   Toll Free: (800) 657-3866
Fax: (651) 642-0675   TDD: (800) 627-3529
E-mail: Ginny.Dodds@state.mn.us
Web: www.ohe.state.mn.us

Summary To provide financial assistance for college or graduate school in the state to residents of Minnesota who served in the military after September 11, 2001 and the families of deceased or disabled military personnel.

Eligibility This program is open to residents of Minnesota enrolled at colleges and universities in the state as undergraduate or graduate students. Applicants must be 1) a veteran who is serving or has served honorably in a branch of the U.S. armed forces at any time on or after September 11, 2001; 2) a non-veteran who has served honorably for a total of 5 years or more cumulatively as a member of the Minnesota National Guard or other active or Reserve component of the U.S. armed forces, and any part of that service occurred on or after September 11, 2001; or 3) a surviving child or spouse of a person who has served in the military at any time on or after September 11, 2001 and who has died or has a total and permanent disability as a result of that military service. Financial need is also considered in the selection process.

Financial Data The stipend is $1,000 per semester for full-time study or $500 per semester for part-time study.

Duration 1 year; may be renewed up to 4 additional years, provided the recipient continues to make satisfactory academic progress.

Additional data This program was established by the Minnesota Legislature in 2007.

Number awarded Varies each year.

Deadline Deadline not specified.

[790]
MONTANA HONORABLY DISCHARGED VETERAN WAIVER

Montana Guaranteed Student Loan Program
2500 Broadway
P.O. Box 203101
Helena, MT 59620-3101
(406) 444-0638   Toll Free: (800) 537-7508
Fax: (406) 444-1869 E-mail: scholarships@mgslp.state.mt.us
Web: www.mgslp.state.mt.us

Summary To provide financial assistance for undergraduate or graduate studies to selected Montana veterans.

Eligibility This program is open to honorably-discharged veterans who served with the U.S. armed forces and who are residents of Montana. Only veterans who at some time qualified for U.S.

Department of Veterans Affairs (VA) educational benefits, but who are no longer eligible or have exhausted their benefits, are entitled to this waiver. Veterans who served any time prior to May 8, 1975 are eligible to work on undergraduate or graduate degrees. Veterans whose service began after May 7, 1975 are eligible only to work on their first undergraduate degree. They must have received an Armed Forces Expeditionary Medal for service in Lebanon, Grenada, or Panama; served in a combat theater in the Persian Gulf between August 2, 1990 and April 11, 1991 and received the Southwest Asia Service Medal; were awarded the Kosovo Campaign Medal; or served in a combat theater in Afghanistan or Iraq after September 11, 2001 and received the Global War on Terrorism Expeditionary Medal, the Afghanistan Campaign Medal, or the Iraq Campaign Medal. Financial need must be demonstrated.

Financial Data Veterans eligible for this benefit are entitled to attend any unit of the Montana University System without payment of registration or incidental fees.

Duration Students are eligible for continued fee waiver as long as they make reasonable academic progress as full-time students.

Number awarded Varies each year.

Deadline Deadline not specified.

[791]
MONTGOMERY GI BILL (ACTIVE DUTY)

Department of Veterans Affairs
Attn: Veterans Benefits Administration
810 Vermont Avenue, N.W.
Washington, DC 20420
(202) 418-4343   Toll Free: (888) GI-BILL1
Web: www.gibill.va.gov/GI_Bill_Info/benefits.htm

Summary To provide financial assistance for college, graduate school, and other types of postsecondary schools to new enlistees in any of the armed forces after they have completed their service obligation.

Eligibility This program is open to veterans who received an honorable discharge and have a high school diploma, a GED, or, in some cases, up to 12 hours of college credit; veterans who already have a bachelor's degree are eligible to work on a master's degree or higher. Applicants must also meet the requirements of 1 of the following categories: 1) entered active duty for the first time after June 30, 1985, had military pay reduced by $100 per month for the first 12 months, and continuously served for 3 years, or 2 years if that was their original enlistment, or 2 years if they entered Selected Reserve within a year of leaving active duty and served 4 years (the 2 by 4 program); 2) entered active duty before January 1, 1977, had remaining entitlement under the Vietnam Era GI Bill on December 31, 1989, served at least 1 day between October 19, 1984 and June 30, 1985, and stayed on active duty through June 30, 1988 (or June 30, 1987 if they entered Selected Reserve within 1 year of leaving active duty and served 4 years); 3) on active duty on September 30, 1990 and separated involuntarily after February 2, 1991, involuntarily separated on or after November 30, 1993, or voluntarily separated under either the Voluntary Separation Incentive (VSI) or Special Separation Benefit (SSB) program, and before separation had military pay reduced by $1,200; or 4) on active duty on October 9, 1996, had money remaining in an account from the Veterans Educational Assistance Program (VEAP), elected Montgomery GI Bill (MGIB) by October 9, 1997, and paid $1,200. Certain National Guard members may also qualify under category 4 if they served on full-time active duty between July 1, 1985 and November 28, 1989, elected MGIB between October 9, 1996 and July 8, 1997, and paid $1,200. Following completion of their service obligation, participants may enroll in colleges or universities for associate, bachelor, or graduate degrees; in courses leading to a certificate or diploma from business, technical, or vocational schools; for apprenticeships or on-the-job training programs; in correspondence courses; in flight training; for preparatory courses necessary for admission to a college or graduate school; for licensing and certification tests approved for veterans; or in state-approved teacher certification programs. Veterans who wish to enroll in certain high-cost technology programs (life science, physical science, engineering, mathematics, engineering and science technology, computer specialties, and engineering, science, and computer management) may be eligible for an accelerated payment.

Financial Data For veterans in categories 1, 3, and 4 who served on active duty for 3 years or more, the current monthly stipend for college or university work is $1,368 for full-time study, $1,026 for three-quarter time study, $684 for half-time study, or $342 for quarter-time study or less; for apprenticeship and on-the-job training, the monthly stipend is $1,026 for the first 6 months, $752.40 for the second 6 months, and $478.80 for the remainder of the program. For enlistees whose initial active-duty obligation was less than 3 years, the current monthly stipend for college or university work is $1,111 for full-time study, $833.25 for three-quarter time study, $550.50 for half-time study, or $275.75 for quarter-time study or less; for apprenticeship and on-the-job training, the monthly stipend is $833.25 for the first 6 months, $611.05 for the second 6 months, and $388.85 for the remainder of the program. For veterans in category 2 with remaining eligibility, the current monthly stipend for institutional study full time is $1,556 for no dependents, $1,592 with 1 dependent, $1,623 with 2 dependents, and $16 for each additional dependent; for three-quarter time study, the monthly stipend is $1,167.50 for no dependents, $1,194 with 1 dependent, $1,217.50 with 2 dependents, and $12 for each additional dependent; for half-time study, the monthly stipend is $778 for no dependents, $796 with 1 dependent, $811.50 with 2 dependents, and $8.50 for each additional dependent. For those veterans pursuing an apprenticeship or on-the-job training, the current monthly stipend for the first 6 months is $1,128.75 for no dependents, $1,141.13 with 1 dependent, $1,152 with 2 dependents, and $5.25 for each additional dependent; for the second 6 months, the current monthly stipend is $808.78 for no dependents, $818.13 with 1 dependent, $825.83 with 2 dependents, and $3.85 for each additional dependent; for the third 6 months, the current monthly stipend is $502.60 for no dependents, $508.73 with 1 dependent, $513.45 with 2 dependents, and $2.45 for each additional dependent; for the remainder of the training period, the current monthly stipend is $490.70 for no dependents, $496.48 with 1 dependent, $501.73 with 2 dependents, and $2.45 for each additional dependent. Other rates apply for less than half-time study, cooperative education, correspondence courses, and flight training. Veterans who qualify for the accelerated payment and whose entitlement does not cover 60% of tuition and fees receive an additional lump sum payment to make up the difference between their entitlement and 60% of tuition and fees.

Duration 36 months; active-duty servicemembers must utilize the funds within 10 years of leaving the armed services; Reservists may draw on their funds while still serving.

Additional data Further information is available from local armed forces recruiters. This was the basic VA education program, referred to as Chapter 30, until the passage of the Post-9/11 GI Bill in 2009. Veterans who have remaining benefits available from this program may utilize those or transfer to the new program.

Number awarded Varies each year.

Deadline Deadline not specified.

[792]
NAVAL HELICOPTER ASSOCIATION GRADUATE SCHOLARSHIPS

Naval Helicopter Association
Attn: Scholarship Fund
P.O. Box 180578
Coronado, CA 92178-0578
(619) 435-7139   Fax: (619) 435-7354
E-mail: info@nhascholarship.org
Web: www.nhascholarship.org/nhascholarshipfund/index.html

Summary To provide financial assistance for graduate school to students who have an affiliation with the rotary wing activities of the sea services.

Eligibility This program is open to graduate students who are 1) children, grandchildren, or spouses of current or former Navy, Marine Corps, or Coast Guard rotary wing aviators or aircrewmen; 2) individuals who are serving or have served in maintenance or support billets in rotary wing squadrons or wings and their spouses and children. Applicants must provide information on their rotary wing affiliation and a personal statement on their educational plans and future goals. Selection is based on that statement, academic proficiency, scholastic achievements and awards, extracurricular activities, employment history, and letters of recommendation.

Financial Data The stipend is $3,000.

Duration 1 year.

Number awarded 1 each year.

Deadline January of each year.

[793]
NEW MEXICO VIETNAM VETERANS SCHOLARSHIPS

New Mexico Department of Veterans' Services
Attn: Benefits Division
407 Galisteo Street, Room 142
Santa Fe, NM 87504
(505) 827-6374   Toll Free: (866) 433-VETS
Fax: (505) 827-6372   E-mail: alan.martinez@state.nm.us
Web: www.dvs.state.nm.us/benefits.html

Summary To provide financial assistance to Vietnam veterans in New Mexico who are interested in working on an undergraduate or master's degree at a public college in the state.

Eligibility This program is open to Vietnam veterans who have been residents of New Mexico for at least 10 years. Applicants must have been honorably discharged and have been awarded the Vietnam Service Medal or the Vietnam Campaign Medal. They must be planning to attend a state-supported college, university, or community college in New Mexico to work on an undergraduate or master's degree. Awards are granted on a first-come, first-served basis.

Financial Data The scholarships provide full payment of tuition and purchase of required books at any state-funded postsecondary institution in New Mexico.

Duration 1 year.

Deadline Deadline not specified.

[794]
NEW YORK VETERANS TUITION AWARDS

New York State Higher Education Services Corporation
Attn: Student Information
99 Washington Avenue
Albany, NY 12255
(518) 473-1574   Toll Free: (888) NYS-HESC
Fax: (518) 473-3749   TDD: (800) 445-5234
E-mail: webmail@hesc.com
Web: www.hesc.com

Summary To provide tuition assistance to eligible veterans enrolled in an undergraduate or graduate program in New York.

Eligibility This program is open to veterans who served in the U.S. armed forces in 1) Indochina between February 28, 1961 and May 7, 1975; 2) hostilities that occurred after February 28, 1961 as evidenced by receipt of an Armed Forces Expeditionary Medal, Navy Expeditionary Medal, or Marine Corps Expeditionary Medal; 3) the Persian Gulf on or after August 2, 1990; or 4) Afghanistan on or after September 11, 2001. Applicants must have been discharged from the service under honorable conditions, must be a New York resident, must be a U.S. citizen or eligible non-citizen, must be enrolled full or part time at an undergraduate or graduate degree-granting institution in New York State or in an approved vocational training program in the state, must be charged at least $200 tuition per year, and must apply for a New York Tuition Assistance Program (TAP) award.

Financial Data For full-time study, the maximum stipend is 98% of tuition or $4,895.10, whichever is less. For part-time study, the stipend is based on the number of credits certified and the student's actual part-time tuition.

Duration For undergraduate study, up to 8 semesters, or up to 10 semesters for a program requiring 5 years for completion; for graduate study, up to 6 semesters; for vocational programs, up to 4 semesters. Award limits are based on full-time study or equivalent part-time study.

Additional data If a TAP award is also received, the combined academic year award cannot exceed tuition costs. If it does, the TAP award will be reduced accordingly.

Number awarded Varies each year.

Deadline April of each year.

[795]
NGASC SCHOLARSHIPS

National Guard Association of South Carolina
Attn: NGASC Scholarship Foundation
132 Pickens Street
Columbia, SC 29205
(803) 254-8456   Toll Free: (800) 822-3235
Fax: (803) 254-3869   E-mail: nginfo@ngasc.org
Web: www.ngasc.org/ngasc_scholarship_foundation.htm

Summary To provide financial assistance to current and former South Carolina National Guard members and their dependents who are interested in attending college or graduate school in any state.

Eligibility This program is open to undergraduate students who are 1) current, retired, or deceased members of the South Carolina National Guard; 2) their dependents; and 3) members of the National Guard Association of South Carolina (NGASC). Graduate students are also eligible if they are members of the South Carolina National Guard. Applicants must be attending or interested in attending a college or university in any state as a full-time student. Several of the scholarships include additional restrictions on school or academic major; some are granted only for academic excellence, but most are based on both academics and financial need.

Financial Data The stipend is $1,500 or $1,000.

Duration 1 year; may be renewed up to 3 additional years.

Additional data Among the named scholarships included in this program recently were the BG (Ret) C. Norwood Gayle Memorial Scholarship Award, the CMSgt Jim Burgess Scholarship Award, the Mrs. Kaye Helgeson Memorial Scholarship Award, the LTC (Ret) Glenny J. (Jeff) Matthews Memorial Scholarship Awards, the Ron McNair Memorial Scholarship Award, the Darla Moore Scholarship Award, the Sergeants Major Watson Scholarship Award, the SCANG Chiefs Council Scholarship Award, the Chief Shepherd Pitney Bowes Scholarship Award, the Fallen Soldiers' Memorial Scholarship Award, and the South Carolina National Guard Federal Credit Union Awards.

Number awarded Varies each year. Recently, 48 of these scholarships were awarded: 1 at $1,500 and 47 at $1,000. The $1,500 scholarship and 1 of the $1,000 scholarships were based on academic excellence; the remaining $1,000 scholarships were based on both academics and financial need.

Deadline January of each year.

[796]
NGAT SCHOLARSHIP PROGRAM

National Guard Association of Texas
Attn: NGAT Educational Foundation
3706 Crawford Avenue
Austin, TX 78731-6803
(512) 454-7300   Toll Free: (800) 252-NGAT
Fax: (512) 467-6803   E-mail: rlindner@ngat.org
Web: www.ngat.org

Summary To provide financial assistance to members and dependents of members of the National Guard Association of Texas who are interested in attending college or graduate school in any state.

Eligibility This program is open to annual and life members of the association and their spouses and children (associate members and their dependents are not eligible). Applicants may be high school seniors, undergraduate students, or graduate students, either enrolled or planning to enroll at an institution of higher education in any state. Along with their application, they must submit an essay on their desire to continue their education. Selection is based on scholarship, citizenship, and leadership.

Financial Data Stipends range from $500 to $5,000.

Duration 1 year (nonrenewable).

Additional data This program includes the following named scholarships: the Thomas F. Berry Memorial Scholarship, the Len and Jean Tallas Memorial Scholarship, the Texas Military Forces Retirees Scholarship, the T-Mates Scholarship, the LTC Gary W. Parrish Memorial Scholarship, the 1SG Harry E. Lux Memorial Scholarship, the Gloria Jenell and Marlin E. Mote Endowed Scholarship, the Chief Master Sergeants Scholarship, the Sergeants Major Scholarship, and the Texas USAA Scholarship (sponsored by USAA Insurance Corporation).

Number awarded Varies each year. Recently, 10 of these scholarships were awarded: 1 at $5,000, 3 at $2,500, 1 at $2,000, 2 at $1,250, 2 at $1,000, and 1 at $500.

Deadline February of each year.

[797]
NMIA/NMIF SCHOLARSHIP PROGRAM

National Military Intelligence Association
Attn: Scholarship Committee
256 Morris Creek Road
Cullen, VA 23934
(434) 542-5929   Fax: (703) 738-7487
E-mail: admin@nmia.org
Web: www.nmia.org/about/scholarshipprogram.html

Summary To provide financial assistance to undergraduate and graduate students majoring in a field of interest to the intelligence community.

Eligibility This program is open to full- and part-time juniors, seniors, and graduate students who are preparing for a career in a field related to the intelligence community. Applicants must list special activities, internships, prior or current military service, or other activities that provide tangible evidence of career aspirations to serve as a member of the intelligence community. Along with their application, they must submit a 1,000-word essay that covers 1) their intelligence community career goals and objectives; 2) the relationship between courses completed, courses planned, extracurricular activities, and prior work experience (including military service) to identified career goals and objectives; and 3) how this scholarship will make a difference to their efforts to realize their career goals and aspirations. Selection is based primarily on past academic success; financial need is not considered.

Financial Data The stipend is $3,000 for full-time students or $2,000 for part-time students.

Duration 1 year; nonrenewable.

Additional data This program is offered jointly by the National Military Intelligence Association (NMIA) and the National Military Intelligence Foundation (NMIF), P.O. Box 6844, Arlington, VA 22206, E-mail: ffrank54@comcast.net

Number awarded 6 each year: 3 for full-time students and 3 for part-time students.

Deadline November each year.

[798]
PETER CONNACHER MEMORIAL AMERICAN EX-PRISONER OF WAR SCHOLARSHIPS

Oregon Student Assistance Commission
Attn: Grants and Scholarships Division
1500 Valley River Drive, Suite 100
Eugene, OR 97401-2146
(541) 687-7395   Toll Free: (800) 452-8807, ext. 7395
Fax: (541) 687-7414   TDD: (800) 735-2900
E-mail: awardinfo@osac.state.or.us
Web: www.osac.state.or.us/osac_programs.html

Summary To provide financial assistance for college or graduate school to ex-prisoners of war and their descendants.

Eligibility Applicants must be U.S. citizens who 1) were military or civilian prisoners of war or 2) are the descendants of ex-prisoners of war. They may be undergraduate or graduate students. A copy of the ex-prisoner of war's discharge papers from the U.S. armed forces must accompany the application. In addition, written proof of POW status must be submitted, along with a statement of the relationship between the applicant and the ex-prisoner of war (father, grandfather, etc.). Selection is based on academic record and financial need. Preference is given to Oregon residents or their dependents.

Financial Data The stipend amount varies; recently, it was at least $1,150.

Duration 1 year; may be renewed for up to 3 additional years for undergraduate students or 2 additional years for graduate students. Renewal is dependent on evidence of continued financial need and satisfactory academic progress.

Additional data This program is administered by the Oregon Student Assistance Commission (OSAC) with funds provided by the Oregon Community Foundation, 1221 S.W. Yamhill, Suite 100, Portland, OR 97205, (503) 227-6846, Fax: (503) 274-7771. Funds are also provided by the Columbia River Chapter of the American Ex-prisoners of War, Inc. Recipients must attend college on a full-time basis.

Number awarded Varies each year; recently, 4 of these scholarships were awarded.

Deadline February of each year.

[799]
POST-9/11 GI BILL

Department of Veterans Affairs
Attn: Veterans Benefits Administration
810 Vermont Avenue, N.W.
Washington, DC 20420
(202) 418-4343   Toll Free: (888) GI-BILL1
Web: www.gibill.va.gov

Summary To provide financial assistance to veterans or military personnel who entered service on or after September 11, 2001.

Eligibility This program is open to current and former military who served on active duty for at least 90 aggregate days after September 11, 2001. Applicants must be planning to enroll at an accredited college or university as an undergraduate or graduate student; study in a certificate program, on-the-job training, apprenticeship program, flight training, and non-college degree course study do not qualify for support.

Financial Data Active-duty personnel receive payment of tuition and fees, up to the level of tuition and fees at the most expensive public institution of higher learning in their state of residence; the actual amount depends on the state of residence and the length of service completed. Veterans also receive a monthly housing allowance based on the Basic Allowance for Housing (BAH) for an E-5 with dependents if the location of the school they are attending is in the United States (or $1,333 per month at schools in foreign countries); an annual book allowance of $1,000; and (for participants who live in a rural county remote from an educational institution) a rural benefit payment of $500 per year.

Duration Most participants receive up to 36 months of entitlement under this program.

Additional data This program began in 2009 as a replacement for previous educational programs for veterans and military personnel (e.g., Montgomery GI Bill, REAP). Current participants in those programs may be able to utilize benefits under those programs and this new plan. Further information is available from local armed forces recruiters. This is the latest VA education program, referred to as Chapter 33.

Number awarded Varies each year.

Deadline Deadline not specified.

[800]
ROBERT W. NOLAN EMERITUS SCHOLARSHIP

Fleet Reserve Association
Attn: Scholarship Administrator
125 North West Street
Alexandria, VA 22314-2754
(703) 683-1400   Toll Free: (800) FRA-1924
Fax: (703) 549-6610   E-mail: fra@fra.org
Web: www.fra.org

Summary To provide financial assistance for graduate school to members of the Fleet Reserve Association (FRA) and their spouses, children, and grandchildren.

Eligibility This program is open to the dependent children, grandchildren, and spouses of members of the association who are in good standing (or were at the time of death, if deceased). FRA members are also eligible. Applicants should be enrolled in a graduate program. Along with their application, they must submit an essay on their life experiences, career objectives, and what motivated them to select those objectives. Selection is based on academic record, financial need, extracurricular activities, leadership skills, and participation in community activities. U.S. citizenship is required.

Financial Data The stipend is $5,000 per year.

Duration 1 year; may be renewed.

Additional data Membership in the FRA is restricted to active-duty, retired, and Reserve members of the Navy, Marine Corps, and Coast Guard. This program was established in 2001.

Number awarded 1 each year.

Deadline April of each year.

[801]
SAUL T. WILSON, JR. SCHOLARSHIP

Department of Agriculture
Animal and Plant Health Inspection Service
Attn: Human Resources/Recruitment
1400 Independence Avenue, S.W., Room 1710
Washington, DC 20250
(202) 690-4759
Web: www.aphis.usda.gov

Summary To provide scholarship/loans and work experience to undergraduate and graduate students (particularly veterans) who are interested in preparing for a career in veterinary medicine and biomedical sciences.

Eligibility This program is open to U.S. citizens enrolled in an accredited college or university in the United States as a full-time student. Undergraduates must have completed at least 2-years of a 4-year preveterinary medicine or other biomedical science program. Graduate students must have completed not more than 1 year of study in veterinary medicine. All applicants must submit a 500-word essay on why they should receive this scholarship and what contributions they would make to veterinary services of the Animal and Plant Health Inspection Service (APHIS). Preference is given to veterans of the U.S. armed forces. Financial need is not considered in the selection process.

Financial Data The maximum stipend is $5,000 per year for undergraduates or $10,000 per year for graduate students. Funds must be used for tuition, books, tutors, and laboratory fees. During summers and school breaks, scholars receive paid employment as a veterinary student trainee with APHIS at a salary that ranges from $9 to $13 per hour, depending on the student's qualifications. After 640 hours of study-related work with APHIS in the career experience program and graduation with a D.V.M. degree, and at the option of APHIS, the student must become a full-time employee for at least 1 calendar year for each school year of support from this scholarship. If scholarship recipients refuse to accept an APHIS offer of employment, they must reimburse the agency for all financial assistance received. If recipients fail to serve the entire length of the mandatory APHIS employment period, they must reimburse APHIS a prorated share of scholarship funds used.

Duration 1 year; may be renewed.

Number awarded 1 or more each year.

Deadline February of each year.

[802]
SCHUYLER S. PYLE SCHOLARSHIP

Fleet Reserve Association
Attn: Scholarship Administrator
125 North West Street
Alexandria, VA 22314-2754
(703) 683-1400　　　　　　　Toll Free: (800) FRA-1924
Fax: (703) 549-6610　　　　　E-mail: fra@fra.org
Web: www.fra.org

Summary To provide financial assistance for college or graduate school to members of the Fleet Reserve Association (FRA) who are current or former naval personnel and their spouses and children.

Eligibility This program is open to dependent children, grandchildren, and spouses of FRA members who are in good standing (or were at the time of death, if deceased). FRA members are also eligible. Applicants must be working on or planning to work on an undergraduate or graduate degree. Along with their application, they must submit an essay on their life experiences, career objectives, and what motivated them to select those objectives. Selection is based on academic record, financial need, extracurricular activities, leadership skills, and participation in community activities. U.S. citizenship is required.

Financial Data The stipend is $5,000 per year.

Duration 1 year; may be renewed.

Additional data Membership in the FRA is restricted to active-duty, retired, and Reserve members of the Navy, Marine Corps, and Coast Guard.

Number awarded 1 each year.

Deadline April of each year.

[803]
SFC CURTIS MANCINI MEMORIAL SCHOLARSHIPS

Association of the United States Army-Rhode Island Chapter
c/o CSM (Ret) Anthony Ferri, Secretary
47 Spokane Street
Providence, RI 02904
(401) 861-2997　　　　　　　E-mail: afnf458673755@aol.com
Web: www.ausari.org/index.html

Summary To provide financial assistance to members of the Rhode Island Chapter of the Association of the United States Army (AUSA) and their families who are interested in attending college or graduate school in any state.

Eligibility This program is open to members of the AUSA Rhode Island Chapter and their family members (spouses, children, and grandchildren). Applicants must be high school seniors or graduates accepted at an accredited college, university, or vocational/technical school in any state or current undergraduate or graduate students. Along with their application, they must submit a 250-word essay on why they feel their achievements should qualify them for this award. Selection is based on academic and individual achievements; financial need is not considered. Membership in AUSA is open to current and retired Army personnel (including Reserves and National Guard), ROTC cadets, or civilian employees of the Army.

Financial Data The stipend is $1,000.

Duration 1 year.

Number awarded 2 each year.

Deadline March of each year.

[804]
TILLMAN MILITARY SCHOLARSHIPS FOR SERVICEMEMBERS

Pat Tillman Foundation
2121 South Mill Avenue, Suite 214
Tempe, AZ 85282
(480) 621-4074　　　　　　　Fax: (480) 621-4075
E-mail: scholarships@pattillmanfoundation.org
Web: www.pattillmanfoundation.org

Summary To provide financial assistance to veterans and active servicemembers who are interested in working on an undergraduate or graduate degree.

Eligibility This program is open to veterans and active servicemembers of all branches of the armed forces from both the pre- and post-September 11 era whose educational benefits have run out or are insufficient to meet their need. Applicants must be interested in starting, finishing, or furthering their undergraduate, graduate, or postgraduate education at a 2-year, 4-year, or vocational institution (public or private). Along with their application, they must submit 1-page essays on 1) their specific financial need, including any gap in educational benefits they may already be receiving and their reason for applying for this scholarship; 2) their motivation and decision to serve in the U.S. armed forces; and 3) their educational and career goals, how they will incorporate their military service into those goals, and how they intend to continue their service to others and the community. Selection is based on those essays, educational and career ambitions, length of service, record of personal achievement, demonstration of service to others in the community and a desire to continue such service, and unmet financial need.

Financial Data Stipends vary; recently, total awards (including multi-year awards) averaged $12,800.

Duration 1 year; may be renewed, provided the recipient maintains a GPA of 3.0 or higher, remains enrolled full time, and documents participation in civic action or community service.

Additional data This program was established in 2009. The foundation administers the program directly for students at colleges and universities nationwide; it also acts in partnership with 4 universities (the University of Maryland, the University of Arkansas, the University of Idaho, and Mississippi State University) which award scholarships directly to their students.

Number awarded Varies each year; recently, 52 students received a total of $665,820 in these scholarships

Deadline May of each year.

[805]
UTAH TUITION WAIVER FOR PURPLE HEART RECIPIENTS

Utah Division of Veteran's Affairs
Attn: Director
550 Foothill Boulevard, Room 202
Salt Lake City, UT 84108
(801) 326-2372　　　Toll Free: (800) 894-9497 (within UT)
Fax: (801) 326-2369　　　E-mail: veterans@utah.gov
Web: veterans.utah.gov/homepage/stateBenefits/index.html

Summary To provide a tuition waiver to veterans in Utah who received a Purple Heart award and are attending a public institution in the state.

Eligibility This program is open to residents of Utah who received a Purple Heart award as a result of military service. Applicants must be working on an undergraduate or master's degree at a public college or university in the state.

Financial Data Tuition at the rate for residents of the state is waived for qualified veterans.

Duration Tuition is waived until completion of a bachelor's or master's degree.

Number awarded Varies each year.

Deadline Deadline not specified.

[806]
VADM ROBERT L. WALTERS SCHOLARSHIP

Surface Navy Association
2550 Huntington Avenue, Suite 202
Alexandria, VA 22303
(703) 960-6800　　　Toll Free: (800) NAVY-SNA
Fax: (703) 960-6807　　　E-mail: navysna@aol.com
Web: www.navysna.org/awards/index.html

Summary To provide financial assistance for college or graduate school to members of the Surface Navy Association (SNA) and their dependents.

Eligibility This program is open to SNA members and their children, stepchildren, wards, and spouses. The SNA member must 1) be in the second or subsequent consecutive year of membership; 2) be serving, retired, or honorably discharged; 3) be a Surface Warfare Officer or Enlisted Surface Warfare Specialist; and 4) have served for at least 3 years on a surface ship of the U.S. Navy or Coast Guard. Applicants must be studying or planning to study at an accredited undergraduate or graduate institution. Along with their application, they must submit a 200-word essay about themselves; a list of their extracurricular activities, community service activities, academic honors and/or positions of leadership that represent their interests, with an estimate of the amount of time involved with each activity; and 3 letters of reference. High school seniors should also include a transcript of high school grades and a copy of ACT or SAT scores. Applicants who are on active duty or drilling Reservists should also include a letter from their commanding officer commenting on their military service and leadership potential, a transcript of grades from their most recent 4 semesters of school, a copy of their ACT or SAT scores if available, and an indication of whether they have applied for or are enrolled in the Enlisted Commissioning Program. Applicants who are not high school seniors, active-duty servicemembers, or drilling Reservists should also include a transcript of the grades from their most recent 4 semesters of school and a copy of ACT or SAT test scores (unless they are currently attending a college or university). Selection is based on demonstrated lead-

ership, community service, academic achievement, and commitment to pursuing higher educational objectives.

Financial Data The stipend is $2,000 per year.

Duration 4 years, provided the recipient maintains a GPA of 3.0 or higher.

Number awarded Varies each year.

Deadline February of each year.

[807]
VETERANS EDUCATIONAL ASSISTANCE PROGRAM (VEAP)

Department of Veterans Affairs
Attn: Veterans Benefits Administration
810 Vermont Avenue, N.W.
Washington, DC 20420
(202) 418-4343　　　Toll Free: (888) GI-BILL1
Web: www.gibill.va.gov/GI_Bill_Info/benefits.htm

Summary To provide financial assistance for college to veterans who first entered active duty between January 1, 1977 and June 30, 1985.

Eligibility Veterans who served and military servicemembers currently serving are eligible if they 1) entered active duty between January 1, 1977 and June 30, 1985; 2) were released under conditions other than dishonorable or continue on active duty; 3) served for a continuous period of 181 days or more (or were discharged earlier for a service-connected disability); and 4) have satisfactorily contributed to the program. No individuals on active duty could enroll in this program after March 31, 1987. Veterans who enlisted for the first time after September 7, 1980 or entered active duty as an office or enlistee after October 16, 1981 must have completed 24 continuous months of active duty. Benefits are available for the pursuit of an associate, bachelor, or graduate degree at a college or university; a certificate or diploma from a business, technical, or vocational school; apprenticeship or on-the-job training programs; cooperative courses; correspondence school courses; tutorial assistance; remedial, refresher, and deficiency training; flight training; study abroad programs leading to a college degree; nontraditional training away from school; and work-study for students enrolled at least three-quarter time.

Financial Data Participants contribute to the program, through monthly deductions from their military pay, from $25 to $100 monthly, up to a maximum of $2,700. They may also, while on active duty, make a lump sum contribution to the training fund. At the time the eligible participant elects to use the benefits to pursue an approved course of education or training, the Department of Veterans Affairs (VA) will match the contribution at the rate of $2 for every $1 made by the participant.

Duration Participants receive monthly payments for the number of months they contributed, or for 36 months, whichever is less. The amount of the payments is determined by dividing the number of months benefits will be paid into the participant's training fund total. Participants have 10 years from the date of last discharge or release from active duty within which to use these benefits.

Additional data A participant may leave this program at the end of any 12-consecutive-month period of participation and those who do so may have their contributions refunded. Ineligible courses include bartending or personality development courses; farm cooperative courses; non-accredited independent study courses; any course given by radio; self-improvement courses such as reading, speaking, woodworking, basic seamanship, and English as a second language; audited courses; any course that is avocational or recreational in character; courses not leading to an educational, professional, or vocational objective; courses taken and successfully completed previously; courses taken by a federal government employee and paid for under the Government Employees' Training Act; courses paid for in whole or in part by the armed forces while on active duty; and courses taken while in receipt of benefits for the same program from the Office of Workers' Compensation Programs.

Number awarded Varies each year.

Deadline Applications may be submitted at any time.

[808]
VOCATIONAL REHABILITATION FOR DISABLED VETERANS

Department of Veterans Affairs
Attn: Veterans Benefits Administration
Vocational Rehabilitation and Employment Service
810 Vermont Avenue, N.W.
Washington, DC 20420
(202) 418-4343   Toll Free: (800) 827-1000
Web: www.vba.va.gov/bin/vre/index.htm

Summary To provide vocational rehabilitation to certain categories of veterans with disabilities.

Eligibility This program is open to veterans who have a service-connected disability of 1) at least 10% and a serious employment handicap, or 2) at least 20% and an employment handicap. They must have been discharged or released from military service under other than dishonorable conditions. The Department of Veterans Affairs (VA) must determine that they would benefit from a training program that would help them prepare for, find, and keep suitable employment. The program may be 1) institutional training at a certificate, 2-year college, 4-year college or university, or technical program; 2) unpaid on-the-job training in a federal, state, or local agency or a federally-recognized Indian tribal agency, training in a home, vocational course in a rehabilitation facility or sheltered workshop, independent instruction, or institutional non-farm cooperative; or 3) paid training through a farm cooperative, apprenticeship, on-the-job training, or on-the-job non-farm cooperative.

Financial Data While in training and for 2 months after, eligible disabled veterans may receive subsistence allowances in addition to their disability compensation or retirement pay. For most training programs, the current full-time monthly rate is $547.54 with no dependents, $679.18 with 1 dependent, $800.36 with 2 dependents, and $58.34 for each additional dependent; proportional rates apply for less than full-time training. The VA also pays the costs of tuition, books, fees, supplies, and equipment; it may also pay for special supportive services, such as tutorial assistance, prosthetic devices, lipreading training, and signing for the deaf. If during training or employment services the veteran's disabilities cause transportation expenses that would not be incurred by nondisabled persons, the VA will pay for at least a portion of those expenses. If the veteran encounters financial difficulty during training, the VA may provide an advance against future benefit payments.

Duration Up to 48 months of full-time training or its equivalent in part-time training. If a veteran with a serious disability receives services under an extended evaluation to improve training potential, the total of the extended evaluation and the training phases of the rehabilitation program may exceed 48 months. Usually, the veteran must complete a rehabilitation program within 12 years from the date of notification of entitlement to compensation by the VA. Following completion of the training portion of a rehabilitation program, a veteran may receive counseling and job search and adjustment services for 18 months.

Additional data The program may also provide employment assistance, self-employment assistance, training in a rehabilitation facility, or college and other training. Veterans who are seriously disabled may receive services and assistance to improve their ability to live more independently in their community. After completion of the training phase, the VA will assist the veteran to find and have a suitable job.

Number awarded Varies each year.

Deadline Applications are accepted at any time.

[809]
WISCONSIN G.I. BILL TUITION REMISSION PROGRAM

Wisconsin Department of Veterans Affairs
30 West Mifflin Street
P.O. Box 7843
Madison, WI 53707-7843
(608) 266-1311   Toll Free: (800) WIS-VETS
Fax: (608) 267-0403   E-mail: WDVAInfo@dva.state.wi.us
Web: www.dva.state.wi.us/Ben_education.asp

Summary To provide financial assistance for college or graduate school to Wisconsin veterans and their dependents.

Eligibility This program is open to current residents of Wisconsin who 1) were residents of the state when they entered or reentered active duty in the U.S. armed forces, or 2) have moved to the state and have been residents for any consecutive 12-month period after entry or reentry into service. Applicants must have served on active duty for at least 2 continuous years or for at least 90 days during specified wartime periods. Also eligible are 1) qualifying children and unremarried surviving spouses of Wisconsin veterans who died in the line of duty or as the direct result of a service-connected disability; and 2) children and spouses of Wisconsin veterans who have a service-connected disability rated by the U.S. Department of Veterans Affairs as 30% or greater. Children must be between 17 and 25 years of age (regardless of the date of the veteran's death or initial disability rating) and be a Wisconsin resident for tuition purposes. Spouses remain eligible for 10 years following the date of the veteran's death or initial disability rating; they must be Wisconsin residents for tuition purposes but they may enroll full or part time. Students may attend any institution, center, or school within the University of Wisconsin (UW) System or the Wisconsin Technical College System (WCTS). There are no income limits, delimiting periods following military service during which the benefit must be used, or limits on the level of study (e.g., vocational, undergraduate, professional, or graduate).

Financial Data Veterans who qualify as a Wisconsin resident for tuition purposes are eligible for a remission of 100% of standard academic fees and segregated fees at a UW campus or 100% of program and material fees at a WCTS institution. Veterans who qualify as a Wisconsin veteran for purposes of this program but for other reasons fail to meet the definition of a Wisconsin resident for tuition purposes at the UW system are eligible for a remission of 100% of non-resident fees. Spouses and children of deceased or disabled veterans are entitled to a remission of 100% of tuition and fees at a UW or WCTS institution.

Duration Up to 8 semesters or 128 credits, whichever is greater.

Additional data This program was established in 2005 as a replacement for Wisconsin Tuition and Fee Reimbursement Grants.

Number awarded Varies each year.

Deadline Applications must be submitted within 14 days from the office start of the academic term: in October for fall, March for spring, or June for summer.

[810]
WISCONSIN JOB RETRAINING GRANTS

Wisconsin Department of Veterans Affairs
30 West Mifflin Street
P.O. Box 7843
Madison, WI 53707-7843
(608) 266-1311   Toll Free: (800) WIS-VETS
Fax: (608) 267-0403   E-mail: WDVAInfo@dva.state.wi.us
Web: www.dva.state.wi.us/Ben_retraininggrants.asp

Summary To provide funds to recently unemployed Wisconsin veterans or their families who need financial assistance while being retrained for employment.

Eligibility This program is open to current residents of Wisconsin who 1) were residents of the state when they entered or reentered active duty in the U.S. armed forces, or 2) have moved to the state and have been residents for any consecutive 12-month period after entry or reentry into service. Applicants must have served on active duty for at least 2 continuous years or for at least 90 days during specified wartime periods. Unremarried spouses and minor or dependent children of deceased veterans who would have been eligible for the grant if they were living today may also be eligible. The applicant must, within the year prior to the date of application, have become unemployed (involuntarily laid off or discharged, not due to willful misconduct) or underemployed (experienced an involuntary reduction of income). Underemployed applicants must have current annual income from employment that does not exceed federal poverty guidelines. All applicants must be retraining at accredited schools in Wisconsin or in a structured on-the-job program. Course work toward a college degree does not qualify. Training does not have to be full time, but the program must be completed within 2 years and must reasonably be expected to lead to employment.

Financial Data The maximum grant is $3,000 per year; the actual amount varies, depending upon the amount of the applicant's unmet need. In addition to books, fees, and tuition, the funds may be used for living expenses.

Duration 1 year; may be renewed 1 additional year.

Number awarded Varies each year.

Deadline Applications may be submitted at any time.

[811]
WMA SCHOLARSHIP PROGRAM

Women Marines Association
P.O. Box 377
Oaks, PA 19456-0377
Toll Free: (888) 525-1943 E-mail: wma@womenmarines.org
Web: www.womenmarines.org/scholarships.aspx

Summary To provide financial assistance for college or graduate school to students sponsored by members of the Women Marines Association (WMA).

Eligibility Applicants must be sponsored by a WMA member and fall into 1 of the following categories: 1) have served or are serving in the U.S. Marine Corps, regular or Reserve; 2) are a direct descendant by blood, legal adoption, or stepchild of a Marine on active duty or who has served honorably in the U.S. Marine Corps, regular or Reserve; 3) are a sibling or a descendant of a sibling by blood, legal adoption, or stepchild of a Marine on active duty or who has served honorably in the U.S. Marine Corps, regular or Reserve; or 4) have completed 2 years in a Marine Corps JROTC program. WMA members may sponsor an unlimited number of applicants per year. High school seniors must submit transcripts (GPA of 3.0 or higher) and SAT or ACT scores. Undergraduate and graduate students must have a GPA of 3.0 or higher.

Financial Data The stipend is $1,500 per year.

Duration 1 year; may be renewed 1 additional year.

Additional data This program includes the following named scholarships: the WMA Memorial Scholarships, the Lily H. Gridley Memorial Scholarship, the Ethyl and Armin Wiebke Memorial Scholarship, the Maj. Megan Malia McClung Memorial Scholarship, and the LaRue A. Ditmore Music Scholarships. Applicants must know a WMA member to serve as their sponsor; the WMA will not supply listings of the names or addresses of chapters or individual members.

Number awarded Varies each year.

Deadline March of each year.

[812]
WNGEA COLLEGE GRANT PROGRAM

Wisconsin National Guard Enlisted Association
Attn: Executive Director
2400 Wright Street
Madison, WI 53704
(608) 242-3112   E-mail: WNGEA@yahoo.com
Web: www.wngea.org/MAIN/PROG/prosch.htm

Summary To provide financial assistance to members of the Wisconsin National Guard Enlisted Association (WNGEA) and their spouses and children who are interested in attending college or graduate school in any state.

Eligibility This program is open to WNGEA members, the unmarried children of WNGEA members, the spouses of WNGEA members, and the unmarried children and spouses of deceased WNGEA members. WNGEA member applicants, as well as the parents or guardians of unmarried children who are applicants, must have at least 1 year remaining on their enlistment following completion of the school year for which application is submitted (or they must have 20 or more years of service). Applicants must be enrolled at a college, university, graduate school, trade school, or business school in any state. Selection is based on financial need, leadership, and moral character.

Financial Data Stipends are $1,000 or $500 per year.

Duration 1 year; recipients may not reapply for 2 years.

Additional data This program includes 1 scholarship sponsored by the USAA Insurance Corporation.

Number awarded Varies each year. Recently, 4 of these scholarships were awarded: the Raymond A. Matera Scholarship at $1,000 and 3 others at $500 each.

Deadline May of each year.

Military Personnel

[813]
AAAA SCHOLARSHIPS

Army Aviation Association of America Scholarship
  Foundation
Attn: AAAA Scholarship Foundation
755 Main Street, Suite 4D
Monroe, CT 06468-2830
(203) 268-2450   Fax: (203) 268-5870
E-mail: Scholarship@quad-a.org
Web: www.quad-a.org/scholarship.htm

Summary To provide financial aid for undergraduate or graduate study to members of the Army Aviation Association of America (AAAA) and their relatives.

Eligibility This program is open to AAAA members and their spouses, unmarried siblings, unmarried children, and unmarried grandchildren. Applicants must be enrolled or accepted for enrollment as an undergraduate or graduate student at an accredited college or university. Graduate students must include a 250-word essay on their life experiences, work history, and aspirations. Some scholarships are specifically reserved for enlisted, warrant officer, company grade, and Department of the Army civilian members. Selection is based on academic merit and personal achievement.

Financial Data Most stipends range from $1,000 to $4,000. Special scholarships are $11,000.

Duration Scholarships may be for 1 year, 2 years, or 4 years.

Additional data This program includes 3 special scholarships: the GEN Hamilton H. Howze Memorial Scholarship, the Helen

Cribbins Memorial Scholarship, and the Joseph P. Cribbins Scholarship.

Number awarded Varies each year; recently, $268,500 in scholarships was awarded to 171 students. Since the program began in 1963, the foundation has awarded more than $3.3 million to nearly 2,000 qualified applicants.

Deadline April of each year.

[814]
ADVANCED CIVIL SCHOOLING PROGRAM

U.S. Army
Human Resources Command
Attn: OPCF ACS Program
200 Stovall Street
Alexandria, VA 22332
(703) 325-8142   E-mail: tapcopza@hoffman.army.mil
Web: www.hrc.army.mil/SITE/Active/opfamacs/ACS14.htm

Summary To provide financial assistance to Army officers interested in working on an advanced degree in selected fields.

Eligibility This program is open to Army officers who wish to work on an advanced degree at an approved civilian institution on a full-time basis. Applicants must have a regular Army commission or a United States Army Reserve (USAR) commission with Voluntary Indefinite Status (VI). They must have completed a bachelor's degree with a GPA of 2.5 or higher and must have a GMAT score of 500 or higher or a GRE score of 500 or higher in the quantitative and verbal categories plus a 4.0 or higher in the analytical category.

Financial Data The officer continues to receive regular Army salary and allowances. The fellowship pays tuition up to $14,500 per year, a 1-time payment of $600 for application fees, and a book allotment of $200 per year.

Duration 12 to 22 months, depending on the program.

Additional data Participants in this program incur an additional service obligation of 3 days of service for each day of educational leave. Further information and applications are available from the applicant's assignment officer.

Number awarded Approximately 412 each year.

Deadline September of each year.

[815]
AIR FORCE EXCELLENCE SCHOLARSHIPS

Air Force Association
Attn: Scholarship Manager
1501 Lee Highway
Arlington, VA 22209-1198
(703) 247-5800, ext. 4807
Toll Free: (800) 727-3337, ext. 4807
Fax: (703) 247-5853   E-mail: LCross@afa.org
Web: www.afa.org/aef/aid/afa-fcef-rotc.asp

Summary To provide financial assistance for college or graduate school to Air Force personnel and their dependents.

Eligibility This program is open to Air Force active duty, Reserve, or Air National Guard personnel and their spouses and dependent children. Applicants must be entering or enrolled at an accredited college or university to work on an associate, bachelor's, or master's degree. In the selection process, no consideration is given to race, creed, color, sex, religious belief, national origin, rank, length of service, or financial need.

Financial Data The stipend is $3,000.

Duration 1 year.

Additional data This program was established in 2008 by the Air Force Association in partnership with the First Command Educational Foundation.

Number awarded 5 each year.

Deadline April of each year.

[816]
AIR FORCE FINANCIAL ASSISTANCE PROGRAM

U.S. Air Force
Attn: Air Force Institute of Technology
2950 P Street, Building 642
Wright-Patterson AFB, OH 45433-7765
(937) 255-5824, ext. 3036   Toll Free: (800) 588-5260
Fax: (937) 656-7156   E-mail: afit.cimj3@afit.edu
Web: www.airforce.com/opportunities/healthcare/education

Summary To provide financial assistance to future Air Force officers who are currently participating in a medical or dental residency.

Eligibility This program is open to U.S. citizens who are currently at any point in residency training in a medical or dental specialty that meets the needs of the U.S. Air Force. Upon acceptance into the program, applicants are commissioned as officers in the U.S. Air Force Reserve; after completion of school, they must perform active-duty service as a doctor or dentist in the Air Force.

Financial Data This program pays an annual grant of more than $45,000 and a stipend of $1,992 per month.

Additional data Participants must spend 14 days each year in an Active Duty Tour (ADT) assignment. Medical doctors incur an active-duty obligation of 1 year for each year of support plus 1 additional year. Dentists incur an active-duty obligation of 1 year for each year of support, with a minimum of 3 years.

Number awarded Varies each year.

Deadline Applications may be submitted at any time.

[817]
AIR FORCE HEALTH PROFESSIONS SCHOLARSHIP PROGRAM

U.S. Air Force
Attn: Air Force Institute of Technology
2950 P Street, Building 642
Wright-Patterson AFB, OH 45433-7765
(937) 255-5824, ext. 3036   Toll Free: (800) 588-5260
Fax: (937) 656-7156   E-mail: afit.cimj3@afit.edu
Web: www.airforce.com/opportunities/healthcare/education

Summary To provide financial assistance for education in a medical or scientific field to future Air Force medical officers.

Eligibility This program is open to U.S. citizens who are accepted to or already enrolled in a health care professional program. They must be working on a degree that will prepare them for service in Air Force Biomedical Science Corps specialties (pharmacists, optometrists, clinical psychologists, or public health officers), Nurse Corps specialties, Medical Corps, or Dental Corps. Upon acceptance into the program, applicants are commissioned as officers in the U.S. Air Force; after completion of medical school, they must perform at least 3 years of active-duty service in the U.S. Air Force.

Financial Data This program pays full tuition at any school of medicine or osteopathy located in the United States or Puerto Rico, and it also covers the cost of fees, books, and other required equipment. In addition, recipients are awarded a stipend of $1,992 per month for 10 1/2 months of the year; for the other 1 1/2 months of each year, they perform active-duty service, usually at an Air Force medical facility, and receive the normal pay of a Second Lieutenant.

Duration 1 or 2 years for Biomedical Service Corps specialties, 2 or 3 years for Nurse Corps specialties, 3 or 4 years for Medical Corps or Dental Corps.

Additional data Following receipt of the degree, students serve an internship and residency either in an Air Force hospital (in which case they receive Air Force active-duty pay) or, if not selected for Air Force graduate medical education, in a civilian hospital (where they receive only the regular salary paid by the civilian institution). Only after completion of the residency, in either an Air Force or a civilian hospital, do the students begin the active-duty service obligation. That obligation is equal to the number of years of support received plus 1 year.

Number awarded   Approximately 325 each year.

Deadline   Deadline not specified.

[818]
AIR FORCE JUDGE ADVOCATE GENERAL'S DEPARTMENT FUNDED LEGAL EDUCATION PROGRAM

U.S. Air Force
Attn: HQ USAF/JAX
1420 Air Force
Pentagon, Room 5B269
Washington, DC 20330-1420
(703) 614-5941   Toll Free: (800) JAG-USAF
E-mail: afsana.ahmed@pentagon.af.mil
Web: www.jagusaf.hq.af.mil/EDprgrms/flep.htm

Summary   To provide financial assistance to Air Force officers interested in attending law school.

Eligibility   This program is open to commissioned officers in the U.S. Air Force who have at least 2 but no more than 6 years of active-duty military service (including both enlisted and commissioned time) and have graduated from an accredited college or university with a bachelor's degree. Applicants must be currently in the pay grade of O-3 or below. They must submit transcripts from undergraduate (and/or graduate) schools, their LSAT results, and proof of an application or acceptance to an ABA-accredited law school.

Financial Data   Selectees continue to receive their regular pay and allowances during participation in this program. They also receive payment of tuition (to a maximum of $12,000 per year) and a book allowance.

Duration   Until completion of a law degree.

Additional data   Selectees are required to perform legal internships each summer they are in law school. Following completion of law school and passage of a bar examination, they enter service as an Air Force judge advocate with an active-duty obligation of 2 years for each year of legal training supported by this program.

Number awarded   Varies each year; recently, 8 officers received support from this program.

Deadline   February of each year.

[819]
AIR FORCE ONE-YEAR COLLEGE PROGRAM (OYCP)

U.S. Air Force
Attn: HQ USAF/JAX
1420 Air Force
Pentagon, Room 5B269
Washington, DC 20330-1420
(703) 614-5941   Toll Free: (800) JAG-USAF
E-mail: afsana.ahmed@pentagon.af.mil
Web: www.jagusaf.hq.af.mil/EDprgrms/oycp.htm

Summary   To provide financial assistance to law students who are willing to join Air Force ROTC and serve as Air Force Judge Advocates following completion of their studies.

Eligibility   This program is open to students in their second year at an ABA-approved law school that has, or is located near, an AFROTC detachment. Applicants must be in good academic standing and able to meet AFROTC entry standards (U.S. citizenship, weight and medical qualifications, and Air Force Officer Qualification Test minimum score). They must be younger than 35 years of age upon commissioning and entering active duty. Selection is based on academic performance, extracurricular activities, community service, prior military record (if any), work experience,

and a recommendation by a staff judge advocate following an interview.

Financial Data   Participants receive a stipend for 10 months of the year at $400 per month and a salary during summer field training. No other scholarship assistance is available.

Duration   1 year.

Additional data   Selectees with no prior military experience attend field training encampment during the summer prior to entering the AFROTC program as contract cadets. Upon completion of their degree and legal licensing requirements, participants enter active duty as first lieutenants in the U.S. Air Force Judge Advocate General's Department. After 6 months of active duty, they are promoted to captain. The initial required active-duty service obligation is 4 years.

Number awarded   Varies each year.

Deadline   January of each year.

[820]
AIR FORCE RESERVE TUITION ASSISTANCE

U.S. Air Force Reserve
Attn: Air Reserve Personnel Center
Directorate of Personnel Services
6760 East Irvington Place
Denver, CO 80280-4000
(303) 676-7037   Toll Free: (800) 525-0102
Fax: (478) 327-2215
E-mail: arpc.contactcenter@arpc.denver.af.mil
Web: www.arpc.afrc.af.mil/library/education/index.asp

Summary   To provide financial assistance for college or graduate school to members of the Air Force Reserve.

Eligibility   This program is open to Air Force Reserve members interested in working on an undergraduate or graduate degree either through distance learning or on-campus courses from an accredited postsecondary institution. Applicants must be actively participating (for pay and points) and in good standing (not have a UIF, not placed on a control roster, not pending or issued an Article 15, and/or not pending court martial). They must submit a degree plan specifying all classes for which they are seeking assistance. Enlisted students must have retainability that extends beyond the last course approved for assistance or they must extend or re-enlist; commissioned officers must have a mandatory separation date of not less than 24 months of service commitment starting at the end of the last course completed.

Financial Data   Undergraduates receive 100% of tuition, to a maximum of $250 per semester hour or $4,500 per year; graduate students receive 75% of tuition, to a maximum of $250 per semester hour or $4,500 per year.

Duration   1 year; may be renewed.

Number awarded   Varies each year.

Deadline   Applications may be submitted at any time.

[821]
AIR FORCE ROTC GRADUATE LAW PROGRAM

U.S. Air Force
Attn: Headquarters AFROTC/RRUC
551 East Maxwell Boulevard
Maxwell AFB, AL 36112-5917
(334) 953-2091   Toll Free: (866) 4-AFROTC
Fax: (334) 953-6167   E-mail: afrotc1@maxwell.af.mil
Web: afrotc.com

Summary   To provide financial assistance for law school to individuals who are interested in joining Air Force ROTC and are willing to serve as Air Force officers following completion of their professional degree.

Eligibility   Applicants must be U.S. citizens who are currently enrolled in the first year of law school at a college or university with an Air Force ROTC unit on campus or a college with a cross-enrollment agreement with such a school. They may be veterans, current military personnel, or first-year law students without military experience. The law school must be accredited by the American Bar Association. Applicants must agree to serve for at least 4 years as active-duty Air Force officers following graduation from law school. Selection is based on academic performance, extracurricular activities, work experience, community service, military record (if appropriate), and recommendations.

Financial Data Students are paid during summer field training and also receive a tax-free stipend of $400 per month during the last 2 years of their legal education. No other scholarship assistance is provided.

Duration 2 years.

Additional data Participants attend a field training encampment (4 weeks for students with prior military service, 5 weeks for students with no prior military experience) during the summer between their first and second year of law school. They then complete the normal academic requirements for the 2-year AFROTC program while completing law school. After graduation, participants enter active duty as a first lieutenant (with promotion after 6 months).

Deadline March of each year.

[822]
AIR FORCE ROTC PROFESSIONAL OFFICER CORPS INCENTIVE

U.S. Air Force
Attn: Headquarters AFROTC/RRUC
551 East Maxwell Boulevard
Maxwell AFB, AL 36112-5917
(334) 953-2091   Toll Free: (866) 4-AFROTC
Fax: (334) 953-6167   E-mail: afrotc1@maxwell.af.mil
Web: afrotc.com/learn-about/programs-and-scholarships

Summary To provide financial assistance for undergraduate and graduate studies to individuals who have completed 2 years of college and who are willing to join Air Force ROTC and serve as Air Force officers following completion of their degree.

Eligibility Applicants must be U.S. citizens who have completed 2 years of the general military course at a college or university with an Air Force ROTC unit on campus or a college with a cross-enrollment agreement with such a college. They must be full-time students, have a GPA of 2.0 or higher both cumulatively and for the prior term, be enrolled in both Aerospace Studies class and Leadership Laboratory, pass the Air Force Officer Qualifying Test, meet Air Force physical fitness and weight requirements, and be able to be commissioned before they become 31 years of age. They must agree to serve for at least 4 years as active-duty Air Force officers following graduation from college with either a bachelor's or graduate degree.

Financial Data This scholarship provides $3,000 per year for tuition and a monthly subsistence allowance of $450 as a junior or $500 as a senior.

Duration Until completion of a graduate degree.

Additional data Scholarship recipients must complete 4 years of aerospace studies courses at 1 of the 144 colleges and universities that have an Air Force ROTC unit on campus; students may also attend 984 other colleges that have cross-enrollment agreements with the institutions that have an Air Force ROTC unit on campus. Recipients must also attend a 4-week summer training camp at an Air Force base between their junior and senior year.

Number awarded Varies each year.

Deadline Deadline not specified.

[823]
AIR FORCE SERVICES CLUB MEMBERSHIP SCHOLARSHIP PROGRAM

Air Force Services Agency
Attn: HQ AFSVA/SVOFT
10100 Reunion Place, Suite 501
San Antonio, TX 78216-4138
(210) 652-6312   Toll Free: (800) 443-4834
Fax: (210) 652-7041
E-mail: web.clubs-operations@randolph.af.mil
Web: www.afclubs.net/CN_Scholarship.htm

Summary To recognize and reward, with academic scholarships, Air Force Club members and their families who submit outstanding essays.

Eligibility This program is open to Air Force Club members and their spouses, children, and stepchildren who have been accepted by or are enrolled at an accredited college or university. Grandchildren are eligible if they are the dependent of a club member. Applicants may be undergraduate or graduate students enrolled full or part time. They must submit an essay of up to 500 words on a topic that changes annually; a recent topic was "The High Cost of Freedom" Applicants must also include a 1-page summary of their long-term career and life goals and previous accomplishments, including civic, athletic, and academic awards.

Financial Data Awards are $1,000 scholarships.

Duration The competition is held annually.

Additional data This competition, first held in 1997, is sponsored by Chase Bank and the Coca-Cola Company.

Number awarded 25 each year.

Deadline Entries must be submitted to the member's base services commander or division chief by June of each year.

[824]
AIR FORCE TUITION ASSISTANCE PROGRAM

U.S. Air Force
Attn: Air Force Personnel Center
Headquarters USAF/DPPAT
550 C Street West, Suite 10
Randolph AFB, TX 78150-4712
Fax: (210) 565-2328
Web: www.airforce.com/opportunities/enlisted/education

Summary To provide financial assistance for college or graduate school to active-duty Air Force personnel.

Eligibility Eligible to apply for this program are active-duty Air Force personnel who have completed 2 years of their service obligation.

Financial Data Air Force personnel chosen for participation in this program continue to receive their regular Air Force pay. The Air Force will pay 100% of the tuition costs in an approved program, to a maximum of $4,500 per year or $250 per semester hour, whichever is less.

Duration Up to 4 years.

Additional data Applications and further information about this program are available from counselors at the education centers on Air Force bases. Most Air Force personnel who receive tuition assistance participate in the Community College of the Air Force; there, participants earn a 2-year associate degree by combining on-the-job technical training or attendance at Air Force schools with enrollment in college courses at a civilian institution during off-duty hours. In addition, each Air Force base offers at least 4 subject areas in which selected Air Force personnel can receive tuition assistance for study leading to a bachelor's degree, and 2 disciplines in which they can pursue graduate study.

Number awarded Varies each year.

Deadline Deadline not specified.

[825]
AL PONTE SCHOLARSHIP AWARD

Association of Former Intelligence Officers
Attn: Scholarship Committee
6723 Whittier Avenue, Suite 200
McLean, VA 22101-4533
(703) 790-0320   Fax: (703) 991-1278
E-mail: afio@afio.com
Web: www.afio.com/13_scholarships.htm

Summary To provide financial assistance to members or the children or grandchildren of members of the Association of Former Intelligence Officers (AFIO) who are interested in working on a graduate degree in international relations and/or intelligence.

Eligibility This program is open to college seniors who are interested in attending graduate school to work on a degree in international relations and/or intelligence. Applicants must be AFIO members, the children or grandchildren of members, or the children or grandchildren of personnel currently serving in military intelligence. Selection is based on merit, character, estimated future potential, background, and relevance of their studies to the full spectrum of national security interests and career ambitions. U.S. citizenship is required.

Financial Data The stipend is $1,000.

Duration 1 year.

Number awarded 1 each year.

Deadline June of each year.

[826]
ALABAMA NATIONAL GUARD EDUCATIONAL ASSISTANCE PROGRAM

Alabama Commission on Higher Education
Attn: Grants Coordinator
100 North Union Street
P.O. Box 302000
Montgomery, AL 36130-2000
(334) 242-2273   Fax: (334) 242-0268
E-mail: cheryl.newton@ache.alabama.gov
Web: www.ache.alabama.gov/StudentAsst/Programs.htm

Summary To provide financial assistance to members of the Alabama National Guard interested in attending college or graduate school in the state.

Eligibility This program is open to Alabama residents who are enrolled in an associate, baccalaureate, master's, or doctoral program at a public college, university, community college, technical college, or junior college in the state; are making satisfactory academic progress as determined by the eligible institution; and are members in good standing of the Alabama National Guard who have completed basic training and advanced individual training. Applicants may be receiving federal veterans benefits, but they must show a cost less aid amount of at least $25.

Financial Data Scholarships cover tuition, educational fees, books, and supplies, up to a maximum of $1,000 per year. All Alabama Student Grant program proceeds for which the student is eligible are deducted from this award.

Duration Up to 12 years after the date of the first grant payment to the student through this program.

Number awarded Varies each year; awards are determined on a first-in, first-out basis as long as funds are available.

Deadline July of each year.

[827]
ALASKA NATIONAL GUARD STATE TUITION REIMBURSEMENT PROGRAM

Alaska National Guard
Attn: Education Services Officer
P.O. Box 5800
Fort Richardson, AK 99505-5800
(907) 428-6477   Fax: (907) 428-6929
E-mail: les.poletzky@us.army.mil
Web: veterans.alaska.gov/state_benefits.htm

Summary To provide financial assistance to members of the Alaska National Guard who wish to attend a college or university in the state other than the University of Alaska.

Eligibility This program is open to members of the Alaska National Guard (Air and Army) and Naval Militia who are attending a university program in Alaska, other than the University of Alaska. First priority is given to undergraduates; if funding is available, students working on a second bachelor's degree or a master's degree may be supported. Non-prior servicemembers must complete Initial Active Duty for Training (IADT); prior servicemembers are eligible immediately.

Financial Data Recipients are entitled to reimbursement of 100% of the cost of tuition and fees, to a maximum of $2,000 per fiscal year.

Duration 1 semester; may be renewed.

Number awarded Varies each year.

Deadline Applications may be submitted at any time.

[828]
ALASKA NATIONAL GUARD UNIVERSITY OF ALASKA TUITION SCHOLARSHIPS

Alaska National Guard
Attn: Education Services Officer
P.O. Box 5800
Fort Richardson, AK 99505-5800
(907) 428-6477   Fax: (907) 428-6929
E-mail: les.poletzky@us.army.mil
Web: veterans.alaska.gov/state_benefits.htm

Summary To provide financial assistance to members of the Alaska National Guard who wish to take classes at a campus or branch of the University of Alaska.

Eligibility This program is open to members of the Alaska National Guard (Air and Army) and Naval Militia who are interested in attending any institution within the University of Alaska system to work on an associate, bachelor's, or master's degree. Applicants must have completed Initial Active Duty for Training (IADT).

Financial Data Recipients are entitled to reimbursement of 100% of the cost of tuition and fees, to a maximum of 15 undergraduate course units per semester or 9 graduate course units per semester.

Duration 1 semester; may be renewed as long as undergraduates maintain a GPA of 2.0 or higher and graduate students maintain a GPA of 3.0 or higher.

Number awarded Varies each year.

Deadline August of each year for fall semester; December of each year for spring semester.

[829]
ARMED FORCES HEALTH PROFESSIONS SCHOLARSHIPS

U.S. Navy
Attn: Navy Medicine Manpower, Personnel, Education and
Training Command
Code OH
8901 Wisconsin Avenue, Building 1, Tower 13, Room 13132
Bethesda, MD 20889-5611
(301) 295-1217   Toll Free: (800) USA-NAVY
Fax: (301) 295-1811   E-mail: OH@med.navy.mil
Web: www.med.navy.mil

Summary   To provide financial assistance for education in a medical field to future Navy medical officers.

Eligibility   Applicants for this assistance must be U.S. citizens, under 36 years of age, who are enrolled in or accepted at an accredited medical, osteopathic, physician assistant, dental, or optometry school located in the United States or Puerto Rico. Upon acceptance into the program, applicants are commissioned as officers in the U.S. Navy Medical Corps Reserve; after completion of medical school, they must perform at least 3 years of active-duty service in the U.S. Navy.

Financial Data   This program pays full tuition at any school of medicine, osteopathy, dentistry, or optometry or a course leading to a master's degree as a physician assistant located in the United States or Puerto Rico, and also covers the cost of fees, books, and required equipment. In addition, recipients are awarded a stipend of $1,992 per month for 10 1/2 months of the year; for the other 1 1/2 months of each year, they perform active-duty service, usually at a Navy medical facility, and receive the normal pay of an Ensign.

Duration   Assistance under this program continues until the student completes work for a doctorate degree in medicine, osteopathy, dentistry, or optometry or a master's degree as a physician assistant.

Additional data   Following receipt of the doctorate degree, recipients serve an internship and residency either in a naval hospital (in which case they receive Navy active-duty pay) or, if not selected for naval graduate medical education, in a civilian hospital (where they receive only the regular salary of the civilian institution). After completion of the residency, the students must begin the active-duty service obligation. That obligation is 2 years for the first 2 years of participation in the program, plus half a year of service for each additional half-year of program participation; in any case, the minimum service obligation is 3 years regardless of years of participation.

Number awarded   Varies each year.

Deadline   August of each year.

[830]
ARMY FUNDED NURSE EDUCATION PROGRAM (FNEP)

U.S. Army
Attn: Recruiting Command, RCHS-SVD-FNEP
1307 Third Avenue
Fort Knox, KY 40121-2726
(502) 626-0364   Toll Free: (800) 223-3735, ext. 60364
Fax: (502) 626-0952   E-mail: fnep@usarec.army.mil
Web: www.usarec.army.mil/AECP

Summary   To provide financial assistance to Army officers who are interested in completing a bachelor's or master's degree in nursing and continuing to serve in the Army Nurse Corps.

Eligibility   This program is open to active component Army officers who are currently in grade O-3 and have completed at least 38 months but no more than 7 years of active federal service. Applicants must be interested in enrolling full time at an accredited school of nursing to work on a bachelor's or entry-level master's degree. They must agree to serve an additional 2 years for each year of support received for a bachelor's degree or an addi-

tional 3 years for the first year of support for a master's degree plus 1 year for each additional 6 months of support. U.S. citizenship is required.

Financial Data   The stipend is $12,000 per year, including $11,000 for tuition and fees and $1,000 for books. Participants are not allowed to pay tuition in excess of $11,000 per year from other sources. If the university's tuition is more than $11,000, it must either waive the additional amount or direct the participant to another school. Army officers continue to draw their regular pay and allowances while attending nursing school.

Duration   Participants must be able to complete all degree requirements in 24 consecutive months or less. They must remain enrolled full time and maintain a GPA of 2.5 or higher.

Number awarded   Up to 25 each year.

Deadline   February of each year.

[831]
ARMY HEALTH PROFESSIONS SCHOLARSHIP PROGRAM

U.S. Army
Human Resources Command, Health Services Division
Attn: AHRC-OPH-AN
200 Stovall Street, Room 9N47
Alexandria, VA 22332-0417
(703) 325-2330   Toll Free: (800) USA-ARMY
Fax: (703) 325-2358
Web: www.goarmy.com/amedd/hpsp.jsp

Summary   To provide financial assistance to future Army officers who are interested in preparing for a career in medically-related fields.

Eligibility   This program is open to U.S. citizens under 35 years of age. Applicants must be enrolled in or accepted as a full-time student at an accredited professional school located in the United States or Puerto Rico in 1 of the following areas: allopathic or osteopathic medicine, dentistry, clinical or counseling psychology, optometry, veterinary science, or psychiatric nurse practitioner. Upon acceptance into the program, applicants are commissioned as officers in the U.S. Army Reserve; after completion of school, they must perform active-duty service in the U.S. Army Medical Corps, Dental Corps, Medical Service Corps (for clinical psychology and optometry), Nurse Corps, or Veterinary Corps.

Financial Data   This program pays full tuition at any school or college granting a doctoral or other relevant professional degree located in the United States or Puerto Rico and covers the cost of fees, books, and other required equipment. Recipients are also awarded a stipend of $1,992 per month for 10 1/2 months of the year. During the other 1 1/2 months of each year, they perform active-duty service, usually at an Army medical facility, and receive the normal pay of a Second Lieutenant.

Duration   1 to 4 years for the medical program; 1 to 4 years for the dental program; 2 or 3 years for the clinical or counseling psychology program; 2 to 4 years for the optometry program; and 1 to 3 years for the veterinary program.

Additional data   Participants incur an active-duty obligation based on existing Department of Defense and Army Directives in effect at the time they sign their contract accepting support through this program. Recently, the obligation has been 1 year for each year of support and a minimum of 2 years for the medical program or 3 years for the dental, clinical or counseling psychology, optometry, or veterinary programs.

Number awarded   Varies each year.

Deadline   Applications may be submitted at any time.

[832]
ARMY JUDGE ADVOCATE GENERAL CORPS FUNDED LEGAL EDUCATION PROGRAM

U.S. Army
Attn: Judge Advocate Recruiting Office
1777 North Kent Street, Suite 5200
Rosslyn, VA 22209-2194
(703) 588-6774   Toll Free: (866) ARMY-JAG
Fax: (703) 588-0100   E-mail: Yvonne.Caron@us.army.mil
Web: www.jagcnet.army.mil/law.goarmy.com

Summary   To provide financial assistance to Army officers interested in obtaining a law degree.

Eligibility   This program is open to commissioned active-duty Army officers who have graduated from an accredited college or university with a baccalaureate (or equivalent) degree. Applicants must have completed at least 2 but not more than 6 years of active duty (including warrant officer and enlisted service) and currently hold a rank of O-1 through O-3. They must be interested in attending a regular course of instruction leading to a J.D. or LL.B. degree at an approved civilian law school. U.S. citizenship is required. Selection is based on the "total person concept," including an evaluation of undergraduate and graduate school transcripts, LSAT score, ORB, OERs, SJA interview letter, and statement of motivation to attend law school.

Financial Data   While participating in this program, officers continue to receive their regular Army salary. The program also covers tuition, fees, and all other educational costs.

Duration   3 years.

Additional data   Participants normally are expected to attend a state-supported law school where they qualify for in-state tuition or where military members are granted in-state tuition rates. Following completion of their law degree and admission to the bar, they incur a 2-year active-duty service obligation as an attorney in the Judge Advocate General's Corps (JAGC) for each academic year spent in law school. If they fail to pass the bar examination or are not assigned to the JAGC for any other reason, they are returned to their basic branch of assignment for completion of their service obligation. If they refuse to accept appointment in or assignment to the JAGC, they are returned to their basic branch of assignment for completion of their service obligation; they must also reimburse the government for all costs of their advanced education.

Number awarded   The program is authorized to support up to 25 officers each year but normally selects only 15.

Deadline   October of each year.

[833]
ARMY MEDICAL AND DENTAL SCHOOL STIPEND PROGRAM (MDSSP)

U.S. Army
Human Resources Command, Health Services Division
Attn: AHRC-OPH-AN
200 Stovall Street, Room 9N47
Alexandria, VA 22332-0417
(703) 325-2330   Toll Free: (800) USA-ARMY
Fax: (703) 325-2358
Web: www.goarmy.com/amedd/graduate.jsp

Summary   To provide financial assistance to students in designated medically-related fields who are interested in serving in the U.S. Army Reserve after graduation.

Eligibility   This program is open to U.S. citizens under 35 years of age. Applicants must be enrolled in or accepted as a full-time student at an accredited professional school located in the United States or Puerto Rico in 1 of the following areas: allopathic or osteopathic medicine, dentistry, psychology (doctoral level only), optometry, or psychiatric nurse practitioner. Upon acceptance into the program, applicants are commissioned as officers in the U.S. Army Reserve; after completion of school, they must train as part of an Army Reserve unit and serve when needed.

Financial Data   This program pays a stipend of $1,992 per month.

Duration   Until completion of a degree.

Additional data   Participants incur an obligation to serve in the Selected Reserve for 1 year for each 6 months of support received, including 12 days of annual training or active duty for training.

Number awarded   Varies each year.

Deadline   Applications may be submitted at any time.

[834]
ARMY MEDICAL DEPARTMENT FINANCIAL ASSISTANCE PROGRAM

U.S. Army
Human Resources Command, Health Services Division
Attn: AHRC-OPH-AN
200 Stovall Street, Room 9N47
Alexandria, VA 22332-0417
(703) 325-2330   Toll Free: (800) USA-ARMY
Fax: (703) 325-2358
Web: www.goarmy.com/amedd/medical/corps_benefits.jsp

Summary   To provide financial assistance to future Army officers who are currently participating in a medical or dental residency.

Eligibility   This program is open to U.S. citizens who are currently at any point in residency training as a medical resident, oral surgeon, endodontist, periodontist, pedodontist, or orthodontist. Medical doctors must possess a permanent unrestricted license to practice medicine in the United States, the District of Columbia, Puerto Rico, or a U.S. territory. Upon acceptance into the program, applicants are commissioned as officers in the U.S. Army Reserve; after completion of training, they must perform active-duty service in the U.S. Army Medical Corps or Dental Corps.

Financial Data   This program pays an annual grant of more than $45,000 and a stipend of $1,992 per month.

Additional data   Participants also spend 14 days each year in an Active-Duty-For-Training (ADFT) assignment. Medical doctors incur an active-duty obligation of 1 year for each year of support plus 1 additional year. Dentists incur an active-duty obligation of 1 year for each year of support and a minimum of 3 years.

Number awarded   Varies each year.

Deadline   Applications may be submitted at any time.

[835]
ARMY NATIONAL GUARD TUITION ASSISTANCE

U.S. Army National Guard
c/o DANTES
6490 Saufley Field Road
Pensacola, FL 32509-5243
(850) 452-1085   Fax: (850) 452-1161
E-mail: tahelp@voled.doded.mil
Web: www.nationalguard.com/education/payingfor.php

Summary   To provide financial assistance for college or graduate school to members of the Army National Guard in each state.

Eligibility   This program is open to members of the Army National Guard in every state who are interested in attending a college, community college, or university within the state. Applicants must have sufficient time to complete the course before their Expiration Time of Service (ETS) date. They must be interested in working on a high school diploma or equivalent (GED), certificate, associate degree, bachelor's degree, master's degree, or first professional degree, including those in architecture, Certified Public Accountant (C.P.A.), podiatry, dentistry (D.D.S. or D.M.D.), medicine (M.D.), optometry, osteopathic medicine, pharmacy (Pharm.D.), or theology (M.Div. or M.H.L.). Commissioned officers must agree to remain in the Guard for at least 4 years following completion of the course for which assistance is provided, unless they are involuntarily separated from the service.

Financial Data Assistance provides up to 100% of tuition (to a maximum of $250 per semester hour or $4,500 per person per fiscal year).

Duration Participants in Office Candidate School (OCS), Warrant Officer Candidate School (WOCS), and ROTC Simultaneous Membership Program (SMP) may enroll in up to 15 semester hours per year until completion of a baccalaureate degree. Warrant Officers are funded to complete an associate degree.

Additional data Tuition assistance may be used along with federal Pell Grants but not with Montgomery GI Bill benefits. State tuition assistance programs can be used concurrently with this program, but not to exceed 100% of tuition costs.

Number awarded Varies each year; recently, more than 22,000 Guard members received tuition assistance.

Deadline Deadline not specified.

[836]
ARMY NURSE CORPS ASSOCIATION SCHOLARSHIPS

Army Nurse Corps Association
Attn: Education Committee
P.O. Box 39235
San Antonio, TX 78218-1235
(210) 650-3534   Fax: (210) 650-3494
E-mail: education@e-anca.org
Web: e-anca.org/ANCAEduc.htm

Summary To provide financial assistance to students who have a connection to the Army and are interested in working on an undergraduate or graduate degree in nursing.

Eligibility This program is open to students attending colleges or universities that have accredited programs offering associate, bachelor's, master's, or doctoral degrees in nursing. Applicants must be 1) nursing students who plan to enter the active Army, Army National Guard, or Army Reserve and are not participating in a program funded by the active Army, Army National Guard, or Army Reserve; 2) nursing students who have previously served in the active Army, Army National Guard, or Army Reserve; 3) Army Nurse Corps officers enrolled in an undergraduate or graduate nursing program not funded by the active Army, Army National Guard, or Army Reserve; 4) Army enlisted soldiers in the active Army, Army National Guard, or Army Reserve who are working on a baccalaureate degree in nursing not funded by the active Army, Army National Guard, or Army Reserve; or 5) nursing students whose parent(s) or spouse are serving or have served in the active Army, Army National Guard, or Army Reserve. Along with their application, they must submit a personal statement on their professional career objectives, reasons for applying for this scholarship, financial need, special considerations, personal and academic interests, and why they are preparing for a nursing career.

Financial Data The stipend is $3,000. Funds are sent directly to the recipient's school.

Duration 1 year.

Additional data Although the sponsoring organization is made up of current, retired, and honorably discharged officers of the Army Nurse Corps, it does not have an official affiliation with the Army. Therefore, students who receive these scholarships do not incur any military service obligation.

Number awarded 1 or more each year.

Deadline March of each year.

[837]
ARMY RESERVE TUITION ASSISTANCE

U.S. Army Reserve
Attn: Director, USAR Education
ARPC-PS
1 Reserve Way
St. Louis, MO 63132-5200
Toll Free: (800) 452-0201
Web: www.goarmy.com/reserve/nps/education.jsp

Summary To provide financial assistance for college or graduate school to specified members of the U.S. Army Reserve (USAR).

Eligibility This program is open to USAR soldiers in the following categories: TPU, JRU, IMA, ROTC Simultaneous Membership Program Cadets (non-scholarship holders), and Chaplain Candidates. Members of the Active Guard Reserve (AGR) are covered by Regular Army tuition assistance and are not eligible for this program. Soldiers who have been flagged for weight control or because of the results of their Army Physical Fitness Test (APFT) are still eligible, but soldiers who have been flagged for adverse actions cannot receive this assistance. Applicants must be working on their first credential at the diploma, certificate associate, baccalaureate, or graduate level. Commissioned officers must agree to participate actively for 4 years in the Selected Reserve from the date of completion of the course for which tuition assistance is provided. Enlisted soldiers must certify that sufficient time remains within their Time In Service (TIS) to complete the course before their Expiration Term of Service (ETS).

Financial Data Assistance is provided at the rate of $250 per credit hour, to a maximum of $4,500 per fiscal year.

Duration 1 year; may be renewed.

Number awarded Varies each year.

Deadline Applications may be submitted at any time.

[838]
ARMY SPECIALIZED TRAINING ASSISTANCE PROGRAM (STRAP)

U.S. Army
Human Resources Command, Health Services Division
Attn: AHRC-OPH-AN
200 Stovall Street, Room 9N47
Alexandria, VA 22332-0417
(703) 325-2330   Toll Free: (800) USA-ARMY
Fax: (703) 325-2358
Web: www.goarmy.com/amedd/postgrad.jsp

Summary To provide funding for service to members of the United States Army Reserve (USAR) or Army National Guard (ARNG) who are engaged in additional training in designated health care fields that are considered critical for wartime medical needs.

Eligibility This program is open to members of the USAR or ARNG who are currently 1) medical residents (in orthopedic surgery, family practice, emergency medicine, general surgery, obstetrics/gynecology, or internal medicine); 2) dental residents (in oral surgery, prosthodontics, or comprehensive dentistry); 3) nursing students working on a master's degree in critical care or nurse anesthesia; or 4) associate degree or diploma nurses working on a bachelor's degree. Applicants must agree to a service obligation of 1 year for every 6 months of support received.

Financial Data This program pays a stipend of $1,992 per month.

Additional data During their obligated period of service, participants must attend Extended Combat Training (ECT) at least 12 days each year and complete the Officer Basic Leadership Course (OBLC) within the first year.

Number awarded Varies each year.

Deadline Applications may be submitted at any time.

[839]
ARMY TUITION ASSISTANCE BENEFITS

U.S. Army
Human Resources Command
AHRC-PDE-EI
Attn: Education Incentives and Counseling Branch
200 Stovall Street, Suite 3N17
Alexandria, VA 22332-0472
(703) 325-0285   Toll Free: (800) 872-8272
Fax: (703) 325-6599   E-mail: pdeei@hoffman.army.mil
Web: www.goarmy.com/benefits/education_taking_classes.jsp

Summary To provide financial assistance to Army personnel interested in working on an undergraduate or graduate degree.

Eligibility This program is open to active-duty Army personnel, including members of the Army National Guard and Army Reserve on active duty. Applicants must first visit an education counselor to declare an educational goal and establish an educational plan. Applicants may enroll in up to 15 semester hours of academic courses.

Financial Data Those selected for participation in this program receive their regular Army pay and 100% of tuition at the postsecondary educational institution of their choice, but capped at $4,500 per year or $250 per semester hour, whichever is less.

Duration Until completion of a bachelor's or graduate degree.

Additional data This program is part of the Army Continuing Education System (ACES). Further information is available from counselors at the education centers at all Army installations with a troop strength of 750 or more.

Number awarded Varies each year.

Deadline Deadline not specified.

[840]
BART LONGO MEMORIAL SCHOLARSHIPS

National Chief Petty Officers' Association
c/o Marjorie Hays, Treasurer
1014 Ronald Drive
Corpus Christi, TX 78412-3548
Web: www.goatlocker.org/ncpoa/scholarship.htm

Summary To provide financial assistance for college or graduate school to members of the National Chief Petty Officers' Association (NCPOA) and their families.

Eligibility This program is open to members of the NCPOA and the children, stepchildren, and grandchildren of living or deceased members. Applicants may be high school seniors or graduates entering a college or university or students currently enrolled full time as undergraduate or graduate students. Selection is based on academic achievement and participation in extracurricular activities; financial need is not considered.

Financial Data The stipend is $1,000.

Duration 1 year.

Additional data Membership in the NCPOA is limited to men and women who served or are serving as Chief Petty Officers in the U.S. Navy, U.S. Coast Guard, or their Reserve components for at least 30 days.

Number awarded 2 each year: 1 to a high school senior or graduate and 1 to an undergraduate or graduate student.

Deadline May of each year.

[841]
BG BENJAMIN B. TALLEY SCHOLARSHIP

Society of American Military Engineers-Anchorage Post
Attn: BG B.B. Talley Scholarship Endowment Fund
P.O. Box 6409
Anchorage, AK 99506-6409
E-mail: william_kontess@urscorp.com
Web: www.sameanchorage.org/h_about/scholinfo.html

Summary To provide financial assistance to student members of the Society of American Military Engineers (SAME) from Alaska who are working on a bachelor's or master's degree in designated fields of engineering or the natural sciences.

Eligibility This program is open to members of the Anchorage Post of SAME who are residents of Alaska, attending college in Alaska, an active-duty military member stationed in Alaska, or a dependent of an active-duty military member stationed in Alaska. Applicants must be 1) sophomores, juniors, or seniors majoring in engineering, architecture, construction or project management, natural sciences, physical sciences, applied sciences, or mathematics at an accredited college or university; or 2) students working on a master's degree in those fields. They must have a GPA of 2.5 or higher. U.S. citizenship is required. Along with their application, they must submit an essay of 250 to 500 words on their career goals. Selection is based on that essay, academic achievement, participation in school and community activities, and work/family activities; financial need is not considered.

Financial Data Stipends range up to $3,000.

Duration 1 year.

Additional data This program was established in 1997.

Number awarded Varies each year; at least 1 scholarship is reserved for a master's degree students.

Deadline December of each year.

[842]
CANNON ENDOWMENT SCHOLARSHIP

United Church of Christ
Parish Life and Leadership Ministry Team
Attn: Grants, Scholarships, and Resources
700 Prospect Avenue East
Cleveland, OH 44115-1100
(216) 736-3839   Toll Free: (866) 822-8224, ext. 3839
Fax: (216) 736-3783   E-mail: jeffersv@ucc.org
Web: www.ucc.org/seminarians/ucc-scholarships-for.html

Summary To provide financial assistance to seminary students who are interested in becoming a military chaplain.

Eligibility This program is open to students at accredited seminaries who are affiliated with the Christian Church (Disciples of Christ), Presbyterian Church (USA), United Church of Christ, or United Methodist Church. Applicants must be planning to become military chaplains.

Financial Data The stipend is approximately $2,500.

Duration 1 year.

Additional data This program was established in 1992.

Number awarded Varies each year; recently, 3 of these scholarships were awarded.

Deadline Deadline not specified.

[843]
CHAPLAIN SAMUEL GROVER POWELL SCHOLARSHIP

United Methodist Higher Education Foundation
Attn: Scholarships Administrator
1001 19th Avenue South
P.O. Box 340005
Nashville, TN 37203-0005
(615) 340-7385   Toll Free: (800) 811-8110
Fax: (615) 340-7330 E-mail: umhefscholarships@gbhem.org
Web: www.umhef.org/receive.php?id=chap_powell

Summary To provide funding to students interested in preparing for a career as a military chaplain.

Eligibility This program is open to middlers and seniors at accredited theological seminaries who are either involved in the chaplain candidate (seminarian) program or serving in a military Reserve component after having completed an active-duty tour in 1 of the armed forces. Preference is given to students in their senior year who plan to serve in the U.S. Air Force. However, students preparing for chaplaincy in any branch of the military are considered. Applicants must submit a letter that includes a brief personal history and a statement about their decision to choose military chaplaincy as a career, a recent photograph, undergraduate and graduate transcripts, a financial statement, and a report on their ministry in the chaplain candidate (seminarian) program.

Financial Data A stipend is awarded (amount not specified). Funds must be used to pay for tuition. Checks are mailed to the recipient's school.

Duration 1 year; recipients may reapply for 1 additional year (but new applicants are given priority each year).

Additional data This program was established in 1980. Recipients are expected to serve in the U.S. Military Chaplaincy upon completion of seminary and ordination. If this does not happen (due to factors within the recipient's control), the recipient may be asked to repay the scholarship.

Number awarded 1 or more each year.

Deadline June of each year.

[844]
CIVIL ENGINEER CORPS SCHOLARSHIPS

U.S. Navy
Bureau of Navy Personnel
BUPERS-314E
5720 Integrity Drive
Millington, TN 38055-4630
(901) 874-4034 Toll Free: (866) CEC-NAVY
Fax: (901) 874-2681 E-mail: p4413d@persnet.navy.mil
Web: portal.navfac.navy.mil/portal/page/portal/cec/accessions

Summary To provide financial assistance to undergraduate and graduate students in architecture and engineering who are interested in serving in the Navy's Civil Engineer Corps (CEC) following graduation.

Eligibility This program is open to undergraduate and master's degree students who are U.S. citizens between 19 and 35 years of age. Applicants must be enrolled in an engineering program accredited by the Accreditation Board for Engineering and Technology (ABET) or an architecture program accredited by the National Architectural Accrediting Board (NAAB) with a GPA of 3.0 or higher. Eligible majors include civil engineering, electrical engineering, mechanical engineering, ocean engineering, or architecture. For the Exceptional Student Program, they must apply at the end of their sophomore year. For the Collegiate Program, they must apply at the end of their junior year. For the Graduate Program, they must apply upon acceptance to an accredited graduate school and when they are within 6 months of completing a bachelor's degree in engineering. Preference is given to applicants who have engineering or architecture work experience and registration as a Professional Engineer (P.E.) or Engineer-in-Training (EIT). Students majoring in mathematics, physics, non-engineering programs, and engineering or architectural technology are not eligible. Applicants must also be able to meet the Navy's physical fitness requirements.

Financial Data Students accepted as undergraduates receive E-3 pay (approximately $2,000 per month), an allowance, and benefits; after completing 12 months of the program or being referred to other specified programs, they may be advanced to E-4 or E-5 levels. Graduate students receive payment of tuition and fees plus full officers' salary and allowances.

Duration Up to 24 months for the Exceptional Student Program, up to 12 months for the Collegiate Program, and up to 18 months (6 months of undergraduate school plus 12 months of graduate school) for the Graduate Program.

Additional data While in college, selectees have no uniforms, drills, or military duties. After graduation with a bachelor's or master's degree, they enter the Navy and attend 13 weeks at Officer Candidate School (OCS) in Pensacola, Florida, followed by 15 weeks at Civil Engineer Corps Officers School (CECOS) in Port Hueneme, California. They then serve 4 years in the CEC, rotat-

ing among public works, contract management, and the Naval Construction Force (Seabees).

Number awarded Varies each year.

Deadline Deadline not specified.

[845]
COAST GUARD TUITION ASSISTANCE PROGRAM

U.S. Coast Guard Institute
Attn: Commanding Officer
5900 S.W. 64th Street, Room 233
Oklahoma City, OK 73169-6990
(405) 954-1360 Fax: (405) 954-7245
E-mail: CGI-PF-Tuition_Assistance@uscg.mil
Web: www.uscg.mil/hq/cgi/cfa/ta.asp

Summary To provide financial assistance to members and employees of the Coast Guard who are interested in pursuing additional education during their off-duty hours.

Eligibility This program is open to Coast Guard members who are interested in pursuing additional education at the high school, vocational/technical, undergraduate, graduate, or professional level. Civilian employees with at least 90 days of Coast Guard service and Selected Reservists are also eligible. Enlisted members must have at least 12 months remaining on their active-duty contracts or Selected Reserve obligation after completion of the course. Active-duty officers must agree to fulfill a 2-year service obligation following completion of the course; officers of the selected reserve must agree to fulfill a 4-year service obligation following completion of the course. Civilian employees must agree to retain employment with the Coast Guard for 1 month for each completed course credit hour. For military personnel, the command education services officer (ESO) must certify that the course of instruction is Coast Guard mission or career related. The supervisor of civilian employees must certify that the education is career related. All courses must be related to the mission of the Coast Guard or the individual's career or professional development.

Financial Data Active-duty, Reserve, and civilian Coast Guard members receive full payment of all expenses for completion of a high school degree or equivalent. For college courses (vocational/technical, undergraduate, and graduate), 100% of the cost of tuition is reimbursed, to a maximum of $250 per semester hour or $4,500 per fiscal year.

Duration Until completion of a bachelor's or graduate degree.

Additional data Graduate students must earn a grade of "B" or higher to receive reimbursement; undergraduates must earn a grade of "D" or higher.

Number awarded Varies each year; recently, more than 10,000 Coast Guard active-duty members, Reservists, and civilian employees received tuition assistance worth approximately $14.5 million.

Deadline Applications may be submitted at any time.

[846]
COLONEL JERRY W. ROSS SCHOLARSHIP

American Pharmacists Association
Attn: APhA Foundation
2215 Constitution Avenue, N.W.
Washington, DC 20037-2985
(202) 429-7565 Toll Free: (800) 237-APhA
Fax: (202) 783-2351 E-mail: msheahan@aphanet.org
Web: www.pharmacist.com

Summary To provide financial assistance for work on a degree in pharmacy to Air Force pharmacy technicians who are members of the Academy of Student Pharmacists of the American Pharmacists Association (APhA-ASP) and their families.

Eligibility This program is open to full-time pharmacy students who are either 1) Air Force pharmacy technicians working on a degree in pharmacy, or 2) family members of an Air Force pharmacist or technician who is enrolled in an accredited college of pharmacy. Applicants must have been actively involved in their school's APhA-ASP chapter. They must have completed at least 1 year in the professional sequence of courses with a GPA of 2.75 or higher. Along with their application, they must submit a 500-word essay on how they envision their role in health care as a future pharmacist, 2 letters of recommendation, a current resume or curriculum vitae, and a list of pharmacy and non-pharmacy related activities. Preference is given to applicants who indicate further Air Force service.

Financial Data The stipend is $1,000.

Duration 1 year; recipients may reapply.

Number awarded 1 each year.

Deadline November of each year.

[847]
COLORADO NATIONAL GUARD STATE TUITION ASSISTANCE

Department of Military and Veterans Affairs
Attn: CODAG-TA
6848 South Revere Parkway
Centennial, CO 80112-6703
(720) 250-1550   Fax: (720) 250-1559
E-mail: tuition@dmva.state.co.us
Web: www.dmva.state.co.us/page/ta

Summary To provide financial assistance for college or graduate school to members of the Colorado National Guard.

Eligibility This program is open to members of the Colorado National Guard who have completed at least 6 months of military service and are currently in drilling status. Applicants must be enrolled or planning to enroll at a public institution of higher education in Colorado to work on an associate, bachelor's, or master's degree.

Financial Data This program provides payment of up to 100% of the in-state tuition at public institutions in Colorado.

Duration 1 semester; may be renewed as long as the recipient remains an active member of the Guard and maintains a GPA of 2.0 or higher. Assistance is limited to a total of 132 semester hours.

Additional data Recipients must serve 1 year in the Guard for each semester or quarter of assistance received.

Number awarded Varies each year.

Deadline June of each year for the fall semester; November of each year for the spring semester; April of each year for the summer term.

[848]
COUNCIL ON FOREIGN RELATIONS MILITARY FELLOWSHIPS

Council on Foreign Relations
Attn: Fellowship Affairs
58 East 68th Street
New York, NY 10021
(212) 434-9489   Fax: (212) 434-9801
E-mail: fellowships@cfr.org
Web: www.cfr.org/about/fellowships/mil.html

Summary To provide military officers with an opportunity to engage in a program of study in residence at the Council on Foreign Relations in New York or Washington, D.C.

Eligibility The Chiefs of Staff of the Army and the Air Force, the Chief of Naval Operations, and the Commandant of the Marine Corps are invited to nominate an outstanding officer from their respective services as a candidate for these fellowships. Nominees should be interested in broadening their understanding of foreign relations in residence at the council's headquarters in New York or, in special circumstances, at the council offices in Washington, D.C.

Financial Data The stipend is determined according to individual requirements; in general, the program attempts to meet the major portion of the fellow's current income.

Duration 1 year.

Additional data Fellows participate in council programs, meet with council members and staff, and engage in studies in conjunction with the council's studies program. They also assist in arranging several politico-military trips for council members during the year.

Number awarded 2 or 3 each year.

Deadline Deadline not specified.

[849]
CSM ROBERT W. ELKEY AWARD

Army Engineer Association
Attn: Washington DC Operations
P.O. Box 30260
Alexandria, VA 22310-8260
(703) 428-7084   Fax: (703) 428-6043
E-mail: DCOps@armyengineer.com
Web: www.armyengineer.com/AEA_scholarships.html

Summary To provide financial assistance for college or graduate school to enlisted members of the Army Engineer Association (AEA).

Eligibility This program is open to AEA members serving in an active, Reserve, or National Guard component Army Engineer unit, school, or organization within the Corps of Engineers of the United States Army. Applicants must be enlisted personnel (PVT, PFC, SPC, CPL, SGT, or SSG). They must be working on or planning to work on an associate, bachelor's, or master's degree at an accredited college or university. Selection is based primarily on financial need, although potential for academic success and standards of conduct as supported by personal references are also considered.

Financial Data The stipend is $1,000.

Duration 1 year.

Number awarded 3 each year.

Deadline June of each year.

[850]
DARREL PERRY, RN MEMORIAL SCHOLARSHIP

American Association of Nurse Anesthetists
Attn: AANA Foundation
222 South Prospect Avenue
Park Ridge, IL 60068-4001
(847) 655-1171   Fax: (847) 692-7137
E-mail: foundation@aana.com
Web: www.aanafoundation.com

Summary To provide financial assistance to members of the American Association of Nurse Anesthetists (AANA) who are serving in the Army and interested in obtaining further education.

Eligibility This program is open to members of the association who are currently enrolled in an accredited nurse anesthesia education program. Preference is given to members of the U.S. Army (Active or Reserves). First-year students must have completed 6 months of nurse anesthesia classes; second-year students must have completed 12 months of nurse anesthesia classes. Along with their application, they must submit a 200-word essay describing why they have chosen nurse anesthesia as a profession and their professional goals for the future. Financial need is also considered in the selection process.

Financial Data The stipend is $1,000.

Duration 1 year.

Additional data This scholarship was first awarded in 2004. The application processing fee is $25.

Number awarded 1 each year.

Deadline March of each year.

[851]
DEDARNG SCHOLARSHIPS

U.S. Army
ROTC Cadet Command
Attn: ATCC-OP-I-S
55 Patch Road, Building 56
Fort Monroe, VA 23651-1052
(757) 788-4551   Toll Free: (800) USA-ROTC
Fax: (757) 788-4643 E-mail: william.daniels@usaac.army.mil
Web: www.rotc.monroe.army.mil

Summary To provide financial assistance to college and graduate students who are interested in enrolling in Army ROTC and serving in the Army National Guard following graduation.

Eligibility This program is open to full-time students entering their sophomore or junior year of college with a GPA of 2.5 or higher. High school seniors are also eligible if they plan to attend a military junior college (MJC), have a GPA of 2.5 or higher, and have scores of at least 19 on the ACT or 920 on the combined mathematics and critical reading SAT. Graduate students may also be eligible if they have only 2 years remaining for completion of their degree. Students who have been awarded an ROTC campus-based scholarship may apply to convert to this program during their freshman year. Applicants must meet all medical and moral character requirements for enrollment in Army ROTC. They must be willing to enroll in the Simultaneous Membership Program (SMP) of an ROTC unit on their campus; the SMP requires simultaneous membership in Army ROTC and the Army National Guard.

Financial Data Participants receive full reimbursement of tuition, a grant of $1,200 per year for books, plus an ROTC stipend for 10 months of the year at $450 per month during their junior year and $500 per month during their senior year. As a member of the Army National Guard, they also receive weekend drill pay at the pay grade of E-5 during their junior year or E-6 during their senior year.

Duration 2 or 3 years for college students; 2 years for high school seniors entering an MJC.

Additional data After graduation, participants serve 3 to 6 months on active duty in the Officer Basic Course (OBC). Following completion of OBC, they are released from active duty and are obligated to serve 8 years in the Army National Guard.

Number awarded 594 each year (11 in each state or U.S. territory).

Deadline Deadline not specified.

[852]
DISTRICT OF COLUMBIA NATIONAL GUARD TUITION ASSISTANCE

District of Columbia National Guard
Attn: Education Services Office
2001 East Capitol Street
Washington, DC 20003-1719
(202) 685-9825   Fax: (202) 685-9815
E-mail: joanne.thweatt@dc.ngb.army.mil
Web: states.ng.mil/sites/DC/education/Pages/tuition.aspx

Summary To provide financial assistance for college to current members of the District of Columbia National Guard.

Eligibility This program is open to traditional, technician, and AGR members of the District of Columbia Air and Army National Guard. Applicants must have a high school diploma or equivalency and currently be working on an associate, bachelor's, or master's degree at an accredited postsecondary education institution. In some instances, support may also be available for an M.D., D.O., P.A., or J.D. degree.

Financial Data Army National Guard members are eligible for up to $4,500 per year in federal tuition assistance; they may supplement that with up to $1,500 per year in District tuition assistance. Air National Guard members do not have access to federal tuition assistance, so they may receive up to $6,000 in District

tuition assistance. Funds must be used to pay for tuition, fees, and/or books.

Duration 1 semester; recipients may reapply.

Number awarded Varies each year.

Deadline July of each year for the fall session, October of each year for the spring session, or April of each year for the summer session.

[853]
FIRST SERGEANT DOUGLAS AND CHARLOTTE DEHORSE SCHOLARSHIP

Catching the Dream
8200 Mountain Road, N.E., Suite 203
Albuquerque, NM 87110-7835
(505) 262-2351   Fax: (505) 262-0534
E-mail: NScholarsh@aol.com
Web: www.catchingthedream.org

Summary To provide financial assistance to American Indians who have ties to the military and are working on an undergraduate or graduate degree.

Eligibility This program is open to American Indians who 1) have completed 1 year of an Army, Navy, or Air Force Junior Reserve Officer Training (JROTC) program; 2) are enrolled in an Army, Navy, or Air Force Reserve Officer Training (ROTC) program; or 3) are a veteran of the U.S. Army, Navy, Air Force, Marines, Merchant Marine, or Coast Guard. Applicants must be enrolled in an undergraduate or graduate program of study. Along with their application, they must submit a personal essay, high school transcripts, and letters of recommendation.

Financial Data A stipend is awarded (amount not specified).

Duration 1 year.

Additional data This program was established in 2007.

Number awarded 1 or more each year.

Deadline April of each year for fall semester or quarter; September of each year for spring semester or winter quarter.

[854]
FLEET RESERVE ASSOCIATION SCHOLARSHIP

Fleet Reserve Association
Attn: Scholarship Administrator
125 North West Street
Alexandria, VA 22314-2754
(703) 683-1400   Toll Free: (800) FRA-1924
Fax: (703) 549-6610   E-mail: fra@fra.org
Web: www.fra.org

Summary To provide financial assistance for college or graduate school to members of the Fleet Reserve Association (FRA), as well as their spouses, children, and grandchildren.

Eligibility This program is open to members of the FRA and their dependent children, grandchildren, and spouses. The children, grandchildren, and spouses of deceased FRA members are also eligible. Applicants must submit an essay on their life experiences, career objectives, and what motivated them to select those objectives. Selection is based on academic record, financial need, extracurricular activities, leadership skills, and participation in community activities. U.S. citizenship is required.

Financial Data The stipend is $5,000 per year.

Duration 1 year; may be renewed.

Additional data Membership in the FRA is restricted to active-duty, retired, and reserve members of the Navy, Marines, and Coast Guard.

Number awarded 6 each year.

Deadline April of each year.

[855]
FLORIDA NATIONAL GUARD EDUCATIONAL DOLLARS FOR DUTY (EDD) PROGRAM

Department of Military Affairs
Attn: Education Services Officer
82 Marine Street
St. Augustine, FL 32084-5039
(904) 823-0417   Toll Free: (800) 342-6528
Web: www.dma.state.fl.us

Summary   To provide financial assistance for college to members of the Florida National Guard.

Eligibility   This program is open to current members of the Florida National Guard. Applicants must be attending or planning to attend a college or university in Florida to work on an undergraduate or master's degree. College preparatory and vocational/technical programs also qualify. Guard members who already have a master's degree are not eligible.

Financial Data   The program provides for payment of 100% of tuition and fees at a public college or university or an equivalent amount at a private institution.

Duration   1 year; may be renewed.

Number awarded   Varies each year; recently, approximately 765 Florida National Guard members utilized this program.

Deadline   Deadline not specified.

[856]
GEORGE WASHINGTON CHAPTER AUSA SCHOLARSHIPS

Association of the United States Army-George Washington
  Chapter
c/o Bobbie Williams, Scholarship Committee
79 Brush Everard Court
Stafford, VA 22554
(703) 697-6340   E-mail: Bobbie.Williams@us.army.mil
Web: www.gwcausa.org/Scholarship/index.htm

Summary   To provide financial assistance for undergraduate or graduate study at a school in any state to members of the George Washington Chapter of the Association of the United States Army (AUSA) and their families.

Eligibility   This program is open to active members of the AUSA George Washington Chapter (which serves the Washington, D.C. area) and the families of active members. Applicants must have a GPA of 2.5 or higher and be working on an undergraduate or advanced degree at a college or university in any state. Along with their application, they must submit a letter describing any family circumstances they believe are relevant and explaining why they deserve the scholarship. Members must also submit a favorable recommendation from their supervisor. Membership in AUSA is open to Army personnel (including Reserves and National Guard) who are either active or retired, ROTC cadets, or civilian employees of the Army.

Financial Data   Stipends range up to $1,000.

Duration   1 year.

Number awarded   Varies each year; recently, 15 of these scholarships were awarded.

Deadline   April of each year.

[857]
GLADYS MCPARTLAND SCHOLARSHIPS

United States Marine Corps Combat Correspondents
  Association
Attn: Executive Director
110 Fox Court
Wildwood, FL 34785
(352) 748-4698   E-mail: usmccca@cfl.rr.com
Web: www.usmccca.org/awards/gladys

Summary   To provide financial assistance for college or graduate school to regular members of the U.S. Marine Corps Combat Correspondents Association (USMCCCA) or their children.

Eligibility   Eligible are active-duty Marines and certain Marine Corps Reservists who are regular members of the USMCCCA, or the dependent children of such members, as long as the member is in a "dues-paid" status, or died in such status, or is listed as a prisoner of war or missing in action and was in a "dues-paid" status when so listed. Applicants must be high school seniors or graduates, seeking at least a bachelor's degree. Preference is given to students working on degrees in disciplines that will lead to careers in mass media communications, although applications are accepted in any field.

Financial Data   The stipend is $1,000; funds are to be used exclusively for tuition, books, and/or fees.

Duration   1 year; may be renewed, provided the recipient maintains a GPA of 2.0 or higher.

Additional data   Funds for this scholarship were originally provided by a contribution from Kathryne Timmons in honor of her sister, Gladys McPartland, who served as executive secretary of the USMCCCA from its founding until her death in 1985.

Number awarded   1 or more each year.

Deadline   June of each year.

[858]
GLENN F. GLEZEN SCHOLARSHIP

Fleet Reserve Association
Attn: Scholarship Administrator
125 North West Street
Alexandria, VA 22314-2754
(703) 683-1400   Toll Free: (800) FRA-1924
Fax: (703) 549-6610   E-mail: fra@fra.org
Web: www.fra.org

Summary   To provide financial assistance for graduate school to members of the Fleet Reserve Association (FRA) and their spouses, children, and grandchildren.

Eligibility   This program is open to the dependent children, grandchildren, and spouses of members of the association who are in good standing (or were at the time of death, if deceased). FRA members are also eligible. Applicants should be enrolled in a graduate program. Along with their application, they must submit an essay on their life experiences, career objectives, and what motivated them to select those objectives. Selection is based on academic record, financial need, extracurricular activities, leadership skills, and participation in community activities. U.S. citizenship is required.

Financial Data   The stipend is $5,000 per year.

Duration   1 year; may be renewed.

Additional data   Membership in the FRA is restricted to active-duty, retired, and Reserve members of the Navy, Marine Corps, and Coast Guard. This program was established in 2001.

Number awarded   1 each year.

Deadline   April of each year.

[859]
GREEN TO GOLD ACTIVE DUTY OPTION

U.S. Army
ROTC Cadet Command
Attn: ATCC-OP-I-S
55 Patch Road, Building 56
Fort Monroe, VA 23651-1052
(757) 788-3341   Toll Free: (800) USA-ROTC
Fax: (757) 788-5781   E-mail: atccps@usacc.army.mil
Web: www.goarmy.com/rotc/green_to_gold_active_duty.jsp

Summary   To provide an opportunity for soldiers to remain in the Army while they return to college to participate in the Army Reserve Officers' Training Corps (ROTC).

Eligibility This program is open to enlisted soldiers who have served at least 2 but less than 10 years on active duty and have also completed at least 2 years of college so they can complete a bachelor's or master's degree within 21 months. Applicants must have a cumulative high school or college GPA of 2.5 or higher, a General Technical (GT) score of 110 or higher, and a recent (within the past 6 months) Army Physical Fitness Test (APFT) score of 180 or higher (including 60 points in each event). They must be under 35 years of age when they graduate. Soldiers who participate in this program remain on active duty while they attend a college or university that has an Army ROTC unit on campus.

Financial Data Participants continue to receive their current pay and allowances; they are responsible for payment of all educational expenses.

Duration Up to 21 months; may be extended to 24 months upon petition.

Additional data Cadets who had previously qualified for benefits from the Army College Fund and/or the Montgomery GI Bill are still entitled to receive those in addition to any benefits from this program. They are not, however, eligible for Army Tuition Assistance. While in college, participants must successfully complete the prescribed military science classes, professional military education subjects, the Leader Development and Assessment Course (normally between their junior and senior years), and any other requirements for commissioning. Upon graduation, they are commissioned as second lieutenants and are required to serve in the military for 8 years. That obligation may be fulfilled by serving 3 years on active duty and 5 years in the Army National Guard (ARNG), the United States Army Reserve (USAR), or the Inactive Ready Reserve (IRR).

Number awarded Up to 200 each year.

Deadline March of each year.

[860]
GRFD SCHOLARSHIPS

U.S. Army
ROTC Cadet Command
Attn: ATCC-OP-I-S
55 Patch Road, Building 56
Fort Monroe, VA 23651-1052
(757) 788-2782   Toll Free: (800) USA-ROTC
Fax: (757) 788-4643   E-mail: nancy.davis@usaac.army.mil
Web: www.rotc.monroe.army.mil

Summary To provide financial assistance to college and graduate students who are willing to enroll in Army ROTC and serve in a Reserve component of the Army following graduation.

Eligibility This program is open to full-time students entering their junior year of college with a GPA of 2.5 or higher. High school seniors are also eligible if they plan to attend a military junior college (MJC), have a GPA of 2.5 or higher, and have scores of at least 19 on the ACT or 920 on the combined mathematics and critical reading SAT. Graduate students are also eligible if they have only 2 years remaining before completion of their graduate degree. Applicants must meet all other medical and moral character requirements for enrollment in Army ROTC. They must be willing to enroll in the Simultaneous Membership Program (SMP) of an ROTC unit on their campus; the SMP requires simultaneous membership in Army ROTC and either the Army National Guard or Army Reserve.

Financial Data Participants receive full reimbursement of tuition, a grant of $1,200 per year for books, plus an ROTC stipend for 10 months of the year at $450 per month during their junior year and $500 per month during their senior year. As a member of the Army National Guard or Army Reserve, they also receive weekend drill pay at the pay grade of E-5 during their junior year or E-6 during their senior year.

Duration 2 years.

Additional data After graduation, participants serve 3 to 6 months on active duty in the Officer Basic Course (OBC). Following completion of OBC, they are released from active duty and are obligated to serve 8 years in the Army National Guard or Army Reserve.

Number awarded Currently, 416 of these scholarships are awarded each year: 108 (2 in each state or U.S. territory) for members of the Army National Guard, 223 for members of the Army Reserve, and 85 for MJC students (17 at each approved school).

Deadline Deadline not specified.

[861]
ILLINOIS NATIONAL GUARD GRANT PROGRAM

Illinois Student Assistance Commission
Attn: Scholarship and Grant Services
1755 Lake Cook Road
Deerfield, IL 60015-5209
(847) 948-8550   Toll Free: (800) 899-ISAC
Fax: (847) 831-8549   TDD: (800) 526-0844
E-mail: collegezone@isac.org
Web: www.collegezone.com/studentzone/407_626.htm

Summary To provide financial assistance to current or former members of the Illinois National Guard who are interested in attending college or graduate school in the state.

Eligibility This program is open to members of the Illinois National Guard who are 1) currently active or 2) have been active for at least 5 consecutive years, have been called to federal active duty for at least 6 months, and are within 12 months after their discharge date. Applicants must also be enrolled at an Illinois public 2- or 4-year college or university and have served at least 1 full year in the Guard.

Financial Data Recipients are eligible for payment of tuition and some fees for either undergraduate or graduate study at an Illinois state-supported college or university.

Duration This assistance extends for 8 semesters or 12 quarters (or the equivalent in part-time study).

Number awarded Varies each year.

Deadline September of each year for the academic year; February of each year for spring semester, winter quarter, or spring quarter; June of each year for summer term.

[862]
INTERNATIONAL SECURITY AND COOPERATION PROFESSIONAL FELLOWSHIPS

Stanford University
Center for International Security and Cooperation
Attn: Fellowship and Visiting Scholars Program Associate
Encina Hall, Room C223
616 Serra Street
Stanford, CA 94305-6055
(650) 723-9626   Fax: (650) 723-0089
E-mail: mgellner@stanford.edu
Web: cisac.stanford.edu/fellowships

Summary To provide funding to professionals who are interested in conducting research on arms control and international security at Stanford University's Center for International Security and Cooperation.

Eligibility This program is open to military officers or civilian members of the U.S. government, members of military or diplomatic services from other countries, and journalists interested in arms control and international security issues. Applicants must be interested in conducting research on international security and arms control issues at the center. Topics suitable for support might include terrorism and counter-terrorism; regional and global security relationships; the United Nations and global governance; causes and prevention of conflict; organizational success and failure in avoiding or responding to disaster; proliferation of nuclear, chemical, and biological weapons; norms of nonproliferation and nonuse of weapons; and the interaction of science, politics, and policy.

Financial Data The stipend depends on experience and is determined on a case-by-case basis. Additional funds may be available for dependents and travel.

Duration 9 months.

Number awarded Varies each year.

Deadline January of each year.

[863]
JODI CALLAHAN MEMORIAL GRADUATE SCHOLARSHIP

Air Force Association
Attn: Scholarship Manager
1501 Lee Highway
Arlington, VA 22209-1198
(703) 247-5800, ext. 4807
Toll Free: (800) 727-3337, ext. 4807
Fax: (703) 247-5853   E-mail: LCross@afa.org
Web: www.afa.org/aef/aid/callahan.asp

Summary To provide financial assistance for graduate education to Air Force personnel who are members of the Air Force Association.

Eligibility This program is open to active-duty Air Force members and full-time Guard and Reserve personnel (officer or enlisted) who are also members of the association. Applicants must be working on a master's degree in a nontechnical field during off-duty time and have a GPA of 3.0 or higher. Along with their application, they must submit a 2-page essay describing their academic goals and how they expect their degree to enhance their service to the Air Force.

Financial Data The stipend is $1,000. Funds may be used for any reasonable expenses related to working on a degree, including tuition, lab fees, and books.

Duration 1 year; nonrenewable.

Number awarded 2 each year.

Deadline June of each year.

[864]
JOHN CORNELIUS/MAX ENGLISH MEMORIAL SCHOLARSHIP AWARD

Marine Corps Tankers Association
P.O. Box 20761
El Cajon, CA 92021
Web: www.usmarinetankers.org/scholarship-program

Summary To provide financial assistance for college or graduate school to children and grandchildren of Marines who served in a tank unit.

Eligibility This program is open to high school seniors and graduates who are children, grandchildren, or under the guardianship of an active, Reserve, retired, or honorably discharged Marine who served in a tank unit. Marine or Navy Corpsmen currently assigned to tank units are also eligible. Applicants must be enrolled or planning to enroll full time at a college or graduate school. Their sponsor must be a member of the Marine Corps Tankers Association or, if not a member, must join if the application is accepted. Along with their application, they must submit an essay on their educational goals, future aspirations, and concern for the future of our society and for the peoples of the world. Selection is based on that essay, academic record, school activities, leadership potential, and community service.

Financial Data The stipend is at least $2,000 per year.

Duration 1 year; recipients may reapply.

Number awarded 8 to 12 each year.

Deadline March of each year.

[865]
JOSEPH A. MCALINDEN DIVERS' SCHOLARSHIP

Navy-Marine Corps Relief Society
Attn: Education Division
875 North Randolph Street, Suite 225
Arlington, VA 22203-1757
(703) 696-4960   Fax: (703) 696-0144
E-mail: education@nmcrs.org
Web: www.nmcrs.org/education.html

Summary To provide financial assistance to current and former Navy and Marine Corps divers and their families who are interested in working on an undergraduate or graduate degree in a field related to ocean agriculture.

Eligibility This program is open to Navy and Marine Corps active-duty and retired divers and members of their families. Applicants must be enrolled full time in an undergraduate or graduate program in oceanography, ocean agriculture, aquaculture, or a related field; they may also be engaged in advanced diver training, certification, or recertification. Financial need is considered in the selection process.

Financial Data The stipend ranges from $500 to $3,000, depending on the need of the recipient.

Duration 1 year.

Number awarded 1 or more each year.

Deadline Applications may be submitted at any time.

[866]
JOSEPH R. BARANSKI EMERITUS SCHOLARSHIP

Fleet Reserve Association
Attn: Scholarship Administrator
125 North West Street
Alexandria, VA 22314-2754
(703) 683-1400   Toll Free: (800) FRA-1924
Fax: (703) 549-6610   E-mail: fra@fra.org
Web: www.fra.org

Summary To provide financial assistance for graduate school to members of the Fleet Reserve Association (FRA) and their spouses, children, and grandchildren.

Eligibility This program is open to the dependent children, grandchildren, and spouses of members of the association who are in good standing (or were at the time of death, if deceased). FRA members are also eligible. Applicants should be enrolled in a graduate program. Along with their application, they must submit an essay on their life experiences, career objectives, and what motivated them to select those objectives. Selection is based on academic record, financial need, extracurricular activities, leadership skills, and participation in community activities. U.S. citizenship is required.

Financial Data The stipend is $5,000.

Duration 1 year; may be renewed.

Additional data Membership in the FRA is restricted to active-duty, retired, and Reserve members of the Navy, Marine Corps, and Coast Guard. This program was established in 2001.

Number awarded 1 each year.

Deadline April of each year.

[867]
LIFE'S CHOICES FOUNDATION GRADUATE SCHOLARSHIP AWARDS

Association for Intelligence Officers
Attn: Scholarships Committee
6723 Whittier Avenue, Suite 303A
McLean, VA 22101-4533
(703) 790-0320   Fax: (703) 991-1278
E-mail: afio@afio.com
Web: www.afio.com/13_scholarships.htm

Summary To provide financial assistance to graduate students who are members or descendants of members of the U.S. intelligence community and interested in working on a degree in a field related to national security.

Eligibility This program is open to graduate students who apply in their senior undergraduate year or first graduate year. Applicants must be 1) personnel serving in government agencies that are part of the U.S. intelligence community or 2) their children or grandchildren. They must be working on a degree in a field related to national security or intelligence studies and be, or planning to be, serving in the U.S. government. Along with their application, they must submit a cover letter that explains their need for assistance, their career goals and dreams, and their views of U.S. world standing and its intelligence community. Selection is based on merit, character, estimated future potential, background, and relevance of their studies to the full spectrum of national security interests and career ambitions. U.S. citizenship is required.

Financial Data The stipend is $4,000.

Duration 1 year.

Additional data This program is sponsored by the Morris Family Charitable Corporation.

Number awarded 2 each year.

Deadline June of each year.

[868]
MAINE NATIONAL GUARD EDUCATION ASSISTANCE PROGRAM

Maine National Guard
Attn: Education
Camp Keyes
Augusta, ME 04333-0033
(207) 626-4370   Toll Free: (800) 462-3101 (within ME)
Fax: (207) 626-4509
Web: www.me.ngb.army.mil

Summary To provide financial assistance for undergraduate or graduate study to members of the Maine National Guard.

Eligibility This program is open to active members of the Maine National Guard who are interested in working on an undergraduate or graduate degree or certificate at a college or university within the state. Applicants must be Maine residents who have successfully completed basic training or received a commission. They may not have any unsatisfactory record of participation in the Guard. First priority is given to Guard members who do not have a baccalaureate degree and are working on a degree; second priority is given to members without a graduate degree who are working on a degree, teacher certification, principal certification, or superintendent certification; third priority is for all others.

Financial Data This program provides payment of up to 100% of tuition and fees at a Maine accredited public postsecondary institution. Recipients may also attend a private college or university in Maine, but the benefit is capped at the tuition rates at the University of Maine.

Duration 1 semester; may be renewed for a total of 150 credit hours, as long as the recipient maintains satisfactory participation in the Guard and an academic GPA of 2.0 or higher.

Number awarded Varies each year.

Deadline October of each year for college terms beginning from January through April; February of each year for college terms beginning from May through July; June of each year for college terms beginning in August or September.

[869]
MARINE CORPS FUNDED LAW EDUCATION PROGRAM

U.S. Marine Corps
Manpower and Reserve Affairs (MMOA-5)
Attn: Undergraduate and Graduate Education Programs
3280 Russell Road
Quantico, VA 22134-5103
(703) 784-9286   Fax: (703) 784-9844
E-mail: Diane.Rodgers@usmc.mil
Web: www.usmc.mil

Summary To allow selected commissioned Marine Corps officers to earn a law degree by providing financial assistance for full-time study.

Eligibility Eligible to participate in this program are commissioned Marine Corps officers at the rank of captain or below. Applicants must have at least 2 but no more than 6 years of total active service and be able to complete 20 years of active service before their 55th birthday. They must have graduated from an accredited college or university with a bachelor's degree, have taken the LSAT at their own arrangement and expense, and have been accepted at an accredited law school in the United States.

Financial Data Commissioned officers selected to participate in this program receive their regular Marine Corps pay and allowances while attending a college or university on a full-time basis, as well as payment for the cost of tuition (to a maximum of $10,000 per year).

Duration Up to the equivalent of 2 academic years.

Number awarded Varies each year; recently, 3 Marines were selected to participate in this program.

Deadline November of each year.

[870]
MARINE CORPS SPECIAL EDUCATION PROGRAM

U.S. Marine Corps
Manpower and Reserve Affairs (MMOA-5)
Attn: Undergraduate and Graduate Education Programs
3280 Russell Road
Quantico, VA 22134-5103
(703) 784-9286   Fax: (703) 784-9844
E-mail: Diane.Rodgers@usmc.mil
Web: www.usmc.mil

Summary To provide financial assistance to commissioned Marine Corps officers who are interested in earning an advanced degree in selected fields.

Eligibility This program is open to selected commissioned Marine Corps officers at the rank of first lieutenant through lieutenant colonel. Applicants must be interested in earning a postgraduate degree in specified disciplines (recently: aeronautical engineering, computer science, defense systems analysis, electrical engineering, environmental engineering and science, financial management, information systems technology, information warfare systems, joint C4I, leadership development, manpower systems analysis, material logistics support, modeling virtual environmental simulation, operations analysis, ordnance systems engineering, public affairs management, and space systems operations). They must be planning to attend the Naval Postgraduate School, the United States Naval Academy, the Air Force Institute of Technology, or (for designated programs) approved civilian institutions.

Financial Data Commissioned officers selected to participate in this program receive their regular Marine Corps pay while attending a college or university on a full-time basis, as well as full payment for the cost of tuition (to a maximum of $10,000 per year at a civilian institution). Other allowances include reimbursement of up to $150 per academic year for required textbooks and up to $200 for typing a required thesis.

Duration Up to the equivalent of 2 academic years.

Additional data Officers must agree not to tender their resignation or request retirement while enrolled in the program. They must also agree to remain on active duty, after completion of degree requirements or upon separation from the program for any other reason, for 3 years or, if the enrollment in school is longer than 1 calendar year, for 4 years.

Number awarded Varies each year. Recently, 81 officers were selected to participate in this program.

Deadline June of each year.

[871]
MARINE CORPS TUITION ASSISTANCE PROGRAM

U.S. Marine Corps
Attn: Lifelong Learning Center
3098 Range Road
Quantico, VA 22134-5028
(703) 784-9550   E-mail: vernon.taylor@usmc.mil
Web: www.usmc-mccs.org/education/mta.cfm

Summary To provide financial assistance for undergraduate or graduate study to Marine Corps personnel.

Eligibility Eligible for assistance under this program are active-duty Marines who wish to take college courses for academic credit during off-duty time. Funding is available for vocational/technical, undergraduate, graduate, undergraduate development, independent study, and distance learning programs. Commissioned officers must agree to remain on active duty for 2 years after the completion of any funded courses. All students must successfully complete their courses with a satisfactory grade.

Financial Data Those selected for participation in this program receive their regular Marine Corps pay and 100% of tuition at the postsecondary educational institution of their choice, but capped at $4,500 per year or $250 per semester hour, whichever is less.

Duration Until completion of a bachelor's or graduate degree.

Number awarded Varies each year; in recent years, approximately 20,000 Marines availed themselves of this funding.

Deadline Deadline not specified.

[872]
MARYLAND NATIONAL GUARD STATE TUITION WAIVER

Maryland National Guard
Attn: Education Services Office
Fifth Regiment Armory
29th Division Street, Room D24
Baltimore, MD 21201-2288
(410) 576-1467   Toll Free: (800) 492-2526
Fax: (410) 576-6082
E-mail: mdng_education@md.ngb.army.mil
Web: www.mdarmyguard.com/moneyforcollege.htm

Summary To waive tuition for members of the Maryland National Guard at colleges and universities in the state.

Eligibility All state-supported colleges and universities in Maryland have developed a tuition waiver program for members of the National Guard who are taking graduate or university courses.

Financial Data The amount of the waiver ranges from 25% to 50%.

Duration 1 semester; recipients may reapply.

Additional data Some schools also limit the number of credits for which a Guard member can receive waivers during any semester.

Number awarded Varies each year.

Deadline Deadline not specified.

[873]
MASSACHUSETTS NATIONAL GUARD EDUCATIONAL ASSISTANCE PROGRAM

Massachusetts National Guard
Attn: Education Services Office
50 Maple Street
Milford, MA 01757-3604
Toll Free: (888) 301-3103, ext. 6753   Fax: (508) 233-6781
E-mail: ma-education@ng.army.mil
Web: www.mass.gov/guard/education/index.htm

Summary To provide financial assistance to members of the Massachusetts National Guard interested in working on an undergraduate or graduate degree at a college in the state.

Eligibility This program is open to actively participating members of the Army or Air National Guard in Massachusetts. Applicants must have less than 9 AWOLs (Absence Without Leave) at all times and must not ETS (Expiration of Term of Service) during the period enrolled. They must be accepted for admission or enrolled at 1 of 28 Massachusetts public colleges, universities, or community colleges and working on an associate, bachelor's, master's, or doctoral degree. The institution must have a vacancy after all tuition-paying students and all students who are enrolled under any scholarship or tuition waiver provisions have enrolled.

Financial Data Eligible Guard members are exempt from any tuition payments at colleges or universities operated by the Commonwealth of Massachusetts and funded by the Massachusetts Board of Higher Education.

Duration Up to a total of 130 semester hours.

Additional data Recipients may enroll either part or full time in a Massachusetts state-supported institution. This program, commonly referred to as the 100% Tuition Waiver Program, is funded through the Massachusetts Board of Higher Education.

Number awarded Varies each year.

Deadline Deadline not specified.

[874]
MEDICAL CORPS OPTION OF THE SEAMAN TO ADMIRAL-21 PROGRAM

U.S. Navy
Attn: Commander, Naval Service Training Command
250 Dallas Street, Suite A
Pensacola, FL 32508-5268
(850) 452-9563   Fax: (850) 452-2486
E-mail: PNSC_STA21@navy.mil
Web: www.sta-21.navy.mil

Summary To allow outstanding enlisted Navy personnel to complete a bachelor's degree, be accepted to medical school, earn an M.D. or D.O. degree, and be commissioned in the Navy Medical Corps.

Eligibility This program is open to U.S. citizens who are currently serving on active duty in the U.S. Navy or Naval Reserve, including Full Time Support (FTS), Selected Reserves (SEL-RES), and Navy Reservists on active duty except for those on active duty for training (ACDUTRA). Applicants must be high school graduates (or GED recipients) who are able to complete requirements for baccalaureate and medical degrees and then be able to complete 20 years of active commissioned service as a physician by age 62. Within the past 3 years, they must have taken the SAT test (and achieved scores of at least 500 on the mathematics section and 500 on the critical reading section) or the ACT test (and achieved a score of 41 or higher, including at least 21 on the mathematics portion and 20 on the English portion).

Financial Data Awardees continue to receive their regular Navy pay and allowances while they attend college on a full-time basis. They also receive reimbursement for tuition, fees, and books up to $10,000 per year. If base housing is available, they are eligible to live there. Participants are not eligible to receive benefits under the Navy's Tuition Assistance Program (TA), the Montgomery GI Bill (MGIB), the Navy College Fund, or the Veterans Educational Assistance Program (VEAP).

Duration Selectees are supported for up to 36 months of full-time, year-round study or completion of a bachelor's degree, as long as they maintain a GPA of 3.0 or higher. They are then supported until completion of a medical degree.

Additional data Upon acceptance into the program, selectees attend the Naval Science Institute (NSI) in Newport, Rhode Island for an 8-week program in the fundamental core concepts of being a naval officer (navigation, engineering, weapons, military history and justice, etc.). They then enter an NROTC affiliated college or university with a pre-medical program that confers an accredited B.S. degree to pursue full-time study. They become members of and drill with the NROTC unit. After they complete their bachelor's degree, they are commissioned as an ensign in the Naval Reserve. They must apply to and be accepted at medical school, either the Uniformed Services University of Health Sciences (USUSH) or a civilian medical school through the Health Professions Scholarship Program (HPSP). Following completion of medical school, they are promoted to lieutenant and assigned to active duty in the Medical Corps. Selectees incur a service obligation of 5 years for their baccalaureate degree support plus whatever obligation they incur for medical degree support (usually 7 years if they attend USUSH or 4 years if they attend a civilian institution through HPSP).

Number awarded Varies each year.

Deadline June of each year.

[875]
MEDICAL SERVICE CORPS INSERVICE PROCUREMENT PROGRAM (MSC-IPP)

U.S. Navy
Attn: Navy Medicine Manpower, Personnel, Education and
   Training Command
Code O3C
8901 Wisconsin Avenue, 16th Floor, Tower 1
Bethesda, MD 20889-5611
(301) 319-4520   Fax: (301) 295-1783
E-mail: mscipp@nmetc.med.navy.mil
Web: www.med.navy.mil

Summary To provide funding to Navy and Marine enlisted personnel who wish to earn an undergraduate or graduate degree in selected health care specialties while continuing to receive their regular pay and allowances.

Eligibility This program is open to enlisted personnel who are serving on active duty in any rating in pay grade E-5 through E-9 of the U.S. Navy, U.S. Marine Corps, and the Marine Corps Reserve serving on active duty (including Full Time Support of the Reserve). Applicants must be interested in working on a degree to become commissioned in the following medical specialties: health care administration, physician assistant, radiation health, pharmacy, environmental health, industrial hygiene, or entomology. If they plan to work on a graduate degree, they must have scores of at least 1000 on the GRE or 500 on the GMAT; if they plan to work on a bachelor's or physician assistant degree, they must have scores of at least 1000 on the SAT (including 460 on the mathematics portion) or 42 on the ACT. They must be U.S. citizens who can be commissioned before they reach their 42nd birthday.

Financial Data Participants receive payment of tuition, mandatory fees, a book allowance, and full pay and allowances for their enlisted pay grade. They are eligible for advancement while in college.

Duration 24 to 48 months of full-time, year-round study, until completion of a relevant degree.

Additional data Following graduation, participants are commissioned in the Medical Service Corps and attend Officer Indoctrination School.

Number awarded Varies each year. Recently, 36 of these positions were available: 20 in health care administration, 10 in physician assistant, 2 in pharmacy, 2 in environmental health, 1 in industrial hygiene, and 1 in entomology.

Deadline August of each year.

[876]
MG LEIF J. SVERDRUP AWARD

Army Engineer Association
Attn: Washington DC Operations
P.O. Box 30260
Alexandria, VA 22310-8260
(703) 428-7084   Fax: (703) 428-6043
E-mail: DCOps@armyengineer.com
Web: www.armyengineer.com/AEA_scholarships.html

Summary To provide financial assistance for college or graduate school to officers who are members of the Army Engineer Association (AEA).

Eligibility This program is open to AEA members serving in an active, Reserve, or National Guard component Army Engineer unit, school, or organization within the Corps of Engineers of the United States Army. Applicants must be commissioned officers (2LT, 1LT, or CPT) or warrant officers (WO1 or WO2). They must be working on or planning to work on an associate, bachelor's, or master's degree at an accredited college or university. Selection is based primarily on financial need, although potential for academic success and standards of conduct as supported by personal references are also considered.

Financial Data The stipend is $1,000.

Duration 1 year.

Number awarded 1 or 2 each year.

Deadline June of each year.

[877]
MILITARY NONRESIDENT TUITION WAIVER FOR MEMBERS, SPOUSES OR CHILDREN ASSIGNED TO DUTY IN TEXAS

Texas Higher Education Coordinating Board
Attn: Grants and Special Programs
1200 East Anderson Lane
P.O. Box 12788, Capitol Station
Austin, TX 78711-2788
(512) 427-6340   Toll Free: (800) 242-3062
Fax: (512) 427-6127   E-mail: grantinfo@thecb.state.tx.us
Web: www.collegeforalltexans.com

Summary To exempt military personnel stationed in Texas and their dependents from the payment of nonresident tuition at public institutions of higher education in the state.

Eligibility Eligible for these waivers are members of the U.S. armed forces and commissioned officers of the Public Health Service from states other than Texas, their spouses, and dependent children. Applicants must be assigned to Texas and attending or planning to attend a public college or university in the state.

Financial Data Although persons eligible under this program are classified as nonresidents, they are entitled to pay the resident tuition at Texas institutions of higher education, regardless of their length of residence in Texas.

Duration 1 year; may be renewed.

Number awarded Varies each year; recently, 11,600 students received these waivers.

Deadline Deadline not specified.

[878]
MILTON E. COOPER/YOUNG AFCEAN GRADUATE SCHOLARSHIP

Armed Forces Communications and Electronics Association
Attn: AFCEA Educational Foundation
4400 Fair Lakes Court
Fairfax, VA 22033-3899
(703) 631-6149   Toll Free: (800) 336-4583, ext. 6149
Fax: (703) 631-4693   E-mail: scholarship@afcea.org
Web: www.afcea.org

Summary To provide financial assistance to young professionals (especially active-duty officers) who are working on a graduate degree in designated scientific and engineering fields.

Eligibility This program is open to young professionals (35 years of age or younger) already employed in a field related to communications, computer science, or electronics. Applicants must be currently enrolled at an accredited college or university in the United States and committed to working on an advanced college degree (M.S. or Ph.D.) relating to communications, computer science, electronics engineering, electrical engineering, or systems engineering. They must have a GPA of 3.2 or higher and be preparing for a career in science or engineering. U.S. citizenship is required.

Financial Data The stipend is $3,000.

Duration 1 year; may be renewed.

Additional data Since the establishment of this program in 2001, every recipient has been an active-duty officer in the U.S. armed forces.

Number awarded 1 each year.

Deadline March of each year.

[879]
MINNESOTA G.I. BILL PROGRAM

Minnesota Office of Higher Education
Attn: Manager of State Financial Aid Programs
1450 Energy Park Drive, Suite 350
St. Paul, MN 55108-5227
(651) 642-0567   Toll Free: (800) 657-3866
Fax: (651) 642-0675   TDD: (800) 627-3529
E-mail: Ginny.Dodds@state.mn.us
Web: www.ohe.state.mn.us

Summary To provide financial assistance for college or graduate school in the state to residents of Minnesota who served in the military after September 11, 2001 and the families of deceased or disabled military personnel.

Eligibility This program is open to residents of Minnesota enrolled at colleges and universities in the state as undergraduate or graduate students. Applicants must be 1) a veteran who is serving or has served honorably in a branch of the U.S. armed forces at any time on or after September 11, 2001; 2) a non-veteran who has served honorably for a total of 5 years or more cumulatively as a member of the Minnesota National Guard or other active or Reserve component of the U.S. armed forces, and any part of that service occurred on or after September 11, 2001; or 3) a surviving child or spouse of a person who has served in the military at any time on or after September 11, 2001 and who has died or has a total and permanent disability as a result of that military service. Financial need is also considered in the selection process.

Financial Data The stipend is $1,000 per semester for full-time study or $500 per semester for part-time study.

Duration 1 year; may be renewed up to 4 additional years, provided the recipient continues to make satisfactory academic progress.

Additional data This program was established by the Minnesota Legislature in 2007.

Number awarded Varies each year.

Deadline Deadline not specified.

[880]
MINNESOTA NATIONAL GUARD MEDICAL AND DENTAL TUITION REIMBURSEMENT PROGRAM

Department of Military Affairs
Attn: Education Services Officer
JFMN-J1-ARED
20 West 12th Street
St. Paul, MN 55155-2098
(651) 282-4125   Toll Free: (800) 657-3848
Fax: (651) 282-4694   E-mail: education@mn.ngb.army.mil
Web: www.minnesotanationalguard.org

Summary To provide partial tuition reimbursement to medical and dental students who are serving in the Minnesota National Guard.

Eligibility This program is open to Minnesota Army and Air National Guard members admitted to medical or dental school. Applicants must agree to accept a Medical Corps commission in the Guard after graduation.

Financial Data This program provides reimbursement of the tuition charged, not to exceed 100% of the tuition costs at the University of Minnesota Twin Cities campus medical or dental schools. Upon graduation from medical or dental school, officers must serve the same number of years in the Minnesota National Guard that they participated in the program. Failure to fulfill that service obligation will result in recoupment of a prorated portion of the tuition reimbursed.

Duration Until completion of a medical or dental degree.

Number awarded The number of participants at any given time is limited to 11 Army officers and 3 Air Guard officers.

Deadline Participants must request reimbursement within 60 days of the last official day of the term.

[881]
MINNESOTA NATIONAL GUARD STATE TUITION REIMBURSEMENT

Department of Military Affairs
Attn: Education Services Officer
JFMN-J1-ARED
20 West 12th Street
St. Paul, MN 55155-2098
(651) 282-4125   Toll Free: (800) 657-3848
Fax: (651) 282-4694   E-mail: education@mn.ngb.army.mil
Web: www.minnesotanationalguard.org

Summary To provide financial assistance for college or graduate school to members of the Minnesota National Guard.

Eligibility Eligible for this program are members of the Minnesota Army or Air National Guard in grades E-1 through O-5 (including warrant officers) who are enrolled as undergraduate or graduate students at colleges or universities in Minnesota. Reimbursement is provided only for undergraduate courses completed with a grade of "C" or better or for graduate courses completed with a grade of "B" or better. Guard members who served on federal active status or federally-funded state active service after September 11, 2001 are eligible for this assistance for up to 2 years after completion of their service contract (or up to 8 years if they were separated or discharged because of a service-connected injury, disease, or disability).

Financial Data The maximum reimbursement rate is 100% of the undergraduate tuition rate at the University of Minnesota Twin Cities campus (currently, $326.92 per credit to a maximum of $4,250 per term).

Duration 1 semester, to a maximum of 18 credits per semester; may be renewed.

Number awarded Varies each year.

Deadline Deadline not specified.

[882]
MONTGOMERY GI BILL (SELECTED RESERVE)

Department of Veterans Affairs
Attn: Veterans Benefits Administration
810 Vermont Avenue, N.W.
Washington, DC 20420
(202) 418-4343 Toll Free: (888) GI-BILL1
Web: www.gibill.va.gov/GI_Bill_Info/benefits.htm

Summary To provide financial assistance for college or graduate school to members of the Reserves or National Guard.

Eligibility Eligible to apply are members of the Reserve elements of the Army, Navy, Air Force, Marine Corps, and Coast Guard, as well as the Army National Guard and the Air National Guard. To be eligible, a Reservist must 1) have a 6-year obligation to serve in the Selected Reserves signed after June 30, 1985 (or, if an officer, to agree to serve 6 years in addition to the original obligation); 2) complete Initial Active Duty for Training (IADT); 3) meet the requirements for a high school diploma or equivalent certificate before completing IADT; and 4) remain in good standing in a drilling Selected Reserve unit. Reservists who enlisted after June 30, 1985 can receive benefits for undergraduate degrees, graduate training, or technical courses leading to certificates at colleges and universities. Reservists whose 6-year commitment began after September 30, 1990 may also use these benefits for a certificate or diploma from business, technical, or vocational schools; cooperative training; apprenticeship or on-the-job training; correspondence courses; independent study programs; tutorial assistance; remedial, deficiency, or refresher training; flight training; or state-approved alternative teacher certification programs.

Financial Data The current monthly rate is $333 for full-time study, $249 for three-quarter time study, $169 for half-time study, or $83.25 for less than half-time study. For apprenticeship and on-the-job training, the monthly stipend is $249.75 for the first 6 months, $183.15 for the second 6 months, and $116.55 for the remainder of the program. Other rates apply for cooperative education, correspondence courses, and flight training.

Duration Up to 36 months for full-time study, 48 months for three-quarter study, 72 months for half-time study, or 144 months for less than half-time study.

Additional data This program is frequently referred to as Chapter 1606 (formerly Chapter 106). Reservists who are enrolled for three-quarter or full-time study are eligible to participate in the work-study program. The Department of Defense periodically offers "kickers" of additional benefits on behalf of individuals in critical military fields, as deemed necessary to encourage enlistment. Information on currently-available "kickers" is available from Reserve and National Guard recruiters. Benefits end 10 years from the date the Reservist became eligible for the program. The Department of Veterans Affairs (VA) may extend the 10-year period if the individual could not train because of a disability caused by Selected Reserve service. Certain individuals separated from the Selected Reserve due to downsizing of the military between October 1, 1991 and September 30, 1999 will also have the full 10 years to use their benefits.

Number awarded Varies each year.

Deadline Applications may be submitted at any time.

[883]
MONTGOMERY GI BILL TUITION ASSISTANCE TOP-UP

Department of Veterans Affairs
Attn: Veterans Benefits Administration
810 Vermont Avenue, N.W.
Washington, DC 20420
(202) 418-4343 Toll Free: (888) GI-BILL1
Web: www.gibill.va.gov/GI_Bill_Info/benefits.htm

Summary To supplement the tuition assistance provided by the military services to their members.

Eligibility This program is open to military personnel who have served at least 2 full years on active duty and are approved for tuition assistance by their military service. Applicants must be participating in the Montgomery GI Bill (MGIB) Active Duty program and be eligible for MGIB benefits. This assistance is available to servicemembers whose military service does not pay 100% of tuition and fees.

Financial Data This program pays the difference between what the military services pay for tuition assistance and the full amount of tuition and fees, to a maximum of $1,075 per month.

Duration Up to 36 months of payments are available.

Additional data This program was established in 2000.

Number awarded Varies each year.

Deadline Deadline not specified.

[884]
NATIONAL GUARD ASSOCIATION OF CALIFORNIA SCHOLARSHIPS

National Guard Association of California
Attn: Scholarship Committee
3336 Bradshaw Road, Suite 230
Sacramento, CA 95827-2615
(916) 362-3411 Toll Free: (800) 647-0018
Fax: (916) 362-3707
Web: www.ngac.org

Summary To provide financial assistance for college or graduate school to members of the National Guard Association of California.

Eligibility This program is open to members of the association who are also currently serving in the California National Guard. Applicants must be attending or planning to attend a college, university, graduate school, business school, or trade school in California. They may have no record of AWOL or unsatisfactory performance for the previous year or since enlistment. Selection is based on academic merit and financial need.

Financial Data The amount of the award depends on the availability of funds.

Duration 1 year; recipients are ineligible for 2 successive awards.

Number awarded Varies each year; recently, 4 of these scholarships were awarded.

Deadline Applications may be submitted at any time, but recipients are selected in October and April of each year.

[885]
NATIONAL GUARD ASSOCIATION OF COLORADO SCHOLARSHIP PROGRAM

National Guard Association of Colorado
Attn: Education Foundation, Inc.
P.O. Box 440889
Aurora, CO 80044-0889
(303) 677-8387 Fax: (303) 677-8823
E-mail: ed.foundation@earthlink.net
Web: www.ngaco-edufoundation.org

Summary To provide financial assistance to members of the National Guard Association of Colorado (NGACO) and the Colorado National Guard and their families who are interested in attending college or graduate school in any state.

Eligibility This program is open to 1) current and retired members of the Colorado National Guard and the NGACO; 2) dependent unmarried children of current and retired members of the Colorado National Guard and the NGACO; 3) spouses of current and retired members of the Colorado National Guard and the NGACO; and 4) unremarried spouses and unmarried dependent children of deceased members of the Colorado National Guard and the NGACO. Applicants must be enrolled or planning to enroll full or part time at a college, university, trade school, business school, or graduate school in any state. Along with their application, they must submit an essay, up to 2 pages in length, on their desire to continue their education, what motivates them, their financial need, their commitment to academic excellence, and their current situation.

Financial Data　Stipends are $1,000, $750, or $500 per year.

Duration　1 year; may be renewed.

Additional data　Members of the Colorado National Guard must perform at least 1 year of service following the completion of the school year for which the scholarship was received.

Number awarded　Varies each year. Recently, 11 of these scholarships were awarded: 4 at $1,000 to members of the NGACO, 2 at $750 to dependents of members of the NGACO, 2 at $500 to current enlisted members of the Colorado National Guard, 2 at $500 to current officer members of the Colorado National Guard, and 1 at $1,000 to a Colorado National Guard member or dependent working on a graduate degree.

Deadline　August of each year for fall semester; January of each year for spring semester.

[886]
NAVAL HELICOPTER ASSOCIATION GRADUATE SCHOLARSHIPS

Naval Helicopter Association
Attn: Scholarship Fund
P.O. Box 180578
Coronado, CA 92178-0578
(619) 435-7139　　　　　　　　　　　　Fax: (619) 435-7354
E-mail: info@nhascholarship.org
Web: www.nhascholarship.org/nhascholarshipfund/index.html

Summary　To provide financial assistance for graduate school to students who have an affiliation with the rotary wing activities of the sea services.

Eligibility　This program is open to graduate students who are 1) children, grandchildren, or spouses of current or former Navy, Marine Corps, or Coast Guard rotary wing aviators or aircrewmen; 2) individuals who are serving or have served in maintenance or support billets in rotary wing squadrons or wings and their spouses and children. Applicants must provide information on their rotary wing affiliation and a personal statement on their educational plans and future goals. Selection is based on that statement, academic proficiency, scholastic achievements and awards, extracurricular activities, employment history, and letters of recommendation.

Financial Data　The stipend is $3,000.

Duration　1 year.

Number awarded　1 each year.

Deadline　January of each year.

[887]
NAVY ADVANCED EDUCATION VOUCHER PROGRAM

U.S. Navy
Naval Education and Training Command
Center for Personal and Professional Development
Attn: AEV Program Office
6490 Saufley Field Road
Pensacola, FL 32509-5204
(850) 452-7271　　　　　　　　　　　　Fax: (850) 452-1272
E-mail: rick.cusimano@navy.mil
Web: www.navycollege.navy.mil/aev/aev_home.cfm

Summary　To provide financial assistance to Navy enlisted personnel who are interested in earning an undergraduate or graduate degree during off-duty hours.

Eligibility　This program is open to senior enlisted Navy personnel in ranks E-7 and E-8. Applicants should be transferring to, or currently on, shore duty with sufficient time ashore to complete a bachelor's or master's degree. Personnel at rank E-7 may have no more than 16 years time in service and E-8 no more than 18

years. The area of study must be certified by the Naval Postgraduate School as Navy-relevant.

Financial Data　This program covers 100% of education costs (tuition, books, and fees). For a bachelor's degree, the maximum is $6,700 per year or a total of $20,000 per participant. For a master's degree, the maximum is $20,000 per year or a total of $40,000 per participant.

Duration　Up to 36 months from the time of enrollment for a bachelor's degree; up to 24 months from the time of enrollment for a master's degree.

Additional data　Recently approved majors for bachelor's degrees included human resources, construction management, information technology, emergency and disaster management, paralegal, engineering, business administration, leadership and management, nursing, strategic foreign languages, and electrical/electronic technology. Approved fields of study for master's degrees included business administration, education and training management, emergency and disaster management, engineering and technology, homeland defense and security, human resources, information technology, leadership and management, project management, and systems analysis. Recipients of this assistance incur an obligation to remain on active duty following completion of the program for a period equal to 3 times the number of months of education completed, to a maximum obligation of 36 months.

Number awarded　Varies each year. Recently, 20 of these vouchers were awarded: 15 for bachelor's degrees and 5 for master's degrees.

Deadline　February of each year.

[888]
NAVY GRADUATE EDUCATION VOUCHER PROGRAM

U.S. Navy
Naval Education and Training Command
Center for Personal and Professional Development
Attn: GEV Program Office
6490 Saufley Field Road
Pensacola, FL 32509-5204
(850) 452-1001, ext. 2247　　　　　　　Fax: (850) 452-1272
E-mail: marjoriette.dilworth@navy.mil
Web: www.navycollege.navy.mil/gev/gev_home.cfm

Summary　To provide financial assistance to Navy officers who are interested in earning a graduate degree in selected fields during off-duty hours.

Eligibility　This program is open to active-duty unrestricted line (URL) Navy officers in ranks O-3 through O-5. Applicants should be transferring to, or currently on, shore duty with sufficient time ashore to complete a master's degree program. Officers who already have a graduate degree funded through any Department of Defense assistance or veteran's education benefits are not eligible. Officers currently enrolled in a qualifying master's degree program using the Navy Tuition Assistance Program, using any other financial assistance program, or paying privately are eligible to apply for this program, but they are not eligible for reimbursement of any previously paid educational expenses. The area of study must be certified by the Naval Postgraduate School as Navy-relevant.

Financial Data　This program covers 100% of graduate education costs (tuition, books, and fees), up to a maximum of $20,000 per year.

Duration　Up to 24 months from the time of enrollment, provided the student maintains a GPA of 3.0 or higher.

Additional data　This program began in 1999. Recently, support was provided for graduate study in global leadership, international affairs, regional studies, operations research and analysis, financial management, economics, human resource management, science and technology, engineering management, information technology, computer science, information systems management, and computer systems. Recipients of this assistance incur an obligation to remain on active duty following completion of the program for a period equal to 3 times the number of months of education completed, to a maximum obligation of 36 months.

Number awarded Varies each year; recently, 136 of these positions were available.

Deadline Deadline not specified.

[889]
NAVY LAW EDUCATION PROGRAM

U.S. Navy
Attn: Naval Education and Training Command
Center for Personal and Professional Development
Code N2A2
6490 Saufley Field Road
Pensacola, FL 32509-5204
(850) 452-1001, ext. 2219   E-mail: billie.colonna@navy.mil
Web: www.jag.navy.mil

Summary To provide financial assistance to Navy and Marine Corps officers who are interested in working on a law degree on a full-time basis.

Eligibility This program is open to active-duty Navy and Marine Corps commissioned officers in pay grade O-1 through O-3. Applicants must have served at least 2 but not more than 6 years on active duty and be able to complete 20 years of active service as a commissioned officer before their 62nd birthday. They must have a baccalaureate degree from an accredited institution and be interested in working on a degree at an ABA-accredited law school. U.S. citizenship is required.

Financial Data This program provides payment of mandatory tuition and fees, up to $500 per year for required textbooks, and a 1-time payment of $1,500 for a bar examination review course. Recipients continue to earn full pay and benefits while attending law school.

Duration Participants must complete their law degree within 36 months.

Additional data Following completion of their law degree, participants serve as career judge advocates in the Navy for 2 years for each year of legal training from this program.

Number awarded 7 each year.

Deadline November of each year.

[890]
NAVY MEDICAL FINANCIAL ASSISTANCE PROGRAM

U.S. Navy
Attn: Navy Medicine Manpower, Personnel, Education and
   Training Command
Code OH
8901 Wisconsin Avenue, Building 1, Tower 13, Room 13132
Bethesda, MD 20889-5611
(301) 295-1217   Toll Free: (800) USA-NAVY
Fax: (301) 295-1811   E-mail: OH@med.navy.mil
Web: www.med.navy.mil

Summary To provide financial assistance to future Navy officers who are currently participating in a medical or dental residency.

Eligibility This program is open to U.S. citizens who are currently at any point in residency training in a medical or dental specialty that meets the needs of the U.S. Navy. Recently, that included (for doctors) family practice, orthopedic surgery, internal medicine, and general surgery and (for dentists) oral surgery and endodontics. Upon acceptance into the program, applicants are commissioned as officers in the U.S. Navy Reserve; after completion of school, they must perform active-duty service as a doctor or dentist in the Navy.

Financial Data This program pays an annual grant of more than $45,000 and a stipend of $1,992 per month.

Additional data Participants also spend 14 days each year in an Annual Training (AT) assignment. Medical doctors incur an active-duty obligation of 1 year for each year of support plus 1 additional year. Dentists incur an active-duty obligation of 1 year for each year of support and a minimum of 3 years.

Number awarded Varies each year.

Deadline Applications may be submitted at any time.

[891]
NAVY TUITION ASSISTANCE PROGRAM

U.S. Navy
Attn: Naval Education and Training Command
Center for Personal and Professional Development
Code N725
6490 Saufley Field Road
Pensacola, FL 32509-5241
(850) 452-7271   Toll Free: (877) 253-7122
Fax: (850) 452-1149   E-mail: ncc@navy.mil
Web: www.navycollege.navy.mil/nta.cfm

Summary To provide financial assistance for high school, vocational, undergraduate, or graduate studies to Navy personnel.

Eligibility This program is open to active-duty Navy officers and enlisted personnel, including Naval Reservists on continuous active duty, enlisted Naval Reservists ordered to active duty for 120 days or more, and Naval Reservist officers ordered to active duty for 2 years or more. Applicants must register to take courses at accredited civilian schools during off-duty time. They must be working on their first associate, bachelor's, master's, doctoral, or professional degree. Tuition assistance is provided for courses taken at accredited colleges, universities, vocational/technical schools, private schools, and through independent study/distance learning (but not for flight training).

Financial Data Those selected for participation in this program receive their regular Navy pay and 100% of tuition at the postsecondary educational institution of their choice, but capped at $250 per semester hour and 12 semester hours per fiscal year (the 12-semester hour limit may be waived upon application), or a total of $4,500 per fiscal year.

Duration Until completion of a bachelor's or graduate degree.

Additional data Officers must agree to remain on active duty for at least 2 years after completion of courses funded by this program.

Number awarded Varies each year.

Deadline Deadline not specified.

[892]
NEVADA NATIONAL GUARD STATE TUITION WAIVER PROGRAM

Nevada National Guard
Attn: Education Officer
2460 Fairview Drive
Carson City, NV 89701-6807
(775) 887-7326   Fax: (775) 887-7279
Web: www.nv.ngb.army.mil/education.cfm

Summary To provide financial assistance to Nevada National Guard members who are interested in attending college or graduate school in the state.

Eligibility This program is open to active members of the Nevada National Guard who are interested in attending a public community college, 4-year college, or university in the state. Applicants must be residents of Nevada. Independent study, correspondence courses, and study at the William S. Boyd School of Law, the University of Nevada School of Medicine, and the UNLV School of Dental Medicine are not eligible.

Financial Data This program provides a waiver of 100% of tuition at state-supported community colleges, colleges, or universities in Nevada.

Duration 1 year; may be renewed.

Additional data This program was established on a pilot basis in 2003 and became permanent in 2005. Recipients must attain a GPA of at least 2.0 or refund all tuition received.

Number awarded Varies each year.

Deadline Applications must be received at least 3 weeks prior to the start of classes.

[893]
NEW HAMPSHIRE NATIONAL GUARD TUITION WAIVER PROGRAM

Office of the Adjutant General
Attn: Education Office
State Military Reservation
4 Pembroke Road
Concord, NH 03301-5652
(603) 227-1550   Fax: (603) 225-1257
TDD: (800) 735-2964 E-mail: education@nharmyguard.com
Web: www.nh.ngb.army.mil/members/education

Summary To provide financial assistance to members of the New Hampshire National Guard who are interested in attending college or graduate school in the state.

Eligibility This program is open to active members of the New Hampshire National Guard who have completed advanced individual training or commissioning and have at least a 90% attendance rate at annual training and drill assemblies. Applicants may be working on any type of academic degree at public institutions in New Hampshire. They must apply for financial aid from their school, for the New Hampshire National Guard Scholarship Program, and for federal tuition assistance.

Financial Data The program provides full payment of tuition.

Duration 1 year; may be renewed.

Additional data This program began in 1996.

Number awarded Varies each year, depending on availability of space.

Deadline Deadline not specified.

[894]
NEW JERSEY NATIONAL GUARD TUITION PROGRAM

New Jersey Department of Military and Veterans Affairs
Attn: New Jersey Army National Guard Education Center
3650 Saylors Pond Road
Fort Dix, NJ 08640-7600
(609) 562-0654   Toll Free: (888) 859-0352
Fax: (609) 562-0201
Web: www.state.nj.us/military/education/NJNGTP.htm

Summary To provide financial assistance for college or graduate school to New Jersey National Guard members and the surviving spouses and children of deceased members.

Eligibility This program is open to active members of the New Jersey National Guard who have completed Initial Active Duty for Training (IADT). Applicants must be New Jersey residents who have been accepted into a program of undergraduate or graduate study at any of 31 public institutions of higher education in the state. The surviving spouses and children of deceased members of the Guard who had completed IADT and were killed in the performance of their duties while a member of the Guard are also eligible if the school has classroom space available.

Financial Data Tuition for up to 15 credits per semester is waived for full-time recipients in state-supported colleges or community colleges in New Jersey.

Duration 1 semester; may be renewed.

Number awarded Varies each year.

Deadline Deadline not specified.

[895]
NEW MEXICO NATIONAL GUARD ASSOCIATION MASTER'S/CONTINUING EDUCATION SCHOLARSHIPS

New Mexico National Guard Association
Attn: Executive Director
10 Bataan Boulevard
Santa Fe, NM 87508
(505) 474-1669   Fax: (505) 474-1671
E-mail: execdir@nganm.org
Web: www.nganm.org

Summary To provide financial assistance to members of the New Mexico National Guard Association and their dependents who are working on a master's or other advanced degree.

Eligibility This program is open to association members (with paid-up current dues) and their dependents. Applicants must have completed their postsecondary education and be working on their master's or other higher degree. They must submit an official college transcript with a GPA of 3.3 or higher, a completed application, and an original essay (from 800 to 1,200 words) on their past accomplishments and contributions and what contributions they intend to make with this education to better the community or the National Guard.

Financial Data The stipend is $1,000. Funds are paid directly to the recipient's school.

Duration 1 year; nonrenewable.

Number awarded 2 each year.

Deadline April of each year.

[896]
NGANJ SCHOLARSHIP PROGRAM

National Guard Association of New Jersey
Attn: Executive Director
P.O. Box 266
Wrightstown, NJ 08562
(973) 541-6776   Fax: (973) 541-6909
E-mail: jose.maldonado@njdmava.state.nj.us
Web: www.nganj.org

Summary To provide financial assistance to New Jersey National Guard members or their dependents who are interested in attending college or graduate school in any state.

Eligibility This program is open to active members of the New Jersey National Guard; the spouses, children, legal wards, and grandchildren of active members; and the children, legal wards, and grandchildren of retired (with at least 20 years of service) or deceased members. Applicants must be currently attending or entering an approved community college, school of nursing, or 4-year college in any state as a full-time undergraduate or graduate student. Selection is based on academic accomplishment, leadership, and citizenship.

Financial Data Stipends up to $1,000 are available.

Duration 1 year; nonrenewable.

Number awarded Varies each year; recently, 10 of these scholarships were awarded.

Deadline March of each year.

[897]
NGASC SCHOLARSHIPS

National Guard Association of South Carolina
Attn: NGASC Scholarship Foundation
132 Pickens Street
Columbia, SC 29205
(803) 254-8456   Toll Free: (800) 822-3235
Fax: (803) 254-3869   E-mail: nginfo@ngasc.org
Web: www.ngasc.org/ngasc_scholarship_foundation.htm

Summary To provide financial assistance to current and former South Carolina National Guard members and their dependents who are interested in attending college or graduate school in any state.

Eligibility This program is open to undergraduate students who are 1) current, retired, or deceased members of the South Carolina National Guard; 2) their dependents; and 3) members of the National Guard Association of South Carolina (NGASC). Graduate students are also eligible if they are members of the South Carolina National Guard. Applicants must be attending or interested in attending a college or university in any state as a full-time student. Several of the scholarships include additional restrictions on school or academic major; some are granted only for academic excellence, but most are based on both academics and financial need.

Financial Data The stipend is $1,500 or $1,000.

Duration 1 year; may be renewed up to 3 additional years.

Additional data Among the named scholarships included in this program recently were the BG (Ret) C. Norwood Gayle Memorial Scholarship Award, the CMSgt Jim Burgess Scholarship Award, the Mrs. Kaye Helgeson Memorial Scholarship Award, the LTC (Ret) Glenny J. (Jeff) Matthews Memorial Scholarship Awards, the Ron McNair Memorial Scholarship Award, the Darla Moore Scholarship Award, the Sergeants Major Watson Scholarship Award, the SCANG Chiefs Council Scholarship Award, the Chief Shepherd Pitney Bowes Scholarship Award, the Fallen Soldiers' Memorial Scholarship Award, and the South Carolina National Guard Federal Credit Union Awards.

Number awarded Varies each year. Recently, 48 of these scholarships were awarded: 1 at $1,500 and 47 at $1,000. The $1,500 scholarship and 1 of the $1,000 scholarships were based on academic excellence; the remaining $1,000 scholarships were based on both academics and financial need.

Deadline January of each year.

[898]
NGAT SCHOLARSHIP PROGRAM

National Guard Association of Texas
Attn: NGAT Educational Foundation
3706 Crawford Avenue
Austin, TX 78731-6803
(512) 454-7300   Toll Free: (800) 252-NGAT
Fax: (512) 467-6803   E-mail: rlindner@ngat.org
Web: www.ngat.org

Summary To provide financial assistance to members and dependents of members of the National Guard Association of Texas who are interested in attending college or graduate school in any state.

Eligibility This program is open to annual and life members of the association and their spouses and children (associate members and their dependents are not eligible). Applicants may be high school seniors, undergraduate students, or graduate students, either enrolled or planning to enroll at an institution of higher education in any state. Along with their application, they must submit an essay on their desire to continue their education. Selection is based on scholarship, citizenship, and leadership.

Financial Data Stipends range from $500 to $5,000.

Duration 1 year (nonrenewable).

Additional data This program includes the following named scholarships: the Thomas F. Berry Memorial Scholarship, the Len and Jean Tallas Memorial Scholarship, the Texas Military Forces Retirees Scholarship, the T-Mates Scholarship, the LTC Gary W. Parrish Memorial Scholarship, the 1SG Harry E. Lux Memorial Scholarship, the Gloria Jenell and Marlin E. Mote Endowed Scholarship, the Chief Master Sergeants Scholarship, the Sergeants Major Scholarship, and the Texas USAA Scholarship (sponsored by USAA Insurance Corporation).

Number awarded Varies each year. Recently, 10 of these scholarships were awarded: 1 at $5,000, 3 at $2,500, 1 at $2,000, 2 at $1,250, 2 at $1,000, and 1 at $500.

Deadline February of each year.

[899]
NMIA/NMIF SCHOLARSHIP PROGRAM

National Military Intelligence Association
Attn: Scholarship Committee
256 Morris Creek Road
Cullen, VA 23934
(434) 542-5929   Fax: (703) 738-7487
E-mail: admin@nmia.org
Web: www.nmia.org/about/scholarshipprogram.html

Summary To provide financial assistance to undergraduate and graduate students majoring in a field of interest to the intelligence community.

Eligibility This program is open to full- and part-time juniors, seniors, and graduate students who are preparing for a career in a field related to the intelligence community. Applicants must list special activities, internships, prior or current military service, or other activities that provide tangible evidence of career aspirations to serve as a member of the intelligence community. Along with their application, they must submit a 1,000-word essay that covers 1) their intelligence community career goals and objectives; 2) the relationship between courses completed, courses planned, extracurricular activities, and prior work experience (including military service) to identified career goals and objectives; and 3) how this scholarship will make a difference to their efforts to realize their career goals and aspirations. Selection is based primarily on past academic success; financial need is not considered.

Financial Data The stipend is $3,000 for full-time students or $2,000 for part-time students.

Duration 1 year; nonrenewable.

Additional data This program is offered jointly by the National Military Intelligence Association (NMIA) and the National Military Intelligence Foundation (NMIF), P.O. Box 6844, Arlington, VA 22206, E-mail: ffrank54@comcast.net

Number awarded 6 each year: 3 for full-time students and 3 for part-time students.

Deadline November each year.

[900]
NORTH CAROLINA NATIONAL GUARD TUITION ASSISTANCE PROGRAM

North Carolina National Guard
Attn: Education Services Office
4105 Reedy Creek Road
Raleigh, NC 27607-6410
(919) 664-6272   Toll Free: (800) 621-4136
Fax: (919) 664-6520   E-mail: nceso@ng.army.mil
Web: www.nc.ngb.army.mil

Summary To provide financial assistance to members of the North Carolina National Guard who plan to attend college or graduate school in the state.

Eligibility This program is open to active members of the North Carolina National Guard (officer, warrant officer, or enlisted) who have at least 2 years of enlistment remaining after the end of the academic period for which tuition assistance is provided. Applicants must be enrolled in an eligible business or trade school, private institution, or public college/university in North Carolina. They may be working on a vocational, undergraduate, graduate, or doctoral degree.

Financial Data The maximum stipend is based on the highest tuition and fees at the University of North Carolina at Chapel Hill.

Duration 1 year; may be renewed.
Number awarded Varies each year.
Deadline Deadline not specified.

[901]
NORTH DAKOTA NATIONAL GUARD TUITION ASSISTANCE PROGRAM

North Dakota National Guard
Attn: Education Services Office
P.O. Box 5511
Bismarck, ND 58506-5511
(701) 333-3064   E-mail: ngndj1esos@ng.army.mil
Web: www.ndguard.ngb.army.mil

Summary To provide financial assistance to members of the North Dakota National Guard who plan to attend college or graduate school in the state.

Eligibility This program is open to members of the North Dakota National Guard who have a record of satisfactory participation (no more than 9 unexcused absences in the past 12 months) and service remaining after completion of the class for which they are requesting assistance. Applicants must be seeking support for trade or vocational training or work on an associate, baccalaureate, or graduate degree. They must be attending or planning to attend a North Dakota higher education public institution or a participating private institution (currently, Jamestown College, University of Mary in Bismarck, MedCenter One College of Nursing, Rasmussen College, or Trinity Bible College). Full-time AGR personnel do not qualify for this program. This is an entitlement program, provided all requirements are met.

Financial Data Participating colleges and universities waive 25% of tuition for eligible courses (undergraduate only), up to 25% of the tuition at the University of North Dakota. This program provides reimbursement of 75% of tuition for eligible courses (undergraduate and graduate), or up to 75% of the tuition at the University of North Dakota. The program also reimburses 100% of all regular fees, not to exceed 100% of the regular fees charged by the University of North Dakota.

Duration Benefits are available for up to 144 semester credit hours or the completion of an undergraduate or graduate degree, provided the recipient earns a grade of "C" or higher in each undergraduate course or "B" or higher in each graduate course.

Number awarded Varies each year.

Deadline Applications should be submitted at least 30 days before the semester begins.

[902]
PENNSYLVANIA NATIONAL GUARD EDUCATIONAL ASSISTANCE PROGRAM

Pennsylvania Higher Education Assistance Agency
Attn: State Grant and Special Programs
1200 North Seventh Street
P.O. Box 8114
Harrisburg, PA 17105-8114
(717) 720-2800   Toll Free: (800) 692-7392
TDD: (800) 654-5988   E-mail: info@pheaa.org
Web: www.pheaa.org

Summary To provide scholarship/loans for college or graduate school to Pennsylvania National Guard members.

Eligibility This program is open to active members of the Pennsylvania National Guard who are Pennsylvania residents and serving as enlisted personnel, warrant officers, or commissioned officers of any grade. Applicants must accept an obligation to serve in the Pennsylvania National Guard for a period of 6 years from the date of entry into the program. Students who do not possess a baccalaureate degree must be enrolled full or part time in an approved program of education at an approved institution of higher learning in Pennsylvania. Master's degree students are

supported on a part-time basis only. Guard members receiving an ROTC scholarship of any type are not eligible.

Financial Data Full-time undergraduate students receive payment of 100% of tuition at a state-owned university (recently, $5,554 per year). Part-time students receive either actual tuition charged or two-thirds of the full-time tuition charged to a Pennsylvania resident at a state-owned university (recently, $3,702 per year), whichever is less. Graduate students receive either half the actual tuition charged or one-third of the full-time tuition charged to a Pennsylvania resident at a state-owned university (recently, $1,851 per year), whichever is less. Recipients who fail to fulfill the service obligation must repay all funds received within 10 years, including interest at 7%.

Duration Up to 5 years.

Additional data This program, first offered in 1997, is jointly administered by the Pennsylvania Department of Military and Veterans Affairs and the Pennsylvania Higher Education Assistance Agency. Support for summer and graduate school is available only if funding permits.

Number awarded Varies each year; recently, 1,789 members of the Pennsylvania National Guard were enrolled in this program.

Deadline June of each year for fall semester; October of each year for spring semester; May of each year for summer school.

[903]
PLATOON LEADERS CLASS MARINE CORPS TUITION ASSISTANCE PROGRAM

U.S. Marine Corps
Attn: Marine Corps Recruiting Command
3280 Russell Road
Quantico, VA 22134-5103
(703) 784-9449   Fax: (703) 784-9859
E-mail: wendelrf@mcrc.usmc.mil
Web: www.usmc.mil

Summary To provide financial assistance to members of the Marine Corps Reserves interested in working on a bachelor's or law degree.

Eligibility This program is open to members of the Marine Corps Reserves enrolled full time in a bachelor's or law (J.D. or equivalent) degree program. Applicants must be a member of the Marine Corps Platoon Leader Class (PLC) Program and have completed 6 weeks (or more) of military training required by that program. They must agree to accept a commission in the active-duty Marine Corps and serve 5 years following completion of their degree.

Financial Data This program provides reimbursement of tuition, books, and required fees, up to a maximum of $5,200 per academic year. If participants are also members of the Marine Corps Reserves, they may use any Montgomery GI Bill benefits to which they are entitled.

Duration Up to 3 consecutive years, or completion of a bachelor's or law degree.

Additional data Participants who successfully obtain a bachelor's or law degree and complete officer candidate training are commissioned as second lieutenants in the Regular Marine Corps. This program was established in 1999.

Number awarded Up to 1,200 each year.

Deadline December of each year.

[904]
POST-9/11 GI BILL

Department of Veterans Affairs
Attn: Veterans Benefits Administration
810 Vermont Avenue, N.W.
Washington, DC 20420
(202) 418-4343   Toll Free: (888) GI-BILL1
Web: www.gibill.va.gov

Summary To provide financial assistance to veterans or military personnel who entered service on or after September 11, 2001.

Eligibility This program is open to current and former military who served on active duty for at least 90 aggregate days after September 11, 2001. Applicants must be planning to enroll at an accredited college or university as an undergraduate or graduate student; study in a certificate program, on-the-job training, apprenticeship program, flight training, and non-college degree course study do not qualify for support.

Financial Data Active-duty personnel receive payment of tuition and fees, up to the level of tuition and fees at the most expensive public institution of higher learning in their state of residence; the actual amount depends on the state of residence and the length of service completed. Veterans also receive a monthly housing allowance based on the Basic Allowance for Housing (BAH) for an E-5 with dependents if the location of the school they are attending is in the United States (or $1,333 per month at schools in foreign countries); an annual book allowance of $1,000; and (for participants who live in a rural county remote from an educational institution) a rural benefit payment of $500 per year.

Duration Most participants receive up to 36 months of entitlement under this program.

Additional data This program began in 2009 as a replacement for previous educational programs for veterans and military personnel (e.g., Montgomery GI Bill, REAP). Current participants in those programs may be able to utilize benefits under those programs and this new plan. Further information is available from local armed forces recruiters. This is the latest VA education program, referred to as Chapter 33.

Number awarded Varies each year.

Deadline Deadline not specified.

[905]
RESERVE EDUCATIONAL ASSISTANCE PROGRAM

Department of Veterans Affairs
Attn: Veterans Benefits Administration
810 Vermont Avenue, N.W.
Washington, DC 20420
(202) 418-4343   Toll Free: (888) GI-BILL1
Web: www.gibill.va.gov/GI_Bill_Info/benefits.htm

Summary To provide financial assistance for college or graduate school to members of the Reserves or National Guard who are called to active duty during a period of national emergency.

Eligibility Eligible to apply are members of the Reserve elements of the Army, Navy, Air Force, Marine Corps, and Coast Guard, as well as the Army National Guard and the Air National Guard. To be eligible, a Reservist must 1) have a 6-year obligation to serve in the Selected Reserves signed after June 30, 1985 (or, if an officer, agree to serve 6 years in addition to the original obligation); 2) complete Initial Active Duty for Training (IADT); 3) meet the requirements for a high school diploma or equivalent certificate before completing IADT; and 4) remain in good standing in a drilling Selected Reserve unit. Reservists who enlisted after June 30, 1985 can receive benefits for undergraduate degrees, graduate training, or technical courses leading to certificates at colleges and universities. Reservists whose 6-year commitment began after September 30, 1990 may also use these benefits for a certificate or diploma from business, technical, or vocational schools; cooperative training; apprenticeship or on-the-job training; correspondence courses; independent study programs; tutorial assistance; remedial, deficiency, or refresher training; flight training; or state-approved alternative teacher certification programs.

Financial Data For full-time study at a college or university, the current monthly rate is $528.40 for personnel with consecutive service of 90 days but less than 1 year, $792.60 for personnel with consecutive service of more than 1 year but less than 2 years, or $1,056.80 for those with consecutive service of 2 years or more.

Reduced rates apply for part-time college or university study, apprenticeship and on-the-job training, licensing and certification training, cooperative education, correspondence courses, and flight training.

Duration Up to 36 months for full-time study, 48 months for three-quarter study, 72 months for half-time study, or 144 months for less than half-time study.

Additional data This program is frequently referred to as Chapter 1607. Benefits end 10 years from the date the Reservist became eligible for the program. The Department of Veterans Affairs (VA) may extend the 10-year period if the individual could not train because of a disability caused by Selected Reserve service. Certain individuals separated from the Selected Reserve due to downsizing of the military between October 1, 1991 and September 30, 1999 will also have the full 10 years to use their benefits.

Number awarded Varies each year.

Deadline Applications may be submitted at any time.

[906]
RHODE ISLAND NATIONAL GUARD STATE TUITION ASSISTANCE PROGRAM

Rhode Island National Guard
Joint Force Headquarters
Attn: Education Service Officer
645 New London Avenue
Cranston, RI 02920-3097
(401) 275-4109   Fax: (401) 275-4014
E-mail: NGRIeduc@ngb.army.mil
Web: states.ng.mil/sites/RI/education/default.aspx

Summary To provide financial support to members of the National Guard in Rhode Island interested in attending college or graduate school in the state.

Eligibility This program is open to active members of the Rhode Island National Guard in good standing who are currently satisfactorily participating in all unit training assemblies and annual training periods. Applicants must have at least 1 year of service remaining. They must be enrolled in or planning to enroll in an associate, bachelor's, or master's degree program at a public institution in the state.

Financial Data Qualified Guard members receive payment of tuition for up to 5 courses per semester.

Duration 1 semester; may be renewed.

Additional data This program was established in 1999.

Number awarded Varies each year.

Deadline Deadline not specified.

[907]
RHODE ISLAND NATIONAL GUARD STATE TUITION EXEMPTION PROGRAM

Rhode Island National Guard
Joint Force Headquarters
Attn: Education Service Officer
645 New London Avenue
Cranston, RI 02920-3097
(401) 275-4109   Fax: (401) 275-4014
E-mail: NGRIeduc@ngb.army.mil
Web: states.ng.mil/sites/RI/education/default.aspx

Summary To provide financial support to members of the Rhode Island National Guard who attend public institutions in the state.

Eligibility This program is open to active members of the Rhode Island National Guard who attend all required unit training assemblies and annual training. Applicants must be residents of Rhode Island working toward an associate, bachelors, or master's degree at a designated public institution in the state. They must pass the Guard's height and weight standards, weapons qualification, and the APFT. They may not have more than 4 unexcused absences from military duty within a 12-month period or have tested positive for any illegal drug.

Financial Data Qualified Guard members are entitled to tuition-free classes at public institutions in Rhode Island. The waiver does not cover books or fees.

Duration Upon enrollment, Guard members are entitled to 2 tuition-free classes per year.

Additional data This program was established in 1994. The designated institutions are the University of Rhode Island, Rhode Island College, and the Community College of Rhode Island.

Number awarded Varies each year.

Deadline Deadline not specified.

[908]
ROBERT W. NOLAN EMERITUS SCHOLARSHIP

Fleet Reserve Association
Attn: Scholarship Administrator
125 North West Street
Alexandria, VA 22314-2754
(703) 683-1400   Toll Free: (800) FRA-1924
Fax: (703) 549-6610   E-mail: fra@fra.org
Web: www.fra.org

Summary To provide financial assistance for graduate school to members of the Fleet Reserve Association (FRA) and their spouses, children, and grandchildren.

Eligibility This program is open to the dependent children, grandchildren, and spouses of members of the association who are in good standing (or were at the time of death, if deceased). FRA members are also eligible. Applicants should be enrolled in a graduate program. Along with their application, they must submit an essay on their life experiences, career objectives, and what motivated them to select those objectives. Selection is based on academic record, financial need, extracurricular activities, leadership skills, and participation in community activities. U.S. citizenship is required.

Financial Data The stipend is $5,000 per year.

Duration 1 year; may be renewed.

Additional data Membership in the FRA is restricted to active-duty, retired, and Reserve members of the Navy, Marine Corps, and Coast Guard. This program was established in 2001.

Number awarded 1 each year.

Deadline April of each year.

[909]
SCHUYLER S. PYLE SCHOLARSHIP

Fleet Reserve Association
Attn: Scholarship Administrator
125 North West Street
Alexandria, VA 22314-2754
(703) 683-1400   Toll Free: (800) FRA-1924
Fax: (703) 549-6610   E-mail: fra@fra.org
Web: www.fra.org

Summary To provide financial assistance for college or graduate school to members of the Fleet Reserve Association (FRA) who are current or former naval personnel and their spouses and children.

Eligibility This program is open to dependent children, grandchildren, and spouses of FRA members who are in good standing (or were at the time of death, if deceased). FRA members are also eligible. Applicants must be working on or planning to work on an undergraduate or graduate degree. Along with their application, they must submit an essay on their life experiences, career objectives, and what motivated them to select those objectives. Selection is based on academic record, financial need, extracurricular activities, leadership skills, and participation in community activities. U.S. citizenship is required.

Financial Data The stipend is $5,000 per year.

Duration 1 year; may be renewed.

Additional data Membership in the FRA is restricted to active-duty, retired, and Reserve members of the Navy, Marine Corps, and Coast Guard.

Number awarded 1 each year.

Deadline April of each year.

[910]
SECRETARY OF THE NAVY FELLOWSHIP IN OCEANOGRAPHY

U.S. Navy
Attn: Navy Personnel Command (PERS-440B)
5720 Integrity Drive
Millington, TN 38055-4400
(901) 874-4056   Fax: (901) 874-2676
E-mail: p440b@persnet.navy.mil
Web: www.npc.navy.mil

Summary To provide an opportunity for Navy officers to work on a doctoral degree in oceanography or a related field.

Eligibility This program is open to active-duty unrestricted line (URL) Navy officers in grades O-3 and O-4. Applicants must have a master's degree and be interested in working full time on a doctoral degree in oceanography, meteorology, or hydrography at an institution in the United States. Officers who have previously received Navy-funded graduate level education leading to a sub-specialty unrelated to oceanography are ineligible. Selection is based on demonstrated distinguished performance, leadership abilities, academic skill, and clear potential for professional growth.

Financial Data Recipients continue to earn full pay and benefits while attending graduate school. They are entitled to permanent change of station reimbursement. Tuition and fees are paid by the Office of Naval Research (ONR).

Duration Up to 3 years.

Additional data Officers who participate in this program are required to serve on active duty following graduation for a period 3 times the length of the period they were in the program, with a maximum obligation of 5 years.

Number awarded 1 or more each year.

Deadline Deadline not specified.

[911]
SFC CURTIS MANCINI MEMORIAL SCHOLARSHIPS

Association of the United States Army-Rhode Island Chapter
c/o CSM (Ret) Anthony Ferri, Secretary
47 Spokane Street
Providence, RI 02904
(401) 861-2997   E-mail: afnf458673755@aol.com
Web: www.ausari.org/index.html

Summary To provide financial assistance to members of the Rhode Island Chapter of the Association of the United States Army (AUSA) and their families who are interested in attending college or graduate school in any state.

Eligibility This program is open to members of the AUSA Rhode Island Chapter and their family members (spouses, children, and grandchildren). Applicants must be high school seniors or graduates accepted at an accredited college, university, or vocational/technical school in any state or current undergraduate or graduate students. Along with their application, they must submit a 250-word essay on why they feel their achievements should qualify them for this award. Selection is based on academic and individual achievements; financial need is not considered. Membership in AUSA is open to current and retired Army personnel (including Reserves and National Guard), ROTC cadets, or civilian employees of the Army.

Financial Data The stipend is $1,000.

Duration 1 year.

Number awarded 2 each year.

Deadline March of each year.

[912]
TILLMAN MILITARY SCHOLARSHIPS FOR SERVICEMEMBERS

Pat Tillman Foundation
2121 South Mill Avenue, Suite 214
Tempe, AZ 85282
(480) 621-4074 Fax: (480) 621-4075
E-mail: scholarships@pattillmanfoundation.org
Web: www.pattillmanfoundation.org

Summary To provide financial assistance to veterans and active servicemembers who are interested in working on an undergraduate or graduate degree.

Eligibility This program is open to veterans and active servicemembers of all branches of the armed forces from both the pre- and post-September 11 era whose educational benefits have run out or are insufficient to meet their need. Applicants must be interested in starting, finishing, or furthering their undergraduate, graduate, or postgraduate education at a 2-year, 4-year, or vocational institution (public or private). Along with their application, they must submit 1-page essays on 1) their specific financial need, including any gap in educational benefits they may already be receiving and their reason for applying for this scholarship; 2) their motivation and decision to serve in the U.S. armed forces; and 3) their educational and career goals, how they will incorporate their military service into those goals, and how they intend to continue their service to others and the community. Selection is based on those essays, educational and career ambitions, length of service, record of personal achievement, demonstration of service to others in the community and a desire to continue such service, and unmet financial need.

Financial Data Stipends vary; recently, total awards (including multi-year awards) averaged $12,800.

Duration 1 year; may be renewed, provided the recipient maintains a GPA of 3.0 or higher, remains enrolled full time, and documents participation in civic action or community service.

Additional data This program was established in 2009. The foundation administers the program directly for students at colleges and universities nationwide; it also acts in partnership with 4 universities (the University of Maryland, the University of Arkansas, the University of Idaho, and Mississippi State University) which award scholarships directly to their students.

Number awarded Varies each year; recently, 52 students received a total of $665,820 in these scholarships

Deadline May of each year.

[913]
VADM ROBERT L. WALTERS SCHOLARSHIP

Surface Navy Association
2550 Huntington Avenue, Suite 202
Alexandria, VA 22303
(703) 960-6800 Toll Free: (800) NAVY-SNA
Fax: (703) 960-6807 E-mail: navysna@aol.com
Web: www.navysna.org/awards/index.html

Summary To provide financial assistance for college or graduate school to members of the Surface Navy Association (SNA) and their dependents.

Eligibility This program is open to SNA members and their children, stepchildren, wards, and spouses. The SNA member must 1) be in the second or subsequent consecutive year of membership; 2) be serving, retired, or honorably discharged; 3) be a Surface Warfare Officer or Enlisted Surface Warfare Specialist; and 4) have served at least 3 years on a surface ship of the U.S. Navy or Coast Guard. Applicants must be studying or planning to study at an accredited undergraduate or graduate institution. Along with their application, they must submit a 200-word essay about themselves; a list of their extracurricular activities, community service activities, academic honors and/or positions of leadership that represent their interests, with an estimate of the amount of time involved with each activity; and 3 letters of refer-

ence. High school seniors should also include a transcript of high school grades and a copy of ACT or SAT scores. Applicants who are on active duty or drilling Reservists should also include a letter from their commanding officer commenting on their military service and leadership potential, a transcript of grades from their most recent 4 semesters of school, a copy of their ACT or SAT scores if available, and an indication of whether they have applied for or are enrolled in the Enlisted Commissioning Program. Applicants who are not high school seniors, active-duty servicemembers, or drilling Reservists should also include a transcript of the grades from their most recent 4 semesters of school and a copy of ACT or SAT test scores (unless they are currently attending a college or university). Selection is based on demonstrated leadership, community service, academic achievement, and commitment to pursuing higher educational objectives.

Financial Data The stipend is $2,000 per year.

Duration 4 years, provided the recipient maintains a GPA of 3.0 or higher.

Number awarded Varies each year.

Deadline February of each year.

[914]
VIRGINIA NATIONAL GUARD TUITION ASSISTANCE PROGRAM

Virginia National Guard
Attn: Educational Services Officer
Fort Pickett, Building 316
Blackstone, VA 23824-6316
(434) 298-6222 Toll Free: (888) 483-2682
Fax: (434) 298-6296 E-mail: djuana.goodwin@us.army.mil
Web: vko.va.ngb.army.mil/VirginiaGuard

Summary To provide financial assistance to members of the Virginia National Guard who are interested in attending college or graduate school in the state.

Eligibility This program is open to active members of the Virginia National Guard who are residents of Virginia and interested in attending college or graduate school in the state. Awards are presented in the following priority order: 1) enlisted personnel who have previously received assistance through this program; 2) officers who need to complete a bachelor's degree in order to be eligible for promotion to captain; 3) warrant officers working on an associate or bachelor's degree; 4) any member working on an undergraduate degree; and 4) any member working on a graduate degree.

Financial Data The program provides reimbursement of tuition at approved colleges, universities, and vocational/technical schools in Virginia, to a maximum of $2,000 per semester or $6,000 per year. Bookstore grants up to $350 per semester are also provided.

Duration 1 semester; may be renewed.

Additional data This program was established in 1983. Recipients must remain in the Guard for at least 2 years after being funded.

Number awarded Varies each year.

Deadline March of each year for summer session; June of each year for fall semester; October of each year for spring semester.

[915]
WASHINGTON NATIONAL GUARD SCHOLARSHIP PROGRAM

Washington National Guard
Attn: Education Services Office
Building 15, G1-ED
Camp Murray, WA 98498
(253) 512-8899 Toll Free: (800) 606-9843 (within WA)
Fax: (253) 512-8941 E-mail: education@wa.ngb.army.mil
Web: washingtonguard.org/edu

Summary To provide forgivable loans to members of the Washington National Guard who wish to attend college or graduate school in the state.

Eligibility This program is open to members of the Washington National Guard who have already served for at least 1 year and have at least 2 years remaining on their current contract. Applicants must have a rank between E1 and O3. They must be attending an accredited college as a resident of Washington state and must already have utilized all available federal educational benefits. Army Guard members must have completed BCT/AIT and awarded initial MOS; Air Guard members must have completed BMT/initial tech school and been awarded "3-Level" AFSC. Graduate students are eligible, but undergraduates receive preference as long as they are making satisfactory progress toward a baccalaureate degree. The minimum GPA requirement is 2.5 for undergraduates or 3.0 for graduate students.

Financial Data This program provides a stipend that is based on the number of credits completed but does not exceed the amount required for tuition, books, and fees at the University of Washington. Recipients incur a service obligation of 1 additional year in the Guard for the initial scholarship award and 1 additional year for each full year of academic credit completed with this assistance. The grant serves as a loan which is forgiven if the recipient completes the contracted service time in the Washington National Guard. Failure to meet the service obligation requires the recipient to repay the loan plus 8% interest.

Duration 1 year; may be renewed.

Number awarded Varies each year. A total of $100,000 is available for this program annually; scholarships are awarded on a first-come, first-served basis as long as funds are available.

Deadline June of each year.

[916]
WEST VIRGINIA NATIONAL GUARD EDUCATIONAL ENCOURAGEMENT PROGRAM

Office of the Adjutant General
Attn: Education Officer
1703 Coonskin Drive
Charleston, WV 25311-1085
(304) 561-6306   Toll Free: (866) 986-4326
Fax: (304) 561-6307   E-mail: kathy.kidd@us.army.mil
Web: www.wv.ngb.army.mil/education/benefits/default.aspx

Summary To provide financial assistance to members of the National Guard in West Virginia who are interested in attending college or graduate school in the state.

Eligibility This program is open to active members of the West Virginia National Guard who are residents of West Virginia and interested in attending a public or private college in the state. Applicants must have maintained satisfactory participation (90% attendance) in the Guard. They must be interested in working on a vocational, associate, bachelor's, or master's degree. In some instances, support may also be available to Guard members who are interested in working on an M.D., D.O., P.A., or J.D. degree.

Financial Data The program provides payment of 100% of the tuition and fees at participating colleges and universities in West Virginia, to a maximum of $6,000 per year.

Duration 1 academic year; may be renewed.

Number awarded Varies each year.

Deadline Deadline not specified.

[917]
WMA SCHOLARSHIP PROGRAM

Women Marines Association
P.O. Box 377
Oaks, PA 19456-0377
Toll Free: (888) 525-1943 E-mail: wma@womenmarines.org
Web: www.womenmarines.org/scholarships.aspx

Summary To provide financial assistance for college or graduate school to students sponsored by members of the Women Marines Association (WMA).

Eligibility Applicants must be sponsored by a WMA member and fall into 1 of the following categories: 1) have served or are serving in the U.S. Marine Corps, regular or Reserve; 2) are a direct descendant by blood, legal adoption, or stepchild of a Marine on active duty or who has served honorably in the U.S. Marine Corps, regular or Reserve; 3) are a sibling or a descendant of a sibling by blood, legal adoption, or stepchild of a Marine on active duty or who has served honorably in the U.S. Marine Corps, regular or Reserve; or 4) have completed 2 years in a Marine Corps JROTC program. WMA members may sponsor an unlimited number of applicants per year. High school seniors must submit transcripts (GPA of 3.0 or higher) and SAT or ACT scores. Undergraduate and graduate students must have a GPA of 3.0 or higher.

Financial Data The stipend is $1,500 per year.

Duration 1 year; may be renewed 1 additional year.

Additional data This program includes the following named scholarships: the WMA Memorial Scholarships, the Lily H. Gridley Memorial Scholarship, the Ethyl and Armin Wiebke Memorial Scholarship, the Maj. Megan Malia McClung Memorial Scholarship, and the LaRue A. Ditmore Music Scholarships. Applicants must know a WMA member to serve as their sponsor; the WMA will not supply listings of the names or addresses of chapters or individual members.

Number awarded Varies each year.

Deadline March of each year.

[918]
WNGEA COLLEGE GRANT PROGRAM

Wisconsin National Guard Enlisted Association
Attn: Executive Director
2400 Wright Street
Madison, WI 53704
(608) 242-3112   E-mail: WNGEA@yahoo.com
Web: www.wngea.org/MAIN/PROG/prosch.htm

Summary To provide financial assistance to members of the Wisconsin National Guard Enlisted Association (WNGEA) and their spouses and children who are interested in attending college or graduate school in any state.

Eligibility This program is open to WNGEA members, the unmarried children of WNGEA members, the spouses of WNGEA members, and the unmarried children and spouses of deceased WNGEA members. WNGEA member applicants, as well as the parents or guardians of unmarried children who are applicants, must have at least 1 year remaining on their enlistment following completion of the school year for which application is submitted (or they must have 20 or more years of service). Applicants must be enrolled at a college, university, graduate school, trade school, or business school in any state. Selection is based on financial need, leadership, and moral character.

Financial Data Stipends are $1,000 or $500 per year.

Duration 1 year; recipients may not reapply for 2 years.

Additional data This program includes 1 scholarship sponsored by the USAA Insurance Corporation.

Number awarded Varies each year. Recently, 4 of these scholarships were awarded: the Raymond A. Matera Scholarship at $1,000 and 3 others at $500 each.

Deadline May of each year.

[919]
WYOMING NATIONAL GUARD EDUCATIONAL ASSISTANCE PLAN

Wyoming National Guard
Attn: Education Services Officer
5500 Bishop Boulevard
Cheyenne, WY 82009-3320
(307) 772-5053   Toll Free: (800) 832-1959, ext. 5053
Fax: (307) 772-5132   E-mail: poconn@state.wy.us
Web: www.wy.ngb.army.mil/Tuition/assistance.asp

Summary   To provide financial assistance to members of the Wyoming National Guard who are interested in attending college or graduate school in the state.

Eligibility   This program is open to members of the Wyoming Army National Guard and the Wyoming Air National Guard who have spent at least 6 years in the Guard or are currently serving under their initial 6-year enlistment period. New enlistees who commit to serving 6 years are also eligible. Applicants may be pursuing, or planning to pursue, a degree at any level at the University of Wyoming, a Wyoming community college, or an approved technical institution in Wyoming.

Financial Data   The program provides full payment of tuition at eligible institutions.

Duration   Guard members may continue to receive these benefits as long as they maintain a GPA of 2.0 or higher, keep up with Guard standards for drill attendance, and remain in good standing with the Guard.

Additional data   The Wyoming legislature created this program in 2001. Recipients must agree to serve in the Guard for at least 2 years after they graduate or stop using the plan.

Number awarded   Varies each year.

Deadline   Deadline not specified.

Family Members

[920]
100TH INFANTRY BATTALION MEMORIAL SCHOLARSHIP FUND

Hawai'i Community Foundation
Attn: Scholarship Department
1164 Bishop Street, Suite 800
Honolulu, HI 96813
(808) 566-5570   Toll Free: (888) 731-3863
Fax: (808) 521-6286   E-mail: scholarships@hcf-hawaii.org
Web: www.hawaiicommunityfoundation.org

Summary   To provide financial assistance for college or graduate school to descendants of 100th Infantry Battalion World War II veterans.

Eligibility   This program is open to entering and continuing full-time undergraduate and graduate students at 2- and 4-year colleges and universities. Applicants must be a direct descendant of a World War II veteran of the 100th Infantry Battalion (which was comprised of Americans of Japanese descent). They must be able to demonstrate academic achievement (GPA of 3.5 or higher), an active record of extracurricular activities and community service, a willingness to promote the legacy of the 100th Infantry Battalion of World War II, and financial need. Along with their application, they must submit a short statement indicating their reasons for attending college, their planned course of study, and their career goals. Current residency in Hawaii is not required.

Financial Data   The amounts of the awards depend on the availability of funds and the need of the recipient; recently, stipends averaged $4,250.

Duration   1 year.

Number awarded   Varies each year; recently, 2 of these scholarships were awarded.

Deadline   February of each year.

[921]
AAAA SCHOLARSHIPS

Army Aviation Association of America Scholarship
   Foundation
Attn: AAAA Scholarship Foundation
755 Main Street, Suite 4D
Monroe, CT 06468-2830
(203) 268-2450   Fax: (203) 268-5870
E-mail: Scholarship@quad-a.org
Web: www.quad-a.org/scholarship.htm

Summary   To provide financial aid for undergraduate or graduate study to members of the Army Aviation Association of America (AAAA) and their relatives.

Eligibility   This program is open to AAAA members and their spouses, unmarried siblings, unmarried children, and unmarried grandchildren. Applicants must be enrolled or accepted for enrollment as an undergraduate or graduate student at an accredited college or university. Graduate students must include a 250-word essay on their life experiences, work history, and aspirations. Some scholarships are specifically reserved for enlisted, warrant officer, company grade, and Department of the Army civilian members. Selection is based on academic merit and personal achievement.

Financial Data   Most stipends range from $1,000 to $4,000. Special scholarships are $11,000.

Duration   Scholarships may be for 1 year, 2 years, or 4 years.

Additional data   This program includes 3 special scholarships: the GEN Hamilton H. Howze Memorial Scholarship, the Helen Cribbins Memorial Scholarship, and the Joseph P. Cribbins Scholarship.

Number awarded   Varies each year; recently, $268,500 in scholarships was awarded to 171 students. Since the program began in 1963, the foundation has awarded more than $3.3 million to nearly 2,000 qualified applicants.

Deadline   April of each year.

[922]
AFOWC OF WASHINGTON, D.C. CONTINUING EDUCATION SCHOLARSHIPS FOR AIR FORCE DEPENDENTS

Air Force Officers' Wives' Club of Washington, D.C.
Attn: Scholarship Committee
P.O. Box 8490
Washington, DC 20032
E-mail: scholarship@afowc.com
Web: www.afowc.com/making-difference.html

Summary   To provide financial assistance for undergraduate or graduate education in any state to the dependents of Air Force members in the Washington, D.C. area.

Eligibility   This program is open to the dependents of Air Force members residing in the Washington, D.C. metropolitan area in the following categories: active duty, retired, MIA/POW, or deceased. Dependents are eligible if their Air Force sponsor is assigned remote from the area or reassigned during the current school year and the student has remained behind to continue school. Applicants must be currently enrolled full time at an accredited college or university in any state and have a GPA of 3.0 or higher. Along with their application, they must submit a 500-word essay on a topic that changes annually; recently, applicants were asked to write on which book is required reading for all students and why. Selection is based on academic and citizenship achievements; financial need is not considered. Applicants who receive an appointment to a service academy are not eligible.

Financial Data A stipend is awarded (amount not specified). Funds may be used only for payment of tuition or academic fees.

Duration 1 year.

Number awarded Varies each year.

Deadline February of each year.

[923]
AFOWC OF WASHINGTON, D.C. CONTINUING EDUCATION SCHOLARSHIPS FOR NON-MILITARY AIR FORCE SPOUSES

Air Force Officers' Wives' Club of Washington, D.C.
Attn: Scholarship Committee
P.O. Box 8490
Washington, DC 20032
E-mail: scholarship@afowc.com
Web: www.afowc.com/making-difference.html

Summary To provide financial assistance for undergraduate or graduate study in any state to the non-military spouses of Air Force members in the Washington, D.C. area.

Eligibility This program is open to the non-military spouses of Air Force members residing in the Washington, D.C. metropolitan area in the following categories: active duty, retired, MIA/POW, or deceased. Spouses whose Air Force sponsor is assigned remote from the area or reassigned during the current school year are also eligible if they remained behind to continue their education. Applicants must be enrolled or planning to enroll as an undergraduate or graduate student at a college or university in any state. Along with their application, they must submit a 500-word essay on a topic that changes annually; recently, applicants were asked to write on which book is required reading for all students and why. Selection is based on academic and citizenship achievements; financial need is not considered.

Financial Data A stipend is awarded (amount not specified). Funds may be used only for payment of tuition or academic fees.

Duration 1 year.

Number awarded Varies each year.

Deadline February of each year.

[924]
AIR FORCE EXCELLENCE SCHOLARSHIPS

Air Force Association
Attn: Scholarship Manager
1501 Lee Highway
Arlington, VA 22209-1198
(703) 247-5800, ext. 4807
Toll Free: (800) 727-3337, ext. 4807
Fax: (703) 247-5853   E-mail: LCross@afa.org
Web: www.afa.org/aef/aid/afa-fcef-rotc.asp

Summary To provide financial assistance for college or graduate school to Air Force personnel and their dependents.

Eligibility This program is open to Air Force active duty, Reserve, or Air National Guard personnel and their spouses and dependent children. Applicants must be entering or enrolled at an accredited college or university to work on an associate, bachelor's, or master's degree. In the selection process, no consideration is given to race, creed, color, sex, religious belief, national origin, rank, length of service, or financial need.

Financial Data The stipend is $3,000.

Duration 1 year.

Additional data This program was established in 2008 by the Air Force Association in partnership with the First Command Educational Foundation.

Number awarded 5 each year.

Deadline April of each year.

[925]
AIR FORCE SERVICES CLUB MEMBERSHIP SCHOLARSHIP PROGRAM

Air Force Services Agency
Attn: HQ AFSVA/SVOFT
10100 Reunion Place, Suite 501
San Antonio, TX 78216-4138
(210) 652-6312   Toll Free: (800) 443-4834
Fax: (210) 652-7041
E-mail: web.clubs-operations@randolph.af.mil
Web: www.afclubs.net/CN_Scholarship.htm

Summary To recognize and reward, with academic scholarships, Air Force Club members and their families who submit outstanding essays.

Eligibility This program is open to Air Force Club members and their spouses, children, and stepchildren who have been accepted by or are enrolled at an accredited college or university. Grandchildren are eligible if they are the dependent of a club member. Applicants may be undergraduate or graduate students enrolled full or part time. They must submit an essay of up to 500 words on a topic that changes annually; a recent topic was "The High Cost of Freedom" Applicants must also include a 1-page summary of their long-term career and life goals and previous accomplishments, including civic, athletic, and academic awards.

Financial Data Awards are $1,000 scholarships.

Duration The competition is held annually.

Additional data This competition, first held in 1997, is sponsored by Chase Bank and the Coca-Cola Company.

Number awarded 25 each year.

Deadline Entries must be submitted to the member's base services commander or division chief by June of each year.

[926]
AIR FORCE SPOUSE SCHOLARSHIPS

Air Force Association
Attn: Scholarship Manager
1501 Lee Highway
Arlington, VA 22209-1198
(703) 247-5800, ext. 4807
Toll Free: (800) 727-3337, ext. 4807
Fax: (703) 247-5853   E-mail: LCross@afa.org
Web: www.afa.org/aef/aid/spouse.asp

Summary To provide financial assistance for undergraduate or graduate study to spouses of Air Force members.

Eligibility This program is open to spouses of active-duty Air Force, Air National Guard, or Air Force Reserve members. Spouses who are themselves military members or in ROTC are not eligible. Applicants must have a GPA of 3.5 or higher in college (or high school if entering college for the first time) and be able to provide proof of acceptance into an accredited undergraduate or graduate degree program. They must submit a 2-page essay on their academic and career goals, the motivation that led them to that decision, and how Air Force and other local community activities in which they are involved will enhance their goals. Selection is based on the essay and 2 letters of recommendation.

Financial Data The stipend is $2,500; funds are sent to the recipients' schools to be used for any reasonable cost related to working on a degree.

Duration 1 year; nonrenewable.

Additional data This program was established in 1995.

Number awarded Varies each year; recently, 7 of these scholarships were awarded.

Deadline April of each year.

[927]
AL AND WILLAMARY VISTE SCHOLARSHIP PROGRAM

101st Airborne Division Association
32 Screaming Eagle Boulevard
P.O. Box 929
Fort Campbell, KY 42223-0929
(931) 431-0199   Fax: (931) 431-0195
E-mail: 101stairbornedivisionassociation@comcast.net
Web: www.screamingeagle.org

Summary To provide financial assistance to the spouses, children, and grandchildren of members of the 101st Airborne Division Association who are upper-division or graduate students working on a degree in science.

Eligibility This program is open to college juniors, seniors, and graduate students who maintained a GPA of 3.75 or higher during the preceding school year and whose parent, grandparent, or spouse is (or, if deceased, was) a regular or life (not associate) member of the 101st Airborne Division. Preference is given to students working on a degree in a physical science, medical science, or other scientific research field. Applicants must submit a 500-word essay on what it means to be an American and a letter on their course of study, community service, hobbies, interests, personal achievements, and how a higher education for them in their chosen field can benefit our nation. Selection is based on the letter, career objectives, academic record, and letters of recommendation.

Financial Data A stipend is awarded (amount not specified).

Duration 1 year; may be renewed.

Number awarded At least 1 each year.

Deadline May of each year.

[928]
AL PONTE SCHOLARSHIP AWARD

Association of Former Intelligence Officers
Attn: Scholarship Committee
6723 Whittier Avenue, Suite 200
McLean, VA 22101-4533
(703) 790-0320   Fax: (703) 991-1278
E-mail: afio@afio.com
Web: www.afio.com/13_scholarships.htm

Summary To provide financial assistance to members or the children or grandchildren of members of the Association of Former Intelligence Officers (AFIO) who are interested in working on a graduate degree in international relations and/or intelligence.

Eligibility This program is open to college seniors who are interested in attending graduate school to work on a degree in international relations and/or intelligence. Applicants must be AFIO members, the children or grandchildren of members, or the children or grandchildren of personnel currently serving in military intelligence. Selection is based on merit, character, estimated future potential, background, and relevance of their studies to the full spectrum of national security interests and career ambitions. U.S. citizenship is required.

Financial Data The stipend is $1,000.

Duration 1 year.

Number awarded 1 each year.

Deadline June of each year.

[929]
ALABAMA G.I. DEPENDENTS' SCHOLARSHIP PROGRAM

Alabama Department of Veterans Affairs
770 Washington Avenue, Suite 530
Montgomery, AL 36102-1509
(334) 242-5077   Fax: (334) 242-5102
E-mail: willie.moore@va.state.al.us
Web: www.va.state.al.us/scholarship.htm

Summary To provide educational benefits to the dependents of disabled, deceased, and other Alabama veterans.

Eligibility Eligible are spouses, children, stepchildren, and unremarried widow(er)s of veterans who served honorably for 90 days or more and 1) are currently rated as 20% or more service-connected disabled or were so rated at time of death; 2) were a former prisoner of war; 3) have been declared missing in action; 4) died as the result of a service-connected disability; or 5) died while on active military duty in the line of duty. The veteran must have been a permanent civilian resident of Alabama for at least 1 year prior to entering active military service; veterans who were not Alabama residents at the time of entering active military service may also qualify if they have a 100% disability and were permanent residents of Alabama for at least 5 years prior to filing the application for this program or prior to death, if deceased. Children and stepchildren must be under the age of 26, but spouses and unremarried widow(er)s may be of any age.

Financial Data Eligible dependents may attend any state-supported Alabama institution of higher learning or enroll in a prescribed course of study at any Alabama state-supported trade school without payment of any tuition, book fees, or laboratory charges.

Duration This is an entitlement program for 4 years of full-time undergraduate or graduate study or part-time equivalent. Spouses and unremarried widow(er)s whose veteran spouse is rated between 20% and 90% disabled, or 100% disabled but not permanently so, may attend only 2 standard academic years.

Additional data Benefits for children, spouses, and unremarried widow(er)s are available in addition to federal government benefits. Assistance is not provided for noncredit courses, placement testing, GED preparation, continuing educational courses, pre-technical courses, or state board examinations.

Number awarded Varies each year.

Deadline Applications may be submitted at any time.

[930]
ANGELFIRE SCHOLARSHIP

Datatel Scholars Foundation
4375 Fair Lakes Court
Fairfax, VA 22033
(703) 968-9000, ext. 4549   Toll Free: (800) 486-4332
Fax: (703) 968-4625   E-mail: scholars@datatel.com
Web: www.datatelscholars.org

Summary To provide financial assistance to graduating high school seniors, continuing college students, and graduate students who will be studying at a Datatel client school and are veterans, veterans' dependents, or refugees from southeast Asia.

Eligibility This program is open to 1) veterans who served in the Asian theater (Vietnam, Cambodia, or Laos) between 1964 and 1975; 2) their spouses and children; 3) refugees from Vietnam, Cambodia, or Laos; and 4) veterans who served in Operation Desert Storm, Operation Enduring Freedom, and/or Operation Iraqi Freedom. Applicants must attend a Datatel client college or university during the upcoming school year. They must first apply to their institution, which selects 2 semifinalists and forwards their applications to the sponsor. Along with their application, they must include a 1,000-word personal statement that discusses how the conflict has affected them personally, summarizes how the conflict has impacted their educational goals, and describes how being awarded this scholarship will help them achieve their goals. Selection is based on the quality of the personal statement (40%), academic merit (30%), achievements and civic involvement (20%), and 2 letters of recommendation (10%).

Financial Data The stipend is $1,700. Funds are paid directly to the institution.

Duration 1 year.

Additional data Datatel, Inc. produces advanced information technology solutions for higher education. It has more than 725 client sites in the United States and Canada. This scholarship was created to commemorate those who lost their lives in Vietnam or Iraq and is named after a memorial administered by the Disabled American Veterans Association in Angelfire, New Mexico.

Number awarded Varies each year. Recently, 10 of these scholarships were awarded.

Deadline Students must submit online applications to their institution or organization by January of each year.

[931]
ARMY NURSE CORPS ASSOCIATION SCHOLARSHIPS

Army Nurse Corps Association
Attn: Education Committee
P.O. Box 39235
San Antonio, TX 78218-1235
(210) 650-3534   Fax: (210) 650-3494
E-mail: education@e-anca.org
Web: e-anca.org/ANCAEduc.htm

Summary To provide financial assistance to students who have a connection to the Army and are interested in working on an undergraduate or graduate degree in nursing.

Eligibility This program is open to students attending colleges or universities that have accredited programs offering associate, bachelor's, master's, or doctoral degrees in nursing. Applicants must be 1) nursing students who plan to enter the active Army, Army National Guard, or Army Reserve and are not participating in a program funded by the active Army, Army National Guard, or Army Reserve; 2) nursing students who have previously served in the active Army, Army National Guard, or Army Reserve; 3) Army Nurse Corps officers enrolled in an undergraduate or graduate nursing program not funded by the active Army, Army National Guard, or Army Reserve; 4) Army enlisted soldiers in the active Army, Army National Guard, or Army Reserve who are working on a baccalaureate degree in nursing not funded by the active Army, Army National Guard, or Army Reserve; or 5) nursing students whose parent(s) or spouse are serving or have served in the active Army, Army National Guard, or Army Reserve. Along with their application, they must submit a personal statement on their professional career objectives, reasons for applying for this scholarship, financial need, special considerations, personal and academic interests, and why they are preparing for a nursing career.

Financial Data The stipend is $3,000. Funds are sent directly to the recipient's school.

Duration 1 year.

Additional data Although the sponsoring organization is made up of current, retired, and honorably discharged officers of the Army Nurse Corps, it does not have an official affiliation with the Army. Therefore, students who receive these scholarships do not incur any military service obligation.

Number awarded 1 or more each year.

Deadline March of each year.

[932]
BART LONGO MEMORIAL SCHOLARSHIPS

National Chief Petty Officers' Association
c/o Marjorie Hays, Treasurer
1014 Ronald Drive
Corpus Christi, TX 78412-3548
Web: www.goatlocker.org/ncpoa/scholarship.htm

Summary To provide financial assistance for college or graduate school to members of the National Chief Petty Officers' Association (NCPOA) and their families.

Eligibility This program is open to members of the NCPOA and the children, stepchildren, and grandchildren of living or deceased members. Applicants may be high school seniors or graduates entering a college or university or students currently enrolled full time as undergraduate or graduate students. Selection is based on academic achievement and participation in extracurricular activities; financial need is not considered.

Financial Data The stipend is $1,000.

Duration 1 year.

Additional data Membership in the NCPOA is limited to men and women who served or are serving as Chief Petty Officers in the U.S. Navy, U.S. Coast Guard, or their Reserve components for at least 30 days.

Number awarded 2 each year: 1 to a high school senior or graduate and 1 to an undergraduate or graduate student.

Deadline May of each year.

[933]
BG BENJAMIN B. TALLEY SCHOLARSHIP

Society of American Military Engineers-Anchorage Post
Attn: BG B.B. Talley Scholarship Endowment Fund
P.O. Box 6409
Anchorage, AK 99506-6409
E-mail: william_kontess@urscorp.com
Web: www.sameanchorage.org/h_about/scholinfo.html

Summary To provide financial assistance to student members of the Society of American Military Engineers (SAME) from Alaska who are working on a bachelor's or master's degree in designated fields of engineering or the natural sciences.

Eligibility This program is open to members of the Anchorage Post of SAME who are residents of Alaska, attending college in Alaska, an active-duty military member stationed in Alaska, or a dependent of an active-duty military member stationed in Alaska. Applicants must be 1) sophomores, juniors, or seniors majoring in engineering, architecture, construction or project management, natural sciences, physical sciences, applied sciences, or mathematics at an accredited college or university; or 2) students working on a master's degree in those fields. They must have a GPA of 2.5 or higher. U.S. citizenship is required. Along with their application, they must submit an essay of 250 to 500 words on their career goals. Selection is based on that essay, academic achievement, participation in school and community activities, and work/family activities; financial need is not considered.

Financial Data Stipends range up to $3,000.

Duration 1 year.

Additional data This program was established in 1997.

Number awarded Varies each year; at least 1 scholarship is reserved for a master's degree students.

Deadline December of each year.

[934]
CHAN-PADGETT SPECIAL FORCES MEMORIAL SCHOLARSHIP

American Academy of Physician Assistants-Veterans Caucus
Attn: Veterans Caucus
P.O. Box 362
Danville, PA 17821-0362
(570) 271-0292   Fax: (570) 271-5850
E-mail: admin@veteranscaucus.org
Web: www.veteranscaucus.org

Summary To provide financial assistance to children of veterans of the Army Special Forces who are studying to become physician assistants.

Eligibility This program is open to U.S. citizens who are currently enrolled in a physician assistant program. The program must be approved by the Commission on Accreditation of Allied Health Education. Applicants must be children of honorably discharged members of the Army Special Forces. Selection is based on military honors and awards received, civic and college honors and awards received, professional memberships and activities, and GPA. An electronic copy of the sponsor's DD Form 214 must accompany the application.

Financial Data The stipend is $2,000.

Duration 1 year.

Additional data This program was established in 2002.

Number awarded 1 each year.

Deadline February of each year.

[935]
COLONEL JERRY W. ROSS SCHOLARSHIP

American Pharmacists Association
Attn: APhA Foundation
2215 Constitution Avenue, N.W.
Washington, DC 20037-2985
(202) 429-7565   Toll Free: (800) 237-APhA
Fax: (202) 783-2351   E-mail: msheahan@aphanet.org
Web: www.pharmacist.com

Summary To provide financial assistance for work on a degree in pharmacy to Air Force pharmacy technicians who are members of the Academy of Student Pharmacists of the American Pharmacists Association (APhA-ASP) and their families.

Eligibility This program is open to full-time pharmacy students who are either 1) Air Force pharmacy technicians working on a degree in pharmacy, or 2) family members of an Air Force pharmacist or technician who is enrolled in an accredited college of pharmacy. Applicants must have been actively involved in their school's APhA-ASP chapter. They must have completed at least 1 year in the professional sequence of courses with a GPA of 2.75 or higher. Along with their application, they must submit a 500-word essay on how they envision their role in health care as a future pharmacist, 2 letters of recommendation, a current resume or curriculum vitae, and a list of pharmacy and non-pharmacy related activities. Preference is given to applicants who indicate further Air Force service.

Financial Data The stipend is $1,000.

Duration 1 year; recipients may reapply.

Number awarded 1 each year.

Deadline November of each year.

[936]
DAEDALIAN FOUNDATION DESCENDANTS' SCHOLARSHIP PROGRAM

Daedalian Foundation
Attn: Scholarship Committee
55 Main Circle (Building 676)
P.O. Box 249
Randolph AFB, TX 78148-0249
(210) 945-2113   Fax: (210) 945-2112
E-mail: icarus2@daedalians.org
Web: www.daedalians.org/foundation/scholarships.htm

Summary To provide financial assistance to descendants of members of the Order of Daedalians who wish to prepare for a career in military aviation or space.

Eligibility This program is open to descendants of members of the order who are working on or planning to work on a baccalaureate or higher degree. Applicants must be interested in and willing to commit to a career as a commissioned military pilot, flight crew member, astronaut, or commissioned officer in 1 of the armed forces of the United States in a discipline directly supporting aeronautics or astronautics. They must be physically and mentally qualified for flight and/or space; if they intend to pursue a non-flying career as a commissioned officer in a scientific or engineering discipline supporting aviation or space, they must pass a physical examination qualifying for active commissioned duty in the U.S. armed forces. Nominations must be submitted by a local chapter (Flight) of Daedalian. Selection is based on academic achievement and recognition, extracurricular activities, honors, and employment experience. Financial need may be considered if all other factors are equal.

Financial Data The stipend is $2,000.

Additional data The Order of Daedalians was founded in 1934 as an organization of the nearly 14,000 aviators who served as military pilots during World War I and are still listed and designated as Founder Members. In the 1950s, the organization expanded eligibility to include 1) on a sponsorship basis, current and former commissioned military pilots from all services, and 2) on a hereditary basis, descendants of Founder Members.

Number awarded Up to 3 each year.

Deadline July of each year.

[937]
DEPARTMENT OF HOMELAND SECURITY SMALL BUSINESS INNOVATION RESEARCH GRANTS

Department of Homeland Security
Homeland Security Advanced Research Projects Agency
Attn: SBIR Program Manager
Washington, DC 20528
(202) 254-6768   Toll Free: (800) 754-3043
Fax: (202) 254-7170   E-mail: elissa.sobolewski@dhs.gov
Web: www.dhs.gov/files/grants/gc_1247254058883.shtm

Summary To support small businesses (especially those owned by disabled veterans, minorities, and women) that have the technological expertise to contribute to the research and development mission of the Department of Homeland Security (DHS).

Eligibility For the purposes of this program, a "small business" is defined as a firm that is organized for profit with a location in the United States; is in the legal form of an individual proprietorship, partnership, limited liability company, corporation, joint venture, association, trust, or cooperative; is at least 51% owned and controlled by 1 or more individuals who are citizens or permanent residents of the United States; and has (including its affiliates) fewer than 500 employees. The primary employment of the principal investigator must be with the firm at the time of award and during the conduct of the proposed project. Preference is given to women-owned small business concerns, service-disabled veteran small business concerns, veteran small business concerns, and socially and economically disadvantaged small business concerns. Women-owned small business concerns are those that are at least 51% owned by a woman or women who also control and operate them. Service-disabled veteran small business concerns are those that are at least 51% owned by a service-disabled veteran and controlled by such a veteran or (for veterans with permanent and severe disability) the spouse of permanent caregiver of such a veteran. Veteran small business concerns are those that are at least 51% owned by a veteran or veterans who also control and manage them. Socially and economically disadvantaged small business concerns are at least 51% owned by an Indian tribe, a Native Hawaiian organization, a Community Development Corporation, or 1 or more socially and economically disadvantaged individuals (African Americans, Hispanic Americans, Native Americans, Asian Pacific Americans, or subcontinent Asian Americans). The project must be performed in the United States. Currently, DHS has 7 research priorities: explosives; border and maritime security; command, control, and interoperability; human factors; infrastructure and geophysical; chemical and biological; and domestic nuclear detection. Selection is based on the soundness, technical merit, and innovation of the proposed approach and its incremental progress toward topic or subtopic solution; the qualifications of the proposed principal investigators, supporting staff, and consultants; and the potential for commercial application and the benefits expected to accrue from this commercialization.

Financial Data Grants are offered in 2 phases. In phase 1, awards normally range up to $100,000 (or $150,000 for domestic nuclear detection); in phase 2, awards normally range up to $750,000 (or $1,000,000 for domestic nuclear detection).

Duration Phase 1 awards may extend up to 6 months; phase 2 awards may extend up to 2 years.

Number awarded Varies each year. Recently, 61 Phase 1 awards were granted.

Deadline February of each year.

[938]
EDWARD T. CONROY MEMORIAL SCHOLARSHIP PROGRAM

Maryland Higher Education Commission
Attn: Office of Student Financial Assistance
839 Bestgate Road, Suite 400
Annapolis, MD 21401-3013
(410) 260-4563   Toll Free: (800) 974-1024, ext. 4563
Fax: (410) 260-3200   TDD: (800) 735-2258
E-mail: lasplin@mhec.state.md.us
Web: www.mhec.state.md.us

Summary To provide financial assistance for college or graduate school in Maryland to children and spouses of victims of the September 11, 2001 terrorist attacks and specified categories of veterans, public safety employees, and their children or spouses.

Eligibility This program is open to entering and continuing undergraduate and graduate students in the following categories: 1) children and surviving spouses of victims of the September 11, 2001 terrorist attacks who died in the World Trade Center in New York City, the Pentagon in Virginia, or United Airlines Flight 93 in Pennsylvania; 2) veterans who have, as a direct result of military service, a disability of 25% or greater and have exhausted or are no longer eligible for federal veterans' educational benefits; 3) children of armed forces members whose death or 100% disability was directly caused by military service; 4) POW/MIA veterans of the Vietnam Conflict and their children; 5) state or local public safety officers or volunteers who became 100% disabled in the line of duty; and 6) children and unremarried surviving spouses of state or local public safety employees or volunteers who died or became 100% disabled in the line of duty. The parent, spouse, veteran, POW, or public safety officer or volunteer must have been a resident of Maryland at the time of death or when declared disabled. Financial need is not considered.

Financial Data The amount of the award is equal to tuition and fees at a Maryland postsecondary institution, to a maximum of $19,000 for children and spouses of the September 11 terrorist attacks or $9,000 for all other recipients.

Duration Up to 5 years of full-time study or 8 years of part-time study.

Additional data Recipients must enroll at a 2-year or 4-year Maryland college or university as a full-time or part-time degree-seeking undergraduate or graduate student or attend a private career school.

Number awarded Varies each year.

Deadline July of each year.

[939]
EIRO YAMADA MEMORIAL SCHOLARSHIP

Go For Broke Memorial Education Center
P.O. Box 2590
Gardena, CA 90247
(310) 328-0907   Fax: (310) 222-5700
E-mail: Julia@goforbroke.org
Web: www.goforbroke.org

Summary To provide financial assistance for college or graduate school to residents of any state who are descendants of World War II Japanese American veterans.

Eligibility This program is open to residents of any state who are attending or planning to attend a trade school, community college, or 4-year college or university on the undergraduate or graduate school level. Applicants must be 1) a direct descendant of a Japanese American World War II veteran, or 2) a descendant once-removed (such as a grand-niece or a grand-nephew) of a Japanese American serviceman or servicewoman killed in action during World War II. Along with their application, they must submit a short essay on "The Values I Have Learned from My Japanese American Forefathers" or their personal reflections on the Japanese American experience during World War II.

Financial Data Stipends range from $500 to $1,000.

Duration 1 year.

Number awarded Varies each year; recently, 6 of these scholarships were awarded.

Deadline March of each year.

[940]
EXEMPTION FROM TUITION FEES FOR DEPENDENTS OF KENTUCKY VETERANS

Kentucky Department of Veterans Affairs
Attn: Division of Field Operations
321 West Main Street, Room 390
Louisville, KY 40202
(502) 595-4447   Toll Free: (800) 928-4012 (within KY)
Fax: (502) 595-4448   E-mail: Pamela.Cypert@ky.gov
Web: www.veterans.ky.gov/benefits/tuitionwaiver.htm

Summary To provide financial assistance for undergraduate or graduate studies to the children or unremarried widow(er)s of deceased Kentucky veterans.

Eligibility This program is open to the children, stepchildren, adopted children, and unremarried widow(er)s of veterans who were residents of Kentucky when they entered military service or joined the Kentucky National Guard. The qualifying veteran must have been killed in action during a wartime period or died as a result of a service-connected disability incurred during a wartime period. Applicants must be attending or planning to attend a state-supported college or university in Kentucky to work on an undergraduate or graduate degree.

Financial Data Eligible dependents and survivors are exempt from tuition and matriculation fees at any state-supported institution of higher education in Kentucky.

Duration There are no age or time limits on the waiver.
Number awarded Varies each year.
Deadline Deadline not specified.

[941]
FIRST SERGEANT DOUGLAS AND CHARLOTTE DEHORSE SCHOLARSHIP

Catching the Dream
8200 Mountain Road, N.E., Suite 203
Albuquerque, NM 87110-7835
(505) 262-2351　　　　　　　　Fax: (505) 262-0534
E-mail: NScholarsh@aol.com
Web: www.catchingthedream.org

Summary To provide financial assistance to American Indians who have ties to the military and are working on an undergraduate or graduate degree.

Eligibility This program is open to American Indians who 1) have completed 1 year of an Army, Navy, or Air Force Junior Reserve Officer Training (JROTC) program; 2) are enrolled in an Army, Navy, or Air Force Reserve Officer Training (ROTC) program; or 3) are a veteran of the U.S. Army, Navy, Air Force, Marines, Merchant Marine, or Coast Guard. Applicants must be enrolled in an undergraduate or graduate program of study. Along with their application, they must submit a personal essay, high school transcripts, and letters of recommendation.

Financial Data A stipend is awarded (amount not specified).

Duration 1 year.

Additional data This program was established in 2007.

Number awarded 1 or more each year.

Deadline April of each year for fall semester or quarter; September of each year for spring semester or winter quarter.

[942]
FLEET RESERVE ASSOCIATION SCHOLARSHIP

Fleet Reserve Association
Attn: Scholarship Administrator
125 North West Street
Alexandria, VA 22314-2754
(703) 683-1400　　　　　　Toll Free: (800) FRA-1924
Fax: (703) 549-6610　　　　E-mail: fra@fra.org
Web: www.fra.org

Summary To provide financial assistance for college or graduate school to members of the Fleet Reserve Association (FRA), as well as their spouses, children, and grandchildren.

Eligibility This program is open to members of the FRA and their dependent children, grandchildren, and spouses. The children, grandchildren, and spouses of deceased FRA members are also eligible. Applicants must submit an essay on their life experiences, career objectives, and what motivated them to select those objectives. Selection is based on academic record, financial need, extracurricular activities, leadership skills, and participation in community activities. U.S. citizenship is required.

Financial Data The stipend is $5,000 per year.

Duration 1 year; may be renewed.

Additional data Membership in the FRA is restricted to active-duty, retired, and reserve members of the Navy, Marines, and Coast Guard.

Number awarded 6 each year.

Deadline April of each year.

[943]
FLORIDA LEGION AUXILIARY MASTER'S PROGRAM GRANT

American Legion Auxiliary
Department of Florida
1912A Lee Road
P.O. Box 547917
Orlando, FL 32854-7917
(407) 293-7411　　　　　　Fax: (407) 299-6522
E-mail: contact@alafl.org
Web: alafl.org

Summary To provide financial assistance to members of the Florida American Legion Auxiliary who are interested in working on a master's degree in any field at a university in any state.

Eligibility This program is open to residents of Florida who have been members of the American Legion Auxiliary for at least 5 consecutive years. Applicants must be planning to enroll in an accredited master's degree program in any field at a college or university in any state. They must be sponsored by the local American Legion Auxiliary unit. Selection is based on academic record and financial need.

Financial Data The stipend is $2,500 per year. All funds are paid directly to the institution.

Duration 1 year; may be renewed 1 additional year if the recipient needs further financial assistance and has maintained at least a 2.5 GPA.

Number awarded 1 each year.

Deadline January of each year.

[944]
GEORGE WASHINGTON CHAPTER AUSA SCHOLARSHIPS

Association of the United States Army-George Washington
　　Chapter
c/o Bobbie Williams, Scholarship Committee
79 Brush Everard Court
Stafford, VA 22554
(703) 697-6340　　　　　E-mail: Bobbie.Williams@us.army.mil
Web: www.gwcausa.org/Scholarship/index.htm

Summary To provide financial assistance for undergraduate or graduate study at a school in any state to members of the George Washington Chapter of the Association of the United States Army (AUSA) and their families.

Eligibility This program is open to active members of the AUSA George Washington Chapter (which serves the Washington, D.C. area) and the families of active members. Applicants must have a GPA of 2.5 or higher and be working on an undergraduate or advanced degree at a college or university in any state. Along with their application, they must submit a letter describing any family circumstances they believe are relevant and explaining why they deserve the scholarship. Members must also submit a favorable recommendation from their supervisor. Membership in AUSA is open to Army personnel (including Reserves and National Guard) who are either active or retired, ROTC cadets, or civilian employees of the Army.

Financial Data Stipends range up to $1,000.

Duration 1 year.

Number awarded Varies each year; recently, 15 of these scholarships were awarded.

Deadline April of each year.

[945]
GLADYS MCPARTLAND SCHOLARSHIPS

United States Marine Corps Combat Correspondents
  Association
Attn: Executive Director
110 Fox Court
Wildwood, FL 34785
(352) 748-4698   E-mail: usmccca@cfl.rr.com
Web: www.usmccca.org/awards/gladys

Summary   To provide financial assistance for college or graduate school to regular members of the U.S. Marine Corps Combat
Correspondents Association (USMCCCA) or their children.

Eligibility   Eligible are active-duty Marines and certain Marine
Corps Reservists who are regular members of the USMCCCA, or
the dependent children of such members, as long as the member
is in a "dues-paid" status, or died in such status, or is listed as a
prisoner of war or missing in action and was in a "dues-paid" status when so listed. Applicants must be high school seniors or
graduates, seeking at least a bachelor's degree. Preference is
given to students working on degrees in disciplines that will lead
to careers in mass media communications, although applications
are accepted in any field.

Financial Data   The stipend is $1,000; funds are to be used
exclusively for tuition, books, and/or fees.

Duration   1 year; may be renewed, provided the recipient maintains a GPA of 2.0 or higher.

Additional data   Funds for this scholarship were originally provided by a contribution from Kathryne Timmons in honor of her
sister, Gladys McPartland, who served as executive secretary of
the USMCCCA from its founding until her death in 1985.

Number awarded   1 or more each year.

Deadline   June of each year.

[946]
GLENN F. GLEZEN SCHOLARSHIP

Fleet Reserve Association
Attn: Scholarship Administrator
125 North West Street
Alexandria, VA 22314-2754
(703) 683-1400   Toll Free: (800) FRA-1924
Fax: (703) 549-6610   E-mail: fra@fra.org
Web: www.fra.org

Summary   To provide financial assistance for graduate school
to members of the Fleet Reserve Association (FRA) and their
spouses, children, and grandchildren.

Eligibility   This program is open to the dependent children,
grandchildren, and spouses of members of the association who
are in good standing (or were at the time of death, if deceased).
FRA members are also eligible. Applicants should be enrolled in
a graduate program. Along with their application, they must submit an essay on their life experiences, career objectives, and what
motivated them to select those objectives. Selection is based on
academic record, financial need, extracurricular activities, leadership skills, and participation in community activities. U.S. citizenship is required.

Financial Data   The stipend is $5,000 per year.

Duration   1 year; may be renewed.

Additional data   Membership in the FRA is restricted to active-
duty, retired, and Reserve members of the Navy, Marine Corps,
and Coast Guard. This program was established in 2001.

Number awarded   1 each year.

Deadline   April of each year.

[947]
H.S. AND ANGELINE LEWIS SCHOLARSHIPS

American Legion Auxiliary
Department of Wisconsin
Attn: Education Chair
2930 American Legion Drive
P.O. Box 140
Portage, WI 53901-0140
(608) 745-0124   Toll Free: (866) 664-3863
Fax: (608) 745-1947   E-mail: alawi@amlegionauxwi.org
Web: www.amlegionauxwi.org/Scholarships.htm

Summary   To provide financial assistance to Wisconsin residents who are related to veterans or members of the American
Legion Auxiliary and interested in working on an undergraduate
or graduate degree at a school in any state.

Eligibility   This program is open to the children, wives, and widows of veterans who are high school seniors or graduates and
have a GPA of 3.5 or higher. Grandchildren and great-grandchildren of members of the American Legion Auxiliary are also eligible. Applicants must be residents of Wisconsin and interested in
working on an undergraduate or graduate degree at a school in
any state. Along with their application, they must submit a 300-
word essay on "Education-An Investment in the Future." Financial
need is considered in the selection process.

Financial Data   The stipend is $1,000.

Duration   1 year; nonrenewable.

Number awarded   6 each year: 1 to a graduate student and 5 to
undergraduates.

Deadline   March of each year.

[948]
INDIANA CHILD OF VETERAN AND PUBLIC
SAFETY OFFICER SUPPLEMENTAL GRANT
PROGRAM

State Student Assistance Commission of Indiana
Attn: Grant Division
150 West Market Street, Suite 500
Indianapolis, IN 46204-2811
(317) 232-2350   Toll Free: (888) 528-4719 (within IN)
Fax: (317) 232-3260   E-mail: grants@ssaci.state.in.us
Web: www.in.gov/ssaci/2338.htm

Summary   To provide financial assistance to residents of Indiana who are the children or spouses of specified categories of
deceased or disabled veterans or public safety officers and interested in attending college or graduate school in the state.

Eligibility   This program is open to 1) children of disabled Indiana veterans; 2) children and spouses of members of the Indiana
National Guard killed while serving on state active duty; and 3)
children and spouses of Indiana public safety officers killed in the
line of duty. The veterans portion is open to Indiana residents who
are the natural or adopted children of veterans who served in the
active-duty U.S. armed forces during a period of wartime. Applicants may be of any age; parents must have lived in Indiana for at
least 3 years during their lifetime. The veteran parent must also 1)
have a service-connected disability as determined by the U.S.
Department of Veterans Affairs or the Department of Defense; 2)
have received a Purple Heart Medal; or 3) have been a resident
of Indiana at the time of entry into the service and declared a
POW or MIA after January 1, 1960. Students at the Indiana Soldiers' and Sailors' Children's Home are also eligible. The National
Guard portion of this program is open to children and spouses of
members of the Indiana National Guard who suffered a service-
connected death while serving on state active duty. The public
safety officer portion of this program is open to 1) the children and
spouses of regular law enforcement officers, regular fire fighters,
volunteer fire fighters, county police reserve officers, city police
reserve officers, paramedics, emergency medical technicians,
and advanced emergency medical technicians killed in the line of
duty, and 2) the children and spouses of Indiana state police

troopers permanently and totally disabled in the line of duty. Children must be younger than 23 years of age and enrolled full time in an undergraduate or graduate degree program at a public college or university in Indiana. Spouses must be enrolled in an undergraduate program and must have been married to the covered public safety officer at the time of death or disability.

Financial Data Qualified applicants receive a 100% remission of tuition and all mandatory fees for undergraduate or graduate work at state-supported postsecondary schools and universities in Indiana. Support is not provided for such fees as room and board.

Duration Up to 124 semester hours of study.

Additional data The veterans portion of this program is administered by the Indiana Department of Veterans' Affairs, 302 West Washington Street, Room E-120, Indianapolis, IN 46204-2738, (317) 232-3910, (800) 400-4520, Fax: (317) 232-7721, E-mail: jkiser@dva.state.in.us. The National Guard portion of this program is administered by Joint Forces Headquarters, Attn: Education Services Office, 9301 East 59th Street, Lawrence, IN 46216, (317) 964-7023, Fax: (317) 964-7028.

Number awarded Varies each year.

Deadline Applications must be submitted at least 30 days before the start of the college term.

[949]
JOHN CORNELIUS/MAX ENGLISH MEMORIAL SCHOLARSHIP AWARD

Marine Corps Tankers Association
P.O. Box 20761
El Cajon, CA 92021
Web: www.usmarinetankers.org/scholarship-program

Summary To provide financial assistance for college or graduate school to children and grandchildren of Marines who served in a tank unit.

Eligibility This program is open to high school seniors and graduates who are children, grandchildren, or under the guardianship of an active, Reserve, retired, or honorably discharged Marine who served in a tank unit. Marine or Navy Corpsmen currently assigned to tank units are also eligible. Applicants must be enrolled or planning to enroll full time at a college or graduate school. Their sponsor must be a member of the Marine Corps Tankers Association or, if not a member, must join if the application is accepted. Along with their application, they must submit an essay on their educational goals, future aspirations, and concern for the future of our society and for the peoples of the world. Selection is based on that essay, academic record, school activities, leadership potential, and community service.

Financial Data The stipend is at least $2,000 per year.

Duration 1 year; recipients may reapply.

Number awarded 8 to 12 each year.

Deadline March of each year.

[950]
JOSEPH A. MCALINDEN DIVERS' SCHOLARSHIP

Navy-Marine Corps Relief Society
Attn: Education Division
875 North Randolph Street, Suite 225
Arlington, VA 22203-1757
(703) 696-4960   Fax: (703) 696-0144
E-mail: education@nmcrs.org
Web: www.nmcrs.org/education.html

Summary To provide financial assistance to current and former Navy and Marine Corps divers and their families who are interested in working on an undergraduate or graduate degree in a field related to ocean agriculture.

Eligibility This program is open to Navy and Marine Corps active-duty and retired divers and members of their families. Applicants must be enrolled full time in an undergraduate or grad-

uate program in oceanography, ocean agriculture, aquaculture, or a related field; they may also be engaged in advanced diver training, certification, or recertification. Financial need is considered in the selection process.

Financial Data The stipend ranges from $500 to $3,000, depending on the need of the recipient.

Duration 1 year.

Number awarded 1 or more each year.

Deadline Applications may be submitted at any time.

[951]
JOSEPH R. BARANSKI EMERITUS SCHOLARSHIP

Fleet Reserve Association
Attn: Scholarship Administrator
125 North West Street
Alexandria, VA 22314-2754
(703) 683-1400   Toll Free: (800) FRA-1924
Fax: (703) 549-6610   E-mail: fra@fra.org
Web: www.fra.org

Summary To provide financial assistance for graduate school to members of the Fleet Reserve Association (FRA) and their spouses, children, and grandchildren.

Eligibility This program is open to the dependent children, grandchildren, and spouses of members of the association who are in good standing (or were at the time of death, if deceased). FRA members are also eligible. Applicants should be enrolled in a graduate program. Along with their application, they must submit an essay on their life experiences, career objectives, and what motivated them to select those objectives. Selection is based on academic record, financial need, extracurricular activities, leadership skills, and participation in community activities. U.S. citizenship is required.

Financial Data The stipend is $5,000.

Duration 1 year; may be renewed.

Additional data Membership in the FRA is restricted to active-duty, retired, and Reserve members of the Navy, Marine Corps, and Coast Guard. This program was established in 2001.

Number awarded 1 each year.

Deadline April of each year.

[952]
KATHERN F. GRUBER SCHOLARSHIPS

Blinded Veterans Association
477 H Street, N.W.
Washington, DC 20001-2694
(202) 371-8880   Toll Free: (800) 669-7079
Fax: (202) 371-8258   E-mail: bva@bva.org
Web: www.bva.org/services.html

Summary To provide financial assistance for undergraduate or graduate study to spouses and children of blinded veterans.

Eligibility This program is open to dependent children and spouses of blinded veterans of the U.S. armed forces. The veteran need not be a member of the Blinded Veterans Association. The veteran's blindness may be either service connected or non-service connected, but it must meet the following definition: central visual acuity of 20/200 or less in the better eye with corrective glasses, or central visual acuity of more than 20/200 if there is a field defect in which the peripheral field has contracted to such an extent that the widest diameter of visual field subtends an angular distance no greater than 20 degrees in the better eye. Applicants must have been accepted or be currently enrolled as a full-time student in an undergraduate or graduate program at an accredited institution of higher learning. Along with their application, they must submit a 300-word essay on their career goals and aspirations. Financial need is not considered in the selection process.

Financial Data The stipend is $2,000; funds are intended to be used to cover the student's expenses, including tuition, other academic fees, books, dormitory fees, and cafeteria fees. Funds are paid directly to the recipient's school.

Duration 1 year; recipients may reapply.

Additional data Scholarships may be used for only 1 degree (vocational, bachelor's, or graduate) or nongraduate certificate (e.g., nursing, secretarial).

Number awarded 6 each year.

Deadline April of each year.

[953]
LIFE'S CHOICES FOUNDATION GRADUATE SCHOLARSHIP AWARDS

Association for Intelligence Officers
Attn: Scholarships Committee
6723 Whittier Avenue, Suite 303A
McLean, VA 22101-4533
(703) 790-0320   Fax: (703) 991-1278
E-mail: afio@afio.com
Web: www.afio.com/13_scholarships.htm

Summary To provide financial assistance to graduate students who are members or descendants of members of the U.S. intelligence community and interested in working on a degree in a field related to national security.

Eligibility This program is open to graduate students who apply in their senior undergraduate year or first graduate year. Applicants must be 1) personnel serving in government agencies that are part of the U.S. intelligence community or 2) their children or grandchildren. They must be working on a degree in a field related to national security or intelligence studies and be, or planning to be, serving in the U.S. government. Along with their application, they must submit a cover letter that explains their need for assistance, their career goals and dreams, and their views of U.S. world standing and its intelligence community. Selection is based on merit, character, estimated future potential, background, and relevance of their studies to the full spectrum of national security interests and career ambitions. U.S. citizenship is required.

Financial Data The stipend is $4,000.

Duration 1 year.

Additional data This program is sponsored by the Morris Family Charitable Corporation.

Number awarded 2 each year.

Deadline June of each year.

[954]
MAINE VETERANS DEPENDENTS EDUCATIONAL BENEFITS

Bureau of Veterans' Services
117 State House Station
Augusta, ME 04333-0117
(207) 626-4464   Toll Free: (800) 345-0116 (within ME)
Fax: (207) 626-4471   E-mail: mainebvs@maine.gov
Web: www.maine.gov/dvem/bvs/educational_benefits.htm

Summary To provide financial assistance for undergraduate or graduate education to dependents of disabled and other Maine veterans.

Eligibility Applicants for these benefits must be children (high school seniors or graduates under 22 years of age), non-divorced spouses, or unremarried widow(er)s of veterans who meet 1 or more of the following requirements: 1) living and determined to have a total permanent disability resulting from a service-connected cause; 2) killed in action; 3) died from a service-connected disability; 4) died while totally and permanently disabled due to a service-connected disability but whose death was not related to the service-connected disability; or 5) a member of the armed forces on active duty who has been listed for more than 90 days as missing in action, captured, forcibly detained, or interned in the line of duty by a foreign government or power. The veteran parent must have been a resident of Maine at the time of entry into ser-

vice or a resident of Maine for 5 years preceding application for these benefits. Children may be working on an associate or bachelor's degree. Spouses, widows, and widowers may work on an associate, bachelor's, or master's degree.

Financial Data Recipients are entitled to free tuition at institutions of higher education supported by the state of Maine.

Duration Children may receive up to 8 semesters of support; they have 6 years from the date of first entrance to complete those 8 semesters. Continuation in the program is based on their earning a GPA of 2.0 or higher each semester. Spouses are entitled to receive up to 120 credit hours of educational benefits and have 10 years from the date of first entrance to complete their program.

Additional data College preparatory schooling and correspondence courses do not qualify under this program.

Number awarded Varies each year.

Deadline Deadline not specified.

[955]
MARIA C. JACKSON/GENERAL GEORGE A. WHITE SCHOLARSHIP

Oregon Student Assistance Commission
Attn: Grants and Scholarships Division
1500 Valley River Drive, Suite 100
Eugene, OR 97401-2146
(541) 687-7395   Toll Free: (800) 452-8807, ext. 7395
Fax: (541) 687-7414   TDD: (800) 735-2900
E-mail: awardinfo@osac.state.or.us
Web: www.osac.state.or.us/osac_programs.html

Summary To provide financial assistance to veterans and children of veterans and military personnel in Oregon who are interested in attending college or graduate school in the state.

Eligibility This program is open to residents of Oregon who served, or whose parents are serving or have served, in the U.S. armed forces. Applicants or their parents must have resided in Oregon at the time of enlistment. They must be enrolled or planning to enrolled in a college or graduate school in the state. College and university undergraduates must have a GPA of 3.75 or higher, but there is no minimum GPA requirement for graduate students or those attending a technical school. Selection is based on scholastic ability and financial need.

Financial Data A stipend is awarded (amount not specified).

Number awarded Varies each year.

Deadline February of each year.

[956]
MARY PAOLOZZI MEMBER'S SCHOLARSHIP

Navy Wives Club of America
P.O. Box 54022
Millington, TN 38053-6022
Toll Free: (866) 511-NWCA
E-mail: nwca@navywivesclubsofamerica.org
Web: www.navywivesclubsofamerica.org/scholarinfo.htm

Summary To provide financial assistance for undergraduate or graduate study to members of the Navy Wives' Club of America (NWCA).

Eligibility This program is open to NWCA members who can demonstrate financial need. Applicants must be 1) a high school graduate or senior planning to attend college full time next year; 2) currently enrolled in an undergraduate program and planning to continue as a full-time undergraduate; 3) a college graduate or senior planning to be a full-time graduate student next year; or 4) a high school graduate or GED recipient planning to attend vocational or business school next year. Along with their application, they must submit a brief statement on why they feel they should be awarded this scholarship and any special circumstances (financial or other) they wish to have considered. Financial need is also considered in the selection process.

Financial Data Stipends range from $500 to $1,000 each year (depending upon the donations from the NWCA chapters).

Duration 1 year.

Additional data Membership in the NWCA is open to spouses of enlisted personnel serving in the Navy, Marine Corps, Coast Guard, and the active Reserve units of those services; spouses of enlisted personnel who have been honorably discharged, retired, or transferred to the Fleet Reserve on completion of duty; and widows of enlisted personnel in those services.

Number awarded 1 or more each year.

Deadline May of each year.

[957]
MILITARY NONRESIDENT TUITION WAIVER FOR MEMBERS, SPOUSES OR CHILDREN ASSIGNED TO DUTY IN TEXAS

Texas Higher Education Coordinating Board
Attn: Grants and Special Programs
1200 East Anderson Lane
P.O. Box 12788, Capitol Station
Austin, TX 78711-2788
(512) 427-6340   Toll Free: (800) 242-3062
Fax: (512) 427-6127   E-mail: grantinfo@thecb.state.tx.us
Web: www.collegeforalltexans.com

Summary To exempt military personnel stationed in Texas and their dependents from the payment of nonresident tuition at public institutions of higher education in the state.

Eligibility Eligible for these waivers are members of the U.S. armed forces and commissioned officers of the Public Health Service from states other than Texas, their spouses, and dependent children. Applicants must be assigned to Texas and attending or planning to attend a public college or university in the state.

Financial Data Although persons eligible under this program are classified as nonresidents, they are entitled to pay the resident tuition at Texas institutions of higher education, regardless of their length of residence in Texas.

Duration 1 year; may be renewed.

Number awarded Varies each year; recently, 11,600 students received these waivers.

Deadline Deadline not specified.

[958]
MILITARY ORDER OF THE PURPLE HEART SCHOLARSHIP PROGRAM

Military Order of the Purple Heart
Attn: Scholarships
5413-B Backlick Road
Springfield, VA 22151-3960
(703) 642-5360   Toll Free: (888) 668-1656
Fax: (703) 642-2054   E-mail: scholarship@purpleheart.org
Web: www.purpleheart.org/Scholarships/Default.aspx

Summary To provide financial assistance for college or graduate school to members of the Military Order of the Purple Heart (MOPH) and their families.

Eligibility This program is open to 1) members of the MOPH; 2) direct descendants (children, stepchildren, adopted children, grandchildren, and great- grandchildren) of veterans who are MOPH members or who were members at the time of death; 3) direct descendants of veterans killed in action or who died of wounds but did not have the opportunity to join the order; and 4) spouses and widows of MOPH members, veterans killed in action, and veterans who died of wounds. Applicants must be graduating seniors or graduates of an accredited high school who are enrolled or accepted for enrollment in a full-time program of study in a college, trade school, or graduate school. They must have a GPA of 2.75 or higher. U.S. citizenship is required. Along with their application, they must submit an essay of 200 to 300

words on "What it means to be an American." Financial need is not considered in the selection process.

Financial Data The stipend is $3,000 per year.

Duration 1 year; may be renewed up to 2 additional years.

Additional data Membership in MOPH is open to all veterans who received a Purple Heart Medal and were discharged under conditions other than dishonorable. A processing fee of $15 is required.

Number awarded Varies each year; recently, 50 of these scholarships were awarded.

Deadline February of each year.

[959]
MILITARY SPOUSE SCHOLARSHIPS FOR ALL MILITARY SPOUSES

National Military Family Association, Inc.
Attn: Spouse Scholarship Program
2500 North Van Dorn Street, Suite 102
Alexandria, VA 22302-1601
(703) 931-NMFA   Toll Free: (800) 260-0218
Fax: (703) 931-4600 E-mail: scholarships@militaryfamily.org
Web: www.militaryfamily.org

Summary To provide financial assistance for postsecondary study to spouses of active and retired military personnel.

Eligibility This program is open to the spouses of military personnel (active, retired, Reserve, Guard, or survivor). Applicants must be attending or planning to attend an accredited postsecondary institution to work on an undergraduate or graduate degree, professional certification, vocational training, GED or ESL, or other postsecondary training. They may enroll part or full time and in-class or online. Along with their application, they must submit an essay on a question that changes annually; recently, applicants were asked to write about what they like most about the health care they are receiving as a military family member, what they like the least, and what they would recommend to change it. Selection is based on that essay, community involvement, and academic achievement.

Financial Data The stipend is $1,000. Funds are paid directly to the educational institution to be used for tuition, fees, and school room and board. Support is not provided for books, rent, or previous education loans.

Duration 1 year; recipients may reapply.

Additional data This program, is a component of the Joanne Holbrook Patton Military Spouse Scholarship Program, which began in 2004.

Number awarded Varies each year; recently, the program awarded a total of 293 scholarships.

Deadline January of each year.

[960]
MILITARY SPOUSE SCHOLARSHIPS FOR SPOUSES OF THE FALLEN

National Military Family Association, Inc.
Attn: Spouse Scholarship Program
2500 North Van Dorn Street, Suite 102
Alexandria, VA 22302-1601
(703) 931-NMFA   Toll Free: (800) 260-0218
Fax: (703) 931-4600 E-mail: scholarships@militaryfamily.org
Web: www.militaryfamily.org

Summary To provide financial assistance for postsecondary study to spouses of military personnel have been killed as a result of service since September 11, 2001.

Eligibility This program is open to the spouses of military personnel who have been killed as a result of active-duty service since September 11, 2001. Applicants must be able to verify that the death was a result of service in support of the Global War on Terror. They must be attending or planning to attend an accredited postsecondary institution to work on an undergraduate or graduate degree, professional certification, vocational training, GED or ESL, or other postsecondary training. They may enroll part or full time and in-class or online. Along with their application, they must submit an essay on a question that changes annually; recently, applicants were asked to write about what they like most about the health care they are receiving as a military family member, what they like the least, and what they would recommend to change it. Selection is based on that essay, community involvement, and academic achievement.

Financial Data The stipend is $1,000. Funds are paid directly to the educational institution to be used for tuition, fees, and school room and board. Support is not provided for books, rent, or previous education loans.

Duration 1 year; recipients may reapply.

Additional data This program, is a component of the Joanne Holbrook Patton Military Spouse Scholarship Program, which began in 2004.

Number awarded Varies each year; recently, the program awarded a total of 293 scholarships.

Deadline January of each year.

[961]
MILITARY SPOUSE SCHOLARSHIPS FOR SPOUSES OF THE WOUNDED

National Military Family Association, Inc.
Attn: Spouse Scholarship Program
2500 North Van Dorn Street, Suite 102
Alexandria, VA 22302-1601
(703) 931-NMFA   Toll Free: (800) 260-0218
Fax: (703) 931-4600 E-mail: scholarships@militaryfamily.org
Web: www.militaryfamily.org

Summary To provide financial assistance for postsecondary study to spouses of military personnel have been wounded as a result of service since September 11, 2001.

Eligibility This program is open to the spouses of military personnel who have been wounded as a result of active-duty service since September 11, 2001. Applicants must be able to verify that the wound or injury was a result of service in support of the Global War on Terror. They must be attending or planning to attend an accredited postsecondary institution to work on an undergraduate or graduate degree, professional certification, vocational training, GED or ESL, or other postsecondary training. They may enroll part or full time and in-class or online. Along with their application, they must submit an essay on a question that changes annually; recently, applicants were asked to write about what they like most about the health care they are receiving as a military family member, what they like the least, and what they would recommend to change it. Selection is based on that essay, community involvement, and academic achievement.

Financial Data The stipend is $1,000. Funds are paid directly to the educational institution to be used for tuition, fees, and school room and board. Support is not provided for books, rent, or previous education loans.

Duration 1 year; recipients may reapply.

Additional data This program, is a component of the Joanne Holbrook Patton Military Spouse Scholarship Program, which began in 2004.

Number awarded Varies each year; recently, the program awarded a total of 293 scholarships.

Deadline January of each year.

[962]
MINNESOTA G.I. BILL PROGRAM

Minnesota Office of Higher Education
Attn: Manager of State Financial Aid Programs
1450 Energy Park Drive, Suite 350
St. Paul, MN 55108-5227
(651) 642-0567   Toll Free: (800) 657-3866
Fax: (651) 642-0675   TDD: (800) 627-3529
E-mail: Ginny.Dodds@state.mn.us
Web: www.ohe.state.mn.us

Summary To provide financial assistance for college or graduate school in the state to residents of Minnesota who served in the military after September 11, 2001 and the families of deceased or disabled military personnel.

Eligibility This program is open to residents of Minnesota enrolled at colleges and universities in the state as undergraduate or graduate students. Applicants must be 1) a veteran who is serving or has served honorably in a branch of the U.S. armed forces at any time on or after September 11, 2001; 2) a non-veteran who has served honorably for a total of 5 years or more cumulatively as a member of the Minnesota National Guard or other active or Reserve component of the U.S. armed forces, and any part of that service occurred on or after September 11, 2001; or 3) a surviving child or spouse of a person who has served in the military at any time on or after September 11, 2001 and who has died or has a total and permanent disability as a result of that military service. Financial need is also considered in the selection process.

Financial Data The stipend is $1,000 per semester for full-time study or $500 per semester for part-time study.

Duration 1 year; may be renewed up to 4 additional years, provided the recipient continues to make satisfactory academic progress.

Additional data This program was established by the Minnesota Legislature in 2007.

Number awarded Varies each year.

Deadline Deadline not specified.

[963]
MINNESOTA NATIONAL GUARD SURVIVOR ENTITLEMENT TUITION REIMBURSEMENT PROGRAM

Department of Military Affairs
Attn: Education Services Officer
JFMN-J1-ARED
20 West 12th Street
St. Paul, MN 55155-2098
(651) 282-4125   Toll Free: (800) 657-3848
Fax: (651) 282-4694   E-mail: education@mn.ngb.army.mil
Web: www.minnesotanationalguard.org

Summary To provide financial assistance for college or graduate school to survivors of members of the Minnesota National Guard who were killed on active duty.

Eligibility This program is open to surviving spouses and children of members of the Minnesota Army or Air National Guard who were killed while performing military duty. Spouses remain eligible unless they remarry; dependent children are eligible until their 24th birthday. The Guard member's death must have occurred within the scope of assigned duties while in a federal duty status or on state active service. Applicants must be enrolled as undergraduate or graduate students at colleges or universities in Minnesota. Reimbursement is provided only for undergraduate courses completed with a grade of "C" or better or for graduate courses completed with a grade of "B" or better.

Financial Data The maximum reimbursement rate is 100% of the undergraduate tuition rate at the University of Minnesota Twin Cities campus (currently, $326.92 per credit to a maximum of $4,250 per term).

Duration 1 academic term, to a maximum of 18 credits per term; may be renewed for a total of 144 semester credits or 208 quarter credits.

Number awarded Varies each year.

Deadline Participants must request reimbursement within 60 days of the last official day of the term.

[964]
NATIONAL GUARD ASSOCIATION OF COLORADO SCHOLARSHIP PROGRAM

National Guard Association of Colorado
Attn: Education Foundation, Inc.
P.O. Box 440889
Aurora, CO 80044-0889
(303) 677-8387   Fax: (303) 677-8823
E-mail: ed.foundation@earthlink.net
Web: www.ngaco-edufoundation.org

Summary To provide financial assistance to members of the National Guard Association of Colorado (NGACO) and the Colorado National Guard and their families who are interested in attending college or graduate school in any state.

Eligibility This program is open to 1) current and retired members of the Colorado National Guard and the NGACO; 2) dependent unmarried children of current and retired members of the Colorado National Guard and the NGACO; 3) spouses of current and retired members of the Colorado National Guard and the NGACO; and 4) unremarried spouses and unmarried dependent children of deceased members of the Colorado National Guard and the NGACO. Applicants must be enrolled or planning to enroll full or part time at a college, university, trade school, business school, or graduate school in any state. Along with their application, they must submit an essay, up to 2 pages in length, on their desire to continue their education, what motivates them, their financial need, their commitment to academic excellence, and their current situation.

Financial Data Stipends are $1,000, $750, or $500 per year.

Duration 1 year; may be renewed.

Additional data Members of the Colorado National Guard must perform at least 1 year of service following the completion of the school year for which the scholarship was received.

Number awarded Varies each year. Recently, 11 of these scholarships were awarded: 4 at $1,000 to members of the NGACO, 2 at $750 to dependents of members of the NGACO, 2 at $500 to current enlisted members of the Colorado National Guard, 2 at $500 to current officer members of the Colorado National Guard, and 1 at $1,000 to a Colorado National Guard member or dependent working on a graduate degree.

Deadline August of each year for fall semester; January of each year for spring semester.

[965]
NAVAL HELICOPTER ASSOCIATION GRADUATE SCHOLARSHIPS

Naval Helicopter Association
Attn: Scholarship Fund
P.O. Box 180578
Coronado, CA 92178-0578
(619) 435-7139   Fax: (619) 435-7354
E-mail: info@nhascholarship.org
Web: www.nhascholarship.org/nhascholarshipfund/index.html

Summary To provide financial assistance for graduate school to students who have an affiliation with the rotary wing activities of the sea services.

Eligibility This program is open to graduate students who are 1) children, grandchildren, or spouses of current or former Navy, Marine Corps, or Coast Guard rotary wing aviators or aircrewmen; 2) individuals who are serving or have served in maintenance or support billets in rotary wing squadrons or wings and their

spouses and children. Applicants must provide information on their rotary wing affiliation and a personal statement on their educational plans and future goals. Selection is based on that statement, academic proficiency, scholastic achievements and awards, extracurricular activities, employment history, and letters of recommendation.

Financial Data The stipend is $3,000.

Duration 1 year.

Number awarded 1 each year.

Deadline January of each year.

[966]
NAVY/MARINE CORPS/COAST GUARD ENLISTED DEPENDENT SPOUSE SCHOLARSHIP

Navy Wives Club of America
P.O. Box 54022
Millington, TN 38053-6022
Toll Free: (866) 511-NWCA
E-mail: nwca@navywivesclubsofamerica.org
Web: www.navywivesclubsofamerica.org/scholarinfo.htm

Summary To provide financial assistance for undergraduate or graduate study to spouses of naval personnel.

Eligibility This program is open to the spouses of active-duty Navy, Marine Corps, or Coast Guard members who can demonstrate financial need. Applicants must be 1) a high school graduate or senior planning to attend college full time next year; 2) currently enrolled in an undergraduate program and planning to continue as a full-time undergraduate; 3) a college graduate or senior planning to be a full-time graduate student next year; and 4) a high school graduate or GED recipient planning to attend vocational or business school next year. Along with their application, they must submit a brief statement on why they feel they should be awarded this scholarship and any special circumstances (financial or other) they wish to have considered. Financial need is also considered in the selection process.

Financial Data The stipends range from $500 to $1,000 each year (depending upon the donations from chapters of the Navy Wives Club of America).

Duration 1 year.

Number awarded 1 or more each year.

Deadline May of each year.

[967]
NEW JERSEY NATIONAL GUARD TUITION PROGRAM

New Jersey Department of Military and Veterans Affairs
Attn: New Jersey Army National Guard Education Center
3650 Saylors Pond Road
Fort Dix, NJ 08640-7600
(609) 562-0654   Toll Free: (888) 859-0352
Fax: (609) 562-0201
Web: www.state.nj.us/military/education/NJNGTP.htm

Summary To provide financial assistance for college or graduate school to New Jersey National Guard members and the surviving spouses and children of deceased members.

Eligibility This program is open to active members of the New Jersey National Guard who have completed Initial Active Duty for Training (IADT). Applicants must be New Jersey residents who have been accepted into a program of undergraduate or graduate study at any of 31 public institutions of higher education in the state. The surviving spouses and children of deceased members of the Guard who had completed IADT and were killed in the performance of their duties while a member of the Guard are also eligible if the school has classroom space available.

Financial Data Tuition for up to 15 credits per semester is waived for full-time recipients in state-supported colleges or community colleges in New Jersey.

Duration 1 semester; may be renewed.
Number awarded Varies each year.
Deadline Deadline not specified.

[968]
NEW MEXICO CHILDREN OF DECEASED MILITARY AND STATE POLICE PERSONNEL SCHOLARSHIPS

New Mexico Department of Veterans' Services
Attn: Benefits Division
407 Galisteo Street, Room 142
Santa Fe, NM 87504
(505) 827-6374   Toll Free: (866) 433-VETS
Fax: (505) 827-6372   E-mail: alan.martinez@state.nm.us
Web: www.dvs.state.nm.us/benefits.html

Summary To provide financial assistance for college or graduate school to the children of deceased military and state police personnel in New Mexico.
Eligibility This program is open to the children of 1) military personnel killed in action or as a result of such action during a period of armed conflict; 2) members of the New Mexico National Guard killed while on active duty; and 3) New Mexico State Police killed on active duty. Applicants must be between the ages of 16 and 26 and enrolled in a state-supported school in New Mexico. Children of deceased veterans must be nominated by the New Mexico Veterans' Service Commission; children of National Guard members must be nominated by the adjutant general of the state; children of state police must be nominated by the New Mexico State Police Board. Selection is based on merit and financial need.
Financial Data The scholarships provide full waiver of tuition at state-funding postsecondary schools in New Mexico. A stipend of $150 per semester ($300 per year) provides assistance with books and fees.
Duration 1 year; may be renewed.
Deadline Deadline not specified.

[969]
NEW MEXICO NATIONAL GUARD ASSOCIATION MASTER'S/CONTINUING EDUCATION SCHOLARSHIPS

New Mexico National Guard Association
Attn: Executive Director
10 Bataan Boulevard
Santa Fe, NM 87508
(505) 474-1669   Fax: (505) 474-1671
E-mail: execdir@nganm.org
Web: www.nganm.org

Summary To provide financial assistance to members of the New Mexico National Guard Association and their dependents who are working on a master's or other advanced degree.
Eligibility This program is open to association members (with paid-up current dues) and their dependents. Applicants must have completed their postsecondary education and be working on their master's or other higher degree. They must submit an official college transcript with a GPA of 3.3 or higher, a completed application, and an original essay (from 800 to 1,200 words) on their past accomplishments and contributions and what contributions they intend to make with this education to better the community or the National Guard.
Financial Data The stipend is $1,000. Funds are paid directly to the recipient's school.
Duration 1 year; nonrenewable.
Number awarded 2 each year.
Deadline April of each year.

[970]
NGANJ SCHOLARSHIP PROGRAM

National Guard Association of New Jersey
Attn: Executive Director
P.O. Box 266
Wrightstown, NJ 08562
(973) 541-6776   Fax: (973) 541-6909
E-mail: jose.maldonado@njdmava.state.nj.us
Web: www.nganj.org

Summary To provide financial assistance to New Jersey National Guard members or their dependents who are interested in attending college or graduate school in any state.
Eligibility This program is open to active members of the New Jersey National Guard; the spouses, children, legal wards, and grandchildren of active members; and the children, legal wards, and grandchildren of retired (with at least 20 years of service) or deceased members. Applicants must be currently attending or entering an approved community college, school of nursing, or 4-year college in any state as a full-time undergraduate or graduate student. Selection is based on academic accomplishment, leadership, and citizenship.
Financial Data Stipends up to $1,000 are available.
Duration 1 year; nonrenewable.
Number awarded Varies each year; recently, 10 of these scholarships were awarded.
Deadline March of each year.

[971]
NGASC SCHOLARSHIPS

National Guard Association of South Carolina
Attn: NGASC Scholarship Foundation
132 Pickens Street
Columbia, SC 29205
(803) 254-8456   Toll Free: (800) 822-3235
Fax: (803) 254-3869   E-mail: nginfo@ngasc.org
Web: www.ngasc.org/ngasc_scholarship_foundation.htm

Summary To provide financial assistance to current and former South Carolina National Guard members and their dependents who are interested in attending college or graduate school in any state.
Eligibility This program is open to undergraduate students who are 1) current, retired, or deceased members of the South Carolina National Guard; 2) their dependents; and 3) members of the National Guard Association of South Carolina (NGASC). Graduate students are also eligible if they are members of the South Carolina National Guard. Applicants must be attending or interested in attending a college or university in any state as a full-time student. Several of the scholarships include additional restrictions on school or academic major; some are granted only for academic excellence, but most are based on both academics and financial need.
Financial Data The stipend is $1,500 or $1,000.
Duration 1 year; may be renewed up to 3 additional years.
Additional data Among the named scholarships included in this program recently were the BG (Ret) C. Norwood Gayle Memorial Scholarship Award, the CMSgt Jim Burgess Scholarship Award, the Mrs. Kaye Helgeson Memorial Scholarship Award, the LTC (Ret) Glenny J. (Jeff) Matthews Memorial Scholarship Awards, the Ron McNair Memorial Scholarship Award, the Darla Moore Scholarship Award, the Sergeants Major Watson Scholarship Award, the SCANG Chiefs Council Scholarship Award, the Chief Shepherd Pitney Bowes Scholarship Award, the Fallen Soldiers' Memorial Scholarship Award, and the South Carolina National Guard Federal Credit Union Awards.
Number awarded Varies each year. Recently, 48 of these scholarships were awarded: 1 at $1,500 and 47 at $1,000. The $1,500 scholarship and 1 of the $1,000 scholarships were based

on academic excellence; the remaining $1,000 scholarships were based on both academics and financial need.

Deadline January of each year.

[972]
NGAT SCHOLARSHIP PROGRAM

National Guard Association of Texas
Attn: NGAT Educational Foundation
3706 Crawford Avenue
Austin, TX 78731-6803
(512) 454-7300   Toll Free: (800) 252-NGAT
Fax: (512) 467-6803   E-mail: rlindner@ngat.org
Web: www.ngat.org

Summary To provide financial assistance to members and dependents of members of the National Guard Association of Texas who are interested in attending college or graduate school in any state.

Eligibility This program is open to annual and life members of the association and their spouses and children (associate members and their dependents are not eligible). Applicants may be high school seniors, undergraduate students, or graduate students, either enrolled or planning to enroll at an institution of higher education in any state. Along with their application, they must submit an essay on their desire to continue their education. Selection is based on scholarship, citizenship, and leadership.

Financial Data Stipends range from $500 to $5,000.

Duration 1 year (nonrenewable).

Additional data This program includes the following named scholarships: the Thomas F. Berry Memorial Scholarship, the Len and Jean Tallas Memorial Scholarship, the Texas Military Forces Retirees Scholarship, the T-Mates Scholarship, the LTC Gary W. Parrish Memorial Scholarship, the 1SG Harry E. Lux Memorial Scholarship, the Gloria Jenell and Marlin E. Mote Endowed Scholarship, the Chief Master Sergeants Scholarship, the Sergeants Major Scholarship, and the Texas USAA Scholarship (sponsored by USAA Insurance Corporation).

Number awarded Varies each year. Recently, 10 of these scholarships were awarded: 1 at $5,000, 3 at $2,500, 1 at $2,000, 2 at $1,250, 2 at $1,000, and 1 at $500.

Deadline February of each year.

[973]
NWCA NATIONAL SCHOLARSHIPS

Navy Wives Club of America
P.O. Box 54022
Millington, TN 38053-6022
Toll Free: (866) 511-NWCA
E-mail: nwca@navywivesclubsofamerica.org
Web: www.navywivesclubsofamerica.org/scholarinfo.htm

Summary To provide financial assistance for college or graduate school to the children of naval personnel.

Eligibility Applicants for these scholarships must be the children (natural born, legally adopted, or stepchildren) of enlisted members of the Navy, Marine Corps, or Coast Guard on active duty, retired with pay, or deceased. Applicants must be attending or planning to attend an accredited college or university as a full-time undergraduate or graduate student. They must have a GPA of 2.5 or higher. Along with their application, they must submit an essay on their career objectives and the reasons they chose those objectives. Selection is based on academic standing, moral character, and financial need. Some scholarships are reserved for students majoring in special education, medical students, and children of members of Navy Wives Club of America (NWCA).

Financial Data The stipend is $1,500.

Duration 1 year; may be renewed up to 3 additional years.

Additional data Membership in the NWCA is open to spouses of enlisted personnel serving in the Navy, Marine Corps, Coast Guard, and the active Reserve units of those services; spouses of

enlisted personnel who have been honorably discharged, retired, or transferred to the Fleet Reserve on completion of duty; and widows of enlisted personnel in those services.

Number awarded 30 each year, including at least 4 to freshmen, 4 to current undergraduates applying for the first time, 2 to medical students, 1 to a student majoring in special education, and 4 to children of NWCA members.

Deadline May of each year.

[974]
PETER CONNACHER MEMORIAL AMERICAN EX-PRISONER OF WAR SCHOLARSHIPS

Oregon Student Assistance Commission
Attn: Grants and Scholarships Division
1500 Valley River Drive, Suite 100
Eugene, OR 97401-2146
(541) 687-7395   Toll Free: (800) 452-8807, ext. 7395
Fax: (541) 687-7414   TDD: (800) 735-2900
E-mail: awardinfo@osac.state.or.us
Web: www.osac.state.or.us/osac_programs.html

Summary To provide financial assistance for college or graduate school to ex-prisoners of war and their descendants.

Eligibility Applicants must be U.S. citizens who 1) were military or civilian prisoners of war or 2) are the descendants of ex-prisoners of war. They may be undergraduate or graduate students. A copy of the ex-prisoner of war's discharge papers from the U.S. armed forces must accompany the application. In addition, written proof of POW status must be submitted, along with a statement of the relationship between the applicant and the ex-prisoner of war (father, grandfather, etc.). Selection is based on academic record and financial need. Preference is given to Oregon residents or their dependents.

Financial Data The stipend amount varies; recently, it was at least $1,150.

Duration 1 year; may be renewed for up to 3 additional years for undergraduate students or 2 additional years for graduate students. Renewal is dependent on evidence of continued financial need and satisfactory academic progress.

Additional data This program is administered by the Oregon Student Assistance Commission (OSAC) with funds provided by the Oregon Community Foundation, 1221 S.W. Yamhill, Suite 100, Portland, OR 97205, (503) 227-6846, Fax: (503) 274-7771. Funds are also provided by the Columbia River Chapter of the American Ex-prisoners of War, Inc. Recipients must attend college on a full-time basis.

Number awarded Varies each year; recently, 4 of these scholarships were awarded.

Deadline February of each year.

[975]
RED RIVER VALLEY FIGHTER PILOTS ASSOCIATION SCHOLARSHIP GRANT PROGRAM

Red River Valley Association Foundation
Attn: Executive Director
P.O. Box 1553
Front Royal, VA 22630-0033
(540) 639-9798   Toll Free: (866) 401-7287
Fax: (540) 636-9776   E-mail: ExecutiveOffice@river-rats.org
Web: www.river-rats.org/about_us/scholarship.php

Summary To provide financial assistance for college or graduate school to the spouses and children of selected service personnel and members of the Red River Valley Fighter Pilots Association.

Eligibility This program is open to the spouses and children of 1) servicemembers missing in action (MIA) or killed in action (KIA) in combat situations involving U.S. military forces from August 1964 through the present; 2) U.S. military aircrew members killed in a non-combat aircraft accident in which they were performing aircrew duties; and 3) current members of the association and deceased members who were in good standing at the time of their death. Scholarships are also available to students in fields related to aviation and space, even if they have no kinship relationship to a deceased aviator or member of the association. Applicants must be interested in attending an accredited college or university to work on an undergraduate or graduate degree. Selection is based on demonstrated academic achievement, college entrance examination scores, financial need, and accomplishments in school, church, civic, and social activities.

Financial Data The amount awarded varies, depending upon the need of the recipient. Recently, undergraduate stipends have ranged from $500 to $3,500 and averaged $1,725; graduate stipends have ranged from $500 to $2,000 and averaged $1,670. Funds are paid directly to the recipient's institution and are to be used for tuition, fees, books, and room and board for full-time students.

Duration 1 year; may be renewed if the recipient maintains a GPA of 2.0 or higher.

Additional data This program was established in 1970, out of concern for the families of aircrews (known as "River Rats") who were killed or missing in action in the Red River Valley of North Vietnam.

Number awarded Varies each year; since this program was established, it has awarded more than 1,000 scholarships worth more than $1,700,000.

Deadline May of each year.

[976]
REMISSION OF FEES FOR CHILDREN OF INDIANA VETERANS

Indiana Department of Veterans' Affairs
302 West Washington Street, Room E-120
Indianapolis, IN 46204-2738
(317) 232-3910   Toll Free: (800) 400-4520 (within IN)
Fax: (317) 232-7721
Web: www.in.gov/dva/2378.htm

Summary To enable the children of disabled and other Indiana veterans to attend public colleges and universities in the state without payment of tuition.

Eligibility This program is open to natural and legally-adopted children of veterans who served on active duty in the U.S. armed forces during a period of wartime and have been residents of Indiana for at least 36 consecutive months during their lifetimes. The veteran must 1) have sustained a service-connected disability as verified by the U.S. Department of Veterans Affairs or a military service; 2) have received a Purple Heart Medal; or 3) have been a resident of Indiana at the time of entry into the service and declared a prisoner of war (POW) or missing in action (MIA) after January 1, 1960. Students who were veteran-related pupils at the Indiana Soldiers' and Sailors' Children's Home are also eligible. Applicants must be attending or planning to attend a state-supported postsecondary college or university in Indiana as an undergraduate or graduate student.

Financial Data Qualified students receive remission of 100% of tuition and mandatory fees.

Duration Fees are remitted for up to 124 semester hours of education.

Number awarded Varies each year.

Deadline Requests for assistance may be submitted at any time.

[977]
ROBERT W. NOLAN EMERITUS SCHOLARSHIP

Fleet Reserve Association
Attn: Scholarship Administrator
125 North West Street
Alexandria, VA 22314-2754
(703) 683-1400   Toll Free: (800) FRA-1924
Fax: (703) 549-6610   E-mail: fra@fra.org
Web: www.fra.org

Summary To provide financial assistance for graduate school to members of the Fleet Reserve Association (FRA) and their spouses, children, and grandchildren.

Eligibility This program is open to the dependent children, grandchildren, and spouses of members of the association who are in good standing (or were at the time of death, if deceased). FRA members are also eligible. Applicants should be enrolled in a graduate program. Along with their application, they must submit an essay on their life experiences, career objectives, and what motivated them to select those objectives. Selection is based on academic record, financial need, extracurricular activities, leadership skills, and participation in community activities. U.S. citizenship is required.

Financial Data The stipend is $5,000 per year.

Duration 1 year; may be renewed.

Additional data Membership in the FRA is restricted to active-duty, retired, and Reserve members of the Navy, Marine Corps, and Coast Guard. This program was established in 2001.

Number awarded 1 each year.

Deadline April of each year.

[978]
SCHUYLER S. PYLE SCHOLARSHIP

Fleet Reserve Association
Attn: Scholarship Administrator
125 North West Street
Alexandria, VA 22314-2754
(703) 683-1400   Toll Free: (800) FRA-1924
Fax: (703) 549-6610   E-mail: fra@fra.org
Web: www.fra.org

Summary To provide financial assistance for college or graduate school to members of the Fleet Reserve Association (FRA) who are current or former naval personnel and their spouses and children.

Eligibility This program is open to dependent children, grandchildren, and spouses of FRA members who are in good standing (or were at the time of death, if deceased). FRA members are also eligible. Applicants must be working on or planning to work on an undergraduate or graduate degree. Along with their application, they must submit an essay on their life experiences, career objectives, and what motivated them to select those objectives. Selection is based on academic record, financial need, extracurricular activities, leadership skills, and participation in community activities. U.S. citizenship is required.

Financial Data The stipend is $5,000 per year.

Duration 1 year; may be renewed.

Additional data Membership in the FRA is restricted to active-duty, retired, and Reserve members of the Navy, Marine Corps, and Coast Guard.

Number awarded 1 each year.

Deadline April of each year.

[979]
SFC CURTIS MANCINI MEMORIAL SCHOLARSHIPS

Association of the United States Army-Rhode Island Chapter
c/o CSM (Ret) Anthony Ferri, Secretary
47 Spokane Street
Providence, RI 02904
(401) 861-2997   E-mail: afnf458673755@aol.com
Web: www.ausari.org/index.html

Summary   To provide financial assistance to members of the Rhode Island Chapter of the Association of the United States Army (AUSA) and their families who are interested in attending college or graduate school in any state.

Eligibility   This program is open to members of the AUSA Rhode Island Chapter and their family members (spouses, children, and grandchildren). Applicants must be high school seniors or graduates accepted at an accredited college, university, or vocational/technical school in any state or current undergraduate or graduate students. Along with their application, they must submit a 250-word essay on why they feel their achievements should qualify them for this award. Selection is based on academic and individual achievements; financial need is not considered. Membership in AUSA is open to current and retired Army personnel (including Reserves and National Guard), ROTC cadets, or civilian employees of the Army.

Financial Data   The stipend is $1,000.

Duration   1 year.

Number awarded   2 each year.

Deadline   March of each year.

[980]
STANLEY A. DORAN MEMORIAL SCHOLARSHIPS

Fleet Reserve Association
Attn: Scholarship Administrator
125 North West Street
Alexandria, VA 22314-2754
(703) 683-1400   Toll Free: (800) FRA-1924
Fax: (703) 549-6610   E-mail: fra@fra.org
Web: www.fra.org

Summary   To provide financial assistance for college or graduate school to children of members of the Fleet Reserve Association (FRA) who are current or former naval personnel.

Eligibility   This program is open to the dependent children of FRA members who are in good standing (or were at the time of death, if deceased). Applicants must be working on or planning to work on an undergraduate or graduate degree. Along with their application, they must submit an essay on their life experiences, career objectives, and what motivated them to select those objectives. Selection is based on academic record, financial need, extracurricular activities, leadership skills, and participation in community activities. U.S. citizenship is required.

Financial Data   The amount awarded varies, depending on the needs of the recipient and the funds available.

Duration   1 year; may be renewed.

Additional data   Membership in the FRA is restricted to active-duty, retired, and Reserve members of the Navy, Marine Corps, and Coast Guard.

Number awarded   3 each year.

Deadline   April of each year.

[981]
SURVIVORS' AND DEPENDENTS' EDUCATIONAL ASSISTANCE PROGRAM

Department of Veterans Affairs
Attn: Veterans Benefits Administration
810 Vermont Avenue, N.W.
Washington, DC 20420
(202) 418-4343   Toll Free: (888) GI-BILL1
Web: www.gibill.va.gov/GI_Bill_Info/benefits.htm

Summary   To provide financial assistance for undergraduate or graduate study to children and spouses of deceased and disabled veterans, MIAs, and POWs.

Eligibility   Eligible for this assistance are spouses and children of 1) veterans who died or are permanently and totally disabled as the result of active service in the armed forces; 2) veterans who died from any cause while rated permanently and totally disabled from a service-connected disability; 3) servicemembers listed as missing in action or captured in the line of duty by a hostile force; 4) servicemembers listed as forcibly detained or interned by a foreign government or power; and 5) servicemembers who are hospitalized or receiving outpatient treatment for a service-connected permanent and total disability and are likely to be discharged for that disability. Children must be between 18 and 26 years of age, although extensions may be granted. Spouses and children over 14 years of age with physical or mental disabilities are also eligible.

Financial Data   Monthly stipends from this program for study at an academic institution are $925 for full time, $694 for three-quarter time, or $461 for half-time. For farm cooperative work, the monthly stipends are $745 for full-time, $559 for three-quarter time, or $372 for half-time. For an apprenticeship or on-the-job training, the monthly stipend is $674 for the first 6 months, $505 for the second 6 months, $333 for the third 6 months, and $168 for the remainder of the program. For special restorative training by beneficiaries with a physical or mental disability, the monthly stipend for full-time training is $925.

Duration   Up to 45 months (or the equivalent in part-time training). Spouses must complete their training within 10 years of the date they are first found eligible. For spouses of servicemembers who died on active duty, benefits end 20 years from the date of death.

Additional data   Benefits may be used to work on associate, bachelor, or graduate degrees at colleges and universities, including independent study, cooperative training, and study abroad programs. Courses leading to a certificate or diploma from business, technical, or vocational schools may also be taken. Other eligible programs include apprenticeships, on-the-job training programs, farm cooperative courses, correspondence courses (for spouses only), secondary school programs (for recipients who are not high school graduates), tutorial assistance, remedial deficiency and refresher training, or work-study (for recipients who are enrolled at least three-quarter time). Eligible children who are handicapped by a physical or mental disability that prevents pursuit of an educational program may receive special restorative training that includes language retraining, lip reading, auditory training, Braille reading and writing, and similar programs. Eligible spouses and children over 14 years of age who are handicapped by a physical or mental disability that prevents pursuit of an educational program may receive specialized vocational training that includes specialized courses, alone or in combination with other courses, leading to a vocational objective that is suitable for the person and required by reason of physical or mental handicap. Ineligible courses include bartending; audited courses; non-accredited independent study courses; any course given by radio; self-improvement courses, such as reading, speaking, woodworking, basic seamanship, and English as a second language; audited courses; any course that is avocational or recreational in character; courses not leading to an educational, professional, or vocational objective; courses taken and successfully completed previously; courses taken by a federal government employee and paid for under the Government Employees' Training Act; and courses taken while in receipt of benefits for the same program from the Office of Workers' Compensation Programs.

Number awarded   Varies each year.

Deadline   Applications may be submitted at any time.

[982]
TILLMAN MILITARY SCHOLARSHIPS FOR DEPENDENTS

Pat Tillman Foundation
2121 South Mill Avenue, Suite 214
Tempe, AZ 85282
(480) 621-4074   Fax: (480) 621-4075
E-mail: scholarships@pattillmanfoundation.org
Web: www.pattillmanfoundation.org

Summary To provide financial assistance to dependents of veterans and active servicemembers who are interested in working on an undergraduate or graduate degree.

Eligibility This program is open to the dependent children and spouses of veterans and active servicemembers whose educational benefits are not transferable from their parent or spouse, who are survivors of a servicemember, or whose transferable benefits are not sufficient to meet their needs. Their parent or spouse may have served or be serving in any branch of the armed forces from both the pre- and post-September 11 era. Applicants must be interested in starting, finishing, or furthering their undergraduate, graduate, or postgraduate education at a 2-year, 4-year, or vocational institution (public or private). Along with their application, they must submit 1-page essays on 1) their specific financial need, including any gap in educational benefits they may already be receiving and their reason for applying for this scholarship; 2) how their family member's service in the U.S. armed forces has affected their life or influenced their actions; and 3) their previous service to others and the community and how they will incorporate those service experiences into their educational and career goals. Selection is based on those essays, educational and career ambitions, family member's length of service, record of personal achievement, demonstration of service to others in the community and a desire to continue such service, and unmet financial need.

Financial Data Stipends vary; recently, total awards (including multi-year awards) averaged $12,800.

Duration 1 year; may be renewed, provided the recipient maintains a GPA of 3.0 or higher, remains enrolled full time, and documents participation in civic action or community service.

Additional data This program was established in 2009. The foundation administers the program directly for students at colleges and universities nationwide; it also acts in partnership with 4 universities (the University of Maryland, the University of Arkansas, the University of Idaho, and Mississippi State University) which award scholarships directly to their students.

Number awarded Varies each year; recently, 52 students received a total of $665,820 through this program.

Deadline May of each year.

[983]
VADM ROBERT L. WALTERS SCHOLARSHIP

Surface Navy Association
2550 Huntington Avenue, Suite 202
Alexandria, VA 22303
(703) 960-6800   Toll Free: (800) NAVY-SNA
Fax: (703) 960-6807   E-mail: navysna@aol.com
Web: www.navysna.org/awards/index.html

Summary To provide financial assistance for college or graduate school to members of the Surface Navy Association (SNA) and their dependents.

Eligibility This program is open to SNA members and their children, stepchildren, wards, and spouses. The SNA member must 1) be in the second or subsequent consecutive year of membership; 2) be serving, retired, or honorably discharged; 3) be a Surface Warfare Officer or Enlisted Surface Warfare Specialist; and 4) have served for at least 3 years on a surface ship of the U.S. Navy or Coast Guard. Applicants must be studying or planning to study at an accredited undergraduate or graduate institution. Along with their application, they must submit a 200-word essay

about themselves; a list of their extracurricular activities, community service activities, academic honors and/or positions of leadership that represent their interests, with an estimate of the amount of time involved with each activity; and 3 letters of reference. High school seniors should also include a transcript of high school grades and a copy of ACT or SAT scores. Applicants who are on active duty or drilling Reservists should also include a letter from their commanding officer commenting on their military service and leadership potential, a transcript of grades from their most recent 4 semesters of school, a copy of their ACT or SAT scores if available, and an indication of whether they have applied for or are enrolled in the Enlisted Commissioning Program. Applicants who are not high school seniors, active-duty servicemembers, or drilling Reservists should also include a transcript of the grades from their most recent 4 semesters of school and a copy of ACT or SAT test scores (unless they are currently attending a college or university). Selection is based on demonstrated leadership, community service, academic achievement, and commitment to pursuing higher educational objectives.

Financial Data The stipend is $2,000 per year.

Duration 4 years, provided the recipient maintains a GPA of 3.0 or higher.

Number awarded Varies each year.

Deadline February of each year.

[984]
VIRGINIA MILITARY SURVIVORS AND DEPENDENTS EDUCATION PROGRAM

Virginia Department of Veterans Services
270 Franklin Road, S.W., Room 503
Roanoke, VA 24011-2215
(540) 857-7101   Fax: (540) 857-7573
Web: www.dvs.virginia.gov/statebenefits.htm

Summary To provide educational assistance to the children and spouses of disabled and other Virginia veterans or service personnel.

Eligibility This program is open to residents of Virginia whose parent or spouse served in the U.S. armed forces (including the Reserves, the Virginia National Guard, or the Virginia National Guard Reserves) during any armed conflict subsequent to December 6, 1941, as a result of a terrorist act, during military operations against terrorism, or on a peacekeeping mission. The veterans must be at least 90% disabled due to an injury or disease incurred as a result of such service, has died, or is listed as a prisoner of war or missing in action. Applicants must have been accepted at a public college or university in Virginia as an undergraduate or graduate student. Children must be between 16 and 29 years of age; there are no age restrictions for spouses. The veteran must have been a resident of Virginia at the time of entry into active military service or for at least 5 consecutive years immediately prior to the date of application or death. The surviving spouse must have been a resident of Virginia for at least 5 years prior to marrying the veteran or for at least 5 years immediately prior to the date on which the application was submitted.

Financial Data The maximum allowable stipend is $1,500 per year, but current funding permits a maximum of $1,350, payable at the rate of $675 per term for full-time students, $450 per term for students enrolled at least half time but less than full time, or $225 per term for students enrolled less than half time.

Duration Entitlement extends to a maximum of 48 months.

Additional data Individuals entitled to this benefit may use it to pursue any vocational, technical, undergraduate, or graduate program of instruction. Generally, programs listed in the academic catalogs of state-supported institutions are acceptable, provided they have a clearly-defined educational objective (such as a certificate, diploma, or degree). This program was formerly known as the Virginia War Orphans Education Program.

Number awarded Varies each year; recently, funding allowed for a total of 740 of these awards.

Deadline Deadline not specified.

[985]
WISCONSIN G.I. BILL TUITION REMISSION PROGRAM

Wisconsin Department of Veterans Affairs
30 West Mifflin Street
P.O. Box 7843
Madison, WI 53707-7843
(608) 266-1311   Toll Free: (800) WIS-VETS
Fax: (608) 267-0403   E-mail: WDVAInfo@dva.state.wi.us
Web: www.dva.state.wi.us/Ben_education.asp

Summary To provide financial assistance for college or graduate school to Wisconsin veterans and their dependents.

Eligibility This program is open to current residents of Wisconsin who 1) were residents of the state when they entered or reentered active duty in the U.S. armed forces, or 2) have moved to the state and have been residents for any consecutive 12-month period after entry or reentry into service. Applicants must have served on active duty for at least 2 continuous years or for at least 90 days during specified wartime periods. Also eligible are 1) qualifying children and unremarried surviving spouses of Wisconsin veterans who died in the line of duty or as the direct result of a service-connected disability; and 2) children and spouses of Wisconsin veterans who have a service-connected disability rated by the U.S. Department of Veterans Affairs as 30% or greater. Children must be between 17 and 25 years of age (regardless of the date of the veteran's death or initial disability rating) and be a Wisconsin resident for tuition purposes. Spouses remain eligible for 10 years following the date of the veteran's death or initial disability rating; they must be Wisconsin residents for tuition purposes but they may enroll full or part time. Students may attend any institution, center, or school within the University of Wisconsin (UW) System or the Wisconsin Technical College System (WCTS). There are no income limits, delimiting periods following military service during which the benefit must be used, or limits on the level of study (e.g., vocational, undergraduate, professional, or graduate).

Financial Data Veterans who qualify as a Wisconsin resident for tuition purposes are eligible for a remission of 100% of standard academic fees and segregated fees at a UW campus or 100% of program and material fees at a WCTS institution. Veterans who qualify as a Wisconsin veteran for purposes of this program but for other reasons fail to meet the definition of a Wisconsin resident for tuition purposes at the UW system are eligible for a remission of 100% of non-resident fees. Spouses and children of deceased or disabled veterans are entitled to a remission of 100% of tuition and fees at a UW or WCTS institution.

Duration Up to 8 semesters or 128 credits, whichever is greater.

Additional data This program was established in 2005 as a replacement for Wisconsin Tuition and Fee Reimbursement Grants.

Number awarded Varies each year.

Deadline Applications must be submitted within 14 days from the office start of the academic term: in October for fall, March for spring, or June for summer.

[986]
WISCONSIN JOB RETRAINING GRANTS

Wisconsin Department of Veterans Affairs
30 West Mifflin Street
P.O. Box 7843
Madison, WI 53707-7843
(608) 266-1311   Toll Free: (800) WIS-VETS
Fax: (608) 267-0403   E-mail: WDVAInfo@dva.state.wi.us
Web: www.dva.state.wi.us/Ben_retraininggrants.asp

Summary To provide funds to recently unemployed Wisconsin veterans or their families who need financial assistance while being retrained for employment.

Eligibility This program is open to current residents of Wisconsin who 1) were residents of the state when they entered or reentered active duty in the U.S. armed forces, or 2) have moved to the state and have been residents for any consecutive 12-month period after entry or reentry into service. Applicants must have served on active duty for at least 2 continuous years or for at least 90 days during specified wartime periods. Unremarried spouses and minor or dependent children of deceased veterans who would have been eligible for the grant if they were living today may also be eligible. The applicant must, within the year prior to the date of application, have become unemployed (involuntarily laid off or discharged, not due to willful misconduct) or underemployed (experienced an involuntary reduction of income). Underemployed applicants must have current annual income from employment that does not exceed federal poverty guidelines. All applicants must be retraining at accredited schools in Wisconsin or in a structured on-the-job program. Course work toward a college degree does not qualify. Training does not have to be full time, but the program must be completed within 2 years and must reasonably be expected to lead to employment.

Financial Data The maximum grant is $3,000 per year; the actual amount varies, depending upon the amount of the applicant's unmet need. In addition to books, fees, and tuition, the funds may be used for living expenses.

Duration 1 year; may be renewed 1 additional year.

Number awarded Varies each year.

Deadline Applications may be submitted at any time.

[987]
WISCONSIN LEGION AUXILIARY CHILD WELFARE SCHOLARSHIP

American Legion Auxiliary
Department of Wisconsin
Attn: Education Chair
2930 American Legion Drive
P.O. Box 140
Portage, WI 53901-0140
(608) 745-0124   Toll Free: (866) 664-3863
Fax: (608) 745-1947   E-mail: alawi@amlegionauxwi.org
Web: www.amlegionauxwi.org/Scholarships.htm

Summary To provide financial assistance for graduate training in special education at a school in any state to dependents and descendants of veterans in Wisconsin.

Eligibility This program is open to the children, wives, and widows of veterans who are college graduates and have a GPA of 3.5 or higher. Grandchildren and great-grandchildren of members of the American Legion Auxiliary are also eligible. Applicants must be residents of Wisconsin and interested in working on a graduate degree in special education at a school in any state. Along with their application, they must submit a 300-word essay on "Education-An Investment in the Future." Financial need is considered in the selection process.

Financial Data The stipend is $1,000.

Duration 1 year; nonrenewable.

Number awarded 1 each year.

Deadline March of each year.

[988]
WMA SCHOLARSHIP PROGRAM

Women Marines Association
P.O. Box 377
Oaks, PA 19456-0377
Toll Free: (888) 525-1943 E-mail: wma@womenmarines.org
Web: www.womenmarines.org/scholarships.aspx

Summary To provide financial assistance for college or graduate school to students sponsored by members of the Women Marines Association (WMA).

Eligibility Applicants must be sponsored by a WMA member and fall into 1 of the following categories: 1) have served or are serving in the U.S. Marine Corps, regular or Reserve; 2) are a direct descendant by blood, legal adoption, or stepchild of a Marine on active duty or who has served honorably in the U.S. Marine Corps, regular or Reserve; 3) are a sibling or a descendant of a sibling by blood, legal adoption, or stepchild of a Marine on active duty or who has served honorably in the U.S. Marine Corps, regular or Reserve; or 4) have completed 2 years in a Marine Corps JROTC program. WMA members may sponsor an unlimited number of applicants per year. High school seniors must submit transcripts (GPA of 3.0 or higher) and SAT or ACT scores. Undergraduate and graduate students must have a GPA of 3.0 or higher.

Financial Data The stipend is $1,500 per year.

Duration 1 year; may be renewed 1 additional year.

Additional data This program includes the following named scholarships: the WMA Memorial Scholarships, the Lily H. Gridley Memorial Scholarship, the Ethyl and Armin Wiebke Memorial Scholarship, the Maj. Megan Malia McClung Memorial Scholarship, and the LaRue A. Ditmore Music Scholarships. Applicants must know a WMA member to serve as their sponsor; the WMA will not supply listings of the names or addresses of chapters or individual members.

Number awarded Varies each year.

Deadline March of each year.

[989]
WNGEA COLLEGE GRANT PROGRAM

Wisconsin National Guard Enlisted Association
Attn: Executive Director
2400 Wright Street
Madison, WI 53704
(608) 242-3112   E-mail: WNGEA@yahoo.com
Web: www.wngea.org/MAIN/PROG/prosch.htm

Summary To provide financial assistance to members of the Wisconsin National Guard Enlisted Association (WNGEA) and their spouses and children who are interested in attending college or graduate school in any state.

Eligibility This program is open to WNGEA members, the unmarried children of WNGEA members, the spouses of WNGEA members, and the unmarried children and spouses of deceased WNGEA members. WNGEA member applicants, as well as the parents or guardians of unmarried children who are applicants, must have at least 1 year remaining on their enlistment following completion of the school year for which application is submitted (or they must have 20 or more years of service). Applicants must be enrolled at a college, university, graduate school, trade school, or business school in any state. Selection is based on financial need, leadership, and moral character.

Financial Data Stipends are $1,000 or $500 per year.

Duration 1 year; recipients may not reapply for 2 years.

Additional data This program includes 1 scholarship sponsored by the USAA Insurance Corporation.

Number awarded Varies each year. Recently, 4 of these scholarships were awarded: the Raymond A. Matera Scholarship at $1,000 and 3 others at $500 each.

Deadline May of each year.

Loans

Veterans ●

Military Personnel ●

Family Members ●

Described here are 83 programs designed primarily or exclusively for veterans, military personnel, and their family members that provide money which must eventually be repaid—with or without interest. Funds may be used for a variety of purposes, including education, personal emergencies, and purchases. Scholarship/loans, forgivable loans, loans-for-service, and loan repayment programs are also covered here. Of these listings, 26 are set aside specifically for veterans, 31 for military personnel, and 26 for their family members (spouses, children, grandchildren, parents, and other relatives). If you are looking for a particular program and don't find it in this section, be sure to check the Program Title Index to see if it is covered elsewhere in the directory.

Veterans

[990]
AAAA LOAN PROGRAM

Army Aviation Association of America
Attn: AAAA Scholarship Foundation
755 Main Street, Suite 4D
Monroe, CT 06468-2830
(203) 268-2450
E-mail: Scholarship@quad-a.org   Fax: (203) 268-5870
Web: www.quad-a.org/scholarship.htm

Summary To provide educational loans to members of the Army Aviation Association of America (AAAA) and their relatives.

Eligibility This program is open to AAAA members and their spouses, unmarried siblings, and unmarried children. Applicants must be enrolled or accepted for enrollment as an undergraduate or graduate student at an accredited college or university.

Financial Data The maximum loan is $1,000 per year. All loans are interest free.

Duration Up to 4 years.

Number awarded Varies each year; recently, 10 of these loans were granted.

Deadline April of each year.

[991]
AER LOANS/GRANTS

Army Emergency Relief
200 Stovall Street
Alexandria, VA 22332-0600
(703) 428-0000   Toll Free: (866) 878-6378
Fax: (703) 325-7183   E-mail: aer@aerhq.org
Web: www.aerhq.org

Summary To provide loans and grants-in-aid to help with the emergency financial needs of Army veterans, military personnel, and their dependents.

Eligibility Eligible to apply are active-duty soldiers (single or married) and their dependents, Army National Guard and Army Reserve soldiers on continuous active duty for more than 30 days and their dependents, soldiers retired from active duty for longevity or physical disability and their dependents, Army National Guard and Army Reserve soldiers who retired at age 60 and their dependents, and surviving spouses and orphans of soldiers who died while on active duty or after they retired. Applicants must be seeking assistance for such emergency needs as food, rent, and utilities; emergency transportation and vehicle repair; funeral expenses; medical and dental expenses; or personal needs when pay is delayed or stolen. Support is not available to help pay for nonessentials, finance ordinary leave or vacation, pay fines or legal expenses, help liquidate or consolidate debt, assist with house purchase or home improvements, cover bad checks, pay credit card bills, or help purchase, rent, or lease a vehicle.

Financial Data Support is provided in the form of loans or grants (or a combination).

Duration Qualifying individuals can apply whenever they have a valid emergency need.

Additional data This organization was established in 1942.

Number awarded Varies each year; recently, the organization helped more than 66,000 Army people with more than $70 million, including $60 million to 58,820 active-duty soldiers and their families, $7.3 million to 4,914 retired soldiers and their families, and $2.7 million to 2,304 widow(er)s and orphans of deceased soldiers. Since it was established, the organization has helped more than 3.2 million qualifying individuals with more than $1.2 billion in financial assistance.

Deadline Applications may be submitted at any time.

[992]
AFAS FINANCIAL ASSISTANCE

Air Force Aid Society
Attn: Financial Assistance Department
241 18th Street South, Suite 202
Arlington, VA 22202-3409
(703) 607-3072, ext. 51   Toll Free: (800) 429-9475
Fax: (703) 607-3022
Web: www.afas.org/Assistance/HowWeCanHelp.cfm

Summary To provide loans and grants-in-aid to current and former Air Force personnel and their families who are facing emergency situations.

Eligibility This program is open to active-duty Air Force members and their dependents, retired Air Force personnel and their dependents, Air National Guard and Air Force Reserve personnel on extended duty over 15 days, and spouses and dependent children of deceased Air Force personnel who died on active duty or in retired status. Applicants must be facing problems, usually for relatively short periods, that affect their job or the essential quality and dignity of life the Air Force wants for its people. Examples of such needs include basic living expenses (food, rent, utilities), medical and dental care, funeral expenses, vehicle expenses, emergency travel, moving expenses, or child or respite care. Funding is generally not provided if it merely postpones a long-term inability to exist on present pay and allowances, for non-essentials, for continuing long-term assistance commitments, or to replace funds lost due to garnishment.

Financial Data Assistance is provided as an interest-free loan, a grant, or a combination of both.

Number awarded Varies each year.

Deadline Applications may be submitted at any time.

[993]
ALASKA STATE VETERANS INTEREST RATE PREFERENCE

Alaska Housing Finance Corporation
Attn: Communications Officer
4300 Boniface Parkway
P.O. Box 101020
Anchorage, AK 99510-1020
(907) 330-8447   Toll Free: (800) 478-AHFC (within AK)
Fax: (907) 338-9218
Web: www.ahfc.state.ak.us/loans/state_vet.cfm

Summary To provide Alaskan veterans and their spouses with lower interest rates on loans to purchase housing.

Eligibility This program is open to Alaska residents who served at least 90 days on active duty in the U.S. armed forces after April 6, 1917 and received an honorable discharge. Also eligible are 1) honorably-discharged members of the Alaska Army or Air National Guard who served at least 5 years; 2) honorably discharged Reservists who served at least 5 years; and 3) widows and widowers of qualified veterans. Members of the military currently serving on active duty are not eligible. Applicants must be proposing to purchase an owner-occupied single-family residence, condominium, unit within a PUD, duplex, triplex, fourplex, or Type I mobile home using Alaska's taxable, tax-exempt, taxable first-time home buyer, rural owner, or non-conforming programs. Their family income may not exceed specified limits that depend on location within the state and size of family.

Financial Data Qualified veterans and widow(er)s receive a 1% rate reduction on the first $50,000 of the loan amount. Loans greater than $50,000 receive a blended interest rate rounded up to the next 0.125%.

Duration Loans are for either 15 years or 30 years.

Additional data Income limits vary in different parts of the state. Recently, they ranged from $39,250 to $44,800 for families with 1 person, from $44,900 to $51,200 for families with 2 persons, from $50,500 to $7,600 for families with 3 persons, and from $56,100 to $64,000 for families with 4 or more persons.

Number awarded Varies each year.

Deadline Deadline not specified.

[994]
ALASKA VETERANS MORTGAGE PROGRAM

Alaska Housing Finance Corporation
Attn: Communications Officer
4300 Boniface Parkway
P.O. Box 101020
Anchorage, AK 99510-1020
(907) 330-8447   Toll Free: (800) 478-AHFC (within AK)
Fax: (907) 338-9218
Web: www.ahfc.state.ak.us/loans/veterans.cfm

Summary To provide loans to Alaskan veterans who wish to purchase a residence.

Eligibility This program is open to veterans who entered active-duty service prior to January 1, 1977 and have not been out of the service for 25 years or more prior to the date of application for a loan. Active-duty service includes service in the U.S. armed forces, Public Health Service, National Oceanic and Atmospheric Administration, or as a cadet in the U.S. Military, Air Force, Coast Guard, or Naval Academy. Applicants must be residents of Alaska who were discharged under conditions other than dishonorable. They must be interested in purchasing an owner-occupied single-family residence, condominium, unit within a PUD, duplex, triplex, fourplex, or Type I mobile home. Family dwellings of 2 to 4 units must have been in existence and initially occupied as a multi-family residence for at least the preceding 5 years.

Financial Data Maximum loan amounts change frequently. Recently, for conventional and VA loans the maximum was $688,050 for single-family homes, $800,775 for duplexes, $967,950 for triplexes, or $1,202,925 for fourplexes. Other maximums apply to FHA loans. The maximum down payment required is 5% for single-family homes, 10% for duplex properties, and 20% for triplex or fourplex properties. Interest rates also vary but recently were 4.625% on 30 year loans or 4.375% on 15 year loans.

Duration Loans are for either 15 years or 30 years.

Number awarded Varies each year.

Deadline Deadline not specified.

[995]
CALVET CONSTRUCTION LOAN PROGRAM

California Department of Veterans Affairs
Attn: Division of Farm and Home Purchases
1227 O Street, Room 200
P.O. Box 942895
Sacramento, CA 94295-0001
(916) 653-2525   Toll Free: (800) 952-LOAN (within CA)
Fax: (916) 653-2401   TDD: (800) 324-5966
E-mail: Kenn.Capps@cdva.ca.gov
Web: www.cdva.ca.gov/CalVetLoans/Constrct.aspx

Summary To provide loans to California veterans who are interested in constructing a new home.

Eligibility This program is open to veterans currently living in California, regardless of where they lived at the time they entered service or when they served. Applicants must be interested in purchasing land and constructing a new detached, single family home (no townhouses or condominiums) or mobile home on land owned (or to be owned) by the veteran (no mobile homes in rental parks). Other acceptable facilities include a garage, barn, porch, patio, pool, workshop, retaining wall, fencing, landscaping, or other permanent improvement necessary for health, safety, energy efficiency, or dwelling integrity. Improvements to personal property, including removable interior or exterior window coverings, are not eligible. The construction must be done by a licensed contractor.

Financial Data The maximum loan, covering both land purchase and construction, is $521,250. The down payment may be as low as 3%. Interest rates depend on the type of bonds used to finance the program; recently they were 5.75%, 5.95% or 6.2%.

Duration Loans are typically for 30 years, although shorter periods are available.

Number awarded Varies each year.

Deadline Applications may be submitted at any time.

[996]
CALVET HOME IMPROVEMENT LOAN PROGRAM

California Department of Veterans Affairs
Attn: Division of Farm and Home Purchases
1227 O Street, Room 200
P.O. Box 942895
Sacramento, CA 94295-0001
(916) 653-2525   Toll Free: (800) 952-LOAN (within CA)
Fax: (916) 653-2401   TDD: (800) 324-5966
E-mail: Kenn.Capps@cdva.ca.gov
Web: www.cdva.ca.gov/CalVetLoans/improve.aspx

Summary To enable current holders of CalVet Loans to obtain additional funding for home improvements.

Eligibility This program is open to active CalVet contract holders, including unremarried spouses of military personnel who died while on active duty or were designated a prisoner of war or missing in action. The basic CalVet contract must have at least 3 remaining months. Applicants must have a good payment record on the basic CalVet loan. Loans are available to improve the basic livability of the home or property; increase the energy efficiency of the home; perform general maintenance, such as painting, reroofing, and general repairs; add living space; renovate baths, kitchens, plumbing and electrical systems; install or update heating or air conditioning systems; install insulation, weather stripping, or thermal windows; add a garage, fence, landscaping, flatwork, retaining wall, or septic system; or connect to public utilities with water, sewer, or electrical lines from the property line to the dwelling. Unacceptable are improvements for recreational or entertainment purposes (such as swimming pools, saunas, hot tubs, pool houses, cabanas, or tennis courts) and improvements to farm property for the purpose of increasing agricultural productivity.

Financial Data Loans are available up to 90% of loan to value on "improved value," to a maximum of $150,000. A loan origination fee of 1.5% of the loan amount is charged. Recently, the interest rate was 5.75%, 5.95%, or 6.2%, depending on the source of funding for the loans.

Duration The maximum loan term is 10 years for loans up to $15,000, 12 years for loans up to $20,000, 15 years for loans up to $50,000, 20 years for loans up to $100,000, or 25 years for loans up to $150,000.

Number awarded Varies each year.

Deadline Applications may be submitted at any time.

[997]
CALVET LOAN PROGRAM

California Department of Veterans Affairs
Attn: Division of Farm and Home Purchases
1227 O Street, Room 200
P.O. Box 942895
Sacramento, CA 94295-0001
(916) 653-2525   Toll Free: (800) 952-LOAN (within CA)
Fax: (916) 653-2401   TDD: (800) 324-5966
E-mail: Kenn.Capps@cdva.ca.gov
Web: www.cdva.ca.gov/CalVetLoans/BestLoan.aspx

Summary To provide low-cost and low-interest financing to California servicemembers and veterans who are interested in purchasing homes, farms, or mobile homes for use as their primary residence.

Eligibility This program is open to veterans and active-duty servicemembers who are currently residents of California, regardless of where they were born or where they resided when they entered active military service. Applicants must have been released or discharged from active duty under honorable conditions or be currently serving on active duty. They must have served at least 90 days on active duty unless 1) discharged sooner due to service-connected disability, 2) eligible to receive a U.S. campaign or expeditionary medal, or 3) called to active duty from the Reserve or National Guard due to Presidential Order. Members of the California National Guard and the U.S. military Reserves who have served at least 1 year of a 6-year obligation are also eligible if they qualify as first-time home buyers or purchase homes in designated "target areas;" they must meet additional income and purchase price limitations. For loans guaranteed by the U.S. Department of Veterans Affairs (CalVet/VA), applicants must be veterans who served on active duty prior to January 1, 1977, who apply within 30 years from their release from active duty, and who served at least 1 day during a specified war period. Loans guaranteed by other means (CalVet97 and CalVeT80/20) are available to veterans who qualify as first-time home buyers, including those whose entire active-duty service was during peacetime. Veterans who do not qualify for the guaranteed-loan programs may be eligible for the unrestricted bond program, but they must meet the wartime service requirement.

Financial Data The maximum loan on single family homes (including condominiums, townhouses, and mobile homes affixed to land owned by the borrower) is currently $521,250; the maximum purchase price of farmland is $625,500; on mobile homes in approved mobile home parks, it is $175,000. Down payment requirements are 0% for the CalVet/VA program, 3% for the CalVet97 program, or 20% for the CalVeT80/20 program. The funding fee ranges from 1.25% to 3.35% but it may be waived for veterans with disability ratings of 10% or higher. The loan origination fee is 1% of the loan amount. Interest rates recently were 6.2% for CalVet/VA loans, 5.95% for CalVet97 loans, or 5.75% for CalVeT80/20 loans.

Duration Loans are typically for 30 years, although shorter periods are available.

Additional data Veteran contract purchasers who move from the CalVet financed property may qualify to have their CalVet loan transferred to another property or may qualify for a second loan contract. Loans that have been repaid or assigned to an ex-spouse in a divorce action may be obtained again. Information on current purchase price and family income limitations for revenue bond loans is available from the Department of Veterans Affairs state headquarters or local district sales offices. The veteran or a member of the veteran's immediate family must occupy the property within 60 days after signing a CalVet loan contract and must continue to reside on the property as the principal place of residence until the loan is paid in full. Acceptance of a bonus or benefit from another state for the qualifying period of military service disqualifies the veteran from CalVet benefits.

Number awarded Varies each year.

Deadline Applications may be submitted at any time.

[998]
CALVET REHABILITATION LOAN PROGRAM

California Department of Veterans Affairs
Attn: Division of Farm and Home Purchases
1227 O Street, Room 200
P.O. Box 942895
Sacramento, CA 94295-0001
(916) 653-2525   Toll Free: (800) 952-LOAN (within CA)
Fax: (916) 653-2401   TDD: (800) 324-5966
E-mail: Kenn.Capps@cdva.ca.gov
Web: www.cdva.ca.gov/CalVetLoans/NeedWork.aspx

Summary To provide loans to California veterans who are interested in purchasing a home that requires substantial rehabilitation.

Eligibility This program is open to veterans who served at least 90 days consecutively (unless discharged earlier because of a service-connected disability); at least 1 of the days of active duty must have occurred during specified periods of World War II, the Korean period, the Vietnam era, or the Persian Gulf War; release from active duty must have been under honorable conditions. Applicants must currently be California residents; they do not need to have been born in California or have been California residents at the time of entry or reentry into active military service. Qualified veterans must be seeking loans for bringing a property up to decent and sanitary condition, bringing older homes up to contemporary living standards, increasing the energy efficiency of the home, adding additional room to meet their family's needs, or correcting deferred maintenance. As part of the application, veterans must submit a detailed description of the repairs and improvements they plan to make, plus estimates of the costs.

Financial Data The maximum loan is $521,250. The down payment may be as low as 3%. Recently, the interest rate was 5.75%, 5.95%, or 6.2%, depending on the source of funding for the loans.

Duration Loans are typically for 30 years, although shorter periods are available.

Additional data The California Department of Veterans Affairs purchases the home in an "as-is" condition. Funds are then advanced for approved repairs or refurbishment as they are completed.

Number awarded Varies each year.

Deadline Applications may be submitted at any time.

[999]
HOME LOANS FOR NATIVE AMERICAN VETERANS

Department of Veterans Affairs
Attn: Veterans Benefits Administration
Home Loan Guaranty Service
810 Vermont Avenue, N.W.
Washington, DC 20420
(202) 418-4343   Toll Free: (800) 827-1000
Web: www.homeloans.va.gov/VAP26-93-1.htm

Summary To provide home loans to Native American veterans.

Eligibility Eligible Native American veterans may apply for these direct home loans if they wish to purchase, construct, or improve a home on Native American trust land. Veterans who are not Native Americans but who are married to Native American non-veterans are also eligible if they reside on federal trust land and both have a meaningful interest in the dwelling or lot.

Financial Data Loans are limited to the Freddie Mac conforming loan limit for a single-family home, currently set at $417,000 for the continental United States or $625,500 for Hawaii, Alaska, and Guam. A funding fee is payable to the Department of Veterans Affairs (VA); the fee is 1.25% to purchase, construct, or improve a home; 0.5% to refinance an existing loan; and waived for veterans receiving compensation for a service-connected disability. The funding fee may be paid in cash or included in the loan; other closing costs may be included in the loan.

Number awarded Varies each year.

Deadline Applications may be submitted at any time.

[1000]
MISSISSIPPI VETERANS' MORTGAGE LOAN PROGRAM

Mississippi Veterans' Home Purchase Board
3466 Highway 80 East
P.O. Box 54111
Pearl, MS 39288-4411
(601) 576-4800   Fax: (601) 576-4812
E-mail: vhpbinfo@vhpb.state.ms.us
Web: www.vhpb.state.ms.us

Summary To provide loans to veterans, their widow(er)s, and selected military personnel who are interested in purchasing or constructing a house in Mississippi.

Eligibility This program is open to honorably-discharged veterans who were Mississippi residents prior to entering military service or have been residents for at least 2 consecutive years prior to applying for a loan. Reserve and National Guard personnel who currently serve and have at least 6 years of service are also eligible. Active-duty military personnel are eligible if they meet the residency requirements. Reserve and National Guard personnel who have been activated for extended duty under Title 10 of the U.S. Code are also eligible. The unremarried surviving spouse of an eligible veteran who died as a result of service or service-connected injuries also qualifies, as does the unremarried spouse of an eligible veteran who has not purchased a home since the veteran's death. Applicants must be planning to purchase an existing single family home in Mississippi or to construct a new home in the state. Farms, raw land, mobile homes, and condominiums do not qualify.

Financial Data This program provides low-interest mortgage loans in amounts up to $195,000. Interest rates are fixed and are generally 1 to 2 percentage points below market rates (currently, that is 3.75% on 10-, 12- and 15-year loans or 4.0% on 20-, 25-, and 30-year loans).

Duration Available terms are 10, 12, 15, 20, 25, and 30 years.

Number awarded Varies each year.

Deadline Applications may be submitted at any time.

[1001]
NMCRS FINANCIAL ASSISTANCE

Navy-Marine Corps Relief Society
875 North Randolph Street, Suite 225
Arlington, VA 22203-1757
(703) 696-4904   Fax: (703) 696-0144
Web: www.nmcrs.org/intfreeloan.html

Summary To provide emergency assistance, in the form of interest-free loans or grants, to current and former Navy and Marine Corps personnel and their families who need temporary funding.

Eligibility This program is open to active-duty and retired Navy and Marine Corps personnel, their eligible family members, eligible family members of Navy and Marine Corps personnel who died on active duty or in a retired status, Reservists on extended active duty, indigent mothers (65 years of age or older) of deceased servicemembers who have limited resources and no family to provide for their welfare, ex-spouses whose marriage to a servicemember lasted for at least 20 years while the servicemember was on active duty and who have not remarried, and uniformed members of the National Oceanic and Atmospheric Administration (NOAA). Applicants must need emergency funding for funeral expenses, medical or dental bills, food, rent, utilities, emergency transportation, disaster relief, child care expenses, essential vehicle repairs, or other unforeseen family emergencies. Funding is not available to pay bills for non-essentials, finance liberty and vacations, pay fines or legal expenses, pay taxes, finance recreational boats or vehicles or help Navy and Marine Corps families live beyond their means.

Financial Data Funds are provided in the form of interest-free loans or grants.

Number awarded Varies each year.

Deadline Applications may be submitted at any time.

[1002]
NORTH DAKOTA VETERANS' AID LOANS

Department of Veterans Affairs
4201 38th Street S.W., Suite 104
P.O. Box 9003
Fargo, ND 58106-9003
(701) 239-7165   Toll Free: (866) 634-8387
Fax: (701) 239-7166
Web: www.nd.gov/veterans/benefits/loan.html

Summary To loan money to meet the emergency needs of North Dakota veterans and their unremarried surviving spouses.

Eligibility This program is open to North Dakota veterans who served in peacetime, wartime, or the National Guard with active duty and received other than a dishonorable discharge. Surviving spouses of deceased veterans are also eligible if they have not remarried. Applicants must be facing a temporary and unexpected financial emergency, including dental work, education expenses for the applicant or dependents, emergency eyeglasses, first-time home buyer improvements, medical care, repair bills (in certain cases), temporary unemployment, expenses related to purchase of a primary family residence, or waiting for relief or assistance from other agencies.

Financial Data Veterans and surviving spouses may borrow up to $5,000 at 8% interest. If the loan is repaid within 2 years, half of the interest is refunded.

Duration Loans may be granted for periods of 6 to 48 months.

Number awarded Varies each year.

Deadline Applications may be submitted at any time.

[1003]
OHIO HEROES PROGRAM

Ohio Housing Finance Agency
Attn: Office of Homeownership
57 East Main Street
Columbus, OH 43215
(614) 466-9920   Toll Free: (888) 362-6432
Fax: (614) 644-5393   TDD: (614) 466-1940
E-mail: twalker@ohiohome.org
Web: www.ohiohome.org/homebuyer/heroes.aspx

Summary To offer lower interest on loans for home purchases by military personnel, veterans, and other providers of public services in Ohio.

Eligibility This program is open to Ohio residents who are 1) active-duty military personnel, active Reservists, or honorably-discharged veterans of any branch of the U.S. armed forces; 2) fire fighters, emergency medical technicians, or paramedics; 3) health care workers (medical residents and fellows, dental hygienists, nurses, nursing assistants, pharmacists, pharmacy technicians, physician assistants, medical technicians, or therapists); 4) police officers; or 5) teachers (K-12 and higher education). Applicants must be first-time home buyers and able to meet housing price and income standards that depend on their county of residence, family size, and other variables.

Financial Data Qualifying home buyers are able to purchase their home at an interest rate that is 0.25% lower than comparable loans provided by the Ohio Housing Finance Agency. Currently, this rate is 4.75%.

Duration This is a 1-time benefit.

Number awarded Varies each year.

Deadline Applications may be submitted at any time.

[1004]
OREGON VETERANS HOME LOAN PROGRAM

Oregon Department of Veterans' Affairs
Attn: Veterans' Home Loan Program
700 Summer Street N.E., Suite 150
Salem, OR 97310-1285
(503) 373-2051   Toll Free: (888) ORE-VETS (within OR)
Fax: (503) 373-2393   TDD: (503) 373-2217
E-mail: orvetshomeloans@odva.state.or.us
Web: www.oregon.gov/ODVA/HOMELOANS

Summary To help Oregon veterans or their surviving spouses buy homes.

Eligibility This program is open to veterans who 1) served honorably on active duty for purposes other than training for not less than 210 consecutive days; 2) served honorably on active duty for less than 210 days but was discharged or released from active duty because of a service-connected injury or illness; or 3) served in a theater of operations for which a campaign or expeditionary ribbon or medal is authorized by the United States (including Grenada, Libya, Panama, Somalia, Haiti, El Salvador, the Persian Gulf, the Balkans, Kosovo, Afghanistan, or Iraq). Applicants must be Oregon residents at the time of application for the loan. Spouses to be eligible must be Oregon residents who have not remarried and whose spouse either died while on active duty or is listed as a prisoner of war or missing in action. The eligibility of a veteran ends 30 years after the last date of separation from service; the eligibility of a spouse expires 30 years after notification of the veteran's death, capture, or disappearance, or upon remarriage. Applicants must demonstrate sufficient income to make loan repayments and be good credit risks. Loans may be used only to finance owner-occupied, single-family residential housing for qualified eligible veterans or their spouses. The purchase of vacation homes, income properties (such as farms or rentals), commercial property, or bare land cannot be financed.

Financial Data Loans are made up to a current maximum of $417,000 and may be as much as 100% of appraised property value. The loan origination fee is 1.375%. Interest rates are fixed at 4.5% with a .125 discount charge to borrower or 4.625% with a .375 credit to borrower.

Duration The maximum loan term is 30 years and the minimum is 15 years.

Additional data Recipients must live on the property and use it as their primary home within 90 days after the loan has closed.

Number awarded Varies each year.

Deadline Applications may be submitted at any time.

[1005]
PATRIOT EXPRESS LOAN PROGRAM

Small Business Administration
Attn: Office of Veterans Business Development
409 Third Street, S.W.
Washington, DC 20416
(202) 205-6773   Toll Free: (800) U-ASK-SBA
Fax: (202) 205-7292   TDD: (704) 344-6640
E-mail: janet.moorman@sba.gov
Web: www.sba.gov/patriotexpress/index.html

Summary To provide business loan guarantees to veterans and members of the military community.

Eligibility This program is open to veterans, service-disabled veterans, active-duty servicemembers eligible for the military's Transition Assistance Program, Reservists and National Guard members, current spouses of any of those, and widowed spouses of servicemembers and veterans who died during service or of a service-connected disability. Applicants must be interested in borrowing money for business-related purposes, including start-up, expansion, equipment, inventory, or business-occupied real estate purchases.

Financial Data The maximum loan is $500,000. The Small Business Administration (SBA) guarantees up to 85% of loans of $150,000 and less and up to 75% of loans above $150,000. Interest rates are the lowest offered by the SBA, generally 2.25% to 4.75% over the Prime Rate.

Duration Maximum loan maturities are generally 7 years for working capital or 25 years for real estate and equipment.

Additional data This program began in 2007.

Number awarded Varies each year.

Deadline Loan applications may be submitted at any time.

[1006]
SAUL T. WILSON, JR. SCHOLARSHIP

Department of Agriculture
Animal and Plant Health Inspection Service
Attn: Human Resources/Recruitment
1400 Independence Avenue, S.W., Room 1710
Washington, DC 20250
(202) 690-4759
Web: www.aphis.usda.gov

Summary To provide scholarship/loans and work experience to undergraduate and graduate students (particularly veterans) who are interested in preparing for a career in veterinary medicine and biomedical sciences.

Eligibility This program is open to U.S. citizens enrolled in an accredited college or university in the United States as a full-time student. Undergraduates must have completed at least 2-years of a 4-year preveterinary medicine or other biomedical science program. Graduate students must have completed not more than 1 year of study in veterinary medicine. All applicants must submit a 500-word essay on why they should receive this scholarship and what contributions they would make to veterinary services of the Animal and Plant Health Inspection Service (APHIS). Preference is given to veterans of the U.S. armed forces. Financial need is not considered in the selection process.

Financial Data The maximum stipend is $5,000 per year for undergraduates or $10,000 per year for graduate students. Funds must be used for tuition, books, tutors, and laboratory fees. During summers and school breaks, scholars receive paid employment as a veterinary student trainee with APHIS at a salary that ranges from $9 to $13 per hour, depending on the student's qualifications. After 640 hours of study-related work with APHIS in the career experience program and graduation with a D.V.M. degree, and at the option of APHIS, the student must become a full-time employee for at least 1 calendar year for each school year of support from this scholarship. If scholarship recipients refuse to accept an APHIS offer of employment, they must reimburse the agency for all financial assistance received. If recipients fail to serve the entire length of the mandatory APHIS employment period, they must reimburse APHIS a prorated share of scholarship funds used.

Duration 1 year; may be renewed.

Number awarded 1 or more each year.

Deadline February of each year.

[1007]
SPECIALLY ADAPTED HOUSING GRANTS

Department of Veterans Affairs
Attn: Specially Adapted Housing
810 Vermont Avenue, N.W.
Washington, DC 20420
(202) 461-9546   Toll Free: (800) 827-1000
Web: www.homeloans.va.gov/sah.htm

Summary To provide loans, grants, and loan guaranties to certain disabled veterans and servicemembers for a home specially adapted to their needs.

Eligibility These grants are available to veterans and servicemembers who are entitled to compensation for permanent and total service-connected disability due to: 1) the loss or loss of use of both lower extremities, such as to preclude locomotion without the aid of braces, crutches, canes, or a wheelchair; or 2) blindness in both eyes, having only light perception, plus loss or loss of use of 1 lower extremity; or 3) a loss or loss of use of 1 lower extremity together with residuals of organic disease or injury or the loss or loss of use of 1 upper extremity, such as to preclude locomotion without resort to braces, canes, crutches, or a wheelchair. Applicants must be planning to 1) construct a home on land to be acquired for that purpose; 2) build a home on land already owned if it is suitable for specially adapted housing; 3) remodel an existing home if it can be made suitable for specially adapted housing, or 4) apply funds against the unpaid principle mortgage balance of a specially adapted home that has already been acquired.

Financial Data The U.S. Department of Veterans Affairs (VA) may approve a grant of not more than 50% of the cost of building, buying, or remodeling homes for eligible veterans, or paying indebtedness of such homes already acquired, up to a maximum grant of $63,780. Eligible veterans with available loan guarantee entitlements may also obtain a guaranteed loan from the VA to supplement the grant to acquire a specially adapted home. If private financing is not available, VA may make a direct loan up to $33,000 to cover the difference between the total cost of the home and the grant.

Duration This is a 1-time grant, guaranteed loan, or direct loan.

Additional data Veterans who receive a specially adapted housing grant may be eligible for Veterans Mortgage Life Insurance.

Number awarded Varies each year.

Deadline Applications are accepted at any time.

[1008]
TEXAS VETERANS HOME IMPROVEMENT PROGRAM

Texas Veterans Land Board
Stephen F. Austin Building
1700 North Congress Avenue, Room 800
P.O. Box 12873
Austin, TX 78711-2873
(512) 463-5060   Toll Free: (800) 252-VETS (within TX)
TDD: (512) 463-6367   E-mail: vlbinfo@glo.state.tx.us
Web: www.glo.state.tx.us/vlb/vhip/index.html

Summary To assist Texas veterans, National Guard members, and unremarried surviving spouses who wish to maintain older homes but who cannot qualify for the high interest rates of conventional home improvement loans.

Eligibility This program is open to 1) veterans who served for at least 90 consecutive days of active duty after September 16, 1940 in the Army, Navy, Air Force, Marines, Coast Guard, U.S. Public Health Service, or a Reserve component of those services; 2) members of the Texas National Guard or Reserves who have enlisted or received an appointment and have completed all Initial Active Duty for Training (IADT) requirements; and 3) veterans who served in the armed forces of the Republic of Vietnam (ARVN) between February 28, 1961 and May 7, 1975. Applicants may not have been dishonorably discharged and must have listed Texas as their home of record at the time of entry into the military or have been a resident of Texas for at least 1 year prior to filing an application. The unremarried surviving spouses of Texas veterans who are missing in action, died in the line of duty, or died from a service-connected cause may be eligible to participate in the program. Applicants must be interested in making alterations, repairs, and improvements to, or in connection with, their existing residence if, and only if, repairs will 1) substantially protect or improve the basic livability or energy efficiency of the property; 2) correct damage resulting from a natural disaster; or 3) correct conditions that are hazardous to health or safety. Examples of eligible improvements include carpeting, fencing, room additions, patios, driveways, and garages. Examples of ineligible improvements include exterior spas, saunas, whirlpools, tree surgery, ten-

nis courts, swimming pools, and barbecue pits. The home must be in Texas and the veteran's primary residence. In addition to single family dwellings, condominiums, duplexes, triplexes, and fourplexes are eligible as long as 1 of the units is the veteran's primary residence. Duplexes, triplexes, and fourplexes must be at least 5 years old. Modular or manufactured homes that are on a permanent foundation and are a part of the real estate may also be eligible. An interest rate reduction is available to Texas veterans who have a service-connected disability of 30% or greater as verified by the U.S. Department of Veterans Affairs.

Financial Data The maximum loan on a single family residence or a manufactured or modular home is $25,000. The maximum loan on a multi-family residence is $12,000 per dwelling unit or $25,000, whichever is less. Loans over $10,000 are for 2 to 20 years; those for $10,000 or less are for 2 to 10 years. Interest rates recently were 4.89%. An interest rate reduction of 0.50 percentage points is available for the Veterans with Disabilities program.

Number awarded Varies each year.

Deadline Applications may be submitted at any time.

[1009]
TEXAS VETERANS HOUSING ASSISTANCE PROGRAM

Texas Veterans Land Board
Stephen F. Austin Building
1700 North Congress Avenue, Room 800
P.O. Box 12873
Austin, TX 78711-2873
(512) 463-5060   Toll Free: (800) 252-VETS (within TX)
TDD: (512) 463-5330   E-mail: vlbinfo@glo.state.tx.us
Web: www.glo.state.tx.us/vlb/vhap/index.html

Summary To provide low-interest loans to assist Texas veterans, National Guard members, and unremarried surviving spouses in purchasing their own homes.

Eligibility This program is open to 1) veterans who served for at least 90 consecutive days of active duty after September 16, 1940 in the Army, Navy, Air Force, Marines, Coast Guard, U.S. Public Health Service, or a Reserve component of those services; 2) members of the Texas National Guard or Reserves who have enlisted or received an appointment and have completed all Initial Active Duty for Training (IADT) requirements; and 3) veterans who served in the armed forces of the Republic of Vietnam (ARVN) between February 28, 1961 and May 7, 1975. Applicants may not have been dishonorably discharged and must have listed Texas as their home of record at the time of entry into the military or have been a resident of Texas for at least 1 year prior to filing an application. The unremarried surviving spouses of Texas veterans who are missing in action, died in the line of duty, or died from a service-connected cause may be eligible to participate in the program. Applicants must be interested in purchasing a new or existing home, including a duplex, triplex, or fourplex if the structure is more than 5 years old, or a modular or manufactured home if it is on a permanent foundation and meets loan guidelines established by the Federal National Mortgage Association or the Federal Home Loan Mortgage Corporation and has an economic life of at least 30 years. Any home purchased with funds from this program must be the primary residence of the veteran for at least 3 years. An interest rate reduction is available to Texas veterans who have a service-connected disability of 30% or greater as verified by the U.S. Department of Veterans Affairs.

Financial Data There is no limit on the sales price of the house, but the maximum loan available through this program is $325,000. Loans for $45,000 or less may be requested directly from the Texas Veterans Land Board (VLB) and may cover up to 85% of the home's appraised value. Loans over $45,000 are originated through a VLB participating lender. No fees are charged on direct loans; loans available through a VLB-approved lender require an origination fee up to 1% and a participation fee up to

1%. Interest rates recently were 4.89%. An interest rate reduction of 0.50 percentage points is available for the Veterans with Disabilities program.

Duration Loans are available with 15, 20, 25, or 30 year terms.

Number awarded Varies each year.

Deadline Applications may be submitted at any time.

[1010]
TEXAS VETERANS LAND PROGRAM

Texas Veterans Land Board
Stephen F. Austin Building
1700 North Congress Avenue, Room 800
P.O. Box 12873
Austin, TX 78711-2873
(512) 463-5060   Toll Free: (800) 252-VETS (within TX)
TDD: (512) 463-5330   E-mail: vlbinfo@glo.state.tx.us
Web: www.glo.state.tx.us/vlb/land/index.html

Summary To assist Texas veterans, National Guard members, and unremarried surviving spouses interested in purchasing land in Texas.

Eligibility This program is open to 1) veterans who served for at least 90 consecutive days of active duty after September 16, 1940 in the Army, Navy, Air Force, Marines, Coast Guard, U.S. Public Health Service, or a Reserve component of those services; 2) members of the Texas National Guard or Reserves who have enlisted or received an appointment and have completed all Initial Active Duty for Training (IADT) requirements. Applicants may not have been dishonorably discharged and must have listed Texas as their home of record at the time of entry into the military or have been a resident of Texas for at least 1 year prior to filing an application. The unremarried surviving spouses of Texas veterans who are missing in action, died in the line of duty, or died from a service-connected cause may be eligible to participate in the program. Applicants must be interested in purchasing up to 1 acre of land within Texas. It must have legal access to a public road, and such right-of-way must be the minimum width required by the county commissioners. Land must be officially surveyed and appraised.

Financial Data The maximum loan is $80,000. The veteran must pay a 5% down payment. If the purchase price is greater than $80,000, the veteran must pay the difference to the VLB in cash. The VLB then purchases the land directly from the seller and resells the land to the veteran using a 30-year contract of sale and purchase. In addition to the down payment, the veteran must pay a closing fee of $325. The interest rate recently was 7.25%.

Number awarded Varies each year.

Deadline Applications may be submitted at any time.

[1011]
VA HOME LOAN GUARANTY BENEFITS

Department of Veterans Affairs
Attn: Veterans Benefits Administration
Home Loan Guaranty Service
810 Vermont Avenue, N.W.
Washington, DC 20420
(202) 418-4343   Toll Free: (800) 827-1000
Web: www.homeloans.va.gov/veteran.htm

Summary To assist disabled and other veterans, certain military personnel, and their unremarried surviving spouses in the purchase of residences.

Eligibility This benefit is available to 1) veterans who served during specified periods of time and were discharged since September 16, 1940 under other than dishonorable conditions; 2) military personnel who have served at least 90 days; 3) members of the Reserves or National Guard who have completed at least 6 years of honorable service or were discharged because of a service-related disability; 4) unremarried spouses of veterans or Reservists who died on active duty or as a result of service-connected causes; 5) surviving spouses who remarry after attaining 57 years of age; 6) spouses of active-duty servicemembers who have been missing in action or a prisoner of war for at least 90 days; 7) U.S. citizens who served in the armed forces of a U.S. ally in World War II; and 8) members of organizations with recognized contributions to the U.S. World War II effort.

Financial Data The Department of Veterans Affairs (VA) does not lend money; the actual loan must come from a commercial lender. The loan may be for any amount, and the VA will guarantee payment on loans for the purchase of homes, farm homes, condominium units, or refinancing of existing loans. The largest guaranty that the VA can give is an amount equal to 25% of the Freddie Mac conforming loan limit for single family residences (currently $417,000 or $625,500 for Hawaii, Alaska, Guam and the Virgin Islands). Interest rates vary with market conditions but are fixed for the life of the loan, which may be as long as 30 years and 32 days. No down payments are prescribed by the VA. A funding fee must be paid to the VA, although it may be included in the loan amount; the amount of the fee varies, depending on the type of loan and whether the borrower is a veteran or a Reservist, but ranges from 0.5% to 3.3% of the amount of the loan. The funding fee is waived for disabled veterans and unremarried surviving spouses of veterans who died as a result of service.

Additional data In addition to the purchase of a new home, VA Loans may be used to buy a residential condominium; to build a home; to repair, alter, or improve a home; to refinance an existing home loan; to buy a manufactured home with or without a lot; to buy and improve a manufactured home lot; to install a solar heating and/or cooling system or other weatherization improvements; to purchase and improve simultaneously a home with energy conserving measures; to refinance an existing VA loan to reduce the interest rate; or to refinance a manufactured home loan to acquire a lot. Mortgages guaranteed by the VA usually offer an interest rate lower than conventional mortgage rates, require no down payment, provide a long repayment period, allow the VA to appraise the property and inspect it to ensure that it conforms to the plans and specifications, and permit early prepayment without premium or penalty. The VA does not have legal authority to act as an architect, supervise construction of the home, guarantee that the home is free of defects, or act as an attorney if the veteran encounters legal difficulties in buying or constructing a home. Veterans must certify that they intend to live in the home they are buying or building with a VA loan. Veterans who wish to refinance or improve a home must certify that they are actually in residence at the time of application.

Number awarded Varies each year.

Deadline Applications may be submitted at any time.

[1012]
VOCATIONAL AND TECHNICAL TRAINING STUDENT LOAN PROGRAM

Coast Guard Mutual Assistance
4200 Wilson Boulevard, Suite 610
Arlington, VA 20598-7180
(202) 493-6624   Toll Free: (800) 881-2462
Fax: (202) 493-6686   E-mail: ARL-DG-CGMA@uscg.mil
Web: www.cgmahq.org

Summary To provide loans to the members of Coast Guard Mutual Assistance (CGMA) and their spouses and dependent children who require assistance for vocational or technical training.

Eligibility This program is open to members of the organization, their spouses, and dependent children. Applicants should be seeking assistance to help pay the costs of non-college courses that provide the technical knowledge and skills needed for entry into a specific career field. Financial need must be demonstrated.

Financial Data The maximum loan is $1,500.

Additional data CGMA membership is open to active-duty and retired members of the U.S. Coast Guard, civilian employees of the U.S. Coast Guard, U.S. Coast Guard Reserve members, U.S.

Coast Guard Auxiliary members, Public Health Service officers serving with the U.S. Coast Guard, and family members of all of those.

Number awarded　Varies each year.

Deadline　Requests must be submitted within 30 days after the course begins.

[1013]
WISCONSIN HOME IMPROVEMENT LOAN PROGRAM

Wisconsin Department of Veterans Affairs
30 West Mifflin Street
P.O. Box 7843
Madison, WI 53707-7843
(608) 266-1311　　　　　　　Toll Free: (800) WIS-VETS
Fax: (608) 267-0403　　　　　E-mail: loans@dva.state.wi.us
Web: www.dva.state.wi.us/Ben_improvementloans.asp

Summary　To provide low-interest loans to veterans, current National Guard members, Reservists, and their families in Wisconsin to pay for improvements to their homes.

Eligibility　This program is open to current residents of Wisconsin who 1) were residents of the state when they entered or reentered active duty in the U.S. armed forces, or 2) have moved to the state and have been residents for any consecutive 12-month period after entry or reentry into service. Applicants must have served on active duty for at least 2 continuous years or for at least 90 days during specified wartime periods. Also eligible are 1) members and former members of the National Guard and Reserves who have completed at least 6 years of continuous service under honorable conditions; 2) unremarried spouses of deceased veterans; and 3) dependent children under 26 years of age who are attending school full time. Applicants may be planning to use the loan funds for additions, construction, repairs, or alterations of their principal residence. The loan also may be used for garage construction. The applicant must have at least 10% equity in the property to be improved.

Financial Data　Loans up to $50,000 are available if secured by an 80% loan to value mortgage, up to $25,000 if secured by a 90% loan to value mortgage, or up to $3,000 if secured with a guarantor. Currently, for loans secured by a mortgage at 80% loan to value, interest rates are 5.85% for 5-year loans, 6.25% for 7- or 10-year loans, or 6.55% for 15-year loans. For loans secured by a mortgage at 90% loan to value, interest rates are 6.75% for 5-year loans, 7% for 7- or 10-year loans, or 7.25% for 15-year loans. For guarantor secured loans, interest rates are 8.5% for 3-year loans or 10% for 5-year loans. Funds may be used only for qualifying home improvements, not for personal property (such as furniture or certain types of appliances).

Duration　The minimum loan repayment term is 1 year and the maximum term is 15 years.

Number awarded　Varies each year.

Deadline　Applications may be submitted at any time.

[1014]
WISCONSIN VETERANS' PERSONAL LOAN PROGRAM

Wisconsin Department of Veterans Affairs
30 West Mifflin Street
P.O. Box 7843
Madison, WI 53707-7843
(608) 266-1311　　　　　　　Toll Free: (800) WIS-VETS
Fax: (608) 267-0403　　　　　E-mail: loans@dva.state.wi.us
Web: www.dva.state.wi.us/Ben_personalloans.asp

Summary　To provide eligible Wisconsin veterans or their dependents with loans for any purpose, including education.

Eligibility　This program is open to current residents of Wisconsin who 1) were residents of the state when they entered or reentered active duty in the U.S. armed forces, or 2) have moved to the

state and have been residents for any consecutive 12-month period after entry or reentry into service. Applicants must have served on active duty for at least 2 continuous years or for at least 90 days during specified wartime periods. Also eligible are unremarried spouses of deceased veterans and dependent children (adult children must be under 26 years of age and attending school full time). A remarried spouse or parent of a veterans' child may qualify if the loan is used for the child's education. Applicants may borrow money for any purpose. They must meet basic credit and underwriting standards. Loans must be secured by a mortgage on the applicant's property or with a guarantor.

Financial Data　This program provides loans up to $25,000 if secured by a mortgage or up to $5,000 if a guarantor secured loan. For loans secured by a mortgage at 80% loan to value, interest rates are 5.85% for 5-year loans or 6.25% for 7- or 10-year loans. For loans secured by a mortgage at 90% loan to value, interest rates are 6.75% for 5-year loans or 7% for 7- or 10-year loans. For guarantor secured loans, interest rates are 8.5% for 3-year loans or 10% for 5-year loans.

Number awarded　Varies each year.

Deadline　Applications may be submitted at any time.

[1015]
WISCONSIN VETERANS PRIMARY MORTGAGE LOAN PROGRAM

Wisconsin Department of Veterans Affairs
30 West Mifflin Street
P.O. Box 7843
Madison, WI 53707-7843
(608) 266-1311　　　　　　　Toll Free: (800) WIS-VETS
Fax: (608) 267-0403　　　　　E-mail: loans@dva.state.wi.us
Web: www.dva.state.wi.us/Ben_mortgageloans.asp

Summary　To provide housing loans to Wisconsin veterans, current National Guard members, Reservists, and their unremarried spouses or children who cannot obtain the necessary funds from other sources.

Eligibility　This program is open to current residents of Wisconsin who 1) were residents of the state when they entered or reentered active duty in the U.S. armed forces, or 2) have moved to the state and have been residents for any consecutive 12-month period after entry or reentry into service. Applicants must have served on active duty for at least 2 continuous years or for at least 90 days during specified wartime periods. Also eligible are 1) dependent children and unremarried surviving spouses of eligible deceased veterans; and 2) members and former members of the National Guard and Reserves who have completed 6 years of continuous service under honorable conditions. Applicants must be seeking to borrow money for the purchase, or the purchase and improvement, of a single family home or condominium; construction of a new single family home; purchase of certain existing 2- to 4-unit owner occupied residences; or refinance of the balance due on existing mortgage loans used for purchase, construction, or improvement of a residence.

Financial Data　The veteran or dependent may obtain a loan of up to 95% of the total cost of the property, to a maximum of $343,750. The required down payment is 5% and the department pays the loan origination fees for veterans with a disability rating of 30% or more. Other attractive features include: no private mortgage insurance or loan guaranty, no discount points, no interest rate increase, and no prepayment penalty. The current interest rate is 6.25%.

Duration　Loan terms up to 30 years are available.

Number awarded　Varies each year.

Deadline　Applications may be submitted at any time.

Military Personnel

[1016]
AAAA LOAN PROGRAM

Army Aviation Association of America
Attn: AAAA Scholarship Foundation
755 Main Street, Suite 4D
Monroe, CT 06468-2830
(203) 268-2450   Fax: (203) 268-5870
E-mail: Scholarship@quad-a.org
Web: www.quad-a.org/scholarship.htm

Summary To provide educational loans to members of the Army Aviation Association of America (AAAA) and their relatives.

Eligibility This program is open to AAAA members and their spouses, unmarried siblings, and unmarried children. Applicants must be enrolled or accepted for enrollment as an undergraduate or graduate student at an accredited college or university.

Financial Data The maximum loan is $1,000 per year. All loans are interest free.

Duration Up to 4 years.

Number awarded Varies each year; recently, 10 of these loans were granted.

Deadline April of each year.

[1017]
AER LOANS/GRANTS

Army Emergency Relief
200 Stovall Street
Alexandria, VA 22332-0600
(703) 428-0000   Toll Free: (866) 878-6378
Fax: (703) 325-7183   E-mail: aer@aerhq.org
Web: www.aerhq.org

Summary To provide loans and grants-in-aid to help with the emergency financial needs of Army veterans, military personnel, and their dependents.

Eligibility Eligible to apply are active-duty soldiers (single or married) and their dependents, Army National Guard and Army Reserve soldiers on continuous active duty for more than 30 days and their dependents, soldiers retired from active duty for longevity or physical disability and their dependents, Army National Guard and Army Reserve soldiers who retired at age 60 and their dependents, and surviving spouses and orphans of soldiers who died while on active duty or after they retired. Applicants must be seeking assistance for such emergency needs as food, rent, and utilities; emergency transportation and vehicle repair; funeral expenses; medical and dental expenses; or personal needs when pay is delayed or stolen. Support is not available to help pay for nonessentials, finance ordinary leave or vacation, pay fines or legal expenses, help liquidate or consolidate debt, assist with house purchase or home improvements, cover bad checks, pay credit card bills, or help purchase, rent, or lease a vehicle.

Financial Data Support is provided in the form of loans or grants (or a combination).

Duration Qualifying individuals can apply whenever they have a valid emergency need.

Additional data This organization was established in 1942.

Number awarded Varies each year; recently, the organization helped more than 66,000 Army people with more than $70 million, including $60 million to 58,820 active-duty soldiers and their families, $7.3 million to 4,914 retired soldiers and their families, and $2.7 million to 2,304 widow(er)s and orphans of deceased soldiers. Since it was established, the organization has helped more than 3.2 million qualifying individuals with more than $1.2 billion in financial assistance.

Deadline Applications may be submitted at any time.

[1018]
AFAS FINANCIAL ASSISTANCE

Air Force Aid Society
Attn: Financial Assistance Department
241 18th Street South, Suite 202
Arlington, VA 22202-3409
(703) 607-3072, ext. 51   Toll Free: (800) 429-9475
Fax: (703) 607-3022
Web: www.afas.org/Assistance/HowWeCanHelp.cfm

Summary To provide loans and grants-in-aid to current and former Air Force personnel and their families who are facing emergency situations.

Eligibility This program is open to active-duty Air Force members and their dependents, retired Air Force personnel and their dependents, Air National Guard and Air Force Reserve personnel on extended duty over 15 days, and spouses and dependent children of deceased Air Force personnel who died on active duty or in retired status. Applicants must be facing problems, usually for relatively short periods, that affect their job or the essential quality and dignity of life the Air Force wants for its people. Examples of such needs include basic living expenses (food, rent, utilities), medical and dental care, funeral expenses, vehicle expenses, emergency travel, moving expenses, or child or respite care. Funding is generally not provided if it merely postpones a long-term inability to exist on present pay and allowances, for nonessentials, for continuing long-term assistance commitments, or to replace funds lost due to garnishment.

Financial Data Assistance is provided as an interest-free loan, a grant, or a combination of both.

Number awarded Varies each year.

Deadline Applications may be submitted at any time.

[1019]
AIR FORCE ACTIVE DUTY HEALTH PROFESSIONS LOAN REPAYMENT PROGRAM

U.S. Air Force
Attn: Air Force Institute of Technology
2950 Hobson Way
Wright-Patterson AFB, OH 45433-7765
(937) 255-5824, ext. 3015
Toll Free: (800) 543-3490, ext. 3015
Fax: (937) 255-4712   E-mail: enem.adhplrp@afit.edu
Web: www.afit.edu/adhplrp

Summary To repay the educational loans of Air Force officers serving in the health professions.

Eligibility This program is open to 1) commissioned Air Force officers qualified for or holding a position in a health profession; 2) full-time students enrolled in the final year of a course of study at an accredited educational institution leading to a degree in a health profession other than medicine or osteopathic medicine; and 3) students enrolled in the final year of an approved graduate program leading to specialty qualification in medicine, dentistry, osteopathic medicine, or other health profession. Applicants may not have received full support from the Air Force Health Professions Scholarship Program. They must have incurred government or commercial loans for actual costs paid for tuition, reasonable educational expenses, and reasonable living expenses relating to the attainment of a degree in the designated health care discipline.

Financial Data The maximum annual payment is $40,000 per year.

Duration Up to 4 years.

Additional data Participants in this program incur an active-duty obligation of 2 years (3 years for physicians) or 1 year for each annual payment, whichever is greater.

Number awarded Varies each year; recently, the program provided support for 114 nurses, 10 physicians, 32 dentists, 10 psychologists, and 10 public health officers.

Deadline January of each year.

[1020]
AIR FORCE COLLEGE LOAN REPAYMENT PROGRAM

U.S. Air Force
Attn: Air Force Personnel Center
Headquarters USAF/DPPAT
550 C Street West, Suite 10
Randolph AFB, TX 78150-4712
Fax: (210) 565-2328
Web: www.airforce.com/opportunities/enlisted/education

Summary To provide an opportunity for individuals to repay their federally-insured student loans by serving in the Air Force.

Eligibility This program is open to non-prior service Air Force enlistees who utilized any of the following loans to help pay for their college education: Auxiliary Loan Assistance for Students (ALAS), Parent Loans for Undergraduate Students (PLUS), Supplemental Loans for Students (SLS), Stafford Loans, Perkins Loans, William D. Ford Loans, or Consolidated Loans. Private loans, equity loans, state-funded loans, institution loans, and consolidated loans for someone else do not qualify. Enlistees for the Air National Guard are also eligible if they qualify for specific shortage AFSCs.

Financial Data Recipients have their indebtedness reduced by one third or $1,500, whichever amount is greater, for each year of active-duty service. The maximum amount payable under this program is $10,000 for active-duty enlistees or $20,000 for Air National Guard enlistees who qualify.

Duration To qualify for this program, individuals must enlist for 4 years on active duty or 6 years in the Air National Guard.

Additional data Loans that are in default cannot qualify for this program.

Number awarded Varies each year.

Deadline Deadline not specified.

[1021]
ARIZONA NATIONAL GUARD EMERGENCY RELIEF FUND GRANTS

Arizona National Guard Emergency Relief Fund
Attn: Fund Administrator
5636 East McDowell Road
Phoenix, AZ 85008
(602) 267-2731   E-mail: danielle.salomon@azdema.gov
Web: www.aerfund.org

Summary To provide emergency assistance (loans and grants) to members of the Arizona National Guard and their families.

Eligibility This program is open to members of the Arizona Army and Air National Guard who have not been mobilized under Presidential Order. Surviving spouses, children, and orphans of soldiers who died while on active duty are also eligible. Applicants must be seeking assistance for such emergency needs as delay in receiving pay or reimbursement from the government; temporary shelter, lodging, or rent; emergency utility assistance; emergency transportation and vehicle repair; costs incurred for emergency travel due to death of immediate family member; or any other special circumstance deemed appropriate by the fund's directors. Support is not provided to help pay for nonessentials, finance ordinary leave or vacation, pay fines or legal expenses, assist with home purchase or improvements, cover bad checks, or help purchase, rent, or lease a vehicle.

Financial Data Most support is provided in the form of interest-free loans, although outright grants are also available.

Duration These are 1-time grants.

Number awarded Varies each year.

Deadline Applications may be submitted at any time.

[1022]
ARIZONA NATIONAL GUARD FAMILY ASSISTANCE FUND

Arizona National Guard Emergency Relief Fund
Attn: Fund Administrator
5636 East McDowell Road
Phoenix, AZ 85008
(602) 267-2731   E-mail: danielle.salomon@azdema.gov
Web: www.aerfund.org

Summary To provide emergency assistance (loans and grants) to members of the Arizona Reserve Component who have been mobilized and their families.

Eligibility This program is open to members of the Arizona Reserve Component (including the Army and Air National Guard and Reserve units of all 5 branches of service) and their dependents. They must have been mobilized under Presidential Order. Surviving spouses, children, and orphans of soldiers who died while on active duty are also eligible. Applicants must be seeking assistance for such emergency needs as delay in receiving pay or reimbursement from the government; temporary shelter, lodging, or rent; emergency utility assistance; emergency transportation and vehicle repair; costs incurred for emergency travel due to death of immediate family member; or any other special circumstance deemed appropriate by the fund's directors. Support is not provided to help pay for nonessentials, financial ordinary leave or vacation, pay fines or legal expenses, assist with home purchase or improvements, cover bad checks, or help purchase, rent, or lease a vehicle.

Financial Data Most support is provided in the form of interest-free loans, although outright grants are also available.

Duration These are awarded on a 1-time basis.

Number awarded Varies each year.

Deadline Applications may be submitted at any time.

[1023]
ARMY COLLEGE LOAN REPAYMENT PROGRAM

U.S. Army
Human Resources Command
AHRC-PDE-EI
Attn: Education Incentives and Counseling Branch
200 Stovall Street, Suite 3N17
Alexandria, VA 22332-0472
(703) 325-0285   Toll Free: (800) 872-8272
Fax: (703) 325-6599   E-mail: pdeei@hoffman.army.mil
Web: www.goarmy.com/benefits/education_money.jsp

Summary To provide an opportunity for individuals to repay their federally-insured student loans by serving in the Army.

Eligibility This program is open to Army enlistees who utilized any of the following loans to help pay for their college education: Auxiliary Loan Assistance for Students (ALAS), Parent Loans for Undergraduate Students (PLUS), Supplemental Loans for Students (SLS), Stafford Loans, Perkins Loans, William D. Ford Loans, or Consolidated Loans. Private loans, equity loans, state-funded loans, institution loans, and consolidated loans for someone else do not qualify. Applicants must have an Armed Forces Qualification Test score of 50 or higher and must enlist in a critical military occupational specialty.

Financial Data Recipients have their indebtedness reduced by one third or $1,500, whichever amount is greater, for each year of active-duty service. The maximum amount payable under this program is $65,000 for active-duty personnel or $40,000 for Reservists and National Guard members.

Duration To qualify for this program, individuals must enlist for 3 years of active duty or 6 years in the Reserves or National Guard.

Additional data Loans that are in default cannot qualify for this program.

Number awarded Varies each year.

Deadline Deadline not specified.

[1024]
ARMY HEALTH PROFESSIONS LOAN REPAYMENT PROGRAM

U.S. Army
Human Resources Command, Health Services Division
Attn: AHRC-OPH-AN
200 Stovall Street, Room 9N47
Alexandria, VA 22332-0417
(703) 325-2330 Toll Free: (800) USA-ARMY
Fax: (703) 325-2358
Web: www.goarmy.com/amedd/benefits.jsp

Summary To repay the educational loans of health professionals who are willing to serve in the Army on active duty or in the Army Reserve.

Eligibility This program is open to fully-qualified health care professionals, full-time students in the final year of a course of study, and trainees in the final year of an approved graduate program leading to specialty qualification in a designated health care skill. Applicants must have qualified government and commercial loans for actual costs paid for tuition, reasonable educational expenses, and reasonable living expenses relating to the attainment of a degree in the designated health care discipline. Eligible health care professions are determined annually by the Secretary of Defense. U.S. citizenship is required.

Financial Data Health care professionals who serve on active duty are entitled to reimbursement of educational loans up to amounts that vary; recently, the maximum was $40,000 per year. Health care professionals who serve in the Army Reserve are entitled to reimbursement of a total of $50,000 in loans, payable at the rate of $20,000 for the first year, $20,000 for the second year, and $10,000 for the third year.

Duration Up to 3 years of active-duty service or 3 years in the Reserves.

Additional data This program was established in 1998. Recently, this program was available to physicians, dentists, nurses, veterinarians, and pharmacists serving on active duty and to physicians, dentists (general, comprehensive, prosthodontists, and oral surgeons), nurses (community/public health, critical care, medical-surgical, perioperative, and nurse anesthetists), veterinarians, clinical psychologists, entomologists, microbiologists, clinical laboratory professionals, nuclear medicine specialists, and optometrists serving in the Reserves. Participants incur a service obligation of 1 year for each year of loan reimbursement.

Number awarded Varies each year.

Deadline Applications may be submitted at any time.

[1025]
CALVET LOAN PROGRAM

California Department of Veterans Affairs
Attn: Division of Farm and Home Purchases
1227 O Street, Room 200
P.O. Box 942895
Sacramento, CA 94295-0001
(916) 653-2525 Toll Free: (800) 952-LOAN (within CA)
Fax: (916) 653-2401 TDD: (800) 324-5966
E-mail: Kenn.Capps@cdva.ca.gov
Web: www.cdva.ca.gov/CalVetLoans/BestLoan.aspx

Summary To provide low-cost and low-interest financing to California servicemembers and veterans who are interested in purchasing homes, farms, or mobile homes for use as their primary residence.

Eligibility This program is open to veterans and active-duty servicemembers who are currently residents of California,

regardless of where they were born or where they resided when they entered active military service. Applicants must have been released or discharged from active duty under honorable conditions or be currently serving on active duty. They must have served at least 90 days on active duty unless 1) discharged sooner due to service-connected disability, 2) eligible to receive a U.S. campaign or expeditionary medal, or 3) called to active duty from the Reserve or National Guard due to Presidential Order. Members of the California National Guard and the U.S. military Reserves who have served at least 1 year of a 6-year obligation are also eligible if they qualify as first-time home buyers or purchase homes in designated "target areas;" they must meet additional income and purchase price limitations. For loans guaranteed by the U.S. Department of Veterans Affairs (CalVet/VA), applicants must be veterans who served on active duty prior to January 1, 1977, who apply within 30 years from their release from active duty, and who served at least 1 day during a specified war period. Loans guaranteed by other means (CalVet97 and CalVeT80/20) are available to veterans who qualify as first-time home buyers, including those whose entire active-duty service was during peacetime. Veterans who do not qualify for the guaranteed-loan programs may be eligible for the unrestricted bond program, but they must meet the wartime service requirement.

Financial Data The maximum loan on single family homes (including condominiums, townhouses, and mobile homes affixed to land owned by the borrower) is currently $521,250; the maximum purchase price of farmland is $625,500; on mobile homes in approved mobile home parks, it is $175,000. Down payment requirements are 0% for the CalVet/VA program, 3% for the CalVet97 program, or 20% for the CalVeT80/20 program. The funding fee ranges from 1.25% to 3.35% but it may be waived for veterans with disability ratings of 10% or higher. The loan origination fee is 1% of the loan amount. Interest rates recently were 6.2% for CalVet/VA loans, 5.95% for CalVet97 loans, or 5.75% for CalVeT80/20 loans.

Duration Loans are typically for 30 years, although shorter periods are available.

Additional data Veteran contract purchasers who move from the CalVet financed property may qualify to have their CalVet loan transferred to another property or may qualify for a second loan contract. Loans that have been repaid or assigned to an ex-spouse in a divorce action may be obtained again. Information on current purchase price and family income limitations for revenue bond loans is available from the Department of Veterans Affairs state headquarters or local district sales offices. The veteran or a member of the veteran's immediate family must occupy the property within 60 days after signing a CalVet loan contract and must continue to reside on the property as the principal place of residence until the loan is paid in full. Acceptance of a bonus or benefit from another state for the qualifying period of military service disqualifies the veteran from CalVet benefits.

Number awarded Varies each year.

Deadline Applications may be submitted at any time.

[1026]
DEPARTMENT OF THE NAVY STUDENT LOAN REPAYMENT PROGRAM

U.S. Navy
Attn: Navy Recruiting Command
5720 Integrity Drive, Building 784
Millington, TN 38054
(901) 874-9345 Fax: (901) 874-9327
E-mail: CNRC_LRP-EB@navy.mil
Web: www.crnc.navy.mil/EIncentives/NCF_LRP.htm

Summary To repay the educational loans of college students who enlist in the Navy.

Eligibility This program is open to recent college graduates who have outstanding federally-insured student loans made by education institutions or banks and other private lenders. Applicants must enlist in the active-duty Navy. The loan may not be in default and it must be the applicant's first enlistment.

Financial Data　Up to $65,000 of qualified loans may be repaid.

Duration　This is a 1-time benefit.

Number awarded　Varies each year.

Deadline　Applications may be submitted at any time.

[1027]
FEDERAL PERKINS LOANS

Department of Education
Attn: Federal Student Aid Information Center
P.O. Box 84
Washington, DC 20044-0084
(319) 337-5665　　　　　　　　Toll Free: (800) 4-FED-AID
TDD: (800) 730-8913
Web: www.FederalStudentAid.ed.gov

Summary　To provide loans for college or graduate school to students in the United States who demonstrate exceptional financial need.

Eligibility　Applicants must be U.S. citizens or eligible non-citizens who have at least a high school diploma or GED certificate, are registered with the Selective Service if required, are enrolled as regular students working toward a degree or certificate in an eligible program, and have a valid Social Security number. Financial need as calculated by federal formulas must be demonstrated.

Financial Data　Undergraduate students may borrow up to $5,500 per year, to a maximum of $27,500; graduate and professional school students may borrow up to $8,000 per year, to a maximum of $60,000 (including any Federal Perkins Loans borrowed as an undergraduate). The interest rate is 5%. The monthly repayment amount depends on the size of the debt and the length of the repayment period (which may not exceed 10 years). Cancellation of 100% of the loan is provided if the borrower becomes totally and permanently disabled or dies; becomes a full-time teacher in a designated elementary or secondary school serving students from low-income families; becomes a full-time special education teacher of children with disabilities in a public or other nonprofit elementary or secondary school; becomes a full-time qualified professional provider of early intervention services for the disabled; becomes a full-time teacher of mathematics, science, foreign languages, bilingual education, or other teacher shortage areas; becomes a librarian at an eligible elementary or secondary school; becomes a librarian at a public library serving an area containing an eligible elementary or secondary school; becomes a full-time employee of a public or nonprofit child or family service agency providing services to high-risk children and their families from low-income communities; becomes a full-time nurse or medical technician; serves as a full-time law enforcement or corrections officer; or serves as a staff member in the educational component of a Head Start program. Up to 70% of a loan may be cancelled if the student serves as a VISTA or Peace Corps volunteer. Up to 50% of a loan may be cancelled if the student serves in the armed forces in areas of hostilities or imminent danger.

Duration　Up to 5 years of undergraduate study and up to 5 additional years of graduate or professional study.

Additional data　The grace period for Perkins loans is 9 months after graduation, leaving school, or dropping below half-time enrollment. Deferments of loans are available while the recipient is enrolled in an approved graduate or postgraduate program, in an approved rehabilitation training program for the disabled, or for 3 years of unemployment or economic hardship.

Number awarded　Varies each year; recently, more than 750,000 new loans, worth more than $1.6 billion, were provided by this program.

Deadline　Each participating college and university sets its own deadline.

[1028]
MARINE CORPS LAW SCHOOL EDUCATION DEBT SUBSIDY PROGRAM

U.S. Marine Corps
Attn: Manpower and Reserve Affairs (MPP-30)
3280 Russell Road
Quantico, VA 22134-5103
(703) 784-9364　　　　　　　E-mail: Bradley.Davin@usmc.mil
Web: www.usmc.mil

Summary　To repay the law school debts of attorneys (judge advocates) serving in the U.S. Marine Corps.

Eligibility　This program is open to judge advocates who have completed their Initial Active Duty Service Obligation (IADSO), or 42 months, and have not been selected for promotion to Major or have been twice passed for promotion to Major. Officers who accessed into the Marine Corps judge advocate community through such programs as the Marine Corps Funded Law Education Program are not eligible.

Financial Data　Judge advocates approved for this program receive a payment of $10,000 per year.

Duration　Up to 3 years.

Additional data　Officers who accept a payment through this program incur an active-duty service obligation of 3 years.

Number awarded　Varies each year.

Deadline　August of each year.

[1029]
MARYLAND MILITARY RESERVIST NO-INTEREST LOAN PROGRAM

Maryland Department of Veterans Affairs
Attn: Director, Outreach and Advocacy Program
Jeffrey Building, Fourth Floor
16 Francis Street
Annapolis, MD 21401
(410) 260-3842　　　　　　　　Toll Free: (866) 793-1577
Fax: (410) 216-7928
E-mail: mdveteransinfo@mdva.state.md.us
Web: www.mdva.state.md.us/state/employment.html

Summary　To provide no-interest loans to 1) members of the National Guard and Reserves in Maryland who are called to active duty and 2) their employers.

Eligibility　This program is open to Maryland residents who are members of the National Guard or military Reserves and the small businesses (fewer than 50 employees) that employ them. Applicants must need funding to pay costs that result from the Guard member or Reservist's call to active duty.

Financial Data　Loans range from $1,000 to $50,000. No interest is charged.

Duration　Loan maturity ranges from 1 to 8 years.

Additional data　This program, established in 2006, is administered by the Department of Business and Economic Development in consultation with the Maryland Department of Veterans Affairs (MDVA). The MDVA receives and reviews applications; if it determines that an applicant qualifies and that the intended use of the loan proceeds is eligible under the program, it forwards the application to the Department of Business and Economic Development.

Number awarded　Varies each year.

Deadline　Applications may be submitted at any time from the date of the call to active duty through the period ending 6 months after the end of the member's active duty.

[1030]
MINNESOTA NATIONAL GUARD MEDICAL AND DENTAL TUITION REIMBURSEMENT PROGRAM

Department of Military Affairs
Attn: Education Services Officer
JFMN-J1-ARED
20 West 12th Street
St. Paul, MN 55155-2098
(651) 282-4125   Toll Free: (800) 657-3848
Fax: (651) 282-4694   E-mail: education@mn.ngb.army.mil
Web: www.minnesotanationalguard.org

Summary To provide partial tuition reimbursement to medical and dental students who are serving in the Minnesota National Guard.

Eligibility This program is open to Minnesota Army and Air National Guard members admitted to medical or dental school. Applicants must agree to accept a Medical Corps commission in the Guard after graduation.

Financial Data This program provides reimbursement of the tuition charged, not to exceed 100% of the tuition costs at the University of Minnesota Twin Cities campus medical or dental schools. Upon graduation from medical or dental school, officers must serve the same number of years in the Minnesota National Guard that they participated in the program. Failure to fulfill that service obligation will result in recoupment of a prorated portion of the tuition reimbursed.

Duration Until completion of a medical or dental degree.

Number awarded The number of participants at any given time is limited to 11 Army officers and 3 Air Guard officers.

Deadline Participants must request reimbursement within 60 days of the last official day of the term.

[1031]
MISSISSIPPI VETERANS' MORTGAGE LOAN PROGRAM

Mississippi Veterans' Home Purchase Board
3466 Highway 80 East
P.O. Box 54111
Pearl, MS 39288-4411
(601) 576-4800   Fax: (601) 576-4812
E-mail: vhpbinfo@vhpb.state.ms.us
Web: www.vhpb.state.ms.us

Summary To provide loans to veterans, their widow(er)s, and selected military personnel who are interested in purchasing or constructing a house in Mississippi.

Eligibility This program is open to honorably-discharged veterans who were Mississippi residents prior to entering military service or have been residents for at least 2 consecutive years prior to applying for a loan. Reserve and National Guard personnel who currently serve and have at least 6 years of service are also eligible. Active-duty military personnel are eligible if they meet the residency requirements. Reserve and National Guard personnel who have been activated for extended duty under Title 10 of the U.S. Code are also eligible. The unremarried surviving spouse of an eligible veteran who died as a result of service or service-connected injuries also qualifies, as does the unremarried spouse of an eligible veteran who has not purchased a home since the veteran's death. Applicants must be planning to purchase an existing single family home in Mississippi or to construct a new home in the state. Farms, raw land, mobile homes, and condominiums do not qualify.

Financial Data This program provides low-interest mortgage loans in amounts up to $195,000. Interest rates are fixed and are generally 1 to 2 percentage points below market rates (currently, that is 3.75% on 10-, 12- and 15-year loans or 4.0% on 20-, 25-, and 30-year loans).

Duration Available terms are 10, 12, 15, 20, 25, and 30 years.

Number awarded Varies each year.
Deadline Applications may be submitted at any time.

[1032]
NATIONAL GUARD ASSUMPTION PROGRAM OF LOANS FOR EDUCATION

California Student Aid Commission
Attn: Specialized Programs
10811 International Drive
P.O. Box 419029
Rancho Cordova, CA 95741-9029
(916) 526-8276   Toll Free: (888) CA-GRANT
Fax: (916) 526-7977   E-mail: specialized@csac.ca.gov
Web: www.csac.ca.gov/doc.asp?id=1249

Summary To repay the educational loans of residents of California who enlist or reenlist in the National Guard, State Military Reserve, or Naval Militia.

Eligibility This program is open to California residents who 1) have completed a baccalaureate degree; 2) are currently enrolled in a program of undergraduate instruction on at least a half-time basis at an institution of higher education in California; 3) are enrolled in or have completed a program of instruction in a qualified vocational diploma program at an institution in California; or 4) on an academic leave of absence because of active-duty status from an institution or program in California. Applicants must agree to enlist, reenlist, or (in the case of an officer) commit to serve for at least 4 years in the National Guard, the State Military Reserve, or the Naval Militia. They must have received, or have been approved to receive, a student loan to meet the costs for undergraduate work or a qualified vocational diploma program under 1 or more of the following designated loan programs: the Federal Family Education Loan Program (FFEL), the Federal Direct Loan Program, or any program approved on a case-by-case basis. Ineligible loans include lines of credit, home equity loans, credit care debt, and other general consumer loans, business loans, personal loans, or mortgages.

Financial Data Up to $11,000 of educational loans may be assumed.

Duration The maximum loan assumption requires 4 years of service in the National Guard, State Military Reserve, or Naval Militia.

Additional data Applications must be submitted to the Office of the Adjutant General, Joint Forces Headquarters, 9800 Goethe Road, Box 26, Sacramento, CA 95826, (916) 854-3227.

Number awarded Up to 100 each year.
Deadline June of each year.

[1033]
NAVY HEALTH PROFESSIONS LOAN REPAYMENT PROGRAM

U.S. Navy
Attn: Navy Medicine Manpower, Personnel, Education and
   Training Command
Code OH
8901 Wisconsin Avenue, Building 1, Tower 13, Room 13132
Bethesda, MD 20889-5611
(301) 319-4121   Toll Free: (800) USA-NAVY
Fax: (301) 295-1811   E-mail: HPLRP@med.navy.mil
Web: www.med.navy.mil

Summary To repay the educational loans of health care professionals willing to serve as an active-duty officer in the Navy.

Eligibility This program is open to 1) full-time students enrolled in the final year of a course of study at an accredited educational institution leading to a degree in a health profession other than medicine, dentistry, or osteopathic medicine; and 2) residents enrolled in the final year of specialty training in medicine, dentistry, or osteopathic medicine. Applicants must be serving as, or willing to serve as, active-duty Navy officers in the Medical Corps,

Dental Corps, Nurse Corps, or Medical Service Corps. They must have qualified government or commercial loans for actual costs paid for tuition, reasonable educational expenses, and reasonable living expenses relating to the attainment of a degree in allopathic or osteopathic medicine, dentistry, or other health profession.

Financial Data This program provides funding for the repayment of educational loans up to $40,000 per year.

Duration 1 year; may be renewed. Each of the 4 Corps (Medical, Dental, Nurse, and Medical Service) determines the total number of years of repayment that may be authorized.

Additional data In additional to applicants in medicine, dentistry, nursing, and osteopathic medicine, this program provides repayment of educational loans in health profession fields designated as necessary to meet identified skill shortages in the Navy; currently, those are clinical psychologists, physician assistants, podiatrists, pharmacists, social workers, environmental health officers, health care administrators, audiologists, and occupational therapists. Participants incur an active-duty service obligation of 2 years or 1 year for each annual repayment, whichever is greater.

Number awarded Varies each year.

Deadline November of each year.

[1034]
NMCRS FINANCIAL ASSISTANCE

Navy-Marine Corps Relief Society
875 North Randolph Street, Suite 225
Arlington, VA 22203-1757
(703) 696-4904   Fax: (703) 696-0144
Web: www.nmcrs.org/intfreeloan.html

Summary To provide emergency assistance, in the form of interest-free loans or grants, to current and former Navy and Marine Corps personnel and their families who need temporary funding.

Eligibility This program is open to active-duty and retired Navy and Marine Corps personnel, their eligible family members, eligible family members of Navy and Marine Corps personnel who died on active duty or in a retired status, Reservists on extended active duty, indigent mothers (65 years of age or older) of deceased servicemembers who have limited resources and no family to provide for their welfare, ex-spouses whose marriage to a servicemember lasted for at least 20 years while the servicemember was on active duty and who have not remarried, and uniformed members of the National Oceanic and Atmospheric Administration (NOAA). Applicants must need emergency funding for funeral expenses, medical or dental bills, food, rent, utilities, emergency transportation, disaster relief, child care expenses, essential vehicle repairs, or other unforeseen family emergencies. Funding is not available to pay bills for non-essentials, finance liberty and vacations, pay fines or legal expenses, pay taxes, finance recreational boats or vehicles or help Navy and Marine Corps families live beyond their means.

Financial Data Funds are provided in the form of interest-free loans or grants.

Number awarded Varies each year.

Deadline Applications may be submitted at any time.

[1035]
OHIO HEROES PROGRAM

Ohio Housing Finance Agency
Attn: Office of Homeownership
57 East Main Street
Columbus, OH 43215
(614) 466-9920   Toll Free: (888) 362-6432
Fax: (614) 644-5393   TDD: (614) 466-1940
E-mail: twalker@ohiohome.org
Web: www.ohiohome.org/homebuyer/heroes.aspx

Summary To offer lower interest on loans for home purchases by military personnel, veterans, and other providers of public services in Ohio.

Eligibility This program is open to Ohio residents who are 1) active-duty military personnel, active Reservists, or honorably-discharged veterans of any branch of the U.S. armed forces; 2) fire fighters, emergency medical technicians, or paramedics; 3) health care workers (medical residents and fellows, dental hygienists, nurses, nursing assistants, pharmacists, pharmacy technicians, physician assistants, medical technicians, or therapists); 4) police officers; or 5) teachers (K-12 and higher education). Applicants must be first-time home buyers and able to meet housing price and income standards that depend on their county of residence, family size, and other variables.

Financial Data Qualifying home buyers are able to purchase their home at an interest rate that is 0.25% lower than comparable loans provided by the Ohio Housing Finance Agency. Currently, this rate is 4.75%.

Duration This is a 1-time benefit.

Number awarded Varies each year.

Deadline Applications may be submitted at any time.

[1036]
PENNSYLVANIA NATIONAL GUARD EDUCATIONAL ASSISTANCE PROGRAM

Pennsylvania Higher Education Assistance Agency
Attn: State Grant and Special Programs
1200 North Seventh Street
P.O. Box 8114
Harrisburg, PA 17105-8114
(717) 720-2800   Toll Free: (800) 692-7392
TDD: (800) 654-5988   E-mail: info@pheaa.org
Web: www.pheaa.org

Summary To provide scholarship/loans for college or graduate school to Pennsylvania National Guard members.

Eligibility This program is open to active members of the Pennsylvania National Guard who are Pennsylvania residents and serving as enlisted personnel, warrant officers, or commissioned officers of any grade. Applicants must accept an obligation to serve in the Pennsylvania National Guard for a period of 6 years from the date of entry into the program. Students who do not possess a baccalaureate degree must be enrolled full or part time in an approved program of education at an approved institution of higher learning in Pennsylvania. Master's degree students are supported on a part-time basis only. Guard members receiving an ROTC scholarship of any type are not eligible.

Financial Data Full-time undergraduate students receive payment of 100% of tuition at a state-owned university (recently, $5,554 per year). Part-time students receive either actual tuition charged or two-thirds of the full-time tuition charged to a Pennsylvania resident at a state-owned university (recently, $3,702 per year), whichever is less. Graduate students receive either half the actual tuition charged or one-third of the full-time tuition charged to a Pennsylvania resident at a state-owned university (recently, $1,851 per year), whichever is less. Recipients who fail to fulfill the service obligation must repay all funds received within 10 years, including interest at 7%.

Duration Up to 5 years.

Additional data This program, first offered in 1997, is jointly administered by the Pennsylvania Department of Military and Veterans Affairs and the Pennsylvania Higher Education Assistance Agency. Support for summer and graduate school is available only if funding permits.

Number awarded Varies each year; recently, 1,789 members of the Pennsylvania National Guard were enrolled in this program.

Deadline June of each year for fall semester; October of each year for spring semester; May of each year for summer school.

[1037]
SOLDIERS' AND SAILORS' CIVIL RELIEF ACT

Department of Veterans Affairs
Attn: Veterans Benefits Administration
810 Vermont Avenue, N.W.
Washington, D.C. 20420
(202) 418-4343   Toll Free: (800) 827-1000
Web: www.va.gov

Summary To provide financial protection and relief to civilians who are mobilized into the military Reserves.

Eligibility When Reservists are mobilized into the military, they automatically become eligible for the benefits offered under this legislation.

Financial Data During the recipient's period of active duty, the interest rate on credit cards and mortgages is reduced to a fixed rate of 6%. The difference between the note rate and the 6% is forgiven and not added back on the loan balance. Further, borrowers can ask the courts to postpone completely any mortgage payments while they are on active duty. If the stay is granted, the loan balance—plus accrued interest at 6%—is reamortized over the total of the remaining loan term plus time spent on active duty. Foreclosures cannot be started or continued against an eligible servicemember. Other benefits include protection from eviction if rent is $1,200 or less, delay of all civil court actions (bankruptcy, foreclosure, divorce), protection against paying taxes in both the home state and the state in which stationed, exemption from personal property taxes (such as an annual property tax on value of an automobile but not real estate taxes) if assigned to a state other than domicile.

Duration The relief begins when the individual receives orders to report for active duty and ends 3 months after separation from active duty.

Additional data This program began in 1940. The provisions regarding terms, stays, and foreclosures can be altered in 2 ways: 1) by written agreement between the lender and the borrower and 2) by either the borrower or the lender applying to the courts for relief.

Number awarded Varies; recently, approximately 50,000 Reservists could qualify for these benefits.

Deadline Deadline not specified.

[1038]
SPECIALLY ADAPTED HOUSING GRANTS

Department of Veterans Affairs
Attn: Specially Adapted Housing
810 Vermont Avenue, N.W.
Washington, DC 20420
(202) 461-9546   Toll Free: (800) 827-1000
Web: www.homeloans.va.gov/sah.htm

Summary To provide loans, grants, and loan guaranties to certain disabled veterans and servicemembers for a home specially adapted to their needs.

Eligibility These grants are available to veterans and servicemembers who are entitled to compensation for permanent and total service-connected disability due to: 1) the loss or loss of use of both lower extremities, such as to preclude locomotion without the aid of braces, crutches, canes, or a wheelchair; or 2) blindness in both eyes, having only light perception, plus loss or loss of use of 1 lower extremity; or 3) a loss or loss of use of 1 lower extremity together with residuals of organic disease or injury or the loss or loss of use of 1 upper extremity, such as to preclude locomotion without resort to braces, canes, crutches, or a wheelchair. Applicants must be planning to 1) construct a home on land to be acquired for that purpose; 2) build a home on land already owned if it is suitable for specially adapted housing; 3) remodel an existing home if it can be made suitable for specially adapted housing, or 4) apply funds against the unpaid principle mortgage balance of a specially adapted home that has already been acquired.

Financial Data The U.S. Department of Veterans Affairs (VA) may approve a grant of not more than 50% of the cost of building, buying, or remodeling homes for eligible veterans, or paying indebtedness of such homes already acquired, up to a maximum grant of $63,780. Eligible veterans with available loan guarantee entitlements may also obtain a guaranteed loan from the VA to supplement the grant to acquire a specially adapted home. If private financing is not available, VA may make a direct loan up to $33,000 to cover the difference between the total cost of the home and the grant.

Duration This is a 1-time grant, guaranteed loan, or direct loan.

Additional data Veterans who receive a specially adapted housing grant may be eligible for Veterans Mortgage Life Insurance.

Number awarded Varies each year.

Deadline Applications are accepted at any time.

[1039]
TEXAS VETERANS HOME IMPROVEMENT PROGRAM

Texas Veterans Land Board
Stephen F. Austin Building
1700 North Congress Avenue, Room 800
P.O. Box 12873
Austin, TX 78711-2873
(512) 463-5060   Toll Free: (800) 252-VETS (within TX)
TDD: (512) 463-6367   E-mail: vlbinfo@glo.state.tx.us
Web: www.glo.state.tx.us/vlb/vhip/index.html

Summary To assist Texas veterans, National Guard members, and unremarried surviving spouses who wish to maintain older homes but who cannot qualify for the high interest rates of conventional home improvement loans.

Eligibility This program is open to 1) veterans who served for at least 90 consecutive days of active duty after September 16, 1940 in the Army, Navy, Air Force, Marines, Coast Guard, U.S. Public Health Service, or a Reserve component of those services; 2) members of the Texas National Guard or Reserves who have enlisted or received an appointment and have completed all Initial Active Duty for Training (IADT) requirements; and 3) veterans who served in the armed forces of the Republic of Vietnam (ARVN) between February 28, 1961 and May 7, 1975. Applicants may not have been dishonorably discharged and must have listed Texas as their home of record at the time of entry into the military or have been a resident of Texas for at least 1 year prior to filing an application. The unremarried surviving spouses of Texas veterans who are missing in action, died in the line of duty, or died from a service-connected cause may be eligible to participate in the program. Applicants must be interested in making alterations, repairs, and improvements to, or in connection with, their existing residence if, and only if, repairs will 1) substantially protect or improve the basic livability or energy efficiency of the property; 2) correct damage resulting from a natural disaster; or 3) correct conditions that are hazardous to health or safety. Examples of eligible improvements include carpeting, fencing, room additions, patios, driveways, and garages. Examples of ineligible improvements include exterior spas, saunas, whirlpools, tree surgery, tennis courts, swimming pools, and barbecue pits. The home must be in Texas and the veteran's primary residence. In addition to single family dwellings, condominiums, duplexes, triplexes, and fourplexes are eligible as long as 1 of the units is the veteran's primary residence. Duplexes, triplexes, and fourplexes must be at least 5 years old. Modular or manufactured homes that are on a permanent foundation and are a part of the real estate may also be eligible. An interest rate reduction is available to Texas veterans who have a service-connected disability of 30% or greater as verified by the U.S. Department of Veterans Affairs.

Financial Data The maximum loan on a single family residence or a manufactured or modular home is $25,000. The maximum loan on a multi-family residence is $12,000 per dwelling unit or

$25,000, whichever is less. Loans over $10,000 are for 2 to 20 years; those for $10,000 or less are for 2 to 10 years. Interest rates recently were 4.89%. An interest rate reduction of 0.50 percentage points is available for the Veterans with Disabilities program.

Number awarded Varies each year.

Deadline Applications may be submitted at any time.

[1040]
TEXAS VETERANS HOUSING ASSISTANCE PROGRAM

Texas Veterans Land Board
Stephen F. Austin Building
1700 North Congress Avenue, Room 800
P.O. Box 12873
Austin, TX 78711-2873
(512) 463-5060   Toll Free: (800) 252-VETS (within TX)
TDD: (512) 463-5330   E-mail: vlbinfo@glo.state.tx.us
Web: www.glo.state.tx.us/vlb/vhap/index.html

Summary To provide low-interest loans to assist Texas veterans, National Guard members, and unremarried surviving spouses in purchasing their own homes.

Eligibility This program is open to 1) veterans who served for at least 90 consecutive days of active duty after September 16, 1940 in the Army, Navy, Air Force, Marines, Coast Guard, U.S. Public Health Service, or a Reserve component of those services; 2) members of the Texas National Guard or Reserves who have enlisted or received an appointment and have completed all Initial Active Duty for Training (IADT) requirements; and 3) veterans who served in the armed forces of the Republic of Vietnam (ARVN) between February 28, 1961 and May 7, 1975. Applicants may not have been dishonorably discharged and must have listed Texas as their home of record at the time of entry into the military or have been a resident of Texas for at least 1 year prior to filing an application. The unremarried surviving spouses of Texas veterans who are missing in action, died in the line of duty, or died from a service-connected cause may be eligible to participate in the program. Applicants must be interested in purchasing a new or existing home, including a duplex, triplex, or fourplex if the structure is more than 5 years old, or a modular or manufactured home if it is on a permanent foundation and meets loan guidelines established by the Federal National Mortgage Association or the Federal Home Loan Mortgage Corporation and has an economic life of at least 30 years. Any home purchased with funds from this program must be the primary residence of the veteran for at least 3 years. An interest rate reduction is available to Texas veterans who have a service-connected disability of 30% or greater as verified by the U.S. Department of Veterans Affairs.

Financial Data There is no limit on the sales price of the house, but the maximum loan available through this program is $325,000. Loans for $45,000 or less may be requested directly from the Texas Veterans Land Board (VLB) and may cover up to 85% of the home's appraised value. Loans over $45,000 are originated through a VLB participating lender. No fees are charged on direct loans; loans available through a VLB-approved lender require an origination fee up to 1% and a participation fee up to 1%. Interest rates recently were 4.89%. An interest rate reduction of 0.50 percentage points is available for the Veterans with Disabilities program.

Duration Loans are available with 15, 20, 25, or 30 year terms.

Number awarded Varies each year.

Deadline Applications may be submitted at any time.

[1041]
TEXAS VETERANS LAND PROGRAM

Texas Veterans Land Board
Stephen F. Austin Building
1700 North Congress Avenue, Room 800
P.O. Box 12873
Austin, TX 78711-2873
(512) 463-5060   Toll Free: (800) 252-VETS (within TX)
TDD: (512) 463-5330   E-mail: vlbinfo@glo.state.tx.us
Web: www.glo.state.tx.us/vlb/land/index.html

Summary To assist Texas veterans, National Guard members, and unremarried surviving spouses interested in purchasing land in Texas.

Eligibility This program is open to 1) veterans who served for at least 90 consecutive days of active duty after September 16, 1940 in the Army, Navy, Air Force, Marines, Coast Guard, U.S. Public Health Service, or a Reserve component of those services; 2) members of the Texas National Guard or Reserves who have enlisted or received an appointment and have completed all Initial Active Duty for Training (IADT) requirements. Applicants may not have been dishonorably discharged and must have listed Texas as their home of record at the time of entry into the military or have been a resident of Texas for at least 1 year prior to filing an application. The unremarried surviving spouses of Texas veterans who are missing in action, died in the line of duty, or died from a service-connected cause may be eligible to participate in the program. Applicants must be interested in purchasing up to 1 acre of land within Texas. It must have legal access to a public road, and such right-of-way must be the minimum width required by the county commissioners. Land must be officially surveyed and appraised.

Financial Data The maximum loan is $80,000. The veteran must pay a 5% down payment. If the purchase price is greater than $80,000, the veteran must pay the difference to the VLB in cash. The VLB then purchases the land directly from the seller and resells the land to the veteran using a 30-year contract of sale and purchase. In addition to the down payment, the veteran must pay a closing fee of $325. The interest rate recently was 7.25%.

Number awarded Varies each year.

Deadline Applications may be submitted at any time.

[1042]
VA HOME LOAN GUARANTY BENEFITS

Department of Veterans Affairs
Attn: Veterans Benefits Administration
Home Loan Guaranty Service
810 Vermont Avenue, N.W.
Washington, DC 20420
(202) 418-4343   Toll Free: (800) 827-1000
Web: www.homeloans.va.gov/veteran.htm

Summary To assist disabled and other veterans, certain military personnel, and their unremarried surviving spouses in the purchase of residences.

Eligibility This benefit is available to 1) veterans who served during specified periods of time and were discharged since September 16, 1940 under other than dishonorable conditions; 2) military personnel who have served at least 90 days; 3) members of the Reserves or National Guard who have completed at least 6 years of honorable service or were discharged because of a service-related disability; 4) unremarried spouses of veterans or Reservists who died on active duty or as a result of service-connected causes; 5) surviving spouses who remarry after attaining 57 years of age; 6) spouses of active-duty servicemembers who have been missing in action or a prisoner of war for at least 90 days; 7) U.S. citizens who served in the armed forces of a U.S. ally in World War II; and 8) members of organizations with recognized contributions to the U.S. World War II effort.

Financial Data The Department of Veterans Affairs (VA) does not lend money; the actual loan must come from a commercial lender. The loan may be for any amount, and the VA will guarantee payment on loans for the purchase of homes, farm homes, condominium units, or refinancing of existing loans. The largest guaranty that the VA can give is an amount equal to 25% of the Freddie Mac conforming loan limit for single family residences (currently $417,000 or $625,500 for Hawaii, Alaska, Guam and the Virgin Islands). Interest rates vary with market conditions but are fixed for the life of the loan, which may be as long as 30 years and 32 days. No down payments are prescribed by the VA. A funding fee must be paid to the VA, although it may be included in the loan amount; the amount of the fee varies, depending on the type of loan and whether the borrower is a veteran or a Reservist, but ranges from 0.5% to 3.3% of the amount of the loan. The funding fee is waived for disabled veterans and unremarried surviving spouses of veterans who died as a result of service.

Additional data In addition to the purchase of a new home, VA Loans may be used to buy a residential condominium; to build a home; to repair, alter, or improve a home; to refinance an existing home loan; to buy a manufactured home with or without a lot; to buy and improve a manufactured home lot; to install a solar heating and/or cooling system or other weatherization improvements; to purchase and improve simultaneously a home with energy conserving measures; to refinance an existing VA loan to reduce the interest rate; or to refinance a manufactured home loan to acquire a lot. Mortgages guaranteed by the VA usually offer an interest rate lower than conventional mortgage rates, require no down payment, provide a long repayment period, allow the VA to appraise the property and inspect it to ensure that it conforms to the plans and specifications, and permit early prepayment without premium or penalty. The VA does not have legal authority to act as an architect, supervise construction of the home, guarantee that the home is free of defects, or act as an attorney if the veteran encounters legal difficulties in buying or constructing a home. Veterans must certify that they intend to live in the home they are buying or building with a VA loan. Veterans who wish to refinance or improve a home must certify that they are actually in residence at the time of application.

Number awarded Varies each year.

Deadline Applications may be submitted at any time.

[1043]
VOCATIONAL AND TECHNICAL TRAINING STUDENT LOAN PROGRAM

Coast Guard Mutual Assistance
4200 Wilson Boulevard, Suite 610
Arlington, VA 20598-7180
(202) 493-6624　　　　Toll Free: (800) 881-2462
Fax: (202) 493-6686　　E-mail: ARL-DG-CGMA@uscg.mil
Web: www.cgmahq.org

Summary To provide loans to the members of Coast Guard Mutual Assistance (CGMA) and their spouses and dependent children who require assistance for vocational or technical training.

Eligibility This program is open to members of the organization, their spouses, and dependent children. Applicants should be seeking assistance to help pay the costs of non-college courses that provide the technical knowledge and skills needed for entry into a specific career field. Financial need must be demonstrated.

Financial Data The maximum loan is $1,500.

Additional data CGMA membership is open to active-duty and retired members of the U.S. Coast Guard, civilian employees of the U.S. Coast Guard, U.S. Coast Guard Reserve members, U.S. Coast Guard Auxiliary members, Public Health Service officers serving with the U.S. Coast Guard, and family members of all of those.

Number awarded Varies each year.

Deadline Requests must be submitted within 30 days after the course begins.

[1044]
WASHINGTON NATIONAL GUARD SCHOLARSHIP PROGRAM

Washington National Guard
Attn: Education Services Office
Building 15, G1-ED
Camp Murray, WA 98498
(253) 512-8899　　　Toll Free: (800) 606-9843 (within WA)
Fax: (253) 512-8941　　E-mail: education@wa.ngb.army.mil
Web: washingtonguard.org/edu

Summary To provide forgivable loans to members of the Washington National Guard who wish to attend college or graduate school in the state.

Eligibility This program is open to members of the Washington National Guard who have already served for at least 1 year and have at least 2 years remaining on their current contract. Applicants must have a rank between E1 and O3. They must be attending an accredited college as a resident of Washington state and must already have utilized all available federal educational benefits. Army Guard members must have completed BCT/AIT and awarded initial MOS; Air Guard members must have completed BMT/initial tech school and been awarded "3-Level" AFSC. Graduate students are eligible, but undergraduates receive preference as long as they are making satisfactory progress toward a baccalaureate degree. The minimum GPA requirement is 2.5 for undergraduates or 3.0 for graduate students.

Financial Data This program provides a stipend that is based on the number of credits completed but does not exceed the amount required for tuition, books, and fees at the University of Washington. Recipients incur a service obligation of 1 additional year in the Guard for the initial scholarship award and 1 additional year for each full year of academic credit completed with this assistance. The grant serves as a loan which is forgiven if the recipient completes the contracted service time in the Washington National Guard. Failure to meet the service obligation requires the recipient to repay the loan plus 8% interest.

Duration 1 year; may be renewed.

Number awarded Varies each year. A total of $100,000 is available for this program annually; scholarships are awarded on a first-come, first-served basis as long as funds are available.

Deadline June of each year.

[1045]
WISCONSIN HOME IMPROVEMENT LOAN PROGRAM

Wisconsin Department of Veterans Affairs
30 West Mifflin Street
P.O. Box 7843
Madison, WI 53707-7843
(608) 266-1311　　　　Toll Free: (800) WIS-VETS
Fax: (608) 267-0403　　E-mail: loans@dva.state.wi.us
Web: www.dva.state.wi.us/Ben_improvementloans.asp

Summary To provide low-interest loans to veterans, current National Guard members, Reservists, and their families in Wisconsin to pay for improvements to their homes.

Eligibility This program is open to current residents of Wisconsin who 1) were residents of the state when they entered or reentered active duty in the U.S. armed forces, or 2) have moved to the state and have been residents for any consecutive 12-month period after entry or reentry into service. Applicants must have served on active duty for at least 2 continuous years or for at least 90 days during specified wartime periods. Also eligible are 1) members and former members of the National Guard and Reserves who have completed at least 6 years of continuous service under honorable conditions; 2) unremarried spouses of deceased veterans; and 3) dependent children under 26 years of age who are attending school full time. Applicants may be planning to use the loan funds for additions, construction, repairs, or alterations of their principal residence. The loan also may be used for garage construction. The applicant must have at least 10% equity in the property to be improved.

Financial Data Loans up to $50,000 are available if secured by an 80% loan to value mortgage, up to $25,000 if secured by a 90% loan to value mortgage, or up to $3,000 if secured with a guarantor. Currently, for loans secured by a mortgage at 80% loan to value, interest rates are 5.85% for 5-year loans, 6.25% for 7- or 10-year loans, or 6.55% for 15-year loans. For loans secured by a mortgage at 90% loan to value, interest rates are 6.75% for 5-year loans, 7% for 7- or 10-year loans, or 7.25% for 15-year loans. For guarantor secured loans, interest rates are 8.5% for 3-year loans or 10% for 5-year loans. Funds may be used only for qualifying home improvements, not for personal property (such as furniture or certain types of appliances).

Duration The minimum loan repayment term is 1 year and the maximum term is 15 years.

Number awarded Varies each year.

Deadline Applications may be submitted at any time.

[1046]
WISCONSIN VETERANS PRIMARY MORTGAGE LOAN PROGRAM

Wisconsin Department of Veterans Affairs
30 West Mifflin Street
P.O. Box 7843
Madison, WI 53707-7843
(608) 266-1311   Toll Free: (800) WIS-VETS
Fax: (608) 267-0403   E-mail: loans@dva.state.wi.us
Web: www.dva.state.wi.us/Ben_mortgageloans.asp

Summary To provide housing loans to Wisconsin veterans, current National Guard members, Reservists, and their unremarried spouses or children who cannot obtain the necessary funds from other sources.

Eligibility This program is open to current residents of Wisconsin who 1) were residents of the state when they entered or reentered active duty in the U.S. armed forces, or 2) have moved to the state and have been residents for any consecutive 12-month period after entry or reentry into service. Applicants must have served on active duty for at least 2 continuous years or for at least 90 days during specified wartime periods. Also eligible are 1) dependent children and unremarried surviving spouses of eligible deceased veterans; and 2) members and former members of the National Guard and Reserves who have completed 6 years of continuous service under honorable conditions. Applicants must be seeking to borrow money for the purchase, or the purchase and improvement, of a single family home or condominium; construction of a new single family home; purchase of certain existing 2- to 4-unit owner occupied residences; or refinance of the balance due on existing mortgage loans used for purchase, construction, or improvement of a residence.

Financial Data The veteran or dependent may obtain a loan of up to 95% of the total cost of the property, to a maximum of $343,750. The required down payment is 5% and the department pays the loan origination fees for veterans with a disability rating of 30% or more. Other attractive features include: no private mortgage insurance or loan guaranty, no discount points, no interest rate increase, and no prepayment penalty. The current interest rate is 6.25%.

Duration Loan terms up to 30 years are available.

Number awarded Varies each year.

Deadline Applications may be submitted at any time.

Family Members

[1047]
AAAA LOAN PROGRAM

Army Aviation Association of America
Attn: AAAA Scholarship Foundation
755 Main Street, Suite 4D
Monroe, CT 06468-2830
(203) 268-2450   Fax: (203) 268-5870
E-mail: Scholarship@quad-a.org
Web: www.quad-a.org/scholarship.htm

Summary To provide educational loans to members of the Army Aviation Association of America (AAAA) and their relatives.

Eligibility This program is open to AAAA members and their spouses, unmarried siblings, and unmarried children. Applicants must be enrolled or accepted for enrollment as an undergraduate or graduate student at an accredited college or university.

Financial Data The maximum loan is $1,000 per year. All loans are interest free.

Duration Up to 4 years.

Number awarded Varies each year; recently, 10 of these loans were granted.

Deadline April of each year.

[1048]
AER LOANS/GRANTS

Army Emergency Relief
200 Stovall Street
Alexandria, VA 22332-0600
(703) 428-0000   Toll Free: (866) 878-6378
Fax: (703) 325-7183   E-mail: aer@aerhq.org
Web: www.aerhq.org

Summary To provide loans and grants-in-aid to help with the emergency financial needs of Army veterans, military personnel, and their dependents.

Eligibility Eligible to apply are active-duty soldiers (single or married) and their dependents, Army National Guard and Army Reserve soldiers on continuous active duty for more than 30 days and their dependents, soldiers retired from active duty for longevity or physical disability and their dependents, Army National Guard and Army Reserve soldiers who retired at age 60 and their dependents, and surviving spouses and orphans of soldiers who died while on active duty or after they retired. Applicants must be seeking assistance for such emergency needs as food, rent, and utilities; emergency transportation and vehicle repair; funeral expenses; medical and dental expenses; or personal needs when pay is delayed or stolen. Support is not available to help pay for nonessentials, finance ordinary leave or vacation, pay fines or legal expenses, help liquidate or consolidate debt, assist with house purchase or home improvements, cover bad checks, pay credit card bills, or help purchase, rent, or lease a vehicle.

Financial Data Support is provided in the form of loans or grants (or a combination).

Duration Qualifying individuals can apply whenever they have a valid emergency need.

Additional data This organization was established in 1942.

Number awarded Varies each year; recently, the organization helped more than 66,000 Army people with more than $70 million, including $60 million to 58,820 active-duty soldiers and their families, $7.3 million to 4,914 retired soldiers and their families, and $2.7 million to 2,304 widow(er)s and orphans of deceased soldiers. Since it was established, the organization has helped more than 3.2 million qualifying individuals with more than $1.2 billion in financial assistance.

Deadline Applications may be submitted at any time.

[1049]
AFAS FINANCIAL ASSISTANCE

Air Force Aid Society
Attn: Financial Assistance Department
241 18th Street South, Suite 202
Arlington, VA 22202-3409
(703) 607-3072, ext. 51   Toll Free: (800) 429-9475
Fax: (703) 607-3022
Web: www.afas.org/Assistance/HowWeCanHelp.cfm

Summary To provide loans and grants-in-aid to current and former Air Force personnel and their families who are facing emergency situations.

Eligibility This program is open to active-duty Air Force members and their dependents, retired Air Force personnel and their dependents, Air National Guard and Air Force Reserve personnel on extended duty over 15 days, and spouses and dependent children of deceased Air Force personnel who died on active duty or in retired status. Applicants must be facing problems, usually for relatively short periods, that affect their job or the essential quality and dignity of life the Air Force wants for its people. Examples of such needs include basic living expenses (food, rent, utilities), medical and dental care, funeral expenses, vehicle expenses, emergency travel, moving expenses, or child or respite care. Funding is generally not provided if it merely postpones a long-term inability to exist on present pay and allowances, for non-essentials, for continuing long-term assistance commitments, or to replace funds lost due to garnishment.

Financial Data Assistance is provided as an interest-free loan, a grant, or a combination of both.

Number awarded Varies each year.

Deadline Applications may be submitted at any time.

[1050]
ALASKA STATE VETERANS INTEREST RATE PREFERENCE

Alaska Housing Finance Corporation
Attn: Communications Officer
4300 Boniface Parkway
P.O. Box 101020
Anchorage, AK 99510-1020
(907) 330-8447   Toll Free: (800) 478-AHFC (within AK)
Fax: (907) 338-9218
Web: www.ahfc.state.ak.us/loans/state_vet.cfm

Summary To provide Alaskan veterans and their spouses with lower interest rates on loans to purchase housing.

Eligibility This program is open to Alaska residents who served at least 90 days on active duty in the U.S. armed forces after April 6, 1917 and received an honorable discharge. Also eligible are 1) honorably-discharged members of the Alaska Army or Air National Guard who served at least 5 years; 2) honorably discharged Reservists who served at least 5 years; and 3) widows and widowers of qualified veterans. Members of the military currently serving on active duty are not eligible. Applicants must be proposing to purchase an owner-occupied single-family residence, condominium, unit within a PUD, duplex, triplex, fourplex, or Type I mobile home using Alaska's taxable, tax-exempt, taxable first-time home buyer, rural owner, or non-conforming programs. Their family income may not exceed specified limits that depend on location within the state and size of family.

Financial Data Qualified veterans and widow(er)s receive a 1% rate reduction on the first $50,000 of the loan amount. Loans greater than $50,000 receive a blended interest rate rounded up to the next 0.125%.

Duration Loans are for either 15 years or 30 years.

Additional data Income limits vary in different parts of the state. Recently, they ranged from $39,250 to $44,800 for families with 1 person, from $44,900 to $51,200 for families with 2 persons, from $50,500 to $7,600 for families with 3 persons, and from $56,100 to $64,000 for families with 4 or more persons.

Number awarded Varies each year.

Deadline Deadline not specified.

[1051]
ARIZONA NATIONAL GUARD EMERGENCY RELIEF FUND GRANTS

Arizona National Guard Emergency Relief Fund
Attn: Fund Administrator
5636 East McDowell Road
Phoenix, AZ 85008
(602) 267-2731   E-mail: danielle.salomon@azdema.gov
Web: www.aerfund.org

Summary To provide emergency assistance (loans and grants) to members of the Arizona National Guard and their families.

Eligibility This program is open to members of the Arizona Army and Air National Guard who have not been mobilized under Presidential Order. Surviving spouses, children, and orphans of soldiers who died while on active duty are also eligible. Applicants must be seeking assistance for such emergency needs as delay in receiving pay or reimbursement from the government; temporary shelter, lodging, or rent; emergency utility assistance; emergency transportation and vehicle repair; costs incurred for emergency travel due to death of immediate family member; or any other special circumstance deemed appropriate by the fund's directors. Support is not provided to help pay for nonessentials, finance ordinary leave or vacation, pay fines or legal expenses, assist with home purchase or improvements, cover bad checks, or help purchase, rent, or lease a vehicle.

Financial Data Most support is provided in the form of interest-free loans, although outright grants are also available.

Duration These are 1-time grants.

Number awarded Varies each year.

Deadline Applications may be submitted at any time.

[1052]
ARIZONA NATIONAL GUARD FAMILY ASSISTANCE FUND

Arizona National Guard Emergency Relief Fund
Attn: Fund Administrator
5636 East McDowell Road
Phoenix, AZ 85008
(602) 267-2731   E-mail: danielle.salomon@azdema.gov
Web: www.aerfund.org

Summary To provide emergency assistance (loans and grants) to members of the Arizona Reserve Component who have been mobilized and their families.

Eligibility This program is open to members of the Arizona Reserve Component (including the Army and Air National Guard and Reserve units of all 5 branches of service) and their dependents. They must have been mobilized under Presidential Order. Surviving spouses, children, and orphans of soldiers who died while on active duty are also eligible. Applicants must be seeking assistance for such emergency needs as delay in receiving pay or reimbursement from the government; temporary shelter, lodging, or rent; emergency utility assistance; emergency transportation and vehicle repair; costs incurred for emergency travel due to death of immediate family member; or any other special circumstance deemed appropriate by the fund's directors. Support is not provided to help pay for nonessentials, financial ordinary leave or vacation, pay fines or legal expenses, assist with home purchase or improvements, cover bad checks, or help purchase, rent, or lease a vehicle.

Financial Data Most support is provided in the form of interest-free loans, although outright grants are also available.

Duration These are awarded on a 1-time basis.

Number awarded Varies each year.

Deadline Applications may be submitted at any time.

[1053]
CALVET HOME IMPROVEMENT LOAN PROGRAM

California Department of Veterans Affairs
Attn: Division of Farm and Home Purchases
1227 O Street, Room 200
P.O. Box 942895
Sacramento, CA 94295-0001
(916) 653-2525   Toll Free: (800) 952-LOAN (within CA)
Fax: (916) 653-2401   TDD: (800) 324-5966
E-mail: Kenn.Capps@cdva.ca.gov
Web: www.cdva.ca.gov/CalVetLoans/improve.aspx

Summary To enable current holders of CalVet Loans to obtain additional funding for home improvements.

Eligibility This program is open to active CalVet contract holders, including unremarried spouses of military personnel who died while on active duty or were designated a prisoner of war or missing in action. The basic CalVet contract must have at least 3 remaining months. Applicants must have a good payment record on the basic CalVet loan. Loans are available to improve the basic livability of the home or property; increase the energy efficiency of the home; perform general maintenance, such as painting, reroofing, and general repairs; add living space; renovate baths, kitchens, plumbing and electrical systems; install or update heating or air conditioning systems; install insulation, weather stripping, or thermal windows; add a garage, fence, landscaping, flatwork, retaining wall, or septic system; or connect to public utilities with water, sewer, or electrical lines from the property line to the dwelling. Unacceptable are improvements for recreational or entertainment purposes (such as swimming pools, saunas, hot tubs, pool houses, cabanas, or tennis courts) and improvements to farm property for the purpose of increasing agricultural productivity.

Financial Data Loans are available up to 90% of loan to value on "improved value," to a maximum of $150,000. A loan origination fee of 1.5% of the loan amount is charged. Recently, the interest rate was 5.75%, 5.95%, or 6.2%, depending on the source of funding for the loans.

Duration The maximum loan term is 10 years for loans up to $15,000, 12 years for loans up to $20,000, 15 years for loans up to $50,000, 20 years for loans up to $100,000, or 25 years for loans up to $150,000.

Number awarded Varies each year.

Deadline Applications may be submitted at any time.

[1054]
DAVA NATIONAL EDUCATION LOAN FUND

Disabled American Veterans Auxiliary
Attn: National Education Loan Fund Director
3725 Alexandria Pike
Cold Spring, KY 41076
(859) 441-7300   Toll Free: (877) 426-2838, ext. 4020
Fax: (859) 442-2095   E-mail: dava@davmail.org
Web: auxiliary.dav.org/membership/Programs.aspx

Summary To provide loans for college to women who are members of the Disabled American Veterans Auxiliary or to their children or grandchildren.

Eligibility This loan fund is open to women who are paid life members of the auxiliary and to their children and grandchildren. Applicants must be enrolled full time in a college, university, or vocational school. They must demonstrate academic achievement and financial need.

Financial Data The maximum loan is $2,500 per year for full-time students or $1,250 per year for part-time students. The loan is to be repaid within 7 years in installments of at least $100 per month. Repayment must begin upon graduation or leaving school. No interest is charged.

Duration The loan is renewable each year for up to 4 consecutive years, provided the student maintains full-time status and a GPA of 2.0 or higher.

Number awarded Varies; generally, 15 each year.

Deadline February of each year.

[1055]
MARYLAND SERVICE-DISABLED NO-INTEREST LOAN PROGRAM

Maryland Department of Veterans Affairs
Attn: Director, Outreach and Advocacy Program
Jeffrey Building, Fourth Floor
16 Francis Street
Annapolis, MD 21401
(410) 260-3842   Toll Free: (866) 793-1577
Fax: (410) 216-7928
E-mail: mdveteransinfo@mdva.state.md.us
Web: www.mdva.state.md.us/state/employment.html

Summary To provide no-interest loans to veterans in Maryland who have a service-connected disability and to their employers.

Eligibility This program is open to veterans who have a service-connected disability and the businesses that employ them. The veteran must have been renting, owning residential real estate, or living on a long-term basis in Maryland at the time the disability was incurred. Applicants must need funding to purchase tangible personal property that has an anticipated useful life in excess of 1 year and helps make the home, automobile, or place of employment of the veteran accessible to individuals with disabilities. Examples include computers, printers, and related peripherals; software; fax machines; scanners; office machines; telecommunication devices; office furniture; home modifications for accessibility and/or to create home offices; motor vehicle modification for drivers with disabilities; assistive technology; or machinery. For home or automobile modifications, veterans must first apply to the U.S. Department of Veterans Affairs.

Financial Data Loans range from $1,000 to $50,000. No interest is charged.

Duration Loan maturity ranges from 1 to 8 years.

Additional data This program, established in 2006, is administered by the Department of Business and Economic Development in consultation with the Maryland Department of Veterans Affairs (MDVA). The MDVA receives and reviews applications; if it determines that an applicant qualifies and that the intended use of the loan proceeds is eligible under the program, it forwards the application to the Department of Business and Economic Development.

Number awarded Varies each year.

Deadline Applications may be submitted at any time.

[1056]
MISSISSIPPI VETERANS' MORTGAGE LOAN PROGRAM

Mississippi Veterans' Home Purchase Board
3466 Highway 80 East
P.O. Box 54111
Pearl, MS 39288-4411
(601) 576-4800   Fax: (601) 576-4812
E-mail: vhpbinfo@vhpb.state.ms.us
Web: www.vhpb.state.ms.us

Summary To provide loans to veterans, their widow(er)s, and selected military personnel who are interested in purchasing or constructing a house in Mississippi.

Eligibility This program is open to honorably-discharged veterans who were Mississippi residents prior to entering military service or have been residents for at least 2 consecutive years prior to applying for a loan. Reserve and National Guard personnel who currently serve and have at least 6 years of service are also eligible. Active-duty military personnel are eligible if they meet the residency requirements. Reserve and National Guard personnel who have been activated for extended duty under Title 10 of the U.S. Code are also eligible. The unremarried surviving spouse of an eligible veteran who died as a result of service or service-connected injuries also qualifies, as does the unremarried spouse of an eligible veteran who has not purchased a home since the veteran's death. Applicants must be planning to purchase an existing single family home in Mississippi or to construct a new home in the state. Farms, raw land, mobile homes, and condominiums do not qualify.

Financial Data This program provides low-interest mortgage loans in amounts up to $195,000. Interest rates are fixed and are generally 1 to 2 percentage points below market rates (currently, that is 3.75% on 10-, 12- and 15-year loans or 4.0% on 20-, 25-, and 30-year loans).

Duration Available terms are 10, 12, 15, 20, 25, and 30 years.

Number awarded Varies each year.

Deadline Applications may be submitted at any time.

[1057]
MOAA STUDENT LOAN PROGRAM

Military Officers Association of America
Attn: Educational Assistance Program
201 North Washington Street
Alexandria, VA 22314-2539
(703) 549-2311   Toll Free: (800) 234-MOAA
Fax: (703) 838-5819   E-mail: edassist@moaa.org
Web: www.moaa.org/about_scholarship_aboutfund/index.htm

Summary To provide interest-free loans for undergraduate education to children of former, active, or retired officers or active or retired enlisted military personnel.

Eligibility This program is open to children of active, Reserve, National Guard, and retired uniformed service personnel (Army, Navy, Air Force, Marines, Coast Guard, Public Health Service, or National Oceanic and Atmospheric Administration). Applicants must be under 24 years of age. Parents who are officers eligible for membership in the Military Officers Association of America (MOAA) must be members. Children of enlisted personnel are also eligible to apply. Selection is based on scholastic ability (GPA of 3.0 or higher), participation, leadership, and financial need.

Financial Data Loans up to $5,500 per year are available. Repayment at an agreed rate begins 3 to 4 months after graduation or after leaving college, but no interest is charged.

Duration 1 year; may be renewed for 4 additional years as long as the recipient remains enrolled full time and has not yet graduated.

Additional data The MOAA was formerly named The Retired Officers Association (TROA). No loans are made for graduate study.

Number awarded Varies each year; recently, more than 1,600 students received loans through this program, including about 400 first-time recipients.

Deadline February of each year.

[1058]
NMCRS FINANCIAL ASSISTANCE

Navy-Marine Corps Relief Society
875 North Randolph Street, Suite 225
Arlington, VA 22203-1757
(703) 696-4904   Fax: (703) 696-0144
Web: www.nmcrs.org/intfreeloan.html

Summary To provide emergency assistance, in the form of interest-free loans or grants, to current and former Navy and Marine Corps personnel and their families who need temporary funding.

Eligibility This program is open to active-duty and retired Navy and Marine Corps personnel, their eligible family members, eligible family members of Navy and Marine Corps personnel who

died on active duty or in a retired status, Reservists on extended active duty, indigent mothers (65 years of age or older) of deceased servicemembers who have limited resources and no family to provide for their welfare, ex-spouses whose marriage to a servicemember lasted for at least 20 years while the servicemember was on active duty and who have not remarried, and uniformed members of the National Oceanic and Atmospheric Administration (NOAA). Applicants must need emergency funding for funeral expenses, medical or dental bills, food, rent, utilities, emergency transportation, disaster relief, child care expenses, essential vehicle repairs, or other unforeseen family emergencies. Funding is not available to pay bills for non-essentials, finance liberty and vacations, pay fines or legal expenses, pay taxes, finance recreational boats or vehicles or help Navy and Marine Corps families live beyond their means.

Financial Data Funds are provided in the form of interest-free loans or grants.

Number awarded Varies each year.

Deadline Applications may be submitted at any time.

[1059]
NORTH DAKOTA VETERANS' AID LOANS

Department of Veterans Affairs
4201 38th Street S.W., Suite 104
P.O. Box 9003
Fargo, ND 58106-9003
(701) 239-7165   Toll Free: (866) 634-8387
Fax: (701) 239-7166
Web: www.nd.gov/veterans/benefits/loan.html

Summary To loan money to meet the emergency needs of North Dakota veterans and their unremarried surviving spouses.

Eligibility This program is open to North Dakota veterans who served in peacetime, wartime, or the National Guard with active duty and received other than a dishonorable discharge. Surviving spouses of deceased veterans are also eligible if they have not remarried. Applicants must be facing a temporary and unexpected financial emergency, including dental work, education expenses for the applicant or dependents, emergency eyeglasses, first-time home buyer improvements, medical care, repair bills (in certain cases), temporary unemployment, expenses related to purchase of a primary family residence, or waiting for relief or assistance from other agencies.

Financial Data Veterans and surviving spouses may borrow up to $5,000 at 8% interest. If the loan is repaid within 2 years, half of the interest is refunded.

Duration Loans may be granted for periods of 6 to 48 months.

Number awarded Varies each year.

Deadline Applications may be submitted at any time.

[1060]
OREGON VETERANS HOME LOAN PROGRAM

Oregon Department of Veterans' Affairs
Attn: Veterans' Home Loan Program
700 Summer Street N.E., Suite 150
Salem, OR 97310-1285
(503) 373-2051   Toll Free: (888) ORE-VETS (within OR)
Fax: (503) 373-2393   TDD: (503) 373-2217
E-mail: orvetshomeloans@odva.state.or.us
Web: www.oregon.gov/ODVA/HOMELOANS

Summary To help Oregon veterans or their surviving spouses buy homes.

Eligibility This program is open to veterans who 1) served honorably on active duty for purposes other than training for not less than 210 consecutive days; 2) served honorably on active duty for less than 210 days but was discharged or released from active duty because of a service-connected injury or illness; or 3) served in a theater of operations for which a campaign or expeditionary ribbon or medal is authorized by the United States (including

Grenada, Libya, Panama, Somalia, Haiti, El Salvador, the Persian Gulf, the Balkans, Kosovo, Afghanistan, or Iraq). Applicants must be Oregon residents at the time of application for the loan. Spouses to be eligible must be Oregon residents who have not remarried and whose spouse either died while on active duty or is listed as a prisoner of war or missing in action. The eligibility of a veteran ends 30 years after the last date of separation from service; the eligibility of a spouse expires 30 years after notification of the veteran's death, capture, or disappearance, or upon remarriage. Applicants must demonstrate sufficient income to make loan repayments and be good credit risks. Loans may be used only to finance owner-occupied, single-family residential housing for qualified eligible veterans or their spouses. The purchase of vacation homes, income properties (such as farms or rentals), commercial property, or bare land cannot be financed.

Financial Data Loans are made up to a current maximum of $417,000 and may be as much as 100% of appraised property value. The loan origination fee is 1.375%. Interest rates are fixed at 4.5% with a .125 discount charge to borrower or 4.625% with a .375 credit to borrower.

Duration The maximum loan term is 30 years and the minimum is 15 years.

Additional data Recipients must live on the property and use it as their primary home within 90 days after the loan has closed.

Number awarded Varies each year.

Deadline Applications may be submitted at any time.

[1061]
PATRIOT EXPRESS LOAN PROGRAM

Small Business Administration
Attn: Office of Veterans Business Development
409 Third Street, S.W.
Washington, DC 20416
(202) 205-6773   Toll Free: (800) U-ASK-SBA
Fax: (202) 205-7292   TDD: (704) 344-6640
E-mail: janet.moorman@sba.gov
Web: www.sba.gov/patriotexpress/index.html

Summary To provide business loan guarantees to veterans and members of the military community.

Eligibility This program is open to veterans, service-disabled veterans, active-duty servicemembers eligible for the military's Transition Assistance Program, Reservists and National Guard members, current spouses of any of those, and widowed spouses of servicemembers and veterans who died during service or of a service-connected disability. Applicants must be interested in borrowing money for business-related purposes, including start-up, expansion, equipment, inventory, or business-occupied real estate purchases.

Financial Data The maximum loan is $500,000. The Small Business Administration (SBA) guarantees up to 85% of loans of $150,000 and less and up to 75% of loans above $150,000. Interest rates are the lowest offered by the SBA, generally 2.25% to 4.75% over the Prime Rate.

Duration Maximum loan maturities are generally 7 years for working capital or 25 years for real estate and equipment.

Additional data This program began in 2007.

Number awarded Varies each year.

Deadline Loan applications may be submitted at any time.

[1062]
SOUTH DAKOTA LEGION EDUCATIONAL LOAN

American Legion
Department of South Dakota
P.O. Box 67
Watertown, SD 57201-0067
(605) 886-3604   Fax: (605) 886-2870
E-mail: sdlegion@dailypost.com
Web: www.sdlegion.org

Summary To provide loans to children and grandchildren of South Dakota veterans who are interested in attending college in the state.

Eligibility This program is open to residents of South Dakota who are the children or grandchildren of veterans eligible for membership in the American Legion (although Legion membership is not required). Applicants must be interested in attending a South Dakota college or technical school (unless no school in the state offers the professional or technical degree being sought).

Financial Data Loans are available up to $1,500 per year. Repayment begins 90 days after the student leaves school, with interest at 3%.

Duration 1 year; the lifetime maximum that may be borrowed is $3,000.

Number awarded Varies each year.

Deadline April of each year for fall semester; October of each year for spring semester.

[1063]
TEXAS B-ON-TIME LOAN PROGRAM

Texas Higher Education Coordinating Board
Attn: Hinson-Hazlewood College Student Loan Program
1200 East Anderson Lane
P.O. Box 12788, Capitol Station
Austin, TX 78711-2788
(512) 427-6340   Toll Free: (800) 242-3062
Fax: (512) 427-6423   E-mail: loaninfo@thecb.state.tx.us
Web: www.hhloans.com/borrowers/BOTfactsheet.cfm

Summary To provide forgivable loans to students in Texas who are residents of the state or entitled to pay resident tuition as a dependent child of a member of the U.S. armed forces.

Eligibility This program is open to residents of Texas and residents of other states who are entitled to pay resident tuition as a dependent child of a member of the U.S. armed forces. Applicants must 1) have graduated from a public or accredited private high school in Texas or from a high school operated by the U.S. Department of Defense; or 2) earned an associate degree from an eligible Texas institution. They must be enrolled full time in an undergraduate degree or certificate program at an eligible college, university, junior college, or public technical college in Texas.

Financial Data Eligible students may borrow up to $2,640 per semester ($5,280 per year) for a 4-year public or private institution, $865 per semester ($1,730 per year) for a 2-year public or private junior college, or $1,325 per semester ($2,650 per year) for a public technical college. A 3% origination fee is deducted from the loan proceeds. No interest is charged. Loans are forgiven if the students 1) graduate with a cumulative GPA of 3.0 or higher within 4 calendar years after they initially enroll; within 5 calendar years after they initially enroll in a degree program in architecture, engineering, or other field that normally requires more than 4 years for completion; or within 2 calendar years if they initially enroll in a public or private 2-year institution; or 2) graduate with a cumulative GPA of 3.0 or higher with a total number of credit hours that is no more than 6 hours beyond what is required to complete the degree or certificate.

Duration 1 year. May be renewed after the first year if the recipient makes satisfactory academic progress toward a degree or certificate. May be renewed after the second and subsequent years if the recipient completes at least 75% of the semester credit hours attempted and has a cumulative GPA of 2.5 or higher on all course work. Loans are available for a maximum of 150 credit hours.

Number awarded Varies each year.

Deadline Deadline not specified.

[1064]
TEXAS VETERANS HOME IMPROVEMENT PROGRAM

Texas Veterans Land Board
Stephen F. Austin Building
1700 North Congress Avenue, Room 800
P.O. Box 12873
Austin, TX 78711-2873
(512) 463-5060   Toll Free: (800) 252-VETS (within TX)
TDD: (512) 463-6367   E-mail: vlbinfo@glo.state.tx.us
Web: www.glo.state.tx.us/vlb/vhip/index.html

Summary To assist Texas veterans, National Guard members, and unremarried surviving spouses who wish to maintain older homes but who cannot qualify for the high interest rates of conventional home improvement loans.

Eligibility This program is open to 1) veterans who served for at least 90 consecutive days of active duty after September 16, 1940 in the Army, Navy, Air Force, Marines, Coast Guard, U.S. Public Health Service, or a Reserve component of those services; 2) members of the Texas National Guard or Reserves who have enlisted or received an appointment and have completed all Initial Active Duty for Training (IADT) requirements; and 3) veterans who served in the armed forces of the Republic of Vietnam (ARVN) between February 28, 1961 and May 7, 1975. Applicants may not have been dishonorably discharged and must have listed Texas as their home of record at the time of entry into the military or have been a resident of Texas for at least 1 year prior to filing an application. The unremarried surviving spouses of Texas veterans who are missing in action, died in the line of duty, or died from a service-connected cause may be eligible to participate in the program. Applicants must be interested in making alterations, repairs, and improvements to, or in connection with, their existing residence if, and only if, repairs will 1) substantially protect or improve the basic livability or energy efficiency of the property; 2) correct damage resulting from a natural disaster; or 3) correct conditions that are hazardous to health or safety. Examples of eligible improvements include carpeting, fencing, room additions, patios, driveways, and garages. Examples of ineligible improvements include exterior spas, saunas, whirlpools, tree surgery, tennis courts, swimming pools, and barbecue pits. The home must be in Texas and the veteran's primary residence. In addition to single family dwellings, condominiums, duplexes, triplexes, and fourplexes are eligible as long as 1 of the units is the veteran's primary residence. Duplexes, triplexes, and fourplexes must be at least 5 years old. Modular or manufactured homes that are on a permanent foundation and are a part of the real estate may also be eligible. An interest rate reduction is available to Texas veterans who have a service-connected disability of 30% or greater as verified by the U.S. Department of Veterans Affairs.

Financial Data The maximum loan on a single family residence or a manufactured or modular home is $25,000. The maximum loan on a multi-family residence is $12,000 per dwelling unit or $25,000, whichever is less. Loans over $10,000 are for 2 to 20 years; those for $10,000 or less are for 2 to 10 years. Interest rates recently were 4.89%. An interest rate reduction of 0.50 percentage points is available for the Veterans with Disabilities program.

Number awarded Varies each year.

Deadline Applications may be submitted at any time.

[1065]
TEXAS VETERANS HOUSING ASSISTANCE PROGRAM

Texas Veterans Land Board
Stephen F. Austin Building
1700 North Congress Avenue, Room 800
P.O. Box 12873
Austin, TX 78711-2873
(512) 463-5060   Toll Free: (800) 252-VETS (within TX)
TDD: (512) 463-5330   E-mail: vlbinfo@glo.state.tx.us
Web: www.glo.state.tx.us/vlb/vhap/index.html

Summary To provide low-interest loans to assist Texas veterans, National Guard members, and unremarried surviving spouses in purchasing their own homes.

Eligibility This program is open to 1) veterans who served for at least 90 consecutive days of active duty after September 16, 1940 in the Army, Navy, Air Force, Marines, Coast Guard, U.S. Public Health Service, or a Reserve component of those services; 2) members of the Texas National Guard or Reserves who have enlisted or received an appointment and have completed all Initial Active Duty for Training (IADT) requirements; and 3) veterans who served in the armed forces of the Republic of Vietnam (ARVN) between February 28, 1961 and May 7, 1975. Applicants may not have been dishonorably discharged and must have listed Texas as their home of record at the time of entry into the military or have been a resident of Texas for at least 1 year prior to filing an application. The unremarried surviving spouses of Texas veterans who are missing in action, died in the line of duty, or died from a service-connected cause may be eligible to participate in the program. Applicants must be interested in purchasing a new or existing home, including a duplex, triplex, or fourplex if the structure is more than 5 years old, or a modular or manufactured home if it is on a permanent foundation and meets loan guidelines established by the Federal National Mortgage Association or the Federal Home Loan Mortgage Corporation and has an economic life of at least 30 years. Any home purchased with funds from this program must be the primary residence of the veteran for at least 3 years. An interest rate reduction is available to Texas veterans who have a service-connected disability of 30% or greater as verified by the U.S. Department of Veterans Affairs.

Financial Data There is no limit on the sales price of the house, but the maximum loan available through this program is $325,000. Loans for $45,000 or less may be requested directly from the Texas Veterans Land Board (VLB) and may cover up to 85% of the home's appraised value. Loans over $45,000 are originated through a VLB participating lender. No fees are charged on direct loans; loans available through a VLB-approved lender require an origination fee up to 1% and a participation fee up to 1%. Interest rates recently were 4.89%. An interest rate reduction of 0.50 percentage points is available for the Veterans with Disabilities program.

Duration Loans are available with 15, 20, 25, or 30 year terms.

Number awarded Varies each year.

Deadline Applications may be submitted at any time.

[1066]
TEXAS VETERANS LAND PROGRAM

Texas Veterans Land Board
Stephen F. Austin Building
1700 North Congress Avenue, Room 800
P.O. Box 12873
Austin, TX 78711-2873
(512) 463-5060   Toll Free: (800) 252-VETS (within TX)
TDD: (512) 463-5330   E-mail: vlbinfo@glo.state.tx.us
Web: www.glo.state.tx.us/vlb/land/index.html

Summary To assist Texas veterans, National Guard members, and unremarried surviving spouses interested in purchasing land in Texas.

Eligibility This program is open to 1) veterans who served for at least 90 consecutive days of active duty after September 16, 1940 in the Army, Navy, Air Force, Marines, Coast Guard, U.S. Public Health Service, or a Reserve component of those services; 2) members of the Texas National Guard or Reserves who have enlisted or received an appointment and have completed all Initial Active Duty for Training (IADT) requirements. Applicants may not have been dishonorably discharged and must have listed Texas as their home of record at the time of entry into the military or have been a resident of Texas for at least 1 year prior to filing an application. The unremarried surviving spouses of Texas veterans who are missing in action, died in the line of duty, or died from a service-connected cause may be eligible to participate in the program. Applicants must be interested in purchasing up to 1 acre of land within Texas. It must have legal access to a public road, and such right-of-way must be the minimum width required by the county commissioners. Land must be officially surveyed and appraised.

Financial Data The maximum loan is $80,000. The veteran must pay a 5% down payment. If the purchase price is greater than $80,000, the veteran must pay the difference to the VLB in cash. The VLB then purchases the land directly from the seller and resells the land to the veteran using a 30-year contract of sale and purchase. In addition to the down payment, the veteran must pay a closing fee of $325. The interest rate recently was 7.25%.

Number awarded Varies each year.

Deadline Applications may be submitted at any time.

[1067]
VA HOME LOAN GUARANTY BENEFITS

Department of Veterans Affairs
Attn: Veterans Benefits Administration
Home Loan Guaranty Service
810 Vermont Avenue, N.W.
Washington, DC 20420
(202) 418-4343   Toll Free: (800) 827-1000
Web: www.homeloans.va.gov/veteran.htm

Summary To assist disabled and other veterans, certain military personnel, and their unremarried surviving spouses in the purchase of residences.

Eligibility This benefit is available to 1) veterans who served during specified periods of time and were discharged since September 16, 1940 under other than dishonorable conditions; 2) military personnel who have served at least 90 days; 3) members of the Reserves or National Guard who have completed at least 6 years of honorable service or were discharged because of a service-related disability; 4) unremarried spouses of veterans or Reservists who died on active duty or as a result of service-connected causes; 5) surviving spouses who remarry after attaining 57 years of age; 6) spouses of active-duty servicemembers who have been missing in action or a prisoner of war for at least 90 days; 7) U.S. citizens who served in the armed forces of a U.S. ally in World War II; and 8) members of organizations with recognized contributions to the U.S. World War II effort.

Financial Data The Department of Veterans Affairs (VA) does not lend money; the actual loan must come from a commercial lender. The loan may be for any amount, and the VA will guarantee payment on loans for the purchase of homes, farm homes, condominium units, or refinancing of existing loans. The largest guaranty that the VA can give is an amount equal to 25% of the Freddie Mac conforming loan limit for single family residences (currently $417,000 or $625,500 for Hawaii, Alaska, Guam and the Virgin Islands). Interest rates vary with market conditions but are fixed for the life of the loan, which may be as long as 30 years and 32 days. No down payments are prescribed by the VA. A funding fee must be paid to the VA, although it may be included in the loan amount; the amount of the fee varies, depending on the type of loan and whether the borrower is a veteran or a Reservist, but ranges from 0.5% to 3.3% of the amount of the loan. The funding fee is waived for disabled veterans and unremarried surviving spouses of veterans who died as a result of service.

Additional data In addition to the purchase of a new home, VA Loans may be used to buy a residential condominium; to build a home; to repair, alter, or improve a home; to refinance an existing home loan; to buy a manufactured home with or without a lot; to buy and improve a manufactured home lot; to install a solar heating and/or cooling system or other weatherization improvements; to purchase and improve simultaneously a home with energy conserving measures; to refinance an existing VA loan to reduce the interest rate; or to refinance a manufactured home loan to acquire a lot. Mortgages guaranteed by the VA usually offer an interest rate lower than conventional mortgage rates, require no down payment, provide a long repayment period, allow the VA to appraise the property and inspect it to ensure that it conforms to the plans and specifications, and permit early prepayment without premium or penalty. The VA does not have legal authority to act as an architect, supervise construction of the home, guarantee that the home is free of defects, or act as an attorney if the veteran encounters legal difficulties in buying or constructing a home. Veterans must certify that they intend to live in the home they are buying or building with a VA loan. Veterans who wish to refinance or improve a home must certify that they are actually in residence at the time of application.

Number awarded Varies each year.

Deadline Applications may be submitted at any time.

[1068]
VICE ADMIRAL E.P. TRAVERS LOAN PROGRAM

Navy-Marine Corps Relief Society
Attn: Education Division
875 North Randolph Street, Suite 225
Arlington, VA 22203-1757
(703) 696-4960   Fax: (703) 696-0144
E-mail: education@nmcrs.org
Web: www.nmcrs.org/travers.html

Summary To provide interest-free loans for college to the spouses and children of Navy and Marine Corps personnel.

Eligibility This program is open to the dependent children of active-duty and retired Navy and Marine Corps personnel (including Reservists while on active duty over 90 days) and the spouses of active-duty Navy and Marine Corps personnel. Applicants must have a GPA of 2.0 or higher and be able to demonstrate financial need. They must be enrolled or planning to enroll as a full-time undergraduate student at an accredited college, university, or vocational/technical school.

Financial Data The loan amount is determined on the basis of need, from $500 to $3,000 per academic year. No interest is charged on the money borrowed. The loan must be repaid within 24 months by allotment of pay, at a monthly rate of at least $50.

Number awarded Varies each year.

Deadline February of each year.

[1069]
VOCATIONAL AND TECHNICAL TRAINING
STUDENT LOAN PROGRAM

Coast Guard Mutual Assistance
4200 Wilson Boulevard, Suite 610
Arlington, VA 20598-7180
(202) 493-6624   Toll Free: (800) 881-2462
Fax: (202) 493-6686   E-mail: ARL-DG-CGMA@uscg.mil
Web: www.cgmahq.org

Summary To provide loans to the members of Coast Guard Mutual Assistance (CGMA) and their spouses and dependent children who require assistance for vocational or technical training.

Eligibility This program is open to members of the organization, their spouses, and dependent children. Applicants should be seeking assistance to help pay the costs of non-college courses that provide the technical knowledge and skills needed for entry into a specific career field. Financial need must be demonstrated.

Financial Data The maximum loan is $1,500.

Additional data CGMA membership is open to active-duty and retired members of the U.S. Coast Guard, civilian employees of the U.S. Coast Guard, U.S. Coast Guard Reserve members, U.S. Coast Guard Auxiliary members, Public Health Service officers serving with the U.S. Coast Guard, and family members of all of those.

Number awarded Varies each year.

Deadline Requests must be submitted within 30 days after the course begins.

[1070]
WISCONSIN HOME IMPROVEMENT LOAN PROGRAM

Wisconsin Department of Veterans Affairs
30 West Mifflin Street
P.O. Box 7843
Madison, WI 53707-7843
(608) 266-1311   Toll Free: (800) WIS-VETS
Fax: (608) 267-0403   E-mail: loans@dva.state.wi.us
Web: www.dva.state.wi.us/Ben_improvementloans.asp

Summary To provide low-interest loans to veterans, current National Guard members, Reservists, and their families in Wisconsin to pay for improvements to their homes.

Eligibility This program is open to current residents of Wisconsin who 1) were residents of the state when they entered or reentered active duty in the U.S. armed forces, or 2) have moved to the state and have been residents for any consecutive 12-month period after entry or reentry into service. Applicants must have served on active duty for at least 2 continuous years or for at least 90 days during specified wartime periods. Also eligible are 1) members and former members of the National Guard and Reserves who have completed at least 6 years of continuous service under honorable conditions; 2) unremarried spouses of deceased veterans; and 3) dependent children under 26 years of age who are attending school full time. Applicants may be planning to use the loan funds for additions, construction, repairs, or alterations of their principal residence. The loan also may be used for garage construction. The applicant must have at least 10% equity in the property to be improved.

Financial Data Loans up to $50,000 are available if secured by an 80% loan to value mortgage, up to $25,000 if secured by a 90% loan to value mortgage, or up to $3,000 if secured with a guarantor. Currently, for loans secured by a mortgage at 80% loan to value, interest rates are 5.85% for 5-year loans, 6.25% for 7- or 10-year loans, or 6.55% for 15-year loans. For loans secured by a mortgage at 90% loan to value, interest rates are 6.75% for 5-year loans, 7% for 7- or 10-year loans, or 7.25% for 15-year loans. For guarantor secured loans, interest rates are 8.5% for 3-year loans or 10% for 5-year loans. Funds may be used only for qualifying home improvements, not for personal property (such as furniture or certain types of appliances).

Duration The minimum loan repayment term is 1 year and the maximum term is 15 years.

Number awarded Varies each year.

Deadline Applications may be submitted at any time.

[1071]
WISCONSIN VETERANS' PERSONAL LOAN PROGRAM

Wisconsin Department of Veterans Affairs
30 West Mifflin Street
P.O. Box 7843
Madison, WI 53707-7843
(608) 266-1311   Toll Free: (800) WIS-VETS
Fax: (608) 267-0403   E-mail: loans@dva.state.wi.us
Web: www.dva.state.wi.us/Ben_personalloans.asp

Summary To provide eligible Wisconsin veterans or their dependents with loans for any purpose, including education.

Eligibility This program is open to current residents of Wisconsin who 1) were residents of the state when they entered or reentered active duty in the U.S. armed forces, or 2) have moved to the state and have been residents for any consecutive 12-month period after entry or reentry into service. Applicants must have served on active duty for at least 2 continuous years or for at least 90 days during specified wartime periods. Also eligible are unremarried spouses of deceased veterans and dependent children (adult children must be under 26 years of age and attending school full time). A remarried spouse or parent of a veterans' child may qualify if the loan is used for the child's education. Applicants may borrow money for any purpose. They must meet basic credit and underwriting standards. Loans must be secured by a mortgage on the applicant's property or with a guarantor.

Financial Data This program provides loans up to $25,000 if secured by a mortgage or up to $5,000 if a guarantor secured loan. For loans secured by a mortgage at 80% loan to value, interest rates are 5.85% for 5-year loans or 6.25% for 7- or 10-year loans. For loans secured by a mortgage at 90% loan to value, interest rates are 6.75% for 5-year loans or 7% for 7- or 10-year loans. For guarantor secured loans, interest rates are 8.5% for 3-year loans or 10% for 5-year loans.

Number awarded Varies each year.

Deadline Applications may be submitted at any time.

[1072]
WISCONSIN VETERANS PRIMARY MORTGAGE LOAN PROGRAM

Wisconsin Department of Veterans Affairs
30 West Mifflin Street
P.O. Box 7843
Madison, WI 53707-7843
(608) 266-1311   Toll Free: (800) WIS-VETS
Fax: (608) 267-0403   E-mail: loans@dva.state.wi.us
Web: www.dva.state.wi.us/Ben_mortgageloans.asp

Summary To provide housing loans to Wisconsin veterans, current National Guard members, Reservists, and their unremarried spouses or children who cannot obtain the necessary funds from other sources.

Eligibility This program is open to current residents of Wisconsin who 1) were residents of the state when they entered or reentered active duty in the U.S. armed forces, or 2) have moved to the state and have been residents for any consecutive 12-month period after entry or reentry into service. Applicants must have served on active duty for at least 2 continuous years or for at least 90 days during specified wartime periods. Also eligible are 1) dependent children and unremarried surviving spouses of eligible deceased veterans; and 2) members and former members of the National Guard and Reserves who have completed 6 years of continuous service under honorable conditions. Applicants must be seeking to borrow money for the purchase, or the purchase and improvement, of a single family home or condominium; construction of a new single family home; purchase of certain existing 2- to 4-unit owner occupied residences; or refinance of the balance due on existing mortgage loans used for purchase, construction, or improvement of a residence.

Financial Data The veteran or dependent may obtain a loan of up to 95% of the total cost of the property, to a maximum of $343,750. The required down payment is 5% and the department pays the loan origination fees for veterans with a disability rating of 30% or more. Other attractive features include: no private mortgage insurance or loan guaranty, no discount points, no interest rate increase, and no prepayment penalty. The current interest rate is 6.25%.

Duration Loan terms up to 30 years are available.

Number awarded Varies each year.

Deadline Applications may be submitted at any time.

Grants-in-Aid

Veterans ●

Military Personnel ●

Family Members ●

Described here are 325 programs that provide financial assistance for property and income tax liabilities, travel, emergency situations, service in dangerous military zones, and burial costs. Of the programs listed here, 137 are open to veterans, 68 to military personnel, and 120 to their family members (spouses, children, grandchildren, parents, and other relatives). If you are looking for a particular program and don't find it in this section, be sure to check the Program Title Index to see if it is covered elsewhere in the directory.

Veterans

[1073]
AER LOANS/GRANTS

Army Emergency Relief
200 Stovall Street
Alexandria, VA 22332-0600
(703) 428-0000
Fax: (703) 325-7183
Web: www.aerhq.org

Toll Free: (866) 878-6378
E-mail: aer@aerhq.org

Summary To provide loans and grants-in-aid to help with the emergency financial needs of Army veterans, military personnel, and their dependents.

Eligibility Eligible to apply are active-duty soldiers (single or married) and their dependents, Army National Guard and Army Reserve soldiers on continuous active duty for more than 30 days and their dependents, soldiers retired from active duty for longevity or physical disability and their dependents, Army National Guard and Army Reserve soldiers who retired at age 60 and their dependents, and surviving spouses and orphans of soldiers who died while on active duty or after they retired. Applicants must be seeking assistance for such emergency needs as food, rent, and utilities; emergency transportation and vehicle repair; funeral expenses; medical and dental expenses; or personal needs when pay is delayed or stolen. Support is not available to help pay for nonessentials, finance ordinary leave or vacation, pay fines or legal expenses, help liquidate or consolidate debt, assist with house purchase or home improvements, cover bad checks, pay credit card bills, or help purchase, rent, or lease a vehicle.

Financial Data Support is provided in the form of loans or grants (or a combination).

Duration Qualifying individuals can apply whenever they have a valid emergency need.

Additional data This organization was established in 1942.

Number awarded Varies each year; recently, the organization helped more than 66,000 Army people with more than $70 million, including $60 million to 58,820 active-duty soldiers and their families, $7.3 million to 4,914 retired soldiers and their families, and $2.7 million to 2,304 widow(er)s and orphans of deceased soldiers. Since it was established, the organization has helped more than 3.2 million qualifying individuals with more than $1.2 billion in financial assistance.

Deadline Applications may be submitted at any time.

[1074]
AFAS FINANCIAL ASSISTANCE

Air Force Aid Society
Attn: Financial Assistance Department
241 18th Street South, Suite 202
Arlington, VA 22202-3409
(703) 607-3072, ext. 51
Fax: (703) 607-3022
Web: www.afas.org/Assistance/HowWeCanHelp.cfm

Toll Free: (800) 429-9475

Summary To provide loans and grants-in-aid to current and former Air Force personnel and their families who are facing emergency situations.

Eligibility This program is open to active-duty Air Force members and their dependents, retired Air Force personnel and their dependents, Air National Guard and Air Force Reserve personnel on extended duty over 15 days, and spouses and dependent children of deceased Air Force personnel who died on active duty or in retired status. Applicants must be facing problems, usually for relatively short periods, that affect their job or the essential quality and dignity of life the Air Force wants for its people. Examples of such needs include basic living expenses (food, rent, utilities),

medical and dental care, funeral expenses, vehicle expenses, emergency travel, moving expenses, or child or respite care. Funding is generally not provided if it merely postpones a long-term inability to exist on present pay and allowances, for non-essentials, for continuing long-term assistance commitments, or to replace funds lost due to garnishment.

Financial Data Assistance is provided as an interest-free loan, a grant, or a combination of both.

Number awarded Varies each year.

Deadline Applications may be submitted at any time.

[1075]
AIR WARRIOR COURAGE FOUNDATION GRANTS

Air Warrior Courage Foundation
P.O. Box 1553
Front Royal, VA 22630-0033
(540) 636-9798
E-mail: awcf@awcfoundation.com
Web: www.airwarriorcourage.org

Fax: (540) 636-9776

Summary To provide emergency assistance to veterans, military personnel, and their families, especially members of the Red River Valley Fighter Pilots Association (RRVA), who are facing unusual situations.

Eligibility These grants are available to active, Guard, Reserve, retired, and former military and Coast Guard personnel and dependent family members. Applicants must be able to demonstrate financial and material needs unmet by insurance programs, community support, or other service agencies. Special consideration is given to applicants eligible for the RRVA scholarship program (spouses and children of servicemembers missing in action or killed in action in armed conflicts by U.S. forces since August 1964, of U.S. military aircrew members killed in a non-combat aircraft accident in which they were performing aircrew duties, and of current members of the association). Assistance is available through the following activities: the 9/11 Terrorism Memorial Fund, which provides financial assistance, college savings programs, and/or material support to surviving family members of those lost or injured in the war on terror and military units performing humanitarian activities worldwide; the Earl Aman Courage Fund, which provides assistance or equipment to those disabled or in need for medically-related extraordinary expenses; and the Helping Achieve Normal Development (HAND) Fund, which provides assistance for therapeutic activities to children with anatomical, physiological, or mental deficits. Other programs are established from time to time as needs arise.

Financial Data The amount awarded varies. Recent grants included $148,744 for servicemember victims of Hurricanes Katrina and Rita; the Earl Aman Courage Fund awarded a total of $38,400 to provide financial support to veterans and/or their families to meet extraordinary medical or personal expenses beyond their financial resources; and the HAND Fund awarded $41,550 to provide therapeutic riding programs for 88 medically challenged military dependent children.

Duration These are 1-time grants.

Additional data This foundation was established in 1998 as a charitable organization affiliated with the RRVA.

Number awarded Varies each year.

Deadline Applications may be submitted at any time.

[1076]
ALABAMA AD VALOREM TAX EXEMPTION FOR SPECIALLY ADAPTED HOUSES

Alabama Department of Revenue
Attn: Property Tax Division
Gordon Persons Building
50 North Ripley Street, Room 4126
P.O. Box 327210
Montgomery, AL 36132-7210
(334) 242-1525
Web: www.ador.state.al.us

Summary To provide a property tax exemption to the owners of specially adapted housing (housing adapted for disabled veterans) in Alabama.

Eligibility The home of any veteran which is or was acquired pursuant to the provisions of Public Law 702, 80th Congress (specially adapted housing grants for veterans) as amended (38 USC) will be exempted from ad valorem taxation if the house is owned and occupied by the veteran or the veteran's unremarried widow(er).

Financial Data Qualifying houses are exempt from all ad valorem taxation.

Duration This exemption continues as long as the qualifying veteran or the unremarried widow(er) resides in the house.

Number awarded Varies each year.

Deadline Deadline not specified.

[1077]
ALABAMA MILITARY RETIREE INCOME TAX EXEMPTION

Alabama Department of Revenue
Attn: Income Tax Division
Gordon Persons Building
50 North Ripley Street, Room 4212
P.O. Box 327410
Montgomery, AL 36132-7410
(334) 242-1105   Fax: (334) 242-0064
E-mail: erohelpdesk@revenue.state.al.us
Web: www.ador.state.al.us

Summary To exempt a portion of the income of veterans and their survivors from taxation in Alabama.

Eligibility Eligible are Alabama recipients of regular military retired pay or military survivors benefits. Recipients of benefits paid by the U.S. Department of Veterans Affairs (including disability retirement payments) are also eligible for this exemption.

Financial Data All income received as military retired pay, veterans' disability payment, or military survivors benefits is exempt from state, county, or municipal income taxation.

Duration The exemption continues as long as the recipient resides in Alabama.

Deadline Deadline not specified.

[1078]
ALASKA PROPERTY TAX EXEMPTION

Division of Community and Regional Affairs
Attn: Office of the State Assessor
550 West Seventh Avenue, Suite 1790
Anchorage, AK 99501-3510
(907) 269-4605   Fax: (907) 269-4539
E-mail: Steve.VanSant@alaska.gov
Web: www.commerce.state.ak.us/dcra/osa/taxfacts.htm

Summary To exempt from taxation the property owned by veterans with disabilities in Alaska.

Eligibility This exemption is available to veterans in Alaska who have a disability that was incurred or aggravated in the line of duty and that has been rated as 50% or more by the military service or the U.S. Department of Veterans Affairs. Applicants must own and occupy real property that is their primary residence and per-

manent place of abode. Senior citizens who are 65 years of age or older are also eligible for this exemption.

Financial Data Qualified veterans are exempt from taxation on the first $150,000 of assessed valuation on real property.

Duration The exemption continues as long as the veteran with a disability resides in Alaska.

Additional data Applications may be obtained from the local assessor's office. Since 1986, the cost of this program has exceeded the funding available for it. As a result, recipients may be granted a prorated level of payments.

Number awarded Varies each year. Recently, more than 25,000 disabled veterans and senior citizens received an average exemption of $1,851 on their property, which had an average assessed value of $135,486.

Deadline Applications may be submitted at any time.

[1079]
ALASKA VETERANS LAND DISCOUNT

Alaska Department of Natural Resources
Attn: Division of Mining, Land and Water
550 West Seventh Avenue, Suite 1070
Anchorage, AK 99501-3579
(907) 269-8600   Fax: (907) 269-8904
TDD: (907) 269-8411
Web: www.dnr.state.ak.us/mlw

Summary To enable veterans in Alaska to purchase state land at a discount whenever the state has a land auction.

Eligibility This discount is available to veterans who are 18 years of age or older on the date of the sale of land and have been residents of Alaska for at least 1 year immediately preceding the date of sale. Applicants must have served in the Alaska Territorial Guard or on active duty in the U.S. armed forces for at least 90 days unless shortened by a service-connected disability, and received an honorable discharge or a general discharge under honorable conditions.

Financial Data Eligible veterans receive a discount of 25% on the purchase price of state land sold for use other than agricultural, commercial, or industrial.

Duration Veterans are entitled to this discount only once.

Additional data Discounts received under this program apply only to surface rights.

Number awarded Varies each year.

Deadline Applications may be submitted at any time.

[1080]
ARIZONA INCOME TAX EXEMPTION FOR PUBLIC EMPLOYEE RETIRED PAY

Arizona Department of Revenue
1600 West Monroe Street
Phoenix, AZ 85007-2650
(602) 542-3572   Toll Free: (800) 352-4090 (within AZ)
TDD: (602) 542-4021
Web: www.revenue.state.az.us

Summary To exempt a portion of the pay of retired military personnel and other public employees from state income taxes in Arizona.

Eligibility Eligible are retired military personnel classified as Arizona residents for purposes of state income taxation. Retired federal, state, and local government employees also qualify.

Financial Data Exempt from state income taxation is $2,500 of military and other public employee retired pay.

Duration The exemption continues as long as the recipient resides in Arizona.

Deadline Deadline not specified.

[1081]
ARKANSAS DISABLED VETERANS PROPERTY TAX EXEMPTION

Arkansas Assessment Coordination Department
1614 West Third Street
Little Rock, AR 72201-1815
(501) 324-9100   Fax: (501) 324-9242
E-mail: dasbury@acd.state.ar.us
Web: www.arkansas.gov/acd

Summary   To exempt from taxation the property owned by blind or disabled veterans, surviving spouses, and minor dependent children in Arkansas.

Eligibility   This program is open to disabled veterans in Arkansas who have been awarded special monthly compensation by the U.S. Department of Veterans Affairs and who have 1) the loss of or the loss of use of 1 or more limbs, 2) total blindness in 1 or both eyes, or 3) total and permanent disability. The benefit also extends to veterans' unremarried surviving spouses and their minor children.

Financial Data   Qualifying veterans (or their unremarried widows or dependent children) are exempt from payment of all state taxes on their homestead and personal property.

Duration   This exemption continues as long as the qualifying veteran (or dependent) resides in Arkansas.

Number awarded   Varies each year.

Deadline   Applications may be submitted at any time.

[1082]
ARKANSAS INCOME TAX EXEMPTIONS FOR MILITARY COMPENSATION AND DISABILITY PAY

Arkansas Department of Finance and Administration
Attn: Office of Income Tax Administration
Joel Ledbetter Building, Room 110
1800 Seventh Street
P.O. Box 3628
Little Rock, AR 72203-3628
(501) 682-7225   Fax: (501) 682-7692
E-mail: individual.income@rev.state.ar.us
Web: www.arkansas.gov/dfa/income_tax/tax_index.html

Summary   To exempt a portion of the income of military personnel and disabled veterans from state income taxes in Arkansas.

Eligibility   Eligible are residents of Arkansas receiving military compensation or military disability income.

Financial Data   The first $9,000 of U.S. military compensation pay or military disability income is exempt from state income taxation.

Duration   The exemptions continue as long as the recipient resides in Arkansas.

Deadline   Deadline not specified.

[1083]
CALIFORNIA DISABLED VETERAN EXEMPTION FROM THE IN LIEU TAX FEE FOR A MANUFACTURED HOME OR MOBILEHOME

Department of Housing and Community Development
Attn: Registration and Titling
1800 Third Street
P.O. Box 2111
Sacramento, CA 95812-2111
(916) 323-9224   Toll Free: (800) 952-8356
Web: www.hcd.ca.gov

Summary   To provide a special property tax exemption to blind or disabled California veterans and/or their spouses who own and occupy a mobile home.

Eligibility   This program is open to disabled veterans and/or their spouses in California who have a manufactured home or mobile home as their principal place of residence. Veterans must be disabled as a result of injury or disease incurred in military ser-

vice and have been a resident of California 1) at the time of entry into the service and be blind, or have lost the use of 1 or more limbs, or be totally disabled; 2) on November 7, 1972 and be blind in both eyes, or have lost the use of 2 or more limbs; or 3) on January 1, 1975 and be totally disabled. The spouses and unremarried surviving spouses of those disabled veterans are also eligible.

Financial Data   The exemption applies to the first $20,000 of the assessed market value of the manufactured home or mobile home. Veterans and/or spouses whose income falls below a specified level are entitled to an additional $10,000 exemption. The amount of the exemption is 100% if the home is owned by a veteran only, a veteran and spouse, or a spouse only; 50% if owned by a veteran and another person other than a spouse or by a spouse and another person other than the veteran; 67% if owned by a veteran, the spouse, and another person; 34% if owned by a veteran and 2 other people other than a spouse or by a spouse and 2 other people; 50% if owned by a veteran, the spouse, and 2 other people; or 25% if owned by a veteran and 3 other people or by a spouse and 3 other people.

Duration   The exemption is available annually as long as the applicant meets all requirements.

Number awarded   Varies each year.

Deadline   Deadline not specified.

[1084]
CALIFORNIA PROPERTY TAX EXEMPTIONS FOR VETERANS

California Department of Veterans Affairs
Attn: Division of Veterans Services
1227 O Street, Room 101
Sacramento, CA 95814
(916) 503-8397   Toll Free: (800) 952-LOAN (within CA)
Fax: (916) 653-2563   TDD: (800) 324-5966
E-mail: ruckergl@cdva.ca.gov
Web: www.cdva.ca.gov/VetService/Overview.aspx

Summary   To exempt a portion of the property of blind or disabled veterans in California and their spouses from taxation.

Eligibility   This exemption is available to homeowners in California who are wartime veterans in receipt of service-connected disability compensation that is 1) at the totally disabled rate, 2) for loss or loss of use of 2 or more limbs, or 3) for blindness. Unremarried surviving spouses, including registered domestic partners, of veterans who are in receipt of service-connected death benefits are also eligible.

Financial Data   For veterans and spouses whose total household income from all sources is greater than $49,979 per year, up to $111,296 of the assessed value of a home is exempt from taxation. For veterans and spouses whose total household income from all sources is less than $49,979 per year, up to $166,944 of the assessed value of a home is exempt from taxation.

Duration   The exemption is available as long as the veteran or spouse owns a home in California.

Additional data   Information is available from the local county assessors office in each California county.

Number awarded   Varies each year.

Deadline   Applications may be submitted at any time.

[1085]
CGMA GRANTS-IN-AID

Coast Guard Mutual Assistance
4200 Wilson Boulevard, Suite 610
Arlington, VA 20598-7180
(202) 493-6621   Toll Free: (800) 881-2462
Fax: (202) 493-6686   E-mail: ARL-DG-CGMA@uscg.mil
Web: www.cgmahq.org

Summary To provide funding to members of the Coast Guard Mutual Assistance (CGMA) and their families who need temporary assistance.

Eligibility This program is open to CGMA members who are facing special needs. Categories of aid that are available include emergency assistance (basic living expenses, emergency home repair, emergency travel expenses, fire and other disasters, funeral expenses, loss of funds, temporary living expenses); general assistance (adoption, child support, child care, family in-home day care facility, financial counseling, government travel cards, household furnishings, immigration fees, insurance, loss of income, moving expenses, non-emergency travel, non-support or inadequate support, past due bills and expenses, pay and allotment problems, vehicle repair, vehicle other expenses); housing assistance (payment of settlement charges associated with purchasing a residence, rental assistance, utilities); and medical and dental assistance (provider won't proceed without payment; mental health and family counseling; patient's cost share; durable medical equipment; prosthetic devices; rehabilitation, nursing, home, or respite care; orthodontia; long-term dental care; travel, transportation, and incidental expenses; special situations). Applicants must be able to demonstrate their need for assistance.

Financial Data The assistance depends on the nature of the need.

Duration These are 1-time grants. A new application must accompany each request for assistance.

Additional data CGMA membership is open to active-duty and retired members of the U.S. Coast Guard, civilian employees of the U.S. Coast Guard, U.S. Coast Guard Reserve members, U.S. Coast Guard Auxiliary members, Public Health Service officers serving with the U.S. Coast Guard, and family members of all of those.

Number awarded Varies each year.

Deadline Deadline not specified.

[1086]
COLORADO PENSION/ANNUITY SUBTRACTION

Colorado Department of Revenue
Attn: Taxpayer Service Division
1375 Sherman Street, Room 242A
Denver, CO 80261-0005
(303) 232-2446   Toll Free: (800) 811-0172
Web: www.colorado.gov

Summary To exempt a portion of the pensions or annuities of veterans, the disabled, and other persons over the age of 55 from state income taxation in Colorado.

Eligibility This exemption is available to taxpayers over the age of 55 who are classified as Colorado residents for purposes of state income taxation, and to beneficiaries (such as a widowed spouse or orphan child) who are receiving a pension or annuity because of the death of the person who earned the pension. To qualify, the payment must be a retirement benefit that arose from an employer/employee relationship, service in the uniformed services of the United States, or contributions to a retirement plan that are deductible for federal income tax purposes. Disability retirement payments received by persons 55 years of age or older also qualify.

Financial Data For retirees who are at least 65 years of age, up to $24,000 of qualified pension or retirement income may be excluded from income for purposes of Colorado state taxation. For persons who are at least 55 but under 65 years of age, up to $20,000 of qualified pension or retirement income may be excluded.

Duration The exclusion continues as long as the recipient resides in Colorado.

Additional data Disability retirement payments received by persons under 55 years of age do not qualify for the pension exclusion.

Deadline Deadline not specified.

[1087]
COLORADO PROPERTY TAX EXEMPTION FOR DISABLED VETERANS

Division of Veterans Affairs
7465 East First Avenue, Suite C
Denver, CO 80230
(303) 343-1268   Fax: (303) 343-7238
Web: www.dmva.state.co.us/page/va/prop_tax

Summary To provide a partial exemption of taxes on property owned by disabled veterans or their spouses in Colorado.

Eligibility This exemption is open to veterans who reside in Colorado and have been rated 100% service-connected disabled by the U.S. Department of Veterans Affairs. Applicants must have been dishonorable discharged and must own property in Colorado which they use as their primary residence. The exemption also applies to members of the National Guard or Reserves who sustained their injury during a period in which they were called to active duty, property owned by a veteran's spouse if both occupy the property as their primary residence, and property owned by a trust or other legal entity if the veteran or spouse is a major of the trust or other legal entity, the property was transferred solely for estate planning purposes, and the veteran or spouse would otherwise be the owner of record.

Financial Data For qualifying veterans, 50% of the first $200,000 of actual value of the primary residence is exempted from taxes.

Duration The exemption continues as long as the veteran resides in the property.

Additional data This program was approved by Colorado voters in 2006.

Number awarded Varies each year.

Deadline Applications must be submitted by June of the year for which the exemption is requested.

[1088]
COMBAT-RELATED SPECIAL COMPENSATION

U.S. Army
Human Resources Command
Attn: AHRC-DZB-CRSC
200 Stovall Street
Alexandria, VA 22332-0470
Toll Free: (866) 281-3254   E-mail: CRSC.info@us.army.mil
Web: www.defenselink.mil/prhome/mppcrsc.html

Summary To provide supplemental compensation to military retirees who are receiving disability pay from the U.S. Department of Veterans Affairs (VA).

Eligibility This program is open to retirees from the United States uniformed services who either 1) served at least 20 years on active duty; 2) served in the Reserves or National Guard, received a 20-year retirement letter, and are at least 60 years of age; 3) performed reserve service under the Reserve TERA program, completed at least 15 but less than 20 years of combined active and reserve service, and are at least 60 years of age; or 4) are currently entitled to military retired pay for any reason, other than early reserve retirement for physical disabilities not incurred in line of duty. Applicants must have a VA disability rating of 10% or higher, be drawing retirement pay, and be receiving VA disability pay. Their disability must be not just service-connected but also combat-related. Spouses and other dependents are not eligible for this program.

Financial Data Qualified veterans receive compensation that depends on their combat-related disability rating (which may differ from their VA service-connected disability rating). They continue to receive their full military retirement pay (unlike VA disability compensation, which acted as an offset for an equivalent reduction in military retirement pay). The compensation is non-taxable.

Duration This compensation is payable for the life of the veteran.

Additional data The Combat-Related Special Compensation Program (CRSC I) began in June, 2003. The program was revised to offer compensation to a larger group of retirees and CRSC II began in January, 2004. Another revision in January 2008 again expanded eligibility requirements. Military retirees must apply through the armed forces branch in which they served. Navy and Marine Corps personnel should contact the Naval Council of Review Boards, Attn: Combat-Related Special Compensation Branch, 720 Kennon Street, S.E., Suite 309, Washington Navy Yard, DC 20374-5023, (877) 366-2772. Air Force personnel should contact the Disability Division (CRSC), 550 C Street West, Suite 6, Randolph AFB, TX 78150-4708, (800), 616-3775, Fax: (210) 565-1101. The program is also available to retirees from the other uniformed services (Coast Guard, National Oceanic and Atmospheric Administration, and Public Health Service). Information is available from those services.

Number awarded Varies each year. Currently, more than 50,000 retirees are receiving these payments of more than $59 million per month.

Deadline Applications may be submitted at any time.

[1089]
CONNECTICUT PERSONAL PROPERTY TAX EXEMPTION FOR WARTIME VETERANS

Office of Policy and Management
Attn: Intergovernmental Policy Division
450 Capitol Avenue
Hartford, CT 06106-1308
(860) 418-6278   Toll Free: (800) 286-2214 (within CT)
Fax: (860) 418-6493   TDD: (860) 418-6456
E-mail: leeann.graham@ct.gov
Web: www.ct.gov/opm/cwp/view.asp?a=2985&Q=383132

Summary To exempt wartime veterans and their family members from a portion of their personal property taxes if they are Connecticut residents.

Eligibility Eligible to apply for this exemption are veterans with 90 days of wartime service who are residents of Connecticut. Spouses, minor children, and parents of deceased veterans may also be eligible. An additional exemption may be available to veterans and spouses whose total adjusted gross income is less than $30,500 if unmarried or $37,300 if married. If the veteran is rated as 100% disabled by the U.S. Department of Veterans Affairs (VA), the maximum income levels are $18,000 if unmarried or $21,000 if married.

Financial Data Property to the amount of $1,000 belonging to, or held in trust for, an eligible veteran is exempt from taxation. The same exemption is available to the surviving unremarried spouse, minor children, and (if there is no surviving unremarried spouse) parent of a deceased veteran. If the death was service-connected and occurred while on active duty, the exemption for a surviving unremarried spouse or minor child is $3,000. Municipalities may provide veterans and spouses with an additional exemption up to $2,000 of the assessed value of the property, provided their income is less than the qualifying level. The additional municipality exemption for spouses and children of veterans who died on active duty of service-connected causes is $6,000. The additional municipality exemptions for veterans and family members who do not meet the income requirements are $500 and $1,500, respectively.

Duration 1 year; exemptions continue as long as the eligible resident lives in Connecticut.

Number awarded Varies each year; recently, a total of 22,944 veterans received property tax exemptions through this and other programs in Connecticut.

Deadline Applications for the additional municipality exemption must be submitted to the assessor's office of the town of residence by September of every other year.

[1090]
CONNECTICUT REAL ESTATE TAX EXEMPTION FOR DISABLED VETERANS

Office of Policy and Management
Attn: Intergovernmental Policy Division
450 Capitol Avenue
Hartford, CT 06106-1308
(860) 418-6278   Toll Free: (800) 286-2214 (within CT)
Fax: (860) 418-6493   TDD: (860) 418-6456
E-mail: leeann.graham@ct.gov
Web: www.ct.gov/opm/cwp/view.asp?a=2985&Q=383132

Summary To exempt Connecticut veterans with disabilities and their surviving spouses from the payment of a portion of their local property taxes.

Eligibility There are 2 categories of Connecticut veterans who qualify for exemptions from their dwelling house and the lot on which it is located: 1) those with major service-connected disabilities (paraplegia or osteochondritis resulting in permanent loss of the use of both legs or permanent paralysis of both legs and lower parts of the body; hemiplegia with permanent paralysis of 1 leg and 1 arm or either side of the body resulting from injury to the spinal cord, skeletal structure, or brain, or from disease of the spinal cord not resulting from syphilis; total blindness; amputation of both arms, both legs, both hands or both feet, or the combination of a hand and a foot; sustained through enemy action or resulting from an accident occurring or disease contracted in such active service) and 2) those with less severe disabilities (loss of use of 1 arm or 1 leg because of service-connected injuries). Surviving unremarried spouses of eligible deceased veterans are entitled to the same exemption as would have been granted to the veteran, as long as they continue to be the legal owner/occupier of the exempted residence. An additional exemption is available to veterans and spouses whose total adjusted gross income is less than $30,500 if unmarried or $37,300 if married. If the veteran is rated as 100% disabled by the U.S. Department of Veterans Affairs (VA), the maximum income levels are $18,000 if unmarried or $21,000 if married.

Financial Data Veterans in the first category receive an exemption from local property taxation of $10,000 of assessed valuation. Veterans in the second category receive exemptions of $5,000 of assessed valuation. For veterans whose income is less than the specified levels, additional exemptions of $20,000 for the first category or $10,000 for the second category are available from municipalities that choose to participate. For veterans whose income exceeds the specified levels, the additional exemption from participating municipalities is $5,000 for the first category or $2,500 for the second category. Connecticut municipalities may also elect to exempt from taxation specially adapted housing acquired or modified by a veteran under the provisions of Section 801 of Title 38 of the United States Code.

Duration 1 year; exemptions continue as long as the eligible resident (or surviving spouse) owns/occupies the primary residence and lives in Connecticut.

Number awarded Varies each year; recently, a total of 22,944 veterans received property tax exemptions through this and other programs in Connecticut.

Deadline Applications for the additional municipality exemption must be submitted to the assessor's office of the town or residence by September of every other year.

[1091]
CONNECTICUT SOLDIERS', SAILORS' AND MARINES' FUND

Connecticut Department of Veterans' Affairs
Attn: Soldiers', Sailors' and Marines' Fund
864 Wethersfield Avenue
Hartford, CT 06114-3184
(860) 296-0719   Toll Free: (800) 491-4941 (within CT)
Fax: (860) 296-0820   E-mail: john.monahan@po.state.ct.us
Web: www.state.ct.us/ssmf

Summary To provide temporary financial assistance to needy Connecticut veterans.

Eligibility This program is open to veterans who were honorably discharged after at least 90 days of service during wartime (World War I, World War II, Korea, Vietnam, Lebanon, Grenada, Operation Ernest Will, Panama, or the Persian Gulf) and are currently residents of Connecticut. Applicants must be able to demonstrate need for the following types of assistance: medical expenses; emergent dental care; prescription medications; eye examination and purchase of eyeglasses; audiological evaluation and hearing aids; assistance with rental payments or mortgage interest payments; utilities (including gas, water, electric, and fuel oil); funeral expenses; or prosthetic devices and durable medical equipment. Support is not provided for payment of taxes; payment of insurance premiums (except medical insurance); purchase of real estate or payments of principal on mortgages; payment of telephone or cable bills; purchase of equities, bonds, or mutual funds; alimony or child support payments; payment of personal debts, credit card bills, past-due bills, loans, or other obligations; or purchase of furniture, automobiles, or other capital goods.

Financial Data The fund provides payments in the form of short-term grants.

Duration The funds are provided for emergency situations only; the program does not assist with ongoing financial needs.

Additional data This program is subsidized by the state of Connecticut but administered by the American Legion of Connecticut.

Number awarded Varies each year.

Deadline Applications may be submitted at any time.

[1092]
CONNECTICUT VETERANS' ADDITIONAL EXEMPTION TAX RELIEF PROGRAM

Office of Policy and Management
Attn: Intergovernmental Policy Division
450 Capitol Avenue
Hartford, CT 06106-1308
(860) 418-6278   Toll Free: (800) 286-2214 (within CT)
Fax: (860) 418-6493   TDD: (860) 418-6456
E-mail: leeann.graham@ct.gov
Web: www.ct.gov/opm/cwp/view.asp?a=2985&Q=383132

Summary To exempt disabled veterans and their surviving spouses who are residents of Connecticut from a portion of their personal property taxes.

Eligibility Eligible to apply for this exemption are Connecticut veterans who are rated as disabled by the U.S. Department of Veterans Affairs (VA). Unremarried surviving spouses of qualified veterans are also eligible. An additional exemption may be available to veterans and spouses whose total adjusted gross income is less than $30,500 if unmarried or $37,300 if married. If the veteran is rated as 100% disabled by the U.S. Department of Veterans Affairs (VA), the maximum income levels are $18,000 if unmarried or $21,000 if married.

Financial Data The amount of the exemption depends on the level of the VA disability rating: for 10% to 25%, it is $1,500; for more than 25% to 50%, $2,000; for more than 50% to 75%, $2,500; for more than 75% and for veterans older than 65 years of age with any level of disability, $3,000. Municipalities may elect to provide an additional exemption, equal to twice the amount provided, to veterans and spouses whose income is less than the qualifying level. For veterans and spouses who do not meet the income requirement, the additional exemption from participating municipalities is equal to 50% of the basic state exemption.

Duration 1 year; exemptions continue as long as the eligible resident lives in Connecticut.

Number awarded Varies each year; recently, a total of 20,117 veterans received property tax exemptions through this and other programs in Connecticut.

Deadline Applications for the additional municipality exemption must be submitted to the assessor's office of the town of residence by September of every other year.

[1093]
DELAWARE INCOME TAX EXCLUSION FOR RETIRED PERSONS

Division of Revenue
Carvel State Office Building
820 North French Street
P.O. Box 8763
Wilmington, DE 19899-8763
(302) 577-3300
Web: revenue.delaware.gov

Summary To provide a partial exemption from state income taxation to retired persons, including veterans and their spouses, in Delaware.

Eligibility This exemption is available to all residents of Delaware who are receiving a pension from an employer, including the U.S. armed forces. Pensions of a deceased taxpayer also qualify.

Financial Data Persons under the age of 60 may exclude $2,000 or the amount of the pension, whichever is less, from income for Delaware state tax purposes; persons 60 years of age and over may exclude $12,500 or the amount of the pension and all other retirement income, whichever is less.

Duration The exemption continues as long as the recipient remains a resident of Delaware for state income tax purposes.

Number awarded Varies each year.

Deadline Deadline not specified.

[1094]
DELAWARE PENSION BENEFITS FOR PARAPLEGIC VETERANS

Delaware Commission of Veterans Affairs
Robbins Building
802 Silver Lake Boulevard, Suite 100
Dover, DE 19904
(302) 739-2792   Toll Free: (800) 344-9900 (within DE)
Fax: (302) 739-2794   E-mail: antonio.davila@state.de.us
Web: veteransaffairs.delaware.gov

Summary To provide a monthly pension to paraplegic veterans in Delaware.

Eligibility Eligible for this benefit are Delaware residents who are paraplegic as a result of service in the armed forces of the United States while it was officially at war or during a period when the United States was engaged in hostilities with another nation as a member of the United Nations. Applicants must be listed on the rolls of the U.S. Department of Veterans Affairs as totally disabled.

Financial Data The pension is $3,000 per year.

Duration Recipients remain eligible for this pension as long as they reside in Delaware.

Deadline Deadline not specified.

[1095]
DISABILITY PENSION PROGRAM FOR VETERANS

Department of Veterans Affairs
Attn: Veterans Benefits Administration
810 Vermont Avenue, N.W.
Washington, DC 20420
(202) 418-4343   Toll Free: (800) 827-1000
Web: www.vba.va.gov/bin/21/pension/vetpen.htm

Summary   To provide a pension for disabled or elderly veterans who served during wartime.

Eligibility   This program is open to veterans who were discharged under conditions other than dishonorable and who had at least 90 days of active military service, at least 1 day of which was during a period of war. They must be permanently and totally disabled or older than 65 years of age. Veterans who enlisted after September 7, 1980 generally had to have served at least 24 months or the full period for which they were called to active duty. The countable income of veterans must be below specified limits. Veterans of the Mexican Border Period and World War I qualify for additional payment as an Early War Veteran.

Financial Data   The pension program pays the difference, in 12 monthly installments, between countable income and the specified income level. Currently, those limits are the following: veteran with no dependents, $11,830; veteran with a spouse or child, $15,493; veteran in need of regular aid and attendance with no dependents, $19,736; veteran in need of regular aid and attendance with 1 dependent, $23,396; veteran permanently housebound without dependents, $14,457; veteran permanently housebound with 1 dependent, $18,120; 2 veterans married to each other, $14,493; increase for each additional dependent child, $2,020; additional payment for Early War Veterans, $2,686 for each of the preceding categories.

Duration   The pension is paid for the life of the recipient.

Number awarded   Varies each year.

Deadline   Applications are accepted at any time.

[1096]
DISTRICT OF COLUMBIA AND FEDERAL GOVERNMENT PENSION AND ANNUITY EXCLUSION

Office of Tax and Revenue
Attn: Customer Service Center
941 North Capitol Street, N.E., First Floor
Washington, DC 20002
(202) 727-4TAX   Fax: (202) 442-6477
E-mail: otr.ocfo@dc.gov
Web: otr.cfo.dc.gov/otr/site/default.asp

Summary   To exempt a portion of the income received as a pension or annuity, including military retirement pay, from local income taxation in the District of Columbia.

Eligibility   This exemption is available to residents of the District of Columbia who are 62 years of age or older. Applicants must be receiving income as military retired pay, pension income, or annuity income from the District or the federal government.

Financial Data   Qualifying residents are entitled to deduct their military retirement pay from local taxation, to a maximum of $3,000.

Duration   The exclusion continues as long as the recipient resides in the District of Columbia.

Number awarded   Varies each year.

Deadline   The exclusion is claimed as part of the local income return, due in April of each year.

[1097]
DVA AUTOMOBILE ALLOWANCE FOR DISABLED VETERANS

Department of Veterans Affairs
Attn: Veterans Benefits Administration
810 Vermont Avenue, N.W.
Washington, DC 20420
(202) 418-4343   Toll Free: (800) 827-1000
Web: www.vba.va.gov/bin/21/Benefits

Summary   To provide funding to certain disabled veterans and current service personnel who require specially adapted automobiles.

Eligibility   To be eligible for a grant for an automobile, a veteran or current servicemember must have a service-connected loss or permanent loss of use of 1 or both hands or feet or permanent impairment of vision of both eyes to a prescribed degree. For adaptive equipment eligibility only, veterans entitled to compensation for ankylosis of 1 or both knees, or 1 or both hips, also qualify.

Financial Data   The grant consists of a payment by the Department of Veterans Affairs (VA) of up to $11,000 toward the purchase of an automobile or other conveyance. The VA will also pay for the adaptive equipment, its repair, and the replacement or reinstallation required for the safe operation of the vehicle purchased with VA assistance or for a previously or subsequently acquired vehicle.

Duration   This is a 1-time grant.

Number awarded   Varies each year.

Deadline   Applications may be submitted at any time.

[1098]
DVA DISASTER RELIEF FUND

Disabled American Veterans
P.O. Box 14301
Cincinnati, OH 45250-0301
(859) 441-7300   Toll Free: (877) 426-2838
Fax: (859) 441-1416   E-mail: ahdav@one.net
Web: www.dav.org/veterans/DisasterRelief.aspx

Summary   To identify and assist needy disabled veterans who have survived a natural calamity.

Eligibility   At times of natural disaster (e.g., flood, earthquake, tornado, or other calamity) representatives of the Disabled American Veterans (DAV) will search out disabled veterans who need assistance.

Financial Data   The amount of assistance depends on the nature of the disasters and the needs of veterans; recently, an annual total of $191,000 was dispersed to help disabled veterans secure temporary lodging, food, and other necessities.

Duration   These funds are granted to relieve emergency situations only; they are not available on an ongoing basis.

Additional data   Disabled veterans need not be DAV members to receive aid through this program. Since this program began in 1968, it has dispersed more than $7.1 million. DAV formerly operated a separate Emergency Relief Fund but incorporated that into this program.

Number awarded   Varies each year. Recently, more than 200 grants totaling $148,860 were awarded.

Deadline   Funds are made available as soon as the need arises.

[1099]
FLORIDA PROPERTY TAX DISABILITY EXEMPTION FOR EX-SERVICE MEMBERS

Florida Department of Revenue
Attn: Taxpayer Services
1379 Blountstown Highway
Tallahassee, FL 32304-2716
(850) 488-6800　　　　　　　　Toll Free: (800) 352-3671
TDD: (800) 367-8331
Web: www.myflorida.com/dor/property/exemptions.html

Summary　To exempt a portion of the value of property owned by disabled veterans in Florida.

Eligibility　This exemption is available to veterans who have at least a 10% service-connected disability and are Florida residents owning taxable property.

Financial Data　$5,000 of the value of the property is exempt from taxation.

Duration　The exemption applies as long as the taxpayer owns the property in Florida.

Additional data　Initial applications should be made in person at the appropriate county property appraiser's office.

Number awarded　Varies each year.

Deadline　Applications must be submitted by February of the year for which the exemption is sought.

[1100]
FLORIDA SERVICE-CONNECTED TOTAL AND PERMANENT DISABILITY PROPERTY TAX EXEMPTION

Florida Department of Revenue
Attn: Taxpayer Services
1379 Blountstown Highway
Tallahassee, FL 32304-2716
(850) 488-6800　　　　　　　　Toll Free: (800) 352-3671
TDD: (800) 367-8331
Web: www.myflorida.com/dor/property/exemptions.html

Summary　To exempt from property taxation real estate owned by disabled veterans and their surviving spouses.

Eligibility　This exemption is available to Florida residents who have real estate that they own and use as a homestead. Applicants must be honorably-discharged veterans with a service-connected total and permanent disability. Under certain circumstances, the benefit of this exemption can carry over to a surviving spouse.

Financial Data　All real estate used and owned as a homestead, less any portion used for commercial purposes, is exempt from taxation.

Duration　The exemption applies as long as the taxpayer owns the property in Florida.

Additional data　Initial applications should be made in person at the appropriate county property appraiser's office.

Number awarded　Varies each year.

Deadline　Applications must be submitted by February of the year for which the exemption is sought.

[1101]
GEORGIA HOMESTEAD TAX EXEMPTION FOR DISABLED VETERANS

Georgia Department of Revenue
Attn: Property Tax Division
4245 International Parkway, Suite A
Hapeville, GA 30354-3918
(404) 968-0707　　　　　　　　Fax: (404) 968-0778
E-mail: Local.Government.Services@dor.ga.gov
Web: etax.dor.ga.gov

Summary　To exempt from property taxation a portion of the value of homesteads owned by disabled veterans in Georgia and their families.

Eligibility　This program is open to residents of Georgia who qualify as a 100% disabled veteran under any of several provisions of state law. Surviving spouses and minor children are also eligible. Applicants must actually occupy a homestead and use it as their legal residence for all purposes.

Financial Data　The first $50,000 of assessed valuation of the homestead owned by disabled veterans or their family members is exempt from property taxes for state, county, municipal, and school purposes.

Duration　The exemption remains in effect as long as the veteran or family member owns and resides in the homestead.

Number awarded　Varies each year.

Deadline　Applications must be filed with local tax officials by February of each year.

[1102]
HAWAII GRANTS FOR SPECIAL HOUSING FOR DISABLED VETERANS

Office of Veterans Services
Attn: Veterans Services Coordinator
459 Patterson Road
E-Wing, Room 1-A103
Honolulu, HI 96819-1522
(808) 433-0420　　　　　　　　Fax: (808) 433-0385
E-mail: ovs@ovs.hawaii.gov
Web: Hawaii.gov/dod/ovs/benefits/state-provided-benefits

Summary　To provide grants to disabled veterans in Hawaii for purchasing or remodeling a home.

Eligibility　This program is open to totally disabled veterans in Hawaii. Applicants must be proposing to purchase or remodel a home to improve handicapped accessibility.

Financial Data　Grants up to $5,000 are available.

Duration　These are 1-time grants.

Deadline　Deadline not specified.

[1103]
HAWAII INCOME TAX EXCLUSION OF PENSION INCOME

Department of Taxation
Attn: Taxpayer Services Branch
425 Queen Street
P.O. Box 259
Honolulu, HI 96809-0259
(808) 587-4242　　　　　　　　Toll Free: (800) 222-3229
Fax: (808) 587-1488　　　　　　TDD: (808) 587-1418
Web: hawaii.gov/tax

Summary　To exempt the income from certain types of pensions from state income taxation in Hawaii.

Eligibility　The following types of pensions are not taxed by Hawaii: 1) pension or annuity distributions from a public (i.e. government) retirement system, including military pensions for veterans and their families; 2) distributions from a private employer pension plan received upon retirement (including early retirement and disability retirement) if the employee did not contribute to the pension plan; and 3) distributions from a pension plan at age 70 and a half that are made to comply with the federal mandatory payout rule, even if the employee is still working full time.

Financial Data　All such payments and benefits are excluded from income for purposes of state taxation.

Duration　The exclusion continues as long as the recipient resides in Hawaii.

Deadline　Deadline not specified.

[1104]
HAWAII PROPERTY TAX EXEMPTIONS FOR DISABLED VETERANS

Office of Veterans Services
Attn: Veterans Services Coordinator
459 Patterson Road
E-Wing, Room 1-A103
Honolulu, HI 96819-1522
(808) 433-0420   Fax: (808) 433-0385
E-mail: ovs@ovs.hawaii.gov
Web: www.dod.state.hi.us/ovs/benefits.html

Summary To exempt the homes of disabled veterans and surviving spouses in Hawaii from real estate taxation.

Eligibility This program is open to totally disabled veterans in Hawaii and their surviving spouses.

Financial Data The real property owned and occupied as a home is exempt from taxation.

Duration The exemption applies as long as the disabled veteran or his/her widow(er) resides in Hawaii.

Deadline Deadline not specified.

[1105]
IDAHO CIRCUIT BREAKER PROPERTY TAX REDUCTION

Idaho State Tax Commission
Attn: Public Information Office
800 Park Boulevard, Plaza IV
P.O. Box 36
Boise, ID 83722-0410
(208) 334-7736   Toll Free: (800) 972-7660
TDD: (800) 377-3529
Web: tax.idaho.gov/propertytax/pt_homeowners.htm

Summary To reduce a portion of the property tax of disabled and other veterans and other disabled or elderly residents of Idaho.

Eligibility Eligible for this property tax reduction are residents of Idaho who own and live in a primary residence in the state and have an annual income of $28,000 or less (after deducting designated forms of income, including compensation received by a veteran from the U.S. Department of Veterans Affairs for a 40% to 100% service-connected disability). Applicants must be in 1 or more of the following categories: disabled (as recognized by an appropriate federal agency), blind, former prisoner of war or hostage, veteran with at least 10% service-connected disability or receiving a VA pension for a nonservice-connected disability, 65 years of age or older, widow(er) of any age, or fatherless or motherless child under 18 years of age.

Financial Data The maximum amount of reduction is the lesser of $1,320 or the actual taxes on the recipient's qualifying home. The minimum reduction is the lesser of $100 or the actual taxes on the home.

Duration Applications for this reduction must be submitted each year.

Additional data All recipients of this reduction automatically receive Idaho's Homeowner's Exemption, which reduces the taxable value of the home (excluding land) by 50% or $75,000, whichever is less. Solid waste, irrigation, or other fees charged by some counties are not taxes and cannot be reduced by this program.

Number awarded Varies each year.

Deadline April of each year.

[1106]
IDAHO RETIREMENT BENEFITS DEDUCTION

Idaho State Tax Commission
Attn: Public Information Office
800 Park Boulevard, Plaza IV
P.O. Box 36
Boise, ID 83722-0410
(208) 334-7660   Toll Free: (800) 972-7660
TDD: (800) 377-3529
Web: tax.idaho.gov

Summary To deduct the retirement and disability income of certain residents from state income tax in Idaho.

Eligibility Eligible for this deduction are full-year residents of Idaho who are age 65 or older, or disabled and age 62 and older, and who are receiving the following annuities and benefits: 1) retirement annuities paid by the United States to a retired civil service employee or the unremarried widow of the employee; 2) retirement benefits paid from the firemen's retirement fund of the state of Idaho to a retired fireman or the unremarried widow of a retired fireman; 3) retirement benefits paid from the policeman's retirement fund of a city within Idaho to a retired policeman or the unremarried widow of a retired policeman; or 4) retirement benefits paid by the United States to a retired member of the U.S. military service or the unremarried widow of those veterans.

Financial Data The amount of retirement or disability benefits may be deducted from taxable state income in Idaho, to a maximum deduction of $39,330 for married couples or $26,220 for single persons.

Duration 1 year; must reapply each year.

Number awarded Varies each year.

Deadline April of each year.

[1107]
IDAHO WAR VETERAN'S EMERGENCY GRANT PROGRAM

Idaho Division of Veterans Services
Attn: Office of Veterans Advocacy
444 Fort Street
Boise, ID 83702
(208) 577-2300   Fax: (208) 577-2333
E-mail: info@veterans.idaho.gov
Web: www.veterans.idaho.gov/Veterans_Advocacy.aspx

Summary To provide emergency assistance to disabled veterans, wartime veterans, and their families in Idaho.

Eligibility Eligible for these grants are veterans who had at least 90 days of honorable wartime military service while a resident of Idaho. Veterans with a service-connected disability are eligible with earlier separation. Surviving spouses and dependent children are also eligible. Applicants must be current residents of Idaho in need of assistance because of a major catastrophe (e.g., natural disaster or death of a spouse or child), loss of job because of a disability, or other extreme financial emergency (e.g., cut-off notice from a utility company, eviction notice from a landlord, arrears payment notice from the lien holder of a home).

Financial Data The maximum amount available under this program is $1,000, issued in small incremental grants.

Duration The limit of $1,000 applies for the lifetime of each veteran or his/her family.

Additional data This program was established by the Idaho legislature in lieu of granting a wartime bonus to Idaho veterans.

Number awarded Varies each year.

Deadline Deadline not specified.

[1108]
ILLINOIS DISABLED VETERANS' STANDARD HOMESTEAD EXEMPTION

Illinois Department of Revenue
101 West Jefferson Street
P.O. Box 19044
Springfield, IL 62794-9044
(217) 782-9337   Toll Free: (800) 732-8866
TDD: (800) 544-5304
Web: www.revenue.state.il.us

Summary To reduce the value for property taxation of homesteads owned by disabled veterans in Illinois.

Eligibility This exemption is available to veterans who own or lease a homestead in Illinois as their primary residence. Applicants must have a service-connected disability verified by the U.S. Department of Veterans Affairs of at least 50%.

Financial Data Veterans whose disability is rated as at least 50% but less than 75% receive a $2,500 reduction in the equalized assessed value (EAV) of their property. Veterans whose disability is rated as at least 75% receive a $5,000 reduction in the EAV of their property.

Duration Veterans must file an annual application to continue to receive this exemption.

Additional data This program was established in 2007.

Deadline Deadline not specified.

[1109]
ILLINOIS INCOME TAX SUBTRACTION FOR GOVERNMENT RETIREES

Illinois Department of Revenue
101 West Jefferson Street
P.O. Box 19044
Springfield, IL 62794-9044
(217) 782-9337   Toll Free: (800) 732-8866
TDD: (800) 544-5304
Web: www.revenue.state.il.us

Summary To exempt the retirement and disability income of veterans and other government employees from state taxation in Illinois.

Eligibility This exemption applies to the income received from government retirement and disability plans, including military plans.

Financial Data All government retirement and disability income of eligible residents is exempt from state income taxation.

Duration The exemption continues as long as the recipient resides in Illinois.

Deadline Deadline not specified.

[1110]
ILLINOIS RETURNING VETERANS' EXEMPTION

Illinois Department of Revenue
101 West Jefferson Street
P.O. Box 19044
Springfield, IL 62794-9044
(217) 782-9337   Toll Free: (800) 732-8866
TDD: (800) 544-5304
Web: www.revenue.state.il.us

Summary To provide an exemption on the value for property taxation of homesteads owned by veterans in Illinois who are returning from conflict.

Eligibility This exemption is available to veterans who own or lease a homestead in Illinois as their primary residence. Applicants must be returning from active duty in an armed conflict involving the armed forces of the United States.

Financial Data Qualifying veterans receive a $5,000 reduction in the equalized assessed value (EAV) of their property.

Duration This is a 1-time exemption

Additional data This program was established in 2007.

Deadline Deadline not specified.

[1111]
ILLINOIS SPECIALLY ADAPTED HOUSING TAX EXEMPTION

Illinois Department of Veterans' Affairs
833 South Spring Street
P.O. Box 19432
Springfield, IL 62794-9432
(217) 782-6641   Toll Free: (800) 437-9824 (within IL)
Fax: (217) 524-0344   TDD: (217) 524-4645
E-mail: webmail@dva.state.il.us
Web: www.veterans.illinois.gov/benefits/realestate.htm

Summary To provide an exemption on the assessed value of specially adapted housing to Illinois veterans with disabilities and their spouses.

Eligibility Specially adapted housing units for disabled veterans that have been purchased or constructed with federal funds are eligible for this exemption. The exemption is extended to the veteran, the spouse, or the unremarried surviving spouse.

Financial Data Under this program, an exemption is allowed on the assessed value of eligible real property, up to a maximum of $70,000 of assessed valuation.

Duration 1 year; renewable as long as the veteran, or spouse, or unremarried surviving spouse resides in the specially adapted housing in Illinois.

Number awarded Varies each year.

Deadline Applications for the exemption may be submitted at any time.

[1112]
ILLINOIS TAX EXEMPTION FOR MOBILE HOMES

Illinois Department of Veterans' Affairs
833 South Spring Street
P.O. Box 19432
Springfield, IL 62794-9432
(217) 782-6641   Toll Free: (800) 437-9824 (within IL)
Fax: (217) 524-0344   TDD: (217) 524-4645
E-mail: webmail@dva.state.il.us
Web: www.veterans.illinois.gov/benefits/realestate.htm

Summary To provide an exemption on the assessed value of mobile homes to Illinois veterans with disabilities and their spouses.

Eligibility This exemption applies to taxes imposed on mobiles homes in Illinois. The property must be owned and used exclusively by a disabled veteran, spouse, or unremarried surviving spouse as a home. The veteran must have received authorization of the Specially Adapted Housing Grant by the U.S. Department of Veterans Affairs, whether that benefit was used or not. Disabled veterans who currently live in a mobile home and never received the Specially Adapted Housing Grant are not eligible.

Financial Data Qualifying veterans, spouses, and unmarried surviving spouses are exempt from property taxes imposed by the state of Illinois on mobile homes.

Duration 1 year; renewable as long as the veteran, or spouse, or unremarried surviving spouse resides in the mobile home in Illinois.

Number awarded Varies each year.

Deadline Applications for the exemption may be submitted at any time.

[1113]
INDIANA MILITARY RETIREMENT OR SURVIVOR'S BENEFIT INCOME TAX DEDUCTION

Indiana Department of Revenue
Attn: Taxpayer Services Division
Indiana Government Center North
100 North Senate Avenue
Indianapolis, IN 46204-2253
(317) 232-2240   TDD: (317) 232-4952
E-mail: pfrequest@dor.state.in.us
Web: www.in.gov/dor

Summary   To exempt a portion of the income of veterans and surviving spouses from state taxation in Indiana.

Eligibility   This program is open to Indiana residents who are retired from the military or are the surviving spouse of a person who was in the military. Applicants must be at least 60 years of age and receiving military retirement or survivor's benefits.

Financial Data   Up to $5,000 of the income from military retirement or survivor's benefits is exempt from state income taxation in Indiana.

Duration   The exemption continues as long as the recipient resides in Indiana.

Deadline   Deadline not specified.

[1114]
INDIANA PROPERTY TAX DEDUCTIONS FOR DISABLED VETERANS

Department of Local Government Finance
Indiana Government Center North, Room 1058
100 North Senate Avenue
Indianapolis, IN 46201
(317) 232-3777   Fax: (317) 232-8779
E-mail: PropertyTaxInfo@dlgf.in.gov
Web: www.in.gov/dlgf

Summary   To exempt disabled Indiana veterans and their spouses from a portion of their property taxes.

Eligibility   This program is open to the following categories of veterans who are residents of Indiana: 1) served honorably at least 90 days and are either totally disabled (the disability does not need to be service-connected) or are at least 62 years old and have at least a 10% service-connected disability; 2) served honorably during wartime and have at least a 10% service-connected disability; or 3) served during World War I and are disabled. A statutory disability rating for pulmonary tuberculosis does not qualify. A disability incurred during Initial Active Duty for Training (IADT) with the National Guard or Reserves is eligible only if the disability occurred from an event during the period of active duty and that duty was performed during wartime. Surviving spouses of those 3 categories of veterans are also eligible.

Financial Data   Property tax deductions are $12,480 for veterans and spouses in the first category (only if the assessed value of the combined real and personal property owned by the veteran or spouse does not exceed $143,160), $24,960 in the second category, or $18,720 in the third category (only if the assessed value of the real property owned by the veteran does not exceed $206,500; there is no limit on the value of the property owned by a surviving spouse).

Duration   1 year; may be renewed as long as the eligible veteran or surviving unremarried spouse owns and occupies the primary residence in Indiana.

Number awarded   Varies each year.

Deadline   Applications must be submitted no later than May of each year.

[1115]
INDIANA VETERANS' BURIAL ALLOWANCE

Indiana Department of Veterans' Affairs
302 West Washington Street, Room E-120
Indianapolis, IN 46204-2738
(317) 232-3910   Toll Free: (800) 400-4520 (within IN)
Fax: (317) 232-7721
Web: www.in.gov/dva/2343.htm

Summary   To provide a burial allowance for Indiana veterans and their spouses.

Eligibility   This benefit is available to honorably-discharged veterans from Indiana and their spouses. Applications must be filed with the county auditor in the county of residence.

Financial Data   County auditors are authorized to pay up to $1,000 for burial costs of a veteran or the veteran's spouse and up to $100 for the setting of a federal headstone.

Duration   This is a 1-time payment.

Number awarded   Varies each year.

Deadline   Requests for assistance may be submitted at any time.

[1116]
IOWA INJURED VETERANS GRANT PROGRAM

Iowa Department of Veterans Affairs
Camp Dodge, Building A6A
7105 N.W. 70th Avenue
Johnston, IA 50131-1824
(515) 242-5331   Toll Free: (800) VET-IOWA
Fax: (515) 242-5659   E-mail: info@idva.state.ia.us
Web: www.iowava.org/benefits/injured_vets_grant.html

Summary   To provide assistance to Iowa residents who were injured in combat while serving in the armed forces after September 11, 2001.

Eligibility   This assistance is available to members of the U.S. armed forces who are still serving or who have been discharged or released from service under honorable conditions. Applicants must have sustained an injury or illness in a combat zone or hostile fire zone after September 11, 2001. The illness or injury must have been serious enough to require medical evacuation from the combat zone and must be considered by the military to be in the line of duty. The veteran or military servicemember must have been a resident of Iowa at the time of injury.

Financial Data   Qualified veterans or military servicemembers are entitled to the following assistance: $2,500 when they are medically evacuated from the combat zone; $2,500 30 days after evacuation date if still hospitalized, receiving medical treatment, or receiving rehabilitation services from the military or Veterans Administration; $2,500 60 days after evacuation date if still hospitalized, receiving medical treatment, or receiving rehabilitation services from the military or Veterans Administration; and $2,500 90 days after the evacuation date if still hospitalized, receiving medical treatment, or receiving rehabilitation services from the military or Veterans Administration. The maximum assistance is $10,000.

Duration   This is a 1-time bonus.

Additional data   This program was established in 2007.

Number awarded   Varies each year.

Deadline   Deadline not specified.

[1117]
IOWA MILITARY HOMEOWNERSHIP PROGRAM

Iowa Finance Authority
Attn: Military Homeownership Program
2015 Grand Avenue
Des Moines, IA 50312
Toll Free: (800) 432-7230   Fax: (515) 725-4901
E-mail: homebuyer.inquiry@iowa.gov
Web: www.ifahome.com

Summary To provide funding to current and former military servicemembers and those surviving spouses who are interested in purchasing a primary residence in Iowa.

Eligibility This program is open to 1) servicemembers who served at least 90 days on active duty since September 11, 2001; 2) federal status injured servicemembers who served on active duty since September 11, 2001; and 3) surviving spouses of those eligible servicemembers who served honorably. Applicants must be purchasing a home in Iowa (including modular homes, condominiums, townhomes, and duplexes) that will be their primary residence. They must be using an Iowa Finance Authority participating lender and either FirstHome, FirstHome Plus, or (if not eligible for either of those programs) a permanent mortgage loan.

Financial Data The grant is $5,000. Funds may be used toward down payment on a qualifying home purchase and/or closing costs on a qualifying first purchase money mortgage.

Duration These are 1-time grants.

Additional data The Iowa Legislature created this program in 2005.

Number awarded Varies each year.

Deadline Applications may be submitted at any time.

[1118]
IOWA MILITARY SERVICE PROPERTY TAX EXEMPTION

Iowa Department of Revenue
Attn: Property Tax Division
Hoover State Office Building
1305 East Walnut
P.O. Box 10457
Des Moines, IA 50306-0457
(515) 281-4040   Toll Free: (800) 367-3388 (within IA)
Fax: (515) 281-3906   E-mail: idr@iowa.gov
Web: www.iowa.gov/tax

Summary To exempt veterans, military personnel, and their family members from a portion of property taxes in Iowa.

Eligibility This exemption is available to residents of Iowa who are 1) former members of the U.S. armed forces who performed at least 18 months of military service (or for fewer months because of a service-related injury), regardless of the time period, and who were honorably discharged; 2) former members, and members currently serving of the U.S. Reserves and Iowa National Guard who have served at least 20; and 3) current members of the U.S. Reserves and Iowa National Guard who were activated for federal duty for at least 90 days; 4) former members of the armed forces whose enlistment would have occurred during the Korean Conflict but chose to serve 5 years in the Reserves; and 5) honorably discharged veterans who served in a designated eligible service period. Applicants must own a primary residence in the state. Also eligible for the exemption are the spouses, unremarried widow(er)s, minor children, and widowed parent of qualified veterans.

Financial Data The amount of the exemption varies.

Duration 1 year; continues until the qualifying veteran or dependent no longer lives in the residence.

Number awarded Varies each year. Recently, more than $2.8 million in property was exempt from taxation.

Deadline Application must be made by June of the year for which the exemption is first requested. The exemption is provided annually, from then on, as long as the qualifying veteran or dependent resides in the house.

[1119]
KANSAS INCOME TAX EXEMPTION FOR VETERANS AND OTHER FEDERAL RETIREES

Kansas Department of Revenue
Attn: Taxpayer Assistance Center
Robert B. Docking State Office Building
915 S.W. Harrison Street
Topeka, KS 66612-1712
(785) 368-8222   Toll Free: (877) 526-7738
Fax: (785) 291-3614   TDD: (785) 296-6461
Web: www.ksrevenue.org/perstaxtypesii.htm

Summary To exempt the income received by federal retirees, including veterans, from state taxation in Kansas.

Eligibility This exemption applies to all amounts received by residents of Kansas as retirement benefits from employment by the federal government or for service in the U.S. armed forces.

Financial Data All federal retirement income, including that for military service, is exempt from state taxation in Kansas.

Duration This benefit continues as long as the recipient remains a resident of Kansas for state income tax purposes.

Number awarded Varies each year.

Deadline Deadline not specified.

[1120]
KENTUCKY PENSION INCOME EXCLUSION

Kentucky Department of Revenue
Attn: Individual Income Tax
501 High Street
P.O. Box 181
Frankfort, KY 40602-0181
(502) 564-4581   Fax: (502) 564-3875
Web: revenue.ky.gov/individual/incometax.htm

Summary To exempt a portion of the income of public retirees (including veterans) in Kentucky from state income taxation.

Eligibility This exemption applies to Kentucky residents who are required to pay state income taxes and who receive retirement income from state and federal systems, including the U.S. military and the Department of Veterans Affairs.

Financial Data For veterans and others who retired prior to January 1, 1998, all pension income is exempt from taxation in Kentucky. For those who retired after December 31, 1997 and whose retirement income is less than $41,110, all income is exempt; for those whose retirement income is greater than $41,110, the exemption depends on the proportion of service credit earned after December 31, 1997.

Duration The exemption continues as long as the recipient resides in Kentucky.

Deadline Deadline not specified.

[1121]
LOUISIANA INCOME EXEMPTION FOR FEDERAL RETIREMENT PAY

Louisiana Department of Revenue
Attn: Individual Income Tax
P.O. Box 201
Baton Rouge, LA 70821
(225) 219-0102
Web: www.revenue.louisiana.gov

Summary To exempt the retirement income of all federal employees, including the military and their surviving spouses, from state taxation in Louisiana.

Eligibility This exemption is available to all residents of Louisiana who are receiving retirement benefits from the federal retirement system, including veterans and their surviving spouses.

Financial Data All federal retirement income is exempt from state income taxation in Louisiana.

Duration The benefit continues as long as the recipient remains a resident of Louisiana for state income tax purposes.
Number awarded Varies each year.
Deadline Deadline not specified.

[1122]
MAINE PROPERTY TAX EXEMPTIONS FOR VETERANS

Maine Revenue Services
Attn: Property Tax Division
P.O. Box 9106
Augusta, ME 04332-9106
(207) 287-2011   Fax: (207) 287-6396
E-mail: prop.tax@maine.gov
Web: www.maine.gov/revenue/propertytax/homepage.html

Summary To exempt the estates of disabled Maine veterans and selected family members from property taxation.
Eligibility Eligible for this program are veterans who served in wartime during World War I, World War II, the Korean campaign, the Vietnam war, the Persian Gulf war, or other recognized service periods, are legal residents of Maine, and are either older than 62 years of age or are receiving a pension or compensation from the U.S. government for total disability (whether service connected or not). Vietnam veterans must have served 180 days on active duty unless discharged earlier for a service-connected disability. The exemption also includes 1) property held in joint tenancy with the veterans' spouses, and 2) property of unremarried widow(er)s, minor children, and mothers of deceased veterans, if those dependents are receiving a pension or compensation from the U.S. government.
Financial Data Estates of disabled veterans and eligible dependents, including both real and personal property, are exempt up to $6,000 of just valuation. For veterans and dependents who served in wartime prior to World War II, estates up to $7,000 are exempt.
Duration Veterans, spouses, unremarried widow(er)s, and mothers are eligible for this exemption throughout their lifetimes; minor children of veterans are eligible until they reach the age of 18.
Number awarded Varies each year.
Deadline When an eligible person first submits an application, the proof of entitlement must reach the assessors of the local municipality prior to the end of March. Once eligibility has been established, notification need not be repeated in subsequent years.

[1123]
MAINE TAX EXEMPTION FOR SPECIALLY ADAPTED HOUSING UNITS

Maine Revenue Services
Attn: Property Tax Division
P.O. Box 9106
Augusta, ME 04332-9106
(207) 287-2011   Fax: (207) 287-6396
E-mail: prop.tax@maine.gov
Web: www.maine.gov/revenue/propertytax/homepage.html

Summary To exempt the specially adapted housing units of paraplegic veterans or their surviving spouses from taxation in Maine.
Eligibility Veterans who served in the U.S. armed forces during any federally-recognized war period, are legal residents of Maine, are paraplegic veterans within the meaning of U.S. statutes, and have received a grant from the U.S. government for specially adapted housing are eligible. The exemption also applies to property held in joint tenancy with the veteran's spouse and to the specially adapted housing of unremarried widow(er)s of eligible veterans.

Financial Data Estates of paraplegic veterans are exempt up to $50,000 of just valuation for a specially adapted housing unit.
Duration The exemption is valid for the lifetime of the paraplegic veteran or unremarried widow(er).
Number awarded Varies each year.
Deadline When an eligible person first submits an application, the proof of entitlement must reach the assessors of the local municipality prior to the end of March. Once eligibility has been established, notification need not be repeated in subsequent years.

[1124]
MARYLAND INCOME TAX EXEMPTION FOR MILITARY RETIRED PAY

Comptroller of Maryland
Attn: Revenue Administration Division
80 Calvert Street
Annapolis, MD 21411
(410) 260-7980   Toll Free: (800) MD-TAXES (within MD)
Fax: (410) 974-3456   TDD: (410) 260-7157
E-mail: taxhelp@comp.state.md.us
Web: individuals.marylandtaxes.com

Summary To exempt certain portions of military retirement pay from Maryland state income tax.
Eligibility This exemption is available to residents of Maryland who are receiving retirement income as a member of an active or Reserve component of the U.S. armed forces, the Maryland National Guard, the Public Health Service, the National Oceanic and Atmospheric Administration, or the Coast and Geodetic Survey.
Financial Data Up to $5,000 of military retired pay, depending on income, may be excluded from state income taxation.
Duration The exemption is available annually.
Number awarded Varies each year.
Deadline Retired military personnel can claim this exemption when they file their state income tax return, in April of each year.

[1125]
MARYLAND PROPERTY TAX EXEMPTION FOR DISABLED VETERANS AND SURVIVING SPOUSES

Maryland Department of Assessments and Taxation
Attn: Property Taxes
301 West Preston Street
Baltimore, MD 21201-2395
(410) 767-1184   Toll Free: (888) 246-5941
TDD: (800) 735-2258
Web: www.dat.state.md.us/sdatweb/exempt.html

Summary To exempt the homes of disabled veterans and their surviving spouses from property taxation in Maryland.
Eligibility This exemption is available to armed services veterans with a permanent service-connected disability rated 100% by the U.S. Department of Veterans Affairs who own a dwelling house in Maryland. Unremarried surviving spouses are also eligible.
Financial Data The dwelling houses of eligible veterans and surviving spouses is exempt from real property taxes.
Duration The exemption is available as long as the veteran or surviving spouse owns the dwelling house in Maryland.
Number awarded Varies each year.
Deadline Applications may be submitted at any time.

[1126]
MARYLAND REAL PROPERTY TAX EXEMPTION FOR DISABLED VETERANS

State Department of Assessments and Taxation
Attn: Tax Credit Program
301 West Preston Street, Room 900
Baltimore, MD 21201-2395
(410) 767-1184   Toll Free: (888) 246-5941 (within MD)
TDD: (800) 735-2258   E-mail: taxcredits@dat.state.md.us
Web: www.dat.state.md.us

Summary To exempt the homes of disabled veterans and their spouses from property taxation in Maryland.

Eligibility This program is open to Maryland residents who are veterans with a 100% service-connected permanent disability and their surviving spouses.

Financial Data The dwelling houses owned by qualifying disabled veterans and their spouses are exempt from real property taxes in Maryland.

Duration This exemption continues as long as the qualifying disabled veterans or spouses reside in Maryland and own their home.

Deadline Deadline not specified.

[1127]
MASSACHUSETTS INCOME TAX EXEMPTION FOR UNIFORMED SERVICES RETIREMENT PAY

Massachusetts Department of Revenue
Attn: Personal Income Tax
P.O. Box 7010
Boston, MA 02204
(617) 887-MDOR   Toll Free: (800) 392-6089 (within MA)
Fax: (617) 887-1900
Web: www.mass.gov

Summary To exempt the retirement income and survivorship benefits received from the U.S. uniformed services from state income taxation in Massachusetts.

Eligibility Eligible for this exemption are residents of Massachusetts who are receiving noncontributory pension income or survivorship benefits from the U.S. uniformed services (including the Army, Navy, Marine Corps, Air Force, Coast Guard, National Oceanic and Atmospheric Administration, and commissioned corps of the Public Health Service).

Financial Data All uniformed services retirement income and survivorship benefits are exempt from state income taxation.

Duration The benefit continues as long as the recipient remains a resident of Massachusetts for state income tax purposes.

Additional data This exemption became effective with income received in 1997.

Number awarded Varies each year.

Deadline Deadline not specified.

[1128]
MASSACHUSETTS PROPERTY TAX EXEMPTION FOR VETERANS AND THEIR FAMILIES

Massachusetts Department of Revenue
Attn: Division of Local Services
100 Cambridge Street
Boston, MA 02114
(617) 626-2386   Fax: (617) 626-2330
E-mail: juszkiewicz@dor.state.ma.us
Web: www.mass.gov

Summary To provide a property tax exemption to blind, disabled, and other veterans (and their families) in Massachusetts.

Eligibility This program is open to veterans who are residents of Massachusetts, were residents for at least 6 months prior to entering the service, have been residents for at least 5 consecutive years, and are occupying property as their domicile. Applicants must have an ownership interest in the domicile that ranges from $2,000 to $10,000, depending on the category of exemption. Veterans must have been discharged under conditions other than dishonorable. Several categories of veterans and their families qualify: 1) veterans who have a service-connected disability rating of 10% or more; veterans who have been awarded the Purple Heart; Gold Star mothers and fathers; and surviving spouses of eligible veterans who do not remarry; 2) veterans who suffered, in the line of duty, the loss or permanent lose of use of 1 foot, 1 hand, or 1 eye; veterans who received the Congressional Medal of Honor, Distinguished Service Cross, Navy Cross, or Air Force Cross; and their spouses or surviving spouses; 3) veterans who suffered, in the line of duty, the loss or permanent loss of use of both feet, both hands, or both eyes; and their spouses or surviving spouses; 4) veterans who suffered total disability in the line of duty and received assistance in acquiring specially adapted housing, which they own and occupy as their domicile; and their spouses or surviving spouses; 5) unremarried surviving spouses of military personnel who died due to injury or disease from being in a combat zone, or are missing and presumed dead due to combat; 6) veterans who suffered total disability in the line of duty and are incapable of working; and their spouses or surviving spouses; and 7) veterans who are certified by the Veterans Administration as paraplegic and their surviving spouses.

Financial Data Qualified veterans and family members are entitled to an annual exemption from their taxes for the different categories: 1, $400; 2, $750; 3, $1,250; 4, $1,500; 5, full, but with a cap of $2,500 after 5 years; 6, $1,000; or 7, total.

Duration The exemptions are provided each year that the veteran or unremarried surviving spouse lives in Massachusetts and owns the property as a domicile.

Additional data Applications are available from local assessor's offices.

Number awarded Varies each year.

Deadline Applications must be filed with the local assessor by December of each year.

[1129]
MASSACHUSETTS PUBLIC ASSISTANCE FOR VETERANS

Department of Veterans' Services
600 Washington Street, Suite 1100
Boston, MA 02111
(617) 210-5927   Fax: (617) 210-5755
E-mail: mdvs@vet.state.ma.us
Web: www.mass.gov/veterans

Summary To provide financial and medical assistance to indigent veterans and their dependents in Massachusetts.

Eligibility This assistance is open to veterans who are residents of Massachusetts and served in the U.S. armed services on active duty either for 90 days during specified periods of wartime or for 180 days during peacetime. Members of the National Guard and Reserves are also eligible if they have been called to regular active duty. Also eligible are spouses of the veteran, widows or widowers of the veteran, dependent parents of the veteran, any person who acted as a parent to the veteran for 5 years immediately prior to entering wartime service, children of the veteran under 19 years of age, children of the veteran between 19 and 23 years of age who are attending high school or an institution of higher education, children of the veteran 19 years of age or older who are mentally or physically unable to support themselves and were affected by the disability prior to their 18th birthday, and legally adopted children of the veteran. Applicants must be able to demonstrate a need for assistance for food, shelter, clothing, housing supplies, and medical care.

Financial Data Grants depend on the need of the recipient.

Duration These are 1-time grants.

Number awarded Varies each year.
Deadline Applications may be submitted at any time.

[1130]
MASSACHUSETTS VETERANS ANNUITY PROGRAM

Department of Veterans' Services
Attn: Annuities
600 Washington Street, Suite 1100
Boston, MA 02111
(617) 210-5480   Fax: (617) 210-5755
E-mail: mdvs@vet.state.ma.us
Web: www.mass.gov/veterans

Summary To provide an annuity to blind or disabled veterans from Massachusetts and to the parents and spouses of deceased military personnel.

Eligibility This program is open to 1) veterans who are blind, double amputee, paraplegic, or have a 100% service-connected disability; 2) the parents of military personnel who died of service-connected causes; and 3) the unremarried spouses of military personnel who died of service-connected causes. Veterans must have been residents of Massachusetts at the time of entry into military service who served during specified wartime periods and received other than a dishonorable discharge. All applicants must currently be residents of Massachusetts.

Financial Data Recipients are entitled to an annuity of $2,000 per year.

Duration The annuity is paid as long as the recipient continues to reside in Massachusetts.

Deadline Deadline not specified.

[1131]
MASSACHUSETTS WELCOME HOME BONUS

Office of the State Treasurer
Attn: Veterans Bonus Division
One Ashburton Place, 12th Floor
Boston, MA 02108-1608
(617) 367-9333, ext. 859   Fax: (617) 227-1622
E-mail: veteransbonus@tre.state.ma.us
Web: www.mass.gov/treasury

Summary To provide a bonus to Massachusetts veterans and servicemembers who served after September 11, 2001 and their families.

Eligibility This bonus is available to veterans and current servicemembers who had resided in Massachusetts for at least 6 months immediately prior to their entry into service in the armed forces. They must have performed service on or after September 11, 2001 and still be serving or have been honorably discharged. If the veteran or servicemember is deceased, an immediate family member (parent, spouse, child, sibling) may apply.

Financial Data The bonus is $1,000 for active service in Afghanistan or Iraq or $500 for 6 months or more of active service.

Duration This is a 1-time bonus.

Number awarded Varies each year.

Deadline Deadline not specified.

[1132]
MEDAL OF HONOR PENSION

Department of Veterans Affairs
Attn: Veterans Benefits Administration
810 Vermont Avenue, N.W.
Washington, DC 20420
(202) 418-4343   Toll Free: (800) 827-1000
Web: www.va.gov

Summary To provide a monthly payment to veterans who hold the Medal of Honor.

Eligibility This program is open to veterans who hold the Congressional Medal of Honor and are at least 40 years of age.

Financial Data Qualified veterans receive a pension of $1,194 per month.

Number awarded Depends on the number of qualified Medal of Honor holders currently living.

Deadline This is an entitlement program available to all Medal of Honor holders.

[1133]
MICHIGAN HOMESTEAD PROPERTY TAX CREDIT FOR VETERANS AND BLIND PEOPLE

Michigan Department of Treasury
Attn: Homestead Exemption
Treasury Building
430 West Allegan Street
Lansing, MI 48922
(517) 373-3200   Toll Free: (800) 827-4000
TDD: (517) 636-4999   E-mail: treasPtd2@michigan.gov
Web: www.michigan.gov/treasury

Summary To provide a property tax credit to veterans, military personnel, their spouses, blind people, and their surviving spouses in Michigan.

Eligibility Eligible to apply are residents of Michigan who are 1) blind and own their homestead; 2) a veteran with a service-connected disability or his/her surviving spouse; 3) a surviving spouse of a veteran deceased in service; 4) a pensioned veteran, a surviving spouse of those veterans, or an active military member, all of whose household income is less than $7,500; or 5) a surviving spouse of a non-disabled or non-pensioned veteran of the Korean War, World War II, or World War I whose household income is less than $7,500. All applicants must own or rent a home in Michigan, have been a Michigan resident for at least 6 months during the year in which application is made, and fall within qualifying income levels (up to $82,650 in household income).

Financial Data The maximum credit is $1,200. The exact amount varies. For homeowners, the credit depends on the state equalized value of the homestead and on an allowance for filing category. For renters, 20% of the rent is considered property tax eligible for credit.

Duration 1 year; eligibility must be established each year.

Number awarded Varies each year.

Deadline December of each year.

[1134]
MICHIGAN INCOME TAX EXEMPTION FOR DISABLED VETERANS

Michigan Department of Treasury
Attn: Income Tax
Treasury Building
430 West Allegan Street
Lansing, MI 48922
(517) 373-3200   Toll Free: (800) 827-4000
TDD: (517) 636-4999   E-mail: treasIndTax@michigan.gov
Web: www.michigan.gov/treasury

Summary To exempt a portion of the income of disabled veterans and their families in Michigan from state income taxation.

Eligibility Residents of Michigan may claim this exemption if 1) the taxpayer or spouse is a qualified disabled veteran; or 2) a dependent of the taxpayer is a qualified disabled veteran. The qualifying individual must be a veteran of the active military, naval, marine, coast guard, or air service who received an honorable or general discharge and has a disability incurred or aggravated in the line of duty. This exemption may be claimed in addition to any other exemption for which the taxpayer is eligible.

Financial Data Qualifying veterans with disabilities and their eligible family members receive an exemption of $250 from their adjusted gross income for purposes of state taxation.

Duration　The exemption continues as long as the recipient resides in Michigan.

Additional data　This exemption was first available for 2008 income.

Deadline　Deadline not specified.

[1135]
MICHIGAN INCOME TAX EXEMPTION FOR VETERANS AND MILITARY PERSONNEL

Michigan Department of Treasury
Attn: Income Tax
Treasury Building
430 West Allegan Street
Lansing, MI 48922
(517) 373-3200　　　　　　　　Toll Free: (800) 827-4000
TDD: (517) 636-4999　　E-mail: treasIndTax@michigan.gov
Web: www.michigan.gov/treasury

Summary　To exempt the income of military personnel and veterans in Michigan from state income taxation.

Eligibility　Eligible for this exemption are military personnel and veterans considered Michigan residents for purposes of state income taxation.

Financial Data　All active-duty military and retirement pay from the U.S. armed forces is exempt from state income taxation.

Duration　The exemption continues as long as the recipient resides in Michigan.

Deadline　Deadline not specified.

[1136]
MICHIGAN VETERANS TRUST FUND EMERGENCY GRANTS

Department of Military and Veterans Affairs
Attn: Michigan Veterans Trust Fund
2500 South Washington Avenue
Lansing, MI 48913-5101
(517) 483-5469　　　　　E-mail: paocmn@michigan.gov
Web: www.michigan.gov/dmva

Summary　To provide temporary financial assistance to disabled and other Michigan veterans and their families, if they are facing personal emergencies.

Eligibility　Eligible for this assistance are veterans and their families residing in Michigan who are temporarily unable to provide the basic necessities of life. Support is not provided for long-term problems or chronic financial difficulties. The qualifying veteran must have been discharged under honorable conditions with at least 180 days of active wartime service or have been separated as a result of a physical or mental disability incurred in the line of duty.

Financial Data　No statutory limit exists on the amount of assistance that may be provided; a local board in each Michigan county determines if the applicant is genuinely needy and the amount of assistance to be awarded.

Duration　This assistance is provided to meet temporary needs only.

Number awarded　Varies each year.

Deadline　Applications may be submitted at any time.

[1137]
MILITARY FAMILY SUPPORT TRUST FINANCIAL ASSISTANCE

Military Family Support Trust
1010 American Eagle Boulevard
P.O. Box 301
Sun City Center, FL 33573
(813) 634-4675　　　　　　　Fax: (813) 633-2412
E-mail: president@mobc-online.org
Web: www.mobc-online.org

Summary　To provide financial assistance for emergency needs to active-duty, retired, and deceased officers who served in the military or designated public service agencies and to their families.

Eligibility　This assistance is available to 1) retired, active-duty, National Guard, or Reserve officers and former officers of the U.S. Army, Navy, Marine Corps, Air Force, Coast Guard, Public Health Service, or National Oceanic and Atmospheric Administration, at the rank of O-1 through O-10, WO-1 through WO-5, or E-5 through E-9; 2) recipients of the Purple Heart, regardless of pay grade or length of service; 3) World War II combat veterans of the Merchant Marine; 4) federal employees at the grade of GS-7 or higher; 5) Foreign Service Officers at the grade of FSO-8 or lower; 6) honorably discharged or retired foreign military officers of friendly nations meeting the service and disability retirement criteria of their respective country and living in the United States; and 7) spouses, surviving spouses, and dependents (including grandchildren) of those categories. Applicants must be in need of financial assistance for personal care, subsistence, housing, all aspects of health care, or other special circumstances.

Financial Data　Grants depend on the need of the recipient.

Duration　Assistance is provided in the form of 1-time grants or monthly payments.

Additional data　This foundation was established in 1992 as the Military Officers' Benevolent Corporation. It changed its name in 2008.

Number awarded　Varies each year.

Deadline　Applications may be submitted at any time.

[1138]
MINNESOTA INCOME TAX SUBTRACTION FOR THE ELDERLY OR DISABLED

Minnesota Department of Revenue
Attn: Individual Income Tax Division
600 North Robert Street
Mail Station 5510
St. Paul, MN 55146-5510
(651) 296-3781　　　　　　　Toll Free: (800) 652-9094 (within MN)
E-mail: indinctax@state.mn.us
Web: www.taxes.state.mn.us

Summary　To exempt from state taxation a portion of the income received by residents of Minnesota who are disabled or elderly.

Eligibility　This exemption is available to residents of Minnesota who are either 65 years of age or older or permanently and totally disabled and receiving disability income from the Social Security Administration or U.S. Department of Veterans Affairs. Their adjusted gross income must be less than $42,000 if married filing a joint return and both spouses qualify, $38,500 if married filing a joint return and 1 spouse qualifies, $21,000 if married filing a separate return, or $33,700 if filing single, head of household, or qualifying widow(er).

Financial Data　Qualified taxpayers are entitled to subtract from their income for purposes of Minnesota state taxation $18,000 if married filing a joint return and both spouses qualify, $14,500 if married filing a joint return and 1 spouse qualifies, $9,000 if married filing a separate return, or $14,500 if filing single, head of household, or qualifying widow(er).

Duration　This exemption is available as long as the taxpayer resides in Minnesota.

Number awarded　Varies each year.

Deadline　Income tax returns must be submitted by April of each year.

[1139]
MINNESOTA SPECIAL HOMESTEAD CLASSIFICATIONS

Minnesota Department of Revenue
Attn: Property Tax Division
600 North Robert Street
Mail Station 3340
St. Paul, MN 55146-3340
(651) 556-6087
Web: www.taxes.state.mn.us

Summary To provide a property tax benefit to owners of homesteads in Minnesota who are disabled, blind, or paraplegic veterans.

Eligibility This benefit is available to owners of residential real estate that is occupied and used as a homestead in Minnesota. Applicants must be certified as totally and permanently disabled, legally blind, or a paraplegic veteran living in specially adapted housing with a grant from the Veterans Administration.

Financial Data Qualified property is taxed at a rate of 0.45% for the first $50,000 of market value of residential homesteads. That compares to the standard rate of 1.0% on the first $500,000 in valuation and 1.25% on valuation over $500,000.

Duration This benefit is available as long as the property is owned by a qualified person.

Number awarded Varies each year.

Deadline Applications must be submitted by September of each year.

[1140]
MINNESOTA STATE SOLDIERS ASSISTANCE PROGRAM

Minnesota Department of Veterans Affairs
Veterans Service Building
20 West 12th Street, Room 206C
St. Paul, MN 55155-2006
(651) 757-1556   Toll Free: (888) LINK-VET
Fax: (651) 296-3954   E-mail: kathy.schwartz@state.mn.us
Web: www.mdva.state.mn.us/financialassistance.htm

Summary To provide emergency financial assistance to disabled veterans and their families in Minnesota.

Eligibility This assistance is available to veterans who are unable to work because of a temporary disability (from service-connected or other causes). Their dependents and survivors are also eligible. Applicants must also meet income and asset guidelines and be residents of Minnesota.

Financial Data The maximum grant is $1,500. Funds may be used to pay for food and shelter, utility bills, and emergency medical treatment (including optical and dental benefits).

Duration This is a short-term program, with benefits payable up to 6 months only. If the veteran's disability is expected to be long term in nature or permanent, the department may continue to provide assistance while application is made for long-term benefits, such as Social Security disability or retirement benefits.

Number awarded Varies each year. A total of $1.4 million is available for this program annually.

Deadline Applications may be submitted at any time.

[1141]
MISSISSIPPI AD VALOREM TAX EXEMPTION FOR DISABLED VETERANS

Mississippi State Veterans Affairs Board
3460 Highway 80 East
P.O. Box 5947
Pearl, MS 39288-5947
(601) 576-4850   Fax: (601) 576-4868
E-mail: grice@vab.state.ms.us
Web: www.vab.state.ms.us/booklet.htm

Summary To exempt the property of disabled veterans from ad valorem taxation in Mississippi.

Eligibility This exemption applies to homesteads owned by American veterans in Mississippi who were honorably discharged. Applicants must have a 100% permanent service-connected disability.

Financial Data All qualifying homesteads of $7,500 or less in assessed value are exempt from ad valorem taxation.

Duration This exemption applies as long as the disabled veteran owns the homestead in Mississippi.

Number awarded Varies each year.

Deadline Deadline not specified.

[1142]
MISSOURI INCOME TAX GOVERNMENT PENSION EXEMPTION

Missouri Department of Revenue
Attn: Taxation Division
301 West High Street, Room 330
P.O. Box 2200
Jefferson City, MO 65105-2200
(573) 751-3505   Toll Free: (800) 877-6881
TDD: (800) 735-2966   E-mail: income@dor.mo.gov
Web: www.dor.mo.gov/tax/personal

Summary To exempt a portion of the retirement income of federal employees, including veterans, from state taxation in Missouri.

Eligibility This exemption is available to all residents of Missouri who are receiving pension payments from the U.S. government, including the armed forces. Applicants must have state adjusted gross incomes below specified levels, currently $16,000 if married and filing separately; $25,000 if single, head of household, or qualifying widow(er); or $32,000 if married filing jointly.

Financial Data Up to $6,000 of retirement income is exempt from state taxation.

Duration This exemption is available as long as the recipient remains a resident of Missouri for state income tax purposes.

Number awarded Varies each year.

Deadline Deadline not specified.

[1143]
MISSOURI SENIOR CITIZEN, DISABLED VETERAN, AND DISABLED PERSON PROPERTY TAX CREDIT CLAIM

Missouri Department of Revenue
Attn: Taxation Division
301 West High Street, Room 330
P.O. Box 2800
Jefferson City, MO 65105-2800
(573) 751-3505   Toll Free: (800) 877-6881
TDD: (800) 735-2966 E-mail: PropertyTaxCredit@dor.mo.gov
Web: www.dor.mo.gov/tax/personal

Summary To provide a property tax credit to low-income disabled veterans, senior citizens, and other persons with disabilities or their spouses in Missouri.

Eligibility This program is open to residents of Missouri (or their spouses) whose net household income does not exceed certain limits ($27,500 per year if they rented or did not own and occupy their home for the entire year, $30,000 if they owned and occupied their home for the entire year) and have paid property tax or rent on their homestead during the tax year. Applicants must be 1) 65 years of age or older, 2) classified by the U.S. Department of Veterans Affairs as a 100% service-connected disabled veteran, 3) 60 years of age or older and receiving surviving spouse Society Security benefits, or 4) 100% disabled.

Financial Data The tax credit depends on the claimant's income and amount paid in property taxes or rent, up to a maximum of $1,100 per year for property tax or $750 per year for rent.

Duration The tax credit is available annually.

Number awarded Varies each year.

Deadline Eligible veterans, people with disabilities, and senior citizens may claim this credit when they file their state income tax return, in April of each year.

[1144]
MONTANA DISABLED AMERICAN VETERAN PROPERTY TAX BENEFIT

Montana Department of Revenue
Attn: Property Tax
125 North Roberts, Third Floor
P.O. Box 5805
Helena, MT 59604-5805
(406) 444-6900   Toll Free: (866) 859-2254
Fax: (406) 444-1505   TDD: (406) 444-2830
Web: mt.gov/revenue

Summary To reduce the property tax rate in Montana for disabled veterans and their surviving spouses.

Eligibility This benefit is available to residents of Montana who own and occupy property in the state. Applicants must have been honorably discharged from active service in the armed forces and be currently rated 100% disabled or compensated at the 100% disabled rate because of a service-connected disability. They must have an adjusted gross income less than $52,899 if married or $45,846 if single. Also eligible are unremarried surviving spouses with an adjusted gross income less than $39,968 whose spouse was a veteran with a 100% service-connected disability or compensation at the 100% disabled rate at the time of death, died while on active duty, or died of a service-connected disability.

Financial Data Qualifying veterans and surviving spouses are entitled to a reduction in local property taxes on their residence, 1 attached or detached garage, and up to 1 acre of land. The amount of the reduction depends on the status of the applicant (married, single, or surviving spouse) and adjusted gross income, but ranges from 50% to 100%.

Duration The reduction continues as long as the recipient resides in Montana and owns and occupies property used as a primary residence.

Number awarded Varies each year.

Deadline Applications must be filed with the local Department of Revenue Office by April of each year.

[1145]
MONTANA TAX EXEMPTION FOR CERTAIN DISABLED OR DECEASED VETERANS' RESIDENCES

Montana Veterans' Affairs Division
1900 Williams Street
P.O. Box 5715
Helena, MT 59604
(406) 324-3740   Fax: (406) 324-3745
E-mail: lehall@mt.gov
Web: dma.mt.gov/mvad/functions/state.asp

Summary To exempt from taxation the real property of disabled or deceased veterans and their widow(er)s in Montana.

Eligibility This exemption applies to residential property in Montana that is owned and occupied by an honorably-discharged veteran who is rated as 100% disabled or is being paid at the 100% disabled rate by the U.S. Department of Veterans Affairs (DVA). Also eligible are unremarried spouses of deceased veterans who own and occupy a residence in Montana. Spouses must obtain documentation from the DVA that the veteran was rated as 100% disabled or was being paid at the 100% disabled rate at the time of death, or that the veteran died while on active duty.

Financial Data Eligible veterans or spouses are entitled to real property tax relief that depends on their income. Single veterans with an income of $30,000 or less are exempt from all property taxes; if their income is $30,001 to $33,000, they pay 20% of the regular tax; those with income from $33,001 to $36,000 pay 30% of the regular tax; and those with income from $36,001 to $39,000 pay 50% of the regular tax. Married veterans with an income of $36,000 or less are exempt from all property taxes; if their income is $36,001 to $39,000, they pay 20% of the regular tax; those with income from $39,001 to $42,000 pay 30% of the regular tax; and those with income from $42,001 to $45,000 pay 50% of the regular tax. Surviving spouses with an income of $25,000 or less are exempt from all property taxes; if their income is $25,001 to $28,000, they pay 20% of the regular tax; those with income from $28,001 to $31,000 pay 30% of the regular tax; and those with income from $31,001 to $34,000 pay 50% of the regular tax.

Duration The exemption continues as long as the residence in Montana is owned and occupied by the disabled veteran or, if deceased, by the veteran's unremarried spouse.

Number awarded Varies each year.

Deadline Deadline not specified.

[1146]
NEBRASKA HOMESTEAD EXEMPTION

Nebraska Department of Revenue
301 Centennial Mall South
P.O. Box 94818
Lincoln, NE 68509-4818
(402) 471-5729
Toll Free: (800) 742-7474 (within NE and IA)
Web: www.revenue.state.ne.us/homestead.htm

Summary To exempt the property of Nebraska residents who are elderly, disabled, or veterans and their widow(er)s from a portion of taxation.

Eligibility This exemption is available to 3 categories of Nebraska residents: the elderly, certain people with disabilities, and certain disabled veterans and their widow(er)s. Elderly people are those 65 years of age or older who own a homestead with a value less than $95,000 or 200% of their county's average assessed value of single family residential property, whichever is greater. Disabled people are those who 1) have a permanent physical disability and have lost all mobility such as to preclude locomotion without the regular use of a mechanical aid or prosthesis; 2) have undergone amputation of both arms above the elbow, or 3) have a permanent partial disability of both arms in excess of 75%. They must own a homestead with a value less than $110,000 or 225% of their county's average assessed value of single family residential property, whichever is greater. Veterans are those who served on active duty in the armed forces of the United States (or a government allied with the United States) during specified periods of war and received an honorable discharge. They must 1) be drawing compensation from the U.S. Department of Veterans Affairs (VA) because of a 100% service-connected disability; 2) be totally disabled by a nonservice-connected illness or accident; or 3) own a home that is substantially contributed to by VA. Also eligible are unremarried widow(er)s of veterans who died because of a service-connected disability, whose death while on active duty was service-connected, who died while on active duty during wartime, or who drew compensation from VA because of a 100% service-connected disability The homestead maximum value is $110,000 or 225% of the county's average assessed value of single family residential property, whichever is greater. Elderly people must have a household income less than $31,301 if single or $36,801 if married. Disabled persons, veterans, and widow(er)s (except veterans and widow(er)s who own a home that is substantially contributed to by the VA) must have a household income less than $34,401 if single or $39,701 if married.

Financial Data Exemptions depend on the income of the applicant, ranging from 25% to 100% of the value of the homestead. For the elderly, the maximum exemption is the taxable value of the homestead up to $40,000 or 100% of the county's average assessed value of single family residential property, whichever is greater. For disabled people and veterans, the maximum exemption is the taxable value of the homestead up to $50,000 or 120% of the county's average assessed value of single family residential property, whichever is greater. For veterans and widow(er)s whose home was substantially contributed to by the VA, the homestead is 100% exempt regardless of the value of the homestead or the income of the owner.

Duration The exemption is provided as long as the qualifying homestead owner resides in Nebraska.

Number awarded Varies each year.

Deadline Applications must be filed by June of each year.

[1147]
NEBRASKA VETERANS' AID FUND

Department of Veterans' Affairs
State Office Building
301 Centennial Mall South, Sixth Floor
P.O. Box 95083
Lincoln, NE 68509-5083
(402) 471-2458   Fax: (402) 471-2491
E-mail: john.hilgert@nebraska.gov
Web: www.vets.state.ne.us

Summary To assist veterans, their spouses, and their dependents in Nebraska who have a temporary emergency need.

Eligibility This assistance is available to veterans, their spouses, and their dependent children who are residents of Nebraska. The veteran must have served on active duty in the armed forces of the United States, other than active duty for training, and either 1) was discharged or otherwise separated with a characterization of honorable or general (under honorable conditions), or 2) died while in service or as a direct result of such service.

Financial Data The amount of aid awarded varies, depending upon the needs of the recipient. Recently, grants averaged approximately $1,000. Aid can only be used for food, fuel, shelter, wearing apparel, funeral, medical, or surgical items.

Duration The funds are provided for emergency situations only; the program does not assist ongoing financial needs.

Additional data The Nebraska Veterans' Aid Fund was established in 1921 in lieu of a bonus for veterans of wartime service. Applications must be made through the county service officer or post service officer of any recognized veterans' organization in the county nearest the applicant's place of residence and submitted to the Department of Veterans' Affairs.

Number awarded Varies each year. In a recent year, more than $764,000 in aid was provided to 694 veterans.

Deadline Applications may be submitted at any time.

[1148]
NEVADA DISABLED VETERAN'S TAX EXEMPTION

Nevada Office of Veterans' Services
Attn: Executive Director
5460 Reno Corporate Drive
Reno, NV 89511
(775) 688-1653   Fax: (775) 688-1656
Web: veterans.nv.gov/NOVS/Veterans%20Benefits.html

Summary To exempt from taxation in Nevada a portion of the property owned by disabled veterans or their surviving spouses.

Eligibility This program is open to veterans who are residents of Nevada and have incurred a service-connected disability of 60% or more. Applicants must have received an honorable separation from military service. The widow(er) of a disabled veteran, who was eligible at the time of death, may also be eligible for this benefit.

Financial Data Veterans and widow(er)s are entitled to exempt from taxation a portion of their property's assessed value. The amount depends on the extent of the disability and the year filed;

it ranges from $6,250 to $20,000 and doubles over a 4-year period.

Duration Disabled veterans and their widow(er)s are entitled to this exemption as long as they live in Nevada.

Additional data Disabled veterans and widow(er)s are able to split their exemption between vehicle taxes and/or property taxes. Further information is available at local county assessors' offices.

Number awarded Varies each year.

Deadline Deadline not specified.

[1149]
NEVADA VETERAN'S TAX EXEMPTION

Nevada Office of Veterans' Services
Attn: Executive Director
5460 Reno Corporate Drive
Reno, NV 89511
(775) 688-1653   Fax: (775) 688-1656
Web: veterans.nv.gov/NOVS/Veterans%20Benefits.html

Summary To exempt from taxation in Nevada a portion of the property owned by wartime veterans.

Eligibility This program is open to veterans who have been residents of Nevada for at least 6 months and have wartime service (including in-theater service during the wars in the Persian Gulf, Afghanistan, and Iraq). Veterans are entitled to an exemption on their vehicle privilege tax or real property tax, but they cannot split the benefit between the 2 taxes.

Financial Data The exact amount of the exemption is available from the local county assessor. The value of the exemption doubles over a 4-year period.

Duration Wartime veterans are entitled to this exemption as long as they live in Nevada.

Number awarded Varies each year.

Deadline Deadline not specified.

[1150]
NEW HAMPSHIRE PROPERTY TAX EXEMPTION FOR CERTAIN DISABLED VETERANS

New Hampshire Department of Revenue Administration
109 Pleasant Street
Concord, NH 03301
(603) 271-2191   Fax: (603) 271-6121
TDD: (800) 735-2964
Web: revenue.nh.gov

Summary To exempt from taxation certain property owned by New Hampshire disabled veterans or their surviving spouses.

Eligibility Eligible for this exemption are New Hampshire residents who are honorably discharged veterans with a total and permanent service-connected disability that involves double amputation of the upper or lower extremities or any combination thereof, paraplegia, or blindness of both eyes with visual acuity of 5/200 or less. Applicants or their surviving spouses must own a specially adapted homestead that has been acquired with the assistance of the U.S. Department of Veterans Affairs.

Financial Data Qualifying disabled veterans and surviving spouses are exempt from all taxation on their specially adapted homestead.

Duration 1 year; once the credit has been approved, it is automatically renewed as long as the qualifying person owns the same residence in New Hampshire.

Number awarded Varies each year.

Deadline The original application for a permanent tax credit must be submitted by April.

[1151]
NEW HAMPSHIRE SERVICE-CONNECTED TOTAL AND PERMANENT DISABILITY TAX CREDIT

New Hampshire Department of Revenue Administration
109 Pleasant Street
Concord, NH 03301
(603) 271-2191   Fax: (603) 271-6121
TDD: (800) 735-2964
Web: revenue.nh.gov

Summary   To provide property tax credits in New Hampshire to disabled veterans or their surviving spouses.

Eligibility   Eligible for this tax credit are honorably discharged veterans residing in New Hampshire who 1) have a total and permanent service-connected disability, or 2) are a double amputee or paraplegic because of a service-connected disability. Unremarried surviving spouses of qualified veterans are also eligible.

Financial Data   Qualifying disabled veterans and surviving spouses receive an annual credit of $700 for property taxes on residential property. In addition, individual towns in New Hampshire may adopt a local option to increase the dollar amount credited to disabled veterans, to a maximum of $2,000.

Duration   1 year; once the credit has been approved, it is automatically renewed for as long as the qualifying person owns the same residence in New Hampshire.

Number awarded   Varies each year.

Deadline   The original application for a permanent tax credit must be submitted by April.

[1152]
NEW JERSEY INCOME TAX EXCLUSION FOR MILITARY PENSIONS AND SURVIVOR'S BENEFITS

New Jersey Division of Taxation
Attn: Information and Publications Branch
50 Barrack Street
P.O. Box 281
Trenton, NJ 08695-0281
(609) 292-6400
Toll Free: (800) 323-4400 (within NJ, NY, PA, DE, and MD)
TDD: (800) 286-6613 (within NJ, NY, PA, DE, and MD)
E-mail: taxation@tax.state.nj.us
Web: www.state.nj.us/treasury/taxation

Summary   To exclude from income taxation in New Jersey military pensions and survivor's benefits.

Eligibility   This exclusion is available to residents of New Jersey who are receiving 1) a military pension resulting from service in the Army, Navy, Air Force, Marine Corps, or Coast Guard, or 2) survivor's benefits related to such service. It does not apply to civil service pensions or annuities, even if the pension or annuity is based on credit for military service.

Financial Data   All military pensions and survivor's benefit payments are excluded from income for state taxation purposes.

Duration   The exclusion applies as long as the individual resides in New Jersey.

Additional data   This exclusion became effective in 2001.

Number awarded   Varies each year.

Deadline   Deadline not specified.

[1153]
NEW JERSEY INCOME TAX EXCLUSIONS FOR PERSONS WITH DISABILITIES

New Jersey Division of Taxation
Attn: Information and Publications Branch
50 Barrack Street
P.O. Box 281
Trenton, NJ 08695-0281
(609) 292-6400
Toll Free: (800) 323-4400 (within NJ, NY, PA, DE, and MD)
TDD: (800) 286-6613 (within NJ, NY, PA, DE, and MD)
E-mail: taxation@tax.state.nj.us
Web: www.state.nj.us/treasury/taxation

Summary   To exclude from income taxation in New Jersey certain benefits received by veterans and other persons with disabilities.

Eligibility   Residents of New Jersey with disabilities are entitled to this exclusion if they are receiving benefits from public agencies, including compensation from the U.S. Department of Veterans Affairs for permanent and total disability or from the state of New Jersey for temporary disability.

Financial Data   Disability payments are excluded from income for state taxation purposes.

Duration   The exclusion applies as long as the individual receives qualifying disability payments.

Number awarded   Varies each year.

Deadline   Deadline not specified.

[1154]
NEW JERSEY PROPERTY TAX EXEMPTION FOR DISABLED VETERANS OR SURVIVING SPOUSES

New Jersey Division of Taxation
Attn: Information and Publications Branch
50 Barrack Street
P.O. Box 281
Trenton, NJ 08695-0281
(609) 292-6400
Toll Free: (800) 323-4400 (within NJ, NY, PA, DE, and MD)
TDD: (800) 286-6613 (within NJ, NY, PA, DE, and MD)
E-mail: taxation@tax.state.nj.us
Web: www.state.nj.us/treasury/taxation/otherptr.shtml

Summary   To provide a real estate tax exemption to New Jersey veterans with disabilities and certain surviving widow(er)s.

Eligibility   This exemption is available to New Jersey residents who have been honorably discharged with active wartime service in the U.S. armed forces and have been certified by the U.S. Department of Veterans Affairs as totally and permanently disabled as a result of wartime service-connected conditions. Unremarried surviving spouses of eligible disabled veterans or of certain wartime servicepersons who died on active duty are also entitled to this exemption. Applicants must be the full owner of and a permanent resident in the dwelling house for which the exemption is claimed.

Financial Data   A 100% exemption from locally-levied real estate taxes is provided.

Duration   1 year; the exemption continues as long as the eligible veteran remains a resident of New Jersey.

Additional data   This program is administered by the local tax assessor or collector. Veterans who are denied exemptions have the right to appeal the decision to their county and state governments.

Number awarded   Varies each year.

Deadline   Applications may be submitted at any time.

[1155]

NEW MEXICO DISABLED VETERAN PROPERTY TAX EXEMPTION

New Mexico Department of Veterans' Services
Attn: Benefits Division
407 Galisteo Street, Room 142
Santa Fe, NM 87504
(505) 827-6374　　　　　Toll Free: (866) 433-VETS
Fax: (505) 827-6372　　　E-mail: alan.martinez@state.nm.us
Web: www.dvs.state.nm.us/benefits.html

Summary To exempt disabled veterans and their spouses from payment of property taxes in New Mexico.

Eligibility This exemption is available to veterans who are rated 100% service-connected disabled by the U.S. Department of Veterans Affairs, are residents of New Mexico, and own a primary residence in the state. Also eligible are qualifying veterans' unremarried surviving spouses, if they are New Mexico residents and continue to own the residence.

Financial Data Veterans and surviving spouses are exempt from payment of property taxes in New Mexico.

Duration 1 year; continues until the qualifying veteran or spouse no longer live in the residence.

Number awarded Varies each year.

Deadline Deadline not specified.

[1156]

NEW MEXICO VETERANS PROPERTY TAX EXEMPTION

New Mexico Department of Veterans' Services
Attn: Benefits Division
407 Galisteo Street, Room 142
Santa Fe, NM 87504
(505) 827-6374　　　　　Toll Free: (866) 433-VETS
Fax: (505) 827-6372　　　E-mail: alan.martinez@state.nm.us
Web: www.dvs.state.nm.us/benefits.html

Summary To exempt veterans and their spouses from a portion of property taxes in New Mexico.

Eligibility This exemption is available to veterans who served honorably for at least 90 days during wartime (World War I, World War II, Korea, Vietnam, Persian Gulf), are residents of New Mexico, and own a primary residence in the state. Also eligible are qualifying veterans' unremarried surviving spouses, if they are New Mexico residents and continue to own the residence.

Financial Data Veterans and surviving spouses are entitled to a reduction in the value of their property that is currently $4,000. The exemption is deducted from the taxable value of the property to determine net taxable value. Veterans who are entitled to this exemption and do not have sufficient real or personal property to claim the full exemption may be eligible to claim a one third reduction in motor vehicle registration fees.

Duration 1 year; continues until the qualifying veteran or spouse no longer lives in the residence.

Number awarded Varies each year.

Deadline Deadline not specified.

[1157]

NEW YORK ALTERNATIVE PROPERTY TAX EXEMPTIONS FOR VETERANS

New York State Division of Veterans' Affairs
5 Empire State Plaza, Suite 2836
Albany, NY 12223-1551
(518) 474-6114　　　　Toll Free: (888) VETS-NYS (within NY)
Fax: (518) 473-0379　　　E-mail: dvainfo@ogs.state.ny.us
Web: veterans.ny.gov/property_tax_exemption.html

Summary To provide wartime veterans and their spouses who are residents of New York with a partial exemption from property taxes.

Eligibility This program is open to veterans who served during specified periods of wartime. Applicants must have been discharged under honorable conditions; additional benefits are available to those who served in a combat zone and to those who have a service-connected disability. The legal title to the property must be in the name of the veteran or the spouse of the veteran or both, or the unremarried surviving spouse of the veteran. The property must be used exclusively for residential purposes. This program is only available in counties, cities, towns, and villages in New York that have opted to participate.

Financial Data This program provides an exemption of 15% of the assessed valuation of the property, to a basic maximum of $12,000 per year; local governments may opt for reduced maximums of $9,000 or $6,000, or for increased maximums of $15,000 to $36,000. For combat-zone veterans, an additional 10% of the assessed valuation is exempt, to a basic maximum of $8,000 per year; local governments may opt for a reduced maximum of $6,000 or $4,000, or for increased maximums of $10,000 to $24,000. For disabled veterans, the exemption is the percentage of assessed value equal to half of the service-connected disability rating, to a basic maximum of $40,000 per year; local governments may opt for a reduced maximum of $30,000 or $20,000, or for increased maximums of $50,000 to $120,000. At its option, New York City and other high appreciation municipalities may use the following increased maximum exemptions: war veteran, $54,000; combat-zone veteran, $36,000; disabled veteran, $180,000.

Duration This exemption is available annually.

Number awarded Varies each year.

Deadline Applications must be filed with the local assessor by "taxable status date;" in most towns, that is the end of February.

[1158]

NEW YORK "ELIGIBLE FUNDS" PROPERTY TAX EXEMPTIONS FOR VETERANS

New York State Division of Veterans' Affairs
5 Empire State Plaza, Suite 2836
Albany, NY 12223-1551
(518) 474-6114　　　　Toll Free: (888) VETS-NYS (within NY)
Fax: (518) 473-0379　　　E-mail: dvainfo@ogs.state.ny.us
Web: veterans.ny.gov

Summary To provide a partial exemption from property taxes to veterans and their surviving spouses who are residents of New York.

Eligibility This program is open to veterans who have purchased properties in New York with pension, bonus, or insurance money (referred to as "eligible funds"). Specially adapted homes of paraplegics, or the homes of their widowed spouses, are also covered.

Financial Data This exemption reduces the property's assessed value to the extent that "eligible funds" were used in the purchase, generally to a maximum of $5,000. It is applicable to general municipal taxes but not to school taxes or special district levies.

Duration This exemption is available annually.

Number awarded Varies each year.

Deadline Applications must be filed with the local assessor by "taxable status date;" in most towns, that is the end of February.

[1159]

NEW YORK STATE BLIND ANNUITY

New York State Division of Veterans' Affairs
5 Empire State Plaza, Suite 2836
Albany, NY 12223-1551
(518) 474-6114　　　　Toll Free: (888) VETS-NYS (within NY)
Fax: (518) 473-0379　　　E-mail: dvainfo@ogs.state.ny.us
Web: veterans.ny.gov/blind_annuity.html

Summary To provide an annuity to blind wartime veterans and their surviving spouses in New York.

Eligibility This benefit is available to veterans who served on active duty during specified periods of war. Applicants must 1) meet the New York State standards of blindness; 2) have received an honorable or general discharge, or a discharge other than for dishonorable service; and 3) be now, and continue to be, residents of and continuously domiciled in New York State. The annuity is also payable to unremarried spouses of deceased veterans who were receiving annuity payments (or were eligible to do so) at the time of their death, and are residents of and continuously domiciled in New York State.

Financial Data The annuity is currently $1,173.84 per year.

Number awarded Varies each year.

Deadline Deadline not specified.

[1160]
NEW YORK STATE INCOME TAX EXEMPTIONS FOR RETIREMENT INCOME

New York State Department of Taxation and Finance
W.A. Harriman Campus
Tax and Finance Building
Albany, NY 12227-0001
(518) 438-8581   Toll Free: (800) 225-5829 (within NY)
Web: www.nystax.gov

Summary To exempt the pension income of retired New York public employees, including the military, from state income tax.

Eligibility Residents of New York who are receiving a pension from a plan that represents a return of contributions in a year prior to retirement as an officer, employee, or beneficiary of an officer or employee of state, local, and federal public agencies, including the U.S. military, are eligible for this exemption.

Financial Data Qualified pension income, to a maximum of $20,000, is exempt from state income taxation in New York.

Duration The exemption is available as long as the recipient resides in New York.

Number awarded Varies each year.

Deadline Deadline not specified.

[1161]
NMCRS FINANCIAL ASSISTANCE

Navy-Marine Corps Relief Society
875 North Randolph Street, Suite 225
Arlington, VA 22203-1757
(703) 696-4904   Fax: (703) 696-0144
Web: www.nmcrs.org/intfreeloan.html

Summary To provide emergency assistance, in the form of interest-free loans or grants, to current and former Navy and Marine Corps personnel and their families who need temporary funding.

Eligibility This program is open to active-duty and retired Navy and Marine Corps personnel, their eligible family members, eligible family members of Navy and Marine Corps personnel who died on active duty or in a retired status, Reservists on extended active duty, indigent mothers (65 years of age or older) of deceased servicemembers who have limited resources and no family to provide for their welfare, ex-spouses whose marriage to a servicemember lasted for at least 20 years while the servicemember was on active duty and who have not remarried, and uniformed members of the National Oceanic and Atmospheric Administration (NOAA). Applicants must need emergency funding for funeral expenses, medical or dental bills, food, rent, utilities, emergency transportation, disaster relief, child care expenses, essential vehicle repairs, or other unforeseen family emergencies. Funding is not available to pay bills for non-essentials, finance liberty and vacations, pay fines or legal expenses, pay taxes, finance recreational boats or vehicles or help Navy and Marine Corps families live beyond their means.

Financial Data Funds are provided in the form of interest-free loans or grants.

Number awarded Varies each year.

Deadline Applications may be submitted at any time.

[1162]
NORTH CAROLINA INCOME TAX EXCLUSION FOR RETIREMENT PAY

North Carolina Department of Revenue
Attn: Individual Income Tax
501 North Wilmington Street
P.O. Box 25000
Raleigh, NC 27640-0640
(919) 733-4684
Web: www.dornc.com/taxes/individual/index.html

Summary To exclude a portion of the retirement pay of military and other retirees from state income taxation in North Carolina.

Eligibility This exclusion is available to residents of North Carolina who are receiving retirement benefits from any federal, state, or local government retirement plan, including the U.S. armed forces.

Financial Data Eligible residents may exclude $4,000 of qualified retirement pay from income for purposes of state taxation in North Carolina.

Duration The exclusion is available as long as the recipient resides in North Carolina.

Number awarded Varies each year.

Deadline Deadline not specified.

[1163]
NORTH CAROLINA PROPERTY TAX RELIEF FOR DISABLED VETERANS

North Carolina Department of Revenue
Attn: Property Tax Division
501 North Wilmington Street
P.O. Box 871
Raleigh, NC 27602
(919) 733-7711   Fax: (919) 733-1821
Web: www.dornc.com/taxes/property/exemptions.html

Summary To provide property tax relief to disabled North Carolina veterans.

Eligibility Disabled veterans who are residents of North Carolina are eligible for these programs. They must own 1) a vehicle that is altered with special equipment to accommodate a service-connected disability; or 2) specially adapted housing purchased with the assistance of the U.S. Department of Veterans Affairs.

Financial Data Qualifying vehicles are exempt from personal property taxes. Qualifying housing is eligible for an exemption on the first $45,000 in assessed value of the housing and land that is owned and used as a residence by the disabled veteran.

Duration The exemptions continue as long as the eligible veteran is a resident of North Carolina.

Number awarded Varies each year.

Deadline Deadline not specified.

[1164]
NORTH DAKOTA PROPERTY TAX CREDIT FOR DISABLED VETERANS

Office of State Tax Commissioner
State Capitol Building
600 East Boulevard Avenue, Department 127
Bismarck, ND 58505-0599
(701) 328-2770   Toll Free: (800) 638-2901
Fax: (701) 328-3700   TDD: (800) 366-6888
E-mail: taxinfo@state.nd.us
Web: www.nd.gov/tax

Summary To provide property tax credits to disabled North Dakota veterans and their surviving spouses.

Eligibility This property tax credit is available to honorably-discharged veterans who have more than a 50% service-connected disability as certified by the U.S. Department of Veterans Affairs. Applicants must own and occupy a homestead according to state law. Unremarried surviving spouses are also eligible. If a disabled veteran co-owns the property with someone other than a spouse, the credit is limited to the disabled veteran's interest in the fixtures, buildings, and improvements of the homestead.

Financial Data The credit is applied against the first $120,000 of true and full valuation of the fixtures, buildings, and improvements of the homestead, to a maximum amount calculated by multiplying $120,000 by the percentage of the disabled veteran's disability compensation rating for service-connected disabilities.

Duration 1 year; renewable as long as qualified individuals continue to reside in North Dakota and live in their homes.

Number awarded Varies each year.

Deadline Applications may be submitted to the county auditor at any time.

[1165]
NORTH DAKOTA PROPERTY TAX EXEMPTION FOR VETERANS WHO LIVE IN SPECIALLY ADAPTED HOUSING

Office of State Tax Commissioner
State Capitol Building
600 East Boulevard Avenue, Department 127
Bismarck, ND 58505-0599
(701) 328-2770   Toll Free: (800) 638-2901
Fax: (701) 328-3700   TDD: (800) 366-6888
E-mail: taxinfo@state.nd.us
Web: www.nd.gov/tax

Summary To provide property tax exemptions to North Dakota veterans and their surviving spouses who have been awarded specially adapted housing.

Eligibility This exemption is available to paraplegic disabled veterans of the U.S. armed forces or any veteran who has been awarded specially adapted housing by the U.S. Department of Veterans Affairs. The paraplegic disability does not have to be service-connected. The unremarried surviving spouses of such deceased veterans are also eligible. Income and assets are not considered in determining eligibility for the exemption.

Financial Data The maximum benefit may not exceed $5,400 taxable value, because the exemption is limited to the first $120,000 of true and full value of fixtures, buildings, and improvements.

Duration 1 year; renewable as long as qualified individuals continue to reside in North Dakota and live in their homes.

Number awarded Varies each year.

Deadline Applications may be submitted to the county auditor at any time.

[1166]
NORTH DAKOTA STATE INCOME TAX MILITARY RETIREMENT PAY EXCLUSION

Office of State Tax Commissioner
State Capitol Building
600 East Boulevard Avenue, Department 127
Bismarck, ND 58505-0599
(701) 328-2770   Toll Free: (800) 638-2901
Fax: (701) 328-3700   TDD: (800) 366-6888
E-mail: taxinfo@state.nd.us
Web: www.nd.gov/tax

Summary To exempt from state income taxation a portion of the income received by veterans residing in North Dakota.

Eligibility Eligible for this benefit are residents of North Dakota who receive military retirement pay for service in the U.S. armed forces (including the Coast Guard) or any of its Reserve components and are at least 50 years of age.

Financial Data Up to $5,000 per year of military retirement pay may be excluded from income for state income tax purposes.

Duration The exclusion may be taken as long as the recipient resides in North Dakota.

Number awarded Varies each year.

Deadline Deadline not specified.

[1167]
OHIO INCOME TAX DEDUCTION FOR MILITARY RETIREMENT INCOME

Ohio Department of Taxation
Attn: Income Tax Audit Division
30 East Broad Street
P.O. Box 182847
Columbus, OH 43218-2847
(614) 433-5817   Toll Free: (800) 282-1780 (within OH)
Fax: (614) 433-7771
Web: tax.ohio.gov

Summary To deduct from state income taxation in Ohio the pay received by retired military personnel and their surviving spouses.

Eligibility This deduction is available to residents of Ohio who are retired from service in the active or reserve components of the U.S. armed forces. Surviving and former spouses of military retirees who are receiving payments under the survivor benefit plan are also eligible. the state is excluded from income for purposes of Ohio state taxation.

Financial Data All retirement income received by military personnel and their surviving or former spouses is excluded from state income taxation in Ohio.

Duration The exclusion is available as long as the recipient remains an Ohio resident.

Number awarded Varies each year.

Deadline Deadline not specified.

[1168]
OHIO MILITARY INJURY RELIEF FUND GRANTS

Ohio Department of Job and Family Services
Attn: Military Injury Relief Fund
30 East Broad Street, 32nd Floor
P.O. Box 182367
Columbus, OH 43218-2367
(614) 466-2100   Toll Free: (888) 296-7541
E-mail: MIRF@jfs.ohio.gov
Web: jfs.ohio.gov/veterans/new/mirf.stm

Summary To provide funding to Ohio residents who suffered injuries while serving in the U.S. armed forces in Operation Enduring Freedom (OEF) or Operation Iraqi Freedom (OIF).

Eligibility This program is open to residents of Ohio who served in country (including Reservists and National Guard members activated under Title 10) under OEF or OIF. Applicants must have suffered a physical injury in the line of duty or have been diagnosed with post-traumatic stress disorder (PTSD) incurred while serving in country under OEF or OIF. The injury must have occurred while the service member was in receipt of hazardous duty, combat, or hostile fire pay in an OEF or OIF theater of operation. Honorably discharged veterans must submit a copy of their DD214; military personnel still serving must submit proof of service; Reservists and National Guard members must submit a copy of the military orders activating them under Title 10.

Financial Data The amount of the grant depends on the availability of funds.

Additional data This program was established in 2005.

Number awarded Varies each year.

Deadline Applications may be submitted at any time.

[1169]
OHIO VETERANS' FINANCIAL ASSISTANCE

Ohio Department of Veterans Services
77 South High Street, 7th Floor
Columbus, OH 43215
(614) 644-0898   Toll Free: (888) DVS-OHIO
Fax: (614) 728-9498   E-mail: ohiovet@dvs.ohio.gov
Web: dvs.ohio.gov

Summary To provide emergency aid to Ohio veterans, military personnel, and their dependents who, because of disability or disaster, are in financial need.

Eligibility This assistance is available to veterans and active-duty members of the U.S. armed forces, as well as their spouses, surviving spouses, dependent parents, minor children, and wards. Applicants must have been residents of the Ohio county in which they are applying for at least 3 months. They must be able to demonstrate need for relief because of sickness, accident, or destitution.

Financial Data The amount granted varies, depending on the needs of the recipient.

Duration These are emergency funds only and are not designed to be a recurring source of income.

Additional data These grants are made by the various county veterans services offices in Ohio.

Number awarded Varies each year.

Deadline Applications may be submitted at any time.

[1170]
OKLAHOMA FINANCIAL ASSISTANCE PROGRAM

Oklahoma Department of Veterans Affairs
Veterans Memorial Building
2311 North Central Avenue
P.O. Box 53067
Oklahoma City, OK 73152
(405) 521-3684   Fax: (405) 521-6533
E-mail: scylmer@odva.state.ok.us
Web: www.ok.gov/ODVA/Financial_Assistance/index.html

Summary To provide emergency aid to Oklahoma veterans and their families who, because of disability or disaster, are in financial need.

Eligibility This program is open to veterans with at least 90 days of wartime service and an honorable discharge who are current residents of Oklahoma and have resided in the state for at least 1 year immediately preceding the date of application. Applicants must be seeking assistance because of an interruption or loss of job and income resulting from illness, injury, or disaster (such as loss of home due to fire, floor, or storm). Widow(er)s and minor children may also qualify for the benefit.

Financial Data The amount of the grant depends on the need of the recipient.

Duration The grant is available only on a 1-time basis.

Additional data No financial assistance will be granted when regular monetary benefits are being received from other state agencies. The funds cannot be used for old debts, car payments, or medical expenses.

Number awarded Varies each year.

Deadline Applications must be submitted to the local post or chapter of a veterans services organization for initial approval or disapproval. They may be submitted at any time during the year.

[1171]
OKLAHOMA MILITARY RETIREMENT INCOME TAX EXCLUSION

Oklahoma Tax Commission
Attn: Income Tax
2501 North Lincoln Boulevard
Oklahoma City, OK 73194-0009
(405) 521-3160   Toll Free: (800) 522-8165 (within OK)
Fax: (405) 522-0063   E-mail: otcmaster@tax.ok.gov
Web: www.tax.ok.gov/incometax.html

Summary To exclude a portion of the income of military retirees and their spouses from state taxation in Oklahoma.

Eligibility This exclusion is available to residents of Oklahoma and their spouses who are receiving retirement benefits from a component of the U.S. armed forces.

Financial Data Military retirees are entitled to exclude 75% of their retirement benefits or $10,000, whichever is greater, from state taxation.

Duration The exclusion is available as long as the recipient resides in Oklahoma.

Deadline Deadline not specified.

[1172]
OKLAHOMA PROPERTY TAX EXEMPTION FOR DISABLED VETERANS

Oklahoma Tax Commission
Attn: Property Tax
2501 North Lincoln Boulevard
Oklahoma City, OK 73194-0009
(405) 521-3178   Toll Free: (800) 522-8165 (within OK)
Fax: (405) 522-0063   E-mail: otcmaster@tax.ok.gov
Web: www.tax.ok.gov

Summary To exempt the property of disabled veterans and their surviving spouses from taxation in Oklahoma.

Eligibility This program is available to Oklahoma residents who are veterans honorably discharged from a branch of the armed forces or the Oklahoma National Guard. Applicants must have a 100% permanent disability sustained through military action or accident or resulting from a disease contracted while in active service; the disability must be certified by the U.S. Department of Veterans Affairs. They must own property that qualifies for the Oklahoma homestead exemption. Surviving spouses of qualified veterans are also eligible.

Financial Data Qualified veterans and surviving spouses are eligible for exemption of the taxes on the full fair cash value of their homestead.

Duration The exemption is available as long as the veteran or surviving spouse resides in Oklahoma and owns a qualifying homestead.

Additional data This exemption was first available in 2006.

Deadline Deadline not specified.

[1173]
OREGON PROPERTY TAX EXEMPTION FOR VETERANS WITH DISABILITIES AND THEIR SPOUSES

Oregon Department of Revenue
Attn: Property Tax Division
Revenue Building
955 Center Street, N.E.
Salem, OR 97310-2551
(503) 378-4988   Toll Free: (800) 356-4222 (within OR)
TDD: (800) 886-7204 (within OR)
Web: www.oregon.gov/DOR/PTD/IC_310_676.shtml

Summary To exempt disabled Oregon veterans and their spouses from a portion of their property taxes.

Eligibility Qualifying veterans are those who received a discharge or release under honorable conditions after service of either 1) 90 consecutive days during World War I, World War II, or the Korean Conflict; or 2) 210 consecutive days after January 31, 1955. Eligible individuals must meet 1 of these conditions: 1) a war veteran who is officially certified by the U.S. Department of Veterans Affairs (VA) or any branch of the U.S. armed forces as having disabilities of 40% or more; 2) a war veteran who is certified each year by a licensed physician as being 40% or more disabled and has total gross income that is less than 185% of the federal poverty level (currently $18,130 for a family of 1, rising to $62,160 for a family of 8); or 3) a war veteran's surviving spouse who has not remarried, even if the veteran's spouse was not disabled or did not take advantage of the exemption if disabled. Recipients of this exemption must own and live on a property in Oregon.

Financial Data The exemption is $15,450 of the homestead property's real market value.

Duration 1 year; may be renewed as long as the eligible veteran or surviving unremarried spouse owns and occupies the primary residence.

Number awarded Varies each year.

Deadline This exemption is not automatic. Applications must be submitted by March of each year.

[1174]
OREGON PROPERTY TAX EXEMPTION FOR VETERANS WITH SERVICE-CONNECTED DISABILITIES AND THEIR SPOUSES

Oregon Department of Revenue
Attn: Property Tax Division
Revenue Building
955 Center Street, N.E.
Salem, OR 97310-2551
(503) 378-4988   Toll Free: (800) 356-4222 (within OR)
TDD: (800) 886-7204 (within OR)
Web: www.oregon.gov/DOR/PTD/IC_310_676.shtml

Summary To exempt Oregon veterans with service-connected disabilities and their spouses from a portion of their property taxes.

Eligibility Qualifying veterans are those who received a discharge or release under honorable conditions after service of either 1) 90 consecutive days during World War I, World War II, or the Korean Conflict; or 2) 210 consecutive days after January 31, 1955. Eligible individuals must meet 1 of these conditions: 1) a war veteran who is certified by the U.S. Department of Veterans Affairs (VA) or any branch of the U.S. armed forces as having service-connected disabilities of 40% or more; or 2) a surviving spouse of a war veteran who died because of service-connected injury or illness or who received at least 1 year of this exemption. Recipients of this exemption must own and live on a property in Oregon.

Financial Data The exemption is $18,540 of the homestead property's real market value.

Duration 1 year; may be renewed as long as the eligible veterans or surviving spouse owns and occupies the primary residence.

Number awarded Varies each year.

Deadline This exemption is not automatic. Applications must be submitted by March of each year.

[1175]
OREGON RETIREMENT INCOME TAX CREDIT

Oregon Department of Revenue
Revenue Building
955 Center Street, N.E.
Salem, OR 97310-2551
(503) 378-4988   Toll Free: (800) 356-4222 (within OR)
TDD: (800) 886-7204 (within OR)
Web: www.oregon.gov/DOR/PERTAX

Summary To provide an income tax credit to retired veterans and other residents of Oregon.

Eligibility This exemption applies to pension income earned by residents of Oregon from Social Security, Railroad Retirement, the military, or the U.S. Department of Veterans Affairs. Taxpayers must be 62 years of age or older and have household income less than $22,500 (or $45,000 if married filing jointly). They may qualify for this credit or the credit for the elderly or the disabled, but not both.

Financial Data The credit depends on the income of the taxpayer.

Duration The credit is available as long as the recipient resides in Oregon.

Additional data People who claim this credit may not also claim the credit for the elderly or the disabled.

Deadline Credits are filed with state income tax returns in April of each year.

[1176]
OREGON VETERANS' EMERGENCY FINANCIAL ASSISTANCE

Oregon Department of Veterans' Affairs
Attn: Veterans' Services Division
700 Summer Street N.E., Suite 150
Salem, OR 97310-1285
(503) 373-2000   Toll Free: (800) 692-9666 (within OR)
Fax: (503) 373-2362   TDD: (503) 373-2217
Web: www.oregon.gov/ODVA/BENEFITS/statebenefits.shtml

Summary To provide emergency financial assistance to Oregon veterans and their families.

Eligibility This assistance is available to Oregon residents who are veterans and their spouses, children, and grandchildren. Applicants must be in need of assistance for emergency or temporary housing and related housing expenses, such as utilities, insurance, house repairs, rent assistance, or food; emergency medical or dental expenses; emergency transportation; expenses related to starting a business, such as business licenses or occupational licenses; temporary income after military discharge; or legal assistance.

Financial Data Grants depend on the need of the recipient.

Duration These are 1-time grants.

Number awarded Varies each year.

Deadline Applications may be submitted at any time.

[1177]
PENNSYLVANIA BLIND VETERANS PENSION

Office of the Deputy Adjutant General for Veterans Affairs
Building S-0-47, FTIG
Annville, PA 17003-5002
(717) 865-8911   Toll Free: (800) 54 PA VET (within PA)
Fax: (717) 861-8589   E-mail: jamebutler@state.pa.us
Web: www.milvet.state.pa.us/DMVA/196.htm

Summary To provide financial assistance to blind residents of Pennsylvania who lost their sight while serving in the U.S. armed forces.

Eligibility Persons who have 3/60 or 10/200 or less normal vision are eligible if they are honorably-discharged veterans and were residents of Pennsylvania when they joined the U.S. armed forces. Their blindness must have resulted from a service-connected injury or disease.

Financial Data The pension is $150 per month.

Duration The pension is awarded for the life of the veteran.

Number awarded Varies each year.

Deadline Applications may be submitted at any time.

[1178]
PENNSYLVANIA DISABLED VETERANS REAL ESTATE TAX EXEMPTION

Office of the Deputy Adjutant General for Veterans Affairs
Building S-0-47, FTIG
Annville, PA 17003-5002
(717) 865-8907   Toll Free: (800) 54 PA VET (within PA)
Fax: (717) 861-8589   E-mail: jamebutler@state.pa.us
Web: www.milvet.state.pa.us/DMVA/592.htm

Summary   To exempt blind and disabled Pennsylvania veterans and their unremarried surviving spouses from all state real estate taxes.

Eligibility   Eligible to apply for this exemption are honorably-discharged veterans who are residents of Pennsylvania and who are blind, paraplegic, or 100% disabled from a service-connected disability sustained during wartime military service. The dwelling must be owned by the veteran solely or jointly with a spouse, and financial need for the exemption must be determined by the State Veterans' Commission. Veterans whose income is less than $79,050 per year are presumed to have financial need; veterans with income greater than $79,050 must document need. Upon the death of the veteran, the tax exemption passes on to the veteran's unremarried surviving spouse.

Financial Data   This program exempts the principal residence (and the land on which it stands) from all real estate taxes.

Duration   The exemption continues as long as the eligible veteran or unremarried widow resides in Pennsylvania.

Number awarded   Varies each year.

Deadline   Deadline not specified.

[1179]
PENNSYLVANIA PARALYZED VETERANS PENSION

Office of the Deputy Adjutant General for Veterans Affairs
Building S-0-47, FTIG
Annville, PA 17003-5002
(717) 865-8911   Toll Free: (800) 54 PA VET (within PA)
Fax: (717) 861-8589   E-mail: jamebutler@state.pa.us
Web: www.milvet.state.pa.us/DMVA/197.htm

Summary   To provide financial assistance to Pennsylvania veterans who became disabled while serving in the U.S. armed forces.

Eligibility   Applicants must be current residents of Pennsylvania who suffered an injury or disease resulting in loss or loss of use of 2 or more extremities while serving in the U.S. armed forces during an established period of war or armed conflict or as a result of hostilities during combat-related activities in peacetime. They must be rated by the U.S. Department of Veterans Affairs as 100% permanent and service-connected disabled. At the time of entry into military service, applicants must have been residents of Pennsylvania.

Financial Data   The pension is $150 per month.

Duration   The pension is awarded for the life of the veteran.

Number awarded   Varies each year.

Deadline   Applications may be submitted at any time.

[1180]
PENNSYLVANIA VETERANS EMERGENCY ASSISTANCE

Office of the Deputy Adjutant General for Veterans Affairs
Building S-0-47, FTIG
Annville, PA 17003-5002
(717) 865-8905   Toll Free: (800) 54 PA VET (within PA)
Fax: (717) 861-8589   E-mail: jamebutler@state.pa.us
Web: www.milvet.state.pa.us/DMVA/185.htm

Summary   To provide financial aid on an emergency and temporary basis to Pennsylvania veterans (or their dependents) who are disabled, sick, or without means.

Eligibility   Eligible to apply for this assistance are honorably-discharged veterans who served in the U.S. armed forces during wartime and are now disabled, sick, or in financial need. Widow(er)s or orphan children of recently deceased veterans are also eligible if the veteran would have qualified prior to death. Applicants must have been residents of Pennsylvania for 1 year prior to the date of application.

Financial Data   Financial aid for the necessities of life (food, shelter, fuel, and clothing) is provided. The amount depends on the number of persons in the household and the Pennsylvania county in which the veteran or dependent lives; recently, monthly grants for 1-person households ranged from $174 to $215, for 2-person households from $279 to $330, for 3-person households from $365 to $431, for 4-person households from $454 to $514, for 5-person households from $543 to $607, and for 6-person households from $614 to $687.

Duration   Aid is provided on a temporary basis only, not to exceed 3 months in a 12-month period.

Number awarded   Varies each year.

Deadline   Applications may be submitted at any time, but the factors that caused the emergency must have occurred within 180 days prior to the application.

[1181]
PVA DISASTER RELIEF FUND

Paralyzed Veterans of America
Attn: Disaster Relief Fund
801 18th Street, N.W.
Washington, DC 20006-3517
Toll Free: (800) 555-9140   E-mail: info@pva.org
Web: www.pva.org

Summary   To provide emergency assistance to members of Paralyzed Veterans of America (PVA) who have been victimized by natural disasters.

Eligibility   This assistance is available to PVA members whose property has been severely damaged by natural disasters. Applicants may be seeking funding for transportation, temporary shelter, food, home repairs, or modifications that are needed for wheelchair accessibility, medical supplies, or prosthetic appliances.

Financial Data   Grants range up to $2,500; more than $100,000 is available for relief each year.

Additional data   Membership in PVA is open to veterans with spinal cord injury or disease.

Number awarded   2 each year.

Deadline   Applications may be submitted at any time.

[1182]
RED CROSS EMERGENCY FINANCIAL ASSISTANCE

American Red Cross
c/o National Headquarters
2025 E Street, N.W.
Washington, DC 20006
(202) 303-4498   Toll Free: (800) HELP-NOW
Web: www.redcross.org

Summary   To provide funding to active and retired military personnel and their families who are in need of emergency financial assistance.

Eligibility   This program is open to servicemembers, their families, retired military personnel, and widows of retired military personnel. Members of the National Guard and Reserves are also eligible. Applicants must be in need of such emergency financial assistance as travel that requires the presence of the servicemember or his or her family, burial of a loved one, or other assistance that cannot wait until the next business day (food, temporary lodging, urgent medical needs, or the minimum amount required to avoid eviction or utility shut-off).

Financial Data The amount of the assistance depends on the need of the recipient.

Duration These are 1-time grants.

Additional data The Red Cross works with the military aid societies (Army Emergency Relief, Navy-Marine Corps Relief Society, Air Force Aid Society, and Coast Guard Mutual Assistance).

Number awarded Varies each year; recently, more than 5,000 servicemembers and their families received more than $5.3 million in emergency grants.

Deadline Applications may be submitted at any time.

[1183]
SENTINELS OF FREEDOM SCHOLARSHIPS

Sentinels of Freedom
P.O. Box 1316
San Ramon, CA 94583
(925) 353-7100   Fax: (925) 353-3900
E-mail: info@sentinelsoffreedom.org
Web: www.sentinelsoffreedom.org

Summary To provide funding to veterans and current military personnel who became disabled as a result of injuries sustained in the line of duty on or after September 11, 2001.

Eligibility This program is open to members of the U.S. Air Force, Army, Coast Guard, Marines, or Navy who sustained injuries in the line of duty on or after September 11, 2001. Applicants must be rated as 60% or more disabled as a result of 1 or more of the following conditions: amputation, blindness, deafness, paraplegia, severe burns, limited traumatic brain injury (TBI), or limited post-traumatic stress disorder (PTSD); other severe injuries may be considered on a case-by-case basis. They must complete an interview process and demonstrate that they have the skills, experience, and attitude that lead to employment.

Financial Data Assistance is available for the following needs: housing (adapted for physical needs if necessary), new furniture and other household supplies, career-placement assistance and training, new adaptive vehicles, educational opportunities in addition to the new GI Bill, or financial and personal mentorship.

Duration Assistance may be provided for up to 4 years.

Additional data The first assistance granted by this program was awarded in 2004.

Number awarded Varies each year. Since the program was established, it has supported 32 current and former service members.

Deadline Applications may be submitted at any time.

[1184]
SOUTH CAROLINA NATIONAL GUARD PENSION

South Carolina Retirement Systems
202 Arbor Lake Drive
P.O. Box 11960
Columbia, SC 29211-1960
(803) 737-6800   Toll Free: (800) 868-9002 (within SC)
E-mail: cs@retirement.sc.gov
Web: www.retirement.sc.gov

Summary To provide a pension to retired members of the South Carolina National Guard.

Eligibility This benefit is available to veterans who are at least 60 years of age and who served at least 20 years in the military, with at least 15 of those years, including the last 10 years prior to retirement, in the South Carolina National Guard. Applicants must have received an honorable discharge from the South Carolina National Guard. Veterans receiving retirement or disability payments from the armed forces are not eligible for this pension.

Financial Data The pension is $50 per month for 20 years of military service, with an additional $5 per month for each additional year of service, to a maximum pension of $100 per month.

Duration The pension continues as long as the eligible veteran resides in South Carolina.

Additional data No payment is made to beneficiaries.

Number awarded Varies each year.

Deadline Applications may be submitted at any time.

[1185]
SOUTH CAROLINA PROPERTY TAX EXEMPTION FOR DISABLED VETERANS, LAW ENFORCEMENT OFFICERS, AND FIREFIGHTERS

South Carolina Department of Revenue
Attn: Property Division
301 Gervais Street
P.O. Box 125
Columbia, SC 29214
(803) 898-5480   Fax: (803) 898-5822
Web: www.sctax.org

Summary To exempt the residence of disabled South Carolina veterans, law enforcement officers, fire fighters, their unremarried widow(er)s, and others from property taxation.

Eligibility This exemption is available to owners of homes in South Carolina who are veterans of the U.S. armed forces, former law enforcement officers, or former fire fighters (including volunteer fire fighters). Applicants must be permanently and totally disabled from service-connected causes. The exemption is also available to qualified surviving spouses (defined to include unremarried spouses of disabled veterans, law enforcement officers, and fire fighters, as well as surviving spouses of servicemembers killed in the line of duty, law enforcement officers who died in the line of duty, and fire fighters who died in the line of duty).

Financial Data The exemption applies to all taxes on 1 house and a lot (not to exceed 1 acre).

Duration The exemption extends as long as the veteran, law enforcement officer, or fire fighter resides in the house, or as long as the spouse of a deceased veteran, servicemember, law enforcement officer, or fire fighter remains unremarried and resides in the original house or a single new dwelling.

Number awarded Varies each year.

Deadline Applications may be submitted at any time.

[1186]
SOUTH CAROLINA PROPERTY TAX EXEMPTION FOR MEDAL OF HONOR RECIPIENTS AND PRISONERS OF WAR

South Carolina Department of Revenue
Attn: Property Division
301 Gervais Street
P.O. Box 125
Columbia, SC 29214
(803) 898-5480   Fax: (803) 898-5822
Web: www.sctax.org

Summary To exempt the residence of disabled South Carolina veterans who received a Medal or Honor or who were a prisoner of war from property taxation.

Eligibility This exemption is available to owners of homes in South Carolina who are veterans of the U.S. armed forces and who received a Medal of Honor or were a prisoner of war during World War I, World War II, the Korean Conflict, or the Vietnam Conflict. The exemption is also available to qualified surviving spouses.

Financial Data The exemption applies to all taxes on 1 house and a lot (not to exceed 1 acre).

Duration The exemption extends as long as the veteran or the spouse of a deceased veteran resides in the original house or a single new dwelling.

Number awarded Varies each year.

Deadline Applications may be submitted at any time.

[1187]
SOUTH CAROLINA RETIREMENT INCOME TAX DEDUCTION

South Carolina Department of Revenue
301 Gervais Street
P.O. Box 125
Columbia, SC 29214
(803) 898-5000   Toll Free: (800) 763-1295
Fax: (803) 898-5822
Web: www.sctax.org

Summary   To exempt part of the retirement income received by veterans and others (including spouses) from state taxation in South Carolina.

Eligibility   This program is open to residents of South Carolina who are receiving public employee retirement income from federal, state, or local government, including individual retirement accounts, Keogh plans, and military retirement. Spouses are also entitled to the exemption.

Financial Data   The maximum retirement income deduction is $3,000 for taxpayers under 65 years of age and $10,000 in subsequent years. Taxpayers who wait until they are 65 and older until declaring a retirement exemption are entitled to deduct $15,000 per year.

Duration   The exemption continues as long as the eligible veteran or spouse resides in South Carolina and receives the specified income.

Number awarded   Varies each year.

Deadline   Deadline not specified.

[1188]
SOUTH DAKOTA PROPERTY TAX EXEMPTION FOR PARAPLEGIC VETERANS

South Dakota Department of Revenue and Regulation
Attn: Property Tax Division
445 East Capitol Avenue
Pierre, SD 57501-3185
(605) 773-3311   Toll Free: (800) TAX-9188
Fax: (605) 773-6729   E-mail: PropTaxIn@state.sd.us
Web: www.state.sd.us/drr2/propspectax/property/relief.htm

Summary   To exempt from property taxation the homes of disabled veterans in South Dakota and their widow(er)s.

Eligibility   This benefit is available to residents of South Dakota who are 1) paraplegic veterans, 2) veterans with loss or loss of use of both lower extremities, or 3) unremarried widows or widowers of such veterans. Applicants must own and occupy a dwelling (including the house, garage, and up to 1 acre on which the building is located) that is specifically designed for wheelchair use within the structure. The veteran's injury does not have to be service connected.

Financial Data   Qualified dwellings are exempt from property taxation in South Dakota.

Duration   The exemption applies as long as the dwelling is owned and occupied by the disabled veteran or widow(er).

Number awarded   Varies each year.

Deadline   Deadline not specified.

[1189]
SOUTH DAKOTA SALES AND PROPERTY TAX REFUND FOR SENIOR AND DISABLED CITIZENS

South Dakota Department of Revenue and Regulation
Attn: Special Tax Division
445 East Capitol Avenue
Pierre, SD 57501-3185
(605) 773-3311   Toll Free: (800) TAX-9188
Fax: (605) 773-6729   E-mail: specialt@state.sd.us
Web: www.state.sd.us/drr2/propspectax/property/relief.htm

Summary   To provide a partial refund of sales taxes to elderly and disabled residents (including disabled veterans) in South Dakota.

Eligibility   This program is open to residents of South Dakota who either have a qualified disability or are 66 years of age or older. Applicants must live alone and have a yearly income of less than $10,250 or live in a household whose members' combined income is less than $13,250. Veterans must have a disability of 60% or greater. Other people with disabilities must have been qualified to receive Social Security disability benefits or Supplemental Security Income disability benefits.

Financial Data   Qualified residents are entitled to a refund of a portion of the sales or property taxes they paid during the preceding calendar year.

Duration   Residents of South Dakota are entitled to this refund annually.

Additional data   This program has been in effect since 1974. South Dakotans are not entitled to both a sales tax refund and a property tax refund in the same year. The state will calculate both refunds and pay the amount that is greater.

Number awarded   Varies each year.

Deadline   June of each year.

[1190]
SPECIAL HOUSING ADAPTATIONS GRANTS

Department of Veterans Affairs
Attn: Specially Adapted Housing
810 Vermont Avenue, N.W.
Washington, DC 20420
(202) 461-9546   Toll Free: (800) 827-1000
Web: www.homeloans.va.gov/sah.htm

Summary   To provide grants to certain disabled veterans or servicemembers who wish to make adaptations to their home to meet their needs.

Eligibility   These grants are available to veterans and servicemembers who are entitled to compensation for permanent and total service-connected disability due to: 1) blindness in both eyes with 5/200 visual acuity or less; 2) the anatomical loss or loss of use of both hands; or 3) a severe burn injury. Applicants must be planning to 1) adapt a house which they plan to purchase and in which they intend to reside; 2) adapt a house which a member of their family plans to purchase and in which they intend to reside; 3) adapt a house which they already own and in which they intend to reside; 4) adapt a house which is already owned by a member of their family in which they intend to reside; or 5) purchase a house that has already been adapted with special features that are reasonable necessary because of their disability and in which they intend to reside.

Financial Data   Eligible veterans and servicemembers are entitled to grants up to $12,756 to adapt a house.

Duration   Eligible veterans and servicemembers are entitled to up to 3 usages of these grants.

Number awarded   Varies each year.

Deadline   Applications are accepted at any time.

[1191]
SPECIALLY ADAPTED HOUSING GRANTS

Department of Veterans Affairs
Attn: Specially Adapted Housing
810 Vermont Avenue, N.W.
Washington, DC 20420
(202) 461-9546   Toll Free: (800) 827-1000
Web: www.homeloans.va.gov/sah.htm

Summary   To provide loans, grants, and loan guaranties to certain disabled veterans and servicemembers for a home specially adapted to their needs.

Eligibility   These grants are available to veterans and servicemembers who are entitled to compensation for permanent and total service-connected disability due to: 1) the loss or loss of use of both lower extremities, such as to preclude locomotion without the aid of braces, crutches, canes, or a wheelchair; or 2) blindness in both eyes, having only light perception, plus loss or loss of use of 1 lower extremity; or 3) a loss or loss of use of 1 lower extremity together with residuals of organic disease or injury or the loss or loss of use of 1 upper extremity, such as to preclude locomotion without resort to braces, canes, crutches, or a wheelchair. Applicants must be planning to 1) construct a home on land to be acquired for that purpose; 2) build a home on land already owned if it is suitable for specially adapted housing; 3) remodel an existing home if it can be made suitable for specially adapted housing, or 4) apply funds against the unpaid principle mortgage balance of a specially adapted home that has already been acquired.

Financial Data The U.S. Department of Veterans Affairs (VA) may approve a grant of not more than 50% of the cost of building, buying, or remodeling homes for eligible veterans, or paying indebtedness of such homes already acquired, up to a maximum grant of $63,780. Eligible veterans with available loan guarantee entitlements may also obtain a guaranteed loan from the VA to supplement the grant to acquire a specially adapted home. If private financing is not available, VA may make a direct loan up to $33,000 to cover the difference between the total cost of the home and the grant.

Duration This is a 1-time grant, guaranteed loan, or direct loan.

Additional data Veterans who receive a specially adapted housing grant may be eligible for Veterans Mortgage Life Insurance.

Number awarded Varies each year.

Deadline Applications are accepted at any time.

[1192]
TENNESSEE PROPERTY TAX RELIEF FOR DISABLED VETERANS AND THEIR SPOUSES

Tennessee Comptroller of the Treasury
Attn: Property Tax Relief Program
James K. Polk State Office Building
505 Deaderick Street, Room 1600
Nashville, TN 37243-1402
(615) 747-8871   Fax: (615) 532-3866
E-mail: Kim.Darden@state.tn.us
Web: www.comptroller.state.tn.us/pa/patxr.htm

Summary To provide property tax relief to blind and disabled veterans and their spouses in Tennessee.

Eligibility This exemption is offered to veterans or their surviving unremarried spouses who are residents of Tennessee and own and live in their home in the state. The veteran must have served in the U.S. armed forces and 1) have acquired, as a result of such service, a disability from paraplegia, permanent paralysis of both legs and lower part of the body resulting from traumatic injury, disease to the spinal cord or brain, legal blindness, or loss or loss of use of both legs or arms from any service-connected cause; 2) have been rated by the U.S. Department of Veterans affairs (VA) as 100% permanently disabled as a result of service as a prisoner of war for at least 5 months; or 3) have been rated by the VA as 100% permanently and totally disabled from any other service-connected cause. The relief does not extend to any person who was dishonorably discharged from any of the armed services.

Financial Data The amount of the relief depends on the property assessment and the tax rate in the city or county where the beneficiary lives. The maximum market value on which tax relief is calculated is $175,000.

Duration 1 year; may be renewed as long as the eligible veteran or surviving unremarried spouse owns and occupies the primary residence.

Number awarded Varies each year.

Deadline Deadline not specified.

[1193]
TEXAS PROPERTY TAX EXEMPTION FOR DISABLED VETERANS AND THEIR FAMILIES

Texas Veterans Commission
P.O. Box 12277
Austin, TX 78711-2277
(512) 463-5538   Toll Free: (800) 252-VETS (within TX)
Fax: (512) 475-2395   E-mail: info@tvc.state.tx.us
Web: www.tvc.state.tx.us/StateBenefits.html

Summary To extend property tax exemptions on the appraised value of their property to blind, disabled, and other Texas veterans and their surviving family members.

Eligibility Eligible veterans must be Texas residents rated at least 10% service-connected disabled. Surviving spouses and children of eligible veterans are also covered by this program.

Financial Data For veterans in Texas whose disability is rated as 10% through 29%, the first $5,000 of the appraised property value is exempt from taxation; veterans rated as 30% through 49% disabled are exempt from the first $7,500 of appraised value; those with a 50% through 69% disability are exempt from the first $10,000 of appraised value; the exemption applies to the first $12,000 of appraised value for veterans with disabilities rated as 70% to 99%; veterans rated as 100% disabled are exempt from 100% of the appraised value of their property. A veteran whose disability is 10% or more and who is 65 years or older is entitled to exemption of the first $12,000 of appraised property value. A veteran whose disability consists of the loss of use of 1 or more limbs, total blindness in 1 or both eyes, or paraplegia is exempt from the first $12,000 of the appraised value. The unremarried surviving spouse of a deceased veteran who died on active duty and who, at the time of death had a compensable disability and was entitled to an exemption, is entitled to the same exemption. The surviving spouse of a person who died on active duty is entitled to exemption of the first $5,000 of appraised value of the spouse's property. Surviving spouses, however, are not eligible for the 100% exemption. A surviving child of a person who dies on active duty is entitled to exemption of the first $5,000 of appraised value of the child's property as long as the child is unmarried and under 21 years of age.

Duration 1 year; may be renewed as long as the eligible veteran (or unremarried surviving spouse or child) owns and occupies the primary residence in Texas.

Additional data This program is administered at the local level by the various taxing authorities.

Number awarded Varies each year.

Deadline April of each year.

[1194]
TROOPS-TO-TEACHERS PROGRAM

Defense Activity for Non-Traditional Education Support
Attn: Troops to Teachers
6490 Sauffley Field Road
Pensacola, FL 32509-5243
(850) 452-1241   Toll Free: (800) 231-6242
Fax: (850) 452-1096   E-mail: ttt@navy.mil
Web: www.dantes.doded.mil

Summary To provide a bonus to veterans and military personnel interested in a second career as a public school teacher.

Eligibility This program is open to 1) active-duty military personnel who are retired, have an approved date of retirement within 1 year, or separated on or after January 8, 2002 for physical disability; 2) members of a Reserve component who are retired, currently serving in the Selected Reserve with 10 or more years of credible service and commit to serving an additional 3 years, separated on or after January 8, 2002 due to a physical disability, or transitioned from active duty on or after January 8, 2002 after at least 6 years on active duty and commit to 3 years with a Selected Reserve unit. Applicants must have a baccalaureate or advanced degree, the equivalent of 1 year of college with 6 years of work experience in a vocational or technical field, or meet state requirements for vocational/technical teacher referral. A bonus is available to applicants who are willing to accept employment as a teacher in 1) a school district that has at least 10% of the students from families living below the poverty level, and 2) at a specific school within the district where at least 50% of the students are eligible for the free or reduced cost lunch program or where at least 13.5% of the students have disabilities. A stipend is available to applicants who are willing to accept employment as a teacher at 1) any school within a "high need" district that has at least 20% of the students from families living below the poverty level, or 2) at a specific school where at least 50% of the students are eligible for the free or reduced cost lunch program or at least 13.5% of the students have disabilities, as long as that school is in a district that has between 10% and 20% of students who come from poverty-level families. Preference is given to applicants interested in teaching mathematics, science, or special education.

Financial Data A bonus of $10,000 is awarded to recipients who agree to teach for 3 years in a school that serves a high percentage of students from low-income families. A stipend of $5,000 is awarded to recipients who agree to teach for 3 years in a school located in a "high-need" district; stipend funds are intended to help pay for teacher certification costs.

Duration The bonuses are intended as 1-time grants.

Additional data This program was established in 1994 by the Department of Defense (DoD). In 2000, program oversight and funding were transferred to the U.S. Department of Education, but DoD continues to operate the program. The No Child Left Behind Act of 2001 provided for continuation of the program.

Number awarded Varies each year.

Deadline Deadline not specified.

[1195]
UTAH DISABLED VETERAN PROPERTY TAX ABATEMENT

Utah Division of Veteran's Affairs
Attn: Director
550 Foothill Boulevard, Room 202
Salt Lake City, UT 84108
(801) 326-2372   Toll Free: (800) 894-9497 (within UT)
Fax: (801) 326-2369   E-mail: veterans@utah.gov
Web: veterans.utah.gov/homepage/stateBenefits/index.html

Summary To exempt a portion of the property of disabled veterans and their families in Utah from taxation.

Eligibility This program is available to residents of Utah who are disabled veterans or their unremarried widow(er)s or minor orphans. The disability must be at least 10% and incurred as the result of injuries in the line of duty.

Financial Data The exemption is based on the disability rating of the veteran, to a maximum of $219,164 for a 100% disability.

Duration This benefit is available as long as the disabled veteran or family members reside in Utah.

Deadline Tax exemption applications must be filed with the county government of residence by August of the initial year; once eligibility has been established, reapplication is not required.

[1196]
UTAH VETERAN'S PROPERTY TAX EXEMPTION

Utah State Tax Commission
Attn: Property Tax Division
210 North 1950 West
Salt Lake City, UT 84134
(801) 297-3600   Toll Free: (800) 662-4335, ext. 3600
Fax: (801) 297-7699   TDD: (801) 297-2020
Web: www.tax.utah.gov

Summary To exempt from taxation a portion of the real and tangible property of disabled veterans and their families in Utah.

Eligibility This exemption is available to property owners in Utah who are veterans with a disability of at least 10% incurred in the line of duty, along with their unremarried surviving spouses or minor orphans. First year applications must be accompanied by proof of military service and proof of disability or death.

Financial Data The exemption depends on the percentage of disability, up to $228,505 of taxable value of a residence.

Duration The exemption is available each year the beneficiary owns property in Utah.

Number awarded Varies each year.

Deadline Applications must be submitted by August of each year.

[1197]
VERMONT PROPERTY TAX EXEMPTION FOR DISABLED VETERANS

Vermont Department of Taxes
Attn: Property Valuation and Review Division
P.O. Box 1577
Montpelier, VT 05601-1577
(802) 828-5860   Fax: (802) 828-2824
Web: www.state.vt.us/tax/pvrmilitary.shtml

Summary To exempt disabled Vermont veterans and their dependents from the payment of at least a portion of the state's property tax.

Eligibility Entitled to a property tax exemption are veterans of any war (or their spouses, widow(er)s, or children) who are receiving wartime disability compensation for at least a 50% disability, wartime death compensation, wartime dependence and indemnity compensation, or pension for disability paid through any military department or the Department of Veterans Affairs. Unremarried widow(er)s of previously qualified veterans are also entitled to the exemption whether or not they are receiving government compensation or a pension.

Financial Data Up to $10,000 of the assessed value of real and personal property belonging to eligible veterans or their unremarried widow(er)s is exempt from taxation; individual towns may increase the exemption to as much as $40,000.

Duration 1 year; may be renewed as long as the eligible veteran or widow(er) continues to be the owner/occupant of the residence and lives in Vermont.

Additional data Only 1 exemption may be allowed on a property.

Number awarded Varies each year.

Deadline April of each year.

[1198]
VETERANS DISABILITY COMPENSATION

Department of Veterans Affairs
Attn: Veterans Benefits Administration
810 Vermont Avenue, N.W.
Washington, DC 20420
(202) 418-4343   Toll Free: (800) 827-1000
Web: www.vba.va.gov/bin/21/compensation/index.htm

Summary To provide monthly compensation to veterans who have a disability that occurred or was made worse during military service.

Eligibility Disabled persons who are eligible for compensation under this program are those whose disability resulted from injury or disease incurred or aggravated during active service in the U.S. armed forces in the line of duty during wartime or peacetime service. They must have been discharged or separated under other than dishonorable conditions.

Financial Data Disabled veterans who are found to be eligible for disability compensation are entitled to monthly payments, depending on the degree of disability as determined by the Department of Veterans Affairs. Recent monthly rates for veterans living alone with no dependents ranged from $123 for 10%

disability to $2,673 for 100% disability. Veterans whose service-connected disabilities are rated at 30% or more are entitled to additional allowances for dependent children, spouses, and/or parents. The additional amount is determined according to the number of dependents and the degree of disability. Recently, those supplements ranged from $45 to $150 for a spouse, from $30 to $100 for the first child under 18 years of age, from $22 to $75 for each additional child under 18 years of age, from $72 to $240 for each additional child over 18 years of age and enrolled in school, and from $35 to $120 for each parent. In addition, a veteran whose disability is rated at 30% or more and whose spouse is in need of the aid and attendance of another person may receive an additional amount, ranging from $40 to $136.

Duration Compensation continues as long as the veteran remains disabled.

Additional data In addition to monthly compensation under this program, disabled veterans may also be entitled to prosthetic appliances if they are receiving treatment in a facility under the direct jurisdiction of the Department of Veterans Affairs (VA), or outpatient care under certain specified conditions. Blind veterans are eligible for various aids and services, including adjustment to blindness training, home improvements and structural alterations, low vision aids and training in their use, guide dogs, and material for the blind from the Library of Congress. Former prisoners of war who were incarcerated for at least 30 days and have at least a 10% disability are entitled to a presumption of service connection. Persian Gulf veterans who suffer from chronic disabilities resulting from undiagnosed illnesses may receive disability compensation. VA rating boards determine the degree of disability of each veteran, based on an estimate of the extent to which certain disabilities reduce the typical veteran's ability to earn a living. If a veteran has 2 or more disabilities, the rating board will determine a combined rating and base compensation on that figure.

Number awarded Varies each year.

Deadline Applications are accepted at any time.

[1199]
VETERANS SPECIAL MONTHLY COMPENSATION

Department of Veterans Affairs
Attn: Veterans Benefits Administration
810 Vermont Avenue, N.W.
Washington, DC 20420
(202) 418-4343   Toll Free: (800) 827-1000
Web: www.vba.va.gov/bin/21/compensation/index.htm

Summary To provide monthly compensation to veterans who have a disability that exceeds the 100% combined degree compensation or that results from special circumstances.

Eligibility This assistance is available to honorably-discharged veterans who have service-connected disabilities that have resulted in anatomical loss or loss of use of 1 hand, 1 foot, both buttocks, 1 or more creative organs, blindness of 1 eye having only light perception, deafness of both ears, having absence of air and bone conduction, complete organic aphonia with constant inability to communicate by speech, or (in the case of a female veteran) loss of 25% or more of tissue from a single breast or both breasts. Additional assistance is available to veterans who are permanently bedridden or so helpless as to be in need of regular aid and attendance. A special allowance is also available to veterans who have a spouse determined to require regular aid and attendance.

Financial Data Disabled veterans who are found to be eligible for special compensation are entitled to monthly payments, depending on the nature of the disability and the type and number of dependants. Recent monthly rates ranged from $2,993 to $7,650 for veterans living alone with no dependents, from $3,143 to $7,800 for a veteran and spouse, from $3,252 to $7,909 for a veteran with spouse and 1 child, from $3,094 to $7,751 for a veteran and 1 child, $75 for each additional child under 18 years of age, and $240 for each additional child over 18 years of age and

enrolled in school. Other rates are available for veterans who live with 1 or more parents. In addition, a veteran whose spouse is in need of the aid and attendance of another person may receive an additional $136.

Duration Compensation continues as long as the veteran remains disabled.

Number awarded Varies each year.

Deadline Applications are accepted at any time.

[1200]
VIRGINIA INCOME TAX SUBTRACTION FOR CONGRESSIONAL MEDAL OF HONOR RECIPIENTS

Virginia Department of Taxation
Attn: Office of Customer Services
3600 West Broad Street
P.O. Box 1115
Richmond, VA 23218-1115
(804) 367-8031   Fax: (804) 367-2537
Web: www.tax.virginia.gov

Summary To subtract the retirement income received by recipients of the Congressional Medal of Honor from state income taxation in Virginia.

Eligibility This subtraction is available to residents of Virginia who received the Congressional Medal of Honor and receive military retirement income subject to federal taxation. The subtraction is not available to benefits received by surviving spouses.

Financial Data All military income received by Congressional Medal of Honor recipients is exempt from state taxation in Virginia.

Duration The exemption is available as long as the Medal of Honor recipient remains a resident of Virginia and receives military retirement income.

Number awarded Varies each year.

Deadline The request for an exemption is filed with the state income tax return in April of each year.

[1201]
VOCATIONAL REHABILITATION FOR DISABLED VETERANS

Department of Veterans Affairs
Attn: Veterans Benefits Administration
Vocational Rehabilitation and Employment Service
810 Vermont Avenue, N.W.
Washington, DC 20420
(202) 418-4343   Toll Free: (800) 827-1000
Web: www.vba.va.gov/bin/vre/index.htm

Summary To provide vocational rehabilitation to certain categories of veterans with disabilities.

Eligibility This program is open to veterans who have a service-connected disability of 1) at least 10% and a serious employment handicap, or 2) at least 20% and an employment handicap. They must have been discharged or released from military service under other than dishonorable conditions. The Department of Veterans Affairs (VA) must determine that they would benefit from a training program that would help them prepare for, find, and keep suitable employment. The program may be 1) institutional training at a certificate, 2-year college, 4-year college or university, or technical program; 2) unpaid on-the-job training in a federal, state, or local agency or a federally-recognized Indian tribal agency, training in a home, vocational course in a rehabilitation facility or sheltered workshop, independent instruction, or institutional non-farm cooperative; or 3) paid training through a farm cooperative, apprenticeship, on-the-job training, or on-the-job non-farm cooperative.

Financial Data While in training and for 2 months after, eligible disabled veterans may receive subsistence allowances in addition to their disability compensation or retirement pay. For most training programs, the current full-time monthly rate is $547.54

with no dependents, $679.18 with 1 dependent, $800.36 with 2 dependents, and $58.34 for each additional dependent; proportional rates apply for less than full-time training. The VA also pays the costs of tuition, books, fees, supplies, and equipment; it may also pay for special supportive services, such as tutorial assistance, prosthetic devices, lipreading training, and signing for the deaf. If during training or employment services the veteran's disabilities cause transportation expenses that would not be incurred by nondisabled persons, the VA will pay for at least a portion of those expenses. If the veteran encounters financial difficulty during training, the VA may provide an advance against future benefit payments.

Duration Up to 48 months of full-time training or its equivalent in part-time training. If a veteran with a serious disability receives services under an extended evaluation to improve training potential, the total of the extended evaluation and the training phases of the rehabilitation program may exceed 48 months. Usually, the veteran must complete a rehabilitation program within 12 years from the date of notification of entitlement to compensation by the VA. Following completion of the training portion of a rehabilitation program, a veteran may receive counseling and job search and adjustment services for 18 months.

Additional data The program may also provide employment assistance, self-employment assistance, training in a rehabilitation facility, or college and other training. Veterans who are seriously disabled may receive services and assistance to improve their ability to live more independently in their community. After completion of the training phase, the VA will assist the veteran to find and have a suitable job.

Number awarded Varies each year.

Deadline Applications are accepted at any time.

[1202]
WASHINGTON PROPERTY TAX EXEMPTIONS FOR SENIOR CITIZENS AND DISABLED PERSONS

Washington State Department of Revenue
Attn: Property Tax Division
P.O. Box 47471
Olympia, WA 98504-7471
(360) 570-5867   Toll Free: (800) 647-7706
Fax: (360) 586-7602   TDD: (800) 451-7985
Web: dor.wa.gov

Summary To exempt a portion of the property owned by senior citizens and people with disabilities, including veterans, from taxation in Washington.

Eligibility This exemption is available to residents of Washington who are 1) unable to work because of a disability, 2) veterans with a 100% service-connected disability, 3) at least 61 years of age, or 4) a surviving spouse at least 57 years of age of a person who was approved for this exemption. Applicants must own property that they use as their principal home for at least 6 months of the year; mobile homes may qualify as a residence even if its owner does not own the land where it is located. Their annual disposable income may not exceed $35,000 per year.

Financial Data Property owners whose annual income is $25,000 or less are exempt from regular property taxes on the first $60,000 or 60% of their home's assessed value, whichever is greater. Property owners whose annual income is between $25,001 and $30,000 are exempt from regular property taxes on $50,000 or 35% of the assessed value, whichever is greater, not to exceed $70,000 or the assessed value. Property owners whose annual income is $35,000 or less are exempt from all excess levies that have been approved by voters in excess of regular property taxes.

Duration The exemption is available as long as the property owner meets the eligibility requirements.

Number awarded Varies each year.

Deadline Applications for each year are due by December of the preceding year.

[1203]
WEST VIRGINIA HOMESTEAD EXEMPTION

West Virginia State Tax Department
Attn: Property Tax Division
1124 Smith Street
P.O. Box 2389
Charleston, WV 25301
(304) 558-3940   Toll Free: (800) WVA-TAXS (within WV)
Fax: (304) 558-1843   TDD: (800) 282-9833
Web: www.wva.state.wv.us/wvtax/default.aspx

Summary To provide a partial exemption of property taxes on residences owned by disabled or elderly persons and retired veterans in West Virginia.

Eligibility Eligible for this exemption are single-family residences owned and occupied by any person who is permanently and totally disabled or at least 65 years old. Applicants must have been West Virginia residents for 2 consecutive calendar years prior to the tax year to which the exemption relates. Members of the U.S. military forces who maintain West Virginia as their state of residence throughout military service and return to the state to purchase a homestead upon retirement or separation from the military because of permanent and total disability are considered to meet the residency requirement and also qualify for this exemption.

Financial Data The exemption applies to the first $20,000 of the total assessed value of eligible property.

Duration The exemption continues as long as the eligible property is owned and occupied by the qualifying person in West Virginia.

Additional data Applications for this program are submitted to the office of the county assessor in each West Virginia county.

Number awarded Varies each year.

Deadline Individuals with disabilities apply for this exemption during July, August, or September of any year. Once they have filed for the exemption, they do not need to refile in subsequent years if they sign a statement that they will notify the assessor within 30 days if they cease to be eligible for the exemption on the basis of disability.

[1204]
WEST VIRGINIA INCOME TAX EXEMPTION FOR MILITARY RETIREES

West Virginia State Tax Department
Attn: Taxpayer Services Division
P.O. Box 3784
Charleston, WV 25337-3784
(304) 558-3333   Toll Free: (800) WVA-TAXS (within WV)
Fax: (304) 558-3269   TDD: (800) 282-9833
Web: www.wva.state.wv.us/wvtax/default.aspx

Summary To exempt a portion of the income of military retirees and their spouses in West Virginia from state taxation.

Eligibility This exemption is available to residents of West Virginia who are receiving retirement benefits from any branch of the military. Surviving spouses of eligible residents are also entitled to the exemptions.

Financial Data Military retirees and their spouses are entitled to exempt the first $20,000 of annual military retirement income, including survivorship annuities. That exemption is in addition to the $2,000 exemption available to all retired public employees in West Virginia.

Duration The exemption continues as long as eligible residents (or their spouses) remain residents of West Virginia.

Deadline Deadline not specified.

[1205]
WISCONSIN ASSISTANCE TO NEEDY VETERANS AND FAMILY MEMBERS

Wisconsin Department of Veterans Affairs
30 West Mifflin Street
P.O. Box 7843
Madison, WI 53707-7843
(608) 266-1311   Toll Free: (800) WIS-VETS
Fax: (608) 267-0403   E-mail: WDVAInfo@dva.state.wi.us
Web: www.dva.state.wi.us/Ben_emergencygrants.asp

Summary To provide temporary, emergency financial aid to veterans and their families in Wisconsin.

Eligibility This program is open to Wisconsin residents who served either 1) at least 2 years on active duty in the U.S. armed forces; or 2) at least 90 days on active duty during designated periods of wartime (including the Persian Gulf War since August 1, 1990, the Afghanistan War since September 11, 2001, and the Iraq War since March 19, 2003). The unremarried surviving spouse and dependent children of an eligible veteran who died in the line of duty while or active duty or inactive duty for training also qualify. Applicants must have applied for, and been denied or determined to be ineligible for, all other applicable aid programs (e.g., unemployment insurance, Medicaid, Medicare, Badger-Care, federal Veterans Administration health care). The veteran must be a resident of Wisconsin with an income that does not exceed 130% of the federal poverty guidelines (currently, $14,079 for a family of 1, rising to $48,113 for a family of 8). The family must be facing an economic emergency, such as failure of the sole means of transportation; failure of a stove or refrigerator or of heating, electrical, or plumbing systems; a medical emergency; or severe damage to the primary residence as a result of a natural disaster.

Financial Data Grants do not exceed $7,500 in a lifetime.

Duration Grants are awarded as needed.

Number awarded Varies each year.

Deadline Applications may be submitted at any time.

[1206]
WISCONSIN INCOME TAX EXEMPTION FOR MILITARY AND UNIFORMED SERVICES RETIREMENT BENEFITS

Wisconsin Department of Revenue
Attn: Division of Income, Sales and Excise Tax
2135 Rimrock Road
P.O. Box 8933
Madison, WI 53708-8933
(608) 266-2772   Fax: (608) 267-0834
E-mail: income@revenue.wi.gov
Web: www.revenue.wi.gov

Summary To exempt from state taxation in Wisconsin retirement income received for service in the military.

Eligibility This exemption is available to residents of Wisconsin who receive income from 1) a U.S. military retirement system, or 2) the U.S. government that relates to service with the Coast Guard, the commissioned corps of the National Oceanic and Atmospheric Administration, or the commissioned corps of the Public Health Service.

Financial Data All qualified military or uniformed services retirement pay is exempt from state income taxation in Wisconsin.

Duration The exemption is available as long as the recipient resides in Wisconsin.

Number awarded Varies each year.

Deadline Income tax returns must be filed by April of each year.

[1207]
WISCONSIN VETERANS AND SURVIVING SPOUSES PROPERTY TAX CREDIT

Wisconsin Department of Revenue
Attn: Customer Service and Education Bureau
2135 Rimrock Road
P.O. Box 8949
Madison, WI 53708-8949
(608) 266-2776   Fax: (608) 267-1030
Web: www.revenue.wi.gov

Summary To provide an income tax credit to disabled Wisconsin veterans and their surviving spouses equal to the amount of property taxes they pay.

Eligibility This credit is available to Wisconsin veterans who served on active duty under honorable conditions in the U.S. armed forces and have resided in Wisconsin for any consecutive 5-year period after entry into active duty. Applicants must have either a service-connected disability rating of 100% or a 100% disability rating based on individual unemployability. Also eligible are unremarried surviving spouses of such disabled veterans and of members of the National Guard or a Reserve component of the U.S. armed forces who were residents of Wisconsin and died in the line of duty while on active or inactive duty for training purposes.

Financial Data Eligible veterans and surviving spouses are entitled to an income tax credit equal to the amount of property taxes they pay on their principal residence.

Duration The credit is available as long as the recipient resides in Wisconsin.

Number awarded Varies each year.

Deadline Income tax returns must be filed by April of each year.

[1208]
WISCONSIN VETERANS' SUBSISTENCE AID GRANTS

Wisconsin Department of Veterans Affairs
30 West Mifflin Street
P.O. Box 7843
Madison, WI 53707-7843
(608) 266-1311   Toll Free: (800) WIS-VETS
Fax: (608) 267-0403   E-mail: WDVAInfo@dva.state.wi.us
Web: www.dva.state.wi.us/Ben_emergencygrants.asp

Summary To provide temporary, emergency financial aid to Wisconsin veterans or their dependents.

Eligibility This program is open to current residents of Wisconsin who 1) were residents of the state when they entered or reentered active duty in the U.S. armed forces, or 2) have moved to the state and have been residents for any consecutive 12-month period after entry or reentry into service. Applicants must have served on active duty for at least 2 continuous years or for at least 90 days during specified wartime periods. Also eligible are 1) unremarried surviving spouses and dependent children of eligible veterans who died in the line of duty while on active service or inactive duty for training; and 2) spouses and dependent children of eligible servicemembers who are currently activated or deployed. Applicants must have suffered a loss of income because of illness, injury, or natural disaster and be seeking temporary, emergency financial aid. Their income may not exceed 130% of the federal poverty guidelines (currently, $14,079 for a family of 1, rising to $48,113 for a family of 8).

Financial Data Grants do not exceed $3,000 during any consecutive 12-month period or the program limit of $7,500 in a lifetime.

Duration Grants are awarded for subsistence aid for a 30-day period, up to a maximum of 3 months.

Number awarded Varies each year.

Deadline Applications may be submitted at any time.

[1209]
WYOMING VETERANS PROPERTY TAX EXEMPTION

Wyoming Department of Revenue
Attn: Property Tax Relief Program
122 West 25th Street, Second Floor West
Cheyenne, WY 82002-0110
(307) 777-5235　　　　　　　　　　Fax: (307) 777-7527
E-mail: DirectorOfRevenue@wy.gov
Web: revenue.state.wy.us

Summary To provide a partial tax exemption on the property owned by veterans and their surviving spouses in Wyoming.

Eligibility This program is open to honorably-discharged veterans who were Wyoming residents at the time they entered military service and have resided in Wyoming for 3 years prior to applying for this exemption. Applicants must have served during specified periods of wartime or have received an armed forces expeditionary medal or other authorized service or campaign medal for service in an armed conflict in a foreign country. Surviving spouses of qualified veterans are also eligible. The exemption applies to county fees only, not state fees.

Financial Data Veterans and spouses may exempt $3,000 in assessed value of property from taxation per year. Disabled veterans are entitled to additional exemptions that depend on the level of their disability, to a maximum of $2,000 for a 100% disability.

Duration Veterans and spouses are entitled to use these exemptions as long as they reside in Wyoming and own the property as their principal residence.

Number awarded Varies each year.

Deadline Applicants must advise their county assessor of their intent to use the exemption by May of each year.

Military Personnel

[1210]
AER LOANS/GRANTS

Army Emergency Relief
200 Stovall Street
Alexandria, VA 22332-0600
(703) 428-0000　　　　　　　Toll Free: (866) 878-6378
Fax: (703) 325-7183　　　　　　E-mail: aer@aerhq.org
Web: www.aerhq.org

Summary To provide loans and grants-in-aid to help with the emergency financial needs of Army veterans, military personnel, and their dependents.

Eligibility Eligible to apply are active-duty soldiers (single or married) and their dependents, Army National Guard and Army Reserve soldiers on continuous active duty for more than 30 days and their dependents, soldiers retired from active duty for longevity or physical disability and their dependents, Army National Guard and Army Reserve soldiers who retired at age 60 and their dependents, and surviving spouses and orphans of soldiers who died while on active duty or after they retired. Applicants must be seeking assistance for such emergency needs as food, rent, and utilities; emergency transportation and vehicle repair; funeral expenses; medical and dental expenses; or personal needs when pay is delayed or stolen. Support is not available to help pay for nonessentials, finance ordinary leave or vacation, pay fines or legal expenses, help liquidate or consolidate debt, assist with house purchase or home improvements, cover bad checks, pay credit card bills, or help purchase, rent, or lease a vehicle.

Financial Data Support is provided in the form of loans or grants (or a combination).

Duration Qualifying individuals can apply whenever they have a valid emergency need.

Additional data This organization was established in 1942.

Number awarded Varies each year; recently, the organization helped more than 66,000 Army people with more than $70 million, including $60 million to 58,820 active-duty soldiers and their families, $7.3 million to 4,914 retired soldiers and their families, and $2.7 million to 2,304 widow(er)s and orphans of deceased soldiers. Since it was established, the organization has helped more than 3.2 million qualifying individuals with more than $1.2 billion in financial assistance.

Deadline Applications may be submitted at any time.

[1211]
AFAS FINANCIAL ASSISTANCE

Air Force Aid Society
Attn: Financial Assistance Department
241 18th Street South, Suite 202
Arlington, VA 22202-3409
(703) 607-3072, ext. 51　　　　　　Toll Free: (800) 429-9475
Fax: (703) 607-3022
Web: www.afas.org/Assistance/HowWeCanHelp.cfm

Summary To provide loans and grants-in-aid to current and former Air Force personnel and their families who are facing emergency situations.

Eligibility This program is open to active-duty Air Force members and their dependents, retired Air Force personnel and their dependents, Air National Guard and Air Force Reserve personnel on extended duty over 15 days, and spouses and dependent children of deceased Air Force personnel who died on active duty or in retired status. Applicants must be facing problems, usually for relatively short periods, that affect their job or the essential quality and dignity of life the Air Force wants for its people. Examples of such needs include basic living expenses (food, rent, utilities), medical and dental care, funeral expenses, vehicle expenses, emergency travel, moving expenses, or child or respite care. Funding is generally not provided if it merely postpones a long-term inability to exist on present pay and allowances, for non-essentials, for continuing long-term assistance commitments, or to replace funds lost due to garnishment.

Financial Data Assistance is provided as an interest-free loan, a grant, or a combination of both.

Number awarded Varies each year.

Deadline Applications may be submitted at any time.

[1212]
AFAS RESPITE CARE

Air Force Aid Society
Attn: Financial Assistance Department
241 18th Street South, Suite 202
Arlington, VA 22202-3409
(703) 607-3072, ext. 51　　　　　　Toll Free: (800) 429-9475
Fax: (703) 607-3022
Web: www.afas.org/Community/RespiteCareProgram.cfm

Summary To provide financial assistance to Air Force personnel and their families who have a family member with special needs.

Eligibility This program is open to active-duty Air Force members and their families who are responsible for 24 hour a day care for an ill or disabled family member (child, spouse, or parent) living in the household. Applicants must be referred by the Exceptional Family Member Program (EFMP) or the Family Advocacy Office. Selection is based on need, both financial need and the need of the family for respite time.

Financial Data Assistance is provided as a grant that depends on the needs of the family.

Number awarded Varies each year.

Deadline Applications may be submitted at any time.

[1213]
AIR WARRIOR COURAGE FOUNDATION GRANTS

Air Warrior Courage Foundation
P.O. Box 1553
Front Royal, VA 22630-0033
(540) 636-9798   Fax: (540) 636-9776
E-mail: awcf@awcfoundation.com
Web: www.airwarriorcourage.org

Summary To provide emergency assistance to veterans, military personnel, and their families, especially members of the Red River Valley Fighter Pilots Association (RRVA), who are facing unusual situations.

Eligibility These grants are available to active, Guard, Reserve, retired, and former military and Coast Guard personnel and dependent family members. Applicants must be able to demonstrate financial and material needs unmet by insurance programs, community support, or other service agencies. Special consideration is given to applicants eligible for the RRVA scholarship program (spouses and children of servicemembers missing in action or killed in action in armed conflicts by U.S. forces since August 1964, of U.S. military aircrew members killed in a noncombat aircraft accident in which they were performing aircrew duties, and of current members of the association). Assistance is available through the following activities: the 9/11 Terrorism Memorial Fund, which provides financial assistance, college savings programs, and/or material support to surviving family members of those lost or injured in the war on terror and military units performing humanitarian activities worldwide; the Earl Aman Courage Fund, which provides assistance or equipment to those disabled or in need for medically-related extraordinary expenses; and the Helping Achieve Normal Development (HAND) Fund, which provides assistance for therapeutic activities to children with anatomical, physiological, or mental deficits. Other programs are established from time to time as needs arise.

Financial Data The amount awarded varies. Recent grants included $148,744 for servicemember victims of Hurricanes Katrina and Rita; the Earl Aman Courage Fund awarded a total of $38,400 to provide financial support to veterans and/or their families to meet extraordinary medical or personal expenses beyond their financial resources; and the HAND Fund awarded $41,550 to provide therapeutic riding programs for 88 medically challenged military dependent children.

Duration These are 1-time grants.

Additional data This foundation was established in 1998 as a charitable organization affiliated with the RRVA.

Number awarded Varies each year.

Deadline Applications may be submitted at any time.

[1214]
ALABAMA INCOME TAX EXEMPTION FOR MILITARY COMBAT PAY

Alabama Department of Revenue
Attn: Income Tax Division
Gordon Persons Building
50 North Ripley Street, Room 4212
P.O. Box 327410
Montgomery, AL 36132-7410
(334) 242-1105   Fax: (334) 242-0064
E-mail: erohelpdesk@revenue.state.al.us
Web: www.ador.state.al.us

Summary To exempt portions of the income of military personnel who are residents of Alabama from state taxation.

Eligibility Eligible for these exemptions are residents of Alabama who are in the armed forces. The exemptions apply to 1) compensation for service in a combat zone designated by the

president of the United States and 2) military allowances paid to active-duty military, National Guard, and active Reserves for quarters, subsistence, uniforms, and travel.

Financial Data Qualified income received by military personnel who are Alabama residents is not subject to state income tax.

Duration These exemptions continue as long as the servicemember remains a resident of Alabama and receives designated income.

Number awarded Varies each year.

Deadline Deadline not specified.

[1215]
ARIZONA INCOME TAX EXEMPTION FOR COMBAT PAY

Arizona Department of Revenue
1600 West Monroe Street
Phoenix, AZ 85007-2650
(602) 542-3572   Toll Free: (800) 352-4090 (within AZ)
TDD: (602) 542-4021
Web: www.revenue.state.az.us

Summary To exempt the pay of military personnel from state income taxes in Arizona.

Eligibility This exemption is available to Arizona residents who serve on active duty in the U.S. armed forces, including members of the Reserves and National Guard called to active duty.

Financial Data All active duty pay is exempt from state income taxation.

Duration The exemption continues as long as the recipient resides in Arizona and receives active duty pay.

Deadline Deadline not specified.

[1216]
ARIZONA NATIONAL GUARD EMERGENCY RELIEF FUND GRANTS

Arizona National Guard Emergency Relief Fund
Attn: Fund Administrator
5636 East McDowell Road
Phoenix, AZ 85008
(602) 267-2731   E-mail: danielle.salomon@azdema.gov
Web: www.aerfund.org

Summary To provide emergency assistance (loans and grants) to members of the Arizona National Guard and their families.

Eligibility This program is open to members of the Arizona Army and Air National Guard who have not been mobilized under Presidential Order. Surviving spouses, children, and orphans of soldiers who died while on active duty are also eligible. Applicants must be seeking assistance for such emergency needs as delay in receiving pay or reimbursement from the government; temporary shelter, lodging, or rent; emergency utility assistance; emergency transportation and vehicle repair; costs incurred for emergency travel due to death of immediate family member; or any other special circumstance deemed appropriate by the fund's directors. Support is not provided to help pay for nonessentials, finance ordinary leave or vacation, pay fines or legal expenses, assist with home purchase or improvements, cover bad checks, or help purchase, rent, or lease a vehicle.

Financial Data Most support is provided in the form of interest-free loans, although outright grants are also available.

Duration These are 1-time grants.

Number awarded Varies each year.

Deadline Applications may be submitted at any time.

[1217]
ARIZONA NATIONAL GUARD FAMILY ASSISTANCE FUND

Arizona National Guard Emergency Relief Fund
Attn: Fund Administrator
5636 East McDowell Road
Phoenix, AZ 85008
(602) 267-2731   E-mail: danielle.salomon@azdema.gov
Web: www.aerfund.org

Summary   To provide emergency assistance (loans and grants) to members of the Arizona Reserve Component who have been mobilized and their families.

Eligibility   This program is open to members of the Arizona Reserve Component (including the Army and Air National Guard and Reserve units of all 5 branches of service) and their dependents. They must have been mobilized under Presidential Order. Surviving spouses, children, and orphans of soldiers who died while on active duty are also eligible. Applicants must be seeking assistance for such emergency needs as delay in receiving pay or reimbursement from the government; temporary shelter, lodging, or rent; emergency utility assistance; emergency transportation and vehicle repair; costs incurred for emergency travel due to death of immediate family member; or any other special circumstance deemed appropriate by the fund's directors. Support is not provided to help pay for nonessentials, financial ordinary leave or vacation, pay fines or legal expenses, assist with home purchase or improvements, cover bad checks, or help purchase, rent, or lease a vehicle.

Financial Data   Most support is provided in the form of interest-free loans, although outright grants are also available.

Duration   These are awarded on a 1-time basis.

Number awarded   Varies each year.

Deadline   Applications may be submitted at any time.

[1218]
ARKANSAS INCOME TAX EXEMPTIONS FOR MILITARY COMPENSATION AND DISABILITY PAY

Arkansas Department of Finance and Administration
Attn: Office of Income Tax Administration
Joel Ledbetter Building, Room 110
1800 Seventh Street
P.O. Box 3628
Little Rock, AR 72203-3628
(501) 682-7225   Fax: (501) 682-7692
E-mail: individual.income@rev.state.ar.us
Web: www.arkansas.gov/dfa/income_tax/tax_index.html

Summary   To exempt a portion of the income of military personnel and disabled veterans from state income taxes in Arkansas.

Eligibility   Eligible are residents of Arkansas receiving military compensation or military disability income.

Financial Data   The first $9,000 of U.S. military compensation pay or military disability income is exempt from state income taxation.

Duration   The exemptions continue as long as the recipient resides in Arkansas.

Deadline   Deadline not specified.

[1219]
CGMA GRANTS-IN-AID

Coast Guard Mutual Assistance
4200 Wilson Boulevard, Suite 610
Arlington, VA 20598-7180
(202) 493-6621   Toll Free: (800) 881-2462
Fax: (202) 493-6686   E-mail: ARL-DG-CGMA@uscg.mil
Web: www.cgmahq.org

Summary   To provide funding to members of the Coast Guard Mutual Assistance (CGMA) and their families who need temporary assistance.

Eligibility   This program is open to CGMA members who are facing special needs. Categories of aid that are available include emergency assistance (basic living expenses, emergency home repair, emergency travel expenses, fire and other disasters, funeral expenses, loss of funds, temporary living expenses); general assistance (adoption, child support, child care, family in-home day care facility, financial counseling, government travel cards, household furnishings, immigration fees, insurance, loss of income, moving expenses, non-emergency travel, non-support or inadequate support, past due bills and expenses, pay and allotment problems, vehicle repair, vehicle other expenses); housing assistance (payment of settlement charges associated with purchasing a residence, rental assistance, utilities); and medical and dental assistance (provider won't proceed without payment; mental health and family counseling; patient's cost share; durable medical equipment; prosthetic devices; rehabilitation, nursing, home, or respite care; orthodontia; long-term dental care; travel, transportation, and incidental expenses; special situations). Applicants must be able to demonstrate their need for assistance.

Financial Data   The assistance depends on the nature of the need.

Duration   These are 1-time grants. A new application must accompany each request for assistance.

Additional data   CGMA membership is open to active-duty and retired members of the U.S. Coast Guard, civilian employees of the U.S. Coast Guard, U.S. Coast Guard Reserve members, U.S. Coast Guard Auxiliary members, Public Health Service officers serving with the U.S. Coast Guard, and family members of all of those.

Number awarded   Varies each year.

Deadline   Deadline not specified.

[1220]
CONNECTICUT NATIONAL GUARD FOUNDATION ASSISTANCE

Connecticut National Guard Foundation, Inc.
Attn: Assistance Committee
360 Broad Street
Hartford, CT 06105-3795
(860) 241-1550   Fax: (860) 293-2929
E-mail: assistance.committee@ctngfoundation.org
Web: www.ctngfoundation.org

Summary   To provide emergency and other assistance to members of the Connecticut National Guard and their families.

Eligibility   This program is open to members of the Connecticut Army National Guard and Organized Militia, their children under 18 years of age, and their spouses who live with them. Applicants must be in need of assistance for such benefits as clothing, food, medical and surgical aid, and general care and relief. They must be able to demonstrate a need for assistance.

Financial Data   Grants depend on the need of the recipient.

Duration   These are 1-time grants.

Additional data   Applications are available at all State Armories and Family Assistance Centers.

Number awarded   Varies each year.

Deadline   Applications may be submitted at any time.

[1221]
DVA AUTOMOBILE ALLOWANCE FOR DISABLED VETERANS

Department of Veterans Affairs
Attn: Veterans Benefits Administration
810 Vermont Avenue, N.W.
Washington, DC 20420
(202) 418-4343   Toll Free: (800) 827-1000
Web: www.vba.va.gov/bin/21/Benefits

Summary To provide funding to certain disabled veterans and current service personnel who require specially adapted automobiles.

Eligibility To be eligible for a grant for an automobile, a veteran or current servicemember must have a service-connected loss or permanent loss of use of 1 or both hands or feet or permanent impairment of vision of both eyes to a prescribed degree. For adaptive equipment eligibility only, veterans entitled to compensation for ankylosis of 1 or both knees, or 1 or both hips, also qualify.

Financial Data The grant consists of a payment by the Department of Veterans Affairs (VA) of up to $11,000 toward the purchase of an automobile or other conveyance. The VA will also pay for the adaptive equipment, its repair, and the replacement or reinstallation required for the safe operation of the vehicle purchased with VA assistance or for a previously or subsequently acquired vehicle.

Duration This is a 1-time grant.

Number awarded Varies each year.

Deadline Applications may be submitted at any time.

[1222]
GEORGIA INCOME TAX EXCLUSION FOR COMBAT PAY

Georgia Department of Revenue
Attn: Taxpayer Services Division
1800 Century Boulevard, Room 8300
Atlanta, GA 30345-3205
(404) 417-4477　　　　　　　Toll Free: (877) 602-8477
Fax: (404) 417-6628　　E-mail: taxpayer.services@dor.ga.gov
Web: etax.dor.ga.gov/inctax/IndGeneralInfo.aspx

Summary To exclude from state income taxation combat pay received by residents of Georgia.

Eligibility This exclusion is available to residents of Georgia who are members of the National Guard or any Reserve component of the armed services and stationed in a combat zone.

Financial Data All combat pay received by National Guard and Reserve servicemembers is not subject to Georgia income tax. The exclusion applies only to military income earned in the combat zone during the period covered by the soldier's military orders.

Duration The exclusion continues as long as the recipient is assigned to a combat zone as a resident of Georgia.

Deadline Deadline not specified.

[1223]
HAWAII INCOME TAX EXEMPTIONS FOR MILITARY RESERVE AND NATIONAL GUARD DUTY PAY

Department of Taxation
Attn: Taxpayer Services Branch
425 Queen Street
P.O. Box 259
Honolulu, HI 96809-0259
(808) 587-4242　　　　　　Toll Free: (800) 222-3229
Fax: (808) 587-1488　　　　TDD: (808) 587-1418
Web: hawaii.gov/tax

Summary To exempt a portion of the income of members of the Reserves and National Guard from state income taxation in Hawaii.

Eligibility Eligible are members of the Reserve components of the Army, Navy, Air Force, Marine Corps, and Coast Guard, and the Hawaii National Guard who are classified as residents of Hawaii for state income tax purposes.

Financial Data The first $4,484 of income from service in the Reserves or the Hawaii National Guard is excluded.

Duration The exemption continues as long as the recipient resides in Hawaii.

Deadline Deadline not specified.

[1224]
HONORABLE LOUIS L. GOLDSTEIN VOLUNTEER POLICE, FIRE, RESCUE AND EMERGENCY MEDICAL SERVICES PERSONNEL SUBTRACTION MODIFICATION PROGRAM

Comptroller of Maryland
Attn: Revenue Administration Division
80 Calvert Street
Annapolis, MD 21411
(410) 260-7980　　　　Toll Free: (800) MD-TAXES (within MD)
Fax: (410) 974-3456　　　　　　TDD: (410) 260-7157
E-mail: taxhelp@comp.state.md.us
Web: individuals.marylandtaxes.com/incometax/default.asp

Summary To exempt from state income taxation in Maryland a portion of the income of members of the U.S. Coast Guard Auxiliary and other emergency medical services personnel.

Eligibility Eligible are Maryland residents who are members of the U.S. Coast Guard Auxiliary or qualifying volunteers certified by a Maryland fire, police, rescue, or emergency medical services organization.

Financial Data Eligible residents may exclude $3,500 of their income from state taxation.

Duration The exclusion continues as long as the recipient resides in Maryland and remains a member of the organization or a qualifying volunteer.

Deadline Deadline not specified.

[1225]
ILLINOIS INCOME TAX SUBTRACTIONS FOR MILITARY PERSONNEL

Illinois Department of Revenue
101 West Jefferson Street
P.O. Box 19044
Springfield, IL 62794-9044
(217) 782-9337　　　　　　Toll Free: (800) 732-8866
TDD: (800) 544-5304
Web: www.revenue.state.il.us

Summary To exempt the income of military personnel from state taxation in Illinois.

Eligibility Illinois does not tax the income received for: full-time active duty in the armed forces, including basic training; duty in the Reserves or an Illinois National Guard unit, including ROTC; or full-time duty as a cadet at the U.S. Military, Air Force, and Coast Guard academies or as a midshipman at the U.S. Naval Academy.

Financial Data All qualified pay received by military personnel is exempt from state income taxation.

Duration The exemption continues as long as the recipient resides in Illinois.

Additional data Income received under the Voluntary Separation Incentive, from the military as a civilian, as a member of the National Guard of another state, or under the Ready Reserve Mobilization Income Insurance Program, is not subject to this exemption.

Deadline Deadline not specified.

[1226]
INDIANA MILITARY SERVICE INCOME TAX DEDUCTION

Indiana Department of Revenue
Attn: Taxpayer Services Division
Indiana Government Center North
100 North Senate Avenue
Indianapolis, IN 46204-2253
(317) 232-2240　　　　　　　　　　TDD: (317) 232-4952
E-mail: pfrequest@dor.state.in.us
Web: www.in.gov/dor

Summary   To exempt a portion of the income of military personnel from state taxation in Indiana.

Eligibility   Military personnel on active duty or in the Reserves who are classified as Indiana residents for purposes of state income taxation are eligible for this income adjustment.

Financial Data   Qualified military personnel may deduct up to $5,000 of military pay from state income taxation in Indiana. In addition, they may exclude from taxation all re-enlistment bonuses awarded for serving in a combat zone and all pay received for active service in a combat zone or pay received while hospitalized as a result of service in a combat zone.

Duration   The adjustments continue as long as the recipient resides in Indiana.

Deadline   Deadline not specified.

[1227]
INDIANA NATIONAL GUARD AND RESERVE COMPONENT MEMBERS INCOME TAX DEDUCTION

Indiana Department of Revenue
Attn: Taxpayer Services Division
Indiana Government Center North
100 North Senate Avenue
Indianapolis, IN 46204-2253
(317) 232-2240   TDD: (317) 232-4952
E-mail: pfrequest@dor.state.in.us
Web: www.in.gov/dor

Summary   To exempt the income of Indiana National Guard and Reserve members who are called to active duty from state taxation.

Eligibility   This exemption is available to members of the Indiana Army National Guard, the Indiana Air National Guard, and Reserve components of all branches of the armed forces. Income received while the National Guard unit was federalized or the Reserve component was deployed or mobilized for involuntary full-time service.

Financial Data   All qualified income from National Guard or Reserve service is exempt from state income taxation in Indiana.

Duration   The exemption continues as long as the recipient receives full-time active-duty income.

Deadline   Deadline not specified.

[1228]
INJURED MARINE SEMPER FI GRANTS

Injured Marine Semper Fi Fund
c/o Wounded Warrior Center
Building H49
P.O. Box 555193
Camp Pendleton, CA 92055-5193
(760) 725-3680   Fax: (760) 725-3685
E-mail: info@semperfifund.org
Web: www.semperfifund.org

Summary   To provide supplemental assistance to Marines injured in combat and training operations and their families.

Eligibility   This program is open to Marines injured in combat operations and training accidents and their families. Applicants must need financial assistance to deal with the personal and financial disruption associated with leaving their home, their family, and their job during hospitalization, rehabilitation, and recuperation. Applications are available at military hospitals.

Financial Data   Funds are available for such expenses as child care, travel expenses for families, and other necessities. Assistance is also available for the purchase of adaptive transportation, home modifications, and specialized equipment such as wheelchairs, audio/visual equipment for the blind, and software for traumatic brain injuries.

Duration   Grants are provided as needed.

Additional data   This fund was established in 2004 by a small group of Marine Corps spouses.

Number awarded   Varies each year. Since this program was established, it has awarded more than 18,300 grants worth more than $37 million.

Deadline   Applications may be submitted at any time.

[1229]
IOWA INCOME TAX EXEMPTION OF ACTIVE-DUTY MILITARY PAY

Iowa Department of Revenue
Attn: Taxpayer Services
Hoover State Office Building
1305 East Walnut
P.O. Box 10457
Des Moines, IA 50306-0457
(515) 281-3114   Toll Free: (800) 367-3388 (within IA)
Fax: (515) 242-6487   E-mail: idr@iowa.gov
Web: www.iowa.gov/tax

Summary   To exempt the income earned by military personnel in Iraq from state taxation in Iowa.

Eligibility   This exemption applies to the active-duty military pay of persons in the Iowa National Guard or the U.S. armed forces who served or are serving in Operation Iraqi Freedom, Operation Noble Eagle, or Operation Enduring Freedom. Applicants must be residents of Iowa for state income tax purposes.

Financial Data   All eligible income received since January 1, 2003 is exempt.

Duration   The exemption continues as long as the military personnel remain assigned to peacekeeping activities in Iraq and residents of Iowa for state income tax purposes.

Number awarded   Varies each year.

Deadline   Deadline not specified.

[1230]
IOWA INJURED VETERANS GRANT PROGRAM

Iowa Department of Veterans Affairs
Camp Dodge, Building A6A
7105 N.W. 70th Avenue
Johnston, IA 50131-1824
(515) 242-5331   Toll Free: (800) VET-IOWA
Fax: (515) 242-5659   E-mail: info@idva.state.ia.us
Web: www.iowava.org/benefits/injured_vets_grant.html

Summary   To provide assistance to Iowa residents who were injured in combat while serving in the armed forces after September 11, 2001.

Eligibility   This assistance is available to members of the U.S. armed forces who are still serving or who have been discharged or released from service under honorable conditions. Applicants must have sustained an injury or illness in a combat zone or hostile fire zone after September 11, 2001. The illness or injury must have been serious enough to require medical evacuation from the combat zone and must be considered by the military to be in the line of duty. The veteran or military servicemember must have been a resident of Iowa at the time of injury.

Financial Data   Qualified veterans or military servicemembers are entitled to the following assistance: $2,500 when they are medically evacuated from the combat zone; $2,500 30 days after evacuation date if still hospitalized, receiving medical treatment, or receiving rehabilitation services from the military or Veterans Administration; $2,500 60 days after evacuation date if still hospitalized, receiving medical treatment, or receiving rehabilitation services from the military or Veterans Administration; and $2,500 90 days after the evacuation date if still hospitalized, receiving medical treatment, or receiving rehabilitation services from the military or Veterans Administration. The maximum assistance is $10,000.

Duration   This is a 1-time bonus.

Additional data This program was established in 2007.

Number awarded Varies each year.

Deadline Deadline not specified.

[1231]
IOWA MILITARY HOMEOWNERSHIP PROGRAM

Iowa Finance Authority
Attn: Military Homeownership Program
2015 Grand Avenue
Des Moines, IA 50312
Toll Free: (800) 432-7230　　　　Fax: (515) 725-4901
E-mail: homebuyer.inquiry@iowa.gov
Web: www.ifahome.com

Summary To provide funding to current and former military servicemembers and those surviving spouses who are interested in purchasing a primary residence in Iowa.

Eligibility This program is open to 1) servicemembers who served at least 90 days on active duty since September 11, 2001; 2) federal status injured servicemembers who served on active duty since September 11, 2001; and 3) surviving spouses of those eligible servicemembers who served honorably. Applicants must be purchasing a home in Iowa (including modular homes, condominiums, townhomes, and duplexes) that will be their primary residence. They must be using an Iowa Finance Authority participating lender and either FirstHome, FirstHome Plus, or (if not eligible for either of those programs) a permanent mortgage loan.

Financial Data The grant is $5,000. Funds may be used toward down payment on a qualifying home purchase and/or closing costs on a qualifying first purchase money mortgage.

Duration These are 1-time grants.

Additional data The Iowa Legislature created this program in 2005.

Number awarded Varies each year.

Deadline Applications may be submitted at any time.

[1232]
IOWA MILITARY SERVICE PROPERTY TAX EXEMPTION

Iowa Department of Revenue
Attn: Property Tax Division
Hoover State Office Building
1305 East Walnut
P.O. Box 10457
Des Moines, IA 50306-0457
(515) 281-4040　　　　Toll Free: (800) 367-3388 (within IA)
Fax: (515) 281-3906　　　　E-mail: idr@iowa.gov
Web: www.iowa.gov/tax

Summary To exempt veterans, military personnel, and their family members from a portion of property taxes in Iowa.

Eligibility This exemption is available to residents of Iowa who are 1) former members of the U.S. armed forces who performed at least 18 months of military service (or for fewer months because of a service-related injury), regardless of the time period, and who were honorably discharged; 2) former members, and members currently serving of the U.S. Reserves and Iowa National Guard who have served at least 20; and 3) current members of the U.S. Reserves and Iowa National Guard who were activated for federal duty for at least 90 days; 4) former members of the armed forces whose enlistment would have occurred during the Korean Conflict but chose to serve 5 years in the Reserves; and 5) honorably discharged veterans who served in a designated eligible service period. Applicants must own a primary residence in the state. Also eligible for the exemption are the spouses, unremarried widow(er)s, minor children, and widowed parent of qualified veterans.

Financial Data The amount of the exemption varies.

Duration 1 year; continues until the qualifying veteran or dependent no longer lives in the residence.

Number awarded Varies each year. Recently, more than $2.8 million in property was exempt from taxation.

Deadline Application must be made by June of the year for which the exemption is first requested. The exemption is provided annually, from then on, as long as the qualifying veteran or dependent resides in the house.

[1233]
KENTUCKY MILITARY FAMILY ASSISTANCE TRUST FUND

Kentucky Department of Military Affairs
Attn: State Family Program
Boone National Guard Center
100 Minuteman Parkway
Frankfort, KY 40601-6168
(502) 607-1155　　　　Toll Free: (800) 372-7601
Fax: (502) 607-1394
Web: dma.ky.gov/Family+Assistance

Summary To provide emergency financial assistance to Kentucky residents serving in the armed forces outside of the United States and their spouses.

Eligibility This assistance is available to 1) members of the U.S. armed forces who are deployed outside of the United States and who have a Kentucky home of record; and 2 Kentucky resident spouses of eligible military members. Applicants must be facing expenses that create an undue hardship directly related to deployment outside the country. They may not have reasonable access to any other funding source. There is no limitation on the type of expense for which the assistance is requested, only that it create an undue hardship.

Financial Data Grants are limited to $2,500 for a single application or $5,000 per fiscal year.

Duration Assistance is available while the military member is deployed overseas and for 90 days following the end of deployment or deactivation.

Additional data This program was established in 2006.

Number awarded Varies each year.

Deadline Applications may be submitted at any time.

[1234]
LOUISIANA MILITARY PAY INCOME TAX EXCLUSION

Louisiana Department of Revenue
Attn: Individual Income Tax
P.O. Box 201
Baton Rouge, LA 70821
(225) 219-0102
Web: www.revenue.louisiana.gov

Summary To exempt specified income of military personnel from state taxation in Louisiana.

Eligibility This exemption is available to residents of Louisiana who are on active full-time duty as a member of the armed forces performing service outside the state. Applicants must have served 120 or more consecutive days on active duty.

Financial Data Qualifying armed forces members may exempt up to $30,000 of compensation for service outside the state from income taxation in Louisiana.

Duration The benefit continues as long as the recipient remains a resident of Louisiana and serves outside the state for state income tax purposes.

Number awarded Varies each year.

Deadline Deadline not specified.

[1235]
MARYLAND INCOME TAX EXEMPTION FOR MILITARY PERSONNEL

Comptroller of Maryland
Attn: Revenue Administration Division
80 Calvert Street
Annapolis, MD 21411
(410) 260-7980   Toll Free: (800) MD-TAXES (within MD)
Fax: (410) 974-3456   TDD: (410) 260-7157
E-mail: taxhelp@comp.state.md.us
Web: individuals.marylandtaxes.com

Summary   To exempt certain portions of military pay from Maryland state income tax.

Eligibility   Military personnel who are legal residents of Maryland and have earned overseas pay are eligible for this exemption. Personnel whose total military pay exceeds $30,000 do not quality for this exemption.

Financial Data   Military personnel who are legal residents of Maryland must file a resident state income tax return and report all income from all sources. However, if they have earned overseas pay, they may subtract up to $15,000 of that pay (depending upon their total income) from their gross income.

Duration   The exemption is available annually.

Number awarded   Varies each year.

Deadline   Military personnel claim this exemption when they file their state income tax return, in April of each year.

[1236]
MASSACHUSETTS WELCOME HOME BONUS

Office of the State Treasurer
Attn: Veterans Bonus Division
One Ashburton Place, 12th Floor
Boston, MA 02108-1608
(617) 367-9333, ext. 859   Fax: (617) 227-1622
E-mail: veteransbonus@tre.state.ma.us
Web: www.mass.gov/treasury

Summary   To provide a bonus to Massachusetts veterans and servicemembers who served after September 11, 2001 and their families.

Eligibility   This bonus is available to veterans and current servicemembers who had resided in Massachusetts for at least 6 months immediately prior to their entry into service in the armed forces. They must have performed service on or after September 11, 2001 and still be serving or have been honorably discharged. If the veteran or servicemember is deceased, an immediate family member (parent, spouse, child, sibling) may apply.

Financial Data   The bonus is $1,000 for active service in Afghanistan or Iraq or $500 for 6 months or more of active service.

Duration   This is a 1-time bonus.

Number awarded   Varies each year.

Deadline   Deadline not specified.

[1237]
MCCORMICK GRANTS

Society of the First Infantry Division
Attn: 1st Infantry Division Foundation
1933 Morris Road
Blue Bell, PA 19422-1422
Toll Free: (888) 324-4733   Fax: (215) 661-1934
E-mail: Fdn1ID@aol.com
Web: www.bigredone.org/foundation/grants.cfm

Summary   To provide emergency financial assistance to active First Division soldiers and their families.

Eligibility   This assistance is available to soldiers currently serving in the First Infantry Division and their families. Applicants must be facing emergency financial needs that cannot be met through the usual forms of assistance available to them.

Financial Data   Grant amounts depend on the need of the recipient. Recently, they ranged up to $1,500.

Duration   These are 1-time grants.

Additional data   This program was established in 2005 with funding from the Robert R. McCormick Tribune Foundation.

Number awarded   Varies each year; recently, 3 grants were awarded.

Deadline   Applications may be submitted at any time.

[1238]
MICHIGAN HOMESTEAD PROPERTY TAX CREDIT FOR VETERANS AND BLIND PEOPLE

Michigan Department of Treasury
Attn: Homestead Exemption
Treasury Building
430 West Allegan Street
Lansing, MI 48922
(517) 373-3200   Toll Free: (800) 827-4000
TDD: (517) 636-4999   E-mail: treasPtd2@michigan.gov
Web: www.michigan.gov/treasury

Summary   To provide a property tax credit to veterans, military personnel, their spouses, blind people, and their surviving spouses in Michigan.

Eligibility   Eligible to apply are residents of Michigan who are 1) blind and own their homestead; 2) a veteran with a service-connected disability or his/her surviving spouse; 3) a surviving spouse of a veteran deceased in service; 4) a pensioned veteran, a surviving spouse of those veterans, or an active military member, all of whose household income is less than $7,500; or 5) a surviving spouse of a non-disabled or non-pensioned veteran of the Korean War, World War II, or World War I whose household income is less than $7,500. All applicants must own or rent a home in Michigan, have been a Michigan resident for at least 6 months during the year in which application is made, and fall within qualifying income levels (up to $82,650 in household income).

Financial Data   The maximum credit is $1,200. The exact amount varies. For homeowners, the credit depends on the state equalized value of the homestead and on an allowance for filing category. For renters, 20% of the rent is considered property tax eligible for credit.

Duration   1 year; eligibility must be established each year.

Number awarded   Varies each year.

Deadline   December of each year.

[1239]
MICHIGAN INCOME TAX EXEMPTION FOR VETERANS AND MILITARY PERSONNEL

Michigan Department of Treasury
Attn: Income Tax
Treasury Building
430 West Allegan Street
Lansing, MI 48922
(517) 373-3200   Toll Free: (800) 827-4000
TDD: (517) 636-4999   E-mail: treasIndTax@michigan.gov
Web: www.michigan.gov/treasury

Summary   To exempt the income of military personnel and veterans in Michigan from state income taxation.

Eligibility   Eligible for this exemption are military personnel and veterans considered Michigan residents for purposes of state income taxation.

Financial Data   All active-duty military and retirement pay from the U.S. armed forces is exempt from state income taxation.

Duration   The exemption continues as long as the recipient resides in Michigan.

Deadline   Deadline not specified.

[1240]
MICHIGAN MILITARY FAMILY RELIEF FUND GRANTS

Department of Military and Veterans Affairs
Attn: Military Family Relief Fund
3423 North Martin Luther King Boulevard
P.O. Box 30261
Lansing, MI 48909-7761
Toll Free: (866) 271-4404   Fax: (517) 481-7644
E-mail: paocmn@michigan.gov
Web: www.michigan.gov/dmva

Summary To provide temporary financial support to members of the Michigan National Guard and Reserves who have been called to active duty as part of the national response to the September 11, 2001 terrorist attacks and their families.

Eligibility This assistance is available to members of the Michigan National Guard and Reserves and their families. The military member must have been called to active duty as part of the national response to the events of September 11, 2001. Applicants must be able to demonstrate a need for assistance as a result of the military member's service.

Financial Data The maximum grant is $2,000.

Duration This assistance is provided to meet temporary needs only.

Additional data The state of Michigan established this program in 2004.

Number awarded Varies each year.

Deadline Applications may be submitted at any time.

[1241]
MINNESOTA INCOME TAX SUBTRACTION FOR ACTIVE MILITARY SERVICE

Minnesota Department of Revenue
Attn: Individual Income Tax Division
600 North Robert Street
Mail Station 5510
St. Paul, MN 55146-5510
(651) 296-3781   Toll Free: (800) 652-9094 (within MN)
E-mail: indinctax@state.mn.us
Web: www.taxes.state.mn.us

Summary To exempt from state taxation the income received by National Guard members and Reservists on active duty in Minnesota.

Eligibility This exemption is available to members of the National Guard and other Reserves who are Minnesota residents serving in active military service in Minnesota. Applicants must have earned income for state active service (for disasters, riots, etc., but not regular drill pay), federally-funded state active service, or federal active service.

Financial Data Qualifying income earned by National Guard members or Reservists is exempt from Minnesota state taxation.

Duration This exemption is available as long as the taxpayer earns qualifying income.

Additional data This exemption first applied to income earned in 2005.

Number awarded Varies each year.

Deadline Income tax returns must be submitted by April of each year.

[1242]
MISSISSIPPI INCOME TAX EXCLUSION FOR NATIONAL GUARD AND RESERVE FORCE PAY

Mississippi State Tax Commission
Attn: Individual Income Tax Division
P.O. Box 1033
Jackson, MS 39215-1033
(601) 923-7089   Fax: (601) 923-7039
Web: www.mstc.state.ms.us/taxareas/individ/main.htm

Summary To exclude a portion of the income of selected Mississippi military personnel from state income taxation.

Eligibility This deduction is available to Mississippi residents who are currently members of the National Guard or Reserve Forces in the state. Applicants must have received income for inactive duty training (monthly drills), active-duty training (summer camps and special schools), and state active duty (emergency duty for floods, hurricanes, and disasters). Compensation received for full-time active-duty training and compensation as an employee of the National Guard or Reserve Forces is not subject to the exclusion.

Financial Data Excluded from state income taxation is the lesser of $15,000 or the amount received from the National Guard or Reserve Forces as qualified income.

Duration The deduction continues as long as the recipient resides in Mississippi and receives eligible compensation from the National Guard or Reserve Forces.

Number awarded Varies each year.

Deadline Eligible Guard members or Reservists may claim this deduction when they file their state income tax return, in April of each year.

[1243]
MISSOURI MILITARY FAMILY RELIEF FUND GRANTS

Missouri Military Family Relief Fund
Attn: JFMO-J1/DPP-F
2302 Militia Drive
Jefferson City, MO 65101-1203
(573) 638-9827   E-mail: MilitaryRelief@mo.ngb.army.mil
Web: www.mmfrf.mo.gov

Summary To provide emergency financial assistance to members of the National Guard and Reserves in Missouri or their families who are facing difficulties as a result of deployment after September 11, 2001.

Eligibility This program is open to 1) members of the Missouri National Guard who have been on Title 10 orders as a result of the September 11, 2001 terrorist attacks for 30 consecutive days or more or have been off Title 10 orders as a result of the September 11, 2001 terrorist attacks for 120 days or less; 2) Reserve component members who are residents of Missouri and have been on Title 32 orders as a result of the September 11, 2001 terrorist attacks for 30 days or more or have been off Title 32 orders as a result of the September 11, 2001 terrorist attacks for 120 days or less; 3) immediate relatives of members of those National Guard or Reserve units. The Guard or Reserve member must have a rank no higher than O-3 or W-2. Applicants must be in need of emergency financial assistance; funding is not provided for nonessentials, to finance leave or vacations, to pay fines or legal expenses, to help liquidate or consolidate debts, to assist with house purchase or home improvements, to cover bad checks, or to pay credit card bills.

Financial Data Grants up to $1,000 are available.

Duration Grants may be awarded only once in a 12-month period.

Additional data This program was established in 2005.

Number awarded Varies each year.

Deadline Applications may be submitted at any time.

[1244]
MONTANA MILITARY SALARY INCOME TAX EXCLUSION

Montana Department of Revenue
Attn: Individual Income Tax
125 North Roberts, Third Floor
P.O. Box 5805
Helena, MT 59604-5805
(406) 444-6900   Toll Free: (866) 859-2254
Fax: (406) 444-6642   TDD: (406) 444-2830
Web: mt.gov/revenue

Summary To exclude the income of military personnel from state taxation in Montana.

Eligibility This exclusion is available to residents of Montana for purposes of state income taxation who are 1) serving on active duty as a member of the regular armed forces; 2) a member of a Reserve component of the Army, Navy, Marine Corps, Air Force, or Coast Guard serving on active duty in a "contingent operation;" or 3) a member of the Montana National Guard serving on active duty for a period of more than 30 consecutive days for the purpose of responding to a national emergency.

Financial Data All basic, special, and incentive pay for active-duty service is exempt from state income taxation.

Duration The exemption continues as long as the recipient resides in Montana and serves on active duty.

Deadline Deadline not specified.

[1245]
NEW MEXICO TAX EXCLUSION FOR MILITARY ACTIVE DUTY PAY

New Mexico Taxation and Revenue Department
Attn: Tax Information and Policy Office
1100 South St. Francis Drive
P.O. Box 630
Santa Fe, NM 87504-0630
(505) 827-2523
Web: www.state.nm.us/tax

Summary To exclude the income of active-duty military personnel from state income taxation in New Mexico.

Eligibility This exclusion is available to members of the armed forces, including those on active duty, full-time training duty, annual training duty, full-time National Guard duty, and attendance (while in the active service) at a school designated as a service school. Both residents and non-residents of New Mexico are eligible.

Financial Data All pay received in New Mexico for qualifying military service is excluded from income for income tax purposes.

Duration The exclusion continues as long as the service member earns income from the military in New Mexico.

Number awarded Varies each year.

Deadline The qualifying service member claims the exclusion on the New Mexico state income tax return, which is due in April.

[1246]
NEW MEXICO TAX EXEMPTION FOR INDIANS

New Mexico Taxation and Revenue Department
Attn: Tax Information and Policy Office
1100 South St. Francis Drive
P.O. Box 630
Santa Fe, NM 87504-0630
(505) 827-2523
Web: www.state.nm.us/tax

Summary To exempt the income of Indians in New Mexico, including those in military service, from state taxation.

Eligibility This program is open to residents of New Mexico who are enrolled members of an Indian nation, tribe, or pueblo and 1) live on the lands of the nation, tribe, or pueblo of which they are a member, and 2) earn all their income from work on those lands. Lands include formal and informal reservations, dependent Indian communities, and Indian allotments whether restricted or held in trust by the United States. Also eligible are enrolled members who are serving in the U.S. armed forces and whose home of record is the lands of their Indian nation, tribe, or pueblo.

Financial Data All income of qualifying enrolled members is exempt from state taxation in New Mexico.

Duration The exemption continues as long as the qualifying resident remains enrolled and earns all income on the lands of their Indian nation, tribe, or pueblo.

Additional data The income of Indians who worked or lived on lands outside the Indian nation, tribe, or pueblo of which they are members is subject to taxation.

Number awarded Varies each year.

Deadline The qualifying resident claims the exemption on the New Mexico state income tax return, which is due in April.

[1247]
NEW YORK ORGANIZED MILITIA INCOME TAX EXEMPTION

New York State Department of Taxation and Finance
W.A. Harriman Campus
Tax and Finance Building
Albany, NY 12227-0001
(518) 438-8581   Toll Free: (800) 225-5829 (within NY)
Web: www.nystax.gov

Summary To exempt the income of members of the New York organized militia from state income tax.

Eligibility This exemption is available to members of the New York organized militia (including the New York Army National Guard, the New York Air National Guard, the New York Naval Militia, and the New York Guard). Applicants must have received income for the performance of active service within New York state in accordance with active-duty orders issued by the governor or to federal active Guard duty orders. The exemption does not cover income received for regular duties in the organized militia or active duty in the U.S. armed forces.

Financial Data Qualified income is exempt from state income taxation in New York.

Duration The exemption is available whenever the militia member receives qualified income.

Number awarded Varies each year.

Deadline Deadline not specified.

[1248]
NMCRS FINANCIAL ASSISTANCE

Navy-Marine Corps Relief Society
875 North Randolph Street, Suite 225
Arlington, VA 22203-1757
(703) 696-4904   Fax: (703) 696-0144
Web: www.nmcrs.org/intfreeloan.html

Summary To provide emergency assistance, in the form of interest-free loans or grants, to current and former Navy and Marine Corps personnel and their families who need temporary funding.

Eligibility This program is open to active-duty and retired Navy and Marine Corps personnel, their eligible family members, eligible family members of Navy and Marine Corps personnel who died on active duty or in a retired status, Reservists on extended active duty, indigent mothers (65 years of age or older) of deceased servicemembers who have limited resources and no family to provide for their welfare, ex-spouses whose marriage to a servicemember lasted for at least 20 years while the servicemember was on active duty and who have not remarried, and uniformed members of the National Oceanic and Atmospheric Administration (NOAA). Applicants must need emergency funding for funeral expenses, medical or dental bills, food, rent, utilities, emergency transportation, disaster relief, child care expenses, essential vehicle repairs, or other unforeseen family emergencies. Funding is not available to pay bills for non-essentials, finance liberty and vacations, pay fines or legal expenses, pay taxes, finance recreational boats or vehicles or help Navy and Marine Corps families live beyond their means.

Financial Data Funds are provided in the form of interest-free loans or grants.

Number awarded Varies each year.

Deadline Applications may be submitted at any time.

[1249]
NORTH DAKOTA STATE INCOME TAX MILITARY PAY EXCLUSION

Office of State Tax Commissioner
State Capitol Building
600 East Boulevard Avenue, Department 127
Bismarck, ND 58505-0599
(701) 328-2770   Toll Free: (800) 638-2901
Fax: (701) 328-3700   TDD: (800) 366-6888
E-mail: taxinfo@state.nd.us
Web: www.nd.gov/tax

Summary To exempt from state income taxation a portion of the income received by military personnel residing in North Dakota.

Eligibility Eligible for this benefit are members of the U.S. armed forces who are legal residents of North Dakota for state income tax purposes. Applicants must have received pay for active-duty service in the U.S. armed forces.

Financial Data Up to $1,000 of military pay per year may be excluded from income for state tax purposes. The exclusion is allowed only to the extent that military pay is included in federal taxable income.

Duration The exclusion may be taken as long as the recipient resides in North Dakota.

Number awarded Varies each year.

Deadline Deadline not specified.

[1250]
NORTH DAKOTA STATE INCOME TAX MILITARY PAY EXCLUSION FOR OVERSEAS DUTY

Office of State Tax Commissioner
State Capitol Building
600 East Boulevard Avenue, Department 127
Bismarck, ND 58505-0599
(701) 328-2770   Toll Free: (800) 638-2901
Fax: (701) 328-3700   TDD: (800) 366-6888
E-mail: taxinfo@state.nd.us
Web: www.nd.gov/tax

Summary To exempt from state income taxation a portion of the income received by military personnel serving overseas while residents of North Dakota.

Eligibility Eligible for this benefit are members of the U.S. armed forces who are legal residents of North Dakota for state income tax purposes and served overseas for at least 30 days during the tax year. Field grade and general officers (defined as major or higher in the U.S. Army, Air Force, or Marines, or Lieutenant Commander or higher in the U.S. Navy, or Surgeon or higher in the U.S. Public Health Service) are not eligible for this exclusion.

Financial Data Up to $300 of military pay for each month (or fraction of a month) for overseas service may be excluded from income for state tax purposes. The exclusion is allowed only to the extent that military pay is included in federal taxable income.

Duration The exclusion may be taken as long as the recipient resides in North Dakota.

Number awarded Varies each year.

Deadline Deadline not specified.

[1251]
NORTH DAKOTA STATE INCOME TAX NATIONAL GUARD OR RESERVE MEMBER EXCLUSION

Office of State Tax Commissioner
State Capitol Building
600 East Boulevard Avenue, Department 127
Bismarck, ND 58505-0599
(701) 328-2770   Toll Free: (800) 638-2901
Fax: (701) 328-3700   TDD: (800) 366-6888
E-mail: taxinfo@state.nd.us
Web: www.nd.gov/tax

Summary To exempt from state income taxation the income received by members of the National Guard and armed forces Reserves in North Dakota.

Eligibility Eligible for this benefit are North Dakota residents who are members of the North Dakota National Guard or a Reserve unit of the U.S. armed forces. Applicants must have been mobilized for federal active-duty service and received compensation for that service. Compensation received for attending annual training, basic military training, professional military education, or active duty for which they volunteered but did not receive mobilization orders does not qualify.

Financial Data All qualified income may be excluded from income for state tax purposes.

Duration The exclusion may be taken as long as the recipient resides in North Dakota and receives qualified pay.

Number awarded Varies each year.

Deadline Deadline not specified.

[1252]
NORTH DAKOTA STATE INCOME TAX SERVICEMEMBER CIVIL RELIEF ACT ADJUSTMENT

Office of State Tax Commissioner
State Capitol Building
600 East Boulevard Avenue, Department 127
Bismarck, ND 58505-0599
(701) 328-2770   Toll Free: (800) 638-2901
Fax: (701) 328-3700   TDD: (800) 366-6888
E-mail: taxinfo@state.nd.us
Web: www.nd.gov/tax

Summary To exempt from state income taxation the income received by members of the U.S. uniformed services who are nonresidents or part-year residents of North Dakota.

Eligibility Eligible for this benefit are members of the U.S. uniformed services who are nonresidents or part-year residents of North Dakota for state income tax purposes. Applicants must have received compensation in North Dakota for active-duty service in the U.S. armed forces or for active duty in the commissioned corps of the Public Health Service or the National Oceanic and Atmospheric Administration. For part-year residents, only the compensation received for this service while a nonresident of North Dakota qualifies.

Financial Data All qualified income may be excluded from income for state tax purposes.

Duration The exclusion may be taken as long as the recipient earns qualifying income in North Dakota.

Number awarded Varies each year.

Deadline Deadline not specified.

[1253]
OHIO INCOME TAX DEDUCTION FOR MILITARY PAY

Ohio Department of Taxation
Attn: Income Tax Audit Division
30 East Broad Street
P.O. Box 182847
Columbus, OH 43218-2847
(614) 433-5817   Toll Free: (800) 282-1780 (within OH)
Fax: (614) 433-7771
Web: tax.ohio.gov

Summary   To deduct from state income taxation in Ohio the pay received by military personnel who are residents of the state but stationed elsewhere.

Eligibility   This deduction is available to residents of Ohio who are members of an active component of the U.S. armed forces or of a Reserve component or the National Guard under federal mobilization orders. Applicants must be assigned to a permanent duty station outside Ohio.

Financial Data   All military pay received by military personnel stationed outside the state is excluded from income for purposes of Ohio state taxation.

Duration   The exclusion is available as long as the recipient remains an Ohio resident but stationed outside the state.

Additional data   This deduction became effective in 2007.

Number awarded   Varies each year.

Deadline   Deadline not specified.

[1254]
OHIO MILITARY INJURY RELIEF FUND GRANTS

Ohio Department of Job and Family Services
Attn: Military Injury Relief Fund
30 East Broad Street, 32nd Floor
P.O. Box 182367
Columbus, OH 43218-2367
(614) 466-2100   Toll Free: (888) 296-7541
E-mail: MIRF@jfs.ohio.gov
Web: jfs.ohio.gov/veterans/new/mirf.stm

Summary   To provide funding to Ohio residents who suffered injuries while serving in the U.S. armed forces in Operation Enduring Freedom (OEF) or Operation Iraqi Freedom (OIF).

Eligibility   This program is open to residents of Ohio who served in country (including Reservists and National Guard members activated under Title 10) under OEF or OIF. Applicants must have suffered a physical injury in the line of duty or have been diagnosed with post-traumatic stress disorder (PTSD) incurred while serving in country under OEF or OIF. The injury must have occurred while the service member was in receipt of hazardous duty, combat, or hostile fire pay in an OEF or OIF theater of operation. Honorably discharged veterans must submit a copy of their DD214; military personnel still serving must submit proof of service; Reservists and National Guard members must submit a copy of the military orders activating them under Title 10.

Financial Data   The amount of the grant depends on the availability of funds.

Additional data   This program was established in 2005.

Number awarded   Varies each year.

Deadline   Applications may be submitted at any time.

[1255]
OHIO VETERANS' FINANCIAL ASSISTANCE

Ohio Department of Veterans Services
77 South High Street, 7th Floor
Columbus, OH 43215
(614) 644-0898   Toll Free: (888) DVS-OHIO
Fax: (614) 728-9498   E-mail: ohiovet@dvs.ohio.gov
Web: dvs.ohio.gov

Summary   To provide emergency aid to Ohio veterans, military personnel, and their dependents who, because of disability or disaster, are in financial need.

Eligibility   This assistance is available to veterans and active-duty members of the U.S. armed forces, as well as their spouses, surviving spouses, dependent parents, minor children, and wards. Applicants must have been residents of the Ohio county in which they are applying for at least 3 months. They must be able to demonstrate need for relief because of sickness, accident, or destitution.

Financial Data   The amount granted varies, depending on the needs of the recipient.

Duration   These are emergency funds only and are not designed to be a recurring source of income.

Additional data   These grants are made by the various county veterans services offices in Ohio.

Number awarded   Varies each year.

Deadline   Applications may be submitted at any time.

[1256]
OKLAHOMA PARTIAL MILITARY PAY EXCLUSION

Oklahoma Tax Commission
Attn: Income Tax
2501 North Lincoln Boulevard
Oklahoma City, OK 73194-0009
(405) 521-3160   Toll Free: (800) 522-8165 (within OK)
Fax: (405) 522-0063   E-mail: otcmaster@tax.ok.gov
Web: www.tax.ok.gov/incometax.html

Summary   To exempt a portion of the income of military personnel in Oklahoma from state income taxation.

Eligibility   Members of the armed forces who are defined, for state income tax purposes, as residents of Oklahoma are eligible for this exemption. National Guard and Reserve pay also qualifies.

Financial Data   The first $1,500 received as salary for active-duty service in the U.S. armed forces is deducted from taxable income.

Duration   The exemption is available as long as the recipient resides in Oklahoma and receives salary from the military.

Deadline   Deadline not specified.

[1257]
OREGON INCOME TAX EXEMPTION FOR MILITARY ACTIVE DUTY PAY

Oregon Department of Revenue
Revenue Building
955 Center Street, N.E.
Salem, OR 97310-2551
(503) 378-4988   Toll Free: (800) 356-4222 (within OR)
TDD: (800) 886-7204 (within OR)
Web: www.oregon.gov/DOR/PERTAX

Summary   To exempt a portion of the income of military personnel from state taxation in Oregon.

Eligibility   Eligible are military personnel considered Oregon residents for purposes of state income taxation.

Financial Data   Military pay exempt from state income taxation includes 1) all military active-duty income earned outside Oregon during the year of entry into or discharge from military service; 2) up to $6,000 of active-duty pay earned within Oregon, regardless of other military pay exemptions; and 3) all income earned while serving in a combat zone.

Duration   The exemption continues as long as the recipient resides in Oregon.

Deadline   Exemptions are filed with state income tax returns in April of each year.

[1258]
OREGON INCOME TAX NATIONAL GUARD ACTIVE DUTY PAY SUBTRACTION

Oregon Department of Revenue
Revenue Building
955 Center Street, N.E.
Salem, OR 97310-2551
(503) 378-4988   Toll Free: (800) 356-4222 (within OR)
TDD: (800) 886-7204 (within OR)
Web: www.oregon.gov/DOR/PERTAX

Summary To exempt the income of National Guard members called to active duty from state taxation in Oregon.

Eligibility This exemption is available to members of the Oregon National Guard who served on active duty (under U.S. Code Title 32) in Oregon at any time after January 2001. Applicants must have been called to active duty status (under U.S. Code Title 10).

Financial Data All pay received by members of the Oregon National Guard while on active-duty status (under U.S. Code Title 10) is exempt from state income taxation in Oregon.

Duration The exemption continues as long as the recipient serves on active duty as a member of the Oregon National Guard.

Deadline Exemptions are filed with state income tax returns in April of each year.

[1259]
OREGON PROPERTY TAX EXEMPTION FOR ACTIVE DUTY MILITARY SERVICE

Oregon Department of Revenue
Attn: Property Tax Division
Revenue Building
955 Center Street, N.E.
Salem, OR 97310-2551
(503) 378-4988   Toll Free: (800) 356-4222 (within OR)
TDD: (800) 886-7204 (within OR)
Web: www.oregon.gov/DOR/PTD

Summary To exempt members of the Oregon National Guard and military Reserves called to active duty and their survivors from a portion of their property taxes.

Eligibility This exemption is available to members of the Oregon National Guard and Reserves called to federal active duty (U.S. Code Title 10) who serve more than 178 days with that status during the tax year. Applicants must own property that they occupy as their primary residence in Oregon. Occupants of a home owned by a qualified Guard member or Reservist who is killed in action also qualify for this exemption.

Financial Data The exemption was set as $60,000 of the homestead property's assessed value as of July 1, 2006. It increases by 3% annually.

Duration 1 year; may be renewed as long as the eligible Guard member or surviving occupant of the home owns and occupies the primary residence.

Additional data This exemption was first available in 2005.

Number awarded Varies each year.

Deadline This exemption is not automatic. Applications must be submitted by March of each year.

[1260]
PENNSYLVANIA INCOME TAX EXEMPTION FOR MILITARY PERSONNEL

Pennsylvania Department of Revenue
Attn: Bureau of Individual Taxes
Department 280600
Harrisburg, PA 17128-0600
(717) 787-8201   Toll Free: (888) PA-TAXES
Fax: (717) 787-2391   TDD: (800) 447-3020
E-mail: parev@revenue.state.pa.us
Web: www.revenue.state.pa.us

Summary To exempt from state taxation the income received by Pennsylvania residents for military service outside the state.

Eligibility Eligible are military personnel considered to be Pennsylvania residents for the purposes of state income taxation. Reservists and National Guard members ordered to active duty for training are also eligible.

Financial Data All military pay earned on active duty outside of Pennsylvania or while on federal active duty for training outside of Pennsylvania is not taxable.

Duration The exemption continues as long as the recipient resides in Pennsylvania.

Deadline Deadline not specified.

[1261]
PENNSYLVANIA MILITARY FAMILY RELIEF ASSISTANCE PROGRAM

Pennsylvania Department of Military and Veterans Affairs
Attn: Military Family Relief Assistance Program
Building 7-3
Fort Indiantown Gap
Annville, PA 17003-5002
(717) 861-6288   Toll Free: (866) 292-7201
Fax: (717) 861-2389   E-mail: ra-pa-mfrap@state.pa.us
Web: www.milvet.state.pa.us/DMVA/541.htm

Summary To provide emergency financial assistance to members of the armed forces from Pennsylvania and their families.

Eligibility This assistance is available to residents of Pennsylvania who are serving 1) on 30 or more consecutive days of active duty with the Pennsylvania Army or Air National Guard or Reserve components of the armed forces; 2) on 30 or more consecutive days of active duty with the active armed forces; or 3) on 30 or more consecutive days of state active duty for emergencies or duty under the Emergency Management Assistance Compact in the Pennsylvania Army or Air National Guard. Families of qualifying servicemembers are also eligible if they are Pennsylvania residents. Applicants must be able to demonstrate a direct and immediate financial need as a result of military service; that financial need may include, but is not limited to, a sudden or unexpected loss of income directly related to military service; emergency need for child care for which the applicant lacks financial resources; natural or man-made disasters resulting in a need for food, shelter, or other necessities; or the death or critical illness of a parent, spouse, sibling, or child resulting in immediate need for travel, lodging, or subsistence for which the applicant lacks financial resources.

Financial Data The maximum grant is $2,500.

Duration Only 1 grant will be awarded in each 12-month period.

Additional data This program was established in 2005.

Number awarded Varies each year.

Deadline Applications may be submitted at any time.

[1262]
RED CROSS EMERGENCY FINANCIAL ASSISTANCE

American Red Cross
c/o National Headquarters
2025 E Street, N.W.
Washington, DC 20006
(202) 303-4498   Toll Free: (800) HELP-NOW
Web: www.redcross.org

Summary To provide funding to active and retired military personnel and their families who are in need of emergency financial assistance.

Eligibility This program is open to servicemembers, their families, retired military personnel, and widows of retired military personnel. Members of the National Guard and Reserves are also eligible. Applicants must be in need of such emergency financial assistance as travel that requires the presence of the servicemember or his or her family, burial of a loved one, or other assistance that cannot wait until the next business day (food, temporary lodging, urgent medical needs, or the minimum amount required to avoid eviction or utility shut-off).

Financial Data The amount of the assistance depends on the need of the recipient.

Duration These are 1-time grants.

Additional data The Red Cross works with the military aid societies (Army Emergency Relief, Navy-Marine Corps Relief Society, Air Force Aid Society, and Coast Guard Mutual Assistance).

Number awarded Varies each year; recently, more than 5,000 servicemembers and their families received more than $5.3 million in emergency grants.

Deadline Applications may be submitted at any time.

[1263]
SENTINELS OF FREEDOM SCHOLARSHIPS

Sentinels of Freedom
P.O. Box 1316
San Ramon, CA 94583
(925) 353-7100   Fax: (925) 353-3900
E-mail: info@sentinelsoffreedom.org
Web: www.sentinelsoffreedom.org

Summary To provide funding to veterans and current military personnel who became disabled as a result of injuries sustained in the line of duty on or after September 11, 2001.

Eligibility This program is open to members of the U.S. Air Force, Army, Coast Guard, Marines, or Navy who sustained injuries in the line of duty on or after September 11, 2001. Applicants must be rated as 60% or more disabled as a result of 1 or more of the following conditions: amputation, blindness, deafness, paraplegia, severe burns, limited traumatic brain injury (TBI), or limited post-traumatic stress disorder (PTSD); other severe injuries may be considered on a case-by-case basis. They must complete an interview process and demonstrate that they have the skills, experience, and attitude that lead to employment.

Financial Data Assistance is available for the following needs: housing (adapted for physical needs if necessary), new furniture and other household supplies, career-placement assistance and training, new adaptive vehicles, educational opportunities in addition to the new GI Bill, or financial and personal mentorship.

Duration Assistance may be provided for up to 4 years.

Additional data The first assistance granted by this program was awarded in 2004.

Number awarded Varies each year. Since the program was established, it has supported 32 current and former service members.

Deadline Applications may be submitted at any time.

[1264]
SOLDIERS' AND SAILORS' CIVIL RELIEF ACT

Department of Veterans Affairs
Attn: Veterans Benefits Administration
810 Vermont Avenue, N.W.
Washington, D.C. 20420
(202) 418-4343   Toll Free: (800) 827-1000
Web: www.va.gov

Summary To provide financial protection and relief to civilians who are mobilized into the military Reserves.

Eligibility When Reservists are mobilized into the military, they automatically become eligible for the benefits offered under this legislation.

Financial Data During the recipient's period of active duty, the interest rate on credit cards and mortgages is reduced to a fixed rate of 6%. The difference between the note rate and the 6% is forgiven and not added back on the loan balance. Further, borrowers can ask the courts to postpone completely any mortgage payments while they are on active duty. If the stay is granted, the

loan balance—plus accrued interest at 6%—is reamortized over the total of the remaining loan term plus time spent on active duty. Foreclosures cannot be started or continued against an eligible servicemember. Other benefits include protection from eviction if rent is $1,200 or less, delay of all civil court actions (bankruptcy, foreclosure, divorce), protection against paying taxes in both the home state and the state in which stationed, exemption from personal property taxes (such as an annual property tax on value of an automobile but not real estate taxes) if assigned to a state other than domicile.

Duration The relief begins when the individual receives orders to report for active duty and ends 3 months after separation from active duty.

Additional data This program began in 1940. The provisions regarding terms, stays, and foreclosures can be altered in 2 ways: 1) by written agreement between the lender and the borrower and 2) by either the borrower or the lender applying to the courts for relief.

Number awarded Varies; recently, approximately 50,000 Reservists could qualify for these benefits.

Deadline Deadline not specified.

[1265]
SOUTH CAROLINA MILITARY FAMILY RELIEF FUND

South Carolina Division of Veterans Affairs
Attn: SCMFRF Coordinator
1205 Pendleton Street, Suite 477
Columbia, SC 29201-3789
(803) 734-0200   Fax: (803) 734-0197
E-mail: va@oepp.sc.gov
Web: www.govoepp.state.sc.us/va/benefits.html

Summary To provide emergency assistance to members and families of the National Guard and Reserve forces in South Carolina who have been called to active duty as a result of the September 11, 2001 terrorist attacks.

Eligibility This assistance is available to families of South Carolina National Guard members and South Carolina residents serving in the U.S. armed forces reserve units who were called to active duty as a result of the September 11, 2001 terrorist attacks. Status-based grants are available to National Guard and Reserve members and their family members enrolled in the Defense Enrollment Eligibility Reporting System (DEERS); the servicemember must have been on active duty for at least 30 consecutive days, have a rank no higher than O-3 or W-2, and have orders for Operation Nobel Eagle, Enduring Freedom, Iraqi Freedom, Executive Order 13223, or other approved operation. Need-based grants are available to servicemembers and their families who meet those requirements and who also can demonstrate that the servicemember sustained a 30% or greater decrease in income from his or her civilian salary. Casualty-based grants are available to servicemembers who sustained a service-connected injury or illness and to next of kin of servicemembers killed in action, missing in action, or a prisoner of war. The following servicemembers are ineligible: those who are unmarried or have no family members enrolled in DEERS; personnel serving in active Guard, Reserve, or similar full-time unit support programs but not called to Title 10 service; and members who receive a discharge under other than honorable conditions.

Financial Data Status grants are $500; need-based grants range up to $2,000; casualty-based grants are $1,000.

Duration Status grants are available only once in each fiscal year and only 1 time for each active-duty order; need-based grants may be renewed after 180 days have elapsed; casualty-based grants may be awarded only 1 time for each active-duty order.

Additional data This program, which began in 2005, is funded by a voluntary check-off on South Carolina individual income tax forms and by other grants and donations.

Number awarded Varies each year.

Deadline Applications may be submitted at any time.

[1266]
SOUTH CAROLINA NATIONAL GUARD AND RESERVE ANNUAL TRAINING AND DRILL PAY EXEMPTION

South Carolina Department of Revenue
301 Gervais Street
P.O. Box 125
Columbia, SC 29214
(803) 898-5000   Toll Free: (800) 763-1295
Fax: (803) 898-5822
Web: www.sctax.org

Summary To exempt the pay received by military Reserve and National Guard members from state taxation in South Carolina.

Eligibility This exemption is available to members of the military Reserves and National Guard in South Carolina who receive income for weekend drills and customary training (normally 1 weekend per month and 2 weeks per year). Military personnel on active duty or assigned to the Reserves on a full-time basis are not eligible.

Financial Data Qualified Reserve and Guard income is exempt from state income taxation in South Carolina.

Duration The exemption continues as long as the eligible Reserve or Guard member resides in South Carolina and receives the specified income.

Number awarded Varies each year.

Deadline Deadline not specified.

[1267]
SPECIAL HOUSING ADAPTATIONS GRANTS

Department of Veterans Affairs
Attn: Specially Adapted Housing
810 Vermont Avenue, N.W.
Washington, DC 20420
(202) 461-9546   Toll Free: (800) 827-1000
Web: www.homeloans.va.gov/sah.htm

Summary To provide grants to certain disabled veterans or servicemembers who wish to make adaptations to their home to meet their needs.

Eligibility These grants are available to veterans and servicemembers who are entitled to compensation for permanent and total service-connected disability due to: 1) blindness in both eyes with 5/200 visual acuity or less; 2) the anatomical loss or loss of use of both hands; or 3) a severe burn injury. Applicants must be planning to 1) adapt a house which they plan to purchase and in which they intend to reside; 2) adapt a house which a member of their family plans to purchase and in which they intend to reside; 3) adapt a house which they already own and in which they intend to reside; 4) adapt a house which is already owned by a member of their family in which they intend to reside; or 5) purchase a house that has already been adapted with special features that are reasonable necessary because of their disability and in which they intend to reside.

Financial Data Eligible veterans and servicemembers are entitled to grants up to $12,756 to adapt a house.

Duration Eligible veterans and servicemembers are entitled to up to 3 usages of these grants.

Number awarded Varies each year.

Deadline Applications are accepted at any time.

[1268]
SPECIALLY ADAPTED HOUSING GRANTS

Department of Veterans Affairs
Attn: Specially Adapted Housing
810 Vermont Avenue, N.W.
Washington, DC 20420
(202) 461-9546   Toll Free: (800) 827-1000
Web: www.homeloans.va.gov/sah.htm

Summary To provide loans, grants, and loan guaranties to certain disabled veterans and servicemembers for a home specially adapted to their needs.

Eligibility These grants are available to veterans and servicemembers who are entitled to compensation for permanent and total service-connected disability due to: 1) the loss or loss of use of both lower extremities, such as to preclude locomotion without the aid of braces, crutches, canes, or a wheelchair; or 2) blindness in both eyes, having only light perception, plus loss or loss of use of 1 lower extremity; or 3) a loss or loss of use of 1 lower extremity together with residuals of organic disease or injury or the loss or loss of use of 1 upper extremity, such as to preclude locomotion without resort to braces, canes, crutches, or a wheelchair. Applicants must be planning to 1) construct a home on land to be acquired for that purpose; 2) build a home on land already owned if it is suitable for specially adapted housing; 3) remodel an existing home if it can be made suitable for specially adapted housing, or 4) apply funds against the unpaid principle mortgage balance of a specially adapted home that has already been acquired.

Financial Data The U.S. Department of Veterans Affairs (VA) may approve a grant of not more than 50% of the cost of building, buying, or remodeling homes for eligible veterans, or paying indebtedness of such homes already acquired, up to a maximum grant of $63,780. Eligible veterans with available loan guarantee entitlements may also obtain a guaranteed loan from the VA to supplement the grant to acquire a specially adapted home. If private financing is not available, VA may make a direct loan up to $33,000 to cover the difference between the total cost of the home and the grant.

Duration This is a 1-time grant, guaranteed loan, or direct loan.

Additional data Veterans who receive a specially adapted housing grant may be eligible for Veterans Mortgage Life Insurance.

Number awarded Varies each year.

Deadline Applications are accepted at any time.

[1269]
TROOPS-TO-TEACHERS PROGRAM

Defense Activity for Non-Traditional Education Support
Attn: Troops to Teachers
6490 Sauffley Field Road
Pensacola, FL 32509-5243
(850) 452-1241   Toll Free: (800) 231-6242
Fax: (850) 452-1096   E-mail: ttt@navy.mil
Web: www.dantes.doded.mil

Summary To provide a bonus to veterans and military personnel interested in a second career as a public school teacher.

Eligibility This program is open to 1) active-duty military personnel who are retired, have an approved date of retirement within 1 year, or separated on or after January 8, 2002 for physical disability; 2) members of a Reserve component who are retired, currently serving in the Selected Reserve with 10 or more years of credible service and commit to serving an additional 3 years, separated on or after January 8, 2002 due to a physical disability, or transitioned from active duty on or after January 8, 2002 after at least 6 years on active duty and commit to 3 years with a Selected Reserve unit. Applicants must have a baccalaureate or advanced degree, the equivalent of 1 year of college with 6 years of work experience in a vocational or technical field, or meet state requirements for vocational/technical teacher referral. A bonus is available to applicants who are willing to accept employment as a teacher in 1) a school district that has at least 10% of the students from families living below the poverty level, and 2) at a specific school within the district where at least 50% of the students are eligible for the free or reduced cost lunch program or where at least 13.5% of the students have disabilities. A stipend is available to applicants who are willing to accept employment as a teacher at 1) any school within a "high need" district that has at least 20% of the students from families living below the poverty level, or 2) at a specific school where at least 50% of the students are eligible for the free or reduced cost lunch program or at least 13.5% of the students have disabilities, as long as that school is in a district that has between 10% and 20% of students who come from poverty-level families. Preference is given to applicants interested in teaching mathematics, science, or special education.

Financial Data A bonus of $10,000 is awarded to recipients who agree to teach for 3 years in a school that serves a high percentage of students from low-income families. A stipend of $5,000 is awarded to recipients who agree to teach for 3 years in a school located in a "high-need" district; stipend funds are intended to help pay for teacher certification costs.

Duration The bonuses are intended as 1-time grants.

Additional data This program was established in 1994 by the Department of Defense (DoD). In 2000, program oversight and funding were transferred to the U.S. Department of Education, but DoD continues to operate the program. The No Child Left Behind Act of 2001 provided for continuation of the program.

Number awarded Varies each year.

Deadline Deadline not specified.

[1270]
VERMONT INCOME TAX EXEMPTION FOR MILITARY PERSONNEL

Vermont Department of Taxes
133 State Street
Montpelier, VT 05633-1401
(802) 828-2865   Toll Free: (866) 828-2865 (within VT)
Fax: (802) 828-2720   E-mail: indincome@tax.state.vt.us
Web: www.state.vt.us/tax/individual.shtml

Summary To exempt from state taxation the income of military personnel in Vermont.

Eligibility Eligible are military personnel considered Vermont residents for purposes of state income taxation.

Financial Data All full-time, active-duty military pay earned outside of Vermont is exempt from state income taxation.

Duration The exemption continues as long as the recipient resides in Vermont.

Deadline Deadline not specified.

[1271]
VERMONT NATIONAL GUARD INCOME TAX EXEMPTION

Vermont Department of Taxes
133 State Street
Montpelier, VT 05633-1401
(802) 828-2865   Toll Free: (866) 828-2865 (within VT)
Fax: (802) 828-2720   E-mail: indincome@tax.state.vt.us
Web: www.state.vt.us/tax/individual.shtml

Summary To exempt from state taxation a portion of the income of members of the Vermont National Guard and Reserve units of the armed forces.

Eligibility This exemption is available to National Guard and armed forces Reserve personnel in Vermont who 1) were enlisted for the full calendar year, 2) attended all training assemblies for their unit during the training year, and 3) had a federal adjusted gross income of less than $50,000 in the prior tax year.

Financial Data The first $2,000 of military pay for training assemblies is exempt from state income taxation.

Duration The exemption continues as long as the recipient resides in Vermont.

Deadline Deadline not specified.

[1272]
VFW UNMET NEEDS PROGRAM GRANTS

Veterans of Foreign Wars of the United States
Attn: VFW Foundation
Unmet Needs Program
406 West 34th Street, Suite 514
Kansas City, MO 64111
Toll Free: (866) 789-NEED   Fax: (816) 968-2779
E-mail: unmetneeds@vfw.org
Web: www.unmetneeds.com

Summary To provide assistance to military personnel and their families who are facing special circumstances.

Eligibility This assistance is available to members of the 5 branches of service (Army, Navy, Air Force, Marines, and Coast Guard) as well as members of the Reserves and National Guard. Applicants must have served on active duty within the past 3 years. They must be able to demonstrate need for assistance not available from other sources. Examples of needs that may be met include medical bills, prescriptions, and eyeglasses; household expenses (mortgage, rent, repairs, insurance); vehicle expenses (payments, insurance, repairs); utilities; food and clothing; or children's clothing, diapers, formula, or school or childcare expenses.

Financial Data Most grants are less than $1,500.

Duration These are 1-time grants.

Additional data This program was established in 2004 with support from Vermont American Power Tools Accessories.

Number awarded Varies each year. Since this program was established, it has awarded 1,146 grants with a value of $1,640,308.

Deadline Applications may be submitted at any time.

[1273]
VIRGINIA BASIC MILITARY PAY INCOME TAX EXEMPTION

Virginia Department of Taxation
Attn: Office of Customer Services
3600 West Broad Street
P.O. Box 1115
Richmond, VA 23218-1115
(804) 367-8031   Fax: (804) 367-2537
Web: www.tax.virginia.gov

Summary To subtract a portion of the income received by military personnel from state income taxation in Virginia.

Eligibility This subtraction is available to residents of Virginia (as defined by federal income tax law) who receive basic military pay. Applicants must have served on active duty for 90 days or more during the year. They may be stationed inside or outside of Virginia.

Financial Data Up to $15,000 of basic military pay may be exempted from Virginia income tax. The exemption is reduced when military pay exceeds $15,000 and is fully phased out when pay reaches $30,000.

Duration The exemption is available as long as the taxpayer remains a resident of Virginia and receives military pay.

Number awarded Varies each year.

Deadline The request for an exemption is filed with the state income tax return in April of each year.

[1274]
VIRGINIA NATIONAL GUARD INCOME TAX SUBTRACTION

Virginia Department of Taxation
Attn: Office of Customer Services
3600 West Broad Street
P.O. Box 1115
Richmond, VA 23218-1115
(804) 367-8031   Fax: (804) 367-2537
Web: www.tax.virginia.gov

Summary To subtract a portion of the income received by members of the income received by members of the Virginia National Guard from state income taxation.

Eligibility This subtraction is available to members of the Virginia National Guard at the military rank of O3 (captain) or below. Applicants must have received income for active or inactive service in the Guard.

Financial Data Eligible members of the Guard are allowed to subtract income received for up to 39 days of service or $3,000, whichever is less, from their income for purposes of state taxation in Virginia.

Duration The subtraction is available as long as the Guard member receives income for service in Virginia.

Number awarded Varies each year.

Deadline The request for an exemption is filed with the state income tax return in April of each year.

[1275]
WEST VIRGINIA INCOME TAX EXEMPTION FOR ACTIVE DUTY MILITARY PAY

West Virginia State Tax Department
Attn: Taxpayer Services Division
P.O. Box 3784
Charleston, WV 25337-3784
(304) 558-3333   Toll Free: (800) WVA-TAXS (within WV)
Fax: (304) 558-3269   TDD: (800) 282-9833
Web: www.wva.state.wv.us/wvtax/default.aspx

Summary To exempt the income received by members of the National Guard or armed forces Reserves in West Virginia serving on active duty from state taxation.

Eligibility This exemption is available to residents of West Virginia who are Members of the National Guard or armed forces Reserves called to active duty pursuant to an Executive Order of the President of the United States.

Financial Data Qualifying income is not subject to taxation in West Virginia.

Duration The exemption continues as long as the Guard or Reserves members remain on active duty.

Deadline Deadline not specified.

[1276]
WISCONSIN INCOME TAX EXEMPTION FOR NATIONAL GUARD AND RESERVE PAY

Wisconsin Department of Revenue
Attn: Division of Income, Sales and Excise Tax
2135 Rimrock Road
P.O. Box 8933
Madison, WI 53708-8933
(608) 266-2772   Fax: (608) 267-0834
E-mail: income@revenue.wi.gov
Web: www.revenue.wi.gov

Summary To exempt from state taxation the income received by members of the National Guard and Reserves in Wisconsin who are serving on active duty.

Eligibility This exemption is available to residents of Wisconsin who are serving in the National Guard or Reserves. Applicants must have been called into active federal service or special state service.

Financial Data All pay received for active service in the National Guard or Reserves is exempt from state income taxation in Wisconsin.

Duration The exemption is available for all active-duty pay received by residents of Wisconsin.

Additional data This exemption was first available in 2004. The exemption does not apply to pay received for weekend or 2-week annual training.

Number awarded Varies each year.

Deadline Income tax returns must be filed by April of each year.

[1277]
WYOMING MILITARY ASSISTANCE TRUST FUND GRANTS

Wyoming Military Department
Attn: State Family Program Coordinator
5500 Bishop Boulevard
Cheyenne, WY 82009
(307) 772-5208   Fax: (307) 772-5330
Web: www.wy.ngb.army.mil/trust-fund

Summary To provide emergency assistance to residents of Wyoming who are facing financial difficulties because a family member has been deployed to active military service.

Eligibility This assistance is available to 1) members of the Wyoming National Guard or Reserve units based in Wyoming who have been called to active duty or active state service; 2) Wyoming residents who are members of a military Reserve unit not based in Wyoming, if the member has been called to active service; 3) other Wyoming residents performing service in the uniformed forces for any branch of the military of the United States; and 4) members of the immediate family (spouses, children, and dependent parents, grandparents, siblings, stepchildren, and adult children) of those military personnel. Applicants must be facing financial hardship resulting from the military member's active-duty status.

Financial Data The amount of the grant depends on the need of the recipient.

Duration These are 1-time grants.

Additional data The Wyoming Legislature created this fund in 2004. These funds may not be used to replace other funds available from public or private sources.

Number awarded Varies each year. Recently, $300,000 was available for this program.

Deadline Applications may be submitted at any time.

Family Members

[1278]
AER LOANS/GRANTS

Army Emergency Relief
200 Stovall Street
Alexandria, VA 22332-0600
(703) 428-0000   Toll Free: (866) 878-6378
Fax: (703) 325-7183   E-mail: aer@aerhq.org
Web: www.aerhq.org

Summary To provide loans and grants-in-aid to help with the emergency financial needs of Army veterans, military personnel, and their dependents.

Eligibility Eligible to apply are active-duty soldiers (single or married) and their dependents, Army National Guard and Army Reserve soldiers on continuous active duty for more than 30 days and their dependents, soldiers retired from active duty for longevity or physical disability and their dependents, Army National Guard and Army Reserve soldiers who retired at age 60 and their dependents, and surviving spouses and orphans of soldiers who died while on active duty or after they retired. Applicants must be seeking assistance for such emergency needs as food, rent, and utilities; emergency transportation and vehicle repair; funeral expenses; medical and dental expenses; or personal needs when pay is delayed or stolen. Support is not available to help pay for nonessentials, finance ordinary leave or vacation, pay fines or legal expenses, help liquidate or consolidate debt, assist with house purchase or home improvements, cover bad checks, pay credit card bills, or help purchase, rent, or lease a vehicle.

Financial Data Support is provided in the form of loans or grants (or a combination).

Duration Qualifying individuals can apply whenever they have a valid emergency need.

Additional data This organization was established in 1942.

Number awarded Varies each year; recently, the organization helped more than 66,000 Army people with more than $70 million, including $60 million to 58,820 active-duty soldiers and their families, $7.3 million to 4,914 retired soldiers and their families, and $2.7 million to 2,304 widow(er)s and orphans of deceased soldiers. Since it was established, the organization has helped more than 3.2 million qualifying individuals with more than $1.2 billion in financial assistance.

Deadline Applications may be submitted at any time.

[1279]
AFAS FINANCIAL ASSISTANCE

Air Force Aid Society
Attn: Financial Assistance Department
241 18th Street South, Suite 202
Arlington, VA 22202-3409
(703) 607-3072, ext. 51   Toll Free: (800) 429-9475
Fax: (703) 607-3022
Web: www.afas.org/Assistance/HowWeCanHelp.cfm

Summary To provide loans and grants-in-aid to current and former Air Force personnel and their families who are facing emergency situations.

Eligibility This program is open to active-duty Air Force members and their dependents, retired Air Force personnel and their dependents, Air National Guard and Air Force Reserve personnel on extended duty over 15 days, and spouses and dependent children of deceased Air Force personnel who died on active duty or in retired status. Applicants must be facing problems, usually for relatively short periods, that affect their job or the essential quality and dignity of life the Air Force wants for its people. Examples of such needs include basic living expenses (food, rent, utilities), medical and dental care, funeral expenses, vehicle expenses, emergency travel, moving expenses, or child or respite care. Funding is generally not provided if it merely postpones a long-term inability to exist on present pay and allowances, for nonessentials, for continuing long-term assistance commitments, or to replace funds lost due to garnishment.

Financial Data Assistance is provided as an interest-free loan, a grant, or a combination of both.

Number awarded Varies each year.

Deadline Applications may be submitted at any time.

[1280]
AFAS RESPITE CARE

Air Force Aid Society
Attn: Financial Assistance Department
241 18th Street South, Suite 202
Arlington, VA 22202-3409
(703) 607-3072, ext. 51   Toll Free: (800) 429-9475
Fax: (703) 607-3022
Web: www.afas.org/Community/RespireCareProgram.cfm

Summary To provide financial assistance to Air Force personnel and their families who have a family member with special needs.

Eligibility This program is open to active-duty Air Force members and their families who are responsible for 24 hour a day care for an ill or disabled family member (child, spouse, or parent) living in the household. Applicants must be referred by the Exceptional Family Member Program (EFMP) or the Family Advocacy Office. Selection is based on need, both financial need and the need of the family for respite time.

Financial Data Assistance is provided as a grant that depends on the needs of the family.

Number awarded Varies each year.

Deadline Applications may be submitted at any time.

[1281]
AIR WARRIOR COURAGE FOUNDATION GRANTS

Air Warrior Courage Foundation
P.O. Box 1553
Front Royal, VA 22630-0033
(540) 636-9798   Fax: (540) 636-9776
E-mail: awcf@awcfoundation.com
Web: www.airwarriorcourage.org

Summary To provide emergency assistance to veterans, military personnel, and their families, especially members of the Red River Valley Fighter Pilots Association (RRVA), who are facing unusual situations.

Eligibility These grants are available to active, Guard, Reserve, retired, and former military and Coast Guard personnel and dependent family members. Applicants must be able to demonstrate financial and material needs unmet by insurance programs, community support, or other service agencies. Special consideration is given to applicants eligible for the RRVA scholarship program (spouses and children of servicemembers missing in action or killed in action in armed conflicts by U.S. forces since August 1964, of U.S. military aircrew members killed in a non-combat aircraft accident in which they were performing aircrew duties, and of current members of the association). Assistance is available through the following activities: the 9/11 Terrorism Memorial Fund, which provides financial assistance, college savings programs, and/or material support to surviving family members of those lost or injured in the war on terror and military units performing humanitarian activities worldwide; the Earl Aman Courage Fund, which provides assistance or equipment to those disabled or in need for medically-related extraordinary expenses; and the Helping Achieve Normal Development (HAND) Fund, which provides assistance for therapeutic activities to children with anatomical, physiological, or mental deficits. Other programs are established from time to time as needs arise.

Financial Data The amount awarded varies. Recent grants included $148,744 for servicemember victims of Hurricanes Katrina and Rita; the Earl Aman Courage Fund awarded a total of $38,400 to provide financial support to veterans and/or their families to meet extraordinary medical or personal expenses beyond their financial resources; and the HAND Fund awarded $41,550 to provide therapeutic riding programs for 88 medically challenged military dependent children.

Duration These are 1-time grants.

Additional data This foundation was established in 1998 as a charitable organization affiliated with the RRVA.

Number awarded Varies each year.

Deadline Applications may be submitted at any time.

[1282]
ALABAMA AD VALOREM TAX EXEMPTION FOR SPECIALLY ADAPTED HOUSES

Alabama Department of Revenue
Attn: Property Tax Division
Gordon Persons Building
50 North Ripley Street, Room 4126
P.O. Box 327210
Montgomery, AL 36132-7210
(334) 242-1525
Web: www.ador.state.al.us

Summary To provide a property tax exemption to the owners of specially adapted housing (housing adapted for disabled veterans) in Alabama.

Eligibility The home of any veteran which is or was acquired pursuant to the provisions of Public Law 702, 80th Congress (specially adapted housing grants for veterans) as amended (38 USC) will be exempted from ad valorem taxation if the house is owned and occupied by the veteran or the veteran's unremarried widow(er).

Financial Data Qualifying houses are exempt from all ad valorem taxation.

Duration This exemption continues as long as the qualifying veteran or the unremarried widow(er) resides in the house.

Number awarded Varies each year.

Deadline Deadline not specified.

[1283]
ALABAMA MILITARY RETIREE INCOME TAX EXEMPTION

Alabama Department of Revenue
Attn: Income Tax Division
Gordon Persons Building
50 North Ripley Street, Room 4212
P.O. Box 327410
Montgomery, AL 36132-7410
(334) 242-1105   Fax: (334) 242-0064
E-mail: erohelpdesk@revenue.state.al.us
Web: www.ador.state.al.us

Summary To exempt a portion of the income of veterans and their survivors from taxation in Alabama.

Eligibility Eligible are Alabama recipients of regular military retired pay or military survivors benefits. Recipients of benefits paid by the U.S. Department of Veterans Affairs (including disability retirement payments) are also eligible for this exemption.

Financial Data All income received as military retired pay, veterans' disability payment, or military survivors benefits is exempt from state, county, or municipal income taxation.

Duration The exemption continues as long as the recipient resides in Alabama.

Deadline Deadline not specified.

[1284]
AMERICAN LEGION AUXILIARY EMERGENCY FUND

American Legion Auxiliary
8945 North Meridian Street
Indianapolis, IN 46260
(317) 569-4500   Fax: (317) 569-4502
E-mail: alahq@legion-aux.org
Web: www.legion-aux.org

Summary To provide funding to members of the American Legion Auxiliary who are facing temporary emergency needs.

Eligibility This program is open to members of the American Legion Auxiliary who have maintained their membership for the immediate past 2 consecutive years and have paid their dues for the current year. Applicants must need emergency assistance for the following purposes: 1) food, shelter, and utilities during a time of financial crisis; 2) food and shelter because of weather-related emergencies and natural disasters; or 3) educational training because of the death of a spouse, divorce, separation, or the need to become the main source of support for their family. They must have exhausted all other sources of financial assistance, including funds and/or services available through the local Post and/or Unit, appropriate community welfare agencies, or state and federal financial aid for education. Grants are not available to settle already existing or accumulated debts, handle catastrophic illness, resettle disaster victims, or other similar problems.

Financial Data The maximum grant is $2,400. Payments may be made directly to the member or to the mortgage company or utility. Educational grants may be paid directly to the educational institution.

Duration Grants are expended over no more than 3 months.

Additional data This program was established in 1969. In 1981, it was expanded to include the Displaced Homemaker Fund (although that title is no longer used).

Number awarded Varies each year.

Deadline Applications may be submitted at any time.

[1285]
ARIZONA NATIONAL GUARD EMERGENCY RELIEF FUND GRANTS

Arizona National Guard Emergency Relief Fund
Attn: Fund Administrator
5636 East McDowell Road
Phoenix, AZ 85008
(602) 267-2731   E-mail: danielle.salomon@azdema.gov
Web: www.aerfund.org

Summary To provide emergency assistance (loans and grants) to members of the Arizona National Guard and their families.

Eligibility This program is open to members of the Arizona Army and Air National Guard who have not been mobilized under Presidential Order. Surviving spouses, children, and orphans of soldiers who died while on active duty are also eligible. Applicants must be seeking assistance for such emergency needs as delay in receiving pay or reimbursement from the government; temporary shelter, lodging, or rent; emergency utility assistance; emergency transportation and vehicle repair; costs incurred for emergency travel due to death of immediate family member; or any other special circumstance deemed appropriate by the fund's directors. Support is not provided to help pay for nonessentials, finance ordinary leave or vacation, pay fines or legal expenses, assist with home purchase or improvements, cover bad checks, or help purchase, rent, or lease a vehicle.

Financial Data Most support is provided in the form of interest-free loans, although outright grants are also available.

Duration These are 1-time grants.

Number awarded Varies each year.

Deadline Applications may be submitted at any time.

[1286]
ARIZONA NATIONAL GUARD FAMILY ASSISTANCE FUND

Arizona National Guard Emergency Relief Fund
Attn: Fund Administrator
5636 East McDowell Road
Phoenix, AZ 85008
(602) 267-2731   E-mail: danielle.salomon@azdema.gov
Web: www.aerfund.org

Summary To provide emergency assistance (loans and grants) to members of the Arizona Reserve Component who have been mobilized and their families.

Eligibility This program is open to members of the Arizona Reserve Component (including the Army and Air National Guard and Reserve units of all 5 branches of service) and their dependents. They must have been mobilized under Presidential Order.

Surviving spouses, children, and orphans of soldiers who died while on active duty are also eligible. Applicants must be seeking assistance for such emergency needs as delay in receiving pay or reimbursement from the government; temporary shelter, lodging, or rent; emergency utility assistance; emergency transportation and vehicle repair; costs incurred for emergency travel due to death of immediate family member; or any other special circumstance deemed appropriate by the fund's directors. Support is not provided to help pay for nonessentials, financial ordinary leave or vacation, pay fines or legal expenses, assist with home purchase or improvements, cover bad checks, or help purchase, rent, or lease a vehicle.

Financial Data Most support is provided in the form of interest-free loans, although outright grants are also available.

Duration These are awarded on a 1-time basis.

Number awarded Varies each year.

Deadline Applications may be submitted at any time.

[1287]
ARKANSAS DISABLED VETERANS PROPERTY TAX EXEMPTION

Arkansas Assessment Coordination Department
1614 West Third Street
Little Rock, AR 72201-1815
(501) 324-9100   Fax: (501) 324-9242
E-mail: dasbury@acd.state.ar.us
Web: www.arkansas.gov/acd

Summary To exempt from taxation the property owned by blind or disabled veterans, surviving spouses, and minor dependent children in Arkansas.

Eligibility This program is open to disabled veterans in Arkansas who have been awarded special monthly compensation by the U.S. Department of Veterans Affairs and who have 1) the loss of or the loss of use of 1 or more limbs, 2) total blindness in 1 or both eyes, or 3) total and permanent disability. The benefit also extends to veterans' unremarried surviving spouses and their minor children.

Financial Data Qualifying veterans (or their unremarried widows or dependent children) are exempt from payment of all state taxes on their homestead and personal property.

Duration This exemption continues as long as the qualifying veteran (or dependent) resides in Arkansas.

Number awarded Varies each year.

Deadline Applications may be submitted at any time.

[1288]
CALIFORNIA DISABLED VETERAN EXEMPTION FROM THE IN LIEU TAX FEE FOR A MANUFACTURED HOME OR MOBILEHOME

Department of Housing and Community Development
Attn: Registration and Titling
1800 Third Street
P.O. Box 2111
Sacramento, CA 95812-2111
(916) 323-9224   Toll Free: (800) 952-8356
Web: www.hcd.ca.gov

Summary To provide a special property tax exemption to blind or disabled California veterans and/or their spouses who own and occupy a mobile home.

Eligibility This program is open to disabled veterans and/or their spouses in California who have a manufactured home or mobile home as their principal place of residence. Veterans must be disabled as a result of injury or disease incurred in military service and have been a resident of California 1) at the time of entry into the service and be blind, or have lost the use of 1 or more limbs, or be totally disabled; 2) on November 7, 1972 and be blind in both eyes, or have lost the use of 2 or more limbs; or 3) on January 1, 1975 and be totally disabled. The spouses and unremar-

ried surviving spouses of those disabled veterans are also eligible.

Financial Data The exemption applies to the first $20,000 of the assessed market value of the manufactured home or mobile home. Veterans and/or spouses whose income falls below a specified level are entitled to an additional $10,000 exemption. The amount of the exemption is 100% if the home is owned by a veteran only, a veteran and spouse, or a spouse only; 50% if owned by a veteran and another person other than a spouse or by a spouse and another person other than the veteran; 67% if owned by a veteran, the spouse, and another person; 34% if owned by a veteran and 2 other people other than a spouse or by a spouse and 2 other people; 50% if owned by a veteran, the spouse, and 2 other people; or 25% if owned by a veteran and 3 other people or by a spouse and 3 other people.

Duration The exemption is available annually as long as the applicant meets all requirements.

Number awarded Varies each year.

Deadline Deadline not specified.

[1289]
CALIFORNIA PROPERTY TAX EXEMPTIONS FOR VETERANS

California Department of Veterans Affairs
Attn: Division of Veterans Services
1227 O Street, Room 101
Sacramento, CA 95814
(916) 503-8397   Toll Free: (800) 952-LOAN (within CA)
Fax: (916) 653-2563   TDD: (800) 324-5966
E-mail: ruckergl@cdva.ca.gov
Web: www.cdva.ca.gov/VetService/Overview.aspx

Summary To exempt a portion of the property of blind or disabled veterans in California and their spouses from taxation.

Eligibility This exemption is available to homeowners in California who are wartime veterans in receipt of service-connected disability compensation that is 1) at the totally disabled rate, 2) for loss or loss of use of 2 or more limbs, or 3) for blindness. Unremarried surviving spouses, including registered domestic partners, of veterans who are in receipt of service-connected death benefits are also eligible.

Financial Data For veterans and spouses whose total household income from all sources is greater than $49,979 per year, up to $111,296 of the assessed value of a home is exempt from taxation. For veterans and spouses whose total household income from all sources is less than $49,979 per year, up to $166,944 of the assessed value of a home is exempt from taxation.

Duration The exemption is available as long as the veteran or spouse owns a home in California.

Additional data Information is available from the local county assessors office in each California county.

Number awarded Varies each year.

Deadline Applications may be submitted at any time.

[1290]
CGMA GRANTS-IN-AID

Coast Guard Mutual Assistance
4200 Wilson Boulevard, Suite 610
Arlington, VA 20598-7180
(202) 493-6621   Toll Free: (800) 881-2462
Fax: (202) 493-6686   E-mail: ARL-DG-CGMA@uscg.mil
Web: www.cgmahq.org

Summary To provide funding to members of the Coast Guard Mutual Assistance (CGMA) and their families who need temporary assistance.

Eligibility This program is open to CGMA members who are facing special needs. Categories of aid that are available include emergency assistance (basic living expenses, emergency home repair, emergency travel expenses, fire and other disasters, funeral expenses, loss of funds, temporary living expenses); general assistance (adoption, child support, child care, family in-home day care facility, financial counseling, government travel cards, household furnishings, immigration fees, insurance, loss of income, moving expenses, non-emergency travel, non-support or inadequate support, past due bills and expenses, pay and allotment problems, vehicle repair, vehicle other expenses); housing assistance (payment of settlement charges associated with purchasing a residence, rental assistance, utilities); and medical and dental assistance (provider won't proceed without payment; mental health and family counseling; patient's cost share; durable medical equipment; prosthetic devices; rehabilitation, nursing, home, or respite care; orthodontia; long-term dental care; travel, transportation, and incidental expenses; special situations). Applicants must be able to demonstrate their need for assistance.

Financial Data The assistance depends on the nature of the need.

Duration These are 1-time grants. A new application must accompany each request for assistance.

Additional data CGMA membership is open to active-duty and retired members of the U.S. Coast Guard, civilian employees of the U.S. Coast Guard, U.S. Coast Guard Reserve members, U.S. Coast Guard Auxiliary members, Public Health Service officers serving with the U.S. Coast Guard, and family members of all of those.

Number awarded Varies each year.

Deadline Deadline not specified.

[1291]
CHILDREN OF WOMEN VIETNAM VETERANS ALLOWANCE

Department of Veterans Affairs
Attn: Veterans Benefits Administration
810 Vermont Avenue, N.W.
Washington, DC 20420
(202) 418-4343   Toll Free: (800) 827-1000
Web: www1.va.gov/opa/ls1/11.asp

Summary To provide support to children of female Vietnam veterans who have birth defects.

Eligibility This program is open to biological children of female veterans who served in the Republic of Vietnam and were conceived after the date the veteran first served, which must have been between February 28, 1961 and May 7, 1975. Applicants must have certain birth defects identified as resulting in permanent physical or mental disability. Conditions that are a family disorder, a birth-related injury, or a fetal or neonatal infirmity with well-established causes are not included.

Financial Data Support depends on the degree of disability. The monthly rate for children at the first level is $131, at the second level $286, at the third level $984, or at the fourth level $1,678

Additional data Applications are available from the nearest VA medical center. Recipients are also entitled to vocational training and medical treatment.

Number awarded Varies each year.

Deadline Applications are accepted at any time.

[1292]
COLORADO PROPERTY TAX EXEMPTION FOR DISABLED VETERANS

Division of Veterans Affairs
7465 East First Avenue, Suite C
Denver, CO 80230
(303) 343-1268   Fax: (303) 343-7238
Web: www.dmva.state.co.us/page/va/prop_tax

Summary To provide a partial exemption of taxes on property owned by disabled veterans or their spouses in Colorado.

Eligibility This exemption is open to veterans who reside in Colorado and have been rated 100% service-connected disabled

by the U.S. Department of Veterans Affairs. Applicants must have been dishonorable discharged and must own property in Colorado which they use as their primary residence. The exemption also applies to members of the National Guard or Reserves who sustained their injury during a period in which they were called to active duty, property owned by a veteran's spouse if both occupy the property as their primary residence, and property owned by a trust or other legal entity if the veteran or spouse is a major of the trust or other legal entity, the property was transferred solely for estate planning purposes, and the veteran or spouse would otherwise be the owner of record.

Financial Data For qualifying veterans, 50% of the first $200,000 of actual value of the primary residence is exempted from taxes.

Duration The exemption continues as long as the veteran resides in the property.

Additional data This program was approved by Colorado voters in 2006.

Number awarded Varies each year.

Deadline Applications must be submitted by June of the year for which the exemption is requested.

[1293]
CONNECTICUT NATIONAL GUARD FOUNDATION ASSISTANCE

Connecticut National Guard Foundation, Inc.
Attn: Assistance Committee
360 Broad Street
Hartford, CT 06105-3795
(860) 241-1550   Fax: (860) 293-2929
E-mail: assistance.committee@ctngfoundation.org
Web: www.ctngfoundation.org

Summary To provide emergency and other assistance to members of the Connecticut National Guard and their families.

Eligibility This program is open to members of the Connecticut Army National Guard and Organized Militia, their children under 18 years of age, and their spouses who live with them. Applicants must be in need of assistance for such benefits as clothing, food, medical and surgical aid, and general care and relief. They must be able to demonstrate a need for assistance.

Financial Data Grants depend on the need of the recipient.

Duration These are 1-time grants.

Additional data Applications are available at all State Armories and Family Assistance Centers.

Number awarded Varies each year.

Deadline Applications may be submitted at any time.

[1294]
CONNECTICUT PERSONAL PROPERTY TAX EXEMPTION FOR WARTIME VETERANS

Office of Policy and Management
Attn: Intergovernmental Policy Division
450 Capitol Avenue
Hartford, CT 06106-1308
(860) 418-6278   Toll Free: (800) 286-2214 (within CT)
Fax: (860) 418-6493   TDD: (860) 418-6456
E-mail: leeann.graham@ct.gov
Web: www.ct.gov/opm/cwp/view.asp?a=2985&Q=383132

Summary To exempt wartime veterans and their family members from a portion of their personal property taxes if they are Connecticut residents.

Eligibility Eligible to apply for this exemption are veterans with 90 days of wartime service who are residents of Connecticut. Spouses, minor children, and parents of deceased veterans may also be eligible. An additional exemption may be available to veterans and spouses whose total adjusted gross income is less than $30,500 if unmarried or $37,300 if married. If the veteran is rated as 100% disabled by the U.S. Department of Veterans

Affairs (VA), the maximum income levels are $18,000 if unmarried or $21,000 if married.

Financial Data Property to the amount of $1,000 belonging to, or held in trust for, an eligible veteran is exempt from taxation. The same exemption is available to the surviving unremarried spouse, minor children, and (if there is no surviving unremarried spouse) parent of a deceased veteran. If the death was service-connected and occurred while on active duty, the exemption for a surviving unremarried spouse or minor child is $3,000. Municipalities may provide veterans and spouses with an additional exemption up to $2,000 of the assessed value of the property, provided their income is less than the qualifying level. The additional municipality exemption for spouses and children of veterans who died on active duty of service-connected causes is $6,000. The additional municipality exemptions for veterans and family members who do not meet the income requirements are $500 and $1,500, respectively.

Duration 1 year; exemptions continue as long as the eligible resident lives in Connecticut.

Number awarded Varies each year; recently, a total of 22,944 veterans received property tax exemptions through this and other programs in Connecticut.

Deadline Applications for the additional municipality exemption must be submitted to the assessor's office of the town of residence by September of every other year.

[1295]
CONNECTICUT REAL ESTATE TAX EXEMPTION FOR DISABLED VETERANS

Office of Policy and Management
Attn: Intergovernmental Policy Division
450 Capitol Avenue
Hartford, CT 06106-1308
(860) 418-6278   Toll Free: (800) 286-2214 (within CT)
Fax: (860) 418-6493   TDD: (860) 418-6456
E-mail: leeann.graham@ct.gov
Web: www.ct.gov/opm/cwp/view.asp?a=2985&Q=383132

Summary To exempt Connecticut veterans with disabilities and their surviving spouses from the payment of a portion of their local property taxes.

Eligibility There are 2 categories of Connecticut veterans who qualify for exemptions from their dwelling house and the lot on which it is located: 1) those with major service-connected disabilities (paraplegia or osteochondritis resulting in permanent loss of the use of both legs or permanent paralysis of both legs and lower parts of the body; hemiplegia with permanent paralysis of 1 leg and 1 arm or either side of the body resulting from injury to the spinal cord, skeletal structure, or brain, or from disease of the spinal cord not resulting from syphilis; total blindness; amputation of both arms, both legs, both hands or both feet, or the combination of a hand and a foot; sustained through enemy action or resulting from an accident occurring or disease contracted in such active service) and 2) those with less severe disabilities (loss of use of 1 arm or 1 leg because of service-connected injuries). Surviving unremarried spouses of eligible deceased veterans are entitled to the same exemption as would have been granted to the veteran, as long as they continue to be the legal owner/occupier of the exempted residence. An additional exemption is available to veterans and spouses whose total adjusted gross income is less than $30,500 if unmarried or $37,300 if married. If the veteran is rated as 100% disabled by the U.S. Department of Veterans Affairs (VA), the maximum income levels are $18,000 if unmarried or $21,000 if married.

Financial Data Veterans in the first category receive an exemption from local property taxation of $10,000 of assessed valuation. Veterans in the second category receive exemptions of $5,000 of assessed valuation. For veterans whose income is less than the specified levels, additional exemptions of $20,000 for the first category or $10,000 for the second category are available

from municipalities that choose to participate. For veterans whose income exceeds the specified levels, the additional exemption from participating municipalities is $5,000 for the first category or $2,500 for the second category. Connecticut municipalities may also elect to exempt from taxation specially adapted housing acquired or modified by a veteran under the provisions of Section 801 of Title 38 of the United States Code.

Duration 1 year; exemptions continue as long as the eligible resident (or surviving spouse) owns/occupies the primary residence and lives in Connecticut.

Number awarded Varies each year; recently, a total of 22,944 veterans received property tax exemptions through this and other programs in Connecticut.

Deadline Applications for the additional municipality exemption must be submitted to the assessor's office of the town or residence by September of every other year.

[1296]
CONNECTICUT VETERANS' ADDITIONAL EXEMPTION TAX RELIEF PROGRAM

Office of Policy and Management
Attn: Intergovernmental Policy Division
450 Capitol Avenue
Hartford, CT 06106-1308
(860) 418-6278   Toll Free: (800) 286-2214 (within CT)
Fax: (860) 418-6493   TDD: (860) 418-6456
E-mail: leeann.graham@ct.gov
Web: www.ct.gov/opm/cwp/view.asp?a=2985&Q=383132

Summary To exempt disabled veterans and their surviving spouses who are residents of Connecticut from a portion of their personal property taxes.

Eligibility Eligible to apply for this exemption are Connecticut veterans who are rated as disabled by the U.S. Department of Veterans Affairs (VA). Unremarried surviving spouses of qualified veterans are also eligible. An additional exemption may be available to veterans and spouses whose total adjusted gross income is less than $30,500 if unmarried or $37,300 if married. If the veteran is rated as 100% disabled by the U.S. Department of Veterans Affairs (VA), the maximum income levels are $18,000 if unmarried or $21,000 if married.

Financial Data The amount of the exemption depends on the level of the VA disability rating: for 10% to 25%, it is $1,500; for more than 25% to 50%, $2,000; for more than 50% to 75%, $2,500; for more than 75% and for veterans older than 65 years of age with any level of disability, $3,000. Municipalities may elect to provide an additional exemption, equal to twice the amount provided, to veterans and spouses whose income is less than the qualifying level. For veterans and spouses who do not meet the income requirement, the additional exemption from participating municipalities is equal to 50% of the basic state exemption.

Duration 1 year; exemptions continue as long as the eligible resident lives in Connecticut.

Number awarded Varies each year; recently, a total of 20,117 veterans received property tax exemptions through this and other programs in Connecticut.

Deadline Applications for the additional municipality exemption must be submitted to the assessor's office of the town of residence by September of every other year.

[1297]
DEATH GRATUITY FOR MILITARY PERSONNEL

Department of Veterans Affairs
Attn: Veterans Benefits Administration
810 Vermont Avenue, N.W.
Washington, DC 20420
(202) 418-4343   Toll Free: (800) 827-1000
Web: www1.va.gov/opa/ls1/11.asp

Summary To provide a death gratuity for the surviving spouses and dependents of veterans or military personnel.

Eligibility Dependents of military personnel who die of any cause in active service or within 120 days after leaving active duty from specified causes related to service are entitled to this benefit. Payment will be made to the spouse, children, or, if designated by the deceased, parents, brothers, or sisters.

Financial Data This benefit is $100,000.

Duration This is a 1-time payment.

Additional data The last military command of the deceased pays this benefit. If funds are not received within a reasonable time, application should be made to the service concerned.

Deadline Applications may be submitted at any time.

[1298]
DEATH PENSION FOR SURVIVORS OF VETERANS

Department of Veterans Affairs
Attn: Veterans Benefits Administration
810 Vermont Avenue, N.W.
Washington, DC 20420
(202) 418-4343   Toll Free: (800) 827-1000
Web: www.vba.va.gov/bin/21/pension/spousepen.htm

Summary To provide pensions to disabled and other spouses and children of deceased veterans with wartime service.

Eligibility This program is open to surviving spouses and unmarried children of deceased veterans who were discharged under conditions other than dishonorable and who had at least 90 days of active military service, at least 1 day of which was during a period of war. Veterans who enlisted after September 7, 1980 generally had to have served at least 24 months or the full period for which they were called to active duty. The countable income of spouses and children must be below specified limits.

Financial Data The pension program pays the difference, in 12 monthly installments, between countable income and the specified income level. Currently, those limits are the following: surviving spouse without dependent children, $7,933; surviving spouse with 1 dependent child, $10,385; surviving spouse in need of regular aid and attendance without dependent children, $12,681; surviving spouse in need of regular aid and attendance with 1 dependent child, $15,128; surviving spouse permanently housebound without dependent children, $9,696; surviving spouse permanently housebound with 1 dependent child, $12,144; increase for each additional dependent child, $2,020; surviving children who are living alone, $2,020.

Duration For surviving spouse: until remarriage. For surviving unmarried child: until the age of 18, or 23 if attending a VA-approved school. For surviving child with disability: as long as the condition exists or until marriage.

Number awarded Varies each year.

Deadline Applications may be submitted at any time.

[1299]
DEPENDENCY AND INDEMNITY COMPENSATION (DIC)

Department of Veterans Affairs
Attn: Veterans Benefits Administration
810 Vermont Avenue, N.W.
Washington, DC 20420
(202) 418-4343   Toll Free: (800) 827-1000
Web: www1.va.gov/opa/ls1/11.asp

Summary To provide financial support to the spouses and children of servicemembers and veterans who died of disabilities or other causes.

Eligibility This program is open to dependents (surviving spouses, unmarried children under 18, helpless children, and those between 18 and 23 if attending a VA-approved school) of servicemembers who died while on active duty and veterans whose death resulted from a service-related disease or injury.

Also eligible are spouses and children of veterans whose death resulted from a non service-related injury or disease and who was receiving, or was entitled to receive, compensation from the U.S. Department of Veterans Affairs for a service-connected disability that was rated as totally disabling for at least 10 years immediately preceding death, or since the veteran's release from active duty and for at least 5 years immediately preceding death, or for at least 1 year before death if the veteran was a former prisoner of war who died after September 30, 1999.

Financial Data Surviving spouses of veterans who died after January 1, 1993 receive a flat rate of $1,154 per month, regardless of pay grade. For veterans who died before January 1, 1993, the monthly amount of DIC is based on the deceased veteran's highest military pay grade. Monthly payments range from $1,154 for E-1 to $1,419 for E-9, from $1,219 for W-1 to $1,380 for W-4, and from $1,219 for O-1 to $2,643 for O-10. Additional payments include the following: $246 per month if the veteran had been receiving compensation for a service-connected disability for at least 8 years prior to death and the survivor had been married to the veteran for those 8 years; $286 per month if the recipient requires the aid and attendance of another person; $135 per month if the recipient is housebound; and $286 for each child under 18 years of age.

Duration Monthly payments continue for the life of the surviving spouse and until unmarried children reach the age of 18 (or 23 if disabled or attending a VA-approved school).

Number awarded Varies each year.

Deadline Applications are accepted at any time.

[1300]
FLORIDA SERVICE-CONNECTED TOTAL AND PERMANENT DISABILITY PROPERTY TAX EXEMPTION

Florida Department of Revenue
Attn: Taxpayer Services
1379 Blountstown Highway
Tallahassee, FL 32304-2716
(850) 488-6800   Toll Free: (800) 352-3671
TDD: (800) 367-8331
Web: www.myflorida.com/dor/property/exemptions.html

Summary To exempt from property taxation real estate owned by disabled veterans and their surviving spouses.

Eligibility This exemption is available to Florida residents who have real estate that they own and use as a homestead. Applicants must be honorably-discharged veterans with a service-connected total and permanent disability. Under certain circumstances, the benefit of this exemption can carry over to a surviving spouse.

Financial Data All real estate used and owned as a homestead, less any portion used for commercial purposes, is exempt from taxation.

Duration The exemption applies as long as the taxpayer owns the property in Florida.

Additional data Initial applications should be made in person at the appropriate county property appraiser's office.

Number awarded Varies each year.

Deadline Applications must be submitted by February of the year for which the exemption is sought.

[1301]
GEORGIA HOMESTEAD TAX EXEMPTION FOR DISABLED VETERANS

Georgia Department of Revenue
Attn: Property Tax Division
4245 International Parkway, Suite A
Hapeville, GA 30354-3918
(404) 968-0707   Fax: (404) 968-0778
E-mail: Local.Government.Services@dor.ga.gov
Web: etax.dor.ga.gov

Summary   To exempt from property taxation a portion of the value of homesteads owned by disabled veterans in Georgia and their families.

Eligibility   This program is open to residents of Georgia who qualify as a 100% disabled veteran under any of several provisions of state law. Surviving spouses and minor children are also eligible. Applicants must actually occupy a homestead and use it as their legal residence for all purposes.

Financial Data   The first $50,000 of assessed valuation of the homestead owned by disabled veterans or their family members is exempt from property taxes for state, county, municipal, and school purposes.

Duration   The exemption remains in effect as long as the veteran or family member owns and resides in the homestead.

Number awarded   Varies each year.

Deadline   Applications must be filed with local tax officials by February of each year.

[1302]
GEORGIA HOMESTEAD TAX EXEMPTION FOR SURVIVING SPOUSES OF U.S. SERVICE MEMBERS

Georgia Department of Revenue
Attn: Property Tax Division
4245 International Parkway, Suite A
Hapeville, GA 30354-3918
(404) 968-0707   Fax: (404) 968-0778
E-mail: Local.Government.Services@dor.ga.gov
Web: etax.dor.ga.gov

Summary   To exempt from property taxation a portion of the value of homesteads in Georgia owned by surviving spouses of deceased U.S. servicemembers.

Eligibility   This program is open to residents of Georgia who are the unremarried spouse of a U.S. servicemember who was killed in action.

Financial Data   The first $50,000 of assessed valuation of the homestead owned by qualifying spouses is exempt from property taxes for state, county, municipal, and school purposes.

Duration   The exemption remains in effect as long as the spouse owns and resides in the homestead and remains unmarried.

Number awarded   Varies each year.

Deadline   Applications must be filed with local tax officials by February of each year.

[1303]
HAWAII PROPERTY TAX EXEMPTIONS FOR DISABLED VETERANS

Office of Veterans Services
Attn: Veterans Services Coordinator
459 Patterson Road
E-Wing, Room 1-A103
Honolulu, HI 96819-1522
(808) 433-0420   Fax: (808) 433-0385
E-mail: ovs@ovs.hawaii.gov
Web: www.dod.state.hi.us/ovs/benefits.html

Summary   To exempt the homes of disabled veterans and surviving spouses in Hawaii from real estate taxation.

Eligibility   This program is open to totally disabled veterans in Hawaii and their surviving spouses.

Financial Data   The real property owned and occupied as a home is exempt from taxation.

Duration   The exemption applies as long as the disabled veteran or his/her widow(er) resides in Hawaii.

Deadline   Deadline not specified.

[1304]
IDAHO RETIREMENT BENEFITS DEDUCTION

Idaho State Tax Commission
Attn: Public Information Office
800 Park Boulevard, Plaza IV
P.O. Box 36
Boise, ID 83722-0410
(208) 334-7660   Toll Free: (800) 972-7660
TDD: (800) 377-3529
Web: tax.idaho.gov

Summary   To deduct the retirement and disability income of certain residents from state income tax in Idaho.

Eligibility   Eligible for this deduction are full-year residents of Idaho who are age 65 or older, or disabled and age 62 and older, and who are receiving the following annuities and benefits: 1) retirement annuities paid by the United States to a retired civil service employee or the unremarried widow of the employee; 2) retirement benefits paid from the firemen's retirement fund of the state of Idaho to a retired fireman or the unremarried widow of a retired fireman; 3) retirement benefits paid from the policeman's retirement fund of a city within Idaho to a retired policeman or the unremarried widow of a retired policeman; or 4) retirement benefits paid by the United States to a retired member of the U.S. military service or the unremarried widow of those veterans.

Financial Data   The amount of retirement or disability benefits may be deducted from taxable state income in Idaho, to a maximum deduction of $39,330 for married couples or $26,220 for single persons.

Duration   1 year; must reapply each year.

Number awarded   Varies each year.

Deadline   April of each year.

[1305]
IDAHO WAR VETERAN'S EMERGENCY GRANT PROGRAM

Idaho Division of Veterans Services
Attn: Office of Veterans Advocacy
444 Fort Street
Boise, ID 83702
(208) 577-2300   Fax: (208) 577-2333
E-mail: info@veterans.idaho.gov
Web: www.veterans.idaho.gov/Veterans_Advocacy.aspx

Summary   To provide emergency assistance to disabled veterans, wartime veterans, and their families in Idaho.

Eligibility   Eligible for these grants are veterans who had at least 90 days of honorable wartime military service while a resident of Idaho. Veterans with a service-connected disability are eligible with earlier separation. Surviving spouses and dependent children are also eligible. Applicants must be current residents of Idaho in need of assistance because of a major catastrophe (e.g., natural disaster or death of a spouse or child), loss of job because of a disability, or other extreme financial emergency (e.g., cut-off notice from a utility company, eviction notice from a landlord, arrears payment notice from the lien holder of a home).

Financial Data   The maximum amount available under this program is $1,000, issued in small incremental grants.

Duration   The limit of $1,000 applies for the lifetime of each veteran or his/her family.

Additional data This program was established by the Idaho legislature in lieu of granting a wartime bonus to Idaho veterans.

Number awarded Varies each year.

Deadline Deadline not specified.

[1306]
ILLINOIS GLOBAL WAR ON TERRORISM SURVIVORS' COMPENSATION

Illinois Department of Veterans' Affairs
833 South Spring Street
P.O. Box 19432
Springfield, IL 62794-9432
(217) 782-6641   Toll Free: (800) 437-9824 (within IL)
Fax: (217) 524-0344   TDD: (217) 524-4645
E-mail: webmail@dva.state.il.us
Web: www.veterans.illinois.gov/benefits/compensation.htm

Summary To pay a bonus to survivors of Illinois veterans killed by terrorist acts or hostile activities.

Eligibility Eligible to receive this bonus are survivors of persons who had been Illinois residents for 1 year prior to entering military service and who were killed by terrorist acts or hostile activities during performance of military service in periods not recognized as wartime or by U.S. campaign or service medals.

Financial Data The bonus is $3,000.

Duration This is a 1-time payment.

Deadline Deadline not specified.

[1307]
ILLINOIS KOREAN, VIETNAM, PERSIAN GULF, AND GLOBAL WAR ON TERRORISM CONFLICT BONUS

Illinois Department of Veterans' Affairs
833 South Spring Street
P.O. Box 19432
Springfield, IL 62794-9432
(217) 782-6641   Toll Free: (800) 437-9824 (within IL)
Fax: (217) 524-0344   TDD: (217) 524-4645
E-mail: webmail@dva.state.il.us
Web: www.veterans.illinois.gov/benefits/bonuspayment.htm

Summary To provide a bonus to Illinois veterans of the Korean, Vietnam, Persian Gulf, or Iraqi conflicts or their survivors.

Eligibility Eligible for this bonus are veterans who served in Korea between June 27, 1950 and July 27, 1953, or in Vietnam between January 1, 1961 and March 28, 1973 or on April 29 or 30, 1975, the Persian Gulf between August 2, 1990 and November 30, 1995, or in Operation Enduring Freedom or Operation Iraqi Freedom (the Global War on Terrorism) on or after September 11, 2001. They must have received the Korean Service Medal, the Vietnam Service Medal, the Armed Forces Expeditionary Medal Vietnam Era, the Southwest Asia Service Medal, the Global War on Terrorism Expeditionary Medal, or the Global War on Terrorism Service Medal, along with having been honorably discharged and a resident of Illinois for 12 months before entering service. Survivors of deceased veterans are eligible if the veteran's death was service connected and within the specified dates.

Financial Data Veterans are entitled to a bonus of $100; survivors are entitled to $1,000.

Duration This is a 1-time payment.

Deadline Deadline not specified.

[1308]
ILLINOIS SPECIALLY ADAPTED HOUSING TAX EXEMPTION

Illinois Department of Veterans' Affairs
833 South Spring Street
P.O. Box 19432
Springfield, IL 62794-9432
(217) 782-6641   Toll Free: (800) 437-9824 (within IL)
Fax: (217) 524-0344   TDD: (217) 524-4645
E-mail: webmail@dva.state.il.us
Web: www.veterans.illinois.gov/benefits/realestate.htm

Summary To provide an exemption on the assessed value of specially adapted housing to Illinois veterans with disabilities and their spouses.

Eligibility Specially adapted housing units for disabled veterans that have been purchased or constructed with federal funds are eligible for this exemption. The exemption is extended to the veteran, the spouse, or the unremarried surviving spouse.

Financial Data Under this program, an exemption is allowed on the assessed value of eligible real property, up to a maximum of $70,000 of assessed valuation.

Duration 1 year; renewable as long as the veteran, or spouse, or unremarried surviving spouse resides in the specially adapted housing in Illinois.

Number awarded Varies each year.

Deadline Applications for the exemption may be submitted at any time.

[1309]
ILLINOIS TAX EXEMPTION FOR MOBILE HOMES

Illinois Department of Veterans' Affairs
833 South Spring Street
P.O. Box 19432
Springfield, IL 62794-9432
(217) 782-6641   Toll Free: (800) 437-9824 (within IL)
Fax: (217) 524-0344   TDD: (217) 524-4645
E-mail: webmail@dva.state.il.us
Web: www.veterans.illinois.gov/benefits/realestate.htm

Summary To provide an exemption on the assessed value of mobile homes to Illinois veterans with disabilities and their spouses.

Eligibility This exemption applies to taxes imposed on mobiles homes in Illinois. The property must be owned and used exclusively by a disabled veteran, spouse, or unremarried surviving spouse as a home. The veteran must have received authorization of the Specially Adapted Housing Grant by the U.S. Department of Veterans Affairs, whether that benefit was used or not. Disabled veterans who currently live in a mobile home and never received the Specially Adapted Housing Grant are not eligible.

Financial Data Qualifying veterans, spouses, and unmarried surviving spouses are exempt from property taxes imposed by the state of Illinois on mobile homes.

Duration 1 year; renewable as long as the veteran, or spouse, or unremarried surviving spouse resides in the mobile home in Illinois.

Number awarded Varies each year.

Deadline Applications for the exemption may be submitted at any time.

[1310]
INDIANA MILITARY RETIREMENT OR SURVIVOR'S BENEFIT INCOME TAX DEDUCTION

Indiana Department of Revenue
Attn: Taxpayer Services Division
Indiana Government Center North
100 North Senate Avenue
Indianapolis, IN 46204-2253
(317) 232-2240   TDD: (317) 232-4952
E-mail: pfrequest@dor.state.in.us
Web: www.in.gov/dor

Summary   To exempt a portion of the income of veterans and surviving spouses from state taxation in Indiana.

Eligibility   This program is open to Indiana residents who are retired from the military or are the surviving spouse of a person who was in the military. Applicants must be at least 60 years of age and receiving military retirement or survivor's benefits.

Financial Data   Up to $5,000 of the income from military retirement or survivor's benefits is exempt from state income taxation in Indiana.

Duration   The exemption continues as long as the recipient resides in Indiana.

Deadline   Deadline not specified.

[1311]
INDIANA PROPERTY TAX DEDUCTIONS FOR DISABLED VETERANS

Department of Local Government Finance
Indiana Government Center North, Room 1058
100 North Senate Avenue
Indianapolis, IN 46201
(317) 232-3777   Fax: (317) 232-8779
E-mail: PropertyTaxInfo@dlgf.in.gov
Web: www.in.gov/dlgf

Summary   To exempt disabled Indiana veterans and their spouses from a portion of their property taxes.

Eligibility   This program is open to the following categories of veterans who are residents of Indiana: 1) served honorably at least 90 days and are either totally disabled (the disability does not need to be service-connected) or are at least 62 years old and have at least a 10% service-connected disability; 2) served honorably during wartime and have at least a 10% service-connected disability; or 3) served during World War I and are disabled. A statutory disability rating for pulmonary tuberculosis does not qualify. A disability incurred during Initial Active Duty for Training (IADT) with the National Guard or Reserves is eligible only if the disability occurred from an event during the period of active duty and that duty was performed during wartime. Surviving spouses of those 3 categories of veterans are also eligible.

Financial Data   Property tax deductions are $12,480 for veterans and spouses in the first category (only if the assessed value of the combined real and personal property owned by the veteran or spouse does not exceed $143,160), $24,960 in the second category, or $18,720 in the third category (only if the assessed value of the real property owned by the veteran does not exceed $206,500; there is no limit on the value of the property owned by a surviving spouse).

Duration   1 year; may be renewed as long as the eligible veteran or surviving unremarried spouse owns and occupies the primary residence in Indiana.

Number awarded   Varies each year.

Deadline   Applications must be submitted no later than May of each year.

[1312]
INDIANA VETERANS' BURIAL ALLOWANCE

Indiana Department of Veterans' Affairs
302 West Washington Street, Room E-120
Indianapolis, IN 46204-2738
(317) 232-3910   Toll Free: (800) 400-4520 (within IN)
Fax: (317) 232-7721
Web: www.in.gov/dva/2343.htm

Summary   To provide a burial allowance for Indiana veterans and their spouses.

Eligibility   This benefit is available to honorably-discharged veterans from Indiana and their spouses. Applications must be filed with the county auditor in the county of residence.

Financial Data   County auditors are authorized to pay up to $1,000 for burial costs of a veteran or the veteran's spouse and up to $100 for the setting of a federal headstone.

Duration   This is a 1-time payment.

Number awarded   Varies each year.

Deadline   Requests for assistance may be submitted at any time.

[1313]
INJURED MARINE SEMPER FI GRANTS

Injured Marine Semper Fi Fund
c/o Wounded Warrior Center
Building H49
P.O. Box 555193
Camp Pendleton, CA 92055-5193
(760) 725-3680   Fax: (760) 725-3685
E-mail: info@semperfifund.org
Web: www.semperfifund.org

Summary   To provide supplemental assistance to Marines injured in combat and training operations and their families.

Eligibility   This program is open to Marines injured in combat operations and training accidents and their families. Applicants must need financial assistance to deal with the personal and financial disruption associated with leaving their home, their family, and their job during hospitalization, rehabilitation, and recuperation. Applications are available at military hospitals.

Financial Data   Funds are available for such expenses as child care, travel expenses for families, and other necessities. Assistance is also available for the purchase of adaptive transportation, home modifications, and specialized equipment such as wheelchairs, audio/visual equipment for the blind, and software for traumatic brain injuries.

Duration   Grants are provided as needed.

Additional data   This fund was established in 2004 by a small group of Marine Corps spouses.

Number awarded   Varies each year. Since this program was established, it has awarded more than 18,300 grants worth more than $37 million.

Deadline   Applications may be submitted at any time.

[1314]
IOWA MILITARY HOMEOWNERSHIP PROGRAM

Iowa Finance Authority
Attn: Military Homeownership Program
2015 Grand Avenue
Des Moines, IA 50312
Toll Free: (800) 432-7230   Fax: (515) 725-4901
E-mail: homebuyer.inquiry@iowa.gov
Web: www.ifahome.com

Summary   To provide funding to current and former military servicemembers and those surviving spouses who are interested in purchasing a primary residence in Iowa.

Eligibility   This program is open to 1) servicemembers who served at least 90 days on active duty since September 11, 2001; 2) federal status injured servicemembers who served on active duty since September 11, 2001; and 3) surviving spouses of those eligible servicemembers who served honorably. Applicants must be purchasing a home in Iowa (including modular homes, condominiums, townhomes, and duplexes) that will be their primary residence. They must be using an Iowa Finance Authority participating lender and either FirstHome, FirstHome Plus, or (if not eligible for either of those programs) a permanent mortgage loan.

Financial Data The grant is $5,000. Funds may be used toward down payment on a qualifying home purchase and/or closing costs on a qualifying first purchase money mortgage.

Duration These are 1-time grants.

Additional data The Iowa Legislature created this program in 2005.

Number awarded Varies each year.

Deadline Applications may be submitted at any time.

[1315]
IOWA MILITARY SERVICE PROPERTY TAX EXEMPTION

Iowa Department of Revenue
Attn: Property Tax Division
Hoover State Office Building
1305 East Walnut
P.O. Box 10457
Des Moines, IA 50306-0457
(515) 281-4040   Toll Free: (800) 367-3388 (within IA)
Fax: (515) 281-3906   E-mail: idr@iowa.gov
Web: www.iowa.gov/tax

Summary To exempt veterans, military personnel, and their family members from a portion of property taxes in Iowa.

Eligibility This exemption is available to residents of Iowa who are 1) former members of the U.S. armed forces who performed at least 18 months of military service (or for fewer months because of a service-related injury), regardless of the time period, and who were honorably discharged; 2) former members, and members currently serving of the U.S. Reserves and Iowa National Guard who have served at least 20; and 3) current members of the U.S. Reserves and Iowa National Guard who were activated for federal duty for at least 90 days; 4) former members of the armed forces whose enlistment would have occurred during the Korean Conflict but chose to serve 5 years in the Reserves; and 5) honorably discharged veterans who served in a designated eligible service period. Applicants must own a primary residence in the state. Also eligible for the exemption are the spouses, unremarried widow(er)s, minor children, and widowed parent of qualified veterans.

Financial Data The amount of the exemption varies.

Duration 1 year; continues until the qualifying veteran or dependent no longer lives in the residence.

Number awarded Varies each year. Recently, more than $2.8 million in property was exempt from taxation.

Deadline Application must be made by June of the year for which the exemption is first requested. The exemption is provided annually, from then on, as long as the qualifying veteran or dependent resides in the house.

[1316]
KENTUCKY MILITARY FAMILY ASSISTANCE TRUST FUND

Kentucky Department of Military Affairs
Attn: State Family Program
Boone National Guard Center
100 Minuteman Parkway
Frankfort, KY 40601-6168
(502) 607-1155   Toll Free: (800) 372-7601
Fax: (502) 607-1394
Web: dma.ky.gov/Family+Assistance

Summary To provide emergency financial assistance to Kentucky residents serving in the armed forces outside of the United States and their spouses.

Eligibility This assistance is available to 1) members of the U.S. armed forces who are deployed outside of the United States and who have a Kentucky home of record; and 2 Kentucky resident spouses of eligible military members. Applicants must be facing expenses that create an undue hardship directly related to deployment outside the country. They may not have reasonable access to any other funding source. There is no limitation on the type of expense for which the assistance is requested, only that it create an undue hardship.

Financial Data Grants are limited to $2,500 for a single application or $5,000 per fiscal year.

Duration Assistance is available while the military member is deployed overseas and for 90 days following the end of deployment or deactivation.

Additional data This program was established in 2006.

Number awarded Varies each year.

Deadline Applications may be submitted at any time.

[1317]
LOUISIANA INCOME EXEMPTION FOR FEDERAL RETIREMENT PAY

Louisiana Department of Revenue
Attn: Individual Income Tax
P.O. Box 201
Baton Rouge, LA 70821
(225) 219-0102
Web: www.revenue.louisiana.gov

Summary To exempt the retirement income of all federal employees, including the military and their surviving spouses, from state taxation in Louisiana.

Eligibility This exemption is available to all residents of Louisiana who are receiving retirement benefits from the federal retirement system, including veterans and their surviving spouses.

Financial Data All federal retirement income is exempt from state income taxation in Louisiana.

Duration The benefit continues as long as the recipient remains a resident of Louisiana for state income tax purposes.

Number awarded Varies each year.

Deadline Deadline not specified.

[1318]
MAINE PROPERTY TAX EXEMPTIONS FOR VETERANS

Maine Revenue Services
Attn: Property Tax Division
P.O. Box 9106
Augusta, ME 04332-9106
(207) 287-2011   Fax: (207) 287-6396
E-mail: prop.tax@maine.gov
Web: www.maine.gov/revenue/propertytax/homepage.html

Summary To exempt the estates of disabled Maine veterans and selected family members from property taxation.

Eligibility Eligible for this program are veterans who served in wartime during World War I, World War II, the Korean campaign, the Vietnam war, the Persian Gulf war, or other recognized service periods, are legal residents of Maine, and are either older than 62 years of age or are receiving a pension or compensation from the U.S. government for total disability (whether service connected or not). Vietnam veterans must have served 180 days on active duty unless discharged earlier for a service-connected disability. The exemption also includes 1) property held in joint tenancy with the veterans' spouses, and 2) property of unremarried widow(er)s, minor children, and mothers of deceased veterans, if those dependents are receiving a pension or compensation from the U.S. government.

Financial Data Estates of disabled veterans and eligible dependents, including both real and personal property, are exempt up to $6,000 of just valuation. For veterans and dependents who served in wartime prior to World War II, estates up to $7,000 are exempt.

Duration Veterans, spouses, unremarried widow(er)s, and mothers are eligible for this exemption throughout their lifetimes; minor children of veterans are eligible until they reach the age of 18.

Number awarded Varies each year.

Deadline When an eligible person first submits an application, the proof of entitlement must reach the assessors of the local municipality prior to the end of March. Once eligibility has been established, notification need not be repeated in subsequent years.

[1319]
MAINE TAX EXEMPTION FOR SPECIALLY ADAPTED HOUSING UNITS

Maine Revenue Services
Attn: Property Tax Division
P.O. Box 9106
Augusta, ME 04332-9106
(207) 287-2011   Fax: (207) 287-6396
E-mail: prop.tax@maine.gov
Web: www.maine.gov/revenue/propertytax/homepage.html

Summary To exempt the specially adapted housing units of paraplegic veterans or their surviving spouses from taxation in Maine.

Eligibility Veterans who served in the U.S. armed forces during any federally-recognized war period, are legal residents of Maine, are paraplegic veterans within the meaning of U.S. statutes, and have received a grant from the U.S. government for specially adapted housing are eligible. The exemption also applies to property held in joint tenancy with the veteran's spouse and to the specially adapted housing of unremarried widow(er)s of eligible veterans.

Financial Data Estates of paraplegic veterans are exempt up to $50,000 of just valuation for a specially adapted housing unit.

Duration The exemption is valid for the lifetime of the paraplegic veteran or unremarried widow(er).

Number awarded Varies each year.

Deadline When an eligible person first submits an application, the proof of entitlement must reach the assessors of the local municipality prior to the end of March. Once eligibility has been established, notification need not be repeated in subsequent years.

[1320]
MARYLAND PROPERTY TAX EXEMPTION FOR DISABLED VETERANS AND SURVIVING SPOUSES

Maryland Department of Assessments and Taxation
Attn: Property Taxes
301 West Preston Street
Baltimore, MD 21201-2395
(410) 767-1184   Toll Free: (888) 246-5941
TDD: (800) 735-2258
Web: www.dat.state.md.us/sdatweb/exempt.html

Summary To exempt the homes of disabled veterans and their surviving spouses from property taxation in Maryland.

Eligibility This exemption is available to armed services veterans with a permanent service-connected disability rated 100% by the U.S. Department of Veterans Affairs who own a dwelling house in Maryland. Unremarried surviving spouses are also eligible.

Financial Data The dwelling houses of eligible veterans and surviving spouses is exempt from real property taxes.

Duration The exemption is available as long as the veteran or surviving spouse owns the dwelling house in Maryland.

Number awarded Varies each year.

Deadline Applications may be submitted at any time.

[1321]
MARYLAND PROPERTY TAX EXEMPTION FOR SURVIVING SPOUSES OF DECEASED VETERANS

Maryland Department of Assessments and Taxation
Attn: Property Taxes
301 West Preston Street
Baltimore, MD 21201-2395
(410) 767-1184   Toll Free: (888) 246-5941
TDD: (800) 735-2258
Web: www.dat.state.md.us/sdatweb/exempt.html

Summary To exempt the homes of surviving spouses of deceased military personnel from property taxation in Maryland.

Eligibility This exemption is available to surviving spouses of active-duty military personnel who died in the line of duty. Applicants must own a dwelling house in Maryland.

Financial Data The dwelling houses of eligible surviving spouses is exempt from real property taxes.

Duration The exemption is available as long as the surviving spouse owns the dwelling house in Maryland.

Number awarded Varies each year.

Deadline Applications may be submitted at any time.

[1322]
MARYLAND REAL PROPERTY TAX EXEMPTION FOR DISABLED VETERANS

State Department of Assessments and Taxation
Attn: Tax Credit Program
301 West Preston Street, Room 900
Baltimore, MD 21201-2395
(410) 767-1184   Toll Free: (888) 246-5941 (within MD)
TDD: (800) 735-2258   E-mail: taxcredits@dat.state.md.us
Web: www.dat.state.md.us

Summary To exempt the homes of disabled veterans and their spouses from property taxation in Maryland.

Eligibility This program is open to Maryland residents who are veterans with a 100% service-connected permanent disability and their surviving spouses.

Financial Data The dwelling houses owned by qualifying disabled veterans and their spouses are exempt from real property taxes in Maryland.

Duration This exemption continues as long as the qualifying disabled veterans or spouses reside in Maryland and own their home.

Deadline Deadline not specified.

[1323]
MARYLAND REAL PROPERTY TAX EXEMPTION FOR SURVIVING SPOUSES

State Department of Assessments and Taxation
Attn: Tax Credit Program
301 West Preston Street, Room 900
Baltimore, MD 21201-2395
(410) 767-1184   Toll Free: (888) 246-5941 (within MD)
TDD: (800) 735-2258   E-mail: taxcredits@dat.state.md.us
Web: www.dat.state.md.us

Summary To exempt the homes of the spouses of deceased military personnel from property taxation in Maryland.

Eligibility This program is open to Maryland residents who are the surviving spouses of active military personnel who died in the line of duty or of veterans who had a service-connected disability rated 100% by the U.S. Department of Veterans Affairs at the time of death.

Financial Data The dwelling houses owned by qualifying spouses are exempt from real property taxes in Maryland.

Duration This exemption continues as long as the qualifying spouse resides in Maryland and owns their home.

Deadline Deadline not specified.

[1324]
MASSACHUSETTS INCOME TAX EXEMPTION FOR UNIFORMED SERVICES RETIREMENT PAY

Massachusetts Department of Revenue
Attn: Personal Income Tax
P.O. Box 7010
Boston, MA 02204
(617) 887-MDOR   Toll Free: (800) 392-6089 (within MA)
Fax: (617) 887-1900
Web: www.mass.gov

Summary To exempt the retirement income and survivorship benefits received from the U.S. uniformed services from state income taxation in Massachusetts.

Eligibility Eligible for this exemption are residents of Massachusetts who are receiving noncontributory pension income or survivorship benefits from the U.S. uniformed services (including the Army, Navy, Marine Corps, Air Force, Coast Guard, National Oceanic and Atmospheric Administration, and commissioned corps of the Public Health Service).

Financial Data All uniformed services retirement income and survivorship benefits are exempt from state income taxation.

Duration The benefit continues as long as the recipient remains a resident of Massachusetts for state income tax purposes.

Additional data This exemption became effective with income received in 1997.

Number awarded Varies each year.

Deadline Deadline not specified.

[1325]
MASSACHUSETTS PROPERTY TAX EXEMPTION FOR VETERANS AND THEIR FAMILIES

Massachusetts Department of Revenue
Attn: Division of Local Services
100 Cambridge Street
Boston, MA 02114
(617) 626-2386   Fax: (617) 626-2330
E-mail: juszkiewicz@dor.state.ma.us
Web: www.mass.gov

Summary To provide a property tax exemption to blind, disabled, and other veterans (and their families) in Massachusetts.

Eligibility This program is open to veterans who are residents of Massachusetts, were residents for at least 6 months prior to entering the service, have been residents for at least 5 consecutive years, and are occupying property as their domicile. Applicants must have an ownership interest in the domicile that ranges from $2,000 to $10,000, depending on the category of exemption. Veterans must have been discharged under conditions other than dishonorable. Several categories of veterans and their families qualify: 1) veterans who have a service-connected disability rating of 10% or more; veterans who have been awarded the Purple Heart; Gold Star mothers and fathers; and surviving spouses of eligible veterans who do not remarry; 2) veterans who suffered, in the line of duty, the loss or permanent lose of use of 1 foot, 1 hand, or 1 eye; veterans who received the Congressional Medal of Honor, Distinguished Service Cross, Navy Cross, or Air Force Cross; and their spouses or surviving spouses; 3) veterans who suffered, in the line of duty, the loss or permanent loss of use of both feet, both hands, or both eyes; and their spouses or surviving spouses; 4) veterans who suffered total disability in the line of duty and received assistance in acquiring specially adapted housing, which they own and occupy as their domicile; and their

spouses or surviving spouses; 5) unremarried surviving spouses of military personnel who died due to injury or disease from being in a combat zone, or are missing and presumed dead due to combat; 6) veterans who suffered total disability in the line of duty and are incapable of working; and their spouses or surviving spouses; and 7) veterans who are certified by the Veterans Administration as paraplegic and their surviving spouses.

Financial Data Qualified veterans and family members are entitled to an annual exemption from their taxes for the different categories: 1, $400; 2, $750; 3, $1,250; 4, $1,500; 5, full, but with a cap of $2,500 after 5 years; 6, $1,000; or 7, total.

Duration The exemptions are provided each year that the veteran or unremarried surviving spouse lives in Massachusetts and owns the property as a domicile.

Additional data Applications are available from local assessor's offices.

Number awarded Varies each year.

Deadline Applications must be filed with the local assessor by December of each year.

[1326]
MASSACHUSETTS PUBLIC ASSISTANCE FOR VETERANS

Department of Veterans' Services
600 Washington Street, Suite 1100
Boston, MA 02111
(617) 210-5927   Fax: (617) 210-5755
E-mail: mdvs@vet.state.ma.us
Web: www.mass.gov/veterans

Summary To provide financial and medical assistance to indigent veterans and their dependents in Massachusetts.

Eligibility This assistance is open to veterans who are residents of Massachusetts and served in the U.S. armed services on active duty either for 90 days during specified periods of wartime or for 180 days during peacetime. Members of the National Guard and Reserves are also eligible if they have been called to regular active duty. Also eligible are spouses of the veteran, widows or widowers of the veteran, dependent parents of the veteran, any person who acted as a parent to the veteran for 5 years immediately prior to entering wartime service, children of the veteran under 19 years of age, children of the veteran between 19 and 23 years of age who are attending high school or an institution of higher education, children of the veteran 19 years of age or older who are mentally or physically unable to support themselves and were affected by the disability prior to their 18th birthday, and legally adopted children of the veteran. Applicants must be able to demonstrate a need for assistance for food, shelter, clothing, housing supplies, and medical care.

Financial Data Grants depend on the need of the recipient.

Duration These are 1-time grants.

Number awarded Varies each year.

Deadline Applications may be submitted at any time.

[1327]
MASSACHUSETTS VETERANS ANNUITY PROGRAM

Department of Veterans' Services
Attn: Annuities
600 Washington Street, Suite 1100
Boston, MA 02111
(617) 210-5480   Fax: (617) 210-5755
E-mail: mdvs@vet.state.ma.us
Web: www.mass.gov/veterans

Summary To provide an annuity to blind or disabled veterans from Massachusetts and to the parents and spouses of deceased military personnel.

Eligibility This program is open to 1) veterans who are blind, double amputee, paraplegic, or have a 100% service-connected disability; 2) the parents of military personnel who died of service-connected causes; and 3) the unremarried spouses of military personnel who died of service-connected causes. Veterans must have been residents of Massachusetts at the time of entry into military service who served during specified wartime periods and received other than a dishonorable discharge. All applicants must currently be residents of Massachusetts.

Financial Data Recipients are entitled to an annuity of $2,000 per year.

Duration The annuity is paid as long as the recipient continues to reside in Massachusetts.

Deadline Deadline not specified.

[1328]
MASSACHUSETTS WELCOME HOME BONUS

Office of the State Treasurer
Attn: Veterans Bonus Division
One Ashburton Place, 12th Floor
Boston, MA 02108-1608
(617) 367-9333, ext. 859   Fax: (617) 227-1622
E-mail: veteransbonus@tre.state.ma.us
Web: www.mass.gov/treasury

Summary To provide a bonus to Massachusetts veterans and servicemembers who served after September 11, 2001 and their families.

Eligibility This bonus is available to veterans and current servicemembers who had resided in Massachusetts for at least 6 months immediately prior to their entry into service in the armed forces. They must have performed service on or after September 11, 2001 and still be serving or have been honorably discharged. If the veteran or servicemember is deceased, an immediate family member (parent, spouse, child, sibling) may apply.

Financial Data The bonus is $1,000 for active service in Afghanistan or Iraq or $500 for 6 months or more of active service.

Duration This is a 1-time bonus.

Number awarded Varies each year.

Deadline Deadline not specified.

[1329]
MCCORMICK GRANTS

Society of the First Infantry Division
Attn: 1st Infantry Division Foundation
1933 Morris Road
Blue Bell, PA 19422-1422
Toll Free: (888) 324-4733   Fax: (215) 661-1934
E-mail: Fdn1ID@aol.com
Web: www.bigredone.org/foundation/grants.cfm

Summary To provide emergency financial assistance to active First Division soldiers and their families.

Eligibility This assistance is available to soldiers currently serving in the First Infantry Division and their families. Applicants must be facing emergency financial needs that cannot be met through the usual forms of assistance available to them.

Financial Data Grant amounts depend on the need of the recipient. Recently, they ranged up to $1,500.

Duration These are 1-time grants.

Additional data This program was established in 2005 with funding from the Robert R. McCormick Tribune Foundation.

Number awarded Varies each year; recently, 3 grants were awarded.

Deadline Applications may be submitted at any time.

[1330]
MICHIGAN HOMESTEAD PROPERTY TAX CREDIT FOR VETERANS AND BLIND PEOPLE

Michigan Department of Treasury
Attn: Homestead Exemption
Treasury Building
430 West Allegan Street
Lansing, MI 48922
(517) 373-3200   Toll Free: (800) 827-4000
TDD: (517) 636-4999   E-mail: treasPtd2@michigan.gov
Web: www.michigan.gov/treasury

Summary To provide a property tax credit to veterans, military personnel, their spouses, blind people, and their surviving spouses in Michigan.

Eligibility Eligible to apply are residents of Michigan who are 1) blind and own their homestead; 2) a veteran with a service-connected disability or his/her surviving spouse; 3) a surviving spouse of a veteran deceased in service; 4) a pensioned veteran, a surviving spouse of those veterans, or an active military member, all of whose household income is less than $7,500; or 5) a surviving spouse of a non-disabled or non-pensioned veteran of the Korean War, World War II, or World War I whose household income is less than $7,500. All applicants must own or rent a home in Michigan, have been a Michigan resident for at least 6 months during the year in which application is made, and fall within qualifying income levels (up to $82,650 in household income).

Financial Data The maximum credit is $1,200. The exact amount varies. For homeowners, the credit depends on the state equalized value of the homestead and on an allowance for filing category. For renters, 20% of the rent is considered property tax eligible for credit.

Duration 1 year; eligibility must be established each year.

Number awarded Varies each year.

Deadline December of each year.

[1331]
MICHIGAN INCOME TAX EXEMPTION FOR DISABLED VETERANS

Michigan Department of Treasury
Attn: Income Tax
Treasury Building
430 West Allegan Street
Lansing, MI 48922
(517) 373-3200   Toll Free: (800) 827-4000
TDD: (517) 636-4999   E-mail: treasIndTax@michigan.gov
Web: www.michigan.gov/treasury

Summary To exempt a portion of the income of disabled veterans and their families in Michigan from state income taxation.

Eligibility Residents of Michigan may claim this exemption if 1) the taxpayer or spouse is a qualified disabled veteran; or 2) a dependent of the taxpayer is a qualified disabled veteran. The qualifying individual must be a veteran of the active military, naval, marine, coast guard, or air service who received an honorable or general discharge and has a disability incurred or aggravated in the line of duty. This exemption may be claimed in addition to any other exemption for which the taxpayer is eligible.

Financial Data Qualifying veterans with disabilities and their eligible family members receive an exemption of $250 from their adjusted gross income for purposes of state taxation.

Duration The exemption continues as long as the recipient resides in Michigan.

Additional data This exemption was first available for 2008 income.

Deadline Deadline not specified.

[1332]
MICHIGAN MILITARY FAMILY RELIEF FUND GRANTS

Department of Military and Veterans Affairs
Attn: Military Family Relief Fund
3423 North Martin Luther King Boulevard
P.O. Box 30261
Lansing, MI 48909-7761
Toll Free: (866) 271-4404   Fax: (517) 481-7644
E-mail: paocmn@michigan.gov
Web: www.michigan.gov/dmva

Summary   To provide temporary financial support to members of the Michigan National Guard and Reserves who have been called to active duty as part of the national response to the September 11, 2001 terrorist attacks and their families.

Eligibility   This assistance is available to members of the Michigan National Guard and Reserves and their families. The military member must have been called to active duty as part of the national response to the events of September 11, 2001. Applicants must be able to demonstrate a need for assistance as a result of the military member's service.

Financial Data   The maximum grant is $2,000.

Duration   This assistance is provided to meet temporary needs only.

Additional data   The state of Michigan established this program in 2004.

Number awarded   Varies each year.

Deadline   Applications may be submitted at any time.

[1333]
MICHIGAN VETERANS TRUST FUND EMERGENCY GRANTS

Department of Military and Veterans Affairs
Attn: Michigan Veterans Trust Fund
2500 South Washington Avenue
Lansing, MI 48913-5101
(517) 483-5469   E-mail: paocmn@michigan.gov
Web: www.michigan.gov/dmva

Summary   To provide temporary financial assistance to disabled and other Michigan veterans and their families, if they are facing personal emergencies.

Eligibility   Eligible for this assistance are veterans and their families residing in Michigan who are temporarily unable to provide the basic necessities of life. Support is not provided for long-term problems or chronic financial difficulties. The qualifying veteran must have been discharged under honorable conditions with at least 180 days of active wartime service or have been separated as a result of a physical or mental disability incurred in the line of duty.

Financial Data   No statutory limit exists on the amount of assistance that may be provided; a local board in each Michigan county determines if the applicant is genuinely needy and the amount of assistance to be awarded.

Duration   This assistance is provided to meet temporary needs only.

Number awarded   Varies each year.

Deadline   Applications may be submitted at any time.

[1334]
MILITARY FAMILY SUPPORT TRUST FINANCIAL ASSISTANCE

Military Family Support Trust
1010 American Eagle Boulevard
P.O. Box 301
Sun City Center, FL 33573
(813) 634-4675   Fax: (813) 633-2412
E-mail: president@mobc-online.org
Web: www.mobc-online.org

Summary   To provide financial assistance for emergency needs to active-duty, retired, and deceased officers who served in the military or designated public service agencies and to their families.

Eligibility   This assistance is available to 1) retired, active-duty, National Guard, or Reserve officers and former officers of the U.S. Army, Navy, Marine Corps, Air Force, Coast Guard, Public Health Service, or National Oceanic and Atmospheric Administration, at the rank of O-1 through O-10, WO-1 through WO-5, or E-5 through E-9; 2) recipients of the Purple Heart, regardless of pay grade or length of service; 3) World War II combat veterans of the Merchant Marine; 4) federal employees at the grade of GS-7 or higher; 5) Foreign Service Officers at the grade of FSO-8 or lower; 6) honorably discharged or retired foreign military officers of friendly nations meeting the service and disability retirement criteria of their respective country and living in the United States; and 7) spouses, surviving spouses, and dependents (including grandchildren) of those categories. Applicants must be in need of financial assistance for personal care, subsistence, housing, all aspects of health care, or other special circumstances.

Financial Data   Grants depend on the need of the recipient.

Duration   Assistance is provided in the form of 1-time grants or monthly payments.

Additional data   This foundation was established in 1992 as the Military Officers' Benevolent Corporation. It changed its name in 2008.

Number awarded   Varies each year.

Deadline   Applications may be submitted at any time.

[1335]
MINNESOTA STATE SOLDIERS ASSISTANCE PROGRAM

Minnesota Department of Veterans Affairs
Veterans Service Building
20 West 12th Street, Room 206C
St. Paul, MN 55155-2006
(651) 757-1556   Toll Free: (888) LINK-VET
Fax: (651) 296-3954   E-mail: kathy.schwartz@state.mn.us
Web: www.mdva.state.mn.us/financialassistance.htm

Summary   To provide emergency financial assistance to disabled veterans and their families in Minnesota.

Eligibility   This assistance is available to veterans who are unable to work because of a temporary disability (from service-connected or other causes). Their dependents and survivors are also eligible. Applicants must also meet income and asset guidelines and be residents of Minnesota.

Financial Data   The maximum grant is $1,500. Funds may be used to pay for food and shelter, utility bills, and emergency medical treatment (including optical and dental benefits).

Duration   This is a short-term program, with benefits payable up to 6 months only. If the veteran's disability is expected to be long term in nature or permanent, the department may continue to provide assistance while application is made for long-term benefits, such as Social Security disability or retirement benefits.

Number awarded   Varies each year. A total of $1.4 million is available for this program annually.

Deadline   Applications may be submitted at any time.

[1336]
MISSOURI MILITARY FAMILY RELIEF FUND GRANTS

Missouri Military Family Relief Fund
Attn: JFMO-J1/DPP-F
2302 Militia Drive
Jefferson City, MO 65101-1203
(573) 638-9827   E-mail: MilitaryRelief@mo.ngb.army.mil
Web: www.mmfrf.mo.gov

Summary To provide emergency financial assistance to members of the National Guard and Reserves in Missouri or their families who are facing difficulties as a result of deployment after September 11, 2001.

Eligibility This program is open to 1) members of the Missouri National Guard who have been on Title 10 orders as a result of the September 11, 2001 terrorist attacks for 30 consecutive days or more or have been off Title 10 orders as a result of the September 11, 2001 terrorist attacks for 120 days or less; 2) Reserve component members who are residents of Missouri and have been on Title 32 orders as a result of the September 11, 2001 terrorist attacks for 30 days or more or have been off Title 32 orders as a result of the September 11, 2001 terrorist attacks for 120 days or less; 3) immediate relatives of members of those National Guard or Reserve units. The Guard or Reserve member must have a rank no higher than O-3 or W-2. Applicants must be in need of emergency financial assistance; funding is not provided for nonessentials, to finance leave or vacations, to pay fines or legal expenses, to help liquidate or consolidate debts, to assist with house purchase or home improvements, to cover bad checks, or to pay credit card bills.

Financial Data Grants up to $1,000 are available.

Duration Grants may be awarded only once in a 12-month period.

Additional data This program was established in 2005.

Number awarded Varies each year.

Deadline Applications may be submitted at any time.

[1337]
MISSOURI SENIOR CITIZEN, DISABLED VETERAN, AND DISABLED PERSON PROPERTY TAX CREDIT CLAIM

Missouri Department of Revenue
Attn: Taxation Division
301 West High Street, Room 330
P.O. Box 2800
Jefferson City, MO 65105-2800
(573) 751-3505   Toll Free: (800) 877-6881
TDD: (800) 735-2966 E-mail: PropertyTaxCredit@dor.mo.gov
Web: www.dor.mo.gov/tax/personal

Summary To provide a property tax credit to low-income disabled veterans, senior citizens, and other persons with disabilities or their spouses in Missouri.

Eligibility This program is open to residents of Missouri (or their spouses) whose net household income does not exceed certain limits ($27,500 per year if they rented or did not own and occupy their home for the entire year, $30,000 if they owned and occupied their home for the entire year) and have paid property tax or rent on their homestead during the tax year. Applicants must be 1) 65 years of age or older, 2) classified by the U.S. Department of Veterans Affairs as a 100% service-connected disabled veteran, 3) 60 years of age or older and receiving surviving spouse Society Security benefits, or 4) 100% disabled.

Financial Data The tax credit depends on the claimant's income and amount paid in property taxes or rent, up to a maximum of $1,100 per year for property tax or $750 per year for rent.

Duration The tax credit is available annually.

Number awarded Varies each year.

Deadline Eligible veterans, people with disabilities, and senior citizens may claim this credit when they file their state income tax return, in April of each year.

[1338]
MONTANA DISABLED AMERICAN VETERAN PROPERTY TAX BENEFIT

Montana Department of Revenue
Attn: Property Tax
125 North Roberts, Third Floor
P.O. Box 5805
Helena, MT 59604-5805
(406) 444-6900   Toll Free: (866) 859-2254
Fax: (406) 444-1505   TDD: (406) 444-2830
Web: mt.gov/revenue

Summary To reduce the property tax rate in Montana for disabled veterans and their surviving spouses.

Eligibility This benefit is available to residents of Montana who own and occupy property in the state. Applicants must have been honorably discharged from active service in the armed forces and be currently rated 100% disabled or compensated at the 100% disabled rate because of a service-connected disability. They must have an adjusted gross income less than $52,899 if married or $45,846 if single. Also eligible are unremarried surviving spouses with an adjusted gross income less than $39,968 whose spouse was a veteran with a 100% service-connected disability or compensation at the 100% disabled rate at the time of death, died while on active duty, or died of a service-connected disability.

Financial Data Qualifying veterans and surviving spouses are entitled to a reduction in local property taxes on their residence, 1 attached or detached garage, and up to 1 acre of land. The amount of the reduction depends on the status of the applicant (married, single, or surviving spouse) and adjusted gross income, but ranges from 50% to 100%.

Duration The reduction continues as long as the recipient resides in Montana and owns and occupies property used as a primary residence.

Number awarded Varies each year.

Deadline Applications must be filed with the local Department of Revenue Office by April of each year.

[1339]
MONTANA TAX EXEMPTION FOR CERTAIN DISABLED OR DECEASED VETERANS' RESIDENCES

Montana Veterans' Affairs Division
1900 Williams Street
P.O. Box 5715
Helena, MT 59604
(406) 324-3740   Fax: (406) 324-3745
E-mail: lehall@mt.gov
Web: dma.mt.gov/mvad/functions/state.asp

Summary To exempt from taxation the real property of disabled or deceased veterans and their widow(er)s in Montana.

Eligibility This exemption applies to residential property in Montana that is owned and occupied by an honorably-discharged veteran who is rated as 100% disabled or is being paid at the 100% disabled rate by the U.S. Department of Veterans Affairs (DVA). Also eligible are unremarried spouses of deceased veterans who own and occupy a residence in Montana. Spouses must obtain documentation from the DVA that the veteran was rated as 100% disabled or was being paid at the 100% disabled rate at the time of death, or that the veteran died while on active duty.

Financial Data Eligible veterans or spouses are entitled to real property tax relief that depends on their income. Single veterans with an income of $30,000 or less are exempt from all property taxes; if their income is $30,001 to $33,000, they pay 20% of the regular tax; those with income from $33,001 to $36,000 pay 30% of the regular tax; and those with income from $36,001 to $39,000 pay 50% of the regular tax. Married veterans with an income of $36,000 or less are exempt from all property taxes; if their income is $36,001 to $39,000, they pay 20% of the regular tax; those with income from $39,001 to $42,000 pay 30% of the regular tax; and those with income from $42,001 to $45,000 pay 50% of the regular tax. Surviving spouses with an income of $25,000 or less are exempt from all property taxes; if their income is $25,001 to $28,000, they pay 20% of the regular tax; those with income from $28,001 to $31,000 pay 30% of the regular tax; and those with income from $31,001 to $34,000 pay 50% of the regular tax.

Duration The exemption continues as long as the residence in Montana is owned and occupied by the disabled veteran or, if deceased, by the veteran's unremarried spouse.

Number awarded Varies each year.

Deadline Deadline not specified.

[1340]
MONTGOMERY GI BILL (ACTIVE DUTY) DEATH BENEFIT

Department of Veterans Affairs
Attn: Veterans Benefits Administration
810 Vermont Avenue, N.W.
Washington, DC 20420
(202) 418-4343　　　　Toll Free: (800) 827-1000
Web: www1.va.gov/opa/ls1/11.asp

Summary To provide a death benefit to a designated survivor of a serviceperson who was participating in the Montgomery GI Bill at the time of death.

Eligibility This benefit goes to the designated survivor of a serviceperson participating in the Montgomery GI Bill at the time of death, if the serviceperson's death occurred in service or within 1 year after discharge or release and was service connected. The benefit also will be paid if the serviceperson would have been eligible to participate but for the high school diploma requirement or the length-of-service requirement.

Financial Data The amount paid is equal to the participant's actual military pay reduction less any education benefits paid.

Duration This is a 1-time disbursement.

Number awarded Varies each year.

Deadline Deadline not specified.

[1341]
NEBRASKA HOMESTEAD EXEMPTION

Nebraska Department of Revenue
301 Centennial Mall South
P.O. Box 94818
Lincoln, NE 68509-4818
(402) 471-5729
Toll Free: (800) 742-7474 (within NE and IA)
Web: www.revenue.state.ne.us/homestead.htm

Summary To exempt the property of Nebraska residents who are elderly, disabled, or veterans and their widow(er)s from a portion of taxation.

Eligibility This exemption is available to 3 categories of Nebraska residents: the elderly, certain people with disabilities, and certain disabled veterans and their widow(er)s. Elderly people are those 65 years of age or older who own a homestead with a value less than $95,000 or 200% of their county's average assessed value of single family residential property, whichever is greater. Disabled people are those who 1) have a permanent physical disability and have lost all mobility such as to preclude locomotion without the regular use of a mechanical aid or prosthesis; 2) have undergone amputation of both arms above the elbow, or 3) have a permanent partial disability of both arms in excess of 75%. They must own a homestead with a value less than $110,000 or 225% of their county's average assessed value of single family residential property, whichever is greater. Veterans are those who served on active duty in the armed forces of the United States (or a government allied with the United States) during specified periods of war and received an honorable discharge. They must 1) be drawing compensation from the U.S.

Department of Veterans Affairs (VA) because of a 100% service-connected disability; 2) be totally disabled by a nonservice-connected illness or accident; or 3) own a home that is substantially contributed to by VA. Also eligible are unremarried widow(er)s of veterans who died because of a service-connected disability, whose death while on active duty was service-connected, who died while on active duty during wartime, or who drew compensation from VA because of a 100% service-connected disability The homestead maximum value is $110,000 or 225% of the county's average assessed value of single family residential property, whichever is greater. Elderly people must have a household income less than $31,301 if single or $36,801 if married. Disabled persons, veterans, and widow(er)s (except veterans and widow(er)s who own a home that is substantially contributed to by the VA) must have a household income less than $34,401 if single or $39,701 if married.

Financial Data Exemptions depend on the income of the applicant, ranging from 25% to 100% of the value of the homestead. For the elderly, the maximum exemption is the taxable value of the homestead up to $40,000 or 100% of the county's average assessed value of single family residential property, whichever is greater. For disabled people and veterans, the maximum exemption is the taxable value of the homestead up to $50,000 or 120% of the county's average assessed value of single family residential property, whichever is greater. For veterans and widow(er)s whose home was substantially contributed to by the VA, the homestead is 100% exempt regardless of the value of the homestead or the income of the owner.

Duration The exemption is provided as long as the qualifying homestead owner resides in Nebraska.

Number awarded Varies each year.

Deadline Applications must be filed by June of each year.

[1342]
NEBRASKA VETERANS' AID FUND

Department of Veterans' Affairs
State Office Building
301 Centennial Mall South, Sixth Floor
P.O. Box 95083
Lincoln, NE 68509-5083
(402) 471-2458　　　　Fax: (402) 471-2491
E-mail: john.hilgert@nebraska.gov
Web: www.vets.state.ne.us

Summary To assist veterans, their spouses, and their dependents in Nebraska who have a temporary emergency need.

Eligibility This assistance is available to veterans, their spouses, and their dependent children who are residents of Nebraska. The veteran must have served on active duty in the armed forces of the United States, other than active duty for training, and either 1) was discharged or otherwise separated with a characterization of honorable or general (under honorable conditions), or 2) died while in service or as a direct result of such service.

Financial Data The amount of aid awarded varies, depending upon the needs of the recipient. Recently, grants averaged approximately $1,000. Aid can only be used for food, fuel, shelter, wearing apparel, funeral, medical, or surgical items.

Duration The funds are provided for emergency situations only; the program does not assist ongoing financial needs.

Additional data The Nebraska Veterans' Aid Fund was established in 1921 in lieu of a bonus for veterans of wartime service. Applications must be made through the county service officer or post service officer of any recognized veterans' organization in the county nearest the applicant's place of residence and submitted to the Department of Veterans' Affairs.

Number awarded Varies each year. In a recent year, more than $764,000 in aid was provided to 694 veterans.

Deadline Applications may be submitted at any time.

[1343]
NEVADA DISABLED VETERAN'S TAX EXEMPTION

Nevada Office of Veterans' Services
Attn: Executive Director
5460 Reno Corporate Drive
Reno, NV 89511
(775) 688-1653 Fax: (775) 688-1656
Web: veterans.nv.gov/NOVS/Veterans%20Benefits.html

Summary To exempt from taxation in Nevada a portion of the property owned by disabled veterans or their surviving spouses.

Eligibility This program is open to veterans who are residents of Nevada and have incurred a service-connected disability of 60% or more. Applicants must have received an honorable separation from military service. The widow(er) of a disabled veteran, who was eligible at the time of death, may also be eligible for this benefit.

Financial Data Veterans and widow(er)s are entitled to exempt from taxation a portion of their property's assessed value. The amount depends on the extent of the disability and the year filed; it ranges from $6,250 to $20,000 and doubles over a 4-year period.

Duration Disabled veterans and their widow(er)s are entitled to this exemption as long as they live in Nevada.

Additional data Disabled veterans and widow(er)s are able to split their exemption between vehicle taxes and/or property taxes. Further information is available at local county assessors' offices.

Number awarded Varies each year.

Deadline Deadline not specified.

[1344]
NEW HAMPSHIRE PROPERTY TAX EXEMPTION FOR CERTAIN DISABLED VETERANS

New Hampshire Department of Revenue Administration
109 Pleasant Street
Concord, NH 03301
(603) 271-2191 Fax: (603) 271-6121
TDD: (800) 735-2964
Web: revenue.nh.gov

Summary To exempt from taxation certain property owned by New Hampshire disabled veterans or their surviving spouses.

Eligibility Eligible for this exemption are New Hampshire residents who are honorably discharged veterans with a total and permanent service-connected disability that involves double amputation of the upper or lower extremities or any combination thereof, paraplegia, or blindness of both eyes with visual acuity of 5/200 or less. Applicants or their surviving spouses must own a specially adapted homestead that has been acquired with the assistance of the U.S. Department of Veterans Affairs.

Financial Data Qualifying disabled veterans and surviving spouses are exempt from all taxation on their specially adapted homestead.

Duration 1 year; once the credit has been approved, it is automatically renewed as long as the qualifying person owns the same residence in New Hampshire.

Number awarded Varies each year.

Deadline The original application for a permanent tax credit must be submitted by April.

[1345]
NEW HAMPSHIRE SERVICE-CONNECTED TOTAL AND PERMANENT DISABILITY TAX CREDIT

New Hampshire Department of Revenue Administration
109 Pleasant Street
Concord, NH 03301
(603) 271-2191 Fax: (603) 271-6121
TDD: (800) 735-2964
Web: revenue.nh.gov

Summary To provide property tax credits in New Hampshire to disabled veterans or their surviving spouses.

Eligibility Eligible for this tax credit are honorably discharged veterans residing in New Hampshire who 1) have a total and permanent service-connected disability, or 2) are a double amputee or paraplegic because of a service-connected disability. Unremarried surviving spouses of qualified veterans are also eligible.

Financial Data Qualifying disabled veterans and surviving spouses receive an annual credit of $700 for property taxes on residential property. In addition, individual towns in New Hampshire may adopt a local option to increase the dollar amount credited to disabled veterans, to a maximum of $2,000.

Duration 1 year; once the credit has been approved, it is automatically renewed for as long as the qualifying person owns the same residence in New Hampshire.

Number awarded Varies each year.

Deadline The original application for a permanent tax credit must be submitted by April.

[1346]
NEW HAMPSHIRE SURVIVING SPOUSE TAX CREDIT

New Hampshire Department of Revenue Administration
109 Pleasant Street
Concord, NH 03301
(603) 271-2191 Fax: (603) 271-6121
TDD: (800) 735-2964
Web: revenue.nh.gov

Summary To provide property tax credits in New Hampshire to surviving spouses of servicemembers who died while on active duty.

Eligibility Eligible for this tax credit are New Hampshire residents who are the unremarried surviving spouses of persons who were killed or died while on active duty in the armed forces.

Financial Data Qualifying spouses receive an annual credit of $700 for property taxes on residential property. In addition, individual towns in New Hampshire may adopt a local option to increase the dollar amount credited to surviving spouses of deceased veterans, to a maximum of $2,000.

Duration 1 year; once the credit has been approved, it is automatically renewed as long as the qualifying person owns the same residence in New Hampshire.

Number awarded Varies each year.

Deadline The original application for a permanent tax credit must be submitted by April.

[1347]
NEW JERSEY INCOME TAX EXCLUSION FOR MILITARY PENSIONS AND SURVIVOR'S BENEFITS

New Jersey Division of Taxation
Attn: Information and Publications Branch
50 Barrack Street
P.O. Box 281
Trenton, NJ 08695-0281
(609) 292-6400
Toll Free: (800) 323-4400 (within NJ, NY, PA, DE, and MD)
TDD: (800) 286-6613 (within NJ, NY, PA, DE, and MD)
E-mail: taxation@tax.state.nj.us
Web: www.state.nj.us/treasury/taxation

Summary To exclude from income taxation in New Jersey military pensions and survivor's benefits.

Eligibility This exclusion is available to residents of New Jersey who are receiving 1) a military pension resulting from service in the Army, Navy, Air Force, Marine Corps, or Coast Guard, or 2) survivor's benefits related to such service. It does not apply to civil service pensions or annuities, even if the pension or annuity is based on credit for military service.

Financial Data All military pensions and survivor's benefit payments are excluded from income for state taxation purposes.

Duration The exclusion applies as long as the individual resides in New Jersey.

Additional data This exclusion became effective in 2001.

Number awarded Varies each year.

Deadline Deadline not specified.

[1348]
NEW JERSEY PROPERTY TAX EXEMPTION FOR DISABLED VETERANS OR SURVIVING SPOUSES

New Jersey Division of Taxation
Attn: Information and Publications Branch
50 Barrack Street
P.O. Box 281
Trenton, NJ 08695-0281
(609) 292-6400
Toll Free: (800) 323-4400 (within NJ, NY, PA, DE, and MD)
TDD: (800) 286-6613 (within NJ, NY, PA, DE, and MD)
E-mail: taxation@tax.state.nj.us
Web: www.state.nj.us/treasury/taxation/otherptr.shtml

Summary To provide a real estate tax exemption to New Jersey veterans with disabilities and certain surviving widow(er)s.

Eligibility This exemption is available to New Jersey residents who have been honorably discharged with active wartime service in the U.S. armed forces and have been certified by the U.S. Department of Veterans Affairs as totally and permanently disabled as a result of wartime service-connected conditions. Unremarried surviving spouses of eligible disabled veterans or of certain wartime servicepersons who died on active duty are also entitled to this exemption. Applicants must be the full owner of and a permanent resident in the dwelling house for which the exemption is claimed.

Financial Data A 100% exemption from locally-levied real estate taxes is provided.

Duration 1 year; the exemption continues as long as the eligible veteran remains a resident of New Jersey.

Additional data This program is administered by the local tax assessor or collector. Veterans who are denied exemptions have the right to appeal the decision to their county and state governments.

Number awarded Varies each year.

Deadline Applications may be submitted at any time.

[1349]
NEW MEXICO DISABLED VETERAN PROPERTY TAX EXEMPTION

New Mexico Department of Veterans' Services
Attn: Benefits Division
407 Galisteo Street, Room 142
Santa Fe, NM 87504
(505) 827-6374   Toll Free: (866) 433-VETS
Fax: (505) 827-6372   E-mail: alan.martinez@state.nm.us
Web: www.dvs.state.nm.us/benefits.html

Summary To exempt disabled veterans and their spouses from payment of property taxes in New Mexico.

Eligibility This exemption is available to veterans who are rated 100% service-connected disabled by the U.S. Department of Veterans Affairs, are residents of New Mexico, and own a primary residence in the state. Also eligible are qualifying veterans' unremarried surviving spouses, if they are New Mexico residents and continue to own the residence.

Financial Data Veterans and surviving spouses are exempt from payment of property taxes in New Mexico.

Duration 1 year; continues until the qualifying veteran or spouse no longer live in the residence.

Number awarded Varies each year.

Deadline Deadline not specified.

[1350]
NEW MEXICO VETERANS PROPERTY TAX EXEMPTION

New Mexico Department of Veterans' Services
Attn: Benefits Division
407 Galisteo Street, Room 142
Santa Fe, NM 87504
(505) 827-6374   Toll Free: (866) 433-VETS
Fax: (505) 827-6372   E-mail: alan.martinez@state.nm.us
Web: www.dvs.state.nm.us/benefits.html

Summary To exempt veterans and their spouses from a portion of property taxes in New Mexico.

Eligibility This exemption is available to veterans who served honorably for at least 90 days during wartime (World War I, World War II, Korea, Vietnam, Persian Gulf), are residents of New Mexico, and own a primary residence in the state. Also eligible are qualifying veterans' unremarried surviving spouses, if they are New Mexico residents and continue to own the residence.

Financial Data Veterans and surviving spouses are entitled to a reduction in the value of their property that is currently $4,000. The exemption is deducted from the taxable value of the property to determine net taxable value. Veterans who are entitled to this exemption and do not have sufficient real or personal property to claim the full exemption may be eligible to claim a one third reduction in motor vehicle registration fees.

Duration 1 year; continues until the qualifying veteran or spouse no longer lives in the residence.

Number awarded Varies each year.

Deadline Deadline not specified.

[1351]
NEW YORK ALTERNATIVE PROPERTY TAX EXEMPTIONS FOR VETERANS

New York State Division of Veterans' Affairs
5 Empire State Plaza, Suite 2836
Albany, NY 12223-1551
(518) 474-6114   Toll Free: (888) VETS-NYS (within NY)
Fax: (518) 473-0379   E-mail: dvainfo@ogs.state.ny.us
Web: veterans.ny.gov/property_tax_exemption.html

Summary To provide wartime veterans and their spouses who are residents of New York with a partial exemption from property taxes.

Eligibility This program is open to veterans who served during specified periods of wartime. Applicants must have been discharged under honorable conditions; additional benefits are available to those who served in a combat zone and to those who have a service-connected disability. The legal title to the property must be in the name of the veteran or the spouse of the veteran or both, or the unremarried surviving spouse of the veteran. The property must be used exclusively for residential purposes. This program is only available in counties, cities, towns, and villages in New York that have opted to participate.

Financial Data This program provides an exemption of 15% of the assessed valuation of the property, to a basic maximum of $12,000 per year; local governments may opt for reduced maximums of $9,000 or $6,000, or for increased maximums of $15,000 to $36,000. For combat-zone veterans, an additional 10% of the assessed valuation is exempt, to a basic maximum of $8,000 per year; local governments may opt for a reduced maximum of $6,000 or $4,000, or for increased maximums of $10,000 to $24,000. For disabled veterans, the exemption is the percentage of assessed value equal to half of the service-connected disability rating, to a basic maximum of $40,000 per year; local governments may opt for a reduced maximum of $30,000 or $20,000, or for increased maximums of $50,000 to $120,000. At its option, New York City and other high appreciation municipalities may use the following increased maximum exemptions: war veteran,

$54,000; combat-zone veteran, $36,000; disabled veteran, $180,000.

Duration   This exemption is available annually.

Number awarded   Varies each year.

Deadline   Applications must be filed with the local assessor by "taxable status date;" in most towns, that is the end of February.

[1352]
NEW YORK "ELIGIBLE FUNDS" PROPERTY TAX EXEMPTIONS FOR VETERANS

New York State Division of Veterans' Affairs
5 Empire State Plaza, Suite 2836
Albany, NY 12223-1551
(518) 474-6114   Toll Free: (888) VETS-NYS (within NY)
Fax: (518) 473-0379   E-mail: dvainfo@ogs.state.ny.us
Web: veterans.ny.gov

Summary   To provide a partial exemption from property taxes to veterans and their surviving spouses who are residents of New York.

Eligibility   This program is open to veterans who have purchased properties in New York with pension, bonus, or insurance money (referred to as "eligible funds"). Specially adapted homes of paraplegics, or the homes of their widowed spouses, are also covered.

Financial Data   This exemption reduces the property's assessed value to the extent that "eligible funds" were used in the purchase, generally to a maximum of $5,000. It is applicable to general municipal taxes but not to school taxes or special district levies.

Duration   This exemption is available annually.

Number awarded   Varies each year.

Deadline   Applications must be filed with the local assessor by "taxable status date;" in most towns, that is the end of February.

[1353]
NEW YORK STATE BLIND ANNUITY

New York State Division of Veterans' Affairs
5 Empire State Plaza, Suite 2836
Albany, NY 12223-1551
(518) 474-6114   Toll Free: (888) VETS-NYS (within NY)
Fax: (518) 473-0379   E-mail: dvainfo@ogs.state.ny.us
Web: veterans.ny.gov/blind_annuity.html

Summary   To provide an annuity to blind wartime veterans and their surviving spouses in New York.

Eligibility   This benefit is available to veterans who served on active duty during specified periods of war. Applicants must 1) meet the New York State standards of blindness; 2) have received an honorable or general discharge, or a discharge other than for dishonorable service; and 3) be now, and continue to be, residents of and continuously domiciled in New York State. The annuity is also payable to unremarried spouses of deceased veterans who were receiving annuity payments (or were eligible to do so) at the time of their death, and are residents of and continuously domiciled in New York State.

Financial Data   The annuity is currently $1,173.84 per year.

Number awarded   Varies each year.

Deadline   Deadline not specified.

[1354]
NEW YORK VETERANS SUPPLEMENTAL BURIAL ALLOWANCE

New York State Division of Veterans' Affairs
5 Empire State Plaza, Suite 2836
Albany, NY 12223-1551
(518) 474-6114   Toll Free: (888) VETS-NYS (within NY)
Fax: (518) 473-0379   E-mail: dvainfo@ogs.state.ny.us
Web: veterans.ny.gov/supplemental_burial_allowance.html

Summary   To provide a burial allowance for New York veterans killed in combat.

Eligibility   This benefit is available to the families of New York military personnel killed in combat or while on active duty in hostile or imminent danger locations on or after September 29, 2003.

Financial Data   This program provides a supplemental burial allowance of up to $6,000. Funds are paid to the family member responsible for funeral and burial expenses.

Number awarded   Varies each year.

Deadline   Applications may be submitted at any time, but they must be received within 2 years of permanent burial or cremation of the body.

[1355]
NMCRS FINANCIAL ASSISTANCE

Navy-Marine Corps Relief Society
875 North Randolph Street, Suite 225
Arlington, VA 22203-1757
(703) 696-4904   Fax: (703) 696-0144
Web: www.nmcrs.org/intfreeloan.html

Summary   To provide emergency assistance, in the form of interest-free loans or grants, to current and former Navy and Marine Corps personnel and their families who need temporary funding.

Eligibility   This program is open to active-duty and retired Navy and Marine Corps personnel, their eligible family members, eligible family members of Navy and Marine Corps personnel who died on active duty or in a retired status, Reservists on extended active duty, indigent mothers (65 years of age or older) of deceased servicemembers who have limited resources and no family to provide for their welfare, ex-spouses whose marriage to a servicemember lasted for at least 20 years while the servicemember was on active duty and who have not remarried, and uniformed members of the National Oceanic and Atmospheric Administration (NOAA). Applicants must need emergency funding for funeral expenses, medical or dental bills, food, rent, utilities, emergency transportation, disaster relief, child care expenses, essential vehicle repairs, or other unforeseen family emergencies. Funding is not available to pay bills for non-essentials, finance liberty and vacations, pay fines or legal expenses, pay taxes, finance recreational boats or vehicles or help Navy and Marine Corps families live beyond their means.

Financial Data   Funds are provided in the form of interest-free loans or grants.

Number awarded   Varies each year.

Deadline   Applications may be submitted at any time.

[1356]
NORTH DAKOTA PROPERTY TAX CREDIT FOR DISABLED VETERANS

Office of State Tax Commissioner
State Capitol Building
600 East Boulevard Avenue, Department 127
Bismarck, ND 58505-0599
(701) 328-2770   Toll Free: (800) 638-2901
Fax: (701) 328-3700   TDD: (800) 366-6888
E-mail: taxinfo@state.nd.us
Web: www.nd.gov/tax

Summary   To provide property tax credits to disabled North Dakota veterans and their surviving spouses.

Eligibility   This property tax credit is available to honorably-discharged veterans who have more than a 50% service-connected disability as certified by the U.S. Department of Veterans Affairs. Applicants must own and occupy a homestead according to state law. Unremarried surviving spouses are also eligible. If a disabled veteran co-owns the property with someone other than a spouse, the credit is limited to the disabled veteran's interest in the fixtures, buildings, and improvements of the homestead.

Financial Data The credit is applied against the first $120,000 of true and full valuation of the fixtures, buildings, and improvements of the homestead, to a maximum amount calculated by multiplying $120,000 by the percentage of the disabled veteran's disability compensation rating for service-connected disabilities.

Duration 1 year; renewable as long as qualified individuals continue to reside in North Dakota and live in their homes.

Number awarded Varies each year.

Deadline Applications may be submitted to the county auditor at any time.

[1357]
NORTH DAKOTA PROPERTY TAX EXEMPTION FOR VETERANS WHO LIVE IN SPECIALLY ADAPTED HOUSING

Office of State Tax Commissioner
State Capitol Building
600 East Boulevard Avenue, Department 127
Bismarck, ND 58505-0599
(701) 328-2770 Toll Free: (800) 638-2901
Fax: (701) 328-3700 TDD: (800) 366-6888
E-mail: taxinfo@state.nd.us
Web: www.nd.gov/tax

Summary To provide property tax exemptions to North Dakota veterans and their surviving spouses who have been awarded specially adapted housing.

Eligibility This exemption is available to paraplegic disabled veterans of the U.S. armed forces or any veteran who has been awarded specially adapted housing by the U.S. Department of Veterans Affairs. The paraplegic disability does not have to be service-connected. The unremarried surviving spouses of such deceased veterans are also eligible. Income and assets are not considered in determining eligibility for the exemption.

Financial Data The maximum benefit may not exceed $5,400 taxable value, because the exemption is limited to the first $120,000 of true and full value of fixtures, buildings, and improvements.

Duration 1 year; renewable as long as qualified individuals continue to reside in North Dakota and live in their homes.

Number awarded Varies each year.

Deadline Applications may be submitted to the county auditor at any time.

[1358]
OHIO BURIAL ALLOWANCE FOR INDIGENT VETERANS

Ohio Department of Veterans Services
77 South High Street, 7th Floor
Columbus, OH 43215
(614) 644-0898 Toll Free: (888) DVS-OHIO
Fax: (614) 728-9498 E-mail: ohiovet@dvs.ohio.gov
Web: dvs.ohio.gov

Summary To provide an allowance for the burial of indigent Ohio veterans and certain of their dependents.

Eligibility Eligible to receive this allowance are the survivors of Ohio veterans, their spouses, widow(er)s, or mothers.

Financial Data This allowance is $1,000.

Additional data These grants are made by the various county veterans services offices in Ohio.

Number awarded Varies each year.

Deadline Applications may be submitted at any time.

[1359]
OHIO INCOME TAX DEDUCTION FOR MILITARY RETIREMENT INCOME

Ohio Department of Taxation
Attn: Income Tax Audit Division
30 East Broad Street
P.O. Box 182847
Columbus, OH 43218-2847
(614) 433-5817 Toll Free: (800) 282-1780 (within OH)
Fax: (614) 433-7771
Web: tax.ohio.gov

Summary To deduct from state income taxation in Ohio the pay received by retired military personnel and their surviving spouses.

Eligibility This deduction is available to residents of Ohio who are retired from service in the active or reserve components of the U.S. armed forces. Surviving and former spouses of military retirees who are receiving payments under the survivor benefit plan are also eligible. the state is excluded from income for purposes of Ohio state taxation.

Financial Data All retirement income received by military personnel and their surviving or former spouses is excluded from state income taxation in Ohio.

Duration The exclusion is available as long as the recipient remains an Ohio resident.

Number awarded Varies each year.

Deadline Deadline not specified.

[1360]
OHIO VETERANS' FINANCIAL ASSISTANCE

Ohio Department of Veterans Services
77 South High Street, 7th Floor
Columbus, OH 43215
(614) 644-0898 Toll Free: (888) DVS-OHIO
Fax: (614) 728-9498 E-mail: ohiovet@dvs.ohio.gov
Web: dvs.ohio.gov

Summary To provide emergency aid to Ohio veterans, military personnel, and their dependents who, because of disability or disaster, are in financial need.

Eligibility This assistance is available to veterans and active-duty members of the U.S. armed forces, as well as their spouses, surviving spouses, dependent parents, minor children, and wards. Applicants must have been residents of the Ohio county in which they are applying for at least 3 months. They must be able to demonstrate need for relief because of sickness, accident, or destitution.

Financial Data The amount granted varies, depending on the needs of the recipient.

Duration These are emergency funds only and are not designed to be a recurring source of income.

Additional data These grants are made by the various county veterans services offices in Ohio.

Number awarded Varies each year.

Deadline Applications may be submitted at any time.

[1361]
OKLAHOMA FINANCIAL ASSISTANCE PROGRAM

Oklahoma Department of Veterans Affairs
Veterans Memorial Building
2311 North Central Avenue
P.O. Box 53067
Oklahoma City, OK 73152
(405) 521-3684 Fax: (405) 521-6533
E-mail: scylmer@odva.state.ok.us
Web: www.ok.gov/ODVA/Financial_Assistance/index.html

Summary To provide emergency aid to Oklahoma veterans and their families who, because of disability or disaster, are in financial need.

Eligibility This program is open to veterans with at least 90 days of wartime service and an honorable discharge who are current residents of Oklahoma and have resided in the state for at least 1 year immediately preceding the date of application. Applicants must be seeking assistance because of an interruption or loss of job and income resulting from illness, injury, or disaster (such as loss of home due to fire, floor, or storm). Widow(er)s and minor children may also qualify for the benefit.

Financial Data The amount of the grant depends on the need of the recipient.

Duration The grant is available only on a 1-time basis.

Additional data No financial assistance will be granted when regular monetary benefits are being received from other state agencies. The funds cannot be used for old debts, car payments, or medical expenses.

Number awarded Varies each year.

Deadline Applications must be submitted to the local post or chapter of a veterans services organization for initial approval or disapproval. They may be submitted at any time during the year.

[1362]
OKLAHOMA MILITARY RETIREMENT INCOME TAX EXCLUSION

Oklahoma Tax Commission
Attn: Income Tax
2501 North Lincoln Boulevard
Oklahoma City, OK 73194-0009
(405) 521-3160   Toll Free: (800) 522-8165 (within OK)
Fax: (405) 522-0063   E-mail: otcmaster@tax.ok.gov
Web: www.tax.ok.gov/incometax.html

Summary To exclude a portion of the income of military retirees and their spouses from state taxation in Oklahoma.

Eligibility This exclusion is available to residents of Oklahoma and their spouses who are receiving retirement benefits from a component of the U.S. armed forces.

Financial Data Military retirees are entitled to exclude 75% of their retirement benefits or $10,000, whichever is greater, from state taxation.

Duration The exclusion is available as long as the recipient resides in Oklahoma.

Deadline Deadline not specified.

[1363]
OKLAHOMA PROPERTY TAX EXEMPTION FOR DISABLED VETERANS

Oklahoma Tax Commission
Attn: Property Tax
2501 North Lincoln Boulevard
Oklahoma City, OK 73194-0009
(405) 521-3178   Toll Free: (800) 522-8165 (within OK)
Fax: (405) 522-0063   E-mail: otcmaster@tax.ok.gov
Web: www.tax.ok.gov

Summary To exempt the property of disabled veterans and their surviving spouses from taxation in Oklahoma.

Eligibility This program is available to Oklahoma residents who are veterans honorably discharged from a branch of the armed forces or the Oklahoma National Guard. Applicants must have a 100% permanent disability sustained through military action or accident or resulting from a disease contracted while in active service; the disability must be certified by the U.S. Department of Veterans Affairs. They must own property that qualifies for the Oklahoma homestead exemption. Surviving spouses of qualified veterans are also eligible.

Financial Data Qualified veterans and surviving spouses are eligible for exemption of the taxes on the full fair cash value of their homestead.

Duration The exemption is available as long as the veteran or surviving spouse resides in Oklahoma and owns a qualifying homestead.

Additional data This exemption was first available in 2006.

Deadline Deadline not specified.

[1364]
OREGON PROPERTY TAX EXEMPTION FOR ACTIVE DUTY MILITARY SERVICE

Oregon Department of Revenue
Attn: Property Tax Division
Revenue Building
955 Center Street, N.E.
Salem, OR 97310-2551
(503) 378-4988   Toll Free: (800) 356-4222 (within OR)
TDD: (800) 886-7204 (within OR)
Web: www.oregon.gov/DOR/PTD

Summary To exempt members of the Oregon National Guard and military Reserves called to active duty and their survivors from a portion of their property taxes.

Eligibility This exemption is available to members of the Oregon National Guard and Reserves called to federal active duty (U.S. Code Title 10) who serve more than 178 days with that status during the tax year. Applicants must own property that they occupy as their primary residence in Oregon. Occupants of a home owned by a qualified Guard member or Reservist who is killed in action also qualify for this exemption.

Financial Data The exemption was set as $60,000 of the homestead property's assessed value as of July 1, 2006. It increases by 3% annually.

Duration 1 year; may be renewed as long as the eligible Guard member or surviving occupant of the home owns and occupies the primary residence.

Additional data This exemption was first available in 2005.

Number awarded Varies each year.

Deadline This exemption is not automatic. Applications must be submitted by March of each year.

[1365]
OREGON PROPERTY TAX EXEMPTION FOR VETERANS WITH DISABILITIES AND THEIR SPOUSES

Oregon Department of Revenue
Attn: Property Tax Division
Revenue Building
955 Center Street, N.E.
Salem, OR 97310-2551
(503) 378-4988   Toll Free: (800) 356-4222 (within OR)
TDD: (800) 886-7204 (within OR)
Web: www.oregon.gov/DOR/PTD/IC_310_676.shtml

Summary To exempt disabled Oregon veterans and their spouses from a portion of their property taxes.

Eligibility Qualifying veterans are those who received a discharge or release under honorable conditions after service of either 1) 90 consecutive days during World War I, World War II, or the Korean Conflict; or 2) 210 consecutive days after January 31, 1955. Eligible individuals must meet 1 of these conditions: 1) a war veteran who is officially certified by the U.S. Department of Veterans Affairs (VA) or any branch of the U.S. armed forces as having disabilities of 40% or more; 2) a war veteran who is certified each year by a licensed physician as being 40% or more disabled and has total gross income that is less than 185% of the federal poverty level (currently $18,130 for a family of 1, rising to $62,160 for a family of 8); or 3) a war veteran's surviving spouse who has not remarried, even if the veteran's spouse was not disabled or did not take advantage of the exemption if disabled. Recipients of this exemption must own and live on a property in Oregon.

Financial Data The exemption is $15,450 of the homestead property's real market value.

Duration 1 year; may be renewed as long as the eligible veteran or surviving unremarried spouse owns and occupies the primary residence.

Number awarded Varies each year.

Deadline This exemption is not automatic. Applications must be submitted by March of each year.

[1366]
OREGON PROPERTY TAX EXEMPTION FOR VETERANS WITH SERVICE-CONNECTED DISABILITIES AND THEIR SPOUSES

Oregon Department of Revenue
Attn: Property Tax Division
Revenue Building
955 Center Street, N.E.
Salem, OR 97310-2551
(503) 378-4988   Toll Free: (800) 356-4222 (within OR)
TDD: (800) 886-7204 (within OR)
Web: www.oregon.gov/DOR/PTD/IC_310_676.shtml

Summary To exempt Oregon veterans with service-connected disabilities and their spouses from a portion of their property taxes.

Eligibility Qualifying veterans are those who received a discharge or release under honorable conditions after service of either 1) 90 consecutive days during World War I, World War II, or the Korean Conflict; or 2) 210 consecutive days after January 31, 1955. Eligible individuals must meet 1 of these conditions: 1) a war veteran who is certified by the U.S. Department of Veterans Affairs (VA) or any branch of the U.S. armed forces as having service-connected disabilities of 40% or more; or 2) a surviving spouse of a war veteran who died because of service-connected injury or illness or who received at least 1 year of this exemption. Recipients of this exemption must own and live on a property in Oregon.

Financial Data The exemption is $18,540 of the homestead property's real market value.

Duration 1 year; may be renewed as long as the eligible veterans or surviving spouse owns and occupies the primary residence.

Number awarded Varies each year.

Deadline This exemption is not automatic. Applications must be submitted by March of each year.

[1367]
OREGON VETERANS' EMERGENCY FINANCIAL ASSISTANCE

Oregon Department of Veterans' Affairs
Attn: Veterans' Services Division
700 Summer Street N.E., Suite 150
Salem, OR 97310-1285
(503) 373-2000   Toll Free: (800) 692-9666 (within OR)
Fax: (503) 373-2362   TDD: (503) 373-2217
Web: www.oregon.gov/ODVA/BENEFITS/statebenefits.shtml

Summary To provide emergency financial assistance to Oregon veterans and their families.

Eligibility This assistance is available to Oregon residents who are veterans and their spouses, children, and grandchildren. Applicants must be in need of assistance for emergency or temporary housing and related housing expenses, such as utilities, insurance, house repairs, rent assistance, or food; emergency medical or dental expenses; emergency transportation; expenses related to starting a business, such as business licenses or occupational licenses; temporary income after military discharge; or legal assistance.

Financial Data Grants depend on the need of the recipient.

Duration These are 1-time grants.

Number awarded Varies each year.

Deadline Applications may be submitted at any time.

[1368]
PARENTS' DEPENDENCY AND INDEMNITY COMPENSATION (DIC)

Department of Veterans Affairs
Attn: Veterans Benefits Administration
810 Vermont Avenue, N.W.
Washington, DC 20420
(202) 418-4343   Toll Free: (800) 827-1000
Web: www.va.gov

Summary To provide financial support to the parents of servicemembers and veterans who died of disabilities or other causes.

Eligibility This program is open to parents (biological, adoptive, and foster) of servicemembers and veterans who died from a disease or injury aggravated while on active duty or active duty for training, an injury incurred or aggravated in the line of duty while on inactive duty for training, or a service-connected disability. If the parent is the sole surviving parent or 1 of 2 parents not living with a spouse, their countable income may not exceed $13,456 per year; if the parent is the sole surviving parent living with a spouse, or 1 of 2 parents living with a spouse, their countable income may not exceed $18,087 per year.

Financial Data Benefits depend on the income and current marital status of parents. For sole surviving parents unremarried or remarried and living with a spouse, the maximum benefit is $569 per month. For 1 of 2 parents not living with a spouse, the maximum benefit is $412 per month. For 1 of 2 parents living with a spouse, the maximum benefit is $387 per month. All categories of parents are entitled to an additional payment of $308 per month if they are receiving aid and assistance.

Duration Monthly payments continue for the life of the parent.

Number awarded Varies each year.

Deadline Applications are accepted at any time.

[1369]
PENNSYLVANIA DISABLED VETERANS REAL ESTATE TAX EXEMPTION

Office of the Deputy Adjutant General for Veterans Affairs
Building S-0-47, FTIG
Annville, PA 17003-5002
(717) 865-8907   Toll Free: (800) 54 PA VET (within PA)
Fax: (717) 861-8589   E-mail: jamebutler@state.pa.us
Web: www.milvet.state.pa.us/DMVA/592.htm

Summary To exempt blind and disabled Pennsylvania veterans and their unremarried surviving spouses from all state real estate taxes.

Eligibility Eligible to apply for this exemption are honorably-discharged veterans who are residents of Pennsylvania and who are blind, paraplegic, or 100% disabled from a service-connected disability sustained during wartime military service. The dwelling must be owned by the veteran solely or jointly with a spouse, and financial need for the exemption must be determined by the State Veterans' Commission. Veterans whose income is less than $79,050 per year are presumed to have financial need; veterans with income greater than $79,050 must document need. Upon the death of the veteran, the tax exemption passes on to the veteran's unremarried surviving spouse.

Financial Data This program exempts the principal residence (and the land on which it stands) from all real estate taxes.

Duration The exemption continues as long as the eligible veteran or unremarried widow resides in Pennsylvania.

Number awarded Varies each year.

Deadline Deadline not specified.

[1370]
PENNSYLVANIA MILITARY FAMILY RELIEF ASSISTANCE PROGRAM

Pennsylvania Department of Military and Veterans Affairs
Attn: Military Family Relief Assistance Program
Building 7-3
Fort Indiantown Gap
Annville, PA 17003-5002
(717) 861-6288 Toll Free: (866) 292-7201
Fax: (717) 861-2389 E-mail: ra-pa-mfrap@state.pa.us
Web: www.milvet.state.pa.us/DMVA/541.htm

Summary To provide emergency financial assistance to members of the armed forces from Pennsylvania and their families.

Eligibility This assistance is available to residents of Pennsylvania who are serving 1) on 30 or more consecutive days of active duty with the Pennsylvania Army or Air National Guard or Reserve components of the armed forces; 2) on 30 or more consecutive days of active duty with the active armed forces; or 3) on 30 or more consecutive days of state active duty for emergencies or duty under the Emergency Management Assistance Compact in the Pennsylvania Army or Air National Guard. Families of qualifying servicemembers are also eligible if they are Pennsylvania residents. Applicants must be able to demonstrate a direct and immediate financial need as a result of military service; that financial need may include, but is not limited to, a sudden or unexpected loss of income directly related to military service; emergency need for child care for which the applicant lacks financial resources; natural or man-made disasters resulting in a need for food, shelter, or other necessities; or the death or critical illness of a parent, spouse, sibling, or child resulting in immediate need for travel, lodging, or subsistence for which the applicant lacks financial resources.

Financial Data The maximum grant is $2,500.

Duration Only 1 grant will be awarded in each 12-month period.

Additional data This program was established in 2005.

Number awarded Varies each year.

Deadline Applications may be submitted at any time.

[1371]
PENNSYLVANIA PERSIAN GULF CONFLICT VETERANS' BENEFIT PROGRAM

Office of the Deputy Adjutant General for Veterans Affairs
Building S-0-47, FTIG
Annville, PA 17003-5002
(717) 865-8911 Toll Free: (800) 54 PA VET (within PA)
Fax: (717) 861-8589 E-mail: jamebutler@state.pa.us
Web: www.milvet.state.pa.us/DMVA/2564.htm

Summary To provide an bonus to veterans from Pennsylvania who served in the Persian Gulf Conflict or to their survivors.

Eligibility Eligible to receive this bonus are veterans who served on active duty in the Persian Gulf Theater of Operations during the period from August 2, 1990 to August 31, 1991 and received the Southwest Asia Service Medal. Applicants must have been a resident of Pennsylvania at the time of military service and must have served under honorable conditions.

Financial Data The bonus is $75 per month for each month (or major fraction) of active service in the Gulf, to a maximum of $525. For veterans who died in active service, a bonus of $5,000 is paid to the family. In addition, $5,000 is paid to Persian Gulf Conflict prisoners of war.

Duration This is a 1-time benefit.

Additional data This program was authorized in 2006.

Number awarded Varies each year.

Deadline Applications may be submitted at any time prior to August 31, 2015.

[1372]
PENNSYLVANIA VETERANS EMERGENCY ASSISTANCE

Office of the Deputy Adjutant General for Veterans Affairs
Building S-0-47, FTIG
Annville, PA 17003-5002
(717) 865-8905 Toll Free: (800) 54 PA VET (within PA)
Fax: (717) 861-8589 E-mail: jamebutler@state.pa.us
Web: www.milvet.state.pa.us/DMVA/185.htm

Summary To provide financial aid on an emergency and temporary basis to Pennsylvania veterans (or their dependents) who are disabled, sick, or without means.

Eligibility Eligible to apply for this assistance are honorably-discharged veterans who served in the U.S. armed forces during wartime and are now disabled, sick, or in financial need. Widow(er)s or orphan children of recently deceased veterans are also eligible if the veteran would have qualified prior to death. Applicants must have been residents of Pennsylvania for 1 year prior to the date of application.

Financial Data Financial aid for the necessities of life (food, shelter, fuel, and clothing) is provided. The amount depends on the number of persons in the household and the Pennsylvania county in which the veteran or dependent lives; recently, monthly grants for 1-person households ranged from $174 to $215, for 2-person households from $279 to $330, for 3-person households from $365 to $431, for 4-person households from $454 to $514, for 5-person households from $543 to $607, and for 6-person households from $614 to $687.

Duration Aid is provided on a temporary basis only, not to exceed 3 months in a 12-month period.

Number awarded Varies each year.

Deadline Applications may be submitted at any time, but the factors that caused the emergency must have occurred within 180 days prior to the application.

[1373]
RED CROSS EMERGENCY FINANCIAL ASSISTANCE

American Red Cross
c/o National Headquarters
2025 E Street, N.W.
Washington, DC 20006
(202) 303-4498 Toll Free: (800) HELP-NOW
Web: www.redcross.org

Summary To provide funding to active and retired military personnel and their families who are in need of emergency financial assistance.

Eligibility This program is open to servicemembers, their families, retired military personnel, and widows of retired military personnel. Members of the National Guard and Reserves are also eligible. Applicants must be in need of such emergency financial assistance as travel that requires the presence of the servicemember or his or her family, burial of a loved one, or other assistance that cannot wait until the next business day (food, temporary lodging, urgent medical needs, or the minimum amount required to avoid eviction or utility shut-off).

Financial Data The amount of the assistance depends on the need of the recipient.

Duration These are 1-time grants.

Additional data The Red Cross works with the military aid societies (Army Emergency Relief, Navy-Marine Corps Relief Society, Air Force Aid Society, and Coast Guard Mutual Assistance).

Number awarded Varies each year; recently, more than 5,000 servicemembers and their families received more than $5.3 million in emergency grants.

Deadline Applications may be submitted at any time.

[1374]
REIMBURSEMENT OF BURIAL EXPENSES

Department of Veterans Affairs
Attn: Veterans Benefits Administration
810 Vermont Avenue, N.W.
Washington, DC 20420
(202) 418-4343   Toll Free: (800) 827-1000
Web: www1.va.gov/opa/ls1/7.asp

Summary To provide reimbursement of burial expenses for wartime and certain peacetime veterans.

Eligibility Survivors are eligible for reimbursement if the veteran, at the time of death, was entitled to receive a pension or compensation or would have been entitled to compensation but for receipt of military pay. Eligibility is also established if the veteran died while hospitalized or domiciled in a U.S. Department of Veterans Affairs (VA) facility or other facility at VA expense. The veteran must have been discharged under conditions other than dishonorable.

Financial Data Up to $300 is provided for the veteran's burial expenses. The costs of transporting the remains may be allowed if the veteran died while hospitalized or domiciled in a VA hospital or domiciliary or at VA's expense or died in transit at VA's expense to or from a medical facility. Up to $300 is also paid as a plot or interment allowance (in addition to the $300 basic burial allowance) when the veteran is not buried in a national cemetery or other cemetery under the jurisdiction of the U.S. government. For veterans who died of service-connected causes, the payment is $2,000.

Duration For service-connected deaths, the claim may be filed at any time. For other deaths, the claim must be filed within 2 years after permanent burial or cremation.

Number awarded Varies each year.

Deadline Applications may be submitted at any time.

[1375]
RESTORED ENTITLEMENT PROGRAM FOR SURVIVORS (REPS)

Department of Veterans Affairs
Attn: Veterans Benefits Administration
810 Vermont Avenue, N.W.
Washington, DC 20420
(202) 418-4343   Toll Free: (800) 827-1000
Web: www1.va.gov/opa/ls1/11.asp

Summary To provide benefits to survivors of certain deceased veterans.

Eligibility Survivors of deceased veterans who died of service-connected causes incurred or aggravated prior to August 13, 1981 are eligible for these benefits.

Financial Data The benefits are similar to the benefits for students and surviving spouses with children between the ages of 16 and 18 that were eliminated from the Social Security Act. The exact amount of the benefits is based on information provided by the Social Security Administration.

Additional data The benefits are payable in addition to any other benefits to which the family may be entitled.

Number awarded Varies each year.

Deadline Applications may be submitted at any time.

[1376]
SOUTH CAROLINA MILITARY FAMILY RELIEF FUND

South Carolina Division of Veterans Affairs
Attn: SCMFRF Coordinator
1205 Pendleton Street, Suite 477
Columbia, SC 29201-3789
(803) 734-0200   Fax: (803) 734-0197
E-mail: va@oepp.sc.gov
Web: www.govoepp.state.sc.us/va/benefits.html

Summary To provide emergency assistance to members and families of the National Guard and Reserve forces in South Carolina who have been called to active duty as a result of the September 11, 2001 terrorist attacks.

Eligibility This assistance is available to families of South Carolina National Guard members and South Carolina residents serving in the U.S. armed forces reserve units who were called to active duty as a result of the September 11, 2001 terrorist attacks. Status-based grants are available to National Guard and Reserve members and their family members enrolled in the Defense Enrollment Eligibility Reporting System (DEERS); the servicemember must have been on active duty for at least 30 consecutive days, have a rank no higher than O-3 or W-2, and have orders for Operation Nobel Eagle, Enduring Freedom, Iraqi Freedom, Executive Order 13223, or other approved operation. Need-based grants are available to servicemembers and their families who meet those requirements and who also can demonstrate that the servicemember sustained a 30% or greater decrease in income from his or her civilian salary. Casualty-based grants are available to servicemembers who sustained a service-connected injury or illness and to next of kin of servicemembers killed in action, missing in action, or a prisoner of war. The following servicemembers are ineligible: those who are unmarried or have no family members enrolled in DEERS; personnel serving in active Guard, Reserve, or similar full-time unit support programs but not called to Title 10 service; and members who receive a discharge under other than honorable conditions.

Financial Data Status grants are $500; need-based grants range up to $2,000; casualty-based grants are $1,000.

Duration Status grants are available only once in each fiscal year and only 1 time for each active-duty order; need-based grants may be renewed after 180 days have elapsed; casualty-based grants may be awarded only 1 time for each active-duty order.

Additional data This program, which began in 2005, is funded by a voluntary check-off on South Carolina individual income tax forms and by other grants and donations.

Number awarded Varies each year.

Deadline Applications may be submitted at any time.

[1377]
SOUTH CAROLINA PROPERTY TAX EXEMPTION FOR DISABLED VETERANS, LAW ENFORCEMENT OFFICERS, AND FIREFIGHTERS

South Carolina Department of Revenue
Attn: Property Division
301 Gervais Street
P.O. Box 125
Columbia, SC 29214
(803) 898-5480   Fax: (803) 898-5822
Web: www.sctax.org

Summary To exempt the residence of disabled South Carolina veterans, law enforcement officers, fire fighters, their unremarried widow(er)s, and others from property taxation.

Eligibility This exemption is available to owners of homes in South Carolina who are veterans of the U.S. armed forces, former law enforcement officers, or former fire fighters (including volunteer fire fighters). Applicants must be permanently and totally disabled from service-connected causes. The exemption is also available to qualified surviving spouses (defined to include unremarried spouses of disabled veterans, law enforcement officers, and fire fighters, as well as surviving spouses of servicemembers killed in the line of duty, law enforcement officers who died in the line of duty, and fire fighters who died in the line of duty).

Financial Data The exemption applies to all taxes on 1 house and a lot (not to exceed 1 acre).

Duration The exemption extends as long as the veteran, law enforcement officer, or fire fighter resides in the house, or as long as the spouse of a deceased veteran, servicemember, law enforcement officer, or fire fighter remains unremarried and resides in the original house or a single new dwelling.

Number awarded   Varies each year.

Deadline   Applications may be submitted at any time.

[1378]
SOUTH CAROLINA PROPERTY TAX EXEMPTION FOR MEDAL OF HONOR RECIPIENTS AND PRISONERS OF WAR

South Carolina Department of Revenue
Attn: Property Division
301 Gervais Street
P.O. Box 125
Columbia, SC 29214
(803) 898-5480   Fax: (803) 898-5822
Web: www.sctax.org

Summary   To exempt the residence of disabled South Carolina veterans who received a Medal or Honor or who were a prisoner of war from property taxation.

Eligibility   This exemption is available to owners of homes in South Carolina who are veterans of the U.S. armed forces and who received a Medal of Honor or were a prisoner of war during World War I, World War II, the Korean Conflict, or the Vietnam Conflict. The exemption is also available to qualified surviving spouses.

Financial Data   The exemption applies to all taxes on 1 house and a lot (not to exceed 1 acre).

Duration   The exemption extends as long as the veteran or the spouse of a deceased veteran resides in the original house or a single new dwelling.

Number awarded   Varies each year.

Deadline   Applications may be submitted at any time.

[1379]
SOUTH CAROLINA RETIREMENT INCOME TAX DEDUCTION

South Carolina Department of Revenue
301 Gervais Street
P.O. Box 125
Columbia, SC 29214
(803) 898-5000   Toll Free: (800) 763-1295
Fax: (803) 898-5822
Web: www.sctax.org

Summary   To exempt part of the retirement income received by veterans and others (including spouses) from state taxation in South Carolina.

Eligibility   This program is open to residents of South Carolina who are receiving public employee retirement income from federal, state, or local government, including individual retirement accounts, Keogh plans, and military retirement. Spouses are also entitled to the exemption.

Financial Data   The maximum retirement income deduction is $3,000 for taxpayers under 65 years of age and $10,000 in subsequent years. Taxpayers who wait until they are 65 and older until declaring a retirement exemption are entitled to deduct $15,000 per year.

Duration   The exemption continues as long as the eligible veteran or spouse resides in South Carolina and receives the specified income.

Number awarded   Varies each year.

Deadline   Deadline not specified.

[1380]
SOUTH DAKOTA PROPERTY TAX EXEMPTION FOR PARAPLEGIC VETERANS

South Dakota Department of Revenue and Regulation
Attn: Property Tax Division
445 East Capitol Avenue
Pierre, SD 57501-3185
(605) 773-3311   Toll Free: (800) TAX-9188
Fax: (605) 773-6729   E-mail: PropTaxIn@state.sd.us
Web: www.state.sd.us/drr2/propspectax/property/relief.htm

Summary   To exempt from property taxation the homes of disabled veterans in South Dakota and their widow(er)s.

Eligibility   This benefit is available to residents of South Dakota who are 1) paraplegic veterans, 2) veterans with loss or loss of use of both lower extremities, or 3) unremarried widows or widowers of such veterans. Applicants must own and occupy a dwelling (including the house, garage, and up to 1 acre on which the building is located) that is specifically designed for wheelchair use within the structure. The veteran's injury does not have to be service connected.

Financial Data   Qualified dwellings are exempt from property taxation in South Dakota.

Duration   The exemption applies as long as the dwelling is owned and occupied by the disabled veteran or widow(er).

Number awarded   Varies each year.

Deadline   Deadline not specified.

[1381]
SPINA BIFIDA PROGRAM FOR CHILDREN OF VETERANS

Department of Veterans Affairs
Attn: Veterans Benefits Administration
810 Vermont Avenue, N.W.
Washington, DC 20420
(202) 418-4343   Toll Free: (800) 827-1000
Web: www1.va.gov/opa/ls1/11.asp

Summary   To provide support to children of certain veterans who have spina bifida.

Eligibility   This program is open to spina bifida patients whose veteran parent performed active military, naval, or air service 1) in the Republic of Vietnam during the period from January 9, 1962 through May 7, 1975; or 2) in or near the Korean demilitarized zone during the period from September 1, 1967 through August 31, 1971. Children may be of any age or marital status, but they must have been conceived after the date on which the veteran first served in Vietnam or Korea. The monthly allowance is set at 3 levels, depending upon the degree of disability suffered by the child. The levels are based on neurological manifestations that define the severity of disability: impairment of the functioning of the extremities, impairment of bowel or bladder function, and impairment of intellectual functioning.

Financial Data   Support depends on the degree of disability. The monthly rate for children at the first level is $286, the second level $984, or at the third level $1,678.

Additional data   Applications are available from the nearest VA medical center. Recipients are also entitled to vocational training and medical treatment.

Number awarded   Varies each year.

Deadline   Applications are accepted at any time.

[1382]
TENNESSEE PROPERTY TAX RELIEF FOR DISABLED VETERANS AND THEIR SPOUSES

Tennessee Comptroller of the Treasury
Attn: Property Tax Relief Program
James K. Polk State Office Building
505 Deaderick Street, Room 1600
Nashville, TN 37243-1402
(615) 747-8871   Fax: (615) 532-3866
E-mail: Kim.Darden@state.tn.us
Web: www.comptroller.state.tn.us/pa/patxr.htm

Summary To provide property tax relief to blind and disabled veterans and their spouses in Tennessee.

Eligibility This exemption is offered to veterans or their surviving unremarried spouses who are residents of Tennessee and own and live in their home in the state. The veteran must have served in the U.S. armed forces and 1) have acquired, as a result of such service, a disability from paraplegia, permanent paralysis of both legs and lower part of the body resulting from traumatic injury, disease to the spinal cord or brain, legal blindness, or loss or loss of use of both legs or arms from any service-connected cause; 2) have been rated by the U.S. Department of Veterans affairs (VA) as 100% permanently disabled as a result of service as a prisoner of war for at least 5 months; or 3) have been rated by the VA as 100% permanently and totally disabled from any other service-connected cause. The relief does not extend to any person who was dishonorably discharged from any of the armed services.

Financial Data The amount of the relief depends on the property assessment and the tax rate in the city or county where the beneficiary lives. The maximum market value on which tax relief is calculated is $175,000.

Duration 1 year; may be renewed as long as the eligible veteran or surviving unremarried spouse owns and occupies the primary residence.

Number awarded Varies each year.

Deadline Deadline not specified.

[1383]
TEXAS PROPERTY TAX EXEMPTION FOR DISABLED VETERANS AND THEIR FAMILIES

Texas Veterans Commission
P.O. Box 12277
Austin, TX 78711-2277
(512) 463-5538   Toll Free: (800) 252-VETS (within TX)
Fax: (512) 475-2395   E-mail: info@tvc.state.tx.us
Web: www.tvc.state.tx.us/StateBenefits.html

Summary To extend property tax exemptions on the appraised value of their property to blind, disabled, and other Texas veterans and their surviving family members.

Eligibility Eligible veterans must be Texas residents rated at least 10% service-connected disabled. Surviving spouses and children of eligible veterans are also covered by this program.

Financial Data For veterans in Texas whose disability is rated as 10% through 29%, the first $5,000 of the appraised property value is exempt from taxation; veterans rated as 30% through 49% disabled are exempt from the first $7,500 of appraised value; those with a 50% through 69% disability are exempt from the first $10,000 of appraised value; the exemption applies to the first $12,000 of appraised value for veterans with disabilities rated as 70% to 99%; veterans rated as 100% disabled are exempt from 100% of the appraised value of their property. A veteran whose disability is 10% or more and who is 65 years or older is entitled to exemption of the first $12,000 of appraised property value. A veteran whose disability consists of the loss of use of 1 or more limbs, total blindness in 1 or both eyes, or paraplegia is exempt from the first $12,000 of the appraised value. The unremarried surviving spouse of a deceased veteran who died on active duty and who, at the time of death had a compensable disability and

was entitled to an exemption, is entitled to the same exemption. The surviving spouse of a person who died on active duty is entitled to exemption of the first $5,000 of appraised value of the spouse's property. Surviving spouses, however, are not eligible for the 100% exemption. A surviving child of a person who dies on active duty is entitled to exemption of the first $5,000 of appraised value of the child's property as long as the child is unmarried and under 21 years of age.

Duration 1 year; may be renewed as long as the eligible veteran (or unremarried surviving spouse or child) owns and occupies the primary residence in Texas.

Additional data This program is administered at the local level by the various taxing authorities.

Number awarded Varies each year.

Deadline April of each year.

[1384]
UTAH DISABLED VETERAN PROPERTY TAX ABATEMENT

Utah Division of Veteran's Affairs
Attn: Director
550 Foothill Boulevard, Room 202
Salt Lake City, UT 84108
(801) 326-2372   Toll Free: (800) 894-9497 (within UT)
Fax: (801) 326-2369   E-mail: veterans@utah.gov
Web: veterans.utah.gov/homepage/stateBenefits/index.html

Summary To exempt a portion of the property of disabled veterans and their families in Utah from taxation.

Eligibility This program is available to residents of Utah who are disabled veterans or their unremarried widow(er)s or minor orphans. The disability must be at least 10% and incurred as the result of injuries in the line of duty.

Financial Data The exemption is based on the disability rating of the veteran, to a maximum of $219,164 for a 100% disability.

Duration This benefit is available as long as the disabled veteran or family members reside in Utah.

Deadline Tax exemption applications must be filed with the county government of residence by August of the initial year; once eligibility has been established, reapplication is not required.

[1385]
UTAH VETERAN'S PROPERTY TAX EXEMPTION

Utah State Tax Commission
Attn: Property Tax Division
210 North 1950 West
Salt Lake City, UT 84134
(801) 297-3600   Toll Free: (800) 662-4335, ext. 3600
Fax: (801) 297-7699   TDD: (801) 297-2020
Web: www.tax.utah.gov

Summary To exempt from taxation a portion of the real and tangible property of disabled veterans and their families in Utah.

Eligibility This exemption is available to property owners in Utah who are veterans with a disability of at least 10% incurred in the line of duty, along with their unremarried surviving spouses or minor orphans. First year applications must be accompanied by proof of military service and proof of disability or death.

Financial Data The exemption depends on the percentage of disability, up to $228,505 of taxable value of a residence.

Duration The exemption is available each year the beneficiary owns property in Utah.

Number awarded Varies each year.

Deadline Applications must be submitted by August of each year.

[1386]
VERMONT PROPERTY TAX EXEMPTION FOR DISABLED VETERANS

Vermont Department of Taxes
Attn: Property Valuation and Review Division
P.O. Box 1577
Montpelier, VT 05601-1577
(802) 828-5860   Fax: (802) 828-2824
Web: www.state.vt.us/tax/pvrmilitary.shtml

Summary To exempt disabled Vermont veterans and their dependents from the payment of at least a portion of the state's property tax.

Eligibility Entitled to a property tax exemption are veterans of any war (or their spouses, widow(er)s, or children) who are receiving wartime disability compensation for at least a 50% disability, wartime death compensation, wartime dependence and indemnity compensation, or pension for disability paid through any military department or the Department of Veterans Affairs. Unremarried widow(er)s of previously qualified veterans are also entitled to the exemption whether or not they are receiving government compensation or a pension.

Financial Data Up to $10,000 of the assessed value of real and personal property belonging to eligible veterans or their unremarried widow(er)s is exempt from taxation; individual towns may increase the exemption to as much as $40,000.

Duration 1 year; may be renewed as long as the eligible veteran or widow(er) continues to be the owner/occupant of the residence and lives in Vermont.

Additional data Only 1 exemption may be allowed on a property.

Number awarded Varies each year.

Deadline April of each year.

[1387]
VFW UNMET NEEDS PROGRAM GRANTS

Veterans of Foreign Wars of the United States
Attn: VFW Foundation
Unmet Needs Program
406 West 34th Street, Suite 514
Kansas City, MO 64111
Toll Free: (866) 789-NEED   Fax: (816) 968-2779
E-mail: unmetneeds@vfw.org
Web: www.unmetneeds.com

Summary To provide assistance to military personnel and their families who are facing special circumstances.

Eligibility This assistance is available to members of the 5 branches of service (Army, Navy, Air Force, Marines, and Coast Guard) as well as members of the Reserves and National Guard. Applicants must have served on active duty within the past 3 years. They must be able to demonstrate need for assistance not available from other sources. Examples of needs that may be met include medical bills, prescriptions, and eyeglasses; household expenses (mortgage, rent, repairs, insurance); vehicle expenses (payments, insurance, repairs); utilities; food and clothing; or children's clothing, diapers, formula, or school or childcare expenses.

Financial Data Most grants are less than $1,500.

Duration These are 1-time grants.

Additional data This program was established in 2004 with support from Vermont American Power Tools Accessories.

Number awarded Varies each year. Since this program was established, it has awarded 1,146 grants with a value of $1,640,308.

Deadline Applications may be submitted at any time.

[1388]
VIRGINIA INCOME TAX SUBTRACTION FOR MILITARY DEATH GRATUITY PAYMENTS

Virginia Department of Taxation
Attn: Office of Customer Services
3600 West Broad Street
P.O. Box 1115
Richmond, VA 23218-1115
(804) 367-8031   Fax: (804) 367-2537
Web: www.tax.virginia.gov

Summary To subtract military death gratuity payments from state income taxation in Virginia.

Eligibility This subtraction is available to residents of Virginia who received military death gratuity payments after September 11, 2001 that were included as income subject to federal taxation.

Financial Data Income received as military death gratuity payments is exempt from state taxation in Virginia.

Duration The exemption is retroactive to taxable year 2001.

Number awarded Varies each year.

Deadline The request for an exemption is filed with the state income tax return in April of each year.

[1389]
WASHINGTON PROPERTY TAX ASSISTANCE PROGRAM FOR WIDOWS OR WIDOWERS OF VETERANS

Washington State Department of Revenue
Attn: Property Tax Division
P.O. Box 47471
Olympia, WA 98504-7471
(360) 570-5873   Toll Free: (800) 647-7706
Fax: (360) 586-7602   TDD: (800) 451-7985
Web: dor.wa.gov

Summary To exempt from taxation in Washington a portion of the assessed valuation of property owned by senior citizens and people with disabilities who are widows or widowers of veterans.

Eligibility This exemption is available to residents of Washington who are either 62 years of age or older or who have a disability that prevents them from being gainfully employed and is expected to last for at least 12 months. Applicants must be the unmarried widow or widower of a veteran who 1) died as a result of a service-connected disability; 2) was 100% disabled for 10 years prior to his or her death; 3) was a former prisoner of war and rated as 100% disabled for at least 1 year prior to death; or 4) died in active duty or in active training status. They must own property that they use as their principal home for at least 6 months of the year; mobile homes may qualify as a residence even if its owner does not own the land where it is located. Their annual disposable income may not exceed $40,000 per year.

Financial Data The exemption is $100,000 of the home's assessed value if disposable income is $30,000 or less, $75,000 if disposable income is $30,001 to $35,000, or $50,000 if disposable income is $35,001 to $40,000.

Duration The exemption is available as long as the widow or widower meets the eligibility requirements.

Additional data This program offered assistance beginning with the 2006 tax year.

Number awarded Varies each year.

Deadline Applications are due 30 days before taxes are due.

[1390]
WEST VIRGINIA INCOME TAX EXEMPTION FOR MILITARY RETIREES

West Virginia State Tax Department
Attn: Taxpayer Services Division
P.O. Box 3784
Charleston, WV 25337-3784
(304) 558-3333 Toll Free: (800) WVA-TAXS (within WV)
Fax: (304) 558-3269 TDD: (800) 282-9833
Web: www.wva.state.wv.us/wvtax/default.aspx

Summary To exempt a portion of the income of military retirees and their spouses in West Virginia from state taxation.

Eligibility This exemption is available to residents of West Virginia who are receiving retirement benefits from any branch of the military. Surviving spouses of eligible residents are also entitled to the exemptions.

Financial Data Military retirees and their spouses are entitled to exempt the first $20,000 of annual military retirement income, including survivorship annuities. That exemption is in addition to the $2,000 exemption available to all retired public employees in West Virginia.

Duration The exemption continues as long as eligible residents (or their spouses) remain residents of West Virginia.

Deadline Deadline not specified.

[1391]
WEST VIRGINIA VETERANS BONUS

West Virginia Division of Veteran's Affairs
Charleston Human Resource Center
1321 Plaza East, Suite 101
Charleston, WV 25301-1400
(304) 558-3661 Toll Free: (888) 838-2332 (within WV)
Fax: (304) 558-3662 E-mail: wvdva@state.wv.us
Web: www.wvs.state.wv.us/va/forms.htm

Summary To provide a bonus to living veterans in West Virginia who served in Kosovo, Afghanistan, or Iraq and to the families of deceased veterans.

Eligibility This bonus is available to veterans who were residents of West Virginia when they entered into active duty and for at least 6 months previously. Applicants must have been members of the armed forces of the United States or of Reserve components called to active duty. They must have 1) received a campaign badge or expeditionary medal for Kosovo between November 20, 1995 and December 31, 2000; 2) served in Afghanistan between October 7, 2001 and a date to be determined; or 3) served in Iraq between March 19, 2003 and a date to be determined. A bonus is also available to veterans who had active service outside the combat zone during the time periods specified for Afghanistan and Iraq. Surviving family members of a deceased veteran are also eligible if the veteran's death was connected with the service during the specified time periods.

Financial Data Bonuses are $600 for veterans who served in the specified combat zone, $400 for veterans who served outside the combat zone but during the specified time periods, or $2,000 for surviving relatives of deceased veterans. The amount of the bonus is not considered income for state taxation purposes in West Virginia.

Duration This is a 1-time bonus.

Number awarded Varies each year.

Deadline Applications may be submitted at any time.

[1392]
WISCONSIN AID TO MILITARY FAMILIES

Wisconsin Department of Veterans Affairs
30 West Mifflin Street
P.O. Box 7843
Madison, WI 53707-7843
(608) 266-1311 Toll Free: (800) WIS-VETS
Fax: (608) 267-0403 E-mail: WDVAInfo@dva.state.wi.us
Web: www.dva.state.wi.us/Ben_emergencygrants.asp

Summary To provide temporary, emergency financial aid to families of activated or deployed servicemembers in Wisconsin.

Eligibility This program is open to spouses and dependent children of activated or deployed military servicemembers of the U.S. armed forces or of the Wisconsin National Guard. Applicants must have suffered, or be suffering, a loss of income because of the activation or deployment, although there is no maximum income limitation. The servicemember must be a resident of Wisconsin. The family must be facing an economic emergency, such as failure of the sole means of transportation; failure of a stove or refrigerator or of heating, electrical, or plumbing systems; a medical emergency; or severe damage to the primary residence as a result of a natural disaster.

Financial Data Grants do not exceed $7,500 in a lifetime.

Duration Grants are awarded as needed.

Number awarded Varies each year.

Deadline Applications may be submitted at any time.

[1393]
WISCONSIN ASSISTANCE TO NEEDY VETERANS AND FAMILY MEMBERS

Wisconsin Department of Veterans Affairs
30 West Mifflin Street
P.O. Box 7843
Madison, WI 53707-7843
(608) 266-1311 Toll Free: (800) WIS-VETS
Fax: (608) 267-0403 E-mail: WDVAInfo@dva.state.wi.us
Web: www.dva.state.wi.us/Ben_emergencygrants.asp

Summary To provide temporary, emergency financial aid to veterans and their families in Wisconsin.

Eligibility This program is open to Wisconsin residents who served either 1) at least 2 years on active duty in the U.S. armed forces; or 2) at least 90 days on active duty during designated periods of wartime (including the Persian Gulf War since August 1, 1990, the Afghanistan War since September 11, 2001, and the Iraq War since March 19, 2003). The unremarried surviving spouse and dependent children of an eligible veteran who died in the line of duty while or active duty or inactive duty for training also qualify. Applicants must have applied for, and been denied or determined to be ineligible for, all other applicable aid programs (e.g., unemployment insurance, Medicaid, Medicare, BadgerCare, federal Veterans Administration health care). The veteran must be a resident of Wisconsin with an income that does not exceed 130% of the federal poverty guidelines (currently, $14,079 for a family of 1, rising to $48,113 for a family of 8). The family must be facing an economic emergency, such as failure of the sole means of transportation; failure of a stove or refrigerator or of heating, electrical, or plumbing systems; a medical emergency; or severe damage to the primary residence as a result of a natural disaster.

Financial Data Grants do not exceed $7,500 in a lifetime.

Duration Grants are awarded as needed.

Number awarded Varies each year.

Deadline Applications may be submitted at any time.

[1394]
WISCONSIN VETERANS AND SURVIVING SPOUSES PROPERTY TAX CREDIT

Wisconsin Department of Revenue
Attn: Customer Service and Education Bureau
2135 Rimrock Road
P.O. Box 8949
Madison, WI 53708-8949
(608) 266-2776   Fax: (608) 267-1030
Web: www.revenue.wi.gov

Summary To provide an income tax credit to disabled Wisconsin veterans and their surviving spouses equal to the amount of property taxes they pay.

Eligibility This credit is available to Wisconsin veterans who served on active duty under honorable conditions in the U.S. armed forces and have resided in Wisconsin for any consecutive 5-year period after entry into active duty. Applicants must have either a service-connected disability rating of 100% or a 100% disability rating based on individual unemployability. Also eligible are unremarried surviving spouses of such disabled veterans and of members of the National Guard or a Reserve component of the U.S. armed forces who were residents of Wisconsin and died in the line of duty while on active or inactive duty for training purposes.

Financial Data Eligible veterans and surviving spouses are entitled to an income tax credit equal to the amount of property taxes they pay on their principal residence.

Duration The credit is available as long as the recipient resides in Wisconsin.

Number awarded Varies each year.

Deadline Income tax returns must be filed by April of each year.

[1395]
WISCONSIN VETERANS' SUBSISTENCE AID GRANTS

Wisconsin Department of Veterans Affairs
30 West Mifflin Street
P.O. Box 7843
Madison, WI 53707-7843
(608) 266-1311   Toll Free: (800) WIS-VETS
Fax: (608) 267-0403   E-mail: WDVAInfo@dva.state.wi.us
Web: www.dva.state.wi.us/Ben_emergencygrants.asp

Summary To provide temporary, emergency financial aid to Wisconsin veterans or their dependents.

Eligibility This program is open to current residents of Wisconsin who 1) were residents of the state when they entered or reentered active duty in the U.S. armed forces, or 2) have moved to the state and have been residents for any consecutive 12-month period after entry or reentry into service. Applicants must have served on active duty for at least 2 continuous years or for at least 90 days during specified wartime periods. Also eligible are 1) unremarried surviving spouses and dependent children of eligible veterans who died in the line of duty while on active service or inactive duty for training; and 2) spouses and dependent children of eligible servicemembers who are currently activated or deployed. Applicants must have suffered a loss of income because of illness, injury, or natural disaster and be seeking temporary, emergency financial aid. Their income may not exceed 130% of the federal poverty guidelines (currently, $14,079 for a family of 1, rising to $48,113 for a family of 8).

Financial Data Grants do not exceed $3,000 during any consecutive 12-month period or the program limit of $7,500 in a lifetime.

Duration Grants are awarded for subsistence aid for a 30-day period, up to a maximum of 3 months.

Number awarded Varies each year.

Deadline Applications may be submitted at any time.

[1396]
WYOMING MILITARY ASSISTANCE TRUST FUND GRANTS

Wyoming Military Department
Attn: State Family Program Coordinator
5500 Bishop Boulevard
Cheyenne, WY 82009
(307) 772-5208   Fax: (307) 772-5330
Web: www.wy.ngb.army.mil/trust-fund

Summary To provide emergency assistance to residents of Wyoming who are facing financial difficulties because a family member has been deployed to active military service.

Eligibility This assistance is available to 1) members of the Wyoming National Guard or Reserve units based in Wyoming who have been called to active duty or active state service; 2) Wyoming residents who are members of a military Reserve unit not based in Wyoming, if the member has been called to active service; 3) other Wyoming residents performing service in the uniformed forces for any branch of the military of the United States; and 4) members of the immediate family (spouses, children, and dependent parents, grandparents, siblings, stepchildren, and adult children) of those military personnel. Applicants must be facing financial hardship resulting from the military member's active-duty status.

Financial Data The amount of the grant depends on the need of the recipient.

Duration These are 1-time grants.

Additional data The Wyoming Legislature created this fund in 2004. These funds may not be used to replace other funds available from public or private sources.

Number awarded Varies each year. Recently, $300,000 was available for this program.

Deadline Applications may be submitted at any time.

[1397]
WYOMING VETERANS PROPERTY TAX EXEMPTION

Wyoming Department of Revenue
Attn: Property Tax Relief Program
122 West 25th Street, Second Floor West
Cheyenne, WY 82002-0110
(307) 777-5235   Fax: (307) 777-7527
E-mail: DirectorOfRevenue@wy.gov
Web: revenue.state.wy.us

Summary To provide a partial tax exemption on the property owned by veterans and their surviving spouses in Wyoming.

Eligibility This program is open to honorably-discharged veterans who were Wyoming residents at the time they entered military service and have resided in Wyoming for 3 years prior to applying for this exemption. Applicants must have served during specified periods of wartime or have received an armed forces expeditionary medal or other authorized service or campaign medal for service in an armed conflict in a foreign country. Surviving spouses of qualified veterans are also eligible. The exemption applies to county fees only, not state fees.

Financial Data Veterans and spouses may exempt $3,000 in assessed value of property from taxation per year. Disabled veterans are entitled to additional exemptions that depend on the level of their disability, to a maximum of $2,000 for a 100% disability.

Duration Veterans and spouses are entitled to use these exemptions as long as they reside in Wyoming and own the property as their principal residence.

Number awarded Varies each year.

Deadline Applicants must advise their county assessor of their intent to use the exemption by May of each year.

Indexes

Program Title Index

If you know the name of a particular funding program and want to find out where it is covered in the directory, use the Program Title Index. Here, program titles are arranged alphabetically, word by word. To assist you in your search, every program is listed by all its known names or abbreviations. In addition, we've used a two-character alphabetical code (within parentheses) to help you determine if the program falls within your scope of interest. The first character (capitalized) in the code identifies program type: S = Scholarships; F = Fellowships/Grants; L = Loans; G = Grants-in-Aid. The second character (lower cased) identifies eligible groups: v = Veterans; m = Military Personnel; f = Family Members. Here's how the code works: if a program is followed by (S–v) 241, the program is described in the Scholarships section under Veterans, in entry 241. If the same program title is followed by another entry number—for example, (L–m) 680—the program is also described in the Loans section, under Military Personnel, in entry 680. Remember: the numbers cited here refer to program entry numbers, not to page numbers in the book.

S—Scholarships
v—Veterans

F—Fellowships/Grants
m—Military Personnel

L—Loans

G—Grants-in-aid
f—Family Members

385

S—Scholarships   **F—Fellowships/Grants**   **L—Loans**   **G—Grants-in-aid**

v—Veterans   **m—Military Personnel**   **f—Family Members**

S—Scholarships	F—Fellowships/Grants	L—Loans	G—Grants-in-aid
v—Veterans	m—Military Personnel		f—Family Members

S—Scholarships F—Fellowships/Grants L—Loans G—Grants-in-aid
v—Veterans m—Military Personnel f—Family Members

S—Scholarships   **F—Fellowships/Grants**   **L—Loans**   **G—Grants-in-aid**

v—Veterans   **m—Military Personnel**   **f—Family Members**

S—Scholarships   **F—Fellowships/Grants**   **L—Loans**   **G—Grants-in-aid**
v—Veterans   **m—Military Personnel**   **f—Family Members**

S—Scholarships   **F—Fellowships/Grants**   **L—Loans**   **G—Grants-in-aid**
v—Veterans   **m—Military Personnel**   **f—Family Members**

S—Scholarships   **F—Fellowships/Grants**   **L—Loans**   **G—Grants-in-aid**
v—Veterans   **m—Military Personnel**   **f—Family Members**

S—Scholarships   **F—Fellowships/Grants**   **L—Loans**   **G—Grants-in-aid**

v—Veterans   **m—Military Personnel**   **f—Family Members**

S−Scholarships   F−Fellowships/Grants   L−Loans   G−Grants-in-aid
v−Veterans   m−Military Personnel   f−Family Members

Wirth Scholarship. *See* Navy League Foundation Scholarships, entry (S—f) 618

Wisconsin Aid to Military Families, (G—f) 1392

Wisconsin Assistance to Needy Veterans and Family Members, (G—v) 1205, (G—f) 1393

Wisconsin Eagle Scout of the Year Scholarship, (S—f) 750

Wisconsin G.I. Bill Tuition Remission Program, (S—v) 116, (S—f) 751, (F—v) 809, (F—f) 985

Wisconsin Home Improvement Loan Program, (L—v) 1013, (L—m) 1045, (L—f) 1070

Wisconsin Income Tax Exemption for Military and Uniformed Services Retirement Benefits, (G—v) 1206

Wisconsin Income Tax Exemption for National Guard and Reserve Pay, (G—m) 1276

Wisconsin Job Retraining Grants, (S—v) 117, (S—f) 752, (F—v) 810, (F—f) 986

Wisconsin Legion Auxiliary Child Welfare Scholarship, (F—f) 987

Wisconsin Legion Auxiliary Department President's Scholarship, (S—f) 753

Wisconsin Legion Auxiliary Merit and Memorial Scholarships, (S—f) 754

Wisconsin Legion Auxiliary Past Presidents Parley Health Career Scholarships, (S—f) 755

Wisconsin Legion Auxiliary Past Presidents Parley Registered Nurse Scholarships, (S—f) 756

Wisconsin National Guard Enlisted Association College Grant Program. *See* WNGEA College Grant Program, entries (S—v) 120, (S—m) 362, (S—f) 759, (F—v) 812, (F—m) 918, (F—f) 989

Wisconsin National Guard Tuition Grant, (S—m) 360

Wisconsin Part-Time Study Grants. *See* Wisconsin Veterans Education (VetEd) Reimbursement Grants, entry (S—v) 118

Wisconsin Sons of the American Legion Scholarship, (S—f) 757

Wisconsin Tuition and Fee Reimbursement Grants. *See* Wisconsin G.I. Bill Tuition Remission Program, entries (S—v) 116, (S—f) 751, (F—v) 809, (F—f) 985

Wisconsin Veterans and Surviving Spouses Property Tax Credit, (G—v) 1207, (G—f) 1394

Wisconsin Veterans Education (VetEd) Reimbursement Grants, (S—v) 118

Wisconsin Veterans' Personal Loan Program, (L—v) 1014, (L—f) 1071

Wisconsin Veterans Primary Mortgage Loan Program, (L—v) 1015, (L—m) 1046, (L—f) 1072

Wisconsin Veterans' Subsistence Aid Grants, (G—v) 1208, (G—f) 1395

Wives of the U.S. Submarine Veterans of World War II Scholarship. *See* Dolphin Scholarships, entry (S—f) 459

WMA Memorial Scholarships. *See* WMA Scholarship Program, entries (S—v) 119, (S—m) 361, (S—f) 758, (F—v) 811, (F—m) 917, (F—f) 988

WMA Scholarship Program, (S—v) 119, (S—m) 361, (S—f) 758, (F—v) 811, (F—m) 917, (F—f) 988

WNGEA College Grant Program, (S—v) 120, (S—m) 362, (S—f) 759, (F—v) 812, (F—m) 918, (F—f) 989

Women Marines Association Scholarship Program. *See* WMA Scholarship Program, entries (S—v) 119, (S—m) 361, (S—f) 758, (F—v) 811, (F—m) 917, (F—f) 988

Women's Army Corps Veterans' Association Scholarship, (S—f) 760

Women's Overseas Service League Scholarships for Women, (S—m) 363

Wyoming Combat Veteran Surviving Orphan Tuition Benefit, (S—f) 761

Wyoming Combat Veteran Surviving Spouse Tuition Benefit, (S—f) 762

Wyoming Military Assistance Trust Fund Grants, (G—m) 1277, (G—f) 1396

Wyoming National Guard Educational Assistance Plan, (S—m) 364, (F—m) 919

Wyoming Overseas Combat Veteran Tuition Benefit, (S—v) 121

Wyoming Veterans Property Tax Exemption, (G—v) 1209, (G—f) 1397

Wyoming Vietnam Veteran Surviving Child Tuition Benefit, (S—f) 763

Wyoming Vietnam Veteran Surviving Spouse Tuition Benefit, (S—f) 764

Wyoming Vietnam Veteran Tuition Benefit, (S—v) 122

Y

Yamada Memorial Scholarship. *See* Eiro Yamada Memorial Scholarship, entries (S—f) 468, (F—f) 939

Yancey Scholarship, (S—f) 765

Young AFCEAN Graduate Scholarship. *See* Milton E. Cooper/ Young AFCEAN Graduate Scholarship, entry (F—m) 878

Z

Zabierek Memorial Scholarships. *See* Andrew J. Zabierek Memorial Scholarships, entry (S—v) 5

Zais Scholarships. *See* Army ROTC Civilian Sponsored Scholarship Program, entry (S—m) 159

S—Scholarships   **F—Fellowships/Grants**   **L—Loans**   **G—Grants-in-aid**
v—Veterans   **m—Military Personnel**   **f—Family Members**

Sponsoring Organization Index

The Sponsoring Organization Index makes it easy to identify agencies that offer financial aid to veterans, military personnel, or members of their families. In this index, sponsoring organizations are listed alphabetically, word by word. In addition, we've used a two-character alphabetical code (within parentheses) to help you identify which programs sponsored by these organizations fall within your scope of interest. The first character (capitalized) in the code identifies program type: S = Scholarships; F = Fellowships/Grants; L = Loans; G = Grants-in-Aid. The second character (lower cased) identifies eligible groups: v = Veterans; m = Military Personnel; f = Family Members. For example, if the name of a sponsoring organization is followed by (S–v) 241, a program sponsored by that organization is described in the Scholarship section under Veterans, in entry 241. If that sponsoring organization's name is followed by another entry number—for example, (L–m) 680—the same or a different program sponsored by that organization is described in the Loans section, under Military Personnel, in entry 680. Remember: the numbers cited here refer to program entry numbers, not to page numbers in the book.

101st Airborne Division Association, (S—f) 381, 426, (F—f) 927
10th Mountain Division Descendants, Inc., (S—f) 366
11th Armored Cavalry Veterans of Vietnam and Cambodia, (S—v) 1, (S—f) 367
25th Infantry Division Association, (S—f) 368

A

AAFES Retired Employees Association, (S—f) 370
Air Force Aid Society, (S—f) 498, (L—v) 992, (L—m) 1018, (L—f) 1049, (G—v) 1074, (G—m) 1211-1212, (G—f) 1279-1280
Air Force Association, (S—m) 125, 128, (S—f) 375, 379, 566, (F—m) 815, 863, (F—f) 924, 926
Air Force Officers' Wives' Club of Washington, D.C., (S—f) 372-373, 376, (F—f) 922-923
Air Force Sergeants Association, (S—f) 374, 377, 380, 429
Air Warrior Courage Foundation, (G—v) 1075, (G—m) 1213, (G—f) 1281
Airmen Memorial Foundation, (S—f) 380, 429
Alabama Commission on Higher Education, (S—m) 144, (F—m) 826
Alabama Department of Revenue, (G—v) 1076-1077, (G—m) 1214, (G—f) 1282-1283
Alabama Department of Veterans Affairs, (S—f) 382, (F—f) 929
Alaska Department of Natural Resources, (G—v) 1079
Alaska Housing Finance Corporation, (L—v) 993-994, (L—f) 1050
Alaska National Guard, (S—m) 145-146, (F—m) 827-828
Alaska. Office of the State Assessor, (G—v) 1078
Alaska. Office of Veterans Affairs, (S—f) 383
Ambassador College Bookstores, (S—v) 43, (S—m) 229
Americal Division Veterans Association, (S—f) 390

American Academy of Physician Assistants-Veterans Caucus, (S—v) 108, (S—m) 349, (S—f) 705, (F—f) 934
American Association of Nurse Anesthetists, (F—m) 850
American Ex-prisoners of War, Inc. Columbia River Chapter, (S—v) 81, (S—f) 677, (F—v) 798, (F—f) 974
American Legion. Alaska Auxiliary, (S—f) 384
American Legion. Americanism and Children & Youth Division, (S—f) 391, 465, 692
American Legion. Arizona Auxiliary, (S—v) 115, (S—f) 749
American Legion. Arkansas Department, (S—f) 449
American Legion Auxiliary, (S—v) 75, (S—f) 392-393, 550, 652, 692, 704, (G—f) 1284
American Legion. California Auxiliary, (S—v) 13-14, (S—m) 167-168, (S—f) 420-423
American Legion. Colorado Auxiliary, (S—v) 15, (S—f) 439-441
American Legion. Connecticut Department, (S—f) 446, (G—v) 1091
American Legion. Florida Auxiliary, (S—f) 487-488, (F—f) 943
American Legion. Florida Department, (S—f) 484-486
American Legion. Georgia Auxiliary, (S—f) 502-503
American Legion. Georgia Department, (S—f) 501
American Legion. Idaho Auxiliary, (S—v) 30, (S—f) 520
American Legion. Idaho Department, (S—f) 521
American Legion. Illinois Auxiliary, (S—v) 31-32, 54, (S—f) 371, 527-528, 591
American Legion. Illinois Department, (S—f) 529-530
American Legion. Indiana Department, (S—f) 532, 534
American Legion. Iowa Auxiliary, (S—v) 36, (S—f) 537
American Legion. Iowa Department, (S—f) 536
American Legion. Kansas Auxiliary, (S—f) 551
American Legion. Kansas Department, (S—f) 386, 428, 688

S—Scholarships   **F—Fellowships/Grants**   **L—Loans**   **G—Grants-in-aid**
v—Veterans   **m—Military Personnel**   **f—Family Members**

S—Scholarships   **F—Fellowships/Grants**   **L—Loans**   **G—Grants-in-aid**

v—Veterans   **m—Military Personnel**   **f—Family Members**

U.S. Department of Veterans Affairs, (S—v) 61, 82, 109, 113, (S—m) 255-256, 309, 313, (S—f) 576, 710, (F—v) 791, 799, 807-808, (F—m) 882-883, 904-905, (F—f) 981, (L—v) 999, 1007, 1011, (L—m) 1037-1038, 1042, (L—f) 1067, (G—v) 1095, 1097, 1132, 1190-1191, 1198-1199, 1201, (G—m) 1221, 1264, 1267-1268, (G—f) 1291, 1297-1299, 1340, 1368, 1374-1375, 1381

U.S. Marine Corps, (S—m) 171, 235, 308, (F—m) 869-871, 903, (L—m) 1028

U.S. Navy. Civil Engineer Corps, (S—m) 170, (F—m) 844

U.S. Navy. Council of Review Boards, (G—v) 1088

U.S. Navy. Naval Education and Training Command, (S—m) 212, 265, 268-272, 340, (F—m) 887-889, 891

U.S. Navy. Naval Personnel Command, (S—v) 64, (S—m) 266, 298, (F—m) 910

U.S. Navy. Naval Recruiting Command, (L—m) 1026

U.S. Navy. Naval Service Training Command, (S—m) 169, 171, 214, 242, 263, 299-300, 307, 322, 326-334, (F—m) 874

U.S. Navy. Navy Exchange Service Command, (S—f) 402

U.S. Navy. Navy Medicine Manpower, Personnel, Education and Training Command, (S—m) 243, 267, (F—m) 829, 875, 890, (L—m) 1033

U.S. Navy. Office of Naval Research, (F—m) 910

U.S. Small Business Administration, (L—v) 1005, (L—f) 1061

U.S. Submarine Veterans of World War II, (S—f) 459

USAA Insurance Corporation, (S—v) 71, 77, 120, (S—m) 159, 172, 192-193, 279, 288, 301, 316, 362, (S—f) 380, 434, 470-472, 645, 660, 679, 687, 759, (F—v) 796, 812, (F—m) 898, 918, (F—f) 972, 989

USMC/Combat Helicopter Association, (S—f) 568, 587

USO World Headquarters, (S—f) 723

USS Intrepid Association, Inc., (S—f) 725

USS Lake Champlain Foundation, (S—v) 104, (S—m) 343, (S—f) 726

USS Little Rock Association, (S—m) 344, (S—f) 727

Utah Army National Guard, (S—m) 345-346

Utah Division of Veteran's Affairs, (S—v) 105, (S—f) 695, (F—v) 805, (G—v) 1195, (G—f) 1384

Utah State Tax Commission, (G—v) 1196, (G—f) 1385

V

VA Mortgage Center.com, (S—v) 55, (S—m) 246, (S—f) 592

Vermont American Power Tools Accessories, (G—m) 1272, (G—f) 1387

Vermont Department of Taxes, (G—v) 1197, (G—m) 1270-1271, (G—f) 1386

Vermont. Office of Veterans Affairs, (S—f) 733

Vermont Student Assistance Corporation, (S—f) 665

Veterans of Foreign Wars. Ladies Auxiliary, (S—f) 549, 559

Veterans of Foreign Wars of the United States, (G—m) 1272, (G—f) 1387

Veterans of the Vietnam War, Inc., (S—v) 114, (S—f) 743

Vietnam Veterans Group of San Quentin, (S—f) 735

Vietnam Veterans of America, (S—v) 53, (S—f) 590

Vietnam Veterans of America. Chapter 522, (S—f) 510

Vietnam Veterans of America. Chapter 753, (S—f) 656

Vietnam Veterans of America. Wisconsin State Council, (S—f) 686

VII Corps Desert Storm Veterans Association, (S—v) 111, (S—f) 736

Virgin Islands Board of Education, (S—f) 737

Virginia Army/Air National Guard Enlisted Association, (S—v) 112, (S—m) 352, (S—f) 738

Virginia Department of Taxation, (G—v) 1200, (G—m) 1273-1274, (G—f) 1388

Virginia Department of Veterans Services, (S—f) 740, (F—f) 984

Virginia National Guard, (S—m) 353, (F—m) 914

Virginia National Guard Association, (S—m) 355, (S—f) 742

W

Walter Beall Scholarship Foundation, (S—f) 746

Washington, D.C. Office of Tax and Revenue, (G—v) 1096

Washington National Guard, (S—m) 357-358, (F—m) 915, (L—m) 1044

Washington State Department of Revenue, (G—v) 1202, (G—f) 1389

West Virginia Division of Veteran's Affairs, (G—f) 1391

West Virginia. Office of the Adjutant General, (S—m) 359, (F—m) 916

West Virginia State Tax Department, (G—v) 1203-1204, (G—m) 1275, (G—f) 1390

Winston-Salem Foundation, (S—f) 579

Wisconsin Department of Military Affairs, (S—m) 360

Wisconsin Department of Revenue, (G—v) 1206-1207, (G—m) 1276, (G—f) 1394

Wisconsin Department of Veterans Affairs, (S—v) 116-118, (S—f) 751-752, (F—v) 809-810, (F—f) 985-986, (L—v) 1013-1015, (L—m) 1045-1046, (L—f) 1070-1072, (G—v) 1205, 1208, (G—f) 1392-1393, 1395

Wisconsin National Guard Enlisted Association, (S—v) 120, (S—m) 362, (S—f) 759, (F—v) 812, (F—m) 918, (F—f) 989

Wisconsin Veterans of Foreign Wars, (S—v) 44, (S—f) 563

Women Marines Association, (S—v) 119, (S—m) 361, (S—f) 758, (F—v) 811, (F—m) 917, (F—f) 988

Women's Army Corps Veterans' Association, (S—f) 760

Women's Overseas Service League, (S—m) 363

Wyoming Department of Revenue, (G—v) 1209, (G—f) 1397

Wyoming Military Department, (G—m) 1277, (G—f) 1396

Wyoming National Guard, (S—m) 364, (F—m) 919

Wyoming Veterans Commission, (S—v) 121-122, (S—f) 761-764

Residency Index

Some programs listed in this book are restricted to residents of a particular state or region. Others are open to applicants wherever they may live. The Residency Index will help you pinpoint programs available only to residents in your area as well as programs that have no residency restrictions at all (these are listed under the term "United States"). To use this index, look up the geographic areas that apply to you (always check the listings under "United States"), jot down the entry numbers listed after the program types and availability groups that apply to you, and use those numbers to find the program descriptions in the directory. To help you in your search, we've provided some "see also" references in the index entries. Remember: the numbers cited here refer to program entry numbers, not to page numbers in the book.

Tenability Index

Some programs listed in this book can be used only in specific cities, counties, states, or regions. Others may be used anywhere in the United States (or even abroad). The Tenability Index will help you locate funding that is restricted to a specific area as well as funding that has no tenability restrictions (these are listed under the term "United States"). To use this index, look up the geographic areas where you'd like to go (always check the listings under "United States"), jot down the entry numbers listed after the program types and availability groups that apply to you, and use those numbers to find the program descriptions in the directory. To help you in your search, we've provided some "see also" references in the index entries. Remember: the numbers cited here refer to program entry numbers, not to page numbers in the book.

Subject Index

There are more than 250 different subject areas indexed in this directory. Use the Subject Index when you want to identify the subject focus of available funding programs. To help you pinpoint your search, we've also included hundreds of "see" and "see also" references. In addition to looking for terms that represent your specific subject interest, be sure to check the "General programs" entry; hundreds of programs are listed there that can be used to support study, research, or other activities in *any* subject area (although the programs may be restricted in other ways). Remember: the numbers cited in this index refer to program entry numbers, not to page numbers in the book.

A

Administration. *See* Business administration; Education, administration; Management; Personnel administration; Public administration

Aeronautical engineering. *See* Engineering, aeronautical

Aeronautics
Scholarships: **Family Members,** 452
Fellowships/Grants: **Family Members,** 936
See also Aviation; Engineering, aeronautical; General programs; Physical sciences

Aerospace engineering. *See* Engineering, aerospace

Aerospace sciences. *See* Space sciences

African studies
Scholarships: **Military Personnel,** 142
See also General programs

Agriculture and agricultural sciences
Scholarships: **Veterans,** 83
See also Biological sciences; General programs

Anesthetic nurses and nursing. *See* Nurses and nursing, anesthesiology

Aquaculture
Scholarships: **Veterans,** 39; **Military Personnel,** 223; **Family Members,** 545
Fellowships/Grants: **Veterans,** 784; **Military Personnel,** 865; **Family Members,** 950
See also Agriculture and agricultural sciences; General programs

Aquatic sciences. *See* Oceanography

Arabic language. *See* Language, Arabic

Architectural engineering. *See* Engineering, architectural

Architecture
Scholarships: **Military Personnel,** 136, 143, 165, 169-170, 310, 354; **Family Members,** 412, 741
Fellowships/Grants: **Military Personnel,** 841, 844; **Family Members,** 933
See also General programs

Arithmetic. *See* Mathematics

Armed services. *See* Military affairs

Art
Scholarships: **Family Members,** 581
See also General programs; names of specific art forms

Asian studies
Scholarships: **Military Personnel,** 142
See also General programs

Astronautics
Scholarships: **Family Members,** 452
Fellowships/Grants: **Family Members,** 936
See also General programs; Space sciences

Atmospheric sciences
Scholarships: **Military Personnel,** 143, 310
See also General programs; Physical sciences

Attorneys. *See* Law, general

Audiology
Loans: **Military Personnel,** 1033
See also General programs; Health and health care; Medical sciences

Automation. *See* Computer sciences; Technology

Aviation
Scholarships: **Military Personnel,** 183, 205, 220; **Family Members,** 452, 683, 746
Fellowships/Grants: **Family Members,** 936, 975
See also General programs; Space sciences; Transportation

Azerbaijani language. *See* Language, Azeri

Azeri language. *See* Language, Azeri

B

Bengali language. *See* Language, Bengali

Biological sciences
Scholarships: **Veterans,** 83
Fellowships/Grants: **Veterans,** 774; **Family Members,** 937
See also General programs; Sciences; names of specific biological sciences

F

Farming. *See* Agriculture and agricultural sciences

Farsi language. *See* Language, Farsi

Finance
Scholarships: **Military Personnel,** 214, 265
Fellowships/Grants: **Military Personnel,** 870, 887-888
See also Economics; General programs

Flight science. *See* Aviation

Flying. *See* Aviation

Foreign affairs. *See* International affairs

Foreign language. *See* Language and linguistics

Foreign language education. *See* Education, foreign languages

French language. *See* Language, French

G

General programs
Scholarships: **Veterans,** 1-6, 8, 10-12, 14, 16-18, 20-26, 28-29, 33-35, 37-38, 41-43, 46-48, 50-51, 53-72, 74-82, 84-86, 88, 91-94, 96-106, 109, 111-114, 116-122; **Military Personnel,** 123-124, 126-131, 135-137, 139-141, 144-146, 149-151, 154, 156-160, 163-164, 168, 171-175, 177-179, 181-182, 184-185, 187-190, 192-201, 203-204, 206-213, 215-219, 221-222, 225-226, 228-233, 235-241, 245-264, 266, 269-293, 295-297, 301-309, 311-317, 320-327, 335-339, 341-347, 352-353, 355-364; **Family Members,** 365-380, 382-386, 388-406, 408-411, 413-421, 423-434, 436-440, 442-451, 453-461, 463-496, 498-502, 504, 506-519, 521-526, 529-536, 538-544, 547-553, 555-562, 564-565, 567-568, 570-580, 583-603, 605-626, 628-630, 633-634, 637-665, 667-677, 679-689, 691-704, 706-712, 714-738, 740, 742-745, 747-748, 750-754, 757-765
Fellowships/Grants: **Veterans,** 766, 768-769, 771, 773, 777-783, 785-786, 788-796, 798-800, 802-812; **Military Personnel,** 813-815, 820, 822-824, 826-828, 835, 837, 839-840, 845, 847, 851-861, 863-864, 866, 868, 871-873, 877, 879, 881-886, 891-898, 900-909, 911-919; **Family Members,** 920-926, 929-930, 932, 938-949, 951-952, 954-986, 988-989
Loans: **Veterans,** 990-1004, 1007-1015; **Military Personnel,** 1016-1018, 1020-1023, 1025-1027, 1029, 1031-1032, 1034-1046; **Family Members,** 1047-1060, 1062-1072
Grants-in-aid: **Veterans,** 1073-1193, 1195-1209; **Military Personnel,** 1210-1268, 1270-1277; **Family Members,** 1278-1397

Georgian language. *See* Language, Georgian

Geospatial information technology
Scholarships: **Military Personnel,** 333
See also General programs

Government. *See* Political science and politics; Public administration

Grade school. *See* Education, elementary

Graphic design
Scholarships: **Family Members,** 632
See also General programs

Gynecology
Scholarships: **Military Personnel,** 162
Fellowships/Grants: **Military Personnel,** 838
See also General programs; Medical sciences; Obstetrics

H

Handicapped. *See* Disabilities

Hausa language. *See* Language, Hausa

Health and health care
Scholarships: **Family Members,** 755
Loans: **Military Personnel,** 1019
See also General programs; Medical sciences

Health and health care, administration
Scholarships: **Military Personnel,** 243
Fellowships/Grants: **Military Personnel,** 875
Loans: **Military Personnel,** 1033
See also Business administration; General programs; Health and health care

Hebrew. *See* Language, Hebrew

High school librarians. *See* Libraries and librarianship, school

High schools. *See* Education, secondary

Hindi language. *See* Language, Hindi

Homeland security. *See* Security, national

Hospitals. *See* Health and health care

Human resources. *See* Personnel administration

Human services. *See* Social services

Hydrology
Scholarships: **Military Personnel,** 333
Fellowships/Grants: **Military Personnel,** 910
See also General programs

I

Indonesian language. *See* Language, Indonesian

Industrial hygiene
Scholarships: **Military Personnel,** 243
Fellowships/Grants: **Military Personnel,** 875
See also General programs; Health and health care; Safety studies

Information systems
Scholarships: **Veterans,** 19, 27, 49, 107, 110; **Military Personnel,** 186, 202, 234, 332, 348, 350; **Family Members,** 497
See also Business administration; General programs

Information technology
Scholarships: **Veterans,** 19, 107; **Military Personnel,** 148, 186, 265, 326, 348, 351
Fellowships/Grants: **Military Personnel,** 887-888
See also Computer sciences; General programs

Intelligence service
Scholarships: **Veterans,** 19, 27, 49, 73, 107, 110; **Military Personnel,** 152, 186, 202, 234, 294, 326-327, 348, 350; **Family Members,** 497
Fellowships/Grants: **Veterans,** 797; **Military Personnel,** 825, 867, 899; **Family Members,** 928, 953
See also General programs; International affairs; Military affairs

International affairs
Scholarships: **Military Personnel,** 152
Fellowships/Grants: **Military Personnel,** 825, 848, 862, 888; **Family Members,** 928
See also General programs; Political science and politics

International relations. *See* International affairs

J

Japanese language. *See* Language, Japanese

Jobs. *See* Employment

Journalism
Scholarships: **Family Members,** 632
See also Communications; General programs; names of specific types of journalism

Jurisprudence. *See* Law, general

M

Magazines. *See* Journalism

Malay language. *See* Language, Malay

Management
Scholarships: **Military Personnel,** 265
Fellowships/Grants: **Military Personnel,** 870, 887-888
See also General programs

Marine sciences
Scholarships: **Military Personnel,** 333
See also General programs; Sciences; names of specific marine sciences

Marketing
Scholarships: **Veterans,** 89; **Military Personnel,** 319
See also General programs; Public relations

Mass communications. *See* Communications

Mathematics
Scholarships: **Veterans,** 19, 27, 49, 107, 110; **Military Personnel,** 125, 136, 142-143, 152, 165, 186, 202, 234, 298, 310, 328-330, 332-334, 340, 348, 350; **Family Members,** 409, 412, 435, 497, 566
Fellowships/Grants: **Military Personnel,** 841; **Family Members,** 933
Loans: **Military Personnel,** 1027
See also Computer sciences; General programs; Physical sciences

Mechanical engineering. *See* Engineering, mechanical

Media. *See* Communications

Media specialists. *See* Libraries and librarianship, school

Medical sciences
Scholarships: **Military Personnel,** 162, 242; **Family Members,** 381, 409, 581, 631, 635-636, 657, 713
Fellowships/Grants: **Veterans,** 776; **Military Personnel,** 816-817, 829, 831, 833-834, 838, 874, 880, 890; **Family Members,** 927, 973
Loans: **Military Personnel,** 1019, 1024, 1030, 1033
See also General programs; Health and health care; Sciences; names of medical specialties; names of specific diseases

Medical technology
Scholarships: **Veterans,** 44; **Family Members,** 563, 604
Loans: **Military Personnel,** 1027
See also General programs; Medical sciences; Technology

Mental health nurses and nursing. *See* Nurses and nursing, psychiatry and mental health

Meteorology
Scholarships: **Military Personnel,** 136, 142-143, 310, 333
Fellowships/Grants: **Military Personnel,** 910
See also Atmospheric sciences; General programs

Microbiology
Loans: **Military Personnel,** 1024
See also Biological sciences; General programs

Microcomputers. *See* Computer sciences

Microscopy. *See* Medical technology

Middle Eastern studies
Scholarships: **Military Personnel,** 142
See also General programs

Military affairs
Scholarships: **Veterans,** 73; **Military Personnel,** 294
Fellowships/Grants: **Veterans,** 797; **Military Personnel,** 848, 862, 899
See also General programs

Military law
Scholarships: **Military Personnel,** 308
Fellowships/Grants: **Veterans,** 767; **Military Personnel,** 818-819, 821, 832, 903
See also General programs; Law, general

Missionary work. *See* Religion and religious activities

Music
Scholarships: **Veterans,** 7, 45, 119; **Military Personnel,** 361; **Family Members,** 758
Fellowships/Grants: **Veterans,** 811; **Military Personnel,** 917; **Family Members,** 988
See also General programs

Mycology
Scholarships: **Veterans,** 83
See also Botany; General programs

N

National security. *See* Security, national

Natural sciences
Scholarships: **Military Personnel,** 165; **Family Members,** 412
Fellowships/Grants: **Military Personnel,** 841; **Family Members,** 933
See also General programs; Sciences; names of specific sciences

Naval science
Scholarships: **Military Personnel,** 212, 270-272
See also General programs

Newspapers. *See* Journalism; Newsroom management

Newsroom management
Scholarships: **Family Members,** 632
See also General programs

Nuclear science
Scholarships: **Military Personnel,** 299
See also General programs; Physical sciences

Nurses and nursing, anesthesiology
Scholarships: **Military Personnel,** 162
Fellowships/Grants: **Military Personnel,** 838, 850
Loans: **Military Personnel,** 1024
See also General programs; Nurses and nursing, general

Nurses and nursing, critical care
Scholarships: **Military Personnel,** 162
Fellowships/Grants: **Military Personnel,** 838
Loans: **Military Personnel,** 1024
See also General programs; Nurses and nursing, general

Nurses and nursing, general
Scholarships: **Veterans,** 9, 13, 15, 30, 32, 36, 44; **Military Personnel,** 138, 142, 147, 153, 155, 161-162, 167, 265, 267-268, 300; **Family Members,** 407, 422, 441, 503, 505, 520, 528, 537, 546, 563, 569, 582, 604, 627, 631, 666, 690, 739, 756
Fellowships/Grants: **Veterans,** 770; **Military Personnel,** 817, 830, 836, 838, 887; **Family Members,** 931
Loans: **Military Personnel,** 1019, 1024, 1027
See also General programs; Health and health care; Medical sciences; names of specific nursing specialties

Nurses and nursing, operating room
Loans: **Military Personnel,** 1024
See also General programs; Nurses and nursing, general; Surgery

Nurses and nursing, psychiatry and mental health
Fellowships/Grants: **Military Personnel,** 831, 833
See also General programs; Nurses and nursing, general

Calendar Index

Since most financial aid programs have specific deadline dates, some may have already closed by the time you begin to look for funding. You can use the Calendar Index to identify which programs are still open. To do that, go to the recipient category and program type that applies to you, think about when you'll be able to complete your application forms, go to the appropriate months, jot down the entry numbers listed there, and use those numbers to find the program descriptions in the directory. Keep in mind that the numbers cited here refer to program entry numbers, not to page numbers in the book.

Veterans

Scholarships:
January: 6, 29, 63, 70, 99, 111
February: 7, 18, 27, 33, 45, 47, 50, 58, 71, 75, 77, 81, 83, 88, 90-91, 93, 102-103, 106, 108
March: 9, 14, 19, 31, 38, 46, 54, 68, 86, 94, 98, 110, 112, 116, 119
April: 2-4, 13, 15-16, 21, 25, 28, 32, 41, 43-44, 55, 66-67, 69, 76, 80, 92, 99
May: 1, 5, 10, 30, 36, 52-53, 56, 84, 89, 101, 104, 115, 120
June: 11, 33, 35, 40, 48, 62, 72, 116
July: 22-23, 37, 80
August: 49, 99
September: 33
October: 55, 100, 107, 110, 114, 116
November: 19, 73
December: 87
Any time: 8, 34, 39, 64, 95, 109, 113, 117-118, 121-122
Deadline not specified: 12, 17, 20, 24, 26, 42, 51, 57, 59-61, 65, 74, 78-79, 82, 85, 96-97, 105

Fellowships:
January: 769, 792, 795
February: 773-774, 782, 786, 788, 796, 798, 801, 806
March: 767, 770, 803, 809, 811
April: 766, 768, 779-781, 785, 794, 800, 802
May: 771, 787, 804, 812
June: 772, 776, 782, 809
July: 777
September: 782

October: 809
November: 775, 797
Any time: 783-784, 807-808, 810
Deadline not specified: 778, 789-791, 793, 799, 805

Loans:
February: 1006
April: 990
Any time: 991-992, 995-1005, 1007-1011, 1013-1015
Deadline not specified: 993-994, 1012

Grants-in-Aid:
February: 1099-1101, 1157-1158
March: 1122-1123, 1173-1174
April: 1096, 1105-1106, 1124, 1138, 1143-1144, 1150-1151, 1175, 1193, 1197, 1200, 1206-1207
May: 1114, 1209
June: 1087, 1118, 1146, 1189
August: 1195-1196
September: 1089-1090, 1092, 1139, 1203
December: 1128, 1133, 1202
Any time: 1073-1075, 1078-1079, 1081, 1084, 1088, 1091, 1095, 1097-1098, 1111-1112, 1115, 1117, 1125, 1129, 1136-1137, 1140, 1147, 1154, 1161, 1164-1165, 1168-1170, 1176-1177, 1179-1186, 1190-1191, 1198-1199, 1201, 1205, 1208
Deadline not specified: 1076-1077, 1080, 1082-1083, 1085-1086, 1093-1094, 1102-1104, 1107-1110, 1113, 1116, 1119-1121, 1126-1127, 1130-1132, 1134-1135, 1141-1142, 1145, 1148-1149, 1152-1153, 1155-1156, 1159-1160, 1162-1163, 1166-1167, 1171-1172, 1178, 1187-1188, 1192, 1194, 1204

Military Personnel

Scholarships:
January: 147, 185, 193-194, 212-213, 215, 258, 264, 268, 271, 287, 290, 302, 304, 336
February: 137, 142, 152-153, 174, 191, 202, 216, 226, 232, 238, 241, 265, 283, 288, 301, 316, 339, 342, 347, 349, 363

March: 149, 155, 166, 168, 171, 178, 185-186, 188, 207-209, 218, 221, 227, 233, 249, 259, 270, 272, 274, 284, 286, 302, 311, 317, 323, 335, 340-341, 345, 350, 352-354, 356, 361
April: 123-124, 128, 167, 175, 187, 190, 195, 197-198, 203, 225, 229, 239, 246, 257, 261-262, 280, 285, 321, 336

Military Personnel (Continued)

Family Members

Family Members (Continued)